The Palgrave Handbook of Local Governance in Contemporary China

Jianxing Yu • Sujian Guo
Editors

The Palgrave Handbook of Local Governance in Contemporary China

Editors
Jianxing Yu
School of Public Affairs
Zhejiang University
Hangzhou, Zhejiang, China

Sujian Guo
Department of Political Science, and
Center for US-China Policy Studies
San Francisco State University
San Francisco, CA, USA

ISBN 978-981-13-2798-8   ISBN 978-981-13-2799-5   (eBook)
https://doi.org/10.1007/978-981-13-2799-5

Library of Congress Control Number: 2018960928

Cover illustration: © crystal51/shutterstock.com

This Palgrave Macmillan imprint is published by the registered company Springer Nature
Singapore Pte Ltd.
The registered company address is: 152 Beach Road, #21-01/04 Gateway East, Singapore
189721, Singapore

CONTENTS

Notes on Contributors

Anna L. Ahlers is Associate Professor of Modern Chinese Society and Politics at the Institute of Culture Studies and Oriental Languages (IKOS), University of Oslo. Trained in sinology and political science, her current interests include administrative reform and local governance in China, as well as conceptualizations of legitimacy and political inclusion in authoritarian contexts in comparison. She conducts field research on the modes and consequences of China's new air pollution control policies in various municipalities. Anna is a permanent visiting fellow of the Forum Internationale Wissenschaft, University of Bonn, and of the Environmental and Energy Policy Center at Zhejiang University, Hangzhou/China; senior policy fellow for Chinese Domestic Politics at the Mercator Institute for China Studies (MERICS), Berlin; and elected member of the Young Academy of the Berlin-Brandenburg Academy of Sciences. She has, so far, authored two monographs: *Participation and Empowerment at the Grassroots: Chinese Village Elections in Perspective* (2012, with Gunter Schubert) and *Rural Policy Implementation in Contemporary China: New Socialist Countryside* (2014).

Ehtisham Ahmad is visiting senior fellow at the London School of Economics (LSE) (since 2010); member of the Academic Committee, Institute of State Governance, Sun Yat-sen University, Guangzhou, People's Republic of China (PRC, since 2015); and Pao Yu-Kong Professor at Zhejiang University, PRC (since 2016). He holds a B.A. in Mathematics and Statistics from Government College, Lahore (1969); B.A. Honours (1972) and M.A. (1975) in Economics (Cambridge); and M.A. (1976) in Public Policy and D.Phil. in Economics (1980) from University of Sussex. He has worked at the IMF during 1990–2010 in various capacities: senior advisor at the Executive Board (representing Pakistan during July 2008–December 2009) and advisor and division chief of the Fiscal Affairs Department. He also worked as special advisor to the finance minister of Saudi Arabia during 1996–1998 (on leave from the IMF). He was on the World Bank staff team for the 1990 World Development Report

"Poverty," was director of the Development Economics Research Program, The Suntory and Toyota International Centres for Economic and Related Disciplines (STICERD), LSE (1986–1990), and was deputy director of the Development Economics Research Center at Warwick University (1980–1986). Ahmad has written widely on public policy and fiscal reforms, governance, fiscal federalism, and poverty reduction. His recent books include *Fiscal Underpinnings for Sustainable Development in China* (2018, with M. Niu and K. Xiao); *Multi-level Finance and the Crisis in Europe* (2016, with Giorgio Brosio and Massimo Bordignon); *Handbook of Multilevel Finance* (2015); *Handbook of Fiscal Federalism* (2006); and *Does Decentralization Enhance Service Delivery and Poverty Reduction* (2009, with Giorgio Brosio)? Some earlier books include *Theory and Practice of Tax Reform in Developing Countries* (1991, with Nicholas Stern); *Social Security in Developing Countries* (1992, with Jean Drèze, John Hills, and Amartya Sen); *Reforming China's Public Finances* (1995, with Gao Qiang and Vito Tanzi); *Financing Decentralized Expenditures—A Focus on Intergovernmental Grants* (1997); and *Managing Fiscal Decentralization*.

Fabiana Barbi is a sociologist, Ph.D. in Environment and Society, and postdoctoral researcher in the Center for Environmental Studies and Research (NEPAM) at the University of Campinas (UNICAMP), Brazil. She is a research fellow of the Earth System Governance Project.

Jonathan Benney is Lecturer in Chinese Studies at Monash University, Melbourne, Australia. He researches social and political phenomena in contemporary China, with particular emphasis on law and rights, conflict resolution, activism, new media, political discourse, and design and aesthetics. His publications include the monograph *Defending Rights in Contemporary China* (2013) and journal articles in *Asian Studies Review*, the *Journal of Contemporary China*, and the *Journal of Chinese Governance*. He holds a Ph.D. from the University of Melbourne, and has undergraduate degrees in Arts and Law from the same university. He has worked as a lecturer and researcher in Australia, the United States, Singapore, Germany, and Taiwan.

Wei Chen is an assistant research fellow at the Institute of Social Work and Social Policy, East China University of Science and Technology. Her research centers on developmental state and innovation policy. Her articles have appeared in *Sociological Studies* and *Journal of Public Administration*.

Jørgen Delman has been Professor of China Studies in the Department of Cross-Cultural and Regional Studies at Copenhagen University. For 45 years, his research has focused on China. His recent publications on China focus on state-business and state-society interaction, climate change and renewable energy politics, climate governance at city level, urban sustainable development, and energy security. He has extensive experience from working with Chinese, international, and Danish public, private, and societal stakeholders and clients in China. His titles have included head of department (Private Sector Development), senior consultant, and project manager in RAMBØLL during 1991–2001. He was also the director of the Nordic Institute of Asian Studies (NIAS, 2002–2009) and the director of the China–EU Centre for Agricultural Technology (CECAT, 1991–1996) in the Chinese Ministry of Agriculture.

Yanhua Deng is a professor in the School of Social and Behavioral Sciences, Nanjing University, China. Her research centers on contentious politics and environmental sociology. Her articles have appeared in the following journals: *China Journal*, *The China Quarterly*, the *Journal of Contemporary China*, *Modern China*, and *Political Studies*.

Leila da Costa Ferreira is a full professor in the Institute of Philosophy and Human Sciences and in NEPAM, at UNICAMP, Brazil. She is a faculty member of the Earth System Governance Project.

Xiang Gao is an associate professor in the School of Public Affairs at Zhejiang University, secretary general of Zhejiang Society for Public Administration, project manager of Asian Future Leader Scholarship Program in Public Administration, Zhejiang University, and the assistant editor of the *Journal of Chinese Governance*. Her areas of specialization include political behavior, comparative government, public administration, and social survey. Her research interests include local governance, citizen participation, central-local relations, cadre management, and public policy in China's New Urbanization. She is the co-author of the book *From State-Led Development to Endogenous Development: Redefining Rural and Agricultural Development in China* (Beijing Normal University Press, April 2013). Her articles have appeared in such journals as *Daedalus: The Journal of the American Academy of Arts and Sciences, Australian Journal of Public Administration, Journal of Chinese Governance, Social Sciences in China* (in Chinese), and *Chinese Public Administration* (in Chinese).

Edward Gu is professor in the School of Public Affairs, Zhejiang University. He obtained his Bachelor of Science in Biology from Peking University and Ph.D. from Leiden University, the Netherlands. He was postdoctoral fellow at Harvard University and the University of California at Berkeley. He has worked at National University of Singapore, the Australian National University, and Beijing Normal University. His research and teaching focus on developmentalism, social policy, health policy, and non-profit organizations. He has authored a number of books in Chinese on China's health policy, such as *Diagnosis and Prescription: Facing China's Health Care Reforms* (2006), *Towards Universal Coverage of Health Care Security: Strategies and Tactics for China's New Health Care Reforms* (2008), *Institution-Building for the Universal Coverage of Health Care Insurance* (2010), and *Five Roads Towards the Public Interest in China's New Health Care Reforms* (2012). In addition, many of his articles have appeared in leading journals, including more than 20 articles in international journals. In 2014, 2015, and 2016, he was on the list of Most Cited Chinese Researchers compiled by Elsevier.

Ting Guan is a postdoctoral researcher at the School of Public Policy and Management (SPPM), Tsinghua University. She used to be a researcher at the Institute of East Asian Studies (University of Duisburg-Essen) and the Environmental and Energy Policy Center (Zhejiang University). Her research focuses on local environmental and energy governance from a comparative perspective. Guan has been named a Humboldt Scholar, German Chancellor Fellow, Green Talents Fellow, Global Governance 2020 Fellow, and Visiting Academic Fellow at MERICS.

Sujian Guo is a visiting distinguished professor of the Changjiang Scholar Program of the Ministry of Education at the Fudan Institute for Advanced Study in Social Sciences, a Professor of Political Science and director of the Center for US–China Policy Studies at San Francisco State University, editor in chief of the *Journal of Chinese Political Science*, co-editor in chief of the *Journal of Chinese Governance*, editor in chief of the *Fudan Journal of the Humanities and Social Sciences*, executive editor in chief of the *Chinese Political Science Review*, editor of Rowman & Littlefield-Lexington (USA)'s book series "Challenges Facing Chinese political development," and former president of the Association of Chinese Political Studies (USA). His areas of research include comparative politics, Chinese politics and government, democratic transition, governance theories, sustainable energy, and comparative political economy. Over 60 of his academic articles have appeared in various journals, and he has authored and edited 30 books, including *Governance in Transitional China* (2017), *China's Green Low Carbon Transition* (2017), *The Political Economy of China's Great Transformation* (2016), *Global Sustainable Energy Competitiveness Report* (2015), *Democratic Transitions: Modes and Outcomes* (2014), *Chinese Politics and Government: Power, Ideology and Organization* (2012), *The Political Economy of Asian Transition from Communism* (2006), and *Post-Mao China: From Totalitarianism to Authoritarianism* (2000), among others.

Rongbin Han is an assistant professor at the Department of International Affairs, University of Georgia. His research interests center on social activism, media politics, and political participation in authoritarian regimes, with focus on China. He is the author of *Contesting Cyberspace in China Online Expression and Authoritarian Resilience*. His articles have appeared in *The China Quarterly, Journal of Contemporary China, Journal of Current Chinese Affairs*, and *International Journal of Communication*, among others. His co-authored work with Kevin O'Brien on rural democracy in China has won the 2018 John and Vivian Sabel Award for the best article published in the *Journal of Contemporary China*.

Baogang He is Alfred Deakin Professor, Chair in International Relations at the School of Humanities and Social Sciences, Faculty of Arts & Education, Deakin University. He holds a Ph.D. in Political Science from Australian National University (1994), and is widely known for his work in Chinese democratization and politics—in particular the deliberative politics in China— as well as in Asian politics—covering Asian regionalism, Asian federalism, and Asian multiculturalism. His published work includes 6 single-authored books and 70 international refereed journal articles. His work can be found in top journals including *British Journal of Political Science, Journal of Peace Research, Political Theory, Political Studies,* and *Perspectives on Politics.* In Chinese, his published work includes 3 books, 15 book chapters, and 63 journal papers.

Yanling He is a distinguished professor of the Zhujiang Scholar Program of the People's Government of Guangdong Province, Chair of the Department of Public Administration of Sun Yat-sen University, director of the Research Institute for Urban Governance of Sun Yat-sen University, vice president of the Committee for Government Strategy and Public Policy of the Chinese Research Council of Modern Management, and first editorial director of the *Journal of Public Administration* (PRC). Her areas of specialization include public administration, bureaucracy and organization, and transformation theory. Her research interests have focused on urban governance and local governance, civil society, and administrative reform in transformational China. More than 50 of her academic articles have appeared in both English and Chinese, and she has authored and edited more than 10 books, such as *Practical Logic of Institutionalized Urbanization in China* (2013), *State and Society in the Grassroots Community of Urban China* (2007), and *Blue Book of Municipal Capacity* (2013, 2016).

Thomas Heberer is Senior Professor of Politics and Society of China at the Institute of Political Science and the Institute of East Asian Studies, University of Duisburg-Essen. He has been conducting field research in China since the early 1980s on an annual basis and his published work includes more than 50 books on China as author, co-author, editor, and co-editor. His research interests include local governance, institutional and social change, political culture, nationalities' policies, and the behavior of social actors. In recent years, he has been working on the behavior of "strategic groups" (local cadres, private entrepreneurs, etc.) and political representative claims.

Biao Huang is a Ph.D. candidate in the School of Public Affairs at Zhejiang University and a joint Ph.D. student in the Centre for Contemporary Chinese Studies at the University of Melbourne. His research interests lie in innovation in the public sector, policy experimentation, and Chinese local governance.

Qing Huang is an assistant professor at the College of Media and International Culture, Zhejiang University. She received her PhD in Communication from The Chinese University of Hong Kong in 2016. She won the Hong Kong PhD

Fellowship Scheme 2013/14 awarded by the Research Grants Council of Hong Kong. Her research interests include strategic communication in public issues, globalization and risk communication, and digital media use in transitional China. She is the principal investigator of three research grants funded by the Ministry of Education of PRC, China Postdoctoral Science Foundation, and the Social Science Fund of Zhejiang Province. Her work has been published in *Telematics and Informatics, International Journal of Communication, Chinese Journal of Communication, Public Relations Review,* and *China Media Research,* among others.

Linan Jia is a Ph.D. candidate at the Department of International Affairs, University of Georgia. Her research interests include media politics, authoritarianism, institutional change, and comparative political behavior. Her articles have appeared in *Journal of Chinese Governance, Journal of Contemporary Asia-Pacific Studies,* and *Modern China Studies.*

Yuejin Jing is a professor and vice chairman of the Department of Political Science, School of Social Sciences, Tsinghua University. His research interests cover local governance, state and society relationship, politics of bureaucracy in contemporary China, comparative politics, and political sociology. He has authored some books and many articles in Chinese, such as *Contemporary Chinese Government and Politics* (2016), *An Introduction to Political Science* (2015), *Understanding China Politics: The Key Words Approach* (2012), *An Introduction to Comparative Politics* (co-author, 2008), *An Analysis of Changing Relations between Party Branches and Village Committees in Contemporary Rural China* (2004), and *The Transformation of Political Space in China* (2004).

Shu Keng is a research fellow in School of Public Affairs, Zhejiang University. His research centers on comparative political economy, China's political economy, and cross-strait relations. His articles have appeared in *The China Quarterly, Asian Survey,* and *China: An International Journal.*

Genia Kostka is a fellow at the Hertie School of Governance and was Professor of Governance of Energy and Infrastructure before that. Her research and teaching interests are in energy governance, public policy, and political economy, with a regional focus on China. Previously, Kostka was an assistant professor at the Frankfurt School of Finance and Management and a strategic management consultant for McKinsey & Company in Berlin. She has a Ph.D. in Development Studies from the University of Oxford, an M.A. with specializations in International Economics and International Development from SAIS Johns Hopkins University, and a B.Sc. in International Relations from the LSE. In addition to her many publications, she regularly consults for international organizations, such as the Asian Development Bank, AusAID, GIZ, Oxfam, and the World Bank.

Dan Li is a doctoral candidate of School of Government, Sun Yat-sen University. Her research interests are public-private partnerships and government-enterprise relationships.

Shuoyan Li is a Ph.D. candidate at SPPM, Tsinghua University, and his supervisor is Professor Wang Ming, dean of SPPM, Tsinghua University. His research mainly focuses on the Chinese State-NGO relationship, civil society, and policy entrepreneurship. Shuoyan got his undergraduate degree from the School of Sociology and Anthropology, Sun Yat-sen University, in 2013, and started his Ph.D. in Tsinghua. He was a visiting scholar sponsored by the Chinese Scholarship Council (CSC) from 2016 to 2017 and studied at the School of Public Policy, University of Maryland, College Park, Maryland, under the supervision of Professor Angela Bies. Eight academic articles of his have appeared in different journals, both in Chinese and in English, including "Power of Co-optation: Party, Political Capital and the Development of Grassroots NGO" (*Society*), "Does Political Connection Affect Environmental Grassroots NGOs' Policy Advocacy" (*Journal of Public Management*), "Cross-System Mobility and Policy Innovation: Policy Entrepreneurs' Occupation Choice Under the Restriction of Institutional Environment" (*Journal of Public Administration*), "A Case Study of One-Child Policy Change in China" (*Public Administration and Policy Review*), and "International Experience of Co-governance in Occupational Safety" (*Journal of Eastern Asian Study*).

Shenghua Lu is a Ph.D. student at the Department of Land and Resource Management, Zhejiang University, China. His areas of specialization include land use policy and urban economy.

Milton L. Mueller is a professor at the Georgia Institute of Technology, an internationally prominent scholar specializing in the political economy of information and communication. His research focuses on property rights, institutions, and global governance in communication and information industries. He is the co-founder and director of the Internet Governance Project (IGP). He has participated in proceedings and policy development activities of ICANN, the International Telecommunications Union (ITU), and the National Telecommunications and Information Administration (NTIA), and regulatory proceedings of the European Commission, China, Hong Kong, and New Zealand. He led the creation of the Global Internet Governance Academic Network (GigaNet), an international association of scholars.

Kinglun Ngok is Professor of Social Policy at the Center for Chinese Public Administration Research, associate dean of School of Government at Sun Yat-sen University, a professor in the Department of Public Administration, president of East Asian Social Policy Network, director of Institute for Social Policy, and director of the Center for Social Security at Sun Yat-sen University. He is also editor in chief of *Chinese Public Policy Review*, editorial committee member of *Journal of Poverty and Social Justice* (UK) and *Journal of Public Administration*, global advisor of *Journal of Social Policy* (UK), and expert consultant for Social Innovation and Social Work at Guangdong Province. His areas of specialization include Chinese public policy, social security, and public administration. His research interests have focused on Chinese social policy, social innovation, social integration, welfare reform, and labor politics. More than 100 of his academic articles have been published both in English and in Chinese, and he has authored and edited over 20 books, such as *China's Social Policy: Transformation and Challenges?* (2016), *Industrial Democracy in China: With Additional Studies on Germany, South Korea and Vietnam* (2012), *Serving Migrant Workers: A Challenging Public Service Issue in China* (2012), *Welfare Reform in East Asia: Towards workfare?* (2011), *Social Policy in China* (2008), and *The Changes of Chinese Labour Policy and Labour Legislation in the Context of Market Transition* (2008).

Kerry Ratigan is Assistant Professor of Political Science at Amherst College. Her research focuses on social policy, decentralization, and authoritarian governance. She thanks Xiaohui Gui, Hao Liu, Beatrix Wessel, and Alice Yang for research assistance and gratefully acknowledges Amherst College and the Chiang Ching-kuo Foundation for their support.

Xue Lan Rong is a tenured full professor in School of Education at the University of North Carolina at Chapel Hill. Her published work includes 8 research books, 3 journal special issues, and over 40 book chapters and articles in major sociological and educational journals (e.g., *American Sociological Review, American Sociologist, American Educational Research Journal, Harvard Educational Review*, etc.). She has made over 80 presentations at state, national, and international professional conferences. Her research has focused on social science education, educating immigrant children, and international education. She has also contributed to national and international scholarship through her service on the editorial boards of various professional journals, including the *American Educational Research Journal, Sociology of Education Journal*, and the *Journal of Research and Development in Education*, among others. She has received the Outstanding Professional Achievement Alumni Award (2009) from the University of Georgia at Athens and the American Educational Research Association Outstanding Reviewer Award (2010). She is also a recipient of several research grants, including a research grant from Spencer Foundation (2014–2018).

Gunter Schubert is Professor and Chair of Greater China Studies and director of European Research Center on Contemporary Taiwan (ERCCT) at the University of Tübingen. He is a member of the editorial boards of numerous renowned international journals, including *The China Quarterly, Journal of Chinese Political Science, China Perspectives*, and *Issues & Studies*. He is also co-editor of the book series *East Asia in the 21st Century. Politics-Society-Security-Regional Integration*. He specializes in policy implementation in contemporary China from the perspective of steering theory, with a focus on private sector reform and the evolution of state-business relations, particularly in China's local state; the political economy of cross-strait relations, including the changing economic and political environment of Taiwanese entrepreneurs in China; and Taiwanese domestic politics. He also studies regime legitimacy and nationalism in China, Hong Kong politics, and the politics and culture of the Chinese in Southeast Asia. He conducts several months of fieldwork in China, Taiwan, and Hong Kong. His published work includes *The Taiwan Handbook on Contemporary Taiwan* (2016, editor); *Taiwan and the 'China Impact': Challenges and Opportunities* (2016, editor); *Proactive Local Politics: County and Township Cadres as Strategic Group* (2013, edited with Thomas Heberer and Yang Xuedong); and *Participation and Empowerment at the Grassroots: Chinese Village Elections in Perspective* (2012, co-authored with Anna L. Ahlers), among others.

Yongdong Shen is a researcher in the Department of Public Administration at the School of Public Affairs, Zhejiang University. He was a postdoctoral fellow at the University of Oslo and a visiting scholar at the University of Boston. His Ph.D. thesis, entitled "The Strategic Interaction of Business Associations and Local Governments in a Changing China," examines and analyzes how local business associations participate in the process of policy decision-making and policy implementation. His articles have appeared in journals such as *The China Quarterly, China: An International Journal, The China Review: An Interdisciplinary Journal on Greater China, Journal of Chinese Political Science,* and *Journal of Chinese Governance.* He is an editor for *Journal of Chinese Governance.*

Guocan Su is a doctoral candidate in School of Economics, Xiamen University. His research interests are tax policy, indirect tax incidence, infrastructure financing, and public-private partnerships.

Rong Tan is a professor in the Department of Land Management at Zhejiang University. He has two Ph.D. degrees. One is in Land Management obtained from Nanjing Agricultural University, China, and the other is in Agricultural Economics obtained from Humboldt University of Berlin, Germany. He is the executive director of the MPA Education Center at Zhejiang University and the vice dean of the Land Academy for National Development, jointly established by Zhejiang University and the Ministry of Land and Resource of China. His main research area is institutions and governance systems of natural resources and the environment. His research has been widely cited and applied at central and local levels in China. More than 60 of his academic articles have appeared in both English and Chinese, and he has authored 10 books, including *Governing Farmland Conversion in China: Transactions and Institutional Fit* (2015), *Governance Efficiency of Farmland Conversion* (2015), *China Land Security Review* (2014), *The Market for Collective-owned Forest Land: The Transaction Costs of Public Good Provision* (2014), and *Rural Land Institutional Reform in the Context of New-pattern Urbanization* (2013).

Jessica C. Teets is an associate professor in the Political Science Department at Middlebury College. Her research area is governance challenges and policy innovation in authoritarian regimes, with a focus on public participation and the role of civil society. She is the author of *Civil Society Under Authoritarianism: The China Model* (2014) and editor (with William Hurst) of *Local Governance Innovation in China: Experimentation, Diffusion, and Defiance* (2014).

Hui Wang is a professor at the Department of Land and Resource Management, Zhejiang University, China. He received his Ph.D. degree in 2002 from Zhejiang University. His areas of specialization include land use policy, urban economy, and real estate economy. His research interests focus on land development rights, land requisition, and agricultural land tenure. More than 30 academic articles of his have appeared in both English and Chinese, and his publications can be found in major public policy journals, such as *Land Use Policy, China & World Economy, Habitat International, Housing Studies, Journal of Urban Affairs, Economic Research Journal* (in Chinese), *Management World* (in Chinese), *Chinese Rural Economy* (in Chinese), *China Economic Quarterly, Urban Planning*, and so on. He has authored books such as *China's Land Reform: Difficulties, Breakthroughs and Policy* (2013) and *Reform of Land Requisition in China: Theory, Fact and Policy Funding* (2013). He won the First Chinese Rural Development Research Award, first prize for land planning by Ministry of Land and Resource, and many other provincial awards. His research has received support from the National Natural Science Foundation, National Social Science Foundation, UNDP, and so on.

Ming Wang is a professor at SPPM, Tsinghua University; dean of the Institute for Philanthropy, Tsinghua University; director of the NGO Research Center in Tsinghua University; and chief editor of *The China Nonprofit Review*. His areas of specialization include NGO/NPO and civil society, philanthropy, governance, and public policy. His research interests have focused on Chinese NGOs/NPOs and civil society. More than 50 of his academic articles have appeared in Chinese, English, and Japanese, and he has authored and edited more than 20 books, including *A Discussion on Chinese Road of NGOs: Reform and Co-governance by Society* (2017), *NPO Management* (2016), *Oral History for NGOs in China* (Vol. 2, 2014), *Social Organizations and Social Governance* (2014), *Social Organizations* (2013), *Oral History for NGOs in China* (Vol. 1, 2012), *Emerging Civil Society in China, 1978–2007* (2011), *The Introduction to NPO Management* (2010), *Wenchuan Earthquake: China NGOs in Emergency Rescue* (2009), *A General Survey of Non-governmental Organizations* (2004), *The Non-Governmental Sector in China* (2003), *The Introduction to NPO Management* (2002), *NPO in China* (2002), *The Society Reform in China: The Transformation from Government Choice to Social Choice* (2001), *Case-Studies on China's NGOs* (2000), and *Case-Studies on China's NGOs, 2001* (2001).

Shizong Wang is a professor in the School of Public Affairs and chair of the Department of Governance at Zhejiang University. His areas of specialization include local governance theory and practice and social governance in China. His research interests have focused on social organizations and their relations to state, autonomy of urban communities, and street-level bureaucrats' behavior. He has published 5 books and more than 40 papers in Chinese and English, such as "All Roads Lead to Rome: Autonomy, Political Connections and Organisational Strategies of NGOs in China" (*China: An International Journal*, Vol. 13, Issue 3:125–144), "New Agenda for the Study of Chinese Governance" (*Journal of Chinese Governance*, Vol. 1, Issue 1: 21–40), "Characteristics of China's Nongovernmental Organizations: A Critical Review" (*Journal of Chinese Political Science*, Vol. 20, Issue, 4:1–15), "An Institutional Analysis of the Multi-layered Characteristics of Social Organizations in China" (*Social Science in China*, 2016, Vol. 37, Issue 4:93–116), and *Governance Theory and Its Applicability in China* (2009).

Xinxin Wang is a Ph.D. candidate in the strand of Cultural Studies and Literacies at the School of Education, University of North Carolina at Chapel Hill. Her research focuses on educational policy analysis, including areas of international and comparative education, higher education, critical multicultural education, and educational policies' evaluation. Prior to her Ph.D. studies, Xinxin received her master's degree in Public Policy from Rutgers University at New Brunswick in 2015 and a bachelor's degree in Economics and a minor in Japanese from University of International Business and Economics in China.

Fei Wu is a Qiushi Distinguished Professor at Zhejiang University and a Qianjiang Distinguished Scholar in Zhejiang Province. He is the president of Global Communication and the Public Diplomacy Society. He is the advisory board member of several professional institutions, such as the Journalism Branch of the Ministry of Education of China and the Association of Journalists in Zhejiang. He serves as a reviewer for several major funds, such as the National Social Science Foundation, China News Award, and Yangtze Taofen News Award. He is the associate editor of *China Media Reports Oversea* and a member of the editorial board of a number of journals, including *Chinese Journalism Yearbook, China Media Research*, and *Journal of International Communication*. His research interests include media and society, media law, and journalism theories. He is the author and translator of eight books. More than 70 of his articles have appeared in CSSCI-indexed journals, including top journals such as *Sociology Research* and *Journalism and Communication Research*. He was the principle investigator of a number of important projects, including a key project funded by the Ministry of Education between 2009 and 2013 (Theory, Status Quo, and Trend of International Communication Research). He has been honored as the Outstanding Young Author for Social Sciences Research in China. He has also received awards for his excellent research and teaching from the Zhejiang Academy of Social Sciences and the Ministry of Education of China.

Yong Xu is a professor at the Institute of China Rural Studies, one of the key research bases of Humanities and Social Sciences of Ministry of Education, Central China Normal University, and also a professor at the Institute of Chinese Urban Governance of the Central China Normal University. He is the convener of a political discipline group of the State Council Degree Committee, the evaluation expert of the national postdoctoral research stations, a member of the review panel of National Social Science Fund, one of the first "Changjiang Scholar" Distinguished Professors in Social Science by the Chinese Ministry of Education, a member of the Social Science Committee of the Ministry of Education, and a member of the Expert Advisory Committee of the Ministry of Civil Affairs. He is also the vice president of China Political Association and the president of Political Science Association of Hubei Province. In 2006, he was appointed to deliver thematic lectures at a group learning of the Political Bureau of the Central Committee of the Communist Party of China (CPC). His research has focused on grassroots governance and rural China. His selected works are *Imbalance in Chinese Politics: Comparison between Cities and Villages* (1992), *Rural Villagers' Self-Governance in China* (1997), *Modern State, Rural Society and Institutional Construction* (2009), *Advanced Research on Rural China and Farmers* (2009), and *Developmental Approach and Mechanism of Grassroots Democracy* (2015).

Feng Yang is an associate professor at the School of Public Administration, Sichuan University, China, and was a visiting scholar at Syracuse University School of Information Studies, the USA. He holds his Ph.D. in Economics from Sichuan University. He is the author of several books and journal articles, and his work informs not only Internet governance but also government information management, information poverty, and information policy.

Jianxing Yu is a distinguished professor of the Changjiang Scholar Program of Ministry of Education of PRC, and professor and dean of the School of Public Affairs, Zhejiang University. He is also a co-editor in chief of the *Journal of Chinese Governance*, and an editorial board member of the *Journal of Chinese Political Science* and the *Chinese Political Science Review*. His areas of specialization include political science, public administration, and social policy. His research interests have focused on state transformation, modernization of the state governance system and governance capability, government innovation, nonprofit organization and social governance, Chinese rural reform, and Chinese medical reform. More than 100 of his peer-review articles have appeared in both English and Chinese, and he has authored and/or edited more than 25 books, including *Improving Service Capability of Primary-Level Healthcare: Based on the Practice of Zhejiang Province* (2017), *Public Hospital Privatization: Theory and Policy* (2014),

The Development of Business Associations During the Era of Comprehensive Deepening Reforms (2014), *From State-Led Development to Endogenous Development: The Restarting of China's Agriculture and Rural Areas* (2013), *A Path for Chinese Civil Society: A Case Study on Business Associations in Wenzhou, China* (2012), *Public Service-oriented Government* (2012), and *Towards the Age of Social Policy* (2012).

Lina Zhang, Ph.D. student in the Department of Political Science, School of Social Sciences, Tsinghua University, China.

Yang Zhang is assistant professor in the Department of Political Science and a member of the Center for Asian Culture and Public Administration at Southwest Jiaotong University. His main research interests include political methodology and the role of social capital in Chinese elite politics and civil society.

Litao Zhao is senior research fellow at the East Asian Institute, National University of Singapore. He holds his Ph.D. degree in Sociology from Stanford University. His research interests include social stratification and mobility, sociology of education, organizational analysis, and China's social policy. He has served on the editorial board of *Journal of Technology Management in China, China: An International Journal, East Asian Policy*, and *Shantou University Journal* (Humanities and Social Sciences). His research has appeared or is forthcoming in *The China Quarterly, Journal of Contemporary China, Research in Social Stratification and Mobility, International Journal of Educational Development, Social Sciences in China, Built Environment, China: An International Journal, East Asian Policy, Frontiers of Education in China, Issues and Studies,* and so on. He has authored and edited eight books, including *China's Development: Social Investment and Challenges* (2017), *China's Great Urbanization* (2017), *China's Social Development and Policy* (2013), *China's New Social Policy* (2010), *China's Reform at 30* (2009), and *Paths to Private Entrepreneurship: Markets and Mobility in Rural China* (2008).

Xiaocui Zhao is a graduate student in the Public Administration School at East China Normal University. Her major is public administration. Her research interests include nonprofit organizations and policy implementation.

Zhirong Jerry Zhao is an associate professor at the Hubert H. Humphrey School of Public Affairs, University of Minnesota. He is also a research fellow in China Institute for Urban Governance, Shanghai Jiaotong University. His research area is public finance and budgeting.

Jun Zhou is a professor in the Public Administration School and director of the Center for Nonprofits and Society Governance Innovation at East China Normal University. Her areas of specialization include politics theory, public administration, and philosophy. Her research focuses on nonprofit organizations, contracting out, and community development. More than 50 of her academic articles have appeared in both English and Chinese, and she has authored and edited six books, including *Social Organization* *and Charitable Organization Management* (2017), *Nonprofit Organizations Management* (2015), and *The Development of Business Associations in the Era of Comprehensive Reforms of China* (2015).

Xufeng Zhu is professor and associate dean at SPPM and executive director of the Institute for Sustainable Development Goals, Tsinghua University, and director of the Think Tank Research Center of SPPM. His research interests include the policy process, think tank and expert involvement, science and technology policy, environment and climate policy, and public governance in transitional China. He is the author of *The Rise of Think Tanks in China* (2013), *Expert Involvement in Policy Changes*, and *China's Think Tanks: Their Influences in the Policy Process*. Over 20 of his articles in English have appeared in *Journal of Public Administration Research and Theory*, *Governance*, *Public Administration*, *Policy Studies Journal*, *The China Quarterly*, *Policy Sciences*, *Public Management Review*, *Environmental and Planning C*, *Administration & Society*, *Journal of Contemporary China*, *Journal of Comparative Policy Analysis*, *Asian Survey*, *Energy Policy*, and other international journals; dozens of his articles have appeared in Chinese journals such as *Social Sciences in China*, *Sociological Studies*, and *Management World*, which are highly prestigious academic journals in their respective fields in China. He serves as the regional editor of *Asian Journal of Political Sciences* and as an editorial board member for six other international journals.

Wenjia Zhuang is associate professor in the Center for Chinese Public Administration Research and the Department of Public Administration at School of Government, and an editorial committee member of *Journal of Public Administration* at Sun Yat-sen University. His areas of specialization include social conflict resolution, local governance, social innovation, and public opinion. His research interests have focused on collective labor disputes and grand mediation, Chinese politics, social stability, social organizations, and state governance studies. More than 20 of his academic articles have appeared in both English and Chinese, such as "Mediate First: The Revival of Mediation in Labor Dispute Resolution in China" (2015), "Can the Strategy of "Mediation Mediate First" Alleviate Reduce Collective Labor Disputes?—An Empirical Test Based on Province-Level Panel Data from 1999 to 2011" (2015), and "The Survival and Development Space for China's Labor NGOs: Informal Politics and Its Uncertainty" (2010).

List of Figures

LIST OF TABLES

List of Boxes

CHAPTER 1

Introduction: Local Governance in China—Past, Present, and Future

Jianxing Yu

1 Introduction

As China celebrates its 40th anniversary, in 2018, of the reform and opening-up, it is an opportune moment to examine China's development characteristics from the perspective of local governance. From 1978 to 2018, the main focal point of China's reform and opening-up has been the decentralization from the government to the market and the society, as well as the decentralization from the central government to local governments. China's local governments, which directly undertake local economic development, the provision of public services, and social functions, carry out the policies of the central government and perform de facto governmental functions, as well as offer key insights into to Chinese governmental operation. In China, a local governance system—which gives priority to local governments and includes both market participation and social coordination—is taking shape and playing an increasingly important role in national governance. It's worth pointing out that China's reform and opening-up develops along with the global local governance reform, responding to negative effects of globalization in local economic and social development. It plays a key role in a global multilevel governance since it directly deals with a multitude of public issues and services. This shows that local governance in contemporary China, which develops along with globalization, constitutes a key component of the global local governance reform and reflects the application results of governance theories in China.

J. Yu (✉)
School of Public Affairs, Zhejiang University, Hangzhou, Zhejiang, China
e-mail: yujianxing@zju.edu.cn

© The Author(s) 2019
J. Yu, S. Guo (eds.), *The Palgrave Handbook of Local Governance in Contemporary China*, https://doi.org/10.1007/978-981-13-2799-5_1

In the following sections, this introduction first reviews the overall development of local governance in China, including the rise, structural components, and operational mechanism of local governance since the reform and opening-up. It then summarizes the key characteristics of Chinese local governance as government-dominated, institutionally innovative, and adaptive. Finally, the new trends of local governance in contemporary China are discussed.

2   RISE OF LOCAL GOVERNANCE IN CONTEMPORARY CHINA

Chinese local governance in the modern sense started between the late Qing Dynasty and early Republic of China, when local governments had great power over local affairs. Under the influence of nationalism and the tradition of autonomy, many local celebrities flocked to public affairs, such as the promotion of modern education, and even had a hand in the local fiscal system. In the days of wars, local governments even relied on local celebrities to gather public resources for governing public affairs on public resources gathered through local celebrities (Agrawal et al. 1983). At the same time, some public welfare foundations established by home-grown entrepreneurs also got actively involved in social and welfare services (Zi 2015). Studies have shown that business periodicals, as well as self-governing organizations as represented by trade associations and charitable organizations in the late Qing Dynasty, played an important role in expressing and spreading public opinions, giving rise to public domains independent of the state (Rowe 1993). Continuous cooperation between the state and the public was seen and institutionalized in the third realm (Huang 1993). In the 1930s, the KMT Nationalist government weakened the local self-government and participation, and thus government bureaucrats penetrated into "autonomous" governing bodies and turned them into state-led local organizations (Agrawal et al. 1983). This, together with the Japanese War of Aggression against China, seriously held back local governance. While in the revolutionary base of Yan'an, the Communist Party of China (CPC) didn't follow the Soviet Union model, such as centralization, strict hierarchy, and command economy. Instead, they developed a sound system of local governance, and accumulated rich experience, including promoting decentralization, allowing great flexibility in works of local cadres, and enhancing close contact with the masses. "The strict compliance to central orders remains a main feature of CPC operation, but the delegation of power and regional autonomy began to serve as main principles" (Lieberthal 2003).

Since the founding of the People's Republic of China in 1949, Mao Zedong proposed that "it is better to put both central and local initiatives into active use,"[1] and designed a formal governance system based on China's imperial system, practical experience of the Republic of China, and revolutionary base construction. Given a great deal of domestic and global factors, however,

---

[1] Mao Zedong, *On Ten Relationships*, 1956.

China's government administration system in practice learned a lot from the Soviet pattern and emphasized centralization to boost rapid industrial development and social changes. At the same time, China adopted a planned economy and the system of units (单位*Danwei*) for overall control over the market and society. The power of political organizations, thus, penetrated into and controlled without limits every dimension of the society, and China entered the era of totalism (Tsou 1986).

With regard to the relationship between the central and local governments, as China advanced its socialist construction, the central government adopted a highly centralized system, while local governments became subordinate bodies being ordered to implement the policies and plans formulated by the central government. A one-way order-obedience relationship was established between the central government and local governments. With a highly politicized administration system, political means became the major means for China to realize its administration goals. The government took charge of everything to realize large-scale unity. From the founding of the People's Republic of China in 1949 to the reform and opening-up in 1978, China had gone through several rounds of shifts between centralization and decentralization in its fiscal system. In general, these moves to delegate powers to lower levels were made to stimulate local governments in reaching targets set by the central government, while the overall control over economic resources was still in the hand of the latter. In the planned economy system, the relationship between the central and local governments is explained as follows: "If the power is decentralized to the local government, it would get out of control, and then the power would be recentralized, which would stifle the local initiatives" (一放就乱,一收就死 *Yi fang jiu luan, yi shou jiu si*) (Zhou and Tan 2014).

The relationship between the government and the society also changed after 1949. With changes in the social system and ideologies, and the adoption of totalitarianism in the political system, a high degree of politicization was seen in the Chinese society where the system of units dominated by political systems were defined as basic systems to handle public affairs. Private charity organizations and foundations died out and so did business associations that regulate industry operation and economic development. During this period, as a bridge between the governments and the people, All-China Federation of Trade Union (ACFTU), All-China Youth Federation (ACYF), All-China Women's Federation (ACWF), Chinese Academic Association, and All-China Federation of Industry and Commerce (ACFIC) served as political organizations.

As for the relationship between the government and the market, China adopted a highly centralized socialist planned economy that features public ownership and distribution on the basis of labor to ensure total control over economic resources. As market-oriented economy and private ownership were regarded as basic features of capitalism, commodity economy disappeared from the scene, and enterprises were owned by and brought under direct management of the government sector. To sum up, social and economic independence is not allowed under the system of totalism and planned economy. It is worth noting that, despite a highly centralized political and economic system similar to that in the Soviet Union, there was still power decentralization among governments at all levels in China. In 1978, the hierarchical structure which encompasses different levels and regions had developed into an "M-form" multidivisional structure which is totally different from that adopted in Eastern Europe and the Soviet Union (Qian and Xu 1993). In other words, China, before the reform and opening-up, implemented not a Soviet-style central planning system, but an economic system that covers many levels and is more regional and local. The decentralized system developed in the days of Mao Zedong has laid the groundwork for the reform and opening-up sweeping across China since 1978 (Shirk 1993).

2.1   The Rise of Local Governments to a Dominant Role

Beginning in 1978, China started a round of reforms advanced by local governments and approved by senior central leaders, and local governance also started to take center stage. China's process of reform is described as being like a person crossing a river by feeling his way over the stones. It started with trial or pilot operation locally, and the successful experience was next incorporated in "top-level design" and promoted across the country. The reform and opening-up, in terms of its drivers, paths, and forms, grows out of local innovation. It, in fact, includes a cascade of processes of granting decision-making powers to various entities and allowing them to keep more profits. The relationship between the central government and local governments also took on a new look. Amid reforms in the administration, fiscal, and cadre management systems, along with market economy development, local governments obtained autonomy, namely unleashing their vitality from constraints of the unitary system.

China has established, through reforming the administration system, a local government organizational system that delegates powers to local governments in economic and social management. In addition, it has identified, through three amendments to the Constitution and organizational laws of local governments from the late 1970s to early 1980s, the responsibilities and functions of the central government and local governments, and their relationships, and recognized the dominant position of local governments. Several reforms in the fiscal system of the central and local governments have ensured economic autonomy of local governments. In 1980, China adopted a fiscal decentralization system (分灶吃饭 *Fen zao chi fan*), which was then changed to a fiscal contracting system (财政包干制 *Cai zheng bao gan zhi*) in 1988 (Zhou and Tan 2014; Yang and Lai 2009). The fiscal decentralization reform from the 1980s to early 1990s allowed local governments to control their source of revenues, spurred them to act as economic entities, and drove them to boost local economic development. It is widely believed that China's tax-sharing reform in 1994 marks the watershed where the central government recentralized fiscal power (Zheng 2013; Zhou 2006). With the system, the central government enhanced its control over local governments but also prescribed their power in collecting certain taxes. Thanks to extra-budgetary accounts, local governments had independent sources of revenue (Zhou 2006) and also greater administration power within their jurisdictions. The fiscal decentralization reform contributed to a Chinese federalism (Montinola et al. 1995), and further consolidated the decentralization framework, providing economic support to the local governments' rise to governance body. In 1984, China started to explore an alternative framework for its cadre and personnel management system to reduce the number of leading cadres under direct central control and let local government have more power over appointing local leading cadres. This move granted more decision-making powers to local governments over personnel management and resources mobilization, which benefits regional governance and management. The central government adopted the principal-agent approach to delegate certain functions to local governments instead of directly intervening in their performance functions. With independence in their administrative power, fiscal relations, and personnel system, local governments are really likely to take charge of local governance.

The reform and opening-up in China is not only a process of unleashing the vitality of local governments but also aims to promote market economy and social autonomy. With the economic reform, China has ushered in a new stage where local governments, markets, and the society seek common development.

2.2   Market Entities in the Local Governance System

The economic system reform dedicated to invigorating market players follows throughout the reform and opening-up, and incorporates itself into ideologies to make possible a socialist market economy with Chinese characteristics. China's reform in the economic structure focuses on the modern property right system, modern market economy, modern income distribution system, and modern macroeconomics (Wei 2008). With the reform in the modern property right system, China recognized the presence of nonpublic economy and promoted its development, making it possible for the nonpublic sector to participate in local governance. The reform toward a modern market economy has identified the role and status of the market mechanism in economic development. In 1982, the 12th National Congress of the CPC advanced the policy of "maintaining the primary role of the planned economy while giving play to the supplementary role of market forces in economic regulation." At the 13th National Congress of the CPC in 1987, a mechanism whereby "the government regulates the market and the market guides enterprises" was established. In 1992, Deng Xiaoping officially recognized the role of the market economy in his South Tour Speech. At the 14th National Congress of the CPC, the reform target of building a socialist market economy was clearly set. In 1997, the 15th National Congress of the CPC put forward to "continue the reform toward a socialist market economy in order to further give play to the fundamental role of market in the resource allocation under state macro-control." In 2013, at the Third Plenary Session of the 18th Central Committee of the CPC, China stated to "deepen the economic system reform by cantering on the decisive role of the market in allocating resources." As market mechanism underpins economic development with greater vitality, the market entity of the local governance system has been established.

2.3   Rise of Social Organizations in the Local Governance System

The reform in the government administration system and the development of the market economy have a profound impact on such aspects as China's state-society relationship, social hierarchical structure, social welfare system, and employment structure. China's reform and opening-up also witnessed its society's rejuvenation and transformation. With the development of a market economy, China has witnessed interest differentiation, the collapse of the unit system and accompanying fragmentation, and state power also withdrew from the private sector. At the same time, a great number of grassroots organizations reconstruct common interests and public space where national and social power is absent to mitigate the interest shock of the market economy and deal with social issues caused by institutional deficiency in the process of social transformation (Wang 2013). Social organizations in China have, since the reform and opening-up, experienced four stages of development. First, they (mainly academic and research associations of all kinds) came on the scene from 1978 to the late 1980s. Second, they underwent massive regulation and overhaul from 1989 to the late 1990s, during which *Measures for Management of Foundations* and *Regulation on Registration and Administration of Social Group* were released. Under these rules, foundations and social organizations are required to register at the Ministry of Civil Affairs under the system of "dual management." In other words, they require the approval and registration of both the registration authority and competent business departments. Third, they experienced steady development from 1998 to 2013, mainly economic organizations, grassroots organizations dedicated to improving public welfares, and nonpublic offering foundations. The Third Plenary Session of the 18th CPC Central Committee in 2013 proposed to preferentially foster and develop four types of social organizations: industry associations and chambers of commerce, scientific and technological associations, charity and philanthropic organizations, and urban and rural community service organizations, and allow them to directly register in the bureau of civil affairs when they are established. This reflects that non-profit organizations have played a more prominent role in the provision of public services. Fourth, they have entered a new stage of development since 2013. In 2015, China released the *Overall Plan on Separation of Industrial Associations and Chambers of Commerce from Administrative Organizations*, which heralded de-administration reform for trade associations and chambers of commerce. The *Charity Law of the People's Republic of China* passed at the Fourth Session of the 12th National People's Congress (NPC) in 2016 has ushered in a new era for Chinese philanthropy. In 2016, the *Law of the People's Republic of China on the Administration of Activities of Overseas Non-Governmental Organizations within the Territory of China* was passed by the Standing Committee of the 12th NPC to set standards on the operation of overseas NGOs in China.

All in all, local governance has witnessed its rise in China after the reform and opening-up initiative as local governments obtain greater decision-making power, market mechanism forms and improves, and social organizations play a bigger role in the local provision of public services.

3   Components of Local Governance in Contemporary China

3.1   Local Governments

Local government refers to government entities set by the central government to govern a certain part of the country or administer certain social affairs in a geographical area. It includes local legislative authorities and local administrative authorities. As a primary role in local governance, local governments sustain regional economic development and social stability, and manage social affairs. The Constitution of the People's Republic of China defines the national administrative divisions as provinces, counties, and townships. With the "City Governing County" system in 1982, a four-level system—"provinces, cities, counties, and townships"—came into force, with corresponding people's governments at each level. China has 34 provincial-level regions, including 23 provinces, 5 autonomous regions, 4 municipalities, and 2 special administrative regions (SARs). China has a vast system of local governments featuring huge regional differences.[2] The total number of local governments stands at 36,069,[3] including 323 at prefecture level, 2851 at county level, and 32,895 at township level. There are 1340 local governments in minority-populated autonomous prefectures and autonomous counties. In actual operation, the system seems much more complex, with greater differences in the administrative level, type, and administration authority of local governments.

---

[2] Local government, in strict terms, includes all government entities except the central government, but herein refers to those below provincial level, given the close relationship between provincial governments and the central government.

[3] Source: *The Brochure of Administrative Divisions in P.R. China (2017)*, excluding regions, leagues, district offices, and neighborhoods mainly governed by resident agencies of local governments.

3.1.1   Types of Local Governments

City: Chinese cities are of the most complicated levels and types in the government system, and are classified into different levels and subtypes depending on administration relationship, importance, and scale.[4] Prefecture-level city, directly under the administration of provincial government, comes between province and county, and governs county and county-level cities in the "City Governing County" System. Except Dongguan, Zhongshan, Sansha, and Jiayuguan, the vast majority of Chinese prefecture-cities have administrative control over counties and are divided into districts. In 2016, 44.6% of Chinese cities were at prefecture level, mainly as regional centers. The governments of county-level cities and counties have same administrative status. County-level cities may be affiliated to provinces but governed by region, or led by prefecture-level cities, or attached to autonomous prefectures. Geologically close to rural areas, these governments demonstrate distinctive features of agricultural economy in their administrative management. There are several city subtypes between provinces and cities, including cities specifically designated in the state plan, subprovincial cities, and provincial capital. Cities specifically designated in the state plan have province-level power of plan decision and economic management, and they include Dalian, Qingdao, Ningbo, Xiamen, and Shenzhen. Subprovincial cities are half a level below a province and are administrated by the corresponding provincial Party committee and provincial government. Recognized by the State Council and National Development and Reform Commission as a province-level unit to implement national plans for economic and social development, subprovincial municipalities include Guangzhou, Wuhan, Harbin, Shenyang, Chengdu, Nanjing, Xi'an, Changchun, Jinan, Hangzhou, Dalian, Qingdao, Shenzhen, Xiamen, and Ningbo. Provincial capitals are home to the province-level governments of provinces and autonomous regions. Despite the same administrative status as regular prefecture-level cities, provincial capitals (excluding those recognized as subprovincial cities) have greater advantages in terms of development opportunities and resource allocation, given their special positions in economic development, politics, and culture. City-level governments, which manage local public affairs and support and drive the development of surrounding regions, represent a key component of the local governance system in China's urbanization drive.

County: Counties were created more than 2000 years ago, and this earliest regional division level is a basic unit of state structure (Tian et al. 2005). Due to huge differences and unbalanced development, counties, a powerful role in China's administrative management, often exercise differing authorities at their

---

[4] The category also includes municipalities directly under the central government. These cities, including Beijing, Tianjin, Shanghai, and Chongqing, have the same administrative rank as provinces but greater power in political operation. In addition, they have special urban management privileges and institutional advantages. Municipalities are covered briefly as only governments below province levels are discussed in this book.

own discretion, and are quite independent in developing county economy. After 1978, the number of county decreased since the progress of urbanization drive many counties to upgrade into cities or districts. A total of 229 counties have been transformed into districts during 1997–2015, including 47% in Eastern China (Zhang 2016). By 2016, China had 1535 counties, including 117 autonomous counties, 49 banners, and 3 autonomous banners. County-level governments may be ruled by the province-level governments and city-level (prefecture-level city, autonomous prefecture, subprovincial-level city) governments, or supervised by the regional administrative office.[5] The scope of their political authorities is subject to a combination of factors at different levels. County-level governments rank equivalently to 897 district governments and 361 governments at the county level. County-level governments exercise a full range of functions, including economic regulation, market supervision, social management, public service, and environmental protection.

Township: Township is the lowest administrative unit in China. In 2016, there were 32,895 townships, including 1142 ethnic autonomous townships, as well as 8105 neighborhoods (resident agencies of the same rank as that of township). For its direct-to-urban-and-rural-residents focus, township-level governments directly govern local areas, and they are the ultimate implementers of all tasks assigned by the upper-level governments, including the central government. They must exercise integrated management and total leadership and take full responsibility for all administrative affairs of areas under their jurisdiction (Zhou 2007). The township functions are not diversified, but all are closely related to residents' daily life with characteristics of social management (Xu and Gao 2013). The changes in the number of townships offer compelling evidence on the faster urbanization in China. The "merging of towns" reform (撤乡并镇*che xiang bing zhen*) from 2005 to 2015 has reduced the number by 5300 (Chu 2017). Townships mainly divide into central towns and regular ones. Central towns are home to the county-level governments and have an edge over regular townships in terms of political and economic development, and resource allocation. In the context of new urbanization, the central government has implemented new policies of power expansion of strong towns, construction of key towns, characteristic towns, comprehensive pilots of new-type urbanization, and empowered some pilot townships and regions with special authority in economic and social management. In 2017, Chinese ministries and commissions announced 3675 national key townships, 403 characteristic towns, and new-type urbanization pilot towns of all kinds.

---

[5] Refer to resident agencies of the people's governments at provincial and prefecture levels. Since the adoption of the "City Governing County" system in the 1990s, they have been knocked out and now only exist in a small number in Xinjiang and Inner Mongolia.

3.2 Social Organizations

Social organizations are divided into social groups, private nonenterprise units, and foundations as per *Regulation on Registration and Administration of Social Group, Interim Regulations on Registration Administration of Private Non-Enterprise*,[6] and *Regulation on Foundations Administration*. They can be further classified by nature and task into academic, industrial and economic, social welfare, and charity organizations, as well as community social organizations. According to official statistics, social organizations employed 7,348,000 workers in 2015,[7] and the number of social organizations set new record at 725,000 in the second quarter of 2017, including 344,000 social groups, 375,000 private nonenterprise units, and 5919 foundations.[8] However, due to varying governmental policies and long-existing dual-management institutions, social organizations in China are more complex than what the official statistics demonstrate. They exist in various forms, including social organizations registered at industry and commerce departments as legal industrial and commercial enterprises without tax exemption benefits; and social organizations registered at federations of industry and commerce of all levels as membership associations, which, together with industry associations, are called associations of industry and commerce. Some government-supported organizations need only filing instead of registration by law. These organizations, also known as government-organized nongovernmental organization (GONGO), are playing a major role in Chinese society, such as the Red Cross Society of China and China Disabled Persons Federation.

In such a vast and complicated social organization system, governments offer extra support to some social organizations: industrial associations and chambers of commerce, charitable organizations, and foundations that are gaining importance in local governance. In this wave, industrial associations and chambers of commerce, which are prioritized and most developed so far, are crucial to developing a market economy. Well-developed, independent industrial associations and chambers of commerce demonstrate strategic actions and initiative in cooperating with governments (Yu and Shen 2017).

3.3 Market Entities

Market entities in China are classified by public economy and nonpublic economy. Nonpublic economic entities, especially private enterprises, are more flexible and creative in terms of supplying public goods and public services. They can take advantage of technology, experience, and management in administering public affairs and, therefore, play a bigger role in local governance. Private

---

[6] According to Charity Law of the People's Republic of China effective in 2016, private nonenterprises are renamed social service organizations.

[7] *China Statistical Yearbook 2016*.

[8] 2017 Q2 Report of Ministry of Civil Affairs.

economy is now of vital importance to China's economic development. As of September 2017, there were 26,072,900 private enterprises across the country, accounting for 89.7% of the national total. Their registered capital amounts to 165.38 trillion yuan, 60.3% of the total amount.[9] Since the "Three in One and One Code for One License" registration reform came into full swing in 2015, the number of enterprises rocketed, mainly from the private economy. A total of 5,528,000 new enterprises were registered in 2016 alone.

With the establishment and improvement of market economy, the government policy has encouraged the development of non-public economy, which has now increased its ability to participate in industrial governance, and the sphere of public affairs has rapidly expanded. In 2005, the Chinese government first proposed relaxing control over the nonpublic economic market entry, and nonpublic capital was allowed in monopolized industries, public utilities, and infrastructures, along with more support for the nonpublic economy in finance and taxation, credit and loan, fund-raising and banking. In 2010, special documents were issued to allow the nonpublic economy in industries and fields without entry prohibition by laws, and in 2017 the Chinese government decided to simplify the approval procedures on private investment and encourage private capital to participate in Public Private Partnership (PPP) projects. In recent years, 30 policies and documents have been issued on promoting private investment in China,[10] contributing to a policy system that encourages, supports, and guides the development of the nonpublic economy.

4   OPERATING MECHANISMS OF LOCAL GOVERNANCE IN CONTEMPORARY CHINA

4.1   Mechanism of Vertical Intergovernmental Interaction[11]

Local governments, as a dominant role in local governance under the current system, are largely restrained by vertical intergovernmental relationships for their governance goals, development strategies, and ways of actions. Vertical intergovernmental relationships can be divided into central-local, province-county, and county-township. Central-local relationships structure and define the basic form and development space of local governance, while province-county and county-township relationships picture new sights of local governance to suit the transition ignited by economic and social development. By restructuring power and responsibilities, vertical intergovernmental relationships help release the vitality hidden in the institution and enable governments

---

[9] Source: www.saic.gov.cn, Analysis of National Enterprise Development Since the 18th Communist Party of China National Congress.

[10] Source: The State Council–Policies and Documents to Promote Private Investment.

[11] There is also horizontal intergovernmental interaction, which is not covered here.

at all levels to effectively and accurately respond to local residents' needs for public service and social management.

As central-local relationship defines the functions and methods to perform such functions for multilevel governments, it has a crucial impact on the form of local governance and the model of entities' behavior. Central-local relationship covers aspects such as cadre and personnel management, fiscal, and administration. It features "political centralization and administrative decentralization" and creates room for innovation through "authoritarian resilience" for local governments to reform local governance in the background of centralization of authority (Li 2009). Characteristics of political centralization are reflected in the central-local cadre and personnel management. The central government enhances its absolute control over core political and administrative cadres of next-level government through placing cadres under party supervision, position relocation, and setting the term of office, as well as determining procedures and standards on cadres' selection and appointment, in order to guarantee smooth execution of central policies and local obedience to central authority. Central-local fiscal relationship is marked by fiscal decentralization after the reform and opening-up. The decentralized fiscal system, on the one hand, limits the interference of central government in the development of local economy and society and, on the other hand, encourages local governments to develop local economies with all strengths. Decentralization also exists in central-local administrative relationships. A cascade of administrative decentralizations following the reform and opening-up becomes key methods to adjust vertical intergovernmental relationships. As evidenced by the development path of developed coastal regions, the decentralization of economic and social administration authority is an effective incentive motivating local governments in social governance and economic development, therefore, driving regional economic growth and unleashing the vitality of the system. In addition, central-local relationships display great flexibility in supporting innovation by local governments and creating room and impetus for transformation and reform in local governance.

The relationships among local governments are also part of China's vertical intergovernmental relationships, to be specific, province-county and county-township relationships (Yu et al. 2016). The restructuring of relationships between local governments today focuses mainly on adjusting vertical intergovernmental relationships below province level and redividing powers and responsibilities from the bottom-up, for the purpose of better suiting the needs for economic and social development. To start with, the province-county relations should be adjusted as booming county economy is held back by the lack of land planning, poor infrastructure construction, and cumbersome procedures to get approval from higher authorities for foreign investment projects. As a result, local governments miss many opportunities for economic growth. Local governments as represented by those in Zhejiang Province initiated a reform in which county-level governments take proactive measures to gain more administrative authorities, and province-level governments give positive responses. It effectively expands local autonomy in social and economic management and stimulates regional economic growth (Yu and Gao 2013). Next, following "placing township finances under the management of county-level governments" (乡财县管 *xiang cai xian guan*) and the "merging of towns" (撤乡并镇 *che xiang bing zhen*) reforms, township-level governments start to be troubled by "insufficient financial support and authority, but excessive tasks" in local governance. To lift up the restriction on township-level governments to provide public service due to limited authority in economic and social management, community-level governance reform should focus on county/township governments, for example, devolution to township governments (强镇扩权 *qiang zhen kuo quan*), building the national key towns (全国重点镇建设 *quanguo zhongdian zhen jianshe*), and promoting the trials in the new type of urbanization (国家新型城镇化综合试点 *guojia xinxing chenzhenhua zonghe shidian*). The county-level government may delegate to pilot township-level governments powers to approve and record projects on economic development, as well as powers of public security, employment and social security, and household management. Some even enjoy authority in economic and social management almost the same as that of county-level governments. After the reform, township-level governments have more power in economic and social management and receive more support in staffing, land quota, and special fund (Yu et al. 2016).

4.2   *Relations Between Government and Market*

A good government-market relationship is crucial to promoting effective, equitable, and sustainable regional development. It includes two aspects: correctly identifying the role of local governments and the market in regional economic development and drawing on integration strength to improve both quality and efficiency in providing public goods and services.

Both the government and the market play key roles in regional economic development. The market should leverage its strength in resource allocation, while government should foster a stable, sound, and orderly institutional environment for economic development. Local governance remains problematic: excessive government intervention in market operation, inadequate governmental supervision, defective market system, and restricted flow of production factors. It is necessary to improve the relationship in two dimensions. First, governments should leverage the market's decisive role in resource allocation and build an overarching, open, and well-organized market system to fully unleash the vitality of a market economy. Second, governments should continue administrative reform focusing on streamlining administration and delegating power and transferring governmental functions. At the same time, improper administrative intervention in the market and direct governmental participation in resource allocation should be gradually reduced and abolished. In addition, governments should play a bigger role in maintaining macroeconomic stability, improving the social credit system, enhancing market supervision, and keeping the market in order. In this way, market failures will be offset for healthy, orderly development.

In the delivery of public services and public goods, the main form of government-market relations is the cooperation between government and private enterprises through the PPP model (public-private partnership). Current policy support and ways of cooperation for PPP are already well developed. First of all, governments have reached a consensus on promoting and enhancing PPP to maximize supply of public services by private capital and on including PPP in a standardized management framework. Starting from the *Government Procurement Law of the People's Republic of China*, issued in 2002, government projects would be included in unified procurement procedures for contract-based cooperation between the government and the market. In 2014, the Ministry of Finance and National Development and Reform Commission issued respective guideline documents that support cooperation between the government and private capital. Following this, in 2015, the *Measures for the Administration of Concession for Infrastructure and Public Utilities* elaborated the method of constructing and operating infrastructures and public utilities for private capital, requirements on entering into concession agreements, and division of responsibilities for governments at different levels. It marked the formal incorporation of the PPP model into a standardized, institutionalized management framework. Second, the PPP cooperation model can bring the market players' advantages in fund, technology, and operation to best play and leverage market mechanism to supply higher quality public goods and public services and use public finance more efficiently. That's how government and private capital will form a partnership of shared risks and interests. In addition, private enterprises can have access to more investment fields and profit opportunities. Last but not least, PPP projects between government and private capital have already scaled up to gain an edge. By the end of December 2016, there have been 743 national demonstration projects of PPP with a total amount of 1.86 trillion yuan, 11,260 nationwide projects of PPP with a total amount of 13.5 trillion yuan.[12]

4.3   *Relationships Between Government and Social Organizations*

Government-social organization relationships in China can be classified into two groups: conflict and confrontation, and cooperation and interaction. According to some scholars, China has introduced the idea of classified control to social organizations based on their capability to challenge the governments' authority and the specific types of public goods they could provide (Kang and Han 2008). In terms of local governance, government-social organization relations refer to the development strategy that the government designs for social organizations and the development of a new government-social organization relationship in

---

[12] Source of data: http://jrs.mof.gov.cn/ppp/, *Quarterly Report on the Fifth Phase of Project Library of National PPP Information Platform.*

the provision of public goods and services. The major goal is to improve the delivery efficiency and quality by redefining the relations between the government and social organizations.

On the one hand, government holds two types of strategies toward social organizations' development: first, governmental strategies of control by coercive means and persuasive means, using legitimacy resources and financial resources. Second, empowerment by administrative means and market or quasi-market means, which would facilitate and encourage organizational development and service performance, to forge a path of social organizations' development in favor of social organizations that are politically inactive and professionally capable (Jing 2015). On the other hand, the government and social organizations need to establish a new partnership that embraces mutual independence and equality by clarifying the boundary between the two. The partnership shows the advantages of government to provide policy support and institutional environment for social organizations' independent practices. As a result, both government and social organizations will draw on respective strength and work in concert to manage public affairs.

The government purchase of services delivered by social organizations, as a new model of government-social organization cooperation, has been operated under standards and on a scale. First, a policy system that supports local governments to purchase public services from social organizations has been established. China released the *Government Procurement Law* in 2003 to expand government-social organization cooperation in the supply of public services and the *Guidance of General Office of the State Council for Government Procurement of Public Service from Social Entities* in 2013, which presented new opportunities for the government's purchase of services to promote the development of social organizations. Next, multiple central ministries and commissions, including the Ministry of Finance, Ministry of Civil Affairs, and State Administration of Industry and Commerce, promulgated a series of documents with specific regulations on the principles, buyers, sellers, purchasing items, procedures, and catalog, which form a sound policy system for government purchase of services. The introduction of the *Notice of the General Office of the State Council on Establishing Leader Team of Government-Procurement-of-Service Reform* in 2016 marks the start of an all-around reform in the government's purchase of services. Second, the government purchase of services has operated on a large scale. Government procurement of services has already been spread to the nationwide application, covering multiple fields, such as basic public services, social management services, industrial management and coordination services, and technical service. Lastly, government purchase of services has been normalized through opening bidding, invited bidding, competitive negotiation, and commission or contracting (Zhu and Zhu 2016). The process design places emphasis on contract management, diverse competitors, and involvement of third-party evaluation institutions, to guarantee quality and efficient supply of service procured by governments. Zhejiang

Province, for example, released the *Opinions of the Zhejiang Province People's Government Office on Implementing Government Procurement of Services from Private Enterprises and Social Organizations* in 2014 to confirm the overall requirements, goals and tasks, content, and procedures and methods for governments to procure services from social organizations. In 2015, to steadily promote government procurement of services, Zhejiang Provincial Department of Finance promulgated the Provisional Measures for the Management of Government Procurement of Services in Zhejiang, which standardizes the management of procurement budget implementation, procurement methods, project organization and implementation, contract execution and assessment management. In 2016, Zhejiang Provincial Department of Finance introduced the *Guiding Catalog of Zhejiang Government Procurement of Services from Social Organizations (2017)* that makes public, in advance, service items to be purchased by the government for the next year.

5   Characteristics and New Trends of Local Governance in Contemporary China

In contemporary China, a trend of decentralization is witnessed in its vertical government hierarchies, and the restructuring of powers and responsibilities enhances the autonomy of local governments in public affairs. The primary role of the market in resource allocation has been fully recognized, and governments depend increasingly on cooperation with market entities to deliver public goods and services. Social organizations have seen preliminary results in their development, and the social support system developed by the government has provided favorable institutional conditions for their further growth. They have participated in local governance by delivering public services purchased by governments. Though these entities and mechanisms present some problems in practical local governance, China has witnessed such features in local governance as power sharing, the provision of public services by diverse entities, and cooperative governance. In general, a diverse system of collaborative local governance is taking shape. The system, which focuses on solving problems in local governance and fulfilling the public demand, gives full play to the mechanism that prioritizes local governments and includes both market participation and social coordination, and allows all entities to share governance, benefits, and responsibilities in public affairs.

The local governance system in contemporary China has the following characteristics: (1) the local governance model is dominated by governments. In China's political and administration system, the government guides how local governance systems operate—as well as how different entities participate in and play their part in local governance—and builds the platform of cooperation. The operation and direction of the local governance system is influenced by the government's philosophy of governance and planning for local governance and its attitude toward market and social organizations. (2) China's political system, when applied to local governance, has demonstrated a strong capacity in institutional innovation and adjustment, as well as institutional flexibility. On top of regime stability and a focus on solving local governance problems, the Chinese government can adjust and improve systems and mechanisms that may hinder economic and social development in a timely and flexible manner and, thus, create broad development space for local governance. The government can adjust and reconstruct the division of responsibilities in the vertical hierarchies, delegate more powers to lower local governments, and provide more inclusiveness and flexibility to market and social entities to realize growth and promote collaborative governance. (3) Amid decentralization and multi-entity cooperation in local governance, a network for the delivery of public services is established. As local governments delegate more powers to community-level governments from the top-down, and empower the market and the society horizontally, social organizations and private capital are becoming part of local governance systems at different levels. A governance network based on cooperation is formed.

As compared with other countries, China's local governance has another important feature: the CPC has significant impact on the relations between local governments and society. In China, the CPC is not exclusive to governments, but it is also part of the society.[13] The CPC ensures powerful control over government by placing cadres under party supervision, designating them in both government agencies and the Party's working bodies, and deciding main tasks for local governance by releasing basic lines, principles, and policies. With regard to the relations between government and society, the CPC promotes the establishment of party committees in social organizations, self-governing organizations (neighborhood or village committees), and enterprises to maintain close contact with them. Government agencies may have their organizational boundaries, but "the Party can expand its footprints to self-governing organizations and social organizations where government agencies fail to set foot in, and draw on institutional resources to support them. In this way, the Party has exerted great influence on the society".[14] As a special political force, the Party can leverage its powerful organizing capacity to adjust the relations between the Party and society, thus, changing that between local governments and society. The Party, given its relations with government and society, has profound influence on local governance.

Compared to Western countries, the twin goal of the government to ensure both rapid economic development and social stability, however, has contributed to bureaucratization characteristics of local governance (He and Wang 2017). Bureaucratization refers to the fact that governments tend to control local

---

[13] By the end of 2016, China had registered 89,447,000 party members, with only a small fraction in the Party and government offices, and the vast majority in the society.

[14] Jing Yuejin: "The Party's Important Role in Primary-Level Governance," a speech given at Zhejiang University in July 2017.

governance through orders and intervene in different levels of local governance through unitary, monopolistic coordination. In fact, many areas of local governance are supervised by the government. In economic development, the government will introduce policies that aim to promote local industrial development but intervene forcefully in the operation of a market economy. In social governance, self-governing organizations in urban and rural areas, for example, neighborhood and village committees, are subject to profound influence of government agencies in their organizational functions and operation, and even become an extension of government agencies in the nongovernment sector. At the same time, the government will also adopt administrative means to quickly build social organizations desirable to the government or to intervene in their operation. As a result, these social organizations will run in a similar way to that of the government.

Amid quicker globalization and the transformation in the economic and social development, China has developed some new trends in local governance. First, local governments will play a more important dominant role in local governance. As China incorporates itself further into the globalization architecture and enters a deep-water zone in domestic reform, local governance will encounter greater challenges. To better cope with crisis and challenges, and deepen reform smoothly, local governments need to strengthen regional intergovernmental cooperation and improve top-level design, and enhance their capacity in comprehensive administration and risk response. In local governance, in particular, they need to break through the fetters of vested interest, strike a balance in relations between government and market and between government and society, and promote sound cooperation in local governance. Second, social organizations and market entities will play a bigger role in local governance. With a favorable environment, social organizations will embrace new opportunities in strengthening their role in local governance. The social organizational system that improves at a quicker pace will fully mobilize social resources to guarantee much better delivery of diverse public services. Rapid progress will be made in the capacity of market entities to deliver public goods and services through the PPP model. At the same time, private capital will be introduced to improve the efficiency of public infrastructure construction and public service systems, thus, benefiting both local governance and the development of market entities. Third, the booming modern science and technologies, in particular, the advent of the information technology revolution, will cause massive changes in government functions and their performance, as well as the operation of local governance networks made up of governments, market entities, social organizations, and the public. The use of technologies will become a key measure for local governance level and efficiency. Backed by new technologies, such as big data, "Internet +," cloud computing, and artificial intelligence, local governance will become more intelligent and well targeted. In the information era, an array of factors including growing public awareness, unimpeded access to information, the integration of nongovernment actors, and new governing ideas of the government will push for a different mechanism for delivering public services and promote functional changes and organizational adjustments of governments. Fourth, local governance will focus on heightening the public sense of gain. With increasing social diversity and the growing demand of the public, local governments should think more of public demand and adjust their processes and the model of social governance. At the same time, they need to introduce participatory governance by giving full play to social organizations and individuals, so as to increase public satisfaction.

6   ARRANGEMENT AND STRUCTURE OF THE BOOK

This book is divided into nine parts, which consists of 33 chapters, and covers a wide range of important subject matters, such as governance in the Chinese context, local government, civil society organizations and mass media, grassroots governance, citizen engagement, internet governance, social equity and governance, urbanization and governance, and environmental and energy governance.

Part I gives a brief introduction to the local governance in China and discusses the development and new research trends of governance theory in contemporary China. The introduction depicts a general picture of components, characteristics, and the latest trends of China's local governance and briefly presents the structure of the handbook. The overview gives an introduction of governance theory and a comprehensive description of its application in contemporary China at the local level, the critical role of the local governance in China's national governance system, and major research areas and topics on China's local governance study.

Parts II and III introduce the local governance in contemporary China from the perspective of actor and agency, including local governments and civil society organizations, among others. Local governments discuss local government innovation and its implication for reshaping the relationship between government, market, and society; the relations between central and local governments from the perspective of administrative and fiscal systems; characteristics of local cadres and their strategy choices under China's personnel system; as well as the origin and evolution of Chinese local development state. As for social organizations, it explores the development of business associations and philanthropic organizations, and their main functions and the role of mass media in reshaping local governments and its limitations.

Parts IV–VI deal with China's practice in local governance by providing cases of urban and rural community governance, citizen engagement, conflicts in the political and governance systems, and internet governance. Grassroots governance focuses on the interaction among local governments, social organizations, communities, and citizens in urban community governance; the origins and development of villagers' self-government and its influence on rural governance; the development of rural governance from village election to structural adjustment and to procedural standardization, and the corresponding influence; and social governance in public good provision and corresponding effect factors. Civic engagement discusses the following topics: consultative democracy as a new form of local public policymaking under an authoritarian regime and its impact on local governance; the approaches for business associations represented by local private enterprises pursuing policy advocacy and its consequences; the approaches for citizens to participate in public policymaking and the role of societal actors in promoting accountability of local governments. The part of contentious politics and governance covers the influence of the conflicts between citizens and the government on local governance as well as the influence of internet on government behavior and state-society relationship in local governance.

Parts VII–IX discuss the challenges and responses of local governance in contemporary China, including social equality and local governance, urbanization and governance, local energy policy and environmental governance. The part about social equality and local governance explores the topics including inequality and poverty and the responsive strategy applied by local governments, social organizations, and citizens; the collaboration, competition, and confrontation among local governments, social organizations, and citizens in medicare and health policy; labor relation and collaborative governance; educational inequality, and its reform and policy innovation. The part on urbanization and local governance discusses the role of local governments in the shift from state-led urbanization to collaborative governance, and its new model of cooperation in the market and society; PPPs and public finance; and conflicts in land use and the transformation of local governance. The part about environment and energy governance explores local energy policy implementation, local energy policy design and climate governance, climate change challenges and China's responses, and environmental pollution and protests.

REFERENCES

Agrawal, A., J.K. Fairbank, and A. Feuerwerker. 1983. *The Cambridge History of China, Vol. 13: Republican China, 1912–1949. Part 2.* Cambridge: Cambridge University Press.

Chu, T. 2017. Big strategies for small towns from a new perspective: Reasons for backward development in small towns of China and development strategy study. *Urban and Rural Development*, (11): 33–37.

He, Y., and G. Wang. 2017. Order in transitional China and its institutional logic. *Social Sciences in China* 38(2): 56–75.

Huang, P.C.C. 1993. "Public sphere"/"Civil society" in China? The third realm between state and society. *Modern China, 19*(2), 216–240.

Jing, Y. 2015. Between control and empowerment: Governmental strategies towards the development of the nonprofit sector in China. *Asian Studies Review* 39(4): 589–608.

Kang, X., and H. Han. 2008. Graduated controls: The state-society relationship in contemporary China. *Modern China* 34(1): 36–55.

Li, Y. 2009. Multi-Level "collusion" in China's local governance. *Beijing Cultural Review*, (6): 23–26.

Lieberthal, K. 2003. *Governing China: From Revolution through Reform*. New York: W.W. Norton & Company.
Montinola, G., Y. Qian, and B.R. Weingast. 1995. Federalism, Chinese style: The political basis for economic success in China. *World Politics* 48(1): 50–81.
Qian, Y., and C. Xu. 1993. The M-form hierarchy and China's economic reform. *European Economic Review* 37(2–3): 541–548.
Rowe, W.T. 1993. The problem of "civil society" in late imperial China. *Modern China* 19(2): 139–157.
Shirk, S. 1993. *The Political Logic of Economic Reform in China*. Berkeley, CA: University of California Press.
Tsou, Tang. 1986. *The Cultural Revolution and Post-Mao Reforms*. Chicago, IL: The University of Chicago Press.
Tian, S., H. Luo, and W. Zeng. 2005. *The Introduction to Chinese Administration Divisions*. Beijing: Peking University Press.
Wang, M. 2013. *The Introduction to Non-Governmental Organizations*. Beijing: Social Sciences Academic Press.
Wei, J. 2008. The course of Chinese reform in economic system and tasks for different stage: Celebrating the 30th anniversary of reform and opening-up. *Social Science Front*, 154(4): 9–18.
Xu, Y., and B. Gao. 2013. *Local Government*. Beijing: Higher Education Press.
Yang, X., and H. Lai. 2009. *The Revival of the Local*. Beijing: Social Sciences Academic Press.
Yu, J., and X. Gao. 2013. Redefining decentralization: Devolution of administrative authority to county governments in Zhejiang province. *Australian Journal of Public Administration* 72(3): 239–250.
Yu, J., I. Li, and Y. Shen. 2016. Rediscovering intergovernmental relations at the local level: The devolution to township governments in Zhejiang Province. *China Review*, 16(2), 1–26.
Yu, J., and Y. Shen. 2017. Adaptive cooperation: The strategic reform of the government-social organizations relations since the 18th CPC National Congress. *Journal of Political Science* 3: 34–41, 126.
Zhang, Y. 2016. Analysis of the history and current status of country-to-district-transformation. *Legal System and Society*, 24: 216–218.
Zheng, Y. 2013. *De Facto Federalism in China*. Beijing: The Oriental Press.
Zhou, F. 2006. A decade of tax-sharing: The system and its evolution. *Social Sciences in China* 6: 100–115, 205.
Zhou, F., and M. Tan. 2014. *Central-Local Relationship in Contemporary China*. Beijing: China Social Sciences Press.
Zhou, P. 2007. *Local Governments in Contemporary China*. Beijing: People's Publishing House.
Zhu, Q., and C. Zhu. 2016. *Governmental Purchase of Public Services from A Social Organization Perspective*. Beijing: China Social Sciences Press.
Zi, Z. 2015. *The Responsibility of Wealth and Evolution of Capitalism: Revelation of a Century's Development of American Philanthropy*. Shanghai: Shanghai Joint Publishing House.

PART I

Governance in the Chinese Context

CHAPTER 2

The Applicability of Governance Theory in China: A Novel Approach

Jianxing Yu and Shizong Wang

1   INTRODUCTION

As an influential theory of social science, governance theory has played a prominent role in development studies over the past two decades. Because this theory originates from the Western society, Chinese academics have disputed over its applicability in China, which has essentially different conditions in democracy, rule of law, and civil society from the Western society. It is argued in this chapter that Chinese scholars should neither take its applicability for granted based on the strong solicitude for the reality of China nor conclude that the governance theory is not applicable in China based on rigid structural analysis. Jessop's Strategic-Relational Approach (1996) presents an enlightenment of practical value that actors' choice of strategies and actions needs investigating based on an objective understanding of the structural background. Under the existing political-administrative system of fragmented authoritarianism, China's civil society has already developed into "a dynamic force outside the state system," entitled to certain participation in public affairs. Such a novel understanding is of great significance in developing both the study and practice of governance in China.

Governance theory has played a vital role in development studies and exerted a far-reaching effect on the international academic arena of social science over the past two decades. In Western countries, governance theory has grown into a new choice after statism and neoliberalism, and governance (good governance) has been treated as a possible road to modern state building in non-Western countries. The birth of governance theory has attracted immediate

J. Yu • S. Wang (✉)
School of Public Affairs, Zhejiang University, Hangzhou, Zhejiang, China
e-mail: yujianxing@zju.edu.cn

© The Author(s) 2019
J. Yu, S. Guo (eds.), *The Palgrave Handbook of Local Governance in Contemporary China*, https://doi.org/10.1007/978-981-13-2799-5_2

attention from Chinese researchers, and the correlation studies in China start almost at the same time as that in the West. With Chinese institutional reforms in mind, many scholars promptly introduce governance theory and apply it to studies of Chinese administration reforms and political institution changes. A heated dispute naturally arises over whether governance theory, which originates from Western context, can be applied to China, a country with apparently different conditions in democracy, rule of law, and civil society that has long been a goal for non-Western countries like China to obtain in their modern state building. A passionate concern over Chinese reality is understandable, yet it cannot be taken as adequate grounds for the disregard of proper academic reasoning that would lead to casual interpretation of the theory and misleading practice. Conversely, an absolute denial of applicability of governance theory in China merely for the sake of structural analysis, though logically justifiable, may presuppose an implication of rigid structure (such as power structure, institutional structure, and social structure), which would possibly halt the development of economy and society. Therefore, methodological innovation is required for the study on applicability of governance theory in China. In this chapter, we take Jossep's *Strategic-Relational Approach* and attempt to conduct a comprehensive and objective demonstration of the heated dispute over whether governance is applicable in China, with the view to exhibiting revelations valuable for both study and practice.

2   Dispute over Applicability of Governance in China

As Peters (2000) argued, "governance could be said to be shorthand for the predominant view of government in the *Zeitgeist* of the late twentieth century." This suggests that the impact of governance reaches beyond Europe and America. China virtually keeps pace with the West on the popularity of governance theory. Many Chinese scholars show substantial concern with the reform of Chinese institutions, so they introduce governance theory at the first opportunity and apply it to research on China's administrative reform and vicissitudes of China's political system. With the publishing of collection of papers *Zhili yu shanzhi* (*Governance and Good Governance*) (edited by Yu Keping) in 2000, governance has soon grown into a "famous school" in China. Driven by the study logic since the early 1990s, quite a few Chinese scholars have naturally and closely related governance with both state building and reforms of political-administrative systems. According to Kang and Han (2005), the introduction of Western civil society theory and the study on China's civil society serves as an evident manifestation of Chinese academics' increasing attention to the relation between the state and society in line with the ongoing economic reforms and highlighted social issues. A new paradigm places emphasis on a bottom-up approach rather than top-down (Kang and Han 2005). Due to such a shared academic orientation, governance theory has mixed well with the study of China's civil society immediately after its introduction (Wang 2008). Chinese scholars tend to stress the normative value of governance more than their Western counterparts. In light of the abovementioned, governance in China has been endowed with a strongly "teleological" connotation, namely, expecting to achieve good governance involving transformations of politics, society, and administration. It seems to be just such expectations that have directed governance study toward local levels in recent years and have as well inspired great enthusiasm of Chinese scholars in governance theory.

On the opposing side, a number of researchers take a rather skeptical and cautious attitude toward governance in China, which can be tracked in a pen conversation titled *Zhongguo li "shanzhi" you duoyuan* (*How Far Is China from "Good Governance"*), *Zhongguo xingzheng guanli* (*Chinese Public Administration*), No. 9, 2001. Such suspicion can also be located in the essay series by Zang Zhijun et al., *Fansi yu chaoyue—jiedu zhongguo yujin xia de zhili lilun* ("Reflection and Transcendence—Interpretations of Governance Theory in China's Context"), *Lilun wencui* (*Theory Quintessence*), No. 4, 2003. In this series, Zang (2003) holds that governance essentially depends on two prerequisites, that is, mature pluralistic management bodies cooperating with each other and the spirit of democracy, coordination, and compromise. Liu (2003) argued that without fully developed modern politics as a guarantee, an untimely appeal for transferring state powers back to the society may again lead China into a trap of political romanticism. Yang (2002) has mentioned that it is just like building a castle in the air to solve government failure or market failure through governance wherever modern state building is far from complete.

It appears to these scholars that the application of governance to China would likely commit a fundamental error in the political-administrative development, for, they argue, China still has a long and tough way to go to become a modern state (or perfect the political system) and to cultivate civil society and citizenship. Though rarely given a frontal mention, such concerns may also haunt the advocators but be represented in other forms in their own favor. Their study may be categorized into certain theory orientations, viewed as indirect responses to the suspicion of Zang, Yang et al., and listed as follows: the first focuses on the development of nongovernmental organizations (NGOs), certain third sectors, and civil society to shoulder governance of public affairs (He 2007; Chen and Ma 2004; etc.); the second proposes governance be achieved by reforms on communication mechanism, as well as hierarchical structure within the government (Xu 2004; Li and Zheng 2007; etc.); the third is a combination of the above two—governance can't be achieved without mutual interaction among bodies with diverse interests (Liu 2007; Yu 2008). The orientations vary in their analysis and emphasis, perhaps due to a vague notion of governance and a mass of complex theories. However, it is self-evident that, being aware of the differences between China and developed countries, these scholars are trying to search for some practical theory for governance development in China.

Obviously, some Chinese scholars have shaped unique denotations of governance. First, as an essential premise, civil society is supposed to develop to achieve governance in China, which is an orientation rarely seen in the West but frequently mentioned among Chinese scholars. Second, governance also calls for corresponding reforms on structure and system within the government, which in the West is known as "state rebuilding." To be different, Chinese scholars focus more on government initiative in reforms beneficial to social cooperation, also being a representation of their hidden worry about "the state."

3   THE STRATEGIC-RELATIONAL APPROACH

Comparatively, the advocators' excessive expectations of governance unconsciously draw them away from an overall investigation over its applicability in China; the opponents, who place too much emphasis on structural analysis, may conclude that China, compared with Western countries, lacks essential conditions for governance, such as an advanced democratic system, a sound legal system, and a mature civil society.

The advocators have to admit that relevant system reform is required to guarantee civil society and citizenship, and that social support serves as a motivation for governmental reform, and a logic cycle, thus, comes into being: governance may bring a mature civil society, which in turn is regarded as a prerequisite for governance. In other words, a developed civil society serves as both the basis and the product of modern state building. Frankly speaking, such a logic cycle is not uncommon. If reasonable, it's at least a proof that just a cause-effect description may fail to see how governance relates to a civil society and state building. As for the opponents, on the one hand, they may fail to recognize that the so-called conditions are what China aims to gain through governance[1]; on the other hand, actors, in their perspectives, are not so competent as to break through the so-called fixed structural background. Therefore, governance inapplicability can easily be justified only by intuitive reasoning that China bears no such political and administrative system as in Western developed countries and has not yet formed an elementary paradigm for democracy and public administration, let alone a better one for governance, and that China even has no clear description in the existence of civil society, much less a mature one as it is in the West, and so on. However, provided that any behavior is determined by structure, how can power or social structure sustain its progress in the end, since it is behaviors that structural changes only depend on? This naturally constitutes another logical deadlock.

---

[1] With regard to the objective of governance in non-Western countries, just as Chhotray and Stoker (2009, p. 97) mention, "since the 1990s, the idea of 'governance' has come to occupy the centre stage in thinking of development. ... Development studies has been described as an 'unusual enterprise,' for it appears to be committed at the same time to the principle of 'difference,' in treating the 'Third World' as different from the West, and that of 'similarity,' in development's mission to make the peoples and processes of the developing world more like that of the developed world."

Rather than a sharp opposition in values, the previous two views reflect their own judgments on how China's civil society is developing and where governmental reforms will lead. Anyhow, neither a logic cycle nor rigid structural analysis should be included in governance study. Hereby, an introduction of Jessop's points is of great value, reading: the state is guaranteed by its power, while power goes dependently hand in hand with economy and civil society. In some developing countries, balance between strong state power and other forces has exerted an active effect on economy and civil society. However, such discussions are unfortunately weakened because they lack an agreed division in "strong" and "weak" and risk falling into a trap of circular demonstration. Accordingly, a *Strategic-Relational Approach* can be employed as a potential solution—taking into account the variability in state capacity with specific policies and phases (Jessop 2002). Rigid structural analysis and ignorance of agency and strategy may prevent any possible development. Jessop points out that, unlike rigid structural analysis, the *Strategic-Relational Approach*, alternatively, stresses corresponding strategies implied by the structure, or, analyze strategies in terms of the structural form, content, and performance. Thus, actions in question can be studied under a restricted structural background brought by the employed strategies. Also, the approach can be understood on two levels: on the one hand, rather than absolute or unconditional, structure is often restricted by strategy to be ever changing with time, space, and agency; on the other hand, actors are often so self-reflective as to hunt for new strategies based on a second identification of their roles and benefits under a restricted structure (Jessop 1996).

The *Strategic-Relational Approach* displays a practical methodology: actors' choice of strategy and performance should rely on an objective analysis of the specific structural background, which allows a certain degree of "flexibility" instead of total rigidness. According to Sun (2004, p. 26), social network in general serves as a synonym for governance and the most direct reflection of its essence and features, and citizenship and participation in governance are preconditions for the network. To be specific in China, the issues to be discussed should involve both the potential development for the unsound civil society under the existing system and its chance in participating public affairs and influencing the political-administrative system. Just as Grindle (2004) states that it is of greater significance to identify "what's working rather than focusing solely on governance gaps." Due to the dynamics and concreteness, it is impossible to fully interpret the current system and civil society just through a theoretical deduction, which, however, is indispensable for the *Strategic-Relational Approach* to describe the status quo and potential development of China's civil society, as well as the possible citizen participation under the existing political-administrative system.

4   Chinese Civil Society: "A Dynamic Force Outside the State System"

As soon as governance was introduced, the emerging civil society's prominent role in governance changes was acknowledged in Yu (2005), followed by its combination with a great deal of study on governance in China. Obviously, a clarification on whether there is a civil society in China and how it will develop and function, among other things, has a far-reaching effect on the issue of governance applicability in China. According to Yu (2005), it is "governance" rather than "being governed" if the social management is conducted by CSOs (Citizen Social Organizations) or operated in the form of cooperation between the government and CSOs. More directly, Han (2008) points out that the concept of governance will not be of real significance without participation of independent social organizations.

To free civil society from its long-standing implication of being "against the state," Deng and Jing (2002) put forward the benign interaction between the state and civil society, and they further justify necessary intervention of the state for its role in alleviating contradictions and conflicts within civil society. Gan (1998) argues against the popular one-sided emphasis on extreme opposition (the so-called civil society vs. state) but instead calls for mutual promotion between the state and civil society. Tang (1996) holds that rather than a zero-sum game, reform on state-society relations should be targeted for a win-win situation, that is, a more developed nation and a more harmonious society. Besides, Gu and Wang (2005) illustrate civil society in China as corporatism. Since then, it is the interpretation of the interaction-cooperation theory as a development path and corporatism as its relation with the state that has dominated the study of China's civil society.

Corporatism is a special kind of social-political process, in which a limited number of monopolies with different functional interests bargain in the output of public policies with the government. In other words, under corporatism, the formulation of public policies is subject somewhat to a particular structure, noncompetitive but hierarchical, composed of a limited number of social organizations with diverse functions and obligations. Such a structure, even if not state-established, enjoys absolute authority within a certain domain but may in turn be somewhat controlled by the state in terms of requirements, appointment of leaders, application for supports, and so on (Schmitter 1979). Evidence is not difficult to locate for the description of China's civil society in terms of corporatism. As is shown in Solinger's study, the newly born business class with city economy, since reform and opening up, is still dependent on bureaucracy for survival, and its increasing expectation for independence is constantly dismissed by a haunting concern that a totally free competition may drive them away from where they are (Solinger 1992). White's case study on Xiaoshan of Zhejiang Province also exemplifies that China's civil society should be more corporate than communal. Social organizations in Xiaoshan are unqualified as "pressure groups" or "interest groups" due to their failure in achieving full independence and their functional dependence on the bureaucratic protectors.

To some extent, they do take effect in the structural construction and policy implementation on behalf of their members; however, "from the viewpoint of social organizations, there is a trade-off between autonomy; their leaders often feel that the best way to increase their influence is to go closer to, and more intermeshed with state and Party organs, compromising their autonomy in the process" (White 1993).

However, corporatism of China's civil society gets involved in a twofold attack. One is Wakeman's denial of the existence of China's civil society by arguing that none of the Chinese NGOs are autonomic. Since the beginning of the twentieth century, despite the expansion of NGOs in the form of village communities, trade associations, townsmen associations, and so on, they have not yet been endowed with corresponding civil rights. Besides, suffering from an ever-growing social constraint by the government, a majority of Chinese citizens are drawn away from their due rights and duties. Thus, it's impractical to apply the theory of civil society to China since there is no similar Western-style civil society that is corresponding to the state (Wakeman 1993). Unger and Chan (1995) also construe Chinese social organizations as state corporatism (of an Eastern Asian model), that is, corporatism-directed but state-controlled, as some organizations actually perform as the extension or "transmission belt" of the state under the veil of corporatism. On the other hand, case studies on China's civil society by researchers feature some of the organizations, like Wenzhou Chamber of Commerce, as being more pluralistic than corporate However, pluralism is not a sign of independence of NGOs from the government; on the contrary, by means other than laws or regulations—for example, through chambers of commerce—the state even extends its intervention into NGOs to ensure their political loyalty (Wang 2005).

In terms of the complex status quo in China, corporatism, together with its parallel theories, appears to be Utopian because of the necessity of a strict boundary between the state and society, and a mechanical copy of such theories may consequently lead to a conclusion of there being no civil society in China. Chinese NGOs fail to meet the minimum standard of independence for civil society by Charles. Taylor—social organizations are free from the state authority.[2] Saich (2009, pp. 414–415) points out that, with no satisfying concept system ever created, to some extent, Chinese empirical pegs are being tried to fit Western theoretical holes, and the resulting analysis, though of some value, is far from enough for reality in China. Thus, some novel framework is required.

Having reached an early consensus on the lack of independence in Chinese NGOs, Chinese researchers introduced to their study "interaction-cooperation"

---

[2] Reference to Charles Taylor. "shimin shehui de moshi" (Modes of Civil Society). In: J.C. Alexander and Deng Zhenglai (eds.). *Guojia yu shimin shehui—yizhong shehui lilun de yanjiu lujing* (*State and Civil Society—A Research Approach for Social Theory*). Beijing: zhongyang bianyi chubanshe, 2002. In fact, Unger, Walkman, Kang, et al. have denied the existence of civil society in China.

theory and attached great importance to the theories such as "the state in society" or "state and society in coordination". Being a long-standing complex, developing independence is given priority in the construction of China's civil society. In the view of Deng and Jing (2002), such construction may undergo two phases: the preliminary action is to achieve a dual structure of the state and civil society; the second is a phase of further improvement, in which NGOs strive for participation on the basis of independence to exercise an active impact on government decision-making via a variety of means. Similarly, the two phases are defined by Yu (1999) as formation and maturation. Independence is being viewed as the landmark of the initial success in a civil society and matches the assumption that a dual structure is a prerequisite for a civil society, the relative independence of which then acts as a precondition for citizen participation (Yu and Zhou 2008). Therefore, chances are slim that any promising development of civil society can be achieved through an attempt of the state-society binary differentiation, which will risk arousing a deadlock of structural rigidness.

Objectively speaking, an insistent judgment by independence on current China's civil society can only result in a pessimistic end. Even in European and American countries, the binary differentiation was an ever-gone product of a particular historical era and will never appear at present when the state and society mutually assimilate; even studies on their clear boundary are neglected in some developed and developing countries. In case studies on low-income countries, Migdal discusses the disadvantages of the state-centered theory and proposes improving both "stated-centered" and "society-centered" theories by understanding the conflict, compromise, and promotion in-between instead of being inclined to either, the limitations of which are also dealt with in their analysis. Unchanged is neither the state nor society, both of which will take a new form in their structures, goals, regulations, and supporters (Migdal 2001, p. 57). After analyzing the history and reality of the civil society in developed countries, Baker (1998) argues against the structural achievability for a normalized argument of civil society being totally independent and calls for a careful redocking between the core of democracy and civil society. Based on empirical studies on the functional role of the US civil society, Uphoff and Krishna (2004) regard the civil society to be a social buffer zone and transition layer bridging the state and citizens, and that between state institutions and civil society no clear boundary lies. A variety of institutions consist of a "continuum." There is a huge fuzzy zone between the core layer of the state and NGOs that are highly self-autonomous, besides which many of the institutions bear dual functions and characteristics of either.

The *Strategic-Relational Approach* can possibly survive in Chinese state-society relation study, given the ignorance of a strict state-society boundary. An innovative insight by Ma is to shift to a more positive attitude toward how NGOs perform as a dynamic force outside the state system from whether they have been totally independent (Ma 2002). Case studies on the performance and effect of Chinese NGOs further provide a possible path for China's civil society of "developing through participation." It is the participation in public affairs that goes before and later strengthens its independence. Rather than a by-product of politics and ideology, system improvement is produced only by game between the state and civil society (Yu and Zhou 2008). Such an argument can not only get out of the trap of the binary state-society differentiation but also avoid a logic cycle of demonstrations among applicability of governance theory, modern state building, and civil society development.

In view of this, it can be initially asserted that already-existing social forces besides the state will omit the necessity to dwell on whether there is a totally independent civil society in China. Therefore, only governance inapplicability shouldn't be accounted for the temporary dependence on the government of social organizations that are likely to develop into a potential but irreplaceable force. Since China's civil society grows through participation, the realization of which depends on the government, how can social organizations effectively participate in public affairs under the existing political-administrative system? Correspondingly, the strategic cooperation between government and social organizations is well worth taking to demonstrate.

5   CITIZEN PARTICIPATION UNDER CHINESE POLITICAL-ADMINISTRATIVE SYSTEM

The Chinese political system is often characterized as totalitarian, authoritarian, and so on. Totalism refers to a basic principle of the state's governing society, according to which, the state as a living unity composed of all social members justifies their social membership and meaning of being, and, thus, calls for their absolute obedience, loyalty, devotion, and sacrifice of their own interests or even lives for its sake. In all, "totalism means the power of political institutions are free to invade and control the guiding ideology of any social class or area" (Tsou 1994, p. 3). Under the authoritarian system, citizens and social organizations should also strictly comply with the government, social control is often realized with repressive means, and the state authority even infiltrates citizens' personal freedom. But different from totalism, where the state and society are totally unified, authoritarianism may allow a certain degree of ideological divergence, as well as independence of some social organizations, though the state occasionally acts as a controller or substitute for society (Ting 1999, pp. 28–29). Undoubtedly, an assumption of totalism and authoritarian characteristics being immutable is enough to assert that governance is not applicable in China. However, what should be taken into account is the variability in the state capacity with specific policies and phases.

Even totalism or authoritarianism itself exists in an ever-changing reality. On the one hand, China, once a total state-society unity with highly integrated politics, economy, and society, has undergone two major changes since the reform and opening up: the first is more freedom in economy brought by marketization; the other the initial development of democratic politics, especially grassroots democracy. In the market-oriented reform, individuals as consumers are entitled to a certain degree of free choice in lifestyles or cultures, among other things, which opens the door for the development of social organizations, as well as for individual participation in community-based public affairs (Jia and Huang 2007). As for members within certain organizations, more participation can be realized through democratic consultation, public hearings, councils, and so on. On the other hand, the bureaucratic administrative system with a totalitarian or authoritarian tendency is not that monolithic to destroy. The functional separation among levels of institutions and the usual tension between them often result in dispersion of decision-making, then bargaining for disputes, and finally a fragmented hierarchical structure, which Lieberthal (1988) describes as *fragmented authoritarianism*. According to Wang (2006), the government has brought social communities under its total control through its direct or indirect interference in resources that social communities rely on, as well as drafting relevant laws and regulations, such as *shehui tuanti denji guanli tiaoli* (*Regulations on Registration of Social Communities*) and *minban feiqiye danwei denji guanli zanxing tiaoli* (*Provisional Regulations on Registration of Private Non-enterprise Units*), aided by the intrinsic permeability of its political-administrative system. Meanwhile, grassroots NGOs have won a lease of life out of fragmentation in the hierarchical structure, which is supported by his demonstration that a negative bureaucratic competition makes it possible for nongovernmental environmental organizations to play an active role in *A Suspension of Nu River Hydropower development* and *the EIA Storm (Environmental Impact Assessment)* (Wang 2006). Possibly, the "dynamic force outside the state system" can participate in public affairs even in a strongly totalitarian or authoritarian society, which confirms an important argument of Gray's, that is, the civil society can be associated with either democracy or authoritarianism (Gray 1993).

As is shown in all previous studies, social groups in China are deprived of necessary autonomy or at most bear the so-called embedded autonomy because of the state's long-lasting strict control. In the study of Kang and Han (2005), the government strategy for social organizations may vary from ban to indulgence based on their challenge capacity and provisions of public goods. The state now shifts its attention only to "political field" and "public domain" from an all-around control over economic activities and citizens' personal affairs, known as *fenlei kongzhi* (graduated control), a basic strategy for public control by the state, under which the state overall intervention is replaced with a limited degree of freedom in economic and individual activities, followed by a number of social organizations springing up. With regard to provisions of public goods, the state begins to distribute its responsibilities among social organizations in spite of their trivial role of making good omissions and deficiencies. The Graduated Control System, in the negative sense, illustrates a dilemma faced by China's civil society and citizen participation, but optimistically, it's an implication of the state permission to a certain degree of autonomy by social organizations as well as its expectation of intensive cooperation with them to promote its capability and interests (such as legitimacy, economic growth, and public service). Moreover, together with the state and the society, the study on their relation is somewhat abstract, while, as a concrete manifestation of the state authority, the government shoulders diverse interests and identities at all levels and sectors. As for NGOs, central or local government has its own inclinations. For example, the central government may put more emphasis on their political loyalty, whereas local government may attach more importance to their role in economic growth or public service (Wang 2005). Thus, the bureaucratic fragmentation is likely to appear between the central and local government. Given certain independence, local government can possibly provide chances for citizen participation.

Corresponding to totalitarian or authoritarian politics, the Chinese administrative system tends to be centralized rather than decentralized. However, since reform and opening up, local government and organizations have been the creative driving force for institutional innovation in China. For example, the contract responsibility system originated from among the populace; in Wenzhou, where Chinese private-owned economy originated, decentralized market economic groups act as pioneers of the economic system reform, followed by the local government as the secondary.

Meanwhile, local government is subject to higher levels or central government, giving rise to some new concepts in the field, such as *yalixing tizhi* (pressurized system) or "political contract system". A pressurized system originally refers to the management of quantifying and delegating tasks and a materialized evaluation system, which an elementary political institution (usually county or town) employs to achieve economic catchup and the indicators appointed by its higher authorities (Rong et al. 1998, p. 1). Accordingly, party committees and governments at all levels commonly quantify, decompose, and appoint to the lower levels or individuals various economic tasks and indicators, and those who perform better within a specified period of time will be rewarded with political or economic incentives. Since the "one-vote veto" system is often taken to evaluate the major indicators, organizations at all levels actually fulfill their tasks under the pressure of such an evaluation system. Apart from its role in economic tasks, in the control over lower levels by the senior, the pressurized system frequently works in other forms, such as "one-vote veto for security production," "one-vote veto for serious accidents," and "one-vote veto for group petitions". However, just as is shown in the study by Shi et al. (2002, pp. 33–34), since the 1980s when local government won its financial independence from the central government, its own pursuit of interests has been a substitute for the previous 100% obedience to central policies. Saich (2009) also agrees that the economic reform has exerted a far-reaching influence on the Chinese system, weakening the control of government over economy, increasingly strengthening the role of market in configuration and production, giving local government more control over local economy, and distributing economic prosperity.

Comprehensively speaking, the current political-administrative system in China does differ a lot from that in the West. Nevertheless, neither the exotic totalism or authoritarianism nor the local pressure-type system is sufficient to cover all characteristics of the Chinese system. Fragmentation within the unified political-administrative system provides space for citizen participation. Possibly developed from the private domain created in the market-oriented process, a "public domain" between the state and individuals prepare objects for participation. Despite stressing on the value of social network, governance is never a purely society-centered hypothesis (Stoker 2007) and, thus, likely to break through the system limitations. More importantly, with certain independence and especially driven by a tough task of public service, local government will show its long-lasting power in carrying out new policies and cooperating with other social forces.

6   Conclusion

Under the *Strategic-Relational Approach*, the chapter demonstrates Chinese NGOs as being "a dynamic force outside the state system," analyzes the possibility of citizen participation under the existing political-administrative system, and argues for governance applicability in China. The conclusion, albeit basically theoretical, is sufficient to deny governance inapplicability in China (but admittedly insufficient for an overall demonstration of its applicability). In spite of that, we argue that currently neither the state-society relation nor the political-administrative system should necessarily exclude citizen participation in China, and the realignment is likely to appear or even has appeared among the government, society, and market. It should be noted that more factual elements should and must be taken into consideration to fully demonstrate governance applicability in China, as well as its limitations.

The *Strategic-Relational Approach* has important revelations for both the study and practice of governance in China. First, governance researchers in China should be fully aware of the characteristics and facts in the transitional period instead of eclipsing the truth to conform with literally popular concepts. On the one hand, since NGOs unquestionably depend on the government in a political system similar to authoritarian integration, governance actors in non-Western countries shouldn't be assessed by Western standards of communalism, pluralism, and social corporatism. On the other hand, because of the complexity between actors, it is necessary to allow "exceptions," even from the popularly acceptable concepts or analysis in certain non-Western countries, and to interpret from both angles of structure and agency to identify space and opportunities for governance. Second, in practice, as Grindle (2004) has pointed out, governance in developing countries should not only explain what "must be done" but also accept "a more nuanced understanding of the evolution of institutions and government capabilities; being explicit about trade-offs and priorities in a world in which all good things cannot be pursued at once." In other words, only by adopting initiative and appropriate strategies can governance be effectively applied in China to facilitate modern state building.

REFERENCES

Baker, G. 1998. "Civil Society and Democracy: The Gap between Theory and Possibility." *Politics*, 18(2): 81–87.

Chen, Shengyong, and Bin Ma. 2004. "Wenzhou minjian shanghui de zizhu zhili zhidu fenxi" [An institutional analysis of Wenzhou Chamber of Commerce's self-governance: A typical study on Wenzhou's Clothing Chamber of Commerce]. *Guanli shijie* [*Management World*], 2004 (12): 31–49.

Chhotray, V., and G. Stoker. 2009. *Governance Theory and Practice: A Cross-Disciplinary Approach*. London: Palgrave Macmillan.

Deng, Zhenglai, and Jing Yuejin. 2002. "Jiangou zhongguo de shiminshehui" ["Constructing Civil Society in China"]. In: Zhenglai Deng (ed.). *Shiminshehui de lilun yanjiu* [*Study on Civil Society Theory*], pp. 1–25. Beijing: Zhongguo zhengfa daxue chubanshe.

Gan, Yang. 1998. "'Minjian shehui' gainian pipan" ["Criticism on the concept 'Civil Society'"]. In: Zhang Jing (ed.). *Guojia yu shehui* [*State and Society*], pp. 24–35. Hangzhou: Zhejiang renmin chubanshe.

Gray, J. 1993. *Post Liberalism: Studies in Political Thought*. London: Routledge.

Grindle, M.S. 2004. Good enough governance: Poverty reduction and reform in developing countries. *Governance: An International Journal of Policy, Administration, and Institutions*, 17(4): 525–548.

Gu, Xin and Wang Xu. 2005. Cong guojiazhuyi dao fatuanzhuyi: zhongguo shichang zhuanxing guocheng zhong guojia yu zhuanyetuanti de guanxi yanbian ["From statism to corporatism: Evolution of the relationship between the state and professional organizations in the process of marketization in China]. *Shehuixue yanjiu* [*Sociological Studies*] 2005(2): 145–175.

Han, Hen. 2008. Shutu tonggui de gongmin shehui?—yu yujianxing zhoujun erwei xiansheng shangque. [All roads lead to civil society?—Discussion with Mr. Yu Jianxing and Zhou Jun]. *Ershiyi shiji* [*The Twenty-first Century*] 2008 (Oct.): 126–130.

He, Zengke. 2007. Zhongguo difang zhengfu chuangxin yu zhengzhi hefaxing: yixiang chubu de jingyanxing yanjiu [Chinese local government's innovation and political legitimacy: A preliminary empirical study]. *Yunnan xingzheng xueyuan xuebao* [*Journal of Yunnan Administration College*] 2007(2): 8–13.

Jessop, B. 1996. Interpretive sociology and the dialectic of structure and agency. *Theory of Culture Society* 13(1): 119–128.

Jessop, B. 2002. Guojia lilun de xinjinzhan—gezhong taolun zhenlundian he yicheng(xu) [New developments of state theory—Various discussions, arguments and agenda (continued)]. *Shijie zhexue* [*World Philosophy*] 2002(2): 22–26.

Jia, Xijin, and Aili Huang. 2007. "Chengshi shequ de canyushi zhili—yi ningboshi haishuqu weili" [Participatory Governance in Urban Community—A Case Study of Haishu District, Ningbo City]. In: *Difang zhengfu chuangxin yu gongmin shehui fazhan guoji yantaohui lunwenji* [*Collection of the International Symposium on Local Government Innovation and Development of Civil Society*], pp. 217–231. Hangzhou: Zhejiang University.

Kang, Xiaoguang, and Hen Han. 2005. Fenlei kongzhi: dangqian zhongguo dalu guojia yu shehui guanxi yanjiu [Graduated controls: The state-society relationship in contemporary China]. Shehuixue yanjiu [*Sociological Studies*] 2005(6): 73–89.

Li, Wenxing, and Haiming Zheng. 2007. Lun difangzhili shiye xia de zhengfu yu gong-zhong hudongshi goutong jizhi de goujian [On the construction of an interactive communication mechanism between the government and the public from the per-spective of local governance]. *Zhongguo xingzheng guanli* [*Chinese Public Administration*] 2007(5): 69–72.

Lieberthal, K. 1988. "Introduction: The 'Fragmented Authoritarianism' Model and Its Limitations." In: K. Lieberthal and M. Oksengerg (eds.) *Policy Making in China: Leaders, Structures, and Processes*, pp. 1–30. Princeton, NJ: Princeton University Press.

Liu, Jianjun. 2003. Zhili huanxing: tiaochu guojia quanli huigui shehui de xianjin [Governance retards: Out of the trap of state powers back to society]. *Lilun wencui* [*Theory Quintessence*] 2003(4): 16–18.

Liu, Zhichang. 2007. Caogen zuzhi de shengzhang yu shequ zhili jiegou de zhuanxing [The growth of grass-roots organizations and the transformation of community gov-ernance structure]. *Shehui zhuyi yanjiu* [*Socialist Studies*], 2007(4): 94–96.

Ma, Q. 2002. Defining Chinese nongovernmental organizations. *Voluntas: International Journal of Voluntary and Nonprofit Organizations*, 13(2); 113–130.

Migdal, J. 2001. *State in Society*. New York: Cambridge University Press.

Peters, G. B. 2000. "Governance and Comparative Politics." In: J. Pierre (ed.) *Debating Governance*. New York: Oxford University Press, pp. 36–53.

Rong, Jingben, et al. 1998. "*Cong yalixing tizhi xiang minzhu hezuozhi de zhuanbian*"["*The Transformation from Pressurized System to Democratic Cooperation System*"]. Beijing: Zhongyang bianyi chubanshe.

Saich, A. 2009. "Mangrenmoxiang: zhongguo difang zhengfu fenxi" ["The Blind Man and the Elephant: Analyzing the Local State in China"]. In: Xuedong Yang and Hairong Lai (eds.) *Difang de fuxing: difang zhili gaige 30nian* [*Bring the Local Back in: Reform and Changes of China Local Governance since 1978*], pp. 383–415. Beijing: Shehui kexue wenxian chubanshe.

Schmitter, P.C. 1979. "Still the Century of Corporatism?" In: P.C. Schmitter and G. Lehmbruch (eds.) *Trends Toward Corporatist Intermediation*, pp. 7–52. London: Sage Publications.

Shi, Jinchuan, et al. 2002. *Zhidu bianqian yu jingji fazhan: Wenzhou moshi yanjiu* [*Institutional Changes and Economic Development: Study on Wenzhou Model*]. Hangzhou: Zhejiang daxue chubanshe.

Solinger, D.J. 1992. "Urban Entrepreneurs and the State: The Merger of State and Society." In: A.G. Rosenbaum (ed.) *State and Society in China: The Consequences of Reform*, pp. 121–141. London: Westview Press.

Stoker, G. 2007. Difang zhili yanjiu: fanshi, lilun yu qishi [Local governance: Paradigm, theories and implications]. *Zhejiang daxue xuebao (renwen shehui kexue ban)* [*Journal of Zhejiang University (Humanities and Social Sciences)*] 2007(2): 5–15.

Sun, Baiying. 2004. *Dangdai difang zhili* [*Contemporary Local Governance*]. Beijing: Zhongguo renmin daxue chubanshe.

Tang, Shiqi. 1996. 'Shimin shehui,' xiandai guojia ji zhongguo de guojia shehui guanxi ['Civil society,' modern state and state-society relationship in China]. *Beijing daxue xuebao (zhexue shehuikexue ban)* [*Journal of Peking University (Philosophy and Social Sciences)*] 1996(6): 65–71.

Ting, Jenfang. 1999. *Weiquan tonghezhuyi: lilun, fazhan yu zhuanxing* [*Authoritarian Corporatism: Theory, Development and Transformation*]. Taipei: Shiying chubanshe.

Tsou, Tang. 1994. *Ershi shiji zhongguo zhengzhi: cong hongguan lishi yu weiguan xingdong jiaodu kan* [*Twentieth Century Chinese Politics: From the Perspective of Macro-History and Micro-Mechanism Analysis*]. Hong Kong: Oxford University Press, 1994.

Unger, J. and A. Chan. 1995. China, corporatism, and the East Asian Model. *The Australian Journal of Chinese Affairs*, 33 (Jan.): 29–53.

Uphoff, N., and N. Krishna. 2004. Civil society and public sector Institutions: More than a zero-sum relationship. *Public Administration and Development*, 24(4): 357–372.

Wakeman, F., Jr. 1993. The civil society and public sphere debate. *Modern China*, 19(2): 108–138.

Wang, Shinshien. 2006. *Zhengbian zhong de zhongguo shehui zuzhi yanjiu: guojia-shehui guanxi de shijiao* [*Chinese Social Organizations in Debate: A Perspective of State-Society Relationship*]. Taipei: Weibo wenhua guoji chuban youxiangongsi.

Wang, Shizong. 2005. Hangye zuzhi de zhengzhi yunhan: dui wenzhou shanghui de zhengzhi hefaxing kaocha [The political content of trade association: An exploration to chambers of commerce in Wenzhou from the viewpoint of political legitimacy]. *Zhejiang daxue xuebao(renwen shehuikexue ban)* [*Journal of Zhejiang University (Humanity and Social Science)*] 2005(2): 158–165.

Wang, Shizong. 2008. Zhili lilun de neizai maodun jiqi chulu [The internal contradiction of governance theory and its future approach]. *Zhexue yanjiu* [*Philosophical Researches*] 2008(2): 83–89.

White, G. 1993. Prospects for civil society in China: A case study of Xiaoshan city. *Australian Journal of Chinese Affairs* 29 (Jan.): 63–87.

Xu, Yong. 2004. Jingxiangkuozhen, xiangpaizhenzhi: xiangji zhili tizhi de jiegouxing gaige [Village-reduction and town-expansion and town governance in village: The structural reform of rural governance system]. *Jiangxi shehuikexue* [*Jiangxi Social Sciences*], 2004(1): 24–29.

Yang, Xuedong. 2002. Lun zhili de zhidu jichu [On institutional foundations of governance]. *Tianjin shehuikexue* [*Tianjin Social Sciences*] 2002(2): 43–46.

Yu, Jianxing. 2008. Zhili yu guojia jiangou zhijian de zhangli [Tensions between governance and state building]. *Makesi zhuyi yu xianshi* [*Marxism and Reality*] 2008(1): 86–93.

Yu, Jianxing, and Jun Zhou. 2008. Gonggong shiwu guanli zhong de gongminshehui—zhongguo gongminshehui fazhan lujing de pipan yu fansi [Civil society in administration of public affairs: Criticism and reflection on paths of China civil society development]. *Ershiyi shiji* [*The Twenty-First Century*] 2008 (Apr.): 11–18.

Yu, Keping. 1999. Zhongguo gongmin shehui de xingqi yu zhili de bianqian [The rise of China civil society and governance changes]. *Zhongguo shehuikexue jikan* [*Chinese Social Sciences Quarterly*] 1999 (Autumn): 105–117.

Yu, Keping. 2005. "Zhongguo gongmin shehui de xingqi jiqi dui zhili de yiyi" ["The Rise of China Civil Society and Its Significance in Governance"]. In: Keping Yu (ed.) *Zengliang minzhu yu shanzhi* [*Incremental Democracy and Good Governance*], pp. 188–199. Beijing: Shehui kexue wenxian chubanshe.

Zang, Zhijun. 2003. 'Zhili': wutuobang haishi xianshi? ['Governance: Utopia or reality?']. *Lilun wencui* [*Theory Quintessence*] 2003(4): 10–11.

CHAPTER 3

Governance Models and Policy Framework: Some Chinese Perspectives

Ehtisham Ahmad

1 INTRODUCTION

Governance systems not only reflect the political and constitutional arrangements in different countries, including the administrative, legal, and regulatory frameworks, but also the underlying economic forces, including institutions, policy instruments, and information flows. The interactions are important, as is the sequencing of measures. The tendency of international experts and agencies to assume that more junior levels of government in China behave as they might in the US, often leads to inappropriate analyses and policy prescriptions. Similarly, focusing on the political or administrative aspects in isolation from the economic underpinnings may be a mistake.

There is a presumption that countries tend to follow a common development trajectory, and that there is a close linkage between economic and political systems (Rostow 1960). The policy prescriptions from this framework were largely driven by the US-centric "normative" literature developed after World War II, during the Cold War era. Together with the economic and political underpinnings, this was designed to illustrate that the superiority of the eco-

This chapter reflects an ongoing work program on multilevel finance and sustainable development being undertaken by the author at the London School of Economics and Political Science (LSE). Many of the ideas have been presented at seminars at the LSE, Bonn, Turin, Peking, Sun Yat-Sen, and Zhejiang Universities. Helpful comments from Gao Xiang are acknowledged, and the usual disclaimer applies.

E. Ahmad (✉)
Zhejiang University, Hangzhou, China

Grantham Research Institute, London School of Economics, London, UK
e-mail: s.e.ahmad@lse.ac.uk

© The Author(s) 2019
J. Yu, S. Guo (eds.), *The Palgrave Handbook of Local Governance in Contemporary China*, https://doi.org/10.1007/978-981-13-2799-5_3

nomic outcomes is due to the democratic electoral process that permits preference matching and accountable governance. However, the normative policy prescriptions were seen not to apply even to other "western democracies in Europe" for example. Indeed, the development of the second-generation "positive" or "political economy" models is due largely to the divergence of the European experience from the normative prescriptions. Of importance is the role of yardstick competition across jurisdictions to keep the politicians honest. But the process can be compromised when there is asymmetric information that masks the true cost of public actions by shifting liabilities typically to other higher jurisdictions or "kicking the can down the road" to future administrations. In some cases, the automatic checks and balances, including between the legislative and executive branches, and the judiciary may be "captured" through vested interests, xenophobia, or demagoguery.

Normative views, however, based on the presumed superiority of a specific "ideal type," underlie a principal critique of the Chinese model. This leads to the assertion that a potential trade-off between actions to address environmental considerations and generating prosperity and economic growth could lead to a collapse of the Chinese governance model (see, e.g., Fukuyama 2016). However, such a conclusion is unwarranted and stems from a basic misunderstanding of the institutional and informational underpinnings of the "administrative progression" model being developed in China. Moreover, China's commitment to a clean environment and to improve the quality of life for its citizens also has major implications for the global climate change agenda, as formalized in the Paris agreement.

China operates under a governance model that could be broadly categorized as falling under the class of "administrative progression" systems. Indeed, the historical application of the model over two millennia since the Han Dynasty is well documented, including by Fukuyama (2016). However, the model is not static, given the rapid institutional change that has taken place in China, especially since Deng Xiao Ping's Responsibility System[1] and the fundamental structural changes in organizational capabilities since 1993–1994, and the acceleration in governance reforms instituted by Xi Jingping. Indeed, while China has received a great deal of US-centric normative policy advice, including from some international agencies, the 1993–1994 reform by focusing on gainers and losers from a major structural reform, represented an example of the "positive" or second-generation intergovernmental reforms that have become widespread since the turn of the century (see the reviews in Ahmad and Brosio 2006, 2015).

Comparisons between China and advanced market-based economies are often made without fully understanding that China is, in many respects, an

---

[1] This refers to the general principle that characterized a series of reforms, starting with agriculture, then state-owned enterprises (SOEs) and local governments, and the associated fiscal arrangements.

emerging market economy and often lacks the institutional arrangements and policy instruments that are often taken for granted by Western commentators. For instance, China did not have a central tax administration and the full panoply of tax policies before the early 1990s. Nonetheless, the progress on both counts since 1993–1994 has been very rapid, and in many respects China has managed to deal with the legacy systems at the subnational level much better than countries like India, that are struggling to implement a national value-added tax (VAT) to consolidate a common economic space and minimize the costs of doing business. However, like India and in most other emerging market economies, the personal income tax (PIT) in China does not yield as much as might be expected in the UK or US. Consequently, the comparisons of China with the UK on the PIT, for example, by Brown (2016, p. 16), can be misleading, without a full understanding of the fiscal and institutional constraints or the dynamics of shifting revenue bases in the course of development (see, e.g., Hinrichs 1966 or Tanzi 1987).

In some respects, China benefits from newcomer's advantage—especially with budget and treasury institutions that directly affect governance outcomes. Particularly important are new international standards on general government balance sheets consistent with the International Monetary Fund's (IMF's) Government Financial Statistics Manual 2001–2014, and International Public Sector Accounting Standards (IPSAS) standards on Public-Private Partnerships (PPPs) that require liabilities to be placed on the balance sheets of the relevant contracting governments. These have proved difficult to implement in several European countries, and consequently the basis for yardstick competition has been weakened. Further, political economy constraints, as subnational entities compete with the central government or each other when benefits do not accrue to a single jurisdiction, limit the operations of yardstick competition, including in the US. China, on the other hand, has accepted the standards and has begun implementation at the higher levels—although the process is far from complete, the beginnings have been made. Similarly, the use of new information technologies makes it easier to adapt feedback mechanisms that can lead to further a refinement of the "administered progression model."

It is important to emphasize that the administrative progression model is not a static phenomenon. Indeed, many of the developments in institutions and information sharing in China have opened up new possibilities for improving governance as well as living standards. We examine several of the potential next steps in achieving sustainable growth and improvements in living standards.

2 ALTERNATIVE GOVERNANCE MODELS

It is useful to set out the key elements of the reference governance model that is used to judge the performance of other countries. Since the political-economic reference point is the US **"normative" model**, it is useful to juxtapose the political discussion of Fukuyama (2016) with the considerable literature on the multilevel finance issues, including the discussions leading to the formulation of the US constitution and the assessments of the model over time. In particular, it is helpful to examine the **"positive" models** that have arisen largely since the mid-1990s, given the divergence between the European Commission (EC) policy evolution and the policy recommendations of the normative model.

It is useful also to keep in mind that much of the discussion leading to the US constitution was of a "positive nature," as we describe later. The "normative" perspectives were largely driven by post-World War II political considerations. In any case, the Chinese reforms of 1993–1994 explicitly rejected the prescriptions of the "normative school" and adopted a package that offset gainers and losers to set the foundations for a sustained period of very rapid growth. This was an example of the "positive" approach, as we shall argue later. However, the underlying Chinese governance model is different from that operating in Western countries. The evolution of this "administrative progression" structure is continuing, with the establishment of new institutions, adoption of global norms, and use of modern information technology.

2.1   Normative US-Centric Approaches

The framers of the US constitution, for example, James Madison and Alexander Hamilton among others, were very concerned about the possibilities of "capture" of the benefits of governance by "factions" or lobbies (see *Federalist Papers*, 1787). This also reflects fundamental modern precepts underlying the political economy or positive approaches to governance. Yet the basic premise of the post-World War II "normative" literature lies on the assumption of "benevolent" policymakers intending to maximize the welfare of their communities.

Richard Musgrave's characterization of the multilevel governance process was "to permit different groups living in various states to express different preferences for public services; and this, inevitably, leads to differences in the levels of taxation and public services" (Musgrave 1959, p. 179). This leads to the normative assignments on spending, and that tax assignments and financing arrangements follow the spending functions. The role of the central government would then lie mainly on externalities, such as defense, and addressing spillovers generated by local government policies. Thus, the central government would ensure full internalization of spillovers, while decentralization will accomplish preference matching. In fact, neither conclusion is warranted. Central governments may be able to vary policies to meet local preferences but may not be able to ensure internalization of spillovers generated by local governments (Breton 1965)—and see later.

Given the very pervasive nature of the literature and public policy based on the normative US-centric model, it is useful to examine a few policy instruments that have been very influential. A common recommendation is to devolve, say basic (primary and secondary) education to subnational levels.

This has been the typical reform measure in Latin America, from unitary countries like Colombia and Peru, to federations such as Argentina as well as in the transition economies in Eastern Europe. However, with falling Pisa rankings, the US had to resort to a Federal transfer to schools during the Bush Administration, with the No-Child-Left-Behind program, to improve educational outcomes that were the responsibility of the lower-level governments but with a major impact on longer-term growth potential. Given the difficulties with monitoring such programs, it has been of limited success, and the US remains relatively low in the Pisa rankings.

A second issue relates to the system of subnational income and property taxes. The US system of surcharges or a piggy-back on a central income tax base provides jurisdictions with own-source revenues—over which they have control at the margin (in terms of setting the marginal tax rates). This is relatively simple to replicate in multilevel countries, whether unitary or federal in structure.

An altogether trickier proposition relates to US-style property taxes that typically finance the education function—and the quality of schooling is reflected in property prices, so that there is a close link with spending, financing, and revenues. There is emphasis on maintaining property titles, driven largely by owners and the mortgage lenders. Thus, both ownership and valuations are generally relatively up to date. The ability to vary the property tax rates also affects the ratings of local governments and cities for the issuance of local government bonds. However, it has proved difficult to export the US property tax model to emerging market economies—and in China, the experimentation in Shanghai and Chongqing has been largely unsuccessful. Even the UK has abandoned the ownership-valuation model for residential property, although it is maintained for businesses.

A final set of issues relates to the issuance of local government bonds. This is an important tool for financing local infrastructure in the US and is widely copied elsewhere, including in China. The US system functions, albeit imperfectly,[2] and the linkage with the local own-source revenue system is critical, as they provide flexibility to meet additional spending if needed without jeopardizing the hard budget constraints. Note that shared revenues should be treated as transfers for the debt management strategies, as the subnational jurisdictions have no control over the amounts to be collected. No explicit public financial management (PFM) standards are imposed in the US, partly because the individual states are sovereign and have their own constitutions, and also because the markets have generally accurate information to be able to

---

[2] The US investment financing system functions, although the adequacy is open to question with the crumbling infrastructure in most major cities, highways, and bridges. The amounts of financing required far exceed the amounts linked to local tax bases and has led to the arguments for additional federally financed or guaranteed investments. This introduces game-play considerations into the US governance model that have yet to play out.

punish infractions by specific lower-level jurisdictions. Again, it has proven problematic to extrapolate from the US-institutional framework, and trying to implement subnational fiscal rules in the EC without requiring common accounting and reporting frameworks has not really worked very well.

In the next subsection, we focus on some European and non-US critiques of the model and then examine the specifics of the Chinese context.

2.2   Positive or Political Economy Models

Breton (2002) criticizes two main pillars of the normative approach: that central governments provide uniform levels of goods and services and that local administrations provide a better matching of service delivery to citizens' preferences—and that the more junior the government, the better the ability to meet demands. Yet, the uniform provision may be needed, especially for cross-regional infrastructure as well as the environment, where externalities are particularly great, and the central government is perfectly able to tailor the infrastructure or environmental considerations to the needs of different regions. The second proposition assumes that smaller jurisdictions reflect more homogenous preferences than larger ones. Yet, in the Canadian context, large provinces such as Newfoundland and Prince William Island are fairly homogenous, but the city of Toronto has to deal with 120 different ethnic groups.

When applied to the bottom-up processes of federalization, such as the European Union, the US-style normative assignments have not worked because of missing *political economy* considerations. There are also *information costs* at the lower levels, including with respect to the buildup of liabilities. *Diminishing supply costs* exist for many goods and services and particularly for tax collection and bond finance. There is also *dynamic instability, or a race to the bottom*, that would be particularly marked in the case of the environment. In the latter case, the remedy is to have a national policy—and this is facilitated, for example, by an international agreement—such as the Paris Agreement that would not have been possible without active Chinese support. Of course, in multilevel terms, this involves a national policy to prevent the race to the bottom but with the possibility of additional local action for the more polluted and congested cities, such as Beijing and Shanghai. While some dislocation is clearly likely, this is a far cry from arguing that the governance model is jeopardized because of actions to address the environment. Indeed, adjustment costs are likely also in the Organisation for Economic Co-operation and Development (OECD) countries that are signatories to the Paris agreement.

Defense and foreign policy have not been reassigned to the EC, contrary to the theory. And while education is the prime example from the normative models to be devolved under the subsidiarity principle, in the UK it is financed through a direct special purpose grant from the central government, and local governments have very little to do with the function. Countries in Latin America have been most exposed to the US-normative models and are experimenting with devolving education. However, more recently, countries from

Chile to Mexico have been centralizing the main aspects of the basic education function, to address the poor Pisa outcomes.

Outside Latin America and the EC, the Nigerian Constitutional reform in 1999 and Pakistan's 18th Constitutional Amendment also required devolution of education to lower levels of government. However, it is easier to devolve spending than tax powers, and there is seldom adequate local financing. Typically, this process results in either unfunded mandates or the need for special purpose transfers from higher levels of government that limit "local autonomy," negating the idea of devolution or subsidiarity.

Perhaps the biggest set of problems arises in relation to a transplant of the local borrowing of the US subnational governments to other jurisdictions, including in the European Union. Part of the problem has been that the jurisdiction with taxation powers does not always correspond to the economic unit—including at the city level. This is often a legacy of inefficient sizes of the legal jurisdictions that are impervious to change (Ahmad and Brosio 2006).

A more significant issue has been the lack of uniform recognition of liabilities, such as GFSM2001/14 standards for balance sheets. The anticipation that the "markets would take care of matters," as in the US, has just not worked and hidden liabilities, including from PPPs, exacerbated the 2008 economic crisis. Further, without a full accounting for the liabilities, the basic criteria for yardstick competition needed to keep jurisdictions honest is not met.

2.3   Administrative Progression Models and the Chinese Context

In China, from antiquity or the Han dynasty onwards, a system of administrative progression has been in operation. Officials are appointed through an arms' length examination or set of procedures and performance evaluated through a variety of mechanisms. Several levels of administration were needed in order to act as cross-checks on information flows and on governance.

Further, the administrative progression governance structure precludes Salmon-type yardstick competition (formalized by Besley and Case (1995) and many political economy models—see Lockwood (2015)). While there have been attempts to impute political cycles to the spending patterns in China, these are based on the very imperfect data that cannot distinguish between local own-spending and mandated spending directed by the central government (see Pi-Han Tsai 2016). The models and standards used to evaluate intergovernmental fiscal relations in market economies have to be adapted to the Chinese context. However, some of the international standards that are used to monitor spending and liabilities are not only relevant in China but may need to be strengthened. In order to prevent misappropriation of resources by local officials, much tighter information is needed on the sources and flows of funds and buildup of liabilities than might be required in Western-style yardstick competition models.

The primary focus of public policy in China in recent decades has been on sustainable growth to ensure full employment. The reforms underpinning the Responsibility System, initiated by Deng Xiao Ping in the late 1970s, led to increasing reliance on the private initiative in coastal provinces, like Guangdong. There was also an increasing devolution of decision-making power on spending and investment decisions to local officials. The Responsibility System led to a reduction in tax rates on enterprises to leave more potentially investable resources in the hands of firms. However, this led to a reduction in the overall revenues generated, generating pressures at the local level that were transmitted up to the center.

Prior to 1993–1994, a critical constraint was that the fiscal institutions had been largely centered around local governments, including for raising revenues and actual spending, even though policy was largely determined by the center. The central government did not have a tax administration capable of managing modern taxes and relied on locally administered taxes with upward revenue-sharing. Such an institutional arrangement was common in the middle ages in China and Central and South Asia. The upward-sharing arrangement worked with officials appointed by and loyal to the center with more or less satisfactory success rate over the centuries. However, with the responsibility reforms, the shrinking total resource pie meant that there was insufficient financing for local spending, and reduced incentives to share upwards with the central government.

A major tax cum transfer was needed by the early 1990s, to: (1) reverse the decline in the general government tax/gross domestic product (GDP) ratio, (2) create modern tax instruments and administration, and (3) lay the foundations for rapid growth (see Ahmad 2008, 2012). The tax-transfer nexus was particularly important to garner the support from the provinces for the reform that entailed ceding tax administration authority to the center (for the first time since the middle ages). This permitted the operation of economy-wide taxes, like the VAT, while at the same time avoiding losses for individual local governments because of the reforms.

The origin-based (downward) revenue-sharing mechanism implemented from 1994, ensured buy-in from the well-off provinces that stood to gain from additional revenues generated. An equalization system preserved the interests of the poorer provinces with more limited tax bases and higher costs of provision of public services. The most innovative measure, given the limited domestic connectivity in China at that time, was a "revenue-returned" transfer that greatly helped in preserving and encouraging the growth of the coastal "hubs" for rapid export-led growth. The fiscal measures very strongly supported the overall strategy with great success—and largely maintained full employment, facilitating major rural-to-urban and interior-to-coastal migrations, with one of the largest reductions in poverty in the world within a decade.

The consequences of the success of the strategy have led to new challenges, including considerable imbalances between coastal and interior provinces and the appearance of significant interpersonal inequalities, as well as environmental distress that threatens the sustainability of China's future development. The growth of megacities along the coast has led to increasing congestion and pollution, putting living standards under stress. Far from shying away from the environmental issues as they involve a degree of adjustment, the three-year economic plan issued in December 2017 firmly places the priorities on (1) managing risks, (2) addressing income distribution and minimum standards, and (3) the environment and the quality of life of the citizens.

3   CHINA'S CHANGING INSTITUTIONAL AND GOVERNANCE FRAMEWORK

With one of the most decentralized spending systems in the world, given the size and complexity of the country, the Chinese system of appointed officials with overlapping responsibilities worked well over the centuries, with upward revenue sharing, provided the officials remained honest.

When the officials were honest and governed responsibly, and without resorting to extortions, the country remained strong and prosperous, and able to withstand natural disasters and exogenous shocks. However, with the size of the country, and limitations on the flow of information and connectivity (despite the old silk route), there were periods when governance weakened, and corruption and rent-seeking made the country more vulnerable to shocks. This can be seen in the cyclical periods of prosperity and hardship throughout Chinese history (see Jing Zhang 2015). A complex institutional arrangement has evolved over time in China, and this system cannot be described as purely autocratic, as in many of the successor states of the Former Soviet Union.

The cyclical governance pattern was also evident during the first half of the twentieth century—which was one of the most turbulent periods in Chinese history. Stability was restored with the establishment of the People's Republic in 1950, and the traditional governance model has been used, with some interesting variations, since then. The fundamental trade-off has been that very tight central control reduces incentives to invest, against a greater degree of autonomy that can generate rapid growth. But a very decentralized alternative, with poorly developed institutions of fiscal management—with weak or absent national taxes and administration, as well as weak budget allocation and management/monitoring systems—risks the loss of macroeconomic control, as well as generation of spatial and interpersonal inequalities. The system also generates a potential for irresponsible investments and potential for rent-seeking. There has been considerable emphasis by President Xi's Administration in addressing the rent-seeking behavior by officials at all levels, and we see this as a critical element in the efficient functioning of the administrative hierarchy model. However, a greater role for tax policy and administration in dealing with inequalities and environmental damage, and the budget and treasury institutions dealing with the flow and use of resources and cash, can make the system "automatic" and less prone to Fukuyama's "bad emperor syndrome."[3]

---

[3] It should be noted that the democratic electoral process does not preclude "bad decisions," such as Brexit, or periodic capture by nondemocratic and xenophobic forces, such as during the 1930s.

Some critical elements of the administrative progression model include (1) rigorous selection process of the officials and (2) arms' length evaluation criteria, with full information or independent verifiable feed-back mechanisms, to prevent extortion and unfair treatment of the masses, as well as rent-seeking behavior by the local officials. The model is evolving, as the Chinese economy has undergone a period of extraordinary structural change, especially since the 1980s, relying increasingly on local incentives and initiatives with the Responsibility System. The current emphasis in China to ensure that increasing public resources are not misappropriated by local officials is critical in ensuring that the administrative progression governance structure continues to function efficiently. The key elements of this process include taxes to affect incentives, and budget institutions and full information on the sources and uses of public funds to minimize "game-play" and ability to evade regulations on the misuse of public monies.

As pointed out in Ahmad et al. (2018a), tax reforms were needed to consolidate the growth and rapid development that came about as a result of the Responsibility System. Additional tax reforms are needed for the next stages of the structural reforms. Indeed, in this chapter, we argue that tax reforms are necessary to provide the right incentives, but not sufficient, especially if there is uncontrolled access to credit.

In 1993–1994, the Chinese government established a package of reinforcing measures, including the establishment of a central tax administration (the State Administration of Taxation—SAT) that administered a national VAT with "downward" revenue-sharing, and a concomitant equalization system. The VAT was of the "investment type" that did not provide credits for taxation on capital goods, and the business tax largely on services was left in the hands of local administration. While these measures added to the cost of doing business, these were all that were politically or administratively feasible at the time and have been addressed gradually since then.

Measures were also needed to strengthen information flows and governance to ensure that the incentive structures actually work. Since the late 1990s, there has been a progressive improvement in PFM instruments, such as treasury single accounts and the use of international standards for budget classification and accounting and tracking public spending, particularly at the central and provincial levels. While significant and possibly better than in some other G20 countries, this process is far from complete, especially at the lower levels of government where most of the spending transactions take place—see Ahmad and Zhang (2018).

This evolution of policies and institutions since 1993 has implications for the governance model. The first relates to the overall incentives facing local officials and whether the risks and opportunities of their actions can be linked to their relevant jurisdictions or whether these are likely to spread to higher levels, particularly to the central government (see Liu Shangxi and Li Chengwei 2018). This is critical in establishing hard budget constraints and ring-fencing liabilities, and in addressing the new challenges of rebalancing of the economy and generating sustainable and equitable growth.

Full information on sources and uses of public funds and possible risks associated with public policy are critical in the effective operation of the administrative progression model. These measures are integral to establishing clean governance that has come to the center of public policymaking under the current administration.

Both own-source taxes and improved governance are critical in establishing proper incentives for local officials, also to prevent the buildup of liabilities and rent-seeking behavior. Indeed, ad hoc measures such as the issuance of bonds at the provincial level, while desirable in themselves, may not function as expected, whether the focus is on China or Germany (see Färber and Wang 2018). Indeed, if municipal bonds are implemented before ensuring ability to service debt, there is likely to be a loss of reputation for an essential instrument that will be needed in due course.

A combination of national infrastructure policies with local connectivity and improved public services is critical in generating incentives for sustainable local "hubs." One of the objectives of the Belt and Road Initiative (BRI) is to develop lagging regions and ensure sustainable growth, especially in the Western and interior regions of China. While the nationally financed physical infrastructure is a necessary condition, we argue that a package of measures, including subnational taxes and transfers and improved local services in less well-endowed areas, is needed. This is to better access credit for sustainable investment and make full use of opportunities for utilizing the new connectivity, to achieve the productive rebalancing and a more equal distribution of opportunity throughout China.

Additional tax reforms are needed to generate incentives for further structural change (following Ahmad et al. 2013). The VAT for business tax reform, completed in May 2016, was designed to reduce the cost of doing business and maintain the competitive advantages in an increasingly difficult external environment. However, the removal of the last tax handle under the control of the local governments makes them entirely dependent on transfers and shared revenues—with no room to raise additional resources in case of need, for example, to pay for any debts incurred by them. This reduces the "accountability" of local officials for decisions that they take, particularly in relation to investments and liabilities incurred.

Changes in governance and institutions need to be accelerated or completed for an orderly financing of the new "sustainable hubs." The experience of Guangdong provides a very useful example of the sorts of measures needed for the rebalancing agenda—both within provinces and within China (Luo and Nong 2018; Xiao 2018). The wider realization of substantially expanding production possibility frontiers depends on both new technologies that will be greatly influenced by the tax reforms and the investment in connectivity infrastructure implied by the BRI.

3.1   The Responsibility System

The Responsibility System was designed in the late 1970s to allow a greater role for production incentives in generating growth and employment, to better unleash the investment and growth potential, or "animal spirits" that are critical in structural transformation. This was achieved by reducing the effective tax on profits, while maintaining the governance system of appointed local administrators. It had a significant impact on growth and unleashing the latent productive capabilities of the Chinese economy.

While there was a positive impact on producers, the declining overall revenue generation had a negative impact on local finances—with the total tax/GDP ratio falling from 25% at the start of the reforms to around 10% by 1992–1993 (see Fig. 3.1). This initiated a "game-play" between local officials and the central government. Consequently, the central government *share of total revenues* also fell precipitously, despite various attempts to incentivize local officials (Gao Qiang 1995). The central share, which had been around 55% of total revenues at the start of the Responsibility Reform, fell to well under 30% by 1993 (see Fig. 3.1). The implication was that, although nominally responsible to the central government, local officials focused on local welfare and

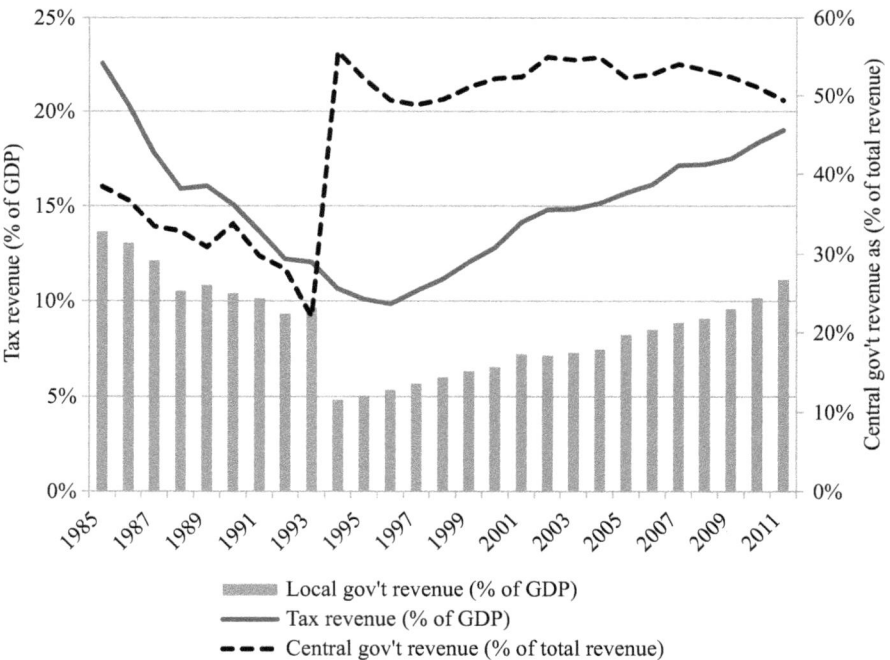

Fig. 3.1 Evolution of tax/GDP ratios and central-local shares (Source: Ahmad et al., China Development Forum 2013)

interests—especially since promotion prospects depended on local growth performance. The expansion of local public activities along with private investments, despite "grey property rights," led to significant growth opportunities. However, the consequence was that there was a reduced incentive at the local levels to share revenue upwards.

By 1992–1993, the plummeting tax/GDP ratio, as well as the decline in the share of revenues going to the center, meant that the central government's ability to maintain macroeconomic stability, ensure redistribution, or meet the fundamental responsibilities of a nation-state were seriously compromised. The constraints on resources led to highlighting the tensions that typically exist in a large multilevel country between those responsible for service delivery and investments at the lower levels and those at more senior levels of government—even if the latter may have been responsible for the appointments of local officials.

3.2   Structural and Tax and Transfer Reforms: 1993–1994—A "Positive" Reform Agenda

By the early 1990s, it was clear that major reforms would be needed to bolster the public finances in China, and with the collapse of the USSR, it was important to bolster the state. An option recommended by many was the normative prescription following on the US model: to fix the spending assignments and then figure out how to finance them. However, the Chinese government chose a pragmatic "positive solution" to focus on taxes and transfers to strengthen central coordination and redistribution functions. This was endorsed by the IMF (see Ahmad et al. 1995) and was a precursor of the "positive approaches" that were popularized in the literature almost a decade later (Ahmad and Brosio 2015).[4]

Subsequently, it became clear that China had to turn attention to budget institutions and processes to develop information flows, with a view improving governance and developmental outcomes. As we shall argue in the final part of the chapter, both tax and governance institutions and policies need to be strengthened further to continue to achieve sustainable structural change. This will also lead to a further evolution in the administrative progression model.

To maintain the center's ability to conduct macroeconomic policy and redistribution, as well as a consistent public investment strategy, the focus was initially to address the critical domestic resource mobilization shortcomings. A central tax administration—the SAT—was established, and a "package of policy reforms was introduced by 1994. The key elements were to establish a VAT on goods, accompanied by a system of revenue-sharing and equalization transfers designed to prevent a negative impact on provinces, and give them incentives

---

[4] See also Ahmad and Brosio (2015) for more recent developments in the positive literature.

to operate efficiently. However, the VAT was of the investment type that did not provide credits for taxes on capital purchases.[5]

This institutional transformation was to have far-reaching effects. This reform was not just imposed from the center, as might have been the case in a purely autocratic institutional arrangement. The very careful balancing of gainers and losers because of the reform was a masterly illustration of the new "positive" approaches to institutional change in a multilevel economy (see Ahmad and Brosio 2015, for a review).[6] This approach could provide lessons for more "market-based" countries in the OECD that rely on "yardstick" competition, at least in principle, or in emerging market countries facing the need for structural change.

The objective was to restore macroeconomic balances as well as to improve the business climate. The reform worked well in restoring revenues for general government, with the central government's share increasing to just over half within a very short period, ensuring financing for redistribution and investment (Ahmad et al. 2002). The shared revenues and "revenue returns" permitted the development of coastal hubs, such as in the Pearl River Delta, and provided connectivity for a successful export-led growth strategy. However, the coastal hubs, attracting migrants from the interior, have become megametropolises with attendant problems of congestion and pollution. And both interregional and interpersonal inequalities have widened significantly.

The key measures adopted by the Chinese government in 1993–1994 were designed to persuade local governments to cede tax collection powers to the center. The SAT was designed to manage wide-area tax instruments, such as the VAT. This was not done by diktat but involved an admirable consultation process that generated a "package" of tax administration and policy reforms designed to minimize losses and share benefits across rich and poor provinces alike. The key elements of the "package" included the following:

- Prevention of losses among local governments by a "hold harmless" clause—this guaranteed all provinces 1993 levels of revenues in absolute terms in perpetuity;
- Providing a share of the (increasing) revenues from the VAT with the provinces that generated the value added—these were mainly the richer ones;
- Introducing a modern "equalization framework"—this enabled all provinces to provide similar levels of services at similar levels of effort. The

---

[5] This was dictated by both administrative constraints and revenue concerns, and while it created an additional cost for exporters, lower Chinese wage levels more than compensated for the disadvantage. This lacuna was addressed in the move toward crediting of input taxation on investments, or the shift from an investment-type to a consumption-type VAT, in the reforms of 2006.

[6] For a review of the positive theories of multilevel finance that address gainers and losers of alternative institutional and policy arrangements in relation to various interest groups, and associated policy implications, see *Handbook of Multilevel Finance* (2015).

version adopted in China was based on the Australian model, but with simpler factors,[7] and provided a "buy-in" from the poorer provinces; and
- Providing, through a most innovative measure, for a revenue-returned policy to provide additional funds to the better-connected provinces, but on a gradually decreasing basis—this measure was criticized by some international agencies at the time as generating regional inequalities. However, this measure was critical in providing for a concentration of resources in existing "production hubs," largely along the coast, making use of the existing connectivity in the short run to generate investment, exports, and employment opportunities.

The 1993–1994 reforms considered incentive effects, not just on local governments but also on firms. As described in Xu Shanda and Ma Lin (1995), one of the main objectives of the introduction of the VAT was to remove cascading from the indirect tax system to make Chinese manufacturing more competitive. This was to be achieved eventually by a "wide base and simple rates" (Xu Shanda and Ma Lin 1995, p. 144).

Similarly, rationalizing and reducing rates of the Enterprise Income Tax (EIT) was critical in removing distortions facing firms (Shi Yao Bin 1995) and separating profits from tax payments in SOEs. The 1994 reforms reduced the EIT rate from 55% to 33%, and this was further reduced to 25% in the aftermath of the 2008 crisis and applied uniformly across types of enterprises— regardless of ownership (foreign, central, or local).

This "package" approach adopted in China to introduce major tax reforms, together with intergovernmental transfers and revenue-sharing arrangements, has been very influential, including in other G20 countries. Countries such as Mexico have begun to pay a great deal of attention to the gainers and losers of major reform initiatives and adopting a "package" to address the political economy considerations. These principles were the foundation for the Mexican fiscal reforms in 2007 and the very major fiscal overhaul in 2013. The approach made it possible to address very important tax reforms that had been blocked individually by strong vested interests.

3.3   Effects of the Measures Adopted

The success of the reforms was spectacular (see Fig. 3.1), with an improvement in the overall tax/GDP ratio as well as the central government's share. Double-digit growth was maintained for over two decades, and with the freeing up of the labor market more than 150 million migrated to the coastal hubs (see Fig. 3.2) and more than 700 million people were taken out of poverty.

However, there were several drawbacks. The VAT was applied only to manufacturing, largely because of administrative constraints (recall that the SAT

---

[7] See Lou Jiwei, 1997.

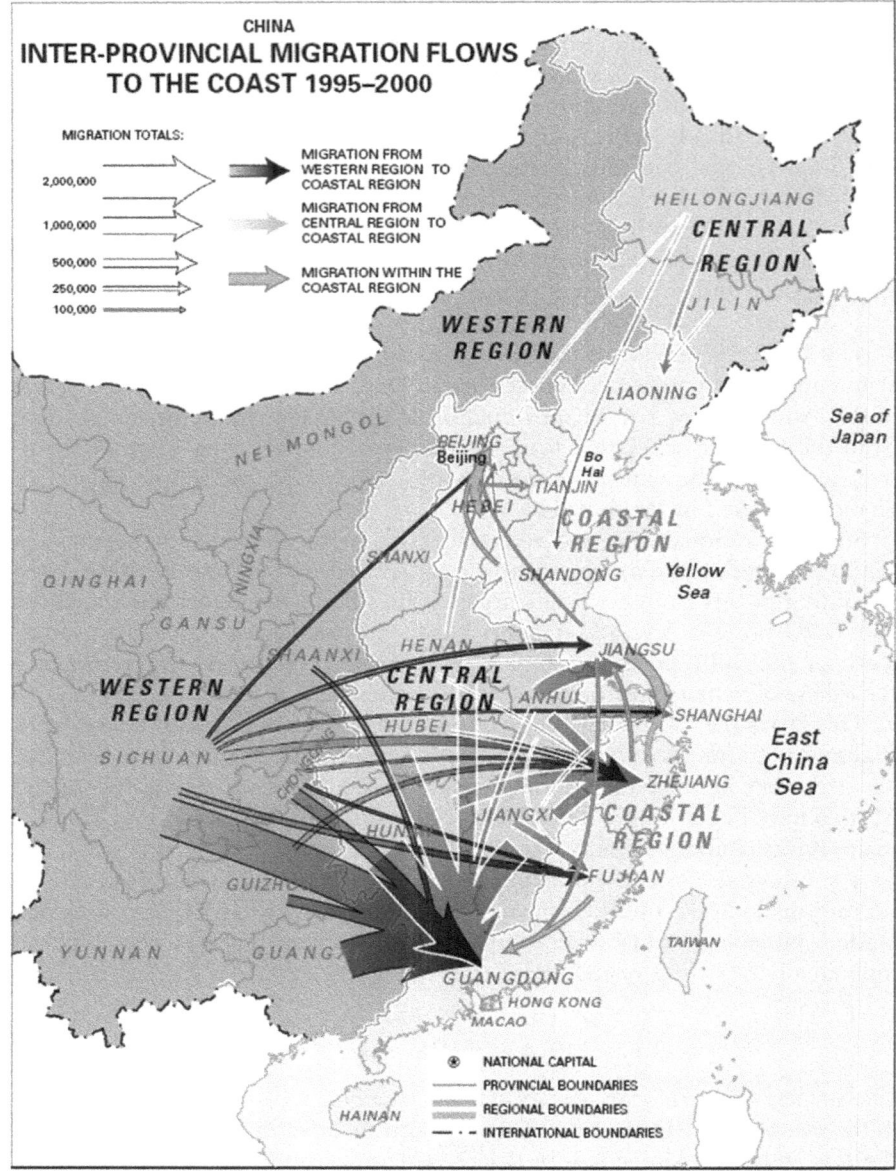

Fig. 3.2   Growing reliance on coastal "hubs"

had just been created), and because of the need to leave at least some tax handles in the hands of local governments (the local business tax mainly on services was one of the main instruments available). Further, the VAT was of "investment type"—that is, the VAT on capital purchases could not be offset against VAT on sales. This again was to meet the revenue targets of the government and was simpler to administer with the nascent SAT. Almost 15 years later, in the aftermath of the 2008 global economic crisis, to reduce the cost of doing business and protect Chinese competitiveness, the investment-type VAT was converted to a consumption-type VAT, with VAT on capital purchases permitted to be offset against VAT on sales.

Moreover, the origin-based revenue-sharing arrangements imposed differential burdens on different governments, falling more heavily on the predominantly industrial provinces. This made it more difficult to push through the integration of the business tax with the VAT, especially since the same provinces were likely to face revenue losses.

With the growing competitive pressures heightened by the economic crisis in the recent past, many trading partners, including the EU and Latin America, have moved to reduce the cost of doing business by shifting from payroll and other taxes (that cannot be refunded on exports) to a "reformed" VAT. The Mexican 2013 reform integrated the taxation of services, an increasingly important base of production, with the VAT on goods. In other words, the reformed VAT fully removed the tax element in the price of exports, and the whole country became an effective tax-free zone. To maintain competitiveness, China has had to speed up the VAT for business tax reform that was initiated over five years ago on a pilot basis, for specific sectors. However, the sector-by-sector approach led to protracted discussions with the local governments and line agencies, generating complex industry-specific arrangements. China undertook the full replacement of the business tax by the VAT in May 2016, accompanied by adjustments in revenue-sharing transfers to ensure that no province would lose revenues, because of the reform.

Widening personal income and regional disparities pose problems for the long-term sustainability of the Chinese development strategy. As pointed out in IMF (2016), the increase in the Chinese level of inequality has been particularly high—rising from around 0.4 in 1992 to around 0.52 in 2013. This is now at levels in the market-based emerging economies in Latin America, such as Chile, that have relied on the service sector to generate "rebalancing" opportunities. Given the implicit social contract in China, high levels of inequality are likely to be less sustainable than in Chile, although the absence of adequate employment opportunities have begun to pose problems in Chile.

A major consequence of the success of the coastal hub phenomenon in China (as in Chile) is the high levels of pollution and congestion in the metropolitan areas, for example, Beijing, Guangzhou-Shenzhen, and Hangzhou-Shanghai corridor. The congestion makes it costlier to do business. And rising pollution levels seriously degrade the quality of life. Beijing's fine particle air pollution level remains well above acceptable health standards despite constant high-level political attention that has led to some improvement in recent years. There are, however, adjustment costs that need to be factored in—including moving polluting industries out of major population centers, closing coal-powered power plants, and building solar-powered renewable sources of energy and clean vehicles.

3.4   Tax Reforms for Structural Change: Improving Competitiveness and Accountability

With a fully integrated VAT to replace the local business tax, the cost of doing business will be reduced, especially since the focus of structural reforms emphasizes the development of the service sector. A VAT on a complete base should also generate full information on value added (wages and profits) and would be critical in providing a cross-check to reduce evasion and avoidance in the income taxes. This was a key element in the structural fiscal reforms implemented in Mexico in 2013 (Ahmad 2017). Additional VAT revenues could also compensate for reductions in the payroll tax that adds to the cost of doing business and more efficiently finance social benefits.

Following the 1993–1994 reforms, the business tax is the last major source of revenues in the hands of provinces and generates significant revenues in the more advanced coastal provinces like Guangdong, and is even more important in relative terms in the middle-income provinces. However, it meant that the VAT chain was incomplete with loss of information on the production process. Also, the business tax generates a cascading effect and adds to the cost of doing business in China. Replacing the business tax by a VAT, while improving overall efficiency would generate losses, especially in the middle-income provinces (see Fig. 3.3; Ahmad et al. 2004; Lou Jiwei and Shulin Wang 2008).

In China, the replacement of the business tax by the VAT was dictated by the structural reform agenda. Given the rising wages in China and greater international competition, it has become important to reduce the competitive burden on enterprises, especially vis à vis imports and for removing taxation from exports. The main services (such as transport, construction, banking, and insurance) form a critical part of most productive activities.

Experimentation of the replacement of the business tax by the VAT for selected services was initiated in Shanghai in 2012. It was followed in other metropolitan areas for selected services including telecommunications, transport, and construction. However, the service-by-service approach has proved to be difficult, as it generates gainers and losers, including state service suppliers. The response has been to "negotiate" VAT rates with the sectors. But the sector-by-sector approach to the VAT makes it complicated and loses the simplicity needed for the tax to be an efficient generator of revenues as well as information.

The VAT for business tax reforms will generate a complex set of gains and losses among local governments, as seen in Fig. 3.3. In general, central revenues will increase (depending on the rate applied, and the rate of the business tax replaced), but provincial revenues will decline. Although the relative losses in the middle-income provinces are large relative to overall revenues, the absolute losses in provinces like Guangdong will be very large and likely greater than the losses in the poorer provinces. It is interesting that rather than the expected revenue losses due to the VAT for business tax reforms, overall revenues actually increased—reflecting the information flow advantages of the VAT

Loss as % of VAT and Business tax revenue

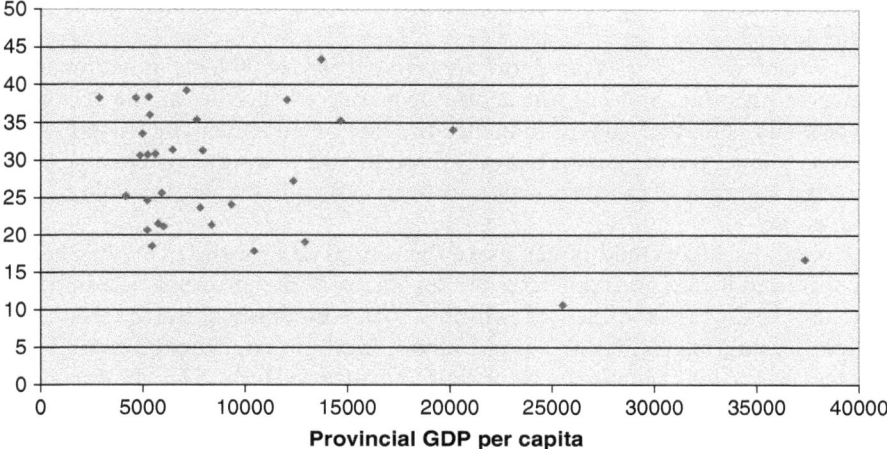

Fig. 3.3 Final stage of the VAT reform: provincial losses (Source: Ahmad et al. 2005; Ahmad 2008)

in closing loopholes in the income taxes. This parallels the experience of Mexico with the 2013 fiscal reform and the main example for China prior to the 2016 reforms (Ahmad 2017).

The Chinese government correctly decided to complete the VAT for business tax in one go in May 2016, paralleling the Mexican reforms of 2013. This was facilitated by "positive measures" to offset gainers and losers, including an adjustment in the origin-based sharing ratios, as well as a lump-sum transfer to compensate provinces for any losses incurred. A complex set of transfers could be involved with higher amounts going to the middle-income provinces. Yet the absolute losses in provinces, like Guangdong, will be very large and likely require greater "lump-sum transfers" than the losses in the poorer provinces.

The problem with the compensation mechanism is that the transfers are seldom "lump sum." Typically, they operate as "gap-filling" transfers and add to the incentives for local administrations to "game" the central government. This certainly does not add to greater accountability or generate incentives to shift to more sustainable "hubs."

3.5   Addressing Inequality: More Effective Use of the Pit and a Local "Piggy-Back"

Increasing inequality has emerged as a major issue in China. The typical instrument to address interpersonal inequality is the PIT. However, the Chinese PIT is not equipped to perform this role. This is because it is largely a tax based on withholding from wages—and may exacerbate inequalities by taxing middle-income groups more heavily than the richest groups. The richest people of course benefit from largely untaxed asset-based income—both from physical (property related) and financial instruments, including capital gains and dividends.

The Chinese PIT is shared on an origin basis with local governments. However, this does not constitute an "own-source" revenue as the recipient government is neither able to influence the rate or the base. The shared tax is effectively like a transfer and is typically discounted by ratings agencies in examining the strength of the jurisdiction in financing its liabilities, including local bond issues.

A piggy-back tax could be set above the central rate for the PIT while keeping the overall rate constant to avoid an increase in the overall tax burden. Further, setting of a local rate within a band established by the National People's Congress (NPC) would incentivize local governments to expand the relevant bases, for example, by providing information to the SAT on the major untapped assets (e.g., luxury homes and expensive cars). This may permit a *reduction* in the total rate available to a local government as the base is expanded, while additional revenues might be generated if there is an increase in the high value-added activity levels. More importantly, this feature becomes a critical element determining the eligibility of a local government in access to credit, given relevant own-sourced revenues.

It is clear that the coastal provinces would benefit from the "piggy-back" on the income tax arrangements more than the interior provinces. Consequently, it would be necessary to recalibrate the equalization framework. To avoid creating disincentives for provincial governments, the equalization system would have to be based on estimates of standard bases across the country and not actual revenues collected in any region. This would also make the equalization system introduced in 1994 work more efficiently—as it is based on the principle of providing all relevant governments the capability to provide similar levels of service at similar levels of tax effort. Operating on the spending part of the equation in isolation, as is largely the case at present in China, does not provide full incentives for efficient operations at the subnational level (see Ahmad and Brosio 2006).

3.6   *Congestion and Environmental Damage and a Carbon Tax*

Given the emphasis being placed by the Chinese government on climate change and structural reforms, a proposal is to develop a carbon tax, including an excise on petroleum products (see Ahmad et al. 2013). As with the PIT, a piggy-back rate with a "band" (e.g., up to 5% points), legislated by the NPC on a central base, would give an incentive to local governments to aggressively pursue the taxation of emissions, while avoiding the risk of a race to the bottom and ineffective implementation of the tax.

A carbon tax simply introduces a wedge above the international price of carbon-based products, such as coal, petroleum, and natural gas, to both reduce consumption and encourage more efficient and sustainable alternatives.

The difficulty is that carbon taxes fall on intermediates and would affect the price element of other goods. Thus, it is important to evaluate "effective taxes" and consequently the effects on producers and consumers as well. Some of the additional revenues should be earmarked toward R&D for new technologies and support for industrial restructuring in the Rust Belt in China.

It is desirable to maintain a uniform base for the carbon tax, if not a central tax. This would help to avoid a race to the bottom and also address externalities across local governments. A piggy-back arrangement for local governments would be possible, as in the income tax case, and this permits a higher rate in the more polluted cities.

In theory, the revenues generated by a system of cap-and-trade can replicate those generated by a carbon tax. The popularity of cap-and-trade is largely due to the difficulty, rather impossibility, of passing any new tax through the US Congress. Nonetheless, a carbon tax may be more transparent and therefore more likely to generate the production and consumption responses that are needed for reducing emissions and ensuring structural change. The experience with cap-and-trade systems in Europe has been mixed at best. Yet most European countries maintain high excises on petroleum products—mimicking a carbon tax that generates a great deal of revenue and has contributed, with other measures such as congestion charges and restrictions on emissions, to improvements in the air quality of cities such as London.

In China, there has been experimentation with seven regional cap-and-trade exchanges, but the revenues generated appear to have been meager. In due course, as the regional exchanges are integrated with the proposed national exchange and the cap-and-trade system begins to operate more effectively, there should be a possibility of discontinuing some of the measures described earlier—such as the quantitative restrictions on emissions. But in the medium term, a tax on petroleum products (or a carbon tax) and a cap-and-trade system are likely to continue in tandem.

A range of taxes is possible in relation to polluting motor vehicles—these would be both environmentally friendly and strongly redistributive. For instance, both purchase tax and annual registration fee could be made a function of engine size, hence corresponding to the likely emissions generated. Hybrid or electric vehicles could be exempted or subject to lower rates. The vehicle taxes could be determined and collected by third-tier governments that have to deal with the consequences of the vehicle pollution. The larger metropolitan areas, for example, Shanghai and Beijing, may also want to consider congestion charges, as practiced in London, or rationing by license plate numbers, as in Singapore.

Natural resource taxes are common as part of an array of instruments that also include production excises or a carbon tax, royalties, production-sharing arrangements, as well as standard VAT and corporate income taxes. A proper assessment would include all the taxes, which may have different components or objectives. As with the case of the VAT and excises described earlier, different objectives come into play vis à vis the taxation of natural resources that would require different instruments. The use of the VAT in the natural resource sector is taking on greater relevance as both private firms and SOEs may have incentives to cheat and hide transactions. Thus, the full VAT chain is of great importance, even in the natural resource sector. The Chinese practice of requiring the VAT on capital purchases to be offset against the VAT on sales of petroleum products is an example that should be more widely adopted in countries that have suffered from diversion of natural resource, such as Nigeria.

It may be appropriate to design a specific local resource tax that is based on the quantities extracted. This has the advantage that it would provide resources in proportion to the environmental damage inflicted by the extraction. And it would not be subject to the vagaries of international prices. However, as resources are depleted, the responsibility for restructuring or retraining would fall to the higher levels, which would also have access to the ad valorem revenues needed for stabilization in the medium term. As suggested in the Third Plenum directive, there should be a review and rationalization of all the charges associated with environmental purposes in China, together with the evaluation and introduction of a carbon tax.

The issue of depleted mineral reserves and affected enterprises and cities is an increasingly important issue for China. Clearly, resources have to be generated to finance the restructuring of industries and retraining of affected workers—this is receiving considerable attention at the present time as the restructuring is being implemented.

A number of "environmental taxes" are appropriate for the city/municipal level—ranging from vehicle registration and annual use permits, together with congestion charges. There could also be local excises on the exploitation and transmission of natural resources, for example, on pipelines that could defray the costs of the environmental damage. Similarly, there could be taxes on the discharge of polluted water or fees for the water treatment facilities. There are thus a range of taxes and fees and charges for environmental purposes that could be assigned to different levels of government.

3.7   Municipal/Community Charges for Local Benefits

Traditional US-style property taxes levied on ownership of property based on established records and up-to-date valuations typically perform poorly in emerging market economies, including in the more advanced Latin American countries. There are several reasons for this, as surveyed in Ahmad et al. (2015), including ownership titles and the difficulty in establishing a proper cadastre as well as valuation. Moreover, the tax is very visible and generates a lot of opposition. Finally, there are opportunities for rent-seeking when the tax is administered locally, especially when rates are set at higher levels (as in Mexico). Local officials are not then accountable and often do "deals" with friends and relatives.

Many of these problems are not confined to emerging markets, and the issue of valuation was one of the reasons that the UK abandoned the property tax system under Margaret Thatcher—although the poll tax that replaced it was even more unpopular and regressive.

A "beneficial tax" linked to the delivery of local public services is a possible alternative to a property tax, as described in Ahmad et al. (2015), an idea developed by Alfred Marshall that links the tax or charge to be paid to the benefits that are provided at the local level. These could include local services and connectivity, although user charges are appropriate for water and electricity.

The "beneficial tax" or "community charge" could operate on a system of bands, linked, for example, to the size and location of the property and the number of inhabitants—this is the logic of the system now in operation in the UK. The bands are linked to the cost and quantities of services consumed and are linked to the number of inhabitants and not necessarily ownership. This mechanism gets around both the cadastre and valuation difficulties that are legendary in emerging market countries with "fuzzy" property rights.

The community charge would also get around the issue of local resistance and would generate accountability on the part of local officials if they do not deliver the services that the community effectively pays for. The discipline of "yardstick competition" operates in countries with local elections. And in bureaucratic progression models, the promotion criteria could be linked to the satisfaction of local inhabitants with the quality of services provided. The big advantage of this system of community-based charges is that it can be put in place relatively quickly, without the need for a top-heavy bureaucratic apparatus or the need for a cadastre and tracking of property prices.

While a judicious choice of bands could reflect the variations in property valuations in metropolitan areas, equity considerations could be enhanced by a stamp duty on sales above a particular valuation. This is also the practice in the UK—and relate particularly to high-priced London properties.

The community charge is an effective "own-source" revenue and would qualify as the basis for an orderly access to credit or borrowing. This, in turn, would be reflected in the quality of public services provided.

It should be possible to begin a pilot project in, for instance, a city like Guangzhou or Shenzhen. These cities would generate much of the community charge in Guangdong, and there would be a need to establish a within-province equalization framework that would not disadvantage the poorest municipalities that may have relatively poor services or lower value bands.

3.8   Governance Changes

China was too large and diverse a country to be managed efficiently by diktat, especially in the presence of poor information available to the center on subnational operations on both revenue generation, which was in the hands of provinces, and public spending. The evolution continues, especially as institutions and information generation are modernized, representing one of the most significant structural transformations in modern times. However, the process needs to be further strengthened to provide the right incentives at the subnational level for a sustainable rebalancing and better utilization of the investment opportunities for lagging regions, across provinces inherent in the BRI, as well as within provinces such as Guangdong.

3.8.1   Budget Institutions and Governance

Although the 1993–1994 reforms constituted a significant "recentralization" on the revenue side (Ahmad et al. 2002, in Ahmad and Tanzi 2002), spending continued to be increasingly decentralized. This was financed by limited and decreasing revenue handles assigned to the local governments but also by equalization (untied) as well as earmarked transfers. As with the reluctance to share upwards a declining revenue pool in the 1980s, it became quickly evident to the central government that it was largely futile to impose conditions on local spending if the categories for spending were vaguely defined, or if there was poor information on the actual spending as well as the flow of funds.

With the realization that there would be limited influence over local governments without full information on the allocation and use of resources and the flow of cash, a fundamental reform of the budget institutions and processes was initiated in the late 1990s. China became one of the first major countries to adopt the IMF's Government Financial Statistical Manual 2001 (GFSM2001, recently revised to 2014). The main advantage of the GFSM2001/14 format is the generation of standardized fiscal data consistent with the System of National Accounts (SNA). The links with the SNA are critical in verifying and ensuring consistency of the data with the real estate sector. And without standardized and consistent data, it is hard to prevent local governments from "playing games."

The absence of standardized information across levels of government has been identified as a contributing factor in the ongoing crisis in Europe (see Ahmad et al. 2016). In particular, it facilitated the generation of liabilities at the local level that were hidden as arrears (e.g., in the Portuguese region of Madeira) or implicit liabilities associated with PPPs[8] and only surfaced with the pressure on the banking system as a result of the crisis. In many cases, for example, in Spain, quasi-private activities associated with local governments— for example, building apartments and holiday resorts—that were not counted as debt either at the central or local levels, also very quickly became public liabilities because of the crisis, leading to a sharp rise in the total general government debt. The ability to "hide" local liabilities or pass them on to other jurisdictions vitiates many of the perceived advantages of the electoral competition models.

Although China does better than the European countries, in that it has adopted the GFSM2001/14 standards, given the complexity of the measures and the time it takes to record and value assets and liabilities in the balance

---

[8] For a recent review of PPPs and incentive issues at multiple levels of government, see Ahmad et al. (2018a, b) (G24 Working Paper).

sheet, the government decided to focus initially on cash basis. This standard is being rolled out to lower levels of government. Consequently, the provisions on accruals and the establishment of the full balance sheets are not yet implemented, especially at the local levels, and consequently for general government (see Ahmad and Zhang 2018).

3.8.2   Number of Levels of Government

Multiple levels of government were useful as a mechanism of information generation and control in a medieval institutional context. This was also the case in Europe and has been one of the main constraints in the modernization of state functions, say in Italy (see Ambrosanio et al. 2016), and has been the focus of the rationalization attempts that were given a fillip by the current economic crisis. The main reasons for this reform are that the overlapping functions make it difficult to assign responsibilities and reduce costs, and also accountability is made more diffuse since it is harder to assign meaningful "own-source" revenues to more than three levels. A final point is that modern budget management and information generation systems become unwieldy at multiple levels and difficult to implement, say with the full GFSM2014 framework. Indeed, the existence of modern Government Financial Management Information Systems (FMIS) that can generate accurate and timely information on government operations at all levels makes the multiple levels of administration redundant.

In the European case, it has been observed that there is a tendency for liabilities to be telescoped down to the lower levels. These governments tend to have weaker financial information management systems, so that the liabilities are easier to disguise. Moreover, the ability of lower levels to manage PPPs efficiently is considerably reduced, accentuating the information asymmetries that exist anyway between the private parties and the lower levels of government or their entities involved. Similar considerations will apply in China (see Färber and Wang 2018, for a comparison between the Chinese and German cases).

3.8.3   Managing Subnational Risks and Liabilities

The Chinese budget law revised in the early 1990s did not permit local governments to borrow directly. However, to encourage investment, a 1992 provision allowed subnational borrowing through local urban development investment corporations. Implicitly, this was designed to encourage investment and would have corresponded to the "golden rule" of borrowing for investment only if the local companies had performed as anticipated. However, in the absence of full information on borrowing and the buildup of liabilities, it has not been possible for the central government to ensure that funds raised ostensibly for "productive" capital spending were not utilized for less productive current spending of local governments or by local enterprises—including for keeping on the right side of local officials.

The estimate of local government debt for June 2013, at around 31% of GDP, by the Audit Bureau was not large in relation to the reserves held by the central government. However, the liabilities appear to have been growing fastest at the county and township level that have very limited tax handles to be able to service the debt, much of which is relatively short term. Consequently, many local governments would likely have difficulty in servicing their debt in the medium term. To address the issue, some international agencies recommended the issuance of US-style local government bonds. And this indeed would be a component of a fully fledged system of local government financing and tax reforms. The Budget Law was revised in 2015 to permit local governments to issue bonds, including for existing liabilities. However, unlike US States and local governments, Chinese local administrations do not have access to own-revenue handles in the sense that rates could be raised on a specified base (or band; explained later). Consequently, it is not surprising that the response from banks and financial institutions to the local government bond issue was not particularly enthusiastic.

Indeed, the option for the central government to assume some of the local debt may be the only solution in the short run, as announced in March 2016, especially in relation to the counter-cyclical spending on behalf of the central government that was needed after the start of the 2008 crisis. However, this may generate disincentives that would need to be addressed through the creation of an own-source revenue-generation mechanism for each level of responsible government. And as mentioned earlier, responsible levels may relate to only the provincial level and county/townships.

4   NEXT STAGE OF GOVERNANCE AND FISCAL REFORMS FOR SUSTAINABLE GROWTH

Both short-term stabilization measures and structural changes for sustained development pose challenges for China and need to be coordinated. Indeed, rebalancing is proposed to move production away from the congested and polluted coastal metropolitan areas toward smaller cities in the interior and opening lagging regions, as well as enhancing connectivity with neighboring regions through the BRI initiative. This provides opportunities to both meet the short-term adjustment needs and the longer-term structural changes to ensure cleaner growth, and sustained employment in China, together with reduced spatial and interpersonal inequalities.

This ambitious restructuring agenda will require that incentives for the private sector and local governments are properly aligned to prevent wasteful spending, including on non-productive construction projects, but focus on "new sustainable hubs" with improved service delivery and improved governance. Consequently, it is useful to examine the role to be played by both tax policy and more effective spending and generation of information on budget processes. As we shall see, the incentive effects for firms and households are closely linked to those for local governments/officials.

The evolution of the Chinese governance model over the past 25 years has illustrated the importance of a balance between incentives and sanctions that keep local officials honest. As in the medieval systems in South Asia and Europe, trusted officials were assigned regions, although multiple layers and overlapping responsibilities ensured some oversight in distant capitals. The creation of a modern tax administration in the hands of the central government, to administer the most modern of tax instruments, was a true revolution, and has changed the dynamics of intergovernmental fiscal relations in China, although as noted earlier, the policy agenda is far from complete.

The difficulty in assigning meaningful own-tax handles and spending responsibilities has led to a three-layer structure that many countries are trying to achieve. Consequently, if the present 5+ layers administrative structure is maintained, two of the layers could become "deconcentrated" organs for say the provinces (prefectures) and counties/townships (village bodies).

The same three-tier arrangement would simplify spending assignments, including a needed recentralization of social security responsibilities, and the maintenance of minimum standards, to the central level as in most advanced countries. This reassignment would considerably reduce the spending pressures, including of unfunded mandates, at the lower levels of administration, and it would also become easier to hold officials accountable for the performance of assigned tasks, particularly effective service delivery and adhering to potential subnational fiscal responsibility legislation. The current aggregate growth targets are much too broad, create significant disincentives, and open up the possibility of diversion of resources and rent-seeking.

Of course, there is no point in establishing detailed performance targets for locally appointed officials if these cannot be monitored on a timely basis. It is also not sufficient just to track outcomes. Consider the case of two identical local governments. Government A manages to achieve all the performance targets, but at the cost of pushing liabilities to other jurisdictions or to the future (e.g., through opaque PPP contracts), so that the true costs of provision are not clearly delineated. Government B manages its finances prudently and does not incur debts. It may have a lower level of absolute performance, but the services are delivered more efficiently than in A. A simple performance-based system would reward officials in A and reduce the incentives for B to manage spending efficiently.

The same criticism applies to models of "yardstick competition" based on electoral evaluations of outcomes in neighboring jurisdictions. As pointed out in Ahmad et al. (2016), the overlapping responsibilities in many European countries, together with considerable "game-play" at the subnational level, resulted in passing on liabilities to other jurisdictions (typically in the end to the central government, although the initial response is to move the liabilities downwards where they might be less visible). Consequently, the electoral process ceases to perform the discipline that the yardstick or electoral competition models suggest. Weak information flows remove the advantage that the electoral models are assumed to have over appointed officials. In general, however, the governance based on appointed officials is likely to involve the need for considerable detail and accuracy of information flows on budgetary transactions and outcomes.

4.1   Fiscal Institutions and Governance with Modern Instruments

Fiscal institutions in China have evolved with changing technology, and with greater emphasis on managing information flows in both tax administration and budget management. The tax administration innovations, particularly the SAT's Golden Tax Project in the 1990s that enabled VAT invoices to be matched electronically, have become the standard being replicated from Mexico to Portugal in recent years. The technological developments open possibilities to streamline and tighten the governance possibilities that were just not available through the centuries and had led to an overlapping and complex structure of governments in order to establish appropriate checks and balances.

As seen earlier, the tax design and assignments affect incentives and costs facing producers and consumers but also local government officials—even if they are nominally appointed by the center. Both the resources available to local governments and a proper evaluation of their effectiveness in meeting public service delivery requirements are critical in ensuring good local governance.

In the context of budget systems, while China has made good progress with the GFSM2001 framework in the early years of the twenty-first century in China (Brazil is only just beginning this reform at the subnational level), significant work is needed to generate full information on liabilities within local balance sheets for the benefit of markets and investors (Ahmad and Zhang 2018). The process will become more complicated with the emphasis on PPPs (Ahmad et al. 2015). While the involvement of the private sector is an important step in financing public investments, this has to be managed carefully.

Treasury systems in China were modernized at the same time as the introduction of the GFSM2001 framework, with the establishment of a nested system of Treasury Single Accounts (TSAs) for the central and provincial governments. Again, this is a critical reform made feasible using modern banking and clearing mechanisms, as well as (eventually) electronic payments and receipts. This way, all cash flows in the economy can be tracked, minimizing the possibilities for diversion of funds.

With the full GFSM2001/14, as well as a TSA, a central government should be able to establish more detailed targets for local officials and be able to monitor outcomes on a real-time basis. In principle, this also applies to arrears and the buildup of liabilities. With the full balance sheets, it should be possible to ensure compliance by local governments of (potential) fiscal responsibility targets in their jurisdictions, as well as monitoring of the effectiveness of service delivery. Although China had moved toward the GFSM2001 format almost ten years ago, together with a system of TSAs, local operations are mainly managed on a cash basis, and liabilities are not recorded effectively in the budget and treasury systems, or in local balance sheets. As argued in Ahmad and Zhang (2018), recording full information on liabilities in the local level balance sheets, while desirable, will take many years to become fully operational.

4.2   Financing Productive Subnational Investments and Management of Liabilities

As mentioned earlier, although local governments were unable to borrow directly, they could establish companies to do so. In the absence of information on sources and uses of the funds, and the full extent of liabilities, it had become very difficult to ensure that the resources were being used effectively. Issues are complicated in borrowing from shadow banks, arrears, as well as potential losses of local SOEs.

It is more difficult to manage future liabilities generated through PPPs. These have been very problematic in Europe (Ahmad et al. 2016). There is an incentive for local governments to use PPPs to "kick the can down the road"—as part of "game-play" with the center. Also, as there is asymmetric information between the private party and the government, or between different levels of government, that could lead to renegotiation of terms and higher incidence of liabilities than contracted. IPSAS Rule 32 requires that the buildup of PPP liabilities should be reflected in the local government balance sheet with appropriate provisioning—this is very hard to achieve in the short run.

Without the full information, consistent with GFSM2001/14 and IPSAS standards (and this will take time to generate), it is not evident that the local governments or their companies would be able to service the debt without having to pass it on to Beijing. Clearly, the central government has the capability to handle local debt easily, but it would create a moral hazard and weaken the budget constraints if it were to do so on a regular basis.

The revision of the Chinese budget law in 2015 now permits local governments to issue bonds. This is a welcome and needed step and needs to be part of the financing arsenal of local governments. However, the measure is unlikely to be sufficient to generate a solution to local government indebtedness in China without the development of own-source revenues at the provincial and municipal levels.

Two components are critical for local bond markets. The most important is that local governments should have own-source revenues against which their ability to pay can be judged by the bondholders and markets. Consequently, the ability to contract debt at the local level and pass on the liabilities to higher levels of government reduces the incentives to either utilize own sources of revenues or manage spending efficiently. The second is that there should be full information available on the nature and magnitude of the liabilities concerned.

5   Conclusions

The Chinese governance model is evolving with the advent of modern institutions and information flows. Additional progress on tax reforms to reduce the costs of doing business leading to more sustainable investment decisions is dependent on new revenue assignments at all levels of government. This reform needs to be coordinated with rationalization of numbers of tiers, clarity in spending assignments, as well as the institutions and information generation capabilities of modern tax and budget systems. In this manner, the appointed officials can be held accountable for more effective service delivery and maintaining fiscal responsibility together with sensible complementary investments needed to make sustainable "rebalancing" a reality and make full use of BRI connectivity.

While rebalancing involves generating new activities in the interior provinces, the within-province differentials are significant enough to warrant a similar consideration as at the national level in China. For instance, restructuring of activities outside the Pearl River Delta, but within the province of Guangdong, also provides a microcosm of the fiscal reforms and investments needed at the national level in China. This related both to the connectivity within China and with neighboring countries under the BRI, as well as local linkages to connect "lagging" regions to the new "hubs." Thus, the fiscal institutions and policy options that could be used in Guangdong may be examples for the rest of the country.

In the final analysis, adapting policies and institutions to deal effectively with risk, income distribution, and the environmental challenges will strengthen the Chinese governance model, not weaken it.

References

Ahmad, Ehtisham, Niu Meili and Xiao Kezhou, eds., 2018a, *Fiscal underpinnings for sustainable development in China—rebalancing in Guangdong*. Springer.

Ahmad, Ehtisham, Amar Bhattacharya, Annalisa Vinella and Kezhou Xiao, 2018b, "Involving the Private Sector and PPPs in Financing Public Investments," in Ahmad, Niu and Xiao (2018).

Ahmad, Ehtisham and Xiaorong Zhang, 2018, "Towards monitoring and managing subnational liabilities in China: lessons from the balance sheet for county K," in Ahmad, Niu and Xiao (2018).

Ahmad, Ehtisham (2017), "Political Economy of Tax Reform for the SDGs: Improving the investment climate, addressing inequality; stopping the cheating." Intergovernmental Group of 24, Working Paper, Washington DC.

Ahmad, Ehtisham, Massimo Bordignon and Giorgio Brosio, eds., 2016, *Multilevel Finance and the Euro Crisis*, Edward Elgar.

Ahmad, Ehtisham and Giorgio Brosio, eds., 2015, *Handbook of Multilevel Finance*, Edward Elgar.

Ahmad, Ehtisham, Giorgio Brosio and Caroline Pöschl, 2015, "Local property taxation and benefits in developing countries: overcoming political resistance", in Ahmad and Brosio 2015, op cit.

Ahmad, Ehtisham, James Rydge and Nicholas Stern, 2013, "Structural change leads to tax reforms leads to structural change," China Development Forum March 2013.

Ahmad, Ehtisham, 2008, "Tax reforms and the sequencing of intergovernmental reforms in China: preconditions for a Xiaokang society," in Lou Jiwei and Shulin Wang, eds., 2008.

Ahmad, Ehtisham and Giorgio Brosio, eds., 2006, *Handbook of Fiscal Federalism*, Edward Elgar.

Ahmad, Ehtisham, Ben Lockwood and Raju Singh, 2004, "Financial Consequences of the Chinese VAT Reform." *International VAT Monitor* May/June: 181–86.

Ahmad, Ehtisham and Vito Tanzi, eds., 2002, *Managing Fiscal Decentralization*, Routledge.

Ahmad, Ehtisham, Li Keping and Tom Richardson, 2002, "Recentralization in China?" in Ehtisham Ahmad and Vito Tanzi, 2002, eds.,

Ahmad, Ehtisham, Gao Qiang and Vito Tanzi, 1995, *Reforming China's Public Finances,* International Monetary Fund.

Ambrosanio, Flavia, Paolo Balduzzi and Massimo Bordignon, 2016, "Economic crisis and fiscal federalism in Italy," in Ahmad, Bordignon and Brosio, eds., 2016, *op cit.*

Besley, Tim and Ann Case, 1995, "Incumbent behavior, vote-seeking, tax-setting and yardstick competition," *American Economic Review*, 85(1), 25–45.

Breton, A., 1965, "A theory of government grants," *Canadian Journal of Economics and Political Science,* 31, 175–87.

Breton, A., 2002, "An introduction to decentralization failure," in Ehtisham Ahmad and Vito Tanzi, eds., (2002).

Brown, K., 2016, "A response to Francis Fukuyama's 'Reflections on Chinese Governance'," *Journal of Chinese Governance*, September 2016.

Färber, Gisela and Zhijie Wang, 2018, "Subnational public debt in China and Germany—a comparative assessment," in Ahmad, Niu and Xiao 2018.

Fukuyama, F., 2016, "Reflections on Chinese Governance," *Journal of Chinese Governance*, September 2016.

Gao Qiang, 1995, "Problems in Chinese intragovernmental fiscal relations, tax-sharing system and future reforms," in Ahmad, Gao and Tanzi, 1995, *op cit.*

Hamilton, Alexander, John Jay and James Madison, 1787–88, *The Federalist Papers,* reprinted in Penguin Classics, 1987.

Hinrichs, H., 1966, *A General Theory of Tax Structure During Economic Development,* Harvard University Press. Mass.

IMF, 2016, China: Article IV Consultation Report, Washington DC.

Liu Shangxi and Li Chengwei, 2018, "Public services evaluation from the perspective of public risk management", in Ahmad, Niu and Xiao (2018).

Lockwood, B., 2015, "The Political Economy of Decentralization," in Ahmad and Brosio, 2015, op cit.

Lou Jiwei and Shulin Wang, eds., 2008, *Fiscal Reforms in China*, Oxford University Press.

Luo, Xubei and Zhu Nong, 2018, "Hub-periphery development pattern and inclusive growth: case study of Guangdong province," in Ahmad, Niu and Xiao, 2018, op cit.

Musgrave, R., 1959, *The Theory of Public Finance,* McGraw-Hill.

Pi-Han Tsai, 2016, "Fiscal incentives and political budget cycles in China," *International Tax and Public Finance.*

Rostow, W.W., 1960, *The Stages of Economic Growth: A Non-Communist Manifesto,* Cambridge University.

Shi Yao Bin, 1995, "Unifying the Enterprise Income Tax and reforming profit distribution between Government and State Owned Enterprises," in Ahmad, Gao and Tanzi 1995.

Tanzi, V., 1987, "Quantitative characteristics of the tax systems of developing countries," in D. Newbery and N. Stern, eds., *The Theory of Taxation for Developing Countries*, Oxford University Press.

Xiao, K., 2018, "Managing subnational liability for sustainable development: a case study of Guangdong Province," in Ahmad, Niu and Xiao (2018).

Xu Shanda and Ma Lin, 1995, "Reform and the market economy and tax in China," in Ahmad, Gao and Tanzi, 1995, op cit.

Jing Zhang, 2015, "Government Finances and Public Interests: Perspectives on State Building," *Journal of Chinese Governance*.

CHAPTER 4

The Critical Role of Local Governance in China's Political System

Anna L. Ahlers, Thomas Heberer, and Gunter Schubert

1 Introduction

Why and how do the tiers of local government, and the modes of governance evolving around them, occupy a critical role in China's authoritarian state structure? This chapter approaches this question by looking at one of the core functions embedded in local governance arrangements: policy implementation. The ability of continuously safeguarding a critical degree of output effectiveness amidst ever-increasing complexity and challenges is widely regarded as a pillar of state capacity and a symbol of regime adaptability in contemporary

This chapter is an abbreviated and slightly revised version of an article previously published as Ahlers et al. (2016).

A. L. Ahlers (✉)
University of Oslo, Oslo, Norway
e-mail: a.l.ahlers@ikos.uio.no

T. Heberer
Institute of Political Science and the Institute of East Asian Studies, University of Duisburg-Essen, Duisburg, Germany
e-mail: thomas.heberer@uni-due.de

G. Schubert
European Research Center on Contemporary Taiwan (ERCCT), University of Tübingen, Tübingen, Germany
e-mail: gunter.schubert@uni-tuebingen.de

© The Author(s) 2019
J. Yu, S. Guo (eds.), *The Palgrave Handbook of Local Governance in Contemporary China*, https://doi.org/10.1007/978-981-13-2799-5_4

China.[1] In fact, governance research needs a local perspective to examine ultimate policymaking where the state 'meets the people' and where policy outcomes become immediately relevant. And it is at the local level that the political system seems most flexible and adaptive.

This chapter shows that local governance in the Chinese political system is more than a mere copy or extension of structures and mechanisms found at higher levels of the governmental hierarchy. Although China's local bureaucracies have to obey the upper levels—prefectures, provinces, and the center—they still have substantial maneuvering space to shape the implementation of policies and to determine the political system's capacity to deliver meaningful outcomes (Ahlers 2014b).

We conceptualize local governance as procedural, along the lines of Capano, Howlett, and Ramesh who recently pleaded for applying a contingent perspective and for abandoning the typological tradition in governance research. Their analytical framework for the study of *governance arrangements* includes such aspects as (here in italics): "*dynamics*: due to the fact that they [government arrangements] change over time and very often are characterized by different policy mixes, (…) their *strategic nature*: since they are the products of the actions and interactions of policy actors driven by specific goals, and (…) their *capacity*: that is how likely governance arrangements can be effective in relation to certain important collective goals" (Capano et al. 2015: 8–9 [original parentheses deleted for this quote]).

Although we concentrate on the local tiers of China's political hierarchy in our analysis, we depart from the usual focus on the apparent central-local state dichotomy and an exclusive concentration on one of these perspectives. Local governance research on China must take into account the 'bigger picture', or systemic context, in which such governance happens. Since the launch of 'reform and opening' in the late 1970s, local governments have enjoyed increasing leeway in adapting central policies to local conditions and steering local policy implementation. In the early 2000s, several important reforms, particularly the tax-for-fee reforms, the ensuing expansion of a system of fiscal transfers, and new state-funded programs for developing the countryside and spurring rural-urban integration have changed the nature of local policymaking in China considerably. Local state maneuvering in contemporary China is shaped as much by centrally designed policies and institutional control mechanisms (tax competition, cadre and performance evaluation, promotion) as by strategic agency on the part of local party and government cadres which must

---

[1] We have defined effective policy implementation elsewhere as measuring outcomes according to the objectives, or targets, defined by policy-makers at the outset of the implementation process, while also ensuring that important public needs and demands are met, overall state capacity is enhanced, and critical degrees of system stability and regime legitimacy are generated. *Effective* policy implementation should not be confused with *efficient* policy implementation, as the latter is less concerned with the policy process, but rather focuses on outcomes in terms of Pareto efficiency and high responsiveness to public demands (Ahlers and Schubert 2015: 377–379).

deliver results to the upper levels in order to ensure their future careers or, if promotion is not likely, at least in order to maintain their current rank and social status (Heberer and Schubert 2012). This tension entails, as we argue, the successful reconciliation of local state agents' collective interests with the central state's overarching policy objectives and the maintenance of overall state capacity to master increasing challenges stemming from the political and social environment. Policymaking in China is not determined exclusively either by top-down guidance or by bottom-up collusion and mere 'muddling through', but rather by a delicate mixture of central state 'signaling', institutional constraints, and strategic agency on the part of local cadre bureaucracies across all governmental tiers. In other words, current local governance arrangements and effective policy implementation are the product of central state claims to political steering *and* local responses to these claims, which are increasingly influenced by and take into account relevant non-governmental stakeholders with specific relevance for policy implementation.

To give flesh to these contentions, we draw from years of fieldwork carried out in some 15 counties and cities spread all over China.[2] Without attempting to delve too deeply into different case studies, we bring together a number of observations and key findings from different regions which suggest that certain reconfigurations of local state governance can be observed across China. This chapter is structured as follows: first, we highlight some of the important policy changes and institutional reforms which have been launched by the central government since the early 2000s. Subsequently, we explain how these reforms have impacted on local state governance, and thereby policy implementation, especially at the county and township level. In the last part, we show how local governance has become more inclusive and increasingly tends to mobilize and selectively involve non-governmental actors and the general public in policymaking. In conclusion, we summarize our conceptualization of current local governance in the Chinese political system.

2   Major Shifts in the National Policy Context Since the 2000s

Local governance arrangements were strongly influenced by the political reorientation of the central government in the early 2000s, when significant reforms to the fiscal system were undertaken and a new, comprehensive approach toward rural development was adopted (He 2007; Liu and Tao 2007; Lou and Wang 2008; Zhan 2009; Göbel 2010; Ahlers 2014b). This was the result of a protracted learning process, after the party leadership realized in the late 1990s that the 'peasant burden', accompanied by increasing

---

[2] More specifically, we conducted fieldwork annually between 2008 and 2015 in the provinces of Fujian, Hubei, Guizhou, Guangdong, Jiangsu, Jiangxi, Jilin, Shaanxi, Shandong, Sichuan, and Zhejiang, working mostly at the county and township/district level.

social disparities and a rural-urban divide, was posing a threat to the survival of 'Chinese socialism'. Consequently, the successive elimination of all taxes and fees since the early 2000s was also accompanied by the abolition of the highly symbolic agricultural tax in 2006 and the systematic expansion of the fiscal transfer system, which had been established in the mid-1990s.[3] These were crucial measures that, together with enforced top-down monitoring, 'turned the wheel' in the Chinese countryside. The areas and localities which were experiencing difficulties in making ends meet were specifically targeted and were provided with fresh public funds in order to invest in the local infrastructure and public goods provision. A new phase of rural development was propagated that would soon link up with a strong push for rural-urban integration.

In fact, the Hu-Wen administration embarked on a paradigmatic change in the government's approach to 'socialism with Chinese characteristics' by using the tax system to discriminate against the wealthier provinces and redistribute this money by means of fiscal transfers (including a wide array of earmarked funds), to the less developed parts of the country.[4] At the same time, local cadre bureaucracies were forced to foster more balanced economic growth and to provide better access to public goods—most notably health care, education, and poverty alleviation—in their jurisdictions. Growing peasant unrest throughout the 1990s and the early 2000s had alerted the central government to the urgent need to deal with the combined dangers of illegal taxes and fees, the wastage of (scarce) public money by local governments, and 'land grabs' implemented without adequate compensation against farmers in order to provide local governments with the new money required to make up for their many 'underfunded mandates'.

These policy reforms were accompanied by a new official discourse that introduced the formula of 'Building a Service-oriented Government' (*jianshe*

---

[3] Although the intergovernmental transfer system has been expanded over the years, most local governments still face 'financial stress' because the central government has not decentralized the fiscal system since 1994. As a matter of fact, the fiscal dependence of local governments helps the central state to enforce its policies, since the former must compete for scarce funding by proving that they can bring about effective policy implementation. The Chinese Communist Party (CCP) Central Committee's new reform agenda of November 2013, as well as the central government work plan presented during the National People's Congress in March 2014, announced another circle of thorough reforms in the intergovernmental financial system. According to the new plans, earmarked funds (*zhuangxiang zhuanyi zhifu*) and matching requirements (*peitao zijin*) for local governments will gradually be replaced by general financial transfers (*yibanxing zhuanyi zhifu*) (CCP Central Committee 2013; Li 2014).

[4] There is a much more negative account of this story. Christine Wong has been one of the fiercest critics of Chinese fiscal policy and has repeatedly contested the claim that it helps to equalize regional economic disparities and strengthen public goods provision in the Chinese countryside (Wong 2007; Wong and Bird 2008). For a more recent account of the 'negative narrative', see also Liu 2012. These authors usually demand that the central government change the fiscal system to ensure that local governments do not have to face 'underfunded mandates' which force them to become 'predators' or debtors.

fuwuxing zhengfu). It emphasized the need to enhance administrative efficiency, in particular the provision of public goods, and was also designed to improve the reputation of local officials (Ahlers 2014a).[5] In the official jargon:

> a service-oriented government represents a *governance mode* that places service in the center of government functions, which requires a fundamental transformation of government functions in Chinese public administration. The service-oriented government asks for a sufficient understanding of the needs of citizens and business that is critical to meet the goals of creating a favorable socio-economic environment and providing quality public services. (Wu et al. 2013: 2 [emphasis added])

This connotation can now be found in any national policy initiative as well as in guidelines targeting local governance reform (Xinhua Press 2006; Ahlers 2014a). Moreover, it summarizes the change in rhetoric which has been implicit in official policy speak since the Hu-Wen Administration years and now continuously calls upon local party and government cadres to become 'service providers' and 'explorers', for example, in developing urbanization strategies (*zhongguo tese xinxing chengzhenhua*) (Ahlers 2015), building up and expanding social welfare security systems (Stepan and Müller 2012), and—generally speaking—implementing the CCP's November 2013 reform agenda at the local level (CCP Central Committee 2013). The new discourse represents a stark contrast from the previous decades of decentralization after 'reform and opening', when local state agents were often easy scapegoats for state propaganda and the media and were basically held responsible for all policy failures at the grassroots level (Göbel 2010, 2011, 2012)—ultimately at the risk of alienating them from the political regime. Now, local cadres are expected more than ever before to foster cooperation with the private sector and, for example, to push for local bank reform in order to facilitate credit access for private enterprises. But local governments are called upon not only to treat citizens and 'stakeholders' affected by certain policies like clients but also to streamline their administrative apparatuses by contracting out a growing number of public services to the private sector (Ahlers 2014b; Ahlers and Schubert 2018).

Concurrently with the inflow of more resources and responsibilities, the cadre and performance evaluation regime (*kaohe, kaoping zhidu*) was reformed. Thus, it not only became more pervasive in controlling local bureaucracies but also increasingly sophisticated and flexible in local adoption. While major developmental issues, such as gross domestic product (GDP) growth or birth planning have retained their crucial status over the years, other major targets,

---

[5] The notion was later integrated into the 'Building a Harmonious Society' concept and further promoted by the party propaganda (Wei 2006; CCP Central Committee 2011).

such as 'social stability',[6] environmental protection and UN-defined 'human development' indicators have been included to different degrees and have reshaped local governance arrangements.[7] Additionally, modern technologies such as digital surveillance methods and online platforms for assessing public concerns on specific issues, as well as telephone-based opinion surveys and even random interviews conducted with residents have been incorporated into cadre evaluation systems at all levels. Although these systems operate in roughly the same way in each and every locality, there is space for local adaptation and, as we argue, for strategic—sometimes informal—forms of application conducive to effective policy implementation (Ahlers 2015; Ahlers and Schubert 2009, 2015, 2018; Delman 2015; Heberer 2014; Heberer and Senz 2011; Heberer and Trappel 2013; Landry 2008; Schubert and Ahlers 2011, 2012).

Finally, as local governments are now largely relieved of strained cadre-peasant relations caused by the highly contested exaction of taxes and fees, the expansion of formal and informal public participation has gained more importance in local governance (He and Warren 2011; Manion 2014; Mertha 2009; Schubert and Ahlers 2012; Thøgersen 2009). Public demands and responses are now increasingly taken into account in the process of designing and carrying out local policies, with the overall objective of ensuring 'social stability'. Furthermore, a rising number of new policies and regulations, such as the 'Action Plan on Prevention and Control of Air Pollution' (*daqi wuran fangzhi xingdong jihua*) (State Council 2013) or the "National New-Type Urbanization Plan" (*guojia xinxing chengzhenhua guihua*) (State Council 2014), explicitly call for more public engagement in local policy implementation, thus making local governance evermore complex (Ahlers and Schubert 2018). The effects of these shifts in policy mixes will briefly be portrayed in the following two sections.

3   ADJUSTMENTS IN THE ORGANIZATION OF LOCAL POLICY IMPLEMENTATION

The reforms pushed through since the early 2000s gave rise to important shifts in central-local relations and changed the ways in which the agency of local governments was framed within the overall policy process; they also included incentives for shifts in governance arrangements. This can best be examined by

---

[6] Most prominent of all, 'social stability' as an evaluation indicator means that any occurrence of social unrest, even legal petitions submitted to whatever government level, will seriously diminish the performance record of an official or a government bureau. The 'social stability imperative' severely constrains the behavior of local bureaucracies. For instance, while until recently protests were often crushed by violent means, county and township cadres are now more cautious and try to anticipate and avoid contention, resulting in attempts at more deliberation of policy adjustment and intensified responsiveness to public demands (Ahlers 2014b; Ahlers and Schubert 2015).

[7] Most recently, the national austerity and anti-corruption campaign under Xi Jinping's central leadership seems to be placing serious constraints on local governments (Wedeman 2014). Although there are indications of positive effects on cadres' behavior with regard to the use of public money, its measurable effects on policy implementation and outcomes have yet to be studied in detail.

taking a closer look at the policy process in the local state (i.e., at the county, township, and village level), where upper-level policies must be constantly adjusted and ultimately implemented. Following the restructuring of the fiscal system, the Chinese central government put forward a new strategy for rural development and urban transformation in the 11th Five-Year-Plan (2006–2010), under the heading of 'Building a New Socialist Countryside' (BNSC).[8] A mixture of policy measures was prescribed to spur investment in local infrastructures (roads and highways, electrical power in villages, broadband access, etc.). Along with it came agricultural modernization and specialization, the expansion of social welfare (with a focus on the new rural cooperative medical system and on the minimum living allowance program), the renovation or relocation of villages, and accelerated in situ urbanization (State Council 2006; Ahlers and Schubert 2009). Since we have analyzed the BSNC policy process in great detail elsewhere, we only highlight here what we see as significant shifts in the governance arrangements that have accompanied this new policy mix, which has arguably been the single most comprehensive and momentous development initiative in recent decades.[9]

The new BNSC policy framework was based on rather vague slogans meant to embody the policy's 'spirit' and accompanied by a few rather general policy guidelines, which provincial and city governments then spelled out more precisely. In this way, local leaders were encouraged to act as political entrepreneurs and to come up with policy innovations and their own development strategy or 'model' (*moshi*), which, if successful, could pave the way for successful cadre careers. This obligation to adapt upper-level guidelines to local circumstances and to promote local best-practice solutions for rural development offered generous leeway for finding new implementation strategies and governance arrangements (Ahlers 2014b; Ahlers and Schubert 2015, 2018; Göbel 2012; Schubert and Heberer 2015). Faced with the need to decide and realize coherent policy measures within a large and diverse policy framework such as BNSC or rural-urban integration, local governments have expanded on long-established modes of internal policy coordination and organization. Beyond the formal implementation structure for upper-level guidelines in the counties that we investigated, the internal coherence of policymaking was additionally enhanced by informal regular meetings among the most committed department heads involved in BNSC design and implementation. For example, in Qingyuan County, Zhejiang Province, regular informal gatherings of concerned

---

[8] For example, BNSC is still mentioned in the 12th Five-Year-Plan and in the CCP's new monumental agenda for the 'Comprehensive Deepening of Reforms' of November 2013 (CCP Central Committee 2013).

[9] Although the terminology of the BNSC program is used with less frequency than in the early years after its promulgation, these arrangements can be found in basically all crucial policy initiatives launched ever since, for example, agricultural modernization and industrialization (decentralized), urbanization, private sector development, better public goods provision, and environmental preservation remain the main objectives of the central state and local governments.

officials to discuss rural issues ensured that the final decisions taken were appropriate while keeping friction between government bureaus and agencies (on issues such as budget and personnel allocation) at bay. In general, the dynamics of the internal policy coordination process were strongly conditioned by the leadership style of the county party secretaries and their respective policy preferences. In all counties, the informal coordination of BNSC was interwoven creatively into the formal policy-making process to ensure that policy implementation was not obstructed by inter-bureau competition of any sort.

In particular, and in accordance with the abovementioned reforms of the fiscal system, the allocation of public funds was subjected to considerable change. Budgets for most of the policy measures related to BNSC were only allocated by higher levels after completion of a complex project application process that started in the villages, and this money was never paid fully in advance but rather on a multistep, cash-on-delivery basis. Counties were forced to monitor the implementation of specific projects by setting up indicators for successive performance fulfillment and, accordingly, only provided partial funding (to contracted companies or township and village coffers). Allocating earmarked funds in this way may not deter local governments from diverting public money to other projects targeted by local budgets nor necessarily do away with corruption and nepotism (Gong and Wu 2012; Liu et al. 2009). However, it is safe to say that such undesirable practices have become more difficult today than they were in the early 2000s. Since counties must come up with substantial matching funds (*peitao jijin*) (which may, however, be refunded if project implementation is swift and cost-effective), they have a strong incentive to secure effective policy implementation. Furthermore, county governments pass the pressure of the *peitao* system down to townships and villages in their jurisdictions, ensuring that the latter run on tight budgets and have fewer opportunities to waste money. The logic underlying this system is simple: all actors will strive harder for successful completion of a project if their own financial resources are involved (Ahlers 2014b; Ahlers and Schubert 2015).

As a matter of fact, county governments are surprisingly inventive in implementing policies under conditions of scarce financial resources. The so-called Five Changes (*wuhua*) program[10] initiated by Qingdao municipality (a sub-provincial city) to improve the rural infrastructure in Laixi (a county-level city in Shandong) is a good example. In order to fulfill the *wuhua* targets and keep expenditures low, the local government started by selecting more developed and wealthier villages close to highways for the first year of policy implementation. In the second year (2009), the county requested additional funding from Qingdao City and expanded the program to villages that were at an average stage of development economically, were able to come up with matching funds,

---

[10] The *wuhua* program encompassed the construction of more solid roads (*yinghua*) and the beautification (*meihua*), greening (*lühua*), illumination (*lianghua*), and cleanliness (*jinghua*) of villages.

or whose good connections with local enterprises guaranteed quick and proper project implementation. Concurrently, the county leadership instructed local enterprises and government departments to take over responsibility for specific villages of the second cohort and to contribute to the program from their budgets. The county also diverted money from various funds (e.g., for poverty alleviation) to the *wuhua* program. In the final year (2010), the Laixi government focused on villages with only marginal funding resources, knowing that poor and remote townships and villages would be unable to implement the *wuhua* program without substantial external support. Given the lack of adequate funding for 2010, Laixi entered again into negotiations with Qingdao in order to ensure program fulfillment.[11] This strategy, which was also found in other counties that we investigated, is clearly based on the logic of development by concentric circles: first, provide support for the cluster of better-off villages close to highways. This will probably lead to a positive evaluation by upper levels and open up bargaining space vis-à-vis the prefectural city for obtaining additional funding in order to proceed to the second circle. The most remote and poor villages are the last to be included in the program on hand, and if targets have been successfully met in the second cohort, there will be more bargaining space for obtaining supplementary funding for the poorest villages, too. Hence, the relationship between counties and municipalities is flexible enough to be exploited by adept county party secretaries to implement policies under 'financial stress' (Heberer and Senz 2011).[12]

4   MULTILEVEL GOVERNANCE IN THE LOCAL STATE

The earlier example alone indicates that altered governance arrangements stretch across different levels of government. In fact, effective policy implementation in contemporary China is also positively linked to specific downwards relationships, that is, between counties and townships. Although there is plenty of competition and friction between these tiers (Hsing 2006; Smith 2010; Wu 2007; Zhao 2006a, b), counties and townships are not fierce antagonists. On the contrary, they are well aware of their interdependence when it comes to being able to fulfill upper-level requirements, realize local developmental goals, and secure the good performance records that are critical for avoiding upper-level interference and securing individual cadre promotion.

While county governments clearly have the upper hand over the townships in their jurisdictions, they also need them to ultimately implement policies at

[11] As a leading official on Laixi's Agricultural Commission stated, Qingdao was under an obligation to increase the funding for the program because the poorer villages were either unwilling or unable to pay for it. Thus, if Qingdao wanted to have the program implemented, more money would have to be provided. Interview, Agricultural Commission of Qingdao, September 8, 2008.

[12] A similar, but slightly more formalized, tool, employed by local governments that contributes to the effective allocation of scarce funds, is what Ahlers and Schubert (2013) have called 'strategic modelling'.

the grassroots. Townships prepare, oversee, and assess the villages' project implementation on behalf of the counties. Quite naturally, the township government exerts a crucial influence on the eventual preference order of villages. In practice, the townships have usually selected the villages they deemed most suitable to apply for funding, taking into account the overall economic situation in a village, the past performance of village leaders (particularly their ability to manage village affairs and project implementation), and the degree of township control over them. The name of the group of villages that would qualify for specific policy measures was then forwarded to the county, where the final decisions were made on project applications and the allocation of funds. These decisions were oriented to the overall development strategy of a county government, the quality of applications from subordinate levels, the scope of available financial resources (often coming down from upper levels as earmarked funds), and, inevitably, informal factors, such as personal access of township leaders to county officials.

At the same time, there was little evidence of conflict between townships and villages in the localities that we visited. Since villages and townships are financially dependent on the county government, they had strong incentives not to risk falling out with their superiors and, as a consequence, see much-needed money flow in other directions. Moreover, the fact that villages did not all receive the same amount of project funding was viewed positively by county and township cadres as being conducive to inter-village competition and resulting in more effective policy implementation. Also, county cadres claimed that they took care to distribute scarce funds evenly across their jurisdictions over time in order to achieve the balanced development of villages and townships—something that their superiors could not and would not ignore in the regular evaluation of county government performance. Respondents at all levels—county, township, and village—reported that the process of applying for projects had become more transparent, that funding had visibly increased each year, and that public goods provision had strengthened since the promulgation of BNSC (Ahlers 2014b; Ahlers and Schubert 2009, 2015; Schubert and Ahlers 2012).[13]

In addition, special BSNC project-related bodies were created in many counties that we visited, mostly at the village level, in order to enhance application cohesiveness and public legitimation, implementation oversight, and communication between different administrative tiers and between authorities and residents (see below). For instance, village group heads, as in Dingnan County (Jiangxi), were made special envoys of their village (group)'s cause (*liancun*) and thus had direct access to the relevant departments within the county government, bypassing the more intermediate township-level authorities. At the same time, in most of the localities studied, leading party and bureau cadres at the county and township level were assigned 'tutorship' for individual villages (*bao-*

---

[13] This assessment is corroborated by other research on the topic (Stepan et al. 2016).

cun zhidu) in their jurisdictions and were given the task of providing guidance and mediation in village affairs and project implementation. All these crisscrossing institutions, which had often started out informally before being formally put in place, both served the purpose of implementation enforcement and acted as a double-check mechanism (Ahlers 2014b; Ahlers and Schubert 2015).

5   INTERNAL EVALUATION OF LOCAL POLICY IMPLEMENTATION

Our empirical analyses in the field of BNSC show that the cadre and performance evaluation system has developed into an influential incentive and communication system that has encouraged local cadres to ensure the sound implementation of upper-level policy guidelines, policy innovation, and 'social stability' (*shehui wending*). In all the localities that we investigated, the county governments adjusted the evaluation sheets for subordinate levels according to their development strategies. They tailored catalogues of target indicators passed down earlier by city governments to match their specific policy preferences. In Dingnan County, for instance, it was decided that 'civilized road building' (a program promoted by superior Ganzhou City) could be discarded for the purpose of converting the evaluation points originally allocated for performance in this category to the urban development section (an important element of Dingnan's BNSC blueprint). Also, county governments accentuated certain policy requirements they deemed important, for instance, by upgrading performance in financial management to 'one veto item' status (*yi piao fou jue*)—a status reserved for political requirements of the highest priority, with the implication that violation of or failure to fulfill these requirements nullifies all other achievements in the annual evaluation process (Ahlers and Schubert 2015). This took place in the case of financial management, for example, in Yulin City, Shaanxi Province, and regarding environmental protection in Qingyuan County and Deqing County, Zhejiang Province; Nanfeng County, Jiangxi Province; Shouguang County, Shandong Province; and in Meigu County, Sichuan Province.

Collusion doubtlessly could and did occur between government bureaus and across administrative tiers in order to 'streamline' the measurement of outcomes,[14] but this apparently did not seriously hamper the soundness of the evaluation process as such in our field sites. Although local governments will always try to cover up dismal policy implementation and try to hide unsatisfactory outcomes from their superiors, the evaluation system cannot be fully sabotaged or manipulated. The reason for this is simple: local governments need performance evaluation to ensure the compliance of their subordinates because this is critical for implementing policies which have to be delivered and

---

[14] On this topic, see also the studies by Hillman (2014), Smith (2009), Zhou (2010), and Zhou et al. (2012).

avoiding pressure from upper levels. Evaluation sheets and performance rankings reflect the extent to which announced policy measures have produced results and thus serve both as a means of measurement and as a tool for sanctioning those who have failed in their duties. No matter whether sanctions are finally employed or not, cadre evaluation entails the stigmatization of nonperformers, which impacts on their future careers. At the same time, the evaluation regime serves as a feedback mechanism for local governments regarding public responses to policy outcomes—even if this influence is (still) minor. We argue that the evaluation regime makes for more effective policy implementation in the sense that local governments are forced to make good on what they have promised to achieve, even if the measurement of outcomes is open to negotiation and compromise (Ahlers and Schubert 2015; Heberer and Schubert 2012; Heberer and Trappel 2013).

Overall, policy shifts since the early 2000s have entailed an ideological and institutional environment that reconciles central state objectives—first and foremost, balanced and sustainable development and urbanization—with those of local governments, most notably the safeguarding of political autonomy from upper levels and cadre promotion. This does not mean that effective policy implementation is guaranteed all over the country. However, local governments can hardly legitimize themselves in present-day China if they do not implement policies in such a way that positive outcomes, as defined by the central state and spelled out in the various development blueprints set up by each administrative level, are achieved, no matter how difficult this may be. As a result, local governments often turn to innovative arrangements to internally communicate across functional bureaucracies and solve problems of policy implementation. But they also redefine their relationship with other crucial *external* policy stakeholders in their domain, as the following section explains.

6   INCLUSION OF EXTERNAL ACTORS

As mentioned earlier, a further reason for changing governance arrangements in China's local state has been the increasing need to mobilize public support for policy implementation. The official 'public participation imperative', inherent in contemporary national policy terminology in China, was met affirmatively in most localities we studied but clearly was not the driving factor behind policy innovation. Rather, practical issues connected with the implementation process, such as lack of funding or public contribution and support, encouraged the inclusion of local public actors in the policy process.

In the case of the BNSC policy, local governments employed new strategies in informal communication with villages and in working more systematically through the closely knit village community in order to neutralize opposition and mobilize support. Public consent to village development blueprints and bottom-up initiatives to gain project approval and funding were regarded as necessary, as villagers had to come up with part of the matching funds that were needed for the realization of many projects. In many localities we investigated, this often seemed more promising for effective policy implementation than an inclusion via the established formal institutions of village self-administration, that is, villagers' assemblies (*cunmin dahui*) and village committees (*cunmin weiyuanhui*).[15] If this strategy does not bear fruit and villagers' support and compliance cannot be ensured, local governments are forced into negotiations, have to make compromises, increase project funding, hand out more compensation, reconsider their development agenda, and even give up on specific projects, at least for the time being. 'Authoritarian bargaining' (Lee and Zhang 2013) or the "bureaucratic absorption" (Chuang 2014) of potential or real protest, not suppression, is typical for everyday policymaking in the local state, since the fallout resulting from suppression impacts negatively on local cadres' performance records and would not help the sustainability of projects after their implementation in any case. Public demands, especially those by the addressees of policies, are thus increasingly being accommodated by local governments; this enhances the legitimacy of policies and makes a meaningful contribution to effective policy implementation (Ahlers 2014b; Ahlers and Schubert 2015; Schubert and Ahlers 2011, 2012).

Local governments in China also increasingly rely on development of the private sector and public-private partnerships—a distinct shift in local governance modes over those in the recent past. Since the early Hu-Wen administration, the fostering of private entrepreneurship has become an important component in the overall approach to the rural-urban integration of local governments. It shapes the local economy by setting priorities in the conversion of scarce land to commercial use, encouraging the development of new product brands and trademarks, providing access to market information, and pushing forward the implementation of environmental standards.[16] Consequently, government interaction and cooperation with private entrepreneurs have also become a crucial feature of local governance and effective policy implementation in contemporary China.

The private sector is a pivotal component of local economic policies, even more so today, as only a few sectors are the exclusive domain of state-owned enterprises (such as, energy, tobacco, crude oil, etc.), and private investment is urgently needed to develop a locality. Recently, the central leadership emphasized that without developing the private sector, the 'Chinese Dream' could not be realized,[17] and that this sector is the most crucial force of innovation

---

[15] For many scholars, the lack of more meaningful 'democratic participation' in local policy implementation is a crucial problem (e.g., Guo and Han 2007; Ye 2006), while others see quite some positive potential in these newly emerging types of limited, goal-oriented inclusion (e.g., He 2010; Tang 2015).

[16] On all our fieldwork sites, local governments attempted to attract or develop *longtou* companies ('dragonhead enterprises'), advocated and subsidized the development of brand-name products, and claimed that they were closing down labor-intensive and polluting industries.

[17] *Minying qiyejia yu Zhongguo meng* (Private entrepreneurs and the Chinese Dream), http://finance.people.com.cn/GB/8215/356561/370131/ (accessed November 10, 2017).

(State Council 2017). Moreover, quantitative economic development is still the most important indicator for assessing the performance of leading cadres and deciding on their individual career trajectories. Particularly in the aftermath of the global financial crisis in 2008–2009, with its negative impact on the Chinese export economy, local governments have tightened their private sector policies to bring about structural change in the local economy, a precondition for more taxes and better public goods provision. Local governments invest continuously in the development of the local infrastructure, communications, and the public goods crucial for private enterprise, such as local development zones, special service centers for small and medium-sized enterprises, and schemes calculated to attract skilled labor and professionals. They also organize vocational training for enterprise personnel, provide information on marketing strategies and new models of business administration, grant money for 'product innovation', and set up communication channels between private enterprises and government bureaus to help them resolve all sorts of technical and financial problems. Moreover, local governments provide financial support for firms with economic difficulties, most notably by adjusting their tax burden.

The entire range of measures undertaken by local governments strongly impacts on private entrepreneurship in their respective jurisdictions: they grant subsidies and earmarked funding, allocate land and land-use rights, act as intermediaries in negotiating bank loans for private enterprises, provide the infrastructure for a sound business environment (e.g., access to major transportation routes, well-equipped development zones, etc.), and attract skilled labor and private investment (*zhaoshang yinzi*) to expand existing local businesses or set up new enterprises. At the same time, local governments can—and do—force private entrepreneurs to ('voluntarily') support specific policies or projects with money. Our respondents have spelled out unmistakably that local governments expect them to 'donate' money to important local initiatives, often in the fields of poverty alleviation and public goods provision, for example, the building of new schools or health-care facilities.[18] Local governments even make contact with private entrepreneurs, who have moved their companies and now operate in other localities, to persuade them to invest in their native places. For their part, entrepreneurs (whether party members or not[19]) cannot but bind themselves closely to the Party State, from which they expect political protection and support. Of course, regional differences and development trajectories produce different state-business relations,[20] and the more important the private sector economy has become for a given locality, the greater the bargaining power of private entrepreneurs vis-à-vis local governments, possibly even culminating in government capture.

---

[18] Other scholars have pointed at such mandatory payments as well (Sun et al. 2014). Ahlers (2014b) described this with regard to private entrepreneurs at the village level.

[19] Most of the private entrepreneurs we interviewed were not CCP members themselves, although party organizations had been established in most of the companies we visited.

[20] For a more detailed description, see Schubert and Heberer (2015).

In addition to steering the political agency of private entrepreneurs by controlling their much-needed economic resources, local governments also dominate local trade and industrial branch associations (*shanghui, hangye xiehui*). None of these are autonomous interest organizations that represent private enterprises or entrepreneurs. On the one hand, they function as transmission belts to help the Party State so as to maintain its political supremacy over the private sector; on the other hand, they act as mediators between private entrepreneurs and local governments, for example, when labor issues are at stake. Their principal task is to provide for a steady flow of communication between local governments and private entrepreneurs in order to ensure continuous economic development and market expansion to the benefit of the local economy. At the same time, however, entrepreneurs often prefer to communicate informally with the relevant government bureaus and local officials, whom they know personally,[21] to solve their problems and rarely rely on business associations to assist them. Associational autonomy, it seems, is not possible in an authoritarian system where the factors of production—labor, capital, and land—are closely monitored by the state, and private entrepreneurship is perpetually coopted by governments at each and every administrative tier. Yet private entrepreneurs pursue strategies of their own for influencing policies, mostly by means of lobbying, networking through chat groups, joining entrepreneurial clubs, setting up informal chambers of commerce, or working as delegates of formal organizations (e.g., local People's Congresses and Political Consultative Conferences) (Heberer and Schubert 2018; Schubert and Heberer 2017).

But Party State control also becomes increasingly organized within the private sector itself. In most of the larger private enterprises, we came across party organizations which were often headed by the founder and boss of the company or a leading manager. The success of this policy is ambivalent at best. Party cells may arguably facilitate the communication of local development policies at the company level, although it is difficult to discern precisely how these processes work out, because they are highly informal and lack transparency. But it is a reasonable assumption that party organizations within private enterprises are useful tools for controlling leading company staff and implementing official policies related to private sector development.

No matter how local private entrepreneurship initially emerged, local governments in all the places that we investigated provided effective leadership and guidance for the private sector, resulting in a rather hierarchic mode of governance.

[21] Local government units, such as the Bureaus of Industry and Commerce (*gongshangju*), assist smaller private enterprises in gaining access to microcredits by organizing special 'dialogue platforms' to bring together entrepreneurs and local financing institutions, thus facilitating credit negotiations. Sometimes, local governments even pay bonuses to banks for providing credit for enterprises. And they may request larger and healthier private companies to act as guarantors for smaller companies that are in need of credit. This is where business associations then have a role to play, since they often serve as platforms to communicate these requests by local governments to the wealthier enterprises in the locality.

This, as we argue, contributes positively to effective policy implementation within the existing context in contemporary China: the local state enjoys sufficient autonomy from the private sector, exclusively controls the access to land, funding, public projects, information, and, although more circumspectly, credit, and therefore can and does bring entrepreneurial interests—most notably, profit increase and company expansion—in line with its specific goals to develop the local economy.[22] At the same time, local state supremacy helps to mobilize private capital, making up for insufficient financial resources (due to the discriminatory tax system), helping local governments to provide public goods, and funding poverty alleviation programs, which has now once again become a priority national policy area (Schubert and Heberer 2015, 2017).

7   CONCLUSIONS

In this chapter, we have discussed the critical role of local governance in China's state structure. Even though we are talking about an authoritarian one-party state with a high degree of top-down political control and initiative, we have argued that the local tiers of the Chinese party and government bureaucracy have (and have always had) plenty of opportunities to shape, steer, or hinder the ultimate implementation of policies and thus to strongly influence the political system's capacity to deliver meaningful outcomes. Since the early 2000s, China's political leadership has focused increasingly on improving and expanding public goods provision in the country's vast rural areas. This has led to new policy initiatives and the introduction (or refurbishment) of powerful institutions to ensure the compliance of local cadre bureaucracies in implementing upper-level guidelines. At the same time, local governments must come up with policy innovations and find alternative ways to make up for insufficient upper-level funding in order to implement policies effectively and demonstrate their strong 'service orientation' to both their superiors and important stakeholders in the society. Sub-standard performance, incompetence, and corruption have become increasingly unacceptable and are likely to be punished one way or another by the Party State at each administrative level (Göbel and Heberer 2017).

This dynamic, we argue, has led to reconfigurations of governance arrangements in China's local state, which we have highlighted here using as examples the rural development and rural-urban integration policies launched in the early 2000s. In the localities we visited, local governments largely succeeded in finding new ways to promote, legitimate, coordinate, and evaluate policies under conditions of continuous institutional change, and to increasingly integrate

---

[22] Naturally, the vertical interrelationships between local governments and private entrepreneurs may also lead to ineffective or non-sustainable policy implementation. The persistent focus on GDP development and the related career advancement opportunities of local cadres, on the one hand, and 'promotion mobility' that favors short-term development strategies, on the other, are obstacles to effective development planning and implementation.

external stakeholders and their demands. These developments clearly represent a shift from pure vertical *government* to a more horizontal and problem-focused *governance* in China's local state.

Still, the governance *re*arrangements we described also reflect the Party State's claim to extensive steering by recentralizing and standardizing policy goals and by enforcing the principle of organizational hierarchy. State actors dominate the policy implementation process by virtue of their almost exclusive access to resources, information, and problem-solving authority and by not having to accommodate fully autonomous interest organizations. However, the limited but increasing inclusion of non-governmental actors arguably helps to better adapt public policy to local needs and preferences. We hypothesize that these reconfigurations in Chinese local governance arrangements will continue to shape local politics. However, taking into account recent developments, the tension between indispensable local discretion to implement upper-level policies, on the one hand, and reinforced central steering in Chinese governance under Xi Jinping, on the other hand, will even become more pronounced in the foreseeable future (Ahlers and Yu 2016; Chen 2017).[23]

Finally, although we highlighted the high degree of adaptability and the consequential shifts in Chinese local governance, this is not meant to downplay local governments' shortcomings in ensuring that public policies reflect all public demands, entail an efficient allocation of public money, or provide meaningful cadre accountability and democratic participation. It shows, however, that the Chinese political system is undergoing a dynamic learning process and succeeds fairly well in safeguarding and even improving arrangements for the effective implementation of policies that reconcile central state objectives with local state strategic agency and generates outcomes that maintain critical degrees of state capacity and regime stability—at least for the time being.

REFERENCES

Ahlers, A. L. 2015. Weaving the Chinese dream on the ground? Local government approaches to "new-typed" rural urbanization. *Journal of Chinese Political Science* 20(2): 121–142.

Ahlers, A. L. 2014a. Lokales Regieren und administrative Interessenvermittlung in China [Local governance and administrative interest mediation in China]. In *Modernes Regieren in China* [Modern governing in China], ed. H. Heinelt. Baden-Baden: Nomos, 89–115.

Ahlers, A. L. 2014b. *Rural policy implementation in contemporary China: New Socialist Countryside*. London: Routledge.

---

[23] For instance, hierarchical control was recently reinforced in processes of local policy experimentation, piloting, and modelling. That means, policy experiments, as an implementation mechanism, persist, but they now have to be authorized by higher level governments, limiting local discretion in this realm.

Ahlers, A. L., T. Heberer, and G. Schubert. 2016. Whither local governance in contemporary China? Reconfiguration for more effective policy implementation. *Journal of Chinese Governance* 1(1): 55–77.

Ahlers, A. L., and G. Schubert. 2018. Local cadre elites and policy implementation in contemporary China. In *Local elites in Post-Mao China*, ed. Y. Guo. London: Routledge, 17–38.

Ahlers, A. L., and G. Schubert. 2015. Effective policy implementation in China's local state. *Modern China* 41(4): 372–405.

Ahlers, A. L., and G. Schubert. 2013. Strategic modelling: "Building of a New Socialist Countryside" in three Chinese counties. *The China Quarterly* 216: 831–849.

Ahlers, A. L., and G. Schubert. 2009. "Building a New Socialist Countryside"—Only a political slogan? *Journal of Current Chinese Affairs* 38(4): 35–62.

Ahlers, A. L., and J. Yu. 2016. Comment on "What Does Xi Jinping's Top-Down Leadership Mean for Innovation in China?". *ChinaFile Conversation*, 26. October. New York: Asia Society.

Capano, G., M. Howlett, and M. Ramesh (eds.). 2015. *Varieties of governance. Dynamics, strategies, capacities.* London: Palgrave Macmillan.

CCP Central Committee. 2013. Zhonggong zhongyang guanyu quanmian shenhua gaige ruogan zhongda wenti de jueding [CCP central committee's decision on major issues concerning comprehensively deepening reforms]. Available at http://news.xinhuanet.com/politics/2013-11/15/c_118164235.htm

CCP Central Committee. 2011. Zhongyang zhengwu gongkai "yijian" zhuli fuuxing zhengfu jianshe ("Suggestions" on the transparency of central government's administrative affairs support the construction of a service-oriented government). Available at http://cpc.people.com.cn/GB/64093/64103/15323011.html

Chen, X. 2017. A u-turn or just pendulum swing? Tides of bottom-up and top-down reforms in contemporary China. *Journal of Chinese Political Science*, Online first (doi.org/10.1007/s11366-017-9515-6).

Chuang, J. 2014. China's Rural land politics: Bureaucratic absorption and the muting of rightful resistance. *The China Quarterly* 219: 649–669.

Delman, J. 2015. Performance assessment, social accountability and sustainability governance in Hangzhou: Leveraging the implementation gap? Paper presented at the workshop on *Governance for urban sustainability in China: Challenges and practices*, University of Copenhagen, October 31–November 01.

Göbel, C. 2010. *The politics of rural reform in China.* London: Routledge.

Göbel, C. 2011. Paving the road to a Socialist New Countryside: China's rural tax and fee reform. In *Politics and markets in rural China*, ed. B. Alpermann. London: Routledge, 155–171.

Göbel, C. 2012. Government propaganda and the organization of rural China. In *Organizing rural China—Rural China organizing*, ed. by A. Bislev, and S. Thøgersen, Lanham: Lexington Books, 51–68.

Göbel, C., and T. Heberer. 2017. The policy innovation imperative: Changing techniques for governing China's local governors. In *To Govern China: Evolving Practices of Power*, ed. V. Shue and P.M. Thornton. Cambridge: Cambridge University Press, 283–308.

Guo, H., and L. Han. 2007. *Zhongguo xinnongcun jianshe: jiyu cunguan he cunmin de fangtan yu wenjuan diaocha [New countryside construction in China: Based on the opinion of village leaders and farmers].* Hangzhou: Zhejiang daxue chubanshe.

Gong, T., and A. M. Wu. 2012. Central mandates in flux: Local noncompliance in China. *Publius. The Journal on Federalism* 42(2): 313–333.

He, B., and M. E. Warren. 2011. Authoritarian deliberation: The deliberative turn in Chinese political development. *Perspectives on Politics* 9(2): 269–289.

He, X. 2010. *Xiangcun shehui guanjian ci. Jinru 21 shiji de zhongguo xiangcun sumiao* [Keywords of rural society. A sketch of China's rural society in the early 21st century]. Jinan: Shandong renmin chubanshe.

He, X. 2007. New rural reconstruction and the Chinese path. *Chinese Sociology and Anthropology* 39(4): 26–38.

Heberer, T. 2014. The contention between Han "civilizers" and Yi "civilizees" over environmental governance: A case study of Liangshan Prefecture in Sichuan. *The China Quarterly* 219: 736–759.

Heberer, T., and G. Schubert. 2012. County and township cadres as a strategic group. A new approach to political agency in China's local state. *Journal of Chinese Political Science* 17(3): 221–249.

Heberer, T., and G. Schubert. 2018. Weapons of the rich: Strategic behavior and collective action of private entrepreneurs in China. *Modern China*. https://doi.org/10.1177/0097700418808755.

Heberer, T., and A. Senz. 2011. Streamlining local behaviour through communication, incentives and control: A case study of local environmental policies in China. *Journal of Current Chinese Affairs* 3: 77–112.

Heberer, T., and R. Trappel. 2013. Evaluation processes, local cadres' behaviour and local development processes. *Journal of Contemporary China* 22 (84): 1048–66.

Hillman, B. 2014. *Patronage and power: Local state networks and party-state resilience in rural China*. Stanford: Stanford University Press.

Hsing, Y. 2006. Brokering power and property in China's townships. *The Pacific Review* 19(1): 103–124.

Landry, P. 2008. *Decentralized authoritarianism in China. The Communist Party's control of local elites in the Post-Mao era*. Cambridge: Cambridge University Press.

Lee, C. K., and Y. Zhang. 2013. The power of instability: Unraveling the microfoundations of bargained authoritarianism in China. *American Journal of Sociology* 118(6): 1475–1508.

Li, K. 2014. Zhengfu gongzuo baogao [Central government work report]. Available at http://news.xinhuanet.com/politics/2014-03/14/c_119779247.htm

Liu, M., and R. Tao. 2007. Local governance, policy mandates and fiscal reform in China. In *Paying for progress in China. Public finance, human welfare and changing patterns of inequality*, ed. V. Shue, and C. P.W. Wong. London: Routledge, 166–189.

Liu, M., J. Wang, R. Tao, and R. Murphy. 2009. The political economy of earmarked transfers in a state-designated poor county in western China: Central policies and local responses. *The China Quarterly* 200: 973–994.

Liu, Y. 2012. From predator to debtor: The soft budget constraint and semi-planned administration in rural China. *Modern China* 38(3): 308–345.

Lou, J., and S. Wang (eds.). 2008. *Public finance in China: Reform and growth for a Harmonious Society*. Washington: The World Bank.

Manion, M. 2014. Authoritarian parochialism: Local congressional representation in China. *The China Quarterly* 218: 311–338.

Mertha, A. C. 2009. "Fragmented authoritarianism 2.0": Political pluralization in the Chinese policy process. *The China Quarterly* 200: 995–1012.

Schubert, G., and A. L. Ahlers. 2011. "Constructing a New Socialist Countryside" and beyond: An analytical framework for studying policy implementation and political stability in contemporary China. *Journal of Chinese Political Science* 16(1): 19–46.

Schubert, G., and A. L. Ahlers. 2012. County and township cadres as a strategic group: "Building a New Socialist Countryside" in three provinces. *The China Journal* 67: 67–86.

Schubert, G., and T. Heberer. 2015. Continuity and change in China's "local state developmentalism". *Issues & Studies* 2: 1–38.

Schubert, G., and T. Heberer. 2017. Private entrepreneurs as a "strategic group" in the Chinese polity. *The China Review* 17(2): 95–122.

Smith, G. 2010. The hollow state: Rural governance in China. *The China Quarterly* 203: 601–618.

Smith, G. 2009. Political machinations in a rural County. *The China Journal* 62: 29–59.

State Council. 2017. Guanyu yingzao qiyejia jiankang chengzhang huanjing hongyang youxiu qiyejia jingshen geng hao fahui qiyejia zuoyongde yijian [Opinion on creating a healthy environment for the growth of entrepreneurs and promote outstanding entrepreneurial spirit in order to develop the function of entrepreneurs], Available at http://news.xinhuanet.com/politics/2017-09/25/c_1121722103.htm

State Council. 2014. Guojia xinxing chengzhenhua guihua (2014–2020 nian) [National new-type urbanization plan (2014–2020)]. Available at http://politics.people.com.cn/n/2014/0317/c1001-24649809.html

State Council. 2013. Daqi wuran fangzhi xingdong jihua" [Action plan for the prevention and control of air pollution]. Available at http://www.gov.cn/zhengce/content/2013-09/13/content_4561.htm

State Council. 2006. Quanmian zhengque lijie shehui zhu yi xin nongcun jianshe" [Fully and correctly understand BNSC]. Available at http://www.gov.cn/node_11140/2006-03/15/content_227640.htm

Stepan, M., E. Han, and T. Reeskens. 2016. Building the New Socialist Countryside: Tracking public policy and public opinion changes in China. *The China Quarterly* 226: 456–476.

Stepan, M., and A. Müller. 2012. Welfare governance in China? A conceptual discussion of governing social policies and the applicability of the concept to contemporary China. *Journal of Cambridge Studies* 7(4): 54–72.

Sun, X., J. Zhu, and Y. Wu. 2014. Organizational clientelism: An analysis of private entrepreneurs in Chinese local legislatures. *Journal of East Asian Studies* 14: 1–26.

Tang, B. 2015. The discursive turn: Deliberative governance in China's urbanized villages. *Journal of Contemporary China* 24(91): 137–57.

Thøgersen, S. 2009. Revisiting a dramatic triangle: The state, villagers and social activists in Chinese rural reconstruction projects. *Journal of Current Chinese Affairs* 38(4): 9–33.

Wedeman, A. 2014. Xi Jinping's tiger hunt and the politics of corruption. *China Currents* 13(2). Available at http://www.chinacenter.net/2014/china_currents/13-2/xi-jinpings-tiger-hunt-and-the-politics-of-corruption/

Wei, L. 2006. Guowuyuan yanjiushi zhuren Wei Liqun: dali jianshe fuwuxing zhengfu" [State council research office director Wei Liqun: Strong efforts to build a service-oriented government], *Qiushi*. Available at http://www.gov.cn/zwhd/2006-11/01/content_429890.htm

Wong, C. P.W. 2007. Can the retreat from equality be reversed? An assessment of redistributive fiscal policies from Deng Xiaoping to Wen Jiabao. In *Paying for progress in*

China. Public finance, human welfare and changing patterns of inequality, ed. V. Shue, and C. P.W. Wong. London: Routledge, 12–28.

Wong, C. P.W., and R. M. Bird. 2008. China's fiscal system: A work in progress. In *China's great economic transformation*, ed. L. Brandt, and T. G. Rawski. Cambridge: Cambridge University Press, 429–466.

Wu, W., W. Yu, T. Lin, J. Wang, and W. Tam. 2013. Evaluating public service performance in urban China. Findings from the 2011 Lien Chinese cities service-oriented government project. In *Buildings service-oriented government: Lessons, challenges and prospects*, ed. W. Wu. Singapore: World Scientific, 1–26.

Wu, Y. 2007. *Xiaozhen xuanxiao. Yi ge xiangzhen zhengzhi yunzuo de yanyi yu chanshi* [Tumult in a small town: Interpretation of a township's political operation]. Beijing: Sanlian shudian.

Xinhua Press (n.a.). 2006. *Jianshe shehui zhuyi xinnongcun. Xuexi duben* [Study book for the construction of a new socialist countryside]. Beijing: Xinhua chubanshe.

Ye, J. 2006. *Nongmin shijiao de xin nongcun jianshe* [*Construction of the New Countryside: Farmers' perspectives*]. Beijing: Shehui kexue wenxian chubanshe.

Zhan, J. V. 2009. Decentralizing China: Analysis of central strategies in China's fiscal reforms. *Journal of Contemporary China* 18 (60): 445–62.

Zhao, S. 2006a. Obligatory interactions in the affairs of township governments. *Chinese Sociology and Anthropology* 39(2): 17–25.

Zhao, S. 2006b. The power system of township governments. *Chinese Sociology and Anthropology* 39(2): 8–16.

Zhou, X. 2010. The institutional logic of collusion among local governments in China. *Modern China* 36(1): 47–78.

Zhou, X, Y. Ai, and H. Lian. 2012. The limit of bureaucratic power in organizations: The case of the Chinese bureaucracy. *Research in the Sociology of Organizations* 34 (34): 81–111.

CHAPTER 5

New Agenda for the Study of Chinese Governance

Jianxing Yu and Shizong Wang

Governance theory originated in the West, but China may well be the biggest "consumer" of this theory. Quite a few Chinese scholars have high expectations of this theory, either in delivery of public services or in political progress. Since the 1990s, public governance has undergone a distinct shift from centralized government to pluralistic cooperation. Moreover, the term governance has attained universal recognition because it can be applied in myriad domains and in any sense. Even within academic communities, there has been a long-existing controversy regarding the understanding of governance and the applicability of governance theory in China. After the Third Plenary Session of the 18th Central Committee of the Chinese Communist Party (CCP), the Central Government officially employed the modern state governance system, the modernization of governance capacity, and social governance, which have contributed to the discord between official discourse and academic concept. All of these are a fair reflection of core contradictions between governance and state building and between state governance and social governance in contemporary China. Future research on Chinese governance may need to revolve around these core contradictions. This chapter attempts to review major research progress and disputes after the introduction of governance theory into China, reflect on the dilemma between state governance and social governance in China, and ultimately propose the research agenda of Chinese governance.

J. Yu • S. Wang (✉)
School of Public Affairs, Zhejiang University, Hangzhou, Zhejiang, China
e-mail: yujianxing@zju.edu.cn

© The Author(s) 2019
J. Yu, S. Guo (eds.), *The Palgrave Handbook of Local Governance in Contemporary China*, https://doi.org/10.1007/978-981-13-2799-5_5

1   Introduction of Governance Theory and Latent Conflicts

The earliest introduction of governance or *Zhidao*[1] in China may be traced back to a paper titled *Governance: A New Concept of Modern 'Zhidao'* by Zhixian published in the first volume of *Public Forum* in 1995. Literature about governance has emerged afterwards. In 2000, Yu Keping edited *Governance and Good Governance*, which included papers about governance theory by Stoker, Kooiman, Jessop, Rhodes, et al. and appealed for the achievement of governance and good governance in China. This book held immense attention to governance in China's academia. Sun Baiying (2004) sorted the complex threads of governance and local governance theories into a coherent and concise system. All this work is in essence overflowing with the vision for China's governance. While Yu Keping et al. introduced governance theory, they integrated previous research on China's civil society and governance, implying their unique opinions in regard to the evolutionary path of China's political system and the orientation of public administration reform.

With the inception of governance theory in China, some researchers endeavored to interpret the application of governance theory in the Chinese context. They sought for the corresponding referents of hierarchy, market, and network in China and explored the likelihood of interaction and collaboration among the three (Lou Chengwu and Zhang Jianwei 2007; Guo Daohui 2006). With the realization that the network is an integral ingredient of governance, scholars researched the relationship between social organizations and government in China (Yu Keping et al. 2006; Wang Hsin-Hsien 2006), policy tools related to the network (Wang Shizong 2007), and the interaction between local government and society in China (Chen Shengyong and Wu Xingzhi 2007; He Baogang and Lang Youxing 2008). It is justifiable to conclude that the introduction of governance theory spurs the striking expansion of knowledge in these fields.

Although governance is an alien concept, it has successfully refreshed the notion of Chinese scholars and officials since its entry into China. Such concepts as local governance, governance of local government, and community governance have gained wide acceptance in China's academic circle and gradually penetrated into the discourse system of local government. This phenomenon may be attributable to the inclusiveness of the concept of governance, which is intimately related to internal conflicts. As a matter of fact, since the introduction of governance theory, the applicability of it in Chinese context implies a principal conceptual conflict between governance and good governance.

---

[1] The translation of governance into *Zhidao* entails the assimilation of Mou Tsung-san's viewpoint. According to Mou Tsung-san, *Zhengdao* refers to the tangible form of corresponding political power while *Zhidao* can be defined as the way of adopting certain measures to deal with public affairs. We can roughly compare *Zhidao* and *Zhengdao* to administration and politics. See Mou Tsung-san (2006).

There is a wide spectrum of definitions on governance.[2] To clarify this concept in the most concise manner, we need to trace it back to early advocates. As a leader of the Anglo-Governance school,[3] Rhodes (1996) classified governance into six types: governance as the minimal state, corporate governance, governance as new public management, good governance, governance as a socio-cybernetic system, and governance as self-organizing networks. Similarly, Paul Hirst identified five versions of governance (Hirst 2000): (1) good governance—it means an effective political framework conducive to private economic actions in non-Western developing countries; (2) international institutions and regimes; (3) corporate governance; (4) governance concerning new public management strategy in the 1980s—it introduces a new model of public services distinct from that of classical public administration; and (5) governance relating to the new practices of coordinating activities through networks, partnerships, and deliberative forums that have grown up on the ruins of the more centralized and hierarchical corporatist representation.

The meaning of governance, which those Western scholars advocated, is almost certain, if we rule out corporate governance that apparently does not fall under the umbrella of governance theory and suspend governance in the field of international affairs, as well as, good governance in developing countries. In contrast, Rhodes (1997) concisely defined governance as the new ways of interaction between state, society, and market to deal with the growing complexity, diversity, and dynamics in social and policy problem. This definition receives immense support from a host of representative scholars, including Stoker (1998) and Peters (2000). Peters (2000) contended that state-centric "old governance" is focused on steering—the capacity of the center of government to exert control over the rest of the government and over the economy and society, while society-centric "new governance"[4] is primarily concerned with how core governmental agencies interact with society and formulate mutually acceptable policies or how society gains self-regulation instead of being dictated by government, particularly central government.

These scholars highlighted social self-governance, the role of society in public administration and the multiple collaborations between the society and government; thus, governance theory is distinguished from any previous school of public administration. Meanwhile, they described good governance as a concept differentiated from governance.

Unlike new governance, the concept of good governance was directly derived from a series of documents on international organizations, particularly

---

[2] Such as co-governance (Toonen 1990), collaborative governance (Huxham 2000), and multiple governance (Hupe and Hill 2006).

[3] See Marinetto (2003).

[4] According to Peters (2000), new governance or modern governance was first proposed by Kooiman (1993) and Rhodes (1996).

the report of the World Bank (1989).[5] Good governance was to a great extent geared toward developing countries. Many people think that it is a term in the nature of strategy and policy, but there has been much discernment about it from the perspective of administrative management or from the angle of Western countries (a more political understanding). The World Bank did not confine its interpretation of good governance to policy orientation. In the 1992 World Bank report entitled *Governance and Development*, the World Bank deciphered governance as a synonym for reliable development management (World Bank 1992: 1). This policy document focused on four primary elements: responsibility, a rule of law framework congenial to development, information, and transparency (Leftwich 1994). Yu Keping, who was one of the first to advocate governance theory in China, also pointed out that "good governance is a process of social administration, which aims to maximize public interests," and its fundamental components include legitimacy, transparency and accountability, rule of law, responsiveness, and effectiveness (Yu Keping 2000). Apparently, these elements are pillars of classical public administration or key factors to be prioritized in the campaign of reshaping government. In one word, good governance requires that public administration in developing countries be characterized by modernity. Both the World Bank and Yu Keping believe that good governance entails good government or can even be equated with good government. Yu Keping (2000) stressed that "there are striking resemblances in the content of good government, whether in China or in foreign countries, in ancient times or in modern times. As a general rule, it includes a suite of factors as follows: stringent laws, uncorrupt officials, high administrative efficiency, and adequate administrative services." We find no remarkable distinction between good governance and good government by comparing Yu's statements.

It is far from appropriate to simply equate good governance with good government. In fact, good governance invariably encompasses another connotation—the notion of new governance in the West. It is emphasized in the World Development Report 1997—*The State in a Changing World* by the World Bank that if the government of a country is lacking the capacity in a certain aspect, it needs to become a reliable partner so as to boost its capability. In theoretical research, the concept of good governance seems to be more directly endowed with multiple and correlated contents: modern political system, modern public administration system, market economy system, and civil society, which are relatively independent of and interact with the state. Hirst (2000) points out that the strategy of good governance is based on creating a version of societal architecture of classical liberalism, including a limited state, a largely self-regulating civil society, and market economy. Leftwich (1994) maintains

---

[5] This report also catalyzes the popularity of new governance. In the 1998 special issue of the *Journal of International Social Sciences* (Volume 50, Issue 155), most of the papers about governance mention the relevant work of the World Bank.

that the yardstick of governance and good governance follows the Weber style, and that good governance needs to be determined and sustained by certain political factors. Yu Keping also asserts that good government and civil society are two keys to achieving good governance (Wang Qinghua and Guo Gang 2015). These viewpoints demonstrate that it is far from enough to decipher good governance simply as good government. Even if good government is the ultimate goal, it also calls for the support of other relevant elements (democracy, civil society, etc.). In this sense, the contents of good governance are bound to be multiple, and good government, one of the aspects in good governance, cannot be isolated from other aspects. Hence, governance and good governance are overlapping.

It is noteworthy that new governance is originally targeted at Western countries and that its foundation is an existing modern state. In comparison, the goals of good governance are good government and new governance; on the other hand, new governance is also regarded as a prerequisite for good government (Yu Jianxing and Wang Shizong 2011). This ambiguous and contradictory logic may account for the fact that Yu Keping consciously or unconsciously blurs the distinction between governance and good governance or between *Zhengdao* and *Zhidao*. Nonetheless, this kind of ambiguity fails to eliminate the dispute in academia over whether governance theory applies to China, which stems from the latent conflict between governance and good governance.

2   Disputes and Progress

Although governance is usually reckoned as theory, it does not offer a new normative theory (Stoker 1998), thus leaving plenty of space for disputes, especially in China. While advocating governance, Western scholars focus their research on improving the modes of administration and public service delivery and increasing direct participation due to the predicaments of public services. In other words, new governance is primarily concerned with *Zhidao*. In contrast, Chinese scholars pay more attention to *Zhengdao*, namely, the achievement of the historical mission of state building. Therefore, when governance theory was initially introduced in China, Chinese scholars placed high expectations of governance, associating it with the modern state building and the evolution of Chinese political and administrative system. China laid more emphasis on the normative values of governance. As can be seen from the intimate relationship between governance theory and studies of civil society in China, the concept of governance is tinted with an apparent teleological connotation of a paradigm shift in politics, society, and administration, which is manifestly associated with the goal of good governance.

From the perspective of scholars who cast doubt over the applicability of governance in China, the adoption of governance may not only appear to be rough and shallow but also bring about fundamental problems in political and administrative development. These doubts are rarely mentioned by the advocators of the introduction of governance theory into China. Almost certainly, they share the similar doubt, but they expressed the concerns in a more positive manner. Research by the proponents of governance theory can be summarized into the following types as an indirect response to those who are skeptical of the applicability of governance in China. The first type focuses on developing a Chinese civil society and achieving the governance of public affairs through nongovernmental organizations (NGOs) and the third sector (Guo Daohui 2006; He Zengke 2007). The second type asserts that governance can be achieved through the reforms on the internal communication mechanism or the hierarchical structure (Xu Yong 2004; Li Wenxing and Zheng Haiming 2007). The scholars who hold this view predominantly are concerned with reforms within the government, maintaining that reform on the behavioral mode of government is the only pathway for the achievement of governance in a real sense. The third type of view is more comprehensive, contending that reforms should be carried out simultaneously, and that governance can only be achieved through the interaction between multi-agents that have a tense relationship (Liu Zhichang 2007; Yu Jianxing 2008). These theoretical assertions place emphasis on different aspects. This may be related to the ambiguity of the concept of governance and a hodgepodge of theories, but it can also be noted that scholars have realized the distinctions between China and the West and developed their unique understanding of governance. First, in the course of its achievement, governance should include the development and shaping of civil society. It is stressed that governance should be promoted by means of the development and cultivation of the third sector. Second, because of the current systematic problem, governance should include reforms on the internal structure of government or the system. This viewpoint highlights the achievement of governance through reforms on government systems (*Zhengdao*) and reflects a degree of concern about the role of the state in governance.

It cannot be denied that although the proponents of governance theory in China have high expectations of the role of governance in state building, there is inadequate awareness of how governance promotes the evolution of the political system.

In the West, as the wave of romantic advocacy faded away, research on governance shifted to an exploration of its pragmatism.[6] In China, scholars expand their research to a wider scope. Figures 5.1 and 5.2 show the rising amount of relevant literature.

In comparison with that in the early period, research on Chinese governance has become more patient in recent years. Research entails the following major aspects: (1) the mode of and the approach to shifts in China's governance macro-picture, which is the constant focus of some scholars. Yu Jianxing, Zhou Jun, and Jiang Hua (2012) carried out a case study on industrial associations in Wenzhou, and argued for the significance of industrial associations in civil society, and contended that the development of industrial associations in Wenzhou

---

[6] See Svensson et al. (2008); Alford and Hughes (2008); and so on.

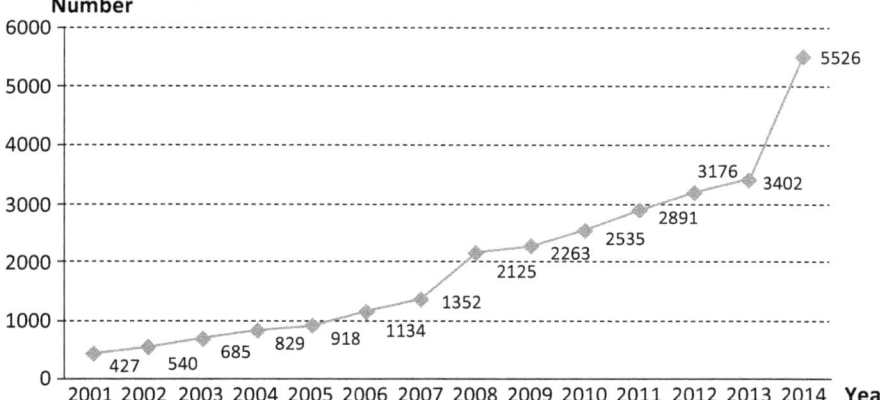

Fig. 5.1 Number of papers about research on Chinese governance in CSSCI journals (2001–2014) (Note: It is based on search results at http://www.cnki.net by input keywords, including "Subject Terms: (governance) and NOT Subject Terms: (Corporate governance)," "Source Category: (CSSCI)," and "Discipline: (philosophy and humanities/social sciences/economy and management sciences)." (Accessed at 2:31 p.m. on December 10, 2015))

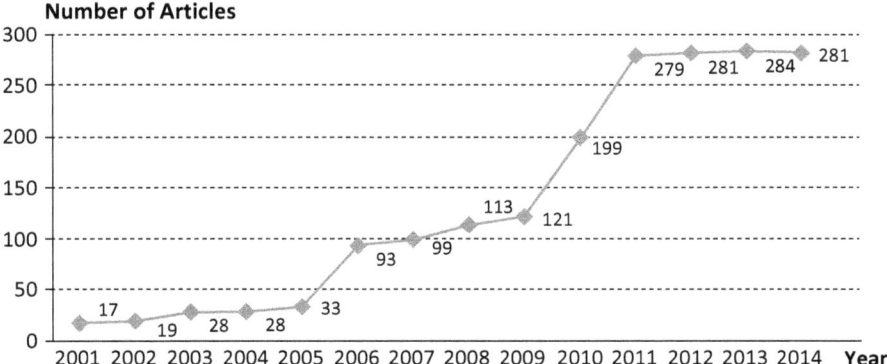

Fig. 5.2 Number of papers about research on Chinese governance in international journals (2001–2014) (Note: It is based on search results at http://zju.summon.serialssolutions.com/en/#!/search by input keywords, including "Subject Terms: (China) OR (Chinese) AND (Subject Terms: (Governance) NOT Subject Terms: (Corporate governance)," "Source Category: (Journal)," and "Discipline: (Not Limited)." (Accessed at 22:40 p.m. on November 17, 2015))

not only demonstrates that Chinese civil society can develop through participation in public affairs but also displays marked values in public governance. Lin Shangli (2011) stressed that the adjustment of government's internal functions plays a crucial role in achieving state governance and put forward the idea of adjusting and rebuilding the intergovernmental relationship so as to promote the transformation of government functions and the governance of the whole country. Chao Yung-mau (2011) contrasted the development of China's Taipei and the United Kingdom in terms of system and history, sorting out the connotations of democratic governance and the problems in different phases. (2) Evaluation of governance performance or quality: in order to present the richness of the connotation of governance and the width of its extension, He Zengke (2008) proposes the assessment of governance performance by combining three complementary approaches. There has been much progress since then in the construction of a more integrated evaluation system for governance performance and quality. For example, Yu Keping led a research team to establish the China Social Governance Index (CSGI), indicative of important values and notions of social governance, including democracy, rule of law, equality, justice, stability, participation, transparency, and self-governance (Research Group of "China's social management evaluation system" and Yu Keping 2012). (3) Chinese social organizations: social organizations receive continuous attention from Chinese researchers because they should assume pivotal roles in governance. Some scholars explore the characteristics of Chinese social organizations and judge China's state-society relationship from the perspective of civil society and corporatism (Spires 2011). Some scholars are more concerned with the behavioral strategies of social organizations while they cooperate with other agents (Tang Wenyu 2012). Other scholars researched the impact of the cooperation between NPOs and enterprises (Cai Ning et al. 2015). Researchers gain a more profound insight into the complicated connotations of Chinese social organizations' independence and reject the either-or judgment, which lays a foundation for the evaluation of the future trend of the relationship between government and social organizations and the proclivity of governance. (4) Grassroots governance and community governance: this type of research covers a diversified array of topics and focuses more on current concerns than prospects. On community governance, research is largely concentrated on the meta-analysis (Chen Tianxiang and Yang Ting 2011; Zheng Hangsheng and Huang Jialiang 2012), as well as community governance from the perspective of polycentricity and social capital (Yan Jirong 2010; Li Huifeng 2010). In terms of rural governance, the dominant focus is fixed on the participation of peasants in rural affairs and the adjustment of the traditional power structure (Xu Yong and Zhao Dejian 2014). (5) The collaborative pattern of government and society in public services: Wang Puqu and Salamon (2013) combined China's specific realistic system and indicators in international research to analyze the partnership between government and social organizations, particularly the purchase of service contracting, and based on the analysis they discovered social organizations' strategy of existence and development when government functions are not fully fulfilled. Some scholars examined a hybrid form of social innovation combining government engineering and citizen participation as the Chinese government's strategy to cope with the rise of nonprofit organizations (Jing Yijia and Gong Ting 2012). (6) Countermeasures for ungovernability, such as governance of letters and visits of the people (Tian Xianhong 2012), environmental governance (Zheng Siqi et al. 2013), governance in media (Yang Deming and Zhao Can 2012), and governance in education (Chu Hongqi 2014). (7) New technologies in governance: some researches advocate the incorporation of the sophisticated network (Fan Ruguo 2014) and big data (Tang Huangfeng and Tao Jianwu 2014) into governance by combining the features of multi-agent participation in governance.

In the aggregate, aforementioned studies became less related to such general theories as civil society. Scholars are less eager to defend the applicability of governance in China or to prove that governance can promote China's political reform. This situation continues well into the convocation of the Third Plenary Session of the 18th Central Committee of CCP where state governance and social governance are officially emphasized and form a dynamic political stream. Since 2013, there has been another explosive growth in the number of papers regarding Chinese governance, and scholars have regained their enthusiasm about macroscopic *Zhengdao* in academia. Figure 5.3 shows the bandwagon phenomenon after 2013 on the researches about state governance system and governance capacity. A host of researchers expound the connotation of state governance and its relationship with social governance (He Zenke 2014; Yan Jirong 2014; Hu Angang 2014; Tang Yalin 2014; Xue Lan 2014; etc.). There is little pronounced discrepancy in terms of social governance, which is primarily compatible with the underlying viewpoint of new governance in the West, but the connotation of state governance is open to much contention. Nevertheless, outside academia, government, and official media seem to deem the modern-

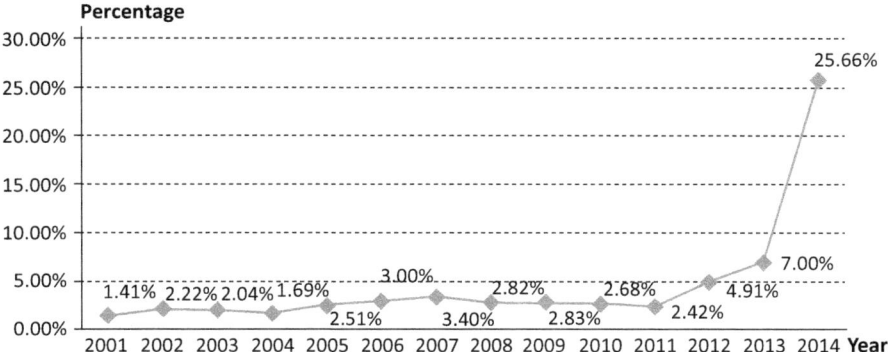

Fig. 5.3 Ratio of literature about "State Governance" to that about Chinese Governance in CSSCI journals (2001–2014) (Note: It is based on search results at www.cnki.net by input keywords, including "Subject Terms: (topic = governance) and NOT Subject Terms: (Corporate governance) (excluding corporate governance)," "Source Category: (CSSCI)," and "Discipline: (philosophy and humanities/social sciences/economy and management sciences)." (Accessed at 14:35 p.m. on December 10, 2015.) In research results, another condition "topic = state governance" is added so as to calculate the ratio)

ization of the state governance system and governance capacity as government capacity characterized by a strong and absolute state.

It is apparent that since the introduction of governance theory into China, there has been, to quote Frederickson (2005), a "governance, governance everywhere" situation. A massive body of researches and progresses convinces us that the field of Chinese governance will remain teeming with dynamism and passion in the future. However, it is worth noting that there are some attention-grabbing issues in post-2010 studies. First, the concept of governance remains messy. There is an abundance of studies unrelated to new governance or good governance, which is quite normal per se, but these researchers often claimed that their views are guided and backed up by governance theory. "Anti-governance" also appears in the form of governance mostly in grid governance (*wangge zhili*), Internet-based rumor governance, and governance for stability maintenance (*weiwen*). Second, the contents of existing studies are mostly focused on fragmental experience, descriptive explanation, value advocacy, and, sometimes, excessive generalization. In contrast, research on institutionalization of governance innovation and causal mechanisms of governance change is far from adequate. Third, from the perspective of methods, Chinese governance researchers have noticed the necessity to combine normative and empirical research. Nonetheless, obvious gaps between macroscopic theories and microscopic evidence can be found frequently in explanations based on causal mechanism. Fourth, *Zhengdao* grabbed little attention and was perceived as an exogenous variable or an established condition for *Zhidao* reforms for a period. Since state governance became a hot research topic, the relationship between *Zhengdao* and *Zhidao* or new governance seems to be weaker in researches.

It should be pointed out that such political issues as state building have been deliberately obscured or dodged by most of scholars during a long period. Although research on state governance has been confined to normative deduction and value judgment after the Third Plenary Session of the 18th Central Committee of CCP, there has been a wave of disputes. Every viewpoint signifies the status and role of social governance in the future. Because of the role of the state in "meta-governance" (Jessop 2002a), the understanding of the connotation of state governance and its relationship with social governance will exert a profound impact on the agenda of Chinese governance research. This relationship can be interpreted through the tension between governance and state building.

3   Conflicts Between Governance and State Building

As mentioned earlier, good governance aimed at developing countries encompasses more complicated connotations than new governance. One of good governance's pivotal items is good government, which fundamentally follows the Weber style (Hirst 2000). Put it differently, good governance assumes the dual responsibilities for modern state building and governance, which are contingent upon each other and form a logic loop. Candidly speaking, this kind of logic circle is quite pervasive.[7] Even if this logic loop is not a complete mistake, it should be recognized that a tense relationship between governance and state building exists and viewing them as mutually conditional fails to work in pure logics.

State building is one of the paramount topics in the contemporary international community. Regarding state building, Fukuyama (2004: 15) suggests that "the problem for many countries was that in the process of reducing state scope, they either decreased state strength or generated demands for new types of state capabilities that were either weak or nonexistent." A modern state possesses two basic features: "nation-state" and "democracy-state." In the course of state building in developing countries, there is always severe imbalance between "nation-state" and "democracy-state." Due to the demonstration effect and the unique characteristics of developing countries, the process of state building is riddled with conflicts between political and cultural integration (Yu Jianxing 2008). Furthermore, if developing countries want to achieve economic progress in the context of economic and capital globalization, they should address various challenges, such as global economic risks, regional strategic cooperation, and national economic competitiveness. While transferring power to market, the state should be armed with the ability to strategically guide and regulate, the ability to fight against external factors, and the ability to formulate game rules between countries. Thus, many developing countries preserve the characteristics of strong state in fiscal and taxation systems, as well as in banking and financial systems. Some proponents believe that building a strong state is the prerequisite for building an affluent and democratic state.

State building is remarkably distinguished from governance. State building intrinsically emphasizes stability, order, and regulation; therefore, it is marked by toughness, controllability, and procedural rationality. In comparison, governance attaches more importance to multiplicity, negotiations, and collaborations; thereby, it is characterized by flexibility, interaction, and reflective rationality. In terms of institutional goals, state building, as a modern feat, revolves around state capability in organizational form and institutional system, whereas governance emphasizes the multiplicity and decentralization of authority, aimed at removing absolute sovereignty of a state, abolishing the notion of the supremacy of the state, requiring the state to change governing modes and share authority and power resources with other governance agents, thus, characterized by salient postmodernism. Governance theory goes beyond classical liberalism designating constitutional counterbalance to state power. Scholars put forward a polycentric governance viewpoint, rendering it necessary that the internal sovereignty of a state, including executive power, is open to individuals and other agencies.

---

[7] As the leading advocates of governance in China, Yu Keping (1999) is a prime example of circular demonstration. See Wang Shizong (2009: 131).

However, a centralized state is needed to not only construct and safeguard free markets but also utilize and ameliorate extensive welfare policies so as to achieve social equality. Moreover, the acceleration of globalization involves states in practically every major policy domain at regional or global levels, and they have to encounter a suite of cross-border mediation issues. If a state wants to implement policies successfully, it has to regain power and expand new functions. In the face of a multi-authority governance system, the challenge that policymakers are confronted with is not to depart from the governance domain but to adapt to and manipulate it. "As the state becomes overloaded with demands on its national and local administrative capacities, it continues to delegate and disperse regulatory and distributive powers to quasi-public corporations, trade associations, professional organizations, social service corporations, labor unions, chambers of commerce, scientific associations, and many other private nonprofit organizations" (Barrow 2005). Thus, state building in the contemporary era cannot rule out governance; rather, it needs to be aided by governance.

There is no escaping the fact that the state governance system and governance capacity include the connotations of modern state building and government capability development, and that social governance stresses decentralization and multiple collaboration in China. The 2014 *Report on the Work of the Government* also specifies the connotation of decentralization in social governance.[8] Therefore, the tension between state building and governance manifests itself as the tension between state governance and social governance in contemporary China. Unfortunately, China's state governance and social governance are in their infancy, but the tension between the two is no more visionary but realistic. As stated earlier, there is a large discrepancy in the understanding of state governance in academia. Several types of viewpoints demonstrate that social governance has been recognized as a role that receives high expectation or has to be treated cautiously. What is more noteworthy is the attitude of leaders and official media as well as the contradictions between official discourses and academic viewpoints. Reflections on democracy and civil society are consciously turned by some into defiance and suppression through Fukuyama's newly published book, *Political Order and Political Decay*, stressing state building and state capacity and other negative evidence collected from those countries that start to adopt democracy.[9] Such an understanding of Fukuyama's viewpoint may well be ascribed to the invention of a pretext for rejecting democracy, which necessarily entails the denial of social governance that is similar to new governance. This, in turn, reflects the importance of social governance to political progress and state building.

---

[8] The 2014 *Report on the Work of the Government* by Li Keqiang stresses that "We will promote innovation in social governance. We will focus on law-based governance and involve all parties in social governance."

[9] This proclivity is extremely noticeable in official media. For example, *Global Times* published an article by Wang Xiaoshi entitled "Reflections on Fukuyama: Construction of State Governance Capacity" on October 23, 2014. Actually, there are numerous similar viewpoints on the Internet.

We agree with Fukuyama's measurement about the priority sequence of state capacity. However, as Fukuyama (2014: 9–15) puts it, rule of law and democratic accountability are needed to limit and check state power and discretion, or bureaucratic autonomy without accountability is equal to corruption. Accountability relies not only on substantial democracy but also on the social accountability generated by civic engagement (Rhodes 1997: 101–103). Hence, if there is no social governance and substantial democracy associated with it, sound government capacity is no more than an illusion. Meanwhile, Fukuyama fails to define government capacity in a lucid manner, which may easily contribute to the confounding of such concepts as capacity and bureaucratic autonomy, order and centralization, governance quality and government function ranges. To our knowledge, government capacity can be encapsulated as the capability of implementing policies effectively in its territory, which is not restricted to legitimate monopoly of violence over the society. The basic capacity of a state is to penetrate into society, organize social relations, and implement policies by means of negotiation and cooperation (Onis 1991). In other words, the expansion of modern state governance capacity cannot be separated from social governance. Social governance may lead to the predicaments of inadequate government, but it may also become one of the cornerstones of effective state governance.

A detailed discussion about Fukuyama's new book is not the focus of this chapter. We want to highlight that even if we consent to Fukuyama's new viewpoint, democracy cannot be rejected and social governance cannot be excluded under the pretext of "a strong government" or "government capacity." Otherwise, state building may well be inclined to absolute state. However, the clarification of the aforementioned views does not necessarily follow that we have resolved the tension of governance and state building. In fact, this problem calls for our conscientious response. It is hardly acceptable that the logic loop is used to confirm the applicability of governance in China. On the other hand, if an analysis on Chinese governance concludes that governance is impossible in China simply because China does not possess prerequisites for governance, it is most likely an obstinate structural analysis. This approach misses the agency and strategy of actors. If we accept this analysis, we must agree that there is no progress in history—a ridiculous view about the end of history.

The strategic-relational approach provides us with a very strong methodological enlightenment (Jessop 1996, 2002b). While confronted with structural ingredients, we should accept a certain kind of "flexibility" to look into strategic options and behavior of actors in a specific structural context. Based on this, we propose three assumptions: (1) the orientation of the state governance system and the modernization of governance capacity will influence the development of social governance; (2) the benign development of social governance can facilitate the construction of the state governance system and the promotion of governance capacity; and (3) it is hard to predict what the future holds for the situation of Chinese governance, but it is certain to be contingent upon the interaction between state governance and social governance. The strategic interaction between state and social actors at various levels will help shape the future picture of Chinese governance.

4   AGENDA OF FUTURE RESEARCH

Just because it is impossible to preestablish the future institutional state and the specific evolutionary pathway does not mean there is no value orientation. We are fully aware that the term governance cannot be confined to new governance, and that it can be employed in various senses. Meanwhile, various kinds of ungovernability in China cannot be solved by new governance or social governance. Different kinds of research on Chinese governance are important and essential. However, the value of new governance and good governance, in a narrow sense, incorporate an expectation of a better life, a better society, and a better system. Therefore, research on China's state governance and social governance should not bypass the connotation of governance and good governance. In accordance with the three assumptions mentioned earlier, state governance, social governance, and their interaction and coevolution should form the core of future research. As a consequence, we put forward the agenda of research into Chinese governance as follows:

1. Research into the state governance system and governance capacity. Major questions include: what are the ingredients of a modern state governance system? What is state governance capacity? What are the sources of contemporary governance capacity? What is the relationship between strong capacity and such concepts as bureaucratic autonomy and centralization? Research in this aspect is aimed to clarify the referent of the state governance system and governance capacity. Notwithstanding an abundance of previous studies, a more insightful and comprehensive dispute is called for.

2. Social governance mechanism in grassroots organizations and communities. Although this area has riveted appreciable attention from scholars, preceding studies are more focused on new forms and functions of governance. Research on the generative and evolutionary mechanism for governance should be high on the agenda. The generative and evolutionary mechanism must be able to explain how actors make decisions and interact and how the decisions and interactions contribute to the evolution of grassroots governance in the political and social structure.

3. Social capital, social traditions, and societal development. In reality, new governance is always associated with traditions.[10] Some Chinese scholars also place a lot of stress on traditional factors in social governance, but they tend to describe traditions as those chronicled in ancient documents and give their own interpretation in the context of modernization. What are real traditions in contemporary social domains? What is the real state of existing social culture and social capital? Can they be helpful to or be

---

[10] See Peters and Pierre (1998).

integrated into the modern social governance system? There is a realistic need to answer these questions, and it may also make significant theoretical contributions to Chinese governance research.

4. The way societal forces seek opportunities and channels for participation. There is empirical evidence that while overcoming a myriad of ungovernability, government may introduce societal forces and even offer stable channels for their participation. A closer look may be taken at the initiative of citizens, as it is indicative of the agency of society. In the long run, researchers should explore the motives and patterns of citizens' active participation in public affairs, whether actors strive for participation by means of social conflicts and protests and whether social conflicts and protests can contribute to participation, cooperation, and order.[11]

5. The way that government mobilizes and integrates social forces. Not only should researchers be concerned about specific collaborative patterns, but they should also care about the strategy of government in integrating and utilizing social forces. For example, apart from public service delivery, grid management, and campaigns are also employed to mobilize society in China in order to achieve government goals. Researchers need to pay persistent attention to the possible impact of these practices on the development of social forces and social governance.

6. Institutional environment for social governance. The institutional structure is very complicated and possesses a degree of flexibility. The regulative institution logic from the state, the normative institution logic of agents, and the cognitive institution logic of social individuals tangle with each other and affect organizational and individual behavior. The regulative institution logic has long captured the attention of researchers,[12] but in future research, researchers should judge and explain state institutions in an integrated sense.[13] State institutions should be accentuated, but diversity and versatility of institutions cannot be overlooked, thereby a better picture about the real situation and function of state institutions can be obtained.

7. The positive impact of social governance on state institutions. It is far from enough to simply realize the beneficial effect of social governance on state institutions conceptually. How social governance affects political institutions and culture, and administrative contents and means should be further observed, and its mechanism further analyzed.

---

[11] Lily L. Tasi (2015) suggests that some noncompliant behaviors may be intended to communicate policy feedback and constructive criticism about the fit between policies and local conditions.

[12] See Yu Keping et al. (2006).

[13] In this respect, importance should be attached to the work of Li Wenzhao and Cai Changkun (2012).

8. Social governance as a new type of policy instrument, applications of social governance to ungovernability, governance quality of Chinese government,[14] and performance of various government tools. This kind of research is aimed at microscopic accumulation, by which researchers can discover modes from contingent phenomena and extract general knowledge from the modes. Knowledge accumulation may help guide practices, provide evidence for the abovementioned items on the agenda, and even make contributions to a general theoretical paradigm of public administration.

These items on the agenda are centered on state governance, social governance, and the interaction between the two. The proposal of the agenda mirrors value identity of the authors. As a matter of fact, although new governance cannot provide a set of normative theories, it is a very powerful discourse and a trend of thought well equipped with the endorsement of society. In the process of promoting governance, developing countries are bound to face conflicts between state building and governance. In spite of the fact that China has achieved governance in certain fields and at particular levels, it has also been confronted with the contradictions between state governance and social governance while endeavoring to propel governance. However, the structure-agency two-dimensional thinking mode may not leave us at a loss or desperate in the tension of state governance and social governance. In future, research on Chinese governance needs to be oriented toward various kinds of ungovernability, but an academic ideology based on the interaction and coevolution of state and society should be at hand. Not only is better social governance an integral part of modern state governance, but it may also be a powerful propeller for the modernization of state governance.

It is beyond dispute that we should not reject governance research unrelated to new governance arbitrarily, but Chinese governance research that stresses the role of society and citizens should be given high priority at present. Moreover, we are firmly convinced that it is difficult to foresee the future state of Chinese governance and the precise evolutionary path due to the complexity of the existing structure and the initiative factor. We believe that by observing various actors in terms of the space of strategic options and the modes of interaction in different structures and contexts, we will be able to better diagnose realistic situations and reflect on potential strategies in a timely manner. The core objective of this research agenda lies on stronger adaptive rational capacity.

---

[14] Research on governance quality may not necessarily be directly related to governance or social governance, but it is instrumental to diagnosing problems with Chinese governance. The research by Tony Saich falls into this category. See Tony Saich (2013).

REFERENCES

Alford, J., and O. Hughes. 2008. "Public value pragmatism as the next phase of public management." *American Review of Public Administration*, 38(2):130–148.

Barrow, C. W. 2005. "The return of the state: Globalization, state theory, and the new imperialism." *New Political Science*, 27(2):123–145.

Cai, Ning, Chengcheng Song, and Ying Zhou. 2015. "Zhengfu hui yingxiang feiyingli zuzhi yu qiye de hezuo ma?" ["Dose government influence the cooperation between NPOs and enterprises?"]. *Gonggong xingzheng pinglun* [*Journal Public Administration*]. (5):114–128.

Chao, Yung-mau. 2011. "Minzhu zhili de jiangou jichu yu wenti" ["The foundation and problems of democratic governance construction"]. In: Xunda Yu and Siqin Xu (eds.), *Minzhu minzhuhua yu zhili jixiao* [*Democracy, Democratization, and Governance Performance*]. Hangzhou: Zhejiang University Press, 106–116.

Chen, Shengyong, and Xingzhi Wu. 2007. "Gongmin canyu yu difang gonggong zhengce de zhiding—Yi zhejiang sheng wenling shi minzhu kentanhui weili" ["Citizen participation and formulation of local public policy—A typical study on the democratic consultation of Wenling in Zhejiang province"]. *Xueshu jie* [*Academy in China*], (5):30–39.

Chen, Tianxiang, and Ting Yang. 2011. "Chengshi shequ zhili: Juese mishi jiqi genyuan—Yi H shi weili" ["Urban community governance: Role failure and its causes: A case study of City H"]. *Zhongguo renmin daxue xuebao* [*Journal Renmin University China*], (3):129–137.

Chu, Hongqi. 2014. "Jiaoyu zhili: Yi gongzhi qiu shanzhi" ["Education governance: Achieving good governance through shared governance"]. *Jiaoyu yanjiu* [*Education Research*], (10):4–11.

Fan, Ruguo. 2014. "Fuza wangluo jiegou fanxing xia de shehui zhili xietong chuangxin" ["Collaborative innovation in social governance in a complex network structural paradigm"]. *Zhongguo shehui kexue* [*Social Science in China*], (4): 105–125.

Frederickson, H. G. 2005. "Whatever Happened to Public Administration? Governance, Governance Everywhere." In: Evan Ferlie, Lawrence E. Lynn, and Christopher Pollitt (eds.), *The Oxford Handbook of Public Management*. New York: Oxford University Press, 282–304.

Fukuyama, F. 2004. *State-Building: Governance and World Order in the 21st Century*. New York: Cornell University Press.

Fukuyama, F. 2014. *Political Order and Political Decay: From the Industrial Revolution to the Globalization of Democracy*. New York: Farrar, Straus and Giroux.

Guo, Daohui. 2006. "Zhengfuzhili yu gongminshehui canyu" ["Governance of government and civil society participation"]. *Hebei Faxue* [*Journal of law in Hebei*], (1):12–16.

He, Baogang, and Youxing Lang. 2008. "Xieshang minzhu zai zhongguo jiceng de shenhua" ["The deepening of deliberative democracy in Chinese grass roots"]. *Xuexi shibao* [*Study Times*]: 03:10005.

He, Zengke. 2007. "Zhengzhi hefaxing yu Zhongguo difang zhengfu chuangxin: yixiang chubu de jingyanxing yanjiu" ["Political legitimacy and Chinese local government's innovation: A preliminary empirical study"]. *Yunnan xingzheng xueyuan xuebao* [*Journal of Yunnan Administration College*], (2):8–13.

He, Zengke. 2008. "Zhongguo zhili pingjia tixi kuangjia chutan" ["A preliminary study of China's governance evaluation system"]. *Beijing xingzheng xueyuan xuebao* [*Journal of Beijing Administration College*], (5):1–8.

He, Zenke. 2014. "Lijie guojia zhili jiqi xiandaihua" ["Understanding state governance and its modernization"]. *Makesi zhuyi yu xianshi* [*Marxism and Reality*], (1):11-15.

Hirst, P., 2000. "Democracy and Governance." In: J. Pierre (ed.), *Debating Governance*. Oxford: Oxford University Press, 13–35.

Hu, Angang, 2014. "Guojia zhili xiandaihua bushi xifanghua" ["State governance modernization is not Westernization"]. *Lilun xuexi* [*Theory study*]. (1): 42–43.

Hupe, P. L., and M. J. Hill, 2006. "The Three Action Levels of Governance: Re-Framing the Policy Process beyond the Stages Model." In: B. G. Peters and J. Pierre (eds.), *Handbook of Public Policy*, London: Sage, 13–30.

Huxham, C., 2000. "The challenge of collaborative governance." *Public Management: An International Journal of Research and Theory*, 2(3):337–57.

Jessop, B., 1996. "Interpretive sociology and the dialectic of structure and agency." *Theory, Culture and Society*, 13(1):119–128.

Jessop, B., 2002a. "Governance and Metagovernance: On Reflexivity, Requisite Variety, and Requisite Irony", http://www.lancs.ac.uk/fss/sociology/papers/jessop-governance-and-metagovernance.pdf (Accessed Oct. 5, 2004).

Jessop, B., 2002b. "Guojia lilun de xinjinzhan—gezhong taolun, zhenlundian he yicheng(xu)" ["Recent developments in state theory—Various discussions, arguments and agenda (continued)"]. *Shijie zhexue* [*World Philosophy*], (2):22–26.

Jing, Yijia, and Ting Gong. 2012. Managed social innovation: The case of government-sponsored venture philanthropy in Shanghai. *Australian Journal of Public Administration*, 71(2):233–245.

Kooiman, 1993. *Modern Governance*. London: Sage.

Leftwich, A., 1994. "Governance, the state and development." *Development and Change*, 25(2):363–386.

Li, Huifeng, 2010. "Shequ zhili yu shehui guanlitizhi chuangxin—Jiyu Ningbo shequ anli yanjiu" ["Community governance and social management system innovation—Case study of Ningbo City"]. *Gonggong guanli xuebao* [*Journal Public Management*], (1):67–72.

Li, Wenxing, and Haiming Zheng, 2007. "Lun difangzhili shiye xia de zhengfu yu gongzhong hudongshi goutong jizhi de goujian" ["On the construction of interactive communication mechanism between government and public from the perspective of local governance"]. *Zhongguo xingzheng guanli* [*Chinese Public Administration*], (5):69–72.

Li, Wenzhao, and Changkun Cai, 2012. "Zhengzhi zhidu jiegou, shehui ziben yu gonggongzhili zhidu xuanze" ["Political institution structures, social capitals and the choice of public governance systems"]. *Guanli shijie* [*Management World*], (8): 43–54.

Lin, Shangli, 2011. "Chonggou fuji guanxi yu guojia zhili" ["Reconstructing intergovernmental relations and state governance"]. *Tansuo yu zhengming* [*Exploration and Free Views*]. (1): 34–37.

Liu, Zhichang, 2007. "Caogen zuzhi de shengzhang yu shequ zhili jiegou de zhuanxing" ["The growth of grass-roots organizations and the transformation of community governance structure"]. *Shehui zhuyi yanjiu* [*Socialism Studies*], (4):94–96.

Lou, Chengwu, and Jiangwei Zhang, 2007. "Cong difangzhengfu dao difangzhili—Difangzhili zhi neihan yu moshi yanjiu" ["From local government to local governance: The study of local governance and its model"]. *Zhongguo xingzheng guanli* [*Chinese Public Administration*], (7):100–102.

Marinetto, M., 2003. "Governing beyond the centre: A critique of the Anglo-governance school." *Political Studies*, 51(4):592–608.

Mou, Tsung-san, 2006. *Zhidao yu zhengdao* [*Governance and Politics*]. Nanning: Guangxi Normal University Press.

Onis, Ziya, 1991. "The logic of the developmental state." *Compar Pol*, 24(1):109–126.

Peters, B. G., and J. Pierre, 1998. "Governing without government? Rethinking public administration." *Journal of Public Administration Research and Theory*, 8(2):223–243.

Peters, G. B., 2000. "Governance and Comparative Politics." In: J. Pierre (eds.), *Debating Governance*. New York: Oxford University Press, 36–53.

Rhodes, R. A. W., 1996. "The new governance: Governing without government?" *Political Studies*, 44(4):652–667.

Rhodes, R. A. W., 1997. *Understanding Governance*. Buckingham and Philadelphia: Open University Press.

Saich, T., 2013. "Zhongguo de zhili zhiliang: Gongmin de shijiao" ["The quality of governance in China: The citizens' view"]. *Zhongguo zhili pinglun* [*China Govern Review*], (1):1–27.

Spires, A. J., 2011. "Contingent symbiosis and civil society in authoritarian state: Understanding the survival of China's Grassroots NGOs." *American Journal of Society*, 117(1):1–45.

Stoker, G., 1998. "Governance as theory: Five propositions." *International Social Science Journal*, 155: 17–28.

Sun, Baiying, 2004. *Dangdai difang zhili* [*Contemporary Local Governance*]. Beijing: Zhongguo renmin daxue chubanshe.

Svensson, J., W. Trommel, and T. Lantink, 2008. "Reemployment services in the Netherlands: A comparative study of bureaucratic, market, and network forms of organization." *Public Administration Review*, 68(3):505–515.

Tang, Huangfeng, and Jianwu Tao, 2014. "Dashuju shidai de zhongguo guojia zhili nengli jianshe" ["China national governance capacity building in the era of big data"]. *Tansuo yu zhengming* [*Exploration and Free Views*], (10):54–58.

Tang, Wenyu, 2012. "Ruhe shenshi zhongguo shehuizuzhi yu zhengfu guanxi" ["How to examine Chinese NGO-State Relations"]. *Gonggong xingzheng pinglun* [*Journal of Public Administration*], (4):145–162.

Tang, Yalin, 2014. "Xiandai guojia zhili zai zhongguo de dengchang jiqi fangfalun jiazhi" ["National governance comes on the stage in contemporary China and its methodological value"]. *Fudan xuebao (Shehui kexueban)* [*Fudan Journal (Social science Edition)*], (2):128–137.

Tasi, L. L., 2015. "Constructive noncompliance." *Comparative Politics*, 47(3):253–279.

Tian, Xianhong, 2012. "Jiceng xinfang zhilizhong de 'baobaozerenzhi': Shijian lujing yu xianshi kunjing" ["The accountability system in the grassroots petition governance: The practical logic and realistic dilemma: A case study of Town Qiao, Mid—Hubei Province"]. *Shehui* [*Journal of Society*], (4):164–193.

Toonen, T. A. J., 1990. "The unitary state as a system of co-governance: The case of The Netherlands." *Public Administration*, 68(3):281–96.

Wang, Hsin-Hsien, 2006. *Zhengbian zhong de zhongguo shehui zuzhi yanjiu: guojia-shehui guanxi de shijiao* [*Chinese Social Organizations in Debate: A Perspective of State-Society Relationship*]. Taipei: Weber Publication International.

Wang, Puqu, and Lester Salamon, 2013. *Zhengfu xiang shehuizuzhi goumai gonggong fuwu yanjiu: Zhongguo yu Quanqiu jingyan fenxi* [*Outsourcing Government-financed Social Services to Civil Society Organizations: Lessons from China and Abroad*]. Beijing: Peking University Press.

Wang, Qinghua, and Gang Guo, 2015. "Yu Keping and Chinese intellectual discourse on good governance." *The China Quarterly*, (7):1–21.

Wang, Shizong, 2007. "Difangzhili zai zhongguo de shiyongxing jiqi xiandu—yi ning-boshi haishuqu zhengfugoumai jujiayanglao zhengce weili" ["The applicability of local government in China and it's limitation—A case study of purchasing services for the aged home by the government in Haishu District"]. *Gonggong guanli xuebao* [*Journal of Public Management*], (4): 45–52.

Wang, Shizong, 2009. *Zhili lilun jiqi zhongguo shiyongxing* [*Governance Theory and its Applicability in China*]. Hangzhou: Zhejiang University Press.

World Bank, 1989. *Sub-Saharan Africa: From Crisis to Sustainable Growth*. Washington, DC: World Bank.

World Bank, 1992. *Governance and Development*. Washington, DC: World Bank.

Xu, Yong, 2004. "Jingxiangkuozhen, xiangpaizhenzhi: xiangji zhili tizhi de jiegouxing gaige" ["Village-reduction and town-expansion and town governance in village: The structural reform of rural governance system"]. *Jiangxi shehuikexue* [*Jiangxi Social Science*], (1):24–29.

Xu, Yong, and Dejian Zhao, 2014. "Zhaohui zizhi: Dui cunmin zizhi youxiao shixian xingshi de tansuo" ["Finding autonomy: Exploration of effective realization form of villager autonomy]. *Huazhong shifan daxue xuebao (Renwen shehui kexueban)* [*J Huazhong Normal University (Human and Social Science)*], (4):1–8.

Xue, Lan, 2014. "Dingceng sheji yu nining qianxing: Zhongguo guojia zhili xiandai-hua" ["Top-level design and moving on hardly: The path of China's state governance modernization"]. *Gonggogn guanli xuebao* [*Journal of Public Management*], (4):1–6.

Yan, Jirong, 2010. "Shequ zhili yu shehui ziben touzi" ["Community governance and social capital investment"]. *Tianjin shehui kexue* [*Tianjin Social Science*], (3):59–64.

Yan, Jirong, 2014. "Xiandai guojia zhili yu zhidu jianshe" ["National governance and institutional building"]. *Zhongguo xingzheng guanli* [*Chinese Public Administration*], (5):58–63.

Yang, Deming, and Can Zhao, 2012. "Meiti jiandu, meitizhili yu gaoguan xinchou" ["Media monitoring, media governance and managers' compensation"]. *Jingji yan-jiu* [*Economy Research Journal*], (6):116–126.

Yu, Jianxing, 2008. "Zhili yu guojia jiangou zhijian de zhangli" ["Tensions between governance and state building"]. *Makesi zhuyi yu xianshi* [*Marxism and Reality*], (1):86–93.

Yu, Jianxing, and Shizong Wang, 2011. "The applicability of governance theory in China." *Fudan Journal of Humanity and Social science*, 4(1):22–36.

Yu, Jianxing, Jun Zhou, and Hua Jiang, 2012. *A Path for Chinese Civil Society: A Case Study on industrial associations in Wenzhou, China*. Lanham, MD: Lexington Books.

Yu, Keping, 1999. "Zhongguo gongminshehui de xingqi yu zhili de bianqian" ["The rise of Chinese civil society and transition of governance"]. *Zhongguo shehuikexue jikan. [Chinese Social Science Quarterly]*. (fall):105–117.

Yu, Keping, 2000. "Introduction: Governance and Good Governance." In: Yu Keping (ed.), *Zhili yu Shanzhi* [*Governance and Good Governance*]. Beijing: China Social Science Press, 1–15.

Yu, keping, Zengke He, and Xiuli Xu, 2006. *Zhongguo gongmin shehui de zhidu huanjing* [*Institutional Environment of Chinese Civil Society*]. Beijing: Peking University Press.

Zheng, Hangsheng, and Jialiang Huang, 2012. "Dangqian woguo shuihui guanli he shequ zhili de xinqushi" ["New trend of social management and community governance in China"]. *Gansu shehui kexue* [*Gansu Social Science*], (6):1–8.

Zheng, Siqi, Guanghua Wan, Weizeng Sun, and Dangluo Lun, 2013. "Gongzhong suqiu yu chengshi huanjing zhili" ["The demand of the public and the control over the city environment"]. *Guanli shijie* [*Management World*], (6):72–84.

PART II

Local Government

CHAPTER 6

Mapping the Progress of Local Government Innovation in Contemporary China

Jianxing Yu and Biao Huang

1 Rise of Practice and Study on Local Government Innovation in Contemporary China

Local government innovation is a key variable in explaining China's economic and social development. What is local government innovation? Government innovation means government adopts a program or policy that is new to the organization, regardless of how old the program or policy may be or how many other organizations may have adopted it (Walker 1969). Correspondingly, local government innovation means a local government's adoption of a new (to such local government) program or policy. Hence, local government innovation not only covers the "spontaneous exploration" of local government but also involves "top-down experimentation" which is appointed by upper-level governments and implemented by local governments.[1]

The Third Plenary Session of the 11th Central Committee of the Communist Party of China (CPC hereafter) in 1978 marked the beginning of the "reform and opening up." Since then, China's economic and social development has entered a new historic stage. At the beginning of the reform, China lacked state-building and effective governance experience. Extensive local government

---

[1] In this chapter, "upper-level governments" means people's governments and their departments at provincial level and above, and "local governments" means people's governments and their departments at municipal level and below.

J. Yu • B. Huang (✉)
School of Public Affairs, Zhejiang University, Hangzhou, Zhejiang, China
e-mail: yujianxing@zju.edu.cn

© The Author(s) 2019
J. Yu, S. Guo (eds.), *The Palgrave Handbook of Local Governance in Contemporary China*, https://doi.org/10.1007/978-981-13-2799-5_6

innovations originated from such lack of institutions and practices. That is because in the Chinese hierarchical system, central government was not directly engaged in the management of local affairs. General institutional design, if directly promoted by the central government, usually would not be applicable in practice. Therefore, Deng Xiaoping (1994), the chief designer of China's reform and opening up, pointed out in the Central Working Conference before the Third Plenary Session of the 11th Central Committee of CPC that "[p]ending the introduction of a unified national program of modern management, we can begin with limited spheres, say, a particular region or a given trade, and then spread the methods gradually to others. The central government departments concerned should promote such experiments." As an important strategy when CPC faced uncertainty, top-down experimentation at local level was given a new mission for reform and opening up.[2]

Local government innovation in the early stage of the reform and opening up was mainly concentrated in the economic field, such as a series of intensive decentralization reforms targeted at mixed functions of governments and enterprises and low efficiency, "special economic zone" and "economic development zone" to encourage foreign investment and attract advanced technologies and management, labor contract reform for building modern employment system, and so on. In 1987, the 13th CPC National Congress extended the function of top-down experimentation from economic reform to other aspects of socioeconomic development and put forward that: "In pursuing reform, we must stress experimentation, encourage exploration, seek practical interim methods and measures, and advance one step at a time." Later, local government innovation gradually extended to social governance, public service, and other areas.

Entering the 1990s, with continuous advancing of marketization and urbanization, Chinese society witnessed diversified development. Facing the increasing complexity in local economic and social development, policy orders from upper-level governments could hardly meet specific requirements of local governance. As a result, local governments needed to explore new policy instruments to respond to increasingly stronger public demands. Meanwhile, globalization and informatization also made it possible for horizontal propagation of the local governance experience. Therefore, local government communication across countries and regions became frequent and convenient. Apart from "top-down" supply, local governments had more experience for reference. Therefore, more and more local governments started to seek solutions for specific problems beyond existing policies. Representative examples included "Service Center for Joint Examination and Approval"

---

[2] According to Sebastian Heilmann (2008a), CPC innovative experimentation can be traced back to the Period of Land Reform during 1928–1943. The experiments with alternative approaches to land reform that were undertaken by Mao Zedong in Jinggangshan and by Deng Zihui in Minxi in 1928 constitute a pioneering experience for later Communist land policy.

established in 1995 in Shenzhen, "Social Conflict Mediation Center" founded in Pudong New Area, Shanghai, and "Home for Migrant Workers" set up in 1997 in Longhua District, Haikou.

Correspondingly, early studies of Chinese local government innovation began with economists' focus on institutional changes and innovations after the reform and opening up. For instance, in 1993, Qian and Xu (1993) discussed the establishment of the household contract responsibility system and off-budget accounts of local governments, surrounding the relationship between innovations of administrative decentralization and China's economic development; in 1994, Zhou (1994) and Cui (1994) also studied the household contract responsibility system in their articles published in the *Chinese Social Sciences Quarterly* and the *21st Century* (Hong Kong), respectively; other innovations included the joint-stock system reform of township collective assets and the election of village committees are mentioned; in the same year, Lin et al. (1994), in *The China Miracle: Development Strategy and Economic Reform*, reviewed the economic reforms since 1978 and explained China's speedy economic growth from the perspective of institutional innovation. Later, as local government innovation became diversified, an increasing number of researchers in politics and public administration started to focus on and discuss innovative experimentation of local governments.

In 2000, under advocacy and promotion of scholars like Keping Yu and Changjiang Wang, "Chinese Local Government Innovation Award" (CLGIA hereafter) has been jointly set up by Center for Comparative Politics and Economics of Central Compilation and Translation Bureau, Center of Comparative Studies on Political Parties of Party School of the CPC Central Committee, and the Center for Chinese Government Innovation of Peking University.[3] The concept of "Government Innovation" was officially introduced into China and became one of the key "buzzwords" in the practice and study of Chinese government reform in the new century. To this day, CLGIA has been held for eight sessions, and more than 2000 innovative programs in total have been evaluated, including 170 finalist programs and 80 winning programs, covering such fields as government service, social service, environmental protection, culture and education, health care, and poverty relief. Representative examples included "Administrative Approval System Reform" in Shenzhen City, Guangdong Province; "Open Recommendation and Direct Election of Township Party Committee" in Pingchang County, Sichuan Province; "Democratic Consultation" in Wenling City, Zhejiang Province; "Government Purchase of Home Care Services" in Haishu District, Ningbo City; and so on. These cases were widely discussed in literatures and became an important window for observing Chinese government and politics. In December 2015, *The China Quarterly*, the most influential overseas journal

---

[3] Since its fifth session, "Chinese Local Government Innovation Award" has been independently held by Center for Chinese Government Innovation, Peking University.

about contemporary Chinese studies, published an article reviewing Keping Yu (the main initiator of CLGIA) and Chinese intellectual discourse on good governance. This article argues that political reform in post-Mao China is mainly about government innovation and has been as successful as China's economic reform (Wang and Guo 2015).

In this chapter, we discuss the following aspects: First, we review studies on local government innovation in contemporary China; second, we present recent arguments about local government innovation since Xi Jinping took over power; third, we make a case study on local government innovation after the 18th National Congress of the CPC. On this basis, we attempt to put forward a new concept to describe the new form of local government innovation during the Xi Era; and lastly, we briefly analyze the further development of Chinese government and politics from the perspective of government innovation in combination with the discussion about power centralization and decentralization.

2   TWO RESEARCH APPROACHES ABOUT LOCAL GOVERNMENT INNOVATION

Existing literature has discussed local government innovation in contemporary China from two approaches.

The first approach is Discipline Study. It summarizes types and characteristics of local government innovation, discusses influential factors of local government innovation, and describes its process. For example, Wu et al. (2007, 2011, 2013), after analysis of several sessions of CLGIA, found that local government innovation in contemporary China can be divided into five categories: management innovation, service innovation, cooperation innovation, technological innovation, and governance innovation. A majority of local government innovation appears in East China and is concentrated at prefecture and county level. Yu (2012) puts forward that the main influential factors of Chinese local government innovation include public stress, pressure from superiors, pursuit of political achievement, crisis and emergency, and new technology and ideas. Zhu et al. (2015) analyze the health insurance policy innovation of local governments through the theory of policy entrepreneur. These researches mostly pay their attention to spontaneous exploration, that is, local governments spontaneously put innovative will into practice to seek solutions for specific problems, which assumes or reveals autonomy and motility of local governments during innovation. It probably stems from some popular arguments made by organizers of CLGIA and practitioners of innovation at a local level. For example, when introducing the setup background of CLGIA, Yu (2003), the main initiator, points out that "[r]ecently, as political ideas and environments change, there emerges a powerful impetus for institutional innovation among local governments, in particular among grassroots governments. Innovation becomes a conscious action among many local party committees and governments."

He (2003), the executive director of CLGIA, states that local governments are the suppliers for innovative arrangements and the pushers for innovation as well. Local government innovation tends to be a result of spontaneous and internal drive. Chen and Yang (2009), key members of the executive committee of CLGIA, also focus analytical object on "innovations that are predominated by local government" at the beginning of their articles. In practice, practitioners of local government innovation generally take spontaneity and creativity as important criteria for innovating. For example, among local government innovation cases surveyed by Zhou (2003) and Chen (2004), et al., most of the innovation decisions are made by local officials spontaneously; according to another survey for finalist programs of the fourth and fifth CLGIA by Yang (2011), government officials in charge of innovation programs prefer to repeatedly highlight "originality" as the prior characteristic of innovation.

The second approach is Area Study. It explains China's economic and social changes and government and political reforms by observing the innovative behaviors of local governments, taking study of local government innovation as an instrument. These studies mainly focus on top-down experimentation, that is, to seek an approach for realizing general policy targets, upper-level governments would authorize one or several local governments for pilot practice before comprehensive promotion of such institutional change. Heilmann (2008b) first conceptualizes and theorizes the top-down experimentation (or as he called it, policy experimentation), on which basis, he explains the rise of Chinese economy. Mei et al. (2015) argue that the mechanism of top-down experimentation is that the central government, who holds the top-down authority, decides policy goals, and selects some local governments as experimental points to test different policy instruments. They believe that top-down experimentation is a process for seeking effective policies dominated by central governments, and appointing some local governments as experimental points is the method for policy seeking. Liu (2015) explains top-down experimentation as exploratory and experimental reforms by upper-level governments in specific places within a certain period. In addition, Zeng (2015), Shin (2013) et al. also had several discussions centering on this type of innovation.

3   New Progress of Chinese Local Government Innovation During the Xi Era

Pervious research has discussed two types of characteristics and properties of local governments when acting as local governance dominator and agent of upper-level governments, revealing two main innovation mechanisms: spontaneous exploration and top-down experimentation. Subsequent studies, conscientiously or unconsciously, have followed this cognition.

There is no doubt that the pursuit of conceptualization and theorization usually helps researchers analyze problems clearly and make succinct conclusions. However, if researchers pay too much attention to constructing simple theoretical models, they may ignore the complexity of reality and even be blind to the difference between existing models and the real world. As Ostrom (1990, p. 216) puts it: "The theoretical enterprise requires social scientists to engage in model-building, but not limit theoretical inquiry to that specific level of discourse." There has already formed a clear and consistent understanding among studies on Chinese local government innovation. However, when the objective world experiences tremendous changes, existing understandings may limit researchers' theoretical assumptions and observation perspectives, thus affecting the accuracy and explanatory power of the theory. This condition is particularly evident in the explanation of local government innovation under Xi Jinping's administration in China.

After the 18th National Congress of CPC, when Xi Jinping took over power, several scholars have argued that the impetus of local government innovation in China has been greatly faded, and local governments have not been active in innovation any more (Yu 2015a; Yang 2015). For example, Yu (2015b) claims that local government innovation impetus is greatly weakened. Once there is a lack of motivation, government reform may be seriously harmed. In a review in the *New York Times*, Sebastian Heilmann said that openness to experimentation contributed to China's success in recent decades. However, local innovative experimentation has largely ended with the central government's idea of "top-level design." This has taken a lot of energy out of China's political system (Johnson 2017). These judgments are based on facts in two aspects. The first aspect is that the number of applications for CLGIA has decreased after the 18th National Congress of CPC. According to Yu (2015b), the number of applications for the 7th CLGIA (2013) decreased by one-third compared with that of the 6th session (2011); the 8th CLGIA (2015)[4] saw a totally different status from that of the past, when local governments were enthusiastic when applying; in this session, however, the executive committee of CLGIA would take the initiative to ask local governments for application. In the other aspect, after the 18th National Congress of CPC, a series of centralization reforms were carried out across China, and autonomy of local governments is greatly limited (see Zheng 2014, 2015). In the words of Sebastian Heilmann, after the 18th National Congress, with Chinese government's emphasis on hierarchy and discipline, the courage to experiment at the local level was squeezed out (Johnson 2017). Also, He points out that the central government's highlight of the status and function of top-level design poses higher requirements on the sense of discipline. Under this context, local governments have limited autonomy to take one step ahead in many circumstances, resulting in insufficient innovation impetus (Zhang 2015).

Do the above judgments correctly reflect actual conditions of current local government innovation in China? On the one hand, the decreasing number and initiative for CLGIA is not equivalent to the decreasing number and initiative of

---

[4] In later period, the eighth "Chinese Local Government Innovation Award" was renamed the eighth "Best Practice in China Government Innovation."

local government innovations. There are other possible factors attributing to the change of application for CLGIA. For example, the manifestation of innovation projects is no longer the target of many local governments, and many innovative polices or projects of local governments are not named after "innovation." On the other hand, stricter regulation, restriction, and even punishment to local governments are structural factors of innovation. Logically, this can only be inferred as a narrowed scope and decreasing the possibility of local governments' spontaneous exploration, but it does not amount to weakening the motivation of local government innovation. As actors, local governments can still have innovation impetus, for example, responding to public demands.

More importantly, the discussion about increase or decrease in innovation impetus has originated from an inaccurate assumption: the more local government innovation, the better. Many studies have already made clarifications. De Ven (1988) has reviewed the way in which innovation and success have been seen as interchangeable. According to de Ven, innovation is often viewed as a good thing because the new idea must be useful. He argues that innovations that do not produce such a normative improvement are subsequently redefined as mistakes. As Hartley (2005) has noted, while innovation and improvement have often been assumed to be synonymous, this is by no means always the case. In a research review, Osborne and Brown (2011) also point out that many organizations involved in innovation and literature studying innovation highlight the attributes of innovation, such as "the need to improve public service" and "to respond to public demands better," yet with no clear statement of what this means. Contained within this discourse has been the enduring assumption that any particular innovation must, a priori, be "a good thing." According to them, one may consider "innovation" as a process essential for the improvement of public service but that is not the same as asserting any specific innovation must therefore be positive. Such overreaching assertions about "innovation" do little to facilitate innovation, nor do they acknowledge the potential for negative effects of innovation and for the understanding of support and management required by innovation. What is worse is that this may give the mistaken guidance to the policymakers. They repeatedly emphasize the point of view that support and management of innovation requires a nuanced approach that acknowledges both that not all positive changes are always innovative in nature and that not all innovative changes are always beneficial. Recognizing this, based on the facts among local government innovations, such as freewheeling innovation, illegal innovation, or innovating for the sake of innovation, we can conclude that for local government innovation, it is not that more is better.

Therefore, the decreasing number of applications for CLGIA or limited autonomy of local governments is not sufficient to judge a weakening impetus of local government innovation. Compared with such discussions, we are more in need of observing and interpreting what has happened to Chinese local government innovation during the Xi era.

4   "SEEKING APPROVAL": NEW NORMAL OF LOCAL GOVERNMENTS' INNOVATIONS

In November 2013, the Third Plenary Session of the 18th CPC Central Committee examined and approved the *Decision of the CPC Central Committee on Some Major Issues Concerning Comprehensively Deepening the Reform*, indicating that China has entered a new historical stage of comprehensively deepening reform. By observing local government innovations during this period, we find that a new model of local government innovation has emerged. In this chapter, we take the reform of comprehensive administrative law enforcement system in Jiaxing City, Zhejiang Province, as an example.[5]

In recent years, with a booming economic and social development, new problems have emerged in Jiaxing City during administrative law enforcement practice, such as complex law enforcement due to disordered rural and urban planning and unsmooth connection, difficulty in cross-department coordination due to ever-changing law enforcement standards, and barriers between higher and lower levels or between different departments and regions and overlapping management. Meanwhile, as an important foodstuff-producing area in Zhejiang Province, Jiaxing city saw common pollution in large-scale farming and illegal occupation of land. Local governments lack the law enforcement authorities and functions, while the frontline law enforcement bodies are dispersed in multiple departments. Many illegal behaviors cannot be found in time and effectively banned. Therefore, to improve management and establish an authoritative and effective administrative law enforcement system, Jiaxing Municipal Party Committee and Government have undertaken a comprehensive reform for the administrative law enforcement system. In summary, the process of this innovation mainly includes four stages (Fig. 6.1).

In July 2013, Jiaxing Municipal Party Committee and Government drafted the *Working Plan for Pilot Work of Comprehensive Administrative Law*

Design plan → Ask superior for approval → Officially authorize → Practice

Fig. 6.1 Reform process of comprehensive administrative law enforcement system in Jiaxing City. Source: Sorted in accordance with the *Summary of Comprehensive Administrative Law Enforcement Reform Documents in Jiaxing City* (unpublished documents)

[5] In October 2014, the delegation of State Commission Office for Public Sectors Reform visited Jiaxing City for survey about this reform. In October 2015, People's Government of Zhejiang Province held a promotion conference about comprehensive administrative law enforcement for Zhejiang Province in Jiashan County, Jiaxing City, to summarize and promote Jiaxing City's experience. In March 2016, the Ministry of Housing and Urban-Rural Development of the People's Republic of China and the Office of Housing and Urban-Rural Development in Zhejiang Province carried out a special survey about the comprehensive administrative law enforcement reform in Jiaxing City. It can be seen that the comprehensive administrative law enforcement reform in Jiaxing City shows the high manifestation and influence across China.

Enforcement in Jiaxing City (Working Plan hereinafter) after repeated surveys and discussions. However, this Working Plan was not immediately issued and implemented.

In September 2013, Jiaxing Municipal Party Committee and Government submitted the Working Plan and pilot application to the CPC Zhejiang Provincial Committee and reported to principal leaders of the Zhejiang Provincial Party Committee and Government in the hope that the upper-level government would approve this Working Plan and authorize Jiaxing as the pilot city. However, the CPC Zhejiang Provincial Party Committee and Government didn't give an official reply immediately, given that no recent policy goals were mentioned by the central government about the administrative law enforcement system.

In November 2013, the Third Plenary Session of the 18th Central Committee of CPC set the goal of "deepening reform of the administrative law enforcement system" and expressly mentioned "integrating major law enforcement bodies, relatively centralizing the law enforcement power, pressing ahead with comprehensive law enforcement, and resolving problems, such as overlapping functions and duplicate law enforcement to establish an authoritative and efficient administrative law enforcement system with the integration of power and responsibility." After that, the leadership in Zhejiang Provincial Party Committee and Government agreed and approved the Working Plan of Jiaxing City. On August 8, the Commission Office for Public Sector Reform of Zhejiang Province issued the *Reply to the Working Plan for Pilot Work of Comprehensive Administrative Law Enforcement in Jiaxing City* and officially authorized Jiaxing City as an experimental point to practice.

By reviewing the innovating process of comprehensive administrative law enforcement in Jiaxing City, we can find that this local government innovation is neither a typical top-down experimentation that should be initiated by upper-level government nor a spontaneous exploration where local governments spontaneously and conscientiously explore new policy goals or instruments. We can call this new form of local government innovation as "seeking approval." "Seeking approval" describes that local governments tend to draft the practice proposal of an innovative intention for universal local problems first and report to upper-level governments to seek for approval; once formally confirmed and approved, this program then would be implemented by local governments. The difference of spontaneous exploration, top-down experimentation, and "seeking approval" is mainly reflected in three dimensions (Table 6.1).

4.1   Subject Dimension

Throughout the general process from generation, implementation, examination, and evaluation of local government innovation, the innovation subject can be divided into initiating subject, executive subject, and responsible subject. Spontaneous exploration is initiated and executed by local governments and the responsible subject is also local governments. In general, top-down

Table 6.1 Comparison of three forms of local government innovations

Dimensions	Items		Spontaneous exploration	Top-down experimentation	"Seeking approval"
Subject dimension	Initiating subject		Local government	Upper-level government	Local government
	Executive subject		Local government	Local government	Local government
	Responsible subject		Local government	Upper-level government	Local governments, upper-level government
Content dimension	Justification source		Self-justification by local governments	Initiative authorization by upper-level governments	Authorization by upper-level governments based on local governments' application
	Degree of institutionalization	Restraint	Low	High	Medium
		Sustainability	Low	High	Medium
		Diffusivity	Low	High	Medium
Functional dimension	Normative value basis		Particularism	Specialization of universalism	Universalization of particularism
	Expected targets		Solve specific local governance issues	Seek for general policy programs through practice in some regions	Attempt to seek for general policy programs while solving specific problems
	Positive externality		Provide knowledge and experience for state-building	Institutional dividend due to institutional difference	Sound interaction between local and upper-level governments
	Negative externality		Short-term behaviors of local governments	Institutionally worsen regional inequality	Excessive circumvention of responsibilities and risks by local governments

experimentation is initiated by, and under the charge of, upper-level governments. Local governments are responsible for executing. The will of "seeking approval" is from local governments. Upper-level governments are responsible for deciding the implementation of such innovation. Therefore, this type of innovation is initiated by local governments and is under the charge of both local governments and upper-level governments. Local governments are responsible for practicing.

4.2   *Content Dimension*

The content difference of three types of innovations can be described in two aspects: justification source and degree of institutionalization. In terms of justification source, because spontaneous exploration mainly handles specific issues in a given case, its justification usually is self-justified by local governments in combination with macro-policy objectives set by upper-level governments. The justifications of top-down experimentation and "seeking approval" are from explicit authorization by upper-level governments. However, from the authorization process, these two forms of innovations differ a lot. Generally, top-down experimentation is initiatively authorized by upper-level governments in the form of an official document. On the contrary, "seeking approval" is applied by local governments. Upper-level governments make authorization selectively based on application, usually in the form of official approval or reply. In terms of degree of institutionalization, it is gradually decreased from top-down experimentation, "seeking approval" to spontaneous exploration. Institutionalization is an essential guarantee for effective implementation of local government innovation (Yu and Guan 2013). Institutionalization has three core elements: Restraint, continuity, and diffusivity (Yu and Qin 2015). The implementation of top-down experimentation is from mandatory requirements of upper-level governments. Under the "Rule of Mandates" system (Birney 2014), this kind of innovation has greater restraint. In addition, top-down experimentation needs to consider subsequent "proceeding from point to surface" (*youdian daomian*) to form regional and even national policy. Therefore, it has higher requirements on continuity and diffusivity. Compared with "seeking approval" and spontaneous exploration, top-down experimentation tends to have higher degree of institutionalization. As for "seeking approval," though the innovative will is from local governments, it needs authorization of upper-level governments and is incorporated with some policy objectives of upper-level governments, thereby having high restraint, continuity, as well as possibility and feasibility for diffusion. Spontaneous exploration, carried out by local governments independently, has a fragile source of justification, and is more prone to be influenced by capability and preference of local reformers. Moreover, most spontaneous exploration is a kind of "stress-response" behavior only for handling specific issues, and diffusion applicability is often not considered in innovation (Yu and Huang 2015). For these reasons, this type of innovation shows relatively low restraint, continuity, and diffusivity.

4.3   Functional Dimension

The differences in functional dimension are mainly reflected in the normative value basis, expected goals, and positive and negative externalities of innovation. Spontaneous exploration is based on the value basis of particularism in public governance, that is, universal institutional arrangements are unable to fully meet the complex and differential local governance requirements. The expected goal of this type of innovation is to break the current governance dilemma and solve specific local governance issues. Top-down experimentation embodies more about the value basis of universalism specialization. The core goal of this type of innovation is to explore general policy. On the other hand, in order to achieve this goal, the innovation must first go through a special process for mutual coordination, adjustment, and combination with local governance conditions and even local culture; by selecting several "experimental points," policymakers can test the universality of policy design and keep implementation risks under control. The normative value basis of the "seeking approval" initiative is in contrast to that of top-down experimentation, which follows the logic of universalization of particularism, that is, making efforts to find general policy programs while handling specific local issues. This type of innovation carries local governments' requirements for solving specific public issues and embodies the consideration of upper-level governments' pursuit of a wider range of institutional changes. As to externality, spontaneous exploration of local governments can bring rich knowledge and experience to state-building. However, this may lead to free-wheeling innovation and innovation for the sake of innovation by local governments. In particular, when innovation is excessively encouraged, this negative externality is more significant. For top-down experimentation, if an area is selected by upper-level governments, it can usually enjoy more institutional bonus and access greater resources, which means better conditions for development. A good example of such benefits is the rapid socioeconomic development in southeast coastal provinces after the reform and opening up. However, selective experimentation enables differential treatment of same public affairs in different regions, resulting in worse regional inequity. Compared with the above two models of innovation, the core characteristic of "seeking approval" is formal interaction between local and upper-level governments, whose continuation, institutionalization, and effect may lead to a new type of vertical intergovernmental relationship. This is discussed later. Of course, local governments may escape from necessary local governance responsibilities by overly "seeking approval."

It should be noted that the earlier judgments are mainly from the flow of local government innovation at a formal level. In fact, the process of local government innovation is much more complex. For example, before the implementation of spontaneous exploration, local reformers may have already reported to their superiors in private and obtained informal approval; before officially publishing "experimental points," upper-level governments may have already reached an agreement with local governments accepting "experimental points" at an unofficial level. There are a small number of studies that have already noted these informal aspects during local government innovation. This informal interaction between governments is even thought to play a key role in innovation. For instance, according to several studies on local government innovation by Yang and Chen, the support and acquiescence by upper-level governments and unofficial approval and instruction by upper-level leadership are thought to be a vital drive for local government innovation (see Yang 2011; Yang and Chen 2010; Chen and Yang 2009). Heilmann (2008b) also noted that before policy innovation, local policymakers may seek the informal backing by higher-level policy patrons. He argues that encouragement and protection extended by senior leaders to local reformers, a mechanism of informal "policy hedging," is a major determinant of pioneering behavior on the local level. When we investigated the "Democratic Consultation" in Zeguo Township, Wenling City, Zhejiang Province, we also found that superior's support was of great importance to smooth implementation of local government innovation.[6] However, it is the formal communication and approval between local and upper-level governments in "seeking approval" that significantly distinguishes this type of innovation from spontaneous exploration and top-down experimentation.

After the 18th National Congress of CPC, "seeking approval" has been empirically demonstrated and has become a new innovating path clearly stated by several party committees and governments at the provincial level. By the end of September, 2017, Hunan, Shandong, Shanxi, and Zhejiang provinces and Inner Mongolia Autonomous Region have issued the methods or circulars (reporting methods hereinafter) to direct local governments reporting innovative programs to the comprehensively deepening reform-leading group (deepening reform group hereinafter) comprised of provincial leaders for deliberating, as shown in Table 6.2.

These reporting methods mainly target planning and coordinating local government innovation, regulating innovative behaviors of local governments, and improving reform programs' quality. Their reporting scopes are largely identical, which basically cover all possible local government innovations. In addition, in these reporting methods, miscellaneous provisions are provided to define absolute power of interpretation of the deepening reform group in reporting scope. For approved reform programs, all five reporting methods require formal document issuance for authorizing.

---

[6] When we conducted a survey in Zeguo Township, Wenling City, Zhejiang Province in August 2015, the president of People's Congress Presidium of Zeguo Township repeatedly mentioned a speech of the director of the People's Congress Standing Committee of Wenling City in a closing ceremony of municipal people's congress. In this speech, the director gave oral support for "Democratic Consultation" work of the People's Congress of Zeguo Township. The president believed that the director's approval was of great importance to the subsequent innovation practice.

Table 6.2 Comparison of "reporting methods" in Hunan, Shandong, Shanxi, and Zhejiang provinces and Inner Mongolia Autonomous Region

Province	Document name	Conference and time	Objective	Miscellaneous provisions within reporting scope	After approval by deepening reform group
Hunan	Circular on Further Defining and Regulating the Scope and Process about Requesting for Approval, Document Filing, and Important Matter Reporting of Reform	The Sixth Conference of Comprehensively Deepening Reform-Leading Group of Hunan Provincial Party Committee in November 2014	Enhance coordination and dispatch of reform matters across Hunan Province and ensure smooth and orderly advancing of various reforms.	Matters deemed to be submitted to the leading group conference for deliberation by the leading group and the Reform Office of CPC Hunan Provincial Committee.	Directly enter the document handling process for reporting, checking, and issuing reform programs according to procedures.
Shandong	Reporting Methods for Reform Plans to Be Submitted to the Comprehensively Deepening Reform-Leading Group of Shandong Provincial Party Committee for Deliberation	The 14th Conference of Comprehensively Deepening Reform-Leading Group of Shandong Provincial Party Committee in September 2015	Regulate reporting and approval of reform programs and comprehensively improve the quality of reform programs	Other reforms to be submitted to the Comprehensively Deepening Reform-Leading Group of CPC Shandong Provincial Committee for deliberation	Report, check, and issue reform programs according to procedures.
Shanxi	Reporting Methods for Major Reform Programs to Be Submitted to the Comprehensively Deepening Reform-Leading Group of CPC Shanxi Provincial Committee for Deliberation	The 19th Conference of Comprehensively Deepening Reform-Leading Group of CPC Shanxi Provincial Committee in February 2016	Enhance coordination and guidance of major reform tasks and initiatives across Shanxi province and make major reform programs more targeted and effective.	Other reform programs that need to be submitted for deliberation.	Report, check, and issue reform programs according to procedures and organize its implementation.

(continued)

Table 6.2 (continued)

Province	Document name	Conference and time	Objective	Miscellaneous provisions within reporting scope	After approval by deepening reform group
Zhejiang	Administrative Reporting Methods for Major Reform Programs to Be Submitted to the Comprehensively Deepening Reform-Leading Group of CPC Zhejiang Provincial Committee for Deliberation	The 11th Conference of Comprehensively Deepening Reform-Leading Group of CPC Zhejiang Provincial Committee in July 2016	Advance practice of reform initiatives and make reform decisions scientific and democratic.	Other major reform programs concerning the overall situation.	Enter the document handling process for reporting, checking, and issuing reform programs according to procedures.
Inner Mongolia	Reporting Methods for Reform Programs to Be Submitted to the Comprehensively Deepening Reform-Leading Group of Inner Mongolia Autonomous Region Party Committee for Deliberation	The 18th Conference of Comprehensively Deepening Reform-Leading Group of Inner Mongolia Autonomous Region Party Committee in January 2017	Advance reform programs being implemented strictly and optimize the reform decision-making process.	Other reform documents to be prepared for major reforms concerning the overall situation of social and economic development of Inner Mongolia Autonomous Region and public benefits	Submit the document to the preparation and issuance department for performing the document issuance procedures.

Source: Sorted based on "reporting methods" of Hunan, Shandong, Shanxi, and Zhejiang provinces and Inner Mongolia Autonomous Region

It is easy to get that when upper-level governments exhibit a clear attitude toward innovating approach, local governments would tend to select the form preferred and encouraged by upper-level governments, that is, "seeking approval" for carrying out innovation. This new form is very likely to become a new trend of local government innovation since the 18th National Congress of CPC. Though, as mentioned earlier, change of structure conditions doesn't necessarily bring about complete change in function. There is no conclusion that "seeking approval" will, in place of spontaneous exploration and top-down experimentation, become the only form in local government innovation in China. Yet, we can at least argue that after the 18th National Congress of CPC, there might emerge a new form of local government innovation in contemporary China called "seeking approval." It is an important supplement to, and integration of, spontaneous exploration and top-down experimentation.

5   Conclusion and Discussion

Local government innovation plays an essential part in Chinese government and politics. It substantiality improves local governance performance, brings knowledge and experience for system changes, and helps explore national policy at low cost. All of these practices represent innovation capacity and governance wisdom of local governments: The household-responsibility system at the beginning of the reform and opening up, the exploration for administrative service center in the middle of the 1990s, the supervision committee for village management, "Open Recommendation and Open Election," and "Open Recommendation and Direct Election" since the twenty-first century. For this reason, local government innovation is highly concerned by both academics and practitioners. Since the reform and opening up, two representative local government innovation mechanisms have come into being in China: spontaneous exploration and top-down experimentation. For general issues, upper-level governments seek a solution through top-down experimentation, where some local governments are selected for a pilot program. For specific problems or public demands in certain places, spontaneous exploration is widely used by local governments. Still, there exist some uncertainties. On the one hand, there is no clear boundary of authority between local and upper-level governments. This means that exiting systems fail to explicitly define the scope of local governments' autonomy and the degree and methods for which upper-level governments intervene in local affairs. On the other hand, upper-level governments overcome the lack of incentives and accountability of local governments caused by "centralized financial power and decentralized authorities of governance" by holding the power of appointment and removal of personnel at hand (Yu et al. 2016). For this reason, key variables that affect innovation tend to be personal characters of the reformer, such as preference, bargaining power, and risk aversion awareness. In a very long period of time, this uncertainty has been offset by informal interaction between local and upper-level governments (such as private contact between local reformers and upper-level leaders, bottom-up lobbying by local reformers, unofficial support and approval of upper-level leaders) to some extent.

Since the 18th National Congress, China has ushered in a new era of comprehensively deepening reform. The comprehensively deepening reform not only carries noteworthy features of centralization, as most of observers noted but also embodies significant characters of decentralization. As a result, the structural conditions and institutional foundations of local government innovation have been altered a lot. In terms of centralization reform, central government's highlight of "top-level design" has limited autonomy of local governments and then narrowed the scope of spontaneous exploration. In addition, with increasing emphasis on legitimacy in public administration, and long-lasting anticorruption campaign, local government behavior has been regulated and limited, decreasing the possibility for spontaneous exploration. In terms of decentralization reform, since the 18th National Congress of CPC, Chinese government has promoted a series of reforms for which the core is to "streamline administration and institute decentralization" (*jianzheng fangquan*) to "streamline administration, delegate more powers to the lower levels, enhance regulation, and improve services of government affairs." Many administrative powers are delegated and cut, thus imposing new requirements for the performance of the supervision function and service quality of local governments, which in turn forces local governments to respond with more innovations. Under these reforms, the unstable balancing status between spontaneous exploration and top-down experimentation has been gradually broken up. Local governance in China has a lack of policy supply to some extent because local governments cannot freely innovate by spontaneous exploration anymore. As a response, "seeking approval," a new form of local government innovation, comes into being in China, which has been empirically demonstrated in some provinces. Compared with spontaneous exploration and top-down experimentation, this new form of innovation has three possible advantages: First, "seeking approval" coordinates the relationship between systematization and the particularity of reform. This satisfies the needs of local governments to handle specific issues and combines some requirements of upper-level governments, thus cutting organizational costs and trial-and-error costs caused by repeat innovation or blind innovation due to information asymmetry. Second, "seeking approval" balances the tension between innovation and legality. Through "seeking approval," local governments can sufficiently obtain authorities for innovation, improve justification of innovative behavior, and remove possible system constraints and law risks (for instance, some contents of local government innovation are not within the jurisdiction of local government, or some contents lack a clear law basis) to the maximum, even when authoritative boundary is unclear. Finally, "seeking approval" improves feasibility and continuity of innovation. With official approval by upper-level governments, local governments can have greater authority to motivate much needed resources to ensure the smooth proceeding of innovative programs. Moreover, the formalization and officialization of these "seeking approval" programs can weaken the impact on innovation continuation from personal characters as well.

What's more, the popularity of "seeking approval" could probably reconstruct a new vertical intergovernmental relationship. Since the reform and opening up, the dialectics between centralization and decentralization has been haunted in China. The adjustment of vertical intergovernmental relationship has often come across a vicious circle earlier: "whenever the Central Government tightens its control, everything will stop working, but when the Central Government relaxes its control, everything will run into great disorder." As for local government innovation, it is also the case that the highlights of coordination and uniformity of reform may hinder initiatives of local governments, and national government running without the support of the local governance experience may get stuck; however, if greater autonomy is given to local governments, it may cause fragmentation of local policies and an increase in localism and departmental protectionism. Shambaugh (2016, pp. 11 and 136) called this spiral evolution an alternation of hard authoritarianism and soft authoritarianism. Undoubtedly, the boundary between centralization and decentralization cannot be obtained a priori. The significance of "seeking approval" for vertical intergovernmental relationships is through this type of local government innovation, upper-level governments and local governments can further define their scope of responsibilities in practice, reducing uncertainty of power boundary among different levels of governments and achieving positive interaction between "top-level design" and "local exploration." "Seeking approval" and the expansion of it may break through the nonbenign circulation of overall and alternating advancement and retreatment during centralization and decentralization reform, thus building a power distribution system based on the division of responsibilities. Of course, to achieve this objective, other reforms are urgently needed at the same time, especially reform of the financial system.

REFERENCES

Birney, M. 2014. Decentralization and veiled corruption under China's "Rule of Mandates." *World Development* 53: 55–67.

Chen, J. 2004. Local governments innovations and governance changing: A comparative case study of two Chinese local governments. *Journal of Public Management* (in Chinese) (4): 22–28.

Chen, X., and X. Yang. 2009. Promoting local government innovations: Local cadres' view. *Journal of Public Management* (in Chinese) (3): 1–11.

Cui, Z. 1994. Institutional innovation and the second thought liberation. *Twenty-First Century* (in Chinese) 24: 5–16.

De Ven, V. 1988. Central Problems in the Management of Innovation. In: Michael L. Tushman, and William L. Moore (eds.). *Readings in the Management of Innovation*. MA: Ballinger.

Deng, X. 1994. "The Reform of Party and State's Leadership System." In: Literature Editing Committee of Central Committee of the Communist Party of China (eds.) *The Selected Works of Deng Xiaoping* (Volume II) (in Chinese), Beijing: People's Publishing House.

Hartley, J. 2005. Innovation in governance and public services: Past and present. *Public Money & Management* 25(1): 27–34.

He, Z. 2003. Rural governance transition and institutional innovation: Investigation and reflection on "Yi Zhi San Hua" experience of Wu'an City in Hebei Province. *Comparative Economic & Social Systems* (in Chinese) (6): 74–82.

Heilmann, S. 2008a. From local experiments to national policy: The origins of China's distinctive policy process. *The China Journal* 59: 1–30.

Heilmann, S. 2008b, Policy experimentation in China's economic rise. *Studies in Comparative International Development* 43(1): 1–26.

Johnson, I. 2017. How the Communist Party Guided China to Success. The *New York Times*. Available at https://www.nytimes.com/2017/02/22/world/asia/china-politics-xi-jinping.html.

Lin, J.Y., F. Cai, and Z. Li. 1994. *The China Miracle: Development Strategy and Economic Reform* (in Chinese). Shanghai: Shanghai Sanlian Press.

Liu, W. 2015. Policy experiments: Start-up mechanisms and internal logic—Case studies on the performance management policies in China's public sectors. *Chinese Public Administration* (in Chinese) (5): 113–119.

Mei, C., X. Wang, L. Liao, et al. 2015. Patterns of "experimentation point": Evidence from *People's Daily*'s 1992–2003 Reports on policy experimentation point. *Journal of Public Administration* (in Chinese) (3): 8–24.

Osborne, S.P., and L. Brown. 2011. Innovation, public policy and public services delivery in the UK: The word that would be king? *Public Administration* 89(4): 1335–1350.

Ostrom, E. 1990. *Governing the Commons*. Cambridge: Cambridge University Press.

Qian, Y., and C. Xu. 1993. Why China's economic reforms differ: The M-form hierarchy and entry/expansion of the nonstate sector. *Comparative Economic & Social Systems* (in Chinese) (1): 29–40.

Shambaugh, D. 2016. *China's Future*. Polity Press.

Shin, S. 2013. China's failure of policy innovation: The case of sulphur dioxide emission trading. *Environmental Politics* 22(6): 918–934.

Walker, J.L. 1969. The diffusion of innovations among the American states. *American Political Science Review* 63(3): 880–899.

Wang, Q., and G. Guo. 2015. Yu Keping and Chinese intellectual discourse on good governance. *The China Quarterly* 224: 985–1005.

Wu, J., L. Ma, T. Su, et al. 2011. Typology and characteristics of government innovations: A multi-case study of winning programs of the "Innovations and Excellence in Chinese Local Governance." *Journal of Public Management* (in Chinese) (1): 94–103.

Wu, J., L. Ma, and Y. Yang. 2007. The local governments' impetus for innovations, their characteristics and the related performance: An analysis of the test of cases adopted from "The Awards for Innovation to China's Local Governments." *Management World* (in Chinese) (8): 43–51.

Wu, J., L. Ma, and Y. Yang. 2013. Innovation in the Chinese public sector: Typology and distribution. *Public Administration* 91(2): 347–365.

Yang X. 2011. China local government reform in the past decade: An evaluation based on Chinese local governance innovations awards. *Journal of Public Administration* (in Chinese) (1): 81–93.

Yang, X. 2015. Why local governments are lack of innovation impetus. *Decision-making* (in Chinese) (11): 12.

Yang X., and X. Chen. 2010. Social conditions and developing status of Chinese government innovations: The vision of local cadres. *Journal of Social Sciences* (in Chinese) (2): 12–23.

Yu, J., and B. Huang. 2015. The applicability of the diffusion of local government innovation. *Comparative Economic & Social Systems* (in Chinese) (1): 171–181.

Yu, J., E. Cai, and X. Gao. 2016. Functions and limits of selection and appointment mechanism of cadres among vertical intergovernmental relationship—Based on questionnaire of party and government leaders of cities and counties in Zhejiang Province. *Journal of Zhejiang Party School of C. P. C.* (in Chinese) (1): 12–21.

Yu, J., and S. Guan. 2013. The function of social governance in local governments: Measurement and institutionalization. *Academic Monthly* (in Chinese) (6): 17–26.

Yu, J., and S. Qin. 2015. Institutionalization: Connotation, mold, formation mechanism and evaluation. *Academic Monthly* (in Chinese) (3): 109–117.

Yu, K. 2003. Reforms and innovations in Chinese local governments, *Comparative Economic & Social Systems* (in Chinese) (4): 31–34.

Yu, K. 2012. Government innovations in China and the United States—A comparative survey based on Chinese and American government innovation awards programs. *Academic Monthly* (in Chinese) (3): 5–15.

Yu, K. 2015a. Lack of innovation impetus among grassroots governments. *Honesty Outlook* (in Chinese) (5): 12.

Yu, K. 2015b. *Insufficient Innovation Impetus among Grassroots Governments.* http://www.chinareform.org.cn/people/Y/yukeping/Article/201504/t20150417_223255.htm.

Zeng, J. 2015. Did policy experimentation in China always seek efficiency? A case study of Wenzhou financial reform in 2012. *Journal of Contemporary China* 24(92): 338–356.

Zhang, W. 2015. Scholar Suggests Central Government's Sustainable Encourage of Local Innovation and Permit Local Government's Making Mistakes. *The Paper* (in Chinese): Dec 12th. Available at http://www.thepaper.cn/newsDetail_forward_1408150.

Zheng, Y. 2014. The Political Risk if China Does not Reform. *Lianhe Zaobao* (in Chinese): July 1st. Available at http://www.zaobao.com/forum/views/opinion/story20140701-360971.

Zheng, Y. 2015. How to Advance Reform under New Normal. *Lianhe Zaobao* (in Chinese): May 12th. Available at http://www.zaobao.com/forum/expert/zheng-yong-nian/story20150512-479161.

Zhou, H. 2003. Let rural Democracy work—Evidence from "two-vote system" Guangshui City, Hubei Province. *Marxism & Reality* (in Chinese) (4): 94–103.

Zhou, Q. 1994. Reform in China's countryside: Changes to the relationship between the state and ownership. *Chinese Social Sciences Quarterly* (in Chinese) 8: 61–84.

Zhu, Y., and D. Xiao. 2015. Policy entrepreneur and social policy innovation. *The Journal of Chinese Sociology* 2(1): 1–17.

CHAPTER 7

Central-Local Relations in China

Xufeng Zhu

1   Introduction

As China is a great power with a large population, area, and gaps in regional development, how to deal with the relationship between the central and local governments has bothered rulers for a long time and attracted the attention of scholars in the field of political science and public management. In general, the central and local relations refer to the basic ones of power and allocation of resources vertically in the state system (Jing et al. 2016: 185). China's *Constitution* describes the division of authority between the central and local state organs as follows: "to follow the principle of sticking to the leadership of the central government and giving full play to the initiative and enthusiasm of local governments". China is characterized by centralization, but from the practical point of view, China's central and local relations appear more complex.

Since the reform and opening up, the central and local relations with the Chinese characteristics are generally regarded by scholars as the key elements to explain China's economic miracle. The current academia has not reached a consensus, however, on how to interpret China's central and local relations. From the legal point of view, the local governments, under the leadership of the central government, are highly centralized, which endow China with a typical unitary system. In practice, however, scholars have found that China's central and local relations differ from that in the unitary system, mainly

X. Zhu (✉)
School of Public Policy and Management (SPPM), Tsinghua University,
Beijing, China
e-mail: zhuxufeng@tsinghua.edu.cn

© The Author(s) 2019
J. Yu, S. Guo (eds.), *The Palgrave Handbook of Local Governance in Contemporary China*, https://doi.org/10.1007/978-981-13-2799-5_7

reflected in the decentralization of the central decision-making power. As long as the political stability and economic growth are maintained, local governments will be able to make policies in accordance with their own conditions and preferences as acquiesced by the central government (Lieberthal 2004; Chung 2016). Thus, some scholars believe that China's central and local relations have certain de facto federalism, and even at the practical level, local governments in China have much greater power than those in federal countries (Zheng 2007: 4).

Academics have three views on how to explain China's central and local relations. First, Qian Yingyi and others have proposed the fiscal federalism with Chinese characteristics. They believe that the decentralization reform with Chinese characteristics has led to a "market-preserving federalism" (Qian and Weingast 2011). The core of how the Chinese government achieves success can be known from the effective financial arrangement between the central and local governments (Jin et al. 2005). The second view comes mainly from the highly centralized authoritarianism in China and explains how China, through the establishment of regional competition mechanism, solves the incentive problems of local governments. The typical points of view include the pressurized system (Rong et al. 1997), promotion tournament (Li and Zhou 2005), centralized authoritarian system (Cai and Treisman 2006), regional decentralized authoritarianism (Xu 2011), and so on. The "experimentation under hierarchy" that stresses on "crossing the river by feeling the stones" is the third. The central government has helped local governments accumulate experience in various ways, such as pilot projects and experiment zones, so as to cope with changes and uncertainty in reform and successfully avoid the large-scale turbulence (Heilmann 2008). These discussions provide good perspectives for us to understand how China's central and local relations have contributed to its economic and social development.

In this chapter, the author first reviews the changes in China's central and local relations since 1949, divides them into three stages of development, and describes the basic characteristics of each stage. Then, in the third part, the author illustrates the allocation of rights and resources between China's central and local governments and their development trends from four dimensions: legislative power, power of office, power over financial resources, and power over personnel. The changes in China's central-local relations since the founding of the People's Republic of China (PRC) have been summarized as a "dynamic and flexible system of alternated centralization and decentralization". During the over 20 years from the late twentieth century, the contemporary Chinese central and local relations have been adjusted and have displayed the following two distinct characteristics: (1) selective centralization (or decentralization) with heterogeneity in different policy areas and (2) differentiated centralization (or decentralization) in different policy tools.

2   HISTORICAL DEVELOPMENT OF CENTRAL-LOCAL RELATIONS

Scholars tend to generally divide the changes in China's central and local relations after the establishment of new China into three stages with distinctive characteristics (Li and Liu 2013). The first stage lasts from the founding of the PRC to reform and opening up. During this period, China's central and local relations in this stage saw several major adjustments, showing great fluctuation. The other two stages are separated by the establishment of the socialist market economic system in 1992. The previous stage is characterized by the central government delegating powers to local levels, and the latter by the concurrence of delegating and taking back powers.

2.1   Two Centralization-Decentralization Cycles During the Planned Economy (1949–1978)

After the founding of the PRC, with the socialist transformation and the establishment of the Soviet-style highly centralized economic system, China's central and local relations saw a high degree of centralization (Song 2013). The drawbacks of this system, however, soon emerged. The leaders of the new China made theoretical and practical attempts at building proper central and local relations. Mao Zedong pointed in his important speech *On the Ten Major Relations* in 1956 that "it is now important to note that we should consolidate the central leadership, expand the local power and endow the local areas with higher degree of independence to facilitate their work … unlike the Soviet Union, we should not centralize in any way or hold all powers from local areas" (Mao 1999: 31). Afterwards and before the reform and opening up, China's central and local relations witnessed two cycles of centralization and decentralization.

From 1956 to 1966 for the first time, and after the socialist transformation, the structure of the power distribution between the central and the local shifted from large-scale decentralization to "Party's leadership". From 1956 onwards, decentralization began to sweep across China—the administrative power, economic management power, financial power, and the management power of a large number of enterprises and institutions were decentralized to the local governments, which greatly drove their enthusiasm and initiative but also had the characteristics of the "Great Leap Forward". Consequently, the decentralization reform led to blind production and redundant construction, causing not only serious waste of resources but also great damage to the central command.

In February 1959, *People's Daily* published an editorial entitled "The Whole Country is a Single Entity", emphasizing "the need to strengthen the centralized leadership and unified arrangements", which marked the end of the large-scale decentralization. In 1961, the central government issued *Several Interim Provisions on the Adjustment of the Management System* to re-emphasize the leadership of the central government over the economic management in all areas. Thus, the central government reestablished six central offices directly under the Central Committee of the Communist Party of China (CPC). The management powers were centralized and held by the central government and offices. At the same time, some powers over financial affairs such as those over allocation of materials and commodity price control were taken back by the central government. The establishment of the central offices subjected all the political power to the Party and the leadership of the Party Central Committee. The Party committees at all levels held the leadership over the governments, organizations, and units at all levels. It is important to note that after this cycle, the powers decentralized in the early 1950s were returned to the Party system instead of the central government and its affiliated departments. Therefore, the decentralization was featured by the shift to "Party's leadership".

The second cycle lasts from 1966 to 1978, in which the structure of the power distribution between the central and local governments shifted from the disordered decentralization during the Cultural Revolution to the subsequent centralization. With the outbreak of the Cultural Revolution in 1966, China once again saw large-scale decentralization since the Great Leap Forward. The central government decided to decentralize the powers of a large number of enterprises directly under it to the local governments. It also expanded the powers of local governments over financial affairs, planning management, material distribution, price management, and personnel appointment and removal.

During this period, the allocation of power for the Chinese central government was as chaotic as its political environment then. The aimless decentralization of power led to serious regional and sectoral division. Until the shattering of the gang of four in 2004, in order to restore the production affected by the political movement and especially to establish an independent and complete defense industry system, the central government launched large-scale centralization of power by taking back certain powers over economic management and many key enterprises under the slogan "down the direct and exclusive control of enterprises".

However, after Deng Xiaoping hosted the Central Working Conference, a series of political and economic reforms centered on strengthening the central power were carried out. The central government once again began to collect power. In the late 1970s, the central government further strengthened the management over railway, civil aviation, post, telecommunications, and other important public service sectors such as railway, civil aviation, post, telecommunications and so on, and retook the control of some key enterprises.

In general, from the founding of the PRC to the reform and opening up, China's central-local relations as a whole showed high degree of centralization but also experienced several major adjustments. Some scholars regard the Chinese government as falling into a cycle of "failure upon centralization, decentralization upon failure, chaos upon decentralization, and centralization again upon chaos".

2.2   Decentralization of Power and Transfer of Profits in Initial Stages for Reform and Opening up (1978–1992)

During the over ten years since the reform and opening up in 1978 to 1992 when the goal of establishing a market-oriented economic system was set up, China's central-local relations revolved around high centralization to local decentralization. During this period, the main principle of the adjustment was to grant decision-making power to enterprises and allow them to keep more profits, that is, more power over financial affairs and economic management.

In 1979, the State Council promulgated *Several Provisions on Trial Financial Management of "Linking Income and Expenses, Total Profit Sharing, Proportion on a Contract Basis and Staying Unchanged for Three Years.* The central government started to launch the new fiscal system with "division of revenue and expenditure between the central and local governments and with contracts at different levels" in 1980 and established the four-level system in 1984—central government, province (municipality, autonomous region), city (county), and district (township, town) to further figure out the power and responsibility at all levels. A few years later, decentralization of power over financial affairs, mainly in the form of financial contracting system allowed the beginning of the "decentralization of power and transfer of profits". The financial contracting system divided revenue and expenditure between the central and local governments. The central government implemented various forms of contracting for different regions with different financial and economic developments, such as "turning over fixed income", "turning over income on an ascending contract basis", and "sharing in the total revenue plus sharing in the profits". It aimed to adopt different policies according to the financial conditions in different regions, in order to expand the local financial autonomy and mobilize the enthusiasm of local governments in developing their economy.

The central government expanded the local powers over financial affairs and economic management. The additional power of office includes that of examination and approval of fixed assets investment projects and economic construction plans, foreign investment, foreign exchange management, price control, material allocation, that of external liaison for tourism and visa notification, and so on. In addition, the central government reformed the investment management system and decentralized part of the authority of examination and approval of fixed asset investment projects to the local governments. The state also allowed enterprises and farmers to conduct most of the major economic activities, narrowed down the scope of the national mandatory plan, and improved the function of the market for economic adjustment. In terms of Party-government relations, the power structure with "undivided Party and government" had been adjusted and the division of labor between the Party and the government carried out since the Third Plenary Session of the 11th Central Committee. The division of labor expanded the scope of authority of governments at all levels and enhanced the administrative autonomy of local governments.

This decentralization reform stimulated the enthusiasm of local governments in economic development but led to many drawbacks. On the one hand, the interregional tournament in economic growth resulted in vicious competition and local protectionism; on the other hand, with the declining proportion of the state revenue and expenditure in gross domestic product (GDP), the central government was seriously weakened in carrying out macro-control and balancing the regional capacities (Hu et al. 2014: 179). In the late 1980s, the separate powers of local governments aroused great attention from the Party Central Committee. In a speech on September 12, 1988, Deng Xiaoping stressed that "the central government should boast the authority, and the macro management in charge of the central government" (Deng 1993: 277). It laid a foundation for the adjustment of China's central-local relations later.

2.3   Trend Since Market-Oriented Reform: Concurrence of Centralization and Decentralization (1992–Present)

Following the South Tour Speech by Deng Xiaoping in 1992, the Party Central Committee had identified the development of market-oriented economy and the establishment of a socialist market economic system as the main objectives of China's economic reform. Since then, as the market-oriented reform continued to advance, China's central-local relations ushered in a new period of adjustment.

Although the adjustment of central-local relations during this period was still limited by the cycle, the power distribution between the central and the local displayed more complex and dynamic characteristics. It can be observed that the central government of China adjusted the central-local relations with different focuses, in different phases, and in a differentiated and orderly way. The features are particularly evident in the 1990s in the following four areas:

First of all, the central and local administrative authority over economic management was planned for the future and the local management of the real economy further strengthened. The 14th National Congress of the CPC in 1992 put forward the principle of "figuring out the distribution between the central and local, and gradually implementing the separated system with taxes and profits and the tax sharing system". At the same time, the central government proposed ideas on reforms aimed at further sorting out the central and local economic management powers and pushing them forward in practice. In November 1993, the Third Plenary Session of the 14th CPC Central Committee proposed to establish a modern enterprise system of "clear property rights, clear rights and responsibilities, separation of government and enterprises, and management science" in order to deepen the reform of enterprises, especially that of state-owned enterprises, and separate government from enterprises. During the economic reform, many enterprises had been in charge by local governments because the central authorities no longer directly managed most state-owned enterprises but formed relations with them through financial channels. With the decentralization of power to local governments and enterprises, the local government's power in management of the real economy was greatly enhanced.

Second, the reform of the tax-sharing system was launched and the power of the central government over financial affairs enhanced. In order to enhance the ability of the central government in financing and redistribution, the central government decided to formally implement the reform of the tax-sharing system between the central and local levels nationwide since 1994. The main measures include: (1) dividing the tax into the central tax, local tax, and shared tax according to the principle of combining the power of office and power over financial affairs; (2) reasonably dividing the respective scope of expenditure for the central and local governments and the revenue mainly for the expense on national security and foreign affairs, macroeconomic regulatory, and national regulatory according to the relevant provisions of the tax-sharing system; (3) establishing the central and local taxation systems, with the central and local tax agencies collecting the central tax and local tax, respectively; and (4) developing a standardized tax return and transfer payment system.

Third, the investment system was reformed and the scope of the investments by local governments expanded. The reform of the investment system in 1994 clarified the investment scope and investment responsibility of the central and local governments. Based on the investment in regional basic projects and public welfare projects, local governments enjoyed wider authority to invest in cross-regional basic projects. The expansion changed the situation of excessive central investments in the past.

Finally, the financial system was reformed and the centralization of financial control strengthened. Because of the financial system reform in 1998, the provincial branches were revoked and cross-provincial ones set up in nine central cities. Each branch was, within the scope authorized by the central bank, specifically responsible for the central monetary policy, while monitoring the management of financial businesses in the relevant areas. In the cities with no branch where provincial governments were located, the central government would set up financial supervision offices to implement the financial supervision function of the central bank. The reform of the financial system enhanced the effectiveness of macroeconomic regulation and control of the central government, reduced the local government's intervention in local financial institutions, strengthened the independence of financial institutions, and also highlighted the centralized financial control by the central government.

It can be seen from these four aspects that during this period China's central-local relations can **no longer be summarized simply as decentralization or centralization**. The central government put forward different policies based on specific objectives. Thus, **after the implementation of market-oriented reform, China's central-local relations have shown both decentralization and centralization simultaneously**.

3   FOUR DIMENSIONS IN THE CENTRAL-LOCAL RELATIONS

This part further states the allocation of power and resources between China's central and local governments from four dimensions: legislative power, power over financial affairs, power of office, and power over personnel, respectively.

3.1   Legislative Power

In China, the division of legislative authority between central and local governments did not appear until the late 1970s. This is because, from the founding of the PRC in 1949 to 1978, **China had been implementing a centralized model of legislation**. The *Constitution* of 1954 established the primary legislative system of China, that is, the National People's Congress (NPC) is the only organ to exercise the national legislative power. Therefore, during this period, except for ethnic autonomous areas, the local state organs in China had no legislative power, and all legislative powers were exercised by the central state organ (NPC).

On July 1, 1979, the *Organic Law on Local People's Congresses at All Levels and Local People's Governments at All Levels* was promulgated and China's mode of lawmaking changed to a two-level legislative system (the central and local legislative power). The *Local Organization Law* in 1979 stipulates that "the people's congresses of provinces, autonomous regions and municipalities directly under the central government and their standing committees can formulate and promulgate local laws with no contradiction against the national constitution, laws, policies, decrees and orders", which **endowed the local authorities at the provincial level with legislative power**. Then, it was once again confirmed in the *Constitution* of 1982 and China's secondary legislative system formally formed.

Subsequently, the Standing Committee of the NPC twice amended the *Local Organization Law* in 1982 and 1986 and **endowed the cities where the provincial people's governments are located and large cities approved by the State Council with the power to develop local laws or regulations**. In addition, the NPC and its Standing Committee **invested the people's congresses and their standing committees and governments in Shenzhen, Zhuhai, Shantou, Xiamen, and other special economic zones in 1992, 1994, and 1996 with the power to develop authorized rules and regulations**.

In 2000, in order to standardize legislation and improve the national legislative system, China formulated and promulgated the *Legislation Law of the People's Republic of China* and defined the division of legislative power between the central and local authorities in many respects. First of all, the exclusive legislative matters of the NPC and its Standing Committee were identified; second, the "no conflict" principle was clarified for local people's congresses and their standing committees when developing local laws and regulations; and finally, the scope of legislative authority of the local government was defined, including the enforceable and creative local government's regulations.

In 2015, China again revised the *Legislation Law*, which adjusted the division of legislative power between the central and local authorities in the following two aspects: (1) the entity with the power to develop local government regulations changed from "large cities" to "cities with districts" and (2) the authorities figured out that the cities with districts can make local regulations on "urban and rural construction and management, environmental protection, and historical and cultural protection".

Therefore, concerning the division of legislative authority, China ended the centralized legislative model in 1979. Since then, the power was gradually decentralized from the provincial-level state power organs to the cities where the provincial people's governments are located and the large city approved by the State Council, and then to the cities with districts. It can be seen that the legislative power is held by more authorities at lower levels in China, and the legislative authority of the central government and local governments becomes increasingly clear and institutionalized.

3.2 Power Over Financial Affairs

3.2.1 High Centralization Before Reform and Opening up

China established a highly centralized financial management system after its founding, and the "unified collection and allocation of funds by the state" were implemented, which means that local finance is only an extension of the central finance, and the vast majority of local revenue should be turned over to the central government. The local financial expenditure should also be approved by the central government within the scope of the national plan and earmarked after the central government checked and ratified the indicators.

3.2.2 1980–1993: The System of Dividing Revenue and Expenditure Between the Central and Local Governments

This highly centralized fiscal model was not broken until the 1980s. In 1979, the State Council promulgated *Several Provisions on Trial Financial Management of "Linking Income and Expenses, Total Profit Sharing, Proportion on a Contract Basis and Staying Unchanged for Three Years"*. The central government started to launch the new fiscal system with "division of revenue and expenditure between the central and local governments and with contracts at different levels" in 1980. This system meant that the scope of the central and local fiscal revenue and expenditure was to be clearly divided and the contracting base for local finance identified in accordance with certain ways. In localities where the income was greater than the expenditure, certain proportion of the excess part would be turned over. In localities where the expenditure was greater than the income, the central government would issue the income for adjustment with the industrial and commercial tax or additional subsidies. It meant that the remaining part of the local revenue after handing over certain part to the central government based on respective base was disposable. The financial autonomy had greatly encouraged the local government to increase the fiscal revenue by developing the economy. In addition, the central government implemented various forms of contracting for different regions with different financial and economic development, such as "turning over fixed income", "turning over income on an ascending contract basis", and "sharing in the total revenue plus sharing in the profits". It aimed to adopt different policies according to the financial conditions in different regions, in order to expand the local financial autonomy and mobilize the enthusiasm of local governments in developing their economy.

Nevertheless, the shortcomings of the financial management system were exposed soon. Local governments, especially the wealthy ones that were required to provide financial revenue to the central government, chose to reduce tax in order to minimize the amount handed over and maximize the local revenue, which greatly reduced the central fiscal revenue, even reaching a crisis level (Zhang 2017). From 1979 to 1993, the proportion of the central fiscal revenue in the total fell from 46.8% to 31.6%. The central financial power was substantially weakened, for which it had to rely on local financial revenue to maintain the balance of payments, and even twice set up foundations to "borrow money" from the local governments (Zhou 2006). The tax-sharing system reform in 1994 was the response of the central government to the crisis with institutional changes.

3.2.3   Since the Tax Sharing System Reform: Gradually Centralized with Weakened Local Financial Power

In December 1993, the State Council formally decided to implement the tax-sharing system since 1994. The system is still in effect today and is regarded as the most important part of China's central-local relations adjustment.

The most important part of the tax-sharing system is that the central and local revenue are divided according to different types of tax—central tax, local tax, and central-local shared tax. Tax revenue is stable. The larger share of the consumption tax is handed over to the central; the local business, corporate, and personal income taxes to the local; and the value-added tax (VAT) closely related to economic development is seen as the central-local shared tax. The tax-sharing system is divided into two subsystems—the central and local tax bureaus. The former is responsible for the collection of central taxes and central-local shared taxes and the latter only for the collection of local taxes. The central-local shared taxes are issued to the local by the central in the form of tax returns or transfer payment. Therefore, after the implementation of the tax-sharing system, the local financial resources are made up of two parts including the local taxes and the shared taxed allocated by the central. When the system was launched, the proportion of the central fiscal revenue in the total was set to increase to 55%, which greatly enhanced the central government's macro-control capacity.

During the over two decades since the tax distribution system was introduced in 1994, China's central government has repeatedly adjusted the type of taxes or proportions to ensure its financial centralization and sufficient financial resources as the basis for the transfer payments. Also due to these institutional arrangements, since 1994, the proportion of the central fiscal revenue in the gross public revenue has always been maintained at around 50%.

In 2002, China began to launch new reforms for sharing income tax, for which the corporate and personal income taxes included in the local taxes were counted as shared taxes. Since 2002, the taxes were equally divided between the central and the local. Since 2003, the proportion was changed to 60% and 40%, respectively. Since the business taxes in some pilot sectors in Shanghai were changed to VAT in 2012, more fields ushered in the pilot projects. The central government decided to launch more pilot projects across China since May 1, 2016. In order to basically maintain the original financial structure between the central and local governments, the VATs were divided in a ratio of 50:50 instead of 75:25. **Although the change from business tax to VAT had not influenced the financial structure between the central and local governments, the tax revenue source for local governments is undoubtedly greatly affected, and its share of local revenue will be significantly reduced**.

3.3   Power of Office

The power of office refers to the administrative and public service functions that the government undertakes, and the distribution of such power refers to the extent to which the central and local governments share the functions of administration and public services, which is manifested in proportion of fiscal expenditure in the two areas. Under the long-term framework of "corresponding duties and responsibilities for upper and lower levels" in China, there is no division of power of office between the central and the local except for several areas such as foreign affairs and national defense (Zhu and Zhang 2005). In terms of the adjustment of the allocation of power between the central and local governments, the tax-sharing system can still be divided into two stages. Before the reform for the tax-sharing system in 1994, the central and local governments mainly resorted to the distribution of economic management authority, that was, the redistribution of the economic management authority by adjusting the relationship of administrative subordination for various types of enterprises and public institutions. After the reform, the adjustment of power of office was obviously featured by "economic decentralization", mainly reflected in the central and local responsibilities for fiscal expenditure through the reform of fiscal and tax system (Jing et al. 2016: 196–197). In *Guidance on the Promotion of Central and Local Power of office and Reform for Division of Expenditure Responsibilities* (GF [2016] No. 49), the power of office measuring the responsibilities for fiscal expenditure is called "financial power of office", used to indicate the duties and responsibilities of the primary government for providing basic public services with the financial resources.

The *State Council's* 1993 *Decision on the Implementation of the Financial Management System of the Tax Sharing System* (GF [1993] No. 85) stipulates that "the central government shall bear the expenditure for the national security, diplomatic affairs and the operation of central state organs, the expense on national economic structure and coordination of regional development, the necessary expenditure for the implementation of macro-control and that directly under the central government for the development of undertakings," and "local finance is mainly responsible for the expenditure for the operation of local authorities and the development of regional economy and business". This general division essentially reflected the separate implementation of the power of office by central and local governments. Therefore, unlike the allocation of financial power between the central and local governments with significant impact, the tax-sharing system followed convention rather than innovation in allocating the power of office (Zhang 2017).

However, with the centralization of the financial power after the reform of the tax-sharing system, the demerits of the blurred division were gradually exposed, shown in the discordance between the financial power and the power of office. After the tax-sharing reform, although the proportion of central fiscal revenue had increased to about 50%, the expenditure from the central government did not increase. On the contrary, the new responsibilities of the government for expenditure, especially the social welfare-related expenditure, were almost entirely borne by local governments. As a result, the proportion of the local fiscal expenditure in the total public expenditure increased from 70% in the mid-1990s to 85% in the mid-2010s (Fan 2015).

Thus, local governments had to bear an increasing burden of financial expenditure, which could only be achieved through the transfer payments by the central government. Transfer payments had also become the basic means for the central government to digest their huge fiscal revenue surplus and for the local governments to fill their huge fiscal deficits. It also meant that it, originally a mechanism for "omission check and leakage remedying", had played a key role in allocating the financial resources between the central and local governments. The non-standardized regulations of the Chinese government on payment transfer and especially the special payment transfer made it difficult to play a proper role. The huge regional differences greatly aggravated the conflict between the local government's power of office and financial power.

In response to this problem, China explicitly proposed in 2006 in the 11th Five-year Plan to establish and improve a fiscal tax system that matches the power of office. The report of the 17th National Congress of the CPC also proposed to improve the system for matching powers of financial and office between the central and local governments. The *Decision of the CPC Central Committee on Several Important Issues concerning the Overall Deepening of the Reform* passed at the Third Plenary Session of the 18th CPC Central Committee clearly states: "National defense, diplomacy, national security and relations with the unified national market rules and management fall under the category of the central power of office; some issues related to social security and cross-regional major project construction and maintenance the common power of office for central and local governments". The framework indicates that the central authority should assume more responsibilities for expenditure in some areas such as social security and the construction and maintenance of major projects across regions. Under the current fiscal system, the central government can only take the form of payment transfer. The reform removes the situation of "only centralizing financial power" by the central government since the launch of the tax-sharing system in 1994. Instead "centralizing financial power" is accompanied by centralizing power of office. The central government's responsibility for expenditure will also effectively alleviate the contradiction between local government's power of office and financial power.

Moreover, the centralization since the 18th National Congress of the CPC is shown in the strengthening of the leadership over the local discipline inspection commission. The commission has become semi-vertically managed instead of the complete territorial administration. The newly established National Security Council has integrated the forces to maintain the social stability; the newly established Leading Group for Comprehensive Reform Deepening strengthened the leadership over the reform. As a result, the central government has been responsible for the overall design of the reform, coordination, overall advancement, supervision, and implementation.

It should be noted that China's central government, with the collection and strengthening of certain power, has also delegated power. For example, the *Decision* clearly pointed towards "minimizing the administration of microeconomic affairs by the central government" by reducing the administrative licensing of various projects—in particular, reducing the management of prices and expanding the provincial government's educational coordination and autonomy of school running (Nie 2014).

3.4   Power over Personnel

The core of the power over personnel lies in the appointment and removal of cadres. China's cadre and personnel system was established following the fundamental principles of managing the cadres (placing cadres under Party supervision) by the CPC. "Placing cadres under Party supervision" is the core content of China's cadre and personnel system, referring to the leading position of the Party and the Party's organization system in the appointment and management of officials (Zhu 2008: 127). According to the *Regulations of the Communist Party of China on the Selection and Appointment of Party and Government Leading Cadres* (revised in 2014), the system is applicable to the cadres in the Party committees, the people's congresses, the governments, the Chinese People's Political Consultative Conference (CPPCC), the discipline inspection commissions, the people's courts, and the people's procuratorate above the county level. In other words, the Party and government leading cadres in China are appointed after being proposed, recommended, inspected, discussed, and determined by the Party committees at all levels in accordance with the management authority of cadres and nominated or recommended to the people's congress, the NPC Standing Committee, and the government.

Thanks to the system of "placing cadres under Party supervision", the central government holds the right and power to appoint officials, which is different from the distribution of the power of office and financial power. Even so, the cadre and personnel system has changed, slightly though, concerning the allocation between the central and local governments in the following three aspects.

First, the local power over personnel has expanded to some extent. For a long period of time after the founding of the PRC, China implemented the cadre and personnel system with "two or even three levels of subordinates", and the power over personnel shows a high degree of centralization. It lasted until the 1980s. With the decentralization of the central economic management authority, the cadre and personnel management authority was adjusted as corresponding to the development needs. In October 1983, the Central Organization Department issued the *Provisions of the CPC Central Committee Organization Department on Reforming the Administrative System of the Cadres*, and put forward the spirit of "less management, vital management and effective management", so as to limit the central management cadres to the Party and government cadres at the provincial level. Then in 1984, the Central Organization Department further issued the *CPC Central Committee Organization Department on the Revision of the List of Titles of Cadres under the Central Management*, for which the system of "one level of subordinates and one level for the record" was officially formed. The reform effectively expanded the management authority of the lower Party committee cadres and achieved the vertical decentralization of power over personnel to some extent.

Second, the exchange of cadres between the central and local governments is becoming more frequent. The reform has expanded the local cadre's management authority and enhanced the local authority on the appointment and removal of cadres but along with the emergence of localism. In order to curb this tendency, the central government has established a cadre exchange system since 1999. Cadre exchange refers to the adjustment of the posts for Party and government leading cadres by the Party committees at all levels and their organizational departments in accordance with the cadre management authority through transfer. In 2006, the *Regulations on Exchanges of Party and Government Leading Cadres* stipulated the inclusion of the leaders of central and local Party organizations, government agencies, people's congresses and CPPCC, persons in charge of the functional departments, and the leaderships of commissions for discipline inspection, courts, and procuratorate into the scope of exchanges. From June to December 2010, the Central Organization Department, in accordance with the central requirements, sent 66 young and middle-aged cadres from the central and state organs to provinces, cities, and autonomous regions, and vice versa (China Political Affairs Monitoring Center 2011).

Third, the criteria for the selection of cadres were adjusted. For a long time, the academic circles have focused on the criteria of the government for cadre's selection (or official's promotion mechanism) about how the central government of China achieves the success of governance through the appointment and removal of cadres. There are two popular views—the economic performance-based promotion championship (Li and Zhou 2005) and political selection based on relational networks (Choi 2012; Shih et al. 2012). With China's economic and social changes, the criteria for cadre election by which the central government takes charge of local ones have changed. The economic indicators in the central government's assessment of the local government have been weakened. Instead, the comprehensive performance-based criteria have been brought forward including the economy, society, and environmental protection (Fang and Zhang 2009). In addition, some scholars suggested that due to shrinking profits for local governments from the economic growth and in order to obtain a relative competitive advantage, Chinese local governments have competed for "social innovation" (He and Li 2017). The adjustment of these standards naturally caused changes in competition among local governments.

In general, since the founding of the PRC, the central government has always held the power over personnel, which is the most centralized area in the central-local relations. Although we can observe that the central authorities have relaxed some control over the personnel management, the center still tries to avoid the local protectionism through the system of cadre rotations and exchanges and ensure their absolute leading position in the power structure. At the same time, the central government has given full play to its leading role by adjusting the criteria for cadre selection and achieved the central leadership over the local governments.

4   CONCLUSION

Through the review of the three stages of the changes in central and local relations in China, we may conclude that the power distribution between the central and local authorities has four dimensions—legislative power, power over financial affairs, power of office, and power over personnel. It can be seen that the development and adjustment of the central and local relations since the founding of the PRC are featured by complexity and flexibility.

It is complicated because China's central and local relations cannot be simply summarized as a centralized or decentralized (or unitary or federal) system. It saw the alternation of "centralization and decentralization" during different stages according to the needs for economic and social development, and also a combination of both from different dimensions so as to realize multidimensional allocation of power and resources.

It is flexible because the highly authoritative central government can adjust the central and local allocation of power and resources in almost all areas according to the needs for economic and social development at any time. When there is the need to strengthen macro-control and break the local protectionism, the central authorities will centralize the power. When there is the need to mobilize the local enthusiasm and bring the advantages of local information into full play, the decentralization is conducted.

In the author's view, the "complexity and flexibility" of the central-local relations in China can be understood as the efforts of the Chinese leaders to "give full play to both the central and local initiative" and balance the central and local allocation of power and resources. Every time the dynamic adjustment can be regarded as the correction after wrong attempts, until a new and satisfactory balance is struck.

During the gradual adjustment, we can see that after the reform for the tax-sharing system in 1994, China's central-local relations as a whole have become more stable and more modest in adjustment. The rulers rarely conducted large-scale decentralization or centralized reform as before but mainly resorted to fine-tuning. In addition, the author believes that contemporary central-local relations in China showed the following two distinctive features during the adjustment and changes:

(1) **Selective (de-)centralization with heterogeneity in different policy areas**. Over the past two decades, China's adjustments of central-local relations through centralization or decentralization were not uncommon. On the one hand, the centralized departments with vertical management experienced two obvious climaxes, respectively, from 1997 to 1998 and from 2005 to 2006 since the reform for the tax-sharing system. They involved the ministries in finance, safe production, statistics, territorial resources, and environmental protection. On the other hand, the reform and decentralization for the administrative licensing authority have become the main tasks of the Chinese government in the twenty-first century. As of October 2014, the State Council abolished 2277 items for the administrative licensing by various departments and decentralized powers for 373 items (excluding partial cancellation or decentralization), both accounting for more than 70% of the total items originally (Li and Lu 2015).

(2) **Differentiated (de-)centralization in different policy tools**. It can be observed that with the economic and social development and the diversity of goals, China has boasted more measures of adjustment of the central and local relations. It is possible to affect the local financial power through the division of taxation and the local financial power of office through transfer payments. It is able to adjust the goals of local officials for competition through the performance-based evaluation and eliminate the local protectionism through the exchanges among cadres. It can increase the local power through decentralization of authority according to the actual needs and limit the improper legislation by determining the authority. It can fortify the central management of local governments through the vertical management and endow the governments at the provincial level with more powers through the semi-vertical management system (vertical management for those below).

In summary, in the Chinese modernization state governance system, the "complexity and flexibility" of the central-local relations in China will persist for quite a long time.

References

Cai, Hongbin, and Daniel Treisman. 2006. "Did Government Decentralization Cause China's Economic Miracle?" *World Politics*, 58(4): 505–535.

China Political Affairs Monitoring Center. 2011. "'Central Version' and 'Local Version' of Post Exchanges of Cadres". *Leader Decision Information*, (20): 22–23.

Choi, Eun Kyong. 2012. "Patronage and Performance: Factors in the Political Mobility of Provincial Leaders in Post-Deng China". *The China Quarterly*, 212: 965–981.

Chung, Jae Ho. 2016. *Centrifugal Empire: Central-Local Relations in China*. Columbia University Press.

Deng, Xiaoping. 1993. The Central Leadership Must Have the Authority. *Selected works of Deng Xiaoping* (volume third). Beijing: People's Publishing House.

Fan, Yongmao. 2015. "The Centre Decides and the Local Pays: Mandates and Politics in Local Government Financial Management in China." *Local Government Studies*, 41 (4): 516–533.

Fang, Hongsheng, and Jun Zhang. 2009. "Competition of Local Governments in China, Soft Budget Constraints and the Expansion-biased Fiscal Behavior". *Economic Research*, 44 (12): 4–16.

He, Yanling, and Ni Li. 2017. "Competition for Innovation: A New Mechanism of Competition for Local Governments". *Journal of Wuhan University (Philosophy and Social Sciences)*, 70 (1): 87–96.

Heilmann, Sebastian. 2008. "From Local Experiments to National Policy: The Origins of China's Distinctive Policy Process". *The China Journal*, 59: 1–30.

Hu, Angang, Xiao Tang, and Zhusong Yang. 2014. *Modernization of National Governance in China*. Beijing: China Renmin University Press.

Jing, Yuejin, et al. 2016. *Contemporary Chinese Government and Politics*. Beijing: China Renmin University Press.

Lieberthal, Kenneth. 2004. *Governing China: From Revolution through Reform* (2nd edition). New York and London: W.W. Norton.

Jin, H., Qian, Y., and Weingast, B. R. 2005. "Regional Decentralization and Fiscal Incentives: Federalism, Chinese Style". *Journal of Public Economics*, 89 (9–10): 1719–1742.

Mao, Zedong. 1999. "On the Ten Major Relations", *Collected Works of Mao Zedong (Volume 7)*. Beijing: People's Publishing House.

Li, Hongbing and Zhou, Li-An. 2005. "Political Turnover and Economic Performance: The Incentive Role of Personnel Control in China". *Journal of Public Economics*, 89 (9–10): 1743–1762.

Li, Zhen, and Yu Lu. 2015. "Selective Mode of (De-)centralization in China – A Case Study of the Vertical Management of Departments and the Reform of Administrative Examination and Approval Authority". *Journal of Public Management*, 12 (3): 13–22 + 155.

Li, Zhilan, and Chengli Liu. 2013. "Contemporary China's Central and Local Relations: Trends, Processes and Their Impact on Policy Implementation". *Foreign Theoretical Trends*, (4): 52–61.

Nie, Huihua. 2014. "New Changes in the Relationship between Central and Local Governments". *Theory Studies*, (1): 42.

Shih, Victor, Christopher Adolph, and Mingxing Liu. 2012. "Getting Ahead in the Communist Party: Explaining the Advancement of Central Committee Members in China". *American Political Science Review*, 106 (1): 166–187.

Song, Lin. 2013. "Selective Centralization and Transition of State Governance – Based on the Investigation of the Relationship between Central and Local Governments". *Journal of Shaanxi Normal University (Philosophy and Social Sciences)*, 42 (4): 121–126.

Qian, Yingyi, and Barry R. Weingast. 2011. "China's Transition to Markets: Market-Preserving Federalism, Chinese Style". *Journal of Policy Reform*, 1 (2): 149–185.

Rong, Jingben, et al. 1997. "Political System Reform at County and Township Levels, How to Establish a New System of Democratic Cooperation – Investigation Report on the Operation Mechanism of the People's Congress System at the County and Township Levels in Xinmi City". *Comparative Economic & Social Systems*, (4): 6–28.

Xu, Chenggang. 2011. "The Fundamental Institutions of China's Reforms and Development". *Journal of Economic Literature*, 49 (4): 1076–1151.

Zhang, Guang. 2017. "Policy for Division of Power of office and Financial Power in China since the 18th National Congress of the Communist Party of China: Breakthrough or Convention?". *Local Finance Research*, (4): 12–18.

Zheng, Yongnian, 2007. *De Facto Federalism in China: Reforms and Dynamics of Central-Local Relations*. Singapore: World Scientific Publishing.

Zhou, Feizhou. 2006. "Ten Years of Tax Distribution System: Institution and Its Impact". *Chinese Social Sciences*, (6): 100–115 + 205.

Zhu, Guanglei. 2008. *Contemporary Chinese Government Process*. Tianjin: Tianjin Peoples Publishing House.

Zhu, Guanglei, and Zhihong Zhang. 2005. "Criticism on 'Corresponding Duties and Responsibilities for Upper and Lower Levels'". *Journal of Peking University (Philosophy and Social Sciences)*, (1): 101–112.

CHAPTER 8

Local Cadres

Thomas Heberer

1 INTRODUCTION

This chapter examines the function, role, and administration of local cadres. Here, the term "local cadres" refers particularly to officials at the county (city), township, and village levels. The chapter is structured as follows: first, China's cadre system, in general, is briefly explained. Second, the discretionary power of county governments is examined. We then consider the role of three levels of officials: county, town and township, and village cadres. In addition, we introduce the analytical concept of "strategic groups" (SGs) to illustrate how to capture local cadres and their behavior from a theoretical perspective. Finally, we deal with the evaluation of cadres' performance by superior bodies and the role of policy piloting at the local level.

2 CHINA'S CADRE SYSTEM

In China, the term "cadre" (*ganbu*) refers, first, to all party officials and civil servants in administrative institutions, public organizations, and armed forces and, second, to persons in leadership positions. It is important to differentiate between party, administrative, and military cadres. A party secretary is a party cadre, a government official an administrative cadre, and an officer a military cadre. As the term covers party and state leaders as well as village officials and ordinary police officers, it does not refer to a homogeneous group (Fan et al. 2015). Originally, the term referred to people in leading positions in the revolutionary struggle. After 1949, it was used for officials in the party and state apparatus funded by the state budget. Due to their power and authority, cadres

T. Heberer (✉)
Institute of Political Science and the Institute of East Asian Studies, University of Duisburg-Essen, Duisburg, Germany
e-mail: thomas.heberer@uni-due.de

© The Author(s) 2019
J. Yu, S. Guo (eds.), *The Palgrave Handbook of Local Governance in Contemporary China*, https://doi.org/10.1007/978-981-13-2799-5_8

differ from the "masses". Sociologically, they constitute a status group enjoying specific privileges.

The cadre system that had been in existence since the 1950s (Schurmann 1968) was remodeled in 1993 by the Provisional Regulations for Public Service into 15 grades, starting with the prime minister at grade 1 and running down to ordinary officials at grades 10 through 15. The grading is the same on each level of the party, the People's Congresses (parliaments), and the Political Consultative Conferences (consultative bodies). This grading also regulates salaries and privileges. State cadres, that is, civil servants paid by the state, are put on the official schedule by the responsible personnel offices. Organizational departments of the Party are responsible for party cadres. State cadres are paid out of the official budgets, whereas other rural (village) cadres have to be paid from extra-budgetary resources. Each cadre grade is treated differently, with privileges increasing as grade level rises. "High cadres" (grade 5 and above) enjoy the greatest privileges as far as salaries, labor conditions, size and standard of accommodation, medical treatment, and pensions are concerned. They also receive a better standard of official car with driver, the right to travel first class in trains and planes on official trips, and, last but not least, access to detailed information on China and foreign countries (Brodsgaard and Zheng 2006).

The current hierarchical system is similar to China's traditional civil service hierarchy, which was also divided into grades in what was known as the *ji* hierarchy. There were two main categories: civil and military service. From the Tang dynasty (618–907) onward, each category was divided into 9 grades, each grade being subdivided into 2 classes, upper (*shang*) and lower (*xia*), for a total of 18 ranks. Each grade was characterized by special insignias and salaries. The higher the rank, the greater the incumbents' privileges and nonmaterial advantages (Marsh 1961; Bodde and Morris 1973).

Nowadays, cadres are generally referred to as officials or public servants (*gongwuyuan*). The Civil Servant Law of the People's Republic of China (2005) defines "civil servants" as "those personnel who perform public duties according to laws and have been included into the state administrative staffing with wages and welfare borne by the state public finance" (The Civil Servant Law 2005; Chan 2016).

3   Local Cadres

The role of China's local state for governance capacity and authoritarian resilience has long been underestimated. However, it is not only the central state which acts as a developmental agency; so does the local state (cities, counties, towns, and townships). The local state and local cadres not only have the task of implementing the policies designed by higher authorities (central and provincial level) within the bounds of the central guidelines, they have also gained more discretionary powers in policy implementation, that is, to execute development according to specific local resources and conditions. The implementation of policies depends primarily on cadres. Arguably, the local state has to solve local problems and ensure social stability. In this way, the central state transfers decision-making power to the local level while at the same time closely monitoring the performance of leading local cadres. Hence, the latter serve as both agents and principals. They act as agents of the central state at the local level and as principals with regard to the lower levels of townships and villages.

Cadres in counties, townships, and villages constitute the absolute majority of all Chinese cadres. This cadre segment has to be understood in terms of its function in the Chinese political system. Local interests are not identical with central ones. The local level is primarily concerned with the implementation of decisions made by superior echelons. Flexibility is needed to implement the Center's policies, building in substantial degrees of political autonomy at the local level. This can be well observed in the realm of agricultural or environmental policy or if local governments have to implement a broad policy framework like "Constructing a New Socialist Countryside" (a program during the Hu-Wen period), which was formulated and framed in a rather general and vague mode, setting standards instead of providing clear-cut directives. Although implementation was required, it was meant to be attuned to local conditions, giving local cadres some leverage for the implementation of their program and thus for flexibility.

Sociologist Zhou Xueguang discerns three categories of flexibility for local cadres in policy processes: (a) "flexibility by purposive design", that is, a flexible central policy in a given policy field; (b) "flexibility of unintended design", that is, action by the local authorities in accordance with specific local conditions; and (c) "flexibility by special interests", which means that the policy of the Center is undermined by individual interests (Zhou 2010). Obviously, on the one hand, such flexibility allows the implementation of policies according to local conditions, while, on the other hand, it might facilitate the pursuit of individual interests (in terms of corrupt practices, rent-seeking, nepotism, or buying of formal positions).

Graeme Smith argues that county governments only take the initiative to act proactively if four conditions are met: (a) a policy is important for annual performance evaluation and career advancement; (b) it increases the county's income; (c) it serves the cadres' individual interests; (d) it can be realized with the existing resources (Smith 2013).

Party secretaries and county mayors are appointed by the next higher echelon, while other leading county cadres are appointed by the Standing Committee of a county's party committee. However, organizational departments of the next higher level have to approve these appointments. Town and township cadres at and above the rank of deputy section chief (*fukeji*) are also appointed by the Standing Committee of a county's party committee.

In 2010, a revised regulation for the selection, appointment, and monitoring of cadres was adopted (Dangzheng lingdao ganbu xuanba 2010). On each administrative level, there is an age limit for members of the Standing

Committee of the party committee: at provincial level it is 55 years. Four to five members have to be below the age of 50, and at least two below 45. At the city level, the age limit of the core group is 50 years, whereas three to four must be below 45 and at least two of them younger than 40 years (2004–2008 nian quanguo dangzheng lingdao 2004).

According to the Regulations on the Appointment of Cadres (2007), leading county cadres have to have five years' work experience in an administrative body plus two years' experience "at the grassroots" (township, village, enterprise, etc.) in addition to a diploma from an institution of higher learning. As a rule, both leading county and township cadres remain in office for at least five years (Dangzheng lingdao ganbu zhiwu 2006). At the city level, the maximum average age of the core group is set at 45; at the county level, it is 40 years.[1]

Finally, at the township level, the age limit for the core group is below 40 or even below the age of 35, and at least one should be younger than 30.[2] As a rule, leading cadres of townships must have previously gained experience in a key organization (such as a county's organizational department, the general office of a county's party committee, or in the county government), thus getting access to county leadership networks. In addition, a diploma from an institution of higher education is required. The latter can also be acquired through distance learning or graduation from a higher-level party school. At least one member has to be female (2009–2013 nian quanguo dangzheng lingdao 2009). Thus, the time span for obtaining a leading cadre position is strictly limited (Dangzheng lingdao ganbu xuanba 2014).

Yang Zhong differentiates between "promotable" and "terminal" officials. Age limits and minimum education requirements have a significant impact on officials' careers. Promotable officials are young and sufficiently well educated to be transferred to higher positions, whereas older and less educated cadres face dead-end careers. Zhong argues that the majority of county cadres belong to the second group, whereas most township cadres are promotable officials (Zhong 2015). Xiang in turn discovered that in Zhejiang Province, a large percentage of cadres have little prospect of being promoted due to age restrictions and local origins. The majority remain in the same location where they were born or commenced their careers (Xiang 2017).

However, even Chinese experts doubt that there has been any major change in recent years since the existing regulations are lacking a system of independent checks and balances (Gao 2010). Provinces adopt different methods to examine cadres' way of life prior to a promotion: Jiangxi Province, for example, decided in 2010 to check a candidate's working and living behavior, assets, and family members' employment status (Renmin Ribao 15 April 2010). In Hunan Province, promotion was accompanied by the signing of a "moral contract" (*daode jiandingshu*) on the working style, lifestyle, and leisure time behavior of

---

[1] See http://www.waizi.org.cn/law/17037.html (accessed 24 April 2017).
[2] http://cpc.people.com.cn/GB/64093/64103/13186087.html (accessed 16 April 2017).

the person to be promoted (Renmin Ribao 8 September 2010). Also in 2010, the Party leadership introduced an obligation for leading officials to provide information on personal matters (Guanyu lingdao ganbu baogao 2010). However, this not only met with strong resistance from cadres at different administrative levels but also did not produce any significant outcomes.

The behavior of county cadres is often criticized. Conflict researcher Yu Jianrong from the Chinese Academy of Social Sciences, for instance, criticized that, in many cases, county cadres would strip peasants of their land and evict residents from their homes. Due to selfish motives, they would violate people's legal rights, suppress critical media reports, and crush criticism and petitions by the local population (Yu 2009).

On the other hand, local cadres are facing tremendous pressure from higher echelons to fulfill salient national tasks. To give just one specific example, during the author's fieldwork in a county in southern Jiangxi province in 2009, he was able to observe the endeavors by which counties strove to overcome the financial crisis at the local level in order to maintain stability. The local leadership had the task of solving the problem of migrant workers who had become unemployed due to the breakdown of their enterprises in coastal areas and had returned to their relatively poor hometowns. The central government had ordered that all counties facing such a problem had to take the following steps: (a) counties had to approach successful entrepreneurs—who originated from a given county but had meanwhile become successful elsewhere—in a bid to attract external investment to create new jobs. These entrepreneurs were asked to invest in new local branch enterprises in their hometowns. By doing so, they gained special access to local credit facilities and loans, a preferential choice of land, tax relief or redemption, and government allowances and subsidies. The central leadership provided local governments with specific target numbers of jobs they had to create. These targets were to be met under all circumstances in order to ensure the career advancement of local government leaders. Accordingly, the leading officials of the county being studied travelled to various parts of the country to convince entrepreneurs who had originally come from that county to invest in their home areas. Fulfillment of the targets by local cadres was rewarded, while non-fulfillment resulted in salary reductions. Local officials told the author that these targets put tremendous pressure on them, since success in meeting them was a precondition for further promotion. (b) Local enterprises were ordered to employ additional people (jobless migrant workers). (c) The county government had to organize professional and skills training to qualify jobless migrant workers for work in local enterprises or for self-employment. Arguably, these (authoritarian) steering measures rather rapidly contributed to solving the unemployment problem of returning migrant workers in that county in 2009.

A general and major challenge for local cadres is the fiscal issue (Zhao 2013, 2017). On the one hand, local governments have to offer social services, but, on the other, they are heavily underfunded by the higher echelons. The fiscal reform after 2002 and the abolition of rural taxes, in particular, reinforced the power of the central government while at the same time weakening the financial capacity and thus the bargaining power of the local level vis-à-vis higher authorities (Kennedy 2016). Local governments attempted to compensate for this problem through acquisition of rural land; trading rural land for infrastructure projects and industrial, residential, and commercial purposes; and selling condominiums (Takeuchi 2013).

In 2013, a new program was adopted by the Chinese leadership, which aimed to pursue a modified reform model. Implementing this new reform program at the local level seemed to be a difficult task. Premier Li Keqiang several times expressed his annoyance with local authorities' reluctance to carry out central directives, which has led to a stalemate in policy implementation. Inspection teams were sent to all provinces to check the situation (Li 2014). The inspection teams, however, found out that the local resistance was less related to policy implementation but rather to the anti-corruption drive and the fear among local cadres that any mistake in policy implementation might be classified as "corrupt behavior". Accordingly, local cadres were reluctant to make decisions for fear of committing political mistakes or being accused of "corrupt practices".

4   County Cadres and the Predominance of the County Party Secretary

In 2017, China had 2862 county-level divisions. In fact, county governments play a key role in maintaining rural development and stability. They serve as a link between the higher administrative echelons and the rural populace.[3] This means solving possible conflicts and contradictions caused by policies that have to be implemented.

Political scientist Hu Wei has enumerated three factors that shape the behavior of county governments and cadres: (a) upper-level (central, provincial, city) guidelines; (b) limited local resources (finance, industry, acreage); and (c) evaluation requirements, mostly focusing on economic success. Since the late 1970s, according to Hu, county governments have undergone a change of role, from leading (*lingdao*) economic development, then figuring as political entrepreneurs and brokers, and finally guiding and steering (*yindao* or *zhidao*) development. Since the mid-1980s, there had been a further change related to pushing privatization of state enterprises and the promotion of market incentives. Finally, since 2002, this push function has been replaced by a new orientation of county governments: providing services for private enterprises and, more generally, for rural development (Hu 2007).

Political scientist Fan Hongmin conceptualizes county cadres as a group with a common way of life based on daily meetings. According to Fan, party secretaries spend one-third of their time in various meetings (Fan 2008). Local

---

[3] A total 60% of party members live in China's counties. See Renmin Ribao, 12 June 2010.

cadres occupy their time listening to (and internalizing) high-flown leadership speeches, reporting regularly to higher levels and dealing with the continuous challenge of upper-level inspections. In addition, local cadres suffer from a negative public image, from peer competition, and the fact that promotion is not always granted to the most qualified among their colleagues (Fan 2008). For promotion, qualifications and effective performance are not the only crucial factors—so too are personal networks (*guanxi*). The higher a position, the more important *guanxi* are to those leaders who decide on the assignments of local cadres. Moreover, previous work experience is helpful in gaining promotion. Those cadres who have worked in an important government or party organization are statistically more likely to be rapidly promoted to a leadership position in a county or township government than those who have not (Fan 2008). The closer a cadre works to the center of local power (e.g. in the Standing Committee of a county's party committee), the higher the probability of early promotion (Yang 2002).

Counties have the same set of party and administrative bodies as the central and provincial governments. The decisive body at the county level is the Standing Committee of the Party Committee. In 2017, in most counties, this core group (*lingdao banzi*) consisted of the following cadres: the party secretary; the mayor; the secretary for political-legal affairs (*zhengfa shuji*), responsible for procuratorial, judicial, and public security matters; the vice-mayor responsible for industry or rural development; the director of the Organization Department of the Party Committee; the Chairman of the Discipline Inspection Commission; the commander of the local armed forces (*wuzhuang buzhang*); and the secretary in charge of the work of the Party Committee (*dangwei mishuzhang*). The party secretary has the final say. Accordingly, party secretaries of counties are called "yi ba shou", that is "number one hands". They are at the top of the local political elite. They are also the persons with the strongest local power, having the final decision-making power in their county (Fan 2013).

The functions of a party secretary cover a wide spectrum. She or he is not only responsible for the county's comprehensive development but even has to take care of the day-to-day life of her or his subordinates, including their family problems.

In order to become a party secretary of a city or county, a person is (officially) expected to display not only political leadership qualities and loyalty to the Party but also social skills such as conflict resolution competence, assertiveness, or responsibility. Individual qualities such as charisma and developmental performance are also deemed to be important (Fan 2008).

Fan identifies three groups of county party secretaries: (a) those dispatched by higher authorities (quickly moving up the career ladder but often lacking grassroots experience); (b) those being promoted from the grassroots; (c) persons with a reputation gained through important local innovations (Fan 2008). Therefore, we find different paths to becoming a party secretary. The central leadership perceives "visionary leadership" as crucial, that is, implementing central policies in an innovative way and combining this with a focus on broad local interests. In many cases, however, this appears to be an almost insoluble task.

Since party secretaries are appointed for a specific term only, the "supreme leader" of a county may frequently change. After the appointment of a new one by higher authorities, such a change has major implications. All government offices of a given county and all its townships are expected to attune their activities to the way in which the new party secretary is thinking and acting. Concurrently, the new leader has to enforce policies through instruments such as evaluations, monitoring, and replacement of personnel. A salient instrument of disciplining is the expectation of county cadres to be promoted or at least to avoid being removed. To achieve this goal, they have themselves to bow to the leadership line of the new party secretary. This gives the latter an enormous amount of power.

For many years, some intellectuals have been criticizing the fact that county party secretaries have too much power, and that their activities lack transparency (Xiao 2009). And indeed, since 2003, party secretaries have concurrently held the post of chair of the local People's Congresses as well, thus combining both the highest political power and the highest state power at the local level.

Interestingly, a web-based survey among county party secretaries revealed that the latter regarded corruption as the main problem at the local level. Researcher Yu Jianrong even argued that the subordination of all local organizations under the leadership of the local party was the main reason for this. Since party secretaries are appointed by superior authorities, they do not feel responsible for issues affecting the local populace but only toward the appointing institution (party committee of a prefectural city or a province) (Yu 2009).

5   Town and Township Cadres

In 2017, China had about eight million town/township cadres in 41,034 township-level administrations. Townships (*xiang*) and towns (*zhen*) are the lowest level of state authority. They are the connecting link between county and village.

As with counties, we often find significant developmental gaps and income disparities among the townships and villages. The reasons are the different endowment with local and fiscal resources, the level of infrastructural development (street and traffic connections), proximity to markets and customers (in the county town or townships), and the existence or lack of industrial facilities and of capable village leaderships (Perkins 2003; Jiang 2004).

According to the annual "responsibility contracts" (Edin 2003b; Heberer and Trappel 2013) assigned by county governments, township cadres are responsible for fulfilling a large number of complex tasks within a given year. These tasks encompass dozens of domains such as maintaining public order, ensuring economic development, maintaining irrigation facilities, birth planning, public security, production and foodstuff safety, and prevention of epidemics and animal diseases. The "*yipiao foujue*" ("one item veto rule") items play an important role; these are periodic political "hard" targets which must be successfully fulfilled or prevented in all circumstances. But in many instances, townships lack the financial resources for the fulfillment of these tasks. They do not have their own fiscal budget but are mostly dependent on financial allowances from the county, although there are great differences among counties and their townships (Smith 2013).

A Chinese study among township party secretaries on major problems, conducted some years ago, revealed the main difficulties township cadres are facing in their area of jurisdiction: funding problems (72.8%); issues of social instability (41.1%); increasing self-awareness of the rural population (35.5%); lack of public services and facilities (31.1%); poor quality of village cadres (23.9%); and conflicts over land-use rights (11.4%) (Zhang and Wei 2009).

Superior levels are not always well aware of township problems. Since the abolition of the agricultural tax in 2005 and the following phasing out of fees to be extracted from villagers, township debts have increased considerably. Today, township governments have very meager operating budgets. In order to provide basic public goods, they have to apply for project funding from the higher levels (Zhao 2013). Moreover, township cadres are not paid well and, in some localities, have to wait for salary payment for many months. They are also exposed to pressure from three sides: (a) increasing demands and control by county governments; (b) increasing demands by the rural populace; and (c) self-imposed and peer pressure to gain promotion.[4] Finally, township cadres are often the target of violent attacks by villagers who hold them responsible for any kind of problem arising at the grassroots.

Many township cadres complain about this "pressure system" (*yalixing tizhi*). Pressure comes from three sides. First, the number of tasks assigned to them by the counties has increased enormously; at the same time, the implementation of these tasks is more strictly monitored and evaluated by county leaderships. Second, local people are more assertive in demanding their rights collectively (village communities, clans); at the same time, the protest potential among peasants has increased, the latter blaming the township officials for any problems. Assaults targeting township governments are therefore not unusual. Third, career advancement and promotion by county governments are highly dependent on both effective policy implementation and good relations to the county leadership.

In addition, township cadres possess little decision-making power, have low prestige, and in many instances see themselves as second-class officials (*erdeng gongwuyuan*) or just a weak group (*ruoshi qunti*). High performance pressure, little respect for their performance, and little hope of gaining promotion, as Chinese studies have shown (Jia 2012), mean that township cadres suffer from

---

[4] Interview with a county party secretary in Xifeng County, Guizhou Province, 6 September 2010.

depression, sleeping disorders, aggressive behavior in the family, and other problems at rising rates (Zhongguo jiceng ganbu 2010; Juece neican 2009).[5]

On the other hand, the number of township officials has tremendously increased (Zhao 2013). In his book *Talking to the Prime Minister*, a former township party secretary in Hubei Province complained that the number of township cadres has mushroomed, that cadres were lacking responsibility toward the people, and that this situation would massively increase the townships' debts (Li 2009).

Town and township cadres, for their part, are often seen as exploiting the people, disobeying existing laws, violating cadre discipline, and causing disorder and chaos in rural areas (Liao 2007). They are perceived to be backward in their thinking, irresponsible and careless, "alienated from the masses", wasting township resources, and falsifying statistics (Li 2005). Alvin Y. So called the township level a "predatory state" (So 2007), and a former township party secretary equated township cadres with "peasant-eating parasites" (Li Changping, op. cit. in Thogersen 2003). Chinese scholars have added negative terms such as "passive" (*mei dongli, beidongde*) to characterize township cadres who would only do what was decreed by higher administrative bodies.

The latter is the result of a number of structural factors: similar to county officials, township cadres are not elected. Hence, they feel responsible only to their superiors at the county level and have no incentive to deal with the needs of the populace.[6] The common people, as a former township party secretary noted, believe that the work of township cadres is just a show set up for higher governments in order to be promoted. Hence, cadres do not fear the people but only their superiors.[7] However, and along the same lines, such negative branding leaves the tangible rural development achieved in many townships and villages all over China over the recent past unexplained. There must be more to township cadres and governments to make sense of the contradiction between their negative public image and the fact that many things are getting done. To respond to this conundrum, some authors have identified five categories of township cadres, that is, learning, developing, democratic, serving and non-corrupt cadres (Guangxi Ribao 8 November 2008). However, such (in this case positive) simplifications explain little because local cadres often represent more than one of these categories: They can be corrupt but still contribute to local development; they can be undemocratic but still be capable of learning (e.g. with respect to attracting external investment and dealing efficiently with local enterprises) (Zhao 2017).

---

[5] The anti-corruption drive after 2014 also intensified pressure on local cadres.

[6] Interviews with scholars at Sichuan University and the Chengdu Academy of Social Sciences, 23 September 2007.

[7] Interview with a former township secretary in Qingdao, 20 August 2009.

6   VILLAGE CADRES

In 2017, China had 703,382 village-level subdivisions. According to the law, villages are not part of the state structure but are "autonomous" and own their land collectively. However, they are strictly monitored by their respective townships. The latter supervise the village finances, decide upon villages' development plans, approve the outcome of village elections, appoint village party secretaries, and monitor fulfillment of major issues such as birth planning, economic development, or fighting religious cults.

Currently, China has about 3.2 million village cadres. Under the Organic Law of Village Committees adopted in 1998, villages were guaranteed administrative self-governance and elections of Village Administration Committees (VACs) every three years. Any villager who has reached the age of 18 has the right to vote and be elected. As a rule, the age of village leaders (party secretary, village head) must not exceed 50 years; for other village cadres, the maximum age is 55 years.

VACs are responsible for economic development, maintaining public security, mediation, land administration, public welfare, birth planning, and so on.

Legally, townships are not allowed to intervene in village affairs. Nonetheless, township interference in village affairs is a hot topic in China. In some instances, township leaderships reinterpret village autonomy as "autonomy under the leadership of the township", thus restricting or violating the villages' legal rights to self-administration.[8] Accordingly, they continuously interfere in the selection and nomination of village election candidates and the outcome of elections. Sometimes, they oppose the election of undesirable candidates or arrest candidates selected and elected by a village. Even elected village leaders have been removed on the grounds that peasants were not "sufficiently qualified to elect the right persons" (Jin 2008).

By establishing stricter control over village finances and village development, the townships concurrently reinforce their control over the villages. Village expenses above a certain amount have to be approved by the township government. This is intended to prevent financial mismanagement and embezzlement by village cadres and further indebtedness. However, many village cadres and villages regard this as a violation of village autonomy. In addition, increasing interference and pressure by the townships have significantly reduced the enthusiasm and incentives of village cadres. At the same time, villages' resistance has increased, making their administration evermore difficult.

From the 1980s onwards, a large number of capable people left the villages or were unwilling to become village cadres. The Chinese government tried to counterbalance this development by dispatching graduates from institutions of higher learning to take over leading positions in villages lacking qualified

---

[8] Interview, Anju, 4 September 2009.

cadres. It also began to raise village cadres' salaries and in less developed areas to cover their allowances out of the higher authorities' budgets.

The lack of village cadres provided the townships with the opportunity to dispatch township cadres to villages in order to fill vacant village cadre positions. This is also meant to guarantee that the villages prescribe to the higher authorities' rules.

The policy of dispatching township cadres to villages has officially been called "*baocun*", that is, to take over responsibility for a village. We find three different types of *baocun*: (a) township cadres taking over the responsibility for a village but intervening only in cases of major problems; (b) cadres regularly inspecting "their" village, and discussing solutions to problems with village cadres; (c) deployment of township cadres as village party secretaries (*guazhi*).[9] In many cases, village cadres and villagers regard such measures as encroachment into both village affairs and village autonomy. Such interference frequently leads to conflicts with villages, for example, in cases where dispatched township cadres intervene in internal village affairs, alter village decisions, or attempt to enforce township policies. According to a Chinese survey among village cadres in a township in Beijing on the usefulness of dispatching township cadres to villages, only 34.9% of the respondents believed that this would serve to support village cadres. A total of 49.2% believed that this was merely an order from superior authorities and had little value, whereas 10.9% responded that the primary goal was to control the village cadres (Di 2009).

Dispatching township cadres to work in villages also has the function of providing new jobs for redundant township cadres. *Renmin Ribao* reported, for instance, that abolishing agricultural taxes in 2005 had the effect that many cadres became redundant and therefore were dispatched to villages as village Party secretaries.

On the other hand, the large number of villages and a lack of capable village cadres intensified the trend by higher authorities to merge several natural villages (*zirancun*) into "administrative" ones (*xingzhengcun*). The official idea was that such mergers would not only reduce the number of cadres required but would also contribute to greater policy efficiency and a reduction of administrative expenses. The outcome, however, was quite different: (a) in many cases, administrative villages became too big, thus complicating villagers' participation in village affairs; (b) many conflicts among villages over projects and project funding emerged due to their different interests; (c) village cadres elected were primarily those of larger villages so that smaller villages no longer felt represented; (d) candidates who wanted to be elected had to buy votes from voters in other villages who did not know them but wanted to be paid for electing an unknown candidate; (e) natural villages still needed administrative staff to handle everyday administration, but compared to the remuneration of

---

[9] *Guazhi* means to serve in a lower-level unit (to gain experience) for a certain period of time while retaining one's position in the previous unit.

administrative villages, these cadres were poorly paid, thus losing their incentive and interest. In this way, village mergers are perceived as a classic example of how administrative thinking at higher levels ultimately fails to solve the real problems in villages, according to village governance expert Shen Duanfeng (2017).

Researcher He Xuefeng argues that peasants tend to believe that all village cadres are corrupt. At times, a strongman emerges in a village pretending to represent the interests of the villagers and convincing them to elect him as a village chief. But the villagers are fully aware that village chiefs have to collaborate with the township leaders in order to avoid removal by the township. And in the end, the villagers are interested in a village chief being able to successfully negotiate and cooperate with the township to safeguard the interests of the village. Accordingly, the issue whether a village leader is corrupt or not is not of primary concern to villagers (He 2008).

7   Local Cadres As Strategic Groups

As noted earlier, in many instances, local cadres are perceived as highly corrupt, pursuing merely selfish interests, opposing the policies of central authorities, and violating the legal rights of the local people. This is why some authors characterize the local state as a predatory state (Pei 2009; So 2007).

Without doubt, such phenomena do exist. But the reduction of local cadres to negative components makes it almost impossible to explain why policies are implemented effectively in many places and why local development processes can result in improved living conditions for local people. Heberer and Schubert explained this with the concept of "SGs" (2012). This concept characterizes SGs as a group of people connected by a common interest in the maintenance or expansion of their shared acquisitive chances, where acquisition refers not only to material goods but also to immaterial factors such as power, prestige, or knowledge. Other features of the members of SGs are common and long-term strategies of action as well as a shared self-perception of being a crucial social actor. SGs form alliances with others in order to protect their long-term interests and to mold the political system accordingly.

Heberer and Schubert argue further that the behavior of both county and township cadres is decisive for successful local implementation of central reform initiatives. SGs are further characterized by shared interests which are pursued strategically (in our case, the interest in career advancement within the nomenclature system and a positive evaluation by superior authorities as a major precondition for this advancement); the existence of a shared collective identity (defining themselves as "avant-garde" with a specific esprit de corps and a distinct "mission"), thus delineating themselves from other social groups and actors. In addition, local leading cadres developed a shared habitus (way of life and lifestyle) and have a specific organization at their disposal (i.e. the local party organization) in order to coordinate and control the members of the SGs. Finally, they display a kind of learning capacity, that is, the readiness to advance innovative ideas for local development and policy implementation. At the level of a county and its townships, all "leading cadres" (from the level of vice-head of a government bureau at county level, *fukeji*, upwards; this also includes the township leaders) constitute such a group.

However, this group of local leading cadres is by no means homogeneous but is based rather on a hierarchical structure with a core group at its top. This leadership group consists of the abovementioned members of the Standing Committee of a county's party committee with the county party secretary at the top. The latter elaborates the strategies and ensures that all SG members participate in implementing these strategies effectively. The behavior of the group is strategic since a long-term, goal-oriented roadmap for policy implementation exists. Policy processes are steered by the leadership core. Concurrently, the core group coordinates and streamlines the behavior of the entire SG. It also ensures that if the strategic objectives (such as effective policy implementation and, accordingly, positive evaluations by superior authorities) are achieved, all group members share in the material and non-material benefits.

An SG is not a homogeneous entity. Its members compete with one another for promotion and career advancement, power, and status. They may also belong to different factions. Due to shared interests (such as a positive evaluation of the performance of all county and township officials by superior authorities), career expectations (partly decided by the core group of a county), and income (dependent on the performance of the entire SG, e.g. in terms of bonus payments by higher authorities for task fulfillment), the SG members are interested in close collaboration. The party discipline as a supervising instrument contributes to their commitment. If a member of the SG is reluctant to collaborate in achieving the group targets, she or he runs the risk of being ostracized by the group, thus losing her or his status.

Although there are certain conflicts of interest among county cadres, the alignment of interests predominates. Township cadres want to become county cadres, and the latter primarily depends on the decision of a given county leadership. Village cadres in turn are not state cadres and are therefore not part of the SG of leading county and township cadres.

Leading cadres act differently in different locations. This can be traced to differences in the endowment with natural and fiscal resources and environmental endowment, the incentives and quality of local leading cadres but also to vague instructions by higher authorities. Since no fixed rules and modus operandi exist and the targets to be achieved are often equivocal, decision-making within a county leadership takes place in an environment of uncertainty. The more vague the preferences and decisions by superior authorities are, the more choices for local decisions do leading local cadres have. They are given unclear instructions but have to act and react. An example of this kind of uncertainty in policy implementation was the abovementioned program "Constructing a new socialist countryside" in the Hu-Wen era (Ahlers 2014). The central leadership provided 20 Chinese characters only, translated as develop agrarian production; improve living conditions (of the local people); civilize rural areas, create esthetic and clean villages; and establish democratic village administrations. The local level had to decide by itself how to implement some of these policies and to select those which were most suitable to local conditions. Local leaderships can focus, for instance, on establishing social security systems, renovation of villages, ecology and environmental protection, developing the rural infrastructure, the rural economy or social housing, the commercialization of land, the conversion of agricultural land to nonagricultural land, urbanization of rural areas, modernizing agrarian production, urban-rural integration, providing services for rural inhabitants, and so on. Counties should select policy fields that are appropriate to local circumstances and for which they can apply for funding.

The concept of SGs is an analytical tool, which assists in capturing and explaining the behavior of local cadres from a theoretical perspective. It also helps in understanding why effective policy implementation at the local level is possible, and that the local state is not necessarily a "predatory" one.

8   EVALUATION OF CADRES

Since the 1990s, the "responsibility contracts" (*zerenshu*), mentioned earlier, between superior and subordinate echelons are concluded on an annual basis. These contracts stipulate in detail the tasks of a local administration in an upcoming year. At the local level, such agreements exist between prefectural cities and counties, between counties and townships, and between townships and villages. Within a given county, the county leadership enters into separate contracts with each bureau and township under its jurisdiction. Inspection teams dispatched by superior authorities examine and assess the fulfillment of the respective targets and tasks. The outcome of the evaluation is decisive for awarding a location or an office and the promotion of cadres. The evaluation process is highly competitive. For instance, the leaderships of three townships at the top of the ranking are awarded and rewarded. The leaderships of the three townships at the bottom of the ranking are penalized by salary deductions, lose their bonuses, and are excluded from promotion.

These comprehensive and multiple evaluations of both party and government offices and individual cadre performance at the local level are an important pillar of China's political system. By means of these "responsibility contracts" and evaluation criteria, higher echelons communicate the targets of their policies to subordinate levels, thus attempting to ensure the implementation of their policies.

The "responsibility contracts" encompass "hard" policy fields (such as gross domestic product—GDP—growth, preserving social stability or birth planning; in the case of environmental models, the implementation of environment policies), which have to be implemented under all circumstances, and "soft" policy fields, which are secondary factors (counted by superior authorities as less important). The realization of the "hard" targets is a must and—at least formally—a necessary precondition for cadre promotions and the payment of bonuses. The "soft" targets in turn should or may be realized. In the latter case, non-implementation does not have any severe consequences.

Two basic types of evaluation exist: (a) program evaluation, that is, assessing the implementation of single policies or policy programs (*mubiao kaohe*) and (b) assessment of the performance of cadres, including the general behavior of local leading cadres (*kaoping*). At the end of an evaluation process, the individual counties of a prefecture, the townships of a county, and the villages of a township are ranked according to their performance in the past year (Heberer and Trappel 2013).

In addition, the abovementioned "periodic priorities" (*yipiao foujue*) exist, items that have to be implemented under all circumstances. As a rule, these items include preserving social stability (no occurrence of mass protests or mass petitions at higher echelons, etc.), the avoidance of industrial or environmental casualties, and the adherence to birth planning regulations. In more and more counties, specific local policy domains such as environmental policies are becoming part of *yipiao foujue*.

If local authorities fail to realize just one of these *yipiao foujue* items, the entire performance of a local leadership is evaluated as void, at least in theory. In such cases, a locality cannot be classified as "advanced", and such an assessment will have a negative impact on the career advancement of its leading cadres. Yu et al. inform us, however, that *yipiao foujue* is not always really binding, and that its violations may not in any case constitute an obstacle to career advancement (Yu et al. 2016).

It is frequently argued that evaluation processes are primarily intended to improve the effectiveness and efficiency of administrative behavior and the control of subordinate authorities, thus figuring as a mechanism for adjusting the interrelationship between the central and the local level (Edin 2003a). However, there are some further features. Evaluations are an instrument of the party state for both political communication and internalizing social control. Accordingly, we can discern four primary functions. (a) By means of the responsibility system and the evaluation of target fulfillment, they serve as an instrument of political communication between the counties and superior administrative entities. The "responsibility contracts" communicate the expectations of superior authorities toward the counties. (b) Evaluations figure as an incentive and steering mechanism since it is only by fulfilling the prescribed tasks that cadres can be positively evaluated, thus preserving their career advancement opportunities. (c) By rating performance of locations or offices, evaluations function as a monitoring and pressure instrument. Formally, only those cadres are promoted whose performance has repeatedly been rated as "excellent" (the highest rating level). Moreover, the target agreements imply not only rewards but also disciplinary measures in the case of non-fulfillment. (d) Evaluations figure as a mechanism for internalizing social and political control, on the one hand, and for disciplining, on the other: disciplining in the sense that local leading cadres proactively implement the central leadership's development concept.

Undoubtedly, the evaluation processes display significant weaknesses: even now, the focus of evaluation is characterized by the priority given to quantitative economic output (GDP), a rather flexible interpretation of the evaluation outcome, and insufficient control by the public sphere. Furthermore, in order to avoid any demotivation of leading local cadres, superior echelons are not really interested in punishing performance deficiencies. Sanctions are only applied in cases in which the public has become aware of blatant mismanagement.

To make cadres more accountable, evaluations should focus on pursuing long-term sustainable development instead of quantitative GDP growth. The latter favored high pollution, tremendous indebtedness, and neglect of people's concerns. Moreover, local and regional circumstances and the provision of public goods should be given more consideration in evaluation processes.

9   Policy Modeling and Experimentation

Since quite some time, policy modeling and policy experimentation at the local level were crucial for China's local cadres in order for them to be noticed by higher authorities and improve their opportunities to be promoted to higher positions. Accordingly, they were under considerable pressure from the higher authorities to create local "models". From the perspective of the Center, local governments should be innovative and produce effective policy experiments that can be replicated elsewhere. Policy experiments are meant to lead to the creation of "models" (*shifan*) and "experiments" (*shidian*), that is, the formal pursuit of political innovation (Heilmann 2008; Heberer 2016; Göbel and Heberer 2017).

Evaluation reinforces the pressure to devise such policy experiments locally and to copy from successful ones, since they indicate how "advanced" a locality and its leadership are. Models are evaluated by higher authorities in an annual process of program evaluation, and the creation of successful models may positively affect the standing of a local leadership and its evaluation scores (Heberer and Trappel 2013).

Meanwhile, in order to become a model, the modeling concept and the respective plan have to be approved by the superior level. In addition, a location must abide by the relevant rules and regulations issued by the Center, the province, or the prefectural city, whereby the latter will regularly check the "model character" and its development (ChinaFile 2016). This re-hierarchization, aimed at the reinforcement of hierarchical decision-making and increased top-down monitoring, negatively affects the incentives and willingness of policy piloting and policy experimenting among local cadres (Ahlers and Stepan 2016).

Models and/or experiments inform higher echelons about the development path which a local government intends to follow. Thus, they are crucial for acquiring resources, political appreciation, and optimal evaluation by higher authorities. As has been argued elsewhere, "leaders have to identify a problem, come up with a policy, and, most importantly, market this policy by convincing other departments and the general public to participate" (Göbel and Heberer 2017).

In the end, effective local developmentalism contributes to effective policy implementation both in tackling crises and in generating stability and legitimacy in the political system. Nevertheless, Chinese people distinguish between the legitimacy of the central authorities and that of local authorities. As the perceived "benign state", the central government possesses trust, while the "malign" local authorities are frequently blamed for all grievances and enjoy only a minimum of trust or none at all. Of course, such a dichotomy is far too superficial. Heberer, Schubert, and Ahlers have shown that in many locations of rural China, effective policy implementation and trust in local governments are undeniably present (Heberer and Schubert 2012; Ahlers 2014; Ahlers et al. 2016).

References

2004–2008 nian quanguo dangzheng lingdao banzi jianshe guihua gangyao (Outline for the establishment of leadership groups of party and government in 2004–2008). 2004. http://www.mzdj.gov.cn/bencandy.php?fid=16&id=53 (accessed 5 May 2017).

2009–2013 nian quanguo dangzheng lingdao banzi jianshe guihua gangyao (Outline for the establishment of leadership groups of party and government 2009–2013). 2009. http://wenda.tianya.cn/wenda/thread?tid=5cedd389b7b84b54 (accessed 5 May 2017).

Ahlers, A. 2014. *Rural Policy Implementation in Contemporary China: New Socialist Countryside*. London, New York: Routledge.

Ahlers, A., Heberer, T., and Schubert, G. 2016. Whither local governance in contemporary China? Reconfiguration for more effective policy implementation. *Journal of Chinese Governance* 1: 55–77.

Ahlers, A., and Stepan, M. 2016. Top-level design and local-level paralysis: Local politics in times of political centralisation. *MERICS Papers on China* 1 (June): 34–39.

Bodde, D., and Morris, C., 1973. *Law in Imperial China. Exemplified by 190 Ch'ing Dynasty Cases*. Cambridge, MA: Harvard University Press.

Brodsgaard, K.E., and Zheng Y. (eds.). 2006. *The Chinese Communist Party in Reform*. London, New York: Routledge.

Chan, H.S. 2016. The Making of Chinese Civil Service Law: Ideals, Technicalities, and Realities. *American Review of Public Administration* 46(4): 379–398.

ChinaFile (ed.). 2016. *What does Xi Jinping's top-down leadership mean for innovation in China? A File conversation*, 27 October. http://www.chinafile.com/conversation/what-does-xi-jinpings-top-down-leadership-mean-innovation-china (accessed 18 April 2017).

Dangzheng lingdao ganbu xuanba renyong gongzuo tiaoli (Regulation for the selection and appointment work of leading cadres). 2014. http://renshi.people.com.cn/n/2014/0116/c139617-24132478.html (accessed 24 May 2017).

Dangzheng lingdao ganbu xuanba renyong gongzuo zeren zhuijiu banfa (Method for selecting, appointing and monitoring the work of leading party and government officials). 2010. *Renmin Ribao* 1 April.

Dangzheng lingdao ganbu zhiwu renqi Zanxing guiding. 2006. http://news.12371. cn/2015/03/12/ARTI1426126246992108.shtml (accessed 27 October 2018).

Di, J. 2009. *Zhongguo de yige zhen: Zhaoquanying diaocha* (A town in China: Investigation in Zhaoquanying). Beijing: Zhongguo shehui kexue chubanshe.

Edin, M. 2003a. State Capacity and Local Agent Control in China: CCP Cadre Management from a Township Perspective. *The China Quarterly* March: 35–52.

Edin, M. 2003b. Remaking the Communist Party-State: The Cadre Responsibility System at the Local Level in China. *China. An International Journal* March: 1–15.

Fan, H. 2008. *Xianyu zhengzhi quanli shijian yu richang chengxu* (Politics on county level. Power practice and daily procedures). Beijing: Shehui kexue chubanshe.

Fan, H. 2013. *Zhuanxing zhongde xianyu zhili: jiegou, xingwei yu biange* (County governance under transformation: structures, behavior, and reform. Beijing: Zhongguo shehui kexue chubanshe.

Fan, J., Heberer, T., and Taubmann, W. 2015. *Rural China. Economic and Social Change in the Late Twentieth Century.* Armonk, London: M.E. Sharpe.

Gao, S. 2010. Dangzheng lingdao ganbu xuanba renyong xingui fabu (New regulations for selecting and appointing leading party and government officials). *Caizheng* (Finance and Politics), 31 March. http://www.caijing.com.cn/ajax/print.html (accessed 18 May 2017).

Göbel, C., and Heberer, T. 2017. The Policy Innovation Imperative: Changing Techniques for Governing China's Local Governors, in: *To Govern China. Evolving Practices of Power.* Edited by Vivienne Shue and Patricia M. Thornton. Cambridge: Cambridge University Press: 279–304.

Guangxi Ribao (Guangxi Daily). 2008. Nanning.

Guanyu lingdao ganbu baogao geren youguan shixiang de guiding (Regulation on the reporting of individual matters of leading cadres). 2010. *Renmin Ribao*, 12 July.

He, X. 2008. *Shenme nongcun, shenme wenti* (What kind of village, what kind of problems). Beijing: Falü chubanshe.

Heberer, T. 2016. The Chinese "Developmental State" 3.0 and the Resilience of Authoritarianism. *Journal of Chinese Governance* 4: 611–632.

Heberer, T., and Schubert, G. 2012. County and Township Cadres as a Strategic Group. A New Approach to Political Agency in China's Local State. *Journal of Chinese Political Science* 17: 221–249.

Heberer, T., and Trappel, R. 2013. Evaluation Processes, Local Cadres' Behaviour and Local Development Processes. *Journal of Contemporary China*. Number 84, November: 1048–1066.

Heilmann, S. 2008. From Local Experiments to National Policy. *The China Journal* No. 59: 1–30.

Hu, W. 2007. *Zhidu bianqian zhongde xianji zhengfu xingwei* (County government behavior amidst institutional change). Beijing: Zhongguo shehui kexue chubanshe.

Jia, J. 2012. *Quntixing shijian zhongde xiangzhen ganbu* (Mass incidents and township cadres). 2012. http://www.snzg.cn/article/2008/0103/article_8708.html (accessed 10 April 2017).

Jiang, X. 2004. 'Rich Brothers' and 'Poor Cousins': the political economy of post-reform rural disparity in a Chinese township. *Journal of Contemporary China* 13 (41) November: 801–817.

Jin, T. 2008. *Cunli zhili yu quanli jiegou* (Village governance and power structure). Guangzhou: Guangdong renmin chubanshe.

Juece neican. Da guo "gan kao" (Decision-making, internal reference. Big country, imperial examinations). 2009. Beijing: Huawen chubanshe.

Kennedy, John J. 2016. Finance and rural governance: centralization and local challenges. Yeh, Emily T., O'Brien, Kevin, and Ye, Jingzhong (eds.), *Rural Politics in Contemporary China*. London and New York: Routledge: 93–110.

Li, C. 2009. *Wo xiang zongli shuo hua*. Xi'an: Shaanxi renmin chubanshe.

Li, D. 2005. *Guanyu dangqian xiangzhen ganbu sixiang zhuangkuang de sikao* (Considerations on the ideological situation co current township cadres). http://theory.people.com.cn/GB/40537/3525699.html (accessed 21 May 2017).

Li, K. 2014. Guowuyuan jue bu fa kongtou wenjian (The State Council absolutely does not issue empty documents). http://finance.sina.com.cn/china/20140601/201919289611.shtml (accessed 20 April 2017).

Liao, X. 2007. Huanyuan yige zhenshi de xiangzhen ganbu (Once again become a genuine township cadre). *Xiangcun Zhongguo Guancha*. http://www.snzg.cn/article/show.php?itemid-7817/page-1.html (accessed 21 May 2017).

Marsh, R.M. 1961. *The Mandarins. The Circulation of Elites in China, 1600–1900*. New York: Crowell-Collier.

Pei, M. 2009. *China's Trapped Transition*. Cambridge, MA and London: Harvard University Press.

Perkins, T. 2003. "Entrepreneurial Fiends and Honest Farmers": Explaining Intravillage Inequality in a Rural Chinese Township. *Economic Development and Cultural Change* 51 (3): 719–751.

Renmin Ribao (People's Daily). 2010. Beijing.

Schurmann, F. 1968. *Ideology and Organization in Communist China*. Berkeley and Los Angeles: University of California Press.

Shen, Duanfeng. 2017. *How Village Mergers Hinder China's Grassroots Governance*. http://www.sixthtone.com/news/2107/village-mergers-restrict-local-governance (accessed 2 May 2017).

Smith, G. (2013). Measurement, promotions and patterns of behavior in Chinese local government. *The Journal of Peasant Studies* 6: 1027–1050.

So, A.Y. 2007. Peasant Conflict and the Local Predatory State in the Chinese Countryside. *The Journal of Peasant Studies* 34 (3–4): 560–581.

Takeuchi, H. 2013. Survival Strategies of Township Governments in Rural China: from predatory taxation to land trade. *Journal of Contemporary China* 22: 755–772.

The Civil Servant Law of the People's Republic of China. 2005. http://www.asianlii.org/cn/legis/cen/laws/tcslotproc462/ (accessed 27 October 2018).

Thogersen, S. 2003. Parasites or Civilisers: The Legitimacy of the Chinese Communist Party in Rural Areas. *China: An International Journal* September: 200–223.

Xiang, G. 2017. Promotion prospects and career paths of local party-government leaders in China. *Journal of Chinese Governance* 2 (2): 223–234.

Xiao, P. 2009. Rang xianwei shuji zouhao quanli zhetiao "dao" (Let the county party secretary walk on the "path" of power in a benign way. *Renmin Ribao* 15 December.

Yang, X. 2002. *Shichang fayu, shehui shengchang yu gonggong quanli goujian – yi xian wie weiguan fenxi danwei* (Market development, social growth and the structure of public power – county as a micro-analytical unit). Zhengzhou: Henan renmin chubanshe.

Yu, J. 2009. Jianli xianji gaige shiyanqu de shexiang (Concept for establishing reform experimental zones at county level. *Nanfang Zhoumo* (Southern Weekly) 10 September.

Yu, J., Cai E., and Gao X. 2016. Difang zhengfu wen guanxi zhongde zuoyong yu xiandu. Jiyu Zhejiang shengshixian dangzheng fuzeren wenjuan diaocha (Local governments on the function and limitation of guanxi. Questionnaire investigation among responsible persons in cities and counties of Zhejiang province). *Zhonggong Zhejiang Sheng Dangxiao Xuebao* (Journal of the Party School of the CCP in Zhejiang province) 1: 12–21.

Zhang, T., and Wei, A. 2009. 710 wei xiangzhen "yi ba shou" de zhuangtai (Situation of party secretaries in 710 towns and townships). *Renmin Ribao* 9 February.

Zhao, S. 2013. *Township Governance and Institutionalization in China*. Singapore and London: World Scientific.

Zhao, S. 2017. *Regeneration of Peasants*. Berlin and New York: Springer.

Zhong, Y. 2015. *Local Government and Politics in China: Challenges from Below*. London and New York: Routledge.

Zhongguo jiceng ganbu quan xiao ze da, jingshen yali da xinli wenti tuchu (Grassroot cadres in China have little power but large obligations, the mental pressure is enormous, psychic problems tremendous). http://internal.dbw.cn/system/2010/04/12/052447662.shtml (accessed 18 April 2017).

Zhongguo jiceng ganbu. 2010. = Zhongguo jiceng ganbu quan xiao ze da, jingshen yali da xinli wenti tuchu (Chinese grassroots cadres have little power but great responsibilities, their mental psychic pressure is big as are psychic problems). http://politics.people.com.cn/GB/1026/11341830.html (accessed 27 October 2018).

Zhou, X. 2010. The Institutional Logic of Collusion among Local Governments in China. *Modern China* 36: 47–78.

CHAPTER 9

China's Developmental State in Transition: In Light of the East Asian Experiences

Wei Chen and Shu Keng

1   INTRODUCTION: CHINA AT THE CROSSROADS

In the second half of 2016, a heated debate attracted widespread attention in China.[1] Two eminent economists, Prof. Justin Yi-Fu Lin, former Chief Economist of the World Bank, and Prof. Wei-Ying Zhang, former Dean of the Guanghua School of Management, Peking University, thoroughly debated the effectiveness of industrial policy (reports). Putting this debate in a larger context, it originates from the growing concerns with China's development strategy. Looking back, China's economic success has greatly benefited from its heavy state intervention. But looking forward, China is likely to be caught in the "middle-income trap," given the slowdown in growth rates and draining in production factors in recent years. So, shall China stick to its old state-led development strategy (Lin's suggestion) or shift to the market-enhancing approach (Zhang's point)?

To answer the question, the chapter suggests us to refer to the development experiences of China's neighbors, the newly industrializing economies (NIEs) in East Asia. As we know, almost all of them have taken a similar development

[1] The debate is on the Sina Website, http://finance.sina.com.cn/focus/lyfvszwy/.

W. Chen
Institute of Social Work and Social Policy, East China University of Science and Technology, Shanghai, China

S. Keng (✉)
School of Public Affairs, Zhejiang University, Hangzhou, Zhejiang, China

© The Author(s) 2019
J. Yu, S. Guo (eds.), *The Palgrave Handbook of Local Governance in Contemporary China*, https://doi.org/10.1007/978-981-13-2799-5_9

strategy long before China did and have achieved enormous success.[2] But, after these economies bid farewell to previous status of late developers, they have abandoned their state intervention strategy one after another.[3] Then, what can China learn from their experiences? In the authors' opinion, the country needs to gradually adjust its existing development strategy from state-led model to market-enhancing approach. Otherwise, China may be caught in the "middle-income trap," when the institutions a country used to achieve earlier-stage success later became its own constraints on its way to move on.

To develop that argument, the authors of this chapter first establish the similarities between the case of China in the reform era and the experiences of other East Asian developmental states in Sect. 2. We then move on to Sect. 3 to address the wave-like pattern of state intervention in East Asia: countries first take on but later give up the interventionist strategy on their way to climbing the ladder of economic development. In Sect. 4, in light of Chinese case studies and the experiences of East Asian NIEs, we argue about the limitations of the state-led approach in encouraging innovations, which is the primary source of sustainable growth. In Sect. 5, we conclude our research and claim that these findings not just shed new light on the general associations between development stages and development strategies but also offer some references for China and other countries on their way bidding farewell to economic backwardness.

2   Is China a Developmental State?

Does China also follow the model of state-led development, and is it a member of the family of the East Asian developmental states? There are still controversies over the issue.[4] In our opinion, the best approach is to contrast the similarities and differences between China and other East Asian cases. The more similarities they have, the more reasonable for China to learn from the experiences of its East Asian predecessors.

---

[2] The development model of these countries is called "Developmental State" which was prevailing between the 1980s and 1990s. See Johnson, *MITI and The Japanese Miracle: The Growth of Industrial Policy, 1925–1975*; Amsden, *Asia's Next Giant: South Korea and Late Industrialization*; Wade, *Governing the Market: Economic Theory and the Role of Government in East Asian Industrialization*; Woo-Cumings, *The Developmental State*.

[3] See Minns, "Of Miracles and Models: The Rise and Decline of the Developmental State in South Korea"; Cherry, "'Big Deal' or Big Disappointment? The Continuing Evolution of the South Korean Developmental State"; Pirie, *The Korean Developmental State: From Dirigisme to Neo-Liberalism*; Radice, "The Developmental State under Global Neo-Liberalism"; Chu, "Eclipse or Reconfigured? South Korea's Developmental State and Challenges of the Global Knowledge Economy"; Stubbs, "What Ever Happened to the East Asian Developmental State? The Unfolding Debate."

[4] Some scholars hold the same argument, such as Oi, "The Role of the Local State in China's Transitional Economy"; Leftwich, "Bringing Politics Back In: Towards a Model of the Developmental State"; Unger & Chan, "Corporatism in China: A Developmental State in an East Asian Context", some don't agree with us, such as Breslin, "China: Developmental State or Dysfunctional Development?"

The concept of developmental state originated from Chalmers Johnson's (1982) study of the Japanese experiences in the post-war era.[5] After setting economic growth as the country's first priority, the Japanese government adopted a series of "industrial policies," including expanding export market, protecting domestic market, and subsidizing favored industries, among others. These state intervention measures then brought deep industrial transformation and fast economic growth. In other words, it was the state that was behind the Japanese economic miracle. Following the same approach, Korea, Taiwan, and Singapore all achieved similar economic success.[6] This strategy, known as the "developmental state" model, has later gained considerable currency in academia. The strategy is of course centered on the role of the state. But it is still not very clear what would qualify as a developmental state? In this section, after reviewing the literature, the authors propose a two-dimensional definition of the developmental state: one being state capacity and the other industrial policy. The former refers to the political foundation, while the latter refers to policy tool of the state to take initiatives effectively. We can then use these qualifications to evaluate the development strategy and draw the boundary of developmental state.

To begin with, since we have both the capitalist developmental state and the socialist developmental state,[7] the distinction in political systems is not a critical criterion. What makes a developmental state then? In our opinion, all developmental states have the following two features. The first is the industrial policy the government used to achieve the compliance of the enterprises and individuals so as to follow its guidance to assure fast development.[8] Because almost all the developmental states are economically late developers, they need to mobilize their limited resources and concentrate them on strategic sectors/ industries, and industrial policy is the policy tool to attain the goal. If they fail to do so, it is difficult for them to survive the competition with advanced developers and let along to catch up with them quickly.[9] The key measures of industrial policy are: (1) pick up the strategic sectors/industries, which can produce long-term growth or generate spillovers to the economy and (2) intentionally "set the relative price wrong,"[10] so as to channel all their resources into those sectors/industries. Therefore, industrial policy is in this sense the state intervention itself and specific practices—such as direct subsidies, preferential loans, or trade protectionism—are but the manifestations of industrial policy.

---

[5] See Johnson, *MITI and The Japanese Miracle: The Growth of Industrial Policy, 1925–1975.*

[6] See Amsden, *Asia's Next Giant: South Korea and Late Industrialization*; Wade, *Governing the Market: Economic Theory and the Role of Government in East Asian Industrialization*; Huff, "The Developmental State, Government, and Singapore's Economic Development since 1960."

[7] White, *Developmental States in East Asia.*

[8] See Johnson, *MITI and The Japanese Miracle*; White, "Developmental State and socialist Industrialization in the Third World"; Amsden, *Asia's Next Gian*; Wade, *Governing the Market*; Öniş, "The Logic of the Developmental State."

[9] List, *The National System of Political Economy.*

[10] Amsden, *Asia's Next Gian*, 139–155.

But not every state can formulate the appropriate industrial policy and implement them faithfully and adequately. The country thus needs strong state capacity—the second feature of the developmental states—so that their industrial policy could be effectively carried out. In terms of state autonomy in bureaucratic decision-making and state strength in breaking social resistance, the state capacity is the political foundation for the successful developmental states. In his modern classic, Peter Evans illustrates the characteristics of state capacity, that is, embedded autonomy, the internal cohesion, and external connectedness of the state.[11] The internal cohesion helps insulate the bureaucratic elite from the special interests so as not to set the policy benefits them. The external connectedness helps bureaucratic elite to impose their will and overcome any resistance to the policy agenda. For all the developmental states, like Japan, Korea, and Chinese Taiwan, state capacity plus industrial policy constitute the two prerequisites for the mobilization, concentration, and coordination of the efforts toward economic development.

China's developmental strategy in the reform era is very similar to the model of developmental state, perfectly demonstrating the significance of industrial policy and state capacity. To begin with, the Chinese government loosened up regulations and encouraged the development of rural industries to meet the demands for consumer goods and to promote the market competition with state-owned enterprises (SOEs). The government then adopted the policy to effectively exploit the country's abundant factors (e.g., labor and land) and successfully attract the scarce factors (e.g., capital and technology), and turned itself as the manufacturing giant.[12] In recent years, the government went further to promote industrial upgrading, indigenous innovations, and the development of high-tech industry, seeking a transition from "made in China" to "created in China." Of course, all these policies and measures are backed up by the strong state ability to freely mobilize and allocate almost all the financial, human, and natural resources in the country and able to insulate itself from the penetration or capture of any special interests of the society.

Judging from these features, China is a typical case of developmental state and has little difference with its East Asian neighbors. But, of course, there are scholars who do not agree with this idea.[13] According to them, China's development experiences are fundamentally different from other East Asian cases, mainly due to following three aspects: (1) China's fragmented regulatory system, (2) China's inconsistent industrial policy, and (3) China's heavy reliance on foreign investment—thus, it should be considered a case of foreign direct investment (FDI)-driven industrialization. The authors of this chapter do not agree with these views and would like to go through the issues being raised.

---

[11] See Johnson, *MITI and The Japanese Miracle*; Evans, *Embedded Autonomy: States and Industrial Transformation* 1995.

[12] Lin et al., *The China miracle: Development strategy and economic reform*.

[13] Tsai, "Off Balance: The Unintended Consequences of Fiscal Federalism in China"; Breslin, China: Developmental State or Dysfunctional Development?"

To begin with, the Chinese state is being criticized as a "fragmented regulatory system," which is quite different from the coherent regulatory systems found in other East Asian developmental states. But for us, this has a lot to do with the sheer size of China. Compared with its East Asian neighbors, China is obviously too large and regional differences too huge. As a result, the central government of China has to devolve power and assign responsibilities to these local governments.[14] After all, these local governments are the only agents that can adjust the central policies to the local settings and address to local demands. There then emerges the division of labor between the central and local governments in China: the latter implements policy while the former, on the one hand, encourages the latter to take initiatives and, on the other hand, monitors them for any abuse of power. The central monitoring, however, normally has limitations, and therefore, local governments often have both the necessities and autonomy to do what they want. This is the reason why the "regulatory system" looks quite fragmented.

But there are two reasons that the Chinese case is still very similar to other East Asian cases. First is that the central government can still hold the local government under its strict control. In a centralized politic system like China, the central government has the full power to appoint and replace the leadership of the local government.[15] The local government can only somehow deviate from but can never change the policy agenda set by the central government. Second, if we look closer, China's local governments actually play the role of developmental state, just like the central government in other East Asian neighbors. This is the reason why the Chinese model is often characterized as the case of "local developmental state."[16] The central-local relations in China thus constitute the "developmental state with Chinese characteristics," but, based on the two core elements specified earlier, the Chinese system is still a case of developmental state.

Third, as for the issue of "inconsistent industrial policy," in our opinion, this has more to do with the uniqueness of the Chinese economic environment and less to do with the strategy of economic development. As a late-latecomer, China faces worse foreign competition and has less time to go through the economic catch-up. Also different from most other East Asian economies, all being capitalist systems ever since and all emerging in the stable post-war bipolarity, China has made a difficult transition from plan to market economy and its catch-up has gone through the transformation from the pre- to the post-globalization era. In this sense, the Chinese case is typically a case of "compressed development,"[17] and thus require for more flexibilities to cope with the

---

[14] Harding, *China's Second Revolution: Reform after Mao*; Baum, *Burying Mao: Chinese Politics in the Age of Deng Xiaoping*.

[15] Li and Zhou, "Political turnover and economic performance: The incentive role of personnel control in China."

[16] White, *The Chinese State in the Era of Economic Reform*; Oi, "The Role of the Local State in China's Transitional Economy"; Blecher & Shue, *Tethered Deer: Government and Economy in a Chinese County*.

[17] Whittaker et al., "Compressed development."

fast-changing environment.[18] Therefore, the fast adjustments of industrial policy should be understood as the appropriate responses to the outside environment rather than the "inconsistency in industrial policy." If put in the same situation as China, in our opinion, every other East Asian developmental state would very likely act just like China does. In other words, the issue of "inconstant industrial policy" has more to do with the situations of the late-late developers and transitional economy, and not much to do with the nature of being a developmental state.

The final issue has to do with the China's reliance on FDI and being considered as a case of FDI-led industrialization. This, of course, has to do with the timing and environment of China's economic takeoff. Unlike other East Asian developmental states—they all emerged from 1950s to 1980s, that is, the pre-globalization era—China initiated its post-Mao reforms in the December of 1978 and thus placed its economic catch-up in the context of expanding globalization. Therefore, all the keywords in the global era, such as capital flow, module production, and economy outsourcing, are associated with China's economic development. Being placed in such a context, of course, China has to make best use of the foreign capital and technology and then expand its exports to occupy foreign markets so as to facilitate its economic development.[19] Therefore, the exploitation of FDI again has more to do with the timing of China's economic takeoff and almost nothing to do with being a developmental state.

In a nutshell, no matter the use of industrial policies or the reliance on state capacity, China is a typical case of developmental state. The differences between China and other East Asian developmental states—such as the role of local government, the changes in economic policy, and the dependence of foreign capital—are just the responses of the Chinese government to its situations and environment. As we know, there are also major variations among the classical cases of developmental state, like Japan, Korea, and Taiwan. These variations are also the response of each economy when dealing with their own conditions. These variations thus should not be understood as the reasons to deny China as another case of the developmental state.

Once we confirm that China is one of the members of the East Asian family of developmental states, the next question is: can China learn from the development experiences of other members? This is the topic of the following section.

3   The Transformations of the Developmental States in East Asia

Looking back, China has greatly benefited from its interventionist strategy and has achieved enormous economic success. But looking forward, given the economic slowdown in recent years, China is very likely to be caught in the

---

[18] Zhu, "Compressed development, flexible practices, and multiple traditions in China's rise."

[19] Zweig, *Internationalizing China: Domestic Interests and Global Linkages.*

"middle-income trap." So, should China still stick to its old state-led development strategy or shall the country shift to a new market-oriented approach? In our opinion, since China is one of the families of East Asian developmental states, China certainly can learn from those who are "one step ahead" of the country. As we can see, after a decade of fast growth, after entering into the 1990s, the economic performance of these East Asian economies was not all that shining any more: they faced financial crisis, economic stagnation, and, in some cases, political turnovers and turmoil. In the end, they have all adjusted their earlier interventionist policy.

When confronting the decline of East Asian developmental states, some other scholars stress the limitations of industrial policy, the policy tools of state intervention. In this regard, Paul Krugman first addresses the issue and claims that the state intervention strategy in East Asia is essentially input-driven rather than efficient-driven, and the strategy can only bring about short-term growth and prosperity.[20] Similarly, the study of the Japanese case also found that the country's industrial policy in the early post-war era (the "catch-up stage") played an important and positive role, but when shifting to the new contest in the 1980s, the same set of industrial policies soon lost its significance and effectiveness.[21] In other words, the similar state capacity and the similar industrial policy may exert different influences and end up with completely different consequences at different stages of development.

The significance of development stage can also be seen in the development experiences of the three East Asian cases. To begin with, Japan has been very successful by relying on the guidance and supervision of the bureaucratic elite (like the Ministry of Foreign Trade, MITI) during the post-war years until the 1980s. However, after reaching the position of economic leader, the Japanese bureaucrats soon lost their effectiveness: they made major mistakes in the development of Information Technology (IT) industry and other areas. As a result, the industrial policy was no guarantee for Japan's economic success and the country then fell into the years of long recession, often referred to as "the lost 20 years."

Similarly, Korea's early development strategy is very similar to that of Japan's, only the state intervention is more extensive and direct in Korea. And this development strategy has brought the countries the fastest growth in the world. However, when Korea also climbed the ladder and reached close to the position of economic leader, the country still stuck to the "scale-first policy." The policy to promote innovations is not very effective, and the country is soon running out of growth momentum. Consequently, Korea was threatened by the economic slowdown in 2010s. Finally, the Taiwanese case is similar, but it draws economic dynamics mainly from small- and medium-sized enterprises. As a result, the Taiwanese enterprises are very good at the original equipment manufacturer (OEM) model of production. The model of government-led

[20] Krugman, "The Myth of Asia's Miracle."
[21] Vestal, *Planning for Change: Industrial Policy and Japanese Economic Development*, 1945–1990.

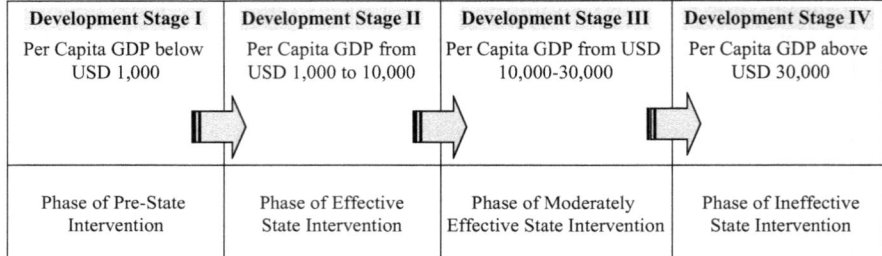

Development Stage I	Development Stage II	Development Stage III	Development Stage IV
Per Capita GDP below USD 1,000	Per Capita GDP from USD 1,000 to 10,000	Per Capita GDP from USD 10,000-30,000	Per Capita GDP above USD 30,000
Phase of Pre-State Intervention	Phase of Effective State Intervention	Phase of Moderately Effective State Intervention	Phase of Ineffective State Intervention

Fig. 9.1 The relationship between development stage and the effectiveness of state intervention. Note: when setting the stages, the authors refer to the pattern of "middle-income trap." For that pattern, please refer to Indermit Singh Gill, Homi J. Kharas and Deepak Bhattasali, *An East Asian Renaissance: Ideas for Economic Growth*, Washington, DC: World Bank, 2007

technological innovations used to work in the 1970s and 1980s but soon failed when entering the new millennium. After that, although the Taiwanese government has kept trying but none of the policies worked. And the economic growth has also been slowing down.

To summarize the experiences of these East Asian developmental states, we find that the state intervention has its strengths and limitations. It applies only to the economies at the "catch-up phase" but not the "leading phase." In this sense, even though we can maintain a strong state and can keep the interventionist policy, it won't work forever. As the economy moves along the ladder and a state becomes a leader, we still have to give it up and shift to other strategies more capable of encouraging innovations. This is the logic behind the wave-like pattern of the state intervention and the rises and falls of developmental states. The relationship between development stage and the effectiveness of state intervention is illustrated in Fig. 9.1.

4   Limitations of the State Intervention in Promoting Innovations

Why development stages matter, if they do make the differences? To answer the question, we can draw examples from the Chinese case. As we can see from the abovementioned wave-like pattern of state intervention, China is about to cross the ladder from Stage II to Stage III. In other words, the interventionist strategy used to create the "China miracle" is about to lose its effectiveness and significance. But without knowing that, the country is still relying on the same strategy for sustainable growth: the primary focus is state-led technological upgrading and innovations. In this section, we are going to use two case studies from the solar energy industry to show why the state intervention may not work well in the promotion of innovations.

4.1   Two Case Studies from China's Solar Energy Industry

Similar to other East Asian developmental states, China also heavily relies on state intervention and industrial policy for economic growth. But different from their neighbors, China is much bigger than all of them, even when all are put together. Therefore, in China, the apparatus that formulate and implement industrial policy is local government. They have been widely accepted as the generator of China's economic miracle in the 1990s. When China was ready for industrial upgrading from labor-intensive and OEM-driven growth (about mid-2000s), the Chinese local government started to propose new initiatives calling for "technological upgrading and indigenous innovations." One of their new foci is the solar energy/photovoltaic (PV) industry, converting solar energy through silicon materials into electricity. The PV system is considered to be a safe, reliable, and cleanest way to generate power. Following the IT and microelectronics, the PV industry is increasingly becoming the primary concern of China's central and local governments: it becomes the symbol of high-tech industry and China's new hope for sustainable growth.

In year 2012, under the leadership of former Premier, Wen Jiabao, the State Council announced a complete policy package to encourage the development of PV industry. Soon after that, when facing all kinds of disadvantages, on June 14, 2013, the State Council again announced the Six Measures to Promote the Photovoltaic Industry (known as the *Guoliutiao*, the Six Measures of the State). It is very rare, if not unprecedented, to set a full policy agenda for just one single industry, meaning that the Chinese government has set the development of PV industry as the top priority in the country's National Strategic Development Plan. Under the sponsorship of the government, the PV industry is growing fast. To cite the statistics provided by the Ministry of Industry and Information Technology, the industry has increased 30% in just the first half of 2015. The average of net profit margin of all the 29 PV companies has increased by 6.5%. This is the reason why we chose the PV industry as our research topic. In the past several years, we have conducted field research on some of the PV companies and have still been following them closely. Most of the companies we have studied fall into the two categories. We thus pick one from each pattern as example to illustrate the problem of state-led technological innovations.

4.2   Shangde Photovoltaic: Concentration of Resources and Amassing Risks

Shangde is a company located in the Wuxi, a prefectural-level city, in Jiangsu Province. It is registered as a joint-venture high-tech enterprise in the new energy sector, but most of the investment comes from China, via bank loans and stock market. In the mid-2000s, the company was the biggest PV manufacturer in China and the fourth largest solar cell producer in the world. It started in 2001 and declared bankruptcy in 2013; in the short span of ten years, Shangde moved from being a nobody to the industry leader position—was successfully listed in the New York Stock Exchange in 2005 in just four years—and finally a disaster. The ups and downs of the company have a lot to do with the support of the government of Wuxi.

It is the support of the Wuxi government that created Shangde's PV empire. In 2001, the founder of the enterprise, with technical expertise and professional experience, returned to China and contacted the Wuxi government, seeking support from the government to establish a PV factory in the locality. It was about time that the idea of Green Energy was introduced to China—the ideal looked great, full of potential. The Wuxi government then decided to offer full support for the new industry, hoping to make itself the leader of the industry in China. The government not just used the government fund but also forced the local SOEs to make their first investment of US$ 6.5 million: this was how the Shangde was created. After that, Wuxi government mobilized several additional investments and, to let the company run healthily, asked the SOE to withdraw from Shangde. With these helpful and positive efforts, the company finally got good reviews and successfully listed itself on New York Stock Exchange, the first non-state enterprise that has ever done so in China.

However, it is also the government's unlimited support that affected the decision of Shangde and finally brought down the promising company. With the strong support of local governments, Shangde bid on the future markets and underestimated the risks, continuing to attract investment and expand productivity, trying to use scale rather than technology to create profits and deter competitors. However, PV manufacturing was a new industry: both technology and costs involved enormous amount of uncertainty. The company soon made two big mistakes. First, it invested a huge amount of money on the R&D of the non-mainstream thin-film battery. This resulted in repeated failures. But all the failures later led to even larger investments. The other mistake was being too optimistic about the future market; Shangde signed a ten-year fixed-priced contract with one of the major suppliers for the required silicon material. Later, abrupt recession in the PV industry made this contract a disaster for the company.

After many failures and facing mounting financial pressures, most other companies would have learnt from their past experiences and would have been conservative in expansion. But with the support of local government, the company tried to make itself "too big to fall" and thus kept expanding even during hard times. Once, the mayor of Wuxi city had to call for a meeting in Shangde, asking the local banks to stop collecting debts and offer more short-term loans. With unlimited support like this, Shangde repeatedly borrowed loans, expanded production capacity, and put itself at high risk. In the end, even the Wuxi government could not bail it out. Shangde declared bankruptcy.

4.3 Linuo Photovoltaic: Difficulties in Monitoring and Failed Policy Implementation

Linuo Ruite, located in Jinan City in Shandong Province, is registered as a joint venture with Chinese and German investments in the solar energy industry. The company is also one of the major producers in the PV industry. Different from Shangde, which produced upstream products only, Linuo was famous for its consumer products, especially the solar water heater. The company introduced the technology of solar heater from Germany and thus won over international recognition, such as the certification of ISO9001, ISO14001 and the European Solar Keymark, Australian AS2712, German TUV, and the United States SRCC, among others. In addition, Linuo also applied and won over the "China Famous Brand," "National Customer Satisfaction Product," and other honors in China. All these seem to suggest that Linuo was a high-tech company specializing in technological innovation to pursue its competitiveness.

Actually, a close look suggests that Linuo was not just a high-tech company, it was especially good in its relationship with the local government. As a result, the company always had access to almost every preferential policy for innovations offered by national or provincial government and that was where Linuo drew its profits from. For example, Linuo was the only company in the solar energy industry that had obtained the status of "State Base of Housing Commercialization," the only company in the field of new energy industry winning the honor of "National Torch Prize," and one of the few companies supported by the special fund of the "Special Grants for the High-Tech Industries in the field of Renewable and New Energy." These grants did not just bring subsidies to the company but also empowered it to gain the support of local government, especially on raising loans and procure land. The most miraculous achievement of Linuo was that the company lobbied the local government to pass the "Regulations on Compulsory Installation" (of clean energy) in all the new buildings in Jinan city. Understandably, with all these government support, Linuo soon became a monster in the field.

But, again, a closer look at the company suggests that Linuo, although greatly benefitting from different kinds of preferential policies, was not involved in technological innovations. The company spent a lot of time and effort on promoting its reputation and lobbying for government-channeled resources. Linuo built a magnificent multipurpose exhibition hall, hosting visitors from all over the world every day. Its executives would take the trouble to introduce the company and let the visitors meet each other, with various photos of CEOs meeting VIPs hanging in every corner of the enterprise. In order to enhance its visibility, Linuo also spent a lot of money signing a contract with Cuba to export solar water heaters to that "Chinese friend," as a sign of the international recognition of Linuo's solar energy technology. However, our interviews suggest that their so-called innovations were cheap and just for the purposes of decoration: the key technology was purchased from Germany and its hundreds of "technical patents" were mostly about the design of the look of the products. There were no real innovations in their products.

Although Linuo was a very successful company for some time, all the government's efforts to encourage innovative ideas had obviously failed. The company relied on the "Regulations on Compulsory Installation," and its capability of getting loans and land soon turned it into a real estate developer. Supported by the slogans like "green energy" and "high technology," Linuo built some "Exemplary Projects" (*shifan jidi*) and soon became a super successful housing developer. But, of course, in the end, Linuo had expanded too fast and got involved in several cases of corruption. Its CEO was later sent to prison, and the company went down with these cases.

4.4   The Effectiveness of State Intervention in Different Stages of Development

The two cases described earlier suggest the two mechanisms of how government support" might not be effective in promoting innovations. In the first case, a capable government offered support for the development of a promising industry. It was a case of "right time, right place, and right people," only difference being that the high-tech industry was also a high-risk sector. The government's support encouraged Shangde to expand the scale of production and to improve its competitiveness. But when a new technology is not mature yet, the investment in high-tech could be very risky and, consequently, the larger the scale/investment of the company is, the more risky the company becomes. The strategy of "contraction and scale" used to work very well in the "catch-up" stage, but can only lead to the mounting risks in the "leading stage."

The second one is a typical case of "monitoring failure." The subsidies provided by the government attract a group of corporations chasing for policy rents. But the real question is even with some rent-seekers, the government used to work pretty effectively and crated remarkable economic growth. Why has the same policy totally lost its effectiveness now? This has a lot to do with its development stage. In the "catch-up stage," the government can borrow from successful experiences, and it should know what should be encouraged and how to implement these preferential policies. When it moves up to the "leading stage," there are no predecessors anymore and the government does not really know what should be invested and has no clear standards to assess and monitor the innovations. And weak monitoring then encourages the companies to chase the rents generated from government efforts for economic development.

Based on the East Asian country experiences and Chinese case experiences, we can establish a framework for the association and the mechanism linking the "development stages" to the "effectiveness of state intervention." In the "catch-up stage," the government of late developers can learn from the successful experiences of predecessors, and thus have clear direction of what to

Table 9.1   The effectiveness of state intervention in two different stages of economic development

The catch-up stage of economic development		The leading stage of economic development	
Informational advantages	Clear direction and effective monitoring	Informational disadvantages	Unclear direction and ineffective monitoring
Economy of scale	Concentration of resources and large-scale production	Diseconomy of scale	Path-dependence and amassing risks

encourage and develop and have much clearer standards for policy implementation. But when moving on to the "leading stage," the government can no longer be sure of what should be encouraged and how to monitor to guarantee its realization. The state intervention can work well in the former stage and lose its effectiveness in the latter stage.

On the other hand, during the "catch-up stage," the government of the late developers, after learning from the successful experiences and being sure about the direction, can mobilize and concentrate all the resources to one or few strategic sectors that most effectively contribute to the country's development. The concentration leads to scale and then greatly improves the competiveness of the country's industry so that the country can survive and catch up. But once moving forward to the "leading stage," the concentration of resources and the scale of production become a really risky business and end up with disastrous results.

Based on these analyses, we can come up with an analytical framework, showing why state interventions tend to be effective (and is probably the only way out) at the earlier stage of development but may not be that effective in the latter phase of development (as being summarized in Table 9.1). Based on this, we can gain insights about the abovementioned wave-like pattern of state intervention and the rises and falls of the developmental state in East Asia.

5   Looking Forward to China's Future Economy Strategy

In the latter half of 2016, a debate attracted widespread attention in China. Two eminent economists, Justin Yi-Fu Lin and Wei-Ying Zhang, had a heated debate over the effectiveness of industrial policy. Putting it in a larger context, we shall know that the debate originates from the concern with China's future development strategy. Looking back, China's economic success has greatly benefited from its heavy state intervention. But looking forward, however, China may very likely be caught in the so-called middle-income trap, given the slowdown in economic growth and draining of demographic dividends in the past decade. Then, should today's China still stick to its previous state-led development (Lin's view) or shift to the market-enhancing strategy (Zhang's point)?

To answer the question, this chapter compares the development experiences of China and other East Asian economies. Many of these economies have taken the similar development strategy long before China, but most of them have now given up that strategy one after another. Judging from their experiences and also taking into account the historical experiences of the five waves of catch-up countries, the authors conclude that a wave-like pattern of state intervention is desirable, similar to Friedrich List's "first use the ladder and then kick the ladder" metaphor. Following List's rationale, the authors then divide the development experiences into two development stages: the "catch-up stage" and the "leading stage." In the former phase, facing intense competition from foreign countries, the late-developers' only option was to introduce heavy state intervention. But after years of growing and upgrading, these latecomers have been promoted to the "leading stage." These economies then do not need and cannot be greatly benefited from the state intervention strategy, and many of them have started to abandon the interventionist policy.

To sum up, in this chapter, the authors seek to establish an analytical framework to show why and how development stages matter, and use the East Asian countries and Chinese PV enterprises as examples to illustrate its validity. The findings of the chapter then not just shed new light on the general associations between development stages and development strategies but also offer additional references for the countries that are on their way to bidding farewell to economic backwardness. For the authors, today's China is struggling with both the advantages and disadvantages of heavy state intervention. But we believe that as China keeps climbing the ladder of development, the country still has to give up the state patronage approach and focus more on the institutional infrastructure paving the way for healthy market completion. This is what China can learn from its East Asian neighbors.

References

Amsden, A., *Asia's Next Giant: South Korea and Late Industrialization*, New York: Oxford University Press, 1989.

Baum, R., *Burying Mao: Chinese Politics in the Age of Deng Xiaoping*, Princeton University Press, 1996.

Blecher, M. J., & V. Shue, *Tethered Deer: Government and Economy in a Chinese County*, Stanford University Press, 1996.

Breslin, S. G., "China: Developmental State or Dysfunctional Development?" *Third World Quarterly* 17, No. 4 (1996): 689–706.

Cherry, J., "'Big Deal' or Big Disappointment? The Continuing Evolution of the South Korean Developmental State," *Pacific Review* 18, No. 3 (2005): 327–354.

Chu, Yin-wah, "Eclipse or Reconfigured? South Korea's Developmental State and Challenges of the Global Knowledge Economy," *Economy and Society* 38, No. 2 (2009): 278–303.

Evans, P., *Embedded Autonomy: States and Industrial Transformation*, Princeton: Princeton University Press, 1995.

Harding, H., *China's Second Revolution: Reform after Mao*, Brookings Institution Press, 1987.

Huff, W. G., "The Developmental State, Government, and Singapore's Economic Development since 1960," *World Development* 23, No. 8 (1995): 1421–1438.

Johnson, C., *MITI and The Japanese Miracle: The Growth of Industrial Policy, 1925–1975*, Stanford, CA: Stanford University Press, 1982.

Krugman, P., "The myth of Asia's miracle." *Foreign Affairs* 73, No. 6 (1994): 62–78.

Leftwich, A., "Bringing Politics Back In: Towards a Model of the Developmental State," *Journal of Development Studies* 31, No. 3 (1995): 400–427.

Li, Hongbin, & Li-An Zhou, "Political Turnover and Economic Performance: The Incentive Role of Personnel Control in China", *Journal of Public Economics* 89 (2005): 1743–1762.

Lin, Justin Yifu, Fang Cai, & Zhou Li, *The China miracle: Development strategy and economic reform*. Chinese University Press, 2003.

List, Friedrich, *National system of political economy: The Two Narratives of Political Economy*. New York: Wiley, 2011.

Minns, J., "Of Miracles and Models: The Rise and Decline of the Developmental State in South Korea", *Third World Quarterly* 22, No. 6 (2001): 1025–1043.

Oi, J. C., "The Role of the Local State in China's Transitional Economy," *China Quarterly* 144 (1995): 1132–1149.

Öniş, Ziya, "The Logic of the Developmental State," *Comparative Politics* 24, No. 1 (1991): 109–126.

Pirie, I., *The Korean Developmental State: From Dirigisme to Neo-Liberalism*. Routledge, 2007.

Radice, H., "The Developmental State under Global Neo-Liberalism," *Third World Quarterly* 29, No. 6 (2008): 1153–1174.

Stubbs, R., "What Ever Happened to the East Asian Developmental State? The Unfolding Debate," *Pacific Review* 22, No. 1 (2009): 1–22.

Tsai, K.S., "Off Balance: The Unintended Consequences of Fiscal Federalism in China," *Journal of Chinese Political Science* 9, No. 2 (2004): 7–26.

Unger, J., & A. Chan, "Corporatism in China: A Developmental State in an East Asian Context," in Jonathan Unger & Anita Chan eds., *China after Socialism: In the Footsteps of Eastern Europe or East Asia*, M. E. Sharpe (1996): 95–129.

Vestal, J., *Planning for Change: Industrial Policy and Japanese Economic Development, 1945–1990*, Oxford: Clarendon, 1993.

Wade, R., *Governing the Market: Economic Theory and the Role of Government in East Asian Industrialization*, Princeton, NJ: Princeton University Press, 1990.

White, G., "Developmental State and socialist Industrialization in the Third World", *Journal of Development Studies* 21, No. 1 (1984): 97–120.

White, G., ed., *Developmental States in East Asia*, Springer, 1988.

White, G., ed., *The Chinese State in the Era of Economic Reform: The Road to Crisis*, Armonk, NY: M.E. Sharpe, 1991.

Whittaker, D. Hugh, et al., "Compressed development," *Studies in Comparative International Development* 45, No. 4 (2010): 439–467.

Woo-Cumings, Meredith, ed., *The Developmental State*, Ithaca: Cornell University Press, 1991.

Zhu, Tianbiao, "Compressed development, flexible practices, and multiple traditions in China's rise." *Sinicization and the rise of China: Civilizational processes beyond East and West* (2012): 99–119.

Zweig, D., *Internationalizing China: Domestic Interests and Global Linkages*, Ithaca and London: Cornell University Press, 2002.

CHAPTER 10

The Behavioral Logic and Institutional Basis of Chinese Local Developmental Government

Jianxing Yu and Xiang Gao

1 Introduction

The local government is the key to understanding the Chinese government. After the reform and opening-up in the 1980s, China has implemented decentralization by delegating socioeconomic authorities and fiscal autonomy to local governments. Since then, local governments, referring to the prefectural and county-level governments, have not only become the main implementer of central policies but have been in charge of local governance as well. To enhance state capacity, the central government aims to recentralize its power by introducing the tax-sharing system in 1994 and vertical management of key areas, such as the banking system, the administration for industry and commerce, the administration of quality supervision, and so on. However, the central government also made a few concessions in order to convince provinces to accept the new taxation system, which resulted in a consolidation of administrative decentralization. According to the National Bureau of Statistics, local governments' expenditure accounted for 85% of the national public budget expenditure in 2015, and the proportion of local expenditure even exceeded 90% in the item of general public services; education; culture, sports, and media; social safety net and employment effort; environmental protection; agriculture, forestry, and water conservation; as well as transportation. Local governments' expenditure for medical care, health services, and family planning, and for urban and rural community affairs, even exceeded 99% of the national government expenditure.

J. Yu • X. Gao (✉)
School of Public Affairs, Zhejiang University, Hangzhou, Zhejiang, China
e-mail: yujianxing@zju.edu.cn; gaoxiang0327@zju.edu.cn

© The Author(s) 2019
J. Yu, S. Guo (eds.), *The Palgrave Handbook of Local Governance in Contemporary China*, https://doi.org/10.1007/978-981-13-2799-5_10

Yet the role of the Chinese local government in economic and social development has received two different evaluations. On the one hand, the role of the local government in promoting economic development has been widely praised and is considered an important driving factor in promoting China's rapid economic development (White 1991). It was shown that there is a positive correlation between fiscal decentralization and economic growth (Lin and Liu 2000; Zhang and Zou 1998; Wong 1992), and that administrative decentralization helps improve economic efficiency (Shi and Zhou 2007) On the other hand, the provision of public services by the Chinese local government has been criticized. After the decentralization, the level of public expenditure for basic public services, such as education, medical care, and health services has not been increased correspondingly, and this is regarded as an important factor contributing to social disparity and causing social injustice (Riskin 2010). Since the 1990s, the proportion of expenditures on social services, culture, and education has been maintained at approximately 25%, whereas expenditures on economic construction, although gradually decreasing, were still as high as 26.56% in 2006. Moreover, the level of rural public service supply has been rather low (Tsai 2007). Based on the behavior of local governments described earlier, some scholars proposed the concepts of "local developmental government," "local entrepreneurial state" (Blecher 1991), and "local state corporatism" (Oi 1995). We generally refer to the local government with the abovementioned behavioral characteristics as "local developmental government," referring to the "government in developing countries that takes promoting the economic development as the main target, acts as the main force of economic development as the main way, and uses economic growth as the main source of political legitimacy in the process of transforming into a modern industrial society" (Yu and Xu 2004).

Why does the local government ignore the responsibility to provide public services while actively performing the function of economic development? What causes local governments to experience difficulties in changing the behavior patterns associated with developmental government? To answer these questions, we first examine two competing interpretations of the Chinese local government: "fiscal federalism with Chinese characteristics" and "decentralized authoritarianism." The former focuses on the influence of the decentralized fiscal system on local government behavior and argues that local governments have gained some autonomy after decentralization and has become a local developmental government under the guidelines of maximizing financial returns. The latter emphasizes the effectiveness of the central government's control over local governments and holds that the central government, after decentralization, still maintains a vertical accountability mechanism through the mastery of the power of appointment and removal of personnel, thus, ensuring that the local government's behavior falls within the limits prescribed by the central authorities. Therefore, the local developmental government is the reflection of the central government's developmentalist ideology.

Undoubtedly, both the decentralized fiscal system and the vertical accountability mechanism are the key institutional arrangements that affect the local government's behavior. However, do they have the same impact on the local government? To discern the behavioral logic of the local developmental government and its institutional basis, we choose two cases of local government's social policy innovation under the background of New Countryside Construction is a project initiated by the central government policy agenda on the behavior of local governments. In both cases, the fiscal system remains unchanged, so we could identify the primary and secondary relationships of the vertical accountability mechanism and the fiscal system in forming local government behavior. Both cases show that the change in the central government's policy agenda is not always the root of the local governments' social policy innovation; instead, promoting economic growth and increasing fiscal revenue are the priorities of local governments, and through these priorities local governments have formed a new type of developmental government that uses social policy innovation as an instrument.

Why is it difficult for local governments to transform from a developmental government to a service-oriented government? By examining the institutional basis of local developmental government, we find that decentralization of the fiscal system is not a necessary and sufficient condition for the formation of the local developmental government. After decentralization, the horizontal accountability mechanism has not been well developed, while the vertical accountability mechanism has obvious limitations. Without effective restrictions from both sides, local governments' independent behavior expands continuously, ultimately resulting in "decentralization with limited accountability." This has caused the maximization of fiscal revenue to gradually assume a dominant position and has led to local governments' selective function fulfillment, thereby giving rise to local developmental government.

Compared with the existing literature on China's local developmental government, our findings confirm the dominant position of maximization of fiscal revenue in shaping local government behavior. It shows that changes in the higher levels of government's policy agenda have not brought about changes in the behavior patterns of local governments but rather have resulted in the formation of a new type of local developmental government. Regarding the viewpoint of "decentralized authoritarianism," we find that the vertical accountability mechanism is limited and that although the central government has a strong despotic power at the local level, the infrastructural power of high-level government is obviously insufficient due to some factors, such as information asymmetry. Therefore, although the central government has a certain impact on local government behavior, changes in its policy agenda do not fundamentally reverse the behavior patterns of local governments. While recognizing the explanatory power of "fiscal federalism with Chinese characteristics," we also note that the decentralized fiscal system does not necessarily improve the level at which public services are supplied nor does it represent the root cause of the creation of local developmental government. "Decentralization with limited accountability," that is, local government behavior lacking external restraints, including unsophisticated horizontal accountability mechanisms, such as the local People's Congress, the judicial system, and so on, and the limitations of the vertical accountability mechanism with the power of appointment and removal of personnel at the core, is the institutional basis for local governments' selective implementation of functions.

2   The Formation of Local Developmental Government in China: Two Competing Theories

Decentralization offers a starting point for discussing local developmental government in contemporary China. However, regarding the factors that influence the behavior patterns of local governments under the background of decentralization, there are two different viewpoints. The first viewpoint emphasizes the autonomy of local government and argues that fiscal decentralization has caused local governments to form local interests that are relatively independent of the central government and, thus, to selectively implement government functions that are beneficial to maximizing local financial returns. The second viewpoint focuses on the regulation and guidance of local governments by the central government and points out that by controlling the power of appointment and removal of personnel and constructing the political tournament mechanism, the central government achieves effective control over local governments; thus, local governments' selective implementation of functions is essentially the reflection of the priority of the policy targets of high-level government.

The theory of "fiscal federalism with Chinese characteristics" holds that decentralization after the reform and opening-up has reconstructed China's central-local relations and achieved a check on the power of the central government (Montinola, Qian and Weingast 1995). Indeed, the fiscal contract system implemented in the 1980s has greatly weakened the central government's financial capacity; in 1993, the central government accounted for only 22% of the national fiscal revenue and lacked sufficient capacity to exercise macro-control, let alone to interfere in local economic and social affairs. The decline in the central government's ability to gather revenues weakened the state's ability to regulate and legitimize, leading to a situation in which the central government lost support (Wang and Hu 1994). Since then, tax-sharing reform has often been regarded as an important symbol of the fiscal recentralization of the central government. However, affected by factors, such as tax returns, the central government's revenue not only failed to increase significantly but slightly decreased in 1994 and did not reach and maintain a level of 40% until after the 16th National Congress of the Communist Party of China (CPC). More importantly, the reduction in budgetary income has led local governments to begin to seek more additional budgetary income from other sources, such as land leasing and creating the area of "land finance" (Li and Luo 2010).

Since then, although the central government stipulated that land-transferring fees should be included in budget management, it still failed to grasp the extent of the revenue and expenditure of local governments' land-transferring fees. After 2008, local governments were allowed to have their own financing platforms, an arrangement that further enhanced the autonomy of local governments' financial management and weakened the ability of the central authorities to regulate and guide local governments' behavior by means of financial instruments (Zhao 2013). Under the condition that the central authority is checked, local governments have gradually evolved into "a subject with special interest and preference" in the process of marketization (He 2007) and have been able to realize their administrative goals according to their own wills, giving rise to "de facto federalism." It is also difficult for the central government to unilaterally impose its will on the provinces and to change the distribution of power at all levels of the local government (Zheng 2007).

So what is the "unique interest and preference" of local governments? Scholars believe that under the decentralized fiscal system local governments face constraints due to limited budgets and must manage local finance in a more reasonable way. However, fiscal reform also assigned to local governments' property rights over increased income and, thus, created strong incentives for local officials to pursue local economic development (Oi 1992). In the 1980s, under a financial structure in which the main sources of government income were enterprise income tax, circulation tax, and industrial and commercial taxes, local governments made the promotion of industrial and commercial development the focus of governance and "acting as the equivalent of a board of directors," thereby engaging in "local state corporatism" (Oi 1992). After the reform of the tax-sharing system, the contribution of the value-added tax (VAT) to the local financial income shrunk, local governments' motivation for enriching enterprises no longer existed, and township enterprises were also dying (Zhou 2006). Accordingly, because of the increasing contribution of sales tax (mainly from construction and tertiary industries) and land finance to local revenue, local governments changed from "managing enterprises" to "managing cities" (Zhou 2010). On the whole, although local governments participated in different forms of economic development in different periods, the essence of their "seizing the initiative of economic development," from which the behavior pattern of the local developmental government was reconstructed, has not fundamentally changed (Cao and Shi 2009).

Another theory emphasizes that the central government still exercises strong control over local governments by firmly grasping the power of appointment and removal of personnel, giving rise to decentralized authoritarianism (Landry 2008). In practice, the central government has indeed never given up its intervention in, and guidance of, local government behavior. First, in the 1980s, the central government began to stress adherence to the principle of the "Party Manages Cadre." In the more than 30 years that have elapsed since then, the central government repeatedly reiterated this principle; for example, in the "Regulation of the Selection and Appointment of Party and Government Leaders" issued in January 2014, the leadership position of the party committee in cadre appointment was once again stressed. Second, the tax-sharing reform implemented in the mid-1990s increased the total revenue of the central government and strengthened its regulatory capacity. As a result, the central government has been able to use its resources to reward "better-performing" areas using intergovernmental transfer payments (Naughton 2008) and direct local governments to implement certain specific policies based on funded mandates (Qu 2012). Third, since the mid-1990s, the central government has begun to test the centralization of administrative power by creating a vertical administration of local branches and agencies that had been set up by the central government or the provincial governments (Shen 2009). Although the executive branches that were included in the vertical management were situated at the local level, their formulation, funding, personnel, and operations were directly managed by the central authorities and, thus, detached from the management sequence of local governments to ensure effective implementation of the central government's policies and regulations. Therefore, decentralization generated the "principle-agent" mode of Chinese government functions; at the same time, the central government has never given up the supervision and control of local governments but has merely adopted various methods to improve the vertical accountability mechanism in such a way as to target local governments (Landry 2008).

Both "fiscal federalism with Chinese characteristics" and "decentralized authoritarianism" have some explanatory power with respect to the formation of China's local developmental government. However, which logic, local autonomy-based revenue maximization or vertical accountability to the high-level government, dictates the behavior pattern of local governments? According to the interpretation of "decentralized authoritarianism," once the central government is determined to adjust the priority of its policies, the transformation of the local government to a service-oriented government is just around the corner. But, if the interpretation of "fiscal federalism with Chinese characteristics" is adopted, how can the decentralized fiscal system shape the local developmental governments but not effectively improve local governments' public service delivery? Is centralization the only way to ensure the full implementation of government functions? Undoubtedly, deciphering the dominant logic that governs the behavior patterns of local governments is not only of theoretical significance but is also a precondition for promoting the transformation of the Chinese government function. Based on such an understanding, we choose two cases of local government innovation in the social policy field against the background of New Countryside Construction, focusing on the relationship between the central government policy orientation and local government policy innovation, especially the extent to which local governments respond to the central government's policies.

3 PROMOTING ECONOMIC DEVELOPMENT WITH SOCIAL POLICIES: A NEW TYPE OF LOCAL DEVELOPMENTAL GOVERNMENT

Implementing New Countryside Construction is an important measure that was adopted by the central government to narrow the gap between urban and rural areas and promote social equity and justice, highlighting the government's emphasis on the public service function. In October 2005, the 5th Plenum of the 16th CPC Central Committee adopted the proposal of developing "the 11th Five-Year Plan" and for the first time put forward the goal and task of building the Socialist New Countryside. In March 2006, the National People's Congress passed the "Outline of the 11th Five-Year Plan for National Economic and Social Development in the People's Republic of China" and began to regard "building the Socialist New Countryside" as the government's important policy agenda. The plan emphasized that "promoting coordinated urban–rural development" is a basic principle of economic and social construction and clearly requested "coordinated urban-rural development" and "a curb on the trend of widening disparities on interregional public services, per capita income, and living standards between urban and rural areas." In the plan, public services, including rural roads, rural drinking water safety, rural biogas, rural medical and health service systems, rural family planning, and rural labor force transfer constitute the key projects of the New Countryside Construction.[1] In fact, since 2004, the central government has issued 14 consecutive agricultural development-related "Documents No. 1 of the Central Authorities" and has repeatedly emphasized the importance of fulfilling public service functions, with the "three Nongs," that is, Nongye (agriculture), Nongcun (countryside), and Nongmin (farmers) as the main targets.

Local governments at all levels responded instantly to the change in the central government's policy agenda. With no exceptions, the "11th Five-Year Plans" of 31 provinces, municipalities, and autonomous regions of the Mainland China included "building the Socialist New Countryside" (some worded it as "coordinating urban and rural development" or "coordinating the development of urban and rural areas") as an important part of the plan. Similar responses were also manifested at the county level. In this regard, precisely as expected based on the theory of "decentralized authoritarianism," the central government maintains strong control over local governments, and when the central government changes its policy objectives and priorities, local government's behavior follows suit, thereby altering the behavior pattern of the developmental government.

However, the actual process of local governments' implementation of social policy innovation in the context of New Countryside Construction has not been effective. Although some local governments have claimed that their social

---

[1] Outline of the 11th Five-Year Plan for National Economic and Social Development of the People's Republic of China, http://news.xinhuanet.com/misc/2006-03/16/content_4309517.htm.

policy innovations were made in response to the central government's call, the basic logic of their policy formulation and implementation has been dominated by the goal of maximizing financial returns. In the case of the reform of the endowment insurance system in Huzhou, Zhejiang Province, the main impetus for the local government's expansion of endowment insurance was resolution of the problem of the pension fund operation. In the case of the reform of the household registration system in Chongqing City, which involved a shift from curbing the urbanization of the rural population to actively promoting its urbanization, the local government made the policy choice under the double inducement of urbanization and land finance.

4   Case 1: The Reform of the Endowment Insurance System in Huzhou, Zhejiang Province—The Expansion of Civil Rights Under the Pressure of Fund Operation

Providing endowment insurance for rural residents is an important part of the New Countryside Construction. In September 2009, the State Council issued the "Guidance on Conducting the Pilot Project of New Rural Social Endowment Insurance" (State Council Document [2009] No. 32) and requested "the gradual solving of the problem of providing for the elderly in accordance with the requirement of accelerating the establishment of a social security system that covers urban and rural residents." In the past, except for the retirement scheme for civil servants, China's endowment insurance system mainly consisted of basic endowment insurance for urban workers; this insurance system mostly covered urban employees in various enterprises and private laborers, and rural residents were excluded from coverage. In the early 1990s, the Ministry of Civil Affairs issued the "Basic Scheme of Rural Social Endowment Insurance at the County Level (draft)," which established an endowment insurance system, aiming at guaranteeing the basic livelihood of the elderly in rural areas and included the rural population of "nonurban hukou and residents without the state-supplied grain commodity scheme," that is, the rural residents, as well as employees of township enterprises (including village enterprise workers), the self-employed, community-supported teachers, township recruitment cadres and employees, and so on, in the system coverage. However, due to the lack of state financial support for this system, it was difficult for the management of the fund, which had been dominated by the buying of national bonds and depositing them in the bank, to keep or add value to the fund, resulting in extremely low pensions; in some areas, the pension was only 3 yuan per month.[2] Rural Social Endowment Insurance (now referred to as "Laonongbao") was practically dead, effectively excluding the vast majority of rural residents from coverage by the endowment insurance system.

---

[2] See "The most outstanding pension: three RMB yuan per month," *Nanfang Metropolis Daily*, August 25, 2009.

Unlike many other rural residents, rural residents of Huzhou, Zhejiang Province, in the eastern coastal region were covered by the same basic endowment insurance as urban workers as early as the late 1990s. In 2005, when New Countryside Construction was elevated to a national strategy, 47,456 rural residents of Huzhou City were already enrolled in the urban worker basic endowment insurance system, accounting for 21.17% of the total insured population. The situation was the result of two local policy documents issued by the local government in 1998 and 2003.

In China, local governments (generally the county-level government because the city-level government is mainly responsible for the areas excluding the counties within its jurisdiction) are the main executives and fund managers of the endowment insurance system and may formulate their own endowment insurance policies in their jurisdiction areas within the framework of the existing system. In 1998, the Huzhou municipal government issued the No. 90 [1998] Document, which extended the basic endowment insurance coverage of urban workers to employees and temporary employees of state-owned enterprises, collective enterprises, urban joint-stock enterprises, joint ventures, cooperative enterprises, foreign-invested enterprises, and other enterprises, as well as to employees of urban private-owned enterprises that were registered in the municipal industrial and commercial administration and to self-employed individuals, helpers, and community jobholders. For the first time, the government went beyond the limitations of the urban and rural household registration system to enroll a large number of rural residents that had been employed in township enterprises in the endowment insurance coverage. In 2003, the municipal government issued the No. 1 [2003] Document entitled "Notice on Further Improvement on the Collection of Workers' Basic Endowment Insurance Payment." This document once again expanded the coverage of basic endowment insurance of urban workers and included various types of enterprises, private non-enterprise units, enterprise-managed institutions, and personnel who had formed labor relationships with the institutions, as well as self-employed individual workers[3] in the urban worker basic endowment insurance system. At this point, the urban worker basic endowment insurance system of Huzhou at the implementation level has eliminated the difference in urban and rural household registrations, achieving "full coverage" by endowment insurance. In 2003, 37,704 rural residents participated in the urban worker basic endowment insurance system, accounting for 18.56% of the total insured population. Thereafter, the system continued to grow at a rate of not less than 5000 persons per year. In 2007, 64,220 rural residents were insured, accounting for 25% of the total insured population.

---

[3] According to this document, only "urban professional workers" are eligible for the urban worker basic endowment insurance system. However, according to the staff of the Huzhou City Labor and Social Security Bureau, in the implementation, even workers with the rural hukou can be enrolled in the urban worker basic endowment insurance system as long as they make the payments for the insurance premiums.

Obviously, the central government was not the main cause of the expansion of the urban workers basic endowment insurance system to rural residents. The expansion preceded not only the instruction of the central government requesting the "solving of the problem of providing for the elderly among rural residents" but also the New Countryside Construction strategy. So, what was the impetus for Huzhou City to implement policy innovation at the local level? The economic and social development background of Huzhou in the mid- and late 1990s provides the answer to this question.

Huzhou is an old industrial base with silk and building materials as its pillar industries, and it houses a large number of state-owned enterprises. However, from the late 1980s to the mid-1990s, its industrial development encountered bottlenecks due to the inevitable restructuring of state-owned enterprises. In the first quarter of 1995, for example, 11 of the 18 state-owned enterprises in the silk industry lost money, with accumulated losses amounting to 17 million RMB yuan (Ye 1995). In this context, Huzhou began to implement the restructuring of state-owned enterprises, and in just a few years generated a large number of laid-off workers and retirees, causing tremendous pressure on local governments in the areas of employment and social security. According to the data provided by the Huzhou Labor and Social Security Bureau, during 1999–2002, the municipal government organized 60,000 laid-off workers to participate in reemployment projects. In addition, there were a large number of retirees. The provisions of the time stipulated that the endowment insurance for retired workers of state-owned enterprises was to be maintained at a level comparable to that of workers in institutions rather than at a level that was based on pension premium and years of payment. In fact, a large number of retirees had never paid the pension premium. As a result, Huzhou's ability to pay the endowment insurance has faced an enormous challenge. In the most difficult period, the fund's ability to pay lasted only a few months. If new sources of funding cannot be found, the pension funds will be unsustainable.

Facing the overstretched pension fund, Huzhou began to initiate the expansion of the urban workers' basic endowment insurance and attempted to increase the source of the endowment insurance payments to enrich the endowment insurance fund and increase the ability of the fund to make payments. In the mid-1990s, similar to other coastal areas, Huzhou's private sectors experienced booming development, and township enterprises, in particular, underwent rapid development, solving the problem of employment for a large number of laborers, especially rural ones. This portion of the employees of the enterprises naturally became the focus of expansion in terms of endowment insurance coverage, as they had not yet been included in the system. In 1998, Huzhou loosened the eligibility for the urban workers basic endowment insurance coverage by adding a provision that all workers entering the nonagricultural sector are eligible to participate in the urban workers basic endowment insurance regardless of their household registration type. In 2003, the government went further by including self-employed individuals in the endowment insurance coverage to maximize the range of pension premiums that could be collected. However, the vast majority of enterprises and individuals lacked motivation to enroll in the endowment insurance, as personal and corporate contributions accounted for approximately 20% of personal monthly wages.[4] Such high payment levels of endowment insurance premiums led to a slow progress in the endowment insurance expansion. To increase the collection range of the endowment insurance premium, Huzhou separated the enterprise payment from the employee's payment and provisioned that an enterprise must make the insurance premium payment based on "the total wage paid by the enterprise" rather than the "number of actual insured employees." In other words, regardless of whether or not the workers are enrolled, the enterprise must first assume "the enterprise responsibility." In 2005, to ensure the collection of the insurance premium, Huzhou began to implement the program of "five-insurance-in-one," that is, combining five types of insurance (endowment insurance, medical insurance, unemployment insurance, job-related injury insurance, and maternity insurance) into one insurance category and assigned the task of premium collection to the tax bureau. The tax bureau collected the payments for the five types of insurance while collecting the monthly taxes, ensuring that the enterprises made full and timely insurance premium payments.

Through the expansion of the insurance system and through innovations in the method of collecting premiums, Huzhou's ability to pay for the endowment insurance fund has been continuously improved. In October 2008, Huzhou's payment capability reached 17 months, and the endowment insurance fund has since been operating normally.

5   CASE 2: REFORM OF THE HOUSEHOLD REGISTRATION SYSTEM IN CHONGQING—THE DOUBLE INDUCEMENT OF URBANIZATION AND LAND FINANCE

The "Hukou Registration Ordinance of the People's Republic of China," which was promulgated in 1958, made a distinction between agricultural and nonagricultural hukous, thereby defining individuals' eligibility for public services. After the reform and opening-up, although a large number of rural residents accepted urban employment, the hukou system resulted in a significant deficiency in the rights of migrant workers with respect to employment, children's education, social security, and medical services. Many scholars have focused on the economic and social consequences of the hukou system, and

---

[4]According to the relevant provisions regarding the contributions to the urban worker basic endowment insurance of Huzhou City, enterprises in Huzhou are generally required to pay 14–20% of the basic contribution for their employees, and the individuals are required to pay 8% of the basic contribution. During the most difficult period of the operation of the urban worker basic endowment insurance system, the Huzhou municipal government requested a special grant from the Zhejiang Provincial Department of Labor and Social Security to increase the enterprises' payment for their employees to 24% of the basic contribution.

many consider that the system creates disparities in employment opportunity and wages at the microscopic level among citizens, and that it, thus, constitutes an important factor leading to social unfairness (Li 2011; Zhao and Howden-Chapman 2010); at the macroscopic level, it causes the problem of "ternary structure" (i.e., urban residents, rural residents, and migrant workers) and restricts urbanization of the population, thereby exerting a negative impact on China's modernization process. Therefore, "strengthening the protection of the rights and interests of migrant workers and guaranteeing their equal treatment as urban residents regarding wage, children's schooling, public health, housing rental and purchasing, etc." and "promoting the reform of the hukou system in such a way as to relax migrant workers' settling conditions in small and medium-sized cities so that farmers who have stable employment and residence can be transformed into urban residents" constitute an important policy orientation of the central government in promoting rural reform and development. However, although the central government issued the "Scheme of a Pilot Project for the Reform of the Household Registration System in Small Towns and Guidelines for the Rural Household Registration Management System" (State Council Document [1997] No. 20) as early as 1997, local governments, as the main providers of various public services, did not relax the hukou system, making the availability of public services to rural and urban residents significantly different.

However, some subtle changes in the above situation have occurred in recent years. A number of local governments have begun to implement policy innovations aimed at promoting the urbanization of rural residents within their areas of jurisdiction. To understand the internal logic of local governments in promoting the reform of the household registration system, we chose the reform plan of the household registration system of Chongqing City, which was launched in 2010, as a case study.

Compared with that of other large cities in China, the urbanization rate of the population of Chongqing has been lower. According to the city's 2010 Statistical Yearbook, the total population of agricultural households in Chongqing City was 23.2692 million, accounting for 71.03% of the city's total household population, whereas the rural resident population was only 13.8408 million, accounting for 48.41% of the city's total resident population. In terms of employment, the total number of rural people employed was 9.5095 million, accounting for 56.98% of the city's total employment. However, the number of persons in the primary industry labor force was only 7.3368 million, accounting for 43.96% of the city's total employment. This shows that despite being employed in nonagricultural sectors and migrating to new residences, a large number of agricultural laborers have not changed hukou status and have, thus, been dissociated from the government's public service delivery system.

Therefore, transforming the household registration status of the rural residents who have been employed in nonagricultural sectors and have changed their residence locations became an important goal of the reform of the household registration system in Chongqing in 2010. In the reform plan, the municipal government made it clear in the guidelines for coordination on the urban and rural household registration system reform that "we need to guide rural residents to transfer in an orderly manner into cities and towns by settling qualified migrant workers, especially the new generation of migrant workers, in cities as a breakthrough ... and ultimately form a scientific and orderly mechanism of population urbanization." At the same time, the city put forward a clearly phased goal of transforming the rural population household registration status, for example, "in 2010–2011, focusing on promoting the transformation of migrant workers and the new generation migrant workers into urban residents ... striving to add 3 million new urban residents and to increase the proportion of nonagricultural households in the population from the current 29% to 37%" and "in 2012–2020, further relaxing the requirements for urban household registration and striving to add 800,000–900,000 new urban residents each year, thereby adding 7 million new urban residents by 2020 and increasing the proportion of nonagricultural households in the population to 60%." To achieve these goals, the Chongqing municipal government proposed lowering the threshold for urban household registration and promoting the migration and settlement of key populations; it relaxed the requirements for settlement in the main urban area and in the 31 counties and districts of the outer suburb and provisioned that the city's rural residents may relocate and settle in cities once they have worked or operated a business in a main urban area for a certain number of years, purchased commodity housing, or invested in enterprises that meet certain requirements. The relaxation of the eligibility requirements for urban household registration increased the number of rural residents who were eligible to settle in towns and provided a basis on which Chongqing City was able to implement the strategy of population urbanization. As the key content of the reform, after the transformation, rural residents began to enjoy public services including "employment, social security, housing, education, and medical care" in the same manner as urban residents, thereby gaining the benefits of citizenship.

So, was the reform of the Chongqing household registration system an active response to the central government's agricultural and rural policies since 2004? Superficially, the measures that were established to transform rural residents' household registration status were consistent with the statements in the central government's documents that emphasized the extension of public services to both migrant workers and urban residents and the protection of residents' rights and interests from infringement. It is noteworthy that although the central government's policies were also concerned with "assimilating migrant workers from a different place," the reform of the Chongqing household registration system targeted the "migrant workers of Chongqing City" and did not include migrant workers from other areas in its policy coverage scope. In addition, compared with the central government's call for pertinent and rational promotion of migrant workers' urbanization, Chongqing's policy goal was far more ambitious, aiming at increasing the proportion of the non-farm population to 60% by 2020; this seems to be an overreach for a city in which the proportion of the nonfarm employed population was less than 60% at the time of the policy introduction.

Therefore, Chongqing's reform of the household registration system is only a selective response to the central government's policy agenda, and at the specific implementation level, it is inconsistent with the descriptions in the central government's documents. However, if the policy advocacy of the central government did not provide the motivation for Chongqing Municipality to actively promote farmers' urbanization in terms of household registration status, what factors caused this reform?

From the perspective of the reform plan of the Chongqing household registration system, the relocated and resettled rural residents, in the process of obtaining various public services, were also faced with the possibility of "losing their land." According to the reform plan, rural residents whose entire households are resettled in urban residences "are allowed to continue to retain the income rights or use rights of their family land plots, homestead land, and residence for three years starting from the day of the transformation." During the three-year period, if the farmers voluntarily give up the right to use the homestead and the rural residence, they will be "reasonably compensated" according to the "Scheme of Rural Land Withdrawal and Utilization of the Chongqing Household Registration System Reform (draft)." Some scholars have noted that although the scheme adopted "legal and voluntary withdrawal" as one of the principles of homestead withdrawal, "legal and voluntary withdrawal" can be understood as "voluntarily surrendering the land within three years; after three years, the farmers are required to make a choice between the urban hukou and the rural land, and if they want to keep the land, they must transfer their hukou back to the countryside" (Huang and Liu 2011). In this regard, this scheme was considered to have the typical characteristic of exchanging "property rights" for "welfare rights." In other words, acquiring "land" is the government's endogenous motive for promoting the reform of the household registration system.

"The Land Law of China" divides land in China into two main categories. The land in the urban area belongs to the state, while the land in the rural and suburban areas, including homestead land and family land plots and hills, except for those that are provisioned to belong to the state, collectively belongs to villagers. After the reform and opening-up of China and with the development of Chinese industrialization and urbanization, the demand of local governments for land has been increasing; since the 1990s, local governments have continuously increased the urban construction land resources required for urbanization through the reconstruction of old cities and through land reclamation, demolition, and land expropriation, in the process developing the field of "land finance," that is, land transferring fee has become an important source of local government budget finance. In cities, such as Beijing, Shanghai, and Hangzhou, the income obtained through land finance even exceeded the total amount of local revenue; for example, in 2010, the land-transferring fee of Shanghai reached 151.343 billion RMB yuan, surpassing the city's total financial revenue (139.32 billion yuan). At the national level, the total national transaction price of land transfer in 2010 was 2.7 trillion yuan, with a year-to-year increase of 70.4%. Although Chongqing was not among the top three cities in terms of land finance, its income from land transfer should not be underestimated. Its land transfer income in 2010 reached 98 billion yuan, which, together with the real estate tax, accounted for 60–70% of the local total revenue (199.1 billion yuan). Because of the large amount of land finance, local governments have a strong incentive to increase the amount of land available for urban construction.

Although local governments were greatly motivated to increase the amount of urban construction land, they were only able to expand the construction land peripheral to cities and towns through land expropriation, that is, through so-called urban management before 2008 because of the system of urban and rural dualism. However, in 2008, the Ministry of Land and Resources issued the "Urban and Rural Construction Land Increase- and Decrease-Linked Management Measures" (Ministry of Land and Resource Document [2008] No. 138), which specifies that "after reclaiming rural construction land to farmland, urban construction land plots of the same acreage can be increased." This means that as long as the local government can obtain rural collective construction land, it can increase the urban construction land needed for urban development through the construction land increase- and decrease-linked measures without being restricted to the actual locations of the plots. As a result, local governments have a strong motivation to decrease rural collective construction land and increase urban construction land. By reforming the household registration system in such a way as to reduce the number of rural residents, local governments reclaim the rural homesteads of the farmers to arable land, which undoubtedly becomes the best way to increase urban construction land. This can also be regarded as an important part of the background of the reform of the household registration system in Chongqing, in which the government attempted to reconstruct the urban and rural household registration population to increase the amount of usable urban construction land, thereby not only meeting the needs of urbanization but also increasing the financial resources available for the local government's use in performing urban management.

6   Conclusions Drawn from the Case Studies

By examining the above two cases, we attempted to answer the following questions: after the central government put forward the view of scientific development and called for building a harmonious society, would local governments transform from developmental governments to service-oriented governments? According to the theory of "decentralized authoritarianism," local developmental government is the reflection of the central government's developmentalist ideology. After the implementation of local decentralization, the central government established a vertical accountability mechanism with the power of appointment and removal of personnel as the core and, thus, continued to maintain effective control over local governments. Therefore, as long as the central government adjusts its policy priorities, local governments would change their behavior patterns and achieve the transformation to a service-oriented government. In this respect, the cases mentioned earlier show that a change in the central government's policy agenda is not always the root of the local government's social policy innovation. Although local governments changed their behavior in certain ways, their behavior patterns did not change radically; financial income maximization was still the primary goal of local governments, and social policy often became an instrument in the service of economic development.

First, in the cases mentioned earlier, the central government's policies were not at the root of local governments' social policy innovations. The Huzhou Municipal Government issued documents as early as 1998 that opened the endowment insurance system to rural residents who had been employed in township enterprises and other enterprises; this occurred much earlier than the proposal for the construction of the unified urban-rural social security system in 2009 and also earlier than the proposal for the New Countryside Construction in 2005. Although the reform of the household registration system in Chongqing occurred after the central government's policy advocacy and was similar in some ways to the policies outlined in the central government's documents, the similarity was only partial. Compared with the central government's policies, the Chongqing Municipal Government differentiated "migrant workers with Chongqing hukou" from "migrant workers" focused the policy innovation on the former population. Therefore, the social policy innovations conducted by local governments in the context of the New Countryside Construction cannot be regarded as changes in governance that were made under the guidance of the central government.

Second, the social policy innovations implemented by local governments imply another type of "development" logic and still manifest the typical characteristics of developmental government, indicating the dominant influence of financial income maximization on local governments' behavior. In the case of Huzhou, the reform of state-owned enterprises were the inevitable choice that was made to promote the development of the regional economy, and the local government was asked to solve the problem of the laid-off and retired workers of the state-owned enterprises. In this context, the local government was forced to implement the expansion of the endowment insurance coverage. In this process, the acquirement of eligibility for endowment insurance by farmers, especially migrant workers, was only a by-product of the reform. In the process of policy implementation, the attention of the local government was mainly focused on solving the problem of funding operations by enlarging the scope of the collection of endowment insurance premiums rather than on ensuring that individual workers were indeed enrolled in the urban workers' basic endowment insurance system. We found in the fieldwork that some migrant workers (including those with local hukou, as well as alien ones) were not enrolled in the endowment insurance system because they were unable to pay the endowment insurance premium 15 years in succession; when taking a transfer, these workers were only able to claim the endowment insurance from their personal accounts. According to the staff of the local social security department, in the case of transfers from the urban worker basic endowment insurance to the new rural social endowment insurance, as well as in the case of transfers to the cross-regional urban worker basic endowment insurance, joint accounts (i.e., the portion paid by the enterprise) cannot be entirely transferred. Obviously, in the practice of endowment insurance expansion, solving the insurance premium payment problems was the fundamental impetus of the policy innovation, its origin being the reform of state-owned enterprises.

In the case of Chongqing, the features of the developmental government were manifested more obviously. The development of urbanization required that the local government increase the amount of urban construction land, while financial income maximization further underscored the importance of land finance. After the Ministry of Land and Resources introduced the policy on rural and urban construction land increase- and decrease-linked rationing, the rural collective construction land became the local government's most important source for obtaining land and increasing its extra-budgetary revenue. Therefore, the reform of the household registration system in Chongqing did not focus on abolishing the institutional barrier to the movement of population between urban and rural areas but continued the government-controlled population policy to ensure that the government was able to acquire the construction land needed for this process. In fact, because the reform of the household registration system in Chongqing required the resettled farmers to exchange their property rights for welfare rights, they were not initially enthusiastic. As a result, the Chongqing municipal government allowed the government to have a full play in promoting the "transforming of rural residents to urban ones," and, in addition to formulating the phased population urbanization goal, it also actively intervened in the redistribution of the population group by group and batch by batch. For example, the reform program treated "2.256 million migrant workers who had worked or done business for more than 5 years in the main urban area or for 3 years in the cities of the suburban counties," "667,000 college and middle-school students who had the rural hukou of the city and were attending school in the city," and "18,000 newly discharged veterans who were originally from the rural areas or petty officers who had served for less than 10 years" as the key targets of the "transforming of rural residents to urban ones," a goal that was promoted through certain discretionary administrative actions.

Therefore, although the central government put forward the important goal of building a service-oriented government in 2005 and set a target to reform the government management system with the establishment of a service-oriented government by 2020, it was still rather difficult to promote changes in local government functions. Local governments responded nominally to the central government's policy requirements, but their actual behavior still exhibited the characteristics of developmental government, and their social policy innovations were mainly designed to promote local economic development, especially the need for maximizing the local financial revenue rather than meeting the demands of the local public. Thus, local governments have not transformed into service-oriented governments, and the essence of the change is that a new type of local developmental government with social policy as an instrument has become a new state of Chinese local governments.

7   INSTITUTIONAL BASIS OF THE LOCAL DEVELOPMENTAL GOVERNMENT: DECENTRALIZATION WITH LIMITED ACCOUNTABILITY

Since the 16th National Congress of CPC in 2002, which was symbolized by proposals for scientific development and the construction of a harmonious society, the construction of a service-oriented government has become an important part of China's reform and development. After the 18th National Congress of CPC, the central government put forward the idea of a "people-centered" development and further took "people's sense of gain" as a starting point and a foothold for the construction of government reform. In this context, some local governments have also begun to experiment government reform and aimed to fully fulfill government functions (He 2010). However, the two cases mentioned earlier show that the change in the policy agenda of the higher-level government has not brought about an overall transformation of the governments' behavior patterns. As the theory of "fiscal federalism with Chinese characteristics" indicates, under the guidance of financial revenue maximization, local governments will not "absolutely follow the orders of the central government," that is, they are more prone to act in ways that are based on the actual needs of local economic and social development than to unconditionally implement the policy directives issued by the central government. It should be noted that financial revenue maximization does not necessarily lead to the weakening of the public service function of the local government, and that it is still possible for such revenue maximization to benefit local people. In our fieldwork of Jinjiang, Fujian Province, in 2016, we note that the local government has taken the measure of "boosting the city with talents" as an important goal of government work and that it has encouraged persons of talent to settle in Jinjiang by improving the level of public services, such as education and medical care. Building new schools and introducing quality medical resources by local governments can also benefit residents. However, compared with the central government's "people-centered" development concept, these "benefits" represent only an associated product of economic development rather than the fundamental goal that drives local government actions. In Jinjiang, the local government's "investment" in the abovementioned public services has been driven by the urgent need for the high-level talent that is required for transforming and upgrading local industries, as well as by a fierce competition for high-level talent with the neighboring city of Xiamen. Local cadres made it clear that unlike the elements of traditional economic development, such as capital and land, high-level talent presents a strong demand for quality public services in addition to economic interests. To this end, local governments need to focus on improving the quality of local public services to avoid the loss of human talent to Xiamen, which is currently richer in high-quality education and medical resources. In other words, the key to the "development" of local developmental government is that it may not necessarily respond to the central government's ideas of "building a service-oriented government" and "performing people-centered development," nor provide public services based on the actual needs of the public, but instead may determine the focus of the implementation of government functions according to the actual needs related to economic development. As a result, despite the fact that at the local level quite a few excellent examples of building a service-oriented government indeed emerged, we still generalize the behavioral logic of local governments as developmental government.

So why has the decentralized fiscal system failed to force local governments to respond better to the needs of residents for public services? The theory of "fiscal federalism with Chinese characteristics" argues that fiscal decentralization has created a powerful motive for local governments to participate in economic development, but it has failed to explain why local governments do not supply public services. On the contrary, many published works clearly indicate that decentralization helps increase the level of public services that are offered. For example, Tiebout (1956) argued that intergovernmental competition for fiscal revenue would force local governments to respond to public needs and improve the efficiency of public service delivery. Ostrom (1974) also stressed that the development of a multicentered, decentralized administrative system is an important way to strengthen the responsiveness of government and achieve democratic administration. Therefore, although fiscal decentralization does not necessarily lead to the selective fulfillment of government functions, it is not a sufficient condition for improvement in the level of nonpublic services.

The answer to the earlier question lies outside the fiscal system. Against the background of decentralization, ensuring the full implementation of government functions is the core of the government system design. The theory of "decentralized authoritarianism" took note of the vertical accountability mechanism centered on the power of appointment and removal of personnel and indicated that this is an important tool that the central government can use to intervene in local governments, but it neglected the fact that at the local level horizontal accountability mechanisms, such as the local People's Congresses and judicial systems, are also key institutional arrangements that guide and regulate local government behavior. Since the reform and opening-up, the People's Congresses and judicial system of local governments have developed rapidly and have shown great potential of horizontal accountability mechanisms. First, since the 1980s, the People's Congress has gradually become an important force in China's political participation. With the progress of marketization reform, the legislative and supervisory functions of the local People's Congresses have been strengthened; the function of the representation has also been strengthened to some extent, and it has started to get actively involved in the formulation and implementation of public policies and no longer acts as just a "rubber stamp." In some localities, the People's Congresses have played an important role in anticorruption, political participation, and consulting activities (Cho 2009). Second, the rule of law as a tool to restrain government's power has also been developed to a certain extent. After 1978, the Chinese government enacted many laws and gradually achieved the rule of law. At the same time, the law has gradually developed into a valuable tool for restraining public power. For example, the Administrative Procedure Law enacted in 1989, for the first time, endowed Chinese citizens with the right to challenge the power of public authorities and put government departments under the restriction of law (Horsley 2010).

Needless to say, the development of the People's Congresses and of the judicial system of local governments is still quite unsophisticated. The local People's Congresses typically assumes the functions of representing, legislating, supervising, and maintaining the rules and is an important mechanism through which the public can express demands, safeguard citizens' rights, and coordinate pluralistic interests. In practice, however, the fulfillment of the function of the local People's Congresses is highly dependent on the support of the local party and government leaders, and it lacks real influence on local governments. Since the mid- and late 1980s, the central government has begun to promote autonomy at the village level and has endowed villagers with the power to participate in the appointment of village leaders; in some areas, grassroots democratic tests, such as "public recommendation, public election" and "public recommendation, direct election," have been conducted at the township level. The practices described earlier have significantly promoted the fulfillment of the functions of townships and villages and have yielded remarkable achievements in standardizing the behavior of grassroots government, improving the supply of public services, and reducing corruption. However, at the higher levels of governments, the nomination of candidates and the results of elections were still tightly controlled (Perry and Goldman 2007), and the grassroots democratic experiments were mostly stalled at the township level and were not expanded (Li 2002). The latter development undoubtedly restricted further development of the local People's Congresses and maintained them in an unsophisticated state. To seek further development, the local People's Congresses chose to be "embedded" in and to cooperate with the local government; as a result, its main role in the formulation and implementation of public policies was manifested as providing information (Manion 2015), and its relationship with the local government should be seen as a division of work rather than a separation of power (O'Brien 1994).

The difficulty encountered by the local People's Congresses in engaging in full participation in government also makes it more difficult for the public to participate in the development of public policies, and the public's demands of public goods also lack appropriate channels for expression. Thus, local governments have also lost a scientific, effective mechanism for the coordination of interests; as a result, it is impossible for their public policies to reflect and balance the competing demands of increasingly diverse groups. This gives rise to a situation in which the interests of the disadvantaged groups are dependent on the local financial income, thus reinforcing the logic of developmental government. The reform of the social insurance system in Huzhou described earlier in essence involves sacrificing and transferring the social insurance rights and interests of the employed rural labor force to protect the benefits of retired workers and the financial interests of the local government, whereas the reform of the household registration system in Chongqing tends to sacrifice the property rights of the resettled farmers to make it possible for the local government and real estate developers to gain more financial benefits. Since the beginning of the twenty-first century, many local governments and their departments have tended to attract investors using low-priced land as a means of gaining a financial advantage and have ignored the interests of urban and rural residents in the process of land expropriation while responding more favorably to the demands of private sector operators (Cai 2007). It is worth noting that after the introduction of the hukou reform scheme, the Chongqing municipal government began to allow the resettled farmers to retain their homestead land indefinitely in the face of public and media questioning and criticism, showing the responsiveness of the government. However, the cost of the ex post facto response mechanism as shown in this case is much higher than that of the local People's Congresses, the ex-ante and formal interest coordinating mechanism.

Compared with the local People's Congresses, the rule of law is an ex post facto corrective mechanism for local governments' misconduct, emphasizing the limitations of the law on private and state power, albeit not easy to implement. On the one hand, China's legal system is still in the process of development, and some of its legal provisions have not been well developed, as in many cases of land expropriation; problems, therefore, arise from the lack of basic legal protection of private property, which is undoubtedly an important cause of the unconstrained public power. On the other hand, when local governments misbehave, the higher-level governments are more inclined to apply vertical accountability mechanisms, such as the suspension and dismissal of the main party and government cadres in the local area rather than adjudication of the specific case through the judicial system based on the existing law. In terms of individual cases, the monopolized personnel power empowers high-level governments to implement their own will by exerting strong control at the local level, and the intervention of the high-level governments can correct the local government's behavior more rapidly and effectively. However, in the long run, the abovementioned practice weakens the role of the judicial system as the arbiter of administrative litigation and makes it difficult for local public power to be bound by the law. At the same time, because of the limitation of the vertical accountability mechanism itself, the high-level governments can hardly correct the daily behavior of local governments while weakening the external constraint of local governments. In terms of Mann's distinction between two types of state power, the vertical accountability mechanism gives the central government a strong despotic power over local governments, while it still obviously lacks infrastructural power (Mann 1984).

Then why is the vertical accountability mechanism so obviously restrictive in constraining local government behavior? To guide local government behavior, the central government has set up evaluation methods for the local leading cadres and adopted an evaluation system that is used to make personnel appointments and to administer rewards and punishments according to the evaluation results, thus providing an incentive to the local party and government leaders. In 2009, the Organization Department of the CPC Central Committee issued the "Guidance on the Implementation of Establishing the Evaluation and Assessment Mechanism for Party and Government Leaders and Leading Cadres to Promote the View of Scientific Development" and the "Implementation Measures for the Evaluation and Assessment Mechanism for Local Party and Government Leaders and Leading Cadres Reflecting the Requirements of the View of Scientific Development" and attempted to encourage local governments to change their behavior patterns by improving the cadre evaluation mechanism. However, the effectiveness of the vertical accountability mechanism is based on the central government's ability to obtain accurate information and to make an accurate assessment of the performance of local government functions. Compared with the economic development goal, it is very difficult to conduct a quantitative assessment of public service functions; this also makes it difficult for the high-level governments to make comprehensive evaluations and comparisons of the performance of local government functions.

In 2010, we conducted an empirical study of the evaluation mechanism of cadres in a county of Zhejiang Province. In the county's 2010 Evaluation System, the proportion of public service functions, including ecological environment and social welfare, was already rather high, with a cumulative level of 35%, while the proportion of the economic development functions had decreased to less than 50%. However, compared with the economic development indicators that were fully quantitative, for example, "total revenue," "local revenue," "state tax revenue," "added value of designed size enterprises," "added value of service industry," and so on, the quantification level of public service functions was extremely low, and these functions were described using fuzzy descriptive indicators, such as "the development of cultural causes," "the development of sports causes," "the development of educational causes," and "the development of health causes." Because of the lack of sufficient information that could be used to make a horizontal comparison of the performance of the local government's public service functions, the economic functions that were easier to quantify had the most real impact on the final evaluation result. Under such circumstances, impacted dually by the evaluation mechanism and the maximization of financial income, local governments tend to indulge in actions that enhanced the economic development indicators, that is, "what the superior favors will receive excessively enthusiastic responses from his subordinates" and to compete to raise the goal. In the "12th Five-Year Plan," in which the central government proposed a goal of 8% annual GDP (gross domestic product) growth, the GDP growth goal for each of the provincial governments, except those of Shanghai, Beijing, Zhejiang, and Guangdong, was higher than that of the central government, and some provinces and cities even put forward the goal of "GDP doubling in five years." Based on the limitations of the vertical accountability mechanism, local governments lack corresponding incentives for public service indicators and only selectively pursue projects that are easily noticed by high-level governments, for example, infrastructure construction or specific public service or social governance innovation projects, so that the overall performance can be represented by high performance in some individual areas. Investigations have shown that rural residents think that living infrastructure and production infrastructure are the two aspects on which local governments have delivered in building the new countryside, whereas other public services, including environmental protection, social security, and medical services, have been neglected by local governments. In general, the vertical accountability mechanism is naturally selective in shaping local government behavior, encouraging the local government to pay more attention to economic development indicators that are easier to quantify and observe, and to attach less importance to vague indicators, such as public services, thus making it difficult to promote the transformation from developmental government to service-oriented government.

In short, at present, the horizontal accountability mechanisms, such as China's local People's Congresses and the judicial system, have limitations, and it is difficult for their functions to receive full play. At the same time, although the vertical accountability mechanism with personnel power as the core gives the central government the despotic power to intervene in the specific actions of local governments, due to factors such as information asymmetry, the infrastructural power of the high-level governments over local governments is still weak. The imperfectness of the horizontal accountability mechanism and the limitations of the vertical accountability mechanism lead to "decentralization with limited accountability," which further expands the autonomous behavior space of local governments and causes the maximization of financial revenue to become the dominant logic of local government behavior, thus forming and solidifying the behavioral logic of local developmental government.

It is worth noting that following the 18th National Congress of CPC, the central government and the provincial governments have begun to implement more centralized reforms, including the strengthening of the leading role of the high-level party committee in the selection and appointment of cadres, and to reinforce their monitoring of local governments' functioning in various areas, such as environmental protection. This has been accomplished through changes in the methods used for central government supervision and inspection and through the assignment of more specific directive policy tasks that allow high-level governments to directly intervene in the allocation priorities of local government resources. However, we cannot simply view these latest practices as reflecting the dualism of "centralization-decentralization" and regard the central-local relationship as a type of a zero-sum game of power allocation, thus neglecting the high-level government's efforts in regulating and guiding local government behavior. It is true that the issuing of more key tasks with more specified goals directly by higher-level governments is indeed an important manifestation of the reduction of autonomy of local governments, that is, the recentralization of power. In a short period of time, the high-level government can influence local government behavior in the realm of decision-making by exerting its authority, and this has the conspicuous advantage of achieving the goal more rapidly with respect to promoting the transformation of government functions. However, as noted earlier, the key to the cause of the local developmental government does not lie in the decentralization itself but in the "decentralization with limited accountability," that is, the inadequacy of the horizontal and vertical accountability mechanisms. As a result, the promotion of changes in local government functions via the centralization of authority is only a short-term solution that cures the symptoms but not the disease. In the long run, determination of how to improve the horizontal and vertical accountability mechanisms to restrain local government behavior is the key to ensuring the full implementation of government functions. In this respect, the content that really deserves our attention in the reconstruction of China's central-local relations after the 18th National Congress of the CPC is the strengthening of the vertical accountability mechanism in the form of central government supervision. These methods, which have effectively overcome the dilemma of asymmetric information between superior and subordinate governments and strengthened the vertical accountability faced by local governments, should be regarded as a new form of China's central-local relations adjustment. Of course, after strengthening the vertical accountability mechanism, whether or not the local government can succeed in transcending the behavioral logic of developmental government is still uncertain and is worthy of continuous observation.

REFERENCES

Blecher, M. 1991. Development state, entrepreneurial state: The political economy of socialist reform in Xinju municipality and Guanghan county. In: *The Chinese State in the Era of Economic Reform*. United Kingdom: Palgrave Macmillan.

Cai, Y. 2007. Civil resistance and rule of law in China: The case of defending home owners' rights. In: *Grassroots Political Reform in Contemporary China*, pp. 174–195.

Cao, Z., and J. Shi. 2009. The strategy of coping with marketization reform of China's local government: Seize the initiative of economic development: Theoretical hypotheses and empirical verification (*Zhongguo Difang Zhengfu Yingdui Shichanghua Gaige de Celue: Zhuazhu Jingji fazhan de Zhudong Quan, Lilun Jiashuo yu Anli Yanzheng*). *Sociological Research* (4): 1–27.

Cho, Y. 2009. *Local People's Congresses in China: Development and Transition*. New York: Cambridge University Press.

He, X. 2007. The role of local government in the process of marketization and its behavior logic: From the perspective of local government autonomy (*Shichanghua JInchengzhong de Difang Zhengfu Juese jiqi Xingwei Luoji: Jiyu Difang Zhengfu Zizhuxing de Shijiao*). *Journal of Zhejiang University (Humanities and Social Sciences Edition)* (6): 25–35.

He, X. 2010. The path selection of building the post-crisis era service-oriented government (*Hou Weiji Shiqi de Fuwuxing Zhengfu Jianshe de Lujing Xuanze: Yi Zhejiang Weili*). *Journal of Party School of CPC Ningbo Municipal Committee* 32(5): 29–37.

Horsley, J. 2010. The rule of law, pushing the limits of Party rule. In: *China Today, China Tomorrow: Domestic Politics, Economy and Society*. Lanham, MD: Rowman & Littlefield Publishers, Inc. 51–68.

Huang, Z., and C. Liu. 2011. The exploration of the Chongqing model of household registration system reform (*Huji Zhidu Gaige de Chongqing Moshi Tansuo*). *Journal of China National School of Administration* (2): 90–94.

Landry, P.F. 2008. *Decentralized Authoritarianism in China: The Communist Party's Control of Local Elites in the Post-Mao Era*. Cambridge University Press.

Lin, J., and Z. Liu. 2000. Fiscal decentralization and economic growth in China. *Economic Development and Cultural Change* 49: 1–21.

Li, L. 2002. The politics of introducing direct township elections in China. *China Quarterly* 171(171): 704–723.

Li, S., and B. Luo. 2010. The estimate of China's land finance scale (*Woguo Tudi Caizheng Guimo Gusuan*). *Journal of the Central University of Finance and Economics* (5): 12–17.

Li, X. 2011. Household registration system and social differences of contemporary China: A quantitative research based on China's comprehensive social survey data (*Huji Zhidu yu Dangdai Zhongguo Shehui Chabie Guanxi de Shizheng Fenxi*). *Journal of Huazhong University of Science and Technology* (Social Science Edition) (3): 98–105.

Manion, M. 2015. *Information for Autocrats: Authoritarian Parochialism*. Cambridge University Press.

Mann, M. 1984. The autonomous power of the state: Its origins, mechanisms and results. *Archives Européennes De Sociologie* 25(2): 185–213.

Montinola, G., Y. Qian, and B.R. Weingast. 1995. Federalism, Chinese style: The political basis for economic success in china. *World Politics* 48(1): 50–81.

Naughton, B. 2008. Analysis of the political economy of China's economic transition. In: *China's Great Economic Transformation*. Cambridge University Press.

O'Brien, K.J. 1994. Chinese people's congresses and legislative embeddedness: Understanding early organizational development. *Social Science Electronic Publishing* 27(1): 80–107.

Oi, J.C. 1992. Fiscal reform and the economic foundations of local state corporatism in China. *World Politics* 45(1): 99–126.

Oi, J.C. 1995. The role of the local state in China's transitional economy. *China Quarterly* 144(144): 1132–1149.

Ostrom, V. 1974. *The Intellectual Crisis in American Public Administration*. Tuscaloosa, AL: University of Alabama Press.

Perry, E., and M. Goldman. 2007 Introduction: Historical reflections on grassroots political reform in China. In: *Grassroots Political Reform in Contemporary China*. Cambridge, MA: Harvard University Press.

Qu, J. 2012. The project system: A new state governance system (*Xiangmu Zhi: Yizhong Xin de GUojia Zhili Tizhi*). *Chinese Social Science* (5): 113–130.

Riskin, C. 2010. Inequality: Overcoming the great divided. In: *China Today, China Tomorrow: Domestic Politics, Economy and Society*. Lanham, MD: Rowman & Littlefield Publishers, Inc.

Shen, R. 2009. The vertical management of government under the background of decentralization: Patterns and ideas (*Fenquan Beijignxia de Zhengfu Chuizhi Guanli: Moshi yu Silu*). *China Administration* (9): 38–43.

Shi, Y., and I. Zhou. 2007. Regional decentralization and economic efficiency: A case study on specially designated in the state plan (*Diqu Fangquan yu Jingji Xiaolv: Yi Jihua Danlie Weili*). *Economic Research* 1: 17–28.

Tiebout, C.M. 1956. A pure theory of local expenditures. *Journal of Political Economy* 64(5): 416–424.

Tsai, L.L. 2007. *Accountability without Democracy: Solidary Groups and Public Goods Provision in Rural China*. Cambridge University Press.

Wang, S., and A. Hu. 1994. The decline of the Chinese government's extractive capacity and its consequences (*Zhongguo Zhengfu Jiqu Nengli de Xiajiang jiqi Houguo*). *Twenty-first Century* 1: 5–14.

White, G. 1991. *The Road to Crisis: The Chinese State in the Era of Economic Reform*. *The Chinese State in the Era of Economic Reform*. United Kingdom: Palgrave Macmillan UK.

Wong, C. 1992. Fiscal reform and local industrialization: The problematic sequencing of reform in post-Mao China. *Modern China* 18: 197–227.

Ye, L. 1995. The plight of state-owned silk enterprises in Huzhou City and thoughts on deepening the reform (*Huzhoushi Guoyou Sichou Qiye de Kunjing yu Shenhua Gaige de Sikao*). *China Textile* (9): 42–44.

Yu, J., and Y. Xu. 2004. From development-type government to public service-type government: A case study of Zhejiang Province (*Cong Fazhanxing Zhengfu dao Fuwuxing Zhengfu: Yi Zhejiang Sheng Wei Ge'an*). *Marxism and Reality* (5): 65–74.

Zhang, T., and H. Zou. 1998. Fiscal decentralization, public spending and economic growth in China. *Journal of Public Economics*: 221–240.

Zhao, P., and P. Howden-Chapman. 2010. Social inequalities in mobility: The impact of the hukou system on migrants' job accessibility and commuting costs in Beijing. *International Development Planning Review* 32(3): 363–384.

Zhao, S. 2013. The crisis and change of the governance of county and township governments: The structural adjustment of power distribution and interactive mode (*Xianxiang ZHengfu ZHili de Weiji yu Biange: Shiquan Fenpei he Hudong Moshi de Jiegouxing Tiaozheng*). *People's Forum* (21): 14–30.

Zheng, Y. 2007. *De Facto Federalism in China: Reforms and Dynamics of Central-Local Relations*. Hackensack, NJ: World Scientific.

Zhou, F. 2006. Ten years of tax distribution system: Institution and its influence (*Fenshuizhi Shinian: Zhidu ji Yingxiang*). *Chinese Social Science* (6): 100–115.

Zhou, F. 2010. Building boom: Land finance and local government behavior (*Daxing Tumu: tudi Caizheng yu Difang Zhengfu Xingwei*). *Economic and Social System Comparison* (3): 77–89.

PART III

Civil Society Organizations and Mass Media

CHAPTER 11

The Development and Prospects of Business Association Since 1978

Jun Zhou and Xiaocui Zhao

1   INTRODUCTION

A wide variety of nonprofit organizations mushroomed during the global "associational revolution" in the 1970s and 1980s (Salarmon et al. 2002, p. 4) and China was no exception. Since China's reform and opening up in 1978, its government has gradually loosened the control over the society, allowing some civil society organizations to develop under its supervision. Under such circumstances, business associations revived along with the booming economy in China and grew into a force in civil society that could not be ignored. Their influence over Chinese economic development, industry, and market governance, and even social governance, is increasing. Therefore, it makes great sense to look back and study the history of business associations in China— right from the start of reform and opening up—understand the background, and locate the impetus of their development, as it will no doubt inform us about the relationship between China's social organizations and the government.

In this chapter, business associations are defined as industry organizations initiated by industrial and commercial businesses and devoted to service provisions for members and self-discipline, communication, and coordination among industry peers. As legal persons, they are reorganized from existing economic organizations and mainly take the forms of industry associations, chambers of commerce, guilds, industry promotion associations, industry confederations, and nonlocal chambers of commerce, in which industry associations and chambers of commerce are the majority.

J. Zhou (✉) • X. Zhao
Public Administration School, East China Normal University, Shanghai, China

© The Author(s) 2019   225
J. Yu, S. Guo (eds.), *The Palgrave Handbook of Local Governance in Contemporary China*, https://doi.org/10.1007/978-981-13-2799-5_11

2   RENAISSANCE OF BUSINESS ASSOCIATIONS
AT THE BEGINNING OF REFORM AND OPENING UP

Business associations have a long history in China. As early as the Spring and Autumn Period (770–476 BC), there emerged "shops" (*Si* in Chinese) under the centralized operation of industrialists and businessmen; in the Song and Yuan Dynasties (960–1368 AD) "peddlers" (*Hang* in Chinese) were spread across the country, and the Ming and Qing Dynasties (1368–1800 AD) witnessed the emergence of various clubs and club houses. Also, Chinese governments started regulations on business associations in early times. For example, in 1904, the Qing government issued the *Brief Rules for Chambers of Commerce,* and during the Republic of China, the Beiyang government and Nanjing government issued *the Law of Chambers of Commerce, the Law of Industrial and Commercial Trade Associations,* and *Laws of Industrial Trade Associations,* successively (Yu et al. 2010, p. 8; Zhu 2014).

Since its foundation in 1949, the government of the People's Republic of China (PRC) began to reform old business associations. In 1952, the Preparatory Committee of the All-China Federation of Industry and Commerce was established, and the *General Rules for the Organization of All-China Federation of Industry and Commerce* was published. Later, federations of industry and commerce were formed across China. As one of the eight "Mass Organizations" subordinate to the government, the Federations of Industry and Commerce mainly served to assist the Communist Party of China (CPC) and the government to implement socialist economic policies and clear and transform private economy. After completion of socialist transformation at the end of 1956, private economy no longer existed. Due to the loss of economic foundation, business associations either stopped operation or were transformed to quasi-government sectors (Jia et al. 2004, p. 88).

Since the reform and opening up in 1978, extensive and profound changes have taken place in China. With the development of commodity economy and private economy, the need to reform the old Industry management system was urgent (Yu et al. 2010, p. 10). In this case, the Federation of Industry and Commerce (General Chamber of Commerce) was revived and industry associations gradually developed with drive from the government.

On December 24, 1977, the United Front Work Department of the CPC Central Committee invited representatives of democratic parties and All-China Federation of Industry and Commerce (ACFIC) principals to attend discussions at the site of the Chinese People's Political Consultative Conference (CPPCC). On January 17, 1979, Deng Xiaoping met with five leaders from ACFIC and the Democratic Construction Party in the Fujian Hall of the Great Hall of the People. Later, the ACFIC was engaged in the recovery of the policies of original industrialists and businessmen and policy implementation of the Rightists among original industrialists and businessmen; the ACFIC resumed its function during "bringing order out of chaos and returning to the rectitude (of the past)" (the Chinese expression is *bo luan fan zheng*). During October 10–22,

1978, the Fourth Membership Reprehensive Conference of ACFIC was held in Beijing, where a *Political Decision* and the new *Articles of Association of All-China Federation of Industry and Commerce* were passed. This conference promoted a great shift in ACFIC work. According to the new *Articles of Association*, municipal federations of industry and commerce shall be established in provincial capitals and capitals of the autonomous regions. Other medium-sized cities can also establish federations of industry and commerce. After the conference, the work of Federation of Industry and Commerce began to recover across China. By March 1983, 280 Federations of Industry and Commerce were recovered. Meanwhile, grassroots Federations of Industry and Commerce below the municipal level were recovered and developed successively (All-China Federation of Industry and Commerce Press 2013, pp. 102–131).

During the Planned Economy period, China ran a highly centralized department management system. All enterprises must strictly accord to directives of superior industrial authorities and lost operational autonomy and independent interests. To adapt to commodity economic development, the Chinese government launched the Reform of the Economic System in 1979. The main thoughts were to weaken the government's administrative interference in enterprises and to promote a separation of enterprise from the government. Attempts were made to change from department management to industry management (Zhou and Song 2011, pp. 36–46), and industry associations were back to the stage of history again.

In March 1979, the first nationwide industry association, China Enterprise Management Association (later renamed China Enterprise Confederation), was established; then, several industrial and professional associations were founded successively, including China Quality Control Association (1979), China Packaging Technology Association (1980), China Food Industry Association (1981), and China Audio Industry Association (1983). This first batch of industry associations were mainly established directly by, or transformed from, government departments. For example, the National Ministry of Textile Industry was transformed to the China Textile Industry Association, and the National Ministry of Light Industry was reconstructed to the China Light Industry Association. These industry associations, funded by governments, were endowed with administrative functions, government posts, and government-determined ranks, featuring strong government-run characters (Jia and Zhang 2016, pp. 99–105).

In addition to setting up new industry associations, original business associations were experiencing a role shift. For instance, the China Council for Promotion of International Trade (CCPIT), whose original functions were of great political implications, changed its main functions in 1979 to foreign trade promotion, utilization of foreign capital, introduction of advanced foreign technologies, and promotion of Sino-foreign economic and technological cooperation in various forms.

In the early years of its reform and opening up, the main features of China's business associations were as follows: first, the Federation of Industry and

Commerce (General Chamber of Commerce) resumed its work after the reform and opening up and became an important subject in the United Front and a main force in "four modernization constructions." Second, the industry associations were mainly generated from within the system and were highly dependent on governments in terms of functions, human resource, and finance (Xu 2010, pp. 57–58). Third, business associations started to play roles in economic development and industrial governance. Federations of Industry and Commerce gave the impetus for private economy development and industry associations bridged the enterprises and governments. Of course, as a whole, business associations at that period featured small quantity and limited functions. Governments remained the major force in economic development and industrial governance.

3   Emergence and Development of Civil Chambers of Commerce During the Mid- to Late 1980s

Since the reform and opening up, with the development of private economy, civil chambers of commerce appeared in Guangdong and Zhejiang provinces. Different from nongovernmental industry organizations in history (such as guilds and guild halls) and business associations separated from the state, civil chambers of commerce were products of market economy and civilian associations. After the reform and opening up, Wenzhou City in Zhejiang Province ranked among the fastest-growing cities in private economy and among the first batch of cities in developing civil chambers of commerce. Civil chambers of commerce in Wenzhou were formed during the mid-1980s and became the key civil chambers of commerce in China by building up their own brands during the mid- to late 1990s.

3.1   Emergence and Development of Wenzhou Chambers of Commerce

When restoring its normal operation in 1979, Wenzhou Federation of Industry and Commerce immediately initiated membership registration to revive private economy. In 1988, Wenzhou Federation of Industry and Commerce started the reorganization of guilds and helped enterprises build three guilds for foreign-funded enterprises, department stores, and food enterprises, respectively. In 1989, the "Wenzhou Guild for Private Enterprise" was founded under the guidance of the Federation of Industry and Commerce and related government authorities. In 1990, Wenzhou Federation of Industry and Commerce was listed as General Chamber of Commerce, further highlighting its role in the development of private economy and civil chambers of commerce. However, due to ongoing debates on "Socialist or Capitalist" in this period, Wenzhou Federation of Industry and Commerce and civil chambers of commerce had their activities confined (Yu et al. 2008, p. 45).

Deng Xiaoping's South Tour Speech in 1992 ended the nationwide debates on "Socialist or Capitalist." Since then, Wenzhou has witnessed unprecedented development, and Wenzhou Chambers of Commerce mushroomed and bloomed rapidly. During this period, 19 nongovernmental trade organizations and trade associations were set up within the industrial and commercial system, spanning fields of furniture, clothing, glasses, hardware, synthetic leather, and so on. The Wenzhou Economic and Trade Commission system and other government authorities also launched a series of industry associations, and chambers of commerce appeared in some villages and towns. These industry associations, trade associations, and nongovernmental trade organizations were collectively referred to as the "Wenzhou Chamber of Commerce." Therefore, "Wenzhou Chamber of Commerce" is a general term for industry associations organized by governments from high to low levels and trade associations spontaneously formed by civil societies. However, the "Wenzhou Chamber of Commerce" gradually became synonymous with civil chambers, due to the dominant status of the latter.

Private economic development provided an ideal breeding ground for fast development and great achievements of the Wenzhou Chamber of Commerce. Apart from this, support from local governments and great efforts of civil chambers of commerce were also crucial. During improvement of regional economic development, with great faith in civil force, the Wenzhou government endowed rights to and worked together with civil chambers of commerce to correct market failure (Yu et al. 2008, p. 185). For instance, in 1993, the Wenzhou government granted four management rights to the Wenzhou Smoking Set Association: primary jurisdiction for business registration, supervision and inspection right for product quality, peer bargaining right, and maintenance right for new products. The last three rights were generally endowed to various industry associations.

With rights empowered by the government, the Wenzhou Chamber of Commerce improved its autonomous capacity and actively took its advantages in policy advocacy and engagement of public policy (Jiang et al. 2011; Kennedy and Deng 2012). For example, the Wenzhou Mold Industry Association, after establishment, has submitted proposals and plans to the Wenzhou Municipal People's Congress and Wenzhou Municipal People's Political Consultative Conference. Thanks to its great efforts, the mold industry was finally listed in the "Tenth Five-Year" development plan of Wenzhou City. Wenzhou Mold Industrial Park was among the characteristic industry parks with government's dedicated support.

3.2   Main Functions of Civil Chambers of Commerce

Most civil chambers of commerce (like the Wenzhou Civil Chamber of Commerce) are founded to meet private entrepreneurs' pursuits to adapt to market economic development, which are different from those industry associations established with the drive of governments at all levels since the beginning. Civil chambers of commerce help governments to conduct industrial governance but are not dependent on governments. Their sources are mainly from the market; therefore, their functions adapt more to market requirements. As a result, functions of civil chambers of commerce also change and expand with market development. Around the 1990s, civil chambers of commerce mainly served to rectify the market order, improve product quality, and protect intellectual property; in the mid- and late 1990s, new functions arose, such as promotion of industrial clusters, enhancement of industrial brand construction, and breakthrough of international trade barriers. The main functions of civil chambers of commerce are listed below:

1. Provide services for member enterprises. This is a basic function for civil chambers of commerce, with main forms such as delivering information to member enterprises, promoting communication between member enterprises and other organizations, delivering technology services for enterprises through innovation platforms and technical R&D centers, cultivating talents through professional and technical training, and so on.
2. Promote product quality. Faced with disorder competition in early market economy, civil chambers of commerce take product quality improvement as a priority. Main measures include preparation of industrial standards, quality certification, and quality detection.
3. Protect product development interests. During market economy development, intellectual property and patent protection are critical to encourage and promote enterprise innovation. Fully aware of this, chambers of civil commerce have done considerable work in preparing regulations and rules and in conflict reconciliation.
4. Strengthen industry brand building. Industry brand is the key for industries and enterprises to win market competition. Through certification and promotion of famous enterprise brands, well-known trademarks, and brand products, civil chambers of commerce play critical roles in building industrial and regional brands. Taking the Wenzhou Chamber of Commerce as an example, by the end of 2007, Wenzhou has 35 national brand-characteristic industrial bases and several professional brand bases at the provincial level such as "China Shoes City" and "China Electrical City," greatly improving the influence and popularity of Wenzhou economy.
5. Break through international trade barriers. Since the 1990s, as China established its status as the "World Factory," Chinese products have taken up an increasing proportion of the international market and, meanwhile, encountered international trade barriers several times. Compared with government- or system-oriented industry associations, civil chambers of commerce are more likely to earn equal status with foreign business associations. Therefore, with support of governments, civil chambers of commerce become major actors in filing antidumping lawsuits, establishment of early-warning information systems, and defending

antidumping cases. For example, from 2002 to 2006, the Wenzhou Smoking Set Association has initiated several negotiations with related European countries with regard to CR Law[1] and finally succeeded.

4   Renovation of Business Associations Since 1990s

In the early 1990s, with the establishment of the market economy status, great importance was attached on roles of various types of business associations. However, at that time, business associations faced many urgent problems. For instance, official and semiofficial industry associations were highly dependent on governments and showed insufficient governance capacity. Civil chambers of commerce, restricted by a "dual-management system," were hardly registered and had a lack of autonomous right. Considering this, since the mid- and late 1990s, the Chinese government has taken measures to reform business associations. Main reform objects included industry associations and chambers of commerce (based on name change in policies, which were named "industry associations, chambers of commerce" and "industry associations and chambers of commerce"). The core theme of reform was "de-administration." Details included separation of industry associations and chambers of commerce from the administrative organ, improvement of management system of industry associations and chambers of commerce, and establishment of a new relationship between governments and industry associations and chambers of commerce.

4.1   Pilots of Industry Associations in Four Cities

In 1997, the State Economic and Trade Commission issued the *Plans for Selecting Several Cities as the Pilots of Industry Associations* (G.J.M. [1997], No. 139). According to this plan, Shanghai, Guangzhou, Xiamen, and Wenzhou were selected in the hope to define status, functions, and roles of industry associates and to explore a basic mode of industry associations with Chinese characters. Later, industry association construction was advanced in pilot cities. For example, in Wenzhou, a "Pilot Leadership Group for Industry Associations" was established, and six representative industry associations in the fields of food

---

[1] As early as 1994, the United States had implemented the CR Law ("CR" is an acronym for "Child Resistant" and was developed by the European Committee for Standardization). According to this law, all lighters below US$2, before entry to the US market, must be mounted with a safety lock to prevent accidental use by children. However, the CR patent was mainly owned by US and European manufacturers, and Wenzhou lighter manufactures failed to take corresponding measures. As a result, most Wenzhou lighters had to exit the US market. In September 2001, as requested by some European lighter manufacturers, the European Union also issued the CR Law, requiring a safety lock for all lighters below €2. In this case, the Wenzhou Smoking Set Association and membership enterprises made several negotiations with related European countries with regard to the CR Law.

industry, packaging technology, and the shoe leather industry were put under centralized management of the Wenzhou Economic and Trade Commission; in 1999, the *Administrative Measures for Wenzhou Industry Associations* was issued; in 2002, Shanghai issued the *Interim Measures for Shanghai Industry Associations*, which specified government support and promotion policies for industry associations, proposed to transfer out to industry associations those functions that should have been under the management of the industry and guarantee independent work of industry associations.

4.2   Early Exploration of "Separation of Associations from Governments"

Given the initial success of pilot programs for industry associations, in 1999, the State Economic and Trade Commission issued the *Several Opinions about Accelerating the Cultivation and Development of Industry and Commerce Associations (Trial)* (G.J.M.C.Y. [1999] No. 1016), which proposed that industry associations shall follow the principles of "self-reliance, self-governance, and self-development" and actively explore management modes of industry associations and chambers of business in the principle of "separation of associations from governments." Later, "separation" of associations from governments was undertaken in some places. For example, in 2003, Nanjing announced complete separation of associations from governments within one year. Public servants and those with reference to the management of public servants shall not hold posts concurrently in industry associations and chambers of commerce. Those who already hold a concurrent post must resign from the industry associations and chambers of commerce or the public office (Zhou 2015a, p. 75).

In March 2005, the *Some Opinions about Promoting the Reform and Development of Industry Associations and Chambers of Commerce* (exposure draft) was issued, which put forward that the industry associations and chambers of commerce shall be completely separated from governments and their instrumentalities, as well as enterprises and public institutions in four aspects including functions, institutions, staff, and finance. This exposure draft has clearly defined the policy thoughts for separation of associations from governments. Later, the separation of associations from governments in four aspects was initiated across China and reached a peak around 2007. Guangdong and Zhejiang provinces announced a basic completion of separation during this period (Zhou 2015b, pp. 26–27). However, as a whole, this work was unbalanced and incomplete. "Unbalanced" means that some places failed to completely implement the separation policies, even in the clear issue of leadership concurrent posts. "Incomplete" means that in terms of policy, the separation of associations from governments included four aspects. However, separation in functions in some places was less than satisfactory.

4.3   Promoting Function Transfer and Government Procurement of Services

Function transfer is the difficulty and key in the reform of "separation of associations from governments." To advance this, in 2007, the *Some Opinions of the General Office of the State Council about Accelerating and Promoting the Reform and Development of Industry Associations and Chambers of Commerce* (G.B.F. [2007] No. 36) was issued, which pointed out that "the people's governments at various levels and their instrumentalities shall further transform their functions, entrust or transfer out to the industry associations those functions suitable for them." Later, local governments promulgated related polices. For instance, in 2010, Wuxi in Jiangsu Province issued the *Implementing Measures on the Wuxi Municipal Government Procurement of Public Services from Industry Associations and Chambers of Commerce* (Trial) and the *Implementing Opinions on the Undertaking of Related Government Functions by Wuxi Industry Associations and Chambers of Commerce*; in April 2010, Wenzhou in Zhejiang Province issued the *Implementing Opinions on the Pilots of Transferring Technical Service Functions of Governments to Industry Associations and Chambers of Commerce*; and in June 2010, Shaoxing City in Zhejiang Province issued the *Implementing Opinions on the Pilots of Transferring Some Government Functions to Industry Associations and Chambers of Commerce*. All localities have promoted the pilot work of function transfer and have obtained sound achievements.

On September 26, 2013, the *Guiding Opinions of the General Office of the State Council for the Government Procurement of Services from the Social Forces* was issued, which clearly required the utilization of social forces in public service fields and strengthening of government procurement. After that, many local governments have issued related guiding opinions or policies on government procurement of services from social organizations, including some provisions on function transfer to industry associations and chambers of commerce. Those provisions have strongly promoted the transfer of partial government functions to industry associations and chambers of commerce and the government purchase of services from industry associations and chambers of commerce. For example, in 2014, Wenzhou initiated a pilot program for the undertaking of government functions by industry associations and chambers in Ouhai District in the forms of government procurement of service and administrative entrustment. The industry associations in building and automobile parts and motorcycle parts have undertaken 25 functions transferred from 7 government departments. In 2015, pilot work has blossomed in another 10 counties (cities and districts) of Wenzhou City. After two years of exploration and practice, Wenzhou municipal governments have accelerated the "simplification, improvement, and transfer of functions," and industry associations and chambers of commerce have been "upgraded."

4.4   Management System Reform

At the turn of the century, social organizations, including industry organizations, have made great progress and played a strong role in economic and social development. However, restricted by traditional systems of "Dual Management" and "one association in one industry," industry associations and chambers of commerce have faced problems, such as difficult registration, lack of market competition, and innovation capacity, which restricted their development. Guangdong, Zhejiang, and Shanghai have always explored the reform and improvement of the management system of industry associations and chambers of commerce. For instance, since January 1, 2012, Guangzhou City in Guangdong Province has implemented the *Notice on Promoting Development of Social Organizations by Further Deepening the Registration Reform*, which specifies that except those requiring preadministration approval according to national laws and regulations, eight categories of organizations, such as industry associations and nonlocal chambers of commerce,[2] can directly apply for registration to the registration authority. In addition, the Notice also specifies to shorten the registration period and lower registration threshold of social organizations.

In 2012, giving full respect to local policy innovation and considering actual development requirements of social organizations, the report at the 18th Party Congress pointed out that "we should quicken the pace of building a system of modern social organizations in which functions of the government are separated from those of social organizations, rights and responsibilities are clearly established, and social organizations exercise autonomy in accordance with the law to guide health and orderly development of social organizations." In 2013, the *Plan for the Institutional Restructuring of the State Council and Transformation of Functions Thereof* put forward that the separation of industry associations and chambers of commerce from administrative authorities shall be gradually advanced, and self-discipline shall be strengthened; "many associations in one industry" shall be explored and a competitive mechanism shall be introduced; and four categories of social organizations, such as industry associations and chambers of commerce, can directly apply for registration to the Civil Affairs Department without approval by the business authority. For industry associations and chambers of commerce, these are major policy breakthroughs, which, if implemented, will overcome huge restraints faced by the industry associations and chambers of commerce and help them return to the essence of a social entity organization (Zhou 2014).

With clear policies of CPC and National People's Congress (NPC), the State Council further advanced the reform of the management system for industry associations and chambers of commerce. In 2014, the State Council

---

[2] Eight categories of organizations include industry associations, nonlocal chambers of commerce, social organizations in public service, social service, economy, technology, sports, and culture.

cancelled three approval items for "establishment filing of social organizations and branches and representative institutions," "establishment registration, change registration, and cancellation registration of national social organizations and branches and representative institutions," and "preapproval for foreign chambers of commerce in China by the Ministry of Commerce." This marked the autonomy of industry associations, and chambers of commerce further developed with the improvement of the management system.

4.5   A New Round of Separation Reform

Despite the remarkable progress in the reform of industry associations and chambers of commerce, the most important target, "separation of associations from governments," is yet to be fully realized, in particular at the central-government level. For historical reasons, it is hard to separate national-level industry associations and chambers of commerce from governments. In addition, in some economically undeveloped areas, industry associations and chambers of commerce still carry a strong administrant implication for lagging reform (Jia and Zhang 2016). To this end, on July 8, 2015, the General Office of the CPC Central Committee and the General Office of the State Council issued the *General Plan for the Separation of Industry Associations and Chambers of Commerce from Administrative Organs* (hereinafter referred to as the General Plan). As required, a clear functional boundary between industry associations and chambers of commerce shall be defined so that the latter can be real service-oriented social organizations established in accordance with laws, featuring autonomous organization, regulated management, and self-discipline conducts. According to the General Plan, main bodies for the separation of associations from governments include administrative authorities at all levels and "other authorities managed in accordance with, or with reference to, the Civil Servant Law" and industry associations and chambers of commerce sponsored by, or managed by, attached to, or connected to those authorities. Specifically, industry associations and chambers of commerce shall meet these conditions: economic organizations whose membership subjects are organizations, persons of same trade engaged in economic activities of similar nature or in a same region; names are suffixed by "industry association," "association," "chamber of commerce," "guild," "joint association," and "promotion association"; and registered as social entity organizations in Civil Affairs departments. According to the reform directions for transforming industry associations and chambers of commerce into civil, social, and marketized organizations, the General Plan puts forward "five separations and five regulations."[3]

---

[3] Organizational separation: regulate comprehensive supervision relationship; functional separation: regulate administrative entrustment and division of responsibilities; financial separation: regulate property relationship; separation of personnel management: regulate employment relationship; and separation of party construction and foreign affairs: regulate management relationship.

To implement the new round of separation plans, the State Council and related departments have prepared and formulated a series of supporting policies. For example, in July 2015, the General Office of the State Council issued the *Circular on Establishing a Joint Working Group for the Separation of Industry Associations and Chambers of Commerce from Administrative Organs* (G.B.F. [2015] No. 53), according to which a special working group was established to promote this work; in September 2015, the Ministry of Finance issued the *Circular on the Undertaking of Government Procurement Service by Industry Associations and Chambers of Commerce (Trial)* (C.Z. [2015] No. 73) and the *Circular on the Reform of Funding Support Method for the Separation of Industry Associations and Chambers of Commerce from Governments (Trial)* (C.J. [2015] No. 788); in the same year, the *Circular of the Ministry of Civil Affairs on Issuing the Administrative Measures for Required Qualifications for Persons-in-Charge of National Industry Associations and Chambers of Commerce* (Trial) (M.F. [2015] No. 166) was issued. In December 2016, nine departments jointly issued the *Comprehensive Supervision Measures for Industry Associations and Chambers of Commerce* (Trial) (F.G.J.T. [2016] No. 2657). Those policy documents gradually formed a comprehensive system, jointly supporting the reform of the industry of associations and chambers of commerce.

In November 2015, the joint working group published the pilot list of the first batch of national industry associations and chambers of commerce to be separated from governments. After that, local governments speeded up the reform and conducted related work in accordance with central-government policies. In October 2016, Shanghai initiated the first batch of pilot work and established a leading group for the separation of industry associations and chambers of commerce from administrative organs, with details governed by the Civil Affairs Department. The separation is mainly to clear the relationship between industry associations and chambers of commerce and business authorities; and regulation is mainly to strengthen party construction and to improve supervision mechanisms.

This round of reform is still in progress and the reform results remain to be seen. Compared with the separation in 1990s, no doubt, this vigorous reform is a typical administration-oriented reform driven from the central government to local governments with a high level and wide coverage. In general, characterized by "mobilized" management, this type of reform can achieve results in a short period under normal circumstances. However, the accomplishment of goals is yet to be tested by practice.

It is noteworthy that apart from the above reforms, with the support of CPC Central Committee and the State Council, and efforts of related functional departments, the preferential tax policies, personnel policies, and policies for participating in society management are constantly optimized. In addition, governments have carried out several special rectification actions for unauthorized charges among industry associations and chambers of commerce,[4] which are of great importance to their development.

5   OPPORTUNITIES AND CHALLENGES FOR BUSINESS ASSOCIATIONS

The 18th CPC National Congress provided the new direction for economic and social development, ushering in a new stage of comprehensively deepening reform in China. In the economic field, surrounding the goals of "leaving the market to play the decisive role in allocation of resources," the governments have taken a number of reform initiatives, such as encouraging the development of "Internet +" and information networking; created various conditions for promoting mass entrepreneurship and innovation; and put forward "the Belt and Road Initiative." In the social field, strengthening and innovating social management is deemed as a crucial foothold for realizing the "13th Five-Year" plan. Governments have created platforms for social management innovation in all aspects. Under new economic and social situations, industry organizations face both development opportunities and challenges, and their future depends on whether they can grasp opportunities and address the challenges.

The industry organization is an amphibious organization of economy and society. It is a reorganized organization based on economic organizations, which are of great importance in economic development. In addition, as a social group, the industry organization also has a crucial impact on civil society. In turn, change of economic or social environment will also impact the industry organization. In this era of comprehensive deepening reform, the new opportunities for industry organizations include the following.

First of all, the Party and government's repositioning of the market puts forward again the requirement to determine the functional boundary between the government and the market. This provides the policy backbone for governments' transfer of functions and industrial organizations actively seeking market opportunities. After nearly 40 years of development, though industry organizations in China have played a certain role, given excessive market intervention by the government, the function of industry organizations is unable to be brought into full play as it should have been. The new requirement on the relationship between the government and the market will surely change this situation. With the industrial management function required by the market economy back in hand, industry organizations will have more space to develop. Meanwhile, as the government-market relationship is increasingly standardized, governments will no longer directly intervene in microeconomic affairs.

---

[4] For example, on September 13, 2017, the executive meeting of the State Council required that related departments shall be urgent to issue measures to rectify repeat, high, and excessive charges and resolutely ban illegal charges.

As the club organization of enterprises, the industry organization can get close to the enterprise and learn industry advantages and make considerable contributions to serving membership enterprises and promoting industry development.

Second, the main economic tasks of the Party and government are to transform the mode of economic development, optimize and upgrade the industrial structure, and improve international economic competition. Therefore, industry organizations are required to play their due roles in these aspects. Under new circumstances, industry organizations shall play important roles in promoting industrial scientific innovation, promoting industrial clusters, establishing a common industrial service platform, strengthening and improving industry management, leading and promoting the quality and efficiency for the improvement of the industry, participating in the international economic competition, and dealing with international trade friction; they shall become a main impetus for economic transformation and upgrading and development of an export-oriented economy. Moreover, some industry organizations have an indispensable role in new undertakings, such as all-people innovation and "the Belt and Road," and become a vital force in leading China's economic innovation and development and "going out."

Lastly, the transformation and innovation of social management bring numerous opportunities for industry organizations to participate in the process. As an aggregation of entrepreneurs, the industry organization must fulfill its function for cohesion of industry enterprises and for giving back to the society on behalf of the later. In history, industry organizations like guilds, commercial groups, and guild halls have been playing a key role in supporting entrepreneurs, industry public benefit, and charities. However, after the founding of the PRC, these functions have been gradually weakened as a result of overall control of society by the government. Under new circumstances, industry organizations shall take on greater social responsibilities. Despite traditional functions, they shall make a difference in credit construction and social responsibilities of industry enterprises and development of industry philanthropy.

While seeing the opportunities, we should also notice that industry organizations are facing a number of challenges. With nearly 40 years of development after the reform and opening up, industry associations in China amounted close to 70,000 in June 2015, which was far from enough compared with China's mammoth economy. In terms of structure, about 90% industry organizations in China are government-run or semigovernment-run, while those spontaneously formed by the private sector only take up a very small proportion. After rounds of "separations of associations from governments," government-run or semigovernment-run industry associations and chambers of commerce have moved toward independence. However, this process is yet to be finished. The market properties of these industry associations and chambers of commerce still have to be improved. These problems are greatly related to the original "Dual Management" and "one association in one industry." Reforms in recent years, such as "direct registration" and "many associations in one industry," are not a complete success. Despite great achievements, many problems are caused or left over. In this era of comprehensive deepening reform, the main challenges for industry organizations are listed as follows:

1. In terms of the external environment, business associations are lacking national legal regulations. In the Late Qing Dynasty and the Republic of China era, there were once laws on business associations in China. However, after the founding of new China, related legislative work lagged behind, and until now no related law has been issued. Due to a lack of laws, some fundamental problems surrounding business associations remain unsolved. For example, internationally, the relationship between business organizations and governments has always been divided into "Pluralist Model," "Corporatism Model," and "Mixed Model." Under different positionings, the statuses, roles, and functions of business associations, and their relationship with governments, are totally different. Under which positioning should Chinese business associations be selected for development? With no clear legal positioning, how should a government manage business associations? How should it conduct its relationship with business associations? If these problems are not solved, it will inevitably influence the development of industry associations and chambers of commerce.

2. Systems such as "direct registration" and "many associations in one industry" have not been fully put in place. Despite significant progress in the management system of industry associations, and chambers of commerce, and cancellation of the original "Dual Management" system in policy, the "direct registration" system is only implemented in cities like Shenzhen and Wenzhou. The preapproval for establishment of industry associations and chambers of commerce and "one association in one industry" still prevails in most places. Some places only implement these two policies for newly established industry associations and chambers of commerce. The management system reform has a limited role in promoting development of business associations and competitive environment is not formed. A number of industry associations and chambers of commerce still enjoy a monopolistic position, and it is not easy to form new organizations.

3. Functional transfer from governments to industry organizations is slow and even stagnated. A clear functional boundary between governments and business associations is the primary premise for the development of the latter. Aware of this, the Chinese government has made several reforms in promoting "the separation of associations from governments." However, the separation in the form of person, finance, and property is easy, but functional separation, which is the essence, can hardly be promoted as scheduled. Many departments are very concerned about functional transfer to or service procurement from business associations for fear of the loss of power or fear that industry organizations

are not mature enough for fulfilling related functions or because those departments are not capable for clearing the function boundary. In places where function transfer is vigorously advanced, problems still exist. For example, some governments seem to have transferred functions, but the truth is the opposite, or, some governments only transfer indifferent functions or those that are difficult to implement. As a whole, many functional transfers are formalistic with crucial issues being evaded. The functional space expansion for business associations remains a daunting task.

4. Lastly, in the Internet era, the meaning of business associations is under threat. As a joint organization for entrepreneurs, it mainly serves to overcome the dilemma of collective action, enhance information exchange of members, and share resources. In traditional periods, these works must be completed by organizing a physical organization, which can now be done by a network virtual association, where entrepreneurs can form a fellowship and jointly discuss and settle problems in a network platform and can combine online work with offline work to achieve entity cooperation from a virtual association. All these do not necessarily need a formal organization at high costs. For industry organizations, this technical change brings huge challenges, which is very likely to eliminate the meaning of existing business associations. Therefore, business associations must rethink and reform the traditional management mode, take full advantage of Internet technologies, and create a new working mode to provide services for members in a more convenient and economic manner and timely achieve transformation and upgrading of the organization and management.

Besides the external environment, business associations still face some internal challenges. Many business associations have acted as the "second government" and enjoyed the monopoly position from "one association in one industry" for a long time and, therefore, have been used to the bureaucratic style of work (Ni 2016), with lagging self-construction ability and insufficient member service capacity. This is specifically manifested by an incomplete management structure of industry associations and chambers of commerce, a limited role of the board of directors, and a lack of supervision mechanism; an incomplete financial and personnel management system and serious patriarchal style; a lack of strategic management and transform consciousness; a lack of core functions and competitiveness; and so on. In general, internal management for business associations is far from achieving expectations and requirements of economic and social development.

6   Development Prospects of Business Associations

The Chinese government has been aware of the great significance of developing business associations, and has made numerous efforts that bring new changes, which increases quantity and improves the roles of business associations to some extent. However, compared with the actual development requirement in China, these efforts are far from enough, and further development still needs to be driven by new policies. It can be expected that the reform in Chinese business associations will continue until a relative mature development mode is established. Based on the requirements of business associations and the main problems in their development, future reform might include focusing on the following aspects:

1. Define the development mode of business associations. In terms of the present reform of Chinese business associations, we will not follow the development direction of the "Corporatism Model," which features compulsory membership and grants industry organizations with a public entity identity (Yu 2008, p. 37). Instead, China adopts a free membership system, and the government grants industry associations and chambers of commerce a corporate identity; this is somewhat similar to the Pluralist Model, but entrustment of public functions, service procurement, and party construction strengthening are not part of the "Pluralist Model." China seems to follow a "Mixed Model" path. On the one hand, industry organizations are defined as autonomous organizations with the principle of voluntary membership; on the other hand, governments will grant industry organizations with a large number of management functions; however, the Chinese government cannot get rid of authoritarian regime awareness and has strengthened flexible regulation for business associations while advancing their "legal autonomy." Therefore, on the basis of the "Mixed Model," China may explore a "Chinese Model" for the development of business associations and select a development path with Chinese characters.

2. Further regulate the relationship between governments and industry organizations. The separation of associations from governments, not yet ended, has made a great impact on Chinese industry organizations. On the one hand, this reform will completely break the dependence of industry associations and chambers of commerce on governments to achieve independent development and legal autonomy; on the other hand, if transfer of government functions and cultivation and support policies are not in place, industry associations and chambers of commerce with little market experience can hardly survive in the market, and old organizations will also become extinct. If new industry organizations are to be generated based on market requirements, the undertaking of Chinese business associations must start from the beginning, which is not the best solution. Therefore, the Chinese government is extremely likely to speed

up improving the supporting policies for "separating associations form governments" and to further promote the transfer of government functions and reform of government purchase services and put these two key works into practice. Meanwhile, Chinese governments may issue policies to cultivate and support business associations and further practice the system of "many associations in one industry." This will guarantee a certain transformation period for organizations forced to be "separated" and help them smoothly adapt to the market environment. Moreover, this will be helpful to enhance market competition and the upgrading of business associations.

3. Strengthen comprehensive supervision for business associations. The Chinese government has always emphasized "separation of functions but not separation of management" for industry associations and chambers of commerce. In a new round of separation reform, comprehensive supervision measures for industry associations and chambers of commerce are issued. However, at present, comprehensive supervision is an abstract concept, and related policies and regulations are principle contents. How to put comprehensive supervision in place remains an urgent problem. Therefore, for future development, the Chinese government should focus on the management of business associations for the establishment of a comprehensive system and determination of a comprehensive supervision system. No doubt, the key is to determine specific supervision functions and a mode of realization of each supervision department; to establish department linkage mechanisms; to play a self-supervision role of business associations; and to make the most of non-administrative supervision like industry supervision and social supervision. For the Chinese government, the last work is difficult yet important.

4. Prepare laws for business associations. There has been a long-lasting call for laws in business associations from all social circles. Since the 18th CPC National Congress, a series of reforms have been taken around business associations, with the aim of specifying positioning, role, and function of industry organizations and their relationship with governments. With the advance of reform, some important problems need to be clarified in practice, which also provide a rich practice foundation for preparation of laws for industry organizations. From another aspect, to reinforce reform achievements, legislative departments may also actively promote legislative work for business associations and define a structural system, management system, main functions, the relationship between business associations and governments, and supporting policies by law.

Besides government efforts, self-renovation of business associations is also essential to maintain their sustainable development. For most business associations, the most important thing is to stick to organizational principles and establish a management structure based on modern nonprofit organization requirements and realize good governance on the basis of independence. On this basis, business associations shall serve members and engage in industry management and create core competitiveness and brand image surrounding main functions of the organization.

All in all, with the development of the market economy and with government policy backing and self-effort, Chinese business associations, with industry associations and chambers of commerce as the main bodies, have witnessed fast development and made certain contributions in promoting economic development and improving industry management after the reform and opening up, and have become a nonnegligible force in Chinese civil society. Currently, comprehensively deepening reform in China has provided a rare chance for the development of business associations. However, due to various reasons, business associations also face many challenges. Whether business associations can overcome challenges and seize the chance finally depends on governments' determination and actions of advancing business associations' reform and efforts of business associations in improving organization governance and management.

References

All-China Federation of Industry and Commerce. 2013. *Brief History of All-China Federation of Industry and Commerce* (1953–2013). Beijing: All-China Federation of Industry and Commerce Press.

Jia, X.J., H. C. Shen, and W.A. Hu, et al. 2004. *Industrial Associations under Transition Period: Roles, Functions and Management Systems*. Beijing: Social Sciences Academic Press.

Jia, X.J., and J. Zhang. 2016. Reform strategies and challenges of separating industry associations and chambers of commerce from government. *Social Governance* 1: 99–105.

Jiang H., J.J. Zhang, and Y. Zhou. 2011. Interests alignment: An analytical framework of the state and society relations in transitional China. *Sociology Studies* 2: 136–152.

Kennedy, S., and G.S. Deng. 2012. Analysis of the factors shaping the lobbying behavior of industry associations. *Comparative Economy and Social System* 4: 147–156.

Ni, X. L. 2016. Study on improving internal management after separation of industry associations and chambers of commerce from governments. *Administrative Management Reform* 10: 41–45.

Salarmon, L.M., et al. 2002. *Global Civil Society: Dimensions of the Nonprofit Sector*. Beijing: Social Sciences Academic Press.

Xu, J.I. 2010. *Mutual Beneficial Organization: Study of Industry Associations in China*. Beijing: Beijing Normal University Press.

Yu, H. 2008. Model election for the management system of business association. *Research on Financial and Economic Issue* 8: 31–39.

Yu, J.X., H. Jiang, and J. Zhou. 2008. *A Path for Chinese Civil Society: A Case Study on Business Associations in Wenzhou, China*. Hangzhou: Zhejiang University Press.

Yu, J.X., W.L. Zhang, and X.Q. Song. 2010. *Trade Association Management*. Hangzhou: Zhejiang People's Publishing House.

Zhou, J. 2014. Autonomy and law-based autonomy of industry associations and chambers of commerce. *Journal of Zhejiang Provincial Party School* 5: 38–44.

Zhou, J. 2015a. *Social Organization Management*. Beijing: China Renmin University Press.

Zhou, J. 2015b. Function separation determines the success of separation of associations from governments. *China Social Organization* 19: 26–27.

Zhou, J., and X.Q. Song. 2011. Public functions of industrial associations and their reconstruction: Cases of Hangzhou and Wenzhou industrial associations. *Journal of Zhejiang University* 6: 36–46.

Zhu, Y. 2014. The amendment of the law on chambers of commerce in the 1920s and Its effects. *History Researches* 2: 91–107.

CHAPTER 12

The Development of Charitable Organizations in China Since Reform and Opening-Up and a New Layout for State-Society Relations

Ming Wang and Shuoyan Li

1 Introduction

This chapter briefly straightens out the development of China's social organizations since the reform and opening-up and the corresponding boom of charities. It then focuses on the newly emerged social organizations—charitable organizations brought about by the newly issued *Charity Law* in 2016. With the implementation of the *Charity Law* and the development of charitable organizations, a new state-society system has been formulated. This new system, based on the Internet as the platform, has three characteristics, including information transparency, social regulation, and charitable big data. Social organizations in China have entered a new era with charitable organizations as the major players. There is a new layout for state-society relations, which is based on charity and social values playing the dominant role, and collaboration between social organizations and the market has been set up.

Since 1978, China adopted the reform and opening-up policy; various social organizations have been actively engaged in social service concerning various fields at all levels of government. It is no doubt that social organizations are playing a significant part in the transformation of the state-society relationship. In recent years, with the support from the government, public services, as well as

M. Wang (✉)
School of Public Policy and Management, Tsinghua University, Beijing, China
e-mail: oumei@mail.tsinghua.edu.cn

S. Li
School of Sociology and Political Science, Shanghai University, Shanghai, China
e-mail: shuoyan.li@qq.com

J. Yu, S. Guo (eds.), *The Palgrave Handbook of Local Governance in Contemporary China*, https://doi.org/10.1007/978-981-13-2799-5_12

245

other charity activities, has been the most vigorous sector in tackling social problems, reconciling social conflicts, and improving social governance. The *Charity Law of the People's Republic of China*, which was released in 2016, specifies that charitable organizations share the same highest legitimacy and preferential policies as other social organizations and establishes a new institutional framework that takes information disclosure as its primary task. It places charitable organizations under the supervision of the whole society and, thus, sets the government and the society free. The *Charity Law* also enables the gradual formation of a new state-society relationship system, which is based on information disclosure, social monitoring, and big data and relies on the Internet platform. The essence of this system can be summarized as "government control, platform-based organization, all-around social supervision and operation by law." It is impossible for a newly formed system to skip a transitional period. However, we are firmly convinced that the new system, backed by extensive legal support and prevailing charity momentum, will advance step by step steadily, and that it will in turn deepen the reform of the entire social system. A new state-society relationship landscape is increasingly taking shape. This landscape gives priority to public services, charities, and social values and advocates the coordinated development of various social organizations, government authorities, and the market.

2   THE DEVELOPMENT OF SOCIAL ORGANIZATIONS IN CHINA SINCE THE REFORM AND OPENING-UP

The most profound change for China since 1978 is its embrace of the market economy. First, as China's rural reform (characterized by the household contract responsibility system) proceeded, the commodity economy started to make its way into vast rural areas and domains of agricultural production and product circulation and then penetrated every aspect of the entire society via the market. Soon afterward, the curtain of the urban economic system reform was also lifted, where the state-owned enterprises transformed step by step; private enterprises gradually emerged; and limitations concerning various elements and fields of market economy were removed little by little. When the market has the final say in the economy, it is only reasonable to expect a wealth difference among different people and, therefore, differentiated social class. Among these groups, those entrepreneurs have stood out on the historical stage because they own means of production, capital, and wealth. Other occupational groups also start to enrich the whole society, including the accountants, auditors, lawyers, teachers, and doctors. Meanwhile, a large group of grassroots laborers termed "migrant workers" or "peasant workers" have also offered their shares of contribution to the whole society. Social organizations with an intermediary nature, which are indispensable in the development of market economy, have made their appearances on the market economy stage, including all kinds of trade associations, chambers of commerce, professional associations, federations, promotion associations, and rights protection or mutual aid organizations, which are the voice for the abovementioned "migrant workers" or "peasant workers." These social organizations work as the interest expression and rights protection agencies simultaneously for different interest groups. The government, under such circumstances, also accelerates the reform process. The reform, under the guide principle of making economic development the central task, has gradually shifted its main focus from direct management over all the economic fields to macroeconomic regulation and market supervision. In addition, the reform has given more priorities to social management and public services. Many economic and social functions that were previously carried out by the government are being transferred to intermediary trade associations. The development of the market economy and its external effect on a harmonious society have assisted in the booming of various social organizations.

Alongside China's development of a market economy is a tough social transformation. The Chinese society prior to 1978 was highly politicized. As its market economy developed and reform in the government system progressed, the established "unit" system (including the people's commune system in rural China) was about to collapse. The "unit," once being the "carrier" of people's social life, along with a variety of unit-based social relations, ethics, value systems, and codes of conduct, gradually lost its functions and significance of existence, thus, bringing about a process of "fragmented" social disruption. On the other hand, with the proceeding of government reform, state power decreased its social control. Yet, whether in urban communities or rural societies, no new model of social integration was established, leaving a huge vacuum between the state and the society. It is precisely in the context of social disruption and state power withdrawal that social reconstruction was initiated alongside the development of the market economy. In the vast urban communities and rural societies, a large number of grassroots social organizations sprang up in the form of independent operations at the primary level. Voluntarily founded by the masses, those organizations prioritized the needs and values of the grassroots society and, to some extent, replaced the established social network and gave rise to new common interests and public spaces. Meanwhile, they strove to strike a balance among the profit pursuit of a market economy, the administrative promotion of community building by governments at all levels, the public call for residents' self-governance, as well as a range of social needs. By doing so, they managed to form a diversified landscape of interests and a mix of interactions. Social transformation-enabled social reconstruction (particularly urban community and rural society-centered grassroots social reconstruction) helped to facilitate the vigorous development of social organizations in various forms.

Against the backdrop that the market economy develops and the society undertakes reconstruction, the original planned economy gradually loses its functions, and it still takes time for a new society to be built. Besides, governmental organizations are undertaking trial and error in reform, and the market economy has its intrinsic defects. Under such circumstances, the deficiency of related regulations and mechanisms in social transformation has been amplified, leading to increasingly severe social problems concerning ecological environment, poverty, education, and public health. Subsequently, the disparity between the wealthy and the poor is becoming more serious and social conflicts are intensifying. In the face of all these prominent social problems, many citizens have taken the initiative in the cause of charity to protect the environment, help the poor, support education, enable AIDS prevention and control, and so on. On the other hand, in the context of the market economy, some new charitable organizations, such as private foundations that are dominated by the rich and entrepreneurs, have come to the fore. Charity in China has assumed a similar development path to that of China's economy, as China gradually alleviates its economy out of poverty and keeps accumulating wealth. Charity in China has experienced a historical transition from "charity by the masses," which features mass participation, to "charity by the rich," which is led by the elites.

It has been almost 40 years since China launched its reform and opening-up. During this period, social organizations in China have gone through two phases. The first one starts from the beginning of the reform and opening-up to 1992. Social organizations in China experienced a period of primitive growth from scratch. The tremendous power released by the reform and opening-up, coupled with a lack of corresponding regulations, gave rise to the explosive growth of social organizations during this period. Among all the organizations, academies and institutes took up a large proportion, associations in various forms grew steadily, and foundations developed from nothing. By the end of 1992, social organizations registered in civil administration departments at all levels totaled 154,500, which was 22 times that of 1978. This period of time was identified as the "emergence of social organizations." The second phase, starting from 1993 and continuing to the present day, is regarded as the "climax of standardized management and further development of social organizations." During this phase, social organizations in China have experienced two distinct development stages. The first stage features the standardized management of social organizations by the Communist Party of China (CPC) and the government and the resulting slow development of those social organizations. The second stage, benefiting from a more developed market economy, in-depth reform and opening-up, and all-around social transformation, gradually brings the development of social organizations to a new height. Compared with those of 1992, social organizations registered in civil administration departments by the end of 2000 saw a decrease, rather than increase. Its total number was only 85% of the 1992 figure, showing the arduous development of Chinese social organizations within the standardized regulation framework. Around 2000, there was a new upsurge in social organizations. According to the statistics from the Ministry of Civil Affairs, the annual cumulative number of all social organizations registered in civil administration departments at all levels reached 200,000 in 2001; 300,000 in 2005; 400,000 in 2008; 500,000 in 2012; and 600,000 in 2014. By the end of 2016, this number had exceeded 702,000, which was 4.5 times that of 1992. During this stage, social organizations, foundations, and private nonprofit organizations have grown rapidly and more importantly, a large group of unregistered social organizations, or organizations registered as a business entity, emerged in all walks of life. They are particularly active in the following areas: environmental protection, poverty alleviation and development, safeguarding the rights and interests of women and children, education support, public health, social welfare, industrial governance, and so on. In rural and urban areas and even virtual space, such as the Internet, a growing number of social organizations have kept popping up, playing a significant role in every aspect of current society.

3   The Booming Charity Work in China

Since the beginning of China's reform and opening-up, as the economy advanced and the society progressed, charity work has resumed its development. Especially in the recent decade, charity work in China has seen prosperous growth in many aspects, as demonstrated in the following six sections.

3.1   Increase in Social Donation

The Wenchuan Earthquake in 2008 pushed China's annual social donation from RMB 30.9 billion in 2007 to RMB 107 billion in 2008. Despite a little drop in the number, the Yushu Earthquake in 2010 led to a social donation fever. The number amounted to more than RMB 100 billion again, reaching RMB 103.2 billion. The third time when the number was higher than RMB 100 billion was in 2014, standing at RMB 104 billion. After this, the number increased to RMB 121.5 billion in 2015 and RMB 134.6 billion in 2016 (Yang 2015, 2016, 2017). It is fair to say that social donations in China have generated a huge and stable scale with RMB 100 billion as the unit and have become staunch supporters for China's charity work.

3.2   Fast Development of Charitable Social Organizations

Charitable social organizations are the most active and fastest growing organizations among all kinds of social organizations, especially those private nonenterprise organizations (social service agencies) providing grassroots' social services and foundations. Private nonenterprise organizations took off since the 1990s. According to the statistics of the Department of Civil Affairs, the registered number of those organizations at different civil departments at the end of year exceeded 100,000 in 2002; 150,000 in 2006; 200,000 in 2011; 250,000 in 2013; 300,000 in 2015; and more than 350,000, reaching 361,000, in 2016. As for foundations, they were divided into public-raising and private-raising foundations since 2004. The total registered number of these two types of foundations was 1144 in 2006, and 5559 in 2016, respectively, nearly quadrupling during this period. Among all the foundations, the number of private-raising ones increased by 4000, more than two-thirds that of the aggregate of foundations,[1] becoming a strong power of China's charitable social organizations.

---

[1] Official website of China's social organizations: http://www.chinanpo.gov.cn/index.html.

3.3   Wide Popularity of Volunteering and Social Work

Volunteers and social workers are referred to as "Zhi Gong," "Yi Gong," and "She Gong" in *pinyin*. They are the most fundamental and important human resources in public charity. In recent years, China's volunteers and volunteering services have achieved rapid development, fostering a preliminary and diversified volunteering service system. According to recent in-depth empirical research, 58.0661 million volunteers through 1.1617 million volunteering service organizations took part in 18 major volunteering works, including helping the elderly, the disabled, and the poor and providing community services in 2016. They donated 1.597 billion hours of service and exerted RMB 49.565 billion of economic value. It is estimated that the number of volunteers of all kinds amounted to 135 million, among whom those providing more than ten hours of volunteering services reached 58.06 million, an active rate of 32.5% (Zhai et al. 2016).

At the same time, the professional social work at all levels in China has been prevalent, becoming the most important professional social resources for public charity services. Based on the estimates, the number of certified social workers across the nation stood at 288,000 in 2016, among whom 69,000 were social workers and 219,000 were assistant social workers, 5.3 times that of the number five years earlier, in 2011.[2]

3.4   Reinforcement of Corporate Social Responsibilities

Corporate social responsibility (CSR) is an important support for public charity provided by the market system. It is not only embodied as business donations, but a comprehensive charitable contribution made by the businesses for labors, consumers, the environment, and the community. The corresponding results are shown in the periodic CSR reports. According to the estimates, in 2011, different businesses in China released 32 CSR reports, while the number grew exponentially afterward, mounting to 1703 in 2015 (Zhang et al. 2016). Over the years, businesses of all kinds have actively participated in public undertakings, such as targeting poverty alleviation and development. PetroChina, Sinopec, Wanda Group, Bank of China, Evergrande Group, Hainan Airlines Group, Tencent, and other companies have initiated public charitable strategies by issuing their CSR reports and outlines on poverty alleviation and development. Many renowned entrepreneurs, such as Ma Yun, Ma Huateng, Pan Shiyi, and Lu Zhiqiang, took part in charitable activities with enormous donations, thus, giving rise to a group of large foundations.

3.5   Unprecedented Growth of Innovation in Public Charities

Innovations of all kinds keep popping up, breaking the traditional boundaries of public charity and leading to tremendous social influences. A large number

---

[2] The Department of Civil Affairs website: http://www.mca.gov.cn/.

of social enterprises linking the market and charity have sprung up. With the help of both the mobile Internet and public charity, some charitable platforms, such as "Free Lunch," "Micro Charity," and "99 Public Welfare Day by Tencent Charity Foundation," are emerging; between the media, the new media, and charity, innovative platforms for information transparency are popping up. Between finance and charity, more financial tools are fulfilling stronger social functions and are flourishing: charitable venture capital (VC) investment, trust, microcredit, investment in social influences, and so on. A new industry called "Charity Industry" is emerging.

3.6 The Formation of Academic Camps in Public Welfare Research

In recent years, a number of universities and colleges, including Tsinghua University, Peking University, Renmin University of China, Beijing Normal University, Sun Yat-sen University, Nanjing University, and Zhejiang University, have been competing to set up specialized public-welfare institutions for the research of public services, charity works, as well as relevant personnel training. In April 2015, a research institute of public services and charity works was jointly set up by the Ministry of Civil Affairs and Tsinghua University. This institute was expected to promote the construction of state-level think tanks in the sphere of public services and charity works through "ministry-university cooperation." Thus, related research has become a new "heat" in academic and policy studies. There are an increasing number of academic papers, policy reports, case studies, and specialized periodicals published on a yearly basis. According to relevant statistics, retrievable documents related to public services and charity works in 2006 numbered 7472, of which 1344 pieces were doctoral dissertations and master's theses; in 2014, the two figures rose to 21,821 and 13,832, respectively, representing growth of 192% and 929%.

The five primary reasons for the boom in public services and charity works in China over the past few years are as follows.

1. Since the launch of the reform and opening-up, the Chinese economy has experienced sustained high growth, allowing for the accumulation of immense wealth while laying a solid economic foundation for the development of public services and charity works.
2. As the reform and opening-up and market economy steadily progress, a comprehensive social transformation is taking place, setting the stage for public services and charity works.
3. The all-inclusive deepening of reform, based primarily on government transformation, creates space for the practice of public services and charity works.

4. The explosive growth in the Chinese society's demand for public goods, coupled with a dearth of government's supply of public services, has resulted in a supply-and-demand gap that creates a real need for public services and charity works.

5. A steady flow of manpower and a solid societal foundation for public services and charity works are created by the extensive and increasingly active participation of the general public at large.

Compared with the United States, the United Kingdom, Germany, Japan, and other developed countries, China has four noteworthy characteristics in its development of public services and charity works.

First, there are striking similarities between the present-day vigorous growth in public services and charity works in China and the related upsurge at the beginning of the twentieth century in the United States. This is particularly true for the advances in leaps and bounds of privately endowed foundations made possible by unprecedented accumulation of wealth and for the changes in the organization of nonprofits and the transformation in the development model of public services and charity works led by modern foundations. It can be said that the "Charitable Revolution" staged originally in the United States is presently occurring in China, partially seen in the growth of privately endowed foundations. Indeed, the number of privately endowed foundations in the United States grew from 18 to 505 over a period of time just shy of a half century from 1900 to 1946. In China, nonpublic foundations (of which most are on par with privately endowed foundations in the United States) could be legally registered as of 2005; in the ten years since, their number has exceeded 4000.

Second, with regard to the immense public space that public services and charity works obtain from organizational transformations, the development of public services and charity works in China very closely resembles the pattern of the vigorous development of nonprofit organizations during the United States' "Welfare State" era from the 1930s to the 1970s. The United States of that time had a government that, via the purchase of services, encouraged nonprofit organizations to make greater offerings in areas such as poverty alleviation, education, and public health, thereby building on a large scale a "beautiful society." Similar development presented itself in the postwar United Kingdom, as well as Germany, as the purchase of services became the largest source of capital for nonprofit organizations in these countries. China is currently experiencing a similar process.

Third, when it comes to participating and providing lead in social innovation, public services and charity works in China are only slightly behind, and in some sectors even ahead, of their counterparts in developed countries, such as the United States, the United Kingdom, and Japan. For example, in terms of social enterprises, VC, public finance, social impact investment, and microcharity, China has developed mature forms of innovation, which are not second to those in developed countries in Europe and America, and to some extent can even lead the world. And this is particularly true in venture philanthropy and social finance, of which the United States is a pioneer but now lags behind China in the practice model and policy system.

Fourth, despite a recent tendency to thrive, public services and charity works in China are still far behind those of developed countries and regions in the overall scale, level of development, capacity building, and mechanisms of operation and management. For example, the proportion of social donations in China's GDP (Gross Domestic Product) has witnessed a marked increase in recent years, from 0.05% in 2006 up to 0.16% in 2016, exceeding Japan's 0.14% and Germany's 0.13%. However, there is still a wide gap between China and many other developed countries (the ratios of social donations to GDP in Israel, the United Kingdom, the United States, Sweden, and the Netherlands are, respectively, 1.29%, 1.01%, 0.62%, 0.4%, and 0.37%). Another example is the social organization ownership per 10,000 of population. In China the figure was raised from 2.7 in 2006 to 5.1 in 2016, while the standard is set at 133.3 in Germany, 67.8 in the United States, 40 in the United Kingdom, and 38.5 in Japan. Thus, it can be seen, the disparity between China and the major developed countries is significant.

4 The *Charity Law*: A Whole New Institutional Construction and Its Revolutionary Impact

In early 2014, the legislative work of the *Charity Law* was officially launched in China. After a compact two-year calendar of drafting, discussion, consultation, and repeated revision, in March 2016, the 12th National People's Congress passed the *Charity Law of the People's Republic of China* by large margins. This is the first basic law concerning social organizations that was reviewed, passed, and released by the highest legislative body in China. Prior to that, regulations concerning social organizations were all issued by the Legislative Affairs Office of the State Council of the People's Republic of China. Among them, there are three administrative regulations concerning social organizations, foundations, and private nonenterprise units. The newly released law, which took effect on September 1, 2016, moved social organization-related legislation up a notch in the legal hierarchy, pushed an overhaul of the current relevant regulations, and brought China's construction of social organization-related regulations into a new era. The *Charity Law*, with 112 sections in 12 chapters, formulates an unprecedented set of Chinese regulations concerning philanthropic organizations, which, grounded on a shared institutional vision of "big charity," builds a new institutional system that advocates enabling the public to be better informed, placing charitable organizations under the supervision of the whole society, thereby freeing the government and the society.

4.1   Institutional Consensus: Eight Ideas Running Through the Legislation

The new *Charity Law* was shaped out of a two-year-long open legislation process, in which a raft of experts and scholars specializing in philanthropic research and legislation were involved. After a long period of extensive participation, heated discussion, forceful argumentation, and full confirmation, the Internal and Judicial Affairs Committee of the National People's Congress, who took charge of the drafting work, compiled the final draft on the basis of seven experts' proposals. That was followed by multiple symposiums, two solicitations of public opinion, and dozens of revisions before the draft was finally approved by the National People's Congress. During the whole legislation process, a consensus was also achieved concerning eight aspects, which formed the institutional foundation of the *Charity Law*. The specific concepts are as follows:

1. **Mass charity:** "Mass charity" refers to modern or public charitable activities different from those traditional ones. In the legislative process of the *Charity Law*, experts made multiple rounds of discussions and finally reached a consensus that in Article 3, it has been specified that charitable activities are nonprofit activities on a voluntary basis by natural persons, a view advocated by most experts, thus making mass charity the most salient feature of this law.

2. **Organizations play a dominant role:** This law emphasizes that charitable organizations comprise the most crucial legal subject, a characteristic of organization law. The contest of this legislation is that the *Charity Law* is formulated to make up the vacancy for laws on social organizations. The *Charity Law* is established to safeguard the legitimate rights and interests of charitable organizations and promote the healthy development of social organizations with charitable organizations at their core. At the same time, the *Charity Law* identifies the legitimacy of charitable organizations for their superior status in social organizations, highlighting the legal status of charitable organizations.

3. **Multiple players:** This law shows that charitable activities are open and embracing. Any member of the society can have access to them. This concept has embodied the openness and inclusiveness of the *Charity Law*, that is, an open access to kindness and good deeds and embracing all charitable activities.

4. **Deepening reform:** This law states that the legislation of the *Charity Law* should be included in the deepening of reform and should play an exemplary role in actively advancing comprehensively deepening reform. This is the most important historical background and legal basis. This concept has also put forward the political mission of advancing with times and coexisting with reform for the *Charity Law*.

5. **Meliorism:** This concept advocates and stimulates kindness, encourages and supports charitable causes, tries to spur all social members to do good deeds, and fosters a nice atmosphere and mode of caring for others, volunteering for charity, and striving for kindness.

6. **Public charitable values:** This concept regards public benefits as the core value of charitable organizations and public charity the main values for social organizations. Against the backdrop that charity means public benefits, the *Charity Law* separates public benefit with mutual benefit, common benefit, and private benefit. The *Charity Law* also recognizes that social organizations have multiple values and interest demands. On such basis, to highlight public value is the superior form of social values.

7. **Strict rules:** This concept holds that what the *Charity Law* regulates has restrictions on, and clear legal responsibilities for, social organizations and governmental departments. It can be seen that this law not only advocates and encourages all kinds of players in this society to take an active part in the charitable work but establishes a lot of restrictive clauses and prohibitions, posing clear-cut and rigid restrictions on charitable organizations and governmental departments.

8. **Noninterference from the governments:** This concept stresses that, as the major source of public power, the governments should not directly participate in charitable activities nor interfere in the decision-making of charitable organizations.

4.2   *Systematic Structure: New System Based on Information Transparency*

Based on the eight concepts—mentioned above—the *Charity Law* has established a set of new legal systems and policy structures. There is an important core for these new systems and structures, that is, the institutional foundation for charity information transparency. It is stipulated in the *Charity Law* that through institutional design and policy arrangements, all charitable organizations and governmental departments should provide open access regarding charity-related information to the society through three major charity information platforms. The information needs to be opened to the public and covers at least the following 23 aspects:

1. Registration system: There should be a unified registration system for charitable organizations. These organizations should be managed and registered by civil departments of the people's governments above county level.

2. Accreditation systems: The charitable organizations are accredited by registration and management authorities; those social organizations

that have already been registered as foundations can apply to be accredited as charitable organizations.

3. Annual report submission and openness system: Charitable organizations should submit annual work reports and financial accounting reports to registration and management authorities and open them to the public.

4. Internal transaction restriction and openness system: Stakeholders who have been involved in internal transactions within the charitable organizations should not participate in related decision-making. The transactions concerned should also be open to public in time.

5. Liquidation systems of charity assets: Charitable organizations should conduct liquidation after the termination of its services and activities. The residual assets are transferred to charitable organizations with the same or similar purposes.

6. Public fund-raising certificate systems: Charitable organizations should register for a public fund-raising certificate. Whereupon review, civil affairs departments have not discovered the receipt of any administrative punishments provided for by the law, they shall issue a public fund-raising qualification certificate.

7. Three information platform systems: Charitable organizations that have registered at the civil affairs departments can conduct Internet fund-raising on the charity information platforms designated or established by the civil affairs departments of the State Council at which they have registered.

8. Fund-raising and filing system: Charitable organizations should formulate fund-raising plans before conducting this activity. The design and plan should be filed with registration and management organizations ahead of time.

9. Cooperation systems for fund-raising: Organizations or persons can cooperate with charitable organizations eligible for public fund-raising to conduct public fund-raising.

10. Fund-raising qualification system through platforms: Platforms that can conduct public fund-raising online should verify the registrations and public fund-raising certificates of charitable organizations.

11. Targeted fund-raising system: Fund-raising activities conducted for targeted groups are referred to as "targeted fund-raising." Charitable organizations can conduct targeted fund-raising.

12. Disaster relief and coordination system: When major natural disasters, accidents and disasters, public health incidents, or social security incidents happen, relevant people's governments shall establish coordination mechanisms to provide information on demand and to orderly guide fund-raising and rescue operations.

13. Forbiddance on forcible apportionment: Forcible apportionment or other interferences on charitable work through public power are forbidden.

14. Morals and regulations for charitable donations: Publicity for charity should be regulated. Organizations and individuals must not use charitable donations to publicize tobacco products or the manufacturers or vendors thereof or other matters prohibited from being publicized by laws and regulations.

15. Donors shall fulfill their obligations to donate: The rights and interests of donors should be identified. Donors should also fulfill their obligations in accordance with the donor agreements.

16. Charitable trusts' filing and reporting system: Charitable trusts should be recorded with the Department of Civil Affairs. The trustees should report the status of the handling of the affairs of the trust and state of financial affairs to the civil affairs department at least once per year and shall make the information public.

17. System of minimum proportion of charitable expenditures: The annual charitable expenditures of a charitable organization should be more than 70% of last year's revenue or more than 70% of the average revenue of the past three years.

18. Annual management cost system: Annual management cost for charitable organizations should not exceed 10% of the overall expenditure of the year.

19. Charity information gathering and releasing system: People's governments at the county level or above establish and improve systems for gathering and releasing charity information. Charitable information that should be transparent to the public should be identified.

20. Mechanisms of sharing charity information among departments: The civil affairs departments of the people's governments shall establish mechanisms of sharing charity information with other departments.

21. Preferential policies for poverty relief: China implements preferential policies on activities of poverty relief.

22. System of complaints, reports, and handling for illegal behaviors: Any unit or individual who discovers that a charitable organization has violated the law may complain about or report it to the relevant department or the charitable industry organization. The department or charitable industry organization shall, upon receipt of a complaint or report, promptly investigate and handle it.

23. System of public opinion and social supervision: The state encourages the public and the media to exercise supervision over charitable activities and to expose the obtaining of assets by deception in the name of false charity or violations of the law and regulations by charitable organizations and trusts, giving full play to public opinion and social supervision.

4.3   Revolutionary Feature: Transferring Charitable Organizations to the Society

Viewing from the transition of state-society relations, the revolutionary feature of the *Charity Law* lies in transferring charitable organizations to the society. With the implementation of the *Charity Law*, registration and management authorities at all levels, business governing organizations, and other party and governmental departments will gradually be relieved from the burden of the original supervision of charitable organizations. These authorities then may transfer their concentration to the effective control and efficiency improvement on the three information platforms.

Under the current mechanism, it is the state that mainly supervises and regulates social organizations, including registration and management authorities at all levels, business governing organizations, and other party and government departments. Supervision and management is a complex administrative function, requiring report, issuance, auditing, formulating, and revising a great number of documents. A lot of human and economic resources are also needed. Different kinds of coordination mechanisms should be set up among all political and administrative systems. There were several rounds of changes: The original extensive mechanism where related departments were in charge of their own matters was replaced by one where registration and management authorities and business governing organizations assumed their responsibilities, respectively. Then the mechanism was upgraded to the current version of classified management system, or even in some fields, a reform of a unified direct registration and management system is taking shape. Although the supervision and management mechanism now is more oriented to the social organizations, it has not yet stepped out of the layout where the state should directly confront the society.

On one hand, the issuance and implementation of the *Charity Law* has endowed charitable organizations with the supreme legitimacy, higher than other social organizations. On the other hand, based on the abovementioned systems featuring charitable information transparency, the state no longer has to confront charitable organizations. Instead, through their establishment and operation, the three information platforms have been replaced as the dominant regulator and manager. With the application of the mobile Internet and charity big data, a new layout featuring overall supervision on charitable organizations and their activities has been set up, thus realizing the ultimate goal of charitable organizations conducting charitable activities in accordance with the law. We referred this new type of mechanisms as the new state-society relations featuring "the state controlling the platforms, the platforms confronting the organizations, the organizations acting in accordance with the law."

5   New Mechanism of State-Society Relations and Its Structures

With the implementation of the *Charity Law* and the development of charitable organizations, a new mechanism of state-society relations built on information transparency, social oversight, and charity big data, and dependent on the Internet platform, may be rolled out. Its features can be summarized as "the state controlling the platforms, the platforms confronting the organizations, the organizations acting in accordance with the law." Even though it is inevitable that there may be a transitional mechanism occurring between the old and new mechanisms, thanks to the mainstreaming of legitimacy and public values, new mechanisms will finally come out and pioneer in all social institutional reforms.

5.1   New Mechanism of State-Society Relations

Long after the reform and opening-up, China remains where "the state is strong, but the society is weak." On one hand, marketization promoted economic growth but expedited the diversion of a different social stratum. The governments kept delegating more powers to the market and society. This in return has expanded the social gap. Traditional organizational structures can no longer accommodate people's needs to voice their interests. A society that used to be part of the state has gradually been separated, resulting in a rudiment of dual construction of state and society. But on the other hand, since all kinds of social powers are in their initial development, China is relatively weak compared with the almighty state pursuing gradual reform. In China, the state exerts prevalent control over the society, but the society can still impose limited restrictions on the state. Domestic experts have made a lot of qualified research on state-society relations during this period. Besides learning from overseas frameworks such as civil society and corporatism, the "administration absorbing the society," "classified control," and a lot of other frameworks with local features also appear. These researches acknowledge the background that the state, as the designer and activist of concrete mechanisms, can play a decisive role in the activities of nongovernmental organizations (NGOs) and stress that NGOs have their own autonomy and initiative in concrete contexts. After the 3rd Plenary Session of the 18th CPC National Committee, the policy of comprehensively deepening reform has been rolled out and state-society relations have welcomed new changes. After nearly 40 years of development, social organizations in China have leapfrogged in both quantity and quality. As the authorities started to streamline administration and delegate power to lower-level governments, the society has gained more and more autonomy and more independence in the scale and scope of participating in public governance. Apart from purchasing some public goods through the governments, more

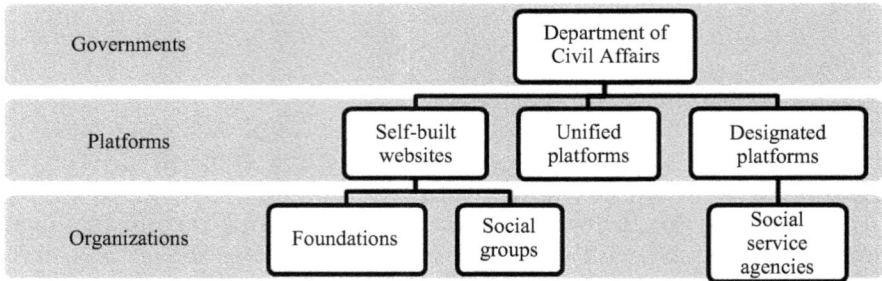

Fig. 12.1 The new layout of state-society relations built on the *Charity Law*

social organizations have begun to take an active part in the supervision of policies. The traditional governing philosophy featuring "managing the society" has been transforming to one that is "participated by multiple players and governed by all." All this has shown that state-society relations have been positively upgrading from the original one of "controlling and being controlled" to one featuring "coordination and cooperation."

In this context, the issuance of the *Charity Law* is undoubtedly of utmost importance to the transformation of state-society relations. The *Charity Law* is the first general law about the charity cause in China, but it is a complete institutional system itself, including related departments of the governments, charitable organizations, and the information platforms mentioned in the *Charity Law;* therefore, the law has basically outlined the blueprint of the future new state-society relations, that is, a new system built on information transparency, social oversight, and charity big data, and dependent on the Internet platform. This bears more weight than charity itself (see Fig. 12.1). The character of this system can be summarized as "the state controlling the platforms, the platforms confronting the organizations, the organizations acting in accordance with the law."

5.1.1   Government Management Platform

The biggest change in state-society relations is the orientation of governments. For previous state-society relations, social organizations were usually supervised and controlled directly by the governments. Whether as stipulated by law or in real operations, social organizations should always confront the governments directly. However, in the new system, the orientation of governments has made considerable changes, from playing in the "front stage" to playing "behind the scenes." The governments also transformed from the original supervisor of social organizations to the provider of mechanisms and the executor of law. On one hand, governments can step away from the busy affairs and devote their energy to the establishment and safeguarding of mechanisms. On the other, this change is conducive that social organizations can strengthen their recognitions of their own roles and responsibilities and enhance their independent operating capabilities. The supervisory duties originally fulfilled by the governments will be assumed by the platforms in the new mechanism.

Meanwhile, governments do not directly control platforms, but guide them indirectly, thus playing an exemplary role of an institution provider at the macro-level. First, governments should clarify the roles and functions platforms play in the new mechanism from both legal and policy perspectives. Second, governments also need to set up effective evaluation systems to regulate activities done through the platform. Governments can set credits and grades for relative platforms and open the results to the public on a regular basis, hence advancing a sound development of the latter and bringing out their potential. Finally, governments should also punish and correct the illegal behaviors of the platforms through administrative enforcement of law, for instance, the malicious correction of charitable information by the platform should be strictly forbidden.

5.1.2 Supervisory Organizations for the Platforms

Platforms are the main supervisors of charitable organizations and are basically the core of the new state-society layout. It is stipulated in Article 8 of the *Charity Law* that "the civil affairs departments of the people's governments at or above the county level shall establish mechanisms of sharing charity information with other departments," and that "charitable organizations and the trustees of charitable trusts shall release charity information on the platforms stipulated by the preceding paragraph, and shall be responsible for the authenticity of the information." It is fair to say that as the collecting and releasing body, the platforms play a crucial role in connecting the links within the mechanisms in the *Charity Law*. According to the *Charity Law*, the civil affairs departments of the people's governments shall establish or designate charity information platforms. All charitable organizations, as long as they upload their relevant information on the platforms, are then accountable for the truthfulness of the information and are willing to accept the supervision of the platforms. The platforms have the following three characteristics.

1. **Flexibility**. The first advantage of platform supervision is that the platforms are flexible. Governments do not interfere in nor regulate the platforms through direct administrative means. The relationship between them is rather similar to "outsourcing of services" instead. The two parties will assume and shoulder the rights and responsibilities in accordance with the contract. Departments of Civil Affairs will design the functions and tasks for the platforms; hand the establishment, operation, and management of the platforms to a third party; and pay it some money to run the platform. The platform operators can use all sorts of means to complete the tasks and requirements of the contracts within the legal boundaries. On the other hand, governmental departments may supervise the management and validate the results in accordance with the contracts. The government purchasing service sets the boundaries between the government and the platform operators clearly. It is beneficial for safeguarding the autonomy and flexibility of platform operators, and avoid-

ing the supervision system from rigidity, so that government functions can be transformed.

2. **Competitiveness**. The operation of platforms is not only flexible but competitive as well, which can be seen from two aspects. First, competition exists between the unified platforms of the Department of Civil Affairs and the designated ones. Both the two platforms should release related information in accordance with the *Charity Law*. However, some specific details, such as the issuance frequency, way of information exposure, and the evaluation of public information, can be decided by themselves, respectively. To some extent, a potential competition has taken shape. Apart from competition between the unified platforms and the designated ones, competition also exists in different designated platforms. Those platforms with high credibility, a large amount of information, fast technological upgrades, and high scientific and technological contents are more likely to gain popularity among charitable organizations and the public. Popularity among charitable organizations and the public means high click rates. For better reputation and social influence, designated platforms will try hard to improve their technological level, so as to make faster and more accurate upgrades for information of charitable organizations.

3. **Sharing**. Platforms are established behind big data and other high technologies. As time passes and the data increase, the platforms will gradually become a large information pool of charitable big data. It is stipulated in the *Charity Law* that charitable organizations should release the information at a certain time. Some information needs to be sent at a certain time, some fluid, some instant, and some that need to be upgraded year after year. After the information is included in the platforms, a big data system that keeps improving and absorbing new information will be generated, conducive to the openness and sharing of information.

5.1.3   *Overall Supervision from the Society*

The establishment of platforms with big data as the foundation is beneficial for realizing the overall supervision by the society. As the designated platforms roll out, better ones will be discovered. The public and the charitable organizations will select good ones through their own behaviors, thus improving the whole regulatory system of the charitable organizations. No matter who, the public, the media, or other charitable organizations can know about an event held by certain organizations, about its time, place, and participants. The charity big data system can also be integrated with reports and supervision systems. The public can report on charitable organizations through modern IT means like SMS or WeChat. All the reports and results can be stored in the information pool as big data, so that they can be made available to people as soon as possible.

5.1.4   *Organizations Acting in Accordance with the Law*

To improve platforms for better regulation of charitable organizations, national or local charitable organizations should provide open access to information on the unified platform as required. This will not only eliminate the unequal access to information but strengthen the society's trust in charitable organizations. Social organizations can be regulated together through other third sectors. For those organizations that fail to obey the regulations of the *Charity Law*, the platforms may record their behaviors and submit the files to related governmental departments to establish penalties. For those organizations that obey the law and provide open access to their information promptly, the platforms may make evaluations of their behavior. Such behavior will form a restricting and eliminating mechanism, conducive to the establishment and upgrading of charitable organizations.

Taking account of the abovementioned four aspects, this chapter has lineated the new layout of state-society relations after the issuance of the *Charity Law*. This new layout is based on big data technology and centers on platforms. Under this new layout, the players turned from traditional ones as governments and social organizations into three major bodies—governments, platforms, and social organizations. These new state-society relations have stepped out of the traditional dual construction of state and society. Taking advantage of the Internet big data, the platforms have been placed at the forefront of supervisory organizations. The governments, acting as the provider of mechanisms and the executor of law, correspondingly stay behind the platforms. Not only has this new layout changed the governments' previous role and facilitated their transformation, it has also regulated the behavior of social organizations by formulating regulations and incorporating the development of social organizations into rule of law.

5.2   *Transition from the Old System into a New One*

After the issuance of the *Charity Law*, it is inevitable that there may be a transitional mechanism occurring between the old and new mechanisms. One of the salient features of this process is that charitable organizations will play an increasingly important role. The old system featuring dual management mainly included traditional social groups, foundations, and public nonenterprise organizations. Such a system highlights the state's control over the society but hinders the development of social organizations and the establishment of modern governance.

As for the transitional system, besides certain social organizations, some old charitable organizations will coexist with the new ones. One of the differences lies in the origin of their legitimacy. The legitimacy of old charitable organizations depends mainly on subordination with dual management at its core and related rights and powers. However, the legitimacy of new ones originates from accreditation of law and social evaluation. With the improvement of related regulations, the old charitable organizations will gradually be replaced by the new ones.

In the ultimate new system, a new form of social organizations with charitable organizations at its core and other social organizations playing an important role will take shape. In this new system, charitable organizations will take charge of allocating charitable resources, while other social organizations will fulfill their distinctive responsibilities in their own fields.

5.3   Two Forces Facilitating the Establishment of the New System

During the transition from the old system into the new one, two forces will play a crucial role in facilitating its development.

The first force is legitimacy becoming mainstream. With the improvement in the *Charity Law* and other regulations and standards, the original legitimacy recognition featuring administrative powers and subordination will gradually be substituted by one featuring legal approval and social recognition. More social and charitable organizations with official backgrounds will have to be supervised by platforms and the society, and administrative powers will gradually exit from the management and operation of social organizations.

The second force is that public values are becoming mainstream. In the process of transition, with the rise of new charitable organizations, public values focusing on public benefits and volunteer spirits will become the mainstream of social values. In return, such a trend will facilitate the development of charitable organizations and activities, and boosting the old charitable and social organizations in becoming more customized, thus fostering a new system with charitable organizations at its core.

5.4   New Directions for Institutional Reform

The core of institutional reform lies in the development of charitable organizations. With the implementation of the *Charity Law* and the ongoing reform of separation of the governments from the businesses, besides supporting the newly emerging charitable organizations, as a state, it is more significant to reform public institutions, mass organizations, and other social organizations. Closely connected to the state, public institutions and mass organizations themselves boast of a lot of administrative resources and social networks. Therefore, they are the important potential players that can be committed to charity works. It is, hence, imperative to accelerate the reform in public institutions, people's groups, and other social organizations, guiding them to transform and develop into charitable organizations, fostering a pillar for a new system in the future.

All in all, a new layout of state-society relations built on information transparency, social oversight, and charity big data and dependent on the Internet platform will gradually take shape. Its characters can be summarized as "the state controlling the platforms, the platforms confronting the organizations, the organizations acting in accordance with the law." A new layout for country-society relations with charity and social values playing the dominant role and a coordinated development between social organizations and the market will be clearly put in place.

REFERENCES

Yang, T. (ed.). 2015. *The Bluebook of Charity: Report on China's Charity Development.* Beijing: Social Sciences Academic Press.

Yang, T. (ed.). 2016. *The Bluebook of Charity: Report on China's Charity Development.* Beijing: Social Sciences Academic Press.

Yang, T. (ed.). 2017. *The Bluebook of Charity: Report on China's Charity Development.* Beijing: Social Sciences Academic Press.

Zhai, Y., H. Xin, and Y. Song. 2016. Index Report on China's Volunteering Services. *The Bluebook of Charity: Report on China's Charity Development* (2017): 75–122.

Zhang, E., M.J. Wang, X. Lin, and X.J. Fang. 2016. *Report on China's Corporate Social Responsibility (2015).* Economic Management Press, January 2016 edition.

CHAPTER 13

The Role of Mass Media in Reshaping Local Governance and Its Limitations

Fei Wu and Qing Huang

1   Introduction

This chapter aims to discuss the potential of mass media, especially social media, for reshaping the mode of local governance in China by examining how social media prevalence influences local government responsiveness to online public inquiries and online civic engagement in 31 provincial-level administrative divisions in China. It first introduces mass media as an indispensable part of governance by briefly reviewing the social function of mass media. Afterward, it focuses on how social media can afford the interactions between local governments, including local governmental agencies and officials, and various social actors in the process of local governance in China. Through the analysis of the aggregate data regarding *social media prevalence, local government responsiveness,* and *civic engagement* in 31 provincial-level administrative divisions in China, the results show that social media in general contributes to local government responsiveness to online public inquiries and online civic engagement. Specifically, local governmental agencies tend to respond to public inquiries more actively than local government officials on social media, and citizens tend to discuss local affairs more frequently with local governmental agencies than with local government officials on social media. The findings indicate the promising role of social media in improving local government responsiveness

F. Wu, Ph.D. • Q. Huang, Ph.D. (✉)
College of Media and International Culture, Zhejiang University, Hangzhou, China
e-mail: wufei0318@zju.edu.cn; qing_huang@zju.edu.cn

© The Author(s) 2019   267
J. Yu, S. Guo (eds.), *The Palgrave Handbook of Local Governance in Contemporary China*, https://doi.org/10.1007/978-981-13-2799-5_13

and advancing civic engagement but reveal that local government officials' underuse of social media might constrain the development of good local governance in China. It concludes with an outlook into the future of digitalized local governance in China.

2   HISTORY OF THE ROLE OF MASS MEDIA

Historically, mass media has played a significant role in influencing the development of societies in different regions across the world. During the Cold War, the press (the predominant mass media then) was used to achieve certain political and social aims. For example, the press was supposed to serve the state by advocating the policies of the government in power in authoritarian countries (Siebert et al. 1956). In democratic societies, in addition to informing, entertaining, and selling, the press was also expected to counterbalance the state power and discover the truth by providing everyone with a forum to voice their opinions (Siebert et al. 1956). Afterward, many scholars started discussing the major societal functions of mass media in Western democracies, including surveillance, sociocultural integration, heritage transmission, and entertainment (Breed 1958; Lasswell 1948; Lazarsfeld and Merton 1948; Wright 1959). Besides, mass media was argued to be an agent of power, representing those who held political, economic, and social power in a given society (Altschull 1984).

Since the economic reform and opening up in China, the development of mass media in transitional China has been driven by and, in turn, promoted the marketization and maintenance of government legitimacy. For instance, news media in the 1980s mainly served as the ideological manager for the state and, meanwhile, provided the public with a wide range of information, especially the economic news reported by a large number of newspapers that were exclusively devoted to economy (Li 1998). During the 1990s, news media, such as the *Beijing Youth News*, represented a propaganda/commercial model of journalism, in which the propaganda needs of the Party were first addressed, accompanied with a certain degree of responsiveness to readers' interests or tastes (Zhao 1996). In the late 1990s, the success of *Jiaodian Fangtan*, a current affairs TV program casted by the China Central Television, showed that mass media offered people a platform to voice opinions, whereas the concerns expressed by the public should not challenge government legitimacy (Chan 2002). Since the twenty-first century, mass media, on the one hand, has continually served to promote government image and legitimacy and has been forced to survive in the competitive market by informing and entertaining the audience in commercial ways (Lee et al. 2006). On the other hand, the rise of professional journalism and investigative journalism in transitional China signals that mass media has been trying to provide factual coverage on news and to expose publicly denounced problems without fundamentally challenging the current political and social order (Pan and Chan 2003; Zhou 2000).

Although not explicitly using the term *governance*, the societal function of mass media in general and the sociopolitical function of mass media in China indicate that mass media is indispensable to the process of governance, including government administration, policy implementation, civic engagement, public service delivery, and so on (Osborne 2010; Peters 2000). From the 1980s to the early 2000s, mass media, such as the printed press and television in China, struggled to find their niche to survive by simultaneously serving the government and catering to the market. However, ordinary people and social organizations had constrained access to negotiating with the government in terms of public and local affairs during that time period. Noticeably, with the fast development of the Internet-based mass media in recent decades, including the wide application of BBS and blogs from 2000, and later the popularization of social media (e.g., Weibo and WeChat) since 2009 (Zhu et al. 2009), the role of the government, news media, ordinary individuals, and other social actors in dealing with local issues in China has changed compared to that when the press and TV prevailed (see detailed illustrations in Table 13.1 in the next section). Moreover, the normative governance theory was first introduced from Western academia to China in the late 1990s and has started to prevail and influence Chinese scholars since the 2000s (Yu and Wang 2016), which parallels the development of Internet-based mass media in China. Given the impact from Western governance theories and the technological advancement, we believe that Internet-based mass media is reshaping the mode of (local) governance in China compared to that in the age of print or electronic media.

In terms of (local) governance, mass media can be seen as news organizations that serve as the mediator between the government/state and civil society in coping with social issues, either in China (Che 2014; Jiang 2015), in Western democracies (Norris 2010), or in global societies (Castells 2008). Meanwhile, mass media can also be considered a means of communication and technology to reach a vast majority of the audience, such as social media used by the government to release information and to interact with the public (Downey and Jones 2012; Yuan 2013), as well as the Web 2.0-based technologies adopted by various social actors to promote discursive participation in public issues (Guo 2013; Linders 2012; Yang 2005). Despite the different understandings of mass media in the extant literature, this study defines mass media as the technology through which a vast amount of information is exchanged among various actors, while news organizations are one type of these multiple actors. Given the increasing significance of social media for dealing with public affairs in China in recent years (Bertot et al. 2010; King et al. 2013), the current study primarily focuses on the role of social media in local governance in China.

The open access to the Internet and the interactivity of social media afford a variety of social actors to participate in the public decision-making process and enable the government to respond to public inquiries effectively, which echoes the very idea of civic engagement and responsive government proposed by the normative governance theory (Denters 2011; Kooiman 1999; Peters 2000; Hirst 2000). By focusing on local govern-

Table 13.1 Local emergencies that occurred in China from 2000 to 2016

Emergency (Time)	Government performance	Civic engagement
SARS outbreak in Guangdong Province (2002)	The local government failed to provide transparent and relevant information at the initial stage.	The public had constrained access to online discussions about the emergency.
Tai Lake pollution in Jiangsu Province (2007)	The local government excused itself from taking responsibility for pollution.	Individuals' online or offline communication about the information related to the pollution was impeded.
Labor abuse in a brick factory in Shanxi Province (2007)	The local government regulated the abuse only after the abuse was exposed to the public.	News media first unveiled the abuse, which later triggered online controversies.
Shishou incident in Hubei Province (2009)	The local government suppressed the mass demonstration and obscured the incident in press releases.	The public tried to organize a demonstration to express dissatisfaction with the government's regulation, but the demonstration was suppressed.
Rainstorm and flood in Beijing (2012)	The local government actively and in a timely manner responded to public inquires on social media.	Citizens, NGOs/NPOs, and news media participated in coping with the crisis through information exchange on social media.
Protest against PX plants in Guangdong Province (2014)	The local government tried to block information and delayed its official statements.	Residents and activist groups utilized social media to organize and mobilize the protest.
Stampede in Shanghai (2015)	The local government released the latest information and took immediate measures to cope with the emergency.	The general public, opinion leaders, and news media questioned the city emergency system through social media posts.
Tainted vaccines from Shandong Province (2016)	The local government released the information about the tainted vaccines on its official website and implemented regulations in a timely manner.	The scandal triggered widespread debates on social media, especially the criticisms from influential social media users.

ments' social media profiles, this study tries to examine how social media affords government responsiveness to online public inquiries and online civic engagement during the process of local governance in China. Moreover, by specifying local governments' social media accounts as those of the agencies and officials, it further attempts to differentiate how local governmental agencies and officials respond to public inquiries and how citizens engage with them on social media. The results are expected to shed some light on the potential and limitations of social media for building a responsive government and advancing civic engagement to achieve good local governance in China.

3   Governance and Local Governance in China

From the late twentieth century, governance theory has been receiving increasing attention from American and European scholars (Pierre 2000). Since the first introduction of the idea of governance to China in 1995 and the publication of the first edited volume on Western governance theories in China in 2000, the quantity of research on Chinese governance has witnessed a steady increase, with a dramatic growth around the year 2011 (Yu and Wang 2016). Accordingly, it is not an exaggeration to say that governance theory has become a fashionable conceptual tool to examine the social issues in contemporary China.

Despite a variety of definitions, *governance* reflects new modes of interactions between the state, society, and market to deal with the growing complexity in social and policy problems (Kooiman 1999). Different from the state-centric public administration, governance highlights the role of society and the cooperation between various social actors and the government to optimize public policy implementation and public service delivery (Osborne 2010; Peters 2000). In summary, compared to the prevalent mode of government, governance is essentially characterized by polycentricism, which indicates that a variety of actors from different domains of political and socioeconomic life take part in the public decision-making process through cooperation, negotiation, or competition (Denters 2011, pp. 313–314).

Given that the governance theory has originated from developed democracies, the applicability of governance theory to China has remained controversial among Chinese scholars, especially the inevitable conflict between the maintenance of the authoritarian regime and the growing need for developing a civil society in transitional China (Yang 2002; Zang 2003). In response, some scholars proposed the idea of local governance as an alternative to advance governance in China through a step-by-step process (Ma and Zhang 2008; Yu and Feng 2011). Compared to the governance at the national level, local governance is more feasible and can involve more actors from different domains of society to cope with regional issues, thus creating more space for civic engagement due to the distance from the central state (Yu and Feng 2011; Yu and Wang 2016). Drawing upon the idea of polycentricism advocated by the Western governance theory and taking into account the state-centric structure of China's politics, local governance in China is considered to be simultaneously characterized by local government interventions and civic engagement.

4   Local Emergencies: The Emerging Role of Social Media in Local Governance

In general, local governance in China involves the making and implementation of public policies and public service delivery in normal settings, as well as the management of incidents, outbreaks, or emergencies that occurred in certain regions (Li 2015). The outbreak of local emergencies presents the critical conditions in which the local government's capability and accountability are tested and, meanwhile, provides opportunities for public participation. With the purpose of examining the role of local governments and other social actors in affecting local governance in China, this section briefly reviews several local emergencies that occurred from the early 2000s to 2016 in China. These local emergencies are selected from the *Annual Report on Online Public Opinions in China* issued by people.com each year. Considering that Sina Weibo was established in 2009 and that the year 2009 witnessed a transition to the social media age (Zhu et al. 2009), the characteristics of local governance reflected through the local emergencies which occurred before and after 2009 are compared, in order to show the potential impact of social media on local governance in China.

According to Table 13.1, the local governments' performances in coping with local emergencies that happened before or in 2009 were mainly characterized by delayed regulations and intentional covering up of information; meanwhile, civic engagement in these events was largely hindered. By contrast, in most of the local emergencies that happened after 2009, local governments played a more active and responsible role in dealing with the consequences through the use of social media. In terms of citizen engagement, social media has become a useful tool for the general public and activists to organize and mobilize offline protests and demonstrations and meanwhile provided a platform for online public discussions. Therefore, the emergence and popularization of social media have more or less changed local governance in China in recent years, manifested by local governments' improved performances and civic engagement in major local emergencies.

5   SOCIAL MEDIA AND LOCAL GOVERNANCE: RESPONSIVE GOVERNMENT AND CIVIC ENGAGEMENT?

In addition to the change in local governance demonstrated through the aforementioned local emergencies, studies have also theoretically indicated that social media has the potential to change the mode of local governance in China, including the ways in which local governments deal with the relationship with their public, as well as the opportunities for advancing civic engagement initiated by various social actors.

Compared to the time when TV and newspapers prevailed, Web 2.0-based applications serve as a bridge between the government and the public by facilitating a dialogue between the two parties (Cheng 2016; Downey and Jones 2012). Accordingly, local governments are expected to respond to public inquiries in a timely and active manner (Yuan 2013). For instance, the open access to the Internet and the interactivity inherent in Weibo help the local government develop a cooperative relationship with Weibo users, so as to mobilize and integrate resources to solve social problems in China (Yan 2013). Besides, the relatively closed social network embedded in WeChat enables the local government to initiate a dialogue with key stakeholders in public events in a relatively private way, thus avoiding the escalation of the event into a crisis (Zhou and Shen 2014).

Meanwhile, social media has been changing the power relations between the government and the public by providing the public with an alternative to voice their opinions about community affairs or urban development in China (Li 2015; Wang 2014; Wang 2016). Moreover, activists use social media to mobilize and organize protests and demonstrations to defend public rights and interests in various local issues, such as the debates on the building of p-xylene plants (also known as PX plants) and waste sites in their neighborhood (Guo 2013; Ren and Yan 2015) or the disputes on the ownership of real estate (Wang 2015). Therefore, the increasing issue visibility on social media tends to attract more social actors, such as news organizations, NGOs/NPOs, corporations, and opinion leaders, to participate in public deliberation.

To sum up, the interactivity of social media provides local governments with a platform to listen to and have a dialogue with the public, thus facilitating them to respond to public inquires more quickly and proactively. Besides, the open access to social media enables people's participation in the construction and communication of public issues, advancing online civic engagement in public affairs. In other words, how local governments respond to public inquiries and how the public interact with local governments in discussing local affairs on social media constitute the process of local governance in the digital age. From the view of affordances, technologies provide the users with the possibility for actions, but it does not necessarily lead to users' actual behaviors (Evans et al. 2017; Gibson 1979). Therefore, by focusing on social media accounts of local governments, including those of the governmental agencies and officials, this study tries to examine whether and how social media influences the process of local governance in China by asking the following questions:

1. How does social media afford local government responsiveness to, respectively, online public inquires and online civic engagement?
2. How do local governmental agencies and officials, respectively, respond to public inquiries on social media?
3. How do citizens interact with local governmental agencies and officials, respectively, on social media?

6   Methods

Compared to the governance at the national level, local governance can be regarded as the governance at the provincial, municipal, or county level. This study focuses on local governance at the provincial level, considering that provincial-level administrative divisions administrate local affairs within their administrative regions. Each of the 31 provincial-level divisions, including 22 provinces, 5 autonomous regions, and 4 direct-controlled municipalities in mainland China, served as a unit of analysis.

Social media functioned as a platform on which local governments and the public interacted with each other. This study considered local governments' Weibo profiles as a typical context to address the research questions proposed earlier. Specifically, the number of local governments' Weibo accounts in a given provincial-level administrative division indicated the level of the prevalence of social media platforms for local governance in that administrative division. Besides, the communicative behaviors of local governments and individual Weibo users presented on local governments' Weibo profiles demonstrated the degree of government responsiveness and civic engagement.

6.1   Measures

Social media prevalence: Social media prevalence in terms of local governance was measured by the total number of Weibo accounts run by the local governmental agencies and officials in each provincial-level administrative division in mainland China in 2016 (CNNIC 2017, p. 75). Among the 31 provincial-level administrative divisions, Guangdong Province ranked the first with 12,707 governmental Weibo accounts in total. The higher the scale, the more prevalent the application of social media in local governance in a given provincial-level administrative division (M = 5267.39, SD = 3444.53).

6.1.1   Government Responsiveness

On a 0–100 scale, government responsiveness was measured by the "service index" of governmental Weibo accounts of each provincial-level administrative division in 2016 released by the Online Public Opinion Monitoring Center (OPOMC) of *People's Daily*, which described the extent to which local governments responded to public inquiries on their official Weibo accounts (OPOMC 2017, p. 64). Guangdong Province ranked the most responsive in terms of the degree to which the local governments responded to public inquiries on Weibo (index = 89.01). A higher score of the "service index" indicated a higher degree of local government responsiveness to public inquires on Weibo in a given provincial-level administrative division (M = 53.65, SD = 25.96).

6.1.2   Civic Engagement

On a 0–100 scale, civic engagement was measured by the "interactivity index" of governmental Weibo accounts of each provincial-level administrative division in 2016, which calculated the extent to which Weibo users reposted, commented, and liked the posts posted by the local governments (OPOMC 2017, p. 64). Weibo users in Jiangsu Province interacted with their local governments on Weibo most frequently (index = 92.60). In general, a higher score of the "interactivity index" demonstrated a higher degree of civic engagement in local affairs on Weibo in a given provincial-level administrative division (M = 55.76, SD = 22.17).

7   RESULTS

7.1   Social Media Prevalence Contributed to Government Responsiveness and Civic Engagement

As the results of the bilateral correlation analysis showed, social media prevalence was positively associated with government responsiveness ($r = 0.72$, $p < 0.001$) and with civic engagement ($r = 0.83$, $p < 0.001$). This demonstrated that the more prevalently social media was used during the process of local governance, the more likely would local governments respond to online public inquires. Meanwhile, the prevalence of social media tended to advance citizens' engagement in public affairs through interactions with their local governments on social media. Table 13.2 described the correlations between the involved variables.

7.2   Responsiveness to Public Inquires on Social Media: Active Local Governmental Agencies and Passive Officials

As shown in Table 13.3, the number of Weibo accounts run by local governmental agencies was positively related to the extent to which local governments responded to public inquires ($\beta = 0.99$, $p < 0.001$), and it accounted for 57.8% of the variance in local governments' responsiveness. By contrast, the quantity of the Weibo accounts run by local officials was negatively associated with the degree to which local governments responded to public inquiries ($\beta = -0.30$, $p = 0.10$), and it explained 2.3% of the variance in local governments' responsiveness.

It was concluded from the results that local governmental agencies considered social media a useful tool to address public concerns, which facilitated the agencies to respond more actively to public inquiries. However, local officials acted passively while responding to public inquiries on social media, with much less or even no feedback to the inquiries raised by the public.

Table 13.2 Correlations between social media prevalence, government responsiveness, and civic engagement

Variables	1	2	3
1. Social media prevalence	–		
2. Government responsiveness	0.72*	–	
3. Civic engagement	0.83*	0.65*	–
M	5267.39	53.65	55.76
SD	3444.53	25.96	22.17

Note: $N = 31$. Pearson's r was reported as the correlation coefficient

*$p < 0.001$

Table 13.3 Hierarchical multiple regression predicting government responsiveness and civic engagement

	Government responsiveness	Civic engagement
Number of agencies' Weibo accounts	0.99***	0.47**
Incremental R^2 (%)	57.8***	61.6***
Number of officials' Weibo accounts	−0.30#	0.43*
Incremental R^2 (%)	2.3#	6.7*
Total R^2	0.60***	0.68***
F	23.62	33.38

Note: N = 31. Standardized regression coefficients and adjusted R^2 were reported

#$p \leq 0.10$; *$p < 0.05$; **$p < 0.01$; ***$p < 0.001$

7.3   Citizens Interacted More with Local Governmental Agencies than with Officials on Social Media

As Table 13.3 demonstrates, the number of the Weibo accounts run by local governmental agencies was positively associated with the extent to which citizens interacted with them on social media ($\beta = 0.47$, $p < 0.01$), and it accounted for 61.6% of the variance in citizen engagement. Besides, the quantity of the Weibo accounts run by local officials was also positively related to the degree to which citizens interacted with them on social media ($\beta = 0.43$, $p < 0.05$), explaining 6.7% of the variance in citizen engagement.

The results indicated that citizens engaged in the discussions about public affairs by interacting with both local governmental agencies and officials on social media. Noticeably, the majority of the variance in citizen engagement was explained by the number of Weibo accounts run by local governmental agencies, implying that citizens were more likely to interact with the agencies than with the officials.

8   Conclusions

The statistical findings suggest that social media has more or less changed the mode of local governance in China compared to that in the predigital age. In general, the wide adoption of social media by local governments during the process of local governance not only improved local government responsiveness to online public inquires but also advanced online civic engagement in public affairs. Local governmental agencies tend to frequently respond to public inquiries, and meanwhile the public are quite willing to interact with the agencies on social media. However, compared to local governmental agencies, local officials behave in a relatively passive manner in addressing public concerns raised on social media, which might impair the public's intentions to further interact with them.

8.1 The Promising Role of Social Media in Advancing Good Local Governance in China

This study demonstrates that social media prevalence contributes to increased government responsiveness and civic engagement, which indicates that social media is playing a promising role in advancing good local governance in China. To some extent, it echoes previous studies that social media can not only facilitate a two-way communication between the government and the public (Cheng 2016; Downey and Jones 2012; Yuan 2013), but also empower citizens to engage in the discussion about public affairs (Li 2015; Wang 2014; Wang 2016). It further implies that local governments and the public are recognizing that social media can and should be fully utilized in dealing with local affairs in everyday life.

Meanwhile, the fast development of information and communication technologies (ICTs) enables individuals to construct and communicate public issues more quickly and frequently, which requires the government to respond to public inquires in a more active and timely way. In order to legitimize the bottom-up government accountability, establishing the institutions to collect public inquiries and disseminate government responses is, however, costly for local governments in China (Lorentzen et al. 2010). Accordingly, social media as a cost-effective platform is expected to facilitate the information exchange between local governments and the public, thus improving the efficiency of local governance in China.

8.2 The Access Point of Local Governments: Negotiating the Role of Agencies and Officials for Good Local Governance

In terms of local government responsiveness to public inquiries, local governmental agencies respond actively on social media, whereas local government officials behave in a passive way. This might result from the different understandings of the function of social media held by local governmental agencies and officials. In most circumstances, local governmental agencies register and manage a verified social media account merely for the sake of improving work efficiency, such as facilitating the process of collecting public opinions, releasing administrative information, and answering questions raised by the public. By contrast, work is not the only reason for local government officials to register a verified social media account. In addition to managing communication with the public regarding public affairs, government officials also post a considerable amount of social media posts related to their personal lives (Zhang 2012). Therefore, the *work-oriented* and *work-and-life mixed* mode of social media use accounts for the difference in government responsiveness to public inquiries between local governmental agencies and officials.

As regards civic engagement, people tend to interact more with local governmental agencies than with local government officials on social media, which indicates that they are more willing to engage in the online discussions about local affairs initiated by the agencies than those initiated by the officials. This might result from the difference between the perceived credibility of the agencies and officials. On the one hand, the public tends to perceive the agencies as more representative of their local governments because agencies serve as branches of the local government and perform by rules. However, individual officials cannot fully represent local governments due to their multiple identities. Consequently, the agencies are considered more credible and representative of the local government than the officials. On the other hand, local government officials lack the proactivity to respond to public inquires on social media, which might undermine the public's willingness to interact with them. In a word, the multiple identities of government officials and their passiveness in responding to public inquiries might explain people's less frequent interactions with them.

Taken together, the difference in government responsiveness between local governmental agencies and officials and the difference between civic engagement with the agencies and officials call us to rethink about the role of agencies and officials in local governance. Local governmental agencies and officials serve as the "access point" from which the public gets to know about the abstract system of local government (Giddens 1990, p. 88). The function of the *access point* becomes more salient in the digital age, in that social media platforms have provided the public and their local governments with more access to know each other, to exchange information more frequently and to maintain relationship more efficiently. In order to achieve good local governance in China, local government officials are advised to actively respond to public inquires on social media and to highlight their identity as a credible representative of the local government. Besides, dialogues between local governmental agencies and officials should be encouraged on social media, with the purpose of leaving the public with an impression that the agencies and officials both represent the local government and work together to improve local governance.

8.3   An Outlook into the Future for Digitalized (Local) Governance in China

It is concluded that social media has more or less changed the mode of local governance in China through improving government responsiveness and advancing online civic engagement. Despite the limitations, such as the underuse of social media by local government officials, social media in general has shown its potential for promoting good local governance in China. Given the fast development of ICTs and the wide application of digital media by local governments at the provincial, municipal, or even county levels in dealing with public affairs in China (CNNIC 2017), it signals that digitalized local governance will become an increasingly significant and indispensable part of local governance in China.

In addition to improving government responsiveness and advancing civic engagement to strive for good governance (Denters 2011; Kooiman 1999; Osborne 2010; Peters 2000), digital media also contributes to (local) governance in China in a unique way. For instance, to boost modernization and economy, the Chinese government is using ICTs to accelerate a decentralized and transparent administration, and in the meantime also to efficiently oversee relevant online information (Ma et al. 2005). Likewise, the Chinese government could forestall collective activities by monitoring social media posts (King et al. 2013). Moreover, leaders in China try to maintain government legitimacy by strategically tolerating online criticism, which serves as a safety valve to release public grievances and dissatisfactions (Wang and Shen 2017). Taken together, in China, digital media could not only be used normatively but also strategically to develop a distinctive mode of digitalized (local) governance in transitional China.

REFERENCES

Altschull, J.H. (1984). *Agents of Power: The Role of the News Media in Human Affairs.* London: Longman Publishing Group.

Bertot, J.C., P.T. Jaeger, and J.M. Grimes. (2010). Using ICTs to create a culture of transparency: E-government and social media as openness and anti-corruption tools for societies. *Government Information Quarterly*, 27(3): 264–271.

Breed, W. (1958). Mass communication and socio-cultural integration. *Social Forces*, 37(2): 109–116.

Castells, M. (2008). The new public sphere: Global civil society, communication networks, and global governance. *The Annals of the American Academy of Political and Social Science*, 616(1): 78–93.

Chan, A. (2002). From propaganda to hegemony: Jiaodian Fangtan and China's media policy. *Journal of Contemporary China*, 11(30): 35–51.

Che, F. (2014). *A Study on the Social Governance of News Media in China.* Beijing, China: Communication University of China Press. [In Chinese].

Cheng, Y. (2016). A comparison between Internet-based administration and TV-based administration. *Contemporary TV*, 11: 85–86. [In Chinese].

CNNIC. (2017). The 29th China statistical report on Internet development. Retrieved from http://www.cnnic.cn/hlwfzyj/hlwxzbg/hlwtjbg/201701/t20170122_66437.htm.

Denters, B. (2011). Local Governance. In: M. Bevir (ed.), *The SAGE Handbook of Governance.* Sage.

Downey, E., and M. Jones (eds.). (2012). *Public Service, Governance and Web 2.0 Technologies: Future Trends in Social Media.* IGI Global.

Evans, S.K., K.E. Pearce, J. Vitak, and J.W. Treem. (2017). Explicating affordances: A conceptual framework for understanding affordances in communication research. *Journal of Computer-Mediated Communication*, 22(1): 35–52.

Gibson, J.J. (1979). *The Ecological Approach to Visual Perception.* Boston: Houghton Mifflin.

Giddens, A. (1990). *The Consequences of Modernity.* Cambridge, UK: Polity.

Guo, X. (2013). New media, citizen journalists, and good governance of environmental civil society in the NIMBY conflict. *Chinese Journal of Journalism and Communication,* 5: 52–61. [In Chinese].

Hirst, P. (2000). Democracy and Governance. In: J. Pierre (ed.), *Debating Governance.* Oxford: Oxford University.

Jiang, Z. (2015). *A Study on Public Governance and Media Services Provision in China.* Beijing, China: Word Book Inc. [In Chinese].

King, G., J. Pan, and M.E. Roberts. (2013). How censorship in China allows government criticism but silences collective expression. *American Political Science Review,* 107(02): 326–343.

Kooiman, J. (1999). Social-political governance. *Public Management Review,* 1(1): 67–92.

Lasswell, H.D. (1948). The Structure and Function of Communication in Society. In: L. Bryson (ed.), *The Communication of Ideas.* New York: Institute for Religious and Social Studies.

Lazarsfeld, P.F., and R.K. Merton. (1948). "Mass Communication, Popular Taste and Organized Social Action." In: L. Bryson (ed.), *The Communication of Ideas.* New York: Institute for Religious and Social Studies.

Lee, C.C., Z. He, and Y. Huang. (2006). 'Chinese Party Publicity Inc.' conglomerated: The case of the Shenzhen press group. *Media, Culture & Society,* 28(4): 581–602.

Li, L. (1998). Reforms of journalism in China: From 1978 to 1998. *Journalism and Mass Communication Monthly,* 6: 11–12. [In Chinese].

Li, M. (2015). City communication studies in the social media age. *China Publishing Update,* 13: 65–68. [In Chinese].

Linders, D. (2012). From e-government to we-government: Defining a typology for citizen coproduction in the age of social media. *Government Information Quarterly,* 29(4): 446–454.

Lorentzen, P., P. Landry, and J. Yasuda. (2010). Transparent authoritarianism?: An analysis of political and economic barriers to greater government transparency in China. In: APSA 2010 Annual Meeting Paper, Washington, DC.

Ma, D., and L. Zhang. (2008). Measuring governance: Overseas studies and their implications for China. *Journal of Public Management,* 5(4): 101–128. [In Chinese].

Ma, L., J. Chung, and S. Thorson (2005). E-government in China: Bringing economic development through administrative reform. *Government Information Quarterly,* 22(1): 20–37.

Norris, P. (ed.). (2010). *Public Sentinel: News Media and Governance Reform.* World Bank Publications.

Online Public Opinion Monitoring Center (OPOMC). (2017). The 2016 annual report on the influence index of governmental Weibo in China. Retrieved from http://yuqing.people.com.cn/n1/2017/0119/c209043-29036185.html.

Osborne, S.P. (ed.). (2010). *The New Public Governance: Emerging Perspectives on the Theory and Practice of Public Governance.* Routledge.

Pan, Z., and J.M. Chan. (2003). Shifting journalistic paradigms: How China's journalists assess "media exemplars." *Communication Research,* 30(6): 649–682.

Peters, G.B. (2000). Governance and Comparative Politics. In: J. Pierre (ed.), *Debating Governance.* Oxford: Oxford University.

Pierre, J. (2000). Introduction: Understanding Governance. In: J. Pierre (ed.), *Debating Governance.* New York: Oxford University Press.

Ren, B., and I. Yan. (2015). NIMBY conflicts in cities: An explanation on the construction of the actors' strategic planning. *Henan Social Sciences*, 23(3): 65–70. [In Chinese].

Siebert, F.S., T. Peterson, and W. Schramm. (1956). *Four Theories of the Press: The Authoritarian, Libertarian, Social Responsibility, and Soviet Communist Concepts of What the Press Should Be and Do*. Champaign, IL: University of Illinois Press.

Wang, B. (2016). The new media-based modes of community-level governance in cities: New approaches. *Jinan Journal* (Philosophy & Social Science Edition), 6: 99–106. [In Chinese].

Wang, R. (2015). The emergence and dissolvement of publicity: A case study of the real estate owners' defense for civil rights and their rights of access to the mass media in City N. *Press Circles*, 15: 4–12. [In Chinese].

Wang, S. (2014). The impact of new media on the governance of intercultural communities. *Academic Research*, 6: 37–40. [In Chinese].

Wang, T., and F. Shen. (2017). The impacts of online grassroots criticism on citizen satisfaction with government: An inconsistent mediation model. *International Journal of Communication*, 11: 113–136.

Wright, C.R. (1959). *Mass Communication: A Sociological Perspective*. New York: McGraw-Hill College.

Yan, J. (2013). A case study of the police department's management of human trafficking on Weibo. *The Journal of Jiangsu Administration Institute*, 4: 98–102. [In Chinese].

Yang, G. (2005). Environmental NGOs and institutional dynamics in China. *The China Quarterly*. 46–66.

Yang, X. (2002). On institutional foundations of governance. *Tianjin Social Sciences*, 2: 43–46. [In Chinese].

Yu, J., and T. Feng. (2011). The governance transition of local government in the process of urbanization: An analytical framework. *Journal of Social Sciences*, 11: 4–11. [In Chinese].

Yu, J., and S. Wang. (2016). New Agenda for the Study of Chinese Governance. *Journal of Chinese Governance*, 1(1): 21–40.

Yuan, D. (2013). Building a responsive government in the new media era. *Editorial Friend*, 6: 79–81. [In Chinese].

Zang, Z. (2003). Governance: Utopia or reality? *Theory Quintessence*: 10–11. [In Chinese].

Zhang, N. (2012). Government officials' Weibo profiles: A new perspective to view government-public relationships. *Modern Communication* (*Journal of Communication University of China*), 7: 100–104. [In Chinese].

Zhao, Y. (1996). Toward a propaganda/commercial model of journalism in China? The case of the Beijing Youth News. *International Communication Gazette*, 58(3): 143–157.

Zhou, T., and D. Shen. (2014). Administration on WeChat: An exploration into the mode of social governance in digital media age. *Press Circles*, 15: 64–68. [In Chinese].

Zhou, Y. (2000). Watchdogs on party leashes? Contexts and implications of investigative journalism in post-Deng China. *Journalism Studies*, 1(4): 577–597.

Zhu, H., X. Shan, and J. Hu. (2009). China's Online Public Opinions Report. Retrieved from http://yuqing.people.com.cn/n/2012/0727/c209170-18615454.html.

PART IV

Grassroots Governance

CHAPTER 14

Villagers' Self-Governance in Rural China

Yong Xu

1 Introduction

Grassroots self-governance has a long history in rural China. The currently implemented villagers' self-governance system was established after the abolishment of the people's commune system in 1978. It is in nature a grassroots governance system, which enables rural residents to directly engage in public affairs. Being of modern democratic significance, villagers' self-governance has been recognized by relevant laws of the People's Republic of China (PRC). And its implementation paves the way for rural residents to exercise their democratic rights and for the Chinese government to organize its rural society. Since its establishment, villagers' self-governance has experienced continuous expansion and deepening. Accordingly, the study of villagers' self-governance has shifted from "value-institution paradigm" to "form-condition paradigm." As the rural society changes, villagers' self-governance is going to exhibit new features during its development process.

2 The Emergence and Progress of Villagers' Self-Governance in Rural China

Villagers' self-governance in rural China is in nature a rural mass system of self-governance at grassroots level, which enables villagers to deal with village affairs concerning their interests through villagers' self-governing organization in accordance with law, and realize self-management, self-education, and self-service. It mainly covers the following four aspects: (a) the subject of self-governance is rural residents who enjoy the democratic right to independently manage the public affairs of their own village; (b) the geographic scope of

Y. Xu (✉)
Institute of China Rural Studies, Central China Normal University, Wuhan, China

J. Yu, S. Guo (eds.), *The Palgrave Handbook of Local Governance in Contemporary China*, https://doi.org/10.1007/978-981-13-2799-5_14

self-governance is village, which is a rural community closely related to the life of rural residents and is also the primary organizational unit of rural society; (c) the content of self-governance is the public affairs and public welfare undertakings of a village, that is, village affairs; (d) the goal of self-governance is to enable rural residents of China to manage, educate, and serve themselves within a village and effectively deal with village affairs concerning their interests.

Villagers' self-governance is a form of direct democracy at grassroots level, which allows villagers to directly participate in the management of village-level public affairs concerning their interests. It includes (a) democratic election—leaders of villagers' self-governing organization are directly elected by villagers; (b) democratic decision-making—major village affairs are collectively decided by villagers; (c) democratic management—villagers participate in the management of their village affairs through organizations and forms such as villagers' assembly, villagers' representative conference, villagers' committee, and villagers' group; (d) democratic supervision—villagers supervise leaders of villagers' self-governing organization and their management of village affairs and exercise self-discipline and self-education during this process.

Grassroots self-governance has a long history in rural China. Historically, grassroots self-governance in rural China was mainly based on the units of family, extended family, clan, and village. Rural residents followed established conventions to practice self-governance. Such a system was dominated by family heads, patriarchs, squires, as well as leaders of village organizations. Although grassroots self-governance in rural China was recognized by the Central Government, it did not enjoy a definite legal protection.

In 1949, the PRC was founded, which marked the beginning of a series of major reforms in the organizations and systems of rural society. Through socialist transformation of agriculture, the Central Government introduced the people's commune system in rural China. Integrating government administration with economic management, people's commune was a rural collective economic organization (RCEO) and a grassroots rural unit of the state power. It adopted a management system of "production team-based three-tiered ownership," which covers the production team, the production brigade, and the people's commune. With the initiation of rural reform in 1978, household contract responsibility system was universally implemented in rural China, making household a basic unit of agricultural production and operation and directly leading to the disintegration of the people's commune system.

Economic reform in rural China gave full play to the production initiative of Chinese farmers. Yet at the same time, it also caused social chaos due to the relaxation of the previous organizational system. Under such circumstances, the organization and governance of rural society became a top priority.

As is known to all, China's household contract responsibility system was originally a spontaneous creation of Chinese farmers. Likewise, villagers' self-governance, a form of rural grassroots governance, was also initiated by Chinese farmers during the process of economic restructuring. In the early

1980s, with the emergence of the household contract responsibility system and the abolishment of the people's commune system, grassroots organization system in some areas was basically in a paralyzed state. Against this background, farmers created a self-governing organization—the villagers' committee, which originated in Luoshan and Yishan of Guangxi Zhuang Autonomous Region (also known by other names such as villagers' management committee, villagers council, and steering group of village public security). As a new form of grassroots organization, villagers' committee immediately drew attention from China's top decision-making level that was considering how to establish a new grassroots organization system to better adapt to the ongoing economic restructuring. Through experience summarizing, villagers' committee was included in national legal and policy agenda.

In December 1982, *the Constitution of the PRC* was passed, whose Article 111 stipulates that "the residents' committees and villagers' committees established among urban and rural residents on the basis of their place of residence are mass organizations of self-governance at the grassroots level. The chairman, vice-chairmen and members of each residents' or villagers' committee are elected by the residents. The relationship between the residents' and villagers' committees and the grassroots organs of state power is prescribed by law." This article also covers the establishment of residents' and villagers' subcommittees and their main functions.

The 1982 Constitution is of great significance to the rise of villagers' self-governance. First, it acknowledged the legal status of villagers' committee by including it in this fundamental law of China and thus enabled this new form of organization, which emerged in rural reform, to be recognized by national laws. This indicates that the villagers' committee, a newly emerged organization form, officially replaced the previous grassroots organization in the people's commune era. Second, it confirmed the nature of villagers' committee as a mass organization of self-governance at the grassroots level and specified the basic functions of villagers' committee, that is, dealing with local public affairs and public welfare undertakings, mediating civil disputes, assisting in maintaining public order, and reporting the masses' opinions, suggestions and requirements to the people's government. This clearly distinguishes the villagers' committee from the grassroots organization in the people's commune era. The latter features an integration of government administration with economic management and a focus on agricultural production. Third, relevant constitutional provision also liberated the villagers' committee from being a subordinate of any organ of state power and recognized its relative independence.

With the advancement of rural reform and national democratization, villagers' self-governance saw increasing improvement in principle, organizational form, and corresponding laws and regulations.

Following the abolishment of the people's commune system, the *Notice on Strengthening the Construction of Grassroots Governance in Rural Areas* was co-released by the Communist Party of China (CPC) Central Committee and the State Council in September 1986. The *Notice* fully affirmed the separation of government administration and economic management and the establishment of township government to be one more reform move of profound significance after the universal implementation of household contract responsibility system in rural China. While calling for further enhancement of grassroots governance in rural China, the *Notice* also attached great importance to the construction of villagers' (residents') committee. After all, the separation of government administration and economic management and the establishment of township government only facilitated the grassroots governance at township level. Without organizational restructuring below the township level (i.e., at the village level), the somewhat chaotic state in rural China would remain. To this end, the Notice specified tasks concerning the construction of villagers' (residents') committee, stressing the importance of giving full play to the self-education, self-management and self-service of the mass organizations of self-governance. Meanwhile, it also instructed the Ministry of Civil Affairs of the PRC to supervise the specific work of villagers' committee construction. The issuance of this Notice signifies that after completing the separation of government administration and economic management and the establishment of township government, the Central Government shifted its focus to the construction of organizations and systems below township level, or rather, at the village level, thus accelerating the rise of villagers' self-governance.

In November 1987, the *Organic Law of the Villagers' Committees of the People's Republic of China* (trial) (hereinafter referred to as the *Organic Law* (trial)) was approved by the 23rd Session of the Sixth National People's Congress (NPC) Standing Committee. It was not until then that the principle of villagers' self-governance was acknowledged and the corresponding form of organization was specified by a national law of China. As aforementioned, the *Organic Law* (trial) explicitly defined villagers' self-governance and villagers' committee. According to its Article 1, the purpose of the *Law* is to "ensure villagers' exercise of self-governance, enable them to deal with their own affairs by law, and promote grassroots socialist democracy, as well as socialist material and cultural progress in rural China." In addition to that, it also further defined the self-governance nature and functions of villagers' committee and clearly specified its formation process, main responsibilities, form of organization, working principles, subcommittees, and so on. In particular, Article 3 of the *Law* specified that the relationship between a township government and corresponding village committees is of a guiding-assisting nature, rather than a leading-being led one. Such stipulation was vital to the establishment of villagers' self-governance principle. The enacting of the *Organic Law* (trial) marked the emergence of villagers' self-governance in rural China.

The *1987 Organic Law* (trial) marked the start of institutionalized operation of villagers' self-governance in rural China. In the beginning, this institutionalized operation featured demonstrative and innovative characteristics, reflecting the dual effect created by the Chinese government's prudent advancement of villagers' self-governance and the Chinese farmers' continual perfection of this system in practice. In September 1990, the Ministry of Civil Affairs of the PRC issued the *Notice on Carrying Out Demonstrative Activities of Villagers' Self-governance in Rural China*. According to the *Notice*, demonstrative activities of villagers' self-governance were to be initiated nationwide to further guide the implementation of the *Organic Law* (trial) and step-by-step gradually popularize villagers' self-governance in a well-planned and organized way. Through such exemplary and demonstrative activities, new forms of self-governance like villagers' representative conference were created by the Chinese farmers.

Through more than one decade's trial implementation, within the framework of the *Organic Law* (trial), farmers in scattered distribution were included in legitimate villagers' committees, through which they were able to directly participate in village governance. Thus, rural China struck a balance between government administration and villagers' self-governance, presenting a "spectacular view" in China's construction of socialist democracy. Just as Peng Zhen put it when pushing through the legislation of the *Organic Law* (trial) in 1987, "eight hundred million Chinese farmers' practice of self-governance, self-management, self-education and self-service would make them true masters of this country, which was extraordinary and unprecedented." And much credit was given to this villagers' self-governance at the 15th CPC National Congress in 1997. In order to further improve villagers' self-governance system and ensure rural mass to directly exercise democratic rights, the Ninth NPC Standing Committee, in the spirit of the 15th CPC National Congress, summarized the implementation experience of the *Organic Law* (trial) over the previous decade, and revised and passed the *Organic Law of the Villagers' Committees of the PRC* in November 1998 to better target existing problems. The approval of the *Organic Law* brought villagers' self-governance in rural China to a new stage featuring state-level integrated development and enabled the establishment of a general framework for villagers' self-governance. The newly passed law deleted the "trial" articles in the *1987 Organic Law* (trial) and increased parts concerning "democratic election, democratic decision-making, and democratic management." It further specified its value orientation, that is, to exercise grassroots democracy through villagers' committee. At the same time, it also defined the role and functions of grassroots CPC organization in the system of villagers' self-governance.

Since 1998, based on the actual situations, the Central Government has released a range of documents in various forms to guide the development of villagers' self-governance. In 2002, the *Notice on Further Improving the Work of Villagers' Committee Election* was jointly issued by the General Office of the CPC Central Committee and the General Office of the State Council. The *Notice* made it clear that "villagers' direct election of a villagers' committee is a basic democratic right conferred by law and is an important manifestation of grassroots democracy." Improving the work of villagers' committee election means fully promoting democracy, effectively safeguarding villagers' rights in the whole process of election, and truthfully reflecting rural mass' will." More importantly, the *Notice* proposed suggestions on the institutional issue of how to engage members of the grassroots CPC organization in the villagers' committee election. To match democratic election with democratic decision-making, democratic management, and democratic supervision, the *Opinions on Improving and Strengthening the Open Management of Village Affairs System and the Democratic Management System* was jointly released by the General Office of the CPC Central Committee and the General Office of the State Council in 2004. The *Opinions* proposed to "further improve the open management of village affairs system to safeguard farmers' right to know; further regulate the mechanism of democratic decision-making to safeguard farmers' right to decide; further perfect the democratic management system to ensure farmers' right to participate; and further enhance the supervision and restriction mechanism of village affairs management to safeguard farmers' right to supervise." While the Central Government was striving to establish a corresponding legislative system, local government also took the initiative to engage in this cause. For example, in the absence of a state-level law of the villagers' committee election, some provinces formulated their provincial-level election laws with local characteristics.

In order to further regulate and advance villagers' self-governance, the NPC Standing Committee revised the *Organic Law of the Villagers' Committees of the PRC* in 2010, thus acknowledging farmers' right to know, right to decide, right to participate, and right to supervise during the practice of villagers' self-governance, as well as corresponding procedures in the form of law.

In addition to institutional norm, local governments and farmers keep exploring and innovating during the practice of villagers' self-governance to enable effective implementation of this governance principle and norm. And this is well demonstrated by the exploration of effective approaches to the realization of villagers' self-governance. Influenced by the people's commune system of "production team-based three-tiered ownership," villagers' committees, which were established after the abolition of the people's commune system, are essentially based on former production brigade with a staff of around 2000. The large population, along with factors like scattered distribution of villagers, makes it difficult to convene a villagers' committee meeting, engage villagers in it, and ensure effective operation of villagers' self-governance system. Such a challenge is particularly highlighted in South China. With the advancement of the "construction of new socialist countryside" program since 2007, some regions began to explore a new basic unit better fitting into villagers' self-governance at or below villagers' committee level and proposed to explore effective approaches to the realization of villagers' self-governance in accordance with the principles of "being interests related, geographically linked, culturally tied, voluntarily engaged and conveniently self-governed." Such efforts made at local and grassroots levels are recognized by the Central Government. The 2014 Document No. 1 of the Central Government proposed to "explore effective approaches to the realization of villagers' self-governance in different contexts." Later, subsequent central documents were introduced to further encourage such an endeavor at the local level.

In 1978, China initiated its rural reform, allowing Chinese farmers to explore possible approaches to villagers' self-governance. Now, it has been nearly 40 years since villagers' self-governance became a national political system, which features a great interaction between and mutual promotion of farmers' exploration and national norm. After the abolishment of the people's commune system in rural China, farmers have such a need to manage public affairs through self-organization; while the state has the intention to reestablish rural organizations for effective governance. It is in this context that villagers' self-governance is established and has developed into a solid system.

Being concrete and vigorous, villagers' self-governance is practiced by hundreds of millions of farmers and is influenced and restricted by specific environments. The advancement of villagers' self-governance as a state system coincides with China's mass industrialization and urbanization, which has brought about a series of new challenges and problems to villagers' self-governance. For example, the substantial outflow of rural population, particularly rural talents, coupled with a range of demanding national tasks such as agricultural tax collection and family planning, fosters increasingly administrated villagers' committees, unsatisfactory villagers' self-governance, and twisted views of villagers' self-governance during the implementation process. These challenges and problems restricted and affected the realization of villagers' self-governance. Nevertheless, villagers' self-governance has been established as a state system and is advancing ahead in practice.

3   STUDIES ON VILLAGERS' SELF-GOVERNANCE IN RURAL CHINA

Studies on villagers' self-governance closely follow the progress of villagers' self-governance. In the 1980s and the first half of the 1990s, villagers' self-governance was still in trial, for which it attracted little academic attention. And this is ridiculed by a sarcastic claim that "there were 900 million Chinese farmers practicing villagers' self-governance, while there were only nine scholars studying it."

Later, the democratic election-oriented villagers' self-governance, which started in 1998, managed to draw extensive attention from the Chinese academics and thus quickly became a hot topic. Political scientists, among many other scholars of different academic areas, participated in this research, contributing numerous essays and publications. This academic heat lasted as long as ten years. Centering on villagers' self-governance system, their studies are regarded as mainstream in the realm of villagers' self-governance. Yet at the same time, there is no lack of different views and voices.

First, there are high expectations on villagers' self-governance. Since 1988, the ruling party, that is, the CPC, has kept advancing villagers' self-governance as "foundation works" of socialist democracy, taking it as a "prototype" to showcase our socialist democracy. Consequently, villagers' self-governance quickly attracted enormous attention from academics. Villagers' self-governance was identified as a "silent revolution" with democratic ideals by the academic circles. For this reason, it was vested with a lot of democratic hopes, expectations, and imagination (Rong 1998). That gave rise to the establishment of the "value-institution" paradigm. Being democracy oriented, this paradigm focuses on the advancement of grassroots democracy by establishing and improving corresponding systems.

Second, there are doubts about villagers' self-governance. Being a hot academic topic does not silence the voice of skeptics, some of whom even hold a completely negative attitude toward it. One of the prominent skeptics is Shen Yansheng, who published a 50,000-word essay the "Rise, Fall and Reconstruction of Village Governance" in *Strategy and Management*. From a broad historical perspective, this essay strongly questioned the mass democracy and election included in the villagers' self-governance system, reminding that a similar system once got Adolf Hitler elected as state head. According to Shen Yansheng, the theory of villagers' self-governance is a "freak," which was never mentioned by Marx, Lenin, Mao Zedong, or Deng Xiaoping (Shen 1998). Another prominent representative is Dang Guoying, who did not consider villagers' self-governance to be the starting point of socialist democracy (Dang 1999). Given the political climate back then, the disapprovals voiced by Shen and Dang were indeed rare and praiseworthy. However, their research paradigm was based on texts and historical experience and lacked practical roots. Not having a thorough understanding or analysis of what had happened, they failed to extend their research in villagers' self-governance further.

Third, there is also no shortage of skepticism. Some scholars attached great importance to field survey, through which they discovered that a substantial gap lay between real practice of villagers' self-governance and institutional design and that villagers' self-governance was far from enough to address the complexity and diversity of rural governance. Because of that, they became skeptical of the efficiency of such a system. They attempted to follow the philosophy of rural governance to understand and analyze the rural society and subsequently extended the scope of rural governance research. That is how these scholars turned away from villagers' self-governance research, resulting in the disappearance of villagers' self-governance from rural governance. Focusing excessively on local and individual experience, none of them developed a paradigm for relevant academic research.

Fourth, there are serious reflections. With more and more sociologists, economists, and humanitarians gradually withdrawing from villagers' self-governance research, political scientists, being a major force in this regard, still hold fast to it and approach it reflectively. These scholars have unveiled the contrast between the institutional supply and the institutional performance of the villagers' self-governance system and thereby raised corresponding questions. Yet, they continue to follow the "value-institution" paradigm, for which they cannot offer any profounder explanation of the "involution" that troubles villagers' self-governance.

Fifth, there is extreme pessimism. When villagers' self-governance was first introduced across China as a state system, many people had high expectations on it and were very optimistic about the development path of socialist democracy—the one about to extend from village and township level to county level and above. In reality, however, things did not develop as expected. In particular, direct election of township head was called off because it was found to be in conflict with existing laws; the advancement of villagers' self-governance became more difficult for various reasons. Such a self-governance dilemma disappointed some scholars. On the other hand, since 1998, China's "three rural issues" (issues concerning agriculture, countryside, and farmers) have been highlighted. People supporting villagers' self-governance for utilitarian purposes feel more and more disappointed because they believe villagers' self-governance, instead of solving the "three rural issues," have exacerbated them. The much longer-than-expected development process of villagers' self-governance stopped the scholars, who initially followed this topic purely out of their faith, ideal, and passion, from further exploration.

Sixth, there are persistent discussions. The designers of villagers' self-governance system place high hopes on it and at the same time are prudent enough. As early as in 1987, when the *Organic Law* (trial) was formulated, Peng Zhen warned, "organizing villagers committee and implementing villagers' self-governance is a long-term challenge and should not be deem an easy task that can be accomplished within a short period of time by simply issuing a document or a decree." As aforementioned, the *Organic Law* (trial) issued back then was a "trial version" and "no definite period of validity is given. It can only be solved in practice. The implementation of this trial version is also a gradual process of experience accumulation and exploration" (Peng 1991). A decade later, villagers' self-governance was implemented across China as a state system. While making significant progress, it was also faced with challenges that even its designers had not expected. Given that, some scholars shifted their focus to the challenges and problems arising during the progress of villagers' self-governance and tried to find feasible solutions.

In 2014, at the "No.1 village of villagers' self-governance," the Institute of China Rural Studies of Central China Normal University held the "Forum on Exploring the Effective Approaches to the Realization of Villagers' Self-governance," calling for a "return to self-governance studies" and having a series of essays published. Central China Normal University's advocacy of an academic "return to self-governance studies" reinvigorated the Chinese scholars' passion for villagers' self-governance research and more importantly, developed a new paradigm in this regard, that is, "form-condition" paradigm. If "value-institution" paradigm is the 1.0 version of villagers' self-governance research paradigm, "form-condition" paradigm should be its 2.0 version. And the 1.0 version is still a natural extension of political science research paradigm, while the 2.0 version exhibits a high degree of academic consciousness.

Since 2010, there have been new views expressed by different scholars concerning villagers' self-governance innovation, such as Prof. Cheng Tongshun's inclusion of villagers' groups in villagers' self-governance system. Still, by and large, there is no real breakthrough in the research paradigm. Below are statistics of villagers' self-governance-themed papers retrieved from the China National Knowledge Infrastructure (CNKI).

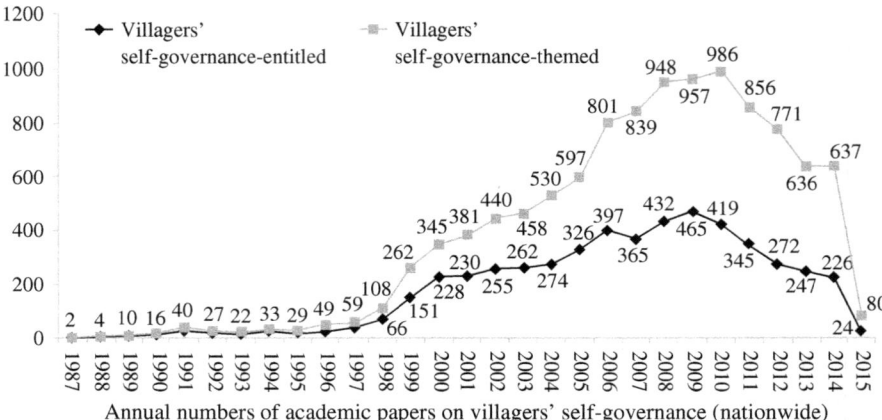

Annual numbers of academic papers on villagers' self-governance (nationwide)

It is true that studies on villagers' self-governance in China are far from mature. However, their significance lies in the fact that they begin to develop research paradigms of their own. To put it another way, they gradually develop a high consciousness of paradigm. How do studies on villagers' self-governance form their own research paradigms distinctive from those of other Chinese social sciences? Fundamentally, they do so by basing themselves on the Chinese practice. It is precisely those concrete and vigorous practices of villagers' self-governance that drive scholars to keep developing and transforming research paradigms, properly explain and answer questions arising from villagers' self-governance practice, and thus adapt to such practices.

The formation of the two research paradigms of villagers' self-governance in rural China is closely related to villagers' practice of self-governance. It is fair to say that such practice lays the basis for the development and transformation of villagers' self-governance research paradigms.

Villagers' self-governance originated in the early 1980s, while rural self-governance has a long history in China. The upgrading of such grassroots self-governance from village-level practice to a state system inevitably required proper value orientation and a reflection of its significance. This, to a large extent, also explains why political science is always accompanied by state building and national system construction. As a state system, villagers' self-governance is vested with democratic value by the government and represents the strategic orientation of state system construction. The political practice, which upgraded villagers' self-governance to a state system, enabled the formation of the "value-institution" paradigm of villagers' self-governance. And such a paradigm has at least four major contributions.

First, it defined the villagers' self-governance as something distinct from traditional rural self-governance, which, rooted deep in history and characterized by rural elite dominance, was more like a kind of self-construction of rural order. Today, villagers' self-governance is set in a modern country and involves all villagers in the self-governance. It well demonstrates the right for the villagers to participate in public affairs administration as a member of the country and collectivity.

Second, through the lens of theory, it clearly expounded on China's unique national conditions which attributed to the villagers' self-governance, namely the collective ownership—the socioeconomic soil in which the rights of villagers reflected in the villagers' self-governance are deeply rooted. Thus villagers' self-governance is viewed as "a grassroots democracy."

Third, it helped improve the overall institutional design. After the villagers' self-governance rose to a state system from mere local experience, scholars were inspired to come out with a "value-system" paradigm which delved into issues relating to the system, including its composition, subsystems, operation, and performance.

Fourth, it diverted the vision of multiple disciplines like politics to China and its practices. Several disciplines of China, like politics, sociology, and law, were mostly resumed after the 1980s by relying on the introduction of foreign theories at the very beginning. But the local attempt in politics to launch the villagers' self-governance has drawn academic attention to China, marking the evolution of Chinese political science from "being enshrined high up in temple" to "being down-to-earth."

When the villagers' self-governance entered people's everyday life as a state system, the "value-institution" paradigm proved deficient. In consequence, the "involution" theory was proposed by some experts to explain why the more mature the system is, the worse its performance becomes. Regrettably, no solution was given in the theory.

As related work advanced, the upgraded 2.0 version of the research paradigm of the villagers' self-governance—"form-condition"—was invented. Its major contributions are as follows:

First, the real villagers' self-governance is recovered. Related practices in the past have proved that when the villagers' committee, the vehicle for the villagers' self-governance, was expected to organize the rural society on behalf of the country, it might stand at the risk of being devastated under excessive tasks. Meanwhile, the "value-institution" paradigm used the villagers' committee, the statutory autonomous institution, as the only measure and placed too much expectation upon it. This is a dilemma the "value-institution" paradigm must face: the system must be proved sensible and evolutionary. If no value comes, the system is doomed to be discouraged. The result is that when the villagers' committee was made an administrative institution, the villagers' self-governance was twisted, and the once too optimistic scholars were let down. In fact, the villagers' self-governance is just one means of rural governance and should not be burdened with too much expectation. During the new countryside construction, the villagers' self-governance was recovered in some places, and what's most important, this time it was weighed by its internal value. Though it was a democracy, it was a more pluralistic one. The "form-condition" research paradigm was a natural outcome of the recovered villagers' self-governance.

Second, it broadens the horizon of the study on the villagers' self-governance. When the villagers' self-governance rose to become part of the national legal system from mere local experience, regulations were not made based on the principles of the villagers' self-governance, but rather on the role of the villagers' committee, which made the villagers' committee the sole statutory autonomous institution, and also the major subject of the "value-institution" paradigm. However, due to its being administrative, it was somehow restraining the villagers' self-governance. In contrast, the "form-condition" paradigm focuses on how to give full play to the villagers' self-governance and largely broadens the horizon of researches. For example, while in some "administrative villages" the villagers' self-governance sinks deep into the mire, it thrives in other "natural villages," which enlightens researchers to the effect that the villagers' self-governance should not be limited to administrative villages with villagers' committees, but rather any form that is sensible is worth a try. The horizon of the studies on the villagers' self-governance is thus broadened.

Third, the focus of research shifts from national institutional arrangement to the internal requirements and conditions of the villages. When the villagers' self-governance rose to become part of the national legal system from mere local experience, it had to be uniform, consistent, and well regulated across the country, as is required by the character of state systems. However, when it landed on different regions as a national transcript, the villagers' self-governance, which was meant to involve millions upon millions of farmers, was challenged by the complexity of different regional conditions and different requirements of farmers. It had to be "down-to-earth." The "value-institution" paradigm, while focused on the institutional side, could hardly provide instructions on that. Thus comes the "form-condition" paradigm, which, focusing on the very value of the villagers' self-governance, especially stresses promoting valid forms to realize it and adjusting the forms to the local idiosyncrasies. The approaches to the realization of the villagers' self-governance are shaped by the conditions, and the "form-condition" paradigm comes from none other than the practices of the villagers' self-governance. For example, the requisites of the villagers' self-governance—"being interests related, geographically linked, culturally tied, voluntarily engaged and conveniently self-governed" were rightly condensed by scholars from local practices which had first posed related theories based on the internal factors and requirements of the villagers' self-governance. Such relevant studies largely make the overall research more scientific and more effective when used in practices.

Fourth, the "form-condition" paradigm not only focuses on the present but also takes into account the continuity of history and the trend of the future, for it emphasizes all variations with the time, location, and conditions. Requiring a deep understanding about the conditions in a certain context, the form makes it an imperative for scholars to delve into the rural social patterns, changes, and current circumstances and get well acquainted with each detail of the diverse local idiosyncrasies.

4   OUTLOOK FOR THE VILLAGERS' SELF-GOVERNANCE IN RURAL CHINA

China is well known for its most ancient agricultural civilization, which throughout history had been characterized by rural self-governance. Into the twentieth century, due to the revolutions and the modern state construction, this tradition had experienced enormous changes, while the villagers' self-governance emerged and evolved. Given the fact that China is experiencing significant historical transformations, the conditions and content of the villagers' self-governance will also undergo considerable changes.

First, there will be urban-rural integration. The villagers' self-governance came into being in an urban-rural dual structure—whereas self-governance fell on urban residents, it also found its way to the rural villagers. As the urban-rural integration advances, the boundaries between cities and villages will be further blurred, contributing to the changes in content and forms of villagers' self-governance in rural China. For example, more public services will be found accompanying the ongoing villagers' self-governance.

Second, rural communities will be built. The urban-rural integration will make the rural society more open. The rural areas will pool an increasing number of public services provided by the country. Rural production mode, lifestyle, and inhabitation mode will also be different, and the rural communities will serve as a new living space for the rural population. The traditional natural villages will gradually give way to new communities. Thus the villagers' self-governance stands to be newly shaped.

Third, there will be more diversity. As China steps into a more modernized society, its rural areas will by degrees feature a diversity trend, whereby the content and forms of the villagers' self-governance will surely be diversified.

No matter how the context changes, the villagers' self-governance will never cease playing a vital role in solving collective issues in rural China and maintaining a benign rural governance.

REFERENCES

Rong, Jingben. "Villagers' Self-governance – the Butterfly of Democracy is Flying," Inside Information on Economic Reform, 1998 (3).

Shen, Yansheng. "The Rise, Fall and Reconstruction of Village Governance", Strategy and Management, 1998 (6).

Dang, Guoying. "Is Villagers' Self-governance the Starting Point of Socialist Democracy?", Strategy and Management, 1999 (1).

Peng, Zhen, "Practicing Direct Democracy at Grassroots Level through Mass Self-governance", *Selected Works of Peng Zhen* (1941–1990), People's Publishing House, 1991: 610–611.

CHAPTER 15

The Changing Institutional Space Regarding Roles and Behavior of Village Leaders: An Evolution from Villagers' Autonomy to the Power List

Yuejin Jing and Lina Zhang

1 Introduction

The rural society in China has undergone dramatic changes in the past four decades since the implementation of reform and opening-up. These changes are reflected in width, depth, and disparity. Width refers to the fact that they cover a wide range of aspects, such as politics, economy, society, culture, and mentality. Depth refers to the fact that a suite of factors, including the market economy, industrialization, urbanization, population flow, and the Internet, alter the way that villagers make a living and the physical configuration of rural areas in a fundamental manner. Disparity refers to the fact that changes in width and depth display a degree of differences in speed and pattern in different areas as well as the structural difference in the process of resource reallocation (many villages may well vanish on the horizon).

At this grand countryside stage, many actors play various roles. Village leaders are brought into the limelight due to their indispensable status, thus becoming the subject of this research. We seek to explore the roles and behavior of

Y. Jing (✉) • L. Zhang
Department of Political Science, School of Social Sciences, Tsinghua University, Beijing, China
e-mail: zln15@mails.tsinghua.edu.cn

© The Author(s) 2019
J. Yu, S. Guo (eds.), *The Palgrave Handbook of Local Governance in Contemporary China*, https://doi.org/10.1007/978-981-13-2799-5_15

village leaders from the perspective of modernization of rural governance within the framework of the state-society relationship. Precisely speaking, we focus our research on those village leaders who grasp opportunities for development or take the lead during the course of dramatic changes.[1]

This chapter comprises three parts. Section 1 presents a brief discussion about the concept of village leaders and outlines a schema delineating their roles and behavior on the grounds of literature review. Unlike existing studies, we focus on the institutional space aimed at normalizing their roles and behavior rather than their specific roles and behavior. It is of vital importance that the behavior of village leaders should be normalized, and effective institutions should be formulated in the modernization of rural governance. Thus, Section 2 is primarily concerned about the institutional construction of the roles and behavior of village leaders. Section 3 serves as a recapitulation and carries out exploratory discussions.

2   LITERATURE REVIEW AND DESCRIPTIVE FRAMEWORK

2.1   Concept of Village Cadres[2]

There is virtually a void in academia with regard to the etymology of "village cadres." Conventional wisdom has it that this concept has existed for more than 100 years.[3] However, it is certain that "village cadres" are an outcome of the penetration of state power into rural society in modern China.[4] Academically speaking, this concept is not only an integral part of Chinese nation-state building but also a symbol of the degree of the penetration of state power into rural society. In demotic terms, this grand historical process commenced in the late Qing Dynasty and has undergone changes in the Republic of China and the People's Republic of China (PRC). In contrast with the late Qing Dynasty and the Republic of China, PRC has transformed rural society on an unprecedented scale and exerted the most appreciable impact on village leaders. Nevertheless, owing to drastic policy adjustments in different periods, the identity and title

---

[1] It is worth noting that there exist enormous distinctions in Chinese rural areas. Resources also vary from village to village. Due to this basic condition in China, we cannot make a generalized analysis of village leaders. This chapter focuses on village leaders in coastal regions or relatively economically dynamic villages with abundant resources. The institutional space of village leaders' behavior embraces two factors: changes in the roles of village leaders and behavioral norms. Their roles should not only be brought into full play but also be checked and harnessed.

[2] "Village cadres" and "village leaders" can be used interchangeably.

[3] The term "village cadres" is said to have made its first appearance while Yan Xishan promoted the construction of the village system. See *Yan Xishan Established Village Leadership System* by Wang Zhai. *Senior Citizens in Shanxi* (2013).

[4] In the 1920s, Yan Xishan, who returned to China from Japan, promoted the construction of the village system in Shanxi Province. On the basis of Japan's village system and China's ancient system, the village became the grassroots unit. See Li Maosheng (2010), *The Biography of Yan Xishan* (p. 223), Shanxi People's Press.

of village heads change accordingly. It is in the 1980s that the image of "village cadres" took shape.[5]

The village leadership system is analogous to the party-government system in structure in contemporary China. Like the party-government system, village leaders also include the party branch committee and the villagers' committee. In accordance with *The Constitution of the Communist Party of China*, grass-roots party organizations, composed of a party branch secretary and several committee members, shall be established in villages.[6] In accordance with *The Organic Law of the Villagers' Committees of the People's Republic of China*, the villagers' committee shall be composed of three to seven members, including the head, the vice head, and other members.[7] It can, thus, be inferred that there are, as a rule, six village leaders in an administrative village (three party branch members and three villagers' committee members), while there are more than ten village leaders in a large village (three to five party leaders and seven villagers' committee members). In order to reduce villagers' burden, village leaders are encouraged to work as party branch member and villagers' committee member at the same time. Therefore, the actual number of village leaders is less than these figures. Generally, the number of the village leaders in an administrative village is around five. Given the tradition of the "number one" leader in China's political culture, there is a need to distinguish between major village leaders and ordinary ones—the former referring to the party branch secretary and the head of the villagers' committee (sometimes including the director of the supervisory committee of village affairs in some villages).[8]

The Constitution of the Communist Party of China and *The Organic Law of the Villagers' Committees of the People's Republic of China* define the boundaries of village leaders and attribute corresponding roles to them, but it is far from enough if the understanding of village leaders is confined to these official rules

---

[5] There are substantial differences in terms of the establishment of villages in South China and North China. The unified establishment of village organizations was completed during the process of the collectivization of villages. During the period of cooperatives, village leaders were incorporated in the people's commune system. Traditional villages were transformed into production brigade. After the collapse of the people's commune system, the production brigade was converted into an administrative village. The villagers' committee was set up on the previous production brigade. The term "village cadres" was put on the historical stage again. In the 1980s and 1990s, the term "village cadres" was commonly used in government documents.

[6] Party branches, general party branches, or party committees may be established depending on the situation of the village or the number of Party members in the village. In most cases, party branches are set up in villages.

[7] The term "cadre" was introduced in China from outside. In the history of the Communist Party of China (CPC), it first appeared in the Party Chart by its 2nd National Congress in 1922. A cadre is a person who holds a public post in this context. In the current time, anyone who plays a crucial role and fulfills administrative roles in national organs, organizations, or public groups is dubbed as a "cadre." Wang Zhengbing and Fu Yongmin (2009). *Research into Village Leaders* (p. 30). China Agriculture Press.

[8] If only one person acts as the leader in both the villagers' committee and the party branch committee in a village, he will definitely be the political core of the village.

and regulations at the institutional level. Rather, it is essential that this concept should be interpreted within a larger framework concerning the cadre personnel management system. Two key indicators should be taken into consideration: whether village leaders have the identity of civil servants and whether they are eligible to exercise authority over the public.

As far as the first indicator is concerned, village leaders are apparently excluded. In accordance with *The Civil Servant Law of the People's Republic of China*, "civil servants" refer to those personnel who perform public duties by law and have been included into the state administrative staffing and whose wages and welfare are borne by the state public finance (Article 2). In this chapter, the identity of civil servants shall comply with three requirements simultaneously: (1) fulfillment of public duties, (2) inclusion into the state personnel system, and (3) wages and welfare from the state public finance. Although "village cadres" are "cadres," their identity remains as farmers who are "cadres" excluded from the state personnel system.[9]

However, the identity of nonstate cadres does not affect village cadres in exercising public powers. This can be deciphered from the following two dimensions. First, Article 32 in *The Constitution of the Communist Party of China* stipulates that "the primary Party committees in communities, townships, and towns and the Party organizations in villages and communities provide leadership for the work in their localities and assist administrative departments, economic institutions, and self-governing mass organizations in fully exercising their functions and powers." In other words, although villages do not fall into the umbrella of a governmental organization, village cadres' exercise of power in their localities is essentially identical to that of leaders in other administrative organs, be it a provincial, municipal, county, and township organ. Second, village cadres perform administrative duties as entrusted by higher-level government. In line with Article 4 of *The Organic Law of the Villagers' Committees of the People's Republic of China*, the people's government of a township, an *ethnic township* or a town shall guide, support, and help the villagers' committees in their work. The villagers' committees, on their part, shall assist the abovementioned people's government in its work. In this sense, village leaders are practically entitled to exercise administrative authority.[10]

---

[9] Village leaders are not included in the official staffing system, nor do they live on national finance. During the period of the people's communes, the income of village leaders was paid in the form of subsidies for the loss of working time. Since the reform and opening-up, their salaries have been paid out of the revenues of the collective economy. At present, township government has undertaken their salaries in different degrees. However, village leaders are not civil servants; rather, their identity remains to be farmers. In the urban-rural residence permit (Hukou) system, they hold the agricultural residence registration.

[10] Aside from administrative power and political leadership, the village, as a common living community, has its own affairs as a self-governing agency. There are also many village affairs within the village. Though they have nothing to do with state authority, they are intimately tied to communal life. Thus, in order to distinguish the two, the former is referred to as state authority, the latter is referred to as public influence of a village.

Thus, the roles of village leaders appear to be awkward, in that they exercise authority in spite of the fact that they are not civil servants. They are not included into the state administrative system, but they are also "the cadres of the state." The structural feature of the roles of village leaders is a prerequisite background for the understanding of their behavior and a vital key to understanding the formulation of relevant institutions.

In China's contemporary political system, the significance of village leaders can be interpreted from different perspectives: they are the mediator between the state and society, the bridge between the Party and the masses, the implementer of Party and government policies, the doorkeeper in the process of up-bottom implementation of policies and bottom-up accumulation and expression of benefits, and so on. As village leaders, they determine major affairs concerning the development of the village; as "agents," they exercise administrative power entrusted by township government; as "patriarchs," they exercise the power of public affairs management in the village. Thus, village cadres play an indispensable role in rural governance, rural order, and village development.

2.2   Review of Relevant Studies

During the long empire period, centralization was reflected in the county system, but the vast rural area could not be governed by the royalty. It was up to the local gentry to govern rural society. There are two different viewpoints in terms of the function of the gentry in academia. Fei et al. (2015) assert that the gentry acted as a buffering cushion between royal power and rural societies. The conventional power system in China is marked by dual-track politics composed of the central government and the self-governing organization administered by gentry (Sun 2009). The lower track could serve as a mechanism for the bottom-up transmission by means of institutional connection between the gentry and central power (Fei 2009), thereby attaining social stability. Zhang also holds a similar viewpoint stating that "the gentry acted as a mediator between government officials and local residents" and "they performed duties on behalf of government, but they were not government agents. The gentry tended to argue with government officials when they pleaded local benefits" (Zhang 2008). Other scholars hold a different viewpoint. For example, Wu maintains that there was no absolute force circumscribing royal power, that the buffering function of the gentry was another aspect of royal power rather than bottom-up expressions, and that these strictures were usually invalid (Fei et al. 2015). Moreover, the gentry used to extort money from farmers claiming that they had the well-being of ordinary people at heart.

In reality, these two situations may well arise. Thus, Hu Qingjun holds that "the behavior of the gentry depends exclusively on individual virtue and training" (Fei et al. 2015). Shi Jingyi stresses that only if the gentry were equipped with necessary virtue and conditions could they gain respect from various classes in a community and support from government (Fei et al. 2015).

The time-honored tradition of the imperial gentry was discontinued in the construction of an early modern nation-state. The "New Deal" in the late Qing Dynasty ruled that "grassroots official posts shall be set up in below-prefecture or below-county government, every prefecture or county shall be divided into several districts and there shall be one official in charge in each district" (Wang 2007). The convention that imperial bureaucracy stops at the county was abolished, so the mediator between the state and rural societies changed as well. Accordingly, Duara (2010) replaces "the paradigm of the gentry" with "the paradigm of brokerage." From his viewpoint, due to the financial pressures, the Qing government and the government in the Republic of China, were eager to establish an effective tax-collection institution in the countryside during the nation-state building. To this end, the cultural ties were demolished in rural societies so that the "protective brokers," whose authority stemmed from the cultural network, could not survive. The "entrepreneurial brokers" gradually became the leaders of rural societies and the tax collectors of the state, thus leading to the "state involution" (Duara 2010). As a consequence, the "state building" failed to achieve the purpose of resolving financial problems; instead, it provided fertile soil for the arbitrary and selfish behavior of the "entrepreneurial brokers."

The PRC altered the social fabric and production relationship in the countryside by means of the land reform and the collectivization campaign, which comprised three stages: precollectivization, in-collectivization, and postcollectivization. In the 1980s, township governments were set up on the basis of previous communes and became responsible for state governance of the countryside. Administrative villages, governed by villagers who elected their own villagers' committees, were established. Thus, village leaders superseded "cadres of the production brigade" and became the mediator between the state and the village.[11] With the aggravating burdens of villagers in the 1990s, the tension of the roles of village leaders loomed large. Research into the roles and behavior of village leaders has, thus, been brought into focus in academia.

Xu carried out pioneering research into the roles of village leaders. In a paper published in 1997, he put forward the dual roles of village leaders, asserting that they were not only the agent of the government but also the patriarch in charge of village affairs. With the development of economy and society, different expectations of village leaders from government and villagers made the conflicts of these two roles increasingly intense. From his perspective, it was in essence a reflection of the relationship between the state and society and that between administrative power and village autonomy (Xu 1997).

Wu made a further analysis of the dual roles. He pointed out that the viewpoint that village leaders served as the agent and the patriarch was a continuation of the dual-track politics and a type of static analysis of "ought to be." In fact, the status of village leaders was marginalized in both ways.

---

[11] Debate over elite replacement and elite transformation.

They were affected by both government and villagers, whereas they were not manipulated and absorbed by either force (Wu 2002). On the one hand, they would not totally become wheeler-dealers in pursuit of their own interest; on the other hand, as the patriarchs of villages, they could not perform the duties either. Therefore, the "bell-ringer" and the "night watchman" became the notable characteristics of these village leaders (Wu 2001). In this sense, there was an evolution from dual roles to three-dimensional roles. This viewpoint was followed by other scholars. For example, in his research, Su shows how the role of village cadres shifted from the protector and the agent of state power to the contractor chasing after personal benefits (Su 2002). Fu also found out that village leaders were also rational men who endeavored to maximize individual interests in addition to the aforementioned dual roles in land expropriation and allocation (Fu 2014).

Some scholars also highlighted that village leaders possessed some degree of autonomy. Although village leaders fell within the specific role structure, they were neither the mechanical device for the implementation of government policies nor the simple mouthpiece for the interests of villagers. Village leaders were somehow independent in playing their own roles[12] (He 2015). Besides, Shen and Chen pointed out that the market economy produced extensive external impacts. On the one hand, village leaders undermined their role as the "custodian" of the village when they pursued personal benefits by utilizing their power. On the other hand, the development of the market economy contributed to the polarization of villagers' interests, thus reducing their reliance on village leaders (Shen and Chen 2001). Put differently, the previous longitudinal and singular state-rural society relationship was affected by the horizontal and diverse network in the economy market. The "honeycomb" (Vivienne 1988) structure gradually collapsed. The penetration of external relationships made villager's interactions dynamic and complex.[13]

---

[12] He Xuefeng (2015). Incomes of Village Leaders and Professionalization. *Social Governance Review*, 11. Although there is a degree of overlap between the agent and the egoist, the logic of the distinction is different. The concept of the egoist stems from the application of the rational man in economics, while the concept of the agent derives from dichotomy in social sciences—the relationship between the structure and the agent. In practice, the agent can be either an egoist or an altruist depending on different variables of behavioral constraint.

[13] If brigade leaders during the people's commune period were a relatively identical group, the development of different rural areas in China since the reform and opening-up has shown remarkable differences. The concept of administrative villages remains unchanged, but the connotation of villages has changed dramatically. Some villages become empty with a lot of villagers migrating to urban areas for job opportunities, whereas there is a huge wave of population into other villages where floating people even outnumber permanent residents. Against this backdrop, "village leaders" in different localities are endowed with completely different connotations: the political ecology in villages is varied and numerous, including the able, the rich and the intelligent, villains, criminal forces, loafers, and the "intermediate farmer."

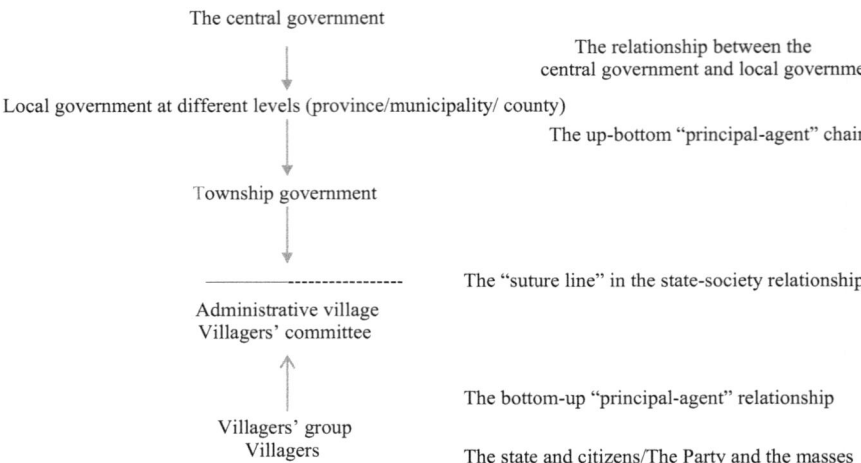

Fig. 15.1 The model of the roles of village leaders in nation-state building

2.3   Construction of the Framework

On the basis of existing studies, we can draw a structure chart in terms of the roles of village leaders (see Fig. 15.1).

Figure 15.1 reflects two different types of the "principal-agent" relationship: the up-bottom relationship governed by the bureaucratic logic (order and compliance) and the bottom-up relationship determined by villagers' autonomy.[14] These two types of relationships intersect between township government and villages, and there emerges a suture line between them. Township government is a crucial dividing line above which there is an intergovernmental relationship and below which there is the state-society relationship. "Township government and villagers' autonomy" is a classical expression of this structural change.[15] In this schema, the role of village leaders as the "agent" of the

---

[14] Besides these two relationships, there are another two relationships: the relationship between the state and citizens (the direct relationship between the state and citizens is emblematic of a modern nation) and the relationship between the Party and the masses (the political leadership of the party branch in a village is deduced from this relationship). These four relationships intersect on the suture line.

[15] In the structure of state institutions, the Constitution sets up the government at five levels: the Central government, provincial government or government in autonomous regions or municipalities directly under the Central government, municipal government, county government, and township government. Under the township government is the administrative village where villagers conduct self-governance. The organizational border between governments and villages is crystal clear, but the functional boundary of government is beyond the organization border. It is up to village leaders to tackle many governmental affairs. How to deal with this relationship has become a fundamental issue in China's grassroots politics. The Report to the 17th National Congress of the Communist Party of China proposed that "to bring about effective connection and beneficial interaction between government administration and primary-level self-governance." The Report

state-society relationship is not endogenous but the outcome of the infiltration of state power into rural society. Meanwhile, village leaders also undertake the bottom-up principal-agent relationship. They have the obligation and responsibility to respond to the requests of villagers and manage village affairs on the basis of public interests instead of personal interests. Consequently, the concept of village leaders as the "patriarch" and the "custodian" is proposed in a normalized manner.

In this sense, whether village leaders perform the role as the agent of township government or the patriarch of the village, their structural status is ascribed rather than self-induced. It is inevitable that they play an awkward role in the relationship between the central government and local government and the relationship between the state and society. They may well be confronted with latent conflicts anytime. At the same time, as a rational actor equipped with personal interest, the village cadres possess some autonomy and a quite scope for options.[16]

Figure 15.2 indicates that the autonomy of village leaders cannot be neglected despite some structural constraints. In terms of governance in rural areas, this kind of autonomy is marked by duality. On the one hand, it has its intrinsic justification because of diversity of the country. When a national policy is formulated, administrative discretion appropriate for different localities should be afforded. In most cases, this is true for village governance. On the other hand, this discretion may also produce negative effects. In reality, it is extremely hard to draw a dividing line between "adaptation to local conditions" and "Tu Zhengce" (policies distorted). Moreover, rural work is intensely informal and, thus, cannot be rigorously carried out in accordance with Weber's bureaucracy theory. When tasks are staggering and pressures are overwhelming, it is common that village leaders are not concerned about means but outcomes. It is also not unusual that they thumb a free ride by taking advantage of

---

to the 18th National Congress of the Communist Party of China advocated that "Community-level organizations of various types should also get involved to integrate government administration and community-level democracy."

[16] In an article entitled "Why is there no fixed rule in counties?" the author offers an impressive statement about local officials: in their actual political careers, county-level officials often deal with three types of responsibilities consciously or unconsciously. They are responsible to the upper-level government primarily by implementing Party and state policies, laws and rules, protecting overall benefits, and fulfilling the particular demands of superiors; they are responsible to the lower-level government by safeguarding local public interests and the interests of local residents or units; and they are responsible to themselves in protecting their own political achievement, reputation, future development, and safety. Most officials seek to strike a balance among these three and pinpoint their own target. The key indicators of losses and profits vary dramatically from official to official, but they share two common things. First, they wish to make the maximum achievement and yield the maximum fruits at the expense of minimum costs. The bottom line is that the balance of losses and gains should be reached. Second, they should do what they should do, deal with things by rule and conflate legitimate administration with flexible and bold practice so as to maximize achievement. In fact, if county officials are supplanted by village leaders in the abovementioned text, this viewpoint still holds true despite the fact that village leaders are not in a real sense officials.

Fig. 15.2 Behavioral model of village leaders: variables and choices. In village politics, three kinds of relationship should be taken into considerations: the relationship with the upper-level government, the relationship with villagers, and the relationship between two committees. There are three types of interest: completing the task as assigned by the upper-level government, safeguarding the interests of villagers, and protecting their own interests maybe at the cost of villagers' or the state's interest

policies. The combination of up-bottom pressures and personal interests of village leaders tends to bring about the imbalance and conflicts between village leaders and the masses. To gain game advantages, villagers usually leapfrog petitions so that they impose pressures on township government. Thus, when it comes to township government, village leaders are also characterized by duality: not only do they act as the reliable force of governmental work and the helper of policy implementation, but they are also the latent troublemakers.[17] Figure 15.3 displays this complicated relationship.

In this interactive model, although village leaders, unlike township officials, exercise public power, they are not civil servants. Therefore, they are lacking in motivation and pressures and are more inclined to adopt opportunist approaches. What's more, the cultural vein of rural society makes village leaders prone to deal with the relationship with upper-level government in a flexible manner (Sun Liping et al.).

As far as township government is concerned, the heavier the task from above is, the more difficult it will be to govern rural areas and, thus, the more intense the need of controlling and manipulating village cadres will

---

[17] While tackling some tricky problems, the township government may have to rely on villains to govern a village. In order to fulfill tasks, the township government has no other alternative but to appoint some "tough" people as village leaders and give them tacit consent to seek for some benefits and adopt some "hard" measures. The reliance of township government on some powerful people or even villains to settle problems has brought about a myriad of political and social problems, thereby leading to the aggravation of the conflicts between leaders and the masses. The relationship between the township government and village leaders is a dynamic and changing process.

Fig. 15.3 The interactive relationship among township governments, village leaders, and villagers

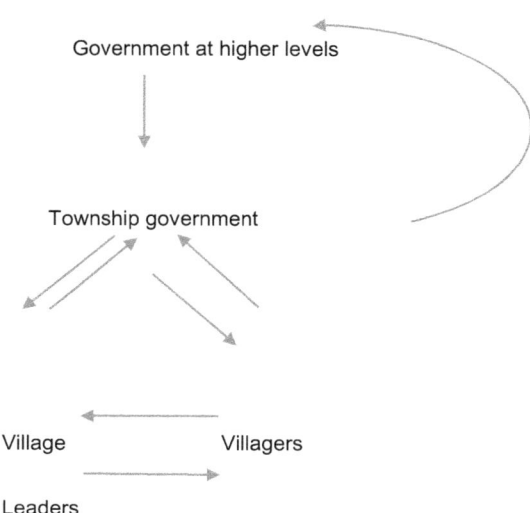

be. In academic terms, there is a positive relationship between the frequency and intensity of the state-rural society interaction and the requirement for behavioral control over village leaders. It is an endogenous structural issue in the construction of a modern country to normalize the autonomous space of village leaders and promote the modernization of rural society and ensure the benefits of villagers. Therefore, like political control of bureaucracy, the governance of village leaders constitutes an essential dimension in the modernization system of state governance.

This chapter perceives the role-behavior model of village leaders as a structural constant and places emphasis on the institutional factors of the structural balance. In other words, we focus on the institutional supply from the perspective of the state—how to normalize the roles and behavior of village leaders via institutional innovation. As the title of this chapter indicates, the analysis framework spans all the changes since the inception of villagers' autonomy.

3 The Institutional Changes in the Roles and Behavior of Village Leaders (1987–2014)

Since the promulgation of The Organic Law of Villagers' Committees in 1987, relevant institutional innovation has unswervingly kept pace with the times in practice. The detailed exploration of this process surpasses the length of this chapter, and it is not our intended purpose. This part is committed to outlining the basic steps in this process in a history-logic pattern.

3.1   Practice of Villagers' Autonomy

3.1.1   Villagers' Election

In the 1980s, China adopted the household contract responsibility system, so the people's commune system on the basis of collective labor could not be maintained. There emerged two schools of thought in terms of how to deal with the issues concerning production brigades. One school of thought asserted that production brigades should be transferred to agencies of the township government and governed in an administrative way. An opposing viewpoint was that they should be self-governed and villagers' committees should be set up. Villagers' autonomy policy was eventually adopted in this wave of debate. "Sea election," open to be a candidate as a tool for fair competition was innovated in Pin'an Village, Shuanghe Town, Lishu County, Jilin Province, in 1991. Villagers entitled to the voting right could nominate any candidate with no interference from leaders at higher levels and the village party branch, which set a precedent for the democratic election of the villagers' committee.

As far as the institutional origin is concerned, election is primarily a matter of "access to power" and at the core is the legitimacy of authorization. However, they also fulfill the power-checking function by punishing disqualified village leaders via the anticipated feedback mechanism. Those who attempt to be reelected will, thus, be urged to respond to the demands of villagers.

The creation of "sea election" leads to three major changes in rural politics. First, the dual roles of village leaders are reconstructed on the basis of elections. Villagers' elections infuse a new variable into rural political life, thereby leading to the breakdown of the unitary structure of rural power. The variable of bottom-up election is embedded in the up-bottom authoritative structure (Jing 2003). At one time, the role as the village patriarch was bound up with clans, reputation, and administration. Villagers' autonomy has based the role as the patriarch in the competitive election, which is protected by law for the first time. Second, the political structure of a village is converted into "two committees" from "one committee." The relationship between the party branch committee and the villagers' committee has taken the stage. Third, the relationship between cadres and the masses in people's communes has been expanded by the principal-agent relationship in the election logic.

Admittedly, the logical possibility at the theoretical level may not be attained in reality. So far, regulating the behavior of village leaders by means of elections has not yet lived up to the expectations.[18] The contributing factors for this

---

[18] There exist considerable controversies in academia in this aspect. Some scholars contend that elections do indeed produce an impact on the behavior of village leaders and make them more concerned about the voice of villagers in their behavioral model. See M. Manion (2006). However, more Chinese scholars do not think elections produce such an immense impact and that the problem with postelections still exists. More importantly, officials in the township government have learned how to manage the election procedure and control the variables of elections, thus reducing the possibility of the "black horse" in elections. In addition, the Central government has increas-

phenomenon are multifaceted. First, there are some problems with elections per se. Village leaders who are elected due to bribery tend to regard their position as a platform for lining their own pockets. Second, in the context of multilateral appeals and various pressures, the dual roles of village leaders will lose their balance. They are apparently more partial toward the township government. Since the implementation of the tax-sharing system in 1991, local revenues have been extremely tense. The township government has incessantly imposed pressures on village-level organizations to ask for money and grain. Many village leaders have thumbed free rides, which have contributed to the tense relationship between cadres and the masses and the frequent occurrence of corruption. Third, since the implementation of the system for villagers' autonomy, Party and government departments still took villagers' committees as village-level administrative organizations and assigned tasks to them. Fourth, power is concentrated in the hands of major village leaders and the corresponding supervisory mechanism is lacking, thus leading to power abuse. Fifth, in some villages, competitive elections result in the tense relationship between the two committees, and the internal waste in rural politics is conducive to the malfunctioning of village governance.

Nonetheless, there is no denying the fact that villagers' autonomy is crucial. It has constituted an underlying platform for rural governance in contemporary China and played an essential role in its political institutions.

3.1.2 The Supervisory Committee of Village Affairs

Since the implementation of villagers' autonomy, there is a constant need for financial supervision in economically dynamic villages. As a systematic institution, the emergence of the supervisory committee of village affairs is intimately related to the accelerating urbanization and the construction of new rural areas in the twenty-first century. As for suburban villages, rapid urbanization would bring great wealth. In this case, it turns out to be exceptionally critical to normalize the behavior of village leaders, develop collective economy, allocate resources fairly, and prevent corruption. It is against this background that the supervisory committee of village affairs has arisen.

In 2004, the Commission for Discipline Inspection in Wuyi County, Zhejiang Province, targeted Houchen Village, where the management of village affairs was trapped in a confused state and the relationship between cadres and the masses was very tense, as an **experimental** village. On June 18, 2014, the first supervisory committee of village affairs was set up in China. Meanwhile, *The rules of Village manage in Houchen Village*, aimed at normalizing the management of village affairs, and *The Supervisory System for Village Affairs in Houchen Village*, aimed at constraining the power of village leaders, were formulated (Zhu 2008). In contrast with other innovative systems for the supervision of

ingly stressed that the pivotal role of grassroots Party organizations in rural areas should be brought into full play in recent years, which has weakened the role of election variables in rural politics.

village affairs in other localities, Wuyi County entrusted village-level agencies with this task and developed a three-dimensional power structure composed of the party branch committee, the villagers' committee, and the supervisory committee. Wuyi County ensured the right of villagers to supervise public power at the institutional level by establishing the village-level supervision committee (Pan 2012). In 2010, the establishment of the supervisory committee of village affairs was officially incorporated into the revised *The Organic Law of the Villagers' Committee*[19] and carried out on a nationwide scale.

Like villagers' elections, the implementation of the system for the supervisory committee of village affairs has also met with a series of problems. First, the villagers lack motivation to engage in the supervision of village affairs[20] (He 2007). This problem looms even larger in those villages that lack collective revenues or have no collective economy at all. As a result, many supervisory committees of village affairs are essentially nominal (Yang and Liu 2014). Second, the other two committees in villages are superior in position to the supervisory committee, which increases the difficulty of supervision. Third, members of the party branch committee at the same time work as members in the supervisory committee, thereby producing the effect of "self-supervision." Fourth, some township governments are concerned that the establishment of the supervisory committee will aggravate the complicated conflicts between different committees. Township officials may undermine the function of the supervisory committee of village affairs by different methods, making it unable to bring into full play the supervisory mechanism (Wei 2014). In addition, members of the supervisory committee may be less educated causing conflicts between different factions and clans, between the supervisory committee, and various departments in the township government may also get in the way of supervision.

3.2   The "Return" of State Power and the Officialization of the Role of Village Leaders

Viewed from modern Chinese history, two kinds of relationships between state and rural societies could be identified: the penetration of state power aimed to resource acquisition and the exercise of state power aimed to resource input.

---

[19] Article 32 of the amended version of *The Organic Law of the Villagers' Committee* stipulates that "A village shall set up a village affairs supervisory committee or a village affairs supervisory organ in any other form to be responsible for the financial management of villagers by democratic means and oversee the implementation of the village affairs disclosure system and other relevant systems. Members of such an organ shall be elected from the villagers by the villagers' assembly or the villagers' representatives assembly and include persons with accounting and management expertise. Members of a villagers' committee and their near relatives may not be members of a village affairs supervisory organ. Members of a village affairs supervisory organ shall be responsible to the villagers' assembly or the villagers' representative assembly, and can observe the meetings of the villagers' committee."

[20] He (2007) pointed out that "there are two conditions for the smooth operation of the supervisory committee of village affairs in Houchen Village: the collective revenues of the village and the influx of resources."

Most developing countries have no alternative but to adopt the former during the process of modernization, especially at the initial stage, while the latter means a historic turning point of the development model. Fortunately, in the first decade of the twenty-first century, we embraced this turning point. During the process of modernization in the past 150 years in China, it is the first time that cities have plowed back into rural areas, that industry has rendered assistance to agriculture, and that developed areas have lent systematic support to backward areas.

This historic turning point offers a wildly different background for our discussion. The acceleration of urbanization contributes to the burgeoning development of suburban villages. In coastal areas, with the development of a market economy and the inflow of population, the configuration of villages has changed beyond recognition. The changes include community construction, village merging, government projects in rural areas, land circulation, financial aids from government agencies, land expropriation, rural planning, and so on. The conflation of these forces has profoundly altered the relationship between the state and rural societies in contemporary China. While the household contract responsibility system, which was adopted in the 1980s, was a passive government response to rural society's crisis. The Chinese government has pursued a more vigorous and positive intervention policy with the development of the market economy in the new century. Thus, state power has been "brought back" into rural areas with new forms and through channels. As an inevitable by-product, the administrative role of village leaders has been augmented. We can analyze this evolving trend in the three aspects that follow.

3.2.1 Construction of New Rural Areas

Suggestions on the Outline of the 11th Five-year Plan, approved at the 5th Plenum of the 16th Central Committee of the CPC in 2005, put forward the idea of building new socialist villages and pinpointed the guideline of "giving more, requiring less and giving more freedom." This guideline reflected different dimensions in policy: the construction project of connecting every village, the establishment of the New Rural Cooperative Medical System, the repealing of the agricultural tax, the reform on the household registration system, the construction of beautiful villages, and so on. Massive fiscal resources were directed into rural areas in the construction of new rural areas. Not only did the implementation of different projects make village-level organizations highly dependent on the township government in financial resources, but it also lead to the officialization of the role of village leaders. In this pressurized system, the township government synergized the assessment of village-level organizations with incomes, which aggravated this trend (Fan et al. 2013). In the very beginning, paying salaries to village leaders was a local practice, but it gradually developed into a state-level policy. It was explicitly pointed out at the 3rd and 4th Plenum of the 17th Central Committee of the CPC that the income and insurance system for village leaders shall be set up via the financial transference of the government. Thus, the "clay rice bowl" (meaning an insecure job) turned into the "iron rice bowl" (meaning a secure job).

3.2.2   Construction of Rural Communities

In 2006, the Central Committee of the CPC formulated Decisions on Several Major Issues in Constructing Harmonious Socialist Societies, which pointed out that "we should carry out the construction of urban communities in a comprehensive way, promote the construction of rural communities in a vigorous way, and improve a new community management and service system." In developed areas, the standardization and professionalization of community construction propelled the administrative role of village leaders from a different angle (Ning et al. 2005). In some villages, the status of officialdom was granted to village or community cadres (Li and Wang 2011). In some rural communities, elections were separated from appointments. By this way, the secretary of the village party branch committee could control the elected village leaders. Meanwhile, it could help township officials control the secretary of the village party branch committee.[21]

3.2.3   Village Merging

The original driving force behind village merging was to alleviate villagers' burdens and allay the financial pressure of township government.[22] With the large-scale national financial investment and the acceleration of urbanization, the land indicator became a strong motive for village merging in many villages. Statistics reveal that the number of administrative villages (villagers' committees) dropped from more than over 730,000 in 2000 to over 580,000 in 2015 (Lin 2012). As a consequence, the scale of villages was considerably expanded. Villagers used to be acquaintances with each other, but with the expansion of villages, villagers' autonomy on the basis of "acquaintance" began to decline, and village leaders were increasingly "disconnected" with villagers. In the context of community construction, village affairs became more administrative.

Apart from the more salient administrative role of village leaders, the up-bottom "first secretary" and grassroots party construction also reinforced the political control of towns over villages from different perspectives.

3.3   External Pressures on the Behavior of Village Leaders: Power Lists

Coupled with the more apparent administrative role of village leaders, normalizing the behavior of village leaders is another essential part of the governance

---

[21] In primary-level governance, strengthening the control of the township government over village leaders is an extremely realistic problem. Township officials are changing very frequently, whereas the chief of the village party branch tends to hold his post for a long time. Therefore, when young township officials command senior Party chiefs, they will encounter some barriers. When university graduates are appointed as the township head of the secretary of the township Party committee, it is far from a sure thing as to whether village leaders will obey them. How to control village leaders is, thus, a complicated matter.

[22] *Opinions of the Central Committee of the CPC and the State Council Concerning Several Policies on Promoting the Increase of Farmers' Income*, promulgated in 2003, pointed out: "We should streamline personnel in township institutions and fiscal dependents, adjust the township system in a vigorous and stable way, and promote the cross-appointment of leaders."

of village leaders in the twenty-first century. Ninghai County, Zhejiang Province, is a prime example of this phenomenon. One of the highlights is a list of 36 power items at the village level.

The power list system was previously a new measure that the government took in the reform of administrative permit. Items on the power list defined the range of lawful administrative power. By sorting out the government-market relationship and the government-society relationship, the power list system imposed restrictions on government's inappropriate intervention in the market and society. Meanwhile, what falls under the legal jurisdiction shall be rigorously enforced in accordance with law in a transparent way. The power list system was intended for the normalization of the arbitrary abuse of power and the inhibition of corruption by clearing the boundary and setting the "right course of action."

Ninghai County innovatively introduced the power list system into village-level governance. In 2014, after a systematic analysis of relevant documents and legal texts, Ninghai County condensed a series of policies, laws, and regulations concerning village-level governance into a list of 36 power items and formulated *Opinions on Promoting the Standardized Exercise of Small and Micro Power in Villages* and *Interim Measures for the Liabilities of Village Leaders in Ninghai County*. The 36 power items defined not only what village leaders should do but how they should exercise power. In legal terms, the behavior of village leaders was normalized from the perspective of both the entity and the procedure. A total of 19 collective items—such as decision-making in major issues, administration of bidding, and financial management—and 17 service items—such as examination and approval of land used for rural housing and family planning, and allotment of land requisition incomes—were displayed in the form of a flow chart, thus enabling villagers to get a clear picture about these items and facilitating their supervision over the routine behavior of village leaders.

The function of the 36 power items system in Ninghai received some fruitful results. However, this practice has not yet been promoted and disseminated. This chapter holds that the significance of these 36 power items lies in the fact that the government adopts measures originally that are applied to the administration of public servants to govern village leaders. This may imply the trend of the administrative roles of village leaders. As a matter of fact, the practice of Ninghai County is not isolated. The newly established local state supervision committee in various villages has integrated "violation of the interests of the masses and corruption" by village cadres into the range of supervision.

4   Discussions

Until now, we have explored the institutional significance of normalizing the roles and behavior of village leaders from the perspective of political science—villagers' autonomy, the administrative role of village leaders, and the power list. Villagers' elections are substantially a kind of bottom-up competition and

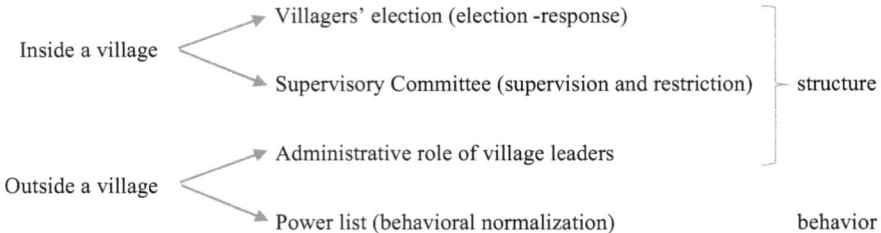

Fig. 15.4 Institutional space of the role and behavior of village leaders

empowerment, and the establishment of the supervisory committee of village affairs reflects organizational supervision,[23] whereas the administrative role of village leaders and the power list are characterized as up-bottom: the penetration of the administrative mechanism and the reform logic of government into rural areas. The former two are perceived as the structural improvement within villages, while the latter two are dedicated to changing the role identity of village leaders and drawing up institutional norms for their behavior from external forces. The combination of internal and external forces alters and shapes the institutional space of the role and behavior of village leaders in various ways (see Fig. 15.4).

Over the past 40 years, the state-rural society relationship has taken a zigzagging path. If the people's commune system is deemed as a peak achievement in the penetration of state power into rural societies, the collapse of people's communes and the implementation of the household contract responsibility system and villagers' autonomy may be viewed as the "withdrawal" of state power. The subsequent process is more dramatic: the tax-sharing system compelled local governments to procure resources from rural areas, thus leading to a nominal village autonomy in different degrees and the tense relationship between the "government agent" and the "village patriarch." Then, the process did a U-turn as China eradicated the rural taxation, pursued policies in favor of farmers, devised plans to support poverty-stricken areas and eliminate poverty, and channeled various resources into rural construction. Industrialization and urbanization contributed to the migration of the population. The construction of new rural areas, village merging and rural planning, and the integrated development of urban and rural areas not only altered the skyline of cities and villages but also enormously revised the cultural landscape of rural areas. Allocating resources to rural areas in the economic dimension and the penetration of power to rural areas in the political dimension have become a beautiful scenic vista in the countryside. Figure 15.5 shows some important polices on rural governance from the year 1987 to 2014.

---

[23] Some scholars attempt to interpret this phenomenon from the perspective of the principle of checks and balances, regarding the party branch, the villagers' committee, and the supervisory committee of village affairs as three core branches.

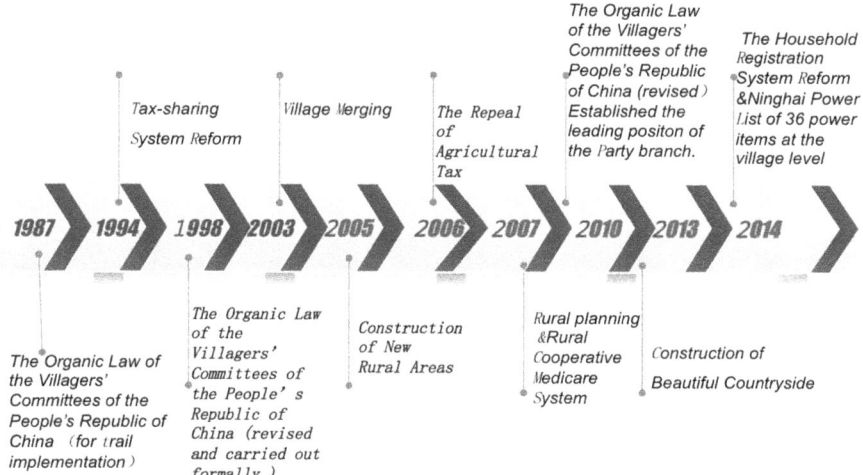

Fig. 15.5   Changes in the state-rural society relationship (1987–2014)

Unlike the people's commune system in the planned economy, the intense penetration of state power into rural societies was conducted in the background of market economy. The government in late-developed countries usually plays a crucial role in promoting modernization. China's experience since the reform and opening-up enriches this viewpoint appreciably. The integrated utilization of the market and administrative measures has become a magic wand in promoting economic and social development. As a natural outcome, the arena of state power has been expanded on an unprecedented scale. We find that the government in various localities has an overwhelming need to control and manipulate village leaders in the modernization of state governance. Two most salient symbols include the administrative role of village leaders and the specialized administration of villages in coastal areas with developed villages that have a large floating population. While cities and industrialization lead to the development of rural areas and agriculture, village leaders have increasingly been incorporated into the state apparatus and become a crucial device for the penetration of state power. As one of the consequences of this process, the boundary of the state-rural society relationship has moved downward (see Fig. 15.6).

Figure 15.6 indicates a major change: the state-society relationship has evolved from a "line" to an "area." The "line" states that there is a clear dividing line between government and villagers' autonomy, and that it can be crossed in function as the government needs village leaders to tackle and implement many things. The "area" denotes that with the increasing administrative role of village leaders, the villagers' committee remains to be a self-governing organization elected by villagers on the surface, but this kind of election is prone to be more nominal. The appointment of the first secretary of the village

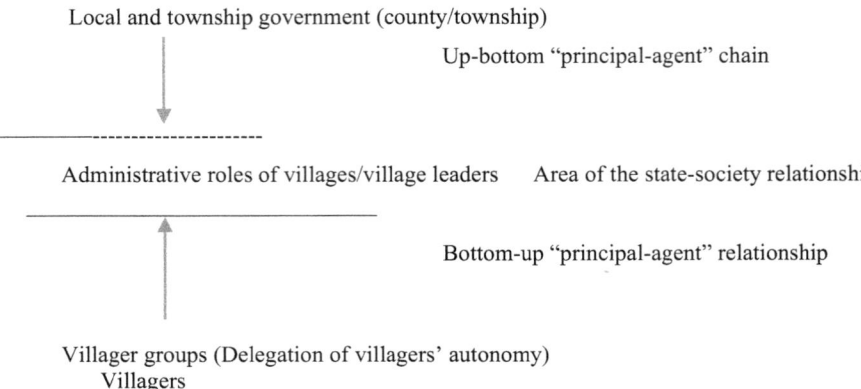

Fig. 15.6 The changing model for the roles of village leaders and the state-society relationship

party branch, income sources of village leaders, the comprehensive utilization of various assessment methods, the selective approach to becoming a public servant, the specialized administration of villages and communities, and so on transform the merged village into a hybrid of the administrative role and villagers' autonomy. This trend leads to the disconnection between village leaders and villagers. The situation of rural areas in the twenty-first century is a far cry from what was expected of villagers' autonomy in the past.

The evolution in the state-rural society relationship has produced dual impacts on village governance. On the one hand, it has exerted an immense effect on the roles and behavior of village leaders. When resource acquisition relies more heavily on local government and work assessment is increasingly contingent upon government officials, the rational option for village leaders is to cooperate with the government. Therefore, they have become a tool for the implementation of national and local policies as grassroots bureaucrats. Meanwhile, the system for villagers' autonomy in the 1980s has been subjected to more impediments. Where does villagers' autonomy go? It is a tough and challenging issue. In 1990, people talked about administrativization of villagers' autonomy that stemmed primarily from the pressures of village leaders and the need for township leaders to acquire resources while the current intensive administrative role of village leaders emerges against a drastically different background. This not only refers to the transformation from resource acquisition to resource input, the large-scale "return" of state power, and above all, the officialization of village management. On this basis, many localities have started to explore the possibility of delegating villagers' autonomy to a villager group level. The previous township-village dichotomy has evolved into a three-level (township-village-villager group) governance structure.

How do we look at the change in China's rural societies since the reform and opening-up? Has China's nation-state building stepped into a new stage from the perspective of history? As Duara (2010) pointed out China was confronted with two basic challenges in the early twentieth century: the modern nation-state building and the development of a market economy. In the twenty-first century, we have a clearer picture about these two historical processes than ever before, which, to some extent, is reflected in the evolution of the institutional space of the roles and behavior of village leaders: despite the fluctuations in the penetration and impact of the state power in rural society, the current era has witnessed more intense penetration and more considerable impacts on the whole. In contrast with any time in history, today's China is, so to speak, at an all-time peak. In official terms, China is closer to achieving the goal of modernization than anytime.

Does the evolution from villagers' autonomy to the power list mean that we are approaching an unfinished cause: the modernization of the roles and behavior of village leaders? In other words, does what has happened in the micro or grassroots domain display the macro-logic of modernization to a large extent? This is yet to be tested by history. However, it is beyond question that after more than 100 years, China's rural areas have accumulated various resources: from new schools of thought, political parties, and cooperative organizations, to rule of law, capital investment, and power supervision. During this overall historical change, village leaders as the "mediator" have been increasingly salient. Will they become public servants in the future as they play a more administrative role? This question is worth pondering.

References

Central Commission for Discipline Inspection website. http://www.ccdi.gov.cn/special/jdbg3/qb_bgt/sffbwt_jdbg3/.

Duara, P. 2010. *Culture, Power, and the State: Rural North China, 1900–1942.* Nangjing: Jiangsu People's Publishing House.

Fan, B., Shao Qing, and Xu Wei. 2013. A study on the functional alienation of village-level organizations in the post-agricultural tax era and its governance. *Journal of Zhejiang University (Humanities and Social Sciences)* 5: 177–188.

Fei, X. 2009. *Gentry in China.* Shanghai: SDX Joint Publishing Company.

Fei, X., Wu Han, et al. 2015. *Imperial Power and Gentry Power.* Shanghai: East China Normal University Press.

Fu, Y. 2014. Triple roles of village leaders and relevant policies: An exploration of land requisition and compensation. *Journal of Tsinghua University (Philosophy and Social Sciences)* 3: 154–163.

He, X. 2007. Interpretation of the experience of Houchen Village. *New Observation* 2: 26–27.

He, X. 2015. Incomes of village leaders and professionalization. *Social Governance Review* 11: 64–66.

Jing, Y. 2003. The two-ballot system: Organizational technology and election pattern – The relationship between the two committees and the power construction in villages. *Journal of Renmin University of China* 3: 124–130.

Li, M. 2010. *The Biography of Yan Xishan.* Tai Yuan: Shanxi People's Press.

Li, Y., and Y. Wang. 2011. The actual impact of the "official" status of village leaders on villagers' autonomy and suggestions on policies: An empirical study of Zhejiang Province. *Probe* 5: 67–72.

Lin, J. 2012. Village merging and development of rural communities. *The Journal of Humanities* 1: 160–164.

Manion, M. 2006. Democracy, community, trust: The impact of elections in rural China. *Comparative Political Studies* 39(3): 301–324.

National Bureau of Statistics of the People's Republic of China website, http://data. stats.gov.cn/search.htm?s=村民委员会.

Ning, Z., H. Liu, Z. Wang, and H. Chai. 2005. Where should village leaders go: The possibility of granting village leaders the status of civil servants? *China Rural Survey* 1: 58–65.

Pan, Z. 2012. Innovation in the primary-level democratic supervisory system in rural areas – An exploration of the supervisory committee of village affairs in Zhejiang Province. *Rural Economy* 3: 11–13.

Shen, J., and Jing Chen. 2001. "Weak custodians" in villages: An analysis of the roles of village leaders from the mass perspective – A case study of rural areas in southern Shandong Province. *China Rural Survey* 5: 53–61.

Su, S. 2002. From "Protector" to "Contractor." In: Yang Shan Hua and Wang Si Bing (eds.) *Social Transformation: The Exploration of Young Scholars at Peking University.* China: Social Sciences Academic Press.

Sun, X. 2009. Democracy in villages – Roles and behavior of village leaders. *Society* 29(1): 66–68.

Vivienne, S. 1988. *The Reach of the State: Sketches of Chinese Body Politic.* Stanford, CA: Stanford University Press.

Wang, F. 2007. *Government of the Republic of China – The Township System in the New County System.* Capital Normal University, 1–52.

Wang, Z. 2013. Yan Xishan established village leadership system. *Senior Citizens in Shanxi* 10: 48.

Wang, Z., and Y. Fu. 2009. *Research into Village Leaders.* Beijing: China Agriculture Press.

Wei, S. 2014. The status quo, problems and solutions concerning the supervision of village affairs. *People's Tribune* 8: 128–130.

Wu, Y. 2001. Dual role, broker model, night watchman, and bell-ringer. *Open Times* 12: 114–117.

Wu, Y. 2002. Dual marginalization: Typological analysis of the roles and behavior of village leaders. *Management World* 11: 78–85.

Xu, Y. 1997. Dual roles of village leaders: The agent and the patriarch. *Twenty-First Century* 8: 151–158.

Yang, Y., and Tong Liu. 2014. The nominalization of the Supervisory Committee of Village Affairs and its solution. *Rural Economy* 2: 109–112.

Zhang, Z. 2008. *Research into Chinese Gentry.* Shanghai: Shanghai People's Press.

Zhu, Y. 2008. CCTV Pays Constant Attention to the Supervisory Committee of Village Affairs in Wuyi County. http://epaper.jhnews.com.cn/site1/jhrb/html/2008-02/26/content_396801.htm.

CHAPTER 16

The Unfulfilled Promise of Collaborative Governance: The Case of Low-Income Housing in Jiangsu

Kerry Ratigan and Jessica C. Teets

In this chapter, we explore the development of urban community governance in China, specifically the interaction of local government, social organizations, community, and citizens in urban community governance. To explore this interaction, we selected the case of collaborative governance in urban housing, because by the 2000s the cost of housing was one of the top concerns of urban residents across the country. In a nationwide survey, including both urban and rural respondents, nearly 40 percent of Chinese agreed that "housing conditions are poor [and they] can't afford to build/purchase housing," and 24 percent thought that the high cost of housing was the most pressing problem facing the country (Chinese Academy of Social Sciences 2012).[1] Based on evidence from affordable housing (AH) policy in Jiangsu, we find that the state continues to dominate the policy process. Despite state rhetoric encouraging

---

[1] As housing costs are a far more severe problem in urban areas, and we can assume that the proportion of respondents concerned about this issue would be even higher if rural respondents were omitted.

K. Ratigan
Amherst College, Amherst, MA, USA
e-mail: kratigan@amherst.edu

J. C. Teets (✉)
Political Science Department, Middlebury College, Middlebury, VT, USA
e-mail: jteets@middlebury.edu

© The Author(s) 2019
J. Yu, S. Guo (eds.), *The Palgrave Handbook of Local Governance in Contemporary China*, https://doi.org/10.1007/978-981-13-2799-5_16

collaborative governance, non-state actors (NSAs),[2] such as business and community organizations, tend to be excluded from AH policymaking and implementation.

Collaborative governance,[3] or the inclusion of NSAs in designing and implementing policy, was introduced in China in the late 1990s and early 2000s as many governments, especially the US and the UK, were pursuing this system of governance due to its promise to cut costs, improve policy effectiveness, and increase citizen satisfaction in government policy. China's central and local governments passed a series of procurement laws legalizing the collaboration between local agencies and NSAs, which applied to both for- and not-for-profit organizations. For example, in September 2013, the State Council General Office issued its "Guiding Opinions on Government Purchase-of-Services from Societal Actors" (国务院办公厅 2013), which was followed by the "Interim Measures for the Administration of Government Purchase-of-Services" published by the Ministry of Finance in 2014 (财政部,民政部,国家工商行政管理总局 2014), and in August 2016, the Chinese Communist Party (CCP) Central Committee and the State Council jointly announced the "Opinion on the Reform of the Social Organization Management System and Promotion of the Healthy and Well-Ordered Development of Social Organizations" (中共中央办公厅 and 国务院办公厅 2016). These regulations encouraged local governments to "contract out" (*goumai fuwu* 购买服务) services, and many scholars posited that increasing government outsourcing might lead to more extensive forms of collaborative governance (Jing and Besharov 2014; Teets and Jagusztyn 2016). The promise of collaborative governance in China was to increase policy effectiveness and citizen satisfaction through more public participation, and also reduce government costs and potential malfeasance by increasing the adaptability of policy (rather than a "one-size-fits-all" approach) and transparency. Moreover, several scholars viewed the promise of collaborative governance as "democratizing" the policy process without needing large-scale political reform:

> While this practice is not yet increasing non-profit participation in the policy process, the creation of access channels that are currently operating solely in one direction may at some future date allow groups to participate in relevant policy areas. Contracting public goods might have the potential of significant effects beyond the term of the contract by increasing pluralism in local public policy and

---

[2] We use the term "non-state actor" to encompass entities that are not officially part of the government, including private enterprise, think tanks, nonprofit organizations, nongovernmental organizations, community organizations, and social organizations.

[3] We do not engage in the ongoing debate about the meaning of the term "governance" in this chapter but simply use it as to mean the collective process of policymaking and implementation or, more specifically, the way that state actors, or any other included stakeholders, collectively decide on specific policies and then implement these policies. In this way, we view governance as an activity or process rather than an outcome.

generating more demand for transparency and accountability of government ser-vices. As such, this is an interesting bellwether for future political change in China. (Teets 2012)

The extant literature on collaborative governance has focused mainly on public management concepts of how to ensure policy effectiveness when introducing new stakeholders into the policy process. Two dominant approaches to collab-orative governance—agency theory and stewardship theory—both predicted that more collaborative governance might be ineffective if the goals between the government agencies and NSAs were not correctly aligned through either positive or negative incentives, or some form of monitoring and evaluation to compel adherence to these goals. Most empirical research in China on collab-orative governance found that agencies were not delegating much authority (Teets 2012) or that the agencies were controlling the NSAs in order to col-lude (Jing 2012). Thus, despite central government regulations encouraging "contracting out" and local government rhetoric promising community involvement in policymaking, we find that policies continue to be implemented primarily by the state with little participation by NSAs.

We selected Jiangsu as our case because this province has several conditions that are conducive to collaborative governance. As AH policy in Jiangsu is more likely to exhibit collaborative governance than other policy areas and other localities, we consider this to be a "crucial" case to test the effectiveness of collaborative governance in China, following Gerring (2007, 115–16). Jiangsu is a wealthy province that has the capacity to change governance mod-els, including human capital, and a history of including NSAs in certain sectors, like commercial regulations. Jiangsu has afforded nongovernmental organiza-tions (NGOs) more opportunities to flourish through early adoption of a streamlined registration process (Zhang 2013). Because the province has severe problems with AH in its large cities, we expect that local leaders are seeking innovative solutions to this policy problem. Moreover, localities in Jiangsu are often chosen for pilot projects, making the province a likely site for policy inno-vation. Thus, Jiangsu should be fertile ground for the growth of successful collaborative governance models, especially in such an important policy area that is being closely monitored by both dissatisfied citizens and the central government.

In response to pressure from the central government in the early 2000s, Jiangsu began to develop provincial policies regarding low-income housing in 2003 in its capital city of Nanjing (Ye et al. 2017). In Jiangsu's adaptation of the central government's policy directive, the provincial government empha-sized the role of NSAs, such as social organizations and private enterprise. However, we find that despite stated intentions to include NSAs, AH projects in Jiangsu have been largely implemented by the government. For example, in Nanjing, one project completed in 2016 comprised 51,100 units of AH on 5.6 km² of land, and although for-profit organizations assisted with financing, NPOs were only peripherally involved, mainly on an intermittent or ad hoc basis (Du et al. 2017). Based on these outcomes, Du, Wang, and Zhu argue that NSAs should take on a larger role in AH, suggesting that the "government needs to shift its role from that of 'rower' to 'helmsman'"(2017, 362).

In the rest of this chapter, we analyze how the provincial government in Jiangsu interacted with NSAs when developing and implementing low-income housing policy. Overall, we find that low-income housing is one of the most important urban governance policy areas for society, and the government intends to work with NSAs, but ultimately does not, except in a very perfunctory way. The outcome of local government's stated intention to work more with NSAs and the subsequent failure of collaborative governance in this case mirrors the findings of other scholars in different provinces and policy areas (Donahue et al. 2013; Jing and Besharov 2014).

This finding is especially important, given the initial hopes of increasing government outsourcing leading to more public participation in local policy-making. In fact, the unfulfilled promise of collaborative governance in Jiangsu, despite the high public profile of the issue and stated intention of the local government to work with NSAs, offers a good corrective for earlier publications that hypothesized that outsourcing might be a channel for more participation in public policy (Teets 2012). Instead, we find evidence that collaborative governance between the local state and NSAs has not met this initial promise because local officials perceive NSAs, and NPOs in particular, as lacking capacity. This perception and the large power imbalance between local government and NPOs result in an unwillingness to collaborate. Reinforcing this view, the concept of Xi Jinping's "top-level design" (*dingceng sheji* 顶层设计) dominates urban governance and reinforces a model of government-led policy design and service provision. If this outcome in Jiangsu is mirrored in other urban municipalities, the initial promise of collaborative governance appears unlikely to materialize.

Although we find that the unfulfilled promise of collaborative governance played a role in the failure of AH policies in China, we suggest several steps that the central government can take that will help encourage more collaborative governance. Based on empirical evidence of successful collaboration, we recommend that the central government develop NPO capacity through incubators and other programs, encourage collaboration between NPOs and local agencies by creating promotion incentives and/or directives, and reinforce the financial support and promotion incentives around AH policy. These actions will help encourage more collaborative governance and the development of more effective AH policies.

In the next section, we review the literature on collaborative governance theoretically in China, and then the literature on our specific case of AH policy. After this review, we analyze the case study of Jiangsu to assess how collaborative governance performed in this policy area and conclude with a discussion of how to encourage more collaborative governance to ameliorate some of the observed policy failures.

1 THE PROMISE OF COLLABORATIVE GOVERNANCE IN CHINA

To meet changing demands for services and in response to central government contracting legislation, local governments in China began collaborating with nonprofits and private companies to deliver services like health care and education in the early 2000s. In its most simple form, this collaboration took the form of outsourcing or contracting (*goumai fuwu* 购买服务), where the government still designed the service or policy, but the NSA delivered the service or implemented the policy. At its most complex, government agencies and NSAs collaborated to design and deliver public services. This new form of governance was imported from Western public management practices and theories and was expected to outperform traditional adversarial and managerial modes of policymaking and implementation with lower costs, more effective outcomes, and more citizen satisfaction (Ansell and Gash 2008).

Collaborative governance, as a concept, is a "governing arrangement where one or more public agencies directly engage non-state stakeholders in a collective decision-making process that is formal, consensus-oriented, and deliberative and that aims to make or implement public policy or manage public programs or assets" (Ansell and Gash 2008, 544). As mentioned above, collaborative governance may take a number of forms, with differing levels of collaboration, such as outsourcing, contracting, and public-private partnerships (PPP). Regardless of the form, all of these governance models involve sharing responsibility to design and implement public policy. In its most advanced form, collaborative governance must meet "six important criteria: (1) the forum is initiated by public agencies or institutions, (2) participants in the forum include nonstate actors, (3) participants engage directly in decision making and are not merely 'consulted' by public agencies, (4) the forum is formally organized and meets collectively, (5) the forum aims to make decisions by consensus (even if consensus is not achieved in practice), and (6) the focus of collaboration is on public policy or public management" (Ansell and Gash 2008, 544).

This collaborative format challenges existing governance models where local governments develop, provide, and evaluate all service provision. Instead, government agencies must partner with a variety of for-profit and NPOs, which differs from both the models of serving as the sole designer and provider of public services, and from the model of merely regulating privately provided services. Changing governance models is challenging for many reasons. Ansell and Gash review 137 cases of collaborative governance across a range of policy sectors and find several variables that influence whether or not collaboration will be successful, including a prior history of conflict or cooperation, the incentives for stakeholders to participate, power and resources imbalances, leadership, and institutional design (Ansell and Gash 2008). As we discuss in the case study of AH in Jiangsu Province, collaborative governance was not successful because the state agencies did not create meaningful roles for NSAs where they could engage directly in decision-making. We evaluate several potential explanations for why this did not happen, but generally, as Ansell and Gash argue, the lack of incentives to include NSAs as well as large imbalances in power and resources between the state and nonprofit sector influenced the failure of collaborative governance in this case.

2   Achieving Effective Collaboration: Goal Alignment

The literature regarding government-NSA collaborative relationships and contract management practices for social services mostly rely on two theories: agency theory and stewardship theory (Van Slyke 2007). These theories mostly focus on one of the largest governance challenges for collaborative governance which is aligning the goals of the agency with NSAs. This challenge is greater in the cases with more collaboration.

Agency theory focuses on conflicting goals on the part of the two actors in a contracting relationship: the principal (government agency) and the agent (NSA) (Dharwadkar, George, and Brandes 2000). Van Slyke, who focuses on NPOs, outlines the two assumptions characterizing this principal-agent (P-A) model: first, there is goal conflict between the budget-maximizing behavior of the principal and the utility-maximizing behavior of the agent; and second, agents have more information than principals, which agents can exploit for self-gain rather than for the collective interests (Van Slyke 2007, 162). These two characteristics highlight the uncertainty and challenges associated with collaborative governance models. As many governments, especially in the US and the UK, pursued extensive contracting based on perceptions of greater efficiency and potential innovation from the private sector, this transformation highlighted these problems and led scholars to develop models for effectively managing relationships between governments and NSAs (Cooper 2003). This transition necessitated the creation of a new model of governance constructed around partnerships with NSAs focused on mitigating P-A problems. The recommended solution was better goal alignment through monitoring the frequency, consistency, and quality of service delivery provided by contractors and using that information to sanction poor performers and/or adjust the policy goals contained in the contract (Brown and Van Slyke 2006). Monitoring and sanctioning are vital because of the "distance" between regulators and agents, which allows for discretion in the implementation of services, often leading to goal divergence between the policy directives of the principal (government) and the implementation practices of the agent (NSA). In response, principals must better align the actions of the agent through monitoring mechanisms and a mix of rewards and sanctions (Eisenhardt 1989, 63). The local government might seek to contract with nonprofits to deliver social services, but this relationship can be difficult for public managers, in that performance is not always easily observed and measured, and competitive bidding mechanisms might be weak if there are few potential partners in local markets (Van Slyke 2007).

Stewardship theory challenges the assumptions of agency theory by contending that agent goals are not always utility-maximizing but often collective, in which a higher value is placed on achieving the goals of the principal. Stewardship theory "defines situations in which managers are not motivated by individual goals, but rather are stewards whose motives are aligned with the objectives of their principals" (Davis et al. 1997, 21). As Van Slyke argues, in the case of the government-NPO collaboration, stewardship theory might be the most "appropriate model because nonprofits by virtue of their organizational form, specialized missions focused on poverty reduction and client stability, governance structures, the resource-interdependent nature of their funding relationship with government, as well as the incomplete nature of social services contracts may well contribute to there being a closer alignment with government's goals" (Van Slyke 2007, 164). According to this theory, the agent (steward) is motivated by intrinsic rewards, such as trust, reputation, and reciprocity, and views the success of the organization as the reward, which results in goal alignment without need for monitoring or financial incentives (Davis et al. 1997). Therefore, instead of relying on monitoring and incentives for achieving goal alignment, the principal invests in developing a trusting relationship with the steward through other types of contractual mechanisms focused on long-term goal alignment. These mechanisms have fewer monitoring and reporting requirements; more involvement in how the contract is defined, structured, and implemented; and trust and reputation are used as incentives for alignment and monitoring as a potential sanction but one that is less coercive and directed toward relational alignment (Van Slyke 2007, 166).

Although both theories stress the importance of goal alignment for the success of any form of collaborative governance, the mechanisms for achieving this differ with agency theory relying on monitoring and incentives and stewardship theory depending on building trust and long-term partnerships to align goals.

3   Creating Collaborative Governance in China

During the process of economic reform in China throughout the 1980s and 1990s, the central government encouraged the downsizing and streamlining of government at all levels through several waves of reform, including public service organizations (*shiye danwei* 事业单位) which previously helped the government design and deliver services. This changing political economy motivated local governments to pass new laws to legalize collaboration between government agencies and a variety of private firms and NPOs, most frequently in the form of contracting. Yijia Jing (2008) estimates that between 2002 and 2004, roughly a third of government service expenditures in China were outsourced, following a trend of 1 percent annual growth. By 2005, many local governments in more developed areas like Shanghai, Beijing, and Shenzhen had experimented with using competitive bidding to deliver social services (Jing and Savas 2009). In Guangzhou, one of the most developed "contracting out" provinces, the municipal government's procurement of public services reached a total of about 330 million yuan in 2014, creating a total of 3800 jobs (including 2500 professional social work jobs), and collaborated with 267 social service organizations (Pan 2015). Although the main goal was cost reduction, central government officials have also stated that contracting and service competition might restructure government-NPO relationships and improve service delivery (Xinhua 2013).

At the national level, regulatory change to support contracting consisted of a series of procurement laws allowing government agencies to contract out selected services, creating a competitive bidding process, mandating an annual review of services, and a financing mechanism. For example, in 2012, the central government allocated 200 million yuan (US$32.08 million) through the Ministry of Civil Affairs (MoCA), and local governments invested another 120 million yuan to finance 377 social service projects (Xinhua (China Daily) 2013). Additionally, to create a larger supply-side market, MoCA encouraged 19 provinces to ease registration regulations to allow for direct registration of nonprofits since 2011 (Xinhua (China Daily) 2013). Wang Jianjun, the director of the Bureau of Administration of NGOs at MoCA at the time, stated that "There is no reliable data to show the exact number of unregistered NGOs, but I know that most NGOs providing services in communities are not licensed, including about 400,000 NGOs dedicated to senior residents. A direct registration policy will greatly boost their development and help these organizations to become better service providers" (He 2013). Guangdong Province adopted the direct registration policy in 2012 and had 4200 NGOs register that year, and direct registration became national law in 2016.

Analyzing the outcomes of collaborative governance experiments, Yijia Jing finds that social service contracting in Shanghai led to collusion between collaborating governments and nonprofits, partially due to a lack of competitive bidding but also as a result of an extreme "stewardship" model (Jing 2012). This result aligns with much of the research on nonprofits in China detailing the prevalence of a corporatism model (Hsu and Hasmath 2013; Foster 2002). The corporatist approach contends that NPOs are used by the state to advance its interests, and that these organizations serve to execute government projects using government resources, such as funding and employees. Although corporatism is a limited form of collaborative governance like outsourcing, more comprehensive collaborative governance aims for the inclusion of a broader range of stakeholders, and the stakeholders often lack a representational monopoly over their sector (Ansell and Gash 2008). In addition to the cooptation or integration of NPOs into state agencies, analyses of other forms of collaborative governance find that local governments are likely to only contract out basic services, like trash removal, and complete most projects solely with government partners in other agencies or levels of government. For example, despite the rhetoric to reduce state debt levels by promoting PPP to fund roads, bridges, and railways, the majority of partners have turned out to be state-owned enterprises (SOEs): 55 percent of the social partners are SOEs, and SOEs take up 74 percent of the projects by value (Bloomberg News 2017).

Therefore, despite the fact that many provinces such as Guangdong and Shanghai created a legal structure for agencies to contract out social services, facilitated the existence of successful collaborations ranging from HIV care to migrant education (Teets and Jagusztyn 2016), and fostered a process of non-profit capacity-building (Jing 2015), the promise of collaborative governance has not been realized. Instead, in many policy areas, the relationship appears to be one of outsourcing, with little responsibility on the part of the NSAs, or what we more appropriately might call "consultative governance" rather than "collaborative governance." Although citizen consultation often improves policy design and outcomes, it falls far short of the promise of collaborative governance, in that it does not strengthen the capacity of a non-state sector capable of social innovation. As we see in the case of AH in Jiangsu, a lack of collaborative governance also creates inferior policies that do not effectively address housing problems and reduces transparency resulting in waste and malfeasance.

In analyzing the unfulfilled promise of collaborative governance in China, we find two potential explanations for this outcome: leadership change and the underdeveloped nonprofit sector. Collaborative governance and the broader trend of small state-big society (*xiaozhengfu dashehui* 小政府, 大社会) began under the leadership of Jiang Zemin and Zhu Rongji and accelerated throughout the Hu Jintao and Wen Jiabao administration (2002–2012). When Xi Jinping assumed leadership, he promoted a new governance concept of "top-level design," which returns the primary responsibility for governance back to the state and might discourage local governments from collaborating with NSAs. This explanation is dissatisfying for two reasons: the timing of reduced collaboration and Xi's continued insistence on using more "market-based" or private forces to make governance decisions. The decline (or stagnation) of collaboration was being documented as early as 2010, and definitely by 2013 when Xi Jinping assumed leadership (Beh 2010). Xi has also repeatedly stressed the important or "dominant" role of market forces in guiding government decisions (Kennedy et al. 2016). Therefore, the second explanation of the presence of an underdeveloped nonprofit sector, or supply-side imperfection (Van Slyke 2007), seems more logical, given the timing of declining collaboration and our findings in the case of AH, where local governments set goals to work with NSAs but then did not find partners with enough perceived capacity, especially in the nonprofit sector. Although the nonprofit sector in China is in a developing stage, with many NPOs lacking many full-time staff and project experience, there are several NPOs in each market that are large enough to handle aspects of collaborative governance (Spires et al. 2014). The perceived lack of capacity and state unwillingness to collaborate might in fact be resulting from the large power imbalance between stakeholders, which is a commonly noted problem in collaborative governance (Tett et al. 2003). Ansell and Gash find that if "some stakeholders do not have the capacity, organization, status, or resources to participate, or to participate on an equal footing with other stakeholders, the collaborative governance process will be prone to manipulation by stronger actors … power and resource imbalances will affect the incentives of groups to participate in collaborative processes" (Ansell and Gash 2008, 551; Imperial 2005). This is the situation in China with such large power imbalances between government agencies and local nonprofits and likely leads to the perception on the part of government agencies that NPOs lack the capacity to collaborate even if the agency states its willingness to collaborate (Teets interview with MoCA representative, Nanjing, Jiangsu, 2010).

In contradistinction to our findings, Shen and Yu find that local governments in Shanghai City and Ningbo City (Zhejiang Province) do collaborate with NPOs, motivated by performance-based decentralization (Shen and Yu 2017). The authors argue that when local governments see how the performance of NPOs can contribute to local development, they begin the collaboration process, and the better the performance, the more authority the NPOs are granted (Shen and Yu 2017). This suggests that local governments can learn to collaborate with NPOs, as officials see this collaboration results in performance improvements. Although we find this argument compelling (and in fact argued something similar in Teets 2012), we are left with the chicken and egg problem, namely that if local governments do not perceive NPO partners as having enough capacity to help govern, how do these organizations demonstrate performance to motivate collaboration? If local governments are not collaborating with NPOs due to perceptions of low capacity, these officials cannot see improvements in measured outcomes that might result if they had in fact worked with the NPOs. Meanwhile, if NPOs lack the opportunity to participate in the policy process, it will be more difficult for them to develop the necessary capacity to be effective partners with the state. Additionally, it is difficult to determine if the perception of low NPO capacity by the local government is in fact the entire problem or if there is a bias toward the government delivering services derived from the Chinese history of public administration, currently being re-emphasized by Xi Jinping's "top-level design" governance concept. In which case, it is hard to imagine even the best performance by NPOs influencing more government collaboration.

However, despite the failure of collaborative governance to change policy-making in China, the relationship between government agencies and NSAs continues to evolve. This dynamism is reflected in many of the case studies of collaborative governance experiments, although theories of collaborative governance tend to describe a static relationship between government agencies and non-state partners. As one public manager interviewed by Van Slyke stated, "Trust is outcome based, based on success. You could have a history, but that history is built on success. We're not a very trusting agency" (Van Slyke 2007, 172). This statement illustrates the development of "trust" as emerging between parties based on repeated interactions over time. Ansell and Gash also identify a series of factors that are crucial within the collaborative process, including face-to-face dialogue, trust building, and the development of commitment and shared understanding (2008). The authors found that a virtuous cycle of collaboration tends to develop when collaborative forums focus on "small wins" that deepen trust, commitment, and shared understanding (Ansell and Gash 2008). These empirical results drawn from China and other comparative cases suggest that collaborative governance requires experience, and that it can only be achieved by practice. If this is the case, the more the central government can encourage local governments to return to a collaborative governance model and truly collaborate with NSAs in both the design and implementation of public services, the more effective this model of governance will be. Due to the power imbalance, local governments are not likely to collaborate with NSAs unless they have a history of doing so and have observed good results; thus, central government encouragement is likely necessary. This is important to address since research shows that more collaboration produces more effective services that meet citizen needs, and this form of governance also better addresses unknown governance and stability challenges. As Donahue and Zeckhauser argue, collaborative governance is a "force multiplier" that leverages the skills in each sector to create synergies between governments and private participants, "allowing them together to produce more than the sum of what their separate efforts would yield" (Donahue and Zeckhauser 2011, 5).

In the next section, we examine how AH policy has developed in China and the role of collaborative governance in the case of implementing this policy in Jiangsu Province.

4   DEVELOPING AFFORDABLE HOUSING POLICY

Housing is the basis for individuals to participate in the community and the economy, and yet, significant numbers of people live in inadequate or unsanitary housing conditions in both developed and developing countries. The problem is so pervasive that the United Nations (UN) included housing as part of the Millennium Development Goals: "Achieve, by 2020, a significant improvement in the lives of at least 100 million slum dwellers" ("United Nations Millennium Development Goals" 2017). In the early 2000s, many slum dwellers experienced improved living conditions, but the UN estimates that more than 880 million people live in slums currently ("United Nations Millennium Development Goals" 2017), a number that may not include inadequate housing conditions in many more developed countries.

In addition to the obvious human rights concerns related to inadequate housing, scholars and policymakers are concerned about societal problems created by slums and lack of decent housing. Socioeconomically segregated neighborhoods can reduce the possibility of upward mobility and population health (Anderson et al. 2003). As a result, many developed countries have attempted policies to design more inclusive, mixed-income AH. Countries have attempted myriad types of AH policies implemented either primarily by the state or by some combination of the state, NSAs, and "self-help" housing (e.g., Newton and Schuermans 2013). Self-help housing entails some degree of state subsidy for individuals to solve their own housing problems and sometimes includes support from NGOs or COs (community organizations). Despite these efforts, some common problems arise in AH implementation cross-nationally, including unsuitable locations, low-quality construction or inappropriate design, lack of community services, and misallocation or inappropriate targeting.

Collaborative governance has the potential to address some of the problems associated with implementing AH policy. First, state- or private-sector-led AH projects are often constructed in undesirable locations or designed without the beneficiary in mind. They are far from prospective residents' employment and the amenities necessary for a decent life, such as grocery stores, health care, and schools. They often lack access to efficient public transportation, which would mean unreasonably long commutes for residents. As a result, AH may be so undesirable that even those desperate for housing are unwilling to live there. However, if the end user is allowed to participate early in the process, these types of mistakes can be avoided. Second, AH projects consistently face difficulty with targeting the appropriate population and avoiding corruption (Huchzermeyer 2008). NGOs or COs could provide a crucial monitoring role to reduce corruption and misallocation of AH units through transparency. Third, NSAs can determine what kind of local services might be needed for the community and contribute to provision of these services. For example, an NGO might provide a day care, job training, or medical services to marginalized populations to serve as a "force multiplier" to government initiatives and subsidies.

Despite these valuable corrective roles, efforts at including NSAs in AH project development have fallen short of stated goals. NGOs and COs typically play a peripheral role in AH policy, even when NGOs are active in other issues. NGO involvement has been hampered by myriad factors (Rahman 2002). First, NGOs often do not consider housing to be a priority issue. Second, the government tends to dominate housing provision and is reluctant to include NGOs. In India, for example, the government prefers that NGOs limit their work to service delivery or assisting with the implementation of a project or policy designed by the government rather than taking a more active role such as advocacy (Baruah 2007, 231). Third, NGOs depend on external funding, often from international sources that may direct their work toward international trends or hot topics. Fourth, NGOs often lack technical expertise and the relevant professional staff to engage in housing provision (Rahman 2002).

Several cross-national cases provide examples of how the same power imbalances and subsequent unwillingness of state agencies to share responsibility, as we find in China, hindered the promise of collaborative governance. First, in the US, the city of Minneapolis has successfully included local communities in a participatory process for neighborhood revitalization, but this approach has also faced difficulties in terms of inclusivity, resistance to new rental housing by current homeowners, and uneven implementation depending on the level of engagement at the neighborhood level (Fagotto and Fung 2006). In the city of Chicago, housing policy (HOPE VI) included provisions for private sector, NGO, and community involvement, including allowing residents to take on some management and for NGOs to provide community services such as "job training and placement, day care, and substance-abuse counseling" (Alexander 2009, 144). However, due to existing power structures and a lack of technical expertise, Alexander finds that residents could not "meaningfully participate" in decisions related to public housing (Alexander 2009, 165). Similar to our recommendations for China, Alexander suggests capacity-building for local communities and a stronger formal legal framework to empower marginalized voices (Alexander 2009). Without support, nonprofit groups have difficulty contributing in a meaningful way, and opportunistic private and state actors tend to dominate the process (Alexander 2009).

In India, new housing policies have emphasized community participation and PPP to improve efficiency and community relations. Kamath finds that the Indian government seeks to change the role of the state in housing from "'builder and provider' to 'facilitator'" (Kamath 2012, 77). Indeed, NSAs took a larger role, with some NGOs even providing technical expertise, such as mapping, surveys, and monitoring and sometimes dealing with community relations (Kamath 2012, 77, 83). Despite these successes, much of the community participation was pro forma and the lack of meaningful community representation led to conflicts (Kamath 2012, 78).

Similarly, programs in South Africa and Ghana also were ineffective due to limited participation by NSAs. South Africa's enhanced People's Housing Process (ePHP) encouraged the beneficiaries and their community to participate in the design and construction process (Newton 2013). In one South African neighborhood, the community formed a cooperative to manage the design and construction of AH, which established a savings scheme for residents to supplement state subsidies. By consulting with professional architects, the beneficiaries provided the labor to build the houses. This process also provided training to interested community members, which could benefit recipients after completion of the project (Newton 2013). Although this case was more successful, the impact of the collaboration was small. Habitat for Humanity Ghana (HFHG) has also achieved important gains through educating beneficiaries and involving local communities, but their model faces challenges. For example, the units are too expensive, and beneficiaries typically cease to contribute sweat equity after their own house is built, despite being required to assist with building others' houses as per the organization's agreement with the recipient (Obeng-Odoom 2009). Moreover, most of the older units developed cracks, and Obeng-Odoom found that HFHG does not provide sufficient quality control during construction, and communities lack training in maintenance (Obeng-Odoom 2009).

As with these comparative cases, AH programs in China consist of a mix of government subsidies and provision of rent-controlled housing. In the Chinese case, housing is also a major policy concern, not because of concerns over social exclusion, but because the cost of housing poses a potential challenge to social stability. The programs, which evolved substantially under the Hu Jintao government, target both low- and middle-income households, and sometimes even qualifying migrants.[4] Local governments were required to adopt these policies as per central government directives; nonetheless, localities chose to implement AH policy quite differently, with some provinces emphasizing the role of private actors in supplying AH, and others taking a more state-led, top-down approach to housing policy.

5   DEVELOPING AFFORDABLE HOUSING POLICY IN JIANGSU: THE CASE FOR COLLABORATIVE GOVERNANCE

During the Maoist period, many urban residents were employed by SOEs that provided housing. With the advent of economic reforms in 1978, housing was gradually marketized. Housing prices rose, particularly as the central government incentivized real estate development in the late 1990s as a driver of economic growth in the wake of the Asian Financial Crisis (Wang et al. 2012, 347). Moreover, migrants increasingly populated the coastal cities, leading to additional demand for AH (Huang 2012). In the early twenty-first century, the central government oscillated between encouraging growth in the real estate market and dampening housing prices, amid concerns of instability. As a result, the Hu Jintao government instituted new policies to expand the availability of AH. Meanwhile, due to concerns about overheating in the real estate market, central and local governments began to experiment with cooling mechanisms, such as instituting a property tax, which was piloted in Chongqing and Shanghai in 2011 (Huang 2012, 959; Wang et al. 2012, 347–48). The central government subsequently required property taxes to be used for AH projects (Zou 2014, 14). In the early 2000s, the central government instituted several waves of new policies to encourage local government to expand the provision of AH. However, the public finance system and localization of policy implementation resulted in a lack of commitment from local governments to low-income housing, complemented by the absence of housing metrics in the performance evaluation system for local officials (Huang 2012). In 2010, the central government increased pressure on localities to increase AH projects, including by adding these metrics to the performance evaluation system.

The provincial government in Jiangsu explicitly encouraged the involvement of NSAs in housing policy through several policy documents. In 2011, Jiangsu issued additional guidelines regarding housing policies in response to

---

[4] Standard AH programs initiated by the central government in the Hu Jintao era include cheap rental housing (CRH), economic and comfortable housing (ECH), and public rental housing (PRH). CRH targets low-income households and makes rental housing accessible through rent control, rent subsidies, and rent reduction. CRH can be provided by public or private entities. ECH is usually a homeownership program for low-income households (and middle-income households before 2007), which utilizes free or low-cost land from the municipal government and dwellings built by developers. PRH is a rental program for lower middle-income households and some qualifying migrants in which the government may provide free land, regulated rents, or reduced fees and taxes. PRH may be provided by public or private entities (Huang 2012).

the central government's heightened emphasis on low-income housing, including *Measures of Jiangsu Province on the Administration of Public Rental Housing* and *Opinion of the General Office of Jiangsu Provincial Government on Accelerating the Construction of Protected Housing* (People's Government of Jiangsu Province 2011; "江苏省政府办公厅关于加快保障性安居工程建设的意见" 2015). In Jiangsu's adaptation of the policy, the provincial government emphasized the role of NSAs, such as social groups and private enterprises. *Measures* suggests involvement of NSAs as both providers and funders of PRH. For example, *Measures* states that sources of public housing could include "housing invested and constructed, reconstructed, purchased and rented by enterprises and institutions, social groups, and other organizations"[5] (People's Government of Jiangsu Province 2011). Funding for AH could include "funds from social donation." The *Opinion* also provides a role for NSAs, mainly private enterprise, by stating: "new commercial housing projects should be built with a proportion allocated to PRH, *as determined by the city and county government*"[6] (emphasis added). The document also encourages industrial parks and corporations to build PRH for migrant workers. Similar to central government directives, Jiangsu established some tax incentives for social organizations who donate properties to be used as AH. Under some circumstances, these organizations could be exempted from various land-related taxes, and some expenses can be used as a tax deduction (Jiangsu Taizhou Local Taxation Bureau 2010; Sina 2011). Furthermore, in 2011, the Jiangsu government published tax policies for reducing the tax burden of social organizations that donate housing stock to be used as AH, presumably to encourage such donations. Specifically, the policies said that:

- When social organizations transfer old housing to be used for renovated resettlement housing (for people who had their homes demolished), land value increment taxes are exempted if the increment is 20 percent or less of the deductions.
- When social organizations transfer old housing to be used as a source of PRH, the deed tax and stamp duty are exempted if the increment is 20 percent or less of the deductions.
- When social organizations donate housing to be used as PRH, contribution expenses up to 12 percent of the total annual profit can be deducted when calculating the taxable income (Sina 2011).

Finally, the provincial government expressed the intention to work with the private sector to increase AH by encouraging real estate developers to build smaller commercial units that the government can then rent for the PRH program, which provides subsidized housing for lower middle-income households.

---

[5] Translation by Alice Yang. Original in Chinese.
[6] Translation by the authors. Original in Chinese.

While the units are leased under PRH, the government would compensate the developer for any interest incurred on loans associated with the construction project. After a predetermined period, the housing units would be returned to the developer for sale on the commercial market ("江苏省政府办公厅关于加快保障性安居工程建设的意见" 2015). Despite these regulations and stated goals, AH policy has fallen short of its stated goals both in providing quality AH and in collaborating with NSAs.

First, initial efforts at AH in the early 2000s stalled as there were no performance targets for local officials to provide low-income housing prior to 2010 (Huang 2012, 952). Therefore, not only did local government vary immensely in their compliance with central government policy, but they generally failed to meet the center's targets for AH. Despite central policies mandating otherwise, in coastal cities, only 1 percent of the revenue generated from land conveyance fees was used for AH, and the wealthiest cities—who had benefited the most from rising real estate prices—used none of this revenue for AH (Huang 2012, 950–51). These cities included Beijing, Tianjin, Shanghai, and cities in Zhejiang and Fujian provinces. Furthermore, Huang notes that many local governments were still not in compliance with directives to use land fees for AH, with only 1.5 percent of this revenue used for housing nationwide (Huang 2012, 950–51).

Cities in wealthy, coastal provinces like Jiangsu in the 2000s had the greatest need in terms of AH and the largest provincial budgets for social policy but have also been the most reticent to subsidize housing. In the early 2000s, real estate prices spiked, particularly along the coast, and migrants flocked to Eastern cities (Wang et al. 2012). However, even after the central government increased monitoring of housing policy in 2010, some provinces resisted adopting AH. Wealthier cities could raise much larger funds for AH than their poorer counterparts, but these localities allocated a relatively small proportion of their provincial budget to housing (Zou 2014, 3). China's National Development and Reform Commission was providing progressive subsidies for housing by the end of the Hu Jintao administration, at RMB 500, RMB 400, and RMB 300 per square meter for the Western, Central, and Eastern regions, respectively (Huang 2012, 958, footnote 76). Nonetheless, despite progressive central subsidies, vast differences in the proportion of funding allocated to housing and how housing policies were implemented remained. Figure 16.1 shows the strong inverse relationship between the percent of the provincial budget allocated to AH and gross regional product (GRP) per capita in 2010.[7] Consistent with other wealthy provinces, Jiangsu allocates less than 1.5 percent of its provincial budget to housing, despite local needs for housing relief.

The potential for revenue from real estate explains most of local government's opposition to AH policies. Land, as a finite resource controlled by the local government, provides ample opportunities for generating revenue (Cai

[7] The correlation coefficient between the percent of the provincial budget allocated to AH and GRP per capita is −0.57.

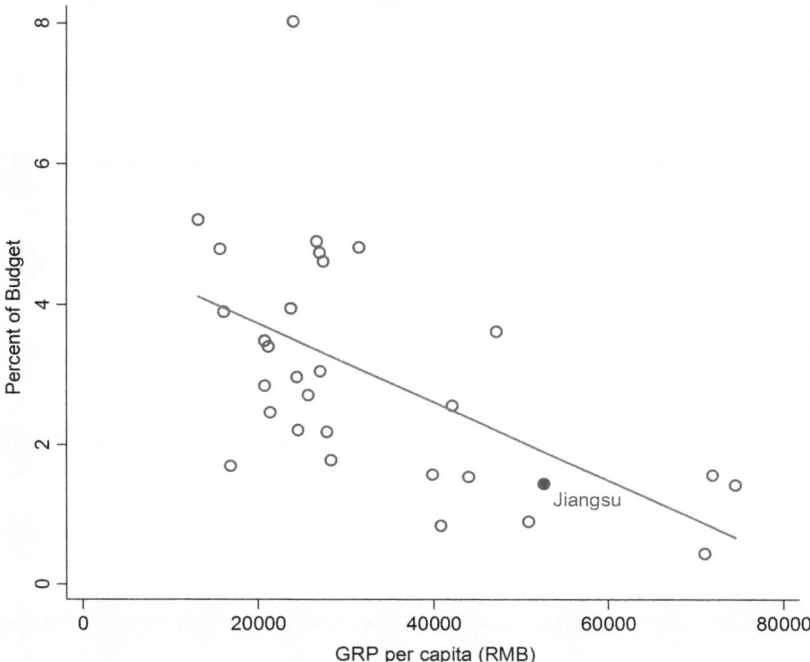

Fig. 16.1 Percent of provincial budget spent on affordable housing (2010). Source: China Statistical Yearbook, 2010. The year 2010 was the first year that the National Bureau of Statistics of China started reporting provincial spending on housing in the national yearbook

2015). Local officials prefer to lease land to investors, preferably manufacturers or others with the potential to produce long-term tax revenue. As China did not begin to introduce a property tax until the end of the Hu Jintao adminis-tration, leasing the land to residential developers, as opposed to manufacturers, would only produce a one-off gain (Zou 2014, 12). Further complicating mat-ters, since land prices impact local government revenue, when land prices decrease, causing local revenue to contract, local government tends to subse-quently reduce funding to AH (Zou 2014, 13). Officials in wealthy, coastal provinces prioritized economic growth over poverty alleviation and focused on managing the real estate market for growth rather than social assistance.

Second, despite stated intentions to include NSAs, AH projects in Jiangsu have been largely implemented by the government. As evidence of this, Du, Wang, and Zhu scored how multiple parties collaborated in AH projects, such as the government, for-profit organizations, and NPOs (2017). They found negligible involvement of NPOs in these projects with the participation model scoring only 60 points: "Only a small number of volunteer associations and other informal nonprofit organizations were involved, and their role was to offer advice to residents, provide physicals, and offer other irregular services"[8] (Du et al. 2017, 360). The authors found more involvement of for-profit organizations but mostly for financing: "The Nanjing municipal government was very supportive of innovative financing by companies. For example, it cooperated with commercial banks and backed corporate trust loans, allowed enterprises to issue targeted bonds, and made full use of social and other measures"[9] (Du et al. 2017, 361). Similarly, Donahue and his co-authors also found minimal involvement of NSAs in AH in two cities in Jiangsu and six other coastal cities (2013). Although private enterprises were involved in a competitive bidding process for the design and construction of AH, Donahue and his co-authors did not observe more meaningful collaboration between NSAs and the government and did not find any involvement of NPOs in AH (Donahue et al. 2013).

Government officials often complain that very few NPOs in China have the capacity to collaborate with the government and few focus on the issue of housing (Teets interview with MoCA representative, Nanjing, 2010; Zhao 2009). As a result, despite stated rhetoric of government intentions to collaborate with NPOs, AH initiatives tend to be state-led, with perhaps some involvement of for-profit companies in the construction phase. However, many of these projects rely mainly on full or partial SOEs for design, construction, management, and maintenance rather than private firms.

As predicted by collaborative governance models, AH projects in China suffer from several shortcomings, due to both local government resistance and lack of community participation. For example, many housing units have been left vacant due to improper and unsafe construction (caijing.com.cn 2013). Moreover, the process for sale or rent of these units has been marred by corruption and fraud. Often, through bribery or connections, the affluent manage to purchase or rent units that are intended for the poor (caijing.com.cn 2013). In some cases, AH is left vacant because it is located in an undesirable location (caijing.com.cn 2013; Tan 2017). AH policy has been unsuccessful because of the lack of goal alignment between central and local governments, with local governments implementing these policies in piecemeal and ineffective ways (Tan 2017). This is a larger governance issue in Chinese politics; however, the expanded use of collaborative governance might ameliorate some of these problems in helping to design more appropriate and effective policies and in monitoring local government actions to provide more transparency in policy implementation to both citizens and central officials.

6   DISCUSSION AND IMPLICATIONS

This case of AH shows the unfulfilled promise of collaborative governance, where despite new policies at the central and local level, housing remains a serious problem in Jiangsu and other coastal provinces (Chen et al. 2013; Soares 2014; Huang 2013).

---

[8] Translation by Alice Yang. Original in Chinese.
[9] Translation by Alice Yang. Original in Chinese.

AH policy was ineffective in Jiangsu for two reasons: the goals of local government diverged from the center and policy design did not incorporate community partners. First, the central government did not provide sufficient funding and promotion incentives to support housing policies, particularly in areas where the problem is most acute. Without a substantial government commitment to the issue, local governments have more incentive to focus on developing more expensive housing projects which return more revenue. Second, the policy implementation process is deeply flawed due to a lack of community collaboration in the design stage. For example, new units are not placed in suitable locations, some do not pass safety inspections, and corrupt practices enable the affluent to purchase units intended for low-income residents. As Du et al. (2017) summarizes:

> In general, the government assumed a relatively singular role, with for-profit and non-profit organizations participating in a fairly inactive way. Lacking are oversight mechanisms and a rational risk-sharing mechanism. The system is marred by low occupancy and allocation rates and poor social and ecological sustainability. The government should change its role to achieve a separation between the owners and operators of affordable housing and strengthen the development and growth of for-profit and non-profit organizations. (361)[10]

Based on their observations in Nanjing, Du, Wang, and Zhu argue that NSAs should take on a larger role in AH, suggesting that the "government needs to shift its role from that of 'rower' to 'helmsman'"[11] (2017, 362). Greater involvement by NSAs could ameliorate some of the implementation problems plaguing these policies. By involving NPOs and COs in the planning process, developers could choose more appropriate locations for new housing projects. Furthermore, NPOs could provide assistance to low-income residents in identifying newly available AH projects and completing the application process. Finally, NSAs could offer oversight for development and management, possibly reducing the incidence of corruption.

This case illustrates the unfulfilled promise of collaborative governance, due to power imbalances between government agencies and nonprofit partners and reinforced by the national trend of "top-level design" of public policy. More centralized policymaking avoids problems of variation in implementation. However, this approach also risks losing the benefits of "collaborative governance" where community participation facilitates policy that meets local needs, enhances local support and cooperation, improves citizen monitoring of implementation and corruption, and, most importantly, provides information about policy effects that could help reform policy to avoid unintended consequences (Teets 2012; Jing and Besharov 2014). Although NPOs in China are still developing and many do lack capacity to partner with the government on equal footing, many do have this capacity or at least the capacity to assist in aspects of policy design and implementation. It is unclear from our research how much

[10] Translation by Alice Yang. Original in Chinese.
[11] Translation by Alice Yang. Original in Chinese.

of local officials' concerns of low capacity were real and how much was a perception based on the traditional concept of Chinese governance of strong state and weak society. Regardless of the source of this perception, power imbalances between agencies and NSAs must be addressed before collaborative governance can be successful in China.

Based on the extant literature and this empirical case, we suggest a three-pronged solution for the central government: develop NPO capacity, encourage collaboration between NPOs and local agencies, and reinforce financial support and promotion incentives around this policy. As Shen and Yu and Van Slyke find, the more NPOs and state agencies collaborate, the more trust is developed and authority is given to the community partners (Shen and Yu 2017; Van Slyke 2007). The central government needs to further encourage (or mandate) the presence of NSAs in these projects. However, theories of evolving relationships are predicated on the ability of NPOs to actually work on these collaborative projects, and so the central government needs to continue to fund and support nonprofit incubators (NPI), like the NPIs active in several cities like Shanghai and Beijing (Han 2016). The NPI trains NPOs that have won government contracts or are working on other collaborative projects with the government, by providing professional development and other capacity-building measures (Han 2016; Jing 2015).

Additionally, the central government needs to reinforce its financial support and promotion incentives around this policy to encourage local alignment with its goals. This is important regardless, but if the trend of more "top-level design" continues and local governments are no longer encouraged to "contract out" with non-state partners, then the governance problems highlighted in this case of AH may only be addressed through substantial political reform focused on changing municipal finance away from a reliance on land transfers and by revising the cadre evaluation system even further to focus on incentives to provide AH. For example, Tan suggests that the evaluation methods for housing policy should be shifted from reporting measures such as the number of units constructed to measures that capture the number of people whose housing challenges were resolved (2017). We concur with this recommendation.

In conclusion, we find that the promises of collaborative governance have not been realized in China, despite some initial success stories in the early 2000s. We find that these unfulfilled promises have played a role in the failure of AH policies in China, and recommend that the central government develop NPO capacity, encourage collaboration between NPOs and local agencies, and reinforce financial support and promotion incentives around this policy. These steps will help encourage more collaborative governance and the development of more effective AH policies.

REFERENCES

Alexander, Lisa T. 2009. "Stakeholder Participation in New Governance: Lessons from Chicago's Public Housing Reform Experiment." *Georgetown Journal on Poverty Law & Policy* 16: 117–86.

Anderson, Laurie M., Joseph St. Charles, Mindy T. Fullilove, Susan C. Scrimshaw, Jonathan E. Fielding, and Jacques Normand. 2003. "Providing Affordable Family Housing and Reducing Residential Segregation by Income." *American Journal of Preventive Medicine* 24 (3): 47–67. https://doi.org/10.1016/S0749-3797(02)00656-6.

Ansell, Chris, and Alison Gash. 2008. "Collaborative Governance in Theory and Practice." *Journal of Public Administration Research and Theory* 18 (4): 543–71. https://doi.org/10.1093/jopart/mum032.

Baruah, Bipasha. 2007. "Assessment of public–private–NGO Partnerships: Water and Sanitation Services in Slums." *Natural Resources Forum* 31 (3): 226–37. https://doi.org/10.1111/j.1477-8947.2007.00153.x.

Beh, LooSee. 2010. "Public-Private Partnerships in China: A Responsive Participation." *Journal of US-China Public Administration* 7 (8): 30–35.

Bloomberg News. 2017. "In China, Public-Private Partnerships Are Really Public-Public." *Bloomberg.com*. Accessed September 11. https://www.bloomberg.com/news/articles/2017-02-27/in-china-public-private-partnerships-are-really-public-public.

Brown, Matthew Potoski, and David M. Van Slyke. 2006. "Managing Public Service Contracts: Aligning Values, Institutions, and Markets." *Public Administration Review* (3): 323–31.

Cai, Meina. 2015. "Flying Land: Institutional Innovation in Land Management in Contemporary China." In *Local Governance Innovation in China: Experimentation, Diffusion, and Defiance,* edited by Jessica C. Teets and William Hurst, 60–83. Routledge Contemporary China Series: 122. New York, NY: Routledge, Taylor & Francis Group.

caijing.com.cn. 2013. "重构住房保障_经济全局_《财经》杂志_杂志频道首页_财经网 – CAIJING.COM.CN." *Caijing.com.cn*. August 25. http://magazine.caijing.com.cn/20130825/2677099.shtml.

Chen, Jie, Juan Jing, Yanyun Man, and Zan Yang. 2013. "Public Housing in Mainland China: History, Ongoing Trends, and Future Perspectives." In *The Future of Public Housing: Ongoing Trends in the East and the West,* edited by Jie Chen, Mark Stephens, and Yanyun Man, 13–35. Heidelberg: Springer.

Chinese Academy of Social Sciences. 2012. "2011 General Survey of Chinese Society (2011 年度中国社会状况综合调查)." http://www.sdccass.cn/pic/Upload/Files/baogao/201203/F6346722794823612054106.pdf.

Cooper, Phillip J. 2003. *Governing by Contract: Challenges and Opportunities for Public Managers*. Public Affairs and Policy Administration Series. Washington, DC: CQ Press.

Davis, James H., David F. Schoorman, and Lex Donaldson. 1997. "Toward a Stewardship Theory of Management." *The Academy of Management Review* 22 (1): 20–47.

Dharwadkar, Ravi, Gerard George, and Pamela Brandes. 2000. "Privatization in Emerging Economies: An Agency Theory Perspective." *The Academy of Management Review* 25 (3): 650–669.

Donahue, Jack, Karen Eggleston, Yijia Jing, and Richard Zeckhauser. 2013. "Collaborative Governance in China and the United States: Theory and Practice."

Donahue, John D., and Richard Zeckhauser. 2011. *Collaborative Governance: Private Roles for Public Goals in Turbulent Times*. Princeton, NJ: Princeton University Press.

Du, Jing, Jiamin Wang, and Lifei Zhu. 2017. "基于IAD的保障房多中心协同供应机制 Multi-Center Collaborative Supply Mechanism of Affordable Housing Based on IAD Framework." 土木工程 *Hans Journal of Civil Engineering* 6 (4): 355–363.

Eisenhardt, Kathleen M. 1989. "Agency Theory: An Assessment and Review." *Academy of Management Review* 14 (1): 57–74. https://doi.org/10.5465/AMR.1989.4279003.

Fagotto, Elena, and Archon Fung. 2006. "Empowered Participation in Urban Governance: The Minneapolis Neighborhood Revitalization Program." *International Journal of Urban and Regional Research* 30 (3): 638–655. https://doi.org/10.1111/j.1468-2427.2006.00685.x.

Foster, Kenneth W. 2002. "Embedded within State Agencies: Business Associations in Yantai." *The China Journal*, no. 47: 41–65. https://doi.org/10.2307/3182073.

Gerring, John. 2007. *Case Study Research: Principles and Practices.* New York: Cambridge University Press.

Han, Jun. 2016. "The Emergence of Social Corporatism in China: Nonprofit Organizations, Private Foundations, and the State." *China Review* 16 (2): 27–53.

He, Dan. 2013. "New Rules for NGOs to Improve Operations." *China Daily*. April 17. http://www.chinadaily.com.cn/china/2013-04/17/content_16413055.htm.

Hsu, Jennifer, and Reza Hasmath. 2013. *The Chinese Corporatist State: Adaption, Survival and Resistance.* Routledge Contemporary China Series: 92. London; New York: Routledge.

Huang, Youqin. 2012. "Low-Income Housing in Chinese Cities: Policies and Practices." *The China Quarterly* 212 (December): 941–964. https://doi.org/10.1017/S0305741012001270.

Huang, Youqin. 2013. "Lack of Affordable Housing Threatens China's Urban Dream." *China Dialogue*. Accessed August 9, 2017. https://www.chinadialogue.net/article/show/single/en/6365-Lack-of-affordable-housing-threatens-China-s-urban-dream.

Huchzermeyer, Marie. 2008. "Slum Upgrading in Nairobi within the Housing and Basic Services Market: A Housing Rights Concern." *Journal of Asian and African Studies* 43 (1): 19–39. https://doi.org/10.1177/0021909607085586.

Imperial, Mark T. 2005. "Using Collaboration as Governance Strategy: Lessons from Six Watershed Management Programs." *Administration & Society* 37 (3): 281–320.

Jiangsu Taizhou Local Taxation Bureau. 2010. "对城市和国有工矿棚户区改造安置住房用地如何免税?." Accessed July 11, 2017. http://tz.jsds.gov.cn/art/2010/8/16/art_4141_265834.html.

Jing, Yijia. 2008. "Outsourcing in China: An exploratory assessment". *Public Administration and Development: The International Journal of Management Research and Practice*, 28 (2), 119–128.

Jing, Yijia. 2012. "From Stewards to Agents? Intergovernmental Management of Public-Nonprofit Partnerships in China." *Public Performance & Management Review* 36 (2): 230–252.

Jing, Yijia. 2015. "Between Control and Empowerment: Governmental Strategies towards the Development of the Non-Profit Sector in China." *Asian Studies Review* 39 (4): 589–608.

Jing, Yijia, and D. J. Besharov. 2014. "Collaboration Among Government, Market, and Society: Forging Partnerships and Encouraging Competition." *Journal of Policy Analysis and Management* 33 (3): 835–842.

Jing, Yijia, and E. S. Savas. 2009. "Managing Collaborative Service Delivery: Comparing China and the United States." *Public Administration Review* 69 (S1): S101–S107.

Kamath, Lalitha. 2012. "New Policy Paradigms and Actual Practices in Slum Housing: The Case of Housing Projects in Bengaluru." *Economic and Political Weekly* 47 (47–48): 76–86.

Kennedy, Scott, Christopher K. Johnson, and Center for Strategic and International Studies (Washington, DC). 2016. *Perfecting China, Inc.: China's 13th Five-Year Plan.* CSIS Reports. Lanham, MD: Center for Strategic & International Studies.

Newton, Caroline. 2013. "The Peoples Housing Process … Getting the Quality in the Quantity?" *Journal of Housing and the Built Environment* 28 (4): 639–651. https://doi.org/10.1007/s10901-013-9349-2.

Newton, Caroline, and Nick Schuermans. 2013. "More than Twenty Years after the Repeal of the Group Areas Act: Housing, Spatial Planning and Urban Development in Post-Apartheid South Africa." *Journal of Housing and the Built Environment* 28 (4): 579–587. https://doi.org/10.1007/s10901-013-9344-7.

Obeng-Odoom, Franklin. 2009. "Has the Habitat for Humanity Housing Scheme Achieved Its Goals? A Ghanaian Case Study." *Journal of Housing and the Built Environment* 24 (1): 67–84. https://doi.org/10.1007/s10901-008-9128-7.

Pan, Li. 2015. "Sustainability Study of Government Procurement of Public Services in Guangzhou – A Perspective Based on the Resources Dependence of Social Work." *Open Journal of Social Sciences* 3 (12): 118–123.

People's Government of Jiangsu Province. 2011. "Measures of Jiangsu Province on the Administration of Public Rental Housing. Decree of the People's Government of Jiangsu Province (No. 73)." http://www.lawinfochina.com/display.aspx?id=12318&lib=law&SearchKeyword=&SearchCKeyword=#.

Rahman, Mohammed Mahbubur. 2002. "Problems of the NGOs in Housing the Urban Poor in Bangladesh." *Habitat International* 26 (3): 433–451. https://doi.org/10.1016/S0197-3975(02)00017-6.

Shen, Yongdong, and Jianxing Yu. 2017. "Local Government and NGOs in China: Performance-Based Collaboration." *China: An International Journal* 15 (2): 177–191.

Sina. 2011. "江苏省地方税务局税收优惠政策系列专题四:住房保障." *blog.sina.com/cn*, June 21. http://blog.sina.com.cn/s/blog_5ed646f701017072.html.

Soares, Isa. 2014. "China's Property Bubble Stalls the Urban Dream." *CNN.com.* February 25. Accessed August 9, 2017. http://www.cnn.com/2014/02/25/business/nanjing-real-estate/index.html.

Spires, Anthony J., Lin Tao, and Kin-man Chan. 2014. "Societal Support for China's Grass-Roots NGOs: Evidence from Yunnan, Guangdong and Beijing." *The China Journal* 71 (1): 65–90. https://doi.org/10.1086/674554.

Tan, Rui. 2017. "中国保障性住房体系的演进、特点与方向 The Evolution, Characteristics and Orientation of China's Affordable Housing System." *Journal of Shenzhen University (Humanities & Social Sciences)* 34 (2): 101–118.

Teets, Jessica C. 2012. "Reforming Service Delivery in China: The Emergence of a Social Innovation Model." *Journal of Chinese Political Science* 17 (1): 15–32.

Teets, Jessica C., and Marta Jagusztyn. 2016. "Evolution of a Collaborative Governance Model: Social Service Outsourcing to Civil Society Organizations in China." In *NGO Governance and Management in China*, edited by Jennifer Hsu and Reza Hasmath. Routledge Studies on China in Transition. Milton Park, Abingdon, Oxon: Routledge.

Tett, Lyn, Jim Crowther, and Paul O'Hara. 2003. "Collaborative Partnerships in Community Education." *Journal of Education Policy* 18 (1): 37–51. https://doi.org/10.1080/0268093032000042191.

"United Nations Millennium Development Goals". 2017. Accessed August 29. http://www.un.org/millenniumgoals/environ.shtml.

Van Slyke, David M. 2007. "Agents or Stewards: Using Theory to Understand the Government-Nonprofit Social Service Contracting Relationship." *Journal of Public Administration Research and Theory* 17 (2): 157–187. https://doi.org/10.1093/jopart/mul012.

Wang, Ya Ping, Lei Shao, Alan Murie, and Jianhua Cheng. 2012. "The Maturation of the Neo-Liberal Housing Market in Urban China." *Housing Studies* 27 (3): 343–359. https://doi.org/10.1080/02673037.2012.651106.

Xinhua. 2013. "China Rolls out Plan to Transform Gov't Functions." *GlobalTimes.com*. March 10. Accessed October 29, 2018. http://www.globaltimes.cn/content/766974.shtml.

Xinhua (China Daily). 2013. "Chinese Government's NGO Funding Peaks in 2012." *China Daily*. February 13. http://www.chinadaily.com.cn/china/2013-02/13/content_16221162.htm.

Ye, Dan, Jingxiang Zhang, and Guoliang Xu. 2017. "Peripherization of Indemnificatory Housing Community under Land-Centered Urban Transformation: The Case of Nanjing, China." *Sustainability (2071–1050)* 9 (4), 656: 1–14.

Zhang, Mingmin 张明敏. 2013. "江苏 从太仓试点到全省推进." *China Philanthropy Times* 公益时报. October 28. http://www.gongyishibao.com/html/yaowen/2411.html.

Zhao, Feifei. 2009. "The Community-Based Partnership Approach for Affordable Housing Development: A Case in Shenzhen, China."

Zou, Yonghua. 2014. "Contradictions in China's Affordable Housing Policy: Goals vs. Structure." *Habitat International* 41 (January): 8–16. https://doi.org/10.1016/j.habitatint.2013.06.001.

中共中央办公厅, and 国务院办公厅. 2016. 中共中央办公厅、国务院办公厅关于改革社会组织管理制度促进社会组织健康有序发展的意见. Retrieved from ChinaLawInfo. CLI.5.278425.

国务院办公厅. 2013. 国务院办公厅关于政府向社会力量购买服务的指导意见. 国办发*[2013]96*号. Retrieved from ChinaLawInfo. CLI.2.210888.

"江苏省政府办公厅关于加快保障性安居工程建设的意见". 2015. Accessed November 24. http://www.law110.com/law/32/jiangsu/law1102006215260.html.

财政部,民政部,国家工商行政管理总局. 2014. 财政部、民政部、工商总局关于印发《政府购买服务管理办法(暂行)》的通知. 财综*[2014]96*号. Retrieved from ChinaLawInfo. CLI.4.240682.

PART V

Citizen Engagement

CHAPTER 17

"Orderly Political Participation" in China

Baogang He

This chapter provides an in-depth examination of Chinese "orderly political participation" so as to develop an understanding of how political participation in China is developed, regulated, and governed, how various forms of political participation function, and the critical issues that political participation currently faces. It selects and examines the three official-sanctioned forms of political participation, that is, village elections, consultative and deliberative forums, and participatory budgeting (PB). It also discusses increasingly citizen-initiated political spaces or non-sanctioned forms of political participation. Finally it briefly investigates the interaction and conflict between the official and citizen forms of political participation and speculates on the future development of political participation in China.

To understand the variety and complexity of Chinese political participation we need to take "公民有序政治参与" ("gongmin youxue zhengzhi canyu", literally, citizen's orderly political participation) seriously. The official discourse on an orderly political participation was written in the reports of the 9th–15th National Party Congresses. Citizen's orderly political participation aims to address Huntington's (1968) problem of too much participation in developing countries with the following key features. First, the goal of strengthening the authority of the Chinese Communist Party (CCP) and improving governance should be the top priority for political participation, while the empowerment of citizens is a secondary goal. Second, all activities associated with political participation are bounded by certain procedures and rules and should remain within such boundaries. Third, political participation should

B. He (✉)

School of Humanities and Social Sciences, Faculty of Arts & Education, Deakin University, Burwood Campus, VIC, Australia
e-mail: baogang.he@deakin.edu.au

© The Author(s) 2019
J. Yu, S. Guo (eds.), *The Palgrave Handbook of Local Governance in Contemporary China*, https://doi.org/10.1007/978-981-13-2799-5_17

result in order and harmony rather than chaos or social unrest. Political participation is thus designed to function as part of the "nuts and bolts" of the authoritarian political system and to prevent citizen-initiated activities from leading to the development of an opposition party. Fourth, while nation building requires widespread and deepening participation, economic development requires controlled political participation so as to reduce political risk. In this context, the CCP has promoted three official-invited political spaces or sanctioned forms of political participation, that is, village elections, consultative and deliberative forums, and PB.

According to the official discourse on citizen's orderly political participation, all activities and forms of participations must be based on an order. Moreover, the CCP has the final power to define what constitutes an order. Thus, any attempt to form an opposition party (a common phenomenon of political participation in many liberal societies) is considered as non-orderly participation and not tolerated. Even political criticism of the CCP is suppressed as a non-orderly form of participation. The party-defined order predetermines the boundaries of an orderly political participation, which is essentially sanctioned and subject to heavy control and regulation. As Heberer (2009) observes, political participation that has gone along with the establishment of neighbourhood communities in urban areas is part of a process of developing citizenship, but this has been activated by the party-state in a top-down process of authoritarian communitarianism.

Citizens' orderly political participation exhibits contradictions and tensions: while it emphasises emancipation, liberation, and the master of country, it has involved a variety of manipulations, regulations and control. Currently the existing models of participation in the field of Chinese studies reflect these contradictions, and each model often reveals one aspect of the orderly political participation in China. The *mobilisation model*, which stresses on mobilisation as the key feature of the orderly political participation, for example, suggests that participation is so mobilised by the party-state that it is largely meaningless. In contrast, the *empowerment model* assesses the value of the orderly political participation in terms of whether citizens are empowered or not or the extent to which citizens are becoming autonomous actors. The *disengagement model* can be seen as a reaction to the orderly political participation in that many citizens adopt non-participatory forms of behaviour as a means of protest.

Tianjian Shi's (1997) study highlights the inadequacy and limitations of the mobilisation model. Kent Jennings's research identifies the emergence of "autonomous" participation. Similarly, this chapter also demonstrates that a growing number of ordinary Chinese are developing citizen-initiated participation through strong rights-based consciousness and activism. Yang Zhong and Jie Chen (2002) suggest that villager participation in elections in Jiangsu fits the disengagement model. Yusheng Yao (2009), however, finds that, contrary to the expectations of the disengagement model, the elite cadres were unable to manipulate the elections; at the same time, contrary to the expectations of the empowerment model, the elections did not improve governance because they did not allow villagers to participate in decision-making once the election was over.

All three existing models hold some degree of validity in some cases and reveal different aspects of the variety and complexity of the orderly political participation in China, in particular the interaction between the official-invited versus citizen-created forms of political participation. This chapter examines an orderly political participation, focusing on the official-sanctioned political participation. The limits of official-invited political space have led to more and more resistance, paradoxically driving Chinese citizens to develop their own political space and forms of participation. In this context, this chapter also discusses increasingly citizen-initiated political spaces or non-sanctioned forms of political participation.

The structure of this chapter is as follows. The first three sections examine the three official-initiated participations, namely village elections, deliberative mechanisms, and PB. Section 4 discusses citizen-initiated activities and new strategies. The conclusion briefly outlines the interaction and conflict between the official- and citizen-initiated forms of political participation.

1   VILLAGE ELECTIONS

Village elections were introduced in 1987 with the promulgation of the Provisional Organic Law of Village Committees. In the wake of the collapse of the People's Commune System, rural China encountered challenging issues regarding local stability and order. In order to fill the organisational vacuum and re-establish local order, villagers in Guangxi created autonomous village organisations and introduced village elections in 1979.

In 2004 there were 652,718 villages and approximately 3 million "village officials" in China. The word "village" (*cun*) has two meanings in Chinese: either a natural village or hamlet composed of residents who live together (*ziran cun*) or an administrative rural area (*xingzhen cun*). An average village has roughly 382 households. The size of villages varies from about 1000 up to 5000–6000 villagers.

In each village there is usually a branch of the CCP, as well as a village committee and a village representatives' assembly. These three organisations generally constitute the village political power structure. According to Article 111 of the Constitution of the People's Republic of China (1982), the village committee is constituted as an autonomous grassroots organisation of the people. And its members are to be elected through regular and fair elections. The village committee is responsible for handling the village's affairs.

1.1   Competitive Elections[1]

Two types of non-competitive elections exist. Muddled elections refer to those in which electors lack information about electoral procedures, and township and villager leaders conduct elections without following a set electoral proce-

---

[1] In this section, I have used some material from He (2007).

dure. In manipulated elections village party secretaries manipulate electoral procedures, select their own favoured candidates, and predetermine the result of elections. Prior to these elections, electors already know who will win and elections lack uncertainty and excitement. These manipulated elections take place in authoritarian villages where competitiveness is absent and popular participation is low (O'Brien 1994).

Both muddled and manipulated elections tend to invite villagers' criticism, scepticism, and resistance and contribute little to good village governance. During the village elections in September 1999 in Shengzhou, the city received over 1900 telephone calls, letters, and personal visits. Approximately 10 per cent of the calls, letters, and visits sought election information, 60 per cent complained about violations of regulations by electorate staff and party secretaries, 20 per cent included the violations of the Organic Laws by election staff, and 10 per cent included financial mismanagement. Petitioners demanded that action be taken before elections could continue. Through villagers' constant struggle, semi-competitive or full competitive elections have been gradually tolerated and adopted by the state (He 2007).

Elections to positions on village committees have become increasingly competitive since they were first introduced. The 1998 election was particularly competitive. The practice of direct and open elections, called *haixuan* (naming from the floor or direct nomination for candidates) in many localities, has dramatically increased the competitiveness of village elections. One indication of this was that there were many more candidates than positions. Between April and July 1999, the ratio of candidates to positions was 48:1 in the Yuyao municipality (He 2007).

The competitiveness of elections is related to the nominating procedures and the number of candidates. The intensity of competition depends on how candidates are nominated, how many can be nominated, and whether the number of candidates is larger than the number of posts. In past elections in the Liuzheng Township, candidates were chosen by the village branch of the CCP and were approved by the township party committee and government leadership before they were introduced to the voters. Voters actually had no right or opportunity to nominate candidates. In addition, in the case of elections for heads of villages, it was official policy to limit the elections to one candidate for one position. Thus, competition was simply not expected (He 2007).

One major difference between the "Organic Law of Village Committee" of 1998 and its 1987 predecessor is that the 1998 law stipulates that the village committee should be directly elected by the villagers. When asked to compare the April 1999 elections in the Laofangqiao Township with earlier elections, villagers stated that during past elections the candidates were all handpicked by the leadership above. The number of candidates was exactly the same as the number of positions open to elections. However, nominating procedures such as *haixuan* involve and encourage much competition. In such cases, the authorities do not try to control or dominate the nominating procedure.

Instead, they allow the villagers to exercise their rights and nominate the candidates of their own choice (He 2007).

1.2   Procedures

Through various forms of protest, villagers have resisted manipulated elections and demanded fair and free elections. They have resisted election procedures they consider unfair, irregular, or corrupt by refusing to pay tax. Such resistance has forced the state to adopt and promote open and transparent procedures. In particular, the state has endorsed *haixuan* to resolve practical problems.

My field trips found that party secretaries appointed candidates in earlier village elections in Zhejiang. In the Jiangxia Village of Chengguan Township, village cadres chose their candidates through negotiation amongst themselves. Beizhang, Pukou, and Cangyan townships each had one village where the candidates were secretly decided. The appointment of candidates by party secretaries, however, faced resistance from villagers who did not vote for the official nominated candidates. Sometimes official nominated candidates lost elections, sometimes elections failed to produce any village leader, thus leading to a vacuum in village governance. To overcome this practical problem, some villages experimented with direct nomination by villagers, and township leaders had to make a compromise in letting villagers nominate candidates (He 2007).

In the process of resisting manipulated elections, villagers invented and practised *haixuan*, which originated in the Lishu County, Jilin Province. In one village, 571 out of 693 eligible voters took part in *haixuan* (Chan 1998). *Haixuan* was quickly adopted in the Xiangtan and Suining counties of the Hunan Province as well as five counties and two districts in the Gansu Province. This was a small minority in national terms (Ma 1999). *Haixuan* was ultimately endorsed in the 1998 Organic Law.

Focusing on election procedures, Tan (2009), however, argues that the current "two-majority rule" for elections means that electoral officials often manipulate voter registration or use other means to artificially create an appearance of participation so that the election is valid. Tan (2009) also argues that fixed election dates that are synchronised across the whole province would encourage voter participation and enhance democratic culture. Björn Alpermann (2009) claims that more research is needed to find out the effects of post-election procedures on village governance, and gives as an example the question of whether or not procedural rules for village representative assemblies affect participation in decision-making.

1.3   The Trends of Political Participation

There is no doubt that villagers now participate in politics with more awareness and interest. It might be hypothesised that those who have three rounds of electoral experience are likely to possess a higher level of participation than those who have only one or two. Nevertheless in recent years voters are becoming more apathetic and cynical. To understand this trend, Kevin O'Brien and Rongbin Han (2009) point out that the focus on village elections needs to shift from procedures to the broader context.

There is a debate on whether a democratic and participatory culture has emerged in China. Jennings (1997) recognises the emergence of a democratic culture at the local level and finds that the autonomous political participation of villagers is higher than commonly expected and that their actions are just as rational and strategic as their Western counterparts. Zweig's (2002) survey confirms that villagers strongly support the "democratic idea" in rural China. Yang Zhong and Jie Chen's (2002) study of non-voting behaviour shows that villagers with higher levels of internal efficacy and democratic orientation tended to avoid village elections. This type of behaviour can be interpreted as evidence of the emergence of a participant culture. Nevertheless, Kuan and Lau (2002) find that Mainland Chinese political culture remains dominantly traditional and authoritarian. Based on three surveys carried out in 40 Chinese cities in 1988, 1991, and 1993, Torstein Hjellum (1998) was unable to reach a definitive conclusion on whether there is an emergent participant culture in China.

My survey found that 843 respondents (67.7 per cent) regarded voting as their right or responsibility and nominated it as their primary motive for voting. The second-ranked motive was "to get those I trust elected" (33.3 per cent). In addition, 30 per cent of respondents regarded voting as a "sacred duty" and almost 90 per cent of respondents saw elections as either "important" or "very important" (He 2007).

The 1999 survey of 2637 individuals in four counties in rural China, conducted by David Zweig (2002), reveals a strong democratic tendency among the respondents. In response to the statement "If the existing cadres are capable and trusted, there is no need for democratic elections", about 55 per cent "disagreed somewhat" or "disagreed strongly". Only 23.9 per cent "agreed somewhat", while only 12.4 per cent "strongly agreed".

Political participation is influenced by election procedures, policy formulation and implementation, and accountability institutions, and participation combines with public responses to feed into regime legitimacy (Schubert 2009). Looking more at the social-psychological context of political participation, Xu et al. (2010) examine the impact of a sense of community, neighbouring behaviour, and social capital on participation in voting in rural and urban local elections. They find that participation is higher among rural, older, and married residents and also among those with primary or high-school education and higher social status; in rural areas it is higher among men than women and those who are involved in neighbouring behaviour, while in urban areas it is higher among residents who simply know their neighbours. They argue that social capital, as defined according to Western understandings, does not predict local political participation in China.

2   THE DEVELOPMENT OF DELIBERATIVE POLITICS IN CHINA[2]

Manipulative, symbolic, consultative, and empowered forms of deliberation exist. "Manipulative deliberation" generates a fake impression of empowerment but in fact disempowers citizens. Often there are sophisticated instances of top-down propaganda and manipulation. Symbolic deliberation goes on in China just for political show when an official will teach people a certain "correct" line of thinking and policy on a certain issue. Marxist theory, critical theory, and also public relations theory may interpret that people give their support to policies because they are subjected to the arts of persuasion and manipulation (Brady 2009). Still, an empowered form of public deliberation has slowly been developing in the last decades.

2.1   The Origin and Development of Public Deliberation

The contemporary wave of deliberative practices dates to the late 1980s, concurrent with the introduction of village elections and other participatory practices (Shi 1997; He 2007) and administrative reforms (Yang 2004). Indicative evidence includes changes in official terminology. In Mao's time, for example, participatory activities were called "political study", and they were ideologically oriented and politically compulsory. Deliberative forums are now often called *kentan* (heart-to-heart talks) or other names with deliberative connotations.

Generally, deliberative venues have become widespread, though they are widely variable in level, scale, design, and frequency. They exhibit a variety of forms such as elite debates in different levels of Peoples' Congress, lay citizen discussions via the internet, formal discussions in the public sphere, and informal debates in non-governmental domains. They can be, and often are, held monthly, bimonthly, or even quarterly in streets, villages, townships, and cities.

While broad data are not available, some cases in rural areas exhibit an impressive density of deliberative devices. From 1996 to 2000 within the Wenling City, a municipality with almost a million residents, more than 1190 of these deliberative and consultative meetings were held at the village level, 190 at the township level, and 150 in governmental organisations, schools, and business sectors. Wenling has by increments developed a form of democracy that combines popular representation with deliberation (Mo and Chen 2005).

A case in point is Zeguo Township in Wenling, where in 2005 officials introduced the mechanism of deliberative polling, using it to set priorities for the township's budget. Deliberative polling uses random sampling in order to constitute small (typically a few hundred) bodies of ordinary citizens that are descriptively representative of the population. These bodies engage in facili-

---

[2] I have used some material from He and Warren (2011) with some updated information.

tated processes of learning and deliberation about an issue, typically over a period of one or two days, and can produce results that represent considered public opinion. Officials at Zeguo elevated the outcomes of the deliberative poll from its usual advisory status to an empowered status, committing in advance of the process to abide by the outcomes (Fishkin et al. 2010; He 2008; chs. 11 and 12). In 2006, 10 out of 12 projects chosen through deliberative polling were implemented. The mechanism has also evolved: in February–March 2008, 2009, and 2010, the government opened every detail of the township budget to participants.

Whereas deliberative venues in rural locales are often related to village elections, in urban locales deliberative and participatory institutions are more likely to emerge as consequences of administrative rationalisation and accountability (Yang 2004; Ogden 2002). Some of these accountability measures generate deliberative approaches to conflict. Local leaders are increasingly using devices such as consultative meetings and public hearings designed to elicit people's support for local projects. Observations from Hangzhou, Fujian, Shanghai, Beijing, and other urban areas suggest that such deliberative practices are becoming more widespread, with more than 100 public hearings per year being held in each district.[3]

2.2   National Deliberation

The practice of holding public hearings—a consultative institution that may sometimes produce deliberation—has also developed within the area of law. In 1996, the first national law on administrative punishment introduced an article stipulating that a public hearing must be held before any punishment is given. More than 359 public hearings on administrative punishment were held in Shanghai alone between 1996 and 2000 (Zhu 2004). Another example is the well-known Article 23 of the Law on Price passed by China's National People's Congress in December 1997, which specified that the price of public goods must be discussed in public hearings. At least 11 provinces developed regulations to implement this provision with 10 referring specifically to the idea of transparency and openness and 9 to the idea of democracy (Peng et al. 2004). More than 1000 public hearings on prices were held across China between 1998 and 2001. The Legislation Law, passed in 2000 by the National People's Congress, requires public hearings to be an integral part of the decision-making process for new legislation (Wang 2003). More than 39 public hearings on new legislation were held at the provincial level between 1999 and 2004 (Chen and He 2006), including, for example, a national public hearing on income taxes. There has also been a trend towards publicly visible deliberation in the National Legislature, as was evident in the deliberations over the Draft New Labor Contract Law in 2006–07.

---

[3] The author's interviews in Hangzhou and Shanghai in 2003 and 2005.

2.3   Trends Towards Empowered Deliberation

There is a slow and incremental tendency for consultation to be pushed towards increasingly empowered deliberation. First, the consideration the authorities give to public views tends to increase over time. In the early stages, public voices would be heard and given some weight, but this will be a fairly minor consideration in decision-making. Officials will pick up on some views but ignore others. Later, however, public views will be given more weight. For example, after Wenling decided to hold public hearings, the influence of public opinion in relation to the input of officials became more equal. Public views had a major impact on the outcome of decision-making after deliberative polling in 2005. Village referenda have also resulted in the full implementation of public opinion. These referenda involve a discussion followed by villagers filling out a form to indicate their support or rejection of various policies.

Second, the nature of topics that are the subject of deliberation can shift over time to become more substantive. At early stages relatively minor issues will be put up for public consideration, such as the discussion in Xi'an over what should be the symbol of the city. Then the scope of discussions gradually expands to encompass the selection of development projects or discussion of plans for the township, with the possibility of citizens' views leading to revisions by the authorities, or the selection of local leaders, with the public effectively vetoing some candidates who are not popular enough. Finally, they deliberate over sensitive issues that relate to resource distribution, such as the public budget. So there is a gradual move towards deliberating on issues that are more substantive. Third, in some areas, such as Wuhan and Fujian, citizens are able to put forward an agenda. If villages can collect 15 household signatures they can call a village meeting.

Empowered deliberation takes place in market relationships where individuals can exercise power through their feet, that is, they will somehow move to other places or refuse to attend any fake deliberative meeting. Empowerment is often buttressed by protests, obstruction, and "rightful resistance" movements that have generated pressure for elites to consult with the people (O'Brien and Li 2006) but which can, in practice, shade into deliberation.

Empowered deliberation is secured through a set of procedural rules which are slowly developing; this marks another significant difference between consultative and deliberative authoritarianism. There are rules and procedures to call for a meeting and to ensure fairness, equality, and full deliberation. The State Council's official documents stipulate that all participants be presented with the pros and cons or themselves present both sides of argument; favourable arguments should be presented first, followed by competing unfavourable arguments; facilitators must summarise all differences and similarities and lead debate; if the government does not adopt or endorse a particular opinion or policy, it must list all the reasons and evidence to show why it has not done so, and, finally, one ought to have faith that when there are conflicts of interest over public policy, deliberation helps to find the right balanced solution.[4]

3   PARTICIPATORY BUDGETING[5]

3.1   Origin

While the idea and practice of PB were only formally introduced into China in the late 1990s, since the early 1990s, Chinese villagers or village representatives have monitored budgeting with the aim of ensuring that village leaders collect money for public goods, distribute village income in a fair way, and invest village money effectively. This was called "the openness of the village account" and "the democratic management of the village account" (He 2011).

In 1991, the local People's Congress in Shenzhen set up a budget committee in which deputies had an opportunity to examine the budget. In 1998, Hebei Province introduced sector budgeting, meaning that partial budgets were disclosed to the people's deputies of the People's Congress for examination and deliberation. In 2004, the Huinan Township in Shanghai undertook an experiment in public budgeting. Similar experiments in Xinhe and Zeguo townships were conducted in 2005; they subsequently spread to 8 neighbouring townships in Wenling in 2009 and to 79 townships in the Taizhou prefecture city in 2010. PB was also introduced by a dozen or so street-level governments between 2006 and 2008 in Wuxi and Heilongjiang.

Strong calls have been made for budgetary transparency and openness throughout China. Success, however, has often been hard won against the reticence of governments. In Shenzhen, for example, three ordinary citizens began demanding access to budget information in 2006. They went through quite a trial, submitting requests to a dozen central governmental agencies and a dozen local governments but were denied each time until in October 2008 the Shenzhen Department of Public Health permitted them to read the health budget (Huang 2008). By the end of 2010, a third of 92 departments in Shenzhen had disclosed budget information (*Southern Metropolis Daily* 2011).

3.2   Variation and Process of Participatory Budgeting

There are significant variations in PB in terms of patterns, institutions, procedures, and methods in China. PB can be categorised into revenue generation, income distribution, and budget monitoring. While village PB projects include all three aspects, township PB projects are limited in most cases to the expense-distributed category.

PB usually involves the following processes: the administrative decision to introduce PB and its theme, the decision on the proportion of the budget that

---

[4] I was invited to a closed-door meeting to discuss these documents in 2010 in Beijing.
[5] I have used some material from He (2011).

will be subject to PB (which can vary from 3 to 10 per cent in most cases), the information collection stage, the proposal and its selection stage, expert consultation stage, citizens' meetings and deliberations, the final decision stage, and the implementation stage. There are also hidden processes involving negotiations between the government and scholars, advice and funding from international donors, and, importantly, monitoring by the Public Security Bureau.

In 2008, in the Xinhe Town, Wenling City, Zhejiang Province, citizens first participated in the early stages of the budget process by expressing their preferences and concerns. Then, 90–110 deputies were divided into three groups examining the budget, followed by heated debates held in the local congress over each budgeting item. As an outcome of these debates, local deputies proposed a revised version of the overall budget. A final budget proposal was then voted on by the local deputies. During one two-hour session in Xinhe on 23 February 2008, the majority of deputies demanded an increase in a certain section of the budget and reduced government expenses on a few items such as cars (Chen 2008).

Jiaozhuo City, Hunan Province, under the supervision of the Ministry of Finance, has introduced a series of public budgeting reforms as part of a World Bank project beginning in 1999. It has established and improved a number of procedures in achieving balanced budgets, monitoring budgeting implementation, and opening up budgets to citizens and deputies for scrutiny and discussion.

In the Wenling City, Zhejiang Province, more than 80 participants from 16 towns discussed the public transportation sector budget on 13 January 2008. Four small group discussions were held in the morning and one plenary session in the afternoon. Many suggestions were made. For example, it was proposed that the maintenance cost of village-to-village roads should be included in the city budget, with the limited funds that are available being used as effectively as possible. It was recommended that the subsidy for senior citizens should not be included in the transportation budget, as this would be seen as corruption (Zhang 2008).

In summary, at the village level, there are thousands of PB projects in place. At the town or township level there are more than a dozen PB projects. More than 20 PB projects are in place at the street level. Only a few PB projects have been at the city level and national level. The number of PB projects is still very small compared to the number of villages, townships, and street-level governments. Nevertheless, the direction of PB is clear: more and more PB experiments are being introduced.

4   New Activism and Strategies of Chinese Citizens

The government crackdown that followed the Arab Spring in 2011 has meant that many organisers or front-runners who advocate for democracy or social causes have been punished. This has led to a situation where the majority of scholars feel hopeless and powerless. Their response has often been to adopt an indifferent attitude or avoid dealing with the issues. However, as a response to the Arab Spring, Chinese citizens have also developed distinctive new strategies and tactics for activism by using social media, direct action, petitioning, and law. These include novel ways of conducting social protests or other forms of activism and promoting their objectives in the struggle against an authoritarian regime. The general trend is for activism to become more individualised, to focus on legitimate interests, and to operate mostly as an internal critique within the bounds of the official discourse.

4.1   Growth of Social Protesters or Dissidents

New activists continue to emerge, despite the government crackdown. Like grass, individuals can be cut down but new activists emerge to take their place. In fact the suppression itself fuels the growth of new generations of activists. High-profile figures such as Fang Lizhi, Liu Junning, Liu Xiaobo, and Ai Weiwei continue to emerge despite government suppression of their activities.

A new phenomenon is the growth in the number of older citizens who are actively engaged in political activism. For example, one editorial board for the book series of Socialist Constitutionalism includes five scholars who are over 80 years old and two who are over 70. These older activists are critical and dare to speak out when middle-aged or younger activists with careers and family might feel threatened. They do not fear suppression and are instead able to exercise more influence in the later part of their life. The older these activists are, the more sense of social justice they have and the more they protest against corruption and unfairness in society.

4.2   Independent Candidates

One aspect of political participation that has been gaining attention in the media recently has been the involvement of independent candidates in the local People's Congress elections. He Junzhi (2010) examines the role of independent candidates as a substitution for opposition parties, divides them into four categories—idealist intellectuals, legal rights defenders, heads of state-owned sectors, and grassroots elites—and argues that they have different styles of campaigning, with the latter two types most likely to be successful. He also points out that the position of the local authorities is also crucial in determining the likely success of such participation. In the recent 2011 local People's Congress elections a number of independent candidates faced a harsh response from the authorities and were forced to quit their electoral campaigns, including in Beijing.

4.3   Using Official Language to Mask Criticism

By operating within the official discourse it is possible for citizens to "critique the system from within the system". For example, promoting democratic mechanisms can be justified in terms of the need to create a "safety valve" with which to release public pressure on the government. Reform of the military can be discussed under the guise of studying China's grand strategy. Rather than talking about constitutionalism scholars instead discuss "socialist constitutionalism", which allows them to borrow the official ideology so as to obtain protection for their critical ideas. Incorporating the phrases and concepts of the official discourse allows activists to gain a certain amount of protection by connecting their activities with the government's "brand".

4.4   New Language

Citizens have also invented their own terms in order to avoid accusations that they are involved in direct conflict with the government. When middle-class activists in Shanghai wanted to protest against plans to put a high-speed rail route through their neighbourhood they talked about taking a "stroll" (*sanbu*) rather than conducting a demonstration. Instead of strikes, workers such as taxi drivers talk about taking "rest" (*xiuxi*) or "drinking tea" (Shan 2008). This allows citizens to deny that they are engaging in political action or "causing trouble", while still getting across their political point.

4.5   Counter-Culture and Anti-government Discourse

Citizen activism has led to the creation of a new counter-culture and anti-government discourse, with its own norms and rules. In this culture those who are supportive of the government are criticised and looked down upon. Overseas Chinese scholars who defend the Chinese government find themselves the target of criticism by Chinese citizens in this counter-culture. In comparison with past underground cultures, such as in the Soviet Union, communications technology allows this culture to spread quickly. Online counter-culture tends towards the radical because extreme statements gain more attention than moderate ones. On microblogs such as Twitter and Sina Weibo sharp criticism will attract more followers for a user than more moderate, measured comments.

4.6   Individualised Activism

Western literature tends to interpret protest and activism as collective action by groups of citizens. In reality, however, Chinese activism and political participation is increasingly individualised (Yan 2010). This trend towards individualised and informal action is largely a self-protection measure by activists in response to government attempts to prevent the emergence of activist organisations.

In examining the participation of the urban middle-income stratum in terms of civic activities, Xin Wang (2008, 68) argues that this group prefers individualistic activities such as travel and education to public-interest activities. Only less than 16 per cent of survey respondents said that in the previous three years they had been involved in activities organised by their community, union, or professional association. Individual activists are often not connected to any particular group and so political participation does not involve any organisation or collective action. Individual scholars write personal blogs and attract large numbers of readers. Activists such as "barefoot lawyers" or independent candidates for local elections conduct individualised campaigns. Some individuals such as Ai Weiwei become celebrity activists who are well known but do not lead any organisation.

4.7   Internet Activism

The internet is increasingly being recognised as a site for political participation in China. Citizens are able to use the internet in sophisticated ways to avoid censorship, spread their message, and critique the government. Activists can use technological tools to "scale the wall" and gain access to blocked websites. Blogs and especially microblogs can rapidly spread information or criticism to networks of concerned citizens. Sullivan and Lei Xie (2009) refer to the internet as a "lifeline" for environmental non-governmental organisations (NGOs), particularly small groups. They point out that social networks of activists can reduce the institutionalised barriers to political participation and resistance in China. Yang (2009) also provides an in-depth account of how people increasingly engage in political activity—particularly activism and resistance—online.

4.8   NGO Activism

NGOs have been working on campaigns related to opening the budgeting process and the taxation system to public scrutiny. They have also been active in trying to support workers in labour disputes or provide support for women's social causes. These NGOs are closely monitored by the government, however. Guo (2007) examines the role of organisations in facilitating political participation and finds that the effects of political organisations on participation depend on their nature and membership and that being a member of a civic organisation is the consistently significant correlate of political participation.

5   Conclusion

Village elections, consultative and deliberative forums, and PB are all official-invited political spaces; they are orderly and heavily regulated forms of participation. While they contribute to the overall pattern of an increasing trend of political participation by empowering domain- and scope-limited forms of voice, they do not add up to regime democratisation. In the context of the fundamental limits of official forms of political participation together with the government's tough political controls, Chinese citizens have created their own political space and a new set of strategies and forms of activism.

The official-invited and citizen-created participation are interactive. Massive social protests lead some local officials to develop some forms of controlled and orderly participation, but the fundamental limits of such an official-invited political space lead to dissatisfaction, suspicion, and further protests. In particular, the government's attempts to prevent organised activism generate individualised activism and spontaneous social protest.

While Chinese officials hold the upper hand at the moment, citizen-initiated participation is inevitable and irresistible, and it is likely to grow stronger. Whether citizen-initiated participation will lead to regime change in the future is uncertain; the official form of participation is unlikely to develop into a liberal democracy; and administrative power is more likely to co-opt citizen movements in various ways.

REFERENCES

Alpermann, B. 2009. Institutionalizing village governance in China. *Journal of Contemporary China* 18(60): 397–409.

Brady, A. M. 2009. *Marketing dictatorship: Propaganda and thought work in contemporary China.* Lanham, Boulder, New York, Toronto and Plymouth: Rowman and Littlefield Publishers.

Chan, S. 1998. Research notes on villagers' committee election: Chinese style democracy. *Journal of Contemporary China* 7(19): 507–521.

Chen, Y. 2008. Canyu shi yusuan de Wenling moshi (The Wenling Model of participatory budgeting). *Jinri zhongguo luntan (China Today Forum)* 5: 95–98.

Chen, S., and B. He (eds.). 2006. *Development of deliberative democracy.* Beijing: China Social Sciences Press.

Fishkin, J. S., B. He, R. C. Luskin, and A. Siu. 2010. Deliberative democracy in an unlikely place: Deliberative polling in China. *British Journal of Political Science* 40(2): 435–448.

Guo, G. 2007. Organizational involvement and political participation in China. *Comparative Political Studies* 40(4): 457–482.

He, B. 2007. *Rural democracy in China: The role of village elections.* New York: Palgrave/Macmillan.

He, B. 2008. *Deliberative democracy: Theory, method and practice.* Beijing: China's Social Science Publishers.

He, B. 2011. Civic engagement through participatory budgeting in China: Three different logics at work. *Public Administration and Development* 31(2): 122–133.

He, B., and M. E. Warren. 2011. Authoritarian deliberation: The deliberative turn in Chinese political development. *Perspectives on politics* 9(2): 269–289.

He, J. 2010. Independent candidates in China's local people's congresses: A typology. *Journal of Contemporary China* 19(64): 311–333.

Heberer, T. 2009. Evolvement of citizenship in urban China or authoritarian communitarianism? Neighborhood development, community participation, and autonomy. *Journal of Contemporary China* 18(61): 491–515.

Hjellum, T. 1998. Is a participant culture emerging in China. In Brødsgaard, K. E., and D. Strand (eds.). *Reconstructing twentieth-century China: State control, civil society, and national identity.* Oxford: Oxford University Press.

Huang, H. 2008. Shenzhen gongmin de gonggong yusuan zhilu (Shenzhen citizens' journey of participatory budgeting). *Nanfang zhoumou (Nanfang Weekend)* 6: 13–14.

Huntington, S. P. 1968. *Political order in changing societies.* New Heaven: Yale University Press.

Jennings, M. K. 1997. Political participation in the Chinese countryside. *American Political Science Review* 91(2): 361–372.

Kuan H., and S. Lau. 2002. Traditional orientations and political participation in three Chinese societies. *Journal of Contemporary China* 11(31): 297–318.

Ma, Y. 1999. *Xiangcun zhengzhi (Rural Politics).* Nanchang: Jiangxi Renmin Chubanshe.

Mo, Y., and Y. Chen. 2005. *Democratic deliberation: The innovation from Wenling.* Beijing: Central Compliance and Translation Press.

O'Brien, K. J. 1994. Implementing political reform in China's villages. *The Australian Journal of Chinese Affairs* 32(32): 33–59.

O'Brien, K. J. and L. Li. 2006. *Rightful Resistance in Rural China.* Cambridge: Cambridge University Press.

O'Brien, K. J., and R. Han. 2009. Path to democracy? Assessing village elections in China. *Journal of Contemporary China* 18(60): 359–378.

Ogden, S. 2002. *Inklings of democracy in China.* Cambridge: Harvard University Press.

Peng, Z., L. Xue, and K. Kan. 2004. *The public hearing system in China.* Beijing: Qinghua University Press.

Schubert, G. 2009. Studying "Democratic" Governance in Contemporary China: Looking at the village is not enough. *Journal of Contemporary China* 18(60): 385–390.

Shan, S. 2008. Gongmin shehui de guaiyi biaoda: "sanbu" yu "hecha" (The strange expression of civil society: "walk" and "drink tea"). *Chongqing Shibao (Chongqing Times)* 3. Available at http://www.chinaelections.org/NewsInfo.asp?NewsID= 138915.

Shi, T. 1997. *Political participation in Beijing.* Cambridge, MA: Harvard University Press.

Sullivan, J., and L. Xie. 2009. Environmental activism, social networks and the internet. *The China Quarterly* 198: 422–432.

Tan, Q. 2009. Building democratic infrastructure: village electoral institutions. *Journal of Contemporary China* 18(60): 411–420.

Wang, Q. 2003. *A Study of Legislative Hearing.* Beijing: Beijing University Press.

Wang, X. 2008. Divergent identities, convergent interests: The rising middle-income stratum in China and its civic awareness. *Journal of Contemporary China* 17(54): 53–69.

Xu, Q., D. D. Perkins, and J. C. C. Chow. 2010. Sense of community, neighboring, and social capital as predictors of local political participation in China. *American journal of community psychology* 45(3–4): 259–271.

Yan, Y. 2010. The Chinese path to individualization. *The British journal of sociology* 61(3): 489–512.

Yang, D. 2004. *Remaking the Chinese leviathan: Market transition and the politics of governance in China.* Stanford: Stanford University Press.

Yang, G. 2009. *The power of the Internet in China: Citizen activism online.* New York: Columbia University Press.

Yao, Y. 2009. Village elections and redistribution of political power and collective property. *The China Quarterly* 197: 126–144.

Zhang, X. 2008. Shenhua gonggong yusuan gaige, zengqiang yusuan jiandu xiaoguo: guanyu Zhejiang Wenlin shi canyu shi yusuan de shijian yu sikao (Deepening the reform of the public budget and enhancing the effect of budget monitoring: the practice and thinking of participatory budgeting in Wenlin city, Zhejiang Province). *Renda yanjiu (People's Congress Study)* 11: 19–22.

Zhong, Y., and J. Chen. 2002. To vote or not to vote: An analysis of peasants' participation in Chinese village elections. *Comparative Political Studies* 35(6): 686–712.

Zhu, M. 2004. *Multiple Dimensions of Administrative Law*. Beijing: Beijing University Press.

Zweig, D. 2002. *Democratic Values, Political Structures, and Alternative Politics in Greater China*. US Institute of Peace.

CHAPTER 18

Lobbying of Private Business Associations in Local China: Targets, Strategies, and Influence

Yongdong Shen and Jianxing Yu

1   Introduction

The formulation of China's economic policies and regulations are no longer in "closed mode" (Wang 2006). As thousands of economic regulations and laws have become key determinants of the fate of industry, all types of enterprises have become active in the policy process. In China, all large enterprises—state-owned and private, Chinese and foreign—have opportunities to participate in the policy-making process and have easy access to lobby government officials (Tsai 2007; Brødsgaard 2012). However, small and medium-sized enterprises are incapable of lobbying independently since they are small and operate in a single locale.

The previous literature of business lobbying in China focused more on state-owned and/or large-sized enterprises[1] and state-level business associations and maintained that large companies and associations have a substantial effect on Chinese public policy (Deng and Kennedy 2010; Kennedy 2005).

---

[1] The large-sized enterprises are those that have annual sales of at least 500 million yuan per year.

Y. Shen • J. Yu (✉)
School of Public Affairs, Zhejiang University, Hangzhou, Zhejiang, China
e-mail: yongdongshen@zju.edu.cn; yujianxing@zju.edu.cn

© The Author(s) 2019   365
J. Yu, S. Guo (eds.), *The Palgrave Handbook of Local Governance in Contemporary China*, https://doi.org/10.1007/978-981-13-2799-5_18

However, there are fewer studies on the lobbying practice of private business associations representing the interests of small and medium-sized private enterprises. Some scholars have noticed the lobbying of private enterprises. For example, Chinese private entrepreneurs have a diversity of political cooperation strategies, including formal channels of political participation and an informal network of individual lobbying, but those individual lobbying efforts are often fragmented and not well organized (Tsai 2007; Dickson 2003; Pearson 1997). In practice, in accordance with national policies and regulations,[2] it is legal and feasible for private business associations[3] to carry out the lobbying practice. Certain private enterprises succeed in negotiating with the government through private business associations, in the name of promoting industry development (White et al. 1996; Wank 1995; Saich 2000). Nevertheless, the existing studies are limited to lobbying by private enterprises. In short, how private business associations lobby in the policy process and what potential factors contribute to the characteristics of their lobbying practice remains significantly under-examined.

This chapter seeks to explore the lobbying targets, strategies, and influences of local private business associations. We argue that the representative interests of private enterprises and the competition for attracting members among different private business associations contribute to the unique initiative of local private business associations in lobbying, which is characterized as diversified lobbying targets and formal lobbying strategies. Based on a survey of 146 business associations in the developed private economy areas, this chapter examines the lobbying targets and strategies of local private business associations. We find that local private business associations not only lobby government but also other agencies, such as the People's Congress, the People's Political Consultative Conference, and the Federation of Industry and Commerce, and local private business associations employ formal channels, such as public hearings or the submission of the proposal to the People's Political Consultative Conference. We also explore that the limited political resources push local private business associations to make full use of formal channels and various lobbying targets for their private membership interests, while the competition among various business associations

---

[2] It is stipulated in *Some Opinions of the General Office of the State Council about Accelerating and Promoting the Reform and Development of Trade Associations and Chambers of Commerce* (No. 36 [2007] of the General Office of the State Council) that a trade association shall endeavor to carry out in-depth investigations into, and the study of, the relevant industry, actively reflect the claims of the industry and its members to the government and the departments thereof, put forward its opinions and suggestions for industrial development and legislation, and so on, actively participate in the study and formulation of the pertinent laws, regulations, macro control, and industrial policies, participate in the formulation and revision of the industrial standards, industrial development plans, industrial entry requirements, improve the industrial management, and promote industrial development.

[3] Private business associations in this chapter include both industry associations and chambers of commerce that were established by private enterprises.

promote their initiatives in trying a wide spectrum of formal channels and a diversity of lobbying targets to attract associations members.

The rest of this chapter is organized as follows. We first begin with a brief review of literature on the lobbying practice of private enterprises and business associations in China. We then present a framework that guides our study. Thereafter we discuss our research design and methodology. Next, we present our findings through providing empirical data for the lobbying of local private business associations from the perspectives of targets, strategies, effects, and factors. Finally, we conclude this chapter with the summary of the contribution and implication of this study.

2   THE INDIVIDUAL AND COLLECTIVE LOBBYING OF CHINESE ENTERPRISES

2.1   *The Individual Lobbying of All Types of Enterprises in China*

The term "lobbying," which was previously only used to refer to the behavior of enterprises in Western capitalist countries, is now increasingly being associated with domestic enterprises' behavior in China. Although China is a socialist country, business lobbying has become indispensable after China's reform and opening up (Kennedy 2005).

Many scholars assert that state-owned enterprises play a primary role in lobbying that influences China's policy process. Those state-owned enterprises occupy China's most important economic sectors and have a monopoly over specific industries, such as oil, steel, electricity, and communications. Furthermore, the majority of CEOs in those state-owned enterprises have a personal connection with leaders of the central government, thus producing a decided impact on the policy-making process in China (Brødsgaard 2012). The lobbying practices of multinational companies (MNCs)—with their influence on China's policies, laws, and regulations in various ways—in China were also studied by certain scholars (Sanyal and Guvenli 2000; Luo 2001; Regina Chen 2004; Gao 2008).

Compared with state-owned enterprises heavily utilizing *Guanxi* to lobby, MNCs draw on a larger toolkit, which includes leveraging their technological expertise and their home-country governments to affect taxation laws and make their voice heard (Regina Chen 2004, 2007; Luo 2001).

The lobbying of Chinese private enterprises is also a concern of certain scholars. They maintain that, in contrast to state-owned enterprises and MNCs, private enterprises do not have sufficient political resources to rely on and, thus, face more difficulty in lobbying. Private enterprises mostly employ a formal setting to lobby, such as participating in policymaking via the People's Congress and/or the Chinese People's Political Consultative Conference (CPPCC). Another way is to achieve collective interest through joining business associations or chambers of commerce to lobby (Gao and Tian 2006; Tian and Deng 2007; Wu 2008).

Scholars believe that the Communist Party of China (CPC) has created various channels of CPC members, the People's Congresses, and the CPPCC for private enterprises and adopted them in the political system (Dickson 2003; Pearson 1997). However, only private enterprises that have significant contributions to the local economic development and fiscal revenues can gain accesses to effective lobbying (Ji 2015; Huang 2013). Kennedy (2005) claims that large companies are likely to have a greater say over political trajectory since they have more capital and a greater variety of channels to support their lobbying. Most private small and medium-sized enterprises are unable to procure influence over the policy process through individual lobbying, so they often attain individual interests by means of collective lobbying.

2.2   The Collective Lobbying of Chinese Private Enterprises

Some scholars argue that Chinese private enterprises are inclined to lobby individually rather than collectively (Tsai 2007). Nevertheless, it is often large-sized private enterprises that are able to lobby individually by creating a dialogue with the government. As a matter of fact, small and medium-sized private enterprises are unable to exert any individual influences on policymaking for their limited resources and capabilities. As organizations representing private enterprises' interests, private business associations are frequently employed for collective lobbying (Kennedy 2005; Zhou 2009; Jiang et al. 2011). The lobbying turns out to be effective when private enterprises rely on business associations to boost their individual interests in the name of the whole industrial development (Gao and Tian 2006; Ji and Fan 2017). Therefore, the lobbying practice of private business associations can reflect the motivation, strategies, approaches, and influences of private enterprises´ collective lobbying.

2.3   The Lobbying of Chinese Business Associations

Most studies on Chinese business associations focus on the lobbying of state-level business associations, showing that Chinese business associations are too weak to make the members' voice heard. The majority of state-level business associations are not active in lobbying and primarily lobby agencies of the State Council by adopting the "*Guanxi*" strategy (Brødsgaard 2012; Deng and Kennedy 2010; Kennedy and Deng 2012).

The limited lobbying predominantly is attributed to business associations' underrepresentation and highly constrained autonomy. Both can be reflected in the following aspects: (1) business associations are initiated by the government, (2) they are required to register and be affiliated with a government agency, (3) they are staffed by government officials, and (4) they are dependent on government financing (Kennedy 2005, 2009; Kennedy and Deng 2012). Most state-level business associations are transformed from certain departments and committees of the State Council, so they are marked by a distinct official background. Put in other words, they have a natural affinity with the government in their establishment, human resources, and financing, and are therefore unable to be autonomous and fully represent the interests of enterprises (Yu 2002).

In contrast, case studies by some domestic scholars find that local private business associations can represent the interests of members and influence the policy-making process by submitting proposals to the People's Congress and the People's Political Consultative Conference, conveying policy propositions through hearings, seminars, and investigations, exerting an indirect influence on policymaking via media reports and participating in the policy advocacy through personal contacts with officials (Zhou 2009; Jiang and He 2012; Cheng et al. 2003; Yu et al. 2014). Local private business associations are established by private enterprises, and their leaders are autonomously elected by members. The financial source of private business associations is primarily from membership fees and private donations (Nevitt 1996; Unger 1996; Yu et al. 2012; White 1993; Tsai 2007).

However, previous studies on the lobbying practice of private business associations are still insufficient. On the one hand, most of them are based on case studies and lack large samples and statistical analysis. On the other hand, they are mainly focused on business lobbying and state-level business associations' lobbying, while the motivation of private business associations for lobbying remains significantly underexamined. This chapter will explore the characters and motivations of private business associations lobbying in China to contribute to the existing literature.

3   Surveying Private Business Associations in Local China

The survey of private business associations in the developed areas of the private economy was conducted by the Civil Society Development Center of Zhejiang University between March 2011 and August 2012. We adopted a mixed method combining qualitative and quantitative in order to ensure an accurate picture of the private business associations' lobbying. Both questionnaire respondents and interviewees are leaders of private business associations, such as secretariats-general and presidents in charge of daily operations.

All surveyed business associations were established by private entrepreneurs in Zhejiang and Jiangsu provinces where private economy is considerably dynamic,[4] so that the roles of private business associations in policymaking could be best reflected (Jiang and He 2012; Cheng et al. 2003). We used the "probability sampling with quotas" process to choose Hangzhou, Ningbo, and

---

[4] In both Zhejiang and Jiangsu provinces, private economy is highly vibrant. In 2011, private economy accounted for 61–62.2% and 53% of the total gross domestic product (GDP) in Zhejiang and Jiangsu provinces, respectively.

Wenzhou cities in Zhejiang Province and Wuxi and Nantong cities in Jiangsu Province in order to have adequate representation of private business associations of different cities and industries. We received a total of 235 responses, of which 146 responses are valid. Of these, 35 (24%) were from Ningbo, 20 (13.7%) were from Wenzhou, 44 (30.1%) were from Hangzhou, 38 (26%) were from Wuxi, and 9 (6.2%) were from Nantong. In order to understand the lobbying motivation of private business associations, we conducted semistructuralized interviews with 15 associations under the structural proportion of the questionnaires. Among them, there are four associations from Ningbo, two from Wenzhou, four from Hangzhou, four from Wuxi, and one from Nantong.

The questionnaire aimed at seeking answers to three sets of questions. The first involved background information of associations, including the associations' establishment time, the affiliated agency, as well as the personnel and incoming resources. The second area revolved around the influence of the lobbying practice of associations. Respondents were asked to answer questions about the influence of lobbying on government policies, including "the promotion of government influence," "making government policies meet the interests of the industry," and "the influence on the policymaking, implementation, and changes," and so on. Respondents were asked to gauge the policy influence of industry generally, including more questions about the associations' appropriate role in certain circumstances (e.g., when its members and the government disagree, which side should the association support).

The third set of questions focused on the lobbying targets and strategies of private business associations. It tried to determine whether associations take a more proactive or passive approach in dealing with officials on policy issues. That is, do they try to set the agenda and influence policy over an extended period or do they react to regulatory problems as they arise. Adapting the framework that Hillman and Hitt (1999) employ with regard to American and European firms, the survey asked a series of questions concerning their lobbying strategies and tactics (Kennedy and Deng 2012).[5] There are also three types of lobbying strategies—information, public relations, and trust. Specific information strategy includes the provision of oral or written policy-relevant information in both informal settings, such as private meetings, and in formal situations, such as public hearings. The public relations strategy refers to the effort of private business associations to improve their image among the general public, including submitting information to mass media, holding press conferences, and participating in charity and public welfare activities. The trust strategy suggests efforts by associations to influence policymakers by gaining their personal trust, including communicating with officials for policy information by treating them to a formal dinner or inviting officials to give a talk on

---

[5] Hillman and Hitt (1999) divide strategies into informational, constituency-building, and financial categories. Constituency strategy involved grass-roots efforts to attract popular support for elections and policy mobilization campaigns.

explaining new policies. Respondents were also asked about the frequency with which they contacted officials in ministries and commissions under the Central Government, the National People's Congress (NPC), the CPPCC, the All-China Federation of Industry and Commerce (ACFIC), as well as the same sectors at the local level.

We also categorized lobbying strategies into formal and informal ones. Formal channels refer to associations' lobbying in an institutionalized and direct manner, including submitting proposals to the People's Congress and the People's Political Consultative Conference, offering suggestions to the Federation of Industry and Commerce, turning in suggestions to the government and upper-level business associations in a formal way, holding public hearings, capturing the attention of the government via mass media, offering suggestions as member of the policy consulting committee, and so on. Informal channels refer to lobbying in an indirect manner through the personal *"Guanxi"* network, including reporting to government officials through personal contacts; building connections with government officials through their family members, town fellows, classmates or friends to strive for the best interests of the associations; recruiting retired officials to lobby for policymaking, and influencing nongovernment officials involved in policymaking.

This chapter attempts to not only investigate private associations' involvement in policymaking but also to make comparisons with state-level business associations in terms of the target, strategy, and influence of lobbying. The data of state-level business associations is derived from Deng and Kennedy's article entitled "Big Business and Industry Association Lobbying in China: The Paradox of Contrasting Styles" (2007).

4 THE LOBBYING CHARACTERISTICS OF PRIVATE BUSINESS ASSOCIATIONS IN CHINA

4.1 The Lobbying Willingness and Influence of Local Private Business Associations

In China, the success of private enterprises is largely dependent on economic policies, laws, and regulations, which enables local private business associations to make an effort to lobby. Our findings indicate that private business associations in the developed private economy area have gained strong lobbying willingness, participated actively in policymaking, and produced great policy effects. Intervention during the process of policymaking or before a policy is unveiled is a crucial step of effective lobbying. More than 70% of the associations "influence the content of a policy to be made or released in various ways" instead of "taking action after a policy is released." In terms of the effect and influence of lobbying, 65.1% of the associations believe that "they have produced a great effect on the government in the past three years." A total of

Table 18.1 Lobbying target of local private business associations in the developed private economy areas (%)

	Business associations in the developed areas of private economy
The Central Government	26.9
NPC	11.5
CPPCC	10.6
Communist Party organs	12.5
ACFIC	1.5
Local government	87.3
Local people's congress	40.4
Local people's political consultative conference	40.4
Local Communist Party committee	31.6
Local federation of commerce and industry	30.3

65.4% of the associations contend that "government policies are more compatible with the interests of the industry after the efforts of associations."

4.2   The Lobbying Target and Strategy of Local Private Business Associations

The local private business associations show a diversity of lobbying targets and strategies (see Table 18.1). The lobbying targets include the government, the People's Congress, the People's Political Consultative Conference, the Communist Party Committee, and the Federation of Industry and Commerce at national and local levels. Among these targets, local government accounts for the largest proportion at 87.3%. Local people's congresses and local people's political consultative conferences take up 40.4%, while the local Communist Party committees and local federations of industry and commerce occupy 31.6% and 30.3%, respectively. In general, the proportion of lobbying toward local agencies is appreciably higher than that to state-level ones. This has a lot to do with the fact that the policy of local governments is more intimately tied with the interests of local private business associations.

Local private business associations are also differentiated from state-level ones in terms of lobbying goals (see Table 18.2). The goals of state-level business associations predominantly focused on submitting policy appeals by means of offering suggestions to the government (98.6%). Not so many state-level business associations (18%) lobby the NPC and the CPPCC. The submission of policy appeals by means of offering suggestions to the government by local private business associations accounts for 87.3%, lower than that by state-level ones (98.6%). Moreover, local private business associations tend to put forward policy appeals via the People's Congress and the People's Political Consultative

Table 18.2 Comparison of lobbying targets between state-level business associations and local private ones (%)

Local private business associations (2012)		State-level business associations (2007)	
Local government	87.3	Various ministries and departments of the State Council	98.6
Local people's congress	40.4	NPC	18.0
Local people's political consultative conference	40.4	CPPCC	18.0

Conference (40.4%), far higher than that of the state-level ones (18%). Unlike state-level business associations that primarily lobby various ministries and departments of the State Council, the proportion of the lobbying targets of local private associations appear to be more balanced and diversified.

In terms of lobbying strategies, private business associations adopt more multiple ways than state-level ones did. In the information strategy, local private business associations are inclined to produce an effect on policymaking via information submission (see Table 18.3). In the first three items of the information strategy, business associations take the initiative in lobbying and the proportion of private business associations is lower than that of state-level ones. A total of 76.6% of the private business associations offer policies or suggestions to the government by means of journals or classified documents account, while 86.3% of state-level ones do that. Inviting officials to deliver a lecture on explaining new policies takes up 55.8% and 76.6% for local private business associations and state-level ones, respectively; and orally reporting information of industrial policies to the government occupies 58.9% and 90.2% for local private business associations and state-level ones, respectively. However, the proportion of "participating in public hearings convened by the government" stands at 29.5% for private business associations, as compared to 8% for state-level ones. By "participating in public hearings convened by the government," business associations engage in lobbying through an institutionalized channel. It can, thus, be seen that private business associations lobby more frequently through institutionalized channels.

In terms of the public relations strategy, 59.7% of the local private business associations choose to provide mass media information, whereas 89.7% of the state-level ones choose to do so. But in other public relations strategies, the proportion of local private business associations is higher than that of the state-level ones, which means that local private business associations are better at taking advantage of charities, press conferences, and training courses for the media. In terms of the trust strategy, there is virtually no significant distinction between local private business associations and state-level ones. A total of 48.1% of the private business associations and 47% of the state-level ones "exchange policy-related information with officials at a dinner party."

In general, state-level business associations tend to employ some "*Guanxi*" tactics. For example, the strategy of "offering policies or suggestions to the

Table 18.3 Comparison of lobbying strategies between state-level business associations and local private ones

	Private business associations (2012)	State-level business associations (2007)
Information strategy		
Offering policies or suggestions to the government by means of journals or classified documents	76.7	86.3
Inviting officials to deliver a lecture on new policies	55.8	76.6
Participating in public hearings convened by the government	29.5	8
Supporting industry-related academic research	60.5	58.6
Offering oral information about industrial policies to the government	58.9	90.2
Public relations strategy		
Providing mass media with information	59.7	89.7
Holding a press conference	29.9	17.5
Participating in charities	49.6	23.3
Offering training courses about policy orientation to the media	26	7.7
Trust strategy		
Exchanging policy-related information with officials at a dinner party	48.1	47

government by means of journals or classified documents" occupies a very high proportion for state-level business associations, while the strategy of "participating in public hearings convened by the government" takes up a very low proportion. On the contrary, private business associations tend to employ more diversified and institutionalized tactics to lobby.

4.3   Lobbying Channels of Local Private Business Associations: Formal Channels Versus Informal Channels

Previous studies on business lobbying in China lay a great deal of emphasis on the importance of "*Guanxi*" (Gao and Tian 2006; Tian and Deng 2007; Wu 2008), but it is not that significant in the lobbying of local private business associations. Although 92.9% of the private business associations agree that "*Guanxi*" is important to have a good relationship with the government officials and 77% of them also believe that a good relationship with the government could help the influence of business associations on policymaking, merely 64.2% of them agree strongly or agree that they actually develop a good relationship with government officials. It demonstrates that local private business associations do not really achieve affective policymaking by developing a good relationship with local officials.

Table 18.4 Formal and informal channels of lobbying of local private business associations in the developed areas of private economy

	Private business associations (2012)
Formal channels	
Submitting bills or proposals through the delegates of the People's Congress or the members of the People's Political Consultative Conference	60.8%
Offering policy-making suggestions to relevant government departments and upper-level business associations in an official manner so as to produce effects	70.5%
Offering suggestions as policy advisors or committee members for government at various levels	33.8%
Participating in public hearings	29.5%
Offering policy-making suggestions to federations of industry and commerce	20%
Appealing to the government at an upper level or the general public for their concern about a particular issue through mass media	46.8%
Informal channels	
Reporting the situation to familiar government officials directly	80.2%
Contacting government officials through their family members, town fellows, classmates or friends	12.7%
Recruiting retired government officials and asking them to offer policy-making suggestions	17.9%
Offering policy-making suggestions to nongovernment officials, such as experts and scholars	20.5%

We categorize the lobbying channel of local private business associations into formal and informal channels (see Table 18.4). Formal channels refer to lobbying in an open and formal manner, whereas informal channels refer to lobbying on the basis of "*Guanxi.*" Our findings show that, among informal channels, the practice of "reporting the situation to familiar government officials directly" by the leaders of local private business associations accounts for 80.2%, while the proportion of all other informal channels takes up no more than 20.5%. It indicates that the informal lobbying of local private associations depends primarily on those who are in charge of these associations. One leader of a particular private business association said that "the current development of local private business associations is largely contingent on the interpersonal network of their leaders."[6]

In contrast, private business associations tend to employ formal lobbying channels. Except for the lower proportion of "offering policy-making suggestions to federations of industry and commerce" (20%) and "offering suggestions as policy advisors or committee members for government at various levels" (33.8%), the other two formal channels occupy very high proportions,

[6]An interview with the president of one business association, Wenzhou, July 2012.

with the percentages of " offering policy-making suggestions to relevant government departments and upper-level business associations in a formal manner" and "submitting bills or proposals through the delegates of the people's congress or the members of the people's political consultative conference" stands at 70.5% and 60.8%, respectively.

5   THE ANALYSIS FOR THE CHARACTERISTICS OF LOCAL PRIVATE BUSINESS ASSOCIATIONS' LOBBYING IN CHINA

5.1   Why Are the Lobbying Targets and Strategies of Private Business Associations More Diversified?

In comparison with state-level industry associations, private business associations display a more balanced and diversified proportion in terms of lobbying targets. A potential reason for explaining it is that local private business associations lack an intimate relationship with the government agencies. Most of the state-level business associations evolved out of national ministries or commissions, thus easily accessing state agencies and influencing national policymaking (Deng and Kennedy 2010). This also accounts for the high proportion of various ministries and commissions of the State Council as lobbying targets and the low percentage of other lobbying targets. In contrast, private business associations are established independent of the government system, so they are lacking a close tie to the government agencies. In order to exert their policy influence, local private business associations must find lobbying targets, such as the local people's congress and the local people's political consultative conference. In some sense, this is the last resort for them. In China, the government possesses abundant resources. Keeping a close relationship with government agencies is most likely to tremendously benefit business associations. However, local private business associations have a great deal of difficulty in forming a bond with the government, so they have to make the most of other available lobbying targets to maximize their interests. Accordingly, the structure distribution of lobbying targets is more balanced and diversified.

5.2   Why Do Private Business Associations Adopt More Formal Channels than Informal Ones in Lobbying?

The balanced lobbying strategy of private business associations reflects their seeking interests from wider approaches apart from the government. State-level business associations are inclined to be content with the conventional channels for engaging in public policy, so seldom do they need to explore other lobbying channels (Deng and Kennedy 2010). For private business associations, it is indeed difficult in developing "*Guanxi*" with government agencies. "*Guanxi* is extremely crucial, but it is not easy to develop as expected in reality. This is heavily dependent on the social capital that the director of a business association owns,"[7] said the head of one private business association. The lobbying behavior of private business associations may vary from one to another due to the difference in social capital of their leaders. However, formal channels are institutionalized and opportunities are open and equal to every private business association. As a legal lobbying organization,[8] every private business association is entitled to "put forward bills or proposals through the delegates of the people's congress or the members of the people's political consultative conference," "offer policy-making suggestions to relevant government departments and upper-level business associations in an official manner," "participate in public hearings," or "offer suggestions as policy advisers or committee members for the government at various levels." This accounts for local private business associations to employ formal channels of lobbying.

5.3 Exploring the Underlying Reasons for Local Private Business Associations' Lobbying Characteristics: The Representatives of Private Enterprises and the Competition Among Business Associations

The lobbying characteristics of private business associations in lobbying targets and strategies have much to do with the interest representativeness and their embedded environment. Based on the questionnaires results and semistructuralized interviews, we find that: interest representatives of private small and medium-sized enterprises and the competition for members among private business associations are two key factors for private business associations to be different from the state-level ones in lobbying.

5.3.1 Interest Representatives of Private Small and Medium-Sized Enterprises

Local private business associations are established to represent the interests of private enterprises. Many members of private business associations in the developed areas of private economy are small and medium-sized enterprises. The survey data shows that 67.9% of their members are small and medium-sized enterprises or micro-enterprises. Some scholars contend that business associations do not just represent the interests of a single party and that sometimes

---

[7] An interview with the president of one business association, Hangzhou, July 2012.

[8] It is stipulated in *Some Opinions of the General Office of the State Council about Accelerating and Promoting the Reform and Development of Trade Associations and Chambers of Commerce* (No. 36 [2007] of the General Office of the State Council) that a trade association shall endeavor to carry out in-depth investigations into, and study of, the relevant industry, actively reflect the claims of the industry and its members to the government and the departments thereof; put forward its opinions and suggestions for industrial development and legislation, and so on; actively participate in the study and formulation of the pertinent laws, regulations, macro control, and industrial policies; participate in the formulation and revision of the industrial standards, industrial development plans, and industrial entry requirements; and improve the industrial management and promote the industrial development.

they can represent interests of the government, as well as their membership enterprises (Unger 1996; Foster 2002). Thus, we also look into the possibility of private business associations' inability to represent the interests of small and medium-sized enterprises. The survey data indicates that when there existed disagreements in policymaking between the government and the majority of membership enterprises, only 10.8% of the private business associations sought to persuade enterprises to make a compromise with the government.

Other scholars also claim that most of the private business associations may have been captured by large or leading enterprises and may have become the lobbying tool of those dominant enterprises, thereby unable to represent the interests of small and medium-sized enterprises (Jiang and Zhang 2009). Our research findings demonstrates that, when there were interest conflicts between leading enterprises and the whole industry, 60.3% of the private business associations opted to lobby or make decisions in the interests of the entire industry. This reflects that the lobbying of private business associations is closely tied to the collective interests of small and medium-sized enterprises rather than the individual interests of leading enterprises. In other words, local private business associations represent the interests of small and medium-sized enterprises.

5.3.2   The Competitive Environment of Local Private Business Associations in Attracting Members

The policy of "one association in one industry" and "one association in one administrative district" substantially reduces competition for state-level business associations,[9] but this policy doesn't reduce the competition for local private business associations. Unlike state-level business associations, the industry that local private business associations serve in one administrative district is not exclusive to other administrative districts in most cases. According to our survey data, 69.9% of the local private business associations contend that their industries are confronted with pressure and competition from similar industries in other districts. Thus, they have to offer policy-making suggestions to the local government agencies so as to improve the local industry policy. Under this highly competitive environment, similar industries in other places will develop faster if their industry policies are more preferential. This will eventu-

---

[9] "One business association in one industry" refers to the rule that there shall be no more than one business association with the same or a similar scope of activity in the same administrative district at a county level and above. It is stipulated in Article 13 of *Regulation on Registration and Administration of Social Organizations* issued in 1998 that "If in the same administrative area there is already a social organization active in the same [xiang tong] or similar [xiang si] area of work, there is no need for a new organization to be established." During the process of implementation, this rule changed into "one business association in one industry in the same administrative district." Although *Regulation on the Administration of the Registration of Social Organizations* issued in 2016 lifted the restrictions of "one business association in one industry," we carried out our research in 2012–2013, during which period China still adhered to the principle of "one business association in one industry."

ally contribute to the degradation of the local industries and accordingly jeopardize the survival of local private business associations.

This can be supported from the following two perspectives. First, our survey data indicates that local private business associations earn 71.3% of their income from the membership fees or donations of their members and 16.6% of their income from their services or investments. The recession of the local industry will directly reduce the income from membership fees, thus adversely affecting the survival of private business associations. Second, the losses of membership enterprises and the unfavorable policy environment will exert a crippling impact on the efficiency and productivity of local enterprises and may well force some enterprises to relocate to other districts. According to our survey data, 29.1% of the private business associations hold that the phenomenon of relocation does exist in their industries. The loss of membership enterprises will definitely lead to the decline in membership fees, donations, and service fees, thereby influencing the survival of private business associations. Therefore, it is of significant importance that local private business associations improve the industrial policy environment by lobbying. To promote the competitive capacity of local industries, local private business associations will make every effort to lobby local agencies for the policy improvement of industry development.

The heavy reliance of local business associations on their members in resource acquisition makes them have to represent the interests of private small and medium-sized enterprises in the competitive environment, which is the driving force for private business associations to employ diversified lobbying targets and lobbying through formal channels.

6   Conclusions

Most research about business lobbying focuses on the lobbying of large enterprises, state-owned enterprises, and state-level business associations, while there are fewer studies on the collective lobbying of small and medium-sized private enterprises. Based on the survey of private business associations in the advanced private economy areas, we find that local private business associations have a very positive lobbying willingness and exert a great impact on local industry policy. Compared with state-level business associations, local private business associations have balanced and diversified lobbying targets and adopt formal channels of lobbying strategy. The above lobbying characteristic of local private business associations can be ascribed to their interest representativeness of private enterprises and the competitive environment for attracting members.

Established by private enterprises rather than the government, local private business associations´ survival and development primarily depend on membership enterprises instead of government, which encourages private business associations to stand up for the right of their membership enterprises. The members of private business associations are predominantly private small and medium-sized enterprises, and most of the private business associations' lobbying activities are carried out for the interests of the entire industry. Meanwhile, the heavy reliance on membership enterprises also involves private business associations in an intensively competitive environment. More often than not, the competition from similar industries in other districts forces private business associations to lobby local government or other agencies to improve the local industrial policy environment, thereby providing an ideal policy environment for the effective development of the local industry.

The government often has great power and policy resources. In order to obtain benefits for membership enterprises, private business associations have to overcome their innate shortage of an intimate relationship with the government. However, establishing "*Guanxi*" depends largely on the social capital of leaders of private business associations. Currently, the formulation and implementation of policies becomes increasingly formal and institutional, which provides the opportunity to the lobbying of private business associations. Local private business associations engage in effective lobbying by employing and reinforcing formal channels.

This chapter has the following two implications. First, in contrast with the claim in previous studies on state-level business associations that lobbying is singular and passive, there does exist substantial distinctions in lobbying between state-level business associations and local private ones. The fact is that state-level business associations and private ones differ from each other in representative interest groups and political resources, so they are distinct from each other in lobbying targets, strategies, and influences. Second, the lobbying practice of local private business associations is characterized by institutionalized participation, diversified targets, and formal channels. It indicates that, although formal channels are built by the state, private small and medium-sized enterprises reinforce existing formal channels, which may well be of profound significance to the whole business of lobbying.

Our research is based on private business associations in the developed areas of the private economy. These associations are spontaneously and independently established by private enterprises. Meanwhile, the relationship between local private business associations and the government lacks innate and intimate relationship, which is one of the underlying reasons for a diversity of lobbying targets and strategies. These samples selected from the developed areas of private economy and vibrant private economy act as a trigger for a strong desire for interest appeals by means of lobbying. Because these business associations are established at the local level, there exists intensive competition between different business associations in different districts.

Due to the limited research data, this chapter focuses on the lobbying of private business associations in the developed areas of private economy—Zhejiang and Jiangsu provinces. We need a larger number of samples on a nationwide basis to test our conclusion. The follow-up research will call for in-depth investigations and interviews to explore how private business associations adopt different lobbying targets and strategies to achieve that end; how they affect the formulation or change of government policies indirectly by lobbying to the agencies other than the government; and how their leaders strive for lobbying interests through their personal relationship as well as how they achieve an effective balance between "*Guanxi*" and "formal channels."

REFERENCES

Brødsgaard, K.E. 2012. Politics and business group formation in China: The Party in control? *The China Quarterly* 211: 624–648.

Cheng, H., W. Huang, and Y. Wang. 2003. Research into China's social interest groups. *Strategy and Management* 4: 63–64.

Deng, G., and S. Kennedy. 2010. Big business and industry association lobbying in China: The paradox of contrasting styles. *The China Journal* 63: 101–125.

Dickson, B.J. 2003. *Red Capitalists in China: The Party, Private Entrepreneurs, and Prospects for Political Change*. Cambridge: Cambridge University Press.

Foster, K.W. 2002. Embedded within state agencies: Business associations in Yantai. *The China Journal* 47: 41–65.

Gao, Y. 2008. Institutional environment and MNEs' strategy in transitional China. *Managing Global Transitions* 6(1): 5–21.

Gao, Y., and Z. Tian. 2006. How firms influence the government policy decision-making in China. *Singapore Management Review* 28(1): 73–85.

Hillman, A.J., and M.A. Hitt. 1999. Corporate political strategy formulation: A model of approach, participation, and strategy decisions. *Academy of Management Review* 24(4): 825–842.

Huang, D. 2013. How do entrepreneurs affect the local policy process: A case study and typology construction from the state-centered perspective. *Sociological Studies* 5: 172–196.

Ji, Y. 2015. The inner differentiation of business associations: How social foundation influences the organizational cohesion. *The Journal of Public Management* 1: 107–116.

Ji, Y., and X. Fan. 2017. Do deep pockets have more political influence? The size of private enterprises and their strategy selection in resolving administrative disputes. *Sociological Studies* 3: 193–215.

Jiang, H., and B. He. 2012. Contrastive research into policy-making participation of business associations: Nanjing and Wenzhou. *Journal of Zhejiang Provincial Party School* 1: 27–36.

Jiang, H., and J. Zhang. 2009. Analysis of the representativeness of business associations and its influence factors: A case study of Wenzhou-based business associations. *Journal of Public Management* 4: 78–88.

Jiang, H., J. Zhang, and Y. Zhou. 2011. Interests alignment: An analytical framework of the state and society relations in transitional China. *Sociological Studies* 3: 136–145.

Kennedy, S. 2005. *The Business of Lobbying in China*. Cambridge: Harvard University Press.

Kennedy, S. 2009. Comparing formal and informal lobbying practices in China: The capital's ambivalent embrace of capitalists. *China Information* 23(2): 195–222.

Kennedy, S., and G. Deng. 2012. Analysis of the factors shaping the lobbying behavior of industry associations. *Comparative Economic & Social Systems* 4: 147–156.

Luo, Y. 2001. Toward a cooperative view of MNC-host government relations: Building blocks and performance implications. *Journal of International Business Studies* 32(3): 401–419.

Nevitt, C.E. 1996. Private business associations in China: Evidence of civil society or local state power? *The China Journal* 36: 25–43.

Pearson, M.M. 1997. *China's New Business Elite: The Political Consequences of Economic Reform*. California: University of California Press.

Regina Chen, Y.R. 2004. Effective public affairs in China: MNC-government bargaining power and corporate strategies for influencing foreign business policy formulation. *Journal of Communication Management* 8(4): 395–413.

Regina Chen, Y.R. 2007. The strategic management of government affairs in China: How multinational corporations in China interact with the Chinese government. *Journal of Public Relations Research* 19(3): 283–306.

Saich, T. 2000. Negotiating the state: The development of social organizations in China. *The China Quarterly* 161: 124–141.

Sanyal, R.N., and T. Guvenli. 2000. Relations between multinational firms and host governments: The experience of American-owned firms in China. *International Business Review* 9(1): 119–134.

Tian, Z., and X. Deng. 2007. The determinants of corporate political strategy in Chinese transition. *Journal of Public Affairs* 7(4): 341–356.

Tsai, K.S. 2007. *Capitalism without Democracy: The Private Sector in Contemporary China*. Ithaca, NY: Cornell University Press.

Unger, J. 1996. Bridges: Private business, the Chinese government and the rise of new associations. *The China Journal* 147: 795–819.

Wang, S. 2006. Public policy agenda-setting patterns in China. *Social Science in China* 5: 86–99.

Wank, D.L. 1995. Private business, bureaucracy, and political alliance in a Chinese city. *The Australian Journal of Chinese Affairs* 35(33): 55–71.

White, G. 1993. Prospects for civil society in China: A case study of Xiaoshan city. *The Australian Journal of Chinese Affairs* 29: 63–87.

White, G., J.A. Howell, and X. Shang. 1996. *In Search of Civil Society: Market Reform and Social Change in Contemporary China*. Oxford: Oxford University Press.

Wu, W. 2008. Influence of political relationship building on the business activity of firms in China. *Singapore Management Review* 30(2): 73–94.

Yu, H. 2002. *Business Associations and Their Development in China: Theory and Cases*. Beijing: Economy and Management Publishing House.

Yu, J., K. Yashima, and Y. Shen. 2014. Autonomy or privilege? Lobbying intensity of local business associations in China. *Journal of Chinese Political Science* 19(3): 315–333.

Yu, J., J. Zhou, and H. Jiang. 2012. *A Path for Chinese Civil Society: A Case Study on Industrial Associations in Wenzhou, China*. Lanham, MD: The Roman & Littlefield.

Zhou, J. 2009. Policy advocacy of industry associations: Actuality, problems and mechanism building. *Chinese Public Administration* 9: 91–96.

CHAPTER 19

Citizen Action and Policy Change

Yanling He

1 INTRODUCTION

Chinese citizens are becoming more conscious of their citizenship rights. As more and more Chinese citizens are involved in different stages of the decision-making process, how decisions are made is changed in contemporary China. Citizen participation has led to more "scientific" policy decisions and better implementation.

In this chapter, we address citizen participatory action in public affairs and demonstrate its relation to policy change. We believe that Chinese citizen action has been one of the most significant forces propelling local policy change. This chapter includes four parts: the historical change of citizen participation, the controversial aspects of citizen participation, the status quo of institutionalized citizen participation, and the relationship between citizen participation and good governance.

Since the beginning of the twenty-first century, the study of China's civil participation has been booming. Strong contributions have been made from scholars in public administration, political science, sociology, and other disciplines. Although the study of contemporary civil participation in China began by referring to modern Western democratic ideals, it is now heavily influenced by traditional Chinese ideas of "people-centered" governance. At its earliest

Y. He (✉)
Chair Professor of the Pearl River Program (珠江学者特聘教授), Guangzhou, China

Department of Public Administration, Sun Yat-sen University, Guangzhou, China

Research Institute for Urban Governance of Sun Yat-sen University, Guangzhou, China

Committee for Government Strategy and Public Policy of the Chinese Research Council of Modern Management, Guangzhou, China

© The Author(s) 2019
J. Yu, S. Guo (eds.), *The Palgrave Handbook of Local Governance in Contemporary China*, https://doi.org/10.1007/978-981-13-2799-5_19

stages, scholars focused on introducing Western democratic theories and research into Chinese academic discourse. Nowadays, scholars tend to concentrate on explaining a participatory phenomenon or practice with the help of the theories and putting forward suggestions for current local governance.

Classical civil participation mainly refers to citizen influence on government and policy through voting and other avenues. Methods were characterized as passive, indirect, voting, or representative. However, the 1960s brought the New Public Involvement movement to the United States and broadened the boundaries of civil participation, thus creating more extensive and varied connotations (Verba et al. 1978).

As the connotations of modern, civil participation expanded, Jia (2007) observed three effects. First, civil participation extends from election to decision-making and administration. In other words, public participation is an indispensable part of policymaking and the administrative process. Second, the scope of participation has expanded beyond government and policy. In this regard, citizens are also able to participate in the governance of those public affairs that are closely linked to their interests. Third, civil participation stresses civil society and citizenship consciousness, guaranteeing the active citizen involvement rather than passive participation.

As we see it, citizenship consciousness is the solid grounding of civil participation. Its prerequisite is active participation and a high level of involvement in public affairs (Young 2000). These actions help to legitimize the decision-making process and prioritize policies. Therefore, in this chapter, we use a perception of citizenship to discuss the development of, and obstacles facing, civil participation in China.

The most widely accepted framework of civil participation is Arnstein's eight-rung ladder of participation. She sees citizen power as the very nature of civil participation and believes that different levels of participation indicate different degrees of citizen power. She classifies citizen power into three levels: Citizen Control, Tokenism, and Therapy and Manipulation. Only the actual establishment of an innate system of civil participation can guarantee sustainable citizen power. In turn, increasing citizen power can guarantee civil participation.

This chapter discusses the development path of citizen participation in China with reference to citizen power. In order to explore the currently existing, newly developing, and future forms and channels for increased civil involvement in China, we divide our discussion into four parts. We first outline the general development path in sequential order. We then discuss the most controversial topics of China's civic participation in recent years. In the third part, we describe the status quo of civic participation in China. Finally, we explain the relationship between citizen participation and governance.

2   The Development Path of Civil Participation in Local China: An Historical Perspective

This section describes the historical view of the development of citizen participation in China and summarizes the development path in chronological order. In this history, 1980 is the pivotal year. Before 1980, the country was marked by totalitarian dominance and a centrally planned economy; after 1980, reforms ushered in an era of marketization and commercialization. Given these radical differences between before and after, the development of civic participation in China must be viewed within the correct historical context. Therefore, we attempt to illustrate the development path of civic participation through the telling of the many changes in China that represent a gradual progression toward citizen power.

2.1   The Era of the Planned Economy

Before the reform and opening-up policy of 1978, China had a planned economy. The country was governed as a totalitarian state, where an almighty government dominated all areas of society and the economy. Enterprises were owned by governments with different levels of ownership, and there was almost no private enterprise. Social services were embedded within the hierarchical administrative system and were involved and organized in people's communes in rural areas and Danwei in urban areas. These two systems functioned as social resource distributors and were burdened with many social functions (Li and O'Brien 1996; Zhou and Yang 1999).

In local urban governance, residents were under rigid control of the Danwei system, one of the most important mechanisms for controlling participation in China. It was invented to dispel social uncertainty and collective protest through its strong resource mobilization, relative deprivation, and political process (Feng 2006). It actively prevented certain types of participation, such as violent protests or aggressive collective actions through the political effects of the Danwei system's rigid hierarchy; citizen participation was strictly controlled (Liu 2000).

Walder (1983) suggested that the Danwei system had two ways to control individuals: organized dependence and principled particularism (Sun 1996; Bian 2010). In prereform China (before 1978), an urban resident's social welfare services were provided mainly through their employment with a state-owned enterprise (commonly known as a work unit). Along with promises of lifelong employment, urban people had for the most part enjoyed secure lifetime medical and retirement benefits, housing, and education. Participants in the system were highly dependent on the state because it controlled all resources. This resulted in a vertical sanctuary-dependency relation. Horizontally, the Danwei system dissolved the organization of the society and created social segregation. This means citizens were reluctant to cooperate with others to achieve their common interests. Consequently, society lacked a horizontal social network to underpin collaboration among citizens, to say nothing of activism in public affairs (Putnam 2000).

Urban governance was also vertical and relied on a hierarchical district/subdistrict residents' committee management system. Urban residents' committees were established throughout the country beginning in 1958 and were designed to provide residential autonomy. However, in actual operation, the committees deviated from this purpose. The subdistricts became the representative organizations of the district government, and residents' committee became the practical representative organization of the subdistrict. Residents' committees were then extended to become extensions of government management, which also harnessed the willingness and ability of residents into participating in public affairs.

The situation in rural areas resembled those in urban China. People's communes gathered all the resources available in their area and redistributed resources equally to each member. Members were led to participate in collective life according to people's commune's regulations, which limited the possibility of other collective activities.

In general, urban China's administrative system resembled an upside-down pyramid. The upper government controlled almost all socioeconomic resources, made decisions, and pushed forward urban development in a "command–obedience" pattern. The participation mode at this time was state mobilization. The state mobilized citizens to participate in policymaking through its local branches. Citizens participated through a strictly controlled and limited channel and were guided to participate by the state. Needless to say, citizen power was quite low during this period. Limited access to civil participation added to state supremacy, further harming the subjectivity of citizens.

2.2   The Reform Era

After China embarked on its market-oriented reforms, large numbers of nonstate-owned enterprises were set up. Likewise, state-owned enterprises became more independent, market-oriented entities. These enterprises gradually broke away from the vertical administrative system, and a market system gradually took its place. Marketization led to the collapse of the "Unit Society" of the Danwei system, thereby breaking the link between workplace and residence in urban China. Work units were unburdened of their former social responsibilities, most importantly the responsibility to provide social security and housing (Cao and Chen 1997).

With economic reform and the collapse of the "Unit Society," demands for autonomy for residents' committees grew out of the expansion of social affairs. In 1989, the National People's Congress enacted "The Law of the Residents' Committee in People's Republic of China," which aimed to guarantee the autonomy of residents' committees. Democratic elections and other deliberative institutions in urban areas transformed residents' committees from government representatives to autonomic organizations. Since then, the local urban governance pattern has been shifting from a vertical administrative pattern toward a civil society-oriented horizontal pattern.

In rural China, with the collapse of the people's communes in the late 1970s, the political structure of the village became institutionally hollow. People's communes were quickly replaced by a grassroots autonomic organization—the villager committee. The villager committee concept was founded to fill the vacuum left by the dissolution of the people's communes. However, what followed the free-to-tax reform in rural China was awakening of the link between the local government and grassroots autonomic organizations. Moreover, villager committees surpassed the residents' committees in becoming relatively more autonomic and democratic institutions by holding direct elections that attracted broad participation. As a result, participatory democracy has been booming in rural China. Villagers have been effectively motivated to participate in public affairs and encouraged to discuss and debate during village deliberations.

Even though decentralization and marketization have weakened the power of the state at the local level, it is a mistake to interpret this as the state in retreat. In response to the broken link between the resident and workplace and between villager and commune, the Chinese government has filled the vacuum by strengthening its grassroots branches (Lin and Ma 2000). The state is still able to manage local affairs through grassroots government agencies, such as street offices (jiedaoban) and residents' committees. This explains why residents' committees still locate themselves inside the administrative "district–subdistrict–resident committee" system; its main function is to carry out government tasks. Therefore, even if grassroots autonomy is designed and stipulated by law, the level of autonomy is still under the control of the government. Participation in China remains politically sensitive and monitored and guided by formal institutions.

Nevertheless, compared to its planned economy years, China's political environment has improved. Citizens have diverse avenues and free environments to participate. With marketization, and the awakening of modernity and subjectivity, China's increasing occupational diversification, population mobility, and the improving quality of life, have led to an upsurge of diversified societal needs. However, the traditional vertical government system had already proven itself incapable of satisfying those needs. Thus, a new carrier—the social organization—was invented to take these expansive social functions under consideration after economic reform.

Social reform will be possible when large numbers of social organizations are built up. Social organizations have more resources, such as time, personnel, and budget, to solve different social problems and to deal with social affairs. As fast growing social forces, social organizations are crucial for better governance. They offer avenues for citizens to participate in various public affairs and their development helps cultivate a sense of citizenship in contemporary China.

To conclude, civil participation since China's reform and opening-up now involves all aspects of social forces in both the traditional and the expanded sense, and is quite different from the pre-1980 totalitarian system that preceded it. First, the new pattern emphasizes plural social strengths and counters an almighty government. Second, China's governance pattern has changed from the "command–obedience" model to a "consultative interaction" model. Third, forces from civil society have been awakened and emphasized in political discourses. Undoubtedly, China has made significant progress in promoting civil participation.

3   CONTROVERSIAL TOPICS IN THE STUDY OF CHINA'S CITIZEN PARTICIPATION

Studies of China's citizen participation are numerous. It is one of the most popular research themes in studies of China, and it attracts the attention of various scholars from different disciplines. Among many others, there are two burgeoning works on China's citizen participation in recent years: contentious politics and deliberative democracy. These two topics represent the most popular noninstitutional participation avenue and institutional participation avenue, respectively. Moreover, they are miniature versions of the development of participatory citizenship. We introduce the political origins of these two studies and their current contributions toward a better understanding of citizen participation in China.

3.1   Contentious Politics in China

China's contentious politics are the most studied research field of citizen participation for both foreign and domestic scholars. Contentious politics include social rebellion, social movements, collective actions, and other activities based on mass citizen mobilization. Unlike the previously mentioned village deliberation, this is a noninstitutionalized participation pathway, one that is widely taken by peasants and residents of both rural and urban China. Examples include homeowners' protests, worker resistance, peasants' resistance, appeals to higher authorities for help (shangfang), and the not in my backyard (NIMBY) movement; all of these mass actions are widely discussed and controversial political topics (Shi 2005; Chen 2006; Wang 2011; Zhang 2005; Cai et al. 2009; Pan et al. 2010; Cai 2008).

Many scholars have studied the peasant resistance movements in recent years (O'Brien 1996; O'Brien and Li 1999, 2006; Li and O'Brien 1999; Yu 2004; Ying 2001; Chen 2003; Li 2010; Cai 2006; Zhou 1993). The various reforms focused on rural China have generated numerous conflicts in society. For instance, the fiscal reform and the resulting financial burdens on peasants have led to the deprivation of rights and, thus, caused continual and widespread resistance. Li and O'Brien (1996) suggested that this type of resistance is characterized by both contention and participation. In other words, the resistance of peasants, which consists of demanding reasonable welfare, lower economic burdens, protection of collective assets, and transparency in their village's public affairs indicates the awakening of civil rights in rural China.

It is also suggested that peasants are more likely to defend their rights following the logic of rightful resistance (struggle by law) when they feel deprived. Rightful resistance is a semi-institutionalized avenue of participation (Yu 2004). Among the many ways of rightful resistance, shangfang is still the most frequently used way for peasants to defend their legal rights. However, the practices of peasants have been given many new meanings as a result of their direct actions, such as the emerging subjectivity. Besides shangfang, advocacy, collective action, refusal to pay taxes and fees, and lawsuits are also common ways for peasants to resist what they believe to be unfair treatment. Despite the numerous disturbances this movement has inspired, thus far they have not seriously disrupted social order in China because most of these disturbances have been short-lived and nonviolent. They seldom use violence because doing so may justify a local government's repression and increase citizen risk (Cai 2008).

Since the beginning of economic and social reforms in 1978, urban China has witnessed significant popular resistance from different groups of people. The impact of China's reforms on community participation has generated great interest among scholars. Based on our understanding, the dynamics of resistance in urban areas should be understood in relation to the different reforms urban China has experienced. For instance, worker resistance was prevalent in the 1980s (Cai 2002). This could be attributed to the reform of state-owned enterprises (SOEs), which resulted in massive layoffs. This group of people felt deprived, so they organized to defend their rights collectively.

Nevertheless, the most typical citizen's resistance in urban China in recent years is the collective action of households. The dissolution of employment units, housing commodification, and increasing labor mobility have forced the dissolution of Danwei communities and greatly strained kinship networks. The new concepts of community and community-based services were introduced and adopted in the mid-1980s; before then, community participation in China typically involved limited roles for community members in programs initiated by the government and led by the Communist Party (Bray 2006). Community members consequently lacked the necessary motivation and organizational infrastructure to participate in community decision-making processes or local politics.

As the housing commodification process deepened in the middle of the 1990s, a new community model, created by households living in commercial housing developments and organized according to geographical propinquity, has continued to emerge as an alternative to the prereform provision of social welfare and urban service delivery (Xu and Chow 2006). The new types of communities and the new community service programs require considerable involvement from local residents for financing services, strengthening the effectiveness of service delivery and meeting the increasing welfare needs of urban citizens (Ge and Li 2012).

In this new circumstance, residents become more willing to participate in community collective action to address their own community. This creates space for the numerous homeowners' collective protests in recent years. Many scholars have been studying homeowners' protests which entail many interesting stories about local participation (He 2005, 2007, 2013). These collective actions are their attempts to protect their living environment and assets, implicating their rights to live and own property.

The most aggressive actions of homeowners may be the NIMBY movement organized to prevent polluting facilities from being locally established. As an emerging social phenomenon, homeowners' protests are the structural products of urbanization and housing commodification. They bring with them the opportunity to overturn residential indifference to local governance. People are more inclined to participate in the communities where they live.

The numerous disturbances of these direct actions have thus far not seriously disrupted the social order in China because most of these disturbances have been short-lived and nonviolent. None of these contentious political actions are antiauthoritarian but rather provide a pathway for citizens to achieve civil rights. These protests are all territorialized and organized in pursuing proper rights, during which citizenship consciousness is also cultivated. Citizenship is achieved through the protection of their civil rights; in this case, their right to own property. But it is also achieved through the practice of their political rights. Therefore, contentious politics are a way for Chinese citizens to realize their citizenship.

3.2   Democratic Deliberation in China

As more and more people defend their rights through the noninstitutionalized pathways, such as resistance, protest, and rebellion, the government is making great efforts to establish institutionalized participation pathways at the same time to reduce social protest and strengthen the government's ruling capacities. It is believed that people choose a noninstitutionalized pathway because they believe they are being ignored. As more and more citizens became eager for the chance to voice their preferences and express their opinions, democratic deliberation that fits in the socialist tradition of political participation was introduced to both rural and urban China in the early 1990s (He 2004).

Democratic deliberation aims to inspire the masses to exert influence on policymaking through public discussion. Deliberation is formal discussion and debate with the purpose of producing thoughtful, reasonable, and well-informed public opinions (Davies and Chandler 2011). Many deliberative, participatory, and consultative institutions have been established in China, such as the consultative and deliberative meetings, citizen evaluation meetings, consensus conferences, urban and village representative assemblies, citizen forums, public hearing, and so on. The Chinese consultative meeting or public hearing is designed to get people's support for local projects and to be a forum for people's opinions. The popular conciliation or mediation meeting is designed to solve various local problems and conflicts. As we see it, these deliberative avenues are created to dispel the social protests through institutional design, such as equal discussion, open access, reason-giving, and other-regarding (Cohen 1997; Young 2000; Dahlberg 2004; Habermas 2006).

In recent years, deliberative democracy has become increasingly significant. The Chinese government has made democratizing public decision-making through deliberation more of a priority, because legitimacy can be boosted through opinion formation based on collective deliberation. In the recently hosted 19th China's National People's Congress, President Xi has raised its profile even further. Since first being mentioned in the 18th China's National

People's Congress, deliberative democracy has been highly emphasized ever since, which is as significant as democratic election and democratic decision-making. Current discussions of deliberative democracy in China are cutting edge issues and meaningful in explaining the development of Chinese citizen participation. As deliberative democracy gradually increases in scope, it is becoming unavoidable in China. Introducing deliberative democracy incrementally can facilitate China's democratization process; it enables the Chinese people to adjust themselves to democracy and learn it gradually (Zhou 2012).

Many scholars have captured this rising trend in their studies of deliberative participation in China. Professor Baogang He is the most outstanding one. He is dedicated to the study of deliberative institutional experiments in rural China. There have been various forms of experimental deliberation at the local level in China, including public hearings, mediation meetings, and deliberative polling. He and Thøgersen (2010) studied one of the most famous pioneering experiments—the deliberative poll in Zeguo Town, Zhejiang Province. In their study, not only did the poll incorporate the ideals of deliberative democracy theory, such as inclusiveness and equality, but it also showed that deliberative democracy does exist in China, a place where deliberative democracy was thought to be unlikely to happen (Fishkin et al. 2010).

The establishment of participatory and deliberative institutions, such as village representative assemblies, has changed the structure of village politics in China. During those assemblies, meetings, hearings, and forums, major decisions on village affairs such as village collective assets and budgets are discussed, debated, and deliberated upon by village representatives. Villagers are willing to participate since being involved in the decision-making process can guarantee them the empowered status that will allow them to protect their own interests. It seems that there is a tendency for the village democratic process to shift from village election to village deliberation (He 2014). The transformation of village politics is worth further, careful study. On the other side, local urban communities have also developed a number of new participatory and deliberative institutions. However, village deliberation has received more attention because it has made greater progress and become transformative.

4   The Status Quo of Legal Citizen Participation in China: A Critical Perspective

In the previous section, we suggested that the noninstitutionalized avenues of participation have been frequently chosen by underprivileged citizens. This phenomenon aroused our attention because if there were better alternatives, they would have resolved their problems within the legal system as contentious politics are always time consuming and sophisticated. So why is legal participation so much more difficult than the contentious options? Why are so many citizens defending their rights through collective action? In answering these questions, we clarify the legalized democratic participation system in China and conclude scholars' criticisms towards current system.

4.1 Overall Description on the Institutionalized Participation Avenues in China

Currently, the four major, legal democratic institutions are: the system of people's congresses, the Chinese political party system, the system of national regional autonomy, and the system of self-governance at the grassroots level. Apart from these, citizens also have many other political rights, such as freedom of speech, association, assembly, and procession. These political rights are all stipulated in the Chinese constitution. Given all this, how do we comprehend the legal political participation rights of Chinese citizens in terms of these regulations?

First, four democratic institutions legalize the civil rights of citizens to participate in the decision-making processes. They are the people's congress system, the national regional autonomy system, the system of multiparty cooperation and political consultations, and the system of grassroots autonomy. The system of people's congress undertakes representative democracy. Members are representatives elected by citizens to express their voices. People's congresses at all levels are meant to involve civic participation in the decision-making process. The system of multiparty cooperation and political consultations gives citizens the freedom to choose to join an approved political party. Parties may express their opinions and influence decision-making through participating in the Chinese people's political consultative conference. After deliberation, opinions from different parties will be seriously considered by the governing party. As for the Chinese grassroots autonomy system, it is meant to be a retreat of state power from local governance. Space is left for residents or villagers to decide their own public affairs through various activities, such as public hearing, deliberative polling, and democratic meeting.

Second, citizens can exercise their civil rights and participate in public affairs to pursue their common interests through joining political parties, associations, or assemblies. In addition, participation includes public supervision of public sectors by civil society. This is a legal avenue of participation. However, it is not intended to change decision-making or pursue public interests. It is meant instead to be an appeal for responsible officials and just governance. The structure of the legal participation institutions is displayed in Fig. 19.1.

4.2 The Existing Problems of the Legal Participation Avenues

Chinese scholars have suggested, and widely discussed, three main problems with institutionalized participation in China today: the representation in local people's congress (LPC), the mobilization of grassroots China, and the reform of the social organization system.

First, the representation of LPC. Limited civil participation adds to state supremacy. Representation provides a better breeding ground for meaningful citizen participation. As is well known, the LPC is a democratic institution, carrying out legislative activities and practicing supervision on public organiza-

Fig. 19.1 The structure of legal participation avenues

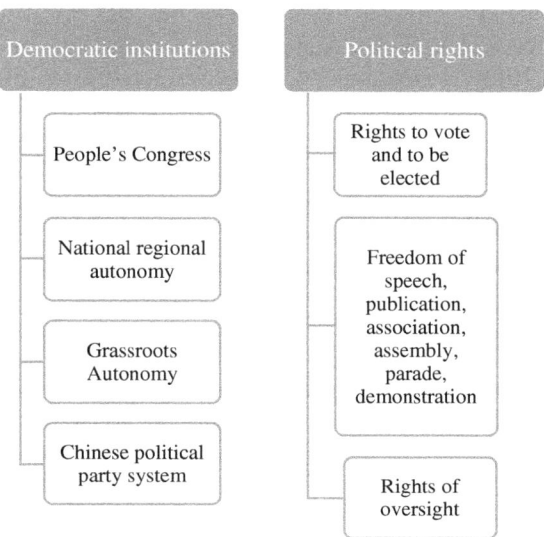

tions through public participation. O'Brien (2009) suggests that the increasing role of LPCs in lawmaking and supervising governmental organizations "has less to do with responsiveness and changing state-society relations and more to do with state-building, restructuring bureaucratic ties, and making Party rule predictable and effective." Nevertheless, there are supposedly three major roles for the LPCs. Apart from lawmaking and oversight, representation constitutes another significant function of the LPC. However, the reality is that it functions selectively. It emphasizes scientific decision-making and oversight rather than representation of public interests. Little attention is devoted to elections, deputy-constituent ties, and speaking out at plenary sessions (O'Brien 2009).

A representative government requires institutional machinery to allow constituents to express their wishes (Hanna 1967). In today's China, the linkage between popular preferences, deputy behavior, and policymaking is tenuous. Local leaders retain a tight grip on LPC elections and there is "minimal electoral connection between the elected and those who elect them" (Xia 2007). The LPC selection system has been criticized for unequally incorporating various social groups into lawmaking and a few underprivileged groups are lumped together with a far larger number of elite groups. This unequal access to the LPC negates the function of the LPC in this area because the interests of society, as a whole, are not reliably taken into account.

Some deputies in higher-level congresses are not even aware of being candidates of LPC until they read about their "election" in the newspaper (Brantly 1982). Many members regard selection as a favor that should be repaid by agreeability rather than by the spirited advocacy of constituent interests (Derleth and Koldyk 2012). LPCs have become places where two interests intersect: the "central" interests represented by the local Communist party committee and the "local" interests represented by the local people's congress delegates. Nevertheless, the state still penetrates into and controls LPCs. As Manion (2008) concluded: "Congresses acted as 'rubber stamps,' ineffectual in the face of powerful Party committees, as well as government institutions."

As a matter of fact, in contemporary grassroots China, delegates of LPCs are required to set up hotlines and reception days and to hold regular meetings with constituents to listen to their opinions. Through these channels, deputies learn of and address requests of the public. Consequently, the electoral ties are becoming closer and public discontents and concerns are being aired. However, the reasons for holding these events are to uncover social discontent and sound an alarm before an explosion occurs (Cho 2008).

To conclude, without institutional mechanisms to ensure it, representation rests on public-spirited members and leadership forbearance and, in a fundamentally unrepresentative system, is precarious, inexact, and occasional.

Second, mobilization of grassroots China. Since the reform and opening-up, urban reform overturned the system that aimed to fix citizens in their Danwei and their specific living places. Rural reform released peasants from their lands in the villages, which facilitated the rural to urban migration. With the collapse of the Danwei system and deepening urbanization, individuals were given larger mobility, including occupational mobility, geographical mobility, and social mobility.

Under these circumstances, a large number of peasants flooded into cities and the number of citizens migrating from cities to cities also surged. Consequently, in order to expand the coverage of grassroots public service, many villages were annexed or withdrawn so as to create a larger administrative village. At the same time, urban areas also promoted the annexation of residents' committees in order to create larger community committees. Obviously, in both urban and rural China, the grassroots autonomic organizations are integrated and condensed. Each grassroots autonomic organization is expected to cover a large geographical area. However, the expanded scope of governance weakened the ties between the committee and the villagers or residents, which also weakened the autonomic organizations' abilities to mobilize and manage public affairs.

Moreover, housing commercialization made housing a product and promoted buying and selling behaviors in the housing market. Thus, residents in a community have higher mobility, and society has shifted from an acquaintance society to a stranger society (Li 2013). Communities are fragmented, comprising many separate cells. Hence, residents become indifferent to public affairs and are reluctant to participate in pursuit of public interests. It seems that after the dissolution of the Danwei, grassroots China still lacks a regime to mobilize residents and promote community participation.

Finally, there has been an administrative involution of grassroots self-governance (Hu 2005; He 2004). Residents' committees and villager committees are still governmental branches extended into grassroots governance. They are still under the command of Jiedaoban, the detached office of the administrative authorities. The essence of autonomy has not yet been put in the right place. Hence, involution results in less citizen participation in grassroots autonomic governance because the public is aware that they are not yet the masters of local affairs. Hence, more and more homeowners and villagers choose to take part in collective actions to achieve their requirements. All these have made the mobilization in grassroots China an urgent but tough task for current authorities.

Third, reform of the social organization system. Not until the 6th Plenary Session of the 16th CPC Central Committee in 2006 was the concept of "social group" officially suggested, thus making the reform of the social organization system both a politically and academically significant topic. Alongside China's reform and opening-up, the central government has realized that society is actually an important partner in improving governance. In response, the government has instituted a system of legal registration to manage, and hopefully control, Chinese social organizations. Following the government's rhetorical appeal for "small state, big society," the registration thresholds and conditions have been lessened in order to promote the development of social organizations to fill gaps left by the retreat of government. Nongovernmental organizations broadened in both number and scope right after the policies were loosened. Compared to government, social organizations are the better organizations to offer public services because they are closer to the public, have lower operating costs, and are more capable of providing diversified services that citizens actually want.

The development of social organizations could advance social empowerment and reshape the state-society relationship so as to achieve better governance. However, the common difficulty faced by social organizations is that they still depend on governments in a noninstitutional way. Ge and Li (2012) suggested that even though Chinese social organizations have a certain degree of autonomy, they are still dependent on the government in informal ways, for instance, fund-raising, goal setting, and leader selection.

First, governments at different levels could help social organizations through indirect financial support, such as by offering free offices or human resources and by paying for part of staff salaries. Apart from this, government could also help social organizations to set up relations with enterprises so that enterprises could donate and sponsor the activities of these social organizations.

Second, social organizations are encouraged by the government because they are expected to fill in the gaps left by governmental functional transformation in China. Therefore, before a social organization matures, it is given a specific goal that meets the managerial needs of the government. Governments have taken a significant role in the birth, operation, and development of social organizations.

Third, the Chinese government will also dispatch the "appropriate" people into relatively large social organizations. These people are closely related to government officials and familiar with government affairs, thus making them the representatives of the governments' intentions in the social sector. By helping social organizations take over the transferred functions and exerting influence on their daily operations, governments become the actual leader of the social organizations (Tang and Ma 2011).

In recent decades, China has made important progress in promoting civil participation. However, participation in China remains politically sensitive and is monitored and guided by formal institutions. Admittedly, social organizations are facing a more flexible policy environment with lower registration thresholds and more preferential policies. However, the leading role of the government has never faded away in the social sector. Social organizations in China are prone to depending on government rather than making decisions on their own. Hence, their participation in public affairs is actually restricted by many factors, for instance, limited funds and resources, lack of networks, and coercive appointments.

5   CITIZEN ACTION AND GOOD GOVERNANCE

The last part of this chapter describes citizen action in China, as well as its relationship to good governance. Chinese governments have long realized that they urgently need to boost their legitimacy by improving their relationship with citizens, and they have made great efforts to promote deliberative participation at local levels. Chinese citizens have more options now than at any time previously to express their demands.

As shown in Fig. 19.2, using Arnstein's eight-rung ladder for levels of participation and Plummer and Taylor's (2004) ladder of community participation in China (left side) as a guide, we have reinterpreted these models in order to account for China's local participation context (right side). Our model takes into consideration Chinese characteristics and displays the different levels of participation in local China.

However, as was demonstrated in the previous section, the effect of institutionalized participation avenues on promoting citizen participation is still much less than expected.

Even though governments at all levels encourage liberal and legal participation through various supportive policies, they still control citizen participation.

Citizen control	Initiative/self-governance
Delegated power	Decision making
Partnership	Deliberation and debate
Placation	Expression
Consultation	Attendance
Informing	Notification
Therapy	×
Manipulation	×
Arnstein's (1969) ladder of citizen participation	**Ladder of local participation in China**

Fig. 19.2   Participation in China

The most common way of managing and controlling it is exerting influence in noninstitutionalized ways. Examples include appointing people for certain positions, offering financial support, informing a narrower group of people deliberately or making the participatory procedures unduly complex. These noninstitutional interferences harness both the scope and quality of citizen participation in China.

For another, as many scholars have argued, the avenues for legal participation in China are designed as specific mechanisms to co-opt and manage key players. Institutions such as LPCs are merely a tool of cooptation by the authoritarian regime, through which social discontent could be dissolved within the institutional routine without destroying the social harmony and threatening governmental authority.

O'Brien (2009) argued that the institutionalization of the people's congress system did not bring liberalization, but instead brought rationalization and inclusion. Rationalization helped improve one-party rule by "legalizing political power and circumscribing the authority of individual leaders." Inclusion helped the regime to "preempt political challenges and protect party rule" by expanding the regime's influence on various forces in the society and the market.

Rationalization and inclusion have severely limited the effect of citizen participation as a way for normal citizens to promote policy change. This explains why there are more and more people choosing to fight for their rights through collective actions or even violent protests. This disorder in society is clearly the result of a lack of effective and efficient legal participation avenues and the misplacement of government in the state-society relationship. Furthermore, the theory of citizenship acknowledges that the public has the right to be proactively involved in a meaningful way in the decision-making process rather than being part of empty ritual participation. Governments are supposed to help citizens to express themselves rather than control and direct policy changes. Therefore, promoting authentic and effective citizen participation is crucial for the Chinese government in its pursuit of good governance and building a harmonious society.

As Arnstein (1969, p. 216) stated, as society becomes more complex and modernized, and people become more citizenship conscious, authentic participation will become a requirement for successful implementation of government policies. In considering good governance, decision-making processes are required to be participatory, consensus oriented, accountable, transparent, responsive, equitable and inclusive, effective and efficient, and obedient to the rule of law. Participation is highly emphasized in the good governance model (see Fig. 19.3). It is assumed that a society moving up Arnstein's ladder of citizen participation is progressing toward a better governance (Enserink and Koppenjan 2007). Citizen participation is considered to be the cornerstone of good governance (Enserink et al. 2007). It is the process through which citizens and stakeholders influence and share control over priority setting, policymaking, resource allocations, and access to public goods and services (World Bank Group 2005).

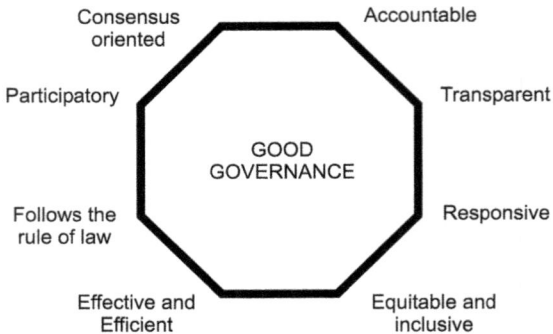

Fig. 19.3 The eight dimensions of good governance (UNESCAP 2005)

Empty, ritualized participation will no longer be accepted by China's awakening citizens. Determining how to involve citizens in the decision-making process is now the crucial question for reaching good governance.

Based on our understanding, Chinese citizen participation should not be merely regarded as a mechanism to promote efficient decision-making, nor should it be merely regarded as a channel to convey public opinions. Instead, citizen participation is also practiced as a form of citizenship consciousness in which consensus is achieved through debates and deliberations (He 2016). The Chinese government should optimize its participation institutions, enlarge participatory access, and make citizens better informed before the decision-making process begins. At the same time, society must be empowered and government must retreat thoroughly from specific sectors and play the role of ombudsmen instead of taking the lead in local governance.

REFERENCES

Arnstein, S. 1969. A ladder of public participation. *Journal of the American Institute of Planners* 35(4), July, 216–224.

Bian, Yanjie. 2010. Relational sociology and other cognate discipline (Guanxi Shehuixue Ji Qi Xueke Diwei).

Brantly Womack. March 1982. The 1980 County-Level Elections in China: Experiment in Democratic Modernization. *Asian Survey* 22(3): 261–277.

Bray, D. 2006. Building 'community': New strategies of governance in urban China. *Economy and Society* 35(4): 530–549.

Cai, Y. 2002. Relaxing the constraints from above: Politics of privatizing public enterprises in China. *Asian Journal of Political Science* (10): 94–121.

Cai, Y. 2006. *State and Laid Off Workers in reform China*. London: Routledge.

Cai, Y. 2008. Power structures and regime resilience: contentious politics in China. *British Journal of Political Science* 38(3): 411–432.

Cai, H., Chaohai Li, and Jianhua Feng. 2009. The collective action of migrant workers—based on the research on enterprises in Pearl River Delta (Liyi Shousun Nongmingong Liyi Kangzheng Xingwei Yanjiu—Jiyu Zhusanjiao Qiye de Diaocha). *Journal of Sociology Study* (1).

Cao, J., and Z. Chen. 1997. *Stepping Outside the Ideal Castle: Research on the Unit in China (Zou Chu Li Xiang Cheng Bao: Zhong Guo Dan Wei Xian Xiang Yan Jiu)*. Shenzhen: Haitian Press.

Chen, Feng. 2003. Between the state and labour: The conflict of Chinese trade unions' double identity in market reform. *The China Quarterly* 176.

Chen, Yinfang. 2006. Action power and institutional limitation—the middle level in urban movement (Xingdongli Yu Zhidu Xianzhi—Dushi Yundong de Zhongchan Jieji). *Journal of Sociology Study* (4).

Cho, Y.N. 2008. *Local People's Congresses in China: Development and Transition*. New York: Cambridge University Press.

Cohen, J. 1997. *Deliberation and Democratic Legitimacy*. Cambridge, MA: MIT Press, pp. 67–91.

Dahlberg, L. 2004. Net-public sphere research: Beyond the first phase. *The Public* 11(1): 27–77, 2004, 29–30.

Davies, T., and R. Chandler. 2011. Online Deliberation Design: Choices, Criteria, and Evidence. In: *Democracy in Motion: Evaluating the Practice and Impact of Deliberative Civic Engagement*. Oxford University Press.

Derleth, J., and Koldyk, D.R. 2002. The district people's congresses and political reform in China. *Problems of Post Communism* 49(2).

Enserink, B., and J. Koppenjan. 2007. Public participation in China: sustainable urbanization and governance. *Management of Environmental Quality: An International Journal* 18(4): 459–474.

Enserink, B., M. Patel, N. Kranz, and J. Maestu. 2007. Cultural factors as co-determinants of participation in river basin management. *Ecology and Society* 12(2): 24. [online] URL: http://www.ecologyandsociety.org/vol12/iss2/art24/.

Feng, S. 2006. Danwei segregation and collective contention (Dan Wei Fen Ge Yu Ji Ti Kang Zheng). *Journal of Sociology Study* (3): 98–134.

Fishkin, J., Baogang He, Robert C. Luskin, and Alice Siu. 2010. Deliberative democracy in an unlikely place: Deliberative polling in China. *British Journal of Political Science* 40(2): 435–444.

Habermas, J. 2006. Towards a United States of Europe. Translated excerpt from Bruno Kreisky Prize Lecture. March 9. Available at: http://www.signandsight.com/features/676.html.

Hanna F. Pitkin. 1967. *The Concept of Representation*. Berkeley: University of California Press, pp. 221–223.

He, B. 2004. Participatory and Deliberative Institutions in China. In: Collection of the Essays Presented at the International Conference on Deliberative Democracy and Chinese Practice of Participatory and Deliberative Institutions. Zhongguo she hui ke xue chu ban she. Beijing, China, pp. 92–108.

He, Y. 2004. The involution of Chinese urban grassroots autonomic organizations and its formation (Zhongguo Chengshi Jiceng Zizhi Zuzhi de Neijuanhua jiqi Chengyin). *Journal of Sun Yat-sen University* (2).

He, B. 2007. *Rural Democracy in China*. New York: Palgrave/Macmillan, pp. 96–97.

He, B. 2014. From village election to village deliberation in rural China: Case study of a deliberative democracy experiment. *Journal of Chinese Political Science/Association of Chinese Political Studies* 19: 133–150.

He, Y. 2016. Revolution without change: The limitation of Chinese local administrative reform (Wu Biange De Biange: Zhongguo Difang Xingzheng Gaige De Xiandu). *Journal of Xuehai* (1): 34–43.

He, B., and S. Thøgersen. 2010. Giving the people a voice? Experiments with consultative authoritarian institutions in China. *Journal of Contemporary China* 19(66): 675–692.

Hu, W. 2005. The reform and reflection on the urban grassroots autonomy institution since late 1990s (20 Shiji 90 Niandai Houqi Yilai Chengshi Jiceng Zizhi Zhidu de Biange yu Fansi). *Journal of Wuhan University* (3).

Jia, X. 2007. An analysis of NGO Avenues for civil participation in China. *Social Sciences in China*. Special issues NGOs and social transition in China.

Li, L. 2010. Rights consciousness and rules consciousness in contemporary China. *The China Journal* 64.

Li, P. 2013. The reform and future of social organization system (Woguo Shehui Zuzhi Tizhi de Gaige he Weilai). *Journal of Sociology* (2).

Li, L., and K.J. O'Brien. 1996. Villagers and popular resistance in contemporary China. *Modern China* 22(1).

Li, L. and K.J. O'Brien. 1999. *The Struggle over Village Elections: The Paradox of China's Post-Mao Reforms*. Harvard University Press, pp. 129–144, 382–389.

Lin, S., and Y. Ma. 2000. *Community Organization and Residents Committee Construction (She Qu Zu Zhi Yu Ju Wei Hui Jian She)*. Shanghai: Shanghai University Press.

Liu, J. 2000. *Unit China: Individual, Organization and Government During Social Reconstruction* (Dan Wei Zhong Guo: She Hui Tiao Kong Ti Xi Chong Gou Zhong De Ge Ren, Zu Zhi He Guo Jia). Taijin: Renmin Press.

O'Brien, K.J., and L. Li. 2006. *Rightful Resistance in Rural China*. Cambridge: Cambridge University Press.

O'Brien, K. 1996. Rightful resistance. *World Politics* 49: 31–55.

O'Brien, K., and L. Li. 1999. Selective policy implementation in rural China. *Comparative Politics* 31: 167–186.

Pan, Y., H. Lu, and H. Zhang. 2010. The formalization of social class: The labor control and collective contention. *Open Times* (5).

Plummer, J., and J.G. Taylor. 2004. The characteristics of community participation in China. In: J. Plummer and J.G. Taylor (eds), *Community Participation in China, Issues and Processes for Capacity Building*. London/Sterling, VA: Earthscan.

Putnam, R.D. 2000. *Bowling Alone: The Collapse and Revival of American Community*. New York: Simon & Schuster.

Shi, F. 2005. Relation network, rightful contention and contemporary urban collective action in China (Guanxi Wangluo, Yi Fa Kangzheng He Zhongguo Chengshi Jiti Xingdong). *Journal of Xuehai* (3):1–27.

Sun Liping. 1996. Relation, social network and social structure (Guanxi, Shehui Guanxi yu Shehui Jiegou). *Journal of sociology study* (5):20–30.

Tang, W., and X. Ma. 2011. Non-political autonomy: Non-governmental organization's living strategy. *Zhejiang Social Sciences* (10).

UNESCAP. 2005. *What is good governance?* United Nations economic and social omission for Asia and the Pacific. Available at: http://www.unescap.org/pdd/prs/ProjectActivities/Ongoing/gg/governance.asp.

Verba, S., N. Nie, and K. Jae-on. 1978. *Participation and Political Equality: A Seven Nation Comparison*. Chicago, IL: University of Chicago Press, pp. 51–52.

Walder. 1983. Organized dependency and cultures of authority in Chinese industry. *Journal of Asian studies* 18(1).

Wang, J. 2011. Internet mobilization and collective contention of OEM workers (Hulianwang Yu Daigongchang Gongren Jiti Kangzheng). *Open Times* (11): 114–128.

World Bank Group. 2005. "*Poverty reduction, strategy formulation organizing participatory processes in the PRSP. What is participation and what role can it play in the PRSP?*" Available at: http://siteresources.worldbank.org/INTPCENG/1143240-1116506251485/20508873/Organizing+Partcipatory+Processes.pdf (accessed Jan 2012).

Xia, M. 2007. *The People's Congresses and Governance in China: Toward a Network Mode of Governance*. London: Routledge.

Xu, Q., and J. Chow. 2006. Urban community in China: Service, participation, and development. *International Journal of Social Welfare* 15(3): 198–208.

Ying, X. 2001. *Dahe Yimin Shangfang de Gushi (A Story of Migrants' Appeals in Dahe)*. Beijing: Sanlian Shudian.

Young, I.M. 2000. *Inclusion and Democracy*. Oxford: Oxford University Press.

Yu, J. 2004. An explanation on peasants' collective action. *Journal of Sociology* (2).

Zhang, L. 2005. Homeowners' collective action: The motivation and mobilisation. *Journal of Sociology Study* (6):1–39.

Zhou, X. 1993. Unorganized interests and collective action in Communist China. *American Sociological Review* 58(1).

Zhou, W. 2012. In search of deliberative democracy in China. *Journal of Public Deliberation* 8(1).

Zhou, Y., and X. Yang. 1999. *Unit Institution in China (Zhong Guo Dan Wei Zhi Du)*. Beijing: Chinese Economy Press.

CHAPTER 20

Selective Use of Political Opportunity: A Case of Environmental Protest in Rural China

Yanhua Deng and Jonathan Benney

1 Introduction

Political opportunity refers to the "dimensions of the political environment" within which movement participants evaluate how their collective action can achieve their goals (Tarrow 1994). The structure of political opportunity, as McAdam (1996, p. 27) has suggested, includes four major components: increasing or decreasing openness in institutionalized political systems, increasing or decreasing instability in the alignment of government elites, changing levels of elite support for collective action, and the capacity of the government to contain collective action.[1]

However, contentious actors may not perceive existing political opportunities or put them to use. The current research has identified three relevant situations: first, where existing political opportunities are clearly perceived and exploited by movement activists (e.g., McAdam 1982; Tarrow 1989; Costain 1992); second, where activists fail to perceive political opportunities which are in fact available (Meyer and Gamson 1996, p. 283; Sawyers and Meyer 1999);

---

[1] Furthermore, some scholars believe that the dimensions of political opportunity should also include "the transnational environment and the role of external actors." See Keck and Sikkink (1998) and Tarrow (2005).

Y. Deng
School of Social and Behavioral Sciences, Nanjing University, Nanjing, China

J. Benney (✉)
Monash University, Melbourne, VIC, Australia
e-mail: jonathan.benney@monash.edu

© The Author(s) 2019
J. Yu, S. Guo (eds.), *The Palgrave Handbook of Local Governance in Contemporary China*, https://doi.org/10.1007/978-981-13-2799-5_20

and finally, where activists stage collective action because they perceive an opportunity that does not in fact exist (Kurzman 1996; Goodwin et al. 1999).

In these three situations, researchers have generally assumed that the strategies of participants in collective action genuinely reflect their assessment of the current political opportunities and that the participants make use of all the political opportunities that present themselves. However, as this chapter argues, a contrasting situation can occur. In certain Chinese collective protests, the activists are fully aware that some of their perceived political opportunities are fake; however, instead of ignoring these opportunities, they act as if they are genuine.

Protest leaders do not equally value all political opportunities, either. They often select those with higher levels of operability. In China, this phenomenon has deeper institutional origins. In a hierarchical political system, different levels of government frequently have different, even contradictory, policy aims. The central government most values regime legitimacy and social stability (Cai 2010), whereas local governments attach more importance to regional economic development. Such differences of position can limit political opportunity for participants in collective action.[2] For example, in pursuing social stability, the central government may propose a policy that would be beneficial to a disadvantaged group, but local governments may be unwilling or unable to implement it. As a result, when political opportunities proposed by the central government reach local levels, they may be limited, modified, or even falsified, which is a process analogous to "leakage of authority" (Downs 1967; Tullock 1987; Cai 2010, p. 70).

All this suggests that, in situations where there is a complex political opportunity structure and different stakeholders with clashing interests, the best strategy for collective action is sometimes not the intuitive one, in which protesters simply make their fundamental demands clear to higher authorities. Rather, they frame their demands so that they are more closely aligned with the existing political opportunity structure than with their real grievance.[3] This leads to the counterintuitive situation where protesters "ask" for something that is not actually what they "want."

This phenomenon brings up the issue of "misframing,"[4] which has received almost no scholarly attention. As an exception, Suh (2001) explores worker resistance in democratizing Korea and identifies a discontinuity between the

---

[2] See Xie (2010). Other research demonstrates that different levels of government pursue their goals in different ways, which might affect the provision of opportunity to activists (Shi and Cai 2006; Shi 2005).

[3] Koopmans (2004) also observes that the "selection processes" of movement participants (i.e., their framing strategy and their choice of political opportunities) may "evolve" as a result of contact with factors, such as the influence of the media, which may not engage "directly" with the core concerns of the participants.

[4] This term builds upon the "frame analysis" paradigm developed by Goffman and Berger in *Frame Analysis* (1986).

factors that movement participants believed to have contributed to their protest outcomes and the factors that were really in action. He argues that this "misframing" of most participants (though some leaders were well aware of it) led to greater "movement vitality" in Korean white-collar labor movements. In contrast, this chapter analyses a case of more *conscious* misframing, where the activists deliberately engineered and exploited a discontinuity between their main concerns and the framing of their action.

2   THE CASE AND DATA SOURCES

The episode of environmental protest we examine took place in Huashui town, Dongyang county, Zhejiang province. The town was home to the Zhuxi Chemical Park, which had been under construction since 2001. By 2004, there were 13 enterprises operating there, most of which were factories emitting high levels of pollution.

The pollution from the Zhuxi Chemical Park was undeniably harmful to the villagers. It was said that in Huashui "the water was muddy, the mountains were dirty, the trees were dead, and crops no longer grew in the fields." According to the deputy town head, who oversaw industry and the environment, some of the chemicals produced by one particular enterprise stunted the growth of plants; some plants, once polluted, stopped growing at half their normal size (Interview, C18, June 29, 2007). A *Dongyang Daily* journalist reported: "Many plants basically rotted from the roots up. There were cabbages that looked like they were healthy, but if you pulled them up from the ground, you could see that the roots were rotten." The proportion of deformed fruit also increased significantly; it went from about 15%, a normal figure, to 40–50% (Interview, p. 9, May 27, 2007). Even worse, produce from Huashui developed a reputation of being "poisonous." One fruit-grower said: "It was almost impossible to sell fruit at the market. When buyers came, they'd ask: 'Where are you from?' If I replied 'Huashui town,' they'd reply, 'I can't eat that, it's poisoned!' We really had no way around it." (Interview, p. 9, May 27, 2007) The town government also admitted that the pollution from the Zhuxi Chemical Park had harmed the surrounding villagers. One of their investigation reports stated: "The three main emissions (gas, water, and industrial residue) from the Chemical Park have disproportionately damaged the health and agricultural production of the local residents. Villagers have been constantly complaining, particularly about the effect of the waste gases from the chemical park on grains, fruit, vegetables, and seedlings, which have led to reduced output or total crop failure" (Huashui Township Government 2004).

Accidents, such as pipeline ruptures, produced sudden increases in pollution, which aggrieved the Huashui villagers immensely. At 3 AM on October 17, 2004, a pipeline in one factory burst, releasing a large amount of noxious gas. Villagers nearby began to feel extremely unwell. One activist recorded the experience of that day: "The whole of Huaxi village was filled with a terrible stench. Everyone's eyes were extremely sore and constantly watering, as if ammonia gas had been released. There were old people at the scene who fainted, and many students on their way to school were crouching by the side of the road, the younger ones wailing and weeping. At the market, more than 500 villagers were gathered; you could hear their complaints and curses everywhere. All in all, the scene was too tragic to describe." (Diary, V11, November 17, 2004) One migrant worker whose child remained in Huaxi said: "When relatives told me that my child couldn't go to school, because he couldn't open his eyes due to the gas and was crying in pain, I felt like I'd been stabbed through the heart, and tears ran down my face."[5]

Facing such serious environmental grievances, Huashui villagers had intensively petitioned higher levels of government from April 2004 onwards, even traveling to Beijing twice, but with no results.[6] In March 2005, disgruntled residents resorted to more confrontational tactics. They put up a tent at the entrance to the chemical park and began a round-the-clock vigil. The tent survived several attempts by the authorities to dismantle it; after a few days there were 18 tents at the entrance. To repress the protest once and for all, at about 3 AM on April 10, the county leadership sent in more than 1500 local cadres and public security personnel to put an end to the encampment. During their efforts to remove the protesters, violence broke out and more than 100 officials or police officers and more than 200 villagers were injured; 68 government vehicles were also burned or damaged. Despite this incident, the protesters still refused to withdraw, and the number of tents grew to about 30, representing 22 villages. The spectacular protest ultimately triggered intervention from the central government,[7] and the local authorities were forced to close the chemical park to placate the contentious villagers. This case of environmental protest was a rare success in contemporary China.[8]

Hardly anyone doubted that Huashui villagers began to protest mainly because of their environmental suffering. However, their resistance, petitioning in particular, was framed more as a land-related protest. As the head of the branch of the Dongyang Bureau of Land and Resources in Huashui stated: "The villagers living in the vicinity of the chemical park are most concerned about problems of environmental protection. The air and water are polluted; the water is not potable, and plants will not grow. The villagers know that the factory cannot operate without their land, so they are demanding the land back."[9] During the 2005 tent encampment, protesters in Huaxi formulated an even more distinctly land-oriented frame of protest, which was shown by a widely circulated poster: "Give back our land, we want to survive; give back

---

[5] An Internet post retrieved by the first author.

[6] There was also a protest against anticipated pollution in October 2001 in the town (see Deng and Yang 2013).

[7] For a discussion of factors that trigger the central government to intervene in protests, and how this contributes to protest success, see Cai (2008).

[8] For more information on this case, see Deng and O'Brien (2013).

[9] An Internet post retrieved by the first author.

our land, we want to be healthy; give back our land, we want our offspring to prosper; give back our land, we want a clean environment." In this frame, "giving back our land" became an indirect approach to achieving the main goals of keeping the environment clean and maintaining the physical health of the town's inhabitants.

Why did Huashui villagers choose to focus on land-related claims? To answer this question, we must analyze the political opportunity structure that the Huashui protesters faced during the period of their resistance. We also have to explore why some opportunities became more important than others and how protesters chose from the various political opportunities at their disposal.

The discussion in this chapter draws on in-depth interviews and archival materials. The first author conducted four months of fieldwork in Huashui town in 2007 and 2008. She carried out 122 semi-structured interviews, with most arranged in a snowball fashion as one person put her in touch with the next. The interviewees ranged from ordinary villagers to protest leaders, village cadres, township cadres, and county officials. She also collected more than 1000 pages of written materials, including petition letters, leaflets, and posters penned by villagers; work diaries and reports written by local officials; official regulations; and meeting records.

3   POLITICAL OPPORTUNITIES: HARD AND SOFT

During the environmental dispute in Huashui, there were a number of political opportunities available to the villagers. Their choice to use particular opportunities, and consequently to frame their discontent in a particular way, was conscious and precise. The "hardness" or "softness" of these political opportunities was a key factor in determining which opportunities they selected, much more than the conceptual relevance of the opportunities to their dispute.

Some opportunities arose from the new central policy orientations (or at least labels) of "scientific development" (*kexue fazhan*) and "people first" (*yi ren wei ben*).[10] Such opportunities, however, are well known to be soft in China, and protesters usually do not take them seriously in practice. In the Huashui case, protest leaders only occasionally referred to the new political language. For example, in one petition letter, entitled "Please Save Us," the petitioners used the "people first" discourse to add legitimacy to their claim: "The Party Central Committee and the State Council have frequently reiterated that illegal use of land cannot be tolerated. You must put the people first, and you absolutely must not destroy the environment at the price of economic development. As General Secretary Hu Jintao has recently said: 'The government must

---

[10] One official from Huashui town, when reflecting on the incident, suggested: "In 2004, the villagers cleverly used the policies the government was advocating at the time: getting close to the people (*qinmin zhengce*), 'putting people first,' and 'scientific development.'"

function by the mandate of the people, empathize with the feelings of the people, and work for the well-being of the people.'"

Other forms of political opportunity arose from changes to environmental policy. From 2002 to 2005, several reforms relating to environmental protection were introduced in China. The most important one was the passing of the Environmental Impact Appraisal Law on October 28, 2002. The then vice-director of the State Environmental Protection Agency, Yue Pan, stated: "The significance of the law is particularly deep … for the first time the environmental rights and interests of Chinese citizens have been written down in law. The law stipulates that the masses have the right to know, to understand, and to supervise the public decision making that may affect their environment. It also signifies that anyone who does not allow the masses to participate in environmental public decision making is violating the law." (Pan 2004). In terms of environmental supervision, the movement known as the "environmental protection storm" (*huanbao fengbao*), which was initiated by the State Environmental Protection Agency and prevailed from late 2004 to early 2005, attracted the most attention. This "storm" was intended to demonstrate that the Environmental Impact Assessment Law was not meaningless in practical terms. As Yue Pan pointed out: "Many people regard the law as a rubber stamp, but I want to emphasize that it is not, and we need to make this clear" (Li 2005).

Naturally, however, the political opportunities arising from changes to environmental policy were very soft. They lacked operability because, as in similar cases, the environmental victims found it difficult to demonstrate the exact extent of the damage, and it was also difficult for them to prove that the pollution had caused that damage (Briggs 2005; van Rooij 2010). For example, considering the Environmental Impact Appraisal Law, Yue Pan once admitted: "Although the right to public participation in environmental supervision is affirmed in this law, there are no detailed regulations for the concrete conditions, means, or processes through which this participation can occur. That is to say, if people face a particular environmental problem, they do not know how to get involved" (Pan 2004). Of 22 petition letters filed by the Huashui villagers, none referred to the Environmental Impact Appraisal Law.[11] Furthermore, the villagers almost never used any other environmental regulations and laws. When accounts of environmental problems were provided in the petition letters, they mainly described the perceived physical harms created by pollution, and never quoted environmental laws to increase the legitimacy of their claims.

---

[11] Until the summer of 2007, of the villagers whom the author interviewed, there was only one activist who—because they had undertaken training in "methods of public participation and temporary measures for environmental impact assessment," provided by a Beijing NGO—knew that there was an Environmental Impact Assessment Law.

Changes to land policy also created political opportunities. In response to the mounting local conflicts caused by requisitioning land to build industrial parks or economic development zones,[12] the central government had issued orders to rectify land misuse from 2003 onwards. One of these regulations, the "Notice Concerning Concrete Standards and Policy Boundaries for the Cleanup and Rectification (*zhengdun*) of Economic Development Zones," jointly issued by several relevant ministries and commissions of the State Council on December 30, 2003, could have been considered a hard political opportunity. This notice stipulated: "All economic development zones established by county and lower levels of government must be cancelled without exception." The Zhejiang provincial government then promulgated a "Public Announcement Regarding the Cleanup and Rectification Scheme of Economic Development Zones (Parks)" and published it in the *Zhejiang Daily* on April 16, 2004, in which the Zhuxi Chemical Park was specifically listed to be canceled.

Compared to the environmental political opportunities, the Huashui activists considered that the opportunities arising from the changes to land policy were much more solid. The regulations for land policy were explicit, and villagers could easily identify violations themselves—unlike the process of environmental pollution appraisal, which required special skills and advanced equipment. It was precisely because the political opportunity created by land policy was hard and implementable that, as soon as they saw the notice in the *Zhejiang Daily*, two activists from Huashui town claimed that their opportunity to address environmental grievances had finally arrived (Interview, p. 3, July 17, 2007). Therefore, during the subsequent contention, they mainly used this type of political opportunity to legitimize their actions, a strategy that they called "pursuing environmental claims by seeking redress for land-related grievances" (*jie tudi wenti, zuo huanbao wenzhang*).

4   Leakage of Political Opportunity

Although the political opportunity arising from the changes to land policy was operable, it faced the problem of "leakage" and ultimately became less "hard." For a policy to be successfully implemented in China, according to Lieberthal (1997), it must satisfy three conditions: (1) high-level leaders recognize that

---

[12] The construction of industrial parks was (and perhaps still is) perceived to be able to improve the reputations and careers of local officials, and consequently all kinds of industrial parks and economic development zones had sprung up everywhere around the year of 2000. In the eastern coastal regions, economic development zones tended to be small and disorganized, and quite a few of these were not really used for development sake. At the same time, because the setup of industrial parks had involved the displacement of many farmers without adequate compensation and assistance with relocation, there were many related mass incidents. According to Chen Xiwen, director of the Central Rural Working Group, in the few years before 2006, mass incidents relating to rural land disputes made up approximately 50% of all rural mass incidents (see Chang 2007).

the policy is desirable; (2) they give the policy priority; and (3) lower levels of government have incentives to implement the policy. By these criteria, the land policies described above could have been implemented successfully. The central government had expressed the need for urgent rectification of the land market, and had repeatedly issued documents stipulating this. Supervisory groups were also dispatched across China to make investigational tours. Furthermore, so that the central government could reduce the burden of supervision, a selective incentive was formulated: if local governments were able to investigate and rectify cases of policy violation internally, they would receive only light penalties; but if they did not, and if the central government identified that there were remaining violations of land policy, the consequences would be harsh.

But for local governments, the Center's attempts to rectify the land market were little different from the incentive schemes of the Great Leap Forward—not realistically applicable. Had the central government's regulations been strictly followed, at least 65% of the industrial parks and economic developmental zones in Zhejiang province would have been canceled. Cancelation might have been possible in areas of land that were still undeveloped; however, in places where industrial parks were already operating and flourishing, it was nigh impossible. So, while the orientation of political discourse and policy implementation could be changed quickly at the central level, it was extremely difficult to create a similarly rapid U-turn in the local economy. Furthermore, local officials often avoided following central policies strictly, because they believed doing so would harm them. One leader in Huashui town suggested: "In China, if the policy asks you to walk, you actually have to fly; if the policy says you have to take one step, you must actually take three steps; and if the policy won't let you move, you have to sneak forward anyway" (Interview, C10, May 23, 2007). The local leaders believed that the parts of Zhejiang that were developing well had all been "disobedient." Under these circumstances, local governments became embroiled in a dilemma. On the one hand, the central land policy, with selective incentives to stimulate implementation, involved strict regulations; on the other hand, local governments were unable or unwilling to actually implement this policy.

Facing this dilemma, most local governments implemented the central land policy symbolically, dealing with cases of illegal land use only superficially.[13] Their goal was simple: making the Center believe that they had implemented the policy and carried out the "self-investigation and self-rectification" (*zicha zijiu*) of illegal land cases. Media reports suggested that whether local governments had done this was mainly demonstrated by whether or not they had

---

[13] From August 8 to September 19, 2003, ten supervision groups were sent to investigate the implementation of the central land policy across China. One investigator found: "What appeared to be vigorous internal investigation and rectification processes were actually quite worrisome. In my view, all local governments did this to take advantage of the regulation that conducting self-investigation and self-rectification would result in more lenient penalties, rather than aiming to genuinely improve the local land markets" (see Tang 2005).

reported on illegal land activities and punished relevant violators. For example, the conclusion that the "self-investigation and self-rectification" in Guangxi and Henan provinces had met the Center's requirements was mainly based on the observations of supervisors sent down by five ministries and commissions: "The Qinzhou city government [in Guangxi] had drawn up a 'Notice on Further Strengthening the Management of Land Use for Construction,' in which they had taken back the right to examine and approve the land used by the Qinzhou harbor economic development zone, as well as the right to supervise its planning. They had also cancelled the Qinzhou Datian Chemical Park. In Henan, the Jiyuan city government published the details of 114 illegal uses of land in the urban area in the news media. Particular emphasis was laid on investigating nine issues, such as commercial use of land by administrative units (*xingzheng shiye danwei*), illegal fencing off of collective land, and land transactions that were against laws and regulations. More than 50 cases of illegal use of state-owned land were set a time limit for rectification" (Tang 2005). The Zhejiang provincial government published its "Public Announcement Regarding the Cleanup and Rectification Scheme of Economic Development Zones (Parks)" in the *Zhejiang Daily* on April 16, 2004, which was also intended to show that local authorities had conducted "self-investigation and self-rectification."

The Dongyang county government, in which Huashui town was situated, and the Bureau of Land and Resources had also been requested to implement internal investigation and rectification. In fact, on October 16, 2003, six months before the promulgation of the Zhejiang provincial government's announcement, the county government had published a notice, which on the surface was intended to cancel the Zhuxi Chemical Park but in fact acted to change its name to "Huashui City and Town Planning Industrial Function Area" (*Huashui zhen chengzhen guihua gongye gongneng qu*). Thus, the Zhuxi Chemical Park had just had its identifying label changed, and the industries in the park continued as before. One Huashui town leader revealed: "After the land policy was tightened up, a county could only have one or two chemical parks, and at town level there could be none. However, Chinese people are smart! If we couldn't call it a chemical park, we would call it a function area. The higher-ups have policies, but the locals have counterstrategies (*shang you zhengce, xia you duice*). When the superiors came to inspect us, we could simply say that we had no chemical parks. The whole province responded with this strategy." (Interview, C10, May 23, 2007).

The ultimate aim of this symbolic implementation of the central policy was to make illegal land use legal. Achieving this goal required a series of administrative procedures. In a reflection on the "Huashui Incident," one local leader wrote: "To legalize the use of the land in the illegal industrial parks requires three conditions: first, the particular land use is consistent with the overall land use plan; second, it is consistent with the overall city plan; and third, there are appropriate legal penalties for the illegal use." Once the Dongyang county government proposed the name change for the Zhuxi Chemical Park, it had basically completed the first two steps, but this still left the question of legal penalties. Hence, on July 26, 2004, the county Bureau of Land and Resources issued 14 versions of a "Written Decision on Administrative Penalties for Illegal Land Use," for each of the companies in the Zhuxi Chemical Park. The penalties for each firm were (1) the confiscation of the buildings and other facilities that had been built on illegally occupied land and (2) a penalty of ¥15 for each square meter of illegally used land. The County Party committee further requested that "the requirements of the penalties be completed by August [2004]."[14]

As can be seen from the above, the outcome of the local government's policy implementation was that the central land policy had been changed into one that functioned in form only. Therefore, from the point of view of the Huashui protest leaders, the political opportunities that had arisen from the changes to land policy had effectively been reduced to "fake" ones by the local authorities. But this process also had an unexpected consequence. In order to make it look to the central government as if the process of internal investigation and rectification was happening, the local government had to call meetings in advance, deal with various opinions, and promote the outcomes of "self-investigation and self-rectification" in the media. This strategy satisfied the demands of the Center, but it also led many locals to develop an understanding of the central policy and objectively reinforced their perception that there were *genuine* opportunities arising from the land policy. For example, the two activists' belief that "our opportunity is here" was formed after the "Public Announcement Regarding the Cleanup and Rectification Scheme of Economic Development Zones (Parks)" was published in the *Zhejiang Daily* on April 16, 2004. But by that time, the process of rectifying the land market, which was organized by ministries and commissions of the State Council, was actually approaching its end. Consequently, the protesters' earlier sense of opportunity did not come directly from any particular notice or provision from the central government but rather from the local government's response to the central government's supervision. However, once the villagers discovered from the provincial announcement that the Zhuxi Chemical Park was to be canceled, they began to focus their attention on land policy, finding all the relevant documents issued by the State Council since 2003 and seizing the subsequent opportunities with increasing skill. For example, after the county Bureau of Land and Resources penalized the 13 firms in the Zhuxi Chemical Park on July 26, 2004, by August 9, one activist had already found out about these penalties, which were not publicly available, from a person inside the government system (Diary, V11, August 9, 2004). That is, once the actors had perceived a form of political opportunity with a high level of operability, they eagerly sought to discover other similar opportunities.

---

[14] Sourced from a reflection report on the Huashui incident written by a key county leader.

5   Fake Opportunities, Instrumental Exploitation

Faced with the leakage and limitation of political opportunities relating to changes in land policy, the Huashui protesters came to understand that these opportunities were essentially fake. According to a key activist's diary, at the time, the statements of some local cadres had led villagers to believe that their land was about to be expropriated. They did not expect that the legal penalties issued by the Dongyang Bureau of Land and Resources would really come into force. They assumed that the Bureau's written legal decisions were no more than "empty documents" (Interview, p. 3, June 11, 2007) with "a few casual penalties" (Interview, p. 1, June 8, 2007).

The petitioning experience also taught the Huashui protesters that the land-related political opportunities were symbolic and that the action taken by the Bureau of Land and Resources was only intended to legitimize the current use of the land. When activists from the town of Huashui went to consult the penalty documents at the Bureau on August 11, 2004, the deputy chief refused their request with the excuse that those documents had already been sent to higher levels (Interview, p. 1, June 8, 2007). They were directly told by a staff member of the Zhejiang Bureau of Land and Resources about the local government's real intention: "Once they have completed the penalties, they can just buy the land back. With some extra procedures, they can requisition it." (Diary, V11, November 16, 2004). The continuing expansion of the Zhuxi Chemical Park further convinced Huashui villagers that the local authorities' written decisions of legal penalties were nothing more than the prelude to making the park legal.[15]

While the Huashui protesters were well aware that the symbolic political opportunity provided by the local government was inherently fake, they grasped and promoted it vigorously. On August 11, 2004, several activists hurried to the Dongyang Bureau of Land and Resources to look at the penalty documents, but their request was refused by the deputy chief. One activist immediately called the office of the Zhejiang Bureau of Land and Resources, in front of the deputy chief, and reported what had happened. The official of the provincial bureau encouraged them to "use the law as a weapon" (Diary, V11, November 16, 2004) to solve their problem. On August 25, the Dongyang county Bureau of Land and Resources, having received many demands from Huashui villagers, went to the Zhuxi Chemical Park to prevent the firms from expanding their factories. To create even more pressure, the activist mentioned above telephoned the provincial Bureau of Land and Resources, again in the presence of the county bureau staff, upon which the provincial official once more urged him to use the law as a weapon, "to bring an administrative lawsuit"

---

[15] One petition letter suggested that after the written decisions of legal penalties were made by the Bureau of Land and Resources, the Zhuxi Chemical Park had not shrunk but was in fact gradually expanding. More than 100 buildings were constructed in the following two months.

(Diary, V11, August 25, 2004). The activist then also called the *People's Daily*, whose staff informed him that the county government's practice was "committing a crime in spite of a law-enforcement campaign" (*dingfeng zuo'an*). This strategy of keeping in constant contact with superior officials is a form of rightful resistance (O'Brien and Li 2006). In this mode of action, the Huashui protesters used modern communications, seeking advice from higher levels of authority in the presence of lower levels. This strategy creates a virtual space containing the three players—higher and lower bureaucratic levels, as well as petitioners—that may eliminate the possibility of collusion between different levels of government. Because the higher levels of government are restrained by political discourse and legal regulations, in this virtual space they must side with the activists and speak for them. With the support of higher levels of government, activists can become more determined in petitioning and may even claim legitimacy to use more radical direct action if local officials continue to disappoint them.

To obtain copies of all the written decisions made by the Dongyang Bureau of Land and Resources, the Huashui petitioners skillfully used the pressure that higher levels had applied to the local government. On October 29, 2004, after returning from petitioning in Beijing, the Huashui petitioners went to the Zhejiang Bureau of Land and Resources, and requested the penalty decisions, which the county office claimed had been "sent to higher levels." The staff said there were no such documents, and that they would need to return to the county office. Extremely disheartened, the activists said, "The Dongyang county government will certainly not give them to us." The provincial staff issued them a letter of introduction and told them that they might call the provincial office if the Zhuxi Chemical Park continued to expand (Diary, V11, October 29, 2004). Once the Huashui activists received this letter, they immediately went to the county bureau and demanded a copy of the written decisions. After arguing for some time, they were permitted to see the documents, but not allowed to make a copy. On November 10, the petitioners returned with the introduction letter, and after many twists and turns, they finally were able to get the documents they sought.

The Huashui activists used the written decisions in an instrumental fashion, though they considered them to have only symbolic significance. On November 11, 2004, the day after the documents of written decisions were obtained, activists printed them out, made many copies, and distributed them around. On November 27, many villagers, holding copies of the written decisions, went to urge the firms to leave their land. On February 28, 2005, several activists from Huangshan, a major village renting land to the Zhuxi Chemical Park, sent a document, "Letter Regarding Assistance to Huangshan villagers in the Return of the Land Illegally Used by the Zhuxi Chemical Park," to the Dongyang county government, the Public Security Bureau, the People's Court, the Bureau of Land and Resources, and the Huashui township government. The letter stated: "The people of Huangshan village, Huashui town, request that the companies withdraw from the land. If the companies fail to do so voluntarily, we hope that the Dongyang county government [or the other relevant organizations to whom the letter was sent] will supervise and urge the industries into compliance as soon as possible, and assist the residents of Huangshan village and Huashui town to reclaim the land."

This practical use of disingenuous official documents constrained the local authorities to some extent.[16] The head of the Huashui branch of the county Bureau of Land and Resources spoke frankly in an internal meeting: "The problems which concerned the villagers are real. It is true that the chemical park was built without proper approval, and consequently they requested that the land be given back to them. The written decisions they hold do exist, which were made according to the request of the State Council. We couldn't arrange the requisitioning of the land last year, since we didn't have a quota of land for industrial use. Consequently, [after knowing the administrative decisions] the villagers requested that the land be given back to them within 20 days."[17] In "Reflections on the Huashui Incident," one town leader revealed: "The chemical park was based on land which was seized illegally or semi-legally. This gave some of the masses in Huaxi No. 5 village (the most important village in the protest) an excuse to file petitions, and it was also the reason why the local government could not use harsh countermeasures during the protest." Another leader affirmed the function of the instrumental use of official documents: "The making of the written decisions was a crucial opportunity for villagers. The events in Huashui town actually all centered around the penalty decisions, and the people felt that these industries were illegal and needed to be removed. They felt that the government had made the decision, and all the firms had to move out of their land. This was indeed a turning point. On February 28, 2005, they brought those penalty decisions to us, sent them to the police, and demanded that the government departments assist them in reclaiming their land, saying 'If the companies don't leave in 20 days, and the land isn't returned to us, we will take the land back by force.' This was all based on the decisions made by the county Bureau of Land and Resources." (Interview, C8, June 28, 2007).

This complex process of negotiation makes it clear that the villagers were applying what has been termed the "wedge" strategy (Benney 2013, p. 116): using the discourse and policy of higher levels of government against lower levels of government to achieve their aims. Consequently, their approach had both an experimental aspect, in which they tried various frames until they found one that best suited their needs, as well as a calculated strategic aspect, where the villagers demonstrated that they used political opportunity and discourse instrumentally, rather than simply as a way of expressing their grievances.

---

[16] Some other factors that contributed to the success of the Huashui environmental protest are described in Deng and O'Brien (2014) and O'Brien and Deng (2015).

[17] From a record of a meeting of cadres in Huashui town on March 4, 2005.

6   CONCLUSION

At the broadest level, the case of Huashui town is an example of Scott's "critique against the hegemony" (Scott 1985). The villagers' disingenuous response to government discourse and policy created a new space in which their "everyday resistance" could manifest itself. But in contrast to Scott's peasants, whose resistance was often both covert and to some extent unconscious, the villagers of Huashui town used disingenuousness as a specific and overt strategy, "taking agency instead of having agency" (Kremmel and Pali 2015).[18]

In this chapter, we have argued that analyzing this seizure of agency allows us to conceptualize political opportunity and frame analysis in new and valuable ways. In terms of framing, when the villagers adopted the strategy of "pursuing environmental claims by seeking redress for land-related grievances," they were engaging in a process of *conscious* "misframing," an approach that was extremely reasonable given the hierarchical structure and fragmented authoritarianism of the Chinese state.

Implementing this misframing strategy required the Huashui villagers to assess and make use of the complex political opportunity structure facing them. Analyzing how they did this allows us to add nuance to much-discussed questions. First, the strategy of conscious misframing leads to "selective use" of political opportunity, where certain perceived opportunities are favored over others. Second, in considering the selection of political opportunities, we distinguish between "hard" and "soft" opportunities. "Hard" opportunities are characterized by high operability, whereas "soft" opportunities, due to disjuncture between their form and their function, lack the potential for practical implementation. That said, the structure of the multilevel Chinese state makes it possible for hard opportunities to "leak" as they make their way downwards from the Center. "Leakage," by which we mean the existence of factors that limit the operability of political opportunities, tends to make political opportunities exist merely in form and become symbolic.

Nonetheless, symbolic political opportunities can still be used by collective actors. The Huashui villagers' response to the leakage of political opportunity illustrates another of our major arguments. We have demonstrated that the villagers went through the process of using political opportunities even when they knew that the opportunities were "fake." In doing so, they played different levels of government against each other, provided themselves with public space for communication and time for negotiation, and demonstrated an intimidating capacity to use the discourse of the state against itself.

---

[18] The authors suggest: "By acting as if they have the rights that they lack, the refugees actualize their political freedom and equality. Even if the public sphere has been defined through their exclusion, they act."

REFERENCES

Benney, J. 2013. *Defending Rights in Contemporary China*. Oxford: Routledge.

Briggs, A. 2005. China's pollution victims: Still seeking a dependable remedy. *Georgetown International Environmental Law Review* 18: 305–333.

Cai, Y. 2008. Power structure and regime resilience: Contentious politics in China. *British Journal of Political Science* 38(3): 411–432.

Cai, Y. 2010. *Collective Resistance in China: Why Popular Protests Succeed or Fail*. Stanford, CA: Stanford University Press.

Chang, H. 2007. "'Yi hao wenjian zuo ban, Chen Xiwen jiedu 'xin nongcun jianshe yuannian'" ("Number one document" issued yesterday, Chen Xiwen analyses "the first year of construction of the new countryside"). *Caijing Wang* (Business and Economics Net). Available at http://www.caijing.com.cn/2007-01-30/10001 6039.html.

Costain, A.N. 1992. *Inviting Women's Rebellion: A Political Process Interpretation of the Women's Movement*. Baltimore: Johns Hopkins University Press.

Deng, Y., and K. J. O'Brien. 2013. Relational Repression in China: Using Social Ties to Demobilize Protesters. *The China Quarterly* 215: 533–552.

Deng, Y., and K.J. O'Brien. 2014. Societies of senior citizens and popular protest in rural Zhejiang. *The China Journal* 71: 172–188.

Deng, Y., and G. Yang. 2013. Pollution and Protest in China: Environmental Mobilization in Context. *The China Quarterly* 214: 321–336.

Downs, A. 1967. *Inside Bureaucracy*. Boston: Little, Brown.

Goffman, E., and B.M. Berger. 1986. *Frame Analysis*. Boston: Northeastern University Press.

Goodwin, J., J.M. Jasper, and J. Khattra. 1999. Caught in a winding, snarling vine: The structural bias of political process theory. *Sociological Forum* 14(1): 27–54.

Huashui Township Government. 2004. "Guanyu yaoqiu xunsu jianli lipei jizhi jiejue zhuxi gongneng qu maodun jiufen de baogao" (Report on the necessity to establish timely compensation mechanism for solving conflicts in the Zhuxi Functional Area), July 6, 2004.

Keck, M.E., and K. Sikkink. 1998. *Activists Beyond Borders*. Ithaca, NY: Cornell University Press.

Koopmans, R. 2004. Movements and media: Selection processes and evolutionary dynamics in the public sphere. *Theory and Society* 33(3): 367–391.

Kremmel, K., and B. Pali. 2015. "Refugee Protests and Political Agency: Framing Dissensus through Precarity." In: R. Sollund (ed.) *Green Harms and Crimes: Critical Criminology in a Changing World*. Basingstoke: Palgrave Macmillan.

Kurzman, C. 1996. Structural Opportunity and Perceived Opportunity in Social-Movement Theory: The Iranian revolution of 1979. *American Sociological Review* 61(1): 153–170.

Li, Y. 2005. Dang zhuiqiu jingji liyi zaoyu huanbao fengbao he nengyuan weiji (The pursuit of economic benefit encounters the environmental protection storm and the energy crisis). *Zhongguo Xin Shidai* (*China's New Era*), February 24, 2005.

Lieberthal, K. 1997. China's governing system and its impact on environmental policy implementation. *China Environmental Series* 1: 3–8.

McAdam, D. 1982. *Political Process and the Development of Black Insurgency*. Chicago: University of Chicago Press.

McAdam, D. 1996. "Conceptual Origins, Current Problems, Future Directions." In: D. McAdam, J.D. McCarthy, and M.N. Zald (eds.) *Comparative Perspectives on Social Movements: Political Opportunities, Mobilizing Structures, and Cultural Framings*. Cambridge, UK: Cambridge University Press.

Meyer, D.S., and W.A. Gamson. 1996. "Framing Political Opportunity." In: D. McAdam, J.D. McCarthy, and M.N. Zald (eds.) *Comparative Perspectives on Social Movements: Political Opportunities, Mobilizing Structures, and Cultural Framings*. Cambridge, UK: Cambridge University Press.

O'Brien, K.J., and L. Li. 2006. *Rightful Resistance in Rural China*. Cambridge: Cambridge University Press.

O'Brien, K.J., and Y. Deng. 2015. Repression backfires: Tactical radicalization and protest spectacle in rural China. *Journal of Contemporary China* 93: 457–470.

Pan, Y. 2004. Huanjing baohu yu gongzong canyu (Environmental protection and public participation). *Zhongguo Jianzai (China Disaster Reduction)* 6 (2004): 24–25.

Sawyers, T.M., and D.S. Meyer. 1999. Missed opportunities: Social movement abeyance and public policy. *Social Problems* 46(2): 187–206.

Scott, J.C. 1985. *Weapons of the Weak: Everyday Forms of Peasant Resistance*. New Haven, CT: Yale University Press.

Shi, F. 2005. Guanxi wangluo yu dangdai Zhongguo jiceng shehui yundong—yi yi ge jiequ huanbao yundong ge'an wei li (*Guanxi* networks and grassroots social movements in modern China—A case study of a street-level environmental movement). *Xuehai (Academia Bimestris)* no. 3 (2005): 76–88.

Shi, F., and Y. Cai. 2006. Disaggregating the state: Networks and collective resistance in Shanghai. *The China Quarterly* 186: 314–332.

Suh, D. 2001. How do political opportunities matter for social movements: Political opportunity, misframing, pseudosuccess, and pseudofailure. *The Sociological Quarterly* 42(3): 437–460.

Tang, X. 2005. Ducha yinxiang lu—yige jizhe de ducha suixing jilu (A record of supervision and inspection—a report from an accompanying journalist). *Zhongguo Tudi (China Land)* 3 (2005): 9–11.

Tarrow, S. 1989. *Democracy and Disorder: Protest and Politics in Italy 1965–1975*. Oxford: Clarendon Press.

Tarrow, S. 1994. *Power in Movement*. Cambridge, UK: Cambridge University Press.

Tarrow, S. 2005. *The New Transnational Activism*. Cambridge, UK: Cambridge University Press.

Tullock, G. 1987. *The Politics of Bureaucracy*. Lanham, MD: University Press of America.

van Rooij, B. 2010. The people vs. pollution: Understanding citizen action against pollution in China. *Journal of Contemporary China* 19(63): 55–77.

Xie, Y. 2010. Cong 'sifa dongyuan' dao 'jietou kangyi'—nongmingong jiti xingdong shibai de zhengzhi yinsu jiqi houguo" (From "judicial mobilisation" to "street protest"—the political factors and consequences of the failure of collective action by migrant workers). *Kaifang Shidai (Open Times)* 9 (2010): 46–56.

PART VI

Internet Governance

CHAPTER 21

Governing by the Internet: Local Governance in the Digital Age

Rongbin Han and Linan Jia

In what ways has the expansion of the Internet transformed local governance in China? Through analysis of over 2000 leaked official emails from a district-level Internet propaganda office, this chapter finds that the Internet has served more as a tool to enhance control rather than to improve governance at the local level. In particular, local authorities have prioritized Internet commentating tasks assigned from upper levels while keeping a close watch on negative publicity of both national and local problems. Their occasional responses to online complaints are often more likely meant to satisfy superiors and pacify the public rather than to address citizens' concerns. Such a "ruling by the Internet" strategy may bring short-term gains such as preserving social stability on the surface but may harm the regime in the long run with accumulated social dissatisfaction.

The rise of the Internet has transformed the dynamics of the state-society interaction in authoritarian regimes such as China (Yang 2003b; Boas 2006). In particular, the new technology has significantly empowered Chinese citizens vis-à-vis the party-state and expanded the scope of socio-political participation by enabling various actors, especially those previously excluded from the governance processes, to engage in politics, through online expression, participation, and mobilization (Esarey and Xiao 2008; Gao and Stanyer 2014; Lagerkvist 2007, 2010; Tai 2006; Yang 2007, 2009; Zheng 2008). Meanwhile, the Chinese party-state, known for its resilience and adaptability, has been actively attempting to tame the Internet and use it to the government's advantage through a series of control, co-optation, and manipulation efforts (Han 2015a, b; King et al. 2013, 2017; MacKinnon 2011; Noesselt 2014; Schlaeger

R. Han (✉) • L. Jia
Department of International Affairs, University of Georgia, Athens, GA, USA
e-mail: hanr@uga.edu; linan.jia25@uga.edu

J. Yu, S. Guo (eds.), *The Palgrave Handbook of Local Governance in Contemporary China*, https://doi.org/10.1007/978-981-13-2799-5_21

421

and Jiang 2014). Based on a rare dataset of leaked emails from a district-level Internet propaganda office, this study explores the impact of the Internet on local governance in the digital age. In particular, it intends to address the following question: have local authorities used the Internet as an opportunity to improve governance—by becoming more responsive and accountable to citizens—or more as a tool to enhance control over the public?

Through analysis of more than 2000 official emails in the dataset, the authors find that while local authorities in China have utilized the Internet to engage the citizenry and improve governance to some degree, they have made more serious efforts to monitor, control, and shape online information flows. More specifically, local authorities have not only prioritized Internet commentating tasks assigned from both the central and local governments but also kept a close watch on online information flows, especially negative publicity. Though local authorities have occasionally responded to citizen complaints, such responsiveness is limited and instrumental in nature as they only accommodate a small number of petitioning citizens, and the responses appear to be more about satisfying the upper levels and pacifying the public than addressing the concerns of citizens. This is not entirely surprising because local authorities likely are not motivated to use the Internet to improve governance, particularly as they are under pressure from above to control the Internet and doing so helps them to use the Internet to their advantage. For instance, in addition to deploying Internet commentators to fulfill tasks of cheerleading for the leadership and opinion manipulation assigned by the central government, local authorities have mobilized the same force to advance local propaganda initiatives, both to maintain their own image and to please upper levels of government.

Close examination of the Internet's impact on local governance is crucial to assess the resilience of Chinese authoritarianism in the digital age. Findings in this study suggest that the Chinese party-state has adopted a "rule by the Internet" strategy that uses the new technology more as an instrument to surveil, control, and manipulate public participation than as a vehicle to improve responsiveness and accountability in local governance. Such emphasis on control bears complicated implications for local governance as well as for the resilience of authoritarian rule. In particular, while granting local authorities the power to watch, control, and shape online information flows may marginalize critical voices, promote official discourse, and even temporarily pacify dissatisfied citizens, this strategy may be ineffective and even counterproductive because local authorities' online activities not only risk alienating citizens but also partially disable the policy feedback function of the Internet by disrupting and distorting the signaling process between the state (the central government) and the citizenry. In short, while utilizing the Internet as a tool to enhance control rather than to improve governance may bring short-term gains, such as preserving a surface appearance of societal harmony, it is likely to harm the regime in the long run: it might logically lead to accumulation of social discontent—which may contribute to social instability and the erosion of regime legitimacy—and weaken the regime's ability to discipline its agents and satisfy social needs.

1   Local Governance and the Digital Impact

The Chinese authoritarian regime has often been depicted as internally fragmented (Lieberthal and Lampton 1992; Mertha 2009; O'Brien and Li 2006). The fragmentation of the party-state clearly has important policy implications, particularly in that this means local officials and government agencies enjoy considerable leeway in policymaking and implementation. Local autonomy may bring about both positive and negative policy consequences. For instance, some argue that local autonomy in policy innovation is a critical factor that can help explain the success of China's economic reforms (Kelliher 1992; Montinola et al. 1995). However, discrepancies in incentive structures and policy goals between central and local authorities have also given rise to the principal-agent problem, often leading to selective policy implementation at the local level (Edin 2003; O'Brien and Li 1999). In fact, many of China's socio-political ills can be attributed to the central-local divide. For instance, the notorious peasant burden issue in the late 1990s largely occurred because local authorities, especially those below the county level, were tasked with numerous unfunded mandates from upper levels of the government (Bernstein and Lv 2003). Similarly, land disputes and soaring housing prices, both important sources of popular discontent in today's China, are at least partially attributable to the fact that local authorities were incentivized to capitalize the land after the 1993 taxation reform which granted most rich revenue sources to the central government. Such central-local divisions also serve as critical opportunity structures for popular protest in China by enabling citizens to lodge rightful resistance—Chinese citizens have often confronted and protested against misconduct of local officials and government agencies by citing laws, policies, and promises from the central government (O'Brien and Li 2006).

It is fair to say that the internal fragmentation of the Chinese party-state conditions local governance in China. In particular, while local authorities, especially those at the grassroots level, play an indispensable role in mediating the state-society interaction, they are often trapped between the central government and the citizenry. As the popular saying goes, "thousands of strings from above, all attached to the single needle at the bottom" (*shangmian qian tiaoxian, xiamian yigen zhen*). Local authorities are held responsible for numerous tasks assigned from above while having to directly deal with citizens. In particular, local officials in today's China are under huge pressure to maintain social stability amidst ever-rising popular dissatisfaction and social unrest (Wang 2015).

However, the pivotal role of local authorities in state-society interaction also allows them to work the system to their advantage. In particular, such a role gives them the incentive and ability to distort the signaling process between the public and upper levels of the government. On the one hand, keeping citizens ill-informed about central policies and commitments can prevent such information from being used by citizens to engage in rightful resistance against local malfeasance. On the other hand, the pressure to achieve performance goals such as stability maintenance means that local officials are motivated to cover up complaints from below. By "hoodwinking those from above and cheating those from below" (*qishang manxia*), local officials may infringe citizens' rights, ignore their grievances, and get away with their misconduct without sanctions and even get rewarded in some cases. This explains why local authorities can be extremely bold in suppressing protesting citizens: through ruthless repression, local authorities hope to prevent protests from escalating by "nipping them in the bud" (*esha zai mengya zhuangtai*).

The Internet may have transformed state-society interaction in China, especially by empowering citizens. Besides enabling a nascent public sphere (Hu 2008; Lagerkvist 2007; Rauchfleisch and Schäfer 2015; Yang 2003b) and promoting the development of civil society (Tai 2006; Yang 2003a), the Internet has also provided alternative channels for civic participation (Xiao 2011; Shi 2014; Jiang et al. 2017). These new options for civic engagement, in particular, constitute a challenge toward local governments in several ways. First, though some argue that certain Internet tools such as social media seem to be "unattractive as a potential outlet for organized social protest" (Qin et al. 2017), the new technology has undoubtedly helped citizens monitor the behavior of local cadres and governments, expose their malfeasance to the public, and even hunt down corrupt officials (Gao and Stanyer 2014; Nip and Fu 2016; Gao 2016; Gorman 2016; Lee and Lio 2014). Second, the Internet also renders it more difficult for local authorities to cover up scandals and suppress protesters as ordinary citizens now have greater influence on agenda-setting using Internet-enabled tools and platforms (Hassid 2012; Tang and Sampson 2012; Wu et al. 2013). Moreover, online experiences often encourage and embolden citizens while also making them more critical toward the government and its agents. Compared to traditional media users and non-media users, Internet users are found to be more politically opinionated, more critical about the political condition, and more likely to participate in collective action (Lei 2011; Tang and Huhe 2013). All these studies suggest that the Internet may empower social actors and help ensure some level of "publicity driven accountability" in local governance (Distelhorst 2012).

The Internet not only challenges the government, it may well help connect it, especially local authorities, with citizens, or at least serve as a tool for the state to engage the citizenry. Indeed, the Chinese government has set up e-government sites at different levels and in different sectors to improve administrative capacity, provide public services, and engage citizens (Damm 2006; Lagerkvist 2005; Lollar 2006; Qiang 2007; Schlæger 2013; Wu and Bauer 2010; Zhang 2002; Zhou 2004). As of December 2016, there are 53,546 government sites across China (CNNIC 2017). Most e-government sites offer not only basic functions such as publicizing state policies, reporting official activities, and providing public services but also include channels such as mayor's boxes that allow citizens to make inquiries, comment on policies, and voice grievances (Hartford 2005). E-government sites are also becoming more interactive as they have begun to embrace popular social media applications such as the mobile instant messenger WeChat and the Twitter-like Weibo as well as mobile web services (Zhao et al. 2016).

Far from passively waiting for citizens to engage with them on e-government sites, local authorities have also begun using social media such as Weibo, WeChat, and Internet forums to actively manage public participation. For example, Schlaeger and Jiang (2014) find that local authorities utilize official microblogs to experiment with ways to improve social management and political legitimacy, enhancing their ability to deliver individualized services and institute state surveillance. Esarey (2015) however, argues that, though official micro-blogging could help cadres win hearts and minds of the public, it may also provide netizens the opportunity to challenge the state. Similarly, local authorities have used WeChat to reach out to their constituents and the public, especially at times of unfolding crises and disasters (Tai and Liu 2015). Though local authorities engage citizens on social media sites only half-heartedly (Wang and Han 2015), it's clear that the Internet, social media in particular, has become a critical factor in local governance. Provided that local authorities utilize it properly, the new technology may help them to more effectively monitor and shape popular opinion, more rapidly address crises online, or at least function as "safety valves" by allowing citizens to vent online (Hassid 2012; Chen 2016).

The Internet has undoubtedly transformed politics, especially local governance. But this process has been accompanied by extensive and growing state monitoring and control efforts. As Boas (2006) points out, being a tool or "medium of communication," the Internet's political influence is largely contingent upon the actors who control it and how they intend to use it. Authoritarian regimes such as China have learned to tame the Internet while exploiting its beneficial aspects. The government does not even attempt to hide its intention to control the Internet and manipulate online expression. State-run media has consistently attempted to justify the state's Internet governance (and control) practices as necessary to protect "moral goodness, personal security, and social stability" (Cui and Wu 2016). In practice, the state has not only established the world's most sophisticated surveillance and censorship system to monitor and control the flow of information online but also deployed more innovative propaganda tactics such as ideotainment—by wrapping official ideological constructs with popular cyber cultural formats—and online astroturfing—by sponsoring state agents to fabricate seemingly spontaneous pro-government voices—to reinvigorate state propaganda in the digital age (Han 2015b; King et al. 2013, 2017; Lagerkvist 2008; MacKinnon 2009, 2011; OpenNet Initiative 2005; Qin et al. 2017). It is argued that though state control (and manipulation) in China may be imperfect, it may be sufficient to maintain authoritarian rule (Boas 2006). In particular, some recent studies argue that by strategically controlling information flow—for instance allowing general criticism but suppressing collective action expressions or tolerating criticism of local officialdom but not top leadership—an authoritarian regime such as the Chinese party-state may benefit from freer expression without risking being overthrown (King et al. 2013; Lorentzen 2014; Qin et al. 2017).

While the party-state as a whole may have attempted to strategize its approach to the Internet to perpetuate its rule, Internet governance in China is by no means designed, implemented, and optimized by a single rational and omnipotent entity. Among all other factors, the process first and foremost well reflects the fragmentation within the regime: Internet governance in China is in fact decentralized, and despite considerable central coordination and organization, local authorities play an indispensable role in controlling and utilizing the Internet as well as media at large (Esarey and Xiao 2011; Han 2018; MacKinnon 2009; Zuckerman 2010). This point, which has yet to be sufficiently discussed, is important to note, as discrepancies and even conflicts of goals, incentives, and interests between the central government and local authorities may affect Internet governance just like in other policy realms in China. From the central government's perspective, strategic censorship—by limiting criticism of top leadership but tolerating attacks on the local officialdom and by adapting controls to social tensions—benefits the regime as a whole (Lorentzen 2014). It should be noted that local authorities are not just willing agents of the central government to implement strategic censorship. Rather, as discussed in the previous section, local officials often have strong motivation to shape, distort, and hinder the signaling process between the central government and the citizenry. For instance, local governments often make their best efforts to prevent the exposure of local scandals, governmental misconduct, and official misbehavior. Plenty of evidence shows that they have gone to great lengths to remove negative publicity online, sometimes even by bribing government censors beyond their own jurisdiction (Xi and Zhang 2014). The same rationale may help explain, at least partially, why local government agencies and individual officials sometimes are actively using popular social media sites such as Weibo, WeChat, and Internet forums to engage citizens, especially given their need to "dilute" negative information and guide public opinion in online crises, though these actions often are also intended to please their superiors (Schlaeger and Jiang 2014; Esarey 2015; Qin et al. 2017; Wang and Han 2015). The pivotal role of local authorities in governing and controlling the Internet is further reinforced by the fact that netizens often post their complaints on local platforms, including local forums and e-government sites that are either subject to direct control or under heavy influence of local governments. All these indicate that, although not perfectly, local authorities will be able to directly monitor, control, and shape online expression, and their effort might not always be in line with directives from the central government.

In sum, the expansion of the Internet may shape local governance in China in at least two ways. First, the new technology enables local governments to better reach and respond to both the upper levels and citizens while making it easier for the latter to engage them, check their behavior, and provide feed-back. Second, the Internet can also serve as an instrument for the state to surveil, control, and manipulate citizens. In particular, as an increasingly important venue of socio-political participation, the Internet itself has become a top target of governance, and local authorities play an indispensable role in this process by undertaking much of the regulating and control responsibility. How do local authorities in China balance these two different functions of the Internet? Have they used the Internet to bring about improved governance at the local level, especially in terms of enhancing government responsiveness to citizens, or have they used the Internet more as a tool to enhance authoritarian control over the public? The following section illustrates an example of local governance in the digital age based on a case study of Z, a county-level district of City G in Province J.[1]

2   The Internet in Local Governance: The Case of District Z

The following analysis is primarily based on a collection of leaked emails from the Internet Propaganda Office of District Z (ZIPO hereafter).[2] Thus far, the only systematic analysis of this dataset is the seminal research by King et al. (2017) on the "50-cent army." However, in addition to revealing activities of the "50-cent army," the dataset is also a valuable resource to study local gover-nance in the digital age. The dataset contains 2370 emails received and sent between February 11, 2013 and November 28, 2014, among which 354 are from the Outbox, and 2016 are from the Inbox. Besides ZIPO, there are 97 agencies involved, ranging from provincial state agencies such as the Propaganda Department of the Chinese Communist Party (CCP) Province J Provincial Committee, to grassroots level social service agencies such as a primary school. In total, there are three superior party/state organs at the city and provincial levels: the Propaganda Department of the CCP's Province J Provincial Committee, the City G Municipal Internet Propaganda Office, and the External Propaganda Office under the CCP City G Municipal Committee. The majority of government agencies in the dataset are 66 district-level bureaus, commis-sions, and offices covering almost every aspect of local governance. These

---

[1] Following the suggestion of a reviewer, this study anonymizes all specific administrative units to avoid potential controversy.

[2] This email archive was released by an anonymous blogger "Xiaolan" in 2014 and has been publicly available since then. Gary King at Harvard University and his colleagues are the first group of political scientists using these data in scholarly research (King et al. 2017). According to them, based on the size and complexity of the archive, as well as the result of reference verification by the researchers, the authenticity of the archive should not be a concern. Since the dataset is publicly available and it provides scholars with unprecedented amount of valuable information, they believe it is appropriate to use the dataset strictly for scholarly research. The authors agree with them on this point.

agencies include the Education Bureau, the Development and Reform Commission, the Foreign Trade and Economic Cooperation Bureau, the Tourism Administration, and the Bureau of Sciences and Technologies, just to name a few. There are also nine sub-district- and township-level agencies, two village-level governments, and ten other communities which appear in the dataset. Interestingly, there are also social service agencies that are normally not considered part of the government apparatus, including local primary schools and local health centers. Overall, the dataset covers an impressive number of government agencies at different administrative levels and in different sectors.

Admittedly, the dataset has two potential limitations. First, it represents only one locality and that makes it hard to generalize the findings. In particular, as one of the famous old revolutionary areas, District Z may demonstrate certain features in local governance that are uncommon in other localities. While the concern is well grounded, findings here should bear broader implications because local governments in China share similar bureaucratic structures despite local variations. The cadre management system ensures that local authorities across China follow similar ways of assigning and implementing tasks (Rothstein 2014). Moreover, though the following analysis is based primarily on the ZIPO dataset, the authors have triangulated sources from District Z with additional data from elsewhere whenever possible.

Second, the Internet Propaganda Office is only a specific branch of the local government, and thus may not show a complete picture of local governance. This is a valid concern, and the discussion here on local governance in the digital age is clearly not exhaustive. For instance, although the dataset does not contain any censorship directives, this by no means implies that local authorities play no role in censoring online expression, as thousands of leaked state censorship directives have suggested otherwise. Rather, it is likely that such tasks are handled by a separate state agency. Having said that, the authors believe that there is no better government agency to study than the Internet Propaganda Office in order to understand local governance in the digital age as this office is the locus of Internet governance for local authorities. Its internal email communications not only reveal much of how the state governs the Internet (and local authorities' role in it) but also show how government agencies at different levels and in different sectors interact with each other and local residents.

Unlike the research of King et al. (2017), which focuses on the "50-cent army," this study explores a broader spectrum of local governance activities. For this purpose, the authors coded all emails in the dataset based on their content and the results show that these emails fall into five categories. The first category, *online publicity*, refers to online propaganda efforts by local authorities, especially activities of Internet commentators (aka the "50-cent army") to guide public opinion in response to online crises or state propaganda initiatives. This category also includes cases in which online commentators fabricated "interactions" with local officials during their online interviews with citizens. The second category is *online monitoring*, which refers to local governments' efforts to monitor online information flows, especially complaints of local residents and media exposure of local problems. The third category is labeled as *online accountability* and includes all cases in which the local government responded to online complaints. This category helps explore whether the Internet has increased government responsiveness or not. The fourth category, *bureaucratic communications*, includes internal directives, notifications, or work reports from subordinate or superior agencies. Emails with unidentifiable content and auto replies are coded as *other*. The last two categories are of less interest here as the authors are more interested in exploring the implications of the Internet for state-society interactions. Table 21.1 summarizes the results. Figure 21.1 plots the categorical distribution of the emails in both inbox and outbox across time, with the "other" category excluded since it is of little relevance to our analysis.

The coding results demonstrate several important features of ZIPO's work. First, online publicity, especially Internet commentating, constitute a highly significant part of its responsibility. Out of the total 2370 emails, 1609 fall into the category of online publicity. Among these emails, 1582 are related to Internet commentating and 27 are self-praising publicity efforts by local government agencies. This is not entirely surprising as the Chinese state, especially since President Xi Jinping came into power, increasingly relies on Internet commentating to produce pro-regime voices and guide popular opinion online (Han 2015a; King et al. 2017; Miller 2016). The propaganda apparatus, especially the Internet propaganda offices, and the Communist Youth League system are the two major sponsors of the "50-cent army" (Han 2018). ZIPO likely only exemplifies how local authorities perform Internet commentating in today's China.

Like King et al. (2017), the authors find that Internet commentators in District Z were mobilized for nationwide propaganda initiatives. The specific topics include online crises, such as riots in Xinjiang, or at politically symbolic moments, such as the Qingming Festival, the National Martyr's Day, the CCP's National Congress, and the National People's Congress (NPC) and Chinese Communist Party Central Community (CCPCC) meetings. Internet commentators were also deployed to promote President Xi Jinping's idea of the China dream and to defame the pro-liberal public intellectuals. Like King et al.

Table 21.1 Coding results of ZIPO dataset

Categories	Inbox	Outbox	Total
Online publicity	1459	150	1609
Online monitoring	87	162	249
Online accountability	20	2	22
Bureaucratic communications	151	37	188
Other	299	3	302
Grand total	2016	354	2370

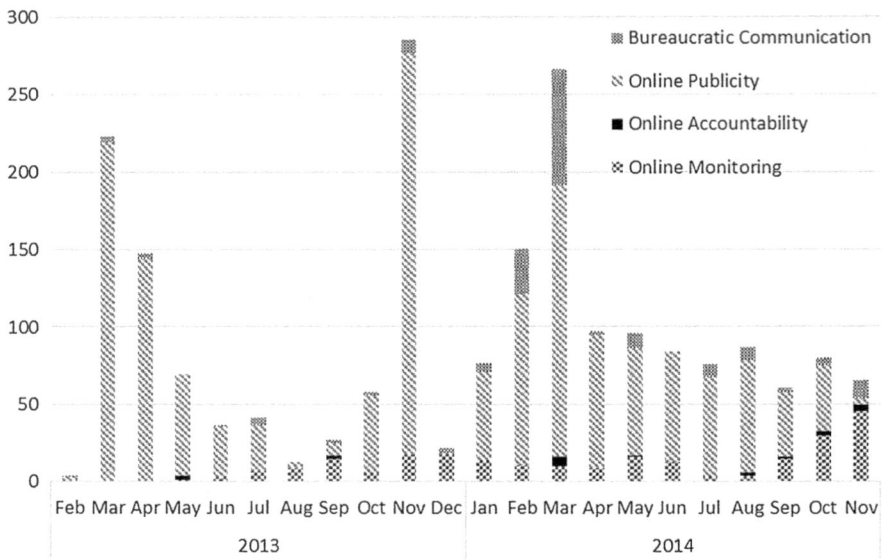

Fig. 21.1 Categorical distribution of emails across time (excluding "other")

(2017), the authors have also observed "distinct spikes" of the Internet commentating activities by ZIPO. However, besides championing national propaganda initiatives, some of ZIPO's Internet commenting work was local in nature. Internet commentators in District Z actively posted about local moral characters such as a primary school teacher who later became one of the top ten "Touching China" moral role models and a cadre who died searching for trapped students in a flood. The 50-cent army forces under ZIPO were also mobilized to promote local culture and local products: in October 2013 and January 2014, they were deployed to promote locally produced navel oranges, first to crack down on fake products from other localities, and then to cheer the "Navel Orange Festival" hosted by the local government. Then in March 2014, they were asked to post about a local opera that tells its revolutionary history using folklore.

Second, the coding results show that monitoring online information is another key area of ZIPO's work, though it may not be as prioritized as Internet commenting tasks. Of the 2370 emails coded, 249 are related to online monitoring. Moreover, among these 249, 222 are about social grievances and citizen complaints, indicating that the local government may have paid special attention to negative publicity. Local authorities monitor online information flows not just for themselves. They have been gathering, compiling, and reporting online information about events that are beyond their jurisdiction for upper levels of the government. In an annual working report dated December 2013, ZIPO proudly claimed that, "as of October 2013, [we] have reported a total of 594 public opinion messages to [upper levels], 123 of which were partially quoted by the Provincial Propaganda Department [to report to the Central Propaganda Department] and 12 pieces were fully adopted."[3]

Figure 21.1 shows that the volume of online monitoring emails seems to be negatively associated with the volume of online publicity emails: from February to May and September to December in 2013, as well as from January to May in 2014, there were three peaks in Internet commentating, while online monitoring recorded relatively low volumes. While this can be a coincidence, it may also indicate that ZIPO focused less on online monitoring when there were more Internet commentating assignments. Another possible explanation is that the government reinforced its censorship during volume bursts of online commentating, thus reducing the amount of negative publicity for it to monitor. In other words, censorship and opinion manipulation may go hand in hand in such cases. Another more intuitive explanation is that local authorities tend to prioritize Internet commentating over online monitoring. While logically the state may enhance both online monitoring and Internet commentating during online crises or politically sensitive moments, the second explanation makes sense for several reasons: (1) not all Internet commentating tasks happened at politically sensitive moments or crises; (2) several Internet commentating tasks such as cheerleading for President Xi's Chinese dream idea and the Party's National Congress were apparently assigned from the central government, and thus likely received priority treatment; and (3) compared to online monitoring, execution of Internet commentating can be more effectively monitored, as the achievement by a particular government agency is much more quantifiable.

Third, the coding results show that local authorities have occasionally responded to citizen complaints, though such cases constitute a very small percentage. There are only 22 such emails in the entire dataset, relating to issues such as land expropriation, environmental problems, and arbitrary education charges. For instance, there are two emails in the dataset about one specific land expropriation case. The first email, dated May 4, 2014, was a report from ZIPO to district leaders about a petition posted one day before on a government-backed petition site for residents across Province J to lodge complaints and provide policy feedback. The petitioner claimed that his land was taken without compensation, and he was stonewalled by village and township cadres. A township deputy director allegedly threatened him, saying that "you will get hurt if you continue to mess with us, and the township government will cover your medical bills; if you win the fight, I'll send the police to arrest you!"[4] The report was also forwarded to the target of the complaint, Township S. The second email, dated May 21, was a follow-up investigation

[3] ZIPO, *2013 niandu Z Qu yuqing xinxi gongzuo qingkuang huibao (District Z 2013 work report on public opinion monitoring)*, December 20, 2013, email communication in ZIPO Dataset.

[4] See Qiugongdao, *Z Qu S Zhen H Cun: Tudi bei zhengyong cunmin yaoqiu buchang (Village H, Township S, District Z: Land expropriated with villager asking for compensation)*, available at: goo.gl/HZf6Gq.

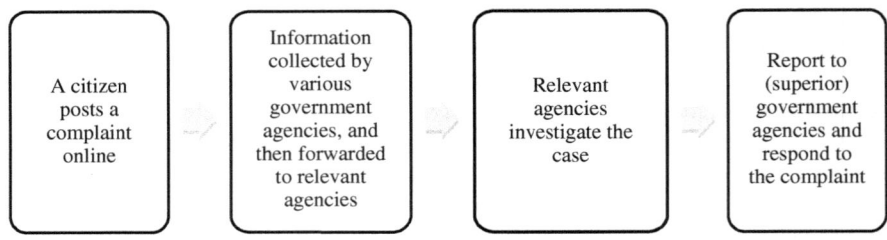

Fig. 21.2   Procedure of local government response to citizen complaints

report sent by ZIPO, on behalf of the district, to the superior municipal information office. The two emails seem to showcase enhanced responsiveness and accountability of local governance in the Internet age. In fact, besides reporting to upper levels, ZIPO also pushed local cadres to engage the petitioner directly online. The authors checked the link of the petition and found two replies from the Township S and its deputy director within a matter of days (on May 5 and 6, 2014) after ZIPO forwarded them the petition.

Local authorities in District Z responded not just to issues like land expropriation that may potentially provoke collective action. They also quickly reacted to a broader array of citizens' complaints. When a resident complained about a school offering extra courses on Saturday for extra charges, the local education bureau replied within two days. The authorities were also not just monitoring governmental platforms. For instance, one of the emails related to a complaint about garbage disposal of a factory on Lebangwang, a local portal site that provides various kinds of online services. The post appeared on August 24, 2014, and an investigation report was submitted the next day to ZIPO by the street-level government that has jurisdiction over the factory.

These cases reveal a procedure of "publicity driven accountability" (Distelhorst 2012) in local governance (see Fig. 21.2). After a citizen posts a compliant online, local authorities, often including multiple local agencies at different levels, may start collecting information. The case will be forwarded to relevant agencies to investigate and then report back to ZIPO, the platform where the complaint was posted, and sometimes to upper levels of government.

3   Discussion

Analysis of the empirical evidence indicates that local government in District Z seems to be preoccupied by surveillance and manipulation tasks. They have only responded to citizen complaints in very few cases. Though their reactions were quite prompt in general, such promptness may not be sufficient evidence of enhanced accountability and responsiveness in local governance. As the Internet enables local authorities to monitor online expression more closely, communicate with other government agencies more efficiently, and engage citizens more directly when necessary, it is only logical to expect quicker responses from them. This point echoes reports on corrupt local officials being punished by the state within a matter of weeks or even days after being exposed online (Gao and Stanyer 2014). However, the limited number of such responses compared to the number of emails on Internet commentating and online monitoring is quite telling about the priorities of the local government.

Moreover, responding to citizens' online complaints promptly does not always mean being more responsive or accountable to the public. Deeper analysis of the dataset reveals that local authorities were more concerned about answering to superiors and pacifying the public rather than truly addressing the problems. As the land expropriation case shows, while local authorities replied to the complaint almost immediately and also provided an explanation to the municipal government, they were highly dismissive both times. The report to the upper-level municipal government dismissed the petition, claiming that local cadres had obtained the petitioner's permission and fully compensated him before taking his land. After detailing the amount of compensation for the petitioner's land, plants, and fruit trees, it concluded that "all due procedures were followed and all compensations were completed."[5] The township's reply to the petitioner on the complaining platform, which was identical to the report to the municipal government, denied all the accusations in the petition, and the deputy township director's reply to the petitioner was a blatant self-defense. Moreover, neither the township government nor the deputy director responded to the petitioner's follow-up post that challenged their responses. The petition essentially ended in the middle of nowhere, though other netizens witnessing the dispute also criticized the governmental responses for being "overly partial and too arbitrary" and demanded further investigation of the case. The very fact that local authorities denied their responsibility completely despite evidence suggesting otherwise betrays their real purpose: they care more about pacifying the public and answering to their superiors than addressing the concerns of the citizens.

Additional evidence from District Z confirms such a rationale of local authorities. For them, responding to online complaints serves primarily as a means to achieve important policy goals such as social stability maintenance. As stressed in a document on Internet propaganda work dated May 14, 2014, ZIPO recommended that local government should strengthen the work of public opinion relevant to the district and improve the coping mechanisms. Specific measures included:

> Enhance surveillance of key websites, forums, blogs and Weibo. Standardize the online information collection and reporting system. All departments (units)

---

[5] ZIPO, *Z Quwei Bangongshi guanyu "Z Qu S Zhen H Cun Cunmin tudi beizhengyong yoaqiu buchang zhengdikuan" de yuqing diaocha qingkuang huibao (Public opinion investigation report by District Z Party Committee Office regarding "Village H, Township S, District Z: Land expropriated with villager asking for compensation")*, May 25, 2014, email communication in ZIPO Dataset.

should establish an online publicity response system to implement the tracking, registration, and recording of online opinion handling and to improve the coping mechanism in cases of major online incidents. [The coping mechanism] should fine-tune the timing, efficacy, and degree when responding to online events, and [government agencies should] act according to the principles of "react promptly, check the facts, and handle properly" to manage scientifically as well as actively and steadily guiding popular opinion during such online incidents.[6]

This was not just a policy recommendation. Rather, it reflected what local authorities had actually done. In its 2013 work report, ZIPO boasted about its achievements in five major areas, including expanding capacity for online publicity work, handling online events, guiding online opinion, better reporting online information to upper levels, and setting up an official Weibo account. The document mentions nothing about enhancing government responsiveness or accountability, and reacting to citizen complaints seems to be covered in the section on handling online events, which states:

[We] established and improved the online opinion response mechanism and the major online events coping mechanism, and also enforced the public opinion work responsibility system. [We] further strengthened the surveillance of key websites, forum, blogs, and Weibo. We collected and compiled online information related to the socio-economic development of our district, especially negative publicity that may cause instability or major mass incidents … and reported to district leaders and the municipal Internet propaganda office. As of November 2013, we have 108 issues of Internet Public Opinion Special Reports, reported 144 online events, and received 21 instructions from the district Party leaders. There was not a single case of omission, false report, or concealment of major online events.[7]

The above two quoted passages again confirm that at least the local government is concerned more about monitoring, controlling, and manipulating online information than becoming more responsive and accountable to citizens.

One may ask if the findings here are only applicable to District Z. Abundant circumstantial evidence suggests that authorities in other localities in Province J are not quite enthusiastic about improving government responsiveness to citizens as well. As Table 21.2 shows, about 70% of the total 45,487 complaints posted on the provincial level government-backed petition site between January 22, 2011 and August 24, 2017 received no government response at all. Several

---

[6] ZIPO, *Guanyu jinyibu jiaqiang quangqu wangluo xuanchuan gongzuo de yijian (Suggestions to further strengthen online propaganda work in our district)*, May 14, 2014, email communication in ZIPO Dataset.

[7] ZIPO, *Qu wangxuanban 2013 nian gongzuo zongjie he 2014 nian gongzuo silu (ZIPO's work report for 2013 and work plan for 2014)*, December 20, 2013, email communication in ZIPO Dataset.

Table 21.2 Government responses to online complaints in Province J

Prefectures	Non-response cases	Total cases	Non-response rate (%)
F	1880	2591	72.56
G	*4658*	*5924*	*78.63*
J	1987	5266	37.73
JD	923	1271	72.62
JJ	4436	6325	70.13
N	9545	12,209	78.18
P	1836	2349	78.16
S	3057	4518	67.66
X	871	1249	69.74
YC	1658	2469	67.15
YT	692	1013	68.31
Other provinces	233	273	85.35
Other	26	30	86.67
Total	**31,802**	**45,487**	**69.91**

Source: Data collected and compiled by the authors

cities, including City G where District Z is located have reported a non-response rate of 78% or above, meaning local authorities responded to less than 22% of all complaints. These numbers are telling, especially considering that the site is specially designated for citizens to lodge complaints. The low response rates clearly confirm one of the key findings of this study: local authorities are not motivated to even engage the public, let alone wholeheartedly address problems for citizens.

The finding also resonates with existing studies. For instance, according to Kluver (1999), one of the most important goals of China's e-governance system is to improve surveillance over government agencies and citizens, as well as to maintain the legitimacy of the ruling regime rather than facilitating efficient communication between citizens and the government. Similarly, based on analysis of government responses to online complaints on China's most popular Internet forum, Wang and Han (2015) find that local authorities often tend to just pay lip services to pacify netizens and to please upper levels rather than actually solving the problems. Such studies show that observation in District Z is unlikely an idiosyncratic case.

4   Conclusion

The expansion of the Internet has brought about both opportunities and challenges in local governance in China. On the one hand, the Internet may improve governance by facilitating local governments to better serve and engage citizens through platforms such as e-government sites and social media platforms. The new technology can also help enhance government responsiveness and accountability in local governance by facilitating public participation and social mobilization. In particular, compared to the pre-Internet era, the

Internet has weakened the ability of local governments to control the information flow or block the signaling process between citizens and the central government, meaning that citizens can have their voices heard by the public or upper levels of the government more easily. However, the Internet has also increased the authoritarian state's capacity to monitor, control, and manipulate social participation. Given that local authorities are incentivized to please upper levels and cover up local malfeasances, they may often be inclined to use the Internet for control purposes rather than governance improvement.

Possibly due to the issue of data availability, previous studies of cyber politics in China tend to focus either on the techniques and behavior of state control, such as censorship and "fifty-cent army," or on how the Internet may enhance government responsiveness and accountability. In general, few studies have attempted to provide a more comprehensive picture of how the Chinese government may balance between these two potentially conflicting functions of the Internet. By using a rarely studied dataset, this study looks systematically into the "black box" of authoritarian state and examines how state's Internet governance works from within. Doing so allows the authors to bridge the gap in existing studies and to integrate the evaluation of the two functions of the Internet as both a tool of state control and a vehicle to improve governance.

Findings in this study show that the Internet has transformed local governance in China, but not so much in the direction of improving government responsiveness and accountability as one may expect or hope. While there are some signs of local authorities reacting to online complaints, much of the evidence has pointed to the enhanced state surveillance, control, and manipulation of public participation via the Internet. In fact, the case of District Z shows that local authorities often only respond to a small portion of citizen complaints online and such responses only constitute a small portion of their online activities. Even in cases when they do respond to citizens, such responses tend to be instrumental and ineffective because the real purpose is usually more about satisfying the superiors or pacifying the public rather than addressing the problems. In contrast, the case of District Z also suggests that local authorities attach much more importance to Internet commentating and online monitoring tasks, both of which are crucial for the party-state, particularly local authorities, to better rule by the Internet. Internet commentating has been utilized by both the central government and local authorities to fulfill propaganda initiatives such as cheerleading for the leaders, promoting state ideology, denigrating regime critics, as well as managing online crises. Such tasks are increasingly important, given that more traditional state propaganda tactics are increasingly ineffective (Tong and Lei 2013). Online monitoring serves as an early-warning mechanism, through which the party-state and local governments keep a close watch on online information flows, especially negative publicity, so that they can choose to intervene when they deem necessary.

This study reveals only an incomplete picture of local governance in the digital age due to limitations of the dataset. Without a more comprehensive dataset that covers multiple localities or multiple government agencies in a given locality, other factors that may impact government response rate can hardly be properly evaluated. In particular, the analysis has focused on how local authorities may utilize the Internet to surveil, manipulate, and sometimes engage citizens but sheds little light on their role in censoring and repressing online expression. Though this is unlikely to affect the key argument of the chapter—local governments use the Internet more as a tool to enhance control over rather than to better serve the people—a more comprehensive study will clearly help better assess the Internet's impact on local governance as well as authoritarian resilience in the digital age. It is likely that utilizing the Internet to enhance control rather than to improve governance may bring short-term gains, but in the long run, it may harm the regime: social dissatisfaction may accumulate while the regime's ability to discipline its agents and respond to social needs may be weakened. Such factors in turn may threaten socio-political stability and contribute to the erosion of regime legitimacy. Thus, unless the state adapts to improve its governance, to what extent the state (and local authorities) can prevent the escalation of citizen activism and maintain its rule depends not only on its capacity to monitor and manipulate online information flows but also on whether it can effectively censor and suppress deviating public expression online.

REFERENCES

Bernstein, T., and X. Lv. 2003. *Taxation without representation in rural China*. New York: Cambridge University Press.

Boas, T.C. 2006. Weaving the authoritarian web: The control of Internet use in non-democratic regimes. In Zysman, J., and A. Newman (eds.). *How revolutionary was the digital revolution: National responses, market transitions, and global technology*. California: Stanford Business Books.

Chen, D. 2016. Review essay: The safety valve analogy in Chinese politics. *Journal of East Asian Studies* 16: 281–294.

CNNIC. 2017. *Di 39 ci Zhongguo hulianwang fazhan zhuangkuang tongji baogao (The 39th China statistical report on Internet development)*. Available at http://www.cnnic.cn.

Cui, D., and F. Wu. 2016. Moral goodness and social orderliness: An analysis of the official media discourse about Internet governance in China. *Telecommunications Policy* 40: 265–276.

Damm, J. 2006. China's e-policy: Examples of local e-government in Guangdong and Fujian. In Damm, J. and S. Thomas (eds.). *Chinese cyberspaces: Technological changes and political effects*. London and New York: Routledge.

Distelhorst, G. 2012. Publicity-driven accountability in China: Qualitative and experimental evidence. *MIT Political Science Department Research Paper Working Paper*.

Edin, M. 2003. State capacity and local agent control in China: CCP cadre management from a township perspective. *The China Quarterly* 173: 35–52.

Esarey, A. 2015. Winning hearts and minds? Cadres as microbloggers in China. *Journal of Current Chinese Affairs* 44(2): 69–103.

Esarey, A., and Q. Xiao. 2008. Political expression in the Chinese blogosphere. *Asian Survey* 48(5): 752–772.

————. 2011. Digital communication and political change in China. *International Journal of Communication* 5: 298–319.

Gao, L. 2016. The emergence of the human flesh search engine and political protest in China: Exploring the Internet and online collective action. *Media, Culture & Society* 38(3): 349–364.

Gao, L., and J. Stanyer. 2014. Hunting corrupt officials online: The human flesh search engine and the search for justice in China. *Information, Communication, & Society* 17(7): 814–829.

Gorman, P. 2016. Flesh searches in China: The governmentality of online engagement and media management. *Asian Survey* 56(2): 325–347.

Han, R. 2015a. Cyberactivism in China: Empowerment, control, and beyond. In Axel B. et al. *The routledge companion to social media and Politics*. London and New York: Routledge.

————. 2015b. Manufacturing consent in cyberspace: China's "fifty-cent army". *Journal of Current Chinese Affairs* 44(2): 105–134.

————. 2018. *Contesting cyberspace in China: Online expression and authoritarian resilience*. New York: Columbia University Press.

Hartford, K. 2005. Dear mayor: Online communications with local governments in Hangzhou and Nanjing. *China Information* 19(2): 217–260.

Hassid, J. 2012. Safety valve or pressure cooker? Blogs in Chinese political life. *Journal of Communication* 62(2): 212–230.

Hu, Y. 2008. *Zhongsheng xuanhua: Wangluo shidai de geren biaoda yu gonggong taolun (The rising cacophoney: Personal expression and public discussion in the Internet age)*. Nanning: Guangxi Normal University Press.

Jiang, J., T. Meng, and Q. Zhang. 2017. *From Internet to social safety net: The policy consequences of online participation in China*. Available at SSRN: https://ssrn.com/abstract=2975456.

Kelliher, D. 1992. *Peasant power in China: The era of rural reform, 1979–1989*. New Haven: Yale University Press.

King, G., J. Pan, and M. Roberts. 2013. How censorship in China allows government criticism but silences collective expression. *American Political Science Review* 107(2): 1–18.

————. 2017. How the Chinese government fabricates social media posts for strategic distraction, not engaged argument. *American Political Science Review* 111(3): 484–501.

Lagerkvist, J. 2005. The techno-cadre's dream. *China Information* 19(2): 189–216.

————. 2007. *The Internet in China: Unlocking and containing the public sphere*. Lund: Lund University.

————. 2008. Internet ideotainment in the PRC: National responses to cultural globalization. *Journal of Contemporary China* 17(54): 121–140.

————. 2010. *After the Internet, before democracy: Competing norms in Chinese media and society*. Switzerland: Peter Lang.

Kluver, R. 1999. The architecture of control: A Chinese strategy for e-governance. *Journal of Public Policy* 25(1): 75–97.

Lee, M., and M. Lio. 2014. The impact of information and communication technology on public governance and corruption in China. *Information Development* 32(2): 127–141.

Lei, Y. 2011. The political consequences of the rise of the Internet: Political beliefs and practices of Chinese netizens. *Political Communication* 28(3): 291–322.

Lieberthal, K., and D. Lampton (eds.). 1992. *Bureaucracy, politics, and decision making in post-Mao China*. Berkeley: University of California Press.

Lollar, X. 2006. Assessing China's e-government: Information, service, transparency and citizen outreach of government websites. *Journal of Contemporary China* 15(46): 31–41.

Lorentzen, P. 2014. China's strategic censorship. *American Journal of Political Science* 58(2): 402–414.

MacKinnon, R. 2009. China's censorship 2.0: How companies censor bloggers. *First Monday* 14(2).

———. 2011. China's "Networked authoritarianism." *Journal of Democracy* 22(2): 32–46.

Mertha, A. 2009. "Fragmented authoritarianism 2.0": Political pluralization in the Chinese policy process. *The China Quarterly* 200: 995–1012.

Miller, B. 2016. Automatic detection of comment propaganda in Chinese media. Available at SSRN: https://ssrn.com/abstract=2738325.

Montinola, G., Y. Qian, and B. Weingast. 1995. Federalism, Chinese style: The political basis for economic success in China. *World Politics* 48(1): 50–81.

Nip, J., and K. Fu. 2016. Networked framing between source posts and their reposts: An analysis of public opinion on China's microblogs. *Information, Communication & Society* 19(8): 1127–1149.

Noesselt, N. 2014. Microblogs and the adaptation of the Chinese party-state's governance strategy. *Governance* 27(3): 449–468.

O'Brien, K., and L. Li. 1999. Selective policy implementation in rural China. *Comparative Politics* 31(2): 167–186.

———. 2006. *Rightful resistance in rural China*. New York: Cambridge University Press.

OpenNet Initiative. 2005. *Internet filtering in China in 2004–2005: A country study*.

Qiang, Z. 2007. *China's information revolution: Managing the economic and social transformation*. Washington: World Bank.

Qin, B., D. Strömberg, and Y. Wu. 2017. Why does China allow freer social media? Protests versus surveillance and propaganda. *Journal of Economic Perspectives* 31(1): 117–140.

Rauchfleisch, A., and M. Schäfer. 2015. Multiple public spheres of Weibo: A typology of forms and potentials of online public spheres in China. *Information, Communication & Society* 18(2): 139–155.

Rothstein, B. 2014. The Chinese paradox of high growth and low quality of government: The cadre organization meets Max Weber. *Governance* 28(4): 533–548.

Schlæger, J. 2013. *E-government in China: Technology, power and local government reform*. Abingdon: Routledge.

Schlaeger, J., and M. Jiang. 2014. Official microblogging and social management by local governments in China. *China Information* 28(2): 189–213.

Shi, L. 2014. Micro-blogs, online forums, and the birth-control policy: Social media and the politics of reproduction in China. *Culture, Medicine, and Psychiatry* 38(1): 115–132.

Tai, Z. 2006. *The Internet in China: Cyberspace and civil society*. London: Routledge.

Tai, Z., and X. Liu. 2015. *The Chinese government hops on the Wechat bandwagon*. China Policy Institute: Analysis. Available at https://cpianalysis.org/2015/05/06/chinese-government-hops-on-the-wechat-bandwagon/.

Tang, L., and H. Sampson. 2012. The interaction between mass media and the Internet in non-democratic states: The case of China. *Media, Culture & Society* 34(4): 457–471.

Tang, M., and N. Huhe. 2013. Alternative framing: The effect of the Internet on political support in authoritarian China. *International Political Science Review* 35(5): 559–576.

Tong, Y., and S. Lei. 2013. War of position and microblogging in China. *Journal of Contemporary China* 22(80): 292–311.

Wang, J. 2015. Managing social stability: The perspective of a local government in China. *Journal of East Asian Studies* 15: 1–25.

Wang Y., and R. Han. 2015 May. Paying lip service or taking it seriously? How Chinese government responds to online complaints. Paper presented at *the 13th China Internet Research Conference*, University of Alberta, Canada.

Wu, Y. et al. 2013. Agenda setting and micro-blog use: An analysis of the relationship between Sina Weibo and newspaper agendas in China. *The Journal of Social Media in Society* 2(2): 8–25.

Wu, Y., and J. Bauer. 2010. E-government in China: Deployment and driving forces of provincial government portals. *Chinese Journal of Communication* 3(3): 290–310.

Xi, Y., and W. Zhang. 2014. Wangjing huilu wangjing: Ti lingdao shantie (Internet police bribing Internet police: Deleting posts for local leaders). *Nanfang Zhoumo (Southern Weekend)*. 17 April.

Xiao, Q. 2011. The rise of online public opinion and its political impact. In Shirk, S. (eds.). *Changing media, changing China*. Oxford: Oxford University Press.

Yang, G. 2003a. The co-evolution of the Internet and civil society in China. *Asian Survey* 43(3): 124–141.

———. 2003b. The Internet and the rise of a transnational Chinese cultural sphere. *Media, Culture & Society* 24(4): 469–490.

———. 2007. How do Chinese civic associations respond to the Internet? Findings from a survey. *The China Quarterly* 189: 122–143.

———. 2009. *The power of the Internet in China: Citizen activism online*. New York: Columbia University press.

Zhang, J. 2002. Will the government "serve the people"? The development of Chinese e-government. *New Media & Society* 4(2): 163–184.

Zhao, J., S. Zhao, M. Alexander, and A. Truell. 2016. E-government use of social media for enhancing democracy in China. *Issues in Information Systems* 17(1): 58–69.

Zheng, Y. 2008. *Technological empowerment: The Internet, state, and society in China*. Stanford: Stanford University Press.

Zhou, X. 2004. E-government in China: A content analysis of national and provincial websites. *Journal of Computer-Mediated Communication* 9(4). Retrieved from https://academic.oup.com/jcmc/article/9/4/JCMC948/4614512.

Zuckerman, E. 2010. Intermediary censorship. In Deibert R., J. Palfrey, R. Rohozinski, and J. Zittrain (eds.). *Access controlled: The shaping of power, rights and rule in cyberspace*. Cambridge: The MIT Press.

CHAPTER 22

Internet Governance in China: A Content Analysis

Feng Yang and Milton L. Mueller

1 Introduction

Using content analysis, this chapter explores the policy-making trends for Internet governance in China. It examines the manner by which policy changes over time, the different policy-making agencies in the country, and the various application scopes and topical focuses of policy. This chapter aims to determine the distribution of key policy decisions over different policy-making agencies and which policy issues receive the most attention from China's government in its efforts to regulate the Internet.

On 14 September 1987, China's first email entitled, "Across the Great Wall we can reach every corner in the world," was sent and marked the beginning of Internet usage in the country.[1] After years of efforts, China became the 71st nation to formally secure linkage to the Internet in 1994; this event was highlighted in the Chinese press as one of the country's top ten scientific news items and one of the major scientific and technological achievements in China's national statistical bulletin that year. Since then, the Internet has become an important medium that considerably influences the public sphere in China.

---

[1] See "Across the Great Wall we can reach every corner in the world" http://tech.sina.com.cn/i/2005-07-19/1038666886.shtml.

F. Yang (✉)
School of Public Administration, Sichuan University, Chengdu, China

M. L. Mueller
Georgia Institute of Technology, Atlanta, GA, USA
e-mail: milton@gatech.edu

© The Author(s) 2019
J. Yu, S. Guo (eds.), *The Palgrave Handbook of Local Governance in Contemporary China*, https://doi.org/10.1007/978-981-13-2799-5_22

The development and usage of the Internet had never before been perceived to bring about a huge difference in the country.

Data from the China Internet Network Information Center (CNNIC 2014) show that by the end of December 2013, the total number of cyber citizens (*wangmin*)[2] in China grew to 618 million, out of which 53.58 million were new users. The penetration rate of Internet use was 45.8%, up 3.7 percentage points over 2012 levels. The total number of Chinese Internet users and the penetration rate has grown dramatically since 2005. The Internet's influence on China's political, economic, and social development has also become increasingly prominent, thereby causing many changes in these spheres. As early as the 1990s, for example, a common occurrence was the use of the Internet for advertising, commercial information exchange, and online shopping (Cullen and Choy 1999). Internet use in business is also gradually shifting from being an aspect of competitive advantage to a necessity (Zhang and Moussi 2007). The country has become fertile ground for the establishment of Internet businesses, as indicated by the rise of numerous domestic Web-based companies, such as Baidu, Sohu, and Taobao; these companies are ranked at the top 75 of global websites by Alexa.com (Lai and To 2012). Furthermore, the Internet has steadily advanced public expression on civil society issues and related activities, thereby endowing power to the Chinese to transform personhood, society, and politics (Yang 2009); additionally, such increasing public participation in state governance matters has strengthened mutual relations between the citizens and the government, as well as political liberalization (Zheng 2007). The Internet is clearly changing the relationship between the state and society in China (Hung 2012).

The development of the Internet enables information sharing, broadens citizens' participation in politics, improves government, promotes economic development, and facilitates cultural exchange. An Internet white paper published by the State Council Information Office (SCIO) elucidates that the Chinese government's basic policy regarding the Internet covers *active use, scientific development, law-based administration, and ensured security* (2010).[3] Despite the advantages associated with the Internet, however, some people have criticized certain facets of China's Internet governance policy. The country has a complex, systematic set of laws, regulations, and technical methods for filtering Internet content, but these programs lack transparency (Zittrain and Edelman 2003). The Chinese state also attempts to control the flow of information through the Internet (Dowell 2006). Arsène (2012) argues that "national sovereignty over the Internet and the existence of the censorship system may be misleading." Even with such spate of criticism, little research has

---

[2] A cyber citizen (wangmin) is defined by the CNNIC as any Chinese citizen aged six or older who has used the Internet in the past half year.

[3] State Council Information Office (2010, June 8). The Internet in China. Retrieved from http://english.gov.cn/2010-06/08/content_1622956_2.htm.

been devoted to the actual substance of China's formal Internet policies and regulations and how these policies have changed over time.

This chapter examines the Internet governance policies in China to determine the policy-making trends in the country. The analysis includes a discussion of policy changes over time, the different agencies that formulate policy, and the different issues that are emphasized in policymaking. The specific aims of this chapter are (1) to understand the distribution of decision-making activities over different policy-making agencies; (2) to explore the topical focus of the policies; and (3) to investigate which policy objectives receive more attention during policy proceedings.

The rest of this study is organized as follows. Section 2 begins with a short summary of the literature on China's Internet governance. Section 3 introduces the research materials used in this chapter, namely, Internet governance policy documents that detail the laws, administrative ordinances, and regulations formulated and enacted in China. This section also introduces our method, which primarily involves quantitative content analysis. Section 4 describes and discusses the analytical findings, including the different policies formulated and the periods at which these were enacted, the various issuing agencies, and the application scopes and themes of the policies. In the concluding section, we use the results as bases for analyzing the fundamental features of current Internet governance policies in China. Our results suggest the need for more attention on Internet policymaking in the country.

2   Literature Review

The relevant literature on China's Internet governance can be divided into five categories: research on the meaning and definition of Internet governance; work on Chinese and global Internet governance; studies on China's institutional development in relation to the information-communications sector; research that describes and analyzes China's Internet filtering and content regulation mechanisms; and research on the effects of the Internet and communications development on China's political development.

Although previous years were characterized by limited progress in terms of realizing coordination and collective agreement on global Internet issues (Mueller et al. 2007), the concept of Internet governance currently enjoys wide recognition and acceptance. Notably, the World Summit on the Information Society led to the creation of the Working Group on Internet Governance (WGIG), which draws from international regime theory in political science in defining "Internet governance" as the "shared principles, norms, rules, decision-making procedures, and programmes that shape the evolution and use of the Internet" (WGIG 2005). It is a term for "how the Internet is coordinated, managed, and shaped to reflect policies" (Mueller 2010), including Internet-related communications and information policy issues. DeNardis (2010) defines Internet governance as the "policy and technical coordination issues related to the exchange of information over the Internet." Chinese scholars agree on the main definitions of Internet governance and affirm that content regulation is a core issue in China (Li 2009; Luo 2012).

Although China's Internet governance policy has elicited considerable criticism in international circles, some states consider it worth imitating (Herold 2011). Regardless of conflicting views regarding Chinese policymaking, the country's rise as an important actor in global Internet governance is inevitable not only because of the sheer number of its Internet users but also because its information technology corporations are prominent shapers of global Internet infrastructure and the device market (Arsène 2012). Yet other scholars caution against overestimating China's role in global Internet governance, even though it has been exerting continual efforts to strengthen influence over Internet-related technology, critical resources, and policymaking (Liu 2012). The dilemma presented by the desire for internal control of the Internet and the need to maintain trade and service links to the external world motivates China to promote sovereignty and collaboration between intergovernmental institutions for global Internet governance (Mueller 2012).

Internet governance is necessarily intertwined with the development of China's information-communications sector, especially when it comes to reform in the telecommunications industry. Mueller and Tan (1997) examine the obstacles that confronted reform in this sector prior to the advent of the Internet; the authors indicate a conflict between economic development and centralized state control. The convergence of information and communication technologies challenges China's segregated, sector-oriented regulatory institutions, which drive the coherent evolution of the regulatory regime (Tan 1999). Although development in China's telecommunications industry is driven by the economic market, such progress ultimately depends on social and political factors (Fu and Mou 2010). A similar argument is maintained by Liu and Jayakar (2012), who analyze the evolution of China's telecommunications policy-making process using the new institutionalism approach. The authors find that "the decision-making is much more affected by the macro level political rearrangement."

China has developed a sophisticated mechanism for controlling Internet use; this mechanism is characterized by four gatekeeping tiers that enable governance over all aspects of information flow (Rayburn and Conrad 2004). It has also launched state-directed self-regulation initiatives, such as the 2002 "Public Pledge on Self-discipline for China's Internet Industry" (Weber and Jia 2007). Dong (2012) reminds us that Internet regulation in China is implemented at five levels: government, service providers, content providers, webmasters, and individual users. Although few official statements regarding content-filtering methods have been issued (Zittrain and Edelman 2003), the Chinese government has deployed many sophisticated technologies that control what happens online; a particularly compelling policy is the 2003 Golden Shield (*Jin Dun* in Chinese) project, commonly known as the "Great Firewall" in Western nations (Fallows 2008). The aborted project, Green Dam Youth Escort, is a filtering software that was slated for installation in all computers in

China—another issue that elicited various discussions from different stakeholders (Tai 2010). The OpenNet Initiative's testing results show that diverse methods—Internet Protocol (IP) blocking, Domain Name System (DNS) tampering, keyword filtering—are deployed to regulate Internet content (Deibert et al. 2011). Beginning 2011, the government has improved the coordination of all regulatory mechanisms for governing Internet platforms and services (MacKinnon 2012). In addition to sensitive political information, obscenity, pornographic content, and other information that the state finds threatening or objectionable are subject to legislative sanctions, stringent law enforcement, and new technological measures (Liang and Lu 2012).

Leibold (2011) dismisses what he calls stereotyped discussions about Internet control as good or evil, claiming that a more interesting issue for consideration is how the Internet and information are reconstituting Chinese society and identity. China's socialist market economy is stimulating a freer flow of information over the Internet—a phenomenon that equally affects the socio-political structure and promotes the empowerment of civil society in the country (Bi 2001). New information and communications technology-driven development of civil society over the Internet facilitates democracy (Marsh and Whalen 2000). The Internet is inevitably intertwined with a specific social context such as habits, beliefs, and values (Tsui 2005). The Internet's political impact depends primarily on "public opinion and civil participation" (Hung 2006). It not only empowers the state and society but also reshapes the relationship between them (Zheng 2007). In other words, the state and civil society exhibit a complicated relationship under China's political development in the information era (Rosen 2010).

The discussion above distinctly indicates that the Chinese government has reinforced its regulation of Internet usage and activities as it undergoes large-scale commercialization. Institutional development in relation to the information and communications field is confronted with a core Internet policy issue: the formulation of strategies for reinforcing both external relations and internal governance. On the one hand, content regulation is the most important concern of the government and has become the central focus of China's legal, technical, and self-regulatory Internet mechanisms. On the other hand, the Internet-enabled strengthening of public participation in civil society challenges the country's current regulatory structure. Research regarding this matter has thus far focused on the implications of Internet governance policies in China, but minimal effort has been directed toward the actual provisions (textual content) of these policies. To address this gap, this study uses content analysis to explore the provisional attributes of China's Internet governance policies and traces the development trajectory of policy-making proceedings in China.

3   MATERIALS AND METHODS

3.1   Materials

Content analysis is intended for textual analysis, by which the basic framework that underlies subject development is identified. The text of Internet governance policy comprises mainly the provisions stated in laws, administrative ordinances, and regulations.

Policy text was collected from three sources published on 3 May 2013. We first obtained Chinese laws, administrative ordinances, and regulations from public sector websites, such as the National People's Congress (NPC), Central People's Government, Supreme People's Court, Supreme People's Procuratorate, Ministry of Industry and Information Technology (MIIT), Ministry of Public Security, State Administration of Radio Film and Television (SARFT),[4] General Administration of Press and Publication (GAPP), National Copyright Administration of China (NCAC), Ministry of Culture (MCPRC), SCIO, Ministry of Education, State Administration for Industry and Commerce, and CNNIC (Table 22.1). Most of the websites contain a page called "Policies and Regulations," which lists the numerous laws, administrative ordinances, and regulations related to corresponding public sector organizations.

Second, we used the Chinese laws and regulations database built by the NPC (http://law.npc.gov.cn) and conducted a full-text search using the keywords "Internet" and "network." We then compared the search results with the list we obtained from the government agency websites. To address gaps in

Table 22.1   Public sector websites

National People's Congress (NPC)	http://www.npc.gov.cn
Central People's Government (CPG)	http://www.gov.cn
Supreme People's Court (SPC)	http://www.court.gov.cn/
Supreme People's Procuratorate (SPP)	http://www.spp.gov.cn/
Ministry of Industry and Information Technology (MIIT)	http://www.miit.gov.cn
Ministry of Public Security (MPS)	http://www.mps.gov.cn
State Administration of Radio Film and Television (SARFT)	http://www.sarft.gov.cn/
General Administration of Press and Publication (GAPP)	http://www.gapp.gov.cn/
National Copyright Administration (NCAC)	http://www.ncac.gov.cn/
Ministry of Culture (MCPRC)	http://www.mcprc.gov.cn/
State Council Information Office (SCIO)	http://www.scio.gov.cn/
Ministry of Education (MOE)	http://www.moe.edu.cn/
State Administration for Industry and Commerce (SAIC)	http://www.saic.gov.cn/
China Internet Network Information Center (CNNIC)	http://www.cnnic.net.cn/

---

[4] In the first plenary session of the 12th National People's Congress in March 2013, the government decided to merge the SARFT and GAPP to form a new regulatory body, the State Administration of Press, Publications, Radio, Film, and Television. The new agency falls under the purview of the NCAC. The SARFT, GAPP, and NCAC have their own websites.

information, we used Google and Baidu to find data that supplement the policy text. Through this method, we identified 63 laws, administrative ordinances, and regulations, which we classified as Internet governance policies.

3.2   Methods

Content analysis is a systematic, objective, quantitative analysis of message characteristics (Neuendorf 2002), which is designed for the examination of message contents to elucidate "what they mean to people, what they enable or prevent, and what the information conveyed by them does" (Krippendorff 2012). Identifying and classifying the contents and characteristics of Internet governance policies necessitates coding the collected textual information on the basis of research questions and hypotheses.

3.2.1   Coding

After the list of laws, administrative ordinances, and regulations on Internet governance was confirmed to be free of duplication or mistakes, the content of the policies was coded in accordance with the following criteria:

1. Year of policy issuance: Period of issuance is motivated by a perceived need. Looking into specific dates enabled us to determine the trend with which Internet governance policies are formulated. The date code was converted into annual units.

2. Issuing government agency: In China, 15 different major agencies are involved in various stages of Internet governance policymaking. Different policy-making agencies impose different effects on enforcement. Some of the policies reviewed were issued by multiple government agencies; thus, a necessary task was to distinguish whether these agencies were also accorded jurisdiction over the provisions to be included in each policy. Every government agency is a coding unit, prompting us to also code whether a single agency or multiple agencies were involved in policymaking.

3. Type of policy: Internet governance policies were categorized into three types: legislation (from the NPC), State Council administrative ordinances, and ministry regulations. The policies were also classified into two categories by application scope: universal and specific policies.

4. Policy theme (e.g. content regulation, cybersecurity, Internet resources, etc.): In this research, the themes were divided into five types for the following reasons—the WGIG (2005) established four key public policy areas: *(1) issues related to the infrastructure and management of critical Internet; (2) issues related to the use of the Internet; (3) issues that are relevant to the Internet, but exert impact on a much wider scale; and (4) issues related to the developmental aspects of Internet governance.* Another debated core issue in relation to Internet governance is freedom of expression (Mueller 2010). The Chinese government's regulation of

Internet content has stimulated both international and domestic discussion regarding this matter (e.g. Dodgson 2000; Li 2008; Luo 2012; Reed 2000; Wu 2009). In consideration of this backdrop, we added another theme to the four initially established by the WGIG. The five themes are described as follows:

(a) Internet resources: As an important component of the Internet, the assignment of domain names and IP addresses must be effectively coordinated. An example of initiatives under this theme would be the 2004 MIIT policy, "China Internet Domain Name Regulations."

(b) Cybersecurity: Security violations are one of the most serious threats encountered over the Internet, making cybersecurity another important regulation domain. One of the endeavors initiated under this theme is the 2000 NPC policy, "The Decision on Internet Security."

(c) Intellectual property: The emergence of the Internet has given rise to the cruciality of protecting intellectual property, thereby driving many regulatory bodies to adopt this issue as one of the exhaustive focal points of policymaking. An example of such policies is the 2005 NCAC and MIIT policy, "Measures on the Administrative Protection of Internet Copyright."

(d) Development: Capacity building is an equally essential component of Internet governance for developing economies and is frequently promoted and supported by relevant policies. An example of the efforts exerted to realize this goal would be the 1996 MIIT policy, "Measures on the Regulation of Public Computer Networks."

(e) Content regulation: The censorship and regulation of messages publicized on the Internet has become a principal issue of debate between governments and users. The 2000 MIIT policy, "Administrative Provisions for Electronic Bulletin Services on the Internet," is one of the policy projects initiated in this regard.

Classification is one of the core components of content analysis. As the counterparts of interview or survey questions, the theme categories identified from analyzed content must accurately correspond with the needs of a study (Budd et al. 1967). A problem is that most of the policies regarding Internet governance are characterized by the multiple themes that we identified for the current work. Therefore, some of the policies exhibit more than one of these themes and a given policy may be coded into two (or more) themes. For more reasonable categorization, a policy document can be categorized as exhibiting certain themes on the basis of its introduction or foreword, which explicitly outlines policy-making objectives and bases. For example, most of the policies are introduced by phrases such as "in order to," "according to," "formulated in accordance with," "to meet the requirement," and "comply with." These phrases served as direct guidelines for categorization.

The format of the coding used for the laws, administrative ordinances, and regulations reviewed in this chapter is explained in Table 22.2.

Table 22.2 Coding format

Title	Year	Issuing agency	Issued jointly	Type	Category	Theme
A_i	B_i	C_i	D_i	E_i	F_i	G_i

Table 22.3 Coding details

Issuing agency (C_i)	C_1: NPC; C_2: CPG; C_3: SPC; C_4: SPP; C_5: MIIT; C_6: MPS; C_7: SARFT; C_8: GAPP; C_9: NCAC; C_{10}: MCPRC; C_{11}: SCIO; C_{12}: MOE; C_{13}: SAIC; C_{14}: NAPSS; C_{15}: CNNIC
Type (E_i)	E_1: NPC legislation; E_2: State Council administrative ordinances; E_3: Regulations by ministries
Theme (G_i)	G_1: Internet resources; G_2: Cybersecurity; G_3: Intellectual property; G_4: Capability development; G_5: Content regulation

In the coding format, A_i refers to the title of laws and regulations on Internet governance (i = 1, 2, 3 … 63); B_i denotes the year of policy issuance (from 1994 to 2012); C_i identifies which of the 15 agencies spearheaded policy formulation and supervised enactment[5]; D_i represents two statuses, yes and no, indicating whether a policy was drafted by one or more government agencies, respectively; E_i pertains to the three categories on which law type is based (NPC, State Council, or Ministry legislation); F_i comprises two categories that point to application scope, that is, universal or specific policy; G_i denotes the five themes (domains) that correspond to the subject matter covered by the policies. These classification types are summarized in Table 22.3.

3.2.2   Coding Reliability

To ensure coding reliability, two coders tested the consistency of categorization for all the policy documents. The formula used to determine the reliability coefficient is $2 * M/N_1 + N_2$, where M denotes the consistent coding numbers derived by the coders; N_1 and N_2 are the first and second coder's coding numbers, respectively. Neuendorf (2002) stated that an agreement coefficient of 0.9 or greater is acceptable. The calculated inter-coder reliability for theme categorization is 0.903, which falls within the range of acceptability. Using the coders' evaluations as bases, we then revised the categorization.

4   Results and Discussion

4.1   Different Types of Policies and Different Periods of Issuance

Over time, the number of Internet governance policies increases in parallel with the growth of the Internet. The first laws were formulated in 1994 when

---

[5] C14: NAPSS, as an institution, is responsible for protecting classified information; it does not have its own website.

the Internet was introduced into China. Our results show that the formulation of policies related to Internet governance steadily increased from 1994 to 2012, especially since the turn of the century (Fig. 22.1).

From 1994 to 1999, almost no major Internet policies were issued, except for several general policies about international network construction and information system security. During this period, China's Internet market was an emerging sector and only a few users accessed the Internet. Such policymaking therefore posed minimal influence on the entire Chinese society. The year 2000, which saw the increased penetration of the Internet into people's lives, marked the establishment of key laws designed to regulate Internet use in the country. Nine policies were formulated, including the "Decision on Internet Security" by the NPC, "Regulations on Telecommunications of the People's Republic of China," and "Measures for the Administration of Internet Information Service" by the State Council. These key early decisions formed the basis of China's contemporary Internet governance policies. Most regulations are intended to exert direct control over Internet websites, Bulletin Board System (BBS) providers, Internet news, and Internet users, with concentration directed principally toward content regulation and cybersecurity. After several years of understanding and assimilating the basic Internet policies put in place in 2000, the government entered a new phase of Internet policy formulation in 2004. At this point, it fully realized that the Internet is an information infrastructure that significantly affects national development and strengthens governance in accordance with the "classification model." The government issued some very concrete governance policies, such as those for email services, audiovisual content, online games, online music, and Web-based printing businesses. Gradually, the widespread adoption of the Internet in China gave rise to serious problems. In 2012, three important Internet policies were issued to establish order in the information services market, information construction, and information protection.

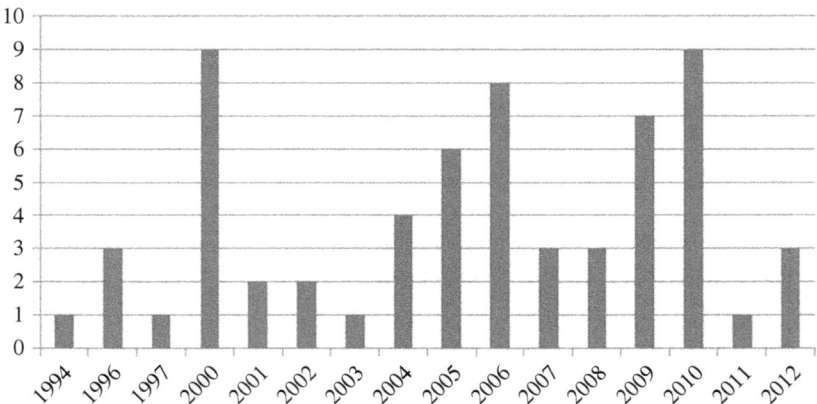

Fig. 22.1 Number of policies issued for Internet governance

Fig. 22.2 Types of policies on Internet governance

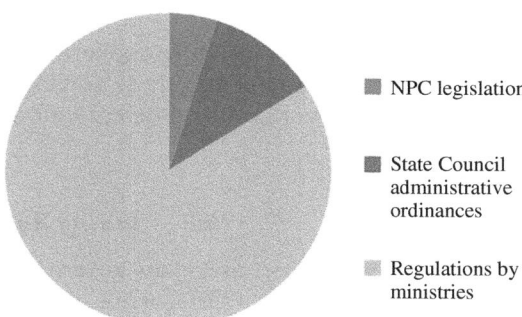

■ NPC legislation

■ State Council administrative ordinances

▨ Regulations by ministries

About 84% of the Internet governance policies and regulations are issued by Chinese ministries. By contrast, the NPC and State Council formulated relatively few legislative and administrative ordinances (Fig. 22.2), indicating the low priority with which the legal system viewed Internet governance (Wu and Bai 2009). This situation is attributed largely to the fact that the Chinese government was more concerned with technology development during the early development of the Internet. Conversely, because the Internet is relatively new in China, numerous legal issues arising from the Internet have not been thoroughly explored. Some of these problems stem from the various conflicts of interest among different ministries and agencies. This disagreement is indicative of an underdeveloped Internet policy regime, in which fundamental laws were the core legislation and administrative regulations served as supplements.

Cybersecurity policies are a good example of how Internet policy formulation developed in China. As indicated by the content of these policies, the primary laws are the "Decision on Internet Security," "Digital Signature Law," "Decision on Strengthening Network Information Protection" by the NPC, and the "Regulations on the Protection of Computer Information System Security" by the State Council. A comparison of these policies indicates a top-heavy trend: an excessive number of policies are issued by Chinese ministries, but only a few are promulgated by the NPC and State Council (Zhang and An 2004). This imbalance emphasizes the necessity of devising a special law on information network security at the national level, instead of focusing on the mass issuance of ministry regulations. The present policies for cybersecurity suffer from obvious gaps and poorly chosen targets; these problems are particularly evident on regulations that revolve around the security of information and network systems—a problem that results from the numerous gaps in the adjustment of network behavior (Ye and Li 2010). More seriously, cybersecurity is supervised by many different line ministries, such as the MPS, MIIT, National Administration for the Protection of State Secrets (NAPSS), and MCPRC. These ministries are engaged in a power struggle, thereby leading to difficult coordination of efforts (Ma 2004). The distribution of authority over cybersecurity across different industries and departments poses a crucial problem: independent efforts may result in a disregard of the functions of other departments and of the need for cooperation. The aforementioned discussion highlights the necessity of effectively developing the policy system for cybersecurity, with consideration for different enforcement levels, policymakers, and content foci.

4.2   Issuing Agencies

Given extensive Internet use, many government agencies in China are involved in Internet governance policymaking. The organizational chart in Fig. 22.3 lists the major agencies involved in the initiatives and the organizational structure. The 15 major agencies are presented in Table 22.4 and Fig. 22.4. The MIIT and SARFT have issued more than half of the policies on Internet governance and continue to dominate the Internet policy-making landscape. The MIIT not only issues independent policies but also spearheads or participates in some other policy-making endeavors. The SARFT concentrates on its audio-visual program service, but it also primarily operates in an independent manner.

The results show that most of the policies (80%) were separately issued by government agencies. Recent years, however, have seen the issuance of regulations by multiple government ministries, given the increasing complexity of Internet problems. The policies jointly issued are shown in Table 22.5. With the popularity of Internet applications and services, an increasing number of fields are becoming intertwined with the Internet, thereby leading to conflicts of interest among multiple policymakers. During cable TV, telecommunications, and Internet network integration, for example, the SARFT was given the authority to regulate radio and television businesses and prohibited the MIIT from overseeing radio and TV network operations. For its part, the MIIT refused to allow the SARFT to regulate Internet and telephone operations. The growing need for agencies to work together may explain the rise in jointly issued policies. This approach not only resolves the complicated problems associated with the Internet environment but also creates a balance of power among agencies.

4.3   Distribution of Universal and Specific Policies

To delve deeper into the provisions (textual content) of the policies, these were classified into categories by application scope. A universal policy is directed toward all or most aspects of a subject area, which is often cited in other policy documents; a specific policy concentrates on an individual aspect of a subject area, providing detailed policy guidance.

Our results show that 15% of the Internet governance policies are universal. Such policies were issued in 1996 for international network construction; in 2000 for information services, telecommunications, and Internet security, and

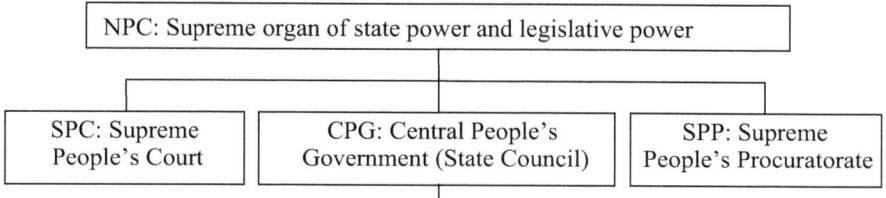

NPC: Supreme organ of state power and legislative power

| SPC: Supreme People's Court | CPG: Central People's Government (State Council) | SPP: Supreme People's Procuratorate |

MIIT: Some of its responsibilities are creating and implementing policy on telecommunications, supervising Internet activities, supervising the information services market, and undertaking network security.

MPS: Some of its responsibilities are ensuring the security of the computer network system and information, and fighting cybercrime.

SARFT: This regulatory body regulates audio-visual program services offered on the Internet.

GAPP: This institution inspects applications for Internet publishing and supervises the content of published information.

NCAC: One of its responsibilities is to protect copyright on the Internet.

MCPRC: Some of its responsibilities are granting approvals for the sale of cultural products on the Internet, granting license for Internet cafes, and regulating services for online gaming.

SCIO: Some of its responsibilities are to supervise Internet news, implement information dissemination policies, and instruct relevant departments to regulate content.

MOE: This institution promotes education and guides behavior on the Internet.

SAIC: This institution regulates trading over the Internet.

NAPSS: This regulatory body manages confidentiality on computer networks.

CNNIC is operated by the Chinese Academy of Sciences and MIIT. It is responsible for the administration of the .cn ccTLD registry and the Chinese domain name system.

Fig. 22.3   Structure of major Internet governance agencies

in 2012 for the Internet services market, informatization, and information protection. These policies mostly cover the themes of cybersecurity, capability development, and content regulation. In all the policy documents, the five most frequently referred to in other policies are the 2002 "Measures for Administration of Internet Information Services," 2000 "Regulations on

Table 22.4 Data on the policies issued by government agencies

Issuing agencies	Total number issued	Issued separately	Issued jointly
MIIT	22	13	9
SARFT	11	9	2
CPG	7	7	0
MPS	7	3	4
MCPRC	7	5	2
SPC	7	4	3
GAPP	5	1	4
NPC	3	3	0
SCIO	3	0	3
SPP	3	0	3
CNNIC	3	3	0
MOE	3	1	2
SAIC	2	0	2
NAPSS	2	1	1
NCAC	1	0	1

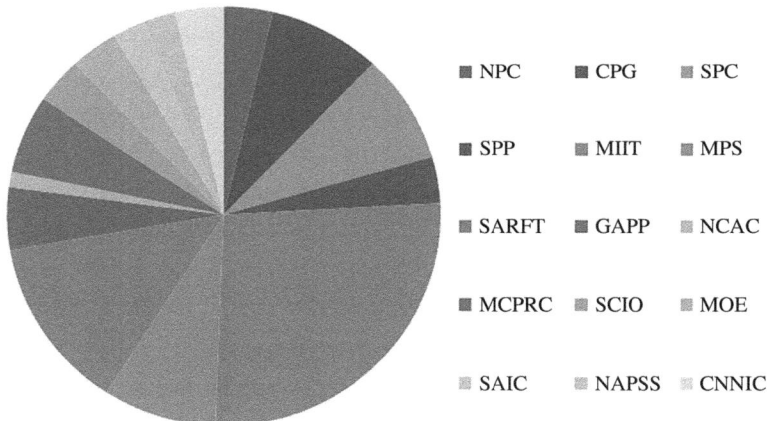

Fig. 22.4 Distribution of policy issuance among issuing agencies

Telecommunications," 2008 "Administrative Rules for Audio-visual Programs Transmitted over Internet," 2000 "Decision on Internet Security," and 2004 "China Internet Domain Name Regulations."

The most important decree for content regulation, cybersecurity, and capacity development is the "Measures for Administration of Internet Information Services" created by The State Council. This policy became the critical basis of later policies for Internet governance. The policy delineates the responsibility of content providers in accordance with the licensing and registration system; it prohibits content providers from creating, replicating,

Table 22.5   Year of issue, topics, and agencies of jointly issued policies

Year	Topic	Agency
2000/2005	Internet news services	SCIO, MIIT
2002	Online publishing	GAPP, MIIT
2004	Control of pornography	SPC, SPP
2005	Copyright on Internet	NCAC, MIIT
2005	Online games	MCPRC, MIIT
2007	Game addiction	GAPP, MOE, MPS, MIIT, etc.
2007	Printing businesses on the Internet	GAPP, MPS, SAIC, MIIT
2008	Audiovisual services	SARFT, MIIT
2009	Website blacklist	MIIT, SCIO, MOE, MPS, MCPRC, SAIC, SARFT, GAPP, NAPSS, etc.
2010	Gambling on the Internet	SPC, SPP, MPS
2011	Computer system crimes	SPC, SPP

retrieving, or transmitting specific types of information in Article 15. Such information pertains to that which[6]

> (1) opposes the fundamental principles determined in the Constitution; (2) compromises State security, divulges State secrets, subverts State power or damages national unity; (3) harms the dignity or interests of the State; (4) incites ethnic hatred or racial discrimination or damages inter-ethnic unity; (5) sabotages State religious policy or propagates heretical teachings or feudal superstitions; (6) disseminates rumors, disturbs social order or disrupts social stability; (7) propagates obscenity, pornography, gambling, violence, murder or fear or incites the commission of crimes; (8) insults or slanders a third party or infringes upon the lawful rights and interests of a third party; or (9) includes other content prohibited by laws or administrative regulations.

We also counted the policy objectives discussed in the documents. Table 22.6 shows the distribution of specific topics which are concerned with Internet governance policies. Audiovisual services, domain names, safety protection, copyright on the Internet, and cybercrimes are ranked the highest in the frequency of discussion. The other topics include online games, online publishing, online music, Internet news service, bulletin board systems, and website records. These policy topics are distinctly paid more attention by policy-making agencies, especially in recent years. At the initial stage of Internet development (from 1994 to 1999), network connection and network security were the key focal points of policy formulation. Given the extensive adoption of the Internet, governance policy during this period gradually emphasized response solutions

[6] State Council (25 September 2000). Measures for the Administration of Internet information services.   Retrieved   from   http://tradeinservices.mofcom.gov.cn/en/b/2000-09-25/18565.shtml.

Table 22.6 Results for specific topics with proportions higher than 3.8%

Rank	Topic	Proportion
1	Audiovisual services	15.1%
2	Domain names	13.2%
3	Safety protection	9.4%
4	Copyright on Internet	9.4%
5	Cybercrime	7.5%
6	Online games	5.7%
7	Online publishing	3.8%
8	Online music	3.8%
9	Internet news services	3.8%
10	Bulletin board systems	3.8%
11	Website records	3.8%

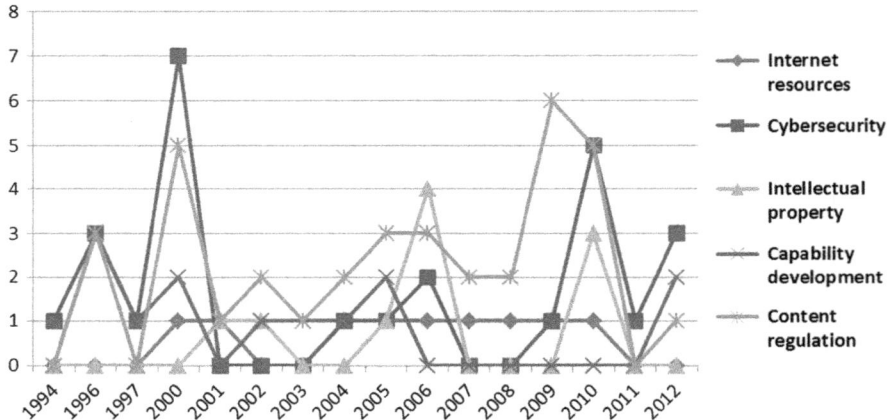

Fig. 22.5 Time distribution of themes

to specific issues, such as online culture construction, which covers online games, music, and videos.

4.4   Theme Distribution

In all the Internet governance policy documents, 57% of the policies revolve around content regulation, accounting for the largest percentage of distribution; 41% of the policies center on cybersecurity. The data also show that 14%, 16%, and 21% of the policies focus on Internet resources, intellectual property, and capacity development, respectively. The number of content regulation and cybersecurity policies increased during the late 2000s (Fig. 22.5).

At the infancy of Internet development, especially from 2000 to 2005, more than one policy on capacity development was issued almost every year, indicating the tremendous importance that the government attached to infrastructure and capacity building. In June 2012, the central government initiated the "Broadband in China" project under the policy "Vigorously Promoting the Development of Informatization and Information Security." This project signifies the national government's recognition and affirmation of the public character of the Internet and the benefits it can provide to public welfare. On the whole, however, the government has more strongly emphasized cybersecurity and content regulation than capacity development since 2006. A large proportion of the policies have revolved around cybersecurity and content regulation in recent years. Frequently, the issue of cybersecurity is addressed in combination with content regulation in a number of policy documents, suggesting that these two themes are considered closely related to each other.

The starting point of effective content regulation is to enable the development of the Internet in a way that does not disrupt political order in China. This type of policy may disadvantage small Internet sites that do not have sufficient resources to monitor content (Boyarski et al. 2001). Present policies on content regulation concentrate on audiovisual services, Internet news services, bulletin board systems, website records, online publishing, music, and games. These clearly delineate requirements and regulations for content control. Meanwhile, one problem is "the definition of state secrets remains vague" (Lapres 2000). A clearer boundary between free expression and state security is needed even as present regulatory mechanisms regulate information transmission via content classification and administrative authority. A difficult task for government agencies is the direct regulation of content; thus, they are more inclined to delegate this responsibility to Internet Service Providers (ISPs) and Internet Content Providers (ICPs). In terms of government agencies' issuance of content regulation policies, the results generally indicate that the MIIT administers over the Internet industry; the SARFT oversees audiovisual program services; the MCP is responsible for the cultural industry; security departments, such as the MPS, manage content legality; and the press and publication department supervises publication and distribution. This complex division of responsibilities for Internet content regulation often causes strife among the different agencies. More importantly, this management system lacks top-down leadership. Various government agencies struggle for power and benefits—a situation that presents difficulties in the formulation and establishment of relevant policies for long-term content governance.

With respect to Internet security, the government attaches great importance to cybersecurity, but serious threats in virtual space remain, including spam, malware, cybercrime, and privacy violation, which are the focal issues of present policies. Nevertheless, the many different aspects of cybersecurity accentuate the importance of constructing a systematic framework. Let us take privacy protection as an example. Present laws, administrative ordinances, and regulations protect privacy to a certain extent. The privacy of correspondence is protected by the Constitution of the People's Republic of China. Core supervisory authorities have also designed regulations that underscore the criticality of protecting users' personal information. These rules, however, lack feasibility and operability because no national act on protecting personal information has been formulated. Despite the progress made in policy proceedings and practices, a complete framework system for privacy and personal data protection has yet to be developed (Ong 2011; Xue 2010). A typical example of this deficiency is what the Chinese refer to as the "human flesh search engine," a collective effort by thousands of Internet users to dig out more information about specific events or people and expose them publicly. However, the "human flesh search engine" is a double-edged sword with a dark side, which inevitably raises the problem of personal privacy infringement. Cheung (2009) calls for putting a stop to its abuse. How exactly do we define personal information? Since the NPC issued the "Decision on Strengthening Network Information Protection" in 2012, privacy protection has been more clearly defined at the national institution level in the policy, where an article presents "the state protects electronic information by which individual citizens can be identified and which involves the individual privacy of citizens." The extensive protection of personal information, however, necessitates a specially designed law on privacy.

The theme of Internet resource is relatively independent, focusing primarily on domain name registration, dispute resolution, Chinese-script domain names, and IP address administration. The series of domestic policies for Internet governance have been established since 2000. One policy for Internet resource has been issued each year from 2004 to 2010, including policies on how to manage DNSs and how to distribute IP addresses. The government adopted measures for content complaint mechanisms, verification of domain name owners, web security, and website record to strengthen governance under the existing regulatory framework (Wong and Chiu 2011). The policies for critical Internet resources mandate registries and registrars to comply with regulations for allocation and content control; the sanctions implementable under these policies include blacklisting websites that have been shut down, ensuring the registry of information, and issuing cease and desist orders for unregistered and illegal websites (Xue 2012).

In the field of intellectual property, the core policies are the "Information Network Transmission Right Protection Ordinance" issued by the State Council in 2006, the "Measures on the Administrative Protection of Internet Copyright" issued by the NCAC and MIIT in 2005, and some regulations and legal interpretations involving intellectual property. These policies were promulgated in 2006 and 2010, but most of them are in the form of judicial interpretations and administrative regulations and rarely take the form of legislation issued by the Standing Committee of the NPC. This committee is of low status in the legal hierarchy for network intellectual property. Given that intellectual piracy has been a serious long-standing problem in China, the government has adopted judicial, administrative, social, and technical modalities to protect intellectual property over the Internet (Tong et al. 2008). Nevertheless, copyright infringement remains a frequent phenomenon—a problem that is attributed to the lack of coordination between multiply managed policymaking and different system types. The starting point of current policies is the regulation of intellectual property over the Internet, but this goal is achieved only through response measures rather than solving the problem at its root.

5   CONCLUSION

The growth and extensive use of the Internet in China have prompted involvement from an increasing number of governance agencies and policies. Policies are formulated to ensure normal operations, develop Internet capacity, reasonably distribute Internet resources, protect intellectual property, improve cybersecurity, and control content. Using content analysis, this chapter examined the circumstances that surround Internet governance policymaking in China.

Current policies focus largely on governance at the national level, with regulations designed for the security of country or industry; individual rights, such as privacy protection, are more or less disregarded. Much of the effort is directed toward strengthening the control and regulatory power of the government, as evidenced by the goals defined in most of the existing policies. These goals emphasize normative order and security rather than governmental obligations and responsibilities. Network operators or Internet users are held liable for violations, and punitive measures include fining, closing down of businesses, cancelation of licenses, and imprisonment. China's structure is currently one of a "powerful government and weak society," as similarly reflected in the architectural structure of Internet governance.

Given the short history of Internet usage in China, regulatory bodies have failed to explore the problems that have arisen from the emergence of this technology. A particularly difficult task is forming a framework for a top-down Internet governance regime—a deficiency that causes the decentralization of political power in the Internet governance realm. Ministries issue a considerably greater number of policies than do the NPC and State Council. The involvement of all kinds of administrative agencies in developing various regulatory policies is inevitable, thereby resulting in conflicts related to the varying levels of Internet governance and the lack of systematic coordination (Chen 2011). The complexity of the Internet has prompted different ministries to jointly promulgate policies in recent years, with such efforts aimed at establishing a coordination mechanism for power balance among multiple policymakers.

In terms of substance, increasing emphasis on content regulation is a remarkable feature of recent Internet governance policies. Although various regulatory mechanisms are in place for monitoring information dissemination, authorities are more inclined to delegate such responsibility to ISPs and ICPs. This approach is insufficient to address Internet-related problems because of the more pressing issue of delineating the boundary between free expression and content regulation. Meanwhile, the participation of multiple stakeholders in content regulation is an essential requirement. Some policy-making processes suffer from a lack of involvement from users; thus, content-related policies, such as those for real-name system which means Internet users are required to offer identifications including real name when they register an account in BBS, have elicited mass opposition. The development of Internet governance is a significant component of China's future; it will entail the formulation of content regulation policies that satisfy social, economic, and political demands, especially those from users.

Certain limitations of this research are worth noting. Content analysis examines the transitions and trends of Internet governance policymaking but does not cover the evaluation of policy effectiveness. Each Internet governance policy in China reflects different benefits and values for stakeholders. Moreover, the materials on Internet governance policies are characterized by certain inadequacies in terms of unified and accurate data under specific research conditions. Some provisions in the laws, administrative ordinances, and regulations (e.g. the relationship between cybercrime and criminal law) were beyond the scope of this research even though their definitions are reflected in some of the policies that we reviewed. The local ordinances influence local jurisdiction rather than the national domain and were therefore excluded from the analysis. Some conventions and treaties issued by the self-regulatory organizations or Internet industry associations were also omitted because they lack compelling enforcement power. Furthermore, the analyzed policies do not discuss special regulations that cater to specific subject matter, such as the administration of share certificates and drug sales over the Internet. Further research should be devoted to local ordinances and self-regulation principles; directing focus to these materials will present different functional mechanisms. Another direction worth exploring is to examine policy application from the perspectives of different stakeholders.

REFERENCES

Arsène, S. 2012 May. The impact of China on global Internet governance in an era of privatized control. Paper presented at *Chinese Internet Research Conference*, Los Angeles, CA.

Bi, J. 2001. The Internet Revolution in China: The Significance for Traditional forms of Communist Control. *International Journal* 56(3): 421–441.

Boyarski, J. R., H. R. Goldstein, J. E. Lawrence, and J. Linn. 2001. China's new Internet regulations may disadvantage small Internet sites. *Intellectual Property & Technology Law Journal* 13(1): 21–22.

Budd, R. W., R. K. Thorp, and L. Donohew. 1967. *Content analysis of communications*. New York: The Macmillan Company.

Chen, X. 2011. *Legal regulation of the Internet service*. Available at http://www.law-time.cn/info/lunwen/qitalw/2011062177439.html.

Cheung, A. S. 2009. China Internet going wild: Cyber-hunting versus privacy protection. *Computer Law & Security Review* 25(3): 275–279.

China Internet Network Information Center. 2014. *The 33rd statistical report on the Internet development in China*. Available at http://cnnic.net/hlwfzyj/hlwxzbg/hlwtjbg/201403/P020140305346585959798.pdf.

Cullen, R., and P. D. Choy. 1999. The Internet in China. *Columbia Journal of Asian Law* 13(1): 99–134.

Deibert, R., J. Palfrey, R. Rohozinski, and J. Zittrain. 2011. *Access contested: Security, identity, and resistance in Asian cyberspace.* Cambridge, MA: MIT Press.

DeNardis, L. 2010. *The emerging field of Internet governance.* Available at http://ssrn.com/abstract=1678343.

Dodgson, C. 2000. Controlling Internet content. *Communications International* 27(5): 24.

Dong, F. 2012. Controlling the Internet in China: The real story. *Convergence: The International Journal of Research into New Media Technologies* 18(4): 403–425.

Dowell, W. T. 2006. The Internet, censorship, and China. *Georgetown Journal of International Affairs* 7(2): 111–119.

Fallows, J. 2008. The connection has been reset. *The Atlantic Monthly* 301(2): 64–69.

Fu, H., and Y. Mou. 2010. An assessment of the 2008 telecommunications restructuring in China. *Telecommunications Policy* 34(10): 649–658.

Herold, D. K. 2011. *An inter-nation-al Internet: China's contribution to global Internet governance?* Available at http://ssrn.com/abstract=1922725.

Hung, C. 2006. The politics of cyber participation in the PRC: The implications of contingency for the awareness of citizens' rights. *Issues and Studies* 42(4): 137–173.

Hung, C. 2012. China's changing state-society relations in the Internet age: Case study of Zhao Zuohai. *International Journal of China Studies* 3(3): 363–381.

Krippendorff, K. 2012. *Content analysis: An introduction to its methodology (3rd ed.).* Thousand Oaks, CA: Sage Publications, Inc.

Lai, L. S., and W. To. 2012. Internet diffusion in China: Economic and social implications. *IT Professional* 14(6): 16–21.

Lapres, D. A. 2000. Legal dos and don'ts of web use in China. *The China Business Review* 27(2): 26–27, 64.

Leibold, J. 2011. Blogging alone: China, the Internet, and the democratic illusion? *The Journal of Asian Studies* 70(4): 1023–1041.

Li, H. 2009. *Internet governance present situation, problems and public policy.* In National Information Center of China (ed.). *Chinese information almanac 2008.* Beijing: Chinese Information Almanac Press.

Li, Y. 2008. Expectation and result of supervision on the content of the Chinese Internet—Facts and evaluation. *Journal of Jiangsu Administration Institute* 2: 90–95.

Liang, B., and H. Lu. 2012. Fighting the obscene, pornographic, and unhealthy—An analysis of the nature, extent, and regulation of China's online pornography within a global context. *Crime, Law and Social Change* 58(2): 111–130.

Liu, C., and K. Jayakar. 2012. The evolution of telecommunications policy-making: Comparative analysis of China and India. *Telecommunications Policy* 36(1): 13–28.

Liu, Y. 2012. The rise of China and global Internet governance. *China Media Research* 8(2): 46–56.

Luo, C. 2012. Freedom of expression and restriction in cyberspace. *Wuhan University Law Review* 30(4): 15–23.

Ma, Z. 2004. Legal system of the information network security. *Science-Technology and Law* 3: 14–18.

MacKinnon, R. 2012. *Consent of the networked: The worldwide struggle for Internet freedom.* New York: Basic Books.

Marsh, C., and L. Whalen. 2000. The Internet, e-social capital, and democratization in China. *American Journal of Chinese Studies* 7(1): 61–81.

Mueller, M. L. 2010. *Networks and states: The global politics of Internet governance*. Cambridge, London: MIT Press.

Mueller, M. L. 2012. *China and global Internet governance: A tiger by the tail*. In Deibert. R., J. Palfrey, R. Rohozinski, and J. Zittrain (eds.). *Access contested: Security, identity, and resistance in Asian cyberspace*. Cambridge, MA: MIT Press.

Mueller, M. L., J. Mathiason, and H. Klein. 2007. The Internet and global governance: Principles and norms for a new regime. *Global Governance* 13(2): 237–254.

Mueller, M. L., and Z. Tan. 1997. *China in the information age: Telecommunications and the dilemmas of reform*. Westport, CT: Praeger.

Neuendorf, K. A. 2002. *The content analysis guidebook*. Thousand Oaks, CA: Sage Publications, Inc.

Ong, R. 2011. Recognition of the right to privacy on the Internet in China. *International Data Privacy Law* 1(3): 172–179.

Rayburn, J. M., and C. Conrad. 2004. China's Internet structure: Problems and control measures. *International Journal of Management* 21(4): 471–480.

Reed, K. M. 2000. From the great firewall of China to the Berlin firewall: The cost of content regulation on Internet commerce. *The Transnational Lawyer* 13(2): 451.

Rosen, S. 2010. Is the Internet a positive force in the development of civil society, a public sphere, and democratization in China? *International Journal of Communication* 4: 509–516.

Tai, Z. 2010. Casting the ubiquitous net of information control: Internet surveillance in China from golden shield to green dam. *International Journal of Advanced Pervasive and Ubiquitous Computing* 2(1): 53–70.

Tan, Z. 1999. Regulating China's Internet: Convergence toward a coherent regulatory regime. *Telecommunications Policy* 23(3–4): 261–276.

Tong, Z., F. Yan, and J. Hao. 2008. Digital copyright protection in China. *Publishing Research Quarterly* 24(1): 48–53.

Tsui, L. 2005. Introduction: The sociopolitical Internet in China. *China Information* 19(2): 181–188.

Weber, I., and L. Jia. 2007. Internet and self-regulation in China: The cultural logic of controlled commodification. *Media Culture and Society* 29(5): 772–789.

The Working Group on Internet Governance. 2005. *Report of the Working Group on Internet Governance*. Available at http://www.itu.int/wsis/docs2/pc3/off5.pdf.

Wong, K., and A. Chiu. 2011. *New domain name developments in China and Hong Kong*. Available at http://www.mayerbrown.com/publications/New-Domain-Name-Developments-in-China-amp-Hong-Kong-01-06-2011/.

Wu, J., and S. Bai. 2009. The policy body and ability enhancement of China's Internet controls. *Heilongjiang Social Sciences* 4: 45–48.

Wu, W. 2009. The separation of Internet content regulation in the face of the convergence of information and communication technologies: The controversies, challenges and solutions for China. *Canadian Social Science* 5(1): 24–43.

Xue, H. 2010. Privacy and personal data protection in China: An update for the year end 2009. *Computer Law and Security Review: The International Journal of Technology and Practice* 26(3): 284–289.

Xue, H. 2012. *China, law enforcement and DNS filtering: Uncertainties, questions and challenges*. Available at http://wsms1.intgovforum.org/sites/default/files/China,%20Law%20Enforcement%20and%20DNS%20Filtering.pdf.

Yang, G. 2009. *The power of the Internet in China: Citizen activism online.* New York: Columbia University Press.

Ye, X., and R. Li. 2010. The status of network information security legal protection. *Theory Research* 11: 117–118.

Zhang, C., and Y. An. 2004. The legal protection of the information networks security. *Computer Security* 2: 1–2.

Zhang, X., and C. Moussi. 2007. Level of Internet use by Chinese businesses: A preliminary study. *Electronic Commerce Research and Applications* 6(4): 453–461.

Zheng, Y. 2007. *Technological empowerment: The Internet, state, and society in China.* Stanford, CA: Stanford University Press.

Zittrain, J., and B. Edelman. 2003. Internet filtering in China. *IEEE Internet Computing* 7(2): 70–77.

CHAPTER 23

The Internet in China: New Methods and Opportunities

Yang Zhang

1   Introduction

This chapter reviews methodological advances in Internet studies in Chinese politics. First, automated text analysis reduces the time and cost of examining texts, and makes it possible to conduct a large-scale analysis of textual data like social media posts. Tools of automated text analysis, such as supervised classification, ReadMe, and topic models, have been applied in Internet studies in Chinese politics. Second, the new methods also bring new opportunities for developing rigorous research designs: (1) the Internet can serve as a platform for online field and survey experiments; (2) in some cases, in particular natural experiments, big data make it easier to conduct causal inference; (3) and with big data, there is potential to make inference with regard to a broader context.

In 2016, the number of netizens reached 710 million, consisting of 51.7% of the Chinese population (CNNIC 2016). China's netizens are relatively young and better educated, and thus the influence of the Internet is likely to keep growing (Yang 2003b: 458). In many ways, the actual society replicates itself on the Internet where private entrepreneurs open shops on e-commerce platforms like Taobao (Liu 2017), netizens and NGOs get involved in political contention in forms of online petitions, campaigns, and protests (Cairns and Carlson 2016; Han 2015; Yang 2009a, b), and local governments receive citizens' questions, complaints, and suggestions through the online Mayor's Mailbox (Chen et al. 2016; Distelhorst and Hou 2017 Online First). Studies of the Internet help us understand a multitude of important issues in Chinese

Y. Zhang (✉)
Department of Political Science, Southwest Jiaotong University, Chengdu, China

© The Author(s) 2019
J. Yu, S. Guo (eds.), *The Palgrave Handbook of Local Governance in Contemporary China*, https://doi.org/10.1007/978-981-13-2799-5_23

politics, which include but are not limited to state control, government responsiveness, nationalism, political support, and social activism.

A variety of research methods have been employed in Internet studies in Chinese politics. On the one hand, due to similarities between online and offline societies, traditional research methods such as social surveys, either online (Pan and Xu 2017; Tai and Truex 2015) or offline (Lei 2011; Mou et al. 2011; Shi et al. 2011; Tang et al. 2017; Yang 2003a, 2007), participant observation (Han 2015; Pang 2008; Yang 2003b), and manual text analysis (Esarey and Qiang 2008; Lee 2016; Shen 2011, 2012; Wang 2013) are readily applicable to the study of the Internet in China. On the other hand, data produced from the Internet are massive, dynamic, and often stored in unstructured formats like text, sound, and image, which pose challenges to researchers but also afford new opportunities for developing novel research designs and data analysis methods. The purpose of this chapter is to review new methodological advances in Internet studies in Chinese politics and to discuss how to utilize these methods to enhance an understanding of the Internet in China.

This chapter begins with a review on how automated text analysis has transformed the way researchers analyze digital textual data such as social media posts. It then explains how the Internet can be used as a platform for experiments and how big data can be used to develop rigorous research designs. Finally, the chapter concludes with a brief summary, talks about the values of network analysis for studying online behavior, and recommends the use of mixed methods for future studies.

2   AUTOMATED TEXT ANALYSIS

Text analysis, also known as content analysis, is a familiar method to China scholars, and it was commonly used before the advent of the Internet. Traditional text analysis involves careful reading for subtle connotations in texts or classification of texts by human coders and has been an important tool for examining sophisticated online expressions such as political satire (Esarey and Qiang 2008; Lee 2016). It has also been used to estimate the distribution of social media posts over a set of predefined categories. For example, Simon Shen analyzed several online forums to learn Chinese netizens' perceptions toward India (2011) and Latin America (2012). Wang (2013) examined distinct frames in Weibo discussions regarding the case of Little Yueyue, a two-year-old toddler who was run over by two cars and ignored by 18 pedestrians passing by her after the accident.

Automated text analysis amplifies our abilities to deal with textual data because of computer assistance and has advantages over traditional text analysis.[1] Automated text analysis reduces the cost and time of analyzing textual

---

[1] Grimmer and Steward (2013) provides a thorough review of automated text analysis methods for political texts.

data, making large-scale text analysis possible (Grimmer and Stewart 2013). And its coding process is more transparent and replicable (Zamith and Lewis 2015: 310).

The simplest method of computer-assisted text analysis is keyword search. Researchers assign texts to different topics based on whether they contain certain keywords (King et al. 2013: 329; Cairns and Carlson 2016). A natural extension of keyword search is dictionary methods, which can be used for classifying and scoring texts (Chen 2011). The second generation of automated text analysis is mainly derived from computer science and focuses on machine learning.

The initial step of automated text analysis is to preprocess unstructured texts. The most common output of text preprocessing is a set of words in which a text is represented by word frequencies and the sequence of words is discarded. Such a representation of textual data is simple but has high performance in practice (Grimmer and Stewart 2013: 272). The procedures of analyzing English and Chinese texts are the same, except that Chinese words are not naturally separated in a sentence in the same way (Lucas et al. 2015: 258). Fortunately, effective tools of Chinese word segmentation have been developed, among which Jieba is free and has convenient packages for R, Python, and Java.[2]

Using preprocessed textual data, computer algorithms help researchers classify online texts into pre-established categories, score texts based on sentiment or policy positions, detect latent topics, or extract named entities like persons, places, and organizations from texts. Despite these methods being new to social scientists, political methodologists have great interest in Internet studies in Chinese politics, and China scholars have quickly recognized the utility of various automated text analysis techniques. This section next briefly reviews applications of three text analysis methods in Internet studies in Chinese politics, which include supervised classification, ReadMe, and topic models.

2.1   Supervised Classification

Classification and clustering are two fundamental problems in machine learning (Bishop 2006; Hastie et al. 2008). In document-level text analysis, a classification algorithm assigns a text to a defined category, and a clustering algorithm, for example, topic models, allocates a collection of texts into different groups that are not defined by the analyst.

However, most classification algorithms are supervised. Using supervised learning to classify texts, we first need to label a number of texts, namely classifying them into predetermined categories by hand. Indeed, this part of supervised classification is the same as traditional text analysis, and high inter-coder

---

[2] The Jieba Chinese word segmentation tool can be downloaded from the following website: https://github.com/fxsjy/jieba.

reliability is required. Online crowdsourcing platforms provide a way to find multiple human coders and finish the labeling task within a short period of time (Wang et al. 2016: 503). Second, the labeled texts are divided into two sets, the training set and the test set. Third, we rely on the training set to build a classifier—for example, a logistic regression—that is able to use word frequencies and some other text features to predict the category of a text. For classifying texts, there are numerous supervised learning algorithms, among which the widely used ones include Naïve Bayes, Support Vector Machine, Random Forest, and Maximum Entropy. Fourth, we validate the classifier by looking at the performance scores for the test set, for example, accuracy, which is the proportion of correctly predicted cases. Since there exists no state-of-the-art classifier for all classification problems, we have to try different algorithms and tune the parameters until the performance scores reach an acceptable level. Finally, we select the best classifier and employ it to classify the texts not manually labeled.

Researchers often first code texts through supervised classification and then input the machine-coded variables into an explanatory or statistical model, as illustrated by two examples. In the first example, Su and Meng (2016) study how local governments respond to citizens' requests. They collected over 200,000 online requests on the Local Leadership Message Board, hosted on people.cn, between 2008 and early 2014. They randomly selected 3000 posts and had two human coders assign them to different topics. A mixed membership classifier, which allows a post to fall into more than one topic, was trained with 1000 labeled posts and validated with the rest of 2000 labeled posts. This classifier was then used to code the entire dataset. Finally, the topics of requests were included as independent variables in two sets of explanatory models, logistic regressions and Cox duration models. The results reveal selective responsiveness of local governments such that they are more responsive to requests from their constituents, expressing collective concerns, or focused on a single issue, especially economic growth (Su and Meng 2016).

In the second example, Pan (2017) studies how Chinese officials use the Internet to construct their public image by examining a random sample of 1.92 million county-level government webpages. Using a multiclass Support Vector Machine, a supervised classification method, Pan classified these webpages into two categories, depending on whether they project images of competence by emphasizing county executives' achievements or images of benevolence by highlighting their attentiveness to citizens. Unlike the aforementioned study, the unit of analysis of this study is county, instead of individual online request. So, webpage-level data were aggregated to create two county-level variables, one indicating the proportion of government webpages dedicated to exhibiting competence and the other benevolence. The two proportion variables then became dependent variables in regression models with official tenure as the independent variable. The models suggest a distinction between early- and late-tenure county executives that the former tend to promote images of benevolence and the latter competence (Pan 2017).

2.2   ReadMe

Supervised machine-learning methods are designed to process individual cases, which is needed in most real-life applications, such as personalized advertisement, document translation, and Go playing. But for many social science studies, the quantities of interest are proportions. Although proportions can be obtained through individual classification and aggregation as Pan did in her study of public image promotion (Pan 2017), such an approach has disadvantages. First, high accuracy of individual classification does not necessarily lead to high accuracy of proportion estimation. Second, it takes time and expertise to obtain a well-performing classifier.

Daniel Hopkins and Gary King (2010) developed a method—colloquially known as ReadMe—that skips the step of individual classification and directly returns proportions of texts over a set of categories. This method rests on relatively weak assumptions and is essentially a simple linear regression. ReadMe is supervised, which means the researchers need to prepare a set of manually coded texts. According to the authors, only 100 manually coded texts would suffice. In measuring proportions of texts, ReadMe substantially outperforms Support Vector Machine, the most widely used supervised classification method.

The very first usage of ReadMe was embedded in studies of China's social media (Cairns and Carlson 2016; King et al. 2013). For instance, Cairns and Carlson (2016) investigated nationalism on Sina Weibo, China's largest microblog platform, as the Sino-Japan conflict over the Diaoyu/Senkaku Islands escalated in 2012. They utilized the data from the WeiboScope project[3] to extract Weibo posts containing the keyword "Diaoyu Islands" and obtained a sample of 145,000 posts. ReadMe was used to estimate the daily distribution of these posts over three types—moderate posts, posts criticizing the government, and posts calling for collective action.

2.3   Topic Models

In machine learning, a topic is represented by a distribution over a vocabulary of words. For example, words like "air", "pollution", and "health" tend to occur frequently in the topic of "environmental protection" but appear rarely in the topic of "state sovereignty". Topic models serve the purpose of clustering texts and are unsupervised machine-learning methods. Topic models do not require manually coded texts but are able to uncover latent topics via a statistical process. However, machine-discovered topics should be labeled by hand. Without proper interpretation by the analyst, such a topic appears to be a group of random words and contains no substantive meaning.

---

[3] The WeiboScope project, maintained by the Journalism and Media Studies Center at the University of Hong Kong, constantly tracks the posts of influential Weibo users (Fu et al. 2013). Another interesting study based on the WeboScope data is Nip and Fu (2016).

One of the most popular topic models is Latent Dirichlet Allocation. This method needs the analyst to first set the total number of topics to be inferred, and it allows mixed membership, that is, different topics can have overlapping keywords and a text can be assigned to more than one topic with varying probability. For example, in the study on public image promotion, Pan utilized a 50-topic Latent Dirichlet Allocation model to analyze the content of county government webpages (Pan 2017: 7).

Invented by Margaret Roberts and her colleagues, the structural topic model adapts Latent Dirichlet Allocation to be an explanatory model, making it resemble regression analysis (Roberts et al. 2014). An important contribution of this method is that it incorporates information about the text, for example, the author's background and treatment assignment (if an experiment), as covariates. In the structural topic model, covariates affect how likely a text is assigned to a particular topic (topical prevalence) and constrain how a vocabulary of words is used to describe the topic (topical content).

Lucas et al. (2015) employ an interesting application of the structural topic model. The researchers wanted to know how people in China and the Middle East perceive the event of Edward Snowden, a former US government employee who disclosed the government's secret surveillance program in June 2013. They gathered thousands of social media posts containing the keyword "Snowden" during that month, consisting of a collection of posts in Chinese from Sina Weibo and a collection of posts in Arabic from Twitter. The posts were all translated to English by computer software, and a 15-topic structural topic model was estimated to fit the textual data, with the language indicator as both topical prevalence and content covariate and date of the post as topical prevalence covariate. Three inferred topics—manually labeled as "attack", "human rights", and "asylum"—were further analyzed. The results show that compared to the tweets in Arabic, the Weibo posts in Chinese were more likely to belong to the topics of "attack" and "human rights" (2015).

2.4   Limitations of Automated Text Analysis

Automated text analysis has limitations in studying the Internet in China. First, automated text analysis has a long learning curve. To master automated text analysis, one needs to understand various machine-learning algorithms and acquire computer programming skills. Second, when the researcher only needs to analyze a small sample of texts, for example, a local party leader's Weibo account, machine coding will actually use more time than manual coding. Third, machine text coding, in theory, cannot outperform manual coding in accuracy. The reason is that the performance of a classifier is validated on how well its predictions accord with human coders' decisions. For example, a classifier makes mistakes when the text analysis requires background knowledge and understanding of satires, puns, or subtle meanings in texts. If the researcher seeks high accuracy of text classification, manual text coding is a better option.

3   DIGITAL DATA AND RESEARCH DESIGN

In the framework of empirical social science research, internal validity and external validity are two crucial concepts for evaluating the quality of a research design. Internal validity refers to the degree to which a study reveals the true causal effect, and external validity refers to the extent to which the results can be generalized to other contexts. For a single study, internal validity should be prioritized over external validity, because strongly biased results are meaningless regardless of their generalizability, and high external validity can be established through a multitude of studies repeated in different contexts (McDermott 2002; Morton and Williams 2010: 264–276).

This section first discusses how the Internet can be utilized as a platform for social experiments, a state-of-the-art method in achieving high internal validity. It then shows the potential of "big data" for discovering causal effects and the efforts of big-data researchers to improve external validity.

3.1   The Internet: An Experiment Platform

In recent years, a host of social experiments—ranging from lab experiments (Gries et al. 2015), to field experiments (Chen et al. 2016; Distelhorst and Hou 2014; Hoffmann and Larner 2013; King 2014; Whiting 2017), to survey experiments (Huang 2015; Lei and Lu 2017; Lu et al. 2012; Mattingly 2016; Meng et al. 2017; Tai and Truex 2015; Tang 2016: 134–151)—have been utilized to study Chinese politics. In contrast to observational research, experimental research has an incomparable advantage at discovering causal effects and ensuring a high level of internal validity in the results. The reason is that the researcher is able to randomly assign the treatment (or the values of the independent variable) to subjects, and as a result the treatment becomes uncorrelated with all of the confounding factors, whether they are observable or unobservable.

Compared to lab and survey experiments, field experiments have a higher degree of mundane realism that the intervention resembles a naturally occurring event and the subjects have no idea that they are part of an academic research project. The Internet is a part of China's public sphere and can serve as a low-cost platform for field experiments. Strict government control over the Internet, along with a number of government websites created in response to the 2007 Open Government Information Ordinance, affords opportunities to study the interactions between the Chinese state and society through online field experiments.

In King et al. (2014), the researchers carried out an online field experiment on censorship in China's social media. The experiment is a two-by-two design. A group of native Chinese speakers were asked to write 1200 unique posts on concurrent high-profile events for four experimental conditions defined by two variables (pro- or anti-government and with or without collective action potential). The researchers created accounts for 100 social media sites, and the posts were submitted on the social media sites in three rounds of online field experiments to investigate how censorship operates. The experiment provides rigorous evidence for the expectation that political criticism is allowed to be published whereas posts with collective action potential are censored. This study is also a good example of mixed-method design in that the participant observation complements the online field experiment. The researchers interviewed many sources with first-hand knowledge about media control and created their own social media website in China to better understand the technological infrastructure of censorship.

Another example of an online field experiment concerns local government responsiveness in China (Chen et al. 2016). The control condition of the experiment entails a request from a Chinese citizen for government assistance with regard to obtaining Minimum Livelihood Guarantee (*Dibao*). Three treatment conditions add additional words to the request so that it contains a threat of collective action, a threat of reporting to a higher-level government, or a claim of loyalty to the Chinese Communist Party. The four types of requests were randomly posted on more than 200 online forums of county governments. The researchers were interested in four outcomes as measures of responsiveness: whether there was a response; if so, when the response was sent; whether the response was publicly viewable; and whether the response is regarded as deferral, referral, or supply of direct information. The experiment results demonstrate that threats of collective action and reporting to upper levels of government render county governments more responsive.

Apart from field experiments, the Internet can also be utilized as a platform for survey experiments (Huang 2015; Tai and Truex 2015). Turning an online survey into an online survey experiment is simple in that the researcher just needs to design two survey questionnaires with a slightly different question as the experimental treatment. For example, Tai and Truex (2015) conducted an online survey experiment on Chinese netizens' perceptions toward returning migrants through China Online Marketing Research, a crowdsourcing website similar to Amazon Mechanical Turk. Of course, like online surveys, online survey experiments have their limitations. The non-response rate is high and the conclusion drawn from an online survey experiment is not generalizable to the population not accessing the Internet. However, online survey experiments have a high degree of internal validity and are a good complement to other types of researches.

3.2   Big Data and Internal Validity

The Internet is the major source of big data. A widely cited Gartner report uses three Vs to describe big data: volume, velocity, and variety (Laney 2001). First, the volume of big data is enormous, which requires new ways to collect, store, and analyze data. Some studies on Chinese social media posts (King et al. 2013), online messages to Mayor's Mailbox (Su and Meng 2016), and local government webpages (Pan 2017) need to deal with tens of thousands of and even millions of data points. Second, big data are generated at an extremely fast speed and need to be processed in real time. In China, because of censorship, many social media posts are removed from the Internet shortly after they are published. Therefore, for unbiased analysis the researcher has to collect social media posts on a very frequent basis (Cairns and Carlson 2016; King et al. 2013; Nip and Fu 2016). Third, big data are represented in complex formats, including both structured databases and unstructured texts, images, speeches, videos, and other objects. Automated text analysis discussed in the previous section was developed in response to this challenge.

Other researchers have identified additional characteristics of big data, for example, variability in that the data are constantly changing (King et al. 2017a), veracity in that the data are naturally occurring (Shah et al. 2015: 7), and granularity in that the data record small details of individual behavior and social interactions.

Social science researchers and China scholars have been debating the promise and perils of big data, but a consensus is that big-data studies should be concerned with internal validity, external validity, measurement reliability, and other key aspects of empirical social science research (Japec et al. 2015; Lazer et al. 2009, 2014; Meng and Guo 2015; Ruths and Pfreffer 2014; Tang 2015). In a 2015 issue of *PS: Political Science & Politics*, a symposium was devoted to bridging two methodological revolutions in political science—the "big-data revolution" that emphasizes how big data can help us better understand the political world and the "causal inference revolution" that emphasizes how causal effects can be unbiasedly estimated through experiments and innovative observational methods (Clark and Golder 2015). Some contributors to the symposium argued that big data are conducive to certain causal inference methods, in particular matching, regression discontinuity design, and heterogeneous treatment effect analysis.

In his book *Bit by Bit: Social Research in the Digital Age*, Matthew Salganik (2017) proposed an interesting equation for digital causal inference: always-on data + unexpected event = natural experiment. Such a natural experiment resembles an online field experiment. Before the unexpected event, the subjects are under the control condition, and after the event, they are under the treatment condition. The researcher can estimate the causal effect by calculating the temporal difference in the quantities of interest. Strictly speaking, a natural experiment is not an experiment, for factors other than the treatment may also change over the course of the unexpected event and affect the experimental results. However, if we narrow the time span of a natural experiment, it will be very close to a real experiment.

The Internet never stops producing data of netizens' opinions and behavior, and unexpected events occur almost on a daily basis in China. Therefore, there are ample opportunities on the Internet for natural experiments. For example, Hobbs and Roberts designed a natural experiment that investigates how sudden censorship changes Chinese netizens' online behavior (2016). Instagram was suddenly blocked in mainland China on September 29, 2014, the third day of the large-scale protest in Hong Kong, and the authors utilized this unexpected censorship for a natural experiment design. Before it was blocked, Instagram was mainly used for entertainment purposes. However, by examining millions of online individual-level actions, the authors found that the sudden censorship inspired many Instagram users to access more sensitive information: millions of Chinese Internet users acquired virtual private networks (VPNs) to evade the Great Firewall and joined social media websites like Twitter and Facebook that have long been blocked. The new users started browsing sensitive political content on Wikipedia, following Chinese political activists on Twitter and posting tweets about the protest in Hong Kong.

3.3   Big Data and External Validity

In the study of Chinese social media, participant observation is an important research approach. It often entails long-time and in-depth observation of a single social media site (Pang 2008) or a small number of online forums (Han 2015; Yang 2003b). Participant observation clarifies complex causal mechanisms and generates novel theories, but it has a limitation of extending the conclusion to a broader context.

To some extent, big-data analytics address this problem. When the research question only concerns the Internet, as in the study of social media versus the study of civic culture, using tools for big data, the researcher can make inference about the universe of all relevant cases. In other words, big data can generalize an anecdotal finding to the Internet-wide level. For instance, in a well-known study, King et al. (2013) conducted a large-scale analysis of censorship in China's social media. The researchers collected all of the posts regarding 85 topic areas from 1382 Chinese websites over a six-month period. From a dataset of more than 3.6 million social media posts, they selected a random sample of about 127,000 posts for further analysis. They analyzed the content of each of the selected posts and repeatedly revisited it to learn whether it was censored.

In another study, King et al. (2017b) took advantage of leaked emails to the Internet Propaganda Office of Zhanggong district in Jiangxi province and developed a method to detect all of the 50-cent posts, the posts fabricated by the Chinese government, on Weibo. They found that for the goal of public opinion guidance, a vast majority of 50-cent posts avoid engaging in arguments with Chinese netizens and instead tend to distract the public via cheerleading for China. The basic procedures for extrapolating the findings from the leaked emails to all Weibo posts go as follows: first, the researchers identified 498 Weibo accounts revealed in the leaked emails and found two simple partition rules to distinguish exclusive accounts dedicated to 50-cent posts from ordinary accounts. The first rule is whether the account comments on or forwards any post on the county/district government Weibo account, and the second rule is whether it has ten or fewer followers. Second, the researchers randomly selected 100 counties, and in accordance with the two partition rules, they identified all of the exclusive Weibo accounts in these counties. Finally, the aforementioned automated text analysis method, ReadMe, was employed to examine the content of the posts from the exclusive Weibo accounts and estimate their distribution over six categories, among which one is cheerleading for China. One thing to note from the above two examples is that for making Internet-wide inference, there is no need to analyze the entire set of big data, and a random sample should be sufficient.

The two examples above demonstrate how big data are suitable for studying issues confined to the scope of the Internet. Big data also have potential to help make inference beyond the Internet. A criticism of online surveys is that they are not representative of the Chinese national population, because netizens tend to be younger, wealthier, and better educated (Tang et al. 2017). But when the online survey is big enough, it is possible to obtain a sample of a considerable size that matches the overall population. For studying political preferences of Chinese citizens, Pan and Xu (2017) obtained an online survey dataset of 460,532 respondents. Because of the large survey size, they are able to construct a new sample of 10,000 observations that is representative of the 2005 One-Percent Intercensal Population Survey, in province, age cohorts, gender, and their interactions. The results from this new sample are consistent with the results from the Asian Barometer Survey conducted through face-to-face interviews.

3.4   Limitations of Big Data

Big data produced on the Internet are certainly not a solution to all problems in Internet studies in Chinese politics, especially when it comes to issues of public opinion. First, heavy Internet censorship in China imposes the problem of missing data and selection bias. Some aforementioned studies deal with this problem by continuously sampling and storing social media posts. However, this method is impractical for most China scholars, who do not have the necessary technological facilities and manpower. It also fails to capture the social media posts censored before they are released to the public the first time, for example, comments on WeChat articles.

Second, many key independent variables in public-opinion studies are not available in social media data. Chinese netizens tend to hide their identities, such as age, gender, and partisanship, when voicing their opinions on the Internet. Thus, social media data are often not suitable for studying how political attitudes are associated with demographic and socioeconomic characteristics. Additionally, although some social media posts are geocoded, a vast majority are not, which makes it difficult to examine China's regional variation in public opinion through social media data.

Third, many Chinese citizens have experience using the Internet, but only a small proportion of them are active in social media. Social media data mostly reflect opinions of active Internet users, which are likely to be different from opinions of those who rarely use social media platforms or prefer to keep silent on the Internet. We should always be cautious when using a finding from social media data to explain public opinion of Chinese citizens in general.

4   Conclusion

Internet studies in Chinese politics is a field where diverse research methods are thriving, and each method has contributed to a better understanding of China's online society. This chapter reviews some new methods in this field of study. First, automated text analysis reduces the time and cost of analyzing texts and makes it possible to systematically examine large amounts of textual data, such as social media posts. Computer-assisted tools, like supervised classification, ReadMe, and topics models, have been applied in studies on the Internet in China. Second, online experiments and big data generated from the Internet offer new opportunities for rigorous research designs. The Internet can serve as a platform for both field and survey experiments. Big data are massive and dynamic, which is conducive to making causal inference and designing natural experiments. Moreover, with big data, we are able to make inference at the Internet-wide level and build an online survey sample representative of the Chinese national population.

Overall, network analysis is useful for examining the structure of online communities and patterns of online communication and should be more widely employed. With the tools of network analysis, for example, we can identify public opinion leaders and information gatekeepers in social media, understand individuals' opinion change over the course of online discussions, visualize divisions in communication networks of online forums, and keep track of the formation and dissemination of viral news. However, when searching the major political science, comparative politics, and China studies journals, I failed to find any study that has employed the tools of network analysis to examine the Internet in China. This type of study in the future would advance an understanding of online behavior and related outcomes.

Moreover, new methods, like automated text analysis, online experiments, and big data analytics, complement rather than substitute for traditional research methods, such as social surveys, discourse analysis, and participant observation. Traditional social surveys reveal how Chinese netizens think and behave in real life and how they differ from other Chinese citizens who have no experience with using the Internet (Lei 2011; Tang et al. 2017). Discourse analysis is able to interpret subtle and sophisticated meanings in human communication (Esarey and Qiang 2008; Lee 2016), which at least in the near future is beyond the capability of any machine-learning algorithm. Online participant observation has great advantages at discovering complex causal mechanisms underlying online communication and activism (Han 2015; Pang 2008).

Thus, a recommendation for future studies on the Internet in China is to take advantage of more than one method for a research project. For example, field experiments can be designed to explore the patterns of online communication networks. Such network-based experiments break the Stable Unit

Treatment Value Assumption (SUTVA) that subjects are independent but make the research design better reflect the reality. In addition, using online experiments and big data, the researcher may obtain a credible estimate of the causal effect between X and Y, but that is not enough. A further step is to understand how X causes Y via participant observation or other qualitative approaches. Put simply, a mixed-method design will enhance the robustness and depth of the empirical findings about the Internet in China.

References

Bishop, Christopher. 2006. *Pattern Recognition and Machine Learning*. Springer.

Cairns, Christopher, and Allen Carlson. 2016. "Real-World Islands in a Social Media Sea: Nationalism and Censorship on Weibo during the 2012 Diaoyu/Senkaku Crisis." *The China Quarterly* 225: 23–49.

Chen, Jidong, Jennifer Pan, and Yiqing Xu. 2016. "Sources of Authoritarian Responsiveness: A Field Experiment in China." *American Journal of Political Science* 60 (2): 383–400.

Chen, Yu-Wen. 2011. "Quantitative Content Analysis of Chinese Texts?: A Methodological Note." *Journal of Chinese Political Science* 16: 431–443.

Clark, William Roberts, and Matt Golder. 2015. "Big Data, Causal Inference, and Formal Theory: Contradictory Trends in Political Science?" *PS: Political Science & Politics* 48 (1): 65–70.

CNNIC. 2016. "CNNIC Fabu Di 38 Ci 'zhongguo Hulianwang Fazhan Zhuangkuang Tongji Baogao.'" http://www.cnnic.cn/gywm/xwzx/rdxw/2016/201608/t20160803_54389.htm.

Distelhorst, Greg, and Yue Hou. 2017 Online First. "Constituency Service Under Nondemocratic Rule: Evidence from China." *The Journal of Politics* 79 (3).

Distelhorst, Greg, and Yue Hou. 2014. "Ingroup Bias in Official Behavior: A National Field Experiment in China." *Quarterly Journal of Political Science* 9: 203–230.

Esarey, Ashley, and Xiao Qiang. 2008. "Political Expression in the Chinese Blogosphere." *Asian Survey* 48 (5): 752–772.

Fu, King Wa, Chung-Hong Chan, and Michael Chau. 2013. "Assessing Censorship on Microblogs in China: Discriminatory Keyword Analysis and the Real-Name Registration Policy." *EEE Internet Computing* 17 (3): 42–50.

Gries, Peter, Matthew Sanders, David Stroup, and Huajian Cai. 2015. "Hollywood in China: How American Popular Culture Shapes Chinese Views of the 'Beautiful Imperialist' – An Experimental Analysis." *The China Quarterly* 224: 1070–1082.

Grimmer, Justin, and Brandon Stewart. 2013. "Text as Data: The Promise and Pitfalls of Automatic Content Analysis Methods for Political Texts." *Political Analysis* 21: 267–297.

Han, Rongbin. 2015. "Defending the Authoritarian Regime Online: China's 'Voluntary Fifty-Cent Army.'" *The China Quarterly* 224: 1006–1025.

Hastie, Trevor, Robert Tibshirani, and Jerome Friedman. 2008. *The Elements of Statistical Learning: Data Mining, Inference, and Prediction (Second Edition)*. Springer.

Hobbs, William, and Margaret Roberts. 2016. "How Sudden Censorship Can Increase Access to Information." Working Paper.

Hoffmann, Robert, and Jeremy Larner. 2013. "The Demography of Chinese Nationalism: A Field-Experimental Approach." *The China Quarterly* 213: 189–204.

Hopkins, Daniel, and Gary King. 2010. "A Method of Automated Nonparametric Content Analysis for Social Science." *American Journal of Political Science* 54 (1): 229–247.

Huang, Haifeng. 2015. "International Knowledge and Domestic Evaluations in a Changing Society: The Case of China." *American Political Science Review* 109 (3): 613–634.

Japec, Lilli, Frauke Kreuter, Marcus Berg, Paul Biemer, Paul Decker, Cliff Lampe, Julia Lane, Cathy O'Neil, and Abe Usher. 2015. "Big Data in Survey Research AAPOR Task Force Report." *Public Opinion Quarterly* 79 (4).

King. 2014. "Reverse-Engineering Censorship in China: Randomized Experimentation and Participant Observation."

King, Gary, Patrick Lam, and Margaret Roberts. 2017a. "Computer-Assisted Keyword and Document Set Discovery from Unstructured Text." Working Paper.

King, Gary, Jennifer Pan, and Margaret Roberts. 2013. "How Censorship in China Allows Government Criticism but Silences Collective Expression." *American Political Science Review* 107 (2): 326–343.

King, Gary, Jennifer Pan, and Margaret Roberts. 2014. "Reverse-Engineering Censorship in China: Randomized Experimentation and Participant Observation." *Science* 345 (6199): 1251722.1–1251722.10.

King, Gary, Jennifer Pan, and Margaret Roberts. 2017b. "How the Chinese Government Fabricates Social Media Posts for Strategic Distraction, Not Engaged Argument." Working Paper.

Laney, Douglas. 2001. "3-D Data Management: Controlling Data Volume, Velocity, and Variety." META Group Research Note. http://gtnr.it/1bKflKH.

Lazer, David, Ryan Kennedy, Gary King, and Alessandro Vespignani. 2014. "The Parable of Google Flu: Traps in Big Data Analysis." *Science* 343 (6176): 1203–1205.

Lazer, David, Alex Pentland, Lada Adamic, Sinan Aral, Albert-László Barabási, Devon Brewer, Nicholas Christakis, et al. 2009. "Computational Social Science." *Science* 323 (5915): 721–723.

Lee, Siu-yau. 2016. "Surviving Online Censorship in China: Three Satirical Tactics and Their Impact." *The China Quarterly* 228: 1061–1080.

Lei, Xuchuan, and Jie Lu. 2017. "Revisiting Political Wariness in China's Public Opinion Surveys: Experimental Evidence on Responses to Politically Sensitive Questions." *Journal of Contemporary China* 26 (104): 213–232.

Lei, Ya-Wen. 2011. "The Political Consequences of the Rise of the Internet: Political Beliefs and Practices of Chinese Netizens." *Political Communication* 28 (3): 291–322.

Liu, Lizhi. 2017. "From Click to Boom: The Political Economy of E-Commerce Growth in China."

Lu, Xiaobo, Kenneth Scheve, and Matthew Slaughter. 2012. "Inequity Aversion and the International Distribution of Trade Protection." *American Journal of Political Science* 56 (3): 638–654.

Lucas, Christopher, Richard Nielsen, Margaret Roberts, Brandon Stewart, Alex Storer, and Dustin Tingley. 2015. "Computer-Assisted Text Analysis for Comparative Politics." *Political Analysis* 23: 254–277.

Mattingly, Daniel. 2016. "Elite Capture: How Decentralization and Informal Institutions Weaken Property Rights in Rural China." *World Politics* 68 (3): 383–412.

McDermott, Rose. 2002. "Experimental Methodology in Political Science." *Political Analysis* 10 (4): 325–342.

Meng, Tianguang, and Fenglin Guo. 2015. "Da Shuju Zhengzhixue: Xin Xinxi Shidai De Zhengzhi Xianxiang Jiqi Tanxi Lujing." *Foreign Theoretical Trends* (1): 46–56.

Meng, Tianguang, Jennifer Pan, and Ping Yang. 2017. "Conditional Receptivity to Citizen Participation: Evidence from a Survey Experiment in China" 50 (4): 399–433.

Morton, Rebecca, and Kenneth Williams. 2010. *Experimental Political Science and the Study of Causality: From Nature to the Lab*. Cambridge University Press.

Mou, Yi, David Atkin, and Hanlong Fu. 2011. "Predicting Political Discussion in a Censored Virtual Environment." *Political Communication* 28 (3): 341–356.

Nip, Joyce, and King Wa Fu. 2016. "Challenging Official Propaganda? Public Opinion Leaders on Sina Weibo." *The China Quarterly* 225: 122–144.

Pan, Jennifer. 2017. "How Chinese Officials Use the Internet to Construct Their Public Image." Working Paper.

Pan, Jennifer, and Yiqing Xu. 2017. "China's Ideological Spectrum." Working Paper.

Pang, Cuiming. 2008. "Self-Censorship and the Rise of Cyber Collectives: An Anthropological Study of a Chinese Online Community." *Intercultural Communication Studies* 17 (3): 57–76.

Roberts, Margaret, Brandon Stewart, Dustin Tingley, Christopher Lucas, Jetson Leder-Luis, Shana Kushner Gadarian, Bethany Albertson, and David Rand. 2014. "Structural Topic Models for Open-Ended Survey Responses." *American Journal of Political Science* 58 (4): 1064–1082.

Ruths, Derek, and Jürgen Pfreffer. 2014. "Social Media for Large Studies of Behavior." *Science* 346 (6213): 1063–1064.

Salganik, Matthew. 2017. *Bit by Bit: Social Research in the Digital Age*. Princeton University Press.

Shah, Dhavan, Joseph Cappella, and Russell Neuman. 2015. "Big Data, Digital Media, and Computational Social Science: Possibilities and Perils." *The ANNALS of the American Academy of Political and Social Science* 659 (1): 6–13.

Shen, Simon. 2011. "Exploring the Neglected Constraints on Chindia: Analysing the Online Chinese Perception of India and Its Interaction with China's Indian Policy." *The China Quarterly* 2017: 541–560.

Shen, Simon. 2012. "Online Chinese Perceptions of Latin America: How They Differ from the Official View." *The China Quarterly* 209: 157–177.

Shi, Tianjian, Jie Lu, and John Aldrich. 2011. "Bifurcated Images of the U.S. in Urban China and the Impact of Media Environment." *Political Communication* 28 (3): 357–376.

Su, Zheng, and Tianguang Meng. 2016. "Selective Responsiveness: Online Public Demands and Government Responsiveness in Authoritarian China." *Social Science Research* 59: 52–67.

Tai, Qiuqing, and Rory Truex. 2015. "Public Opinion towards Return Migration: A Survey Experiment of Chinese Netizens." *The China Quarterly* 223: 770–786.

Tang, Wenfang. 2015. "Da Shuju Yu Xiao Shuju: Shehui Kexue Yanjiu Fangfa De Tantao." *Journal of Sun Yatsen University Social Science Edition* 55 (6): 141–146.

Tang, Wenfang. 2016. *Populist Authoritarianism: Chinese Political Culture and Regime Sustainability*. Oxford University Press.

Tang, Wenfang, Yang Zhang, and Sheri Martin. 2017. "Revolution Postponed: The Limitation of the Internet in Promoting Democracy in China." In *Changing State-Society Relations in Contemporary China*, 169–205. New Jersey, London and Singapore: World Scientific.

Wang, Wilfred Yang. 2013. "Weibo, Framing, and Media Practices in China." *Journal of Chinese Political Science* 18 (4): 375–388.

Wang, Xi, Zhiya Zuo, Yang Zhang, Kang Zhao, Yung-Chun Chang, and Chin-Shun Chou. 2016. "Investigating Regional Prejudice in China Through the Lens of Weibo." In *Proceedings of the 8th International Conference on Social Informatics*, 500–513.

Whiting, Susan. 2017 Online First. "Authoritarian 'Rule of Law' and Regime Legitimacy." *Comparative Political Studies*.

Yang, Guobin. 2003a. "The Internet and Civil Society in China: A Preliminary Assessment." *Journal of Contemporary China* 12 (36): 453–475.

Yang, Guobin. 2003b. "The Internet and the Rise of a Transnational Chinese Cultural Sphere." *Media, Culture & Society* 25: 469–490.

Yang, Guobin. 2007. "How Do Chinese Civic Associations Respond to the Internet? Findings from a Survey." *The China Quarterly* 189: 122–143.

Yang, Guobin. 2009a. "Online Activism." *Journal of Democracy* 20 (3): 33–36.

Yang, Guobin. 2009b. *The Power of the Internet in China: Citizen Activism Online*. Columbia University Press.

Zamith, Rodrigo, and Seth Lewis. 2015. "Content Analysis and the Algorithmic Coder: What Computational Social Science Means for Traditional Modes of Media Analysis." *The ANNALS of the American Academy of Political and Social Science* 659 (1): 307–318.

PART VII

Social Equity and Governance

Predicament of Emerging Collaborative Governance: National Policy, Local Experiments, and Public Hospital Reforms in China

Edward Gu

1   INTRODUCTION

Public hospitals are an important part of the supply side of the health sector around the world, and numerous studies have shown that large majorities of the public, in particular in Europe, support public provision of health care (Wendt et al. 2010; Missinne et al. 2013; Jensen and Naumann 2016). In China, public hospitals play an especially significant role in health-care service delivery system (World Bank 2010a; Qian and Blomqvist 2014). Serving as major facilities for the Chinese people to seek medical care, the capacities, service volumes, and operational revenues of public hospitals hold dominant positions in the hospital sector. Therefore, governance reforms of public hospitals are among the top priorities for improving the overall performance of the health-care sector in China (Yip et al. 2012).

In 2003, the World Bank published a volume of papers on the comparison of innovations in health service delivery, providing an influential analytical framework for studying the governance reforms of public hospitals. According to this framework, public hospitals can be categorized as budgetary, autonomized, and corporatized organizations, and corporatization is identified as a major trend of organizational and governance reform for them (Preker and Harding 2003).

E. Gu (✉)
School of Public Affairs, Zhejiang University, Hangzhou, Zhejiang, China
e-mail: guxin31@zju.edu.cn

J. Yu, S. Guo (eds.), *The Palgrave Handbook of Local Governance in Contemporary China*, https://doi.org/10.1007/978-981-13-2799-5_24

The organizational reform of public hospitals, whether from budgetary to autonomized, corporatized, or even privatized units, involves the interactions of bureaucratic, market, and community governance. Bureaucratic governance occurs in all hierarchical organizations and, in particular, in the public sector, wherein the superiors coordinate the activities of subordinates through "command and control" mechanism (Grand et al. 2007). Market governance is based on voluntary contractual transactions, and its mechanism of coordination is characterized by "choice and competition" (Grand et al. 2007). Being manifested largely in corporate governance and associational life, community governance is characterized as "trust and compliance" in coordinating activities of members through their commitment of and compliance with certain common values and norms (Bowles 2004).

Bureaucratic, market, and community mechanisms, all play a certain role in the governance of economic, social, and political affairs of the human world, but any one of the three rarely works separately or exclusively. Instead, they are embedded in each other. The different modes of combination and embeddedness of the three mechanisms lead to differences in governance modes and in governance performance. State actions or government interventions imposed through bureaucratic mechanism often cast distorting impacts on the proper functioning of market and community mechanisms. If the three mechanisms can complement and reinforce each other, it will form collaborative governance (Donahue and Zeckhauser 2011). Critical to this process is government transformation, namely the transformation from highly bureaucratic interventionist government to what economist Mancur Olson proposed "market-augmenting government" (Olson 2000; Azfar and Cadwell 2003) and/or what social policy scholar Neil Gilbert conceptualizes as "the enabling state" (Gilbert and Gilbert 1989).

In public hospitals, specifically, governance mechanisms are mainly involved in four areas of operational affairs, including the allocation of decision rights and power to control, the sources of funding and financial management, personnel management, and logistics management (in particular, regulations upon pricing, purchase, and sale of pharmaceuticals). Whenever and wherever bureaucratic mechanism dominates in all the four areas, the mode of governance is characterized as bureaucratization. Whenever and wherever the management autonomy is considerably increased, autonomization occurs as the first step of the public hospital governance reform. If hierarchically organized bureaucratic organizations are transformed into parastatal corporations, mostly still non-profit in nature, the corporatization of public hospitals is under way. Autonomization is expected to make hospital managers manage, and corporatization is often associated with an intense use of corporate, managerial, and business-like techniques in management and operation. In this respect, differences between autonomization and corporatization are not always clear-cut (Dan 2017). But the most significant difference between the two reform approaches lies at restructuring the relationship between public hospitals and the government agencies supervising them, making the former organizationally independent from the latter. The most aggressive move for the governance reform is privatization, namely outright divestiture of public hospitals from the public sector (see Fig. 24.1).

In China, a new round of health reforms (hereinafter referred to as "new health reforms"), which was announced in April 2009 and implemented in 2010, proposed the so-called four-separation principles, namely the separation of the government and public service organizations (Qian and Blomqvist 2014), the separation of ownership and management (Huang 2013), the separation of non-profit and for-profit organizations, and the separation of medical services and drug sales (Qian and Blomqvist 2014). No matter how different the principles that have been interpreted and put into practice, the Chinese Party-state was surely determined to push the public hospital reform toward corporatization and privatization on a pilot basis, which has been overlooked by all the publications in reviewing and accessing the 2009 reform policy. "To ascertain the status of independent legal persons for public hospitals" and "to form and perfect the corporate governance of the hospital" were drafted in the eighth and ninth clause of the comprehensive plan for the new health reforms (http://www.gov.cn/jrzg/2009-04/06/content_1278721.htm).

In 2013, China launched its new cycle of reform and vigorously pushed privatization and marketization as a core strategy to reform its public hospitals

	Bureaucratization	Autonomization	Corporatization	Privatization
Decision-making and Control	Vertical stratification: Command and Control	The increase of administrative autonomy from a very limited position & the reduce of governmental controls from infinite to finite;		Full autonomy of administration + markets with different levels of controls
Funding source and Financial Management	Financial allocations from government budget+ (a few) marketized charges government departments fully in charge of financial management	Government subsidies + government contracts (payments from public health insurance) + marketized charges Partial decision-making power delegated for hospitals, but many issues in financial management need to be approved		Government contracts (payments from public health insurance) + marketized charges+ public funding on an occasional and case-by-case basis Full autonomy of financial management
Personnel Management	The government designates managers + controls the recruitment of professionals + controls the salary	The government designates managers Partial autonomy of human resource management + regulated labor market		Full autonomy of human resource management + regulated labor market
Pricing and logistics management	Public pricing for medical services, pharmaceuticals, and consumables	Partial deregulations on price + Price formation based on bargaining between providers and payers		Market pricing + full autonomy of logistics management

4 Areas of Hospital Operation

Bureaucratic governance	Market governance	Community governance

Fig. 24.1 Governance modes and the patterns of public hospitals' organizational reforms

(Yip and Hsiao 2015). On November 12, the Third Plenary Session of the 18th Chinese Communist Party Central Committee promulgated a landmark Decision on comprehensively deepening economic, social, political, and governance reforms. With regard to the health sector's supply-side reform, the Decision made it clear that China would "straighten up the relationship between public organizations and the government's administrative organs supervising them, and promote the de-bureaucratization of public service organizations," "create conditions to gradually rescind the administrative ranks of schools, research institutes and hospitals," "set up corporate governance structure for public organizations," and "transform qualified public organizations into either enterprises or social organizations." The Decision reiterated with regard to health-care reforms that the government would "encourage private funds to flow to medical services, first supporting them to flow to not-for-profit healthcare providers," "allow private funds to invest directly in health services that are short of resources or are to meet diverse demands," and even allow private funds "to participate in in the reform and restructuring of public hospitals in various forms (http://www.gov.cn/jrzg/2013-11/15/content_2528179.htm)."

While having been incorporated into the overall reforming framework of the de-bureaucratization of public service organizations, the corporatization and privatization of public hospitals are staggering in the actual process with the heavy fetters in the existing system. The vast majority of public hospitals are still operated in a way of bureaucratic marketization, that is, on the one hand, their operation highly relies upon marketized funding, and, on the other hand, their decision-making is dominated by multiple bureaucratic forces, and the corresponding market environment is also subject to strict government control (Gu 2011). Although market mechanism has begun to take effect, bureaucratic forces are still dominating the governance of public hospitals by a variety of distortive interventions, leading to both market failure and government failure. As the core of the third mode of governance, community mechanism is still in its infancy.

In short, bureaucratic, market, and community mechanisms have not yet formed a kind of collaborative governance in China's health sector. This study offers an exploitation of the dilemma faced by hardly born collaborative governance in public hospital reforms by examining national and local reform policies in the four areas shown earlier in Fig. 24.1.

2   BUREAUCRATIC MARKETIZATION: THE *STATUS QUO* GOVERNANCE PATTERN OF PUBLIC HOSPITALS IN CHINA

Since the reform and opening-up started from the late 1970s, China's public hospitals have experienced a long and difficult process of the organizational and governance reform. The starting point of the reform process was the so-called *danwei* system, a huge hierarchy of publicly owned workplace units including enterprises, schools, hospitals, research institutes, government agents, and the like, formed during the planned-economy era (Lü and Perry 1997).

The classic work-unit system demonstrates the extreme form of bureaucratization: all the political, social, and economic activities carried out in all work-units relied on and were subject to top-down command and control, and the market and community mechanisms were either insignificant or wiped out. The integration of government administration and public service provision as a phenomenon was found in all work-units (Lu 1993). All work-units were part of various vertical administrative systems and thereby had their own administrative ranks. From a financial point of view, each work-unit was a budgetary unit of the hierarchical system it belonged to. In state socialist countries, public organizations such as universities, hospitals, theaters, museums, and the like are often referred to as "budgetary institutions" (Kornai 1992).

In China, all work-units fell into three categories: administrative agents (xingzheng jiguan), service organizations (shiye danwei), and economic enterprises (qiye danwei). These categories remain nowadays the key concepts for understanding the Chinese state or China's public sector, even after nearly 40 years of the market transition. Of these three categories of organizations, the most unique, and probably the most difficult to understand for international audience, is the service organizations (Lam and Perry 2001). While they may fall into the category of public service organization or simply public organizations around the world, their organizational form and governance mode, namely the extreme bureaucratization of public service provision within a huge hierarchy, finds no parallel in Western countries.

Public hospitals were part of hierarchically organized service organizations. With the huge hierarchical system, the managers of public hospitals had no substantial autonomy of management or decision-making power; as administrative executives, they only carried out the plan or completed the tasks assigned by the government agents who functioned as their superiors. The government's health departments relied on the top-down supervision and evaluation to implement administrative accountability upon public hospitals (Henderson and Cohen 1984).

In the real practice of state socialism, there is a distinction between the centralized and decentralized patterns of bureaucratization in the health sector. In the centralized pattern, the Party chief and the administrative director of the Ministry of Health (MOH) hold the highest decision-making power in allocating health-care resources. Such a "classic socialism" pattern existed mainly in the Soviet Union and Eastern Europe before the transition (Kornai and Eggleston 2001) and is still being implemented in current state socialist countries such as Vietnam, North Korea, and Cuba. In the decentralized pattern, the MOH does not have the complete power of resource allocation regarding health services, of which the power of human resource allocation is shared with the Ministry of Personnel, the power of funds allocation is shared with the Ministry of Finance (MOF), and the power of allocation of materials (including housing, appliances, consumables, etc.) is shared with many other government departments in charge of the distribution of different materials.

In China, the governance structure of public hospitals during the era of planned economy fell in the pattern of decentralized bureaucratization. The vast majority of public hospitals were owned and administered by local governments at different levels, and only a few were administered directly by the MOH. Decentralized bureaucratization was manifested as a huge network of hierarchical organizations: on the one hand, all work-units were organized in a vertical manner according to their functions, forming a number of parallel hierarchical systems; on the other hand, there were cross-unit government bodies at all administrative levels that controlled certain operational aspects of all work-units, such as planning (strategic decision-making), finance, personnel management, and logistics. Despite the market transition for nearly 40 years, China's public sector is still characterized largely by the nested systems of hierarchical organizations inherited from the decentralized past. Due to this institutional legacy, decentralization does not perform as a significantly substantial organizational reform in China as in many other countries (Mills et al. 1990; Saltman et al. 2007) such as in Europe (Dan 2017) and in developing countries (Bossert 1998; Bossert and Beauvais 2002).

The personnel management system of public organizations was a concentrated manifestation of bureaucratic governance. The recruitment and employment of all staff members in public organizations were brought into a so-called "administrative staffing system" (*bianzhi tixi*) administered by the government's personnel department, which expands bureaucratic personnel management targeting from civil servants to all human resources in the public sector (Brødsgaard 2007), including public hospitals. As it has constituted as a significant part of the institutional legacies inherited from the past, *bianzhi* is a keyword for our understanding China's personnel management in the public sector.

Furthermore, the recruitment of managers for all public service organizations was incorporated into the Party's cadre selection and appointment system (Zheng 1997), which was guided by the principle of "the Party assuming the responsibility for cadres' affairs" (*dangguan ganbu*). The Party's organ (*dangzu*) of the administrative system with which the hospital was affiliated was responsible for selection and appointment of the management. The hospital as a public service organization also lacked full managerial autonomy on salary and remuneration, while the government exercised a unified administrative salary system on government agents, public service organizations, and state-owned enterprises (SOEs), where the salary levels were directly linked with administrative ranks.

During the market transition, public hospitals have been delegated some kind of managerial autonomy, moving governance mode from bureaucratization to autonomization. In 1992, the MOH granted substantial financial autonomy to public hospitals, allowing them to charge for their services and to sell drugs (World Bank 2010a). This was similar with the first stage of SOE reform, which was characterized by delegation of management autonomy and creation of operational incentives but without restructuring and corporatization of property rights (Zhang 2008). Financial delegation from the government's administrative agencies to public service organizations was accompanied by state withdrawing from the responsibility of financing public services, including health services (Duckett 2011). Correspondingly, the funding sources for public hospitals' daily operation have considerably changed. Payments from individuals and public health insurance schemes have replaced the government's budgetary appropriations to become the major sources of operational revenue. Actually, this change is global (Preker and Harding 2003); it is never limited to transition countries, not to say being limited to China.

Financially, China's public hospitals have undergone a transformation from public organizations operating on full government funding to ones on self-funding. Since 2003, the proportion of self-generated income in the total revenue of public hospitals has stabilized at 90% or so, while government funding or subsidies merely accounted for 10%. The operations of public hospitals have been highly dependent upon service charges and drug sales, which seemed to bear certain characteristics of "marketization" or "commercialization," incurring widespread criticisms domestically and internationally (Liu and Mills 2002). In this regard, the World Bank's experts wrote, "many public hospitals in China function like private hospitals, and many public-hospital doctors function like private independent practitioners, because both hospitals and doctors obtain significant revenue from charging fees-for-services and earning profits from drug sales on a cost-plus basis" (World Bank 2010a).

With the deepening of the market transition, the old free health-care system embedded in the work-unit-based mini-welfare state became unsustainable, but the new health-care insurance system had not been effectively established for a considerable period of time (Gu 2001) until 2008. Out-of-pocket payment became dominant on the demand-side of the health sector in the late 1990s (Gu 2001), and more than 80% of the population was not covered by health-care insurance or any prepaid plan whatsoever. Against this background, China was ranked fourth worst among all World Health Organization (WHO) member countries in terms of fairness of financing health care when WHO conducted a comprehensive performance evaluation of health systems around the world in 2000 (WHO 2000).

Partially in responding to this embarrassing assessment, the Chinese government since 2003 has once again assumed the organizing and financing responsibilities for building up the basic health insurance system comprised by three public insurance programs, namely Urban Employee Basic Medical Insurance, New Rural Cooperative Medical Scheme, and Urban Resident Basic Medical Insurance (Huang 2013). Universal health insurance coverage was basically achieved in 2011 (Yu 2015). With consolidation of the demand-side reforms, public health-care insurance agents have become the major payers to China's public hospitals (Gu 2010).

However, it would be totally wrong if we consequently thought that China's public hospitals have truly embarked on a path of "genuine" marketization. Except for funding and revenue generating which bear relevance to marketization, the operation of China's public hospitals is dominated by bureaucratic rather than market mechanism in all aspects (Gu 2011), and community mechanism plays little role in either corporate governance or associational governance. Public hospitals might seem to be marketized at the first glace, but in fact they are still highly bureaucratized in nature, which is manifested in the following four aspects.

First, **most public hospitals are the subordinate bodies of the government's health departments at different levels**. According to official statistics, by the end of 2015, there were a total of 27,587 hospitals in China, including 13,069 public hospitals. Of these public hospitals, 9651 were government hospitals, of which 8597 were administered by the health departments, accounting for 89.1% of the government hospitals and 65.8% of all public hospitals (National Health and Family Planning Commission of the People's Republic of China 2016).

The administrative subordinate-superior relationship between most public hospitals and the government's health departments facilitates, to some extent, the implementation of health administration but has led to serious negative consequences in other aspects, especially the institutional ineffectiveness and dysfunction of health-care regulations. In China, the government's health departments act as regulators as well as administrative superiors of the regulated wherein public hospitals are involved. While the neutrality of regulators—a third party to the inter-organizational relationships—serves as a necessary (but not sufficient) condition of regulatory success and governance accountability (Walshe 2003), its absence is one of the institutional roots of inadequate regulations on health-care services and poor governance on hospital-patient conflicts in China.

Second, **with regard to the personnel system, there is a dual labor market within the huge system of public hospitals, that is, the distinction between the "in-staff" (*bianzhi nei*) and "off-staff" (*bianzhi wai*) personnel**. The hospital's plan for position setting and recruitment of the "in-staff" personnel is incorporated in the government's staffing system and needs to be approved by the government's staffing office (*bianzhi ban* or *bianban*), health departments, and personnel departments. Public hospitals hold little managerial autonomy in personnel management of in-staff health professionals, who as formal employees occupy a more significant position in human resources. Public hospitals have the full autonomy in the recruitment of "off-staff" personnel, basically informal employees who are also called "contract employees" (*hetong gong*). Therefore, doctors and other staff under formal employment in public hospitals have continued to be classified as state employees who are paid according to public sector rules and who can only be appointed or terminated by state authorities (Qian and Blomqvist 2014).

The bureaucratized staffing system, or *bianzhi tixi*, is a legacy of the planned economy; hence, it is extremely hard for such a system to fit in the market transition with intensified labor mobility across workplace units and localities. In the localities where the migrant population flows in, the staffing (*bianzhi*) of local public hospitals would turn out to be inadequate to meet the dramatically increasing demand for health-care services, but the government's staffing office at all levels usually responds very slowly to changes in demand for public services in general and health-care services in particular, leading to the shortage of "in-staff" postings. In the localities with a high level of population outflow, the situation is just the opposite.

The distinction between the "in-staff" and "off-staff" personnel has also caused the discrepancy in their employment status, which has not only brought out a lot of problems for the hospital's human resource management, such as the discrepancy in payrolls of people working in the same position (Liu 2014), but also significantly blocked the flow of "in-staff" or "staff-to-be" health-care professionals (who have the opportunity to change their employment status from "off-staff" to "in-staff") to private hospitals, indirectly hindering the development of private hospitals.

Apart from the problem of the dual labor markets bureaucratically imposed in the whole public sector in general and in the health sector in particular, the Chinese government had also implemented the tough regulations on physicians' practice sites until 2017. All the certified Chinese physicians were required to register only one practice site with local health bureaus and re-register when they changed their practice site. The re-registration for changing practice sites needed a lot of paperwork, constituting a heavy burden for labor mobility in the health sector. The strict regulations on practice sites resulted in the legitimization of sole practice; that is to say, physicians were allowed to practice only in health-care institutions where they were officially employed. Such regulations produced a strong incentive for physicians to moonlight, and moonlighting became very popular among senior physicians although the government made it unlawful (Guo and Gu 2016).

Third, **the day-to-day operating revenue of public hospitals are mainly from the payments by individual patients and public health insurance, and all capital investment must be approved by the government's multiple departments including the health department, the finance department, and the development and reform commission**. The operating revenue is generated basically on the basis of fee-for-service payment, while the provider-payment reforms from public health insurance—by introducing various prospective payments such as capitation, global budget, and DRG-based payment—have been sluggish (World Bank 2010b). With regard to capital investment, which is vitally important for the allocation of hardware resources, it is precisely bureaucratic rather than market mechanism that plays the decisive role, which has caused the allocation of medical resources to be significantly tilted toward public hospitals with higher administrative ranks. Due to historical and administrative reasons, such public hospitals are usually concentrated in the municipalities directly under the central government (viz. Beijing, Shanghai, Tianjin, and Chongqing), provincial capitals, and large cities in economically developed areas (Lampton 1979). They always become winners in the process of bureaucratic allocation of resources, leading to increasing disparities of health-care capacities across urban and rural areas, large and medium-sized and small cities, and economically developed and underdeveloped areas.

Fourth, **with regard to logistics, the government, on the one hand, is implementing direct administrative pricing for medical services and price control of pharmaceuticals, and, on the other hand, imposing a bureaucratic bidding system targeting public hospitals on their purchase of most drugs and certain medical consumables and appliances.** Public pricing for medical service is administered by pricing bureaus under the development and reform commissions at the provincial level. A two-tiered price regulation on drugs had been imposed by the pricing department of the National Development and Reform Commission (NDRC) and the provincially administered bidding offices until 2015, when the centrally imposed price-cap regulation was abolished due to almost all related officials being involved in corruption (Qian 2017), while the provincially imposed public pricing for public hospitals' drug purchasing through the bidding system is still in place.

Administrative pricing and/or price control lead to many undesirable results. First, the pricing levels for the vast majority of items deviate significantly from the equilibrium prices set through the market mechanism. For most of major and commonly seen medical services, such as the diagnosis and treatment of normal diseases and nursing care, the charges are set at very (and in many cases excessively) low levels. Second, the prices set through bureaucratic mechanism can never keep up with socioeconomic changes, that is, the pricing levels of medical services implemented around 2010 were set in 1999 and 2000 (Zhou 2008). For more than ten years, the charges for many medical services have only been slightly readjusted. In 2012, the MOH formulated and issued a new catalogue of the chargeable medical service items, but the adjustment of pricing is conducted in a sluggish and fragmented way in most provinces.

With the administrative pricing system, the fees that public hospitals have charged for basic medical services are set at levels that most likely have been below the cost of producing them. Hence, public hospitals have no incentive to supply basic medical services at an adequate level. As the provision of basic medical services produces net losses and drug sale produces net gains anyway under the existing price regulations, public hospitals have no alternative other than the rational choice of over-prescribing of drugs (in particular, expensive drugs). This organizational behavior by public hospitals and individual behavior by physicians that worked for public hospitals can be considered as a form of supply-induced demand, which appears to have been a major problem in China's health sector for a long time (Qian and Blomqvist 2014). By 2008, drug revenue accounted for an average of 40% of gross income of hospitals, far higher than the 15–25% common in most Organisation for Economic Co-operation and Development (OECD) countries. Public hospitals have strong incentives to promote more-profitable higher-technology services and to increase the volume of drug prescription, leading to the rapid increase of health-care expenditures (World Bank 2010a). The financial burdens brought about by the Chinese way of provider-induced over-consumption are borne jointly by patients and public health insurance funds.

In order to curb the rapid increase in drug costs, the government has been exercising multiple regulations on drug pricing and drug sale, targeting all public and nonprofit health-care providers, including regulations on the price cap of most drugs, stock purchasing price, and mark-up rate, as well as the ratio of income generated from drug sale to the total revenue of the hospital, but in the end, all the regulatory measures have neither curbed the over-pricing of drugs nor lowered the expenditure on drug prescription (Zhu 2011). Although the price-cap regulation on drugs was abolished in 2015, the regulatory structure of pharmaceutical purchase and sale for public hospitals remains unchanged. As regulations on the pricing for stock purchase and the mark-up rate for drug sale remain in place, the price levels of most drugs sold through the system of public health-care providers including public hospitals are set by the government.

In brief, the autonomization of China's public hospitals with the dominant functioning of bureaucratic mechanism has eventually led to the formation of a new governance mode, namely bureaucratic marketization. Compared with the mode of bureaucratization, this governance change has added the economic vitality to public hospitals but also resulted in a lot of adverse effects in their social and economic behaviors. Under the governance of bureaucratic marketization, the market mechanism does not play a basic role in the allocation of resources, let alone a "decisive" role as the Party wishes, and the coordinating function of the community mechanism is even not worth mentioning.

Bureaucratic marketization is not at all satisfactory in terms of either promoting efficiency or improving equity, hence producing the imperative need for deepening the reform. Yet, there is no consensus on the direction of public hospital reform, whether among health policy scholars or governments at all levels. Although various specific measures are proposed, they all lack a sense of direction, as well as synchronic coordination across measures and diachronic consistency along the time.

In terms of the direction of the new health reforms in general and public hospital reform in particular, there has been a hot debate between pro-government and pro-market approaches, which burst in 2006 and lasted in one way or another afterward (Hsiao 2007). The pro-government approach, inspired by the British model (largely before the internal market reform), proposes that the government heavily invest in public hospitals to maintain their nature for pursuing "the public interest" and provide cheap public health and basic health care for all. Proponents of the approach include Ge Yanfeng of the Development Research Center (DRC) under the State Council and Professor Li Lin of Peking University. This approach receives support, explicit or implicit, from the MOH. By contrast, the pro-market approach, influenced by the public contract model in general (OECD 1992) or the German model in particular, favors reduced government direct interference in health services provision and the use of third parties largely for social health insurance schemes to purchase health-care services, while the government undertakes major financing responsibility for establishing a national system of basic health-care insurance with universal coverage. The pro-market approach also received support from the Ministry of Labor and Social Security, and the MOF (Hsiao 2007). Proponents of this approach include Professor Liu Guo-en (Gordon Liu) of Peking University and Professor Gu Xin (Edward Gu) of Peking Normal University (Huang 2013), who (the author of this study) has moved to Peking University since 2008.

Based on my participatory observation during the involvement in the debate, it can be affirmed that the pro-government approach is basically inclined to direct the new health reforms toward re-bureaucratization, while the pro-market approach toward de-bureaucratization. The approach of re-bureaucratization is to transform the governance pattern from the Chinese-style decentralized bureaucratization to somehow classical socialist centralized bureaucratization (Gu 2015). Consequently, the power of allocating all the resources involved in operations of public hospitals, which is shared by 14–16 departments of the government (Qian 2015), is expected to be centralized in the hands of the government's health departments, rather than being distributed among different departments. To be specific:

1. In terms of decision-making and power to control, the departments of health at different administrative levels become the executive directors of all public hospitals according to their administrative ranking.
2. In terms of funding sources, the departments of health carry out the "item-line budgeting" for daily operations of public hospitals and hold the exclusive power to approve capital investment.
3. In terms of human resource management, the departments of health are not only responsible for the appointment of managers but also for the staffing and recruitment of all personnel.
4. In terms of material allocation, the departments of health are in charge of the purchase of all drugs, consumables, and appliances through a centralized public procurement system, and the power to decide on public pricing for medical services, drugs, and consumables and appliances is transferred from the pricing bureaus under the development and reform commission to the departments of health.

De-bureaucratization promotes the delegation of power from the government, regardless of which departments and at what levels, to the hospital, namely the corporatization of the majority of public hospitals and the privatization of the rest (Gu 2015). A detailed description of the de-bureaucratized system is as follows:

1. In terms of organizational relations, all public hospitals break off the subordinate-superior affiliation from their corresponding administrative departments and are transformed into independent legal persons. After becoming public corporations, new corporate governance empowered

by the board of directors comprising of stakeholders structures the allocation of strategic decision-making and daily managerial power in public hospitals.

2. In terms of funding sources, the daily operation of public hospitals relies mainly on the payment from all types of health insurers, in particular public health insurance funds, and capital investments may come from private, market-like financing and/or public, government-backed funding. Public hospitals hold the complete right of the residual claim.

3. In terms of human resource management, the staffing and management recruitment of public hospitals should be gradually governed by market mechanism based on the comprehensive labor contract system.

4. In terms of logistical management, public hospitals enjoy full autonomy, especially with the transformation of the bureaucratic bidding system of drugs to marketized and corporatized arrangements, similar to the American model of pharmaceutical benefit management (PBM). The government lifts the price regulations so that health insurance institutions and health-care providers can form a bargaining relationship over provider-payment modes, so as to promote the formation of the public contract model.

Neither set of these reform proposals has been accepted and expressed in an ample, complete, and systematic manner in government documents at any level. Still, many key points of the pro-government approach—such as financially all-inclusive item-line budgetary management over the daily operations and capital investment, continuation of bureaucratic governance over strategic management as well as personnel management, perseverance in price regulations but with only minor adjustments, and centralized bidding and procurement of pharmaceuticals and consumables—are explicitly demonstrated in many policy papers of health-care reforms at national and local levels, as well as in specific local reform practices.

Meanwhile, though bureaucratic governance has been deeply rooted in people's minds and in practices, making it hard to thoroughly deploy de-bureaucratization, many reform measures along with the pro-market approach can always fight their own way out in different times or at different places. This is partly related to the repeated emphasis of the ruling Party and the government on taking full advantage of market mechanism's "basic" and "decisive" role in allocation of resources, namely the legitimization of market governance over the whole public service sector.

3 LOCAL PUBLIC HOSPITAL REFORMS: SWING BETWEEN RE-BUREAUCRATIZATION AND DE-BUREAUCRATIZATION

As a consequence, public hospital reform lacks a definite direction and the local reform practices vacillate between re-bureaucratization and de-bureaucratization across localities and periods. What greatly differ are synchronic incoordination and diachronic incongruity in terms of matters and extents of vacillation.

First and foremost, **the reform in the organizational relationship between public hospitals and the departments of health sinks into ambiguity**. According to the comprehensive "new health reform plan" proposed by the ruling party and the government in April 2009, public hospitals as public service organizations should be separated organizationally from the government bodies with which they were administratively affiliated, and the ownership and management of public hospitals should be separated. Nevertheless, as regulators and general managers of public hospitals, the government's department of health at all levels are themselves the objects of reform. Instead of pushing for the separation of ownership and management, a document drafted by the MOH in April 2010 still bestowed on the health bureaucracy the role of sectoral administration, regulation, and management of hospitals (Huang 2013).

Despite the resistance from the health department of the central government, explicit or implicit, many municipalities selected by the State Council to implement public hospital reform on pilot basis took various measures to push for the separation of ownership and management. The common measures are to set up specialized hospital administration agencies by imitating the Hospital Authority in Hong Kong to carry out administration on public hospitals and to let the existing health bureaus perform as regulators. Unlike the corporatization model of the Hospital Authority of Hong Kong (Gauld 1998), however, the government-run hospital management agencies in the Mainland show three models of organization and governance.

The first is a re-bureaucratized model, featuring the separation of ownership and management functionally but not organizationally, which means to set up the hospital administration authorities (*yiguanju*) under the departments of health. Weifang of Shandong province was the first city selected for this initiative. In 2005, the Weifang Health Bureau established a hospital management center affiliated with itself to manage public hospitals in order to solve the problems resulting from the ambiguous rights and obligations of the government's administrative departments. While the center performs daily administration over public hospitals, the obligations of financing, staffing control, selection and appointment of the management, and provider-payment from public health insurance have been transferred from a number of administrative bodies to the health bureau (World Bank 2010a).

Beijing stands as a new typical example for this model. The Beijing Municipal Administration of Hospitals was set up in 2011, managing over 22 municipal public hospitals. It became a new government agent under Beijing Municipal Health Bureau, but enjoyed the same administrative rank—namely the level of bureau—with the Bureau, an eccentric administrative arrangement officially called "the secondary bureau" (erji ju). The newly formed Municipal Administrations of Hospitals in Luoyang in Henan province and in Ezhou of Hubei province are also subordinated to their municipal health bureaus.

The second is a de-bureaucratized model, featuring the corporatization of hospital administration. In Ma'anshan of Anhui province, an independent Municipal Hospital Group has been formed as a public corporation to perform the function of administration over all public hospitals owned by the municipal government.

The third is in between the above two models, namely making the newly formed public hospital administration bodies affiliated with other local bureaus than health bureaus. In Wuxi and Suzhou of Jiangsu province, Shanghai, specific public organizations have been formed either directly administered by the municipal governments or affiliated with the commission of state-asset management.

In 2001, the Wuxi municipal government launched the reform to separate ownership and management of the health bureau over nine municipally owned hospitals. The management of the hospitals is entrusted to a hospital management center, which serves as an administrative public agent directly administered by the municipal government. Consequently, the local health bureau shifts its function from the owner or even operator of the hospitals to the regulator of the whole health-care sector (Liang et al. 2007).

In 2004, the Suzhou municipal government set up a Hospital Development Center to manage hospitals under government supervision. The council as the governing body comprised the chiefs from a number of government bodies involved in health care, including health, finance, personnel and social security bureau, as well as the administrative staffing office. The council took decisions with respect to the strategic management of the hospitals. The relationship between the health bureau and public hospitals changed from administration to contracting, and the health bureau retained the regulatory and supervisory functions (World Bank 2010a).

In 2005, the Shanghai Shenkang Hospital Development Center was founded. As a public entity responsible for state-owned investment, management, and operation of municipal public hospitals, the Center performed its functions with affiliation to Shanghai State-owned Assets Supervision and Administration Commission (World Bank 2010a).

The provision of corporatization of public hospitals, clearly proposed in the 2009 "new healthcare reform plan," fails to get implemented in many localities and only a number of municipalities such as Zhuzhou of Hunan province, Zhenjiang of Jiangsu province, Xiamen of Fujian province, Luoyang of Henan province, Ma'anshan, Ezhou, Kunming, and Shanghai make some efforts to implement it. Specific institutional arrangements thereof all fall into two categories of re-bureaucratization, without any move toward de-bureaucratization. China's public hospital reform has remained at the stage of autonomization, and the genuine moves toward corporatization are very rare.

Under the centralized re-bureaucratized model, public hospitals set up the board of directors, the board of supervisors, and the board of management under the leadership of local health bureaus. Under the decentralized re-bureaucratized model, the restructuring of corporate governance for public hospitals is undertaken by newly formed hospital administration agencies that are administratively independent from local health bureaus. No matter which model is adopted, superintendents of public hospitals in all pilot cities are mostly appointed by the government, and the board of directors is not granted the power and responsibility to select and appoint the management for public hospitals (Yu 2014).

The first instance of a public hospital implementing corporatization was the "Dongyang case" in Zhejiang province. In 1993, Dongyang People's Hospital was established with the donation of a Taiwanese who was born in Dongyang. With assets being owned by the municipal government, the hospital was accommodated as a non-profit public corporation. According to the proposal of the donor, and under the instructions of Dongyang Municipal Party Committee and Municipal Government, the hospital's board of directors comprised five to nine members, consisting of donors, officials from health and finance bureaus, and hospital management experts. The first batch of directors were nominated through negotiations among Municipal Party Committee, the municipal government, and the donor, and subsequent ones are nominated by the previous board members and are appointed with the endorsement of the organizational department of the Municipal Party Committee. The board of directors enjoys the power of strategic decision-making, the right to nominate the management, and the right to assess and audit finances. In terms of personnel management, the hospital adopts a fully market-oriented labor contract system (Li and Huang 2010). For a long time, the Dongyang model has remained the sole case of corporatization, and the fact that it got ignored within the administrative system of health indicates the huge hindrance that the innovation of corporatized governance has suffered in the face of bureaucratized forces.

In July 2017, the General Office of the State Council promulgated the No. 67 Document on building up "the management system for modern hospitals," reiterating the separation of ownership and management as the primary principle in the de-bureaucratization reform of public hospitals. The focus of the separation lies in properly defining the government's responsibilities as investor rather than manager of public hospitals. The hospital's administrative relationship with the government body should be resolved, and its administrative ranking abolished (http://www.gov.cn/zhengce/content/2017-07/25/content_5213256.htm).

Second, **funding sources have been marketized but financial management remains bureaucratized**. The vast majority of daily operating income of public hospitals comes no longer from the government's fiscal appropriation, but their financial management is still under the control of the government. With the improvement of the government-run basic health-care insurance system, insurance payments account for an increasingly higher percentage in hospital revenues.

For all kinds of health-care providers, there is a global trend that the major funding source for daily operations is the payment from insurers, regardless of whether health financing system is characterized by National Health Service, National Health Insurance, social health insurance, private health insurance, or a mixture of all (Preker and Harding 2003). China is by no means an exception.

Nevertheless, the senior medical professionals often call for the government to increase financial investment in public hospitals in the name of promoting public interest on all possible occasions. This call for reinforcing "subsidizing the supply-side" with public finance is actively echoed by the MOH, which favors the restoration of line-item public budgeting for public hospitals but encounters cool reception from the MOF as well as other government departments. The MOF, which has been backing the pro-market health reform proposal, favors the approach of "subsidizing the demand-side," namely subsidizing the people's enrolment in public health insurance schemes (Gu 2010). By this approach, the MOF wished to create a new third-party purchasing mechanism within which public insurance agents performed the function of strategic purchasing of health services, as a World Bank volume (Preker and Liu 2007) has deliberated. This approach was also acclaimed by the Ministry of Human Resources and Social Security, which plays the administrative role in running two public health insurance schemes targeting urban employees and residents (Blomqvist and Qian 2010).

Although the MOH has been insisting on the re-bureaucratized approach toward line-item public budgeting for public hospitals, it has been rarely adopted in most localities with the only exception being the "Zichang model". In 2008, Zichang county government in Shaanxi province proposed to implement line-item budgeting and financial management over the county's People's Hospital and therefore stood as a "healthcare reform star" strongly recommended by the MOH. But later, due to the growing increase of financial subsides, the Zichang model has become unsustainable and has deviated from its original track as it simply fails to build up a positive financial incentive for the hospital adopting "affordable" health care (Yu 2014).

The restoration toward the item-line public budgeting and "command-and-control" financial management performed by the government belongs to an extreme practice of re-bureaucratization, and its outcomes will inevitably cause health-care delivery to retrogress the bureaucratic governance overwhelmingly which prevailed during the era of the planned economy before the 1980s. Essentially, increasing suspicions on this approach have emerged even within the MOH as well as within health department at local levels, and most managers of public hospitals do not embrace it readily.

Third, **the allocation of human resources remains under tough control through bureaucratic personnel and cadre management**. In February 2010, a multi-department-endorsed guidance on pilot public hospital forms was promulgated, which explicitly stipulates that "measures for registered physicians to practice at multiple sites shall be explored, implemented and standardized, so as to guide the rational flow of medical staff; the personnel staffing in public hospitals shall be checked and ratified in rationalized and scientific way; and the personnel management system featuring employment and posting shall be established and perfected" (http://www.gov.cn/ztzl/ygzt/content_1661148.htm). This official guidance in itself contains elements of re-bureaucratization and de-bureaucratization: on the one hand, it deregulates the control over the practice sites of physicians; on the other hand, the government's personnel departments and staffing offices remain firmly in control of the in-staff personnel of public hospitals.

The breakthrough with the bureaucratized personnel system within the public health-care sector first emerged in deregulation on physicians' practice site. Legitimizing physician dual practice or even multiple jobholding became a widely accepted reform measure for the government at all levels at the beginning of launching "new health reforms." Yet implementation of such reform measures has gone through a tough process of de-bureaucratization. During the stage of "the new health reforms", from 2009 to 2015, most municipal governments adopted a procedural measure of "double examination and approval"; that is to say, physician multisite practice had to fulfill the dual approval by the CEO of the hospital with which the physician was registered and the local health bureau. Kunming was then the sole city to carry out only single examination and approval system, that is, physicians could practice in three places as long as they obtained the approval from the local health bureau. Later on, other cities gradually loosened control over physicians' practice sites. Beijing, Shenzhen (Hu et al. 2012), and other cities, for example, not only shifted from double examination and approval to the single one but have further evolved to the filing system, that is to say, qualified physicians may practice at multiple sites as long as they file to local health bureaus. However, due to the constraints of multilayered administrative system, especially the universal repugnance from the management of the hospitals they are practicing with, the deregulation on physician practice sites did not turn out well in reality (Zhou and Yin 2015). The majority of physicians were still inclined to conduct medical services at the non-registered practice site in the form of moonlighting.

This situation has dramatically changed. On February 28, 2017, the National Health and Family Planning Commission, which was renamed from the MOH in 2013, issued the new edition of *Regulations on Physicians Registration and Practice* (http://www.nhfpc.gov.cn/yzygj/s3576/201703/3f8de749eebd4a1ebf1961c78ad4be7e.shtml). Under the new regulations, once the physician has registered his/her practice site, he/she is allowed to practice at any site without re-registration within the same province, thus realizing the legalization of physicians' free practice. Hence, the year 2017 has been applauded as "the first year for physician free practice" among health-care professionals and by the media.

Compared with deregulations on physician practice site, other deregulations on the personnel management in the public health-care sector have made sluggish progress. While encouraging the free flow of talents has been a strong desire of the Chinese government for many years, the existing bureaucratized personnel management system in the public sector remains to be the most important factor in blocking the formation of the labor market of talents. Though there have been voices among health policy scholars to "abolish the staffing system and free physicians," the reform of the staffing system had never been placed on the central government's policy agenda of the new health-care reforms until 2016.

In some localities, such as Beijing and Shenzhen, some pilot reforms with the staffing system began to be carried out in 2015. Shenzhen became the first city in China to officially promote de-bureaucratization of staffing in public hospitals. In 2016, the policy of staffing de-bureaucratization was finally brought out on the health-care reform agenda of the central government. However, due to the universal opposition of the permanent staff and the fact that the staffing system is entwined with multiple institutional elements, such as financial investment, social security, professional title appraisal, and remunerations, the de-bureaucratized reform is still confronted with many obstacles (Zhang and Huang 2017). It is noteworthy that in the No. 67 Document in 2017 released by the General Office of the State Council, by far the most comprehensive government paper concerning de-bureaucratization reform of public hospitals, abolishing of the staffing system is not mentioned.

Fourth, **the management of logistics in public hospitals, in particular, one involving purchase and sale of drugs, remains strictly and rigidly regulated by the government**. The 2009 "new healthcare reform plan" and 2010 guidelines for hospital reform failed to outline an overall pattern for public hospital reforms in the future, but there has been one area where the plan and guidance targeted is quite clear, namely with respect to the use of pharmaceuticals (Qian and Blomqvist 2014). As drug expenditure is a share of total health expenditure in China and is often double or even threefold of the average of other countries such as OECD member states (Qian 2017), it is not unthinkable that price control over pharmaceuticals is deemed to be the area of the new health-care reforms with the most intensive government concerns. Therefore, there has emerged an ironic and ridiculous saying among the circles that "the healthcare reform" turns out to be "the pharmaceutical reform." The keynote of the measures targeting the use of pharmaceuticals in public hospitals is to intensify the implementation of existing price regulations, on the one hand, and to introduce a series of new regulations, on the other (Qian 2017).

The framework of the existing administrative price control remains little changed, and the central government has made tremendous efforts in imposing a new measure called "zero mark-up rate for medicines" (yaopin lingjiacheng or yaopin lingchalv), namely to transform the existing regulated mark-up rate from 15% to 0%. Since 2015, this policy has become the hallmark measure of public hospital reforms and is considered as the realization of "the separation of medical services and drug sales," one guiding principle proposed by the 2009 new health reforms plan. However, it is controversial whether this measure is coincident with the global practice of separating health services and drug prescription. In essence, the measure of "zero mark-up rate for medicines" is still a kind of mark-up regulation but with a regulated mark-up rate of zero. The new regulatory measure is determined to cast loss of revenue generating from drug sale on the account book of public hospitals. In case of basically unchanged administrative pricing of medical services, the policy of "zero mark-up rate for medicines" compels public hospitals to find out other channels to cover the uncompensated costs of medical services.

The bureaucratic bidding system for pharmaceuticals, since its establishment in various places at the end of the twentieth century, had been implemented based at the municipal level for a long time. Since 2010, this system has been centralized to the provincial level, and the offices in charge of bidding are mostly set up under the health departments. This transformation has come about in a re-bureaucratized way. Though various fine adjustments have been made on the technical aspects of the centralized drug bidding system almost every year, the actual effects of adjustments are minimal since they have never shaken the foundation of price control and the incentive structure of public hospitals.

The distorting effects of price regulations on organizational and individual behaviors in health services had never been reflected in policy thinking, and thereby never been restarted in practice for a long time until 2016. With respect to the pricing system reform, the local health-care reform plans promulgated by the pilot cities implementing public hospital reform basically repeated the guiding opinions appeared in the central government's policy documents, even in largely identical wording and phrasing, and failed to formulate any substantive reform measures. This has been the case because the central government takes the responsibility to formulate the pricing system, while its implementation is carried out by governments at the provincial level, and the municipal governments have basically little authority with price setting and adjustment.

As a matter of fact, the unreasonable prices of health services caused by administrative pricing have evoked endless complaints as well as appeals for adjustment from the health-care profession. Governments at all levels also give a nod of approval for the related appeals, and statements for adjusting the pricing are actually listed in a variety of government documents every year. In 2012, the NDRC released a policy notice on "standardizing" price control over medical services, which stipulated that all the local governments should complete the price adjustment in medical services by the end of 2013. The price levels of the vast majority of normal medical services, such as diagnosis and treatment charges, surgery fees, and nursing fees, were required to be put up, while the prices for medical examinations in particular with large-scale equipment to be lowered down. Nevertheless, due to various reasons, this policy notice for price adjustment of medical services failed to be deployed in the vast majority of localities.

Chongqing, a provincially ranked municipality directly administered by the central government, was an exception. On March 18, 2015, Chongqing Municipal Price Bureau and Chongqing Municipal Health and Family Planning Commission issued a notice, requiring all the public hospitals to implement a new version of pricing, which made adjustment to the prices of 7886 medical service items, among which the cost of kidney dialysis increased from RMB 1000 yuan to RMB 4000 yuan. But Chongqing's administrative price adjustment lasted less than seven days and was rescinded due to the strong protest from the public opposing to the price increase of kidney dialysis and was thus called by the media "the shortest ever" health-care reform (Hu 2015).

The distortions brought about by bureaucratized public pricing of medical services finally got properly addressed on July 1, 2016, when the NDRC issued policy document on the pricing reform (http://www.ndrc.gov.cn/gzdt/201607/t20160706_810596.html). However, the specific measures proposed in this policy document are still stuck in the pattern of administrative adjustment rather than deregulation.

The reason why the majority of local public hospital pilot reforms swing between re-bureaucratization and de-bureaucratization can be attributed to the fact that most local governments are reluctant to make readjustment of power among the departments. But everything has an exception. Since 2012, Sanming of Fujian province has carried out a set of profound health-care reforms through power readjustment, forming the Sanming model extended nationwide by the central government in 2016. The Sanming model is characterized by promoting re-bureaucratization through centralizing the power from more than a dozen departments to a newly formed government body. With the centralization of power, certain measures colored by de-bureaucratization are also carried out in some areas of public hospital governance, that is, imposing provider-payment reform, breaking through the existing personnel and wage management system, and bypassing the administrative pricing. Meanwhile, tough regulations on sale of drugs are imposed. However, the impacts of the Sanming reforms on the operations of public hospital are still limited (Qian 2017), and the sustainability and replicability of Sanming model remain to be seen.

4   Conclusion: From Autonomization to Corporatization—Allowing Market and Community Mechanisms to Play a More Active Role in Public Hospital Governance

Innovation of public hospital governance lies at the core of the supply-side reform in China's health sector. The key to innovation rests in that bureaucratic, market, and community mechanisms can be combined to form collaborative governance where the three are embedded in each other, and supplement and reinforce one another. While market mechanism plays a decisive role in the allocation of resources and community mechanism plays a key role in organizational governance, bureaucratic mechanism takes an enabling, facilitating, and legitimizing part in the operations of the former two. The formation of mutual empowerment among the state, market, and society is critical to public hospital reform. The institutionalization of the public contract system through provider-payment reforms is the key to address the root causes of rapid cost escalation and vast inefficiency in public hospitals (He and Meng 2015).

However, in the reform process, from bureaucratization to autonomization of China's public hospitals, due to governance philosophy and practice preference originating from the historical inheritance of unified bureaucratic mechanisms, the functioning of the market mechanism has been severely distorted in strategic management, personnel management, logistics management, and so on, in public hospitals, while the community mechanism has played little role in organizational coordination (particularly in such areas as strategic decision-making, accountability and self-regulation). Local pilot reforms basically vacillate and oscillate between re-bureaucratization and de-bureaucratization. That is to say, local governments implement the measures of re-bureaucratization in some operational fields, while adopting de-bureaucratization measures in other fields. In spite of local differences, public hospitals across the country have something in common, that is, their operation is largely affected by multiparty, multilevel administrative forces. The dominance of bureaucratic mechanism had failed to bolster the formation of collaborative governance but rather led to the predicament of bureaucratic marketization, thus distorting market mechanism and weakening community mechanism.

Therefore, the only right way for deepening public hospital reform is exactly the reform orientation established during the Third Plenary Session of the 18th CPC Central Committee, which is de-bureaucratization. It is certain that de-bureaucratization does not equal with eliminating the bureaucratic mechanism, which, in fact, is impossible to get removed in any type of governance model. The key to de-bureaucratization lies in allowing market and community mechanism to play a more active role in resource allocation and organizational governance. This applies to all social policies and naturally applies to public hospital reform. Only when de-bureaucratization is thoroughly implemented— that is to say, market mechanism plays a decisive role in allocation of medical resources, community mechanism plays a key role in organizational governance, and bureaucratic mechanism functions itself in market-augmenting and society-enabling manners—can good governance take shape and China's public hospital reform make genuine progress.

REFERENCES

Azfar, O., and C. A. Cadwell (eds.). 2003. *Market-augmenting Government: the Institutional Foundations for Prosperity.* Ann Arbor: The University of Michigan Press.

Blomqvist, Å., and J. Qian. 2010. Direct Provider Subsidies vs Social Health Insurance: A Compromise Proposal. In Zhao Litao and Lim Tin Seng (eds.), *China's New Social Policy: Initiatives for a Harmonious Society.* Singapore: World Scientific Publishing, pp. 41–71.

Bossert, T. 1998. Analyzing the decentralization of health systems in developing countries: Decision space, innovation and performance. *Social Science & Medicine* 47(10): 1513–1527.

Bossert, T., and J. C. Beauvais. 2002. Decentralization of health systems in Ghana, Zambia, Uganda and the Philippines: A comparative analysis of decision space. *Health Policy and Planning* 17(1): 14–31.

Bowles, S. 2004. *Microeconomics: Behavior, Institutions, and Evolution.* Princeton: Princeton University Press.

Brødsgaard, K. E. 2007. Managing China's civil servants. in Gungwu Wang and John Wong (eds.), *Interpreting China's Development.* Singapore: World Scientific Publishing Co., pp. 41–47.

Dan, S. 2017. *The Coordination of European Public Hospital Systems: Interests, Cultures and Resistance.* Cham, Switzerland: Palgrave Macmillan.

Donahue, J. D., and R. J. Zeckhauser. 2011. *Collaborative governance: Private roles for public goals in turbulent times.* Princeton: Princeton University Press.

Duckett, J. 2011. *The Chinese State's Retreat from Health: Policy and the Politics of Retrenchment.* London and New York: Routledge.

Gauld, R. D. C. 1998. A Survey of the Hong Kong Health Sector: Past, Present and Future. *Social Science & Medicine* 47(7): 927–939.

Gilbert, N., and B. Gilbert. 1989. *The Enabling State: Modern Welfare Capitalism in America.* New York: Oxford University Press.

Gu, E. 2001. Market Transition and the Transformation of the Health Care System in Urban China. *Policy Studies* 22(3–4): 197–215.

Gu, E. X. 2001. Dismantling the Chinese Mini-welfare State: Marketization and the Politics of Institutional Transformation. *Communist and Post-Communist Studies* 34(1): 91–111.

Gu, X. 2009. Towards Central Planning or Regulated Marketization? China Debates on the Direction of New Healthcare Reforms. In Zhao Litao and Lim Tin Seng (eds.), *China's New Social Policy: Initiatives for a Harmonious Society.* Singapore: World Science Publishing, pp. 14–25.

———. 2010a. Bureaucratic Marketization and Reforms of Public Hospitals in China. *Journal of Public Administration (Gonggong Xingzheng Pinglun)* 4(3): 15–31 (in Chinese).

———. 2010b. The Transformation of Public Finances and the Return to Government Responsibility for Funding Public Health. *Social Sciences in China* 2: 119–136 (in Chinese).

Guo, K., and X. Gu. 2016. Government Regulation and Incentives of Physician's Moonlighting: A Multitask Principal-Agent Perspective, *Chinese Health Economics* 35 (9): 10–13 (in Chinese).

Henderson, G. E., and M. S. Cohen. 1984. *The Chinese Hospital: A Socialist Work Unit.* New Haven: Yale University Press.

Hsiao, W. C. 2007. The Political Economy of Chinese Health Reform. *Health Economics, Policy and Law* 2(3): 241–249.

Huang, Y. 2013. *Governing Health in Contemporary China.* London and New York: Routledge.

Hu, M., P. Fang, Q. Li, and J. Liu. 2012. An Analysis of the Restricting Factors on Physician Multi-site Practice Policy in Shenzhen. *Medicine and Society* 25(2): 53–55 (in Chinese).

Hu, S. 2015. How to see disturbance caused by price adjustment in Chongqing? *China Health* 5: 43–44.

Jensen, C., and E. Naumann. 2016. Increasing pressures and support for public health-care in Europe. *Health Policy* 120(6): 698–705.

Kornai, J. 1992. *The Socialist System: The Political Economy of Communism.* Oxford: Clarendon Press.

Kornai, J., and K. Eggleston. 2001. *Welfare, Choice and Solidarity in Transition: Reforming the Health Sector in Eastern Europe.* New York: Cambridge University Press.

Lam, T., and J. L. Perry. 2001. Service organizations in China: Reform and its limits. In Peter Nan-shong Lee and Carlos Wing-hung Lo (eds.), *Remaking China's Public Management.* Westport, CT: Quorum Books, pp. 19–39.

Lampton, D. M. 1979. The Roots of Interprovincial Inequality in Education and Health Services in China. *American Political Science Review* 73(2): 459–477.

Li, W., and E. Huang. 2010. The Practice of Governance Reform towards Corporatization: The Corporate Governance of Dongyang People's Hospital in Zhejiang. *Health Economics Research*, 8: 5–8 (in Chinese).

Liang, M., Li Jingwei, Wang Xia, Zheng Xueqian, Chi Baolan, and Deng Liqiang. 2007. Case of Public Hospital Corporate Governance Structure Reform in China. *Chinese Hospitals* 11(5): 11–14 (in Chinese).

Liu, J. 2014. The Management of Hospital Staffing and the Allocation of Human Resource: Analysis and Discussion, *Human Resource Management* 7: 278–279 (in Chinese).

Liu, X., and A. Mills. 2002. Financing reforms of public health services in China: lessons for other nations. *Social Science & Medicine* 54 (11): 1691–1698.

Lu, F. 1993. The origins and formation of the Unit (Danwei) System. *Chinese Sociology and Anthropology* 25(3): 7–92.

Lü, X., and E. J. Perry. 1997. The changing Chinese workplace in historical and comparative perspective. In Xiaobo Lü and E.J. Perry (eds.), *Danwei: The Changing Chinese Workplace in Historical and Comparative Perspective.* Armonk, NY: M.E. Sharpe, pp. 3–17.

He, A. J., and Q. Meng. 2015. An interim interdisciplinary evaluation of china's national health care reform: emerging evidence and new perspectives. *Journal of Asian Public Policy* 8(1): 1–18.

Mills, A., J. P. Vaughan, D. L. Smith, and I. Tabibzadeh. 1990. *Health system decentralization: concepts, issues and country experience.* Geneva: World Health Organisation.

Missinne, S., B. Meuleman, and P. Bracke. 2013. The popular legitimacy of European healthcare systems: a multilevel analysis of 24 countries. *Journal of European Social Policy* 23(3): 231–247.

National Health and Family Planning Commission of the People's Republic of China (ed.). 2016. *The Statistical Yearbook of Health and Family Planning in China.* Beijing: Peking Union Medical College Press.

OECD. 1992. *The Reform of Health Care: A Comparative Analysis of Seven OECD Countries.* Paris: Organisation for Economic Cooperation and Development.

Olson, M. 2000. *Power and Prosperity: Outgrowing Communist and Capitalist Dictatorships.* New York: Basic Books.

Preker, A. S., and A. Harding (eds.). 2003. *Innovations in Health Service Delivery: The Corporatization of Public Hospitals.* Washington, DC: The World Bank.

Preker, A. S., and X. Liu, 2007. *Public Ends, Private Means: Strategic Purchasing of Health Services.* Washington, DC: The World Bank.

Qian, J. Reallocating Authority in the Chinese Health System: An Institutional Perspective. *Journal of Asian Public Policy* 8(1): 19–35.

———. 2017. *The Rise of the Regulatory State in the Chinese Health-Care System.* Singapore: World Scientific Publishing.

Qian, J., and Å. Blomqvist. 2014. *Health Policy Reform in China: A Comparative Perspective.* Singapore: World Scientific Publishing.

Saltman, R. B., V. Bankauskaite, and K. Vrangbæk (eds.). 2007. *Decentralization in health care: strategies and outcomes.* Maidenhead, UK: Open University Press.

Walshe, K. 2003. *Regulating healthcare: a prescription for improvement.* Maidenhead, UK: Open University Press.

Wendt, C., J. Kohl, M. Mischke, and M. Pfeifer. 2010. How do Europeans perceive their healthcare system? Patterns of satisfaction and preference for state involvement in the field of healthcare. *European Sociological Review* 26(2): 177–192.

World Bank. 2010a. *Fixing the Public Hospital System in China.* Washington, DC: The World Bank.

———. 2010b. *Health Provider Payment Reforms in China: What International Experience Tells Us.* Washington, DC: The World Bank.

WHO. 2000. *The World Health Report 2000: Health Systems. Improving Performance.* Geneva: World Health Organisation.

Yip, W. C., and W. C. Hsiao. 2015. What drove the cycles of Chinese health system reforms? *Health Systems and Reform* 1(1): 52–61.

Yip, W. C., W. C. Hsiao, W. Chen, S. Hu, J. Ma, and A. Maynard. 2012. Early appraisal of china's huge and complex health-care reforms. *Lancet* 379: 833–842.

Yu, Hui (ed.). 2014. *The New Healthcare Reforms Exploited by An Independent Think-Tank.* Vol. 2. Beijing: China Fortune Press.

Yu, Hao. 2015. Universal health insurance coverage for 1.3 billion people: what accounts for China's success? *Health Policy* 119(9): 1145–1152.

Zhang, Y. 2008, *Large Chinese State-owned Enterprises: Corporatization and Strategic Development.* Basingstoke, UK: Palgrave Macmillan.

Zhang, X., and H. Huang. 2017. The Difficulties of Abolishing the Staffing System in Public Hospitals and Countermeasures. *Medicine and Society* 30 (4): 43–45, 55 (in Chinese).

Zheng, S. 1997. *Party vs. state in post-1949 China: the institutional dilemma.* New York: Cambridge University Press.

Zhou, X. 2008. *A Study of the Government Regulation on the Pricing of Medical Services in China.* Beijing: China Social Sciences Press (in Chinese).

Zhou, X., and A. Yin. 2015. A Stakeholder Analysis of Physician Multiple-site Practice. *Chinese Health Economics* 34 (6): 48–51 (in Chinese).

Zhu, H. 2011. Endogeneity in Regulation and its Consequences: Taking Healthcare Price Regulations as an Example. *Journal of World Economy* 7: 64–90 (in Chinese).

CHAPTER 25

Variations in Educational Inequalities in China and Policy Implications

Xinxin Wang and Xue Lan Rong

1 INTRODUCTION

As a result of China's rapid economic development, its gross domestic product (GDP) increased by almost 28 times from US$360.9 billion in 1990 to US$11.2 trillion in 2016 (The World Bank 2017). A powerful pillar of China's economic growth is the increase in the educational level of its population. Indeed, a country's economic growth depends on a highly educated workforce. Educational attainment is usually referred to as the measure of human capital obtained through the educational process. Barro and Lee (2001) argued that educational attainment is a significant determinant of economic growth, emphasizing, "A greater amount of education attainment implies more skilled and productive workers, who in turn increase economy's output of goods and services… In addition, the level and distribution of educational attainment has a strong impact on social outcomes, such as child mortality, fertility education of children, and income distribution."

A monumental piece of educational legislation is the Compulsory Education Law of 1986 and the 15 related laws that were subsequently passed. Literacy was made universal, and nine years of compulsory schooling were mandated for children aged 6–16 years throughout China. Through the Compulsory Education Law, which was enacted on 1 July 1986 (The National People's Congress of the People's Republic of China 1986), the central government abolished tuition and fees for students in elementary and junior high schools to

X. Wang • X. L. Rong (✉)
School of Education, University of North Carolina at Chapel Hill,
Chapel Hill, NC, USA
e-mail: xxcheer@live.unc.edu; xrong@email.unc.edu

© The Author(s) 2019
J. Yu, S. Guo (eds.), *The Palgrave Handbook of Local Governance in Contemporary China*, https://doi.org/10.1007/978-981-13-2799-5_25

ensure that they would enjoy a free compulsory education. Because elementary education and junior high education comprise nine years in China's public schools, the fee-free period of compulsory education is also called the nine-year compulsory education period.

According to the China census data for 2010, among the population of young people aged 15–24, the literacy rate was at least 95%, which was a tremendous increase considering that the population was largely illiterate when the People's Republic of China (PRC) was founded in 1949. The 2010 census also revealed that reforms in education, such as the mandatory nine-year education, the recentralization of rural education financing, and the improvement of teacher recruitment and training, have dramatically expanded educational opportunities for children throughout China. Since the mid-1990s, a significant portion of the progress in education in China has been the rapid expansion of the number of senior high schools, colleges, and universities (China Education Daily 2012). Similar to many developing countries with rapidly growing economies, China has experienced many persistent equity-related issues, including equal rights for ethnic minorities, females, and rural residents. In response to one such issue, in August 2012, the State Council announced measures to address the urban-rural divide in education by ensuring no student had to travel more than 40 minutes to and from school (China Daily 2012).

This study focuses on issues in the education of the rural-to-urban migrant population. Although economic development has raised the income level of all Chinese people, the pace and scale have varied in different geo-demographic groups. Consequently, the social economic gap has increased between people who reside in rural and in urban areas. An outstanding issue involves rural residents who migrate to cities for better job opportunities. This group comprises approximately 200 million people or 18–20% of the Chinese population. These rural migrants are without a city *hukou* (a permanent residential permission for long-term urban residents), which is essential to access public school education, fair housing, and governmental employment benefits.

The education of rural migrant children in China has been a public issue since the mid-1990s. Due to the restrictions of their urban *hukou* status, migrant children have often been denied entry to urban public schools, which has raised the question of equal education in China. Although the local schooling policies relevant to migrant children have been changed in various counties, cities, and provinces in recent years, many rural migrant students still face unequal treatments in the urban public school system. Hence, the issue of the education of migrant children remains unresolved (e.g., Liu et al. 2017; Yuan et al. 2017).

The scope of this chapter is confined to the analyses of educational attainment in compulsory education in relation to equality and equity issues. Based on data collected from a national sample in China in 2014, this chapter examines the combined effects of *hukou* status, economic regions, rural and urban residency, and gender on the educational attainment of Chinese people aged 12–43. In this study, educational attainment is defined as the actual number of years of completed schooling and the completion of the mandatory nine years of education, including elementary and junior high school. The results are interpreted with specific regard to the reasons for the disparities in the educational opportunities of rural migrant and urban residents. Based on these findings and the extant literature, several policy recommendations for improvement are suggested.

The following section provides a review of the extant literature on the alleviation of inequality-related concerns in compulsory education in China regarding the population of rural-to-urban migrant youth in the last two decades. The review focuses on *hukou*-related educational issues in addition to other relevant factors, such as gender, rural and urban residency, and economic development regions.

2   LITERATURE REVIEW

First, the literature on macro-level social policy with a focus on the decentralization of educational systems is briefly reviewed. Then the review examines the previous research on several specific issues, including economic-geographical inequality, the rural-urban divide, the gender gap, rural-to-urban migrants, and the *hukou* factor.

2.1   *Social and Policy Context Since the "Opening-Up" Reform*

A remarkable trend in China since the 1980s, when the "opening-up" reform was initiated, has been the decentralization of educational and economic systems at various levels of government. The definition of decentralization has been debated. In general, it means the shifting of governance from one level to another. Qi (2011) described the trend of educational decentralization in China as "the shifting of education policies in China toward devolving education governance over fiscal, administrative, and academic management to the local level". The state had centralized the responsibility to provide education and financial support until the issue of the National Decision on the Reform of the Education Structure in 1985, which claimed for the first time that local governments had become the prime provider of elementary and junior high school education. The landmark legislation of the Compulsory Education Law of the PRC further decentralized the responsibility for the provision of education to lower levels of government.

Since then, instead of receiving educational monies from the central government, local governments have had autonomy in educational finance (Lü 2014). After prioritizing economic development in the national agenda of reform and the opening-up policy, policy goals have emphasized efficiency. Education has been the primary tool for promoting efficiency and productivity. Hence, an increasing number of professionals with specific skills have been educated.

Nevertheless, China's top-down approach to policymaking showed little change after decentralization. The central government maintains the ultimate decision-making power and the overall control of educational provision (Pang and Plucker 2012). Nevertheless, the rapid globalization that increased economic integration and cooperation across countries, which sped the marketization of the Chinese economy, has resulted in the further decentralization of governance to improve efficiency (Qi 2011). Therefore, the educational disparities caused by decentralization in the past recent two decades cannot be overlooked, especially those between rural and urban areas and among regional areas. Such disparities include the policy constraints based on the house registration system (*hukou*).

2.2   Economic-Geographical Inequality in Education in China

In the opening-up and post-reform eras, the shifts in policy from centralization to decentralization in the administration and finance of education at all levels of government boosted the economic growth of China. However, such policy shifts also appeared to exacerbate regional disparities in the funding of schools in locations with a range of GDP levels, and the regional inequalities in China have often been overlooked because of the limited data in educational research (Hannum and Wang 2006). Hannum and Wang (2006) analyzed data from the 2000 Chinese population census to investigate whether a person's province of birth was significantly associated with educational inequality. Their outcomes included years of schooling and levels of educational attainment (primary, secondary, and tertiary). Based on the results of a regression analysis and calculations of indices of dissimilarity, they concluded that regional disparities varied over time. However, geography was found to be an important contributor to disparities in educational attainment at least among persons who were educated in regions with rapid economic development. Zhang and Kanbur (2005) analyzed national-level data and calculated the Gini coefficient in terms of income and illiteracy rate. Their findings showed that since the opening-up reform, educational inequalities had increased between rural and urban areas and between inland and coastal areas. They also investigated health inequality by calculating infant mortality rates. Based on their results, they argued that increased social inequalities in education and health might increase social instability, which could negatively affect socioeconomic development in China.

2.3   Rural-Urban Divide

Disparities in the educational attainment of rural and urban populations have been studied in most developing countries. This section focuses on the review of literature on the rural-urban divide regarding the effects of educational financing and decentralization. Focusing on financing rural compulsory education, Parkhouse and Rong (2016) summarized recent research literature regarding the rural-urban divide in education and explanations for it. Their findings showed that despite the various investment efforts and incentive policies to improve rural education that had been implemented in the last 20 years, significant divisions remained between rural and urban compulsory education.

Among the research on educational financing issues, Parkhouse and Rong (2016) underscored three studies. The first study (Song 2012) found that returns on educational investments (EIs) were typically higher in urban areas and attributed these variations to the poorer quality of rural schools (i.e., unstable and undertrained teachers and long distances to schools). In 2000, China initiated rural taxation reforms (*yi xian wei zhu*) to address the excessive fees levied on farmers to fund newly decentralized government roles in the absence of a sufficient local capacity of taxation.

The second study (Wang and Zhao 2012) focused on the problems in the distribution of counties' educational funds. Their study analyzed the effects of rural tax reform as mentioned earlier, which transferred the responsibility for educational funding from the township to the county. However, because the central government provided more money, it exerted more control. Wang and Zhao found that it succeeded in increasing recurrent spending, particularly on personnel; however, it was less successful in improving capital spending, such as for the renovation of buildings. Overall, their study found no significant reduction in the inequality in the amounts of money spent on rural and urban education.

The third study (Zhao 2009) examined the rural-urban divide in the context of economic-geographic regions. The results showed that inequalities in per-student spending since 2003 had declined, and the rural-urban divide had narrowed more quickly than those between regions. Zhao also found that inequalities in spending on primary education had declined much more rapidly than did the inequalities in spending on junior secondary education. Zhao pointed to the facts that China's overall spending was much more weighted toward primary education between 1997 and 2005 and that the share of government expenditures for junior secondary education had declined during this period. Zhao argued that the shift in funding to the county level allowed poorer rural areas to receive the same level of financial support as urban areas received, but across counties, spending had not been equalized, which had left intact the regional disparities.

2.4 Gender Gap

Although the reform in compulsory education after 1986 was significant for the educational attainment of the entire population in China, the gender gap remained significant. Hannum (2005) used cross-sectional surveys and time-series data to investigate changes in gender inequality in rural China. She found that girls' educational opportunities were associated with household economic circumstances. The reform in 1978 did not accelerate the progress in gender equity in China. Recent research on the gender gap in education has focused on rural China because since the 1990s, disparities based on gender have been more evident in poor, rural areas where children have to compete with siblings for educational resources within the family (Connelly and Zheng 2003). Parkhouse and Rong (2016) compared China's aggregated census data in 1990 and 2000 and found that literacy rates declined significantly for both genders. However, the gender gap ratios had increased. In 2000, the ratio of illiteracy in rural women and urban men was 6.1, which was increased to 8.9 in 2010, although the illiteracy rates for both groups declined during the ten-year period.

Lee (2012) studied the gender gap by focusing on China's one-child policy before 2016 (the two-child policy was implemented in 2016). For the gender analysis, Lee used data from multiple years of the China Health and Nutrition Survey, which includes about 4400 households and 16,000 individuals. He found no significant differences in years of schooling between girls and boys in one-child households. Lee's results suggested that China's one-child policy had contributed to gender equality in education. He found no differences in the number of years of schooling for only-child boys and only-child girls, whereas girls in multiple-child households tended to have fewer years of schooling than boys in multiple-child homes. He found that females in only-child households did not have to compete with male siblings for educational resources, and they had more opportunities to advance in education than females in multiple-child households. Males in only-child households also had more educational opportunities than males in multiple-child homes because they did not have to compete for resources. Lee argued that these findings reflected growing gender equality in education. Nevertheless, gender equality remains a problem in China, which was evidenced by the preference for male children revealed in research literature. Furthermore, the one-child policy was far more prevalent in urban areas than in rural areas. In any case, because the one-child policy ended in 2016, these results may not be relevant to the current situation.

2.5   Rural-to-Urban Migrants and the Hukou Factor

The government's investment in compulsory education led to significant benefits in education and economics. By 2010, the literacy rate was 95.12% among the population aged 15 years and older (UNICEF 2013) compared with 65.51% for the same age group in 1986. The increased education levels have contributed to increasing the productivity and reducing the poverty of farmers in rural areas in the least economically developed areas, who had been among the poorest population in China (Song 2012). According to the Compulsory Education Law, all persons aged 6–16 in 1986 were mandated to receive 9 years of compulsory education for free. However, Song (2012) explained that the law has not been fully implemented for older children in rural areas, which has resulted in their lower educational achievement compared with their peers in urban areas. This disparity has been caused by the fewer governmental subsidies provided to poor rural families, scarce educational resources, poorer schools, and teaching quality in rural areas and less or no regulatory power to enforce the law. There is also an unequal distribution of educational funding by counties. Villages with higher poverty rates and special needs do not receive more funding to improve their education rates, which contributes to maintaining the educational gap between rural and urban areas (Wang and Zhao 2012).

The 'household registration system (*hukou*) is another major factor related to the rural-urban educational divide. After the implementation of the opening-up policy in the 1980s, China accelerated its urbanization. The percentage of China's urban population increased from 18.96% in 1979 to 51.27% in 2011, when the urban population exceeded the rural population. The huge wave of internal rural-to-city migration has contributed to the rapid urbanization of China during the past four decades. Millions of poor peasants from rural areas have migrated to urban areas. By 2016, the number of internal migrant workers had reached 281.71 million, compared to 277.47 million in 2015, an increase of 1.5% (National Bureau of Statistics of People's Republic of China 2017). These "internal migrants" account for about 20.4% of the Chinese population compared to 18% in 2013. Most of them are engaged in basic labor and receive lower wages than urban workers do.

Some migrant workers bring their children ("migrant children") with them while others do not ("left-behind children"). According to the National Bureau of Statistics of People's Republic of China (2016), the number of children of migrant workers who were enrolled in compulsory education in 2015 was 33.86 million, including 20.2 million children who were left behind. According to the literatures, the education of migrant children and left-behind children is questionable. Although all levels of governments have issued policies to ensure free compulsory education for migrant children, because of issues in implementing the policies, many migrant children have difficulty enrolling in local public schools. According to Du (2014), in 2013, there were 12.77 million rural migrant children in the cities. Among them, about 20% did not have access to the local public school system; instead, they either went to low-quality migrant schools or did not attend school at all.

Most migrant children are not able to obtain household registration certificate (*hukou*) in their parents' destination cities because their parents still have a rural *hukou*. Consequently, compared with their urban peers, migrant children often experience unequal treatment in compulsory education, including the right to access city high schools and be admitted to colleges and universities. However, since 2001, the Ministry of Education has required urban public schools to enroll migrant children with a rural *hukou*, and migrant children have had access to public schools in their destination cities. Nevertheless, many migrant children are still enrolled in under-resourced schools with low-quality teachers. For example, in Beijing, 95,000 children were enrolled in more than 130 under-resourced schools that had been established by migrant workers. Only 67 of those schools were certified by the Department of Education; the others were in danger of closing at any time. According to Li (2016), the policy that requires urban schools to enroll migrant children has not been adhered to by urban public schools since 2014 when the access process became much more rigorous. The failure of the policy on the education of migrant children indicates a trend of the denial of equal access to public schools among urban residents against the migrant children population in urban areas (Liu et al. 2017).

In summary, studies in the extant literature have focused on the educational inequalities induced by the rural-urban divide, *hukou* status, disparity in the economic development of regions, and gender gap. Several studies attempted to determine the reasons for these issues. In the last two decades, a significant number of studies focused on the *hukou* problem among migrant children and the attempts to alleviate its effects of educational inequality. However, few studies have examined the combined effects of *hukou*, urban-rural residency, types of region by economic development, and gender. Without considering these combined effects, policymakers may not be able to formulate effective policies and implement them in a specific population stratum. To fill this gap in the research, the present study aims to answer the following questions:

1. Is possessing an urban *hukou* a positive factor in young people's educational attainment?
2. If so, does the significance vary according the four types of regions (classified according to GDP per capita), rural-urban residency, and gender?
3. If disparities exist in educational attainment, how might the current socioeconomic and educational policies explain the disparities? What suggestions could be derived from the present study?

3   DATA AND METHODOLOGY

Educational attainment can be measured through several different proxies. However, three commonly used measures are literacy rate, average years of schooling (AYS), and completion rates of schooling at various levels (elementary, junior high, senior high, two-year, three-year, and four-year colleges, etc.). Based on the availability of the data, in this section, we only use AYS and completion rates of schooling at various levels as indicators to assess the educational attainment of people who are 12–43 years old. We also assess the study sample according to *hukou* status, rural and city residency, economic region, gender, and two or more variables combined. We used the data published by China Family Panel Studies (CFPS) to study educational equality in China. CFPS was launched in 2010 by the Institute of Social Science Survey of Peking University. All variables in the study are based on the most recent CFPS data, which were published in 2014.

In 2014, the CFPS contained four types of surveys: family data, family roster data, adult data (ages 16–104), and child data (ages 0–15). The adult survey included 37,147 individuals in 29 provinces (excluding Hong Kong, Macao, Taiwan, Tibet, and Qinghai). The child survey included 8617 individuals in 29 provinces (excluding Hong Kong, Macao, Taiwan, Tibet, and Qinghai). To investigate the population that is the most affected by the Compulsory Education Law, we used both adult and child data to narrow the age range to 12–43 years.

We used several measures to assess educational attainment: years of schooling completed for the 18–43-year-old age group; completion of six-year primary school for the 13–43-year-old age group; completion of junior high school for the 16–43-year-old age group; completion of senior high school for the 19–43-year-old age group; completion of three years of college for the 22–43-year-old age group; and completion of four years of college for the 23–43-year-old age group. We used the common demographic method of an age-standardized formula to calculate the mean rates of schooling attainment and completion rates. The age-standardized formula,[1] also called age adjustment, is a technique used in epidemiology and demography to calculate the social, health, and educational indexes in populations of wide age ranges (e.g., Grant and Rong 1999; Li 1999; Rong and Brown 2001; Shryock et al. 1980). This technique allows populations to be compared when the *age* profiles of the populations are quite different by taking into account variable age distributions in subgroup populations.

By applying the age standardization formula with the variables of economic region and gender, we constructed cross-tabulations to compare the percentages and means for youth who resided in a city with an urban *hukou*, resided in a city without an urban *hukou*, resided in a rural area with an urban *hukou*, and resided in a rural area with a rural *hukou*. We would like to caution our readers that although the data used in this study were drawn from a large, nationally representative sample, some population segments (e.g., rural residents with an urban *hukou*) are very small. Therefore, the findings for these segments of this study may be seen as references to the patterns of the main findings. For example, the population of this study was

---

[1] We used the standardized age range of the total population on control for variants of age composition across groups. Here is an example of senior high-school completion rate for city migrants (urban residence with rural *hukou*) ages 19–43:

The aged-adjusted high-school completion rate for migrant workers 19–43 years old is calculated by: (a) dividing the numbers of high-school graduates for migrant works in each age category; (b) multiplying the migrant workers' graduation rates by the standard population (total number of people of urban residence with urban *hukou*, urban residence with rural *hukou*, rural residence with urban *hukou*, and rural residence with rural *hukou*) in the corresponding age categories; (c) summing the products; and (d) dividing by the total standard population (people in all age categories combined). The mathematical formula is as follows:

$$\left[\Sigma \left(Ea / Pa \right) \times Psa \right] \div Ps \times 100$$

Ea = Number of city migrants completing senior high schools in age group a
Pa = Number of city migrants in age group a
Psa = Standard population in age group a
Ps = Total standard population in all age categories
We accept age-standardized mean years of schooling and completion rates as indices of educational attainment. These mean scores are, however, different from the means predicted using regression models that control for *hukou*, rural/city residence, economic regions, and gender.

segmented according to type of *hukou* and rural-city residence (four groups), economic development regions (four groups), and gender (two groups). In interpreting the findings, for higher school completion level, the smaller the number of people in each segment, the more cautions we need to take, especially, when the findings for the very small segments are not in line with the main patterns of findings.

To decide the significance of the several factors (economic region, rural/ urban residence, and gender) included in this study and their intersectionalities, we also ran a series of regressions, which showed statistical significance at 0.01 or better levels. For the detailed results from regressions, please read the paper by Wang et al. (2018).[2]

4   Findings

Tables 25.1, 25.2, 25.3, and 25.4 report the average school completion results for the study population (18–43 years). As shown in Table 25.5, we used the age-standardized formula to calculate the AYS and percentages of completion of school at various educational levels for various age ranges.

---

[2] In our paper for the Annual Meeting of American Educational Research Association in 2018 (Wang et al. 2018), we fitted a least squares regression model to the data to examine the significance of each of the major variables under the simultaneous effects of all variables (see Table 6 for Model 1). All major variables are significant at $p \geq 0.001$. Holding other variables equally, an individual with an urban *hukou* has, on average, 3.41 more years of schooling. This aligns with the findings from the research literature that individuals residing in urban areas but with rural *hukou* have generally been disadvantaged in education.

We then ran a multiple regression with total years of schooling as the numerical dependent variable (see Table 7 of Model 2) and two logistic regressions with completion of elementary school and completion of junior high school as the binary categorical dependent variables for the four types of regions separately (see Tables 8 and 9 of Model 3), since we wanted to know if the pattern of impact of *hukou* and location is consistent across the four types of regions.

The results in Table 7 show that people living in the cities with urban *hukou* have higher levels of education than their counterparts living in rural areas, regardless of gender and/or region. Migrants living in cities with rural *hukou* have also received more education than those in rural areas with rural *hukou*. In general, educational gaps are greater between city people with urban *hukou* and migrants (urban residents with rural *hukou*), compared with the gap between migrant people and rural residents with rural *hukou*. Gaps in the educational attainment of people with different types of *hukous* tend to be smaller in wealthier regions (1 and 2) than in poorer ones (3 and 4).

Our next model (Model 3) examines what factors affect people's completion of elementary schooling and junior high school. The interaction effects of *hukou*, location, and gender are estimated as well. Table 8 presents the results of logistic regression analyses with interactions. People with urban *hukou* are more likely to complete elementary education than people with rural *hukou*. In terms of interaction effects, only the effect of male individuals from Region 3 with rural *hukou* is significantly negative. It is likely that migrant males are less likely to complete elementary school than rural men with rural *hukou*. In the same vein, the results in Table 9 indicate that, when holding the other variables constant, urban males in Region 3 (regardless of the types of *hukou*) have a greater possibility of dropping out of junior high schools than their female counterparts do.

Table 25.1 AYS by types of regions and provinces/autonomous regions in 2014 (ages 18–43)

Region and province[a]	AYS	N	Percent
Mainland China	8.55	14,015	100%
Beijing	11.99	119	0.85%
Tianjin	11.49	105	0.75%
Shanghai	11.48	646	4.61%
Jiangsu	9.82	302	2.15%
Region 1 (Average years of schooling)	**11.11**	**1172**	**8.36%**
Liaoning	9.34	1043	7.44%
Zhejiang	10.04	254	1.81%
Fujian	7.61	214	1.53%
Shandong	9.09	524	3.74%
Guangdong	8.92	1394	9.95%
Region 2 (Average years of schooling)	**9.08**	**3432**	**24.49%**
Hebei	9.09	841	6.00%
Jilin	8.55	207	1.48%
Heilongjiang	9.43	405	2.89%
Henan	8.76	1876	13.39%
Hubei	9.90	173	1.23%
Hunan	10.31	338	2.41%
Chongqing	8.22	88	0.63%
Shaanxi	8.84	332	2.37%
Region 3 (Average years of schooling)	**9.04**	**4275**	**30.50%**
Shanxi	8.98	669	4.77%
Anhui	8.90	277	1.98%
Jiangxi	7.93	266	1.90%
Guangxi Zhuang Autonomous Region	7.58	302	2.15%
Sichuan	5.99	629	4.49%
Guizhou	6.28	453	3.23%
Yunnan	6.81	515	3.67%
Gansu	6.90	2025	14.45%
Region 4 (Average years of schooling)	**7.20**	**5136**	**36.65%**

Source: The table is compiled by authors with data and information from CFPS data and The Economist (2016)

[a]There was no data for Ningxia and Tibet. Hainan and Inner Mongolia have only three participants in each province and there were only 12 participants in Xinjiang Autonomous Region; therefore, the statistics for these three provinces/autonomous regions will not be included in our analysis

Table 25.2 AYS by types of regions and genders in 2014 (ages 18–43)

Gender/region	1	2	3	4	Total
Male	11.41	9.27	9.15	7.70	8.84
N	603	1773	2152	2610	7138
Female	10.79	8.88	8.94	6.68	8.25
N	569	1659	2123	2526	6877
Total	11.11	9.08	9.04	7.20	8.55

Source: Data from CFPS, compiled by authors

Table 25.3 AYS by types of regions and locations in 2014 (ages 18–43)

Location/Region	1	2	3	4	Total
Urban residence	11.58	10.05	10.13	8.66	9.95
N	859	1675	2111	1485	6130
Rural residence	9.71	7.92	7.66	6.21	7.13
N	248	1341	1680	2858	6127
Total	11.16	9.10	9.04	7.05	8.54

Source: Data from CFPS, compiled by authors

Table 25.4 AYS by types of regions and *hukou* in 2014 (ages 18–43)

Hukou/*region*	1	2	3	4	Total
Urban *hukou*	12.56	11.38	11.53	11.63	11.71
N	632	816	1173	659	3280
Rural *hukou*	9.26	8.28	7.99	6.42	7.47
N	482	2482	2907	4211	10,082
Total	11.13	9.04	9.01	7.13	8.51

Source: Data from CFPS, compiled by authors

4.1   Regional Division

To investigate the differences in education across provinces, we grouped the provinces and provincial districts into four types from rich to poor based on GDP per capita in 2014. The AYS in the provinces and regions were calculated based on the CFPS data in 2014. Region 1 refers to the municipalities directly under the central government (Beijing, Tianjin, and Shanghai) and one province (Jiangsu) with the highest GDP per capita (above $12,000). Region 2 refers to the provinces (Zhejiang, Inner Mongolia, Liaoning, Fujian, Guangdong) with the second-highest GDP per capita ($10,000–$12,000). Region 3 includes provinces (Shandong, Jilin, Chongqing, Hubei, Shaanxi, Ningxia, Xinjiang, Hunan, Hebei, Qinghai, Heilongjiang, Hainan, Henan) with GDP per capita ranging from $6000 to $10,000. Region 4 refers to the provinces (Sichuan, Shanxi, Jiangxi, Anhui, Guangxi, Tibet, Yunnan, Guizhou, Gansu) with GDP per person under $6000 (the categorization of four regions is adapted from the figure of China's GDP per person in The Economist 2016). Inner Mongolia, Hainan, and Xinjiang autonomous regions were excluded from our data analyses because these provinces had less than 15 participants according to the 2014 CFPS dataset.

Table 25.1 reports the AYS in 2014 by individual provinces and types of regions for adults who were benefited from compulsory education (fully or partially depending on their year of birth). The AYS of China was 8.55 for the entire adult population from 18 to 43 years compared with the AYS of less than 7.5 years in 1996 (Yang et al. 2014). This increase indicates that the compulsory education policy has been effective in the past three decades. In provinces and regional divisions, the gaps in educational attainment measured by AYS

Table 25.5 Educational attainment by region, urban/rural residence, and urban/rural *hukou* status and gender for ages 13–43

	Region 1		Region 2		Region 3		Region 4		Grand total
	Male	Female	Male	Female	Male	Female	Male	Female	
Years of schooling completed (ages 13–43)									
Urban residence and urban *hukou*	12.35	11.88	10.50	10.66	10.59	10.69	10.77	10.39	10.91
Urban residence and rural *hukou*	9.83	8.65	8.58	8.38	8.02	8.19	6.78	6.42	7.84
Rural residence and urban *hukou*	11.00	11.68	10.98	9.00	8.97	9.83	10.74	11.17	10.54
Rural residence and rural *hukou*	8.70	7.76	7.51	6.70	7.34	6.75	5.88	4.93	6.31
Grand Total	11.00	10.36	8.64	8.21	8.41	8.29	6.75	6.05	7.87
% completing primary education (ages 13–43)									
Urban residence and urban *hukou*	99.23%	98.52%	97.84%	98.34%	97.89%	96.73%	97.39%	95.79%	97.70%
Urban residence and rural *hukou*	99.16%	92.00%	96.25%	92.64%	93.05%	93.21%	84.32%	78.59%	90.21%
Rural residence and urban *hukou*	100.00%	100.00%	97.27%	94.36%	95.60%	99.48%	93.76%	99.26%	97.21%
Rural residence and rural *hukou*	95.55%	80.96%	92.58%	85.06%	92.77%	85.89%	76.60%	63.28%	80.07%
Grand Total	98.72%	94.32%	95.13%	90.93%	94.25%	91.27%	81.17%	71.69%	87.42%
% completing junior high education (ages 16–43)									
Urban residence and urban *hukou*	94.69%	92.37%	91.09%	89.20%	90.85%	90.25%	91.96%	88.58%	91.00%
Urban residence and rural *hukou*	87.64%	75.64%	71.67%	73.85%	69.53%	69.92%	61.03%	57.06%	68.56%
Rural residence and urban *hukou*	93.69%	91.99%	83.67%	66.37%	81.44%	85.82%	88.79%	87.94%	86.15%
Rural residence and rural *hukou*	81.29%	67.46%	64.79%	55.73%	61.74%	52.86%	48.63%	36.90%	51.64%
Grand Total	90.74%	84.03%	73.78%	70.06%	72.12%	68.80%	57.68%	49.13%	66.47%
% completing senior high education (ages 19–43)									
Urban residence and urban *hukou*	81.10%	82.16%	67.56%	65.25%	66.52%	68.06%	68.95%	63.72%	69.91%
Urban residence and rural *hukou*	41.54%	36.26%	33.72%	29.71%	25.47%	27.40%	17.14%	14.43%	26.08%
Rural residence and urban *hukou*	66.63%	69.69%	69.41%	43.58%	34.84%	51.40%	66.49%	68.94%	61.12%
Rural residence and rural *hukou*	22.72%	25.71%	19.76%	16.10%	18.25%	12.93%	14.27%	8.78%	14.45%
Grand Total	60.86%	60.14%	37.10%	33.29%	33.59%	33.27%	23.16%	18.29%	32.09%

(*continued*)

Table 25.5 (continued)

	Region 1		Region 2		Region 3		Region 4		Grand total
	Male	Female	Male	Female	Male	Female	Male	Female	
% completing three-year colleges (ages 22–43)									
Urban residence and urban *hukou*	42.52%	37.83%	26.01%	22.20%	26.16%	27.31%	32.57%	28.43%	29.49%
Urban residence and rural *hukou*	13.08%	7.62%	7.55%	6.63%	4.70%	6.37%	3.15%	0.42%	5.37%
Rural residence and urban *hukou*	15.13%	43.08%	31.61%	12.25%	8.97%	13.47%	28.76%	28.16%	23.86%
Rural residence and rural *hukou*	7.10%	7.91%	2.81%	2.99%	3.59%	1.37%	1.73%	1.02%	2.20%
Grand Total	27.24%	25.30%	10.78%	9.19%	10.08%	10.31%	6.67%	4.91%	10.21%
% completing four-year colleges (ages 23–41)									
Urban residence and urban *hukou*	28.57%	24.19%	15.89%	11.11%	16.57%	17.18%	20.26%	19.28%	18.47%
Urban residence and rural *hukou*	7.34%	3.25%	4.91%	2.10%	1.87%	3.43%	1.62%	0.00%	2.62%
Rural residence and urban *hukou*	5.56%	32.14%	26.67%	0.00%	7.14%	6.06%	15.07%	16.98%	14.10%
Rural residence and rural *hukou*	3.28%	1.79%	1.15%	1.17%	1.46%	0.17%	0.89%	0.11%	0.79%
Grand Total	17.31%	15.64%	6.67%	3.91%	5.77%	5.99%	3.83%	2.86%	5.91%

Source: Data from CFPS, compiled by authors

were noticeable, especially in provinces with the highest GDP per capita and the provinces with lowest GDP per capita. Region 1 had the highest AYS (11.11 years), which was about 4 years higher than Region 4 (AYS = 7.2). Region 2 and Region 3 had a difference of only 0.04 years in AYS, which was exceeded by Region 1 in less than 2 years. Region 3 was two years ahead of Region 4. Region 1 has only 8.36% of China's population, but Regions 2 and 3 have more than half of the population. More than one-third (36.65%) live in the poorest region (Region 4), which was the lowest in educational attainment. Although the literature reported that western China is the least developed in economy and education, Table 25.1 indicates that western provinces (Guangxi, Sichuan, Guizhou, Yunnan, Gansu) and some central provinces (Shanxi, Anhui, Jiangxi) are behind in educational attainment. Table 25.1 also reveals that Fujian is among one of the highest GDP per capita provinces in Region 2. However, its AYS was only 7.61, which was much lower than other provinces in the same region. On the contrary, 12 provinces had an AYS higher than 9 years, including 4 provinces in Region 3 (Hebei, Hubei, Hunan, and Heilongjiang). Shanxi and Anhui were categorized in Region 4 in terms of GDP per capita, but their AYS was approximately nine years. This finding may imply that the level of economic development may be a contributor to the pace of educational progress. However, many other factors, such as local cultural beliefs in education, schooling traditions, teachers' quality, and patterns of school financing, may all be contributors to provincial variations in educational attainment.

4.2   Gender Gap

In 2014, males had about 0.6 years more schooling than females did. The gender gap still exists in education but is much narrower than the 1.33 years reported in 1996 (Yang et al. 2014). Regardless of gender, individuals in more economically developed regions stayed in school longer than those in poorer regions. In Regions 1, 2, and 3, males had an AYS higher than nine years, and females in the same regions had an AYS either higher than nine years (Region 1) or slightly less than nine years (Regions 2 and 3). Generally, more economically developed regions showed more gender equality in schooling than the less economically developed regions. The gender gap was widest in the least developed regions. For example, in Region 4, the gender gap in years of schooling was more than one year.

4.3   Urban-Rural Divide

Tables 25.3 and 25.4 present the AYS of individuals in four regions according to residential location and type of *hukou*. Residential location refers to urban or rural residency. People who lived in cities did not necessarily have an urban *hukou*, and most rural migrant workers residing in cities had a rural *hukou*. Based on the extant literature, the distinction between location and type of *hukou* should be included in the analysis of educational inequality in China. As Table 25.3 shows, an educational gap exists between people living in cities and those living in rural areas. On average, people living in cities have stayed in school almost three years longer than those in rural areas have. The gap (4.24 years) is even wider regarding the possession of urban or rural *hukou* (see Table 25.4). People with or without an urban *hukou* was the most distinguishing factor that contributed to gaps in educational attainment compared with the effects of gender and region.

Table 25.3 shows that people in more economically developed regions (Regions 1, 2, and 3), regardless of rural or urban location, had completed the compulsory education (first nine years of education). In 2014, the urban and rural population ratio was 1:1. The difference in years of schooling between urban and rural residents was the smallest in Region 1. On average, people who lived in the poorest region (Region 4) had only elementary education with an AYS of 6.21. In contrast, 75.77% of people who lived in urban areas had more than ten years of schooling. People living in rural areas in three of the four regions had less than nine years of schooling.

Table 25.4 shows that the largest division was between people with urban and rural *hukou*. Although the 2014 data showed that an equal number of Chinese people reside in urban and rural areas, the number of people with a rural *hukou*, including rural residents and rural migrants residing in cities, accounted for more than 75% of the entire Chinese population. People with urban *hukou* in all four economic development regions had not only completed the compulsory nine-year education but also had an AYS of more than 11 years regardless of whether they resided in rural or urban areas. Among people with a rural *hukou*, only those in Region 1 had completed the compulsory education. In Region 3 and Region 4, people with an urban *hukou* had slightly more years of schooling than those with an urban *hukou* in Region 2, a sign showing some minor interactive effects between the regions and *hukou* status on educational attainment. Region 4 showed the largest educational gap between people with different types of *hukou*. In Region 4, people with an urban *hukou* stayed in school 5.21 years longer than people with a rural *hukou* did.

4.4   *The Intersectionality of Educational Attainment*

We used the age standardization formula to calculate the completion rates for each age group by type of region, location, and *hukou*. The age-standardized approach includes variants of age distribution in analyzing different subgroup populations. This procedure is commonly used in the analysis of large datasets based on reliable population samples. Table 25.5 shows the AYS of different age groups and the age standard completion rates of five levels of education (from primary education to four-year college) as indicators of educational attainment. In China, most primary schools take six years to complete, junior high schools take three years to complete, and senior high schools take three years to complete. A typical child starts primary education at 6 years and completes primary school at 12 or 13 years, junior high school around 16 years, senior high school around 19 years, a three-year college by 22 years, and a four-year college at 23 years. The 2014 survey showed that if the people were 43 years or younger (i.e., 15 years or younger in 1986), they were likely to have benefited from free compulsory education laws either fully or partially. To match the age to the educational level, we categorized schooling attainment into five age groups: 13–43 years for primary school, 16–43 years for junior high school, 19–43 years for senior high school, 22–43 years for a three-year college, and 23–43 years for a four-year college. In each age group, we grouped people into four subcategories: urban residents with an urban *hukou*, urban residents with a rural *hukou*, rural residents with an urban *hukou*, and rural residents with a rural *hukou*.

In Regions 1, 2, and 3, people in more economically developed provinces had attained more years of schooling than those in the least economically developed provinces. The largest gap existed between male urban residents with an urban *hukou* in Region 1 and female residents with a rural *hukou* in Region 4, an average difference of 7.42 years. In Region 4, urban males with an urban *hukou* on average completed senior high school, whereas males and females living in rural areas with a rural *hukou* (5.88 for males and 4.93 for females) had finished fewer than six years of primary education. Internal migrants (urban residents with a rural *hukou*) attained more education than those who stayed in rural places with a rural *hukou*. The gap was about 2 years (1.53 years) of schooling. In all regions, people who lived in rural areas with an urban *hukou* had the second-highest level of educational attainment compared with urban residents with an urban *hukou*.

City-to-rural migration is much less common than rural-to-city migration. Many of the city-to-rural migrants with an urban *hukou* is influenced by the national policies that support poor and rural areas in western and central China. For example, the General Office of the State Council of the People's Republic of China (2003) issued a national document to encourage college graduates to work in the least developed western provinces in China to support the development of education, health, agriculture, and technology. By 2015, more than 160,000 college graduates had been assigned to work in 22 provinces in western and central provinces in China (Li 2015).

Overall, 66.47% of the people in the four regions had completed the nine-year compulsory education. Of them, 87.42% had completed primary school, about two-thirds (66.47%) had completed junior high school, one-third (32.09%) had completed senior high school, one-tenth (10.21%) had completed a three-year college, and about 6% had completed a four-year college. Similar to the attainment patterns of the mean years of schooling in the four subcategories of youth, urban residents with an urban *hukou* had the highest completion rates among all levels of education. City-to-rural migrants had the second-highest completion rates, internal migrants had the third-highest completion rates, and rural residents with a rural *hukou* had the lowest completion rates. The mean completion rate of primary education was the highest among all levels of education. More than 87% of the investigated population had completed at least six years of school, including more than 90% of males in Regions 1, 2, and 3. The largest educational gap in the completion of primary education existed between urban males with an urban *hukou* in Region 1 and rural females with a rural *hukou* in Region 4 (the gap was approximately 33%). The same gap was shown in junior high schools, senior high schools, and three-year or four-year colleges. Less than 2% of males and females with a rural residence and a rural *hukou* in Region 4 had completed a four-year college, compared to the 28.6% of urban males with an urban *hukou* who had completed a four-year college in Region 1. In Region 4, only 1% of rural females with a rural *hukou* had graduated from a three-year college. These findings imply that urban residency may enhance the opportunity for both male and female migrants to complete schooling at all levels. However, the gender gap persists for people with a rural *hukou* regardless of the location of their residence.

5   CONCLUSION

The results of this study revealed clear divisions in the AYS and school completion rates for primary and junior high according to type of *hukou*, rural/urban location, economic development region, and gender. It was not surprising that the results showed that male Chinese living in urban areas with an urban household registration system (*hukou*) had the higher educational attainment in the more economically advanced regions. However, the most significant findings were regarding the possession of an urban *hukou* by both rural and urban residents. The findings showed that in 2014, people who lived in urban areas with an urban *hukou* had much higher educational attainment than people without an urban *hukou* regardless of the urban or rural locations of their residence. This trend was particularly prominent in Regions 1 and 4. The findings showed another interesting trend that indicates the importance of urban residency in educational attainment. People who lived in urban areas with a rural *hukou* showed much higher educational attainment than people living in rural areas with a rural *hukou*. This finding is a stronger indicator that rural children who have migrated to cities have an educational advantage over rural children who reside in rural areas.

6   DISCUSSION

In this section, we expand the scope of our discussion in order to help our readers understand our findings. We apply several well-established theoretical frameworks (e.g., Bray 2013; Farrell 2013; Hawkins 2006; Weber 2009; Lieberthal 1997) that are relevant to educational inequity, particularly in

China. We then emphasize the importance of recognizing and understanding intersectionality and its effects on educational inequality. We also provide a comprehensive discussion of the effects of centralization and decentralization on educational inequality and refer to case studies as examples. Finally, we conclude our study by making recommendations for future research.

6.1 Aspects in Education Equality

First, the improvement of educational inequality should not be limited to the outcomes of education because the educational attainment and completion rates at various levels are only one link in the entire process. Instead, as Farrell (2013) noted, the equalization of educational opportunities for adults concerns four interrelated areas. The first area is the equality of access (i.e., enrollment), which concerns the probability of children in different social groups entering the school system. The second area is the equality of survival (i.e., retention and dropout), which concerns the probability that children in various social groups will stay in the school system to a predefined level, such as the end of a complete cycle (e.g., primary, secondary, higher education, etc.). The third area is the equality of output (i.e., attainment), which concerns the probability that all children in various social groups will achieve the same degree of learning at a predefined point in the school system. The fourth area is the equality of outcome (i.e., occupation and career), which concerns the probability that children in various social groups will live relatively similar lives subsequent to and in consequence of their education, such as having equal incomes, similar job status, equal access to sites of political power, and so on (see Fig. 25.1).

According to Farrell (2013), the first three areas refer to the operation of the school system. In the last area (equality of outcome), the educational equity issue concerns the social context because it comprises intersections between the school system, adulthood, and the labor market. Although the focus of our study is on educational attainment, we caution that explaining inequalities and suggesting reforms concern many social, economic, political, and cultural

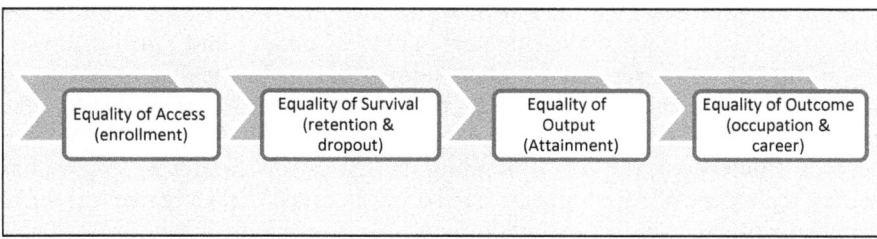

Fig. 25.1 Improvement in educational equality. Source: Figure was made by authors with information from Farrell (2013)

domains. Thus, there is a need to consider all four areas, which are related, including reciprocal inputs and outcomes although the first three areas are directly related to the educational system.

Yuan et al. (2017) conducted a comprehensive literature review of over 40 publications from 1985 to 2013. They concluded that in the first two areas, hindrances contributed to the disadvantages in the third area. That is, the lower educational attainment of rural-to-urban migrants and their children could be attributed to the difficult access to urban public education system from elementary school to college. Furthermore, their unequal treatment in the educational system intersects with academic, emotional, and financial challenges that hinder them from remaining in school. Therefore, they drop out at higher rates and at earlier ages.

6.2   Intersectionality

To study the effects of *hukou* status on educational attainment, we emphasize the importance of being aware of and understanding the concept of intersectionality (see Fig. 25.2) and its relation to the findings of our study. Among all relevant variables, the variables of residential area (i.e., rural-urban and economic-geographic areas) and gender were interrelated, and their effects on education (separate or joint) were created, maintained, and transformed simultaneously at the macro-institutional level. According to Weber (2009), these variables cannot be understood independently of one another. She argued that historically and geographically, intersectionalities exist in contextual power relationships that are simultaneously expressed and experienced at both the macro-level of social institutions and the micro-level of individual lives and small groups. Our findings revealed geographically distributed socioeconomic inequalities within particular populations, which could be exacerbated within socioeconomic groups. Our findings also showed a large number of rural-urban discrepancies in the access to education in China. In certain population groups, these disparities may vary according to structural, political, cultural contexts, or specific policies.

The effects of gender on educational inequalities have been studied in multiple fields. However, we refer to a study that may help our readers better understand the effects of the intersectionality of gender and two other variables: rural or urban residency and economic region. In their investigation of gender inequality in rural China, Song et al. (2006) found no differences in the enrollment of or educational spending on children to the age of 14 years beyond which point, the cost of sending daughters to school was perceived as higher than that of sending sons. These authors also investigated the links between parental educational attainment and investment in schooling. Their findings showed that maternal education had a stronger association with household spending on schooling, specifically on the schooling of daughters, than did paternal education. Based on these findings, the authors recommended that female enrollment could be increased through governmental subsidies,

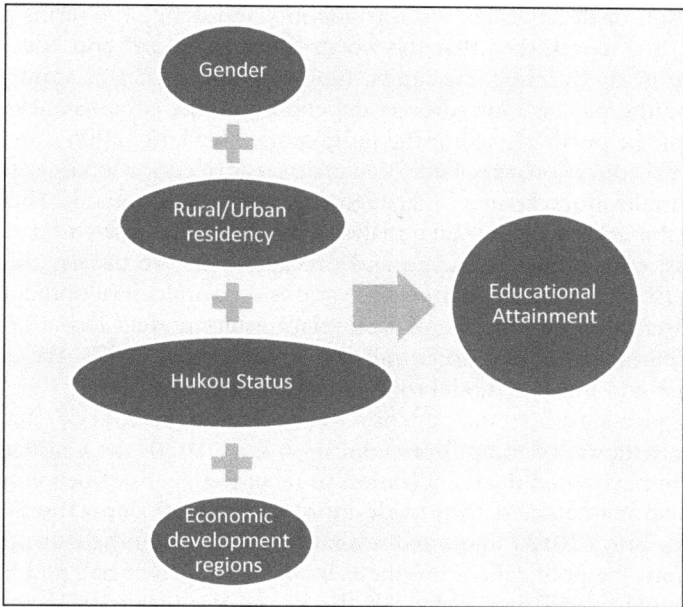

Fig. 25.2 Intersectionality of *hukou*, gender, location, and types of regions contributing to educational inequality

such as making schooling free for girls. These findings indicated that the implementation of compulsory education laws, the effects of generations (e.g., from mother to daughter), rural residency, and the subsidy policies intersected with the variables of gender and educational output.

However, other factors could have been involved in the kinds of intersectionalities discussed here. For example, the findings of our study showed that people who had an urban *hukou* and lived in a rural area did much better than people who had a rural *hukou* and lived in an urban area. There may be two reasons for this finding. First, a substantial portion of the former group (rural residents with an urban *hukou*) consisted of officials in counties and villages, and their employment required them to have a diploma above the high-school level. Second, some high-level, county-level K-12 schools allowed rural students with an urban *hukou* to register. However, as Table 25.5 shows, the effects of the type of *hukou*, region, and gender did not show a clear trend. Instead, they showed complicated discrepancies.

6.3   *Centralization and Decentralization*

In terms of economic and educational reforms, scholars have observed swings in many countries (including China) from centralization to decentralization and back. However, according to Bray (2013), the first task in any review of centralization or decentralization is to identify and define the terms as used in each case. Bray considered that the words "centralization" and "decentralization" have many different meanings. Not only are the terms vague but also their meanings may be contradictory depending on the circumstances and perspectives of the persons making the judgments. Hawkins (2006), an expert in international education, specified three main areas of educational centralization and decentralization: finance, management, and curriculum. In this chapter, based on the results of the data analysis, we focus our discussion on two of these areas: educational financing and management. We discuss the findings regarding EI according to provinces in various economic development regions, and then we apply the central and local relationship model (*Tiao and Kuai*) to examine centralization and decentralization (Lieberthal 1997). We then apply the promise and practice model to a case study (Liu et al. 2017).

We first provide a brief introduction to the decentralization of education. In the implementation of compulsory education since 1980s the Chinese government has implemented decentralization to meet the needs of new internal and international markets and to provide more educational opportunities for the labor force. Bray (2013) suggested several perspectives on the decentralization of education: the political commitment by national, provincial, and local leaders; a tangible model that addressed the issues of educational functions and responsibilities that could be efficiently and effectively delivered at the central level; smaller and decentralized government units; and privatization. The decentralization plan should define the following: the degree of accountability of the different participants; an implementation strategy and schedule; clear operational manuals and procedures; and continuous training of employees at all skill levels in the central and decentralized units of government. Furthermore, relevant performance indicators need to be continuously monitored through a management information system by policymakers and senior government officials. Finally, the most important measure is to identify and provide adequate financial, human, and physical resources to sustain the process.

6.4   Educational Investment

The Organisation for Economic Co-operation and Development (OECD) published an educational report indicating that OECD countries invested an amount equivalent to 5.2% of their GDP on average in primary, secondary, and postsecondary education in 2014 (OECD 2017). However, in the OECD countries, EI had decreased from 6.1% in 2008 after the global economic crisis until 2014. Compared with that of OECD countries, China's EI has been low, but the gap in the ratios of EI of the total GDP has narrowed because of the decreased EI/GDP ratio in OECD countries and the escalated EI/GDP ratio in China (4.25% in 2016), which was 3% in 2008 (Yang et al. 2014). In the 1980s, Deng Xiaoping made the commitment that the Chinese government would raise its EI to 4% (Mok et al. 2009). By 2014, this goal has been achieved.

As indicated in Table 25.6, by 2014, the average EI in the total GDP (US$11,037.89 billion) was 4.25% in China. Table 25.6 shows GDP per capita,

Table 25.6 EI of governmental expenditure in 2014

Region type	Province	GDP per capita 2015 (thousand in USD)	Total GDP (billion in USD)	Educational investment (billion in USD)	EI/GDP[a]	2014 individual income (thousand in USD)
	Mainland China	8.32	11037.89	468.99	4.25%	3.25
1	Tianjin	17.25	253.66	10.20	4.02%	4.65
1	Beijing	16.39	344.05	17.64	5.13%	7.18
1	Shanghai	15.96	380.12	15.96	4.20%	7.41
1	Jiangsu	13.42	1049.81	33.55	3.20%	4.38
2	Zhejiang	11.97	647.95	25.94	4.00%	5.27
2	Inner Mongolia	11.64	286.62	10.31	3.60%	3.32
2	Liaoning	10.69	461.72	14.03	3.04%	3.68
2	Fujian	10.40	388.00	14.40	3.71%	3.76
2	Guangdong	10.40	1093.71	44.12	4.03%	4.14
2	Shandong	9.98	958.49	30.40	3.17%	3.37
3	Jilin	8.22	222.63	8.63	3.88%	2.83
3	Chongqing	7.84	230.04	11.26	4.89%	2.96
3	Hubei	7.73	441.60	15.93	3.61%	2.95
3	Shaanxi	7.69	285.32	14.68	5.15%	2.55
3	Ningxia Hui Autonomous Region	6.86	44.39	2.74	6.17%	2.57
3	Xinjiang Uygur Autonomous Region	6.66	149.57	10.24	6.85%	2.43
3	Hunan	6.60	436.09	18.20	4.17%	2.84
3	Hebei	6.55	474.53	17.52	3.69%	2.69
3	Qinghai	6.50	37.15	3.19	8.58%	2.32
3	Heilongjiang	6.44	242.57	10.13	4.17%	2.81
3	Hainan	6.38	56.46	3.89	6.90%	2.82
3	Henan	6.08	563.52	26.43	4.69%	2.53
4	Sichuan	5.76	460.27	23.40	5.08%	2.54
4	Shanxi	5.75	205.83	11.35	5.51%	2.67
4	Jiangxi	5.68	253.46	14.40	5.68%	2.70
4	Anhui	5.64	336.27	16.87	5.02%	2.71
4	Guangxi Zhuang Autonomous Region	5.42	252.79	13.85	5.48%	2.51
4	Tibet	4.79	14.85	2.47	16.61%	1.73
4	Yunnan	4.47	206.69	14.84	7.18%	2.22
4	Guizhou	4.33	149.46	12.42	8.31%	2.00
4	Gansu	4.33	110.27	8.36	7.58%	1.97

Source: Data compiled from Chinese Statistical Yearbook (2015); National Bureau of Statistics of China (NBSC); and The Economist (2015)

[a]Percentage of total GDP invested in education

the total GDP, the total EI, the percentage of EI in the GDP, and the average individual income by province. It shows information about the entire country as well as about each province and autonomous region. The EIs in absolute numbers in dollars are not comparable because of differences in the sizes of the population and the levels of economic development among the provinces. However, in Table 25.6, the ratio of EI of provincial GDP (EI/GDP) shows that poor provinces had relatively greater EI in their GDP compared with rich provinces. Among the provinces in Region 1 and Region 2, only Beijing had more than 5% of its annual GDP invested in education in 2014. The ratios of the percentage of EI in the GDP varied among the provinces within an economic development region. For example, in Region 3, several provinces (Hebei, Hunan, Heilongjiang, and Henan) historically had better educational attainment, and all had a percentage of EI in the GDP lower than 5%. In contrast, the six provinces and autonomous regions that had an EI of more than 6% in their total GDP had high concentrations of ethnic minorities. The six provinces and autonomous regions were Ningxia Hui Autonomous Region (6.17%), Xinjiang Uygur Autonomous Region (6.85%), Yunnan Province (7.18%), Gansu Province (7.58%), Guizhou Province (8.31%), and Tibet (16.61%).

These findings could explain the reasons as to why better economically developed regions did better educationally than poorer regions in which, although a higher percentage of their total GDP was invested in education, the educational attainment was lower. This finding raises the following question: Should the central government invest more money in the less economically and educationally developed provinces and autonomous regions? Although the answer to this question would likely be "yes," and the Chinese central government invested heavily in education in the provinces with poor rural areas (The State Council 2013), a greater amount of discussion might ensue based on the next question: How will the EI at all levels of government (including the central government) be distributed and managed at and through the province, county, and village levels?

Several previous studies probed the centralized, decentralized, and recentralized educational financing process in their studies. Zhao's study (2009) recommended that the central and provincial governments need to better enforce minimum spending requirements at the county level, particularly poor areas. Wang and Zhao (2012) conjectured that the oversight by high-level governments might primarily result in short-term indicators of economic development, rather than long-term reforms such as education. The authors proposed an improved balance of local governing responsibilities with the local authority to tax as well as a greater priority on financing and administering compulsory education at both the national and provincial levels. Liu et al. (2009) analyzed the effects of fiscal recentralization of rural education specifically on the distribution of management responsibilities across different levels of governments. Their analysis of survey data collected in Gansu (western China), showed that "county reform" resulted in three directions in power shifts: (a) a reduction in "the power sharing arrangements whereby the governor and the township government or the county education bureau and the township government jointly manage the school district"; (b) a shift "from township government to the county education bureau or the county government"; and (c) a shift "from the township government to the governor." Each case affected education differently. The authors contended that in the first case, the ambiguous delineations of authority led to power struggles and the poor coordination of administrative responsibilities. In the second case, decision-making power was excessively situated at the county level and far from the daily activities and concerns of educators and school administrators. The final direction, they concluded, was the most promising of the three.

In the next section, we will discuss the linkages and tensions between centralization and decentralization in educational governance and management.

6.5   The Central-Local Relations Model in China

Since the opening-up reform in the late 1980s, decentralization has been the main theme in the socioeconomic reform of China. Compared with the centralized power system before the 1980s, local governments have had more autonomy in developing local economy and expanding and improving education in terms of making and implementing policies and assessing their outcomes. Lieberthal (1997) conceptualized China's governing system as consisting of many vertical lines (*tiao*) and horizontal pieces (*kuai*). *Tiao* refers to the vertical lines from the authority of the central government to all levels of local authorities. *Kuai* refers to the horizontal levels of the authority of provincial and local governments. The *tiao-kuai* relationship in China's governmental system is distinct compared with many other nations. This two-dimensional arrangement sometimes creates challenges and conflicts. Therefore, it is very demanding for local governments to balance the demands and provisions of *tiao* and *kuai*. According to Lieberthal (1997), "The former [*tiao*] coordinates according to function; the latter [*kuai*] coordinates according to the needs of the locality that it governs." According to Zhou (2009), in China, departments at each level are administered by the governments at the same level, but they also follow the guidelines of the department that is superior to them. For example, the county educational district office takes orders from the county chief administrators and at the same time takes orders from the educational bureau at the provincial level, which follows the guidelines issued by the Ministry of Education. Figure 25.3 explains the influential factors to local educational authorities when implementing reforms through the *Tiao-Kuai* (central-local relation) relationship model. When the goals and implementation strategies of leaders at various levels conflict, it is challenging for local governments to take effective action to meet the requirements of leaders at various levels both vertically and horizontally.

The *tiao-kuai* relationship must be considered in the analysis of the causes of educational inequality that is focused on the relations between the central and the local regions. Policymakers and educators in China have generally been supportive toward educational equality. However, the outcomes of

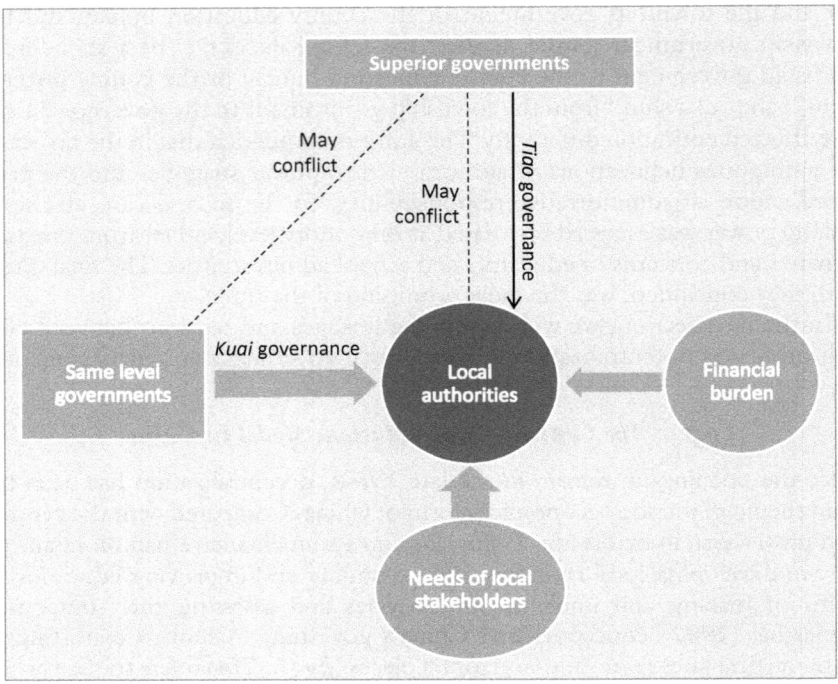

Fig. 25.3 Influential factors to local educational authorities when implementing reforms

policy implementation are mixed because of the *tiao-kuai* relationship between the central government and the local authorities.

Liu et al. (2017) provided an example of the collaboration and tension in educational systems with regard to centralization and decentralization. (See Fig. 25.4) Their case study was based on macroscopic policy analyses and microscopic investigations of policy implementation. It was focused on compulsory education policy and its implementation with regard to rural-to-urban migrant children in Wu City (a pseudonym), where there was a large population of migrant workers. Their study was based on the sociodemographic and academic information as well as interview data collected from participants in Wu City's education department and local schools as well as parents (both migrants and non-migrants).

In Liu et al.'s (2017) study, a promise-practice framework was applied. In this framework, the central government makes promises, and the local education authorities (at both the city and the county levels) are responsible for their implementation. In 2001, China's central government mandated that regional areas with large floating populations of migrant workers must provide migrant children with compulsory education. The State Council's (2001) *Decision on the Improving and Reforming of Basic*

Education highlighted that governments at all levels should pay attention to migrant children's compulsory education, governments in high emigration areas should be the primary providers for migrant children's compulsory education, and full-time public schools should be the primary receivers of migrant children. Subsequently, this mandate became known as the Two Primaries Policy.[3] It has become the standard by which all related issues are judged. This policy was reinforced by the Compulsory Education Law of the PRC in 2006. However, policy implementation is under the jurisdiction of local education authorities, and the central government has no authority over local education practices. Local authorities must navigate the requirements of the Two Primaries Policy, the demands of migrant workers and their children, the discontent of local residents with an urban *hukou*, and the pressure exerted by public schools and teachers. Hence, multiple conflicts of interest can occur at this level. The authors found that among many factors, the dichotomy between the governmental budgetary burden and potential economic prosperity concerns and limited executive powers contributed to an environment of conflict in policy implementation. City governments were usually not able to collect money from the migrant children's home province. In addition, the administrators and educators at city education bureaus and the local schools felt some obligation to continue the exclusion of migrant children from urban public schools based on the local pressure exerted by mainly non-migrant city residents who had an urban *hukou*.

Liu et al.'s (2017) study revealed four kinds of conflicts encountered by local education authorities who had to balance the demands of the central government and of local schools and parents: conflict between local interests and the demands of superiors; conflict between investing more money in economic development and increasing the education budget to fulfill the need for compulsory education; conflict between prioritizing quality or prioritizing equity; and conflict between the uncertainty of migrant labors' geographical flow between cities and local investment in compulsory education.

Figure 25.4 shows the results of Liu, Sun, and Barrow's (2017) case study, which exemplifies the *tiao-kuai* relationship. The left side of Fig. 25.4 illustrates the central government's laws on educational equity (i.e., promises) to the rural-to-urban migrant population to fulfill the obligation of nine years of compulsory education. As indicated by the chart on the right side, the local education authorities faced conflicting demands from community

---

[3] The State Council's (2001) Decision on the Improving and Reforming of Basic Education highlighted that governments at all levels should pay attention to migrant children's compulsory education, governments of high emigration areas should be the primary providers for migrant children's compulsory education, and full-time public schools should be the primary receivers of migrant children. This later became known as the "Two Primaries" Policy and is the standard by which all related issues are judged.

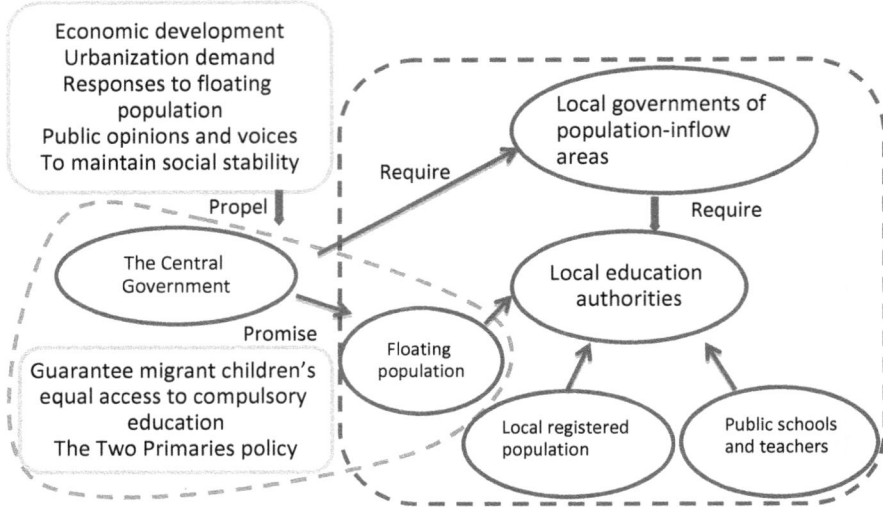

Fig. 25.4   Liu, Sun, and Barrow's promise-practice model. Source: Liu et al. (2017)

stakeholders, including local schools, local long-term residents with an urban *hukou*, and local residents with a rural *hukou*, in their implementation of the central government's policies (i.e., practices).

Similar themes were found in other previous studies. For example, based on a review of over 40 studies in the literature, Yuan et al. (2017) pointed out that the lower years of schooling and completion rates for migrants and their children who stayed in cities without a *hukou* were mainly due to the lack of coordination between various levels of governments in carrying out centralized policies using a decentralized, sometimes recentralized, implementation process. Emphasizing a different aspect, Liu and Dunne (2009) conducted a comparative case study in three different schools in the same region in China. Their study focused on the conflicts between educational equity and the emphasis on testing. The central government advocated for the expansion of the nine-year compulsory education to include all children (including migrant children in cities) and downplayed the roles of testing children of the compulsory education age. However, the findings of Liu and Dunne's study suggested that students' academic scores in the major state examinations remained the top priority of most stakeholders (i.e., teachers, parents, students, schools, and local governments). The process of decentralization and the development of a highly competitive educational market support the prioritization of test-driven academic performance. Although the national policy encourages the systematic reform from an exam-oriented to a quality-oriented focus, the local educational priority is to support exam-oriented education.

To conclude this discussion of centralization and decentralization, our research implies several related educational policies. Both centralization and decentralization involve the distribution of resources. In the education sector, resources provide access to education and its attainment, so it is important to ensure the equitable distribution of resources between rural and urban areas and among various economic regions. Central and provincial governments should increase the amounts of subsidies to compulsory education in poor rural areas based on clear guidelines for budgeting and auditing expenditures. In addition, the equitable distribution of human resources should be ensured in order to improve the quality of rural schools (e.g., school buildings, technological facilities, training, and retaining good teachers) and utilize vocational, adult, and community education to improve the percentage of literacy among rural Chinese parents who will be able to better supervise and facilitate their children's education.

Future research should consider the pros and cons of centralization and decentralization in education. According to Hawkins (2013), some arguments support centralization in countries such as China. It may be easier for centralized authorities to oversee situations and to redistribute resources to geographic locations and educational areas in need. However, the effectiveness may depend on the intentions of those in power. Moreover, centralized regimes are not necessarily more sensitive to the needs of disadvantaged groups than decentralized regimes. Second, the time elements are important to all reforms. The exigencies of political forces sometimes require results before reforms have had time to become fully effective. This is one reason for the swings from centralization to decentralization and back evidenced in some countries. Furthermore, although attempts to empower local communities in decentralization may be laudable, such communities may be dominated by elites and other groups may be as marginalized as they were before the decentralization process. Finally, some previous studies have investigated the problem of recentralization in relation to decentralization (e.g., Liu et al. 2009; Wang and Zhao 2012; Zhao 2009). A potentially negative motivation for decentralization is the desire of the center to reduce its responsibilities for education because of financial stringency. Central governments that realize that they do not have sufficient resources for the adequate provision of services may choose to evade the problem by moving responsibility to lower governmental tiers or to nongovernmental bodies. However, in China, recentralization may allow for a more unified system of standards to be applied in learning, accreditation, and degree granting. Nevertheless, recentralization could be particularly challenging because of the rise in the privatization of education as well as the increase in the disparities among the economic regions in China.

References

Barro, R. J., and J. Lee. 2001. International data on educational attainment: Updates and implications. *Oxford Economic Papers* 53(3): 541–563. DOI:https://doi.org/10.1093/oep/53.3.541.

Bray, M. 2013. Control of education: Issues and tensions in centralization and decentralization. In *Comparative education: the dialectic of the global and the local,* ed. R. F. Arnove, C. A. Torres, and S. Franz. NYC: Rowman and Littlefield Publisher.

China Daily. 2012. China approves new measures to narrow education gap. *China Daily USA.* Retrieved from http://usa.chinadaily.com.cn/china/2012-08/30/content_15718196.htm.

China Education Daily. 2012. Report on reducing illiterate rates and implementing nine years compulsory education among the young generation. Retrieved from http://www.moe.gov.cn/publicfiles/business/htmlfiles/moe/s6832/201209/142013.html.

Connelly, R., and Z. Zheng. 2003. Determinants of school enrollment and completion of 10 to 18 year olds in China. *Economics of Education Review* 22 (4): 379–388.

Du, K. W. 2014. 30 provinces and municipal cities solved the problem of College Entrance Exam for the migrant children in the cities in 2014 (2014年30个省区市解决随迁子女异地高考). Retrieved from http://gb.cri.cn/42071/2014/02/20/5951s4431488.htm.

Farrell, J. P. 2013. Equality of education: Six decades of comparative evidence seen from a new millennium. In *Comparative Education: The Dialectic of the Global and the Local.* ed. R. F. Arnove, C. A. Torres, and S. Franz. New York, NY: Rowman and Littlefield Publisher.

Grant, L., and X. L. Rong. 1999. Gender, immigrant generation, ethnicity and the schooling progress of youth. *Journal of Research and Development in Education* 33(1): 15–26.

Hannum, E. 2005. Market transition, educational disparities, and family strategies in rural China: new evidence on gender stratification and development. *Demography* 42 (2): 275–299.

Hannum, E., and M. Wang. 2006. Geography and educational inequality in China. *China Economic Review* (17): 253–265.

Hawkins, J. N. 2006. Walking on three legs: centralization, decentralization, and recentralization in Chinese education. In *Educational decentralization: Asian experiences and conceptual contributions.* ed. C. Bjork. New York: Springer.

Hawkins, J. N. 2013. Education in Asia-Pacific regions: Some enduring challenges. In *Comparative education: The dialectic of the global and the local.* ed. R. F. Arnove, C. A. Torres, and S. Franz. New York, NY: Rowman and Littlefield Publisher.

Lee, M. H. 2012. The one-child policy and gender equality in education in China: Evidence from household data. *Journal of Family and Economic Issues* 33(1): 41–52.

Li, L. 1999. Standardization of rates and ratios. Retrieved from http://www.epidemiolog.net/evolving/Standardization.pdf.

Li, M. 2016. 不可逾越的"人生起跑线":农民工子女的教育边缘化. Retrieved from http://cul.sohu.com/20160918/n468601964.shtml.

Li, Y. [李彦龙]. 2015. 大学生志愿服务西部计划项目介绍。Retrieved from http://xibu.youth.cn/xmjs/201510/t20151015_7212132.htm.

Lieberthal, K. 1997. China's governing system and its impact on environmental policy implementation. *China Environment Series 1.* Environmental Change and Security Project, Woodrow Wilson International Center for Scholars. Retrieved from http://ecsp.si.edu/ecsplib.nsf.

Liu, M., R. Murphy, R. Tao, and X. An. 2009. Education management and performance after rural education finance reform: Evidence from Western China. *International Journal of Educational Development* 29(5): 463–473.

Liu, S. Y., W. Y. Sun, and E. Barrow. 2017. Promises and practices: A case study on compulsory education policy implementation in a large migrant-inflow city in China. In *International handbook of urban education.* ed. W. Pink and G. Noblit. New York City: Springer.

Liu, Y. and M. Dunne. 2009. Educational reform in China: tensions in national policy and local practice. *Comparative Education* 45(4): 461–476.

Lü, X. 2014. Social policy and regime legitimacy: The effects of education reform in China. *The American Political Science Review* 108(2): 423–437.

Mok, K. H., Y. C. Wong., and X. Zhang. 2009. When marketisation and privatisation clash with socialist ideals: Educational inequality in urban China. *International Journal of Educational Development* (29): 505–512.

National Bureau of Statistics of People's Republic of China. 2016. 21–22 Children of migrant works and children left behind (2015). *China Statistical Yearbook 2016.* Retrieved from http://www.stats.gov.cn/tjsj/ndsj/2016/indexeh.htm.

National Bureau of Statistics of People's Republic of China. 2017. 2016年农民工监测调查报告 Retrieved from http://www.stats.gov.cn/tjsj/zxfb/201704/t20170428_1489334.html.

National Bureau of Statistics of China [NBSC]. 2015. *China Statistical Yearbook 2015.* Beijing: Zhongguo Tongji Chubanshe.

OECD. 2017. Education at a glance 2017: OECD indicators. Retrieved from https://www.hm.ee/sites/default/files/eag2017_eng.pdf.

Pang, W., and J. A. Plucker. 2012. Recent transformations in China's economic, social, and education policies for promoting innovation and creativity. *Journal of Creative Behavior* 46(4): 247–273.

ParkHouse, H., and X. L. Rong. 2016. Inequalities in China's Compulsory Education. In *Spotlight on China.* ed. S. Guo., and Y. Guo. Sense Publishers: Rotterdam.

Qi, T. 2011. Moving toward decentralization? Changing education governance in china after 1985. *International Perspectives on Education and Society* 15(15): 19–41.

Rong, X. L., and F. Brown. 2001. The effects of immigrant generation and ethnicity of educational attainment among young African and Caribbean blacks in the United States. *Harvard Educational Review* 71(3): 536–565.

Shryock, H. S., E. A. Larmon, and J. S. Siegel. 1980. *The methods and materials of demography.* Washington: Dept. of Commerce, Bureau of the Census: for sale by the Supt. of Docs. U.S. Govt. Print. Off.

Song, L., S. Appleton, and J. Knight. 2006. Why do girls in rural China have lower school enrollment? *World Development,* 34(9): 1639–1653.

Song, Y. 2012. Poverty reduction in China: The contribution of popularizing primary education. *China and World Economy* 20(1): 105–122.

The Economist. 2015. Rich province, poor province. The government is struggling to spread wealth more evenly. Retrieved from https://www.economist.com/news/

china/21707964-government-struggling-spread-wealth-more-evenly-rich-province-poor-province.

The General office of the State Council of the People's Republic of China. [中华人民共和国国务院办公厅]. 2003. 国务院办公厅关于做好2003年普通高等学校毕业生就业工作的通知. Retrieved from http://www.gov.cn/gongbao/content/2003/content_62175.htm.

The National People's Congress of the People's Republic of China. [全国人民代表大会]. 1986. 中华人民共和国义务教育法. Retrieved from http://www.npc.gov.cn/wxzl/gongbao/2000-12/06/content_5004469.htm.

The State Council. 2001. Decision on the improving and reforming on the basic education (国务院关于基础教育改革与发展的决定). Reform Data Website (中国改革信息库). Retrieved from http://www.reformdata.org/content/20010529/6183.html.

The State Council. 2013. Aid the Poor in China the past 30 years. Retrieved from http://www.xinhuanet.com/city/zgfp30n/index.htmrs.

The World Bank. 2017. GDP (current US$). Retrieved from https://data.worldbank.org/indicator/NY.GDP.MKTP.CD?locations=CN&view=chart.

UNICEF. 2013. China. Statistics. Retrieved from https://www.unicef.org/infobycountry/china_statistics.html.

Wang, W., and Z. Zhao. 2012. Rural taxation reforms and compulsory education finance in China. *Journal of Public Budgeting, Accounting, and Financial Management* 24(1): 136–162.

Wang, X., Rong, X. L., and Ting, R. X. 2018. Variations in educational inequalities in china and policy recommendations. Paper present at American Educational Research Association annual conference in New York City.

Weber, L. 2009. *Understanding race, class, gender, and sexuality: A conceptual framework*. Oxford University Press.

Yang, J., X. Huang, and X. Liu. 2014. An analysis of education inequality in China. *International Journal of Educational Development* (37): 2–10.

Yuan, S. Z., G. Noblit, and X. L. Rong. 2017. The education issues of the children of internal migrant workers in China. In *International Handbook of Urban Education (Vol 20)*. ed. G. Noblit and W. Pink. New York: Springer.

Zhang, X., and R. Kanbur. 2005. Spatial inequality in education and health care in china. *China Economic Review* 16(2): 189–204.

Zhao, L. 2009. Between local community and central state: Financing basic education in China. *International Journal of Educational Development* 29(4): 366–373.

Zhou, Z. 2009. *Research on the Relationship between the Government Functional Departments and Local Government in Contemporary China* (当代中国政府条块关系研究). Tianjin, China: Tianjin Renmin Publishing House.

CHAPTER 26

Mobilization and Irregularity: Volatile Growth of Educational Expenditure in China

Litao Zhao

1 Introduction

Social policy scholars often take the view that welfare states can be classified into different types based on distinct political philosophies and stable institutional features. It is a challenge to position China in any such taxonomy, however. Using the volatile growth of educational expenditure in recent years as an example, this chapter suggests that China's social policy in general, and educational policy in particular, has not evolved into a stable model. The tension between centralized mandates and decentralized financing generates greater irregularity than any existing theory can sufficiently explain. China often relies on top-down mobilization to achieve unfunded or underfunded policy mandates. Mobilization, however, cannot last long as it stresses and strains local governments. The alternation between mobilization and post-mobilization is highly disruptive for China's welfare state building. Much more needs to be done to replace mobilization with a more regularized, sustainable, and equitable financing mechanism for education and other social programs.

The trajectory of welfare state development is remarkably different in East Asia than in the West. In the post-World War II period, up to the first oil crisis in the early 1970s, welfare states had expanded dramatically in the West. In contrast, government spending on social welfare was kept low in East Asia, where social policy was geared toward economic growth rather than redistributive welfare. This strategy, later described by scholars in terms such as "developmental state" and "productivist welfare capitalism," has worked well to move Japan and the "Four Little Dragons" of South Korea, Taiwan, Hong

L. Zhao (✉)
East Asian Institute, National University of Singapore, Singapore, Singapore
e-mail: eaizlt@nus.edu.sg

© The Author(s) 2019
J. Yu, S. Guo (eds.), *The Palgrave Handbook of Local Governance in Contemporary China*, https://doi.org/10.1007/978-981-13-2799-5_26

Kong, and Singapore from the third world to the first world in terms of economic and social development.

Social policy scholars have debated on whether East Asia falls into the taxonomy of welfare states developed by Esping-Andersen (1990) or deserves a separate category. Nonetheless, they share the assumption that East Asian societies, together with other societies, can be theorized as varieties of welfare state models with stable institutional features and distinct political philosophies. While such classification exercise may help to bring East Asia, including China, into the comparative social policy research, its static view helps little to account for the high level of volatility and irregularity in China's social policy implementation.

Using education as a case, this chapter aims to shed light on how such irregularity is produced in China. In the areas of education, healthcare, and social security, China features centralized policy mandates and decentralized financing. The prevailing literature asserts that as local officials' career advancement relies less on their performance in social development, they lack the incentive to spend on education and other social programs. Consequently, government spending on education (and other social expenditures) cannot grow as fast as GDP (gross domestic product) or government revenue. This chapter argues that the prevailing literature holds in a low-pressure situation, in which there is no strong push from the top leadership. However, there are periods in which top-down mobilization is used to achieve underfunded or unfunded policy mandates in education. Under such high-pressure circumstances, local officials are likely to mobilize government and non-governmental resources for education, resulting in a surge in educational expenditure, considerably higher than the growth of GDP or government revenue. Mobilization, however, cannot last long as it stresses and strains local governments. The alternation between mobilization and post-mobilization involves greater irregularity than any existing theory can sufficiently explain.

Theoretically, this chapter calls for more attention on mobilization as an important feature and dimension of China's social policy implementation. Empirically, it analyzes how China's most recent mobilization resulted in a great leap in educational expenditure in 2012 and how the great leap was followed by a sharp decline in the aftermath. The sharp contrast epitomizes the issue of irregularity in China's social policy process. From the perspective of welfare-state building, China needs to replace mobilization-based policy implementation with a more regularized, sustainable, and equitable financing mechanism for education and other social programs.

2   East Asia in Comparative Perspective

Since the earlier works by Catherine Jones (1990, 1993) and James Midgley (1986, 1995), different scholars have written from different perspectives about the distinctiveness of the East Asian welfare model. Esping-Andersen's (1990) classification of European welfare regimes—the liberal type in Anglo-Saxon

countries, the conservative type in Continental Europe, and the social democratic type in Nordic countries—has added new impetus to the comparative
study of welfare regimes in East Asia.

A number of theorizations have emerged to model East Asia. Some scholars
extend Esping-Andersen's taxonomy to East Asia, arguing that East Asia falls
into the conservative-corporatist category. Aspalter (2001) provides a political
account by stating that the dominance of conservative political parties has
largely determined the development trajectory of welfare states in East Asia.
He points out that Japan, South Korea, Hong Kong, Taiwan, and Singapore
were all governed by conservative political elites in the time of economic takeoff. The welfare state model prevalent in East Asia "rests on the assumption
that social welfare does not need to be redistributive, nor expenditure-oriented"
and features "clear preference to the family and the market in welfare provision,
while limiting the welfare function of the state largely to the regulative role in
social welfare policy" (Aspalter 2006: 298).

Other theorizations tend to see East Asia as a distinctive type that falls outside of Esping-Andersen's taxonomy. The "residual welfare state" model
describes East Asia as a system in which "state welfare is targeted on the most
needy who have no other sources of aid, the means test is widely used and
government social spending is kept low" (Lee et al. 2014: 5). For instance,
Tang (2000) argues that Hong Kong during the early colonial period was best
characterized as a residual welfare system. Wong (2013) believes that China up
to the late 1990s was a residual welfare state. Similarly, Midgley (1986) uses
"reluctant welfarism" to describe East Asia's preoccupation with economic
development as opposed to redistributive welfare.

The "Confucian welfare state" model takes a cultural approach to East Asia.
It notes that in East Asian societies, there is much emphasis on individual
responsibility, work ethic, and filial piety. As family takes on important welfare
functions, the welfare system in East Asia does not rely as much on the state as
is the case in Europe. Recognizing the prominent role of the family in welfare
provision, scholars such as Aspalter (2001) treat East Asia as a type of conservative welfare states within Esping-Andersen's taxonomy. But Jones (1993) sees
East Asia's family-based welfare system as rooted in its Confucian tradition.

The "developmental state" model casts a more positive light on the East
Asian development experience. Some of the salient features of this model
include a ruling elite aspired to elevate their countries from the third world to
the first world at all costs and a technocratic government capable of launching
industrialization and engineering industrial upgrading (Weiss 2000). The
transformative capacity of the developmental state comes from "a relatively
autonomous and determined developmental elite, a powerful, competent and
insulated economic bureaucracy, a weak and subordinated civil society, the ability to quell opposition and sustain legitimacy" (Wong 2013: 211). The "developmental state" model highlights the importance of development rather than
redistribution for general social well-being.

In a similar vein, Midgley's (1995) social development approach is motivated by the quest for social progress in the third world. A leading scholar in promoting the concept of social development, Midgley has long emphasized the need for social programs to support national economic development. Social development as an approach for promoting social welfare has a number of features:

> First, it emphasizes the notion of change, stressing the need for governments, voluntary organizations and communities to bring about progressive social improvements. Second, the commitment to change reveals social development's interventionalism by which resources are mobilized through which a number of agents and institutions of which the state is arguably the most important. Third, social development's interventionalism is based on the idea that economic, social, and other components of the multifaceted development process should be harmonized. (Midgley 2014: 23–24)

Building on the notion of "developmental state" and the social development approach, social policy scholars such as Tang (2000) and Kwon (2002) have used the conception of "welfare developmentalism" to characterize the East Asian welfare systems.

Since the late 1990s, "social investment" has emerged as a new paradigm in European Union (EU) countries. It reformulates social expenditures as investments capable of producing positive returns for households, the economy, and society. European social policy scholars see the social investment model as an alternative not only to the comprehensive, redistributive welfare model that emerged after World War II, but also to the neo-liberal model that emerged since the late 1990s (Esping-Andersen et al. 2002; Morel et al. 2011; Hemerijck 2015). The social investment model aims to reconcile the relationship between social welfare and economic development: social programs promote economic growth by making people more employable and productive, which in turn generates resources for redistribution while reducing reliance on state welfare.

Interestingly, while Europe is where the social investment paradigm has been explicitly formulated and practiced, some scholars argue that East Asia for decades has adopted the productivist approach to social policy. For instance, Ian Holliday (2000) argues that the five East Asian societies—Japan, Korea, Taiwan, Hong Kong, and Singapore—represent a distinctive model of "productivist welfare capitalism." Although they can be further divided into the facilitative, developmental-universalist and developmental-particularistic clusters, they share the two central aspects of productivist welfare capitalism: "a growth-oriented state and subordination of all aspects of state policy, including social policy, to economic/industrial objectives" (Holliday 2000: 709). Notably, Midgley has sought to recast social development through the lens of social investment. As Midgley (1999: 8) puts it, the social development approach "seeks specifically to end the bifurcation of social welfare and economic development and to formulate a conception of social policy as productivist and investment oriented, rather than redistributive and consumption."

Taken together, the existing theorizations share the assumption that East Asia on the whole can be seen as a welfare model with shared experiences and stable institutional features, although they have different views on the determinants as well as uniqueness of the East Asian model. Empirically, they would agree with Wilding's (2000) characterization of the common features of East Asian social policy, including low public expenditure on social welfare, a productivist social policy oriented toward economic growth, hostility to the idea of state welfarism, a residual approach to social protection, a central role for the family, a regulatory and enabling role for the state, piecemeal, pragmatic, and ad hoc welfare development, instrumental use of welfare to build legitimacy, stability and support for the state, weak commitment to the notion of welfare as a citizenship right, and so on.

3   China in Contrast to the East Asian Model(s) of Social Policy

It is tempting to conceptualize China as one of the aforementioned East Asian models. However, as Leung and Xu (2015: 9) argue, while "the success of East Asian countries may provide a number of loosely constructed models and experiences by which to guide China's development," "China's large demographic and geographical size and the complex relationship between local and central government make direct application difficult." This chapter uses education as an example to illustrate the challenge of positioning China within the taxonomy of East Asian welfare model. The reason is twofold. First, all the theorizations of East Asia, from the "Confucian welfare state" model to the "developmental state" model and the "productivist welfare" model, see education as one of the defining features of East Asian social policy. In East Asia, there is wide and strong support for educational development. Second, China also recognizes education as one of its reform and development priorities. The central government has reiterated the importance of education for national economic and social development. By any account, one would expect education to be one of the top priorities and government expenditure on education to grow steadily in tandem with GDP or government revenue growth.

However, a large body of literature on China's education challenges the assertion of either priority funding for education or steady growth of educational expenditure in tandem with GDP or government revenue growth. The prevailing view is that education in China is undersupplied and underfunded. Government expenditure on education has been low by international standards. The World Bank raised this issue in a report published in 1985. It estimated that "China spent slightly more than 3% of its GNP on education in 1979," compared with "a median of 4–5% in other developing countries and 6% or much higher in developed countries" (World Bank 1985: 45). Taking the World Bank's advice into consideration, China decided to increase government spending on education to 4 percent of GDP by 2000. To achieve this target, China passed the Compulsory Education Law, which specified the requirement of "three growths": the growth of government spending on education should be higher than that of regular government revenue; school funding on a per student basis should increase year by year; and teacher salaries and per student recurrent non-personnel expenditure should increase year by year. Also in the mid-1990s, China announced the national strategy of rejuvenating the nation through science and education (*kejiao xingguo zhanlue*). Despite the top leadership's strong commitment to educational development, China never achieved the target of raising government expenditure on education to 4 percent of GDP in the 1990s and 2000s.

China's comparatively low educational expenditure is in sharp contrast to the prediction of the existing East Asian welfare models. It is even more puzzling given that China has rarely missed a development target set by the central leadership year after year. The literature suggests that much of the problem is structurally rooted in China's educational system, which features centralized mandates and decentralized financing (West and Wong 1995; Park et al. 1996; Hannum 1999, 2003; Tsang and Ding 2005; Zhang and Kanbur 2005; Zhao 2009; Xiao and Liu 2014). Decentralized financing has evolved over time. In the 1980s, China's fiscal system featured "each locality eating in their own kitchen" (*fenzao chifan*) in terms of revenue income and expenditure. Each locality under the governance of the province and municipality was required to manage and fund their own compulsory education. As a result, villages were primarily responsible for the financing of primary schools, township governments for junior secondary schools, and county governments for senior secondary schools. In 1994, China overhauled its tax system to increase the revenue share of the central government while continuing to leave social expenditure responsibilities to local governments. It resulted in an extremely decentralized and diversified system of educational financing. In many places, rural schools could not function without contributions from non-governmental sources, such as tuition fees from student families and educational surcharges from farming households and local enterprises. In 2001, as part of a larger reorganization to make the county the primary unit of local government, China began to shift the responsibility from township/town to county government in managing and funding rural education. This was followed by another reform in 2006 to formalize the role of the central and provincial government in funding a number of educational programs (such as free textbooks, free tuition, and subsidies for school boarding fees). Nonetheless, county governments remain the cornerstone of managing and financing compulsory education in China. Despite all the changes since the 1980s, decentralized financing remains an essential feature of China's education (as well as health care and social security).

The literature offers two different but complementary accounts for why China's education has been perennially undersupplied and underfunded. The first one focuses on the limited financial capability of local governments, particularly those in less developed areas; the second one on the lack of strong incentives among local officials to spend on education. Either way, there is a gap between central policy mandate and local implementation.

The fiscal constraint account is particularly pertinent to the 1980s and 1990s. Rural China for long had been expected to provide for itself. However, the dismantling of collective agriculture in the 1980s removed one of the most important financing mechanisms for rural education. Having no formal taxing authority, rural governments had to rely on off-budget funds and a variety of user fees and surcharges to finance education and other social services. West and Wong (1995) find in Shandong that extra-budgetary funds and "self-raised" funds made up 42 percent of the financing for education. The capacity to raise funds locally, however, varied widely across localities. In the 1990s, a major source of off-budget funds was township and village enterprises (TVEs). As West and Wong (1995: 81) point out, "while rural local governments with developed TVEs may have benefited from fiscal decentralization, many in poor regions with weak industrial bases are forced to cut back on basic services and/ or resort to levying *ad-hoc* fees and taxes on farm households." It is not surprising that the growing reliance on off-budget funds to finance public services led to the undersupply of education in places with weak capacity to raise funds locally from TVEs and non-governmental sources. It also gave rise to the increasing regional disparity in education and other social services, since TVEs were concentrated in coastal provinces and/or peri-urban areas.

China started to reduce reliance on off-budgetary funds for rural education in 2001. The 2006 reform went even further with a pledge to establish a public finance-based expense guarantee system for rural education. If the large reliance on off-budget funds is the main cause of undersupplied and underfunded education, one may expect the fiscal constraint account to be less relevant since the 2006 reform. Evidence for this claim is mixed so far. Sun et al. (2010) find that budgetary funds indeed have increased as a share of total educational expenditure and that schools with less government funding prior to the reform received more budgetary funds after the reform. However, they find little evidence that the 2006 reform has substantially increased total educational expenditure. Results from the difference in difference analysis show that counties that implemented the reform did not have a higher growth of educational expenditure than those had yet to implement the reform. Fan and Fu (2009) also conclude that government spending on rural education remains inadequate since the 2006 reform. Zhao et al. (2015) suggest that the concentration of financial transfers from the central and provincial government on lower-spending programs limits the equalization and growth effects of the 2006 reform. Taken together, the fiscal constraint account may be less relevant today than in the 1990s. Nonetheless, the problem of underfunded education still exists in many parts of China.

The weak incentive account shifts attention from fiscal constraint to local officials' unwillingness to prioritize on educational development. A large body of literature has recognized the importance of local officials in shaping local economic and social development. To align the interests and behaviors of local officials with the central state's reform and development agenda, the Chinese Communist Party (CCP) has resorted to the target-based cadre responsibility system (Edin 2003; Landry 2003; Whiting 2004). The system scores local officials based on their performance on a range of indicators. Education is often less important than other performance indicators such as GDP per capita, government revenue, business promotion, birth control, and social stability (Landry 2003; Liu and Tao 2007). The perceived importance of economic performance has induced "tournament competition" among local officials and turned their attention to economic growth (Li and Zhou 2005). Although there is much disagreement on which factors—local GDP growth, revenue growth, or political ties—actually matter for cadre promotion, few would dispute that education has a low priority for local officials. Some scholars have explicitly argued that the weak incentive among local officials toward education is the root cause of China's repeated failure to raise government expenditure on education to 4 percent of the GDP (Zhang and Jiang 2010).

A number of studies have empirically examined the impact of fiscal decentralization on educational expenditure. A common hypothesis in this literature is that fiscal autonomy at the local level has a negative impact on educational expenditure. This hypothesis is supported by a number of empirical studies. Defining local fiscal autonomy as the ratio of county and township self-raised funds to county and township expenditures, Yang and Ren (2015) find that a higher level of local fiscal autonomy is associated with a lower level of educational expenditure. Yin and Zhu (2011) present even more convincing evidence. Using county-level revenue and expenditure data, they find that the share of expenditure on GDP-enhancing activities has been on the rise, in contrast to the declining share of welfare expenditure. In particular, they analyze how county governments allocate what they call "newly disposable government revenue" (*zengliang shouru*), which better reflects the spending preference of local officials than the conventional measure of local fiscal autonomy. Measuring "newly disposable government revenue" as the portion of government revenue for a given year not included in the budget plan made in the beginning of the year, they find that county governments allocate a considerably smaller portion of "newly disposable government revenue" to education, compared to the share of education in the budgeted expenditure. County governments clearly favor investment in areas that promote economic growth. These findings clearly suggest that government expenditure on education cannot grow as fast as the GDP or government revenue. Other studies find similar productivist bias among local officials (Zhang and Jiang 2010).

If the fiscal constraint account applies more to the less developed areas in Central and Western China, the weak incentive account rejects the argument that development would solve the underfunding problem, based on the finding that government expenditure on education increases at a declining rate with GDP or government revenue growth. In China, the central leadership's presumably strong commitment to education is not matched by a strong fiscal capacity or a strong incentive to spend on education at the local level. Such a central-local relationship sets China apart from other East Asian societies and makes the existing East Asian welfare models less tenable for China, insofar as education is concerned.

4 Mobilization in Education

This chapter calls attention to mobilization as an important yet often over-looked dimension of China's central-local relationship. Bringing mobilization back in will shed new light on the nature and features of China's social policy implementation. Different from the weak capacity account or the weak incentive account, the mobilization account highlights the permeability of local officials' behaviors under different circumstances, which vary between a high-pressure situation and a low-pressure one. In a high-pressure situation, where there is tremendous top-down mobilization, local officials tend to adjust their priority and use formal and informal coping strategies to achieve under-funded or unfunded policy mandates. In a low-pressure situation, local officials probably behave in ways described by the weak fiscal capacity or the weak incentive account. The shift from a high-pressure situation (or period) to a low-pressure one will therefore bring about different behaviors of local officials and have different impacts on policy implementation. Taking mobilization into account, this chapter highlights volatility and irregularity as an important feature of China's social policy process, which defies the fixed, monolithic trend implied by the East Asian welfare models, the weak fiscal constraint account, or the weak incentive account.

Top-down mobilization is an intrinsic feature of China's central-local relationship because the CCP's institutionalized efforts to align the preferences and interests of local officials with the central leadership's agenda are at best partially successful. The CCP has relied on its firm control of cadre posts as well as the target-based cadre responsibility system to make local officials responsive to its development agenda. But as a large body of literature suggests, the institutionalized mechanisms do not always work as intended. For instance, based on the analysis of the career paths of prefecture-level mayors, Landry (2003: 51–52) concludes that although "the CCP may want to govern effectively," it is "proving less able to develop incentive mechanisms that reward officials who perform, and penalize those who do not." In a study of determinants of membership in the CCP's Central Committee, Shih et al. (2012) find that factional ties with various top leaders matter more for provincial leaders than their growth performance. They find evidence that the CCP effectively uses the cadre evaluation system to ensure that provincial leaders maximize revenue for the central government but find no evidence that the system rewards those who generate higher-than-average growth or higher-than-expected growth.

Another line of research focuses on local officials' actual behaviors under the cadre evaluation system. It has documented a wide range of gaming behaviors such as unintended consequences, including selective policy implementation, data falsification, and cover-up of problems (O'Brien and Li 1999; Cai 2000; Göbel 2011; Whiting 2004; Tsai 2008; Heberer and Trappel 2013; Gao

2015). Given the problem of information asymmetry across the party-government hierarchy, local officials have demonstrated a variety of gaming behaviors, ranging from benign ones to pernicious ones. They may perform slightly better than the targets although they can perform much better if they do not withhold their efforts. In contrast to such benign gaming behaviors, local officials are also found to engage in a variety of pernicious gaming behaviors, including putting on shows and/or hiding the flaws of sloppy work, and falsifying data (Gao 2015). The prevalence of gaming behaviors among local officials suggest that the cadre evaluation system has its limit in enforcing compliance in a fiscally decentralized system.

When the top leadership comes to realize the large gap between the policy goal and the actual implementation on the ground, a stronger push involving top-down mobilization and even blunt administrative measures often becomes necessary. In the education domain, the latter half of the 1990s featured intensive mobilization to achieve the goal of universalizing nine-year compulsory education nationwide by 2000. The plan was announced in 1993. Tailoring to China's uneven development across regions, the plan separated three policy zones. The first one, mapped to the eastern region, was home to 31 percent of the national population in 1995. It was economically and educationally more developed than other regions. The three centrally administered municipalities in this region—Beijing, Tianjin, and Shanghai—had already universalized nine-year education by 1994; the rest of the region was expected to do so by 1997. The second policy zone, or the central region, was home to 53 percent of the national population. As primary education had already been universalized, the goal for this region was to universalize junior secondary education by 2000. The third policy zone, or the western region, had a greater challenge in expanding education to remote villages in mountainous areas. For poor areas in this region, the goal was to universalize five- or six-year primary education by 2000 or three- or four-year primary education in extremely poor areas. It turned out that the latter half of the 2000s was a high-pressure period for local officials to "bring education up to standard."

A number of studies have documented the coping strategies of local officials since the mid-1990s. These studies cast doubt on the claim that local officials rely on pernicious gaming behaviors such as data falsification to fake achievement. Instead, they find evidence that local officials use a much wider range of formal and informal strategies to achieve the policy mandate assigned from above. Based on a 2004 survey of 20 township governments in ten provinces, Zhao Shukai (2007) finds that the overwhelming majority of surveyed township governments—80 percent—had unrepayable debts that carried forward since the mid-1990s. Bank loans constituted the single largest source of their debts. This strategy was widely used in China, including economically better developed areas. For instance, Kipnis and Li (2010: 331) find in Shandong that "every county we visited had several new schools recently built with loans, and in most counties these included a spectacular new senior middle school for which more than 100 million yuan had been borrowed."

Kipnis and Li (2010) also find other coping strategies. For instance, local governments mobilize resources from local enterprises to build schools. The mobilization is not a one-way process, but "the result of complex negotiations that relate the building of schools to reductions in the tax responsibilities of the enterprise towards the county government, land use deals that the government grants the enterprise, or other advantages" (Kipnis and Li 2010: 334). As part of the mobilization and diversification strategy, local governments allow schools to charge high fees in the name of "donation" or "school choice fee." It is common for highly sought after schools to reserve a number of places for families who are willing to pay a large sum of money. The targeted schools often pick the highest bidders through market-like competition (Wu 2012). It is also a widespread practice for a work unit (*danwei*) to provide a large sum of money or other types of assistance in the name of "joint construction" in exchange for a number of places for children from that work unit (Kipnis and Li 2010; Wu 2012). In some other cases, local governments are forced to spend out of their non-education budget on education if there is still a shortfall. Robinson and Yi (2008) report a case in which a county government had to tap into non-education budget to pay teachers not on government payroll.

Taken together, the preponderance of the evidence from empirical studies suggests that in high-pressure situations where there is tremendous top-down mobilization, local officials do treat education with a high priority. In contrast to the prediction that China's educational expenditure increases at a declining rate of GDP or government revenue growth, this chapter argues that during the mobilization period, China's educational expenditure grows not just in tandem with GDP or government revenue growth but likely at a considerably higher rate. In fact, based on their observation that the educational infrastructure in Shandong "has recently been catching up with, and in many cases exceeding, the facilities at public schools in Australia," Kipnis and Li (2010: 328) go so far as to question whether Chinese education is really underfunded. From the mobilization perspective, there is a need to rethink whether the prevailing perspectives, including the weak capacity account, the weak incentive account, and the gaming behaviors account, can sufficiently explain the growth of educational expenditure amidst intensive top-down mobilization.

5   THE 2012 MOBILIZATION AND ITS AFTERMATH: FINDINGS FROM OFFICIAL DATA

The most recent mobilization for education occurred in the second term of Hu-Wen's leadership, particularly in 2012 when China's government expenditure on education for the first time exceeded 4 percent of GDP. The strong push came from then Premier Wen Jiabao, who was determined to meet the target before he stepped down in 2013. Before 2012, he had already urged government from the central down to the county level to give priority funding to education. After 2012, the new leadership under Xi Jinping placed much less emphasis on education. The shift from mobilization to post-mobilization therefore provides a good opportunity to analyze the growth pattern of educational expenditure in a high-pressure situation versus a low-pressure situation, and to gain new insights on the volatile growth that is not sufficiently explained by the existing theories and models.

This chapter uses data published annually by China's Ministry of Education, National Bureau of Statistics, and Ministry of Finance on educational expenditure. The annual report provides rich information on the level and growth of government expenditure on education for each province as well as the nation. It also separates the contribution of central government from that of lower levels of the government. Two questions guide the analysis. The first one concerns the growth pattern of educational expenditure in China. Competing hypotheses can be derived from different theories and models. The East Asian welfare models would predict a *stable* growth of educational expenditure that is in tandem with GDP or government revenue growth; the gaming behaviors perspective probably makes the same prediction but points to data falsification as the primary reason; the weak capacity or weak incentive perspective would predict a *lower* growth of educational expenditure that lags behind that of GDP or government revenue. In contrast, the mobilizing account predicts a *volatile* growth across mobilization and post-mobilization periods.

The second question concerns the irregularities of educational expenditure as reflected in the official data. In addition to the variation in growth rates over time, this chapter also looks at other dimensions of irregularity, such as statistical adjustments in the scope of educational expenditure and changes in the number of non-compliance provinces over time. The existing theories and models have little to say on such irregularities. By comparison, the mobilization perspective argues that high-powered mobilization can be exhausting for local governments. It is therefore difficult to sustain mobilization for an extended period. Seen in this light, mobilization inevitably involves considerable irregularity in policy implementation.

Table 26.1 presents the growth of fiscal expenditure on education (*caizheng xing jiaoyu jingfei*) between 2010 and 2014. Fiscal expenditure on education includes budgetary expenditure on education, educational surcharges levied by local governments, user fees and social service fees charged by schools, and so on. In terms of the annual growth rate, Table 26.1 clearly shows a contrast between the mobilization period (2010–2012) and the post-mobilization period (2013–2014). During the mobilization period, fiscal expenditure on education grew rapidly year on year, nearly 20 percent in 2010 and 2012 and nearly 27 percent in 2011. This finding challenges the weak fiscal capacity account or the weak incentive account. Interestingly, the highest growth occurred in 2011 rather than 2012. The hyper growth was followed by a sharp decline, however. The year of 2013 registered a much lower growth of 10.1 percent. The slide continued in 2014 at 7.9 percent. Overall, the growth of fiscal expenditure on education has been highly volatile, changing from hyper growth (up to 27 percent) to single-digit growth in a short span of five

Table 26.1 Growth of fiscal expenditure on education in China: 2010–2014

	Total amount (billion yuan)	Annual growth (%)	% of GDP (unadjusted)	% of GDP (adjusted)
2010	1467.0	19.94	3.66	3.59[a]
2011	1858.7	26.70	3.93	3.84[a]
2012	2223.6	19.64	4.28	4.16[a]
2013	2448.8	10.13	4.30	4.16[a]
2014	2642.1	7.89	4.15	4.15

Data Source: "Quanguo jiaoyu jingfei zhixing qingkuang tongji gonggao" (Statistical Communiqué on National Educational Expenditure), jointly issued by the Ministry of Education, National Bureau of Statistics, and the Ministry of Finance

[a]China revised GDP figures for 2013 and preceding years based on the Third National Economic Survey; based on GDP figures from *China Statistical Yearbook 2015*, adjustments are made regarding fiscal expenditure on education as % for GDP for years 2010–2013

years. The volatile growth is not mainly due to economic slowdown. Instead, it is caused by the shift from tremendous mobilization for education to post-mobilization associated with leadership succession.

From Jiang-Zhu's time, China has aimed to raise government expenditure on education to 4 percent of GDP. The goal was never achieved under the Jiang-Zhu leadership. The Hu-Wen leadership also failed in their first term. Table 26.1 shows that the target was finally met in 2012, driven by the hyper growth of educational expenditure in Hu-Wen's second term. After 2012, the Xi leadership did not set any new goal for educational expenditure. China entered the post-mobilization period. The fiscal expenditure on education as a percentage of GDP leveled off, evidenced in the adjusted figures.

Table 26.2 presents the growth of public finance on education (*gonggong caizheng jiaoyu zhichu*) between 2010 and 2014. Public finance on education was identical with budgetary expenditure on education in 2011 and before but was expanded to include educational surcharges levied by local governments in 2012 and after. User fees and service fees charged by schools, which are included in fiscal expenditure on education, are not part of public finance on education. As Table 26.2 shows, the growth pattern of public finance on education closely resembles that of fiscal expenditure on education, except that the decline in 2013 and 2014 was even sharper at 5.4 percent and 5.5 percent, respectively. Notably, the growth of public finance on education was lower than that of GDP and government revenue. As a result, the share of education in total public finance decreased from the peak of 16.31 percent in 2011 down to 14.87 percent in 2012. The downward trend in the post-mobilization period is in line with the weak incentive account, although it cannot explain the upward trend during the mobilization period.

Three more points can be made. First, as explicitly stated in 2006, when the central government decided to establish an expense guarantee system for rural education, China had sought to expand the role of public finance for education while reducing the reliance on non-budgetary sources. The purpose was to cre-

Table 26.2   Growth of public finance on education in China: 2010–2014

	Public finance for education (unadjusted)			Public finance for education (adjusted)		
	Total amount (billion yuan)	Annual growth (%)	% of total public finance	Total amount (billion yuan)	Annual growth (%)	% of total public finance
2010	1349.0	18.13	15.76	1416.4[a]	18.28[a]	15.76
2011	1680.5	24.57	16.31	1782.2[a]	25.83[a]	16.31
2012	2031.4	25.79	16.13	2031.4	13.99[a]	16.13
2013	2140.6	5.37	15.27	2140.6	5.37	15.27
2014	2257.6	5.47	14.87	2257.6	5.47	14.87

Data Source: "Quanguo jiaoyu jingfei zhixing qingkuang tongji gonggao" (Statistical Communiqué on National Educational Expenditure), jointly issued by China's Ministry of Education, National Bureau of Statistics, and the Ministry of Finance

[a]Starting from 2012, China made a change to include educational surcharges as part of public finance for education; annual growth of public finance for education is revised using the 2012 definition for years 2010–2012 by including educational surcharges in public finance on education

ate a more regularized and stable funding mechanism for education. China was moving in this direction under the Hu-Wen leadership, but the trend was reversed under the Xi leadership, evidenced in the considerably lower growth of public finance on education (in Table 26.2) than that of fiscal expenditure on education (in Table 26.1) after 2012. The substantial difference between the two indicates a shaper decline of budgetary expenditure and educational surcharges than user fees and other non-budgetary sources. Instead of moving toward a more regularized funding system for education, China has been moving away from this goal since 2012. Second, the fact that China changed the definition of public finance on education in 2012 to inflate the growth rate of public finance on education is a telling evidence of the looming irregularities resulting from exhausting mobilization.[1] Third, as shown in Table 26.1 and Table 26.2, after years of hyper growth, there were clear signs of stress and strain in 2012, evidenced in the considerably lower growth of either fiscal expenditure or public finance on education. In other words, despite a strong push from then Premier Wen, it was increasingly difficult to sustain the momentum.

Table 26.3 shows the performance of each province in meeting the requirement of "three growths" (sange zengzhang). In 1993, China issued the National Guidelines on Educational Reform and Development, which set the requirement of "three growths": government expenditure on education should grow faster than government revenue; school funding on a per student basis should increase year by year; and teacher salaries and per student recurrent non-

---

[1]When calculating the growth rate of public finance on education, the official report used the expanded definition for 2012 but did not adjust the figure of 2011; thereby it inflated the growth rate to 25.79 percent.

Table 26.3 Provincial performance gap between annual growth rate of public finance for education and that of fiscal revenue: 2010–2014

	2010	2011	2012	2013	2014
Beijing	0.81	5.65	1.57	7.64	0.23
Tianjin	0.56	15.35	6.84	6.55	2.81
Hebei	−3.47	−5.85	15.67	−13.24	1.39
Shanxi	2.86	3.66	0.73	−4.47	−3.16
Inner Mongolia	6.10	−8.57	0.97	−5.69	1.04
Liaoning	−8.83	2.90	15.79	−15.13	−3.71
Jilin	0.08	2.52	12.84	−19.15	−9.04
Heilongjiang	1.27	1.35	34.87	−16.23	−2.14
Shanghai	2.79	7.57	4.05	−0.25	−9.69
Jiangsu	1.78	0.58	8.19	−4.08	−1.72
Zhejiang	1.22	0.55	1.49	0.05	2.74
Anhui	4.07	21.65	10.22	−5.76	−10.51
Fujian	2.34	−3.22	19.70	−9.87	−2.02
Jiangxi	0.14	44.50	17.51	−3.97	0.24
Shandong	4.39	18.74	11.01	−3.50	−2.93
Henan	0.30	18.64	15.76	−5.57	−9.62
Hubei	0.10	0.78	8.96	−7.83	3.98
Hunan	−6.65	2.40	26.99	−2.02	−6.92
Guangdong	0.05	7.55	9.66	1.06	−2.45
Guangxi	15.81	13.35	14.22	−8.96	1.75
Hainan	−18.27	−3.84	10.47	−12.61	−4.43
Chongqing	3.44	5.37	27.87	−13.76	−0.85
Sichuan	−8.41	−1.88	29.11	−6.05	−4.16
Guizhou	0.48	0.65	12.01	−4.84	0.30
Yunnan	−0.72	−1.59	21.94	−11.70	−3.20
Tibet	2.50	0.42	−0.16	0.04	9.97
Shaanxi	−13.40	8.52	7.86	−4.24	−6.88
Gansu	1.77	9.86	13.87	−10.21	−6.54
Qinghai	16.78	19.94	2.02	−36.42	15.93
Ningxia	−6.90	11.77	−2.43	−9.64	−11.75
Xinjiang	0.65	1.24	3.58	0.37	−30.57
Total number of underperforming provinces	8	6	2	25	20

Data source: "Quanguo jiaoyu jingfei zhixing qingkuang tongji gonggao" (Statistical Communiqué on National Educational Expenditure), jointly issued by China's Ministry of Education, National Bureau of Statistics and Ministry of Finance

personnel expenditure should increase year by year. The requirement of "three growths" was later written into the Compulsory Education Law. Among the "three growths," the first one is most crucial, since the other "two growths" to a large extent hinge on the first growth. Theoretically, the first one is also more relevant to the competing perspectives described earlier in this chapter. Table 26.3 therefore focuses on the first growth. It shows the difference between the growth rate of public finance on education and that of government revenue for each province.

Based on Table 26.3, the majority of provinces met the requirement during the mobilization period. In 2010, 8 provinces out of the total 31, or about one quarter, failed to grow their expenditure on education faster than their revenue. The number of underperforming provinces dropped to six in 2011, and further down to two in 2012. It is also worth noting that among those which met the requirement, most of them were slightly higher than the target in 2010. For instance, only three provinces had a higher growth of public finance on education than revenue growth by 5 or more percentage points in 2010; among the three provinces, two had a gap of more than 10 percentage points. The comparable figures increased to 14 and 8, respectively, in 2011, and to 20 and 17, respectively, in 2012. At the height of mobilization in 2012, over half of the provinces managed to grow their expenditure on education faster than their revenue by over 10 percentage points! Table 26.3 therefore shows a strong mobilization effect on the growth of educational expenditure in China.

The situation fundamentally changed after 2012. There was a surge in the number of underperforming provinces in 2013, up to 25 from only 2 in 2012. Despite a considerably lower growth of public finance on education in 2013 (and hence a lower base to calculate the growth for the subsequent year), the situation did not improve in 2014. The majority of provinces—20 out of 31, or nearly two thirds—fell into the category of policy non-compliance. The contrast between the post-mobilization period and the mobilization period is amply clear. Another sharp contrast is that in 2013, only two provinces had a faster growth of public finance on education than that of government revenue by 5 or more percentage points, and no province had a higher growth by 10 percentage points; in 2014, the comparable figures were 2 and 1, respectively. Overall, by the requirement of "three growths," non-compliance was an exception in 2012 and before but became prevalent after 2012. There was much volatility and irregularity in terms of policy conformity between the mobilization period and the post-mobilization period.

6   CONCLUSION AND DISCUSSION

This chapter analyzes the growth pattern of China's educational expenditure in recent years. A major finding is that China's government expenditure on education can grow at an astonishing pace, much higher than GDP or government revenue growth, when the strong push from the top leadership leads to intensive top-down mobilization. Equally important, the hyper growth is followed by a sharp decline, when the top leadership shifts priority from education to other policy areas. The transition from mobilization to post-mobilization involves considerable volatility and irregularity in the growth of educational expenditure. Seen in this light, the existing East Asian welfare models err in overestimating China's growth of educational expenditure in the post-mobilization period, while the weak capacity account and the weak incentive err in underestimating the growth in the mobilization period.

This chapter contributes to the literature by highlighting the need to view mobilization as an important feature of China's social policy process. As widely noted in the literature, China's social policy is jointly shaped by the centralized mandates and decentralized financing. Past research largely focuses on how decentralized financing makes local officials less willing to spend on education. Research in this line, however, overlooks the possibility that centralized mandates, together with centralized personnel control, can lead to intensive top-down mobilization and unprecedented growth of educational expenditure. The weak incentive account holds well in a low-pressure situation. However, it is ill-equipped to account for surging educational expenditures in periods of intensive top-down mobilization. There is a need for the mobilization perspective to sufficiently account for the volatile, irregular growth of educational expenditure between 2010 and 2014 in China.

This chapter also contributes to the debate on welfare state building in China. Much of the debate is centered on whether China should considerably increase its social expenditure or carefully avoid the so-called "high welfare trap". Using educational expenditure as an example, this chapter illustrates that the challenge facing China's welfare state building is not just the level of social expenditure but also the volatility and irregularity within the system caused by the alternation between mobilization and post-mobilization. As is clear in this chapter, both mobilization and post-mobilization are problematic. Too much mobilization can easily exhaust local governments. It is therefore not possible to sustain mobilization for an extended period, making the shift to post-mobilization inevitable. Post-mobilization, however, is also problematic, because local officials lack incentives to prioritize on social development. A prerequisite for welfare state building is a stable and regularized financing mechanism for social programs. Findings in this chapter suggest that China has a big challenge ahead in this regard. Results from official data show that China is not moving toward a more stable and regularized funding system for education.

Education should be one of the central focuses of China's welfare state building. Needless to say, education is among the most important institutions of the modern states. Its importance has not faded away. One of the most consistent findings in social sciences in many decades is the positive economic and social returns to education. Private benefits of education include labor market outcomes such as employability, higher earnings, less unemployment, labor market flexibility, and greater mobility, and nonmarket outcomes such as greater consumer efficiency and better health. Social benefits include higher productivity, higher net tax revenue, less reliance on government financial support, lower crime rates, less spread of infectious diseases, better social cohesion, and so on (Psacharopoulos 2006). In Europe, there is a renewed interest in education as deindustrialization, demographic changes, and fiscal constraints have jointly made the world's most comprehensive and sophisticated welfare regimes less tenable. The search for a viable alternative to the comprehensive, redistributive welfare state model and the neo-liberal approach to social welfare has led to the rise of the social investment approach since the late 1990s, which focuses on human capital investment. For China, the shift to post-mobilization after 2012 should raise concerns about education. Overall, China needs to replace mobilization-based policy implementation with a more regularized, sustainable, and equitable financing mechanism for education and other social programs.

References

Aspalter, Christian. 2001. Conservative Welfare State Systems in East Asia. Westport, CT: Praeger.

Aspalter, Christian. 2006. "The East Asian Welfare Model." *International Journal of Social Welfare* 15: 290–301.

Cai, Yongshun. 2000. "Between State and Peasant: Local Cadres and Statistical Reporting in Rural China." *The China Quarterly* 163: 783–805.

Edin, Maria. 2003. "Remaking the Communist Party-State: The Cadre Responsibility System at the Local Level in China." *China: An International Journal* 1: 1–15.

Esping-Andersen, Gøsta. 1990. *The Three Worlds of Welfare Capitalism*. Cambridge: Polity Press.

Esping-Andersen, Gøsta, Duncan Gallie, Anton Hemerijck, and John Myles. 2002. *Why We Need a New Welfare State*. Oxford: Oxford University Press.

Fan, Xianzuo, and Weidong Fu. 2009. "Nongcun yiwu jiaoyu xin jizhi: chengxiao, wenti ji duice" (The new system of rural compulsory education: effects, problems and solutions) *Huazhong shifan daxue xuebao (renwen shehui kexue ban)* 4: 110–120.

Gao, Jie. 2015. "Pernicious Manipulation of Performance Measures in China's Cadre Evaluation System." *The China Quarterly* 223: 618–637.

Göbel, Christian. 2011. "Uneven Policy Implementation in Rural China." *The China Journal* 65: 53–76.

Hannum, Emily. 1999. "Political Change and the Urban-Rural Gap in Basic Education in China, 1949–1990." *Comparative Education Review* 43: 193–211.

Hannum, Emily. 2003. "Poverty and Basic Education in Rural China: Villages, Households, and Girls' and Boys' Enrollment." *Comparative Education Review* 47: 141–159.

Heberer, Thomas, and Rene Trappel. 2013. "Evaluation Process, Local Cadres' Behaviour and Local Development Processes." *Journal of Contemporary China* 22: 1048–1066.

Hemerijck, Anton. 2015. "The Quiet Paradigm Revolution of Social Investment." *Social Politics* 22: 242–256.

Holliday, Ian. 2000. "Productivist Welfare Capitalism: Social Policy in East Asia." *Political Studies* 48: 706–723.

Jones, Catherine. 1990. "Hong Kong, Singapore, South Korea, and Taiwan: Oikonomic Welfare States". *Government and Opposition* 25(3): 446–462.

Jones, Catherine. 1993. "The Pacific Challenge." Pp. 198–217 in Catherine Jones (ed.) *New Perspectives on the Welfare State in Europe*. London: Routledge.

Kipnis, Andrew, and Shanfeng Li. 2010. "Is Chinese Education Underfunded?" *The China Quarterly* 202: 327–343.

Kwon, Huck-Ju. 2002. "Welfare Reform and Future Challenges in the Republic of Korea: Beyond the Developmental Welfare State?" *International Social Security Review* 55(4): 23–38.

Landry, Pierre F. 2003. "The Political Management of Mayors in Post-Deng China." *The Copenhagen Journal of Asian Studies* 17: 31–57.

Lee, James, James Midgley, and Yapeng Zhu. 2014. "Introduction." Pp. 1–15 in James Lee, James Midgley, and Yapeng Zhu (eds.) *Social Policy and Change in East Asia*. New York: Lexington Books.

Leung, Joe C. B., and Yuebin Xu. 2015. *China's Social Welfare*. Cambridge, UK: Polity.

Li, Hongbin, and Li-An Zhou. 2005. "Political Turnover and Economic Performance: The Incentive Role of Personnel Control in China." *Journal of Public Economics* 89 (9/10): 1743–1762.

Liu, Mingxing, and Ran Tao. 2007. "Local Governance, Policy Mandates, and Fiscal Reform in China." Pp. 166–189 in Vivienne Shue and Christine Wong (eds.) *Paying for Progress in China: Public Finance, Human Welfare, and Changing Patterns of Inequality*. London: Routledge.

Midgley, James. 1986. "Industrialization and Welfare: The Case of the Four Little Tigers." *Social Policy and Administration* 20: 225–238.

Midgley, James. 1995. *Social Development: The Development Perspective in Social Welfare*. Thousand Oaks, California: Sage.

Midgley, James. 1999. "Growth, Redistribution, and Welfare: Toward Social Investment." *Social Service Review* 73(1): 3–21.

Midgley, James. 2014. "Economic Turbulence and Social Welfare: Social Policy and Social Development Perspectives." Pp. 17–33 in James Lee, James Midgley, and Yapeng Zhu (eds.) *Social Policy and Change in East Asia*. New York: Lexington Books.

Morel, Nathalie, Bruno Palier, and Joakim Palme (eds.). 2011. *Towards a Social Investment Welfare State? Ideas, Policies and Challenges*. Bristol: Policy Press.

O'Brien, Kevin J., and Lianjiang Li. 1999. "Selective Policy Implementation in Rural China." *Comparative Politics* 31: 167–186.

Park, Albert, Scott Rozelle, Christine Wong, and Changqing Ren. 1996. "Distributional Consequences of Reforming Local Public Finance in China." *The China Quarterly* 147: 751–778.

Psacharopoulos, George. 2006. "The Value of Investment in Education: Theory, Evidence, and Policy." *Journal of Education Finance* 32: 113–136.

Robinson, Bernadette, and Wenwu Yi. 2008. "The Role and Status of Non-governmental ('daike') Teachers in China's Rural Education." *International Journal of Educational Development* 28: 35–54.

Shih, Victor, Christopher Adolph, and Mingxing Liu. 2012. "Getting Ahead in the Communist Party: Explaining the Advancement of Central Committee Members in China." *American Political Science Review* 106: 166–187.

Sun, Zhijun, Yuhong Du, and Tingting Li. 2010. "Yiwu jiaoyu caizheng gaige: zengliang xiaoguo yu fenpei xiaoguo" (The reform of financing compulsory education: the growth and distributional effects). *Beijing daxue jiaoyu pinglun (Peking University Education Review)* 8: 83–100.

Tang, Kwong-Leung. 2000. *Social Welfare Development in East Asia*. New York: St. Martin's Press.

Tsai, Lily L. 2008. "Understanding the Falsification of Village Income Statistics." *The China Quarterly* 196: 805–826.

Tsang, Mun C., and Yanqing Ding. 2005. "Resource Utilization and Disparities in Compulsory Education in China." *China Review* 5(1): 1–31.

West, Loraine A., and Christine P. W. Wong. 1995. "Fiscal Decentralization and Growing Regional Disparities in Rural China: Some Evidence in the Provision of Social Services." *Oxford Review of Economic Policy* 11: 70–84.

Weiss, Linda. 2000. "Developmental States in Transition: Adapting, Dismantling, Innovating, Not Normalizing." *Pacific Review* 13(1): 21–55.

Whiting, Susan. 2004. "The Cadre Evaluation System at the Grass Roots: The Paradox of Party Rule." Pp. 101–119 in Barry J. Naughton and Dali Yang (eds.), *Holding China Together: Diversity and National Integration in the Post-Deng China Era*. Cambridge: Cambridge University Press.

Wilding, Paul. 2000. "Exploring the East Asian Welfare Model." *Public Administration and Policy* 9: 71–82.

World Bank. 1985. *China: Issues and Prospects in Education*. Washington, DC: The World Bank.

Wong, Chack Kie. 2013. "The Evolving East Asian Welfare Regimes." Pp. 207–229 in Litao Zhao (ed.) *China's Social Development and Policy*. London and New York: Routledge.

Wu, Xiaoxin. 2012. "School Choice with Chinese Characteristics." *Comparative Education* 48: 347–366.

Xiao, Jin, and Zeyun Liu. 2014. "Inequalities in the Financing of Compulsory Education in China: A Comparative Study of Gansu and Jiangsu Provinces with Spatial Analysis." *International Journal of Educational Development* 39: 260–273.

Yang, Liangsong, and Chaoran Ren. 2015. "Sheng yixia caizheng fenquan dui xianxiang yiwu jiaoyu de yingxiang" (How China's sub-provincial fiscal decentralization affect local compulsory education). *Beijing Daxue Jiaoyu Pinglun (Peking University Education Review)* 13: 108–126.

Yin, Heng, and Hong Zhu. 2011. "Xianji caizheng shengchanxing zhichu pianxiang yanjiu" (A study of productive expenditure bias in county-level finance in China). *Zhongguo shehui kexue (Social Sciences in China)* 1: 88–101.

Zhang, Guang, and Yini Jiang. 2010. "Weishenme caizheng jiaoyu touru dabudao zhan GDP baifenzhisi de mubiao" (Why government expenditure on education cannot achieve the target of 4 per cent of GDP). *Gonggong Xingzheng Pinglun (Journal of Public Administration)* 3: 68–94.

Zhang, Xiaobo, and Ravi Kanbur. 2005. "Spatial inequality in education and health care in China." *China Economic Review* 16: 189–204.

Zhao, Litao. 2009. "Between local community and central state: financing basic education in China." *International Journal of Educational Development* 29: 366–373.

Zhao, Litao, Ling Li, Chen Huang, Naiqing Song, and Yiran Zhao. 2015. "Shengji jiaoyu jingfei tongchou gaige de fenpei xiaoguo" (The distributional effects of the provincial-level education finance reform). *Zhongguo Shehui Kexue (Social Sciences in China)* 11: 111–127.

Zhao, Shukai. 2007. "Rural Governance in the Midst of Underfunding, Deception and Mistrust." *Chinese Sociology and Anthropology* 39: 36–44.

CHAPTER 27

Labour Inspection in Contemporary China: Like the Anglo-Saxon Model, but Different

Wenjia Zhuang and Kinglun Ngok

1   Introduction

This chapter examines the lack of enforcement of China's increasing body of labour legislation, showing how, since the 1980s, the country's labour inspection system has evolved into a system resembling the Anglo-Saxon model—characterized by fragmentation and reactive regulatory practices—but with highly selective and non-coercive state enforcement. This "hybrid" labour inspection model stems from the combination of neoliberal reforms with the Leninist legacy of the authoritarian regime. More effective enforcement of labour law would, the authors suggest, require greater tripartite cooperation and social dialogue in the regulatory process and the involvement of an independently organized industrial force.

Since the mid-1990s in China, the role of labour legislation—starting with the 1994 Labour Law—in regulating labour relations has beckers at the Yue Yuen shoe factories in Dongguan exposed the widespread underpayment of legally mandated social insurance contributions in the Pearl River Delta (He and Li 2014). Why, despite the Government's increased efforts in passing labour legislation, has there been no effective enforcement of these laws?

This article seeks to explain this phenomenon by examining the role of labour inspection in China. Labour laws and regulations need to be monitored and enforced if they are to be effective; otherwise, sustainable compliance with labour standards is impossible to achieve. As Francis Blanchard, former Director-General of the International Labour Organization (ILO) said, "labour

W. Zhuang (✉) • K. Ngok
Center for Chinese Public Administration Research, School of Government, Sun Yat-sen University, Guangzhou, China

© The Author(s) 2019
J. Yu, S. Guo (eds.), *The Palgrave Handbook of Local Governance in Contemporary China*, https://doi.org/10.1007/978-981-13-2799-5_27

legislation without inspection is an exercise in ethics, but not a binding social discipline" (Von Richthofen 2002, preface to Part 1). Labour inspection implies the State's responsibility to monitor and enforce labour standards so that workers can enjoy decent working conditions. It is accepted as an effective tool to maintain order and stability in the labour market (Deakin and Wilkinson 2005).

Because of the diverse labour markets and political backgrounds, labour inspection regulatory practices vary across countries. Scholars have identified two contrasting models—the Anglo-Saxon model and the Latin model (see Piore 2005; Schrank and Piore 2007). In the Anglo-Saxon model—found in the United Kingdom and the United States, for example—the labour inspection system is fragmented, with different administrative agencies sharing responsibility for monitoring and implementing labour standards in distinct policy domains. Anglo-Saxon labour inspection is also complaint-driven, reactive, and focused on deterrence, and it opposes inspecting agencies and employers in an adversarial system. By contrast, the Latin model of labour inspection—as followed in France, Spain, and most Latin American countries—"combines a comprehensive body of employment standards and a flexible approach to its implementation" (Teague 2009). Specifically, in the Latin model, labour regulations are implemented and enforced by a single agency; labour inspectors have considerable discretion in implementing labour standards and are more concerned with developing preventive and proactive strategies in order to obtain sustainable compliance with standards. Noticeably, as administrative resources available for labour inspection have shrunk and workplace situations have become more complex and diversified, an increasing number of countries have begun to build "social dialogue" into the traditional top-down labour inspection approach, in an effort to apply innovative and flexible regulations to a rapidly changing labour market (see Amengual 2010; De Baets 2003; Karkkainen 2004; Piore and Schrank 2010; Schrank 2009; Teague 2009). In general, there has been a worldwide shift from the Anglo-Saxon labour inspection model towards more proactive models that are better at reconciling labour regulation with economic flexibility.

The reverse is true of Chinese labour inspection, however. As we show in this article, the Chinese system has been transformed from an integrated, stringent labour inspection model to a fragmented and reactive one—very similar to the Anglo-Saxon model—in which both employers and employees are under-represented and unvoiced in the inspection process. The transformation is incomplete, however, since the Chinese labour inspection model is also highly selective and non-coercive. This "hybrid" labour inspection model stems from the combination of neoliberal reforms with the Leninist legacy of the authoritarian regime. In order to build up an effective labour regulatory framework, however, that is compatible with the operation of a modern market economy, substantial tripartite cooperation and social dialogue should be brought into the regulatory process.

This article consists of five sections. The first describes the general transformation of the Chinese labour inspection system. The second section looks at the administrative restructuring of the system and its impact on the inspection agencies involved. The third section describes the institutional capacity and regulatory practice of the labour inspectorates and the core regulatory agencies involved in monitoring and implementing labour standards. The fourth section looks at the difficulties of building a preventive culture and social dialogue into the inspection process by rethinking the roles of trade unions, multinational corporations, and transnational civil society organizations. The last section contains a brief conclusion and suggests some directions for future reforms of the Chinese labour inspection system.

2   From "Command-and-Control" to "Social" Regulations

Labour inspection in the People's Republic of China first came into being in 1950 when the Government Administration Council, the predecessor of the State Council—that is, the Central Government—released the "Decision on the Working Relationship between Provincial-Government Labour Bureaux and Local State-Owned Enterprises", which authorized provincial labour bureaux to monitor the enforcement of labour standards in state-owned enterprises (SOEs), including in the areas of: occupational safety and health (OSH); social insurance; minimum wages; child and female labour; recruitment and dismissal; and collective contracts. On 17 September 1956, the State Council approved the "General Rule on the Ministry of Labour", making the Ministry of Labour the national agency responsible for labour affairs. The Ministry was tasked with leading and supervising work on labour issues in all State Council departments and guiding local labour bureaux in their work of monitoring compliance with labour standards inside SOEs, cooperative enterprises, joint state-private enterprises, and public institutions. In addition to the Ministry of Labour and its local branches nationwide, competent authorities in different industries—such as enterprise "administrative superiors"—were responsible in the planned economy for the everyday administration of OSH standards. Trade unions were also empowered to supervise compliance with labour standards. These agencies together constituted the "three-in-one" system of labour inspection in the planned economy: implementation of labour laws and regulations was (1) inspected (*jiancha*) by the labour administration on behalf of the State; (2) administrated (*guanli*) by industrial competent authorities; and (3) supervised (*jiandu*) by the trade unions. In this system, the central Ministry of Labour, as well as its local branches, played a leading role in the labour regulation process; by means of bureaucratic command—or even political order—the State successfully regulated labour relations. However, because of their role as the key state apparatus built to support the planned economy, the central Ministry of Labour and its nationwide branches were closely bound up with political goals such as public order and social stability and actually functioned as social control institutions (Burell 2001).

Things changed dramatically with the initiation of economic reform in 1978, after which the State was no longer the sole employer. With the nation-wide implementation of the employment contract system in the 1990s, hierarchical labour relations became contractual ones. Consequently, the daily administration of labour standards—mainly concerned with OSH—was split into two components: industry regulation by industrial competent authorities and self-regulation by enterprises. Then, in 1993, a new "four-in-one" combined system of labour inspection—(1) self-regulation by enterprises; (2) administration by industrial competent authorities; (3) inspection by the labour administration; and (4) supervision by trade unions—was formally introduced, with the issuance of the "Notice of the State Council on Strengthening Production Safety". In subsequent administrative reforms, a fifth layer of inspection was added—that of compliance by workers—thereby turning the system into a "five-in-one" model. Regardless of the changing terminology, the new labour inspection system was still dominated by the State.

However, from the 1990s onwards, the chain of command between the State and enterprises ceased to have much force, and the State gradually ceased to control the labour market, especially in terms of regulating wages and benefits, and working conditions. The resulting lack of regulation led to a revival of "sweat shops" in China (Chan 1993; Solinger 1995), triggering a dramatic spike in labour unrest in the 1990s (Lee 1995). In the face of this social instability, the State was obliged to acknowledge the important role played by laws and regulations and ushered in a wave of labour legislation, from the 1994 Labour Law to the 2007 Labour Contract Law and beyond (Ngok 2008). By 2014, the Chinese Government had set up a relatively comprehensive and multi-layered labour regulatory framework. Meanwhile, the function of labour administration had also been transformed, from micro-level supervision to macro-level guidance and regulation (Table 27.1).

Table 27.1 Transformation of the Chinese labour regulatory framework

Period	1950–1992	1993–2006	2007–2016
Institution	"3-in-1" labour inspection system	"4-in-1" and "5-in-1" labour inspection systems	Social regulation
Target	State-owned enterprises (SOEs)	State and non-state sector	Labour market
Role of state	Monitor	Supervisor	Regulator
Measure	Administrative	Mixed	Legal
Law/ regulation	Decision on the Working Relationship between Provincial-Government Labour Bureaux and SOEs (1950)	Notice of the State Council on Strengthening Production Safety (1993); Labour Law (1994); Law on Prevention and Control of Occupational Diseases (2001); Regulation on Labour Security Supervision (2004)	Labour Contract Law (2007, revised in 2012); Employment Promotion Law (2007); Law on Labour Dispute Mediation and Arbitration (2007); Social Insurance Law (2011); Law on Prevention and Control of Occupational Diseases (revised in 2011)

Generally speaking, the system of labour inspection in China has been trans-formed in two main ways since the initiation of economic reform in the late 1970s. First, China has moved towards becoming a new regulatory state, by reshaping the role of the state as social regulator and building institutions compatible with the operation of a modern market economy. Second, the Chinese Government is seek-ing to set up a labour regulation model that is rule governed and to which the traditionally bureaucratic command of the planned economy no longer applies.

The transformation, however, is incomplete. A series of administrative reforms has established a fragmented system of labour regulation, where differ-ent administrative agencies at the central level compete with each other to consolidate their own policy domains; this fragmentation is repeated at the local level. Also, the labour inspectorate, and its local branches—as the core agency of labour regulation—not only suffer from the same problems of shrink-ing staff and limited financial resources found in other developing countries but must also deal with constant political interventions from local governments.

3   Institutional Fragmentation and Competition for Regulatory Power

Since the late 1990s, "integrated labour inspection systems combining the major functional responsibilities of labour protection such as labour relations, occupational safety and health, general conditions of work and the fight against illegal forms of employment, are being set up in an increasing number of coun-tries" (Von Richthofen 2002, p. 146). An integrated institution has been iden-tified as the main characteristic of the Latin model, where "the whole of the labour code is meant to be enforced by a single agency, and that agency is formally responsible for ensuring compliance with all of the statutes and, typi-cally, with certain provisions of private collective bargaining agreements as well" (Piore 2005). Under the Latin model, labour inspectors can invoke any labour regulation when visiting the workplace (Teague 2009).

Since the late 1980s, however, labour inspection in China has been restruc-tured towards the opposite pole—the Anglo-Saxon model—whose main char-acteristic is institutional fragmentation. Under this fragmented approach, the duties of monitoring and enforcing labour regulations are spread over different administrative agencies, "each with its own system of inspection and with vary-ing types of judicial review and sanctions" (Piore 2005).

In the 1988 administrative restructure, the Ministry of Labour (formerly named the "Ministry of Labour and Personnel") was split into two separate ministries, the Ministry of Labour and the Ministry of Personnel. The new Ministry of Labour was responsible for broad labour protection issues, including matters such as OSH in almost all industries; wages and benefits; and working conditions (State Commission Office for Public Sector Reform 1990, p. 501) and had three separate inspection bureaux: Occupational Safety and Health; Safe Production of Boiler Pressure Containers; and Occupational Safety and Health in the Coalmining Industry (ibid., pp. 165–167).

In the administrative reforms that followed, however, most of the Ministry of Labour's inspection duties were taken over by other ministries. In the 1998 administrative restructuring, inspection related to occupational health (including the prevention and cure of occupational diseases and occupational health in the coalmining industry) was taken over by the Ministry of Health (which in 2013 was to become the National Health and Family Planning Commission—NHFPC); and inspection related to boiler pressure container production was taken over by the General Administration of Quality Supervision, Inspection and Quarantine (GAQSIQ) agency. The remaining inspection duties in the area of occupational safety (including in the coalmining industry) were taken over by the former Occupational Safety Bureau, under the State Economic and Trade Commission. They were subsequently taken over by the newly established State Administration of Occupational Safety agency, which was to become the State Administration of Coal Mine Safety agency in later administrative reforms (Zhu and Ngok 2007). In 2011, the revised Law on Prevention and Control of Occupational Diseases further confirmed this fragmentation, reassigning responsibility in the area of OSH: the NHFPC is now responsible for policy and standard-setting, the Ministry of Human Resources and Social Security (MOHRSS)—which replaced the Ministry of Labour and Social Security in 2008—for work-related injury dispute resolution and compensation and the AQSIQ for workplace inspections.

In addition to matters of OSH, administration of the employee social insurance system has also been fragmented. Although the MOHRSS is the principal agency for social insurance generally, in some areas the collection of social insurance contributions has in practice been carried out by the Local Tax Bureau (Liu 2011). In addition, because of the "Hukou" system of residency permits,[1] most migrant workers continue to be excluded from the basic medical insurance programme for urban employees, relying instead on the New Rural Cooperative Medical Scheme, which was originally targeted at rural residents and administratively managed by the NHFPC (Tian et al. 2013).

As of 2014, there are six central agencies responsible for monitoring the implementation of labour laws and regulations. These agencies (with the exception of the Local Tax Bureau) have been active in promoting legislation aimed at consolidating their power over their own policy domains (Table 27.2) and justifying their demands for larger budgets (Ma and Hou 2005, 2009; Ma 2009a, b). Under the legislation, the agencies are authorized to make separate policies to facilitate the enactment of labour standards in their own policy domains and are thus able to levy considerable non-budgetary and non-institutional funds (Ma and Ni 2008). The trend towards horizontal decentralization was officially endorsed by the State Council in 2004, with the Regulation on Labour Security Supervision, which specified that responsibility

---

[1] For more information on the Chinese "Hukou" household registration system.

Table 27.2 Agencies in the labour inspection system in contemporary China, as of 2014

Policy domain		Responsibility	Agency
	Labour contracts, regulations on wages and working hours, protection of special groups (e.g. child and female labour), job security, and so on.	Policymaking and implementation	Ministry of Human Resources and Social Security
	Transfer payments/Social insurance	Collection, payment and inspection of social insurance contributions	Ministry of Human Resources and Social Security
		Medical insurance for some migrant workers	National Health and Family Planning Commission
		Collection of social insurance contributions in some areas	Local Tax Bureau
Working conditions	Occupational health (including occupational injury and disease)	Evaluation and prevention	National Health and Family Planning Commission
		Dispute resolution and compensation	Ministry of Human Resources and Social Security
		Workplace inspection	General Administration of Quality Supervision, Inspection and Quarantine
	Occupational safety	Coalmining industry	State Administration of Occupational Safety (later became State Administration of Coalmine Safety)
		Agriculture	Ministry of Agriculture
		Construction	Ministry of Housing and Urban-Rural Development
		Special equipment production	General Administration of Quality Supervision, Inspection and Quarantine

for supervising implementation of OSH policies should be taken over by the departments in charge of health, occupational safety, and other departments, in accordance with the relevant laws. The trend was also confirmed in subsequent legislation; in 2007, the Labour Contract Law gave the departments in charge of construction, health, occupational safety, and other departments the power to supervise the implementation of the employment contract system within their administrative mandates.

As a result, Chinese labour regulation, like other segments of the emerging administrative state, suffers from extremely fragmented politics, characterized by protracted bargaining among interested bureaucracies (see Pearson 2005, 2007). In this context, labour inspectorates are assigned only a minor role in the enforcement of employment rights legislation, with considerable constraints being placed on their roles.

The fragmented power structure creates extra administrative and bargaining costs. Firstly, all ministries have set up local branches with their own staff, training programmes, equipment, offices, and budgets. Administrative duplication leads to a waste of human and material resources as well as inefficiency. Secondly, and more importantly, these ministries have split the single issue of labour regulation six ways, which has led to conflicting policies. To overcome such problems, the MOHRSS, which still has principal responsibility for making regulatory policy, has to bargain with the other agencies in order to design policies with them. This process of making collective decisions incurs high transaction costs. For example, competition between the MOHRSS and the Local Tax Bureau over the power to collect social insurance contributions has endured for more than a decade (Liu 2011), as has the fight between the MOHRSS and the health agency for sole competence as the medical insurance authority (Tian et al. 2013). When agencies fail to reach a consensus, the MOHRSS has to appeal to the State Council for political support. At the local level, competition between these agencies has become even fiercer. Agencies with overlapping responsibilities often divide a single case into separate ones, appear to be insensitive to issues that do not fall within their narrow mandate, and shift the blame onto each other. In most cases, workers in difficulty have to struggle to navigate the complicated division of responsibilities and often receive conflicting replies from different agencies.

4   Agency, Institutional Capacity, and Regulatory Practices

As the core agencies in a fragmented system, labour inspectorates at all levels of labour administration are assigned the major responsibility of monitoring the implementation of labour laws and regulations. At the central level, the Labour Inspection Division, under the Legal Department of the former Ministry of Labour and Social Security, had been in charge of nationwide labour inspection for several decades. In 2008, when the Ministry of Personnel and the Ministry of Labour and Social Security were combined to form the MOHRSS, the Labour Inspection Division was upgraded to become the present, relatively independent Labour Inspection Bureau. The upgrade to "bureau" status has brought some changes in vertical governance, facilitating top-down mobilization, training, and supervision. In particular, since 2011—when wage arrears were classified as a criminal offence—the Bureau has been playing an active role in promoting a mechanism for administrative/judiciary collaboration, with the aim of strengthening the coercive power of its local branches. However, the Central Bureau does not have complete control over its local branches, owing to the principle of decentralized management.

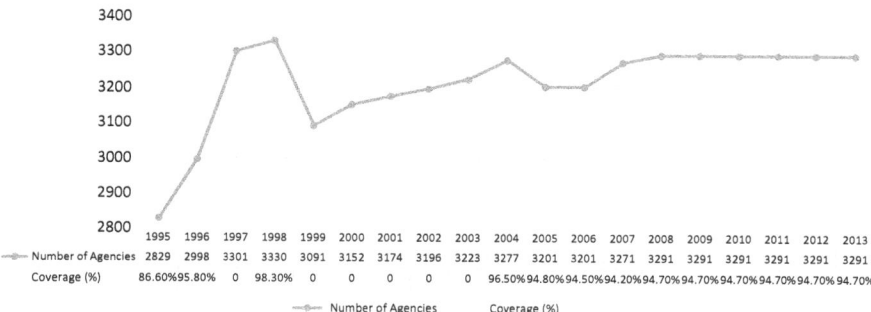

Fig. 27.1 Statistics on labour inspectorates in China, 1995–2013. Source: *Annual Report of Labour Affairs* (Ministry of Labour and Social Security 1997a–2007a; Ministry of Human Resources and Social Security 2008a–2013a). Note: "Coverage" means the percentages of administrative units (e.g. provinces, cities, and counties) that had set up labour inspectorates by the year in question. Missing values are replaced with 0

At local level, in 1993, some 15 provinces had no specific body for labour inspection. City-level and county-level labour administrations did not establish labour inspectorates until 1994. In 1995, the number of local labour inspectorates increased significantly to 2829. And by 1996, local labour inspectorate coverage—that is, the percentage of administrative units such as provinces, cities, and counties that had set up labour inspectorates—exceeded 95 per cent for the first time, bringing the total number of inspectorates to 2998 (Ministry of Labour and Social Security 1997a).[2] In the first decade of this century, a nationwide network of labour inspectorates had finally come into being, with the number of inspectorates maintained at a mean of 3242 and coverage fluctuating between 94.2 and 96.5 per cent (Fig. 27.1).

However, this substantial process of institution building was not as remarkable as the statistical figures seem to indicate. In fact, most of the so-called labour inspectorates were joint agencies (shared with other divisions inside local labour departments) rather than separate agencies. As of June 2005, only 67 per cent of the formal agencies were separate and distinct agencies with special administrative resources. Some provinces, such as Hainan and Tibet, did not have even one separate agency (Table 27.3). The sluggishness in setting up a separate inspection agency in these areas was largely related to underdevelopment of the local labour market, and the focus of local departments on employment creation. With no separate agency, most labour complaints relating to infringement of rights were defused—or even repressed—outside the formal resolution channel.

The increase in the number of labour inspection agencies has not necessarily led to a corresponding improvement in capacity. Institutional capacity, which is claimed to be a critical determinant of service quality (see Ingraham et al. 2003), includes

---

[2] Under the 2004 Regulation on Labour Security Supervision, labour administrations at county level and above were required to establish a corresponding labour inspectorate.

Table 27.3 Local labour inspectorates in China, as of June 2005

Municipality/province/ autonomous region	Required number of agencies	Number of formal agencies	Coverage by formal agencies (%)	Number of separate agencies	Number of joint agencies	Percentage of separate agencies
Beijing	20	20	100.00	20	0	100.00
Tianjin	22	22	100.00	22	0	100.00
Shanghai	20	20	100.00	20	0	100.00
Chongqing	43	43	100.00	37	6	86.05
Gansu	122	122	100.00	104	18	85.25
Guangdong	151	148	98.01	125	23	84.46
Henan	183	159	86.89	134	25	84.28
Anhui	116	67	57.76	56	11	83.58
Hubei	121	106	87.60	85	21	80.19
Shandong	162	125	77.16	100	25	80.00
Fujian	95	94	98.95	70	24	74.47
Guizhou	101	70	69.31	52	18	74.29
Jiangsu	130	120	92.31	87	33	72.50
Hebei	193	191	98.96	138	53	72.25
Inner Mongolia	114	84	73.68	59	25	70.24
Zhejiang	103	93	90.29	65	28	69.89
Guangxi Zhuang	128	119	92.97	78	41	65.55
Yunnan	146	140	95.89	86	54	61.43
Hunan	137	133	97.08	81	52	60.90
Jiangxi	117	97	82.91	59	38	60.82
Heilongjiang	174	112	64.37	66	46	58.93
Liaoning	130	20	15.38	11	9	55.00
Xinjiang Uighur	114	114	100.00	62	52	54.39
Shaanxi	109	88	80.73	46	42	52.27

(continued)

Table 27.3 (continued)

Municipality/province/ autonomous region	Required number of agencies	Number of formal agencies	Coverage by formal agencies (%)	Number of separate agencies	Number of joint agencies	Percentage of separate agencies
Shanxi	136	98	72.06	47	51	47.96
Sichuan	207	192	92.75	88	104	45.83
Jilin	60	50	83.33	21	29	42.00
Qinghai	59	42	71.19	15	27	35.71
Ningxia Hui	28	28	100.00	3	25	10.71
Hainan	27	1	3.70	0	1	0.00
Tibet	82	7	8.54	0	7	0.00
Total	3350	2725	81.34	1837	888	67.41

Source: Report on institution building of local labour inspectorates (Ministry of Labour and Social Security 2005a)

Note: The "number of formal agencies" (i.e. formal labour inspectorates with both offices and staff) is the sum of the number of separate agencies and joint agencies. It differs from the total number of labour inspectorates given in annual reports, which includes agencies without offices or staff

aspects such as financial management, human resource management, and leadership (Honadle 1981; Heckman 2007; Andrews and Boyne 2010). Sufficient and stable budgetary appropriations, well-designed human resource practices, and autonomous leadership all contribute to high organizational performance. Labour inspection agencies in China, however, not only face the fundamental problem of resource limitations, such as diminishing budgets and a reduced staff but also suffer from political interventions from local governments.

4.1   Financial Resources

While actual public expenditure on labour inspection at local level (including the province, county, and city levels) steadily increased overall from 1995 to 2009, when seen as a percentage of expenditure on labour affairs, it has been in dramatic decline since 1999. Indeed, since 2006, the approximate proportion has remained as low as 2.5 per cent (Fig. 27.2). On the one hand, this tendency shows that local institution building has been ongoing. On the other hand, given the overall increase in budget appropriations to labour policy, in the context of promoting a larger labour market, the relative decline in the budget proportion shows that labour inspection was not assigned high priority within local labour

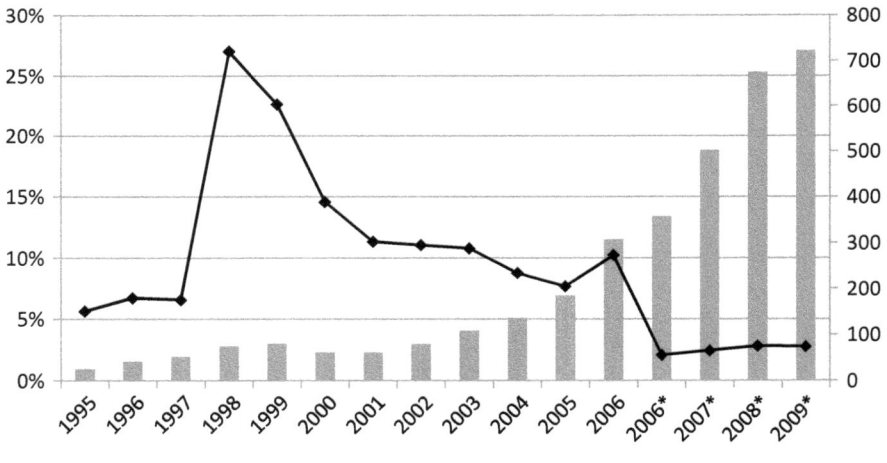

Public Expenditure on Labour Inspection (1 million yuan, inflation-adjusted)

Public Expenditure on Labour Inspection as percentage of Expenditure on Labour Affairs (%)

Fig. 27.2 Public expenditure on labour inspections at local level, 1995–2009. Source: *Statistics of Local Finance* (Department of the Exchequer and Budget Department, Ministry of Finance 1995–2009). Note: For years marked "*", statistics were collected using the 2007 newly adjusted budgetary accounting method, which made the statistics more scientific and precise by using a functional rather than economic classification. See Ministry of Finance (2006) for more details. The expenditure data is inflation-adjusted, using 1995 as the reference year

administrations. In addition, not all local labour inspectorates received financial support from the State. As of June 2005, among the 2419 local labour inspectorates, 141 received budgetary appropriations, while 203 had self-controlled revenue and expenditure. In Hebei Province, only 25 per cent of labour inspectorates were allocated a full appropriation (Ministry of Labour and Social Security 2005a). In fact, most labour inspectorates in China were understaffed, underfinanced, and underequipped at this time (Cao 2006a); in Yunnan Province, for example, most labour inspectors still travel by bicycle when they are on duty, and in some districts of Ningxia Hui Autonomous Region, local labour inspectorates have no equipment, offices, or even staff (Shao and Li 2006).

4.2   Human Resources

Since the 1990s there has been a continuous decrease in the human resources of labour inspectorates. The ratio of workers to labour inspectors has fallen steadily since 1994, dropping in 1998 for the first time below the benchmark level of 20,000 for transition economies (Fig. 27.3).[3] However, more than half the labour inspectors were part-time staff. By 2013, the ratio of workers to *full-time* labour inspectors was still a long way from the 20,000 benchmark, with one full-

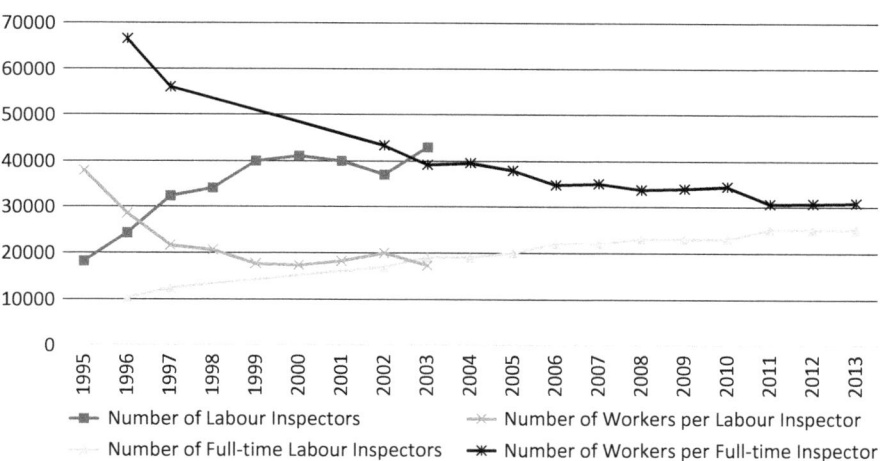

Fig. 27.3   Estimated no. of workers per labour inspector, 1995–2013. Source: *Annual Report of Labour Affairs* (Ministry of Labour and Social Security 1997a–2007a; Ministry of Human Resources and Social Security 2008a–2013a); and *China Labour Statistical Yearbook* (Ministry of Labour and Social Security 1997c–2007c; Ministry of Human Resources and Social Security 2008c–2014c)

[3] The ILO set up benchmarks for the human resources of labour inspectorates according to the stage of economic development of the country: one inspector per 10,000 workers in industrial market economies; one per 15,000 in industrializing economies; one per 20,000 workers in transition economies; and one per 40,000 workers in less developed economies (see ILO 2006, p. 4).

time inspector for 30,791 workers. According to the Administrative Rules Governing Labour Inspectors in China, part-time inspectors are only authorized to handle single-item cases that are relevant to their own jobs. Their powers are highly limited and they can only assign punishments when working with a full-time inspector. In most provinces, municipalities, and autonomous regions, only full-time labour inspectors are empowered to deal with inspection cases.

To get around the official restrictions on personnel quotas, since 2001, the Central Government has allowed local labour departments to recruit assistant labour inspectors, who are authorized to travel in pairs to supervise the enforcement of labour laws and regulations concerning employment contracts, wages and benefits, working hours, social security, workplace regulations, and so on. However, the recruitment criteria are still unclear; most assistant inspectors are unqualified and undertrained, and are not authorized to assign administrative punishments (Cao 2007). Because of these problems, relations between labour inspectorates and employers have become more adversarial in some districts.

4.3   Leadership

The central Labour Inspection Bureau does not, in practice, have a great deal of control over its local branches. Unlike other streamlined and vertically controlled bureaucracies in China, such as the Customs Bureau, Trade and Industry Bureau, Tax Bureau and Transport Bureau, the function of labour administrations (including labour inspectorates) is still based on localized management, which means that their funding, leadership and decision-making are all dominated by local governments. Labour administration chiefs at county level and above must be appointed by the corresponding-level local government. However, local governments have a particular incentive to focus on local economic growth and employment promotion rather than on labour inspection, since their respective leaders are compared and evaluated on the economic results they achieve (see Li and Zhou 2005; Qian et al. 2006). This local protectionism is considered by some to be one of the most challenging obstacles to labour inspectors collecting evidence and enforcing the law in cases of infringement of labour rights (Lai 2014).

Central Government has also tended to assign greater priority to employment promotion than to labour inspection, as demonstrated by the agenda-setting work of the former Ministry of Labour and Social Security (2005b, 2006) over the past decade, and that of the newly established Ministry of Human Resources and Social Security (2011) for the forthcoming years. This is for both economic and political reasons. First, the legitimacy of the current regime relies heavily on economic performance (see Nathan 2003); thus, labour policy is required to be employment-oriented and supportive of economic development (Ngok 2006). Second, unemployment is treated as a potential source of social and even political instability by decision-makers, and employment-promotion policies are accepted as effective preventive measures.

4.4   Regulatory Practices

With limited administrative resources and a lack of qualified staff, coupled with both political and administrative constraints on leadership, the regulatory practices of labour inspectorates at grassroots level are highly selective, reactive and non-coercive.

Since the late 1990s, labour inspectorates have been largely reliant on reactive inspection (see Fig. 27.4). From the late 1990s to the early 2000s, nearly 50 per cent of the cases settled by the labour inspectorates were detected through complaints and reporting. The number of such cases passed the benchmark of 60 per cent in 2003 and continued to rise, reaching a peak of 99 per cent in 2006–2009, when a series of newly enacted labour policies resulted in the exponential growth of labour petitions. During this period, labour inspectorates were mostly interested in reducing their large caseloads. However, the profile of complaints may not accurately map the relative severity of problems across industries, while reactive inspections will not identify unvoiced problems (Weil 2008). With their heavy workload of complaints and reported violations, labour inspectors are unable to actively check for further

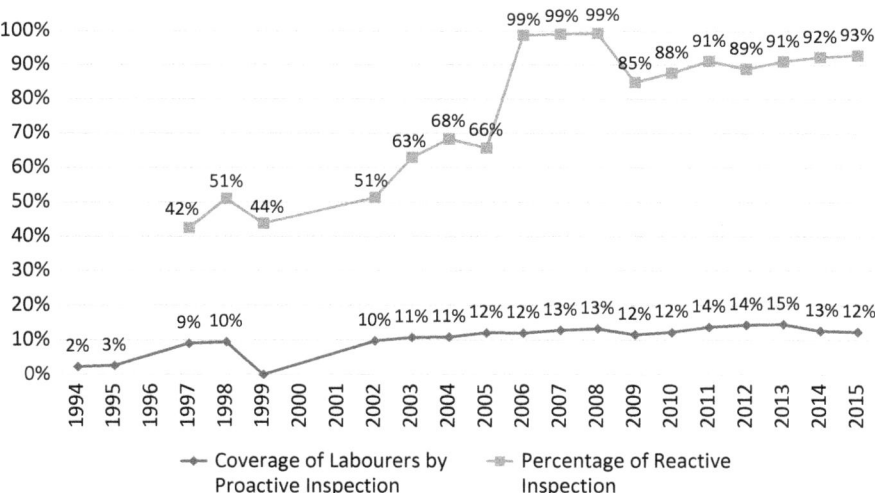

Fig. 27.4 Reactive and proactive labour inspection in China, 1994–2015. Source: *Annual Report of Labour Affairs* (Ministry of Labour and Social Security 1997a–2007a; Ministry of Human Resources and Social Security 2008a–2015a); and *China Labour Statistical Yearbook* (Ministry of Labour and Social Security 1997c–2007c; Ministry of Human Resources and Social Security 2008c–2016c). Note: "Coverage of workers by proactive inspection" is calculated by dividing the number of workers involved in proactive inspection by the total number of workers in the same year. The percentage of reactive inspection is calculated by dividing the number of cases settled through inspection based on reporting (or complaints) by the total number of cases settled

offences by carrying out proactive inspections. From 1994–2015, there was no significant increase in the coverage of workers by proactive inspections (Fig. 27.4). From 2003 to 2015, coverage remained relatively stable, fluctuating between 11 and 14 per cent, with an average of 12 per cent.

With limited administrative resources, labour inspectorates have to schedule proactive inspections according to seasonal changes in the labour market. These include: a rise in labour recruitment after the Chinese Spring Festival, when most migrant workers return to cities looking for work; the employment of illegal workers (mostly child labour) in the summer; working conditions in the autumn; and wages and benefits in the winter.[4] Top-down administrative campaigns are conducted to highlight the need for proactive labour inspections; in some districts, labour inspectorates only carry out proactive inspections during these top-down inspection campaigns.[5] Even during the campaigns, the inspections are highly selective regarding their targets, with small and medium-sized manufacturing firms spared and larger ones targeted.[6] To address this issue, since 2009, MOHRSS has promoted a new programme aimed at improving the human resource management of labour inspectorates. An experiment consisting of building a "twin-network" labour inspection system, consisting of both a physical and virtual inspection network, was carried out in several cities (MOHRSS 2009). The physical network of labour inspectorates reflects the distribution of workers at grassroots level, with each administrative unit allocated one full-time inspector and at least two assistant inspectors, and is linked by computer to MOHRSS. The Ministry, in turn, monitors digitized information collected by the physical labour inspectorates. This initiative has already been placed on the agenda to be promoted throughout the whole country in the *12th Five-Year Plan of Human Resources and Social Security*, covering the period 2011–2015 (MOHRSS 2011). However, due to the shortage of full-time inspectors and the high turnover rate of part-time inspectors, the twin-network system has not significantly increased labour inspection coverage at the lowest local levels of labour administration. By June 2013, the twin-network coverage at municipal level was only 65.77 per cent, while the county-level and township-level allocation of networks was even lower (Zhao 2013).

Besides these reactive and selective characteristics, labour inspection in China also suffers from administrative and political obstacles that discourage coercive, stringent, or punitive enforcement of labour law and regulations. Most of the time, complaints and reports from workers are not immediately taken up by labour inspectors, who try to persuade workers to negotiate with their bosses through labour arbitration panels, in an attempt to reduce their

---

[4] Interview with a labour inspector in a municipal labour bureau on 4 August 2008. Also see Zhao (2010), interview with Chief of Yunnan Provincial Department of Human Resources and Social Security; and Department of Human Resources and Social Security in Fujian Province (2011).

[5] Interview with chief of a county-level labour bureau, 29 July 2008.

[6] Interviews with directors of three manufacturing firms, 25 July 2008.

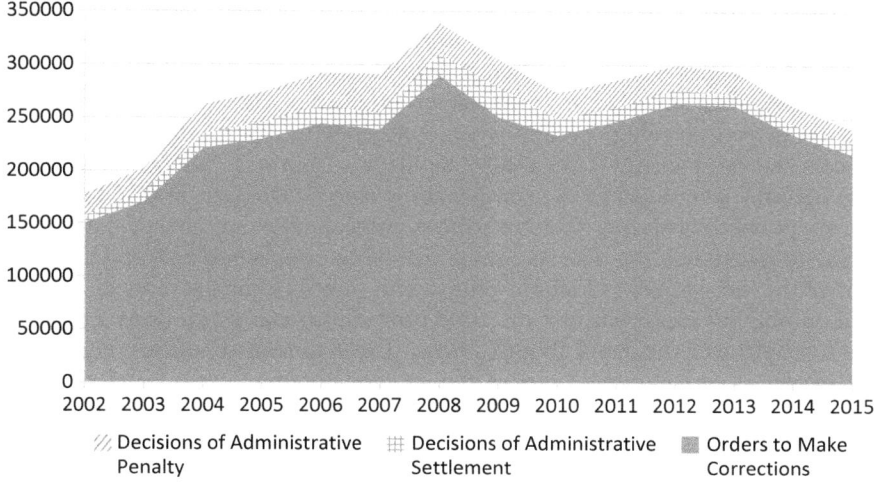

Fig. 27.5 Statistics on settlement of cases by labour inspection, 2002–2015. Source: *China Labour Statistical Yearbook* (Ministry of Human Resources and Social Security 2008c–2016c)

caseloads.[7] Even when cases are accepted by labour inspectors, final settlements often consist of "soft" penalties, which provide a weak deterrent (Fig. 27.5). From 2002–2015, in over 80 per cent of the cases settled by labour inspectorates every year, employers were ordered to correct matters within a specified time limit (so-called improvement notices), while nearly 5.1 per cent of the cases involved an administrative settlement and roughly 9 per cent an administrative punishment. As the chief of a municipal labour inspectorate explained:

"It is nearly impossible to settle with an administrative penalty or other punishment, since there is always a powerful municipal leader behind a large company. Whenever we rule on a case, there is unjustifiable obstruction from the municipal leadership, who claims that making corrections and providing pedagogical advice is more important than punishment, and instructs us not to do anything that might have a negative impact on the functioning of enterprises. Thus, even when we do impose a punishment, it is often the minimum penalty".[8] In Yunnan Province, some county-level governments have even stipulated that all cases involving an administrative penalty of over 2000 yuan should be reported to the chief of the county labour bureau and the head of the county government before the decision is made. In most cases, such applications have been refused by the county governments in a kind of "non-decision".[9]

[7] Interview with the chief of a county-level labour bureau, 29 July 2008.
[8] Interview with the chief of a municipal labour bureau, 4 August 2008.
[9] See interview with the chief of the Yunnan Provincial Department of Human Resources and Social Security, in Zhao (2010).

The pedagogical approach alone is not enough to increase employers' compliance. In most successful cases in other countries, sanctions always serve as a first step before advice/assistance is offered. A balanced combination of sanctions and advice/assistance can lead to sustainable compliance outcomes, in which the improvement of working conditions is reconciled with firms' search for competitiveness and productivity (Pires 2008). Similarly, in Europe, "administrative fines have become operational tools to ensure compliance" (De Baets 2003). However, due to political obstacles, Chinese labour inspectorates are almost completely unable to function in this way. As a result, the labour inspection system is failing to control the infringement of labour rights, with only a negligible reduction in the total number of cases, even after the 2008 campaign entailing top-down mobilization to implement the new Labour Contract Law and related policies (Fig. 27.6). Specifically, issues regarding payment of wages and minimum wage standards so far

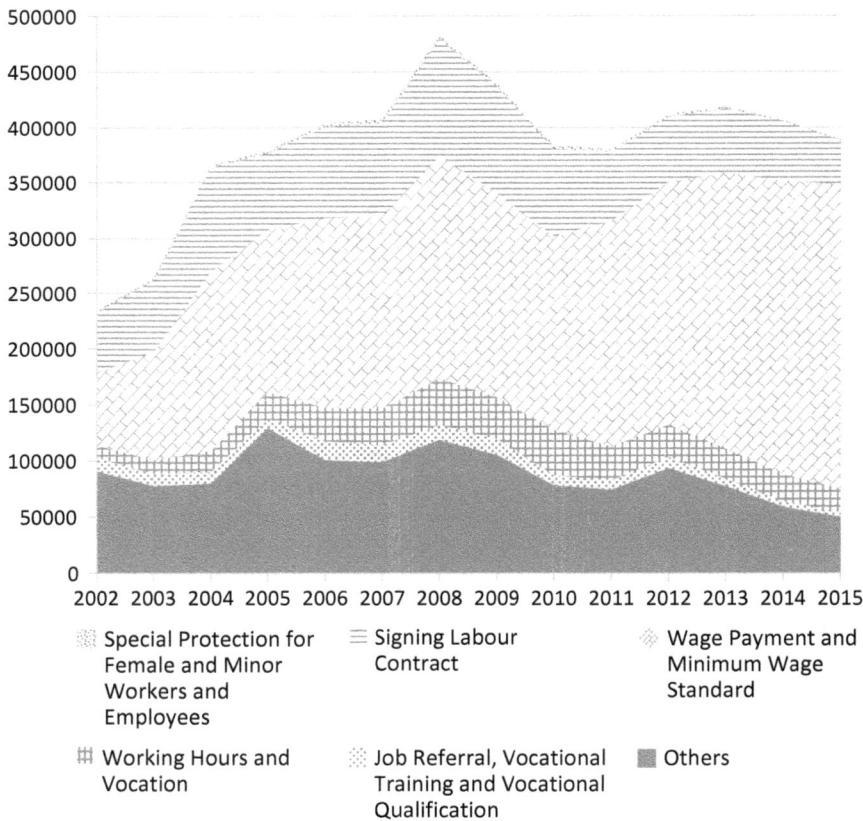

Fig. 27.6 Statistics on type of cases settled by labour inspection, 2002–2015. Source: *China Labour Statistical Yearbook* (Ministry of Human Resources and Social Security 2008c–2016c)

constitute the highest proportion of cases, while the signing of employment contracts remains a serious problem even after the enforcement of the Labour Contract Law (also see Cooney et al. 2012).

To sum up, in the face of limited administrative resources and political obstacles, Chinese labour inspection suffers from the same weaknesses as the Anglo-Saxon model (see Schrank and Piore 2007; Teague 2009); it is complaints-based and reactive, results in conflict between labour inspectorates and employers, and gives "soft sticks" to labour inspectors in cases where an employer is found to have violated labour regulations. It also reveals a dilemma: decentralization has led to a pro-business local political economy and soft enforcement of labour laws, while local labour inspection agencies are confronted with widespread labour grievances and complaints and have to rely on reactive measures to maintain social stability. As Lee (2007) noted, "this tension between accumulation and legitimation, between the interests of the local and the central government, gives rise to endemic violation of labour rights and entitlements".

5   ALLIES OF THE LABOUR INSPECTORS AND TRIPARTITE COOPERATION

In recent years, traditional top-down labour inspection has been labelled ineffective, since it only covers a tiny proportion of worksites (Estlund 2005). In order to move towards a more proactive, flexible, and self-regulated approach, labour inspectors need to "work with employers and employees in setting goals and targets with regard to compliance with labour market standards and then helping them to be met" (Teague 2009). For this reason, an increasing number of countries are establishing a tripartite mechanism in their labour inspection systems at the national, regional, and sectoral levels (Von Richthofen 2002), which aims to institutionalize "social dialogue" among inspectors, employers, and employees in the inspection process and encourages these actors to negotiate with each other in making workplace standards, practices, and policies consistent with the aims of labour regulation. Through tripartite cooperation, workers and employers are more likely to remain committed to complying with laws, regulations, and workplace rules. For this reason, building a tripartite mechanism into the labour inspection system is widely accepted as an innovative approach that can help to overcome the fundamental problems of labour inspection, such as diminishing budgets, a shrinking staff, and an increasingly complicated and difficult regulatory environment.

In China, although the Government has made efforts to establish a tripartite framework for labour relations, the participants (trade unions, employers, and the state) have been "neither independent of one another nor ... the independent participants imagined by labour relations theory" (Ngok 2008). In most resolutions of conflicts of interest in the workplace, trade unions and workers are separate players (Chen 2010). Trade unions only represent workers when there is little risk of accentuating their dual—but contradictory—identity as both state apparatus and labour organization and hence conflicting with the State (Chen 2003). Most of the time, although they are authorized by laws and regulations to monitor the enactment of labour regulations, grassroots trade unions dare not—and in some cases even refuse to—assist labour inspectors (Cao 2006b). Another reason for this is that the presidents of grassroots trade unions are nominated by the managements of enterprises, and the salaries of ordinary members of grassroots trade unions are paid by the employers (Xin 2006). This close relationship between grassroots trade unions and employers makes it impossible to introduce any substantial tripartism into labour relations and build a proactive inspection system.

Trade unions' ambiguous position in labour relations forces workers to seek the involvement of independent labour organizations, outside the framework of the All-China Federation of Trade Unions (ACFTU). In addition, in recent years, multinational corporations with subcontractors in China—such as Reebok, Nike, and Adidas—have entered into a traditional tripartite relationship with global and national labour rights non-governmental organisations (NGOs), in order to better monitor the implementation of labour standards and the principles of corporate social responsibility in their subcontractors' workplaces. These global networks of labour rights NGOs have also been active in promoting Chinese workers' solidarity, by helping them to set up independent and democratically elected trade unions in workplaces in China's coastal provinces. However, these potential allies of government labour inspectors remain unrecognized by the Chinese Government. While the ACFTU pushes for the organization of trade unions and faster expansion of union membership, it strategically tries to incorporate emerging labour organizations into the fold of the ACFTU (see Cheng et al. 2010). The reason for the communist regime's insistence on monopolizing the representation of the working class through the ACFTU network is rooted in "both its entrenched Leninist political tradition and [its] current developmental strategy" (Chen 2007). For the regime, independent unionism equates to a potentially subversive threat to the political order, as well as to the legitimacy of the Communist Party.

Owing to the ambiguous role of trade unions and the exclusion of unofficial labour organizations from the tripartite mechanism, it will be difficult to institutionalize "social dialogue" in the Chinese labour inspection system, which remains bogged down in a reactive model.

6   CONCLUSION

When the labour inspection system was first established in the People's Republic of China in the 1950s, it appeared to be a combination of integrated institutions and stringent regulations in which the former Ministry of Labour took charge of the whole labour regime. In the following three decades, the function of labour inspection developed along the lines of the Latin model, in which the central labour department and its local branches had sole authority in monitoring labour relations under the planned economy. However, the economic reforms since the

Table 27.4 The typology of labour inspection systems and the case of China

Characteristics	Latin model	Anglo-Saxon model	The case of China
Countries	France, Spain and most Latin American countries	United Kingdom, United States, and so on.	China since the late 1980s
Goal	Conciliation	Deterrence	Deterrence
Philosophy	Tutelary	Adversarial	Adversarial
Jurisdictions	Unified authority	Division of labour	Fragmented authorities
Organization	Professional	Bureaucratic	Localized/politicized bureaucratic
Approach	Proactive	Reactive	Reactive
Tools	Carrots and sticks	Sticks	"Soft sticks"
Mechanism	Pedagogical measure	Prosecutorial measure	Selective enforcement

Note: The classification of the Latin and Anglo-Saxon models is an adapted version of the stylized summary by Schrank and Piore (2007, p. 15, Table 1)

late 1970s, along with a series of administrative restructurings, reshaped the Chinese labour inspection system along the lines of the Anglo-Saxon model (Table 27.4). The regulatory institution has become increasingly fragmented, and inspection has become reactive and complaint-based. Lastly, both employers and employees are under-represented in the inspection process. This transformation is in contrast to the Latin model, in which tripartite cooperation and social dialogue are encouraged to facilitate top-down enforcement by the state. Nonetheless, the transformation to the Anglo-Saxon labour inspection model is incomplete; a "hybrid" model has emerged, in which state enforcement of labour law remains non-coercive, with employers who violate labour law often protected from severely punitive sanctions, and selective, with workplace inspections focusing mainly on the most obvious regulatory problem areas.

Although inspectors have refrained from imposing severe penalties, in order to protect capital and promote GDP growth, periodical top-down inspection campaigns have sought to improve the working and living conditions of migrant workers, with the aim of redressing widespread labour grievances and maintaining a harmonious society. These campaigns differ from routine inspections, as they take administrative resources from different bureaucratic agencies and temporarily reallocate them to the most contentious areas. For example, the State has launched a set of special campaigns to inspect cases of migrant workers having their wages reduced, or delayed, before the Chinese Spring Festival each year. Similarly, whenever serious accidents implicating production safety occur, special campaigns are promoted, with all the relevant agencies mobilized by the State Council to collaborate with each other. Although these top-down movements may help improve the system of labour regulation in the short term, they fail to induce sustainable compliance with labour standards in the workplace in the long term, because independent representatives of both employees and employers are absent from the inspection process.

The incomplete transformation to the Anglo-Saxon model stems from the combination of neoliberal reforms with the Leninist legacy of the authoritarian regime. The administrative reforms since the 1980s have been driven by marketization, requiring "the overhaul of the administrative system in order to provide a set of institutions compatible with a market economy" (Ma and Zhang 2009). This is especially true of the administrative reforms carried out since 1998, which have been characterized by the explicit goal of creating a new administrative state to better serve the market economy (Lan 1999; Zhu and Ngok 2007; Yang 2001, 2004; Zheng 2004). This neoliberal reform led the Government to withdraw from direct intervention in the market and limit its administrative control over market operations. In such a context, state-enforced labour inspection is expected to avoid any negative impact on economic growth. The transformation of the labour regulatory framework has thus been driven by the directives of the party-state, leading to an imbalance between labour protection and economic growth (Ngok 2008). The extent of neoliberal reform is restricted by the Leninist legacy of the authoritarian regime; even though the State has undertaken a series of adaptive measures aimed at strengthening its governing capacity and legitimacy, it remains reluctant to allow an independently organized industrial force to become involved in labour policy. Specifically, the Government has been very active in passing legislation stipulating workers' individual rights, but it still refuses to empower them with collective rights, that is, the right to organize and to bargain collectively with their employers (Chen 2007). Although there is a widely established, official network of ACFTU unions, with almost universal membership, it was established not by the workers themselves but by the State, which claimed to represent the working class, as a way of controlling the industrial force (Chen 2007). In the absence of independent representation of the labour force, social dialogue in the regulatory process is virtually impossible. And without the "bottom-up" contribution of the industrial force to labour policy implementation, and substantial tripartite cooperation in the inspection process, the Government's efforts to achieve effective enforcement of labour laws will inevitably be unsuccessful.

With these challenges, any further transformation towards the Anglo-Saxon model will remain limited. Nonetheless, given the recent momentum by China's new leaders, since the 18th National Congress of the Communist Party of China in 2012, in pushing through further neoliberal economic reforms, while sticking firmly to political tradition, it is probable that the Chinese labour regime will continue to develop its own distinctive "hybrid" labour inspection model, which incorporates new ways of managing conflict, the collective power of workers, and the greater presence of multinational corporations.

REFERENCES

Amengual, M. 2010. Complementary labor regulation: the uncoordinated combination of state and private regulators in the Dominican republic. *World Development* 38(3):405–414.

Andrews, R., and Boyne, G. A. 2010. Capacity, leadership, and organizational performance: testing the black box model of public management. *Public Administration Review* 70(3):443–454.

Baets, P. D. 2003. The labour inspection of Belgium, the United Kingdom and Sweden in a comparative perspective. *International Journal of the Sociology of Law* 31(1):35–53.

Burell, M. 2001. The rule-governed state: China's labor market policy, 1978–1998. *Statsvetenskapliga Institutionen.*

Cao, X.H. 2006a. "An analysis of grass roots labour supervision in China", in Journal of China Institute of Industrial Relations (in Chinese) 20(6): 59–62.

Cao, Y.L. 2006b. "Why the trade unions fail to supervise in enterprises", in Modern Miner (in Chinese) (9): 47.

Cao, H.T. 2007. "Assistant inspector, to 'assist' or to 'inspect'?", in People's Daily (in Chinese), 1 November 2007.

Chan, A. 1993. Revolution or corporatism? Workers and trade unions in post-mao China. *Australian Journal of Chinese Affairs* 29(29): 31–61.

Chen, F. 2003. Between the state and labour: the conflict of Chinese trade unions' double identity in market reform. *China Quarterly* 176(176):1006–1028.

Chen, F. 2007. Individual rights and collective rights: labor's predicament in China. *Communist and Post-Communist Studies* 40(1):59–79.

Chen, F. 2010. Trade unions and the quadripartite interactions in strike settlement in China. *China Quarterly 201*(201):104–124.

Cheng, J. Y. S., Ngok, K., and Zhuang, W. 2010. The survival and development space for China's labor NGOs: informal politics and its uncertainty. *Asian Survey* 50(6):1082–1106.

Cooney, S., Biddulph, S., and Zhu, Y. 2012. Law and fair work in China. *Social Science Electronic Publishing.*

Deakin, S., and Wilkinson, F. 2005. *The Law of the Labour Market: Industrialization, Employment, and Legal Evolution.* Oxford University Press.

Department of Exchequer and Department of Budget in the Ministry of Finance. 1995–2007. Statistics of local finance (1995–2007). *Beijing, China Financial & Economic Publishing House.*

Department of Human Resources and Social Security, Fujian Province. 2011. "Outline of labour security inspections in 2011", available at: http://www.fjlss.gov.cn/action/xxgk/xxgk_article_content.action?aid=29588&flag=infoRoot [accessed 20 May 2011].

Estlund, C. 2005. Rebuilding the law of the workplace in an era of self-regulation. *Columbia Law Review 105*(2):319–404.

He, D., and Li, W.F. 2014. "Workers continue strike over unpaid welfare benefits" in *China Daily*, 23 April 2014. Available at http://www.chinadaily.com.cn/china/2014-04/23/content_17455846.htm [accessed 29 September 2014].

Heckman, A. C. 2007. Does management matter? Testing models of government performance.

Honadle, B. W. 1981. A capacity-building framework: a search for concept and purpose. *Public Administration Review* 41(5):575–580.

ILO. 2006. Strategies and practice for labour inspection. Document GB.297/ESP/3. *Governing Body*, 297th Session, Geneva.

Ingraham, P. W., Joyce, P., and Donahue, A. K. 2003. Government performance: why management matters. *Policy Sciences* 38(4):293–298.

Karkkainen, B. C. 2004. New governance in legal thought and in the world: some splitting as antidote to overzealous lumping. *Minnesota Law Review* 89(2):471–497.

Lai, X. 2014. "How difficult to make 'criminal punishment on wage arrears' into enforcement?" in Xinhua News (in Chinese), 16 January 2014. Available at: http://news.xinhuanet.com/legal/2014-01/16/c_118996191.htm [accessed 21 January 2014].

Lan, Z. 1999. The 1998 administrative reform in China: issues, challenges and prospects. *Asian Journal of Public Administration* 21(1): 29–54.

Lee, C. K. 1995. Production politics and labour identities: migrant workers in South China. *China Review* 15.1–15.28.

Lee, C. K. 2007. *Against the Law: Labor Protests in China's Rustbelt and Sunbelt.* University of California Press.

Li, H., and Zhou, L. A. 2005. Political turnover and economic performance: the incentive role of personnel control in China. *Journal of Public Economics* 89(9–10): 1743–1762.

Liu, J.Q. 2011. "Resources, Incentives and Sectoral Interests: A Longitudinal Study of Collecting Systems of Social Insurance Contributions in Urban China (1999–2008)", Social Sciences in China (in Chinese) (3): 139–156.

Ma, J. 2009a. "The dilemma of developing financial accountability without election", in Australia Journal of Public Administration 68(1):62–72.

Ma, J. 2009b. "'If you cannot budget, how can you govern?' A study of the state capacity of China", in *Public Administration & Development* 29:9–20.

Ma, J., and Hou, Y. 2009. Budgeting for accountability: a comparative study of budget reforms in the United States during the progressive era and in contemporary China. *Public Administration Review* 69(s1):S53–S59.

Ma, J., and Ni, X. 2008. Toward a clean government in China: does the budget reform provide a hope? *Crime Law & Social Change* 49(2):119–138.

Ma, J., and Zhang, Z. 2009. Remaking the Chinese administrative state since 1978: the double-movements perspective. *Graduate School of Public Administration Seoul National University, 23.*

Ma, J., and Hou, Y. 2005. "From *budgetary process to policy process: A case study of two Chinese provinces*", in *Comparative Economic and Social Systems (in Chinese),* (5):64–72.

Ministry of Finance. 2006. "Scheme on Reforming the Classification of Governmental Revenue and Expenditure," Available at: http://www.fjlss.gov.cn/action/xxgk/xxgk_article_content.action?aid=29588&flag=infoRoot [accessed 21 January 2014].

Ministry of Human Resources and Social Security. 2008a–2012a. Annual Report of Labour Affairs 2008–2012.

Ministry of Human Resources and Social Security. 2008c–2012c. China Labour Statistical Yearbook 2008–2012. Beijing, China statistics press.

Ministry of Human Resources and Social Security. 2009. "Notice of Conducting Experiment in Building Double-Networks of Labour Inspection".

Ministry of Human Resources and Social Security. 2011. The Twelfth Five-Year Plan of Human Resources and Social Security 2011–2015.

Ministry of Labour and Social Security. 1997a–2007a. Annual Report of Labour Affairs 1997–2007.

Ministry of Labour and Social Security. 1997c–2007c. China Labour Statistical Yearbook 1997–2007. Beijing, China Statistics Press.

Ministry of Labour and Social Security. 2005a. Report on institution building of local labour inspectorates.

Ministry of Labour and Social Security. 2005b. The Tenth Five-Year Plan of Labour and Social Security 2001–2005.

Ministry of Labour and Social Security. 2006. The Eleventh Five-Year Plan of Labour and Social Security 2006–2010.

Nathan, A. J. 2003. Authoritarian resilience. *Journal of Democracy 14*(1):6–17.

Ngok, K. 2006. "Marketization and governance transformation: A case study of the central labour administration", in Jun M. and Hou, Y.L. (eds): Public Management Research, Shanghai, Shanghai People's Press 4: 63–83.

Ngok, K. 2008. The changes of Chinese labor policy and labor legislation in the context of market transition. *International Labor & Working Class History 73*(1): 45–64.

Pearson, M. M. 2005. The business of governing business in China: institutions and norms of the emerging regulatory state. *World Politics 57*(2): 296–322.

Pearson, M. M. 2007. Governing the Chinese economy: regulatory reform in the service of the state. *Public Administration Review 67*(4): 718–730.

Piore, M. J., and Schrank, A. 2010. Toward managed flexibility: the revival of labour inspection in the latin world. *International Labour Review 147*(1): 1–23.

Piore, M.J. 2005. Looking for flexible workplace regulation in Latin America and the United States. Paper presented at conference on Labour Standards Application, Buenos Aires, Nov.

Pires, R. 2008. Promoting sustainable compliance: styles of labour inspection and compliance outcomes in Brazil. *International Labour Review 147*(2–3): 199–229.

Qian, Y., Roland, G., and Xu, C. 2006. Coordination and experimentation in m-form and u-form organizations. *Journal of Political Economy 114*(2): 366–402.

Schrank, A. 2009. Professionalization and probity in a patrimonial state: labor inspectors in the Dominican republic. *Latin American Politics & Society 51*(2): 91–115.

Schrank, A., and Piore, M. J. 2007. Norms, regulations and labor standards in Central America. *Apoptosis An International Journal on Programmed Cell Death 15*(1): 71–82.

Shao, F., and Li, X.Y. 2006. "The formation, development and improvement of labour inspection institution in China", in *The Journal of Finance and Economy in Yunnan* (in Chinese) 21(1): 96–99.

Solinger, D. J. 1995. The Chinese work unit and transient labor in the transition from socialism. *Modern China 21*(2): 155–183.

State Commission Office for Public Sector Reform. 1990. The Chinese governmental institutions. Beijing, China Economic Publishing House.

Teague, P. 2009. Reforming the Anglo-Saxon model of labour inspection: the case of the Republic of Ireland. *European Journal of Industrial Relations 15*(2): 207–225.

Tian, P., Zuo, L., and Hu M. 2013. "Fight Between Two Ministries Intensifies", in *Caijing* (in Chinese), 4 June 2013. Available at: http://english.caijing.com.cn/2013-06-04/112867819.html [accessed 1 October 2014].

Von Richthofen, W. 2002. Labour inspection: a guide to the profession.

Weil, D. 2008. A strategic approach to labour inspection. *International Labour Review* 147(4):349–375.

Xin, S.J. 2006. "The problems of and solutions to trade unions' supervision in labour protection at the enterprise level", in *Trade Union's Tribune* (in Chinese) 12(6): 34–35.

Yang, D.L. 2001. "Rationalizing the Chinese state: The political economy of government reform", in Chao C.M. and Bruce D. (eds): *Remaking the Chinese state: Strategies, society, and security*. London, Routledge 19–45.

Yang, D.L. 2004. Remaking the Chinese leviathan: Market transition and the politics of governance in China. Stanford, CA: Stanford University Press.

Zhao, D.C. 2010. "The dilemma of 'a big cart pulled by a small horse' in regulation", in *Magazine* Oriental Outlook (in Chinese), 26 February 2010. Available at: http:// news.sohu.com/20110226/n279543248_1.shtml [accessed 20 May 2011].

Zhao, X.K. 2013. "Harmonious and stable in general, the long-term mechanism takes shape—a midyear report on national industrial relation and migrant workers," in *China Labour And Social Security News* (in Chinese), 21 August 2013. Available at: http://www.MOHRSS.gov.cn/SYrlzyhshbzb/dongtaixinwen/shizheng-yaowen/201308/t20130821_111042.htm [accessed 21 January 2014].

Zheng, Y.N. 2004. Globalization and state transformation in China. Cambridge, Cambridge University Press.

Zhu, G., and Ngok, K. 2007. Marketization, globalization and administrative reform in China: a zigzag road to a promising future. *Social Science Electronic Publishing* 73(2): 217–233.

PART VIII

Urbanization and Governance

From Local Government-Led to Collaborative Governance: The Changing Role of Local Governments in Urbanization

Hui Wang and Shenghua Lu

1   INTRODUCTION

China has accelerated its urbanization since the 1990s, its urbanization rate leaping from 29.04% in 1995 to 57.4% in 2016. While driving the large-scale migration of rural population to cities, the urbanization has expanded urban entities and urban space. This round of urbanization is a typical local government-led urbanization. As legal subjects of land expropriation and transfer, the local governments levied the land from farmers with low compensation and resettlement costs on the one hand and transferred land use rights to land use developers to obtain extra budgetary income on the other hand. Meanwhile, land has become a key bargaining chip for regional "race-to-bottom" investment attraction as the local governments have deliberately lowered industrial land prices to attract foreign investment, promote local economy, and develop tax bases (Tao et al. 2009; Wang and Tao 2013). It is under this government-led "Land Expropriation—Land Selling" (LELS) Model that China boosted its urbanization and industrialization for more than a decade; therefore, China has become a middle-income country in its urbanization rate, industrial structure, and people's income. However, two major dimensions of China's urbanization, "population urbanization" and "space urbanization," have shown severe contradictions and problems, and they are related to China's traditional local government-led urbanization model, more or less.

H. Wang (✉) • S. Lu
Department of Land and Resource Management, Zhejiang University,
Hangzhou, China
e-mail: wanghuidn@zju.edu.cn

© The Author(s) 2019
J. Yu, S. Guo (eds.), *The Palgrave Handbook of Local Governance in Contemporary China*, https://doi.org/10.1007/978-981-13-2799-5_28

First, under the current land expropriation system, low compensation deprived the farmers, in particular the farmers in underdeveloped areas, of their means of survival when they lost their land, as it meant they lost employment opportunities. More seriously, the landless farmers did not benefit from value-added land benefits or the fruits of urbanization. So, how to compensate the farmers in the expropriation and demolition of land has been a social issue in recent years. Second, administrative power was mainly exercised on "land urbanization," so "population urbanization" obviously lagged behind "space urbanization" in speed, leading to "land urbanization, not population urbanization." It created many desolate cities, which are known as "haunted cities" in China, in urbanization as land resources were wasted to a large extent, and it hindered the flow of labor; therefore, much labor was still in the primary industry. Finally, in the LELS Model, local governments tended to depend heavily on unsustainable land finance. Meanwhile, they were already in heavy debt with land loans, posing a huge risk for the entire financial system.

Governments at all levels have introduced a series of policies, laws, and reforms to address these problems in the land system; however, the focus was on changing the local government-led urbanization model. If the local governments continued to push forward urbanization as leaders with administrative forces, the LELS Model would be maintained and the problems could not be properly tackled. We found out that the changes in government roles actually did not slow down urbanization but, rather, helped solve the problems in current urbanization. The new-type urbanization in the Zhejiang public-private partnership (PPP) model and the urbanization of spontaneous farmers and collaborative governance in the Nanhai Model are successful cases. The former found a solution for the local governments to alleviate their dependence on land finance as the collaboration between the governments and social capital compensated the capital shortage in urban construction, while the latter created a win-win situation for local governments and farmers as farmers benefitted from value-added land benefits. It is our view that China's urbanization would be more healthy and sustainable if local governments transformed from leaders to collaborators and governors to help form mutual promotion and governance between governments and the society.

2   LOCAL GOVERNMENT-LED URBANIZATION AND ITS DRIVING FORCES

2.1   Local Government-Led "Land Urbanization"

In China's rapid urbanization, local governments played a leading role, which had a lot to do with China's special land system. The urban land in China belongs to the country, the rural land to village collectives. Most of the land needed for urban expansion and industrial park construction came from rural collective land, which was expropriated by the governments before it could be developed and sold. The 2004 Amendment to the Constitution endowed local governments with the rights to levy collective land from village collectives and farmers within public interests. Although China had a large population and scarce land, the unequal urban and rural dual land system facilitated local governments to forcibly expropriate land from farmers with low compensation. And due to the land expropriation rights granted by the law, local governments could compensate and place the landless farmers based on the original land uses, with compensation only equivalent to six to ten times the annual returns of farmland. The land expropriation system ensured enough land for construction, which prevented China from falling into economic stagnation with high land price due to land scarcity (Fig. 28.1). With the expansion of urban space and accelerated infrastructure construction since the mid- to late 1990s, more land was expropriated, leading to a huge number of landless farmers. China expropriated land annually that amounted to 2.4–3 million mu (1 mu equaling 0.067 ha) from 1999 to 2002, and about 2–3 million farmers lost or partially lost land each year. By 2006, the number of landless farmers in China was more than 40 million, and it would increase to 70 million in the next 10–15 years.

On the other hand, the local governments monopolized the primary market of land transfer, and the supply of construction land was manipulated by the local governments. The local government first expropriated the land at low cost and transferred the land use rights to land-using units after the leveling of land and building of infrastructure facilities. Between 2000 and 2015, the land for construction experienced an increase of about 35.09 million mu from 543.09 million mu to 578 million mu, that is, an annual increase of 2.34 million mu. Another means of urban expansion by the local governments included

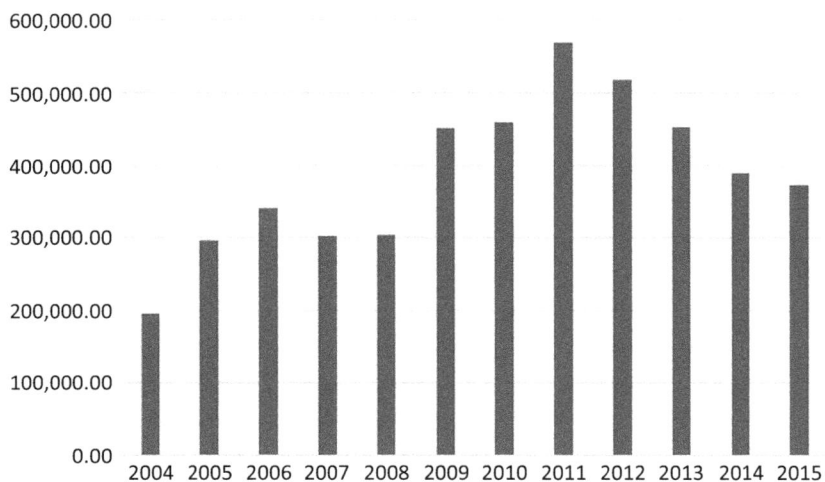

Fig. 28.1 National land expropriation in 2004–2015. Source: *China Land and Resources Statistical Yearbook*

rural and suburban areas into an urban planning circle to expand the urban area by planning revision and administrative division adjustment, namely "urbanization with the outward moving of the urban circle." Between 2000 and 2015, the urban construction area expanded from 22,439.3 to 52,102.3 square kilometers, an increase of 132.2% (see Table 28.1).

In the land supply, the local governments showed a clear preference to industrial land as it would attract businesses and investment or rather, a key stake to attract foreign investment; therefore, a large amount of land was allotted to industrial use to ensure the rapid development of industry. Figures 28.2 and 28.3 show China's land supply structure over the past decade, and it could be seen that the supply of land for industry, mining, and storage, occupying more than 20%, far exceeded that for commerce and services, as well as for residences. This kind of land supply structure led to two consequences. First, there

Table 28.1   China's urban area and construction area in 2006–2015

Year	Urban area	Urban construction area	Year	Urban area	Urban construction area
2006	166,533.5	33,659.8	2011	183,618.0	43,603.2
2007	176,065.5	35,469.7	2012	183,039.4	45,565.8
2008	178,110.3	36,295.3	2013	183,416.1	47,855.3
2009	175,463.6	38,107.3	2014	184,098.6	49,772.6
2010	178,691.7	40,058.0	2015	191,775.5	52,102.3

Source: *China Urban Construction Statistical Yearbook*

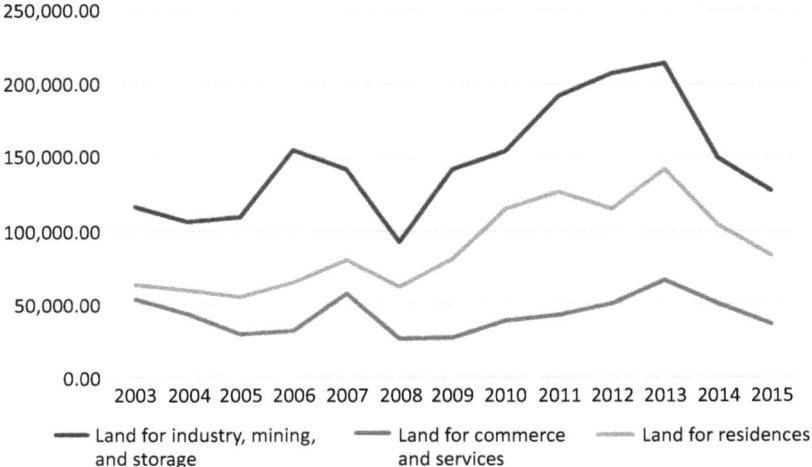

Fig. 28.2   Land supply for different uses in 2003–2015. Source: *China Land and Resources Statistical Yearbook*. Notes: 工矿仓储用地: Land for industry, mining, and storage; 商业服务业用地: Land for commerce and services; 住宅用地: Land for residences

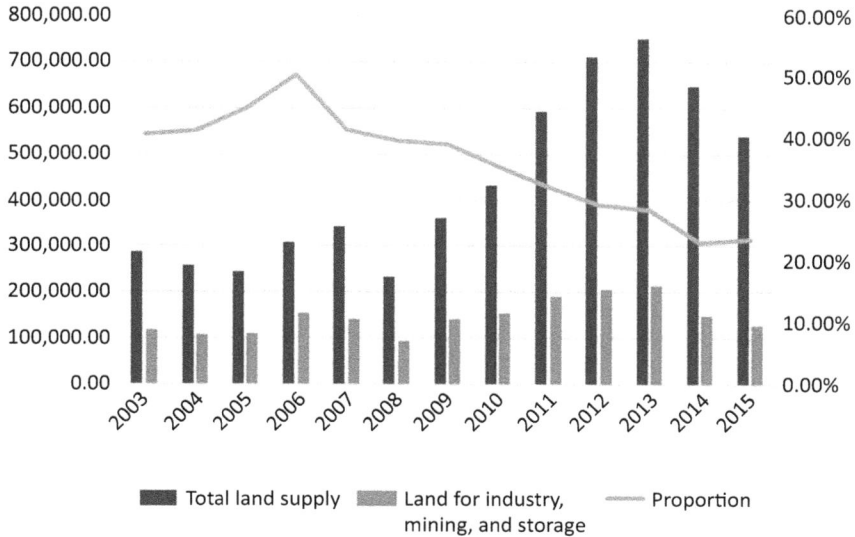

Fig. 28.3 The supply and proportion of the land for industry, mining, and storage in 2003–2015. Source: *China Land and Resources Statistical Yearbook*. Notes: 供地总量: Total land supply; 工矿仓储用地: Land for industry, mining, and storage; 占比: Proportion

is a lot of waste in industrial land. According to the statistics issued by the Ministry of Land and Resources in 2013, the integrated volume rate of national development zones was 0.83, having a building density of 29.28%, and the volume rate in some areas was much lower. Especially in the central and western regions, we saw that development zones had broad roads and good forestation but very light traffic. On the other hand, the local governments had to lower the prices of industrial land for attracting investment, so the prices of industrial land had no significant increase for more than ten years (Fig. 28.4). In fact, the transfer revenues of industrial land for some local governments could not even offset land development costs. In order to compensate that, the local governments had to tighten the supply of commercial land to ensure high-level commercial and residential land transfer revenues. The reduction in the supply of residential land led to output effects and substitution effects, the former decreasing the housing area, while the latter increasing the construction area as real estate developers used commercial capital instead of land. The actual supply of housing was affected by this decrease and increase. Our study showed that the substitution effect between land and capital was less than 1 in reality. In other words, more construction area from the increased investment of real estate developers could not effectively offset the reduction in construction area caused by the reduction in land supply. Such a chain reaction led to high housing prices since the government tightened the supply of residential land, and ultimately, the number of housings in the market became smaller.

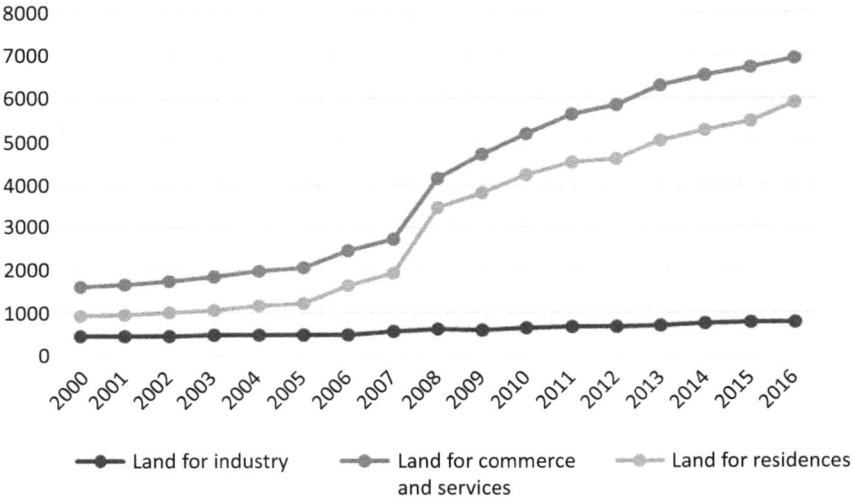

Fig. 28.4 Average prices for the land of different uses in 2000–2016. Source: *Land and Resources Statistical Bulletin* Issued by Ministry of Land and Resources. Notes: 工业用地: Land for industry; 商服用地: Land for commerce and services; 住宅用地: Land for residences

All in all, in the last round of economic growth, the big supply of construction land played a fundamental role. Cheap land expropriation ensured the low cost of land supply. In addition, the big supply of land ensured high investment; the lowered prices of industrial land protected high export. The investment attraction with land led to the accelerated industrialization and urbanization, thus facilitating the rapid growth of the local economy. Therefore, this government-led LELS Model has successfully maneuvered China's rapid urbanization, industrialization, and sustained economic growth.

2.2   The Driving Forces of Local Government-Led Urbanization

Urbanization under this government-led LELS Model embodied deep internal logic, which were the strategic responses of local governments as a weak force in the administrative system and a passive role in policies toward a series of institutional changes. Three motivations were concluded, namely fiscal incentives and development incentives of local governments as organizations and "political incentives" of government officials. In fact, the organizations and individuals, with the same goal and "incentive compatibility" reinforced this government-led LELS Model (see Fig. 28.5).

2.2.1   Fiscal Incentives

China's fiscal system has undergone several major changes since the reform and opening-up. China implemented a system of "serving meals to different diners

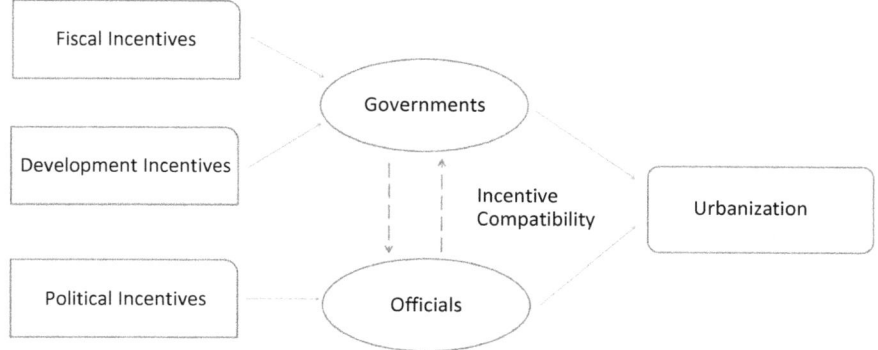

Fig. 28.5 The internal motivation of local governments in driving urbanization. Notes: 财政激励: Fiscal Incentives; 发展激励: Development Incentives; 政治激励: Political Incentives; 政府: Governments; 官员: Officials; 激励相容: Incentive Compatibility; 城市化: Urbanization

from different pots," namely the system of dividing revenue and expenditure between the central and local governments and holding each responsible for balancing their budgets from 1980s to the beginning of 1990s. This system decentralized the power and profits to local governments; meanwhile, a high marginal sharing ratio enjoyed by the local governments in the budget stimulated them to advocate the policies of economic growth (Montinola et al. 1995; Oi 1992). However, this system led to a significant decline in two proportions—the share of fiscal revenue in the GDP (Gross Domestic Product), and the share of central fiscal revenue in total fiscal revenue—with the former falling from 28.4% in 1979 to 12.6%, the latter from 46.8% in 1979 to 31.6% in 1993 (Wu and Li 2010). In this context, in order to stop deteriorating fiscal revenues, the central government implemented a tax distribution system reform in 1994 featured by "the concentration of fiscal revenue rights while keeping the responsibilities of fiscal expenditure unchanged." Local governments, on the one hand, had to pay a higher proportion of budget revenue; on the other hand, large-scale corporate restructuring at that time led to a substantial increase in actual expenditures. In the face of huge fiscal deficits, local governments had to seek new sources of income to relieve financial pressures.

The *Constitution* and *Land Administration Act* in 1988 endowed the local governments the rights to transfer state-owned land use rights, which was a new way for local governments to alleviate financial pressures. From a fiscal point of view, this land transfer brought two kinds of revenues for local governments. First during the land transfer, local governments collected land transfer payments from the land-using units, and the land transfer payments were deemed extra-budgetary income, over which the local governments had free discretion, and after the completion of the transfer, the local governments could levy taxes from the units. We only analyze the benefits from land transfer payments to local governments, that is, the "land finance" we refer to.

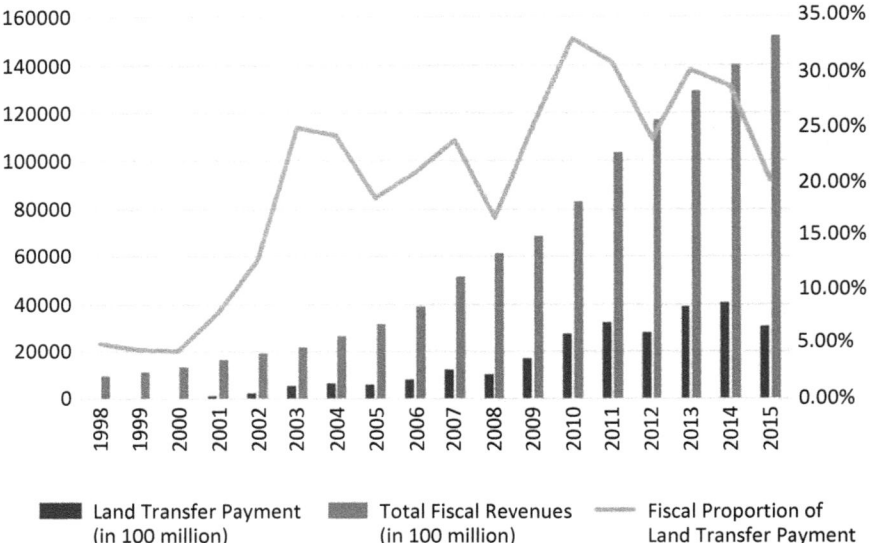

Fig. 28.6 National land transfer payment and its fiscal proportion in 1998–2015. Development incentives. Source: *China Land and Resources Statistical Yearbook* and *China Financial Statistics Yearbook*. Notes: 土地出让金(亿元): Land transfer payment (in 100 million); 总财政收入(亿元): Total fiscal revenues (in 100 million); 土地出让金占比: Fiscal proportion of land transfer payment

Figure 28.6 shows land transfer payment, total fiscal revenues, and the ratio of land transfer payment to total fiscal revenues between 1998 and 2015. At the start of the twenty-first century, land transfer revenues rose rapidly from 59.5 billion yuan in 2000 to 3078.38 billion yuan in 2015, even exceeding 4000 billion yuan in 2014. Simultaneously, land transfer revenues occupied a growing ratio in fiscal revenues, from less than 5% in 2000 to 20% in 2015, or exceeding 30% in some years. It can be seen that the sale of land did provide an important channel for the local governments to relieve financial pressure.

Apart from being a tool to "accumulate wealth," land has become a key chip for local governments to attract investment after the mid-1990s. From late 1970s to early 1990s when China began to adopt its reform and opening-up policy, local governments were not keen on vying for such productive factors of mobility, for example, capital or labor, because the growth of secondary and tertiary industries then was mainly driven by the enterprises invested and controlled by the local governments, including rural community organizations. In other words, state-owned enterprises and township enterprises were the main forces of local economic growth. As owners sharing the resources and profits of the enterprises, the local governments were more motivated to support the development of local enterprises, rather than attracting foreign enterprises to local investment. On the contrary, some places even prevented foreign enterprises entering with local protectionism. Meanwhile, local governments could also evade the central government's taxation by transferring the income of local firms (Che and Qian 1998). However, from the mid-1990s on, the model oriented by the development of local enterprises was no longer applicable, and the regional competition on manufacturing investment started; there are two reasons for this. First, as market-oriented reforms brought about fierce market competition, local governments could not resist market laws, and interregional trade fortresses gradually disintegrated, and local enterprises had to follow the rule of "survival of the fittest" to confront the challenges from the enterprises in domestic markets or even world markets. As a consequence, local state-owned enterprises and township enterprises could not earn more, and the enterprises as financial resources became negative assets of local governments. The second reason is the reforms on the tax division system. The establishment of a national tax system has strengthened the tax supervision system; so the gap for the local governments to evade central taxation by transferring local corporate income became much smaller (Bird and Wong 2005; Wong 1997), which also confined the local governments from supporting local manufacturing with tax tools.

As local governments could neither secure stable financial resources from state-owned and township enterprises nor evade central taxation by operating the government-controlled enterprises, they gradually shifted their attention to private investment and foreign investment, hoping to create a new economic growth point and cultivate new tax bases through foreign capital. So, the local governments would naturally face a problem of how to attract foreign capital to local investments. In addition to the commonly used means of reducing the requirements for labor and environmental protection, as well as providing preferential taxation and policies, a set of "race-to-bottom" capital attraction models by providing industrial land with low prices or even zero prices came to sight in the late 1990s; so land became a key chip to attract investment in the manufacturing sector. In the mid-1990s, when local state-owned and township enterprises completed their restructuring, the local governments began to build industrial development zones on a large scale in the late 1990s, which was most evident in the eastern coastal areas. In order to curb the "industrial zone heat," the State Council launched a national development zone clean-up and rectification in July 2003. The survey showed that there were as many as 6866 development zones with a planned area of 38,600 square kilometers within ten years, which, compared with only 2862 county-level administrative units, meant there are at least two development zones in every county. In most cases, the industrial development zones would first complete infrastructure construction and then provide other support preferential policies, in which governments' fanaticism in attracting investment could be clearly found.

It is worth noting that in the development zone boom at the beginning of the century, land preferential policies, including the agreements on selling industrial land at low prices, returning a certain amount of transfer fees based on investment, were inevitably covered in the investment-inviting policies. More often than not, the industrial land lasting for 50 years with complete infrastructure was transferred to the hands of investors at nominal prices, or so-called zero prices. Figure 28.4 shows the prices of land for different uses from 2000 to 2016. For more than ten years, the industrial land maintained stable low prices, while the land for commerce or services and for residences increased several times. It needed high costs to deliberately control the prices of industrial land, as the local governments not only paid land expropriation costs but ensured sufficient infrastructure investment. Taking southern Jiangsu Province (including Suzhou, Changzhou, and Wuxi) as an example, our field survey showed that the industrial land with an average cost up to 200,000 yuan per mu for its expropriation and construction was sold only at an average price of 150,000 per mu, and even as low as 50,000 or 100,000 per mu in some areas. It was obvious that the local governments spared no efforts to sell their land for investment; however, it helped create the parallel development of high-speed industrialization and urbanization in the late 1990s.

2.2.2   Political Incentives

The political incentives faced by government officials reinforced the above model. The Chinese political institution after the reform and opening-up was mainly characterized by the decentralization of powers; so local governments had discretionary power in economic affairs of the areas (Huang 1997; Lin et al. 2005; Qian and Weingast 1997). Meanwhile, the power for the appointment and removal of local officials was in the hands of superiors. The promotion mechanism of Chinese officials was abstracted by Zhou (2004, 2007) as the theory of promotion tournament, which suggested that under China's centralized political system, superiors assessed and promoted inferior officials mainly based on economic growth of an area (Li and Zhou 2005). In this theory, local officials were considered "political people" who valued political interests, rather than so-called economic people in "fiscal federalism" proposed by Jin, Qian, and Weingast (2005). It was true that the political relations of officials had a significant impact on their promotion, but the relations could not be changed through the efforts of officials themselves; on the contrary, officials could exhibit their governance capacity by boosting local economy. Therefore, with measurable objective indicators and easy comparison of relative competition results, Li'an (2007) maintained that the promotion tournament could be effectively implemented. In addition, Li and Zhou (2005) discovered that the promotion probability of the officials could be predicted with the economic growth rate of a province; Xu (2011) attributed China's economic growth miracle to competitions among local officials. It was speculated that the organization departments of higher CPC committees were apt to measure the individual officials' capacity with the yardstick of the local economic growth rate, so as to influence the promotion of inferior officials.

In this context, local officials had strong incentives to develop local economy, which coincided with the "fiscal incentives" and "development incentives" of local governments. The work organized by the governments for their interests, such as driving urbanization, investing in development zones, and attracting investment just accorded with the political interests of officials. If we viewed the governments as a client, and local officials as agents, both sides obviously had the same goal and incentive compatibility in driving industrialization of urbanization. Therefore, the political incentives of officials strengthened the logic behind the local government-led urbanization.

3   RETHINKING LOCAL GOVERNMENT-LED URBANIZATION

Driven by local governments, China embarked on a road to rapid urbanization. Local governments played a central role in urbanization, industrialization, economic growth, and raising people's living standards. However, some side effects of government-led urbanization emerged, such as the loss of rights and interests of landless farmers and the inefficient use of construction land. Some risks, though not breaking out, need more attention, such as growing local debts and unsustainable land finance. These problems impelled us to reflect on China's urbanization model and the role that local governments should play in urbanization.

3.1   Protecting the Rights and Interests of Landless Farmers

According to the *Constitution*, the government could expropriate land from farmers for public interests, but farmers need to be compensated. Land expropriation and compensation had gone through a historical process. In a planned economy and the start of reform and opening-up, the landless farmers were resettled by the land-using units; so they were recruited by the enterprises using their land. Monetary resettlement was gradually becoming a major one beginning from the mid- and late 1990s. China's "Land Management Law" stipulated that compensation for expropriated cultivated land shall include compensation for land, resettlement subsidies, as well as compensation for attachments and young crops on the requisitioned land. The compensation for the first two was respectively six to ten times and four to six times of the average annual yield value of the land in the previous three years. The lower limit of the sum of these two categories was 10 times, the upper limit 16 times, and the maximum of total compensation may not exceed 30 times, which implied that the maximum compensation was lower than 30,000 yuan if the annual yield value of farmland per mu is 1000 yuan. It was obvious that the *Land Administration Act* implemented the policy of "compensation based on the original uses of the expropriated land," which excluded the farmers from sharing the value-added benefits of farmland converted to other uses. Landless farmers in areas with developed economies could find new employments due to booming second and third industries, while those in underdeveloped areas lost not only land but the opportunities to make a living.

In the land expropriation, local governments acted as decision makers, organizers, and executors, but the image of government officials in the minds of farmers in recent years was seriously damaged in land expropriation, and government credibility was greatly reduced. In order to defend their land and basic rights, the farmers had to rise against the governments. On the other hand, local governments were forced to expropriate land against all pressures, and sometimes resorting to tougher means, ultimately leading to collective confrontations between farmers and the governments. Our large-scale surveys on the 1200 land-expropriated farmers in 12 large and medium-sized cities in the four major metropolitan areas of the Bohai Sea, the Yangtze River Delta, the Pearl River Delta, and the Sichuan-Chongqing region between 2008 and 2009 showed that a total of 63 collective incidents (including obstruction of traffic, resistance, mass fights, demanding statements from the cadres, or police dispatched by superiors) happened. Among them, coming in the first place, 29 cases arose from the dissatisfaction with the compensation for land expropriation and demolition, 6 from unwilling land expropriation, 7 from disputes in land expropriation, and 10 from unsettled compensation placement. Only 11 cases were related to other factors, for example, poor village environments and village conflicts (see Fig. 28.7).

Land is increasing its value in urbanization; so the conflicts on the value-added land are inevitable. Disputes from land expropriation have become major reasons for petition. According to the National Bureau of Letters and Visits, 60% of the mass petitions were related to the land (Liu 2014). Although the compensation for farmers increased, and a social security system provided to landless farmers in recent years, the situation did not substantially improve, that

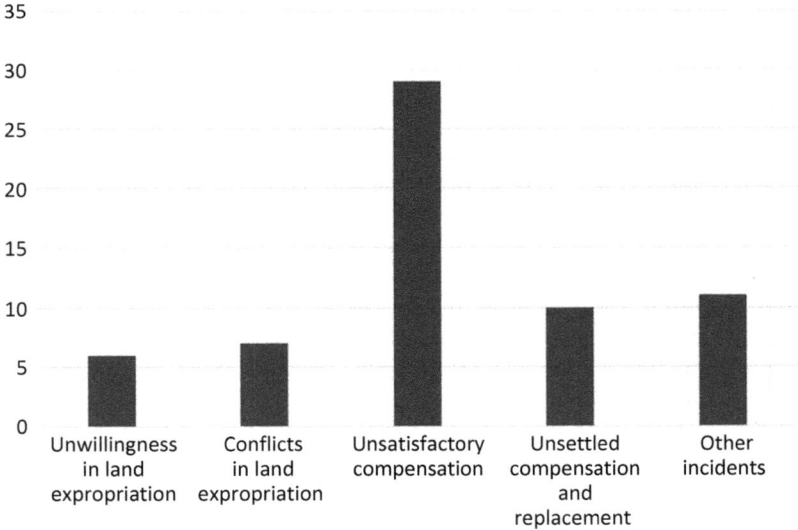

Fig. 28.7 Distribution of collective incidents based on conflict reasons. Source: According to the surveys of land-expropriated farmers in 2008 by authors. Notes: 不愿意征地: Unwillingness in land expropriation; 征地纠纷: Conflicts in land expropriation; 补偿不满: Unsatisfactory compensation. 补偿安置未落实: Unsettled compensation and replacement; 其他事件: Other incidents

is, the farmers were still excluded from the benefits of urbanization or the distribution of value-added land gains. Local development supported by land selling of the governments inevitably led to the conflicts between them and farmers or between officials and civilians. With accelerated industrialization and urbanization, land expropriation was rapidly expanding, depriving more farmers of their land and giving rise to social panic. On the other hand, because farmers had more awareness of power and rights, but were short of effective legal channels to resolve the conflicts, they had to express their demands in extreme ways, and such a large population and prolonged period would definitely endanger social stability. Undeniably, China's current land expropriation system has been a major support for economic development, industrialization, and urbanization. However, unfair distribution of land interests and low-cost forced land expropriation seriously endangered the interests of landless farmers.

3.2   "Space Urbanization, Not Population Urbanization"

Urbanization came in two major dimensions, namely "population urbanization" and "space urbanization." In the local government-led urbanization model, "population urbanization" lagged behind "space urbanization," which was manifested in two main aspects; one was that the growth rate of urban population was lower than the expansion of a constructed urban area, and the second was that the proportion of the primary industry in employment was lower than the decline in output value. World Bank statistics showed that in the last period, China expanded its cities at an annual average rate of 7%, while the average annual growth of urban population was only slightly higher than 3%. Figure 28.8 shows a comparison of urban area expansion and urban population

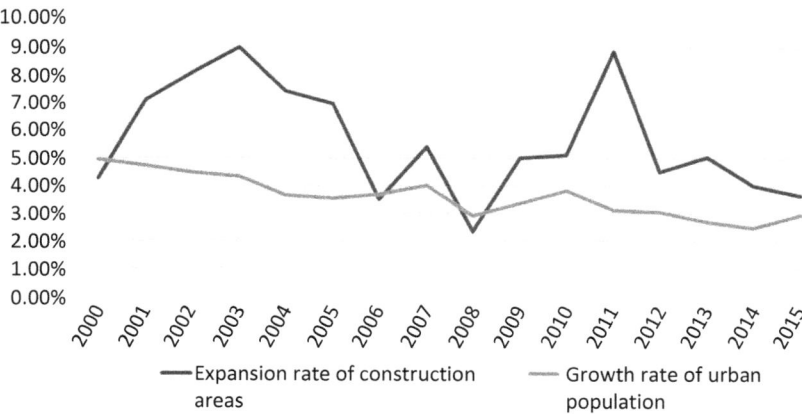

Fig. 28.8 China's "space urbanization" and "population urbanization." Source: *China Statistical Yearbook* and *China Urban Construction Statistical Yearbook*. Notes: 建成区扩张率: Expansion rate of construction areas; 城市人口增长率: Growth rate of urban population

growth from 2000 to 2015, and our conclusion that land urbanization was faster than population urbanization was consistent with the results of the World Bank. This "Space Urbanization, Not Population Urbanization" was clearly not the essence of urbanization (Wen 2014), as in its real sense, urbanization should attract the rural population to settle in cities through strong agglomeration effect, and the population agglomeration should boost industry accumulation and the formation of scale economies. A lot of drawbacks were related to lagging population urbanization, and the urban-rural gap could not be diminished because cities were short of a constant attraction to rural farmers and traditional agriculture of low returns kept the average income of farmers at a low level. On the other hand, the nonmatching land urbanization and population urbanization made a large number of empty cities and ghost cities, leading to the low-efficient use of land and investment waste.

The declining proportion of the primary industry in employment lagging behind that in output value was another manifestation of "Space Urbanization, Not Population Urbanization." The experience of developed countries was that the industrial structure would also be adjusted with industrialization and urbanization, exhibited in the declining proportion of the primary industry and the rising proportion of secondary and tertiary industries. Local government-led urbanization also showed the same pattern. The difference was that the transformation of the employment structure in China's urbanization failed to keep up with the transformation of the industrial structure. In other words, the transfer of the labor force from the primary industry to the second and third industries was too slow. Figures 28.9 and 28.10 show the proportion of different industries according to output value and employment

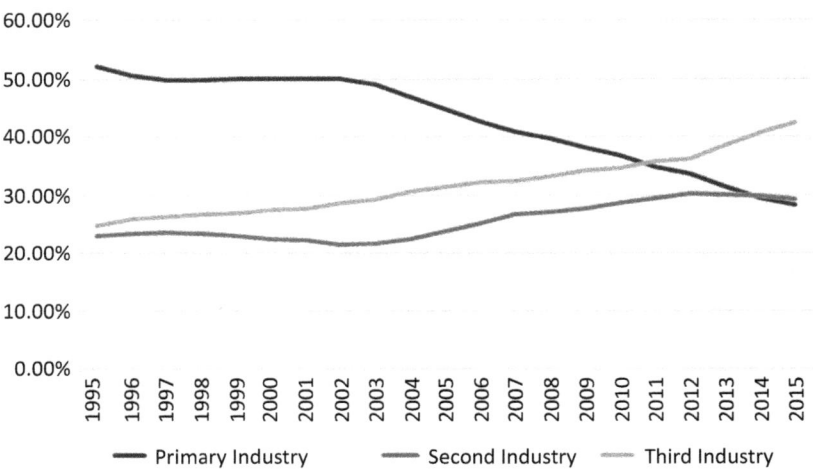

Fig. 28.9 Proportion of industries in China according to output value in 1995–2015. Source: *China Statistical Yearbook*. Notes: 第一产业: Primary industry; 第二产业: Second industry; 第三产业: Third industry

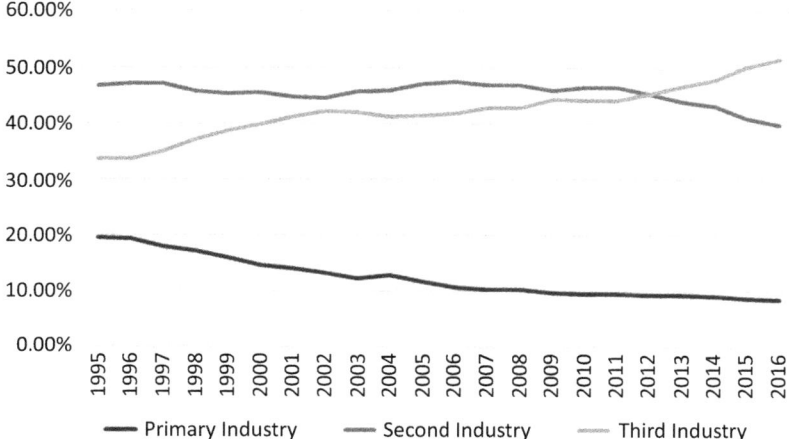

Fig. 28.10 Proportion of industries in China according to employment share in 1995–2015. Source: *China Statistical Yearbook*. Notes: 第一产业: Primary industry; 第二产业: Second industry; 第三产业: Third industry

share from 1995 to 2015. As shown in Fig. 28.9, the share of the primary industry in GDP fell from 50% in 1995 to less than 30% in 2015, while the proportion of secondary and tertiary industries steadily increased. However, the changes in employment share lagged far behind the changes in the output value structure, and the proportion of employment population in the primary industry dropped from 20% to 10% (Fig. 28.10). This meant that in industrialization and urbanization for more than 20 years, the transformation of the employment population failed to keep up with industrial transformation; a lot of labor was still maintained in the primary industry. Of course, the flow of population and labor was also related to the "semi-open" household registration system and the constraints of urban management systems (Knight et al. 1999; Cai 2000; Au and Henderson 2006), but we think our traditional urbanization model was also one of the key factors. Since the government-led urbanization could not attract enough population to cities, many of the people naturally lived in rural areas.

3.3   Unsustainable Land Finance

The value of land has increased with China's rising urbanization in recent years, and farmers have become aware of their rights; so, the costs of land expropriation and demolition have significantly increased and the compensation to the farmers with expropriated land and demolished shelters improved remarkably. The proportion of related compensation costs rose from 42.03% in 2009 to 53.18% in 2015 in total land transfer revenues; in particular, under the "Regulations on the Expropriation and Compensation of Housing on State-

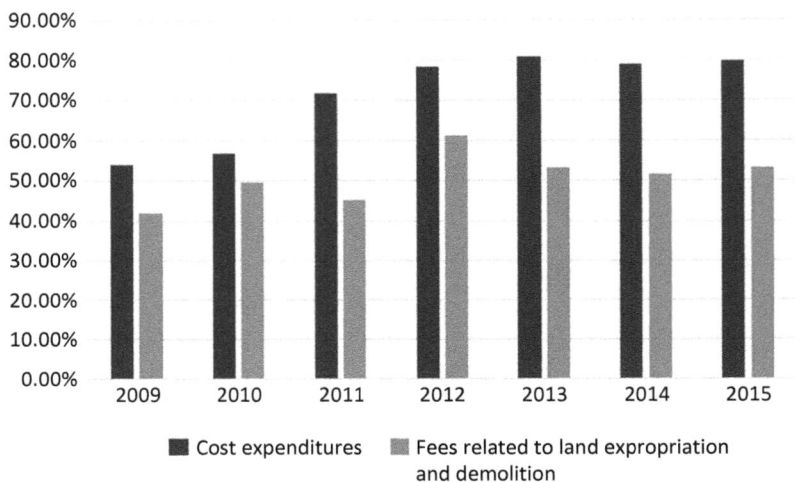

Fig. 28.11 Changes in China's land transfer costs in 2009–2015. Source: *National Land Transfer Revenue and Expenditure* issued by the Ministry of Finance. Notes: 成本性支出: Cost expenditures; 涉及征地拆迁相关费用: Fees related to land expropriation and demolition

owned Land," costs in 2012 were even more than 60% (Fig. 28.11). At the same time, the expenditure prior to land development also increased. In recent years, the costs for land transfer only accounted for 80% of land transfer revenues. It is predictable that, in continuing urbanization, it will be more and more difficult to expropriate land with the compensation on original uses as the compensation costs for land expropriation and demolition continue to grow. It was most evident in the rural-urban continuum and urban expansion areas; so, China's urbanization would slowly bid farewell to the low-cost period supported by low-price land expropriation compensation. This meant the land transfer returns were getting smaller for local governments.

Another risk of relying on land finance was the volatility of land transfer revenues. The total contract price of land transfer in China increased from 60 billion yuan in 2000 to 3.56 trillion yuan in 2015, with an average annual growth rate of 35.62% (Fig. 28.12). Although the land revenue continued to increase at a stable rate for a longer period of time, it showed a large fluctuation between years, for example, more than 50% average annual fluctuation in land transfer revenues between 2000 and 2016. In particular, affected by a macroeconomic situation after 2010, there were obvious fluctuations between years in land transfer revenues. The excessive reliance on land finance would transmit the volatility of land transfer revenues to local finance, which also threatened the stability of fiscal revenues.

As mentioned above, the significance of land to government finance was not only the land transfer revenues and consequent tax revenues but loan finances

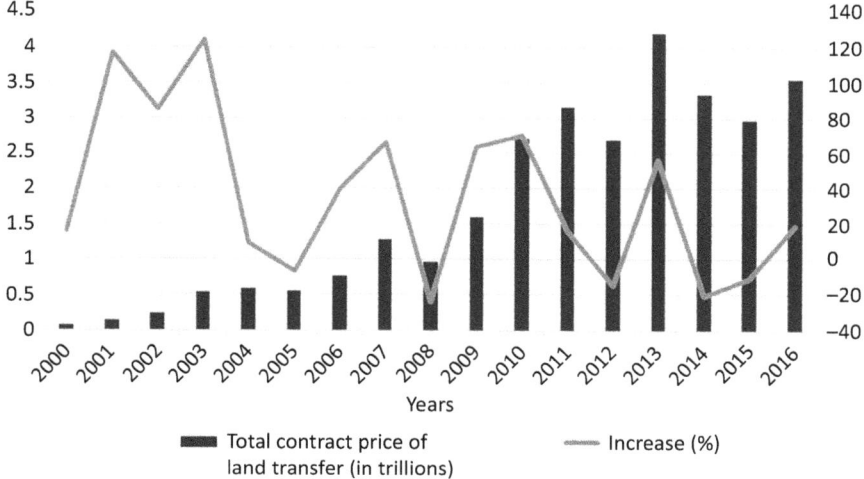

Fig. 28.12 Fluctuations of land transfer revenues in 2000–2016. Source: *Land and Resources Statistical Bulletin* issued by the Ministry of Land and Resources. Notes: 年份: Years; 土地出让合同总价款(万亿元): Total contract price of land transfer (in trillions); 增幅(%): Increase (%)

for local governments with land as collateral. In recent years, China has shown a dramatic increase in its land mortgage area and land mortgages. From 2009 to 2015, the land mortgage area of 84 key cities in China grew from 217,000 ha to 490,800 ha, with an average annual increase of 21%; land mortgage loans increased from 0.259 billion yuan to 1.133 billion yuan, its average annual increase of up to 56.3% (see Fig. 28.13). Land mortgage increased from 6.5% in 2009 to 12.1% in 2015 in total RMB loans from national financial institutions, an increase of about 100%.

The risk of land mortgage loans was first manifested in local debts. According to the report of the National Audit Office, China's local government debt reached a balance of 17.2 trillion yuan at the end of 2016, accounting for 23.1% of GDP in 2016, and if the public sector debt and the financial bonds issued by policy financial institutions were taken into calculation, China's total public debt rate reached 55%. Although this figure was still lower than 60% of the GDP, a warning line set by the European Union, the situation in some areas was not optimistic; especially in China's western areas, the local debt was as high as 36.4%, far more than 16% of the local government debt ratio line set by the United States.

In fact, local governments relied on land for this round of loans, and debt borrowing and paying were both heavily dependent on the land. According to the report released by the National Audit Office in 2014, local governments needed to pay 10.89 trillion yuan for their debt by the end of June 2013, of which 40% was promised to be paid from the land selling and even more than

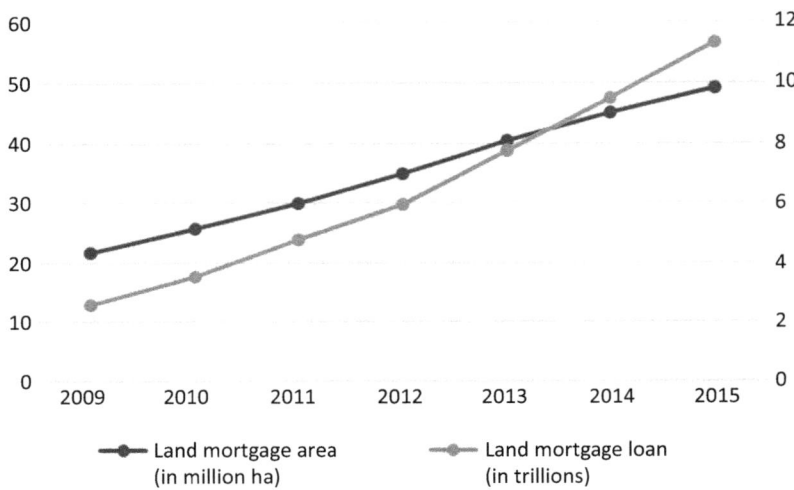

Fig. 28.13 China's land mortgage area and land mortgage loan in 2009–2015. Source: *Land and Resources Statistical Bulletin* issued by the Ministry of Land and Resources. Notes: 土地抵押面积(万公顷): Land mortgage area (in million ha); 土地抵押贷款(万亿元): Land mortgage loan (in trillions)

50% in some areas, for example, close to 65% in Zhejiang and Tianjin. On the other hand, the borrowing with land as the subject matter also increased the financial risk of banks. More than 50% of the total government loan of 10.89 trillion yuan came from bank loans. Local governments would be unable to pay the debt once the land transfer payments continued to fall. Unfortunately, as we mentioned earlier, the net income of local governments from land transfer has declined significantly in recent years, and land transfer revenues were rather unstable; so local governments were bound to have potential debt risk with the declining earning power and unstable land transfer revenues as a major source of debt payment.

4   GOVERNMENT TRANSFORMATION: FROM LEADERS TO COLLABORATORS AND SUPERVISORS

When we reflect on the history of the social governance model of humans, we find out that the social governance structure since modern times tended to regard governments as the only subject of governance, which led to the domination of the social forces from the governments. The governments, as the core of governance of public affairs, provided institutional arrangements to the society and managed social affairs. With the diversification of management subjects in the post-industrial era, nongovernmental organizations (NGOs) have become key participants in social governance and have collaborated with governments in social governance. This governance model was characteristic of cooperative governance. O'Leary et al. (2006) defined it as a common model of collaboration between two or more government agencies, private sectors, and civic groups for addressing the public policy challenges that government agencies were unable to solve on their own. Successful co-governance should satisfy the following points:

1. **Consultation among collaborators**: As Roberts (2016) pointed out, consultations need to be listened to, collaborators' views need be considered, and joint decisions need to be made concerning public affairs.
2. **Effective participation**: A cooperative group should invite the representatives that have different goals, relationships, identities, or institutions to solve problems and resolve conflicts (Lulofs and Cahn 2000).
3. **Abilities of joint action**: A cooperative group should enhance their abilities, and of others, through formal and informal agreements, as well as the designs and rules for institutions to achieve common goals.

Cooperative governance basically eliminated government centralism, which broke the centralist structure of public participation in government affairs by voluntary behaviors of equal subjects. One key point that distinguished co-governance from traditional government-centered social governance was that it broke the singularity of political goals in public policies and put policies out of the single-line linear responsibility for political institutions. One of the inevitable consequences of co-governance was that public policies were influenced by the multiple values of different interest groups. As pointed out by Downs (1967), in the governance system of an industrial society, because the government was the only subject of governance monopoly, internal department measures were taken for the acquisition and allocation of resources, while in cooperative governance, a cooperative organization could make a variety of choices based on its own function, size, and participants, and such a flexibility led to higher efficiency and more equitable results.

It was easy to find that traditional Chinese urbanization was mainly characterized by government-led administrative power. As we have described above, China's urbanization and industrialization from the late 1990s onwards were achieved by government-led LELS Model with legitimate rights. However, many drawbacks were debunked in this model. From the perspective of social governance, these drawbacks may only embody the evils inherent in urbanization from the government-centered governance model. For example, landless farmers lost their rights just because they did not have the power of discourse in land expropriation and the policies were only responsible to government agencies. So the best corresponding solution was transforming government governance to collaborative governance, which required the transformation of local governments from leaders to collaborators and governors in urbanization. However, a common concern was that, with the lessening urbanization in general in China, if the governments reduced stimulation to urbanization, urbanization might be stagnated; in fact, this concern was unnecessary. The successful experience of urbanization in Western countries told us that, apart from administrative powers, urbanization was propelled by market forces more, and urbanization could still be achieved without government leadership. On the contrary, market-oriented urbanization would be more conducive to its real meaning, that is, rural population was attracted to settle down in cities with strong agglomeration effect of cities. The chapter provides two cases in Zhejiang and Guangdong to prove that the transformation of local governments' roles will not hinder urbanization; instead, it will lead to a more healthy and sustainable urbanization in China.

4.1   New Urbanization Under the PPP Model

We mentioned that the major cause for China to have embarked on such a local government-led urbanization was that local governments were facing heavy financial pressure; so, they either sold land to collect land transfer payments or sold industrial land at lower prices to attract investment as tax sources, and then urbanization followed. Meanwhile, the infrastructure construction in cities also needed a lot of investment, so local governments had to depend heavily on land finance. In fact, this vicious circle revealed a problem, that is, "where the money is from" faced by local governments in urbanization. In the expropriation of land transfer revenues in the traditional model, the local governments were also responsible for heavy urban construction expenditure; so the governments of some cities depended on loans to drive urbanization. We think the root cause was that local governments were the leaders monopolizing land, selling it, and constructing the cities. The new urbanization under the Zhejiang PPP model offered a good case in which the local governments no longer served as leaders; instead, they were "collaborators" and "guides."

The PPP model was traced back to the toll road construction in the eighteenth century in Europe, but in a modern sense, it was born and developed out of the market reforms where the private sectors were invited to be active participants of public services in the new public management movement. In order to alleviate the tight financial pressure by the economic recession in the 1970s, Britain and America vigorously introduced private sectors into public projects to operate jointly with government capital, which promoted PPP. To stimulate economy after the debt crises in moderately developed countries in the mid-1980s, many countries managed to lessen their financial burdens by introducing social capital (e.g., Turkey introduced Build-Operate-Transfer (BOT) to build nuclear power plants, which was also a PPP model). With the continuous improvement of norms, PPP has gradually become a key operation model for governments to adopt the joint cooperation of multiple subjects in public construction.

In recent years, the PPP model has been implemented in the urbanization of Zhejiang Province to facilitate the collaboration of government capital and private capital in urban construction. It is written in the "13th Five-Year Plan for Economic and Social Development in New Urbanization in Zhejiang" that "operational fields shall be open legally for the development, construction, and management of markets. Quasi-operational fields are open to social capital with the collaborative mechanism of investment, subsidy, and price based on the PPP model and equity cooperation." A wide range of urban investment projects were involved in the PPP, including the investment in infrastructure roads, municipal green environment, and high-end smart cities. It is worth mentioning that PPP has played a key role in the development of several characteristic towns well-known in China in recent years. In particular, social capital and private capital were quite conducive to those financially weak areas and the areas lacking substantial and continuous capital inflow.

Although the PPP model could provide more funds for urban construction and was a possible alternative for local governments to alleviate financial difficulties, the pivotal question was how to attract private capital in urban construction. It is self-evident that private capital was oriented toward markets and profits, so its participation in urban construction projects was motivated by profits. However, there were obstacles for private capital to flow into PPP at present, and they are shown in the following. First, there lacked a sound legal foundation for private capital to flow into urban infrastructure investments. Second, there were government default risks. As urban construction was featured by large investment and a long payback period, most of the enterprise investment returns were from the financial payment of governments; the enterprises would be in deep waters if governments failed to pay. Currently, local governments were "leaders" in urban construction, so local governments faced rather low penalty costs. Third, there was a shortage of risk-sharing principles. Similarly, since the current governments were "leaders," they were used to shirking their responsibilities while authorizing one project to private investors, which put private investors in unfavorable positions.

We believe the key is that the governments have to change from "leaders" to "collaborators" and strengthen their contract spirit by setting up a contract system. With a sound contract system, the government responsibilities are regulated, penalty for the contract breach made clear, and effective governments monitoring conducted by private departments to dispel the worries of private capital. On the other hand, local governments should play the role of "guides." Through policy guidance, enterprises are given certain tax reductions and land preferential policies, so the investment costs of enterprises are diminished to attract social capital into urbanization. Zhejiang Province did a good job in this area. A professional PPP investment committee, as a platform for the consultation of government and private sectors, was set up in Zhejiang Province in July 2015 to serve the urbanization strategies of the governments.

This kind of government-enterprise cooperation scored achievements in promoting urbanization and urban construction. Ningbo was one typical example. 42 PPP projects with a total social capital of 45.6 billion yuan were approved in Ningbo in 2015, of which, more than 10 projects were included for national demonstration and pilots. For a long time, urbanization and urban construction have been operated by the government alone and the investment on municipal facilities carried out by public sectors, which not only brought heavy financial burdens to local governments but led to low efficiency in urban construction—for example, jelly-built projects due to a government monopoly. Social capital provided sufficient funds for urban construction and also alleviated the governments from heavy construction funds. Meanwhile, with a clear division of responsibilities of government and social capitals stated in contracts, risks can be reduced and distributed so as to share benefits and risks together.

The model of encouraging social capital and private capital into urbanization inspired us a lot. First, local governments can be lifted out of the vicious cycle of "financial pressure–land selling–urbanization–financial pressure," as the governments act as guides to develop reasonable policies to attract private capital for sharing costs, risks, and benefits, without the need for public finance to bear all the construction funds. Second, the Zhejiang model also makes us realize that the key to the above changes is the transformation of local governments in their roles. The local governments would inevitably return to the LELS Model and bear the high cost of urban construction if they promoted urbanization as leaders. On the contrary, if the local governments participated in urbanization as collaborators and guides, it would effectively make up for the funds, resolve the debt crisis, and alleviate them from dependence on "land finance." More importantly, because the urbanization is no longer driven by administrative power alone, but by market forces as well, it will help redress the "land urbanization, not population urbanization," leading urbanization to its true meaning.

4.2   *"Nanhai Model": Spontaneous Urbanization from Farmers*

Nanhai District in Foshan City, located in the heart of the Pearl River Delta, occupies an area of 1073.82 square kilometers. As of 2015, the district had a total population of 3 million with a disposable income of 39,625 yuan per capita, of which urban residents had disposable income per capita of 40,148 yuan and rural residents had net income of 25,909 yuan. Different from the LELS Model, Nanhai stepped onto urban-rural joint development for rural prosperity by inviting farmers to participate in urbanization with their land. The Nanhai Model was mainly characterized by the industrialization and urbanization carried out on collective construction land. According to the results of the second national land survey, Nanhai had a construction area of 797,500 mu, of which 71% (that is, 565.500 mu) was the rural collective construction land.

A large number of enterprises came to Nanhai to look for land and invest in factories in the early 1990s. For satisfying their needs, collective economic organizations at the village and group levels of the Nanhai District applied for land for the establishment of township enterprises, prepared relevant land use right certificates, and then rented the land to the enterprises seeking investment. The establishment of enterprises on collective land avoided national land expropriation; so the land was directly put into industrialization. Most importantly, the differential benefits from the nonfarming land use were kept within the villages, and the farmers could enjoy the value-added land benefits as they had land ownership as a collective. According to statistics, Nanhai District reaped a total industrial output value of 422.6 billion yuan in 2012, and more than half of the industrial land was provided by the collectively constructed land.

In fact, an array of problems appeared in the spontaneous urbanization of the Nanhai District in more than 20 years, such as excessive land development, lack of planning guidance, decentralized layout, and low land use efficiency. In facing these problems, the government played an active role as a governor. With the innovation in the land system and mechanism of profit distribution, a community of shared interests between the government, collective, and farmers was constructed and moderately complete institutional arrangements were made for effective intensive land use, industrial upgrading, and urbanization.

The first step in the cooperative governance of urbanization was to confirm the rights of rural collective land, which ensured its legal use and transaction. First, it was confirmed that collective land included not only the rural collective land except cultivated land, rivers, tidal flats, and fish ponds but nonfarming land for industry and tertiary industry. The second was to define the property rights left over by history. The land that had become collective land but not obtained legal formalities before January 1, 1999, confirmed its rights if only it was the land within the construction land area of overall planning. Third, the certificates of rights were conferred on rural collective economic organizations and landowners after the rights confirmation, and land ownership certificates were conferred directly on the villages in line with the provisions. As of 2013, more than 90% of the collective construction land had confirmed its rights. Clear subjects of rural collective land property laid a foundation for the transfer of collective construction land use rights.

The second step was to standardize rules for the land transactions. In order to standardize and promote the transfer of collective construction land, Guangdong Provincial People's Government introduced the "Methods on the Management of Collective Construction Land Use Rights Transfer in Guangdong Province" in 2005. Based on that, Nanhai District formulated "Methods on the Management of Collective Construction Land Use Rights Transfer and Rent in Nanhai District, Foshan City" and "Methods on the Management of Collective Construction Land Use Rights Transfer, Sublease, and Mortgage," specifying the "same nature, same price, and same rights" of rural collective construction land and state-owned construction land and allowing rural collective construction land to flow into markets through selling, transfer, rental, mortgage, and so on. As for the state-owned reserved land, if the persons owning land use rights did not change or the land did not change its uses, original users had the rights to handle the land, not subject to public transactions. If the rural collective construction land was used for real estate development projects, the procedures were necessary for the transfer of the collective to the state-owned land and for public transaction.

The third step was to draw up the methods for transferring collective to state-owned construction land. Collective construction land in industrial zones was transferred to state-owned construction land within village collectives with legal transfer formalities. Original owners (i.e., original village collectives) whose collective land was transferred to state-owned land could enjoy the distribution and share-holding of property, so their rights were protected. It facilitated the transfer of collective land to state-owned land without the expropriation from local governments.

Fourth, a benchmark land price system was established to regulate the transfer market of collective construction land. Nanhai District spent two years from early 2011 to 2013 in setting up the benchmark land price system for collective construction land. At the beginning of 2013, Nanhai District People's Government promulgated the "Notice on Implementing Benchmark Land Price for Collective Construction Land in Nanhai District," which included the benchmark land price and benchmark rent of collective construction land in existing and planned areas. When a perfect market was not nurtured, the establishment of a benchmark land price system provided an effective reference for the transaction of collective construction land.

Under the abovementioned norms, collective construction land was not only transferred legally but protected technically by the governments. With the establishment of transaction platforms for collective town and village assets, a collaborative pattern of the collectives owning land, farmers enjoying benefits, and governments assisting governance was formed, so that villages and farmers enjoyed the fruits of urbanization and value-added land benefits. Collective land rent increased from 2.26 billion yuan in 2008 to 3.02 billion yuan in 2012; dividends per capita in villages and groups rose from 2347 yuan in 2008 to 3516 yuan in 2012. Farmers' net income per capita grew from 11,158 yuan in 2008 to 25,909 yuan in 2015, an average annual increase of 18%; the urban-rural income ratio was narrowed from 2.33:1 in 2008 to 1.54:1. On the other hand, the economic strength of villages and groups was greatly enhanced. By 2012, their collective assets amounted to 30.6 billion yuan, of which 16.1 billion yuan was reaped by economic communities and 216 villages had a total income of more than 100 million yuan.

The "Nanhai Model" provided a way for farmers to share the value-added land benefits in urbanization, giving rise to a win-win for government and farmers, and urban and rural development. This case made us rethink the roles of governments in urbanization. We believe that the governments did not necessarily play a leading role in urbanization, nor pioneer the way for rapid urbanization. On the contrary, we feel the bottom-up economic vitality of rural collectives in the Nanhai Model. Of course, this spontaneous urbanization was often characterized by collective irrationality, which may lead to the overexploitation of land, the lack of planning, and low utilization. But interestingly, due to the "malfunction" of spontaneous forces, it was essential for the governments to participate in urbanization; however, the governments were not "leaders" at this time but rather "governors." With more talented people, richer resources, and stronger power, the government could develop a series of norms to help village collectives form a complete system of land transfer.

Compared with government-led urbanization, the success of government-governed urbanization was reflected in two aspects. First, the farmers in the Nanhai Model shared the fruits of urbanization. As mentioned above, the urbanization driven by local governments led to a large number of landless farmers, who only received very low compensation and were excluded from value-added benefits of farmland transfer, which tended to become the focus of social contradictions. However, in the Nanhai Model, farmers enjoyed the benefits of urbanization and industrialization, instead of losing their land. Second, because this model was propelled by bottom-up market forces, urbanization was coming along with the transfer of farmer employment; "population urbanization" did not lag behind "space urbanization." To sum up, the Nanhai Model addressed many problems in the urbanization effectively, for example, damaged interests of landless farmers and imbalanced population and employment structures.

5   Conclusions and Prospects

This chapter explored the role of local governments in the traditional urbanization model and the correct role for the governments. We note that China's urbanization since the late 1990s was obviously government-led, that is, the local governments promoted rapid industrialization and urbanization through the LELS Model. Specifically, the local governments first collected farmland from farmers with land-expropriation rights, sold the land to land use units after transferring farmland to state-owned land, which triggered China's industrialization and urbanization. There were fiscal and development motives behind this government model. On the one hand, low-cost land expropriation provided adequate construction land to local governments; low price and sufficient supply of industrial land attracted foreign investors. On the other hand, pressed by fiscal burdens, local governments had to decrease the supply of land for commerce and services to keep its transfer prices at a high level. Meanwhile, motivated by promotions, the officials as the agents of governments were eager to attract foreign investment and boost local economy, which was compatible with the governments as consignors in the incentives. The government-led LELS Model was intensified as the governments and officials had the same goal and compatible incentives.

However, the government-led urbanization pattern exposed many drawbacks. The low-price compensation to landless farmers based on original land uses stirred severe dissatisfaction among farmers and social instability. The "population urbanization" far behind "space urbanization" in speed prevented the potential labor from entering the markets, resulting in sluggish employment transformation and low inefficient land use. In addition, the dependence of local governments on unsustainable land finance, as well as large urban construction investment, accumulated heavy local debts, posing latent risks to the country's financial systems.

The key to stepping out of the traditional urbanization model lay in the transformation of government roles. In the traditional urbanization model, the local governments drove urbanization as leaders, inevitably resulting in many of the problems stated above. However, there was a misconception among many people that China's urbanization would be stagnant without government forces, so the governments delayed in using "visible hand" to promote urbanization. In fact, the spontaneous bottom-up market behaviors could also push forward urbanization, and the Nanhai District in Guangdong Province was a case in point in its urbanization of collective construction land. The governments as governors curbed irrational collective behaviors, for example, overheating land development and lacking planning. This kind of urbanization with spontaneous farmer behaviors and government participation was not only superior to the government-driven urbanization, but more importantly, it created a win-win situation for the governments and farmers, as farmers were entitled to enjoy the fruits of urbanization and value-added land benefits. The participation of governments as collaborators was a new type of urbanization under the PPP model in Zhejiang. The investment in urban construction from government capital, social capital, and private capital eased the shortage of funds and helped local governments alleviate the financial burden from urban construction. Moreover, the urbanization model with the governments and individuals sharing costs, risks, and benefits avoided blind urban expansion driven by administrative power. Generally speaking, we think that only after the transformation of local governments from leaders to collaborators and governors to help form a collaborative governance of governments and the society, as well as governments and markets, can China step onto a healthy road to urbanization, which is also the correct orientation for future urbanization.

References

Au, C.C., and J.V. Henderson. 2006. How migration restrictions limit agglomeration and productivity in China. *Journal of Development Economics*, 80(2): 350–388.

Bird, R.M., and C.P.W. Wong. 2005. China's Fiscal System: A Work in Progress. *International Center for Public Policy Working Paper*, 276(13): 1083–1086.

Cai, F. 2000. Political and economic analysis on the Chinese urban restrictions on migrant workers. *Chinese Journal of Population Science*, 4(4).

Che, J., and Y. Qian. 1998. Insecure property rights and government ownership of firms. *Quarterly Journal of Economics*, 113(2): 467–496.

Downs A. 1967. Inside bureaucracy. *Western Political Quarterly*, 22 (2).

Huang, Y. 1997. Inflation and investment controls in China: The political economy of central-local relations during the reform era. *The China Journal* 70: 236–239.

Jin H, Y. Qian, and B.R. Weingast. 2005. Regional decentralization and fiscal incentives: Federalism, Chinese style. *Journal of Public Economics*, 89(9): 1719–1742.

Knight, J., L. Song, and J. Huaibin. 1999. Chinese rural migrants in urban enterprises: Three perspectives. *The Journal of Development Studies*, 35 (3): 73–104.

Li, H., and L.A. Zhou. 2005. Political turnover and economic performance: The incentive role of personnel control in China. *Journal of Public Economics* 89: 1743–1762.

Lin, J. Y., R. Tao, and M. Liu. 2005. Decentralization and local governance in the context of China's transition[J]. *Perspectives*, 6 (2): 25–36.

Liu, S. 2014. *Land Issue in the Transitional China*. China Development Press.

Lulofs R.S., and D.D.J. Cahn. 2000. *Conflict: From Theory to Action*. Allyn and Bacon.

Montinola, G., Y. Qian, and B.R. Weingast. 1995. Federalism, Chinese style: The political basis for economic success in China. *World Politics*, 48(1): 50–81.

Oi, J.C. 1992. Fiscal reform and the economic foundations of local state corporatism in China. *World Politics*, 45(1): 99–126.

O'Leary, R., C. Gerard, and L. B. Bingham. 2006. Introduction to the Symposium on Collaborative Public Management[J]. *Public Administration Review*, 66 (s1): 6–9.

Qian, Y., and B.R. Weingast. 1997. Federalism as a commitment to preserving market incentives. *Journal of Economic Perspectives* 11: 83–92.

Roberts, N. 2016. Public deliberation in an age of direct citizen participation. *American Review of Public Administration*, 34(4): 315–353.

Tao, R., X. Lu, F. Su, et al. 2009. China's transition and development model under evolving regional competition patterns. *Economic Research Journal*, (7): 21–33.

Wang, H., and R. Tao. 2013. *China's Land System Reform: Difficulties, Breakthroughs and Policy Combination*. Commercial Press.

Wen, G. 2014. *Our People are Landless: Inherent Logic Between Urbanization, Land System and Household Registration System*. Oriental Publishing House.

Wong, C. 1997. "Financing Local Government in the People's Republic of China." *Oup Catalogue*, 19 (vol. 41): 603–605.

Wu, Q., and Y. Li. 2010. Fiscal decentralization, competition and local land revenue. *Finance and Trade Economics*, No. 07.

Xu C. 2011. The fundamental institutions of China's reforms and development. *Journal of Economic Literature*, 49(4): 1076–1151.

Zhou, L. 2004. The incentive and cooperation of government officials in the political tournaments: An interpretation of the prolonged local protectionism and duplicative investments in China. *Economic Research Journal*, 6(1): 2–3.

Zhou, L. 2007. Governing China's local officials: An analysis of promotion tournament model. *Economic Research Journal*, (7): 36–50.

CHAPTER 29

The Rise of Public-Private Partnerships in China

Zhirong Jerry Zhao, Guocan Su, and Dan Li

1 Introduction

China's economic takeoff and rapid urbanization in recent decades have been accompanied by the dazzling growth of the nation's infrastructure system. Take the transportation sector as an example. China's total expressway mileage had reached a staggering 131,000 km by 2016, expanding from merely 20.4 km in 1988 when the first stretch of expressway was completed around Shanghai City (Zaobao 2017). Railroads in operation increased from 22,900 km in 1952 to 124,000 km in 2016, including more than 22,000 km of high-speed rail that moves sleek passenger trains between China's major urban centers at speeds that clock in at over 200 km/h (Xinhua Net 2017a). In China's current subway boom, not only are megacities like Beijing and Shanghai actively adding new lines and extensions, smaller Chinese cities are also racing toward opening their first subway lines. During 2012–2016, the number of cities with subway in operation increased from 17 to 27, with the total ridership climbing from 8.7 billion unlinked passenger trips to about 16.1 billion (Xinhua Net 2017b).

Behind the growth of the infrastructure system is China's massive infrastructure investment. From 1992 to 2013, China's annual infrastructure spending in four major sectors—transportation, power, water, and telecom systems—

Z. J. Zhao (✉)
Hubert H. Humphrey School of Public Affairs, University of Minnesota, Twin Cities, USA
e-mail: zrzhao@umn.edu

G. Su
School of Economics, Xiamen University, Xiamen, China

D. Li
School of Government, Sun Yat-sen University, Guangzhou, China

J. Yu, S. Guo (eds.), *The Palgrave Handbook of Local Governance in Contemporary China*, https://doi.org/10.1007/978-981-13-2799-5_29

accounted for about 8.6% of its national gross domestic product (GDP) (McKinsey Global Institute 2016), in comparison to the global average of about 3.5%. If we define the scope of infrastructure to conclude both economic and noneconomic infrastructure types, according to China Statistical Yearbooks, the share of infrastructure investment in China's GDP rose sharply from about 6.8% in 1992 to about 20% in 2010 and hence remained at the high level until present. The rapid growth of China's infrastructure investment cannot be solely explained by the expansion of fiscal capacity. In China, the majority of general budgetary revenues are used to cover personnel spending for public servants and to maintain the regular operation of public agencies, leaving not much for infrastructure investment. The special governmental fund revenues are mostly spent for infrastructure, but its total amount is far below the scale of investment spending. A large proportion of infrastructure investment in China has to come from untraditional sources of revenue or financial approaches. Some early research points at China's high reliance on debt financing in infrastructure development (Zhao 2014). Since 2014, however, China has seen a sharp expansion of public-private partnerships (PPPs) for infrastructure projects. Limited efforts have been made to understand the background for this PPP movement and its potential effects.

In this chapter, we examine the rise of PPP in the longitudinal context of China's infrastructure finance system. How has the Chinese government financed its unprecedented infrastructure growth? What is the historical background for China's PPP development? How do we characterize the recent PPP expansion? Answering these questions is important not only for decoding China's rapid economic development and urbanization in recent decades but also for addressing concerns that have been raised about the country's long-term financial sustainability. The current literature on the sources of infrastructure investment in China may be divided into two streams. Some studies focus on individual financing approaches that are unique in China. Tsui (2011) ascribes China's infrastructure investment boom to a land-infrastructure-leverage trap created by the country's cadre evaluation system, land management regime, and banking sector. Bo et al. (2017) find out that 17% of borrowing through special purposes vehicle (SPV) companies were in the form of Chengtou bonds and discussed recent policy changes on its development. Zhao (2017) argues that China's land finance, including land transfer fees (LTF) and LTF-backed borrowings such as Chengtou bonds, is a successful example of China-style value capture but also points out that the land-based financing mechanisms have run out of steam and raised increasing concerns. More recently, a lot of discussions are about PPPs in a hope to involve private finance in infrastructure or public service delivery (Yang et al. 2013). These articles shed light on some unique features of China's infrastructure development as local governments experiment on alternative or "innovative" tools.

Another stream of literature examines the structure of financial sources for China's urban infrastructure. Wu (2010) explores patterns and the expanding range of mechanisms for urban infrastructure financing in general and across the country's regions between 1990 and 2006. Wang et al. (2011) explain, contextually and empirically, how Chinese cities finance their infrastructure. Zhao and Cao (2011) trace the history of China's urban infrastructure investment since 1949 and then examine revenue structure and financial approaches for China's urban infrastructure finance. These three articles are based on data from China Urban Construction Statistic Yearbooks, which do not present a full picture about China's infrastructure development, which besides urban facilities also includes regional transportation projects (railroads, highway), major water and power facilities (such as the Three Gorges Dam), as well as health care and educational facilities. Besides, these early studies do not take into consideration the rapid development in China's infrastructure capital structure in recent years.

This chapter is organized as follows. The next section explains key concepts—including traditional mechanisms and alternative financial approaches—in China's infrastructure finance. In Sect. 3, we trace the evolution of the overall infrastructure finance system in China since 1978. In Sect. 4, we begin by briefly reviewing the rise and fall of PPP in China before turning to discuss its recent development. We hope the historical approach can help us understand the nature of PPPs in China and shed light on related policy debates in China and beyond. In the final section, we summarize the features of China's infrastructure finance, conclude about our takes on China's PPP, and provide policy recommendations for its future development. The data come from many sources, including (1) officially published statistical yearbooks and reports, such as China Statistic Yearbook, Finance Yearbook of China, China Urban Construction Statistical Yearbook, and China Land and Resources Yearbook and (2) microlevel databases, consisting of Private Participation in Infrastructure (PPI) Database by World Bank, Wind Financial Database, and National PPP Database by China's Ministry of Finance (MOF).

2   CHINA'S INFRASTRUCTURE FINANCE: TRADITIONAL VERSUS ALTERNATIVE APPROACHES

Infrastructure systems are traditionally provided by the government. The rational for the public provision and regulation of infrastructure is built upon the economic concepts of public goods and market failure. Financial sources for public infrastructure may come from current fiscal revenues (often referred to as "pay-as-you-go" or "pay-go") or governmental debt financing (Wang and Hou 2009). The use of governmental debt is often justified by two reasons: (1) infrastructure investment is lumpy and often involves a very expensive upfront cost that is beyond the annual fiscal capacity of local government and (2) infrastructure facilities have long-term benefits, and thus it is feasible or desirable for them to be paid back gradually over a long period of time. Fiscal revenues for infrastructure development may come from multiple levels of government, through a combination of general or special revenue sources. Governmental debt may involve borrowing by the central government or by local governments. The most common example of local government debt in practice is municipal bonds, which may be guaranteed by the general faith and credit of the local government issuer or by specific revenue streams.

Alternative infrastructure finance refers to non-traditional financial approaches to support infrastructure development. It may include alternative revenue sources, indirect debt financing, and innovative arrangements such as PPPs. Alternative infrastructure finance, also referred to as "innovative" infrastructure finance, is not without controversy in the literature. On the one hand, new and alternative approaches contribute important financial resources for infrastructure development; on the other hand, these non-traditional approaches often lead to policy concerns, in particular, whether the "quick money" involves "kicking the can down the road" that may incur future obligations of the government or whether the financial approaches are used appropriately to advance public interest. Combining traditional and alternative infrastructure finance approaches, we can define the capital structure of infrastructure finance to include fiscal revenues (either traditional and alternative), governmental debts (either traditional or alternative), and PPPs. This is somewhat parallel to the concept of capital structure in the private sector, which involves the combination of internal revenues, debt financing, and equity financing that are used by a firm to make investments (Frank and Goyal 2003).

Fiscal revenues for infrastructure come from both budgetary and extra-budgetary sources. Budgetary sources include more traditional approaches of general revenues and special revenues. General revenues include central and local budgetary allocation, which account for a very small percentage compared to other fiscal sources. Special revenues include local taxes, fees, or surcharges that are earmarked for urban infrastructure development. Special revenues used to play an essential role in China's urban maintenance and construction, but their importance has declined sharply since 1990 (Zhao and Cao 2011). Extra-budgetary sources mainly include LTF. First introduced in the 1980s, LTF involves a lump-sum payment made by developers to obtain the lease of land-use rights for 40–70 years. According to China's land management regime, urban land is owned by the country but directly managed by cities. Rural land is owned collectively by rural residents, but they can be converted into urban use following certain planning and approval process. Local governments can expropriate a large amount of rural land, service it with improved infrastructure, and then lease the land-use right. Local governments can also acquire existing urban land parcels and then transfer the land for an alternative use. These land parcels are consolidated, rearranged, and then strategically re-leased onto the market when the demand is high. Benefitting from the boom in real estate development, local governments have generated a large amount of premium from LTF, which has gradually become the most important revenue source for infrastructure development within cities.

Debt financing consists of borrowing from financial institutions (bank loans) or by issuing bonds. Traditionally, the authority of governmental borrowing was highly centralized in China. According to the 1984 Budget Law, "local governments are not allowed to issue bonds, unless otherwise provided by laws or regulations by the State Council." Borrowing for local governments has been done indirectly, in two general ways. One way is to borrow through the central government. Treasury bonds, for example, are issued by the central government and then lent to local governments under certain terms and interests. Even after the central government selectively opened up local bonds in 2008, the bonds were typically issued, and paid back, by the central government on behalf of local governments. The other way is to issue bank loans or bonds through quasi-governmental organizations, such as local government financing vehicles (LGFVs). Loans are typically provided by state-owned banks. They have low incentive to control the default risk of LGFV loans because these banks may be bailed out by the central government in case of severe fiscal crisis. In recent years, the rapid growth of quasi-governmental borrowing has led to widespread concerns about local government debt crisis. Since 2011, China has pushed forward pilot programs in some localities to allow local government to directly issue municipal bonds, hoping to clean up quasi-government borrowing and to enhance transparency of local government debt (Wildau 2013).

PPP financing refers to the involvement of private finance, either through private debt or through private equity, in the development of public infrastructure. China has rolled out a massive "PPP movement" since 2014, but the use of PPP in China has a long and fluctuated history. One of the most common types in China is build-operate-transfer (BOT). In a typical BOT project, private contractors would spend the upfront cost to build a facility, in exchange for a concession to operate it for a period of time (typically several decades) to recover their initial investment, before transferring the facility back to the government. After several decades of fluctuation and slow growth, PPP suddenly took the center stage of policy discussions after 2014, when China's MOF and several other authorities in China actively promoted "the collaboration between the government and societal capital" (Thieriot and Dominguez 2015). The new wave of PPP includes not only BOT but also other types of partnerships, such as transfer-operate-own (TOT), build-operate-own (BOO), and operating & maintenance (O&M) contract.

3   The Evolution of Infrastructure Finance in China Since 1978

The speeds of infrastructure development in China have seen ups and downs during different periods. Based on macroeconomic backgrounds and historical turning points of significant changes of economic policies, we trace the historical growth of infrastructure investment process in China between 1978 and 2015 and divide the whole trajectory into five periods. For each period, we discuss unique characteristics in the overall capital structure and highlight the

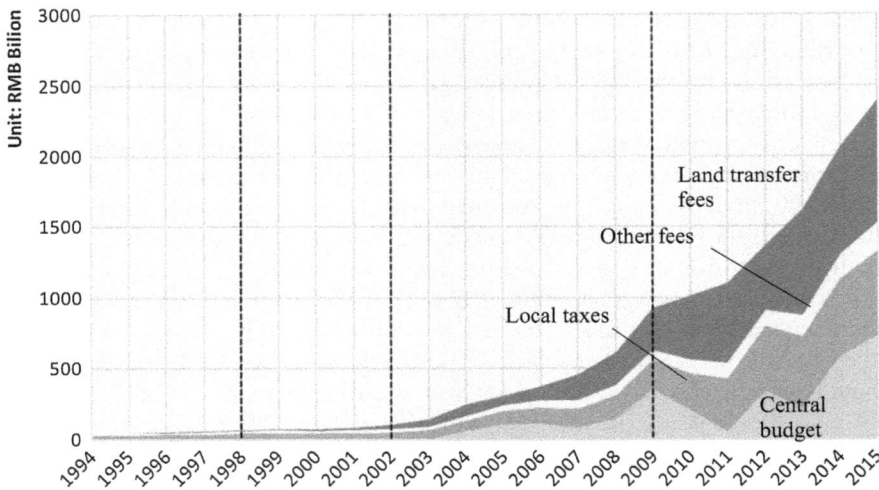

Fig. 29.1   Fiscal revenues in China's infrastructure finance (1994–2015)

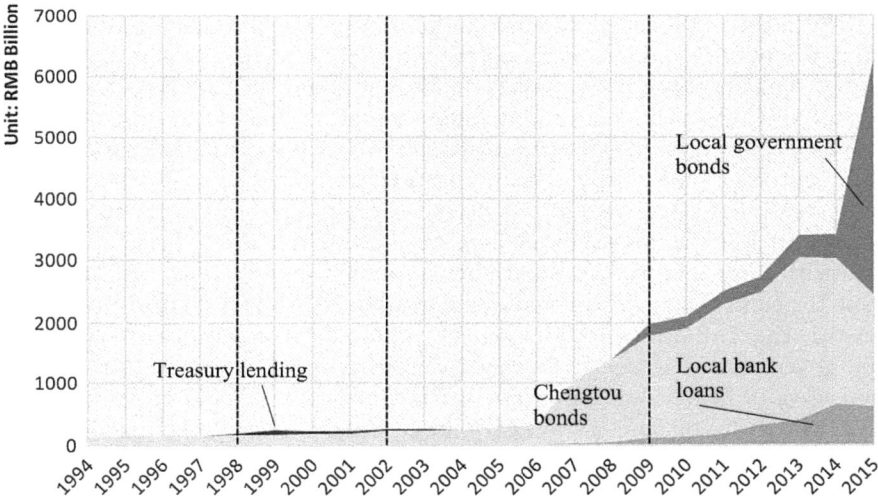

Fig. 29.2   Debt financing in China's infrastructure finance (1994–2015)

development of alternative financial mechanisms and associated policy issues. Figures 29.1 and 29.2 show the evolution of fiscal revenues and debt financing in the last four periods. The first period is not included because the amounts were much smaller in comparison to those in later periods. Likewise, PPPs were not included here because their amounts were too small to show in comparison to fiscal revenues and debt financing.

3.1   1978–1993: The Beginning of Opening-Up

Shortly after the "reform and opening-up" policy that was started in 1978, China's economy was still heavily dominated by central planning. With limited fiscal revenues and a shortage of financing tools, China's infrastructure investment maintained a steady but modest growth. In this period, the capital structure was dominated by fiscal revenues, which accounted for about 96% of China's infrastructure investment, while debt financing accounted for about 4%. Fiscal revenues mostly include direct financial allocation from the central government, but there were also new developments of infrastructure sources at the local level. In 1979, a new urban construction tax was experimented in 57 cities. It then gradually expanded to 150 cities and was later replaced by the special revenue of "Urban Maintenance and Construction Tax" (Chan 1998). This period also saw the infancy of LTF, which started in Shenzhen City in 1981 and then was gradually adopted by many other cities. The first BOT project was also started in Shenzhen City, as localities in southern China began to involve foreign capital in public infrastructure development.

3.2   1994–1997: The Establishment of Socialist Market Economy

It was a major turning point for China's public finance system in 1994, when the country rolled out its tax-assignment reform, which established China's taxation system and intergovernmental fiscal arrangements that have continued to the present (Zhao 2009). China's infrastructure development suddenly turned aggressive, particularly in attracting foreign investment. The typical feature of this period is the boom of BOT. In 1995, Chinese central government launched five pilot BOT projects to promote foreign investment in infrastructure areas, such as energy, water, and transportation. With the central encouragement, local governments cooperated with foreign investors to set up many BOT project companies. Fiscal revenues during this period were mainly levied in the form of traditional taxes, but land transfers were experimented in more and more localities. Initially, the central government claimed 60% of the proceeds from land transfer, but the share was gradually reduced (Peterson 2016). By 1994, all land transfer revenues were assigned to municipal governments, and Tibet was the only province where land-use right had not been implemented (Chan 1998).

3.3   1998–2001: The Adjustment Period After Asian Financial Crisis

The Asian financial crisis in 1997 substantively reduced the availability of private capital in the market, and China's BOT boom braked abruptly in 1998. Meanwhile, the central government realized the problem of hidden local debt associated with the guarantee of fixed rates of return and launched a continuous campaign to "clean up" illegal foreign-invested BOT projects with such arrangements (Shen et al. 2005). To bridge the investment gap, the MOF issued a huge amount of treasury bonds, adding up to 180 billion yuan from 1998 to 2002, and used them for treasury lending. This is a unique example of indirect local borrowing in China through intergovernmental arrangements. With sovereign financial guarantees, treasury bonds were issued at low interest rates, often below 3% annually with a 10-year maturity. The central government designated some proceeds of treasury bonds as revolving loans and lent them to provincial governments—for example, with 5.5% annual interest rate and a six-year maturity to coastal provinces, or 5% annual interest rate and a ten-year maturity to less developed middle and western provinces—on approved projects. Provinces took charge of allocating treasury lending to localities and were responsible for debt services. Comparing to BOT financing, treasury lending enhanced the central government control of local borrowing and reduced the borrowing costs. There were also bank loans that were directly issued by local governments, sometimes done through Chengtou companies (Zhao and Cao 2011). Since infrastructure investment projects usually cannot recover cost within the maturity period of commercial bank loans, local governments often "roll over the loans rather than repay them" (Su and Zhao 2006: 41).

3.4   2002–2008: Rapid Urbanization and the Expansion of Land Finance

The period between 2002 and 2008 was characterized by China's rapid urbanization, which rose sharply from about 39% to about 47%. There was a higher demand for infrastructure in and outside urbanized areas. Moreover, the fact that local government officials were evaluated and held accountable by local economic performance led to intense interlocal competition in infrastructure development, which is especially effective in boosting short-term GDP growth (Wang et al. 2011). This period featured the soaring of land financing, which became a leading approach of infrastructure financing in China. At the beginning, some localities transferred land-use rights of state-owned parcels at low prices to attract private investment. Over time, local governments became more sophisticated in getting revenues or leveraging finance associated with land. In 2003, the Chinese central government promulgated regulations to push for open bidding in land transfer to secure more revenues. In 2007, land finance in China reached a new stage as the Ministry of Land and Resources, the MOF, and the People's Bank of China jointly issued a document allowing local governments to seek land mortgage, that is, bank loans guaranteed with reserved state-owned land that has not yet to be transferred. Promoted by these policy changes, local governments actively engaged in expropriating rural land, leasing part of them through open bidding to fetch high revenues and using other land parcels in reserve as guarantee to seek bank loans. By 2007, LTF had surpassed local taxes and become the top contributor to fiscal revenues for infrastructure finance.

The heavy reliance on land finance in China's local governments—not only for infrastructure investment, but also to support some operating expenses—has drawn heated policy debates. On the one hand, land finance may be considered a successful example of China-style value capture (Zhao 2017). Through the system, China has raised huge amounts of money for urban infrastructure development. The development leads to a significant expansion of urban land and a rapid increase in land value. This process in turn contributes more revenue for further investment through LTF and land mortgage. On the other hand, the system is not financially sustainable because revenues and borrowing associated with long-term leases are used on a one-time basis. Concerns have been raised that conversion of rural land for urban use may have exceeded the real demand, and some local governments may have borrowed more than they can repay.

3.5   Since 2009: Economic Stimulus After the Global Financial Crisis

In response to the global financial crisis in 2008, Chinese government came up with a "4 Trillion Investment Plan" to stimulate the economy development. Most of the funds flooded into infrastructure areas. The infrastructure boom was sustained after the economic stimulus. This period was characterized by the explosion of local government-related bonds, including those issued by local governments, by the central government on behalf of local governments, or by companies for the purpose of local governments.

Since China's 4-trillion stimulus required substantive amounts of local matching, the central government opened up two new doors for local government borrowing. First, it encouraged some "qualified" local governments to set up quasi-governmental entities called LGFVs, which are typically Chengtou companies but may also include other types of quasi-governmental companies, to borrow through bank loans or issue Chengtou bonds. Legally speaking, LGFVs were companies and their borrowing would be corporate debt. But the proceeds were used by urban infrastructure development, with the payback guaranteed by local governments (Zheng 2012). Second, the central government launched a type of local government bonds that were issued by the MOF on behalf of provincial governments. Beginning in 2011, after the experimentation of several pilot programs, some provinces and cities were also allowed to issue local government bonds directly.

The explosive growth of local borrowing soon led to concerns of overborrowing and the risk of debt default. The interest rate of Chengtou bonds increased from 4% in 2009 to 6% in 2013, indicating that the market had perceived the increasing risk associated with LGFVs. Since 2013, China has taken steps to relieve the increasing financial pressure associated with LGFVs. Specifically, banks are prohibited to issue direct bank loans to LGFVs, in order to separate the risk of the financial sector from that of LGFVs. Local governments are encouraged to replace risky and expensive short-term Chengtou bonds with bonds with longer maturity periods. Meanwhile, with the strong encouragement from the central government, local governments plunged into a "PPP movement," hoping to relieve the pressure of local borrowing through PPPs, "the collaboration between the government and societal capital."

Underlying the evolution of China's infrastructure finance, there seems to be a "pecking order" among different sources in the capital structure. For the corporate world, firms are said to show a "pecking order" since they tend to prioritize internal revenues over debt and then equity in capital investment, due to agency costs, information asymmetry, or the consideration of control rights (Jensen and Meckling 1976; Myers and Majluf 1984; Hart 2001). At a first glance, over the course of recent developments, local governments in China follow a similar "pecking order" in raising financial resources for infrastructure. Initially, they used mostly fiscal revenues when most approaches of financing were not available for local governments. Then they gradually developed a high reliance on debt financing after the central government loosened its control. Lastly, they actively pursued PPPs when it was difficult to sustain the growth of fiscal revenues or to incur even more debt. Nevertheless, a closer look of China's infrastructure capital structure reveals unique features that are shaped by the political environment and intergovernmental arrangements in China. While the "pecking order" in corporate finance can also be interpreted as a high reliance on internal revenues over the use of debt or equity, local governments in China tend to rely upon debt financing and alternative revenue sources, especially in recent decades.

The preference of using internal revenues for capital investment may be explained by the information asymmetry theory, since debt financing and equity financing are likely to incur higher financial costs because outside investors are less certain about a company's management and hence require a higher return (Myers and Majluf 1984). In contrast, the high reliance on borrowing in China may be better explained by the agency theory. First, we may see the Chinese government as the agent of the Chinese society. Because of the tendency of budget maximization, the government is likely to invest heavily on infrastructure, due to the country's development orientation and soft budgetary constraint (Qian and Roland 1996). Second, we may see local governments as the agent of the central government. Once allowed, local governments tend to compete with each other in debt financing. Localities with more borrowing enjoy opportunities of development, while the burden and risk associated with borrowing are spread across the whole country, since local borrowing in China are implicitly guaranteed by the central government. Finally, local officials may be considered the agent of local governments. Since officials are often in position with a short tenure and not held accountable for a local government's long-term financial prospect, they have the tendency to use borrowing instead of fiscal revenue, and to use short-term revenue (such as LTF) than traditional revenue sources.

4   The Development of Public-Private Partnerships in China

The rapid development of PPPs in China since 2014 has attracted a lot of attention. Some express enthusiasm and high expectations of it, hoping that the innovative approach not only brings in private capital to sustain China's infrastructure boom but also transforms the way that public services are traditionally delivered in China toward a high level of efficiency. Others, however, raise questions about the appropriate usage of PPP and worry about some potential pitfalls. Similar policy debates are associated with PPP experiences in other places. Commonly used in many developing countries, BOT is often considered a second-best choice for governments when they are constrained by limited fiscal capacity and less developed financial market (Augenblick and Custer 1990). In the UK and some other countries following UK's PFI (Private Finance Initiative) model, PPP has been used in the delivery of infrastructure or public services mainly for the purpose of efficiency gains. In the United States, however, the notion of PPP remains contentious, and the governments are cautious in its adoption (Wang and Zhao 2014). It is worth noting that, with its explosive expansion in recent years, the scale of PPP in China has quickly surpassed those in any other country.

While the official term of "public-private partnerships" suddenly turned in vogue, the use of PPP, in various formats, is not new in China. It has a long and fluctuated history in the past several decades. Figure 29.3 shows the annual PPP projects that were launched each year and the total amounts of PPP finance in China, with data from World Bank's PPI Database, which includes only PPP

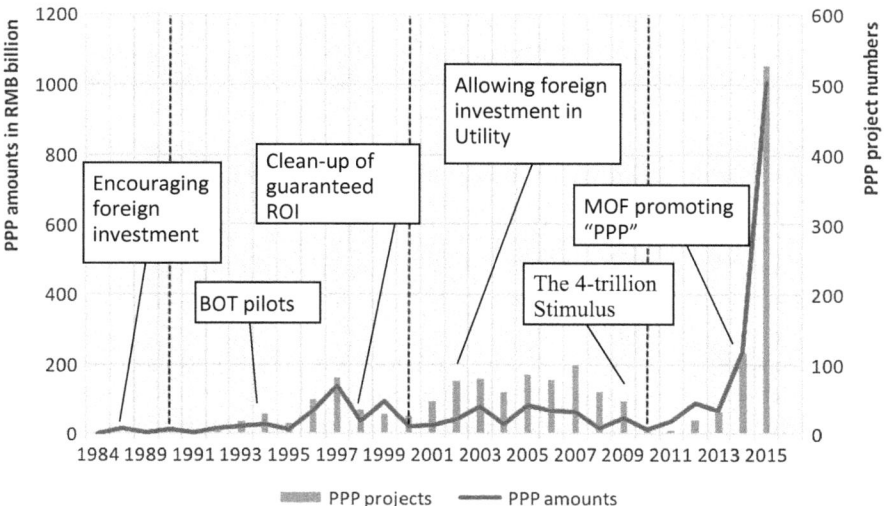

Fig. 29.3   The rise and fall of PPP in China (1980–2015)

projects in transportation, water and sewage, energy, and information technology sectors. We see four waves of PPP activities in these recent decades, signified by some major policy changes from the central government that are highlighted in the figure.

4.1   Early Development of Public-Private Partnerships in China

The first wave of PPP activities occurred in the mid-1980s. At that time, local governments had limited sources of fiscal revenues from taxes and fees. They were not allowed to borrow or issue bonds either. Some localities in southern China began to involve foreign capital in public infrastructure development. A notable example is a power station that was built in Shenzhen City in 1984. This is widely recognized as the first BOT project in China. The experiments received active promotion in 1986, when the central government issued a policy to encourage local governments to attract foreign investment. But the activities were very limited due to the prevalence of ideological barriers and political concerns.

The second wave of PPP activities featured the rise and fall of BOT in the 1990s. The 1994 tax-assignment reform in China further centralized the country's revenue system, while leaving a lot of fiscal responsibilities at the local level. To address the shortfall of infrastructure finance, the central government selected several projects and established pilot BOT projects in 1994. With the central promotion, the number of PPP projects and the amount of investment rose across many places. These experiments, however, achieved mixed results. Since the rules and regulations were not clear and consistent, many BOT projects were developed informally or in ad hoc manner. They were often initiated by private contractors as unsolicited proposals, and the procurement was typically done through closed-door negotiations (Huang and Liu 2015). To attract foreign investment, local governments often fully took up the market risk by guaranteeing fixed rates of return. With the deals reached through closed-door negotiations, these rates were usually set at very high levels, for example, above 12% (Wang 2002). In some sense, such BOT arrangements were used simply as indirect borrowing with high costs to raise money for infrastructure improvement at the period when there were not many other financial tools available. The concern about hidden local government obligations led to a clean-up campaign in 1998, when BOT activities quickly quietened down. In return, local governments received a large amount of treasury lending, and some began to experiment with land sales.

The third wave of PPP activities in 2000s saw several rounds of central encouragement in the use of private finance. In 2001, the central government established a new policy to promote domestic private investment. In 2002, China, in addition, encouraged foreign investments by opening up utility networks that were previously not allowed for them. With these policies, there were a steady increase of PPP activities during the period. After 2008, however, China's infrastructure finance shifted course after the global fiscal crisis. The huge stimulus package of 4-trillion investment came with new ways for local governments to borrow money, such as Chengtou bonds through LGFVs. With the flush of "easy money" flowing to railway, highway, and many other large-scale infrastructure projects, local government's interest about PPP waned.

In general, early development of PPP in China revealed a pattern, that is, attracting private capital—either foreign or domestic—has been used largely to supplement infrastructure finance when other financing approaches were not available. More specifically, PPP activities fluctuated reversely with various types of governmental borrowing: early BOT projects were launched before multiple debt financing approaches became available; the BOT boom was stopped abruptly after local governments received a large amount of treasury lending; the involvement of private capital stayed at a very low level as local governments accumulated a huge amount of local debt.

4.2   Recent Public-Private Partnership Movement in China: "Collaboration Between the Government and Societal Capital"

Since the 1980s, the World Bank's PPI Database has documented about 16,000 PPP projects under implementation across more than 140 countries, with total investment of more than US$2.6 trillion. China accounted for 1440 projects, with a total of US$0.16 trillion (See Fig. 29.3). But these records are dwarfed by China's recent attempt as the country has rolled out a massive "PPP movement" since 2014, when it was formally endorsed by the MOF. According to data from the Government and Social Capital Cooperation (PPP) Research Center, by the end of 2016, China has documented a list of 11,260 PPP projects, across many policy areas, and in different stages of formation, with a total investment target of RMB 13.5 trillion (about UD$2 trillion). Among them, more than 1350 projects have finished the procurement and are under implementation, involving about RMB 2.2 trillion total investment (see Fig. 29.4).[1]

As we discussed earlier, in the 1990s and 2000s, two waves of PPP activities cooled down as China opened up new ways of indirect borrowing for local governments. In the 2010s, however, PPP not only resurrected but claimed the central stage of policy discussion about infrastructure finance because of raising concerns about the risk of financial crisis associated with China's local government debt. According to multiple sources from the government, total local government debt—including all direct and indirect borrowing—have reached RMB 24 trillion by the end of 2014. In some places, the total amount of borrowing that has been accumulated by the local government may have far surpassed its local GDP. In October 2014, the State Council released a special

---

[1] Data for PPP projects come from National PPP Database by Ministry of Finance, available at http://www.pppcenter.org.cn/.

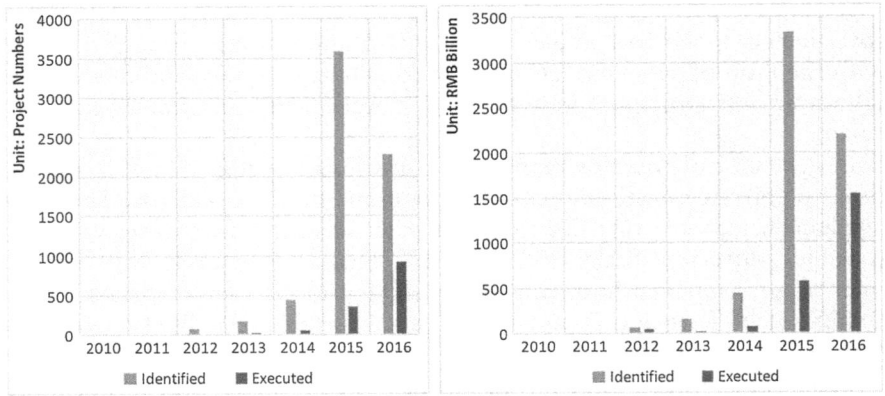

Fig. 29.4 Recent development of PPP in China (2010–2016)

document entitled "On strengthening local government debt management," which aims to gradually remove LGFV's financing function for local governments and to promote "the cooperation of government and social capital (PPP)" as an alternative way of financing. The document "encourages social capital to get involved with urban infrastructure development ... through concession or other suitable arrangements." In 2015, the State Council forwarded a document jointly issued by the MOF, the National Development and Reform Commission (NDRC), and the People's Bank of China, which listed "Guidelines about how to promote PPP in public services sectors" that promote the use of PPP in public service sectors including "energy, transportation, irrigation, environmental protection, agriculture, forestry, science, social housing, medical, senior services, education, culture, etc." While these official documents promote PPP to be a transformative way of public service delivery with many benefits, the intention for relieving the pressure of local debt is explicit. According to the Ministry of Finance (2015), local governments can receive up to 2% of budgetary reward for the amounts of local government debts that are replaced. With the unparalleled level of central support, local governments are actively pursuing PPP in unprecedented scale and scope.

The recent development of PPP in China features a high level of governmental transparency. After a comprehensive information platform for PPP was launched in early 2016, the MOF issued periodical reports with updated information about PPP activities. The projects are categorized into five stages—identification, preparation, procurement, execution, and transferred—according to their different phases in PPP formation and official approval. By the end of 2016, there have been a total of 11,260 projects, among which 6987 projects are in "identification," 1936 in "preparation," 986 in "procurement," and 1351 in "execution" stages. No projects are in the "transferred" stages since none of them have finished the whole cycle of PPP.

Table 29.1   Types of PPP in execution across infrastructure sectors (2017)

	BOT	TOT/ROT	BOO	O&M	Others	Total	%
Utilities	510	120	17	5	106	724	43.0%
Transportation	177	14	8		18	216	12.8%
Environment	102	10	2		26	134	8.0%
Urban development	66	2	7		17	92	5.5%
Education	64	6	4	1	10	84	5.0%
Irrigation	63	7		1	5	73	4.3%
Medical	35	2	7		9	53	3.1%
Energy	34	1	7		2	44	2.6%
Tourism	25	2	7	1	8	42	2.5%
Culture	29	2		1	5	37	2.2%
Senior services	19	2	14		2	36	2.1%
Social housing	30	1	2		2	35	2.1%
Science	24	2	4		3	32	1.9%
Government facility	20	2			6	27	1.6%
Sports	12	1	1		3	17	1.0%
Agriculture	5	0	3		1	9	0.5%
Social security	5	1	2		0	8	0.5%
Forestry	1	1			0	2	0.1%
Others	16	0			2	18	1.1%
Grand Total	*1,237*	*176*	*85*	*9*	*225*	*1,683*	*100.0%*
%	*73.5%*	*10.5%*	*5.1%*	*0.5%*	*13.4%*	*100.0%*	

Data source: National PPP database by China's Ministry of Finance

Table 29.1 shows the types of PPP that are implemented across infrastructure sectors as of early 2017. The most common PPP type is BOT, which accounts for about 74% of total cases. Closely related to BOT are two other PPP types: TOT, which applies to "brownfield projects" that are already built, in comparison to BOT for the new construction of "greenfield projects"; and renovate-operate-transfer (ROT), which is essentially TOT with an additional component of renovation. Projects of TOT and ROT type together account for about 10% of total cases. Then there are about 5% of build-own-operate (BOO) cases, which involve full privatization of the facility and, unlike BOT, would not be transferred back to the government. Accounting for about 0.5%, O&M are cases that only involve private contractors in O&M but not the construction of facilities. There are also about 13% of additional PPP cases with other types of arrangements. Regarding infrastructure sectors, utilities, transportation, and environmental facilities see the most active PPP activities. The three sectors in combination account for more than half of all cases that are in execution. While the BOT type is the most common for all sectors, different sectors may rely on different PPP types. Utilities, for example, seem to have more activities with TOT/ROT proportionally than many other sectors.

The implemented PPP cases are spread across all provinces. Provinces with the highest numbers of cases in execution are Shandong, Xinjiang, Zhejiang, Sichuan, and Henan. Provinces with the highest PPP amounts in execution are

Guizhou, Hebei, Shandong, Beijing, and Yunnan. More studies are needed to explain the adoption of PPP cases in different provinces. The results are likely affected not only by the incentives for a province to use PPP but also by the capacity for a province to reach a deal with private contractors. There are three types of payback mechanisms. About 42% of projects use the "Government Pay" mechanism, in which the government assumes the full operating risk and compensate private contractors directly. About 38% of projects use "Viability Gap Funding," in which the government assumes partial operating risk and subsidizes private contractors in various ways to fill the gap between direct user payment and a reasonable return for private investment. About 20% of projects use "User pay," in which private contractors take up the operating risk and get their returns solely from direct user revenues. With respect to the procurement process, the most commonly used approaches are "Open Tendering" (about 55%) and "Competitive Consultation" (about 35%). Other approaches—including "Competitive Negotiation," "Invited Tendering," and "Single-source procurement"—account for less than 10% of all cases.

Several questions remain about the effectiveness of PPP in attracting private finance to substitute local government borrowing. The first concern is about the low "landing rate" of target PPP projects, that is, the difficulty for a government to reach a deal with partners to actually implement a PPP. The landing rate is commonly measured as the share of PPP projects in execution to all projects that have been identified. By the end of 2016, for example, only about 12% of the projects in the MOF's PPP database have been executed. Note that the landing rate does not accurately reflect the success in PPP implantation for a given year, since the measure does not take into consideration the length of time since a project has been identified. According to the MOF's analysis based on their "Exemplary PPP cases," the average duration between identification and execution used to be about 15 months, but it has been shortened to about 11 months (Renmin Net 2017).

The second concern is about who are the "social capital partners." Data from multiple sources indicate that more than half of the partners are actually state-owned companies, which may account for more than 75% of "social capital" that has been raised through PPP (Southern Weekly 2016). This may happen because the private sector is cautious about getting involved since many local governments do not have a track record of honoring their agreements. It is also possible that state-owned companies, with their close ties to the government, have been able to cherry-pick large and lucrative PPP projects. It seems that the "pecking order" in China's infrastructure capital structure extends well into the selection of PPP partners. Strategically or opportunistically, local governments may have the tendency to establish PPP collaboration with state-owned companies before they work with private sector partners. Among private sector partners, local governments may have a preference for domestic ones instead of foreign companies. In the 1990s and early 2000s, China used to target foreign companies as a source to attract private capital; in the recent

PPP expansion, however, the participation of foreign capital is almost negligible.

A third concern is about the financial costs for PPP projects, which are still understudied but likely to be high. In about 80% of PPP projects, the government either assume the full responsibility to compensate private contractors or guarantee to bridge the revenue gap if private contractors fail to generate sufficient user fees. Based on data of limited coverage, our preliminary analysis shows that most PPP projects have an internal rate of return above 6%, in comparison to a typical interest rate of 3–5% for treasury bonds and local bonds. It is clear that, to be able to attract the investment of "social capital," PPP projects are likely to incur much higher financial costs than direct governmental borrowing. The choice between debt financing versus PPP thus become a tricky policy trade-off between the risk of local government debt crisis, which is more visible now, and a high cost of public service delivery, which is less clear to most for now.

5   Conclusions and Discussions

This chapter put China's recent PPP development in the longitudinal context about the combination of financial sources that has propelled China's infrastructure investment since 1978. Besides traditional revenue sources such as central budget allocation and small local earmarked taxes, the system has been characterized by the use of alternative infrastructure finance, including LTF, and various types of indirect local government borrowing. While accounting for only a tiny percentage of the capital structure, China's PPP has fluctuated over the past several decades. The recent development, or resurrection, of PPPs is a response to two difficulties local governments are facing: dwindling LTF and the increasing pressure of local government borrowing. PPP, however, cannot be an effective way to reduce the high reliance on debt financing because the initial involvement of social capital still needs to be paid back, often with a higher cost.

Our analysis shows that the use of alternative infrastructure finance has contributed significantly to the unprecedented boom of infrastructure development in China. Taking 2015 as an example, LTF, local borrowing, and PPP accounted for more than 85% of total infrastructure spending (see Figs. 29.1, 29.2, and 29.3). It is time for the country to develop a more balanced capital structure with ongoing funding support to keep up its long-term infrastructure development. While some other countries are seeking "innovative" finance to provide supplemental financial resources for meeting their infrastructure needs, China needs to get back to more conventional funding approaches (Zhao 2014).

LTF involves a lump-sum payment made by developers to obtain the lease of land-use rights for 40–70 years. Local governments use LTF to support infrastructure, which boosts land value and in turn contributes more revenue for urban development. It is thus a successful example of China-style value capture. The use of LTF, however, is not financially sustainable in the long run. The lands are transferred for private usage for decades, but the fees are assessed and used at one time. Once the speed to convert rural land to urban use slows down, the revenue stream will dry up. Cities may raise big amounts of money in the short term to build new facilities, but they will face difficulty in operating and maintaining them for the decades to come, and will not able to meet the ongoing service needs associated with expanded urban area, population, and economic activities. Accordingly, scholars call for a local finance reform to replace it with a property tax system that is annually assessed and collected (Zhang and Hou 2016; Zhao 2017). Chinese government experimented with property tax pilot programs in several cities including Shanghai and Chongqing in 2011. But a full implementation of property tax still faces substantial obstacles in China. In addition, China may designate more sources, such as transportation or environmental taxes, as special revenues for particular areas of infrastructure, in addition to the annual assessed property tax.

Local governments in China have heavily relied upon debt financing for infrastructure development, even though they were not allowed to borrow directly from banks or the bond market until recently. Nevertheless, there have been various types of indirect local borrowing, such as treasury lending, bank loans or Chengtou bonds issued by LGFVs, or municipal bonds issued by the MOF on behalf of local governments. Indirect local borrowing such as LGFV debt is less transparent, making it even harder to hold local governments accountable for their borrowing and spending behaviors. Local government borrowing in China is assumed to be implicitly guaranteed by the central government. Because of the skewed incentive system, local governments compete with each other to borrow and overinvest in infrastructure sector in their jurisdictions, while the risks are spread across the whole government. The fact that indirect local borrowing is not transparent to the public further conceals the system-wide risk (Zheng 2012).

China should make its local debt market more open and transparent by fully disclosing borrowing and debt services in the budget and by banning the financing functions of LGFVs as hidden back doors of local government borrowing.

It is advisable for China to address policy concerns over the reliance on LTF and local government borrowing, but the goal of the recent PPP movement is misplaced. The central government intends to substitute debt financing with the involvement of private investments, but the efforts have not been effective. The "pecking order" in China's infrastructure finance shows that local governments started from a reliance on fiscal revenues to the increasing use of debt financing and lastly pursued PPP, as the last resort, when they encountered difficulties to raise additional fiscal revenue or debt financing. Echoing the experiences from the UK and the USA, China's PPP projects are likely to incur higher financial costs than direct governmental borrowing. Private capital may be used to supplement other financial sources but cannot become the mainstay of infrastructure finance.

REFERENCES

Augenblick, M., and Custer, B.S. (1990). *The Build, Operate, and Transfer ("BOT") Approach to Infrastructure Projects in Developing Countries.* Report #. 498. The World Bank.

Bo, L., Mear, F. C., & Huang, J. (2017). New development: China's debt transparency and the case of urban construction investment bonds. Public Money & Management, 37(3), 225–230.

Chan, K Wing. (1998). Infrastructure services and financing in Chinese cities. Pacific Rim Law and Policy Journal, 7(3), 503–528.

Frank, M., & Goyal, V. (2003). Testing the pecking order theory of capital structure. Journal of Financial Economics, 67, 217–248.

Hart, O. (2001), Financial contracting (No. w8285). National Bureau of Economic Research.

Huang, J.W., & Liu, X.P. (2015). Learn from history: China's PPP development and its future, March 2015, http://bond.hexun.com/upload/117.pdf.

Jensen, M. C. and Meckling, W. H. (1976), Theory of the firm: Managerial behavior, agency costs and ownership structure. *Journal of Financial Economics*, 3, 4, pp. 305–360.

McKinsey Global Institute (2016). Bridging global infrastructure gaps, June 2016, http://www.un.org/pga/71/wpcontent/uploads/sites/40/2017/06/Bridging-Global-Infrastructure-Gaps-Full-report-June-2016.pdf.

Ministry of Finance. (2015). Notice on substituting subsidies with rewards for Public-Private Partnership projects, http://jrs.mof.gov.cn/zhengwuxinxi/gongzuodong-tai/201512/t20151217_1618396.html.

Myers, S. C. and Majluf, N. S. (1984), Corporate financing and investment decisions when firms have information that investors do not have. *Journal of Financial Economics*, 13, 2, pp. 187–221.

Peterson, G.E. (2016). Land leasing and land sale as an infrastructure-financing option, World Bank Policy Research Working Paper No. 4043, https://papers.ssrn.com/sol3/papers.cfm?abstract_id=940509.

Qian, Y.Y. and Roland, G. (1996). The Soft Budget Constraint in China. Japan and the World Economy. Vol 8(2): 207–223.

Renmin Net. (2017). Ministry of Finance: The average duration between identification and execution of China's PPP projects start to shorten and the ratio of investment increases more than four times, 07 March, http://finance.people.com.cn/n1/2017/0307/c1004-29128738.html, accessed: 27 October 2017.

Shen, J. Y., Wang, S. Q., & Qiang, M. S. (2005). Political risks and sovereign risks in Chinese BOT/PPP projects: a case study. Chinese Businessman Investment and Finance, 1, 50–53.

Southern Weekly. (2016). How have state-owned companies become the main partici-pators in PPP in China? 02 July 2016, http://www.sohu.com/a/100677261_115812, accessed: 27 October 2017.

Su, M. & Zhao, Q.H. (2006). China: Fiscal Framework and Urban Infrastructure Finance. In George E. Peterson, & Patricia Clarke Annez (Eds.), Financing Cities: Fiscal Responsibility and Urban Infrastructure in Brazil, China, India, Poland and South Africa (2007th ed.) Sage Publications, Log Angeles, USA; World Bank, Washington, DC, USA, 41.

Thieriot, H., & Dominguez, C. (2015). Public-Private Partnerships in China: on 2014 as a landmark year, with past and future challenges. International institute for sustainable development, https://www.iisd.org/sites/default/files/publications/public-private-partnerships-china.pdf.

Tsui, K. Y. (2011). China's infrastructure investment boom and local debt crisis. Eurasian Geography and Economics, 52(5), 686–711.

Wang, W. (2002). Do China's BOT projects experience failure? 26 April, http://business.sohu.com/79/07/article200620779.shtml, accessed: 27 October 2017.

Wang, W., & Hou, Y. (2009). Pay-as-you-go financing and capital outlay volatility: evidence from the states over two recent economic cycles. Public Budgeting & Finance, 29(4), 90–107.

Wang, W., Zheng, X.Y., & Zhao, Z.R. (2011). Fiscal reform and public education spending: A quasi-natural experiment of fiscal decentralization in China. Public: The Journal of Federalism. 42(2): 334–356.

Wang, Y., & Zhao, Z.R. (2014). Motivations, obstacles, and resources: determinants of public-private partnerships in state toll road financing. Journal of Public Performance & Management Review, 37(4): 679–704.

Wildau, G. (2013). China looks to municipal bonds to clean up local-government debt, October 2013, https://www.reuters.com/article/us-china-debt-bonds/china-looks-to-municipal-bonds-to-clean-up-local-government-debt-idUSBRE-99J0AD20131020.

Wu, W. (2010) Urban Infrastructure Financing and Economic Performance in China. *Urban Geography* 31 (5): 648–667.

Xinhua Net. (2017a). Railroads in operation in China reached 124,000 km in 2016, including more than 22,000 km of high-speed rail, 03 January, http://news.xinhuanet.com/politics/2017-01/03/c_129430123.htm, accessed: 27 October 2017.

Xinhua Net. (2017b). Scale of China's subway expands quickly and ten more cities open their subway in five years, 23 June, http://news.xinhuanet.com/politics/2017-06/23/c_1121194913.htm, accessed: 27 October 2017.

Yang, Y., Hou, Y., & Wang, Y. (2013). On the development of public–private partnerships in transitional economies: An explanatory framework. Public Administration Review, 73(2), 301–310.

Zaobao. (2017). China's total expressway mileage had surpassed 130,000 kilometers and ranks as the first all over the world, 17 July 2017, http://www.zaobao.com.sg/realtime/china/story20170717-779768, accessed: 27 October 2017.

Zhang, P., & Hou, Y.L. (2016). A model for the ability-to-pay index of China's real property tax, tax burden distribution and redistributive effects. Economic Research Journal, 51(012), 118–132.

Zhao, J. (2009). Fiscal Decentralization and Provincial-level Fiscal Disparities: A Sino-US Comparative Perspective. Public Administration Review, 69: S67-S74.

Zhao, J. (2017). Funding urban infrastructure: China-style value capture. https://cpi-analysis.org/2017/03/20/funding-urban-infrastructure-china-style-value-capture/.

Zhao, J., & Cao, C. (2011). Funding china's urban infrastructure: revenue structure and financing approaches. Public Finance & Management, 11(3).

Zhao, J., (2014). Making China's urban transportation boom sustainable. http://www.paulsoninstitute.org/think-tank/2014/05/09/making-chinas-urban-transportation-boom-sustainable/.

Zheng, C.R. (2012). The real risk of China's sub-national debt: the risk beyond default. Journal of Public Administration, 5(4): 52–76.

CHAPTER 30

Land Conflict and the Transformation of Local Governance

Rong Tan

1   INTRODUCTION

1.1   Brief Overview of the Land Acquisition System in China

The design of land acquisition system (LAS) is a reflection of antagonisms of government-farmer relationships (GFRs) in China and is a point from which to examine adjustments of local governance. Due to the scarcity and irreplaceability of land resources, inelastic demand cannot be realized by the market or by other means when a nation must use specific land for the public (Zhang 2005). Therefore, LAS has generally been established in all countries worldwide, and the demand for land for national public construction is met by obtaining land from other subjects using national public power (Xu 2011). This arrangement of land use is referred to as the practice of "supreme land rights" in the US; as "compulsory purchasing" in the UK; as "land requisition" in Japan; as "land acquisition" in France, Germany, and Taiwan; and as the "resumption of Crown land" in Hong Kong. In China, land acquisition refers to a form of administrative action through which the state can (for the public) transfer rural collective land into state-owned land in accordance with the law. Land acquisition practices, legal systems, administrative enforcement systems, and acquisition management systems constitute the foundation of the Chinese LAS.

According to the Constitution and the *Land Management Law*, land in urban districts shall be owned by the state and land in the rural and suburban areas shall be owned by the collective except for those portions that belong to the state by law. In addition, any entity or individual who must use land must

R. Tan (✉)

School of Public Affairs, Zhejiang University, Hangzhou, Zhejiang, China

e-mail: tanrong@zju.edu.cn

© The Author(s) 2019

J. Yu, S. Guo (eds.), *The Palgrave Handbook of Local Governance in Contemporary China*, https://doi.org/10.1007/978-981-13-2799-5_30

apply for the state-owned land according to law. The above provisions separate the lands of urban and rural areas and form a unique dual management system of urban and rural land in China. In this context, China's urban expansion driven by urbanization and industrialization has relied on the occupation of rural land. However, rural collective land can only enter the market through land acquisition as state-owned land, forming the primary land market monopolized by the government.

China's land acquisition and dual land management systems have facilitated the country's social and economic development, gradually forming a unique system of land financing. Local governments tightly control land expropriation and land grants as a point of interest. On the one hand, collective land is expropriated at a low cost in accordance with agricultural use. On the other hand, land is assigned at high prices in accordance with construction uses. Thus, local governments capture huge land value-added revenues, which become an important source of funds for urban development and for attracting enterprises. Clearly, this system functions at the expense of the development rights and interests of rural areas. Many social contradictions have been revealed. The most typical concerns the increasingly intensified GFR (e.g., frequent land acquisition and home demolition conflicts). This section thus focuses on the land conflicts resulting from the country's LAS with an emphasis on the GFRs behind its operation and local governance responses (Fig. 30.1).

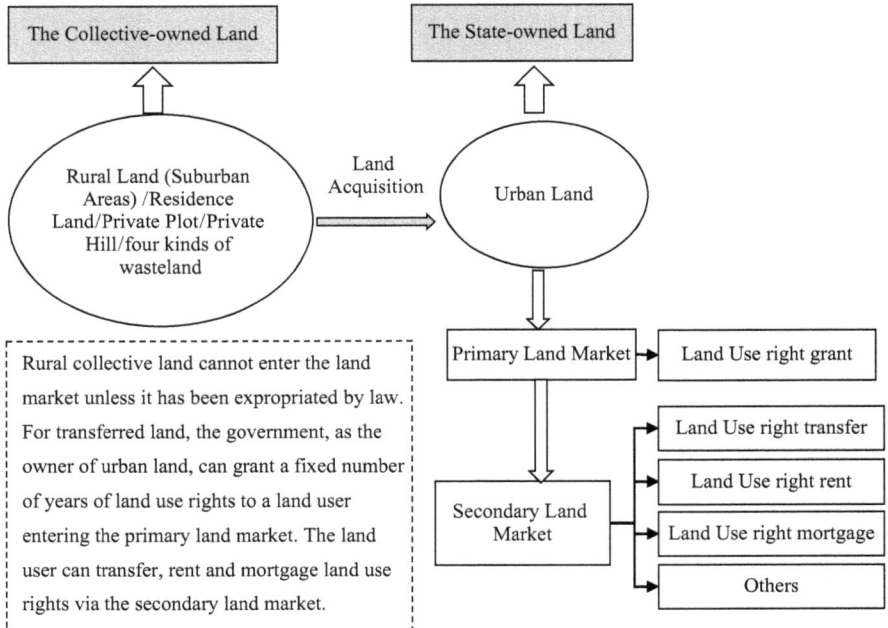

Fig. 30.1   The land acquisition system of the urban-rural dual structure

Main Characteristics

Land acquisition serves as a way for the government to obtain land by coercive means. It is an administrative measure for the adjustment of land use and property rights commonly adopted by governments around the world. Due to the complexities of land resources, urban-rural land systems, and social and economic development in China, the LAS presents distinctive features mainly manifested in the following aspects:

1. The uniqueness of ownership transfers

    Land acquisition involves the transferring of land ownership and land use rights. Under normal circumstances, the nation and government obtain private land ownership by acquisition and convert land into government-owned land. The land expropriator, in turn, loses all rights to the original land after being compensated. In contrast with countries employing private land ownership, ownership transfer is unique in the Chinese LAS, in that land ownership is transferred from the rural collective to the state government. In China, rural land is owned by the rural collective. What is owned by the rural collective is turned over to the state by land acquisition. Finally, the government transfers land use rights to construction land enterprises or entities by means of administrative allocations or grants to realize the transfer of land ownership.

2. Strong planning

    The most striking feature of land acquisition is that the state government can employ mandatory measures for the sake of public interests through forced purchases. China's LAS was formed during the planned economy period following the establishment of the People's Republic of China (PRC). The inherently coercive nature of the system aggravated the irresistible nature of land acquisition under the planned economy. The government obtained land use rights and ownership by executive order to serve the needs for national construction in the planned economy era, constituting the most important institutional arrangement applied in China's formation of its public ownership economy mechanism. With the establishment of relevant legal norms, the planned LAS was determined from a legal perspective (Chai 2008). Interactions between the compulsive LAS and the politically planned economic system at different times finally formed China's current planned LAS.

3. The only source of new urban construction land

    The state completely changed land ownership laws through compulsory land acquisition to obtain land from farmers and the collective. Rural collective-owned land were converted into urban state-owned land for urbanization and industrialization through the application of laws and regulations. As the only source of newly developed urban construction land, the legal status of land acquisition was established (Qian and Ma 2007). This is also essentially why the LAS has long been accompanied by urbanization and industrialization. In addition, the land expropriation system, which is fixed by law, limits the conversion of rural construction land and its entry into the market. This has legally hindered system innovations of relevant construction land and has had a profound impact on the optimal allocation of urban construction land (Gao and Liu 2007).

4. Expanding the scope and low compensation standards

The burden of mandatory land expropriation on public interests should be shared across a whole society. With the acceleration of China's urbanization, contradictions between urban and rural land are becoming more prominent, and the illustration of public interests has been undergoing a gradual expansion. The government has often expropriated land in the name of the public interest to obtain huge prices via land use conversion, driving local government land finance dependence. Compensation standards of land acquisition are currently compensated according to original land uses. This essentially extends the allocation mechanism between agricultural and non-agricultural sectors under the planned economy system, supporting national industrialization construction at the expense of farmers and collective benefits and disregarding the autonomous will and lawful property rights and interests of landowners. Therefore, land acquisition in China is characterized by an expanding scope and low compensation standards, and these trends have been continuously accompanied by the presence of China's LAS (Chai 2008).

5. Low costs and inefficient allocation of land resources

China's planning economy always emphasizes national planning allocation based on production factors. Therefore, restrictions on government land acquisition have become more lax. Low compensation standards reduce land acquisition costs, and land acquisition approval authority is delegated layer upon layer. These factors further the indiscriminate expansion of land acquisition behaviors among local governments of all levels. Issues of land resource waste resulting from land acquisition are very serious, and issues regarding the protection of farmland have also not been taken seriously (Feng 2011), seriously affecting the optimal allocation of land resources.

Statutory Procedures of Land Acquisition
According to laws and regulations currently applied in China, land acquisition procedures mainly involve the following:

1. Formulating and announcing land acquisition plans: Before declaring a land acquisition, a municipal or county government shall draw up a land acquisition plan that specifies information on areas, locations, land boundaries, uses, compensation standards, resettlement modes, and so on. An announce-

ment is made by the rural collective economic organization that has been expropriated.

2. Carrying out condition investigations and reporting results: A land acquisition implementation unit shall investigate the status of the proposed land acquisition plan, must inform rural collective economic organizations and farmers, and must listen to opinions on land acquisition compensation and resettlement.

3. Reviewing investigations and organizing hearings: If there is any objection to the survey results of the proposed land acquisition plan, the administrative department of land resources shall review this in a timely manner. When an application for compensation and the resettlement of land acquisition is submitted, the administrative department of land resources must organize hearings.

4. Approving and reviewing land acquisition plans: In accordance with general land use planning and land use annual planning principles, municipal and county governments shall draw up specifications of an agricultural land conversion scheme, an arable land supplement plan, a land acquisition plan, a land supply scheme and a construction land project and must report this information to administrative departments of municipal or county governments for review.

5. Applying the land acquisition plan: The land acquisition plan shall be announced by municipal and county governments after the approval of legal procedures, and then the plan shall be implemented.

6. Adjudicating disputes on land acquisition compensation: If rural collective economic organizations or farmers who have been expropriated disagree with compensation schemes of a land acquisition plan, this shall be addressed by the municipal or county government. When no coordination exists, they can apply to the next government adjudication entity or bring a lawsuit to the people's court. The dispute over land acquisition compensation and resettlement schemes does not affect the implementation of land acquisition plans.

7. Payment of land acquisition compensation and the resettlement of landless farmers: All forms of land acquisition compensation shall be paid three months from the date of land compensation and resettlement scheme approval. After receiving a compensation fee, farmers must transfer possessions and land by a deadline determined by the government (Fig. 30.2).

The seven steps of land acquisition in China are not clearly defined under China's laws and regulations but rather are defined through various laws, regulations, and acts. The *Land Management Law* and other relevant laws and regulations on land expropriation procedures still use the past government-led management mode of the planned economy system and stress the smooth application of acquisition rights and the comprehensive management of land acquisition. This has ineffectively restrained the expansion and abuse of acquisition rights, and it is also not conducive to protect the legitimate rights and interests of expropriated stakeholders.

Fig. 30.2 Flowchart of land acquisition in China

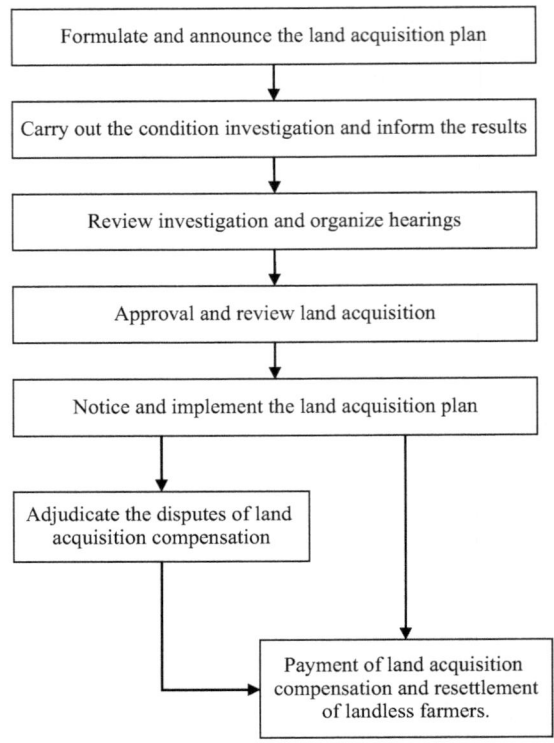

Historical Premises for the Formation of LAS

In the planned economy era, the formation of the LAS has been historically inevitable:

1. Social ideological and institutional reasons: National ideologies determine that the allocation and arrangement of land and especially of construction land should be executed via top-down planning. Through land acquisition, the planning of construction land can be effectively implemented. Limited understanding of market economy and market allocation mechanisms and subjective resistance from society have rendered the market-oriented allocation of urban-rural construction land unfeasible.

2. Restrictions to certain stages of economic and social development: Earlier on, the goals of socialist construction in China had not yet been fully adjusted to processes of economic development. Demand for construction land was low. The planning of LAS arrangements can meet land use demands and can effectively augment national development and strategic propulsion.

3. Impacts of ethical values: There was a common ethical value that individual and collective interests should submit to national interests. National inter-

ests represented the public interests of all members of society. The LAS can garner support from the collective and from individuals.

4. Insufficient understanding of land assets and property rights: The collective and individual understanding of land focused on resource properties. Understanding of assets and capital characteristics was insufficient and had not formed cognitive concepts of property rights, thus failing to develop trading groups of construction land markets.

1.2   Brief History of the LAS and Dynamic Changes in GFR in China

Since the formation of new China in 1949, the LAS has undergone four stages (establishment, adjustment, improvement, and innovation) while the associated GFRs have also transformed from being harmonious to exhibiting contradictions and then to the deterioration of conflicts to the adaptive adjustment of relationships (Fig. 30.3).

Establishment of the LAS and of Harmonious GFR (1949–1955)

During 1949 and 1955, China was faced with unstable political and economic conditions both at home and abroad and with the historical task of resisting interventions from abroad and stabilizing social relations domestically. The promotion of economic development was the inevitable goal of the Chinese central government at the time. In establishing a planned economic system based on Russia's system, the establishment of a relatively complete LAS has become an objective prerequisite for social transformation and economic development, as it is more convenient to collect land resources from farmers, to use such land to spur economic development, and to execute land use management in the name of national construction. For this reason, in 1954, Article 13 of the Constitution of the PRC was written, which stipulated that "for the sake of the public interest, the government can levy both urban and rural land as well as the other production resources in accordance with conditions prescribed by law." This has formed the basis of the establishment of the LAS in China.

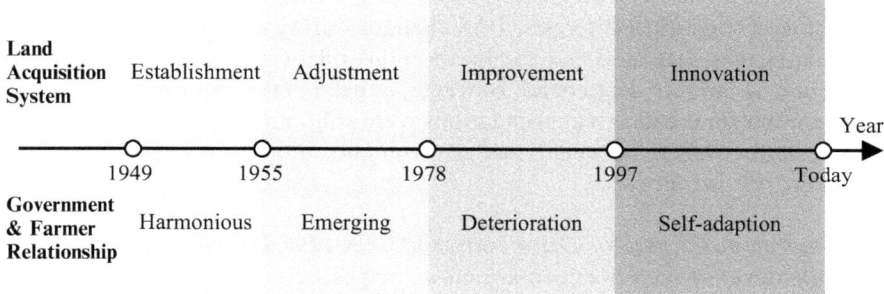

Fig. 30.3   Dynamic changes in the LAS and GFR from 1949 to the present in China

At the time, the socialist transformation of land was not yet fully realized, and most private land in rural areas still belonged to farmers, meaning that the objects of land acquisition were mainly farmers. As farmers enjoyed high social status during this period and to curtail social instability resulting from land acquisition, local governments accounted for the interests of farmers and stressed the principle of "fair and reasonable" compensation in executing land acquisition while the central government also stressed "providing requisite notice to farmers who will lose their land and addressing the interests of farmers as much as possible so that they can consciously follow the interests of the government." Based on a long-standing wish to establish socialist public ownership, farmers had developed a strong sense of public ownership while concepts of private ownership were considered relatively vague. In this historical setting, conflicts between the government and farmers as a result of land acquisition processes did not occur. Rather, the public ownership of land systems combined with the planned economy made large areas of inexpensive land available for industrialization and urbanization, which had considerable effects on development in earlier stages.

Adjustments to the LAS and Emerging GFR Conflicts (1956–1978)

During the period of agricultural cooperation, rural land was transferred from private farmers to collective ownership, and thus collective organizations rather than farmers became the main subjects of land acquisition. However, the relationship between farmers and collective organizations is not clearly defined and collective organizations in rural areas occupy a weak position, as farmers can rarely negotiate with local governments during land acquisition. Simultaneously, shortages of funding and limited means of production were exacerbated during this period, and thus more benefits arising from land acquisition were distributed to local governments in the name of national economic development. As a result, compensation for farmers who had lost land declined. For example, standards of land compensation have been adjusted from "the total value of farm production accumulated over the last 3 or 5 years" to "the total value of farm production accumulated over the last 2 or 4 years." Furthermore, the government states that a land-expropriated farmer can only be relocated to a rural area and not to a city.

From this moment on, with the reduction of land compensation standards, due to the farmers' weak bargaining position, and with the favoring of national interest over individual interests, LAS changes during this period set in place unstable factors that hindered the harmonious relationship between the government and farmers. In general, however, as gaps between the rich and poor and between rural and urban populations were still minor in China during this period, land conflicts between local governments and farmers aroused by the LAS were not yet serious.

LAS Improvements and the Deterioration of GFR (1978–1996)

With the onset of the reform and open-up stages, economic development was at the center of national development, and in response, demand for new construction land increased in every sector. At the same time, to correct for a series of problems that emerged during the earlier operation of the LAS, the central government further standardized procedures by (1) stressing mandatory features of land acquisition, meaning that land acquisition cannot be stopped or hindered in meeting public or national interests; (2) defining collective land as the only object of land acquisition with compensation fees including compensation for land, compensation for crops, compensation for buildings or attachments, and compensation for land-expropriated farmer resettlement; and (3) treating intensive land use as a basic means of land acquisition to curb land losses and the decline of cultivated land through land acquisition.

Adjustments to the LAS aimed at mitigating uncertainties related to land acquisition and at alleviating contradictions between local governments and farmers. Nevertheless, rapid economic development in this period also led to rapid changes in social relations in the country as reflected in the deterioration of land conflicts. Specifically, with the concept of market competition gradually enjoying popular support, property attributes of land resources began to manifest, and farmers and local governments developed a stronger sense of land property rights. Furthermore, land acquisition benefits derived from the difference between low compensation for farmers subjected to land expropriation and the high price of land transactions for the same land became the focus of local governments and farmers. On the one hand, local governments gradually developed land finance dependence, meaning that local governments sought to increase land benefits derived from land acquisition, and compensation for farmers declined correspondingly, causing the relationship between local governments and farmers to become more intensive. On the other hand, value-added land was distributed by local governments and few farmers can determine or monitor its distribution due to the presence of corruption and a lack of transparency, thus escalating conflicts between farmers and local governments, compromising trust in local governments, and precipitating continuous land conflicts across the country.

LAS Innovation and GFR Self-Adaption

In 1997, the socialist market economic system became the basic national policy, and the LAS, which is heavily based on planned economics, appeared to be out of tune. At this time, to alleviate social contradictions caused by land acquisition, the central government promoted several changes to the LAS as follows: (1) limiting the approval authority of local governments on affairs of land acquisition to restrain the land acquisition of local governments; (2) increasing the compensation standard for land acquisition and adjusting the provision stating that "compensation for land acquisition shall not exceed 20 times the average annual output value for three years prior" to "30 times"; (3) implementing a unified price for annual land output value for a defined region to improve the fairness of land acquisition compensation; and (4) choosing several counties as a reform pilot area from the perspective of the central government to narrow the scope of land acquisition, improve compensation mechanisms, and standardize land acquisition procedures. Several provinces and cities, being well positioned for economic development, also attempted to explore LAS changes in line with owners' conditions. For example, Nanjing applied monetization reforms of land requisition compensation and resettlement for farmers subjected to land expropriation; for the long-term development of farmers subjected to land expropriation and collective organizations, during land acquisition execution in Zhejiang Province, reserved land (*liuyongdi*) (e.g., 10% of expropriated land) remained for farmers and collective organizations to use for construction and to enjoy resulting outputs or profits; in Shanghai, with the initiation of land acquisition projects related to highway construction, farmers subjected to land expropriation could share operation profits generated from highways based on the amount of land that had been expropriated from them.

The purpose of such LAS changes imposed by the central and local governments was to limit farmer resistance to land acquisition by "leaving more profits to farmers and collective organizations." Such changes applied by local governments and especially in China's developed regions have been highly successful, as land compensation for farmers has increased rapidly while conflicts between local governments and farmers have been mitigated to some extent. This has been the result of the self-adaptive adjustments of local governments in facing land conflicts stimulated by the LAS. Rather, in considering local conditions of land acquisition compensation, the country's "one size fits all" strategy of land compensation can be avoided, and economic development can be balanced with social stability. From this point of view, the relationship between local governments and farmers in this period was gradually improved through local governments' adaptive adjustment strategies. However, as long as the LAS remains the only means of transforming rural or collective land into state-owned land as the only source of new urban land, conflicts behind political relations cannot be eliminated fully.

2   LAND CONFLICT ANALYSIS OF THE LAS BASED ON CONDITIONS OF NEW URBANIZATION

2.1   *The Internal Relationship Between New Urbanization and the LAS in China*

The counterpoint of new urbanization is traditional urbanization, which refers to urbanization and industrialization occurring in China's reform and opening-up phases. The traditional or earlier style of urbanization development had played a crucial role in promoting social and economic development in China over the short term, as China's urbanization rate increased to over 50% over the past 30 years, and this created strong foundations for long-term development in the country. Traditional urbanization, however, also exposed several fatal problems and eventually could no longer meet development needs. As the most typical example, such development focused on urban expansion while neglecting the quality of urbanization processes, causing other aspects of urbanization such as competitiveness and population quality to remain less developed. Earlier urbanization involved expanding as much as possible, in part because local governments could control land uses via the LAS by easily acquiring land at a relatively low cost while selling land to developers at a high price, and differences between collected costs and selling prices generated major value-added land benefits for local governments. Thus, traditional urbanization is based on the execution of the LAS, and the expansion of urbanization is a direct or indirect result of land acquisition to a large extent via land finance. From this point of view, new urbanization involves reconfiguring urbanization by changing or adjusting the LAS so that it is no longer dependent on land financing.

Of course, new urbanization has new practical implications. Given significant differences between urban and rural areas, the gap between the rich and poor, and the intensive social relationship stimulated by the unfair distribution of wealth, new urbanization has also involved realizing the integrative and coordinated development of rural and urban areas over following years. Therefore, the earlier mode of economic development focused on sacrificing the interests of collectives and farmers for urban growth in the midst of significant condemnation from society on the unfair distribution of land and in the midst of land conflicts between local governments and farmers stimulated by the LAS. From this point of view, to address such problems and to realize the real meaning of new urbanization in China, wealth distribution patterns and relational structures between local governments and farmers needed to be rebuilt. Without a doubt, LAS reforms and GFR adjustments based on land acquisition will inevitably require local governments to change notions of governance and of governance behaviors. If local governments wish to adjust governance ideas or behaviors in a positive way, the land conflicts among local governments and farmers under the backdrop of new urbanization need to be eliminated. To understand the relationship between local governments and farmers and to identify problems confronting local governments faced with land acquisition, it is necessary to analyze the basic characteristics of stakeholders of land acquisition.

2.2   *Analysis of Behavioral Characteristics of Different Stakeholders*

Under the backdrop of new urbanization, the current LAS mainly involves three stakeholders, that is, governments, farmers, and developers. In cases of land acquisition, the attributes, positions, and roles of stakeholders determine their behaviors and rules and affect potential cost-benefit outcomes of different stakeholders.

Governmental entities in China can be divided into central and local governments, which play different roles. According to the *Land Administration Law*, governments have the power to expropriate land from farmers for the public interest, but farmers must be compensated to ensure that their living standards are not compromised. Of course, the central government does not engage in land acquisition directly, and the implementation of the public power thus shifts to local governments at the county level. Therefore, the central government enforces local governments to strictly apply laws and policies of land acquisition to protect the legitimate interests of farmers. For instance, the central government has issued policies on land acquisition several times[1] and has always stressed that local governments must protect the legitimate interests of village collectives and farmers in regard to land acquisition by improving compensation standards, supporting the appropriate resettlement of land-requisitioned farmers, and prohibiting illegal activities (e.g., forced evictions and demolitions). The central government has thus shifted the actual operation of land acquisition to local governments, but it still retains supervisory power.

Local governments have discretion and residual claims for land acquisition. To cater to local interests, they act as a "grabbing hand." After tax distribution reforms were applied in 1994, local governments preferred to adopt "land finance" through land transfers by bidding (*zhaobiao*), auctions (*paimai*), and bulletins (*guapai*). The process of land conversion can generate huge value-added land benefits. In China, the transfer of use rights to converted land to developers is dominated by local governments through the primary urban land market. Local governments secure considerable land-transferring fees as extra-budgetary revenue, increasing their local fiscal revenue. In addition, urbanization and industrialization resulting from land conversion can bring stable tax revenues to local areas, which motivate local governments to take more land from farmers and to sell more land to developers. Under this mechanism of land acquisition and urban development, local governments contend with farmers for land benefits and seize most value-added land benefits through low priced land acquisition and monopoly price land transfers.

To realize the transfer of converted land use rights after land acquisition, local governments must cooperate with developers, which is the reason they are willing to share some value-added land benefits with developers through bargaining and negotiation. However, as the original owners of the land, village collectives and farmers are not as lucky as developers. First, compensation standards of land acquisition are generally set and applied by local governments

---

[1] Examples include *Notice for strengthening the management of land expropriation* issued by the Ministry of Land and Resources in 1999, *Decision on deepening reforms and strict land management* issued by the State Council in 2004, *Urgent notice concerning strict land expropriation and demolition management to effectively protect the legitimate rights and interests of the masses* issued by the State Council in 2010.

under the legal framework, which means that farmers are not involved in decision-making and cannot affect the rules of land compensation. Second, the benefits that farmers derive from land acquisition are marginal, as they are compensated with agricultural prices while the compensation ratio has an upper limit according to compensation rules. Compared to strong local governments, most farmers are relatively weak. They are disadvantaged by information asymmetries and poor action capacities, often forcing them to passively accept compensation plans determined by local governments and to be excluded from the sharing of urbanization benefits. Nevertheless, with greater awareness of farmers' property protections and of constraints on government public power, some farmers, and especially those in developed areas, have increased prices (*zuodiqijia*) and employed nail households (*dingzihu*) to defend their land rights and interests in their engagements with local governments.

Overall, under the current LAS, the central government and developers do not directly engage in land acquisition affairs, and local governments and farmers are the core stakeholders of benefit disputes. Local governments serve as operators of land acquisition affairs and derive the most land benefits in engagements with farmers under incentives of land finance. By contrast, the interests of village collectives and farmers are often compromised. As vulnerable groups, they must adopt resistance strategies, leading to land conflicts. Therefore, under the backdrop of new urbanization, to realize the integration and coordinated development of urban-rural areas, local governments must adjust existing distribution patterns of value-added land benefits and mitigate tensions between local governments and farmers.

2.3   Land Acquisition Conflicts Between Local Governments and Farmers

As noted above, local governments and farmers are the most important stakeholders of land conflicts. The current LAS is not perfect and has many flaws, but it has a strong impact on local governments and farmers as a formal institution. Benefits derived from land acquisitions involving local governments and farmers involve the following four features that can easily lead to land conflicts.

1. The scope of public power over land acquisition: According to *Land Administration Law* Article 2, to support public interests, the state may expropriate or requisition collective land lawfully. *Land Administration Law* Article 43 also states that units and individuals who need land for construction purposes must apply for the use of state-owned land in accordance with the law. The above articles serve as a legal basis for local governments using public power over land acquisition and affect the private rights of farmers. However, the definition of public interests is ambiguous and principles of construction must involve the use of state-

owned land, leading to the abuse of land acquisition power by local governments. In other words, local governments can expropriate land in the name of public interests and can violate farmers' private rights to collective-owned land arbitrarily. Abuses of public power over land acquisition and resulting private rights violations have spurred land conflicts between local governments and farmers.

2. Compensation standards of land acquisition: Compensation standards provided by local governments are related to the willingness and satisfaction of farmers subjected to land acquisition. Unfortunately, compensation standards of land acquisition in China are generally low, meaning that farmers are excluded from value-added land benefit distribution processes. This has been another source of land acquisition conflict. Farmers who have lost land are compensated by low prices for agricultural land use, making it difficult for them to maintain their livelihood and causing them to fall into poverty easily. In addition, to save land acquisition costs, local governments with rights of discretion typically negotiate land acquisition prices with construction project developers and compensate farmers with the minimum legal ratio. According to a survey, via land acquisition for project construction, land acquisition compensation paid to farmers generally accounts for only 10% of a total investment while relevant land taxes and fees (e.g., land-transferring fees) paid to local governments account for 40–50% of a total investment. For the majority of value-added land benefits retrieved by local governments, farmers feel that benefits have been distributed unfairly, causing them to become unsatisfied with local governments. To farmers, local governments take their land and compensate them with hundreds of thousands of *yuan* per hectare and then sell the same land to developers for tens of millions of *yuan* per hectare, which is clearly unfair. To receive expected land compensation funds, some farmers have started to adopt strategies (e.g., nail households and collective petitions) to fight for their legitimate rights. If local governments adopt inappropriate approaches (e.g., armed suppression), conflicts will become more acute.

3. The resettlement plan: A plan imposed with nearly no alternatives regardless of farmers' efforts is another important source of land conflict. From the reform and opening-up phases, many local governments have managed the resettlement of farmers subjected to land acquisition by providing a resettlement fee and then allowing the farmers to fend for themselves. With this unitary monetary compensation, farmers subjected to land acquisition cannot maintain their original living standards or safeguard their livelihoods over the long term. Further, for resettlement after housing demolition, local governments offer house relocation compensation whereby land-expropriated farmers are asked to move to concentrated resettlement areas uniformly planned and

built by local governments. However, to save costs (e.g., land costs), the new resettlement areas are mostly located in less desirable locations such as remote suburban areas with mostly apartments and small high-rise dwellings. Due to a lack of supervision of farmers, inferior materials are used and the quality of housing is poor in most cases. Furthermore, the resettlement standards for average living spaces are also determined by local governments, and farmers have no right to participate in such decisions. As this government-led approach does not consider the actual needs of farmers, the design of resettlement housing may not meet their demands in terms of production and life standards. When farmers subjected to land acquisition are not satisfied with resettlement offerings that local governments force farmers to accept (e.g., farmers forced upstairs (*nongming beishanglou*)), conflicts can arise.

4. Procedures of land acquisition: According to *Regulations for the implementation of Land Administration Law* Article 25, governments of the prefectural or county level must make two announcements and register for land acquisition within ten working days from the date of receiving approval documents from the central or corresponding provincial government (see information listed in Special Column 1 later in the chapter). However, this procedure mentioned presents the following flaws. First, farmers cannot participate in the approval of land acquisition applications. The approval procedure is executed among governmental entities and impacted farmers are fully excluded from this process. Farmers are simply informed that their land will be expropriated through two announcements, resulting in passive acceptance. Second, the consultation mechanism employed is not perfect, reflecting a lack of public participation from farmers subjected to land acquisition. The content of land acquisition announcements (e.g., land areas, compensation standards, and compensation plans) is shaped by local governments and is approved by the central government, meaning that farmers cannot participate in decision-making or comment on announcements. Third, the dispute resolution mechanism employed is unfair, reflecting the unfair court system. Under the current legal system, local courts do not address appeals from farmers subjected to land acquisition with two consequences. Farmers can accept administrative arbitration from superior government departments or they can organize constant collective petitions. Collective petitions are made when local governments do not execute legal procedures (e.g., expropriate farmers' land prior to approval) or when farmers cannot tolerate land acquisition injustices. When local governments employ radical approaches to petitions, this spurs considerable conflict, in turn affecting social stability.

Special Column 1: Two Announcements and One Registration for Land Acquisition

Two announcements:

The first announcement given is the *Land acquisition announcement*. Government entities of the prefecture and county levels are responsible for implementing land acquisition plans approved by superior governmental offices. Land acquisition information ((1) approval authority, approval no., approval date, approval land use; (2) landowners, locations, land use statuses, areas of land acquisition; (3) compensation standards and farmer resettlement approaches; and (4) dates and places for the registration of land acquisition compensation) is publicized to townships and villages where land is to be expropriated.

The second announcement given is the *Announcement for land acquisition compensation and resettlement plan*. Land departments of the prefecture and county levels form a draft of land acquisition compensation and resettlement plans with other departments according to the land acquisition plan approved before. This draft shall be publicized to townships and villages where land is to be expropriated within 45 days from the date of the first announcement to solicit comments from collective economic organizations and farmers. Compensation and resettlement plans for the public include the following information: (1) locations, land use statuses, and acquisition land areas; (2) types and quantities of attachments and young crops relating to requisitioned land; (3) the number of farmers that must resettle; (4) standards, total amounts, payment objects, and land compensation and resettlement fees; (5) compensation standards for attachments or green crops; and (6) the resettlement approach applied for farmers subjected to land acquisition.

One registration:

Landowners and land users must hold a land property certificate (e.g., a land contract) for an assigned place for the delivery of land acquisition compensation within the specified period prescribed by the announcement. Landholders hold different views on land acquisition compensation and resettlement plans and holding hearings shall be held with land departments of the prefecture and county levels ten working days from the date of the second announcement. When a dispute over compensation standards arises, local governments above the county level shall coordinate, and when coordination fails, the governmental entity that approved of the land acquisition plan shall make a final decision. However, disputes over land compensation and resettlement do not affect the implementation of a land acquisition plan.

The rational definition of public interests, the realization of compensation justice, and the normative application of procedures of land acquisition are three major challenges facing the current LAS. Furthermore, the ambiguous definition of public interests has led to rapid urbanization through the use of rural land resources at low costs; the failure of compensation justice has caused value-added land benefits to flow to local governments and developers while farmers have been excluded from the benefits of urbanization; finally, the use of illegal procedures has compromised the basic rights of landowners and users, deepening dual urban-rural structures and differences between local governments and farmers from a distribution perspective. Apparently, the current LAS compromises the integrated and coordinated development of urban-rural areas in the new urbanization era, affords local governments a powerful position, and violates the legitimate rights of farmers subjected to land acquisition. When farmers accept such right infringements passively, land conflicts can arise. Such conflicts could worsen (e.g., farmer collective petitioning vs. armed government suppression, extreme behavior from nail households vs. forced demolitions by local governments), affecting social stability and sustainable economic development.

2.4   The Essence of Land Acquisition Conflicts: Imbalanced Responsibilities, Rights, and Interests

There are two main views on the essence of conflicts of land acquisition as discussed above. Some scholars believe that incompatibilities between the LAS and the economic system are the main causes of land conflicts (e.g., the diversification of investment subjects via land acquisition projects, non-public interest in land acquisition, the deviation of land compensation from market economy laws, and the resettlement of farmers who cannot adapt to the marketization of employment). Other scholars believe that the violation of public and private rights has been the main motivator of land conflicts originating from the LAS (i.e., disregard for collectives' and farmers' rights in the application of administrative authority has led to social contradictions between local governments and farmers, resulting in continuous farmer petitioning on land acquisition issues across the country).

We believe that imbalances of responsibility, rights, and interests among various agents of land acquisition are the main causes of land conflicts occurring between local governments and farmers, and we find some evidence of this from past events. In the initial establishment of the LAS, the country's overall social and economic environment was poor, and as profits generated from land were relatively low, land conflicts between urban and rural areas were rare and farmers were carefully protected by the central government. As a result, the responsibilities, rights, and interests of local governments, farmers, and citizens were relatively balanced, and so the relationship between local governments and farmers was stable and harmonious. With the period of agricultural cooperation, to support the rapid development of the national socialist economy, the notion of sacrificing the interests of rural areas to serve urbanization and industrialization became a reality, and the LAS was branded as an attribute of forced implementation. From that point on, the rights of farmers under the LAS declined while the rights of the government became more powerful. In turn, a strained relationship between local governments and farmers emerged, but as the added value of land was not yet high, land conflicts were less pronounced. With the onset of the reform and opening-up periods, the value of land assets increased each year. The responsibilities of farmers were still heavy while their rights were still violated, and land compensation for farmers subjected to land expropriation remained low. This unfair distribution of land of added value combined with an imbalance of land rights spurred fierce land conflicts between local governments and farmers subjected to land expropriation. By the twentieth century, the central government began to respond to farmers' demands for land acquisition while local governments in some developed areas also tried to alter governance strategies on land acquisition based on local conditions. Such changes were designed to further the rights and interests of farmers in terms of land acquisition, and conflicts between local governments and farmers became less pronounced.

2.5   Effects of Land Conflicts

Under the current LAS, imbalances of responsibilities, rights, and revenues between farmers and governments are the main sources of land conflict, and this contradiction has certain negative effects on both entities.

Effects of Land Conflicts on Farmers and Collectives
The presence of land conflicts has already influenced traditional urban-rural relationships. In some areas, severe land conflicts have occurred when civil servants, collective cadres, and farmers have fought with one another with vicious results. Even in areas not exhibiting direct conflict, negative attitudes toward land acquisition projects obstruct the government's regular work. Among those involved, farmers and collectives, as vulnerable groups, are especially affected.

1. Direct losses: Diminished development opportunities

    In processes of land acquisition, many farmers struggle to alter the government's actions when their interests and demands are not addressed (e.g., a "nail household" that refuses to relocate). They strive to prevent the government from acquiring and developing their land. These long-term actions finally affect the construction of development projects and can even terminate projects owing to the immovable nature of land.

    For the government, the purpose of land acquisition is to meet the land needs of industrial and business enterprises and delivering infrastructure and public services. Firms attracted to land policies not only offer job opportunities to local residents but also have a scale effect that stimulates the development of local economies. Furthermore, new roads, public parks, and public service facilities can improve the living conditions of farmers. However, once land conflicts occur, such prospects no longer exist. When local governments change urban plans and when firms make site decisions, they do not target collectives with a history of land conflict. Under such circumstances, in defending farmers' personal interests, local collectives lose out on development opportunities.

2. High-intensity conflict: Harm to grassroots self-governance

As land conflicts escalate, the government's land acquisition decisions cannot address the interests of farmers, which can lead to violent conflict. "The blue book of China's society: societal analysis and forecast (Ru et al. 2010)" published by the Chinese Academy of Social Sciences shows that 73% of farmers' disputes and petitions are related to land, 40% of which concern land conflicts. Although the Chinese government has gradually increased land acquisition compensation in the twenty-first century, confrontations resulting from land acquisition are still relatively common.

These conflicts inevitably impact the traditional grassroots self-governance regime of rural China. Committee leaders of rural villages are elected directly by farmers, and they are responsible for farmers through collectives. Meanwhile, these leaders also serve as agents of county- and township-level governments. As a result, committee leaders' responsibilities to both sides create dilemmas when land conflicts occur. On the one hand, collectives are required to persuade local farmers to sacrifice their own interests to meet the land acquisition goals of local governments. When severe conflicts such as fights break out, committee leaders must also serve as "pioneers" of acquisition enforcement to fight against villagers. These events can greatly damage the prestige of collective leaders and can decrease the effectiveness of collectives as grassroots self-governance units.

On the other hand, village leaders are elected by villagers according to the *Organic Law of Villager Committees*. Therefore, whether a leader's decisions can complement a collective's interests determines his or her likelihood of reelection. In addition, the leaders themselves are members of their villages, and they share collective interests similar to those of other farmers. In such cases, some leaders are motivated to participate in or even pursue land conflicts. They always conceal the illegal actions of farmers (e.g., sowing additional seeds), causing the government to pay much more attention to issues of compensation.

This double-responsibility regime, wherein collective leaders act as agents of both farmers and local governments, once maintained the sustainability of the urban-rural system and of GFRs. However, as land conflicts have escalated, these leaders' functions have been heavily challenged. The maintenance and reform of the current self-governance system have thus become the central question posed by China's administrative management teams.

3. Confrontation in silence: Crises of government credibility

Government credibility levels affect all aspects of public affairs. In regard to land acquisition, the government's credibility can effectively alleviate the competing interests of farmers, governments, and enterprises and can mitigate losses of process efficiency. Over the 30 years following the reform and opening-up period, the public's trust in the authoritarian system spurred economic development processes referred to as the "Chinese miracle." However, frequent land conflicts gradually affected the government's credibility, and a loss of farmers' trust has, in turn, rendered promoting land acquisition more difficult.

Although the existence of information asymmetries does affect people's likelihood of understanding or misinterpreting the government's land acquisition policies, information asymmetries act as an amplifier. Farmers have lost trust in the government due to the behaviors of local governments in neglecting the interests of farmers in terms of land acquisition (e.g., illegally developing land for commercial use after acquiring land in the name of public utility or rent-seeking action on compensation). In particular, to ease difficulties associated with land acquisition, some local government officials have had to spearhead demolition tasks (e.g., shoveling farmers' crops, demolishing farmers' houses, destroying farmers' ancestral graves, and cutting down trees), in turn tarnishing the government's image. As a result of this loss of government credibility, farmers tend to be more inclined to use violent means to express their interests and demands. As the government cannot protect the interests of farmers, farmers can only declare their rights by struggling fiercely. In recent years, the emergence of opportunistic behaviors (e.g., "nail households") can to some extent be attributed to a loss of government credibility.

Case 1: From "Fertilized Farmland" to "Desolate Wasteland"—A Case of Jinxian County in Nanchang

Jinxian County of the city of Nanchang is well known for food production; the county's annual grain production levels reached 527,500 tons in 2012. With ongoing economic development, local governments have decided to engage in land acquisitions to introduce enterprises and to promote industrial development. In 2008, the county acquired approximately 2000 mu of farmland from 170 villagers of Tujia in the name of constructing logistics parks. The county' government promised local farmers who had lost their land that they would be individually allocated a zone to reconstruct houses.

However, following the demolition of the houses, due to investment difficulties, by 2015, the logistics park had not been completed. With the addition of a new school, more than 1000 acres of land remains in a desolate state and resettlement land promised by the government has not been allocated. According to the *Land Management Law*, acquired land cannot be cultivated, meaning that farmers can only live in temporary living areas after losing their means of production. Worse still, many farmers are forced to make a living by scavenging.

The government's lack of long-term planning and misjudgment of development processes has been the main cause of this tragedy. This not only undermines the normal lives of farmers, but it has also caused them to permanently lose trust in the government. Furthermore, it intensifies conflicts between the government and farmers. This will undoubtedly hinder the government's follow-up land acquisition work.

---

4. Potential contradictions: Changes in lifestyle

Underneath this visible conflict, it cannot be ignored that land acquisition also significantly changes the local farmers' lifestyles. When landless farmers migrate to cities, they suffer from not only increasing costs of living but also a lack of essential skills needed to earn a living. This typically inevitably leads to the decline of farmers' living conditions. Furthermore, even for the small number of landless farmers who still have access to arable land that can be cultivated, resettlement houses are often located in urban areas and such farmers thus face high commute costs, rendering agricultural production unprofitable.

More importantly, social identities and lifestyles differ considerably between rural and urban areas. With land acquisition, the destruction of social networks, changes in neighborhood structures, and changes to leisure and entertainment styles, the gap between farmers and urban residents is aggravated. Traditional folk activities of the countryside have disappeared, leading to the "semi-urbanization" of the farmers.

Case 2: "Be Urbanized"—Densely Residential Districts of Shuangliu County in Sichuan

Shuangliu County has a long history and is positioned conveniently in Sichuan. After the reform and opening-up period, Shuangliu underwent rapid economic development for which it has been continuously ranked as the top county in Sichuan Province for 18 years. From 2007, Shuangliu County has taken the lead in China in terms of reforms "linking urban land taking to rural land giving." This movement encourages collectives to reclaim their construction land as agricultural land and to focus on the construction of high-rise residential buildings to centralize local farmers, thus saving construction land quotas for urban construction.

Reforms in Shuangliu County have achieved prominent results. However, for thousands of rural migrants, such reforms have had a considerable influence on their living conditions. Zhang Liangfu is an ordinary farmer living in Shuangliu County. Since experiencing land acquisition and demolition, he would rather live in a sheep scourge than move to his new house compensated for by the local government. When asked why he did not move to the modern estate, Zhang cited the location of the new house, which is positioned 2 km away from his farmland. If he were to move to the building, he would have "no place to raise sheep or pigs and no place to dry wheat and rice."

Zhang Liangfu's experience is not unique. For farmers who had to leave their homeland, although land acquisition compensation has covered their property losses, they still suffer from changes in lifestyle and living conditions. To continue their agricultural production activities, they must drive a car or ride a motorcycle to their farmland located kilometers away while there is no space available to store their farm tools or to dry their grain. The disappearance of traditional "sunrise to sunset" agricultural production patterns has not only resulted in great losses of efficiency but has also had a profound impact on the social organization of the countryside.

Effects of Land Conflicts on Local Governments' Decision-Making Processes

1. Giving farmers more land exploitation rights

With the intensification of land acquisition trends, it is necessary to find a feasible way to further protect the rights and interests of farmers when land acquisition occurs to alleviate land conflicts. To fully compensate for farmers' losses and to realize the potential value of land, the government must continually improve decision-making on land acquisition compensation and must improve compensation standards. The government must also establish a diverse social security system that covers pension, education, and reemployment provisions.

Such initiatives have become an important facet of land system reforms that the central government has been advocating for in recent years. However, with increases in land acquisition compensation, land conflicts have become more frequent, indicating that land acquisition compensation is not the only factor that determines contradictions of land acquisition. In particular, given the huge gap between incremental land value and land acquisition compensation, farmers often cherish their land and prevent it from being acquired, reinforcing resistance to government land acquisition and demolition. Under the government's monopoly over the first-level land market, standards of land acquisition compensation are often defined according to farmers' losses. Farmers and collectives cannot participate in the land development process nor can they enjoy incremental land revenue derived from land development, which inevitably leads to interest conflicts.

As a result, it is imperative to afford farmers with more land development rights. Some regions carry out policies on "resettlement land," whereby a certain proportion of construction land is reserved for collectives after land acquisition for establishing enterprises or for engaging in business or investment. This resettlement land is subject to tax incentives and administrative support from local governments in terms of policies, capital, industries, and commerce. Other regions have explored "self-acquire and self-develop" policies through which rural collective economic organizations can "self-develop" their construction land for industrial development purposes within the scope of urban planning. Such attempts have overturned the existing system that prevents farmers from participating in land development processes and have truly encouraged farmers to play a more important role in land acquisition and urbanization.

2. Alternative finance systems of land compensation

Land conflicts have not only intensified conflicts between farmers and the government but also raised farmers' expectations in terms of land compensation standards. In particular, some farmers have opportunist views of "overnight riches," and the government's continuous compromises reinforce the idea that "big fights yield big compensation, little fights yield little compensation, and no fights yield no compensation." Undoubtedly, land conflicts are an inevitable result of the unfair distribution of land requisition compensation.

Land acquisition has played an important role in China's low-cost industrialization and urbanization. With the continuous improvement of land acquisition procedures and with the shrinking scale of land acquisition measures, "land acquisition" is gradually transforming into a form of "land purchasing." If local governments gradually withdraw from land acquisition for non-public use, their annual revenues will be greatly compromised. On the other hand, under the farmer-guide land acquisition policy, it is difficult to fully meet farmers' growing expectations of land acquisition compensation, which will further affect local governments' fiscal balances and which will lead to financial difficulties. At the same time, local governments' responsibilities over public affairs and infrastructure are becoming more involved. Such financial pressures pose a major challenge to local governments, which are already suffering from local debt crises.

For the government, it is necessary to develop new sources of finance to provide necessary funds for urban development, and taxation and other alternative financial systems undoubtedly constitute a viable way out. Real estate taxes, for example, have already been applied in many developed countries such as the US and Japan. More importantly, tax regimes can effectively redistribute revenues as compensation for the unfairness of land acquisition schemes and can deliver public services and social welfare for both landless and urban residents.

3   The Direction of the LAS Reforms and the Responses of Local Governments

3.1   The Expectations and Demands of Farmers and Collectives

With the intensification of land acquisition schemes, landowners and the government are facing a "double lose" situation. Local governments must consume more budgets and administrative resources to negotiate with farmers to maintain stability, resulting in the constant extension of land acquisition periods and increases in land acquisition costs. Farmers, who are relatively vulnerable, must constantly fight and petition against local governments and land acquisition departments to express their own interests. This dilemma not only affects farmers' normal lives but also reinforces prejudice and isolation in rural areas. To address these issues, land management departments must carry out reforms of the land requisition system based on the interests of farmers and collectives.

Increasing Land Acquisition Compensation and Diversifying Modes of Social Security
Low compensation is always the focus of land acquisition conflicts. Although, as mentioned above, land acquisition compensation cannot fully reflect the

needs of farmers subjected to land expropriation, many scholars believe that frequent land conflicts can ultimately be attributed to unfair compensation (Zang 2008; Chen and Tong 2013). The "multiple output value method" enshrined under the *Land Administration Law* has become increasingly insufficient at matching the rapid growth of urban commercial housing prices and urban consumption levels, and increases in land acquisition compensation have become a common interest among farmers.

On one hand, farmers are often unable to obtain sufficient compensation based on the formula of 30 times the annual output value of the land. Compared to local governments, which can obtain enormous incomes by transferring construction land to enterprises, farmers only earn tens of thousands of dollars per mu as compensation, which is comparatively very low. For example, in 2014 in Hangzhou, local residential land transfer prices reached approximately 17,400 yuan per square meter. The fact that compensation cannot meet farmers' needs further exaggerates their desires for more compensation.

On the other hand, farmers hope that in addition to a one-time subsidy they may also enjoy access to retirement insurance and to basic living security treatment through a monthly income. At present, eligibility for social security is often based on the area of land that is acquired. However, in economically developed areas, arable land areas per capita are small, making it difficult for farmers to participate in social security after land acquisition. In some rural areas of Zhejiang Province, whether one's parents have retirement insurance has become an important standard on which to judge a farmer's sense of family responsibility. All of these issues reflect farmers' desires for multichannel social security compensation following land acquisition.

From Government-Led to Market-Led Schemes, Allow Collectives to Participate in Land Acquisition Decision-Making Processes

In the land acquisition process, the government is not only the designer of urban planning schemes but also the implementer of land acquisition decisions. In the early stages of Chinese urbanization, the government's public finances were insufficient. Therefore, the government's compulsory use of land acquisition is a cruel but necessary decision. However, this process has led to the loss of farmers' property and social rights, as they cannot fully express their interests through local affairs and affect government decisions. With the expansion of farmers' awareness of rights and with economic development, this government-led mode has gradually become the fuse that has triggered conflicts between the government and farmers.

Therefore, farmers not only want compensation for land acquisition but also hope that following land acquisition they can be afforded with more rights to speak on land development issues, as the development of local projects often has different impacts on prospects. For example, the introduction of polluting industrial enterprises leads to the deterioration of living environments while the introduction of commercial complexes greatly bolsters local commercial vitality. As a result, farmers are more eager to limit government intervention and prefer collectives to serve as main bodies of development so that development is more in line with community interests. Furthermore, farmers tend to participate in collective decision-making on urban construction, which can orient villagers from passive urbanization to active urbanization, thus limiting the chances of the government disregarding farmers' interests and significantly boosting farmers' satisfaction levels.

Case 3: From Resistance to Participation—Collective Decisions on Urbanization in Guangzhou
The village of Liede is located in the Pearl River New City, the central business district of Guangzhou. Within the village, Liede includes numerous "handshake floor" and "veneer floor" living environments while health and security conditions are very poor. In 2007, the Guangzhou government planned to expand urban roads by acquiring land from the village of Liede for 30 million yuan per mu. Although compensation offered was quite high at the time, it was opposed by the villagers.

In this case, the village of Liede spontaneously applied for land acquisition and development projects in the name of collective enterprises of the "Liede Economic Development Corporation." The collective first discussed relevant demolition compensation and resettlement schemes in a shareholders' meeting. It then held a village meeting and collective leaders explained to the villagers how compensation and resettlement programs work. In constructing resettlement housing for the villagers, the village of Liede cooperated with Hong Kong Hopewell Holdings Limited to build a five-star hotel and several commercial buildings. During construction, the local government has only been responsible for approval and has not intervened in project management or in the distribution of incremental land income.

Behind the Liede villagers' active participation in land acquisition work is the power of collective decision-making. After the transformation, the villagers moved into new houses of the same size as their previous houses, and their housing rent increased from 4-fold to 13-fold. While the village collective obtains 120 million yuan as management income each year from commercial real estate transactions, the village of Liede also relies on its own capacities to carry out property management, creating more than 300 job opportunities. Furthermore, Liede has built a new ancestral hall, a primary school, a kindergarten school, a cultural center, a health services center, a meat market, and other public service facilities. Collective decision-making has not only protected the rights and interests of the villagers but also improved the efficiency of land acquisition processes, thus allowing the villagers to take the initiative to participate in urbanization processes.

Realizing Land Development Revenues and Sharing Incremental Value

Land acquisition compensation has not been the only source of conflict. In fact, the most intense land conflicts have occurred in the most economically developed areas with the highest compensation standards (e.g., Guangdong, Zhejiang, and Jiangsu), as farmers not only want compensation for the loss of their houses, cultivated land, and crops but also want to participate in the sharing of incremental land value gains through processes of urbanization.

For farmers, one-time compensation is fixed, but land itself can increase in value with potential for investment and development. In traditional Chinese culture, a "steady income" is very commendable, and thus long-term investments are often favored by farmers as a means of asset management. Therefore, collectives often wish to retain a certain percentage of land or quotas during land acquisition for the independent development of shops, plants, or collective enterprises, in turn profiting from rental and operating income to achieve the sustainable growth of collective assets. This requires local governments to offer collectives some land development and utilization rights through policies, which guarantee that farmers and collectives can participate in the distribution of incremental land value.

3.2   The Future Development of LAS Reforms

Clarification of Public Interests

The experiences of developed countries in Europe and of the US have shown that the strict definition of public interests is key to limiting governmental abuse of land acquisition rights and to protecting private property. This approach can also effectively curb excessive agricultural land conversion to an extent. However, concepts of public interest deteriorated or have been extensively used, as China's constitution and relevant laws employ no clear definition of public interest. The land acquisition policy applies to almost all economic construction projects, causing the scale of land acquisition to be too broad. From a theoretical point of view, this results in the general use of land acquisition rights and in abuse. From a practical point of view, this results in interest structure adjustments and changes and the compromising of farmers' land property rights and interests. To fundamentally protect farmers' legitimate land rights and interests, land acquisition rights must be clearly and strictly defined in accordance with the law.

The Third Plenary Session of the 17th central committee clearly stated that it is important to "strictly define land for public welfare and commercial construction and to gradually narrow the scope of land acquisition." Most studies show that the scope of land acquisition can be compressed by forming a list of items or by adopting elimination methods and that land must not be requisitioned for profit-oriented purposes. Some scholars have further proposed that expropriation rights must only be applied when location decisions for major projects are very demanding. In practice, however, it is not easy to accurately distinguish between public and non-public welfare. Some clearly positive externalities of public infrastructure projects are becoming more diversified, and business and public welfare can coexist. By means of profit motives or business entities, it is difficult to distinguish between public and non-public welfare land.

Case 4: The First Narrowing of the Land Acquisition Scope—Jiangxia, Wuhan

In November 2013, the tourism holiday project of Mozi Island, Jiangxia District, Wuhan, was established as a pilot project to narrow land acquisition schemes. It took more than two years from its launch to identify pilot projects. Over these two years, the goal was to probe into connotations of public and non-public welfare land and to distinguish between public and non-public welfare construction land use projects. Wuhan's Bureau of Land Resources and Planning established a specialized sector to formulate a public welfare land directory based on Standards of Urban Land Classification and Planning Construction Land (GB50137-2011) and the Current Land Use Classification. In addition to adhering to principle of controlling the scope of land acquisition, it applies the principle that a construction project should provide public goods for society and that the land market should be fair and complementary. On this basis, Wuhan identified several land types such as land for institutions, land for state-owned enterprises, land for infrastructures of social capital investment and public service facilities, residential land, land for science and education, and so on. An initial non-public welfare land directory was also drawn up. Residential and commercial land, land for industrial and mining purposes, land for public administration and public services, and land for transportation and land for special uses were listed in the non-public welfare directory. To facilitate operability, these 4 main categories of land use were subdivided into 17 specific types.

The tourism project of Mozi Island of Jiangxia was based on the recommended catalogue as a pilot. Preliminary results of this project not only addressed basic theoretical problems related to narrowing the scope of land acquisition but also created a basis for the selection of pilot projects.

Standardize Procedures for Land Acquisition

Although several measures on land acquisition have been adopted in various regions to improve processes of land expropriation, they do not change the rationale of decision-making mechanisms applied prior to land acquisition, and they only elaborate on and supplement the land requisition procedure itself. Thus, such reforms have made few changes. Therefore, it is necessary to identify core issues in advance based on the further refinement of land acquisition processes (e.g., whether to conform to public interests, income allocation proportions, resettlement modes, compensation methods, etc.). Meanwhile, social supervision mechanisms should improve processes of land acquisition.

Through the establishment of public participation, public inquiries, hearings, and reporting systems, this will strengthen the supervision of society throughout the land acquisition process. Following land acquisition, land use units and land acquisition compensation shall continue to be monitored to regulate land acquisition outcomes. Such procedures have seemingly raised costs and consumed a considerable amount of time. In fact, through the prevention, monitoring, and punitive mechanisms of integrated supervision, property rights have been protected while costs of local governance conflicts on land acquisition have been reduced. It is helpful to properly address disputes in land acquisition compensation.

Case 5: Democracy Land Acquisition Is on the Way—Helin, Inner Mongolia
Helin is the county closest to Hohhot, the capital of the Inner Mongolia Autonomous Region. In 2015, Helin was identified as one of 33 national rural land system reform pilot areas. In accordance with central government goals to further reform the rural land system, Helin has actively explored and promoted reforms and has adopted a series of breakthrough improvement programs via land acquisition procedures.

First, archival records on farmers subjected to land acquisition have been established. Prior to land acquisition, the county department of the Land and Resources Administration confirmed the status of land to be expropriated from farmers. On this basis, archives on farmers were established. Second, farmers subjected to land acquisition participated in the entire process. Heads and representatives of collective economic organizations were invited to participate in the land acquisition process. They solicited the opinions and suggestions of other members to afford farmers the right to know about and participate in the land acquisition process. Third, to expand farmers' demand channels, Helin has established a dispute resolution committee on land acquisition compensation and resettlement that resolves conflicts related to land acquisition, allowing affected farmers to make appeals. Fourth, to prevent the contradiction of land compensation standards during approval periods, land acquisition and conversion are carried out synchronously. Fifth, to disseminate information on land expropriation to the public, the Land and Resources Administrative Department of Helin lists land requisition information on its official website, announcing schemes of land acquisition and conversion in a timely manner and actively establishing public channels for land acquisition information.

Helin has used the legal system as the premise and remedies as a supplement to improve processes, address problems, and innovate from flaws. It has also used innovation to standardize land acquisition procedures to guarantee the legal rights and interests of farmers subjected to land expropriation.

Marketize Compensation Standards

The current compensation standards have been widely criticized first because the land compensation benchmark is used in accordance with the original purposes of expropriated land without considering the particularities of land for Chinese farmers let alone farmers' land property rights. Second, the compensation standard is applied on a non-equivalent basis, and a compensation cap is used. Since the establishment of unified annual output standards for land acquisition and of comprehensive land prices for the zone, the social security function of agricultural land has been gradually normalized under compensation standards.

Whether it is based on the annual output value or unified annual output standards and comprehensive land prices of a zone, it is still based on government pricing. In this unilateral pricing mechanism, farmers still act as passive recipients without negotiating or bargaining power. Standards of land acquisition compensation are seriously incompatible with actual land values, spurring the dissatisfaction of landless farmers and frequent conflicts.

Land system reforms should change land acquisition compensation from the average annual output value to the market value of expropriated land in direct reference to market prices after land use conversion in accordance with the principles of equality and justice. The minimum protection standard for land compensation in the LAS should be implemented. It is possible to use the existing regional price and annual output value as a minimum compensation standard, and this can be directly determined by provincial, autonomous regions and municipal governments according to the actual circumstances of the counties. Meanwhile, negotiation mechanisms for land acquisition units and landless farmers should be introduced, changing traditional unilateral pricing schemes used by the government and affording farmers with a bargaining position as property rights holders. With the advancement of collective construction land market reforms in China, compensation for construction land can be based on the market price of land under similar conditions to correct the parameters of regional and individual factors, and land acquisition compensation should be determined by negotiation.

Diversify the Resettlement of Landless Farmers

The current *Land Management Law* elaborates on requirements and effects of land acquisition resettlement. It states that resettlement must properly settle farmers and maintain farmers' original living standards. However, no corresponding and operable system is in place on how to achieve resettlement requirements and effects, and no evaluative, supervisory, or feedback mechanisms are in place. In the practice of land acquisition compensation and resettlement, most areas still prefer to adopt simple one-off monetary compensation and resettlement methods that are convenient and that offer complete responsibility so that landless farmers can pursue their own livelihoods. The imperfect system lacks guidance and binding on the practice of land acquisition and increases the subjectivity and arbitrariness of local government policies on compensation and resettlement while directly limiting the government's responsibilities and power, spurring psychological comparison and discontent among landless farmers.

Regarding landless farmers' resettlement reforms, we should shift the use of simple one-time monetary methods to the use of multiple market-oriented ways to provide farmers' social security. We must comprehensively consider the skills training and social security issues faced by landless farmers based on the reserved land settlement model, job placements, social insurance, and other resettlement concerns. We must gradually improve landless farmers' normative and security mechanisms. A resettlement approach that addresses farmers' social security can bolster the sustainable livelihoods of landless farmers.

Farmers who have lost land avoid gradually becoming disadvantaged groups in cities and strive to share in the achievements of urbanization so that their long-term livelihoods can be guaranteed.

Case 6: Exploring a New Road to Security—Xi'an
In June 2011, the land ministry officially approved a pilot scheme for the reform of the LAS in Xi'an. Over six years, Xi'an applied compensation and resettlement mechanisms on land acquisition and social security on expropriated land in reforming its rural LAS.

Under the land acquisition resettlement system, resettlement typically occurred after demolition. Malpractice disadvantaged land farmers during the two-year transition. To safeguard the legitimate rights and interests of landless farmers, Xi'an changed its traditional practices. According to the development of regional industries, Xi'an has predicted the scale of housing demolition and of the resettlement of landless farmers for a certain period. Housing placements must be constructed before land acquisition so that expropriated farmers have residences.

It is necessary to improve the social security system for farmers subjected to land expropriation. First, it is essential to actively improve the social security system. Xi'an has created an endowment insurance system and operation mechanisms for farmers subjected to land expropriation, and it has refined methods and standards on the pension funds of farmers subjected to land expropriation. Second, social security standards must be strictly enforced. The Xi'an government has stipulated that the per capita cultivated land area is smaller than 0.3 mu after land acquisition, and original land expropriation compensation and resettlement standards will be increased by 35,000 yuan per mu. The per capita cultivated land area is larger than 0.3 mu but is smaller than 0.5 mu, and the original standard will be increased by 30,000 yuan per mu. The per capita cultivated land area is larger than 0.5 mu, and the original standard will increase by 25,000 yuan per mu. These funds serve as a source of endowment insurance funds for new farmers subjected to land expropriation. Third, improvements to the employment service system are pivotal. Government finances must pay for the employment and training of landless farmers and must help farmers train as water electricians, domestic services workers, computer professionals, and manual workers. To date, Xi'an's pilot area has paid more than 2 million yuan for farmers subjected to land expropriation, which has promoted the employment of this population.

Rationalize Interest Allocation Mechanisms
Under the current land increment income distribution system, collective owners' legal compensation is too low. Local governments obtain initial land increment income but lose future incremental income. Real estate developers and homebuyers pay too much for a one-time land transfer, and land occupiers receive higher returns on future land increments. Above all, institutional factors cause injustices of current land increment distribution.

In reference to the incremental income distribution of land acquisition, Yan (2009) calls for the use of Acquisition–Grant modes rather than Requisition–Taxation modes of construction land allocation under the current LAS. Market mechanisms should be adopted to link land acquisition prices to market prices and to deliver reasonable compensation for landless farmers according to market prices. At the same time, by collecting land increment taxes, value-added land outcomes from social progress should be reverted to the state or to public ownership. In regard to social justice, Yuan et al. (2012) put forward that initial allocations to farmers should be increased as much as possible and that a long-term mechanism for farmers should be established to distribute the added value of land use conversion. Specific measures include land share dividends, land rent collection schemes, and other methods.

Case 7: Benefit Sharing Satisfies Everyone—Dachong, Shenzhen
The village of Dachong is located in the South Mountain District, a high-tech industrial park in Shenzhen. Prior to the village's reconstruction, it was mainly composed of residential and industrial land and parks. A small proportion of land dedicated to commercial services and government groups was located on the north side of Shennan Avenue. The village has been randomly developed into an urban village. The village was dirty and disorderly and local infrastructure was less advanced.

The reconstruction area is located to the east of the high-tech industrial park. Its total land area covers 68.4 hectares. The renovation project involved government-leading marketization operations and included company participation. In 2007, China Resources Land Co. Ltd. signed a letter of renovation intent with the Dachong Joint-Stock Company (Dachong collective economic organization). China Resources Land Co. Ltd. was officially conferred as the developer of the project. Market forces have played an important role in the reconstruction process. Following reconstruction, the collective and villagers received 1.085 million square meters of area compensation, including 34.8 square meters of business area for the village collective, 67.3 square meters of residential area, and 6.4 square meters of commercial area for the villagers. China Resources Land Co. Ltd. acquired 1.6 million square meters of property, including 88,000 square meters of residential property and 750,000 square meters of commercial, office, and hotel space. The government has received 65,000 square meters for school construction and 54,000 square meters for affordable housing, including low-rent housing, to serve surrounding enterprises and to acquire corresponding land price income.

By the end of January 2012, the property contract rate for the villagers had reached 99.7%, and the villagers had agreed to a 100% transfer of property. More than 70,000 temporary residents have undergone a smooth and harmonious departure. From the renovation project, collective industries of the village have enjoyed numerous benefits and the villagers' incomes have improved. Meanwhile, the municipal and overall environments of the region have also greatly improved.

3.3   Responses and Transformations of Local Governments

The current LAS is the main source of land conflict between local governments and farmers, and many land conflicts have spurred the development of antagonistic relationships between local governments and farmers, hindering urbanization in China. In facing potential reforms on land acquisition in the future, local governments, as the main bodies of land acquisition that lead the integrative development of rural and urban areas, must alter their governance behaviors. In recent years, some local governments have begun to adapt their governance in exploring land acquisition reforms.

Modern service-oriented governance philosophies have gradually begun to take shape in local governments. As noted above, sacrificing the interests of rural areas and farmers to meet urbanization and industrialization targets via traditional urbanization processes has led to the development of land conflicts. In this regard, some local governments have begun to actively reverse governance philosophies, and this has clearly been reflected in land acquisition reforms. First, principles that favor "benefiting farmers" through land acquisition and the compensation of farmers subject to land expropriation have altered the unfair distribution of land benefits to some extent. For example, after adjusting for prices of cultivated land in Tianjin, the average price of expropriated land has increased by 179%, and compensation for farmers has clearly improved. Second, in helping farmers who have lost land transform into citizens gradually rather than simply compensating them, the local governments of Guangdong, of Jiangsu, and of other provinces have had to absorb these individuals as members of the social security system for urban residents to pay for pension insurance for urban and rural residents and to offer employment guidance and training. Third, coordinated development in urban and rural areas and equal opportunities for citizens and farmers has been stressed. For example, Yiwu, a city in Zhejiang Province, has constructed new urban communities for farmers subjected to land expropriation to protect their basic housing property rights and interests and to allow them to transfer, rent, or mortgage housing property freely. In short, farmers subjected to land expropriation in Yiwu have equal opportunities to share in the fruits of social and economic development. Fourth, rational decision-making mechanisms that address the interests of stakeholders and especially the rights of farmers have been applied to prevent the development of excessive internal friction. For example, prior to land acquisition, in Jinjiang, a city in Fujian province, local governments must discuss plans with farmers and collective organizations, and only after receiving consent from a certain percentage of farmers can local governments apply a land acquisition and demolition program.

Case 8: The Typical Model of the Coordinated Land Acquisition Program—Reconstruction of a Village in the City of Jinjiang, Zhejiang Province

Guishan is a new community located in Meiling. Once a typical village in the center of Jinjiang, the community has experienced tremendous changes in transforming from a poor village into a modern community over three years as a result of Jinjiang's reconstruction program. The program employed a variety of land acquisition models because the land once belonged to farmers and collective organizations in Guishan, and since the program's implementation, all of the land has been transferred to state owners by the local government. The population of Guishan is currently 3412 with a total of 881 households. More than 3500 individuals are living abroad and more than 1000 are immigrants living within an area of two square kilometers.

During pre-negotiation of land acquisition, local cadres or officers met with every household to help farmers subjected to land expropriation understand the land acquisition project. For instance, they helped farmers account for their home and land assets, evaluate pros and cons of land acquisition, and negotiate land acquisition compensation schemes. At the same time, to unify land expropriation goals, the municipal government stated that only when the overall satisfaction rate of interviewed farmers was greater than 80% could a land acquisition scheme be executed. It was active communication between the local government and farmers and evaluation criteria on satisfaction levels that laid the foundations for the smooth implementation of land acquisition in later periods.

From the start of the negotiations with farmers, Guishan's land acquisition project took only roughly three years to complete (including nine months of consultation with farmers), and almost no land conflicts emerged as a result. Compared to similar cases in China, Jinjiang's land acquisition efficiency has been quite high, and the rare occurrence of land acquisition and anti-demolition events over the course of operations has greatly mitigated internal frictions between the local government and farmers, creating a model for the rapid, stable, and smooth promotion of urban renewal in the area.

Second, in governing land acquisition affairs, local governments have transformed from dominant leaders to guiders and sharers of benefits. In recent years, local governments have begun to act as guides of land acquisition affairs rather than as dominant leaders while emphasizing win-win means of value-added land benefit sharing. In traditional land acquisition affairs, local governments secure most value-added land benefits through excessive government intervention and control often to the detriment of farmers. Conflicts between local government and farmers increase transaction costs (e.g., costs of negotiations between governments and displaced farmers and costs of maintaining social stability in preventing mass disturbances, resulting in inefficient land acquisition schemes). In other words, as decision-making leaders, local governments have not maximized value-added land benefits in more recent waves of urbanization.

To mitigate conflicts and to improve the efficiency of land acquisition governance, local governments have cooperated with farmers and have shared land acquisition benefits to achieve win-win outcomes. Local governments in many areas such as Hangzhou, Wenzhou in Zhejiang Province, and Guangzhou in Guangdong Province have adopted land acquisition policies that deliver compensation (*liuyongdi anzhi*) to endow farmers with the right to land development. Under the reserved land (*liuyongdi*) policy, local governments leave a certain proportion of land to collective economic village organizations through land acquisition. On behalf of farmers, collective economic village organizations can engage in land development independently or transfer land to enterprises to secure land benefits. Farmers making use of reserved land for land development purposes can thus secure more value-added land benefits than can be ensured via traditional land acquisition compensation (see Case 12). Reserved land policies driven by local governments thus transfer more value-added land benefits to farmers to ensure farmers' satisfaction with land acquisition schemes. Compared to those of traditional compensation standards, benefit distribution between local governments and farmers applied under reserved land (*liuyongdi*) policies is relatively fair, making farmers more likely to agree with land acquisition plans and minimizing chances of conflict. In addition, local governments do not dominate decision-making on the development of reserved land. Instead, they make use of planning and policy tools to guide farmers. For instance, some preferential policies address fund shortages and promote community transformation and sustainable development for villages subject to land acquisition. Despite declines in proportions of land benefit distribution, local governments can acquire land efficiently while securing constant tax revenues from land development projects applied in villages subject to land acquisition.

Overall, local governments in China realize that government-led approaches to land acquisition governance are inefficient. Such governments have gradually recognized farmers' roles in value-added land benefit distribution. With the emergence of escalated land conflicts, the delivery of land rights and benefits to farmers and the forging of agreements on land acquisition may optimally support win-win cooperation.

Case 9: Collective Economic Growth Under the Reserved Land (*liuyongdi*) Policy—The Case of a Village in Jianggan District, Hangzhou
Sancha is a village located in the center of Jianggan District, Hangzhou. According to the reserved land (*liuyongdi*) policy, Sancha received 8.7 hectares (with 10% of agricultural land expropriated) of reserved land after land acquisition. Fortunately, Sancha completed land use procedures with the help of the local land department.

To make good use of reserved land, Sancha adopted roll development to accumulate development experience and to mitigate investment risks. The village first pursued an office building project from its own collective funds in 2003. This project attracted the attention of Tesco Supermarket and several other companies, bringing considerable rental income to Sancha. Sancha's village collective then implemented village plans and developed five other projects with great economic benefits.

After nearly a decade of reserved land development, Sancha has transformed from a traditional agricultural economy into a rental property economy, realizing rapid economic growth. In 2014, the rental income of Sancha's collective reached 0.25 billion *yuan* (tax including), which is eight times that for 2002. Development and commercial real estate projects have not only brought about huge economic benefits to Sancha but also promoted the economic development of the Qingchun business circle.

References

Chai, X. T. 2008. Review and prospect on the land requisition system change of China. *China Land Science 22*(2): 69–74. (In Chinese)

Chen, C., and Tong, R. 2013. A Study on the Quantification of Land Acquisition Compensation: Taking Beijing as an Example. *China Land Science* 27: 41–47. (In Chinese)

Feng, C. Z. 2011. The institutional change of China's land requisition. China Land. (In Chinese)

Gao, S. P., and Liu, S. Y. 2007. The market of collective construction land: the reality and legal dilemma. *Management World* (3):158–159. (In Chinese)

Qian, Z. H., and Ma, K. (2007). The land market of urban and rural non-construction in China: monopoly, segmentation and integration. *Management World* (10): 38–44. (In Chinese)

Ru, X., Lu, X., and Li, P. 2010. Blue book of China's society: society of analysis and forecast (2011). Social Sciences Academic Press. (In Chinese)

Xu, Y. C. 2011. A comparative study of system for land expropriation between China and the United States. Northwest A&F University. (In Chinese)

Yan, J. M. 2009. The evolution of land requisition system in China and the choice of reform target and reform path [J]. *Economic theory and economic management* V(1): 39–43. (In Chinese)

Yuan, S. F., Yang, L. X., and Wang, Q. R. 2012. The quantitative study on farmers' welfare change in the farmland conversion in the four towns of Cixi city [J]. *China Land Sciences* 10: 82–90. (In Chinese)

Zang, J. 2008. A Study on the Distribution of Land Revenue and the Protection of Landless Peasants' Rights and Interests in Agricultural Land Conversion: Based on the Analysis of Agricultural Land Development Right. Issues in *Agricultural Economy* 2: 80–85. (In Chinese)

Zhang, H. F. 2005. The study on land expropriation. Beijing: Economic Science Press. (In Chinese)

PART IX

Environmental and Energy Governance

CHAPTER 31

Local Implementation of Energy Conservation Policies in China

Genia Kostka

1   INTRODUCTION

This chapter examines China's national energy policies and the way in which local governments implement policies to reduce energy consumption. It illustrates how Chinese government officials often opt to "kill two (or more) birds with one stone" by choosing implementation pathways that balance local priorities with national energy targets, and how they are more likely to faithfully implement energy conservation policies and projects that also address salient business, economic, safety, pollution, and political legitimacy interests and concerns in their localities. Local governments are less likely to strictly implement energy conservation policies without "bundling" potential and employ foot-dragging measures such as seeking loopholes in the implementation guidelines.[1]

The chapter begins by introducing China's national energy challenges and summarizing national energy conservation policy efforts over the past decade. The subsequent discussion shows how local governments implement national energy conservation policies and identifies barriers to a more comprehensive implementation of energy-saving policies at the local level. The chapter concludes by highlighting the politics of bundling as a common implementation tactic at the local level and offering a brief discussion of recent efforts to address barriers to local implementation.

---

[1] The concept of interest and policy bundling was first discussed in Kostka and Hobbs (2012), and some sections in this chapter draw on this earlier work. The sections on political and economic incentives and state capacities draw on Kostka (2017).

G. Kostka (✉)
Freie Universität Berlin, Berlin, Germany
e-mail: g.kostka@fu-berlin.de

675
J. Yu, S. Guo (eds.), *The Palgrave Handbook of Local Governance in Contemporary China*, https://doi.org/10.1007/978-981-13-2799-5_31

2   NATIONAL CONTEXT: ENERGY-SAVING EFFORTS

One of China's key challenges in the next few decades will be to provide secure, sufficient, appropriate, and affordable energy for its economic and social development. As a result of rising incomes and growing industrial production, China's demand for energy more than doubled between 2005 and 2013 (Stocking and Dinan 2015). In 2010, China became the world's largest energy consumer when it accounted for 19% of global energy consumption (IEA 2010). Energy consumption in China is expected to rise by 47% between 2015 and 2035, while energy production will increase by 38% (British Petroleum 2017). As domestic energy supply continues to be based primarily on fossil fuels, supplying energy is closely related to the emission of carbon dioxide and other gases. Given this unsustainable pace of growth in energy consumption and its severe consequences for energy security and global climate change, China's energy policy has been moved to the top of Beijing's policy agendas.

In response to these developments, China has employed a mix of top-down command and control methods and market-based mechanisms to propel the switch to an energy-secure and energy-efficient growth path. Most importantly, in 2005, the Chinese central government introduced numerous administrative measures and command and control tools in China's fragmented vertical and horizontal (tiao tiao kuai kuai 条条块块) governance structure, the most important of which was a self-imposed national goal of a 20% reduction in energy intensity (i.e., energy consumption per unit of gross domestic product—GDP) against the 2005 levels by 2010.[2] To meet the national goal of a 20% reduction in energy intensity, Beijing introduced mandatory, "hard" (ying xing硬性) energy intensity reduction targets for local government departments and enterprises in its 11th Five-Year Plan (FYP).[3] In concert with the introduction of the hard targets, the central government also published a list of ten key energy-saving projects, ten key "people's projects," energy efficiency guidelines, and industry efficiency standards, along with other government documents to guide government and enterprise implementation of energy efficiency policy (Meidan et al. 2009; Zhou et al. 2010; Lo 2014). One particularly important program was the national Top 1000 Enterprise Program, which required high-energy-consuming enterprises to sign energy intensity reduction contracts with the provincial government (Price et al. 2010). Under the 12th and 13th FYPs, China continued its energy-saving efforts with energy intensity targets set at 16% and 15%, respectively (see

---

[2] The renewed attention by national leaders on energy efficiency was triggered by an increase in energy intensity. Between 2002 and 2005, China's energy intensity increased at an average of 3.8%, reversing a long-term trend of continuous energy efficiency improvements (Zhou et al. 2010).

[3] The majority of these "hard" binding targets have been granted "veto power" (*yipiao foujue*) status, meaning that, if these targets are not met, all of a local leader's other achievements will be rendered null and void. This is a powerful incentive in the context of stiff competition between local cadres for promotion to upper-level positions.

Table 31.1).[4] These targets are generally regarded as ambitious and as putting China in a good position to meet its commitments under the Paris Agreement.

More recently, China has also experimented with a variety of market-based instruments to supplement existing command and control tools, including rolling out a three-tiered electricity pricing system, introducing energy efficiency obligations (EEOs) on Chinese grid companies (Crossley and Wang 2015), and promoting energy service companies (ESCOs) (see Fig. 31.1). Yet

Table 31.1 Major energy targets in the 11th, 12th, and 13th FYPs

Target type	11th FYP (2005–2010)		12th FYP (2010–2015)		13th FYP (2015–2020)
	Target	Actual (by 2010)	Target	Actual (by 2015)	Target
Energy intensity	20% ↓ from 2005	19.1% ↓ from 2005	16% ↓ from 2010	18.2% ↓ from 2010	15% ↓ from 2015
Carbon intensity	–	–	17% ↓ from 2010	20% ↓ from 2010	18% ↓ from 2015
Non-fossil share of primary energy	8.3%	9.6%	11.4%	12%	15%
Hydro power	190 GW	217 GW	260 GW	319 GW	350 GW
Wind power	10 GW	31 GW	100 GW	129 GW	200 GW
Solar power	0.3 GW	0.8 GW	35 GW	43 GW	100 (150) GW
Nuclear power	12.5 GW	11 GW	40 GW	26 GW	58 GW

Source: China News (2007), State Council (2012), Eaton and Kostka (2013), Lewis (2017)

Note: ↓ means decrease

Over the past decade, the NDRC and the Ministry of Finance (MoF), as well as local governments, introduced financial and tax incentives to support the ESCO industry. For example, in 2008, Shanghai set up a special fund to promote ESCO projects. The NDRC and MoF offered 240 RMB for 1 ton of standard coal equivalent as a financial incentive for using ESCOs services and exempted ESCOs from business tax for revenue generated from Energy Performance Contracting (EPC) projects. The NDRC and MoF also issued and repeatedly updated a list of officially approved ESCOs. In 2013, the NDRC and MoF jointly issued the fifth list of 888 newly approved ESCOs, bringing the total number of approved ESCOs in China to 3,210 (estimates suggest that there are over 4,200 ESCOs in China, but only approximately 77% of all ESCOs were officially registered on the NDRC/MoF list).

Despite these numerous initiatives, ESCOs remain marginal players in delivering energy efficiency goals in China. The current list of approved ESCOs lacks transparent and stringent selection criteria and provides neither information about ESCOs technical and financial capabilities nor data on the companies' previous success in implementing energy efficiency projects. A sophisticated accreditation system would be beneficial to ensure confidence in the published list of approved ESCOs. Such an ESCO accreditation system has been successfully adopted in India and helped to build trust and confidence in the country's emerging ESCO industry. Moreover, China's commercial banks need to train their loan officers in developing and using internal energy efficiency saving measures and standards. An introduction of standardized measurements and verification protocols to verify energy savings at the national level would also be helpful.

Fig. 31.1 Policies to support the ESCO industry (Source: Kostka and Shin 2013)

[4] Most of the targets have reportedly been or "almost" been met. Under the 11th FYP, China reduced energy intensity by 19.1%, slightly short of the 20% national energy target. The energy intensity targets for the 12th FYP were met with energy intensity decreasing by 18.2% during the period between 2010 and 2015.

the majority of these market-based instruments have not scaled up to nation-wide programs due to a lack of market preconditions and excessive state intervention in allocation methods and pricing approaches (Lo 2013; Shin 2013). Recent efforts have also gone into developing seven local emissions trading schemes (ETSs), and China will launch a nationwide ETS between 2017 and 2019. Currently, there is large uncertainty regarding the features of a national ETS, especially with regard to the rules for trading and reporting and the role of third-party verifiers (Swartz 2016). With market-based instruments still in their infancy, China's energy governance system continues to rely primarily on top-down command and control instruments.

3   LOCAL CONTEXT: BARRIERS FOR ENERGY EFFICIENCY POLICY IMPLEMENTATION

The energy policies of China's most recent FYPs and the introduction of a variety of market-based mechanisms reflect the great emphasis placed on energy saving by the highest levels of the Chinese Communist Party (CCP) and State Council and can be considered a national reassessment of the "growth at any cost" model previously pursued throughout the country. Yet, the ultimate success or failure of national initiatives continues to depend on local implementation. Most China observers are well aware of gaps between the central government's official national policies and its practical outcomes at the local levels.[5] Often, there is conflict between government levels because national policies sometimes fail to take into account the negative impact that policies can have on local businesses, employment, and taxation revenues. National policies without sufficient local support and legitimacy are only strictly implemented when there is direct and constant attention from the center. Therefore, policy implementation outcomes often directly or indirectly relate to the differences between priorities at the national level and local incentives.

3.1   Economic and Political Incentives for Local Policy Implementation

The incentives provided to local actors via the cadre management system play a crucial steering function in local policy implementation (Whiting 2001; Heberer and Senz 2011). One can differentiate between economic incentives (the economic payoffs that different actions are likely to produce for both political leaders and private actors) and political incentives (political rewards that local bureaucrats can expect).

---

[5] For a discussion of the "environmental implementation gap" in China's highly decentralized and fragmented governing structure, see Lieberthal and Oksenberg (1988), Economy (2004), Van Rooij (2006), Kostka and Hobbs (2012, 2013), Ran (2013), and Kostka and Nahm (2017).

Local cadre behavior is partly determined by *economic* incentives, as severe budget constraints at the local level disincentivize local cadres to faithfully implement national energy mandates. Local governments face increasing pressure to enhance local income since local governments are assigned the main responsibilities for providing public services and infrastructure, yet revenues based on tax revenue sharing and intergovernmental fiscal transfers are insufficient to cover these costs (Wu et al. 2013; Wong 2010, 2013). The revenues received from the sale of land use rights and urban construction projects have become a particularly important source of extra-budgetary income for local governments, but this has often led to urban sprawl and wasteful land use. The revenues received from the sale of land use rights have become the most important source of extra-budgetary income for local governments (Man 2011). The institutional structure of the land transfer process also enables local governments to make significant profits. The compensation required for requisitioned agricultural land, based on the administrative formula, is usually much lower than the conveyance fees governments receive from private developments (Lichtenberg and Ding 2009). Estimates and anecdotal evidence suggest that conveyance fees are approximately 10–20 times the value of compensations (Tian and Ma 2009; Lichtenberg and Ding 2009). In addition, prior to the transfer, the price of the land sale is often intentionally driven up by increasing values through infrastructure construction such as investments in highways, metro stations, or even airports (Wei and Zhao 2009). Given these economic incentives, city expansion "always pays off, whether people end up living there or not" (Kaufman 2012). At its most extreme, these economic incentives can lead to the emergence of ghost cities such as the Kangbashi New Area in Ordos City in Inner Mongolia.

Next to economic incentives, personal *political* incentives play a central role in motivating local cadres to fulfill national energy intensity targets. Like other mandatory targets, binding energy intensity targets have been linked with the annual cadre promotion and evaluation system. Outstanding performances in the annual cadre evaluation are rewarded through promotions (in rank or position), additional wage or bonus payments, or other material benefits, including administrative benefits (e.g., free transport, entertainment, training, and travel) and other allowances for cadres (e.g., subsidized housing, health care, and opportunities for further education). If local leaders fail to meet binding energy intensity targets, they can face punishments through, for example, denial of promotion and formal censure, such as redeployment to a remote region or, in rare cases, expulsion from office. Local leaders (e.g., the Party secretary or the mayor of a province, municipality, or county) also sign individual responsibility contracts that include specific annual energy intensity targets for their locality. The signing of personal responsibility contracts helps to ensure that government officials at each layer of government administration are motivated to at least partially fulfill upper-level government directives.

Managers of state-owned enterprises (SOEs) are also embedded within the same system of annual cadre evaluation, meaning that they are more easily incentivized to comply with energy standards than managers of private enterprises (Kostka and Hobbs 2012; Harrison and Kostka 2014). SOE managers who fall short of their annual goals can be excluded from year-end bonuses and be subject to other political punishments. Managers of certain large SOEs who significantly increase energy efficiency may secure political benefits, including promotions. SOEs have a reputation for shirking regulations and getting away with worse environmental practices (Lo and Tang 2006; Eaton and Kostka 2017), but the example above suggests that the government can sometimes effectively leverage links to SOE managers to achieve energy gains. Informants also reported that SOEs are more easily regulated because local government officials have better information access to them than to private enterprises.

3.2   Target Allocation Practices in China

Energy intensity targets are passed down the administrative hierarchy using a mix of a "one-size-fits-all" approach and differentiated targets, depending on the administrative level and region. Provincial energy intensity targets in the 11th FYP ranged from 12% to 25%, in the 12th FYP from 10% to 18%, and in the 13th FYP from 10% to 17%. In general, to give them room for development, inland provinces were assigned lower energy intensity targets than their eastern counterparts. In the 12th FYP, all coastal provinces, with the exception of Hainan, received an energy intensity target between 16% and 18% while all inland provinces, with the exception of Liaoning, received targets at or below the national target of 16%. Interestingly, the use of differentiated targets declined from the 11th FYP to the 12th FYP. However, a closer look at target differentiation shows that the majority of provinces received targets very close to the national target. Table 31.2 shows that in the 12th FYP, 22 provinces received a target at the same level or plus or minus 1% of the national average.

There is even less differentiation between targets at the municipal level. Some provinces, such as Shandong, have a preference for disaggregating their provincial target into uniform or not highly differentiated municipal targets. For example, almost all municipalities in Shandong received energy intensity targets ranging from 22.02% to 23.09% during the 11th FYP. During the 12th FYP, Shandong's municipalities all received the same energy intensity target: 17%. In other words, provincial leaders in Shandong chose not to differentiate responsibilities between agricultural and industrial municipalities. Table 31.2 shows how other provinces have allocated energy intensity targets. With the exception of Shandong, Shanxi, and Jiangxi, provincial governments adopted a "not highly" differentiated target approach.

The level of differentiation declines even more when examining targets at the county or town level. For example, Jinan municipality, the capital city of Shandong, received an overall target of 22.04% during the 11th FYP and allocated a similar target ranging from 22.00% to 22.10% to all counties and

Table 31.2   Allocation of provincial energy intensity targets, 12th FYP (2011–2015)

Energy intensity	Provincial target (in %)	Target range for municipalities (in %)
National Average	16	–
Jiangsu	18	13–19
Guangdong	18	n/a
Hebei	18	n/a
Shanghai	18	15–18
Beijing	17	16–40[a]
Shandong	17	17[b]
Liaoning	17	n/a
Hubei	16	12–18
Hunan	16	15–17
Henan	16	15–17
Shaanxi	16	12–17
Fujian	16	5–19
Sichuan	16	10–17
Anhui	16	10–17
Shanxi	16	n/a
Jiangxi	16	n/a
Jilin	16	n/a
Inner Mongolia	15	14–16
Guangxi	15	11–19
Guizhou	15	14–16
Gansu	15	12–17
Ningxia	15	n/a
Hainan	10	8–11.5
Tibet	10	6–13

Source: *Author's Municipal Target Database*

[a]Shijingshan District is the only district that received a target of 40%; all other districts received targets ranging from 16% to 19%
[b]Locality adopted a one-size-fits-all approach

districts in the municipality. The maximal differentiation of 0.1% seems very small and arbitrary and lacks a logical pattern. For the 12th FYP, Jinan simply passed on the municipal energy intensity target of 17% to its ten counties and districts. At the county level, some local bureaus passed on additional targets to town governments, but the majority did not. Those officials that did use targets to steer the behavior of town officials have, like their superiors, most often used similar or uniform targets. The examples show that when allocating targets to the lower levels of government, that is, the county or town level, no large differentiations are made.[6]

[6]At each level, local governments are also given flexibility as to how to allocate targets during the five-year planning period. For instance, in one county in Hunan, leaders set the same annual energy intensity targets of −3.43% per year over the entire planning period, while in the neighboring county, energy intensity targets started high with −5% for the first year and declined to −3.5% over time. Leaders selected this descending method because they believed there would be, progressively, lesser room to achieve additional energy savings (Kostka 2016).

In summary, despite the widely acknowledged advantages of a differentiated approach to target allocation, it often happens that Chinese bureaucrats use hardly differentiated energy intensity targets. Especially at the municipal level, the allocation of targets to counties and districts frequently follows a "one-size-fits-all" or "slightly differentiated" approach. This is surprising, as many recent studies highlight the large and growing intra-provincial economic and structural differences (see Yu 2014). Likewise, the municipal unit often encompasses both rural and urban districts and counties, with large variation in energy-saving potentials between them.

3.3   Limitations of the Target-Based Implementation Approach

To date, the heavy reliance on a target-based implementation approach has yielded a number of desirable results. First, energy issues have moved quickly onto the policy agenda of many city mayors and Party secretaries. Second, the target-based system allows for some flexibility in factoring in local circumstances. Energy intensity targets can be allocated through either a "one-size-fits-all" or a "differentiated" approach. And yet, in spite of political incentives woven into the cadre management system, the incentive system does not always work effectively. Leading cadres' pressures for target fulfillment can lead to short-term maximization behavior instead of long-term innovative energy conservation. Many of the energy intensity targets in the 11th FYP were met at the very end of the planning period by using extreme and sometimes socially harmful measures. These included cutting electricity to hospitals, homes, and rural villages. Local governments also temporarily shut down energy-intensive companies for a given period of time, only to allow the same enterprises to reopen again later on—a method known as "sleeping management" (*xiumian guanli*) (Kostka and Hobbs 2012). These low-quality implementation approaches ensured that leading cadres met their energy intensity target outlined in their individual responsibility contracts but effectively put off the difficult matter of economic restructuring. By contrast, after meeting the 11th FYP targets in 2010, many localities went back to "business as usual" and, at the beginning of the 12th FYP in 2011, local governments thought of creative ways to ease their new burden. For example, many localities worked to attract outside companies in the hopes of boosting local growth as a means of manipulating the energy intensity ratio, since energy intensity = energy consumed/GDP.

The existing cadre incentive system is also somewhat problematic as tensions between energy and economic targets result from the different weights allocated to targets in the cadre evaluation forms (*kaohebiao*). Generally, economic targets significantly outweigh social energy and environmental and energy targets. For example, in one county in Shanxi province, government officials could obtain a maximum of 28 points for meeting economic targets in the 2011 evaluation forms, while just 14 points were allocated to resources and environment/energy targets (Eaton and Kostka 2013). Overall, it is clear that energy targets, while substantially more important now than before, compete for space on the crowded agenda of local officials. In these circumstances, most local officials have adopted the attitude of doing the very minimum amount that is required. Naturally, no locality wants to "sacrifice" its economic development and have average or below-average growth. In addition, promotion-seeking cadres will look for projects with high "political accomplishment value" to impress their superiors, but these actions can lead to less optimal outcomes for the locality in the long term (Eaton and Kostka 2014).[7] Figure 31.2 summarizes some general shortcomings of relying on energy intensity targets as a key implementation tool.

A heavy reliance on binding energy intensity targets can be problematic because allocated targets can be unscientific, rigid, arbitrarily inflated as they are passed down through the administrative hierarchy, and difficult to verify.

Unscientific targets: As binding energy intensity targets cascade downward through the administrative hierarchy, bureaucrats need to make decisions as to how to share the burden of implementation. Yet, this decision-making process requires a constant flow of high-quality information in order to identify the "right" target level for subordinate governments and enterprises. In the absence of such information, the use of one-size-fits-all targets can distribute the implementation burden very unequally between different reporting units. For example, within Shanxi province, some municipal governments reported that energy intensity targets were "easy" to achieve, while others felt they were "difficult." Such scenarios can generate resentment and supply incentives for heavily burdened localities to misreport data on difficult targets. With many local governments lacking the technical know-how and resources needed to decide about differentiated energy intensity targets, they are often not allocated in the most optimal way.

Rigid targets: Targets also remain rigid. For example, one urban district in Hunan failed to meet its 11th FYP energy intensity target because a large, central state–owned power enterprise moved into the district. District leaders escaped punishment only because the municipality still managed to meet its overall target despite the shortfall in the district.

Inflated targets: Government officials often inflate energy intensity targets when passing them down the administrative hierarchy in order to allow for slippage as they anticipate that some energy projects and efforts will fail or that the results will be questioned by national inspection teams. For example, in one municipality in Shanxi, energy intensity targets among counties generally ranged from 27 to 30%, despite a municipal overall target of only 25% (Kostka and Hobbs 2012). Receiving unattainable targets demotivates local leaders in charge of implementation and, in extreme cases, can trigger non-cooperation by local leaders.

Verification difficulties: Because energy intensity targets differ widely in terms of their ease of measurability, verifiability, and the extent to which they are tied to vital economic and social issues, the effectiveness and efficiency of binding energy targets can vary widely. Energy intensity outcomes are difficult to measure and verify since there are multiple ways to calculate energy and GDP data and no sophisticated technical equipment to monitor performance. Some localities measure energy intensity per GDP or per value added in large-scale (*guimo yi shang*) enterprises. This measure can be problematic because GDP data for the service sector is often not reliable, especially when it gets down to county-level data.

Fig. 31.2 Limitations of energy intensity targets as the main implementation instrument (Source: Kostka 2016)

[7] It is important to underscore that not all cadres are responsive to the political incentives outlined in the cadre evaluation system. A recent study based on 898 local Party secretaries' biographies shows that county-level cadres face only a slim possibility of being promoted to the municipal government (Kostka and Yu 2015). The study suggests that the importance of political incentives in the cadre evaluation system might be overstated.

In summary, insufficient economic and political incentives at the local level can sometimes disincentivize local cadres to faithfully implement national energy mandates. As a result, local government officials quite rationally invest the majority of time and funds in projects that produce tangible evidence of economic growth within their own tenure. In addition to poor incentives, local agencies' insufficient implementation capacities can be a significant barrier affecting local energy policy outcomes.

3.4   Capacity Constraints

State capacity is of key importance to the implementation of costly and often burdensome energy policies at the local level. Local governments work under certain political, technical, and financial capacity constraints that influence energy policy outcomes.

Political capacity constraints can result from coordination difficulties due to the following three factors: First, the implementation and enforcement of energy mandates at the local level is partly hindered by the fragmented and ambiguous allocation of energy responsibilities. Numerous government agencies are responsible for the implementation of energy mandates but sometimes without a clear division of labor, which in practice ultimately leads to a lack of accountability. For example, at least five departments have a role to play in energy efficiency implementation at subnational levels: the local Development and Reform Commission (DRC), the Economic Commission, the Construction Department, the Transportation Department, and the Environmental Protection Bureau (EPB). Second, implementing agencies face multiple and sometimes conflicting goals within an organization (for a comprehensive table of conflicting priorities, see Ran 2013). For example, the local DRC is in charge of multiple functions; its main interest lies in economic aspects, overseeing planning and investment management, while at the same time it is also responsible for overseeing energy efficiency and climate change issues. In many cases, DRCs' industrial and economic policy goals trump their energy mandates. Third, the importance of providing local bureaucracies with an adequate independent status to enforce energy policies can be illustrated with the example of managing central SOEs. Local officials frequently mention the "central SOE problem" and note that nothing could be done to prevent central SOEs (*yangqi*) from ignoring energy intensity targets in their localities except by bringing this problem to the attention of their superiors on the next administrative level (Eaton and Kostka 2017).

Technical capacity constraints can further hinder the implementation of national environmental mandates. Two pertinent technical constraints commonly cited in the literature are a lack of technical equipment and insufficiently trained local staff (Mol and Carter 2006). First, local agencies in charge of energy conservation report shortages of advanced technical equipment in measuring energy consumption, such as using sensory devices and smart metering technologies. In addition, the local bureaucracy is in chronic need of well-trained staff to strictly monitor the accuracy of reported energy figures and targets. Such skills are needed, for example, in deciding which method is appropriate to estimate energy intensity levels, defined as energy consumption per unit of GDP. Interviewees working in local DRCs frequently admit that sector-specific technical knowledge is needed to enable them to critically check enterprises' self-reported energy consumption reports. The combination of shortages in advanced technical equipment and officials' limited technological know-how leaves ample room for business managers to play a "game about numbers" with the local bureaucracy (Ran 2013), and energy intensity data "becomes more a matter of (political) choice and interpretation than that of showing evidence" (Wu et al. 2017: 209).

Financial capacity constraints refer to insufficient funding available for local implementation. At the national level, China has increased funding for energy conservation and is planning major future investments over the next decade. For instance, during the 11th FYP, the national fund dedicated for Energy Saving and Emission Reduction (ESER) provided more than RMB 220 billion to finance about 5200 major energy-saving projects (State Council 2011). In 2016, the national fund for ESER invested more than RMB 91 billion (China Climate Change Info Net, 2017). Despite the significant increase in funding from Beijing, most of these energy funds are tied to specific programs and projects managed by different central ministries. Local bureaus in charge of energy policy implementation tend to be seriously underfunded, especially as their responsibilities and tasks have multiplied over the past decade.

The financial capacity is further constrained by fiscal and administrative interdependence between local government agencies and top leadership in a locality. As the *de facto* first in charge, local Party secretaries and mayors have substantial influence over local government bureaus through the allocation of resources. From their leadership positions, they can have influence over the comprehensive budget set by the local finance bureau, which includes the annual budget for many energy policy initiatives. This makes the work of many local government bureaus dependent on local finance bureaus for their funding needs; thus, local government officials often worry that their budgets depend on the good graces of local leaders.

To overcome funding shortages, local governments at the county level can apply for project funding and staff expansion from the municipal, provincial, and national governments, but these funding applications are often lengthy and require sustained efforts by the local leadership over several years (Lo and Tang 2006; Kostka 2017). Limited financial capacity can lead to shortages of needed inspection vehicles, up-to-date testing equipment, and skilled staff. In summary, local leaders receive mixed signals: They are asked to fully implement binding energy targets, but these demands by upper-level governments are not always matched with a corresponding increase in financial resources.

4   STRATEGIC RESPONSES FROM LOCAL GOVERNMENTS

This section turns to the strategies that local leaders actually employ to bridge national priorities with local interests. For energy efficiency policy implementation, the clearly defined energy intensity targets, the strict punishments through denial of promotion and formal censure for government officials and enterprise managers if they fail to meet them, and the high cost and at times redistributive nature of energy efficiency improvements make energy policy implementation a site of political contestation (Kostka and Hobbs 2012). To illustrate how local leaders work politically, this section highlights specific implementation tactics that officials use to bring enterprises and the public on board in support of officials' professional objectives.

4.1   Strengthening of Incentives for Local Policy Implementers

Some subnational governments devise *additional* incentives to motivate local policymakers and enterprises to implement national energy policies. Figure 31.3 summarizes the efforts of the Shanxi provincial government to create new incentives and punishments for local governments and enterprises during the 11th FYP. Among other initiatives, Shanxi introduced a tax on provincial coal exports and used part of this money to fund economic restructuring and energy efficiency programs.

4.2   Framing as a Policy Tool

A second tool used frequently during the implementation of costly energy efficiency policies is *framing*, a concept that has its origin in sociological research (Goffman 1974). The linguistic reframing of policies allows officials to shape public perceptions (Scrase and Ockwell 2010). In Shanxi, for instance, research suggests that provincial leaders framed energy efficiency policies by conceptualizing and describing them in ways that played to interests in their localities. This helped to create coalitions to support the implementation of initiatives that were *prima facie* detrimental to interest groups or the public in general. Through these methods, municipal and county officials with unambiguous incentives to meet energy intensity target reductions could balance national and provincial demands with local interests. At the same time, they bundled energy efficiency policy in ways that make it relevant to concerns of greater local importance. Ultimately, local officials frame policies and programs of national and international concern in ways that give them legitimacy at the local level.

4.3   Policy Bundling and Interest Bundling

Local government agencies also built informal and formal coalitions that advanced and sustained their energy efficiency policy objectives. Coalition

Shanxi province mounted a vigorous response to central energy efficiency policy during the 11th FYP. A rich array of implementation incentives was employed, including:

1. Allocation of voluntary targets and signing agreements with the largest industrial enterprises: Shanxi introduced a provincial Top 200 Enterprise Program modeled after the national Top1000 Enterprise Program, which in 2009 was extended to include a provincial Top 1000 Enterprise Program. Under the program, selected provincial enterprises sign voluntary agreements with the provincial government that commit firms to achieving a prescribed amount of energy savings.

2. Strengthening of financial incentives: Shanxi leaders created a *Coal Sustainable Development Fund* by taxing all provincial coal exports to fund energy-saving initiatives:
→ Between 2007 and 2009, the fund collected over 43 billion RMB, of which 1.3 billion RMB was used to phase out inefficient production facilities.
→ The taxation of coal export helps Shanxi to soften the social and economic consequences of plant closures and to eliminate outdated production facilities by providing a pool of funds for city greening initiatives and energy-saving policy implementation.

In 2008, the Shanxi government began to devise a number of financial rewards for municipal governments and larger enterprises with the best record of energy conservation:
→ *Enterprise reward:* A financial reward of 500,000 RMB was granted if enterprises scored 95 points or more, and 200,000 RMB was given if enterprises scored between 80 and 95 points in an annual evaluation.
→ *Government reward:* Municipal governments scoring 95 points or more were rewarded with 300,000 RMB, and those attaining between 80 to 95 points received 200,000 RMB. A proportion of these rewards can be used to provide personal prizes for leaders.

3. Introduction of fines and penalties
Sanctions for non-responsive municipal and county governments/government officials:
→   Localities that repeatedly fell short of energy intensity targets did not receive new land allocations for industrial purposes.
→   In 2006, the Shanxi EPB revoked the right of disobedient localities to conduct environmental evaluations (*quyu xianpi*). The suspension of this right effectively blocks a city's ability to approve industrial projects, as all new projects are required to undergo an environmental evaluation.
→   Fines, excluded from annual provincial personal rewards programs, denied honorary titles, or even demoted or relocated to a remote area.

Provincial leaders used price controls and shut off access to utilities to discipline non-compliant enterprises.
→ Shanxi implemented a differentiated electricity pricing policy by charging higher prices to non-compliant enterprises sorted into two categories:
a) 'Restricted' enterprises on the government's watch list saw their electricity prices rise to between 0.05 and 0.1 RMB/kWh.
b) Flagrant violators in the 'to-be-eliminated' category were charged between 0.2 and 0.3 RMB/kWh.
→ For severe cases, a policy called 'cut electricity, cut water' (*duandian duanshui*) has been used, through which the EPB coordinates with state-owned electricity and water companies to cut off a company's access to utilities.

Fig. 31.3   Strengthening of incentives in Shanxi (Source: Kostka and Hobbs 2012; Harrison and Kostka 2014)

formation can be achieved through deliberate measures to align the interests of diverse local groups, which I refer to as "*bundling.*" Bundling is a strategy used in situations where the support for policies is uncertain given their redistributive, costly, or otherwise contentious nature. It refers to the creation of win–win scenarios so that different policy objectives and/or the priorities of different interest groups can be pursued simultaneously (Kostka and Hobbs 2012; Harrison and Kostka 2014). Bundling can take different forms depending on the level and form of alignment of interests that it is designed to achieve. In the implementation of local energy efficiency policies, we identify and analyze two specific forms of bundling.

The first and more high-level form is *policy bundling*. This refers to a set of techniques that are used to combine different policy objectives to facilitate the implementation of some or all of the policies in the composite bundle. Policy bundling offers two major advantages for implementation. First, less popular policy initiatives can benefit from their association with policies that carry wider political support. For example, in China's 11th five-year planning period, provincial authorities in Shanxi shut down scores of small mining operations in the name of promoting worker safety; in so doing, they achieved energy savings that were often an unstated objective. Second, policy bundling can make it possible for newer initiatives to benefit from the institutional structures and know-how of more established policy issues. For example, some energy-saving policies were implemented as parts of larger campaigns and connected with policies and concerns of more local or immediate interest, like local pollution control.

The second form of bundling—*interest bundling*—refers to deliberate efforts to bring together parties with distinct interests around a particular policy. Examples include linking the implementation of a policy to specific economic or other benefits—such as preferential access to government resources, expedited project approvals, or negotiated agreements of mutual support—in exchange for the implementation of one or more policies. For instance, an enterprise may agree to comply with tough energy efficiency standards in exchange for strict enforcement by the government that company leaders expect will push competing enterprises out of business. For instance, in Shanxi, government officials aligned their interests with those of SOEs and large private enterprise managers by communicating the importance of the ESER policy and indicating the willingness of the local government to provide compensatory benefits such as assurance of uninterrupted business operation and preferential access to land and funds for enterprises that are compliant. The specific incentivization process is often flexible and open to negotiation and depends on an exchange of benefits outside of the formal incentive structure. It hinges on the (explicit or implicit) provision of compensatory benefits and depends on the level of enticement, appeasement, or pressure needed to make enterprises' incentives improve energy efficiency on par with those of the implementing officials who will be rewarded or promoted for the enterprise achievements. Officials also take competing interests such as economic growth and employment into consideration during implementation, as such factors also affect government officials' evaluations (Harrison and Kostka 2014). This interest-bundling approach turns energy efficiency policy implementation into a somewhat cooperative venture and avoids adversarial relationships with important local enterprises.[8]

---

[8] "Interest bundling" is somewhat comparable to "logrolling" in American politics, which occurs when legislators trade votes in exchange for cooperation on other issues (Johnson 2005). The main difference between interest bundling and logrolling is that bundling occurs most often in policy

These two forms of bundling are typically used in conjunction with each other. Together, they form the strategic core of the efforts undertaken in both countries to build informal coalitions capable of pursuing energy efficiency objectives. Through bundling, officials seek to align different interests and build relationships, thereby reconciling competing priorities and increasing their chances of achieving their own objectives.

The bundling potential varies regionally, given different local circumstances. In Shanxi, for instance, many important large industrial enterprises and small competitors offer opportunities for governments to work cooperatively to protect local business interests while at the same time meeting their energy intensity targets. Yet, informal coalitions can quickly dissolve if they are not developed further or maintained (Harrison and Kostka 2017). Triggered by national pressures to lower pollution, Shanxi province was a frontrunner in energy efficiency policy implementation under the 11th FYP (2005–2010). Between 2005 and 2010, provincial leaders in Shanxi province restructured and closed energy-inefficient coke enterprises and coal mines and implemented provincial energy efficiency standards in some industries that were stricter than those set out at the national level (Kostka and Hobbs 2012).[9] However, these company closures and new standards contributed to slowing growth in the province and, when Shanxi's GDP growth dropped dramatically from double-digit growth figures to only 4% at the end of the 11th FYP, making Shanxi one of the slowest-growing provinces in China, provincial leaders reversed many of their energy-saving strategies and started to reopen some of the coal mines that had initially been shuttered, approve new coal projects, and place less emphasis on provincial energy efficiency standards (interviews by author in 2011; The Economist 2015).[10]

5   CONCLUSION

This chapter studied the policy implementation of national energy efficiency policies in China at the local level. The summary highlights a number of institutional barriers for implementation, including shortcomings in the current

implementation rather than during policy formulation. For energy efficiency bundling, local officials and enterprises cooperate on energy efficiency in exchange for compensatory benefits for the enterprises on other issues.

[9] These provincial efficiency standards were created by large provincial enterprises themselves to give them room to take their own interests into account. Although it seems counterintuitive for enterprises to willingly draft tough standards, especially when they are sufficiently stringent to lead to cost increases, many large enterprises have incentives to create high efficiency standards to squeeze small producers out of the industry and increase their market share. One manager of a large magnesium enterprise cited this as a major reason for supporting strict standards.

[10] Interviews conducted by the author in Taiyuan, Shanxi, 2011, reveal that top provincial leadership admitted that Shanxi province experienced negative growth, which triggered the change to sideline energy efficiency policies in favor of maximizing GDP.

energy planning system, insufficient political and economic incentives provided to local implementers, and financial, technical, and political capacity constraints on local implementing agencies. In particular, the analysis shows that reliance on a target-based implementation system as the main instrument has yielded mixed results. Although energy efficiency issues have moved quickly onto the policy agenda of local governments over the past decade, the target system itself produces multiple unanticipated and undesirable results. As binding energy intensity targets cascade downward through the administrative hierarchy, targets can become unscientific and rigid and are routinely inflated. Binding energy intensity targets also aggravate cyclical behaviors among government officials, and pressures for target fulfillment can result in 11th-hour, short-sighted actions.

In addition, weak political and economic incentives for local policymakers further help to explain why there is often insufficient motivation for effective energy efficiency implementation at the local level in China. Energy intensity targets, while substantially more important now than before, compete for space on the crowded agenda of local officials. Under these circumstances, many local officials have adopted the attitude of doing the very minimum required to implement energy targets, while most attention continues to be placed on maximizing GDP growth rate and fiscal income. Among local leaders, the attitude prevails that "no leader will be promoted because of their better achievements in environmental protection and energy savings."

At the most basic level, energy policy implementation at the local level is also constrained by implementing agencies' political, technical, and financial capacities. Political capacity constraints can result from coordination difficulties due to a fragmented bureaucracy, conflicting priorities *within* implementing agencies, and low bureaucratic status and authority granted to the implementing bureaucracies. The main pertinent technical constraints include the lack of advanced technical equipment and insufficiently trained local staff. Finally, upper-level governments' energy conservation demands are also not always matched with a corresponding increase in financial resources, which sends mixed signals to local leaders.

Chinese planners and local governments have recently begun to address some of the barriers for local implementation. Efforts under way include new measures to improve energy efficiency target allocation, implementation, and verification processes. For instance, in order to avoid cyclical implementation behavior among cadres observed at the end of the 11th FYP period, more emphasis was placed in the 12th and 13th FYPs on reaching annual targets instead of accumulated five-year targets (Kostka 2016). In addition, as the case study of Shanxi in this chapter illustrates, some subnational governments have devised additional incentives to motivate local policymakers and enterprises to implement energy efficiency policies. Finally, efforts are underway to address local governments' political, technical, and financial capacity constraints that influence energy policy outcomes. For instance, to improve the energy consumption of central SOEs, the State-owned Assets Supervision and

Administration Commission (SASAC) has included energy savings in the annual performance evaluation of SOEs. These findings contribute to the ongoing debate regarding how China can switch to a more energy-efficient and greener urban growth path, and particular emphasis is needed in the coming years to create additional incentives and increase local implementation capacities.

REFERENCES

British Petroleum. 2017. *British Petroleum Energy Outlook: Country and regional insights – China.* Available at http://www.bp.com/content/dam/bp/pdf/energy-economics/energy-outlook-2017/bp-energy-outlook-2017-country-insight-china.pdf.

China Climate Change Info-Net. 2017.03 *The National Fund Increases Its Support to ESER.* Available at http://www.ccchina.gov.cn/Detail.aspx?newsId=66607&TId=57.

China News. 2007. *Nuclear long-term development plan 2005–2020.* Available at http://www.chinanews.com/gn/news/2007/11-04/1067945.shtml.

Crossley, D. and X. Wang. 2015. *Case Study: China's Grid Company Energy Efficiency Obligation. Beijing, China: Regulatory Assistance Project.* Available at http://www.raponline.org/document/download/id/7711.

Eaton, S. and G. Kostka. 2013. Does Cadre Turnover Help or Hinder China's Green Rise? Evidence from Shanxi Province. In Chinese Environmental Governance Dynamics, Challenges, and Prospects in a Changing Society, *Bingqiang Ren and Huisheng Shou (eds)*, pp: 83–111. Palgrave Macmillan, NY.

Eaton, S. and G. Kostka. 2014. Authoritarian Environmentalism Undermined? Local Leaders' Time Horizons and Environmental Policy Implementation. *The China Quarterly* 218: 359–380.

Eaton, S. and G. Kostka. 2017. Central Protectionism in China: The "Central SOE Problem", *The China Quarterly* 231: 685–704.

Economy, E. C. *The River Runs Black: The Environmental Challenge to China's Future.* Ithaca, NY: Cornell University Press, 2004.

Goffman, E. 1974. *Frame Analysis.* Cambridge: Harvard University Press.

Harrison, T. and G. Kostka. 2014. Balancing priorities, aligning interests: Developing mitigation capacity in China and India, *Comparative Political Studies* 47 (3): 450–480.

Harrison. T. and G. Kostka 2017. Bureaucratic manoeuvres and the local politics of climate change mitigation in China and India, *Development Policy Review*, forthcoming.

Heberer, T. and Senz, A. 2011. Streamlining Local Behaviour through Communication, Incentives and Control: A Case Study of Local Environmental Policies in China. *Journal of Current Chinese Affairs* 40 (3): 77–112.

International Energy Agency (IEA). 2010. China Overtakes the United States to Become World's Largest Energy Consumer, 20 July 2010. Available at http://www.iea.org/index_info.asp?id=1479.

Johnson, P. M. 2005. Logrolling, *Glossary of Political Economic Terms.* Available at http://www.auburn.edu/~johnspm/gloss/logrolling.

Kaufman, B. J. 2012. Drivers and Barriers for Sustainable Urban Form: The Case of China, Unpublished Master's Thesis, *Frankfurt School of Finance and Management.*

Kostka, G. and W. Hobbs. 2012. Local energy efficiency policy implementation in China: Bridging the gap between national priorities and local interests, *The China Quarterly* 211: 765–785.

Kostka, G. and W. Hobbs. 2013. Embedded interests and the managerial local state: the political economy of methanol fuel-switching in China, *Journal of Contemporary China* 22 (80): 204–218.

Kostka, G. and K. Shin. 2013. Energy conservation through energy service companies: Empirical analysis from China, *Energy Policy* 52: 748–759.

Kostka, G. and X. Yu. 2015. Career backgrounds of municipal Party secretaries in China: Why do so few municipal Party secretaries rise from the county level?, *Modern China* 41 (5): 467–505.

Kostka, G. 2016. Command without control: The case of China's environmental target system, *Regulation & Governance* 10: 58–74.

Kostka, G. China's local environmental politics, In E. Sternfeld (ed.), Routledge Handbook of Environmental Policy in China. 2017. Routledge: 31–47.

Kostka, G. and J. Nahm. 2017. Central–Local Relations: Recentralization and Environmental Governance in China (Introduction to Special Section), *The China Quarterly*, 231: 567–582.

Lewis, J. I. 2017. Green energy innovation in China, In E. Sternfeld (ed.), Routledge Handbook of Environmental Policy in China. 2017. Routledge: 280–290.

Lichtenberg, E. and C. Ding. 2009. Local Officials as Land Developers: Urban Spatial Expansion in China. *Journal of Urban Economic* 66: 57–64.

Lieberthal, K. and M. Oksenberg. 1988. *Policy-Making in China: Leaders, Structures, and Processes*. Princeton, N.J.: Princeton University Press.

Lo A. L. 2013. Carbon trading in a socialist market economy: Can China make a difference? *Ecological Economics* 87: 72–74.

Lo, K. 2014. A critical review of China's rapidly developing renewable energy and energy efficiency policies. *Renewable and Sustainable Energy Reviews* 29: 508–516.

Lo W. H. C. and S. Y. Tang. 2006. Institutional Reform, Economic Changes, and Local Environmental Management in China: The Case of Guangdong Province. *Environmental Politics* 15 (2): 190–210.

Man, J. Y. 2011. Local Public Finance in China: An Overview. In J.Y. Man and Y.H. Hong (eds), China's Local Public Finance in Transition. Cambridge, MA: Lincoln Institute of Land Policy: 3–17.

Meidan, M., P. Andrews-Speed, and M. Xin. 2009. Shaping China's Energy Policy: Actors and Processes. *Journal of Contemporary China* 18 (61): 591–616.

Mol, A. P. J. and N. T. Carter. 2006. China's Environmental Governance in Transition. *Environmental Politics* 15 (2): 149–170.

Price, L., X. Wang, and J. Yun. 2010. The Challenge of Reducing Energy-Consumption of the Top-1000 Largest Industrial Enterprises in China. *Energy Policy* 38 (11): 6485–6498.

Ran R. 2013. Perverse Incentive Structure and Policy Implementation Gap in China's Local Environmental Politics. *Journal of Environmental Policy and Planning* 15 (1): 17–39.

Scrase, I. and D. Ockwell. 2010. The Role of Discourse and Linguistic Framing Effects in Sustaining High Carbon Energy Policy: An Accessible Introduction. *Energy Policy* 38 (5): 2225–2233.

Shin S. 2013. China's failure of policy innovation: the case of sulphur dioxide emission trading. *Environmental Politics* 22 (6): 918–934.

State Council. 2011. *China's top ten key energy-saving projects saving 340 million tons of standard coal capacity.* Available at http://www.gov.cn/jrzg/2011-10/01/content_1961479.htm.

State Council. 2012. *China's Energy Policy 2012,* Available at http://news.xinhuanet.com/english/china/2012-10/24/c_131927649.htm.

Stocking, A. and T. Dinan. 2015. *China's Growing Energy Demand: Implications for the United States,* Working Paper Series Congressional Budget Office Washington, D.C., Working Paper No. 2015-05: 1–37.

Swartz, J. 2016. *China's National Emissions Trading System - Implications for Carbon Markets and Trade,* Issue Paper 6. http://www.ieta.org/resources/China/Chinas_National_ETS_Implications_for_Carbon_Markets_and_Trade_ICTSD_March2016_Jeff_Swartz.pdf.

The Economist. 2015. *Shanxi province. King Coal's misrule. The rise and fall of a corrupt coal-fueled economy.* London, 28 November. Available at http://www.economist.com/news/china/21679263-rise-and-fall-corrupt-coal-fuelled-economy-king-coals-misrule.

Tian L. and W. Ma. 2009. Government Intervention in City Development of China: A Tool of Land Supply. *Land Use Policy,* 26 (3): 599–609.

Van Rooij, B. 2006. Implementation of Chinese Environmental Law: Regular Enforcement and Political Campaigns. *Development and Change,* 37 (1): 57–74.

Wei, Y. and M. Zhao. 2009. Urban Spill Over Vs. Local Urban Sprawl: Entangling Land-Use Regulations in the Urban Growth of China's Megacities. *Land Use Policy* 26 (4): 1031–1045.

Whiting, S. 2001. *Power and Wealth in Rural China: The Political Economy of Institutional Change.* Cambridge: Cambridge University Press.

Wong C. 2010. Fiscal Reform: Paying for the Harmonious Society. *China Economic Quarterly* 14 (2): 20–25.

Wong C. 2013. Paying for Urbanization: Challenges for China's Municipal Finance in the 21st Century. In: Bahl R. J. Linn and D. Wetzel eds. 2013. *Metropolitan Government Finances in Developing Countries.* Cambridge, MA: Lincoln Institute for Land Policy.

Wu J., Y. H. Deng, J. Huang, R. Morck and B. Yeung. 2013. *Incentives and Outcomes: China's Environmental Policy.* NBER Working Paper No. 18754, February 2013.

Wu, J., C. Zuidema, K. Gugerell, and G. de Roo, 2017. Mind the gap! Barriers and implementation deficiencies of energy policies at the local scale in urban China. *Energy Policy* 106: 201–211.

Yu, X. 2014. *A Disaggregate Analysis of China's Regional Development, Unpublished Doctoral Thesis,* Frankfurt School of Finance and Management.

Zhou, N., M. Levine, and L. Price. 2010. Overview of Current Energy Efficiency Policies in China. *Energy Policy* 38 (11): 6439–6452.

CHAPTER 32

Energy Policy Design and China's Local Climate Governance: Energy Efficiency and Renewable Energy Policies in Hangzhou

Ting Guan and Jørgen Delman

1   POLICY DESIGN IN CLIMATE CHANGE POLITICS

China's urban climate change politics evolved rapidly during the 2000s,[1] since the central government had quickly recognized that cities are important levels of intervention in relation to climate change. Cities need policy support and incentives to act,[2] and through a short period of time, China's national leadership designed a series of comprehensive low-carbon urban development programs[3] to guide policy development and implementation at local level. The policies designed include a broad array of low-carbon initiatives, including green innovation and new business solutions, not least in relation to energy

---

[1] See Qi and Wu, "Politics of climate change"; CPI, *The policy climate*; Baeumler, Ijjasz-Vasquez and Mehndiratta, *Sustainable Low-Carbon City Development in China*.

[2] See OECD, "Cities and climate change".

[3] Here, based on Chinese practice, we use "low carbon development programs/policies" as a concept that embraces policies that contribute to reducing CO_2 emissions.

T. Guan
School of Public Policy and Management, Tsinghua University, Beijing, China
e-mail: guanting@tsinghua.edu.cn

J. Delman (✉)
Department of Cross-Cultural and Regional Studies, China Studies, University of Copenhagen, Copenhagen, Denmark
e-mail: jorgen.delman@hum.ku.dk

© The Author(s) 2019   695
J. Yu, S. Guo (eds.), *The Palgrave Handbook of Local Governance in Contemporary China*, https://doi.org/10.1007/978-981-13-2799-5_32

efficiency (EE) and renewable energy (RE).[4] Other critical mitigation interventions, such as expanding green coverage for carbon storage, are also important.[5] However, as energy consumption accounted for 78.5% of China's greenhouse gas (GHG) emissions in 2012[6] and since fossils will continue to dominate in the Chinese energy supply for years to come, energy policies focusing on EE and the transition toward clean and renewable energies will remain the dominant political action arena[7] to mitigate CO_2 emissions for a long time.[8]

China's city governments are embedded in a hierarchical party-state system, which is dominated by a top-down, command-and-control approach to policy development and implementation, and therefore they do not control all aspects of GHG emissions on their own. However, like in climate politics elsewhere,[9] they have been prompted to design or adopt instruments of governance that bridge traditional intra-bureaucratic divides as well as gaps between state and non-state stakeholders in order to be able to mitigate the inherent tendency in Chinese politics toward fragmented policy implementation.[10] In addition, within the climate change arena, municipal authorities have been accorded significant flexibility to shape local behaviors in order to reduce GHG emissions.[11] Effectively, the traditional approach of the authoritarian party-state is being renegotiated and redeveloped.

Internationally, the instruments that national and local governments have used to mitigate climate change fall within three distinct categories, that is, command-and-control, market-based, or collaborative governance instruments.[12] These instruments are increasingly being used in different mixes in China as well.[13] These three types of instruments are evidently based on divergent normative assumptions about the role of government and about how to structure economies and societies. Although China is ruled under an authoritarian one-party regime, there does not seem to be a priori normative barriers to the choice of policy instruments. In fact, even in liberal societies, liberal rationalities not only require a certain kind of autonomous individual subject to regulate or facilitate, they also have to employ certain sovereign and authoritarian tactics to sustain themselves.[14] A similar logic applies to China where city leaderships may maintain

---

[4] See Boyd, "China's energy and climate".

[5] See Zhou and Delbosc, "Chinese climate and energy".

[6] Song et al., "China's climate policies".

[7] See Ostrom, "Institutional rational choice".

[8] See Koehn, *China Confronts Climate Change*; Song et al., "China's climate policies"; Odgaard and Delman, "China's energy security challenges".

[9] Cf. Pattberg and Stripple, "Remapping transnational climate governance".

[10] Lieberthal and Oxenberg (1988) argued that China's political system can be seen as a fragmented authoritarian system. Also see Delman, "Urban climate change politics"; Koehn, *China Confronts Climate Change*.

[11] See Koehn, *China Confronts Climate Change*.

[12] See Stavins, "Policy instruments for climate change".

[13] See Guo, "China's Administrative Reform".

[14] See Sigley, "Chinese governmentalities".

their authoritarian approach to government while simultaneously developing a more flexible and adaptive approach to implementation that involves sets of tools and mechanisms aimed to make the policy cycle more effective.[15]

While the city is a crucial level of governance for implementation of climate change mitigation policies,[16] the design of China's urban climate politics[17] is understudied. The few available studies, such as by Schröder, Mai and Francesch-Huidobro, and Koehn,[18] are substantial and informative when it comes to examining and explaining the nature of urban/local climate politics and climate governance, but they do not address the nature and development of the total package of policy designs and instruments systematically.

To address this gap, we wish to analyze the overall implications of specific climate policy instruments at city level. First, we propose a model for policy design analysis to capture the normative choices and preferences in energy policies and the potential for governance innovations. Second, we examine specific climate governance innovations in China based on a case study of energy policy designs in Hangzhou, the capital city of Zhejiang Province. We focus on two core dimensions of climate mitigation policies, namely EE and RE, due to their importance for climate change mitigation.[19] Finally, we discuss the consequences and prospects for climate governance innovations in China.

2   CONTEXTUALIZING THE ANALYSIS OF CLIMATE CHANGE POLICY DESIGN

The examination of city climate change policies provides a basis for explaining the normative assumptions or "frameworks" (more later) underlying these policies and the implications for the institutional architecture of China's urban climate governance. Our analytical approach is anchored in Ostrom's[20] Institutional Analysis and Development (IAD) framework which allows us to reflect on how rules-in-use are designed in the climate change policy arena rather than just rules-in-form.[21] We wish to examine how specific climate change policies socialize climate change mitigation as rules-in-use. We look at five dimensions of policy design: (1) political decisions (frameworks and policy priorities); (2) policy instruments and tools; (3) participants and target groups; (4) implementation modalities; and (5) evaluation. Our analytical model

---

[15] See Heilmann and Perry *Mao's invisible hand*; Yu and Wang, "Applicability of governance theory".

[16] See OECD, "Cities and climate change"; Broto and Bulkeley, "Urban climate change experiments"; Bulkeley, *Cities and climate change*.

[17] We use "climate policies" as another generic term that comprises policies within the fields of climate change, environment, and renewable energy (RE)/energy security.

[18] See Schröder, *Local climate governance*; Mai and Francesch-Huidobro, *Climate change governance*; Koehn, *China Confronts Climate Change*.

[19] See Song et al., "China's climate policies"; IPCC, *Climate change 2014*.

[20] See note 7 above.

[21] See Ostrom, "Institutional rational choice", 23.

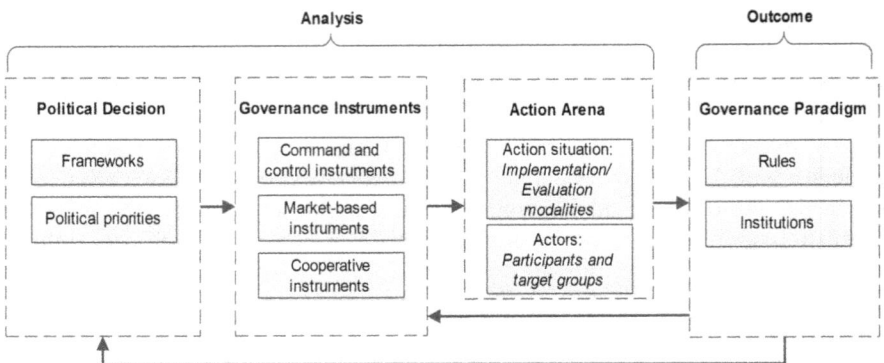

Fig. 32.1 Climate policy design at the city level: Analytical model

(Fig. 32.1) helps us "organize diagnostic, analytical, and prescriptive capabilities. It also aids in the accumulation of knowledge from empirical studies and in the assessment of past efforts in reforms".[22] The model further allows us to follow the institutionalization of the policy design process and the development of rule configurations for policy designs that socialize climate change mitigation efforts through all stages of the policy process.[23] In the following sections, the model is used to contextualize China's existing climate change politics and subsequently to analyze specific policy designs in the subsequent sections.

2.1   *Political Decision*

Frameworks are theoretically or normatively anchored conceptions that can be used to compare not only theories[24] but also underlying conceptual or normative approaches within a political action arena such as climate change policy. Like elsewhere,[25] and as discussed earlier, China's government has had a choice between different types of policy instruments to deal with the climate change challenge, based on distinctly different normative preferences. The preferred instruments have been *Command-and-control approaches* that are associated with hierarchies[26] with distinct preferences for a central planning rationality[27] and *markets*[28] or *market-based instruments* associated with a neo-liberal approach to mobilization of markets for delivery of the required public goods or services.[29] Planning authorities at the apex of the hierarchy, such as the

---

[22] See Ostrom, "Institutional rational choice", 26.

[23] See Ostrom, "Institutional rational choice", 36.

[24] See Ostrom, "Institutional rational choice"; Schlager, "A Comparison of frameworks".

[25] Cf. note 12.

[26] Cf. Ostrom, "Institutional rational choice".

[27] See Chow, "Economic planning in China".

[28] See note 7.

[29] See Sigley, "Chinese governmentalities"; Rhodes, "Governing without government".

National Development and Reform Commission (NDRC), are now working with both types of interventions.[30]

In Fig. 32.1, *policy priorities* relate to basic decisions about what to do and how to do it. China's climate change policies work with climate strategies and legislation, action plans, and detailed regulations and standards. They can provide and enhance incentives for climate change mitigation, they design mechanisms for mainstreaming of climate change interventions, and they provide focal points of interaction for actors, for example, government departments, firms, and nongovernmental organizations (NGOs). China has largely followed what the Organisation for Economic Co-operation and Development (OECD) countries have been doing, and it has taken a lead with other major Asian countries during the period 2007–2012 in relation to nationally binding legislation and action plans.[31] China's national policies are generally based on a mixture of command-and-control and market-based instruments, and a variety of pilot programs have intended to mobilize markets in support of GHG reductions.[32] While *cooperative instruments* are mentioned in policy documents and national plans, they are mainly designed, as we shall see later, at local level to fit the local situation.

2.2   Policy Instruments

Command-and-control instruments: The most common approach used worldwide to address environmental problems is to set standards, for example, technology or design standards, or performance-based standards, for example, emission standards, to directly regulate the activities of firms, organizations, and individuals. Product prohibitions are also used.[33] Generally, an increasing number of such administrative instruments are used in China to ensure compliance with national targets, rules, and standards,[34] and, during the last four decades, China has put out more than 28 environmental and resource laws, 150 national administrative environmental regulations, 1300 national environmental standards, and 200 departmental administrative regulations.[35]

The performance review system based on key performance indicators (KPIs) for party-state organizations and leaders in China is an important intra-bureaucratic command-and-control instrument inspired by neo-liberal thinking. It is used by the central government to control, guide, or incentivize local governments and officials to take responsibility for meeting economic growth and other important policy targets within their territory.[36] Normally,

---

[30] See note 27.
[31] See Dubash et al., "National climate change mitigation".
[32] See CPCCC, "Decision on deepening reforms".
[33] See note 12.
[34] See Xu et al., "Chinese climate change mitigation".
[35] See Kostka, "Barriers of environmental policies".
[36] See Delman, "Urban climate change politics"; Koehn, *China Confronts Climate Change*; Kostka, "Barriers of environmental policies"; CPCCC "Decision on deepening reforms"; Wang, "Search for Sustainable Legitimacy".

KPIs comprise: (1) "guidance targets" (zhidao xing 指导性 or yiban zhibiao—般指标) also considered "soft" indicators, (2) "hard indicators" (ying zhibiao 硬指标), or (3) "indicators with veto power" (yipiao fojue mubiao—票否决目标). "Veto" indicators are the most important and failure to meet them leads to sanctions.[37] From 2011, the responsibility for attaining climate change-related KPIs have been put squarely on the shoulders of leaders at all levels of the party-state. As for EE, KPI obligations were incorporated into the Energy Conservation Law in 2007,[38] and since then, environmental, energy, and climate change-related performance criteria have become increasingly important KPIs for local leaders.[39] There is no doubt that the KPI instrument is important to incentivize and regulate the behavior of the local party-state,[40] and that it is likely to reinforce the authoritarian approach of the party-state.[41]

Market-based instruments. China's "socialist arts of government" increasingly refer to new normative preferences and strategies which "call for governing through autonomy, whether that be through market mechanisms or the autonomous conduct of individuals".[42] Market-based or economic instruments are used widely to encourage behavioral change to reduce GHG emissions. They include charges, fees, and taxes, for example, a carbon tax, taxes on fossil fuels and other energy taxes, trading in carbon rights, and "emission reduction" credits in so-called carbon markets.[43] China's climate and energy policies already use a combination of such instruments, including subsidies, taxation, and market instruments.[44] However, due to weak market preconditions and considerable state intervention in emission trading formats, allocation methods, and pricing approaches, the instruments are not yet widespread. The market-based instruments are still in their infancy, and generally China's environmental governance system continues to rely heavily on top-down command-and-control instruments.[45]

Given the importance accorded to the role of the market in recent years,[46] we do, however, speculate that market-based instruments will stimulate the improvement of capacity in local settings to address climate change issues, for example, leading to higher EE through development of better monitoring, review, and verification systems (MRV). In fact, non-state agents could replace the party-state in providing services and capacity development at the level of enterprises.

---

[37] See Wang, "Search for Sustainable Legitimacy".

[38] See Qi, "Low-Carbon development in China".

[39] See Koehn, *China Confronts Climate Change*; Wang, "Search for Sustainable Legitimacy"; MF, "energy conservation & emission reduction".

[40] See Qi and Wu, "Politics of climate change".

[41] See note 35.

[42] See Sigley, "Chinese governmentalities".

[43] See note 12.

[44] Cottrell et al., "Revenues for green energy"; Zhou and Delbosc, "Chinese climate and energy".

[45] Zhan, "Carbon trading in China"; Kostka, "Barriers of environmental policies".

[46] Culminating with the Communist Party of China (CPC) Central Committee's 2013 reform program. See CPCCC, "Decision on deepening reforms".

Co-operative instruments and co-governance: Governments can also seek to engage with external stakeholders, including third parties (*disanfang* 第三方), through cooperation or interactive/collaborative governance processes to address societal complexities and dynamics, also in relation to climate change. The co-governance approach moderates overlapping and cross-cutting authorities and responsibilities. The parties involved must join hands to address a common purpose and invest their identities and autonomy in the process. However, practices vary considerably across different societal scales, from the local to the global.[47] Mai and Francesch-Huidobro[48] found that the exclusive intra-governmental and hierarchical coordination structure in China is moving toward more cross-sector collaboration. It mobilizes external actors in business and society and thus becomes more inclusive and pluralistic. Co-governance is often based on shared democratic values throughout the policy process, while coordination is still authoritarian. The outcome of such processes is a semi-authoritarian climate change governance regime. The state seeks external support for its policies to make them more effective than under traditional authoritarian coordination.[49] Such developments make it possible to speculate that, while these instruments are still relatively immature and underdeveloped, we may see more of such institutional innovations in the future.

2.3   Participants and Target Groups

Climate change is a political action arena that encompasses different sets of participants or actors.[50] In the context of this study, participants encompass those who issue or formulate policies, often but not necessarily encompassing themselves as acting agents, and target groups that are chosen to participate or to receive benefits or burdens from these policies.[51] In some cases, the study of policy designs will help us identify the chosen potential winners and losers in the local climate politics action arena, for example, those chosen to receive benefits or burdens or to be included or excluded, respectively.

2.4   Implementation Modalities

Policy design entails design of implementation instruments and envisaged outcomes. Two dimensions are particularly important. First, central policies are adapted locally,[52] and local or decentralized "experimentation under hierarchy" has become institutionalized as a key element in policy processes. This implies

---

[47] Kooiman et al., "Interactive governance and governability".
[48] See Mai and Francesch-Huidobro, *Climate change governance*.
[49] See note 48 above.
[50] See note 7.
[51] Cf. Ingram, Schneider, and DeLeon, "Social construction and policy design".
[52] See Guan, Grunow, and Yu, "Improving China's environmental performance".

that novel approaches tested through local experiments are systematically re-adapted into national and local policies.[53] The policy documents examined later in the chapter from Hangzhou contain many provisions for establishing experiments or pilots. Second, evaluation is important for learning and readjustment of policy designs. China has gradually developed its domestic reporting processes for effects of mitigation policies and measures across the multiple arenas and sectors of climate change politics. The Chinese system is mixed and combines provincial, municipal, and national systems. But the system is not fully developed or integrated. In some instances, it is perfectly coordinated, while in others it is uncoordinated.[54] Furthermore, the top-down mode of operation of the party-state system frequently leads to the "gaming" of implementation policies by lower-level governments and businesses, for example, through over-reporting, to avoid problems or even to obtain praise when the actual performance has been less than satisfactory.[55]

3   Hangzhou As a Case

Since the detailed study of climate change policy instruments at the city level in China is new, we have chosen one city as a case to examine how national policies interact with local approaches to governance. While many comparable cities could have been chosen, we have decided to focus on Hangzhou due to its position as a progressive provincial capital that promotes "green city making".[56] We use the analytical dimensions in Fig. 32.1 as entry points to analyze the local EE and RE policy designs to identify and explain the normative conceptions underlying local climate change politics as well as their institutional implications.

The analysis focuses on the three dimensions to the left in Fig. 32.1, whereas the expected outcomes are covered in the right-hand box. In order to implement the 12th Five Year Plan (FYP) 2011–2015, Hangzhou's city authorities elaborated at least 71 general and sector plans.[57] While they cover a broad range of policy arenas, we use EE and RE as exemplary cases within the climate politics action arena in Hangzhou. As discussed earlier, EE and RE represent two different, yet interlinked and critically important, political arenas for climate change mitigation. While we seek for explanations about the normative conceptions and preferences underlying policy design in these two arenas, we also acknowledge that policy designs develop and change over time. Therefore, we focus on the period 2005–2014 as far as the empirical material allows. We primarily examine policy documents of various types from the period. This material is complemented by other official documents and reports, local media coverage, and official statistics. Finally, we also examine the practical implementation measures.

---

[53] See Heilmann, "Local to national policy".

[54] See Boyd, Keen, and Rennkamp, "Emerging arrangements for MRV"; See Zhou and Delbosc, "Chinese climate and energy".

[55] See Qi and Wu, "Politics of climate change".

[56] See Odgaard and Delman, "China's energy security challenges".

[57] See Hangzhou Government, "Preparing the 12th Five-year Plan".

4   ENERGY POLICY DESIGN IN HANGZHOU

4.1   Energy Efficiency

Hangzhou's government has noted that the EE arena is a key to the green transformation of the city's economic growth model, and an increasing number of policies for EE have been formulated and implemented since 2006 based on national policies. The efforts have reduced energy consumption per unit of gross domestic product (GDP) by about 32% from 2006 to 2013, exceeding the average percentage reduction at both provincial and national levels.[58]

4.1.1   Political Decisions

The two most important EE indicators are energy intensity and total energy consumption.[59] In the 11th FYP, Hangzhou's overriding goal for EE was to reduce energy intensity by 20% between 2005 and 2010.[60] A further 15–18% reduction was introduced in the 12th FYP (2010–2015).[61] In 2012, the city government defined total energy consumption as an additional target. Table 32.1 shows the compulsory goals over time and how these targets were gradually disaggregated to the target localities. From 2006 to 2008, all districts and counties in Hangzhou received uniform reduction targets, while the targets were gradually localized from 2009. From 2011, the city districts were all assigned individual reduction targets. Furthermore, based on a target for annual reduction of energy consumption per unit of GDP, three new indicators were added, that is, reduction of electricity consumption per unit of GDP, total energy consumption, and total electricity consumption. This system with four target indicators was initiated as of 2012.

To realize these targets, Hangzhou's government released specific 11th and 12th FYPs for EE and associated annual work plans from 2007. The basic normative framework underlying these interventions were the following: First of all, the policy design combined command-and-control instruments with market-based instruments. Second, the policies provided subsidies and other supporting measures while regulating their use through monitoring and auditing, and, finally, there was a focus on promoting technological innovation through preferential policies.[62]

---

[58] See Hangzhou Government, "Energy reduction report 2014".

[59] Energy intensity, energy consumption per unit of gross domestic product (GDP), has been set as a national indicator for energy conservation since 2006 (State Council of China, 2005). Additionally, total energy consumption was set as a second national indicator for energy conservation in late January 2013, when China's State Council approved an "energy consumption control target" below the equivalent of 4 billion tons of coal per year by 2015 (See State Council of China, 2013).

[60] See Hangzhou Government, "Hangzhou 11th Five Year Plan for energy conservation".

[61] See Hangzhou Government, "Hangzhou 12th Five Year Plan for energy conservation".

[62] See Hangzhou Government, "Hangzhou 11th Five Year Plan for energy conservation"; Hangzhou Government, "Hangzhou 12th Five Year Plan for energy conservation".

Table 32.1   Hangzhou's annual energy efficiency (EE) targets

Year	Annual targets[a]		Annual sub-district targets	
	Reduction of energy intensity (%)	Reduction of total energy consumption (%)	Eight districts and five counties in Hangzhou	
			Reduction of energy consumption per unit GDP (%)	Reduction of electricity consumption per unit GDP (%)
2006	3.2%	–	–	–
2007	4%	–	–	–
2008	4.4%	–	–	–
2009	4.6%	–	• 4.6% in the districts of Xiaoshan, Yuhang, Tonglu, Jiande, Fuyang, and Lin'an • 1% in Chun'an County • 6% in districts of Shangcheng, Xiacheng, Gongshu, Jianggan, Xihu, Binjiang, and the Economic Development Zone	–
2010	3%	–	• 3% in Xiaoshan, Lin'an • 5.2% in Yuhang • 4% in Fuyang, Jiande, Shangcheng, Xiacheng, Gongshu, Jianggan, Xihu, Binjiang, and The Economic Development Zone • 2% in Tonglu • 1% in Chun'an	–
2011	4.1%	–	• 3.8% in Shangcheng, Xiacheng, Gongshu, Jianggan, Xihu, Binjiang, and the Economic Development Zone • 5.0% in Fuyang • 4.8% in Jiande and Xiaoshan • 4.4% in Yuhang • 4.2% in Lin'an, Tonglu • 2.0% in Chun'an	• 3.5% in Shangcheng, Xiacheng, Gongshu, Jianggan, Xihu, Binjiang, and The Economic Development Zone • 4.6% in Fuyang • 4.5% in Jiande and Xiaoshan • 4.1% in Yuhang • 3.5% in Lin'an, Tonglu • 1.0% in Chun'an
2012	5.6%	4.3%	All districts get different targets. The main indicators include annual reduction in percentage of energy consumption per unit GDP, electricity consumption per unit GDP, total energy consumption, and total reduction of electricity consumption.	
2013	4.8%	4.9%	Indicators are the same as above, but with different targets.	
2014	6.4%	1.6%	Indicators are the same as above, but with different targets.	

Sources: Annual Work Plans for Energy Efficiency in Hangzhou 2007–2014 (HG 2007, 2008, 2009, 2010c, 2011a, 2012a, 2013a, 2014c)

[a]Year-on-year percentage reduction

4.1.2   Governance Instruments

During the period since 2005, Hangzhou's government gradually opted for a mix of policy instruments. Command-and-control instruments were seen as critical. The party-state's performance review system with its KPIs functions as the crucial institutional framework to regulate the behavior of the participants.[63] The officials of city-, district-, and county-level governments had to sign responsibility contracts (*zerenshu* 责任书) with the city government. The contracts oblige them to attain energy intensity targets within their jurisdictions, and to do so they sign responsibility contracts with managers of targeted local enterprises who have to commit themselves to specific energy consumption targets. Specific and highly restrictive regulations have been elaborated to link the KPIs of city leaders and officials to the targets set in the contracts.[64]

One of the key command-and-control initiatives for realizing EE goals is the Key Energy-Consuming Enterprises Program. The high-energy-consuming enterprises were selected as target enterprises due to their high levels of emissions of GHGs and pollutants. They were required to employ an energy manager to take charge of energy auditing within the company as well as for reporting to the government. Regulations were designed subsequently to develop supervision and enforcement capacity. An Energy Management Centre in Hangzhou was set up in 2012 to collect energy data from enterprises, establish an energy information network, and introduce a distributed monitoring system.[65] Since 2013, a requirement for mandatory installation of equipment for measuring energy consumption within the companies has been put into force.[66]

The program has had significant results. At the outset, in 2007, the program targeted enterprises with annual energy consumption above 3000 tons of standard coal. A total of 65 enterprises were forced to accept energy auditing.[67] From 2009–2014, the target group was widened to cover enterprises using more than 1000 tons of standard coal annually, and about 190 additional enterprises were included.[68] In 2012, 329 enterprises were enrolled, and they accounted for almost 50% of total energy consumption in Hangzhou.[69]

---

[63] See Delman, "Urban climate change politics".

[64] See Zhejiang Economy and Trade Committee (ZETC) and Zhejiang Statistics Bureau (ZSB). "Guideline for energy consumption".

[65] See Hangzhou Government, "Plan for energy conservation (2012)"; Hangzhou Government, "Plan for energy conservation (2013)".

[66] See General Administration of Quality Supervision (GAQS), "Measuring instrument of energy"; Hangzhou Government, "Plan for energy conservation (2013)".

[67] See Hangzhou Government, "Plan for energy conservation (2007)".

[68] See Hangzhou Government, "Plan for energy conservation (2009)"; Hangzhou Government, "Plan for energy conservation (2010)"; Hangzhou Government, "Plan for energy conservation (2011)"; Hangzhou Government, "Plan for energy conservation (2012)"; Hangzhou Government, "Plan for energy conservation (2013)"; Hangzhou Government, "Energy reduction report 2014".

[69] See Hangzhou Government, "Plans for energy-saving program".

Table 32.2   Annual plans for market-based projects in Hangzhou

Year	Program		
	Cleaner Production	*Power Balance Test*	*Circular Economy*
2007	–	50	36
2008	50	50	100
2009	100	50	120
2010	150	100	130
2011	200	–	100+
2012	500	–	–
2013	400	300	–
2014	300	200	170 projects were designed to be included in
2013–2015	1000 (three-year plan 2013–2015)	No number (three-year plan 2013–2015)	Hangzhou's Circular Economy "770 Project" (2014 plan), with a total investment of RMB 11.9 billion, of which RMB 3.3 billion to be distributed in 2014.

Unit: Number of planned projects
Sources: Annual work plans for EE in Hangzhou 2007–2014; Hangzhou Circular Economy "770 Project"; Hangzhou Three-year Action Plan of Innovation and Development for Energy-saving and Environmental Protection Industries (HG 2007, 2009, 2010c, 2011a, 2012a, 2013a, 2013c, 2014c, 2014d)

Meanwhile, market-based instruments have gained in prominence. Most of the relevant programs prescribe that "third parties" get involved, primarily different types of energy service companies (ESCO), that is, market-based intermediaries like energy consultants and energy-saving service companies. They provide independent technology consultancy and support project implementation. As shown in Table 32.2, a variety of these programs were designed over time, such as a Cleaner Production Programs that employs an integrated preventive environmental strategy to processes, products, and services to increase eco-efficiency and reduce risks to humans and the environment, a Power Balance Test Program that intends to increase production efficiency by testing the power balance systems, and a Circular Economy Program that strives to achieve EE through industrial ecology and life-cycle management approaches. Table 32.2 shows that since 2007 the number of target enterprises has increased sharply which implies a rapid expansion in the use of market-based instruments. To get these programs off the ground, Hangzhou's government provides various subsidies for individual projects, depending on their type, scale, and outcome. At the same time, there has been a rapid development of third-party organizations. Among the 2339 ESCOs approved by authorities across China as of January 2012, 74 were from Hangzhou. Furthermore, the number and size of them are expected to continue growing with support from Hangzhou's government.[70]

[70] See KPMG, "Green economy-invest in Hangzhou".

Generally, the Chinese government sees mechanisms such as standardized measurements, verification protocols, and differentiated support modes as essential to mobilize the market.[71] Although such instruments are designed and implemented by an authoritarian regime and fall under the "competition under hierarchy" approach,[72] nongovernmental actors exert increasing influence on them through their involvement, and the assessment systems are continuously made more transparent and more fair, which suggests a mode of governance that will increasingly combine command-and-control with market-based instruments.

As most programs are designed by the government, there are only few examples in Hangzhou of a cooperative approach with multiple actors. One exception is that Hangzhou's government encourages fund-raising for local EE projects. Local enterprises can raise external funds for EE projects instead of paying the total expense up-front themselves, if they cannot be subsidized by the government. In 2011, Hangzhou's government collaborated with the International Finance Centre to build a risk-sharing pool to provide a fund-raising platform for enterprises.[73] The Hangzhou branch of China Zheshang Bank was the first bank to participate in the scheme. Since it is officially recognized that multiple actors can play more important roles in climate politics, the co-governance mode is expected to become more prominent in Hangzhou in the future.

4.1.3   Implementation Modalities

Hangzhou's government has set a mandatory cap on energy use which combines KPIs for government officials and specific target responsibility contracts for local governments and enterprises. These are tightly linked, and the contracts are compulsory rather than voluntary. These instruments are seen as crucial to incentivize and force officials and leaders of enterprises to attain the EE targets.

Meanwhile, the assigned targets are linked to a variety of regulatory instruments, market-based mechanisms, and capacity-building programs which are increasingly used in combination. The market-based programs are clearly used by the government to increase the capacity for self-management in the market.

4.1.4   Participants and Target Groups

Hangzhou's government seems to spare no effort to incentivize, persuade, or even force enterprises to take action. It has initiated and guided various forms of financial support, established an Energy Conservation Association, and fur-

---

[71] See Kostka and Shin, "Energy conservation service companies".
[72] See Göbel, "Uneven policy implementation in rural China".
[73] See Liu, "Credits for energy conservation".

ther strengthened mandatory auditing.[74] Energy end-users and ESCOs are the main participants in these programs, yet the government is still dominant due to the preference for state intervention and the lack of market preconditions.[75]

4.2   Renewable Energy

Hangzhou's government started to promote RE in 2008.[76] Since then, the so-called new energy industry has developed rapidly. According to a KPMG report, the projected sales volumes of the new energy industry in Hangzhou was planned to increase from RMB 16 billion in 2010 to RMB 32 billion in 2014,[77] with strong guidance and support from the government.

4.2.1   Political Decisions
According to the national 12th FYP on RE, clean energy should account for more than 9.5% of total energy consumption by 2015, including 290 GW of installed hydropower capacity, 100 GW of wind power, and 21 GW of solar power.[78] However, Hangzhou's government only uses sales output from RE industries as a key indicator for RE development, and, since Hangzhou is highly dependent on import of energy, the government mainly focuses on the development of the new energy industry rather than on producing or acquiring RE.[79]

In 2010, Hangzhou's target of new energy industry sales output was set at RMB 100 billion for 2015, of which RMB 40 billion from solar photovoltaic industry, RMB 30 billion from wind power equipment, RMB 15 billion from new battery industry, and RMB 15 billion from other industries.[80] However, in 2012, the ambition had been sharply reduced and the targets for 2015 had been changed to RMB 50 billion, and the sales volume amounted to RMB 25 billion, RMB 15 billion, and RMB 10 billion in solar photo-voltaic (PV), wind power, and new batteries, respectively.[81] Even so, Hangzhou's government continued

[74] See Hangzhou Government, "Plan for energy conservation (2007)"; Hangzhou Government, "Plan for energy conservation (2009)"; Hangzhou Government, "Plan for energy conservation (2010)"; Hangzhou Government, "Plan of strategic industries (2011–2015)"; Hangzhou Government, "Plan for energy conservation (2012)"; Hangzhou Government, "Plan for energy conservation (2013)"; Hangzhou Government, "Plan for energy conservation (2014)"; KPMG. "Green technology–invest Hangzhou".
[75] Cf. Kostka, "Barriers of environmental policies".
[76] The first policies primarily aimed at solar energy and new energy autos.
[77] See KPMG, "New energy".
[78] See National Development and Reform Commission (NDRC) and National Energy Bureau (NEB). "Renewable energy's 12th Five-year plan".
[79] Hangzhou's government has little influence on the acquisition of energy or on determining the sources of its power supply. This responsibility rests with the province (interview with official from Hangzhou Development and Reform Commission, November 13, 2015).
[80] See Hangzhou Government, "New energy industry plan (2010–2015)"; Hangzhou Government, "Plan for major industries (2011–2015)".
[81] See Hangzhou Government, "Three-year plan for energy-saving"; Hangzhou Government, "Development of the photovoltaic industry".

to emphasize that low carbon industries, especially new energy industries should be taken as the backbone of the city's climate change mitigation efforts.[82]

To achieve its goals, the government's RE framework focused on (1) policy reinforcement to institute more market-based instruments within the RE subsectors; (2) promotion of RE development and deployment through pilot and demonstration projects to test and demonstrate pathways for the new energy industry; (3) technology innovation and new production facilities; (4) identification of urban and new rural construction and transportation as the key priority sectors; and (5) government support for research and development (R&D) and innovation in the business sector, including establishment of a platform for RE R&D.[83] Overall, generous subsidies were to be provided through the habitual command-and-control approach.

4.2.2   Governance Instruments

Due to its late development, the conditions in Hangzhou's RE sector are still immature as compared to many other cities in China, and local policy instruments and tools for RE development are different from those within EE. Most prominently, RE has not been included into the KPI system yet. Command-and-control instruments are primarily used to develop infrastructure and considerable support is given to pilot programs based on specific planning initiatives or to adapt best practice cases. Hangzhou's government supports development of auxiliary industrial parks for the new energy industry, such as Hangzhou New Energy Development Zone, and two other key zones, Hangzhou High-tech Industrial Development Zone and Qianjiang Economic Development Zone. There are also other more specialized zones.[84] These dedicated industrial parks are designed to support preferred or targeted industrial sectors and enterprises and to stimulate a cluster effect in relation to development of capacity to produce RE technology.

The pilot programs receive considerable support from the government through preferential policies, financial aid, and allocation of other resources. From 2009, Hangzhou provided subsidies totaling more than RMB 100 million for new energy projects,[85] for example, the Golden Roof Demonstration Project initiated by the national government in 2009. It is estimated that about RMB 10 billion were allocated for this program at the national level. In response, Hangzhou's government decided to cover 700,000 m² of roof tops with solar PV from 2009 to 2013, increasing its solar capacity to 70 MW. This project is considered a pillar for adjusting and optimizing the structure of the energy system.[86] Similar pilot projects can be found in relation to the city's low carbon plan, new energy autos, new batteries, and wind power equipment.

[82] See Hangzhou Government, "'Twelfth Five Year' low carbon plan".
[83] See Hangzhou Government, "New energy industry development (2010–2015)".
[84] See note 83.
[85] See KPMG, "New energy".
[86] See note 82.

The infrastructure projects and the dedicated industrial parks are clearly the dominant policy measures with the RE arena in Hangzhou. In addition, Hangzhou's government also promotes market-based instruments. A typical example is governmental subsidies for distributed solar PV. In addition to subsidies for distributed PV projects from the central and the provincial governments, which amounted to RMB 0.42/kWh and RMB 0.1/kWh, respectively, from 2014 to 2015, Hangzhou's government provides a subsidy of RMB 0.1/kWh for completed projects that comply with specific standards.[87] This policy is based on a demand-side subsidy that is particularly aimed at energy end-users who benefit directly.

Compared to EE polices, cooperative instruments are used even less in RE. However, like in the EE arena, there is also a wish to encourage fund-raising of local private capital to widen the investment channels and secure stable investment.[88]

4.2.3   Implementation Modalities
RE interventions mostly occur through infrastructure programs, pilot projects, and some market-based policies. Unlike EE, RE targets are not linked with the KPIs of organizations and officials, and they are not included in the responsibility contracts of local officials and enterprise leaders. Thus, the targets for the sector are not compulsory and not as constraining as those for EE.

4.2.4   Participants and Target Groups
The major participants in Hangzhou's RE initiatives are (1) the local government; (2) the energy producers and end-users, for example, individual households, enterprises, and government organizations; and (3) appointed ESCOs, especially research institutes and new energy technology companies. Since Hangzhou's preconditions for development of RE were immature, the city government has taken the lead in initiating the programs. It has designed policies, and it distributes subsidies and supervises implementation. Besides, non-governmental actors such as enterprises, appointed ESCOs, and end-users are meant to benefit from engaging in the projects designed by the government. The relevant R&D organizations and technical service companies are expected to develop quickly by relying on generous subsidies for R&D and innovation to support the RE sector. However, unlike with the EE, not many market-based ESCOs can be found in the RE arena and no specific regulations have been identified regarding third-party organizations. Most of the new energy companies have contracts with the government for their projects. Finally, cooperative governance instruments hardly exist.

---

[87] See Hangzhou Government, "Hangzhou Municipal Government opinions on the better development of the distributed photovoltaic industry by accelerating the applications".

[88] See note 87.

5   COMPARING ENERGY POLICY DESIGNS

The two political action arenas examined reveal that local policy design responds loyally to central policies, but they also point to emerging innovative elements developed at the local level. Table 32.3 synthesizes the findings that relate to the policy design dimensions examined.

It is evident from the table that the policy design modalities in the EE and RE arenas differ considerably. Even though both were initiated in recent years, EE policies are more comprehensive and mature than RE policies.

The two cases differ primarily in relation to their preconditions, for example, the nature of the implementing agencies and the conditions in the specific sectors and the sector markets. EE policies are designed with basic standards and rules for sustained market operation, while the RE policy designs mostly promote short-term pilot programs or subsidies to develop local industry. While the capacity and influence of the actors participating in EE are likely to increase in the future due to the chosen approach, the sustainability of the government-dominated mode in the RE arena may be doubtful since activities may be discontinued when the government terminates its support.

The implementation modalities designed are also different. The EE arena is predominantly market-oriented "under hierarchy", while the RE arena is dominated by the government. The analysis allows us to expect that the EE arena is likely to experience more changes in the mode of governance in the future. New policy and institutional mechanisms have already been put in place to shift the focus away from traditional government support to infrastructure and demonstration projects with direct financial allocations.

Furthermore, target indicators within the EE arena are included in the KPIs of government organizations, while this is not the case within the RE arena. KPI fulfillment is an important institutional arrangement. The target responsibility contracts for local governments are linked to individual KPIs, and the performance assessments knit together organizations across the party-state to mitigate the tendency toward fragmented implementation. Contracts function as legally binding instruments that aim to incentivize and pressure local officials to satisfy their higher-ups while also contemplating how to secure and promote their own position by doing what they are told to. Targets are also forced upon enterprise leaders as a quasi-legal obligation.[89]

RE is a new political action arena in Hangzhou. The absence of local market demand has forced the government to support the sector to get off the ground. At the same time, it appears to be considered premature to incorporate this arena under the KPI system. This would, however, not preclude that the sector could follow a development trajectory similar to that of the EE arena at a later stage.

Only few cooperative instruments have been identified, and they are relatively immature due to the asymmetric power relationships between the partici-

---

[89] Cf. note 63.

Table 32.3 Analysis of policy design in energy conservation and renewable energy in Hangzhou

Political decision		Governance instruments			Action arena		Implication
Target	Policy framework	Command-and-control	Market-based	Cooperative	Target groups	Implementation modalities	Implication for governance
Energy conservation							
Energy intensity: 15%–18% (2010–2015)	Target responsibility system; KPIs; Combined instruments	Target responsibility system; Ten Thousand Enterprises Program; Technology promotion (e.g. CWS, industrial boiler technology); Close down outdated production facilities; Energy auditing; Energy conservation assessment; Best practice awards; Power control	Cleaner Production Program; Circular Economy Program; Labelling for energy conservation products; Electricity Balance Program; Demand-side electricity control	Energy performance contracting; Energy conservation fund-raising program	Local government↑; Energy end-users↑; ESCOs↑	Market-oriented under hierarchy	Multi-actor interaction mechanisms are expected to develop and expand in future
Renewable energy							
New energy industry sales output: RMB 50 billion (2015)	Combined instruments; Pilot projects; Financial support	Industrial park planning; Golden Solar Pilot Program; New Energy Automobile Pilot Program; RE use in the countryside	Subsidy for distributed PV program; Subsidy for R&D projects	RE fund-raising program	Local government↑; Energy producer and end-users→; ESCOs→	Government-dominated; Policy experiment	Government-led mode expected to continue

Note: Target groups—arrows are used to indicate the potential winners and losers in the action arenas. "↑" indicates that the actor receives benefits and is expected to play an important role in future. "→" indicates that the actor receives benefits and burdens simultaneously, but the incentive structure for the actor is largely unchanged

pating actors. Hangzhou's government is still in the driver's seat and none of the instruments appear to be designed collaboratively. Yet, with the growing recognition by the government of the need for engaging with non-state actors, we speculate that the few traces of local co-governance based on multiple actor collaboration and the partnerships that we have identified could indicate that such cooperative arrangements may become more prominent in the future as the partners get more familiar with them and with each other.

In summary, the Hangzhou case reflects that new local policy designs and instruments may contribute to gradually transform the local mode of climate governance. First, Hangzhou's government has gradually announced increasingly detailed regulations for interventions to stimulate the role of the market, for example, regulations for energy conservation service organizations and more strict technical standards for equipment using energy. Second, the local market capacity is nurtured by selective government support. As an example, Hangzhou's government introduced an expert evaluation system, and based on the feedback from this system, the government financed targeted enterprises differently according to the effects of their energy conservation actions. The aim is to enhance the energy management capacity of the local enterprises and other actors, as well as it could raise the competitiveness of the enterprises. Third, new market-based mechanisms are firmly promoted by the government. The most illustrative example is fund-raising schemes for energy conservation where the government has increasingly diversified the channels for provision of funds and fund-raising.

Finally, it is noteworthy that the carbon price and the cost-benefit of the proposed interventions do not appear to be a concern in Hangzhou, nor do we find specific requirements for evaluating the policies designed.

6   New Dimensions in Urban Climate Change Politics and Governance

Hangzhou's climate change policy instruments testify to a local climate governance regime that responds loyally to the policies and guidelines issued by the central authorities. While the traditional top-down approach of the city government is still dominant in its climate politics, the study shows that, when dealing with the local economic and social conditions, the city government is willing and able to undertake pilot projects and to experiment. It has flexibly tailored the policies of the central government to the local needs through the use of different types of instruments. This approach has paved the way for new ways to distribute resources and burdens, and it has contributed to empowerment of market players and emerging non-state organizations.

We do not find traces of local debates in Hangzhou about how the use of the diverse policy instruments may affect the local political economy or even the local political system itself. There seems to be an assumed belief that— under the continued control and guidance of the authoritarian party-state— the seemingly incongruous policy preferences will not disrupt or undermine the hegemonic position of the party-state in the local political economy. We would argue, however, that such a conclusion is premature. It is not unlikely that continued experimental designs and piloting that employ more neo-liberally inclined policy instruments may contribute to transform the local mode of governance even more dramatically than is the case now.

Despite the local scope of our study, our findings and conclusions speak to important national issues in China. Most prominently, the performance review system with KPIs is used forcefully to foster greater leadership "attention" to the need for climate change mitigation at the local level. The Qinghua Climate Initiative rightly calls the use of KPI-based performance reviews "the most significant institutional change in the management system of EE and ... the most important institutional innovation in China's low-carbon development in recent decade".[90] In Hangzhou, it has still only been used in the "mature" EE arena until now. It has not been used as yet in the more nascent RE arena.

There is also a strong interest to deploy a variety of market-based instruments that are likely to increasingly empower actors in the market. This may, in turn, lead to the formulation and deployment of more cooperative instruments over time.

On many dimensions, Hangzhou's climate change politics follow patterns that are well known from urban climate governance outside China, not least in OECD countries. This leads us to argue that, just like the national and the local contexts, international experience is also an important driver in climate politics in Hangzhou, and that the three sets of drivers combined may well contribute to further innovations in the approach of the city leadership to climate governance in the future.

Finally, to generalize our findings, we would argue, with reference to Ostrom,[91] that climate change policy designs do not only socialize climate mitigation efforts into an existing rule-ordered system of behavior, but that it also prompts the rule-ordered system to develop in new directions through local rules-in-use. Thus, the approach of Hangzhou's government to the design and implementation of climate change policies seem to gradually become less authoritarian, more market based, and more accountable, due to the inherent complexity of this political action arena. The city government has recognized the need for leveraging information asymmetries to create a multilevel playing field for external non-state stakeholders with whom it enters into contractual relationships to enable them and to ensure that they are able to deliver on their contracts.

The use of instruments with different normative preferences as local rules-in-use may thus tease out new modes of governance that make the relationships between the party-state and the market actors less asymmetric and more collaborative. These developments warrant more comparative research to assess whether such phenomena are observable across China's urban climate governance regimes.

---

[90] See Qi, "Low-Carbon development in China".
[91] See note 7.

Acknowledgments We are grateful to Prof. Yu Jianxing for his support to the project, to Zhang Liyan for her research assistance, and to Andrew Podger for comments on an initial draft.

References

Boyd, Anya, Samantha Keen, and Britta Rennkamp. "A comparative analysis of emerging institutional arrangements for domestic MRV in developing countries." Energy Research Centre, Cape Town: University of Cape Town, 2014. http://www.erc.uct.ac.za/Research/publications/14-Boyd_etal-Comparative_analysis.pdf.

Boyd, Olivia. "China's energy reform and climate policy: the ideas motivating change." *CCEP Working 1205.* Canberra: Centre for Climate Economics and Policy, Crawford School of Economics and Government, the Australian National University, 2012.

Broto, Vanesa C. and Harriet Bulkeley. "A survey of urban climate change experiments in 100 cities." *Global Environmental Change* 23, (2013): 92–102.

Bulkeley, Harriet. *Cities and climate change.* London: Routledge, 2013.

Chow, Gregory C. "Economic planning in China." *CEPS Working Paper*, No. 219, (2011). http://www.princeton.edu/gceps/workingpapers/219chow.pdf.

Cottrell, Jacqueline, Richard Bridle, Zhao Yongqiang, Shi Jingli, Xie Xuxuan, Christopher Beaton, Aaron Leopold, Eike Meyer, Shruti Sharma and Han Cheng. "Green revenues for green energy: environmental fiscal reform for renewable energy technology deployment in China." Winnipeg: International Institute for Sustainable Development and China National Renewable Energy Centre, 2013.

CPCCC (Central Committee of the Communist Party of China). "China's central decision on deepening reforms" [Zhongguo zhongyang guanyu quanmian shenhua gaige ruogan zhongda wenti de jueding.] Xinhua, 2013. http://news.xinhuanet.com/politics/2013-11/15/c_118164235.htm.

Delman, Jørgen. "Urban climate change politics in China: fragmented authoritarianism and governance innovations in Hangzhou." In *Chinese Politics as Fragmented Authoritarianism: Earthquakes, energy and environment,* edited by Kjeld Erik Brødsgaard, 156–180. Routledge, 2016.

Dubash, Navroz K., Markus Hagemann, Niklas Höhne, and Prabhat Upadhyaya. "Developments in national climate change mitigation legislation and strategy." *Climate Policy* 6 (2013): 649–664.

General Administration of Quality Supervision (GAQS), "General principle for equipping and managing of the measuring instrument of energy in organization of energy using" [Yongneng danwei nengyuan jiliang qiju peibei he guanli tongze], 2006. https://www.google.com.hk/url?sa=t&rct=j&q=&esrc=s&source=web&cd=1&cad=rja&uact=8&ved=0ahUKEwihsZzI_L_RAhXLXSwKHbejA9UQFggZMAA&url=http%3A%2F%2Fzjj.lanzhou.gov.cn%2Fjljd%2Fbgxz%2F201210%2FP020121025610810763057.doc&usg=AFQjCNEd21Ob7_BUOGyJ5ie49hdlsOTFXw.

Göbel, Christian. "Uneven policy implementation in rural China." *The China Journal* 65 (2011): 53–76.

Guan, Ting, Dieter Grunow, and Jianxing Yu. "Improving China's Environmental Performance through Adaptive Implementation—A Comparative Case Study of Cleaner Production in Hangzhou and Guiyang." *Sustainability* 6, no. 12 (2014): 8889–8908.

Guo, Baogang. "New Trends in China's Administrative Reform." *China Research Centre Journal* [online], 3(2) (2014). http://www.chinacenter.net/2014/china_currents/13-2/new-trends-in-chinas-administrative-reform/.

Hangzhou Government, "Hangzhou 11th Five Year Plan for energy conservation" [Hangzhoushi "shiyi wu" jieneng zhuanxiang guihua], 2005.

Hangzhou Government, "Annual work plan for energy conservation in Hangzhou (2007)" [Hangzhoushi renmin zhengfu guanyu qieshi zuohao 2007 nian jieneng gongzuo de tongzhi], 2007, http://xmecc.xmsme.gov.cn/2007-5/200751082416.htm.

Hangzhou Government, "Annual work plan for energy conservation in Hangzhou (2009)" [Hanghzoushi 2009 nian jieneng gongzuo shishi fangan], 2009.

Hangzhou Government, "Hangzhou government's decision on preparing the directory of the Twelfth Five-year Plan" [Hangzhoushi renmin zhengfu bangongting guanyu yinfa Hangzhoushi "shier wu" guihua bianzhi mulu de tongzhi], 2010a. http://www.da.hz.gov.cn/xxwj/zxwj/t20100526_21911.htm.

Hangzhou Government, "Hangzhou 12th Five Year Plan for energy conservation" [Hangzhoushi "shier wu" jieneng guihua], 2010b.

Hangzhou Government, "Annual work plan for energy conservation in Hangzhou (2010)" [Hangzhoushi 2010 nian jieneng gongzuo shishi fangan], 2010c. http://www.docin.com/p-100358733.html.

Hangzhou Government, "Hangzhou new energy industry development plan (2010–2015)" [Hangzhoushi xin nengyuan chanye fazhan guihua (2010–2015)] 2010d. http://www.hangzhou.gov.cn/art/2014/6/19/art_964938_286014.html.

Hangzhou Government, "Annual work plan for energy conservation in Hangzhou (2011)" [Hangzhoushi 2011 nian jieneng gongzuo shishi fangan de tongzhi], 2011a. http://www.hangzhou.gov.cn/art/2011/6/29/art_807827_1494.html.

Hangzhou Government, "Development plan of strategic emerging industries of Hangzhou (2011–2015)" [Hangzhoushi zhanluexing xinxing chanye fazhan guihua], 2011b. http://wenku.baidu.com/view/35e409144431b90d6d85c701.html.

Hangzhou Government, "Annual work plan for energy conservation in Hangzhou (2012)" [Hangzhoushi renmin zhengfu bangongting guanyu yinfa hangzhoushi 2012 nian jieneng gongzuo shishi fangan de tongzhi], 2012a. http://www.deqing.gov.cn/art/2012/6/23/art_1801_482.html.

Hangzhou Government, "Development plan for ten major industries of Hangzhou (2011–2015)" [Hangzhoushi shida chanye fazhan zongti guihua (2010–2015)], 2012b. http://www.qianzhan.com/regieconomy/detail/198/130410-22645139.html.

Hangzhou Government, "Annual work plan for energy conservation in Hangzhou (2013)" [Hangzhoushi 2013 nian jieneng gongzuo shishi fangan], 2013a. http://xmecc.xmsme.gov.cn/2013-7/201373145754.htm.

Hangzhou Government, "Implementing plans for 'one thousand ten thousand tons' energy-saving program" [Hangzhoushi "wandun qianjia" jieneng xingdong shishi fangan], 2013b. http://hzjxw.gov.cn/hz/web/ShowInfo_File.asp?ID=22512&TypeID=5&FileID=100.

Hangzhou Government, "Three-year action plan of innovation and development for energy-saving and environmental protection industries in Hangzhou" [Hangzhoushi jieneng huanbao chanye chuangxin fazhan sannian xingdong jihua], 2013c. http://www.hzjxw.gov.cn/hz/web/ShowInfo_File.asp?ID=23398&TypeID=6&FileID=100.

Hangzhou Government, "Conference of energy conservation and consumption reduction report in 2014" [2014 nian quanshi jieneng jianghao gongzuo xingshi tongbao hui], 2014a. http://www.gjjnhb.com/info/detail/37-22322.html.

Hangzhou Government, "Annual work plan for energy conservation in Hangzhou (2014)" [Hangzhoushi 2014 nian jieneng gongzuo shishi fangan de tongzhi], 2014b. http://hangzhouit.gov.cn/hz/web/ShowInfo_File.asp?ID=26148&TypeID=17&FileID=100.

Hangzhou Government, "Hangzhou Municipal Government opinions on the better development of the distributed photovoltaic industry by accelerating the applications" [Hangzhoushi renmin zhengfu guanyu jiakuai fenbushi guangfu fadian yingyong cujin chanye jiankang fazhan de shishi yijian], 2014c. http://www.nea.gov.cn/2014-09/04/c_133620541.htm.

Hangzhou Government, "Hangzhou 'Twelfth Five Year' low carbon urban plan" [Hangzhoushi "shier wu" ditan chengshi fazhan guihua], 2014d.

Heilmann, Sebastian, and Elizabeth J. Perry, eds. *Mao's invisible hand: the political foundations of adaptive governance in China.* Cambridge, MA: Harvard University Asia Center, 2011.

Heilmann, Sebastian. "From local experiments to national policy: The origins of China's distinctive policy process." *The China Journal* 59 (2008): 1–30.

Ingram, Helen, Anne L. Schneider, and Peter DeLeon. "Social construction and policy design." *Theories of the policy process* 2 (2007): 93–126.

Intergovernmental Panel on Climate Change (IPCC). *Climate change 2014: mitigation of climate change.* Vol. 3. Cambridge University Press, 2015.

Koehn, Peter H. *China Confronts Climate Change: A Bottom-up Perspective.* Routledge, 2015.

Kooiman, Jan, Maarten Bavinck, Ratana Chuenpagdee, Robin Mahon, and Roger Pullin. "Interactive governance and governability: an introduction." *Journal of Transdisciplinary environmental studies* 7, no. 1 (2008): 1–11.

Kostka, Genia. "Barriers to the implementation of environmental policies at the local level in China." *World Bank Policy Research Working Paper* 7016. Washington, DC: World Bank Group, 2014. http://documents.worldbank.org/curated/en/2014/08/20144757/barriers-implementation-environmental-policies-local-level-china.

Kostka, Genia, and Kyoung Shin. "Energy conservation through energy service companies: Empirical analysis from China." *Energy Policy* 52 (2013): 748–759.

KPMG. "A green economy on the cutting edge of technology–invest Hangzhou: energy conservation and environment protection industry." 2011. http://www.docin.com/p-1366984124.html.

KPMG. "An emerging centre for the green economy-invest in Hangzhou: energy conservation and environmental protection." 2012.

KPMG, "New Energy: leading the way in Hangzhou's green economy-Invest in Hangzhou: New energy." 2013.

Lieberthal, Kenneth, and Michel Oksenberg. *Policy making in China: Leaders, structures, and processes.* Princeton University Press, 1988.

Liu, Dan. "IFC and Hangzhou government collaboration on supporting bank credits for the energy conservation and emission projects IFC." [Yu Hangzhoushi zhengfu jianli jieneng rouzi hezuo], 2011. http://www.yicai.com/news/2011/02/674274.html.

Mai, Qianqing, and Maria Francesch-Huidobro. *Climate change governance in Chinese cities.* Routledge, 2014.

Ministry of Finance (MF). "Two ministries request to set up examples of energy conservation & emission reduction using fiscal policy" [Liangbumen yaoqiu kaizhan jienengjianpai caizheng zhengce zonghe shifan gongzuo], 2011. http://www.gov.cn/gzdt/2011-06/28/content_1895327.htm.

National Development and Reform Commission (NDRC) and National Energy Bureau (NEB). "Renewable energy development of the 12th Five-year plan." [Kezaisheng nengyuan fazhan "shierwu" guihua], 2012.

Odgaard, Ole, and Jørgen Delman. "China's energy security and its challenges towards 2035." *Energy Policy* 71 (2014): 107–117.

Organisation for Economic Co-operation and Development (OECD). "Cities and Climate Change National governments enabling local action. Policy Perspectives." 2014. https://www.oecd.org/env/cc/Cities-and-climate-change-2014-Policy-Perspectives-Final-web.pdf.

Ostrom, Elinor. "Institutional rational choice. An assessment of the institutional analysis and development framework." In *Theories of the Policy Process*, edited by Paul Sabatier, 21–64. Boulder: Westview Press, 2007.

Pattberg, Philipp, and Johannes Stripple. "Beyond the public and private divide: remapping transnational climate governance in the 21st century." *International environmental agreements: Politics, law and economics* 8, no. 4 (2008): 367–388.

Qi, Ye. "Annual review of Low-Carbon development in China (2013): policy implementation and institutional innovation:" [Zhongguo ditan fazhan baogao (2013): zhengce zhixing yu zhidu chuangxin]. Beijing: Social Sciences Academic Press, 2013.

Qi, Ye, and Tong Wu. "The politics of climate change in China." *Wiley Interdisciplinary Reviews: Climate Change* 4, no. 4 (2013): 301–313.

Rhodes, Roderick Arthur William. "The new governance: governing without government." *Political studies* 44, no. 4 (1996): 652–667.

Schlager, Edella. "A Comparison of frameworks, theories and models of policy processes." In *Theories of the Policy Process*, edited by Paul Sabatier, 293–319. Boulder: Westview Press, 2007.

Schröder, Miriam. ed. *Local climate governance in China: hybrid actors and market mechanisms.* Hampshire, UK: Palgrave Macmillan, 2012.

Sigley, Gary. "Chinese governmentalities: government, governance and the socialist market economy." *Economy and Society* 35, no. 4 (2006): 487–508.

Song, R., W. Dong, J. Zhu, X. Zhao, and Y. Wang. *Assessing implementation of China's climate policies in the 12th 5-year period.* World Resources Institute Working Paper. http://www.wri.org/sites/default/files/15_WP_China_Climate_Policies_final-v2_0.pdf.

Stavins, Robert N. "Policy instruments for climate change: how can national governments address a global problem?" *The University of Chicago Legal Forum*, (1997) 293–330.

Wang, Alex. "The Search for Sustainable Legitimacy. Environmental Law and Bureaucracy in China." *37 Harvard Environmental Law Review* 365 (2013): 367–440.

Xu, Bo, Qie Sun, Ronald Wennersten, and Nils Brandt. "An analysis of Chinese policy instruments for climate change mitigation." *International Journal of Climate Change Strategies and Management* 2, no. 4 (2010): 380–392.

Yu, Jianxing, and Shizong Wang. "The applicability of governance theory in China." In *China's Search for Good Governance*, edited by Deng Zhenlai and Guo Sujian, 35–48. Palgrave Macmillan US, 2011.

Zhang, ZhongXiang. "Carbon emissions trading in China: the evolution from pilots to a nationwide scheme." *Climate Policy* 15, no. sup1 (2015): S104-S126.

Zhejiang Economy and Trade Committee (ZETC) and Zhejiang Statistics Bureau (ZSB). "Implementation guideline for performance appraisal of energy consumption reduction per unit GDP in Zhejiang Province." [Zhejiangshen danwei GDP neng-hao kaohe tixi shishi fangan], 2008. http://www.cnki.com.cn/Article/CJFDTotal-ZJZE200824010.htm.

Zhou, Di, and Anaïs Delbosc. "The economic tools of chinese climate and energy policy at the time of the 12th five-year plan." Climate Report, no. 38, 2013.

CHAPTER 33

Climate Change Challenges and China's Responses: Mitigation and Governance

Fabiana Barbi, Leila da Costa Ferreira, and Sujian Guo

1   INTRODUCTION

China plays a key role in global climate change negotiations with the status of the world's largest emitter of greenhouse gases (GHG), accounting for more than one-third of global emissions in 2014 (Paltsev et al. 2012; Stalley 2015; Wang et al. 2016).

Mitigation responses to climate change, which are part of the analytical focus in this chapter, pursue reduction and stabilization of GHG emissions. They may include biofuels, renewable energy, energy efficiency, low carbon agriculture, carbon market, changes in consumption, and production patterns, among other actions.

These actions are required in order to limit global warming to less than 2 °C above pre-industrial levels according to the Paris agreement from 2015 in

F. Barbi (✉)
Center for Environmental Studies and Research (NEPAM), University of Campinas (UNICAMP), Campinas, Brazil
e-mail: fbarbi@unicamp.br

L. da Costa Ferreira
Institute of Philosophy and Human Sciences and Center for Environmental Studies and Research (NEPAM), University of Campinas (UNICAMP), Campinas, Brazil
e-mail: leilacf@unicamp.br

S. Guo
Department of Political Science, and Center for US-China Policy Studies, San Francisco State University, San Francisco, CA, USA
e-mail: sguo@sfsu.edu

© The Author(s) 2019
J. Yu, S. Guo (eds.), *The Palgrave Handbook of Local Governance in Contemporary China*, https://doi.org/10.1007/978-981-13-2799-5_33

721

order to avoid irreversible climate change. Even though this is considered one of the biggest challenges of this century, scientists claim the mitigation efforts needed for this limitation are economically viable (Field et al. 2015).

In regard to responding to the climate change challenge, governments are important stakeholders in charge of defining regulations, institutional arrangements, and modes of governance to face these changes at different levels and scales and of enforcing the defined rules and regulations (Bulkeley and Kern 2006; Betsill and Bulkeley 2007; Giddens 2009; Bulkeley and Newell 2010).

While a global climate agreement plays a key role in the pursuit of stabilizing GHG emissions,[1] national and local climate policies are central in this process (Harrison and Sundstrom 2007; Bailey and Compston 2012; Dubash et al. 2013; Held et al. 2013). The increase of national and local level policies and actions around climate change worldwide deserves further study and attention (Barbi et al. 2016).

Also, the local dimension of the theme is relevant since most human activities that contribute to global climate change takes place at this level and, at the same time, this level is the most affected by the impacts of these changes (Storbjörk 2007; Dodman 2009; Satterthwaite 2010; Barbi and Ferreira 2013).

Thus, climate change is characterized as a multilevel challenge, permeating different interconnected levels of government (Barbi and Ferreira 2017). Without undermining the role of climate policy at a national level, subnational governments (state, provincial, and municipal) represent important forums and enablers of global climate governance (Bulkeley and Betsill 2003; Gupta 2007).

This chapter analyzes the main Chinese policies and governance structures targeting climate change mitigation over the period 1992–2016 and their influence on Chinese GHG emissions. First, the trajectory of Chinese GHG emissions is presented, using secondary data. Second, mitigation strategies are discussed through literature review and official documents analysis. They are divided in two periods (1992–2006 and 2007–2016), according to their main characteristics. Finally, local Chinese responses to the climate change challenge are explored.

2   Greenhouse Gas Emissions in China: An Overview from 1990 to 2016

The urbanization process and economic growth in China has stimulated an unprecedented surge for energy demand, turning the country into the world's largest energy consumer and producer (Wang et al. 2014). Climate change is closely related to energy issues in China, as the energy sector is largely respon-

---

[1] For more on China's role in international negotiations, see Held et al. (2011) and Stalley (2015).

sible for the country's emissions. Coal is the largest source of energy and, therefore, of GHG emissions—historically and in future projections—even with the increased use of renewable energy, such as hydropower, solar energy, and wind energy. Oil emissions are the second largest, also showing a growth trend. Chinese GHG emissions are estimated to account for about half of global emissions by 2030 (McKibbin et al. 2008).

From 1990 to 2014, China's emissions have quadrupled, as shown in Graph 33.1, surpassing the US emissions in 2006, mainly due to increased industrialization. The country's share in total global CO_2 emissions was 14% in 2000, rising to almost 30% in 2014 (Barbi et al. 2016).

Structural change in the energy mix of China played a key role in the stalling of global GHG emissions in 2016. China's emissions decreased by 0.7% for the first time since 2000. Over the period 2002–2011, Chinese emissions increased by 10% per year on average. The recent average annual growth for 2011–2015 was 3% per year. These data reflect the country's efforts in improving energy intensity and in low carbon energy generation, including, however, the controversial aspect of nuclear power generation. Besides a 1.5% decrease in coal consumption, the country increased the use of nuclear energy (29%), hydropower (5%) and other renewables, such as wind and solar energy (21%) in 2015 (Olivier et al. 2016).

Considering cumulative GHG emissions from 1850 until 2011, China's share of global emissions amounted to only 11%, whereas the USA and the European Union were responsible for 27% and 25%, respectively (WRI 2014). Considering per capita emissions, they were previously lower in China than the world average until 2007; however, today they are above the world average. In 2016, China's per capita carbon emissions were 7.7 t CO_2 per person, below

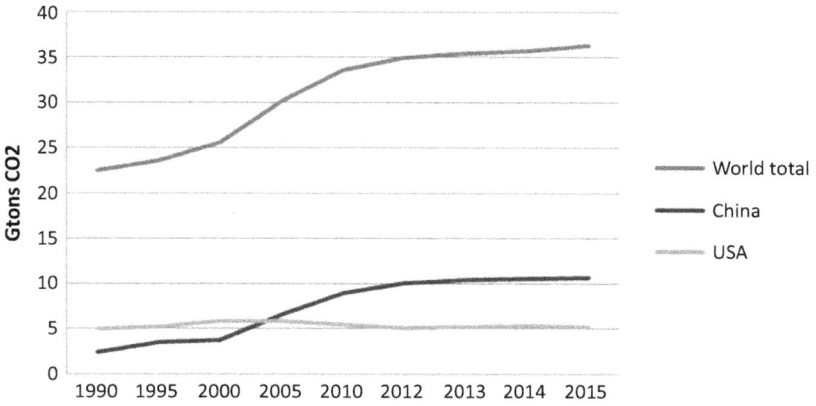

Graph 33.1 GHG emissions in China (1990–2015). Source: Elaborated by the author using Emissions Database for Global Atmospheric Research (http://edgar.jrc. ec.europa.eu/overview.php?v=CO2ts1990-2015, accessed on 05/30/17)

half of the level in the USA, that is, 16.1 t CO_2 per person (Olivier et al. 2016). China has used these measurements to support its decisions in international negotiations on climate change (NDRC 2013).

It is also relevant to consider the fact that about 25% of Chinese emissions are associated with manufacturing products that are consumed abroad. Emissions related to exports are eight times higher than its emissions associated with imports in the country (Barbi et al. 2016).

Another fact to consider is that China's GHG emissions vary regionally in terms of technology, energy mix, and economic development. The distribution of GHG emissions varies among the 30 mainland provinces (Wei and Liu 2011). This requires local and provincial specific mitigation strategies (Barbi et al. 2016).

According to more recent evaluations on China's GHG emissions (Wang et al. 2014), these provinces now face challenges that include inevitable emissions growth, shrinking of mitigation potential from technological progress, difficulty in further adjusting the industrial structure and economic development mode, and continued dominance of coal in the energy mix, among others.

3   MITIGATION AS A TRADE-OFF

During the period from 1992 to 2006, climate change mitigation was treated tangentially as a marginal issue in policymaking by the Chinese government and appeared as a trade-off of policy measures and governmental programs focused on combating environmental pollution and energy conservation (Barbi et al. 2016).

Climate change was perceived as a matter of science rather than politics, economy, and energy (Stalley 2015). This is demonstrated by the fact that China Meteorological Administration (CMA) was the agent responsible for the formulation of climate change-related strategies and international negotiations.

Global climate change was not considered a priority for decision-makers, as domestic problems related to air pollution were seen as more imminent. Therefore, at this point, there were no specific policy responses focused on climate change mitigation. The creation of the National Coordination Committee on Climate Change (NC4) in 1998 (PRC 2008) is perceived as a rhetorical response to the international community, fulfilling the country's commitment to the United Nations Framework Convention on Climate Change (UNFCCC) by presenting reports, such as the National Communications on Climate Change.

Meanwhile, several policy strategies were designed aimed at energy conservation and air pollution that reflected climate change mitigation as a trade-off and prevented Chinese GHG emissions from being even higher. Political attention to environmental problems was intensified with the increased impacts of air and water pollution and degradation of natural resources in the economy and quality of life.

Air pollution and climate change are intimately related in China since the main GHG and major air pollutants come from the same source, that is, fossil fuels (Jiang et al. 2013). Substantial changes in the approach to environmental pollution in general marked the beginning of the 1990s in China. They consisted of the strengthening of environmental laws, programs, and institutional capacity by the central government, provinces, and municipalities. One of the main actions during this period was the revision of the Criminal Law of the People's Republic of China, in 1997. This revision added new articles to the law concerning the possibility of punishment through fines for environmental damage in certain activities (Managi and Kaneko 2010; Ferreira and Barbi 2013).

The main instruments focused on reducing pollutant emissions into the atmosphere and improving air quality were: Law on Prevention and Control of Air Pollution (revised in 1995), Air Quality National Standard (1996), Emission Standard of Air Pollutants for Thermal Power Plants (2003) and Law on Environmental Impact Assessment (2003) (Chan and Yao 2008; Ferreira and Barbi 2013).

The most important policy measures related to energy were the Energy Conservation Law (1998) and the Renewable Energy Law of the People's Republic of China (2005). As a result, the country increased investment in technology and research and development in this area (Richerzhagen and Scholz 2008; Ferreira and Barbi 2013).

The main strategy specifically related to climate change mitigation was part of the 11th Five-Year Plan (FYP) for National Economic and Social Development (2006–2010), which included an ambitious commitment to reduce 20% of energy intensity from 2005 to 2010. It was the first time that climate change was mentioned in the FYPs (Tsang and Kolk 2010). This action targeted the top 1000 energy-consuming industries that accounted for almost half of the industrial consumption in 2004, as well as provincial actions. The goal was almost achieved with a 19% reduction in energy intensity by the end of 2010. Moreover, it is estimated that the mitigation result of this action was the reduction of 1510 million tons of CO_2 emission (Yuan et al. 2011).

4   SPECIFIC CLIMATE-RELATED STRATEGIES: MITIGATION TARGETS

Since China surpassed the USA as the largest GHG emitter, international pressure to reduce the country's carbon emissions has increased. From 2007 on, the Chinese government established specific structures, including governmental agencies related to climate change, implemented accountability systems for the reduction of carbon intensity (carbon emissions per unit of Gross Domestic Product (GDP)), realized studies on climate change, and promoted specific legislation in order to strengthen governance systems and mechanisms dealing with this issue (Barbi et al. 2016).

The first comprehensive policy framework for tackling climate change was approved in 2007—the National Climate Change Program. It included several aspects of climate policy, such as the development of low carbon and renewable energy, planting trees, and family planning. Its importance consisted in setting goals by 2010, including: 20% reduction in energy intensity; raise to 10% the proportion of renewable energy in primary energy supply (compared to the percentage of 3% in 2003) and increase of forest cover to 20% (Huang et al. 2010).

As a result, the National Leading Group on Climate Change (NLGCC) was established, replacing NC4, headed by the premier and headquartered in the ministerial-level National Development and Reform Commission's (NDRC) Department of Climate Change. It is comprised of representatives from 27 ministries and government departments and is responsible for coordinating climate policies within several involved sectors. A scientific advisory committee, the National Advisory Committee on Climate Change (NACCC), represents the only outside participation in the program, although most of its members are from government-funded or owned research institutes, especially the Energy Research Institute of the NDRC.

These goals were practically met (Zhou et al. 2010). By 2010, energy intensity was reduced in 20% all over the country. Renewable energy corresponded to around 13% of energy generation in the country, in 2010 (Irena 2014). China's forest cover has been increasing in the past three decades, and in 2010 it had increased more than 20% (Liu 2015).

However, the Ministry of Science and Technology admitted the difficulty to reverse the increasing trend of energy consumption and GHG emissions in a short time (Most 2007). Moreover, the program is based on the government position of not taking actions that undermine the country's economic growth as it defends that developed countries are primarily responsible for reducing emissions needed to prevent global warming.

In any case, the program had an impact at the provincial level of government and at autonomous regions with the establishment of institutional arrangements related to climate change, energy conservation, and environmental pollution. In addition, all levels of government have to report energy-saving and pollution reduction efforts, since 2008, which led several Chinese local governments to adopt climate policies (NDRC 2013). This is due to the fact that policy-setting is done at the national level, while implementation is left to each provincial government, which in turn delegates most decision-making to lower level governments.

Despite internal targets set by the program, China had never made commitments to the international community. That changed in 2009, during the Conference of the Parties (COP), in Copenhagen, when China announced the target of 40–45% reduction in GHG per unit of GDP by 2020. Moreover, the National GHG Control Work Plan, part of the 12th FYP (2011–2015), released in 2011 by the NDRC, established the following key targets for the period: 17% reduction in carbon intensity, 16% reduction in energy intensity, and increasing non-fossil energy to 11.4% of total energy use.

The 12th FYP also established emissions reduction targets that were decomposed for all provinces (autonomous regions and municipalities). According to the NDRC (2015), China completed 92.3% of its carbon intensity decline target. In 2014, energy intensity had dropped by 13.4%. Also, by the end of 2014, China's non-fossil fuels accounted for 11.2% of primary energy consumption, practically meeting the target.

China consistently refused to accept any reduction targets before industrialized countries took action first according to the principle of "common, but differentiated responsibilities" stipulated in the 1992 UNFCCC. This changed with the "U.S.-China Joint Announcement on Climate Change and Clean Energy Cooperation", in 2014, in which China addressed the cap of total coal consumption by 4 Gt per year, and planned to increase the share of renewable energy by 20% by 2030. According to Liu (2015), further integrated effort is needed to help China meet this goal, an effort that would likely require market-based instruments, technology innovation, energy structure optimization, recycling, and international cooperation.

The latest mitigation commitments in the country refer to the Intended Nationally Determined Contribution (INDC), submitted to the UNFCCC in 2015. It proposed: [i] to achieve the peaking of GHG emissions around 2030, [ii] to increase the share of non-fossil fuels in primary energy consumption to around 20% in 2030, [iii] to lower carbon intensity in 2030 by 60–65% from the 2005 level and [iv] to increase the forest stock volume by around 4.5 billion cubic meters from the 2005 level (NDRC 2015).

Also during this period, Clean Development Mechanism (CDM) projects were implemented. By 2009, the country hosted 2023 of the 4869 global projects, most of them in renewable energy, energy efficiency and energy saving (Heggelund and Buan 2009).

Some authors evaluate that China has made considerable domestic effort to take action on climate change (Held et al. 2011). According to the presented data, the developments within this stage indicate increased policy attention and the building of institutional and political structures and legal framework to meet the challenges of climate change. The main Chinese strategies for reduction of GHG emissions are focused on the energy sector, such as energy efficiency, energy conservation, renewable energy, nuclear energy, industrial emissions control, and increase of carbon sinks. Even though the main motivation for many of these actions is to reduce energy costs and improve energy, they have substantially helped GHG emissions to be higher.

5   Climate Change Institutional Arrangements

From 2007 on, the articulation of several ministries and research institutions in China has resulted in concrete mitigation proposals, based on scientific research findings and technology development, particularly focused on the energy issue.

CMA leads climate change researches in the country, and it is also a key stakeholder in the formulation of climate change strategies and in international negotiations. CMA is the deputy director of the National Climate Change Steering Group Office and leads China's activities related to the Intergovernmental Panel on Climate Change (IPCC), co-chairs the National Climate Center, hosts the National Panel on Climate Change and is the focal point of the China Committee for the Global Climate Observing System. Through its National Climate Center, it is responsible for elaborating the National Assessment on Climate Change and GHG annual reports.

CMA and the Chinese Academy of Social Sciences worked together to establish a simulation laboratory for climate change and economics, responsible for producing the Annual Report on Actions to Address Climate Change (2009), Road to Copenhagen and Annual Report on Actions to Climate Change (2010), Cancun's Challenges and Green Paper on Climate Change China's Actions. Other relevant Chinese institutions involved in climate strategies in the country are: The National Natural Science Foundation, State Oceanic Administration, and China Association for Science and Technology. Non-governmental agents have limited influence on climate strategies in the country.

The main governmental bodies related to climate change strategies in China are shown in Fig. 33.1. The central government retains tight control over most policy decisions in China, including climate change policy. The highest political body dealing with climate change is the NLGCC, under the State Council,

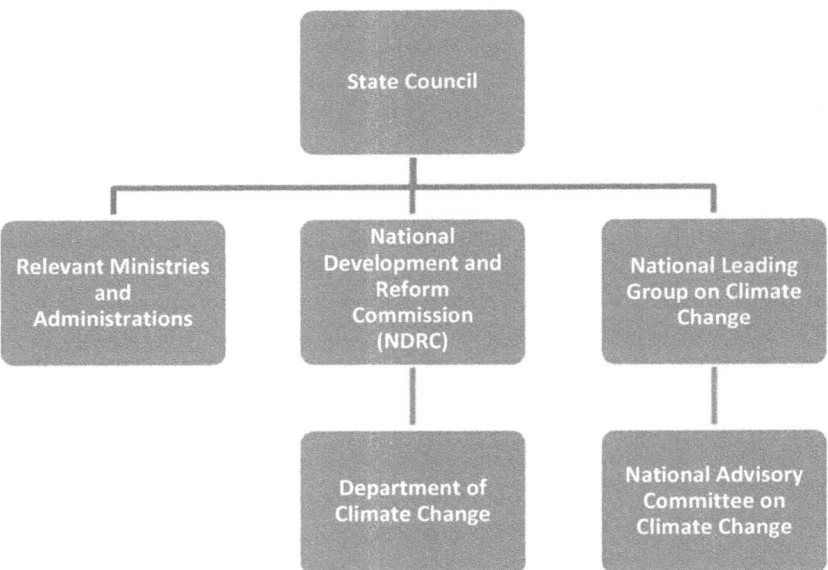

Fig. 33.1 China's main governmental bodies related to climate change strategies. Source: Barbi et al. 2016

which is the top decision-making body, with the final say in case of disagreements or conflicts. Other members are all high-ranking officials of relevant ministries and other political organs, such as Foreign Affairs, Science and Technology, Industry and Information Technology, Finance, Land and Resources, Transport, Water Resources, and Environmental Protection.

NDRC, the primary government institution responsible for climate change governance, is one of the most powerful policymaking bodies in the central government, responsible for all policies related to economic and social development, including the writing of China's FYPs. Daily work is carried out by the NDRC's Climate Change Department. Its mandate ranges from drafting policies and plans to negotiating with international organs. CMA and the Chinese Academy of Sciences (CAS) are represented only in the NLGCC. They jointly chair the National Leading Group's Scientific Assessment Working Group, responsible for scientific advice to the government regarding targets decisions and measures.

Moreover, the National Leading Group also receives information from the NACCC, set up in 2007 and chaired by the CMA and with members from the natural and social sciences. It comprises China's most influential experts on this issue, who provide advice based on a combination of scientific disciplines. The Committee has a direct role in policy development, in international negotiations, and in the FYPs. It also reports to the NDRC and the State Council.

According to the mitigation strategies presented in this session, it is possible to perceive that climate change issues gradually shifted from being solely a scientific issue to increasingly become a political and economic issue, since energy production and consumption, already linked to economy and politics, are also linked to climate change. Therefore, climate change-related issues became the responsibility of the NDRC, the key player influencing Chinese climate change strategies. It is responsible for both economic planning in the country and the design and implementation of climate policies through its Department of Climate Change (Delman 2011).

Climate change is defined primarily as a foreign policy issue in the country, thus, the Ministry of Foreign Affairs (MFA) exercises great influence over China's stance both internationally and nationally. Concurrently, the climate issue permeates all different levels of government, which are interconnected, making climate change a multilevel challenge. In this sense, subnational (provincial) and local (municipal) governments represent important instances in global climate governance. The nation-state remains a central actor in global governance processes, but the role of subnational and local governments cannot be ignored in contributing to policy responses to climate change.

6   Local Responses to Climate Change Mitigation

Following the national movement regarding climate change, the issue has gained priority in the local political agenda of provincial and prefectural governments since mid-2007 (Qi et al. 2008). According to the Chinese unitary governmental system, local governments are expected to implement actions decided by the central government.

Thus, after the creation of the NLGCC, counterparts were also established in the provinces and municipalities. The result of these institutional arrangements was the development of mitigation and adaptation plans at local level. The central government mandate, internalized needs, and the international carbon market were the three main drivers of local governments' mitigation responses to climate change (Qi et al. 2008).

Also at local level, climate change mitigation strategies are combined with energy saving and air pollution reduction actions (Qi et al. 2008). For instance, the 11th FYP (2005–2010) allocated the 20% energy conservation target to the 33 provinces and municipalities. According to Duan and Hu (2014), multiple governmental agencies and officials at different levels are relevant stakeholders mobilizing enterprisers and individuals to meet GHG emissions reduction targets. Local officials are key stakeholders in this process, as they are responsible for action implementation, progress check, and articulation with other stakeholders involving climate policies.

In Beijing, the municipal climate change program and policy was designed in 2008 in response to the National Climate Change Program. The city was an important implementer of the national policy and national targets, since it is the second most energy-consuming Chinese city (behind Shanghai). The actions proposed in the municipal program are related to increasing energy efficiency, changing energy structures, promoting renewable energy, and promoting education and awareness on these issues. Beijing is considered a leading city in China when it comes to improving energy efficiency. Improving air quality for the Olympic Games was the greatest motivation for these actions that produced important co-benefits for addressing climate change mitigation (Zhao 2011).

The Beijing Municipal Development and Reform Commission is the main municipal agency responsible for climate change-related policies, working directly with NDRC. Other stakeholders involved in implementing climate change policies in Beijing are: Beijing Municipal Environmental Protection Bureau, Beijing Municipal Construction Committee, Beijing Municipal Science and Technology Commission, Beijing Council for Promoting Environmental Protection and Energy Saving, Beijing Academy of Environmental Sciences and Tsinghua University (Zhao 2011).

In Beijing's FYPs and other official directives, the city has set several targets related to climate change mitigation, for example: increase to 15% the share of renewable energy by 2020 and 20% by 2030; reduce energy intensity by 16% by 2015; and cap coal use to below 65% of total primary energy consumption by 2017 (Stalley 2015).

Concurrent with these top-down actions, bottom-up decentralized actions also take place through low carbon practices. In this process, central-local interactions are highlighted in the called Collaborative Municipal Networks (CMNs) (Mai and Francesch-Huidobro 2015). CMNs Collaborative Municipal

Networks constitute a specific Chinese arrangement of climate change governance at local level, which have emerged as a response to the country's climate change commitments and to the increasing scientific evidence of the problem. They are based on the interaction among a plurality of state and nonstate actors,[2] focused on achieving climate change mitigation goals through knowledge transfer and resource exchange, "while maintaining municipal autonomy in vertical or horizontal coordination and enhancing municipal capacity in horizontal collaboration" (Mai and Francesch-Huidobro 2015: 52).

Guangzhou, Shenzhen, and Hong Kong are examples that have integrated CMNs connecting the national regime and the global city networks toward climate change mitigation and the transition to a low-carbon environment. In these cases, strong state support and solid resource capacity are incentives for accelerating the development of CMNs (Mai and Francesch-Huidobro 2015).

There are also several international actions focused on climate change mitigation in Chinese cities. For instance, a green electricity project (Jade Electricity), which allows consumers to voluntarily purchase electricity from renewable energy sources, was developed in Shanghai with the World Bank, Energy Sector Management Assistance Program, and the Asia Sustainable and Alternative Energy Program (Schreurs 2008).

7   Final Comments

This chapter analyzed the main policies and governance structures targeting climate change mitigation in China over the past 20 years and their influence on Chinese GHG emissions.

China's potential to contribute towards reduction of global GHG emissions is enormous. The trajectory of Chinese GHG emissions showed that the country is making important efforts toward climate change mitigation. However, Chinese emissions are still high and, combined with other major emitters around the world, they threaten the 2 °C global warming limit.

Climate change mitigation is closely tied to energy saving in China. During the period of 1992–2006, climate change mitigation was a trade-off of air pollution measures and energy conservation efforts. From 2007 on, mitigation strategies have been based on setting targets to reduce emissions, energy intensity, energy consumption, carbon intensity, energy use, and to increase renewable energy generation. Whether these goals will be met is something to be monitored in the coming years. Despite these important measures, the country remains focused on economic growth highly dependent on fossil fuels (especially coal).

The institutional arrangement in charge of climate issues is the same one responsible for economic development, that is, NDRC. This shows that the

---

[2] Nonstate actors include participants from network organizations and NGOs in civil society and corporate actors in the private sector.

climate issue has shifted away from a solely scientific problem toward an economic and foreign affairs matter. The question that remains is whether the proposed actions and the existing political and institutional structures are sufficient to respond effectively to the climate challenge in time to prevent irreversible climate change.

At local level, local governments act mainly as "implementers" of national climate policies. However, there is a growing movement of bottom-up initiatives and international actions in Chinese urban centers, as shown in mitigation actions in Beijing, Shanghai, Guangzhou, Shenzhen, and Hong Kong. They are still isolated measures but with great potential of spreading throughout the country. Local initiatives targeted at climate change mitigation should be more encouraged by the central government since GHG emissions vary regionally.

More research is needed in order to understand how other stakeholders across the country, that is, local authorities, firms, and civil society, are engaged in climate change strategies within the Chinese context.

After all, climate policy should be about the transformation of human activities responsible for causing the problem. Therefore, public involvement in climate policy is essential, encouraging changes in current lifestyle and production and consumption patterns worldwide.

REFERENCES

Bailey, I., and H. Compston (eds.) 2012. *Feeling the Heat*. London: Palgrave Macmillan.

Barbi, F., and L. C. Ferreira. 2017. Governing climate change risks: Subnational climate policies in Brazil. *Chinese Political Science Review*. 2(2): 237–252.

Barbi, F., and L. C. Ferreira. 2013. Climate Change in Brazilian Cities: Policy Strategies and Responses to Global Warming. *International Journal of Environmental Science and Development* 4(1): 49–51.

Barbi, F., L. C. Ferreira, and S. Guo. 2016. Climate change challenges and China's response: mitigation and governance, *Journal of Chinese Governance*, 1(2): 324–339.

Betsill, M., H. Bulkeley. 2007. Looking Back and Thinking Ahead: A Decade of Cities and Climate Change Research. *Local Governments*, 12(5): 447–456.

Bulkeley, H., M. Betsill. 2003. *Cities and Climate Change – Urban Sustainability and Global Environmental Governance*. New York: Routledge.

Bulkeley, H., and K. Kern. 2006. Local Government and the Governing of Climate Change in Germany and the UK. *Urban Studies*, 43(12): 2237–2259.

Bulkeley, H., P. Newell. 2010. *Governing Climate Change*. New York: Routledge.

Chan, C. K., X. Yao. 2008. Air pollution in mega cities in China. *Atmospheric Environment*, 42(1): 1–42.

Delman, J. 2011. China's "Radicalism at the Center": Regime Legitimation through Climate Politics and Climate Governance. *Journal of Chinese Political Science*. 16(1): 183–205.

Dodman, D. 2009. Blaming cities for climate change? An analysis of urban greenhouse gas emissions inventories. *Environment and Urbanization* 21(1): 185–198.

Duan, H., and Q. Hu. 2014. Local officials' concerns of climate change issues in China: a case from Jiangsu. *Journal of Cleaner Production*. 64(1): 545–551.

Dubash, N. K., M. Hagemann, N. Höhne, and P. Upadhyaya. 2013. Developments in national climate change mitigation legislation and strategy. *Climate Policy*, 6(13): 649–664.

Ferreira, L. C., F. Barbi. 2013. *Some issues about environmental concerns in Brazil and China*. Social justice and transitional societies. In: Ferreira, L. C., and J. A. G. Albuquerque (eds.) China & Brazil: Challenges and opportunities. São Paulo: Annablume.

Field, C., P. Cias, W. Cramer, et al. 2015. *Our Common Future under Climate Change*. Outcome Statement. UNESCO, Future Earth e ICSU.

Giddens, A. 2009. *The Politics of Climate Change*. Cambridge: Polity Press.

Gupta, J. 2007. The multi-level governance challenge of climate change. *Journal of Integrative Environmental Sciences* 4(3): 131–137.

Harrison, K., and L. M. Sundstrom. 2007. The Comparative Politics of Climate Change. *Global Environmental Politics* 7(4): 1–18.

Heggelund, G. M., I. F. Buan. 2009. China in the Asia–Pacific Partnership: consequences for UN climate change mitigation efforts? *Int Environ Agreements*, 9(1): 301–317.

Held, D., E. Nag, and C. Roger. 2011. *The Governance of Climate Change in China - Preliminary Report*, LSE-AFD Climate Governance Programme.

Held, D., C. Roger, and E. Nag. 2013. *Climate Governance in the Developing World*. Cambridge: Polity Press.

Huang, X., D. Zhao, C. G. Brown, and Y. Wu. 2010. Environmental Issues and Policy Priorities in China: A Content Analysis of Government Documents. *China: An International Journal*, 8(2): 220–246.

Irena. 2014. *Renewable Energy Prospects: China, REmap 2030 analysis*. IRENA, Abu Dhabi.

Jiang, P., Y. Chen, Y. Geng, W. Dong, B. Xue, B. Xu, and W. Li. 2013. Analysis of the co-benefits of climate change mitigation and air pollution reduction in China. *Journal of Cleaner Production*, 58(1): 130–137.

Liu, Z. 2015. *China's Carbon Emissions Report 2015*. Harvard Kennedy School. Belfer Center for Science and International Affairs.

Mai, Q., and M. Francesch-Huidobro. 2015. *Climate change governance in Chinese cities*. New York: Routledge.

Managi, S., and S. Kaneko. 2010. *Chinese Economic Development and Environment*. Cheltenham: Edward Elgar Publishing Ltd.

Mckibbin, W. J., P. J. Wilcoxen, and W. T. Woo. 2008 China can grow and still help prevent the tragedy of the CO_2 commons.

Song, L. and Woo, W. T. *China's dilemma: economic growth, the environment and climate change*. Asia Pacific Press.

MOST – Ministry of Science and Technology et al. 2007. *China's Scientific & Technological Actions on Climate Change*. Available at: http://english.mep.gov.cn/environmental_education/publications/200801/P020080103476999394910.pdf, accessed on 20/04/2015.

NDRC - *The National Development and Reform Commission. 2012.* China's National Climate Change Programme. 2007.

NDRC - *The National Development and Reform Commission. 2013.* China's Policies and Actions for Addressing Climate Change.

NDRC - *The National Development and Reform Commission. 2015.* China's Policies and Actions on Climate Change.

Olivier J.G.J., G. Janssens-Maenhout, M. Muntean, and J.A.H.W. Peters. 2016. *Trends in global CO₂ emissions*, 2016 Report, The Hague: PBL *Netherlands Environmental Assessment Agency*, Ispra: European Commission, Joint Research Centre.

Paltsev, S., J. Morris, Y. Cai, V. Karplus, and H. Jacoby. 2012. The role of China in mitigating climate change. *Energy Economics* 34(1): 444–450.

PRC – The People's Republic of China. 2008. *China's Policies and Actions for Addressing Climate Change*. Information Office of the State Council of the People's Republic of China. Beijing.

Qi, Y., L. Ma, H. Zhang, and H. Li. 2008. Translating a global issue into local priority: China's local government response to climate change. *The Journal of Environment & Development*. 17(4): 379–400.

Richerzhagen, C., and I. Scholz. 2008. China's Capacities for Mitigating Climate Change. *World Development* 36(2): 308–324.

Satterthwaite, D. 2010. The Contribution of Cities to Global Warming and their Potential Contributions to Solutions. Environment and Urbanization Asia 1(1): 1–12.

Schreurs, M. A. 2008. From the bottom up: Local and subnational climate change politics. The Journal of Environment & Development. 17(4): 343–355.

Stalley, P. 2015. China. In: Bäckstrand, K., and E. Lövbrand. Research Handbook on Climate Governance. Cheltenham: Edward Edgar.

Stensdal, I. China's Carbon-Intensity Target: Climate Actors and Policy Developments. Lysaker: Fridtjof Nansen Institute, 2012.

Storbjörk, S. 2007. Governing Climate Adaptation in the Local Arena: Challenges of Risk Management and Planning in Sweden. *Local Environment* 12(5): 457–469.

Tsang, S., and A. Kolk. 2010. The evolution of Chinese policies and governance structures on environment, energy and climate. *Env. Pol. Gov.*, 20(1): 180–196.

Wang, C., J. Lin, W. Cai, H. Liao. 2014. China's carbon mitigation strategies: Enough? *Energy Policy* 73(1): 47–56.

Wang, S., Q. Li, C. Fang, and C. Zhou. 2016. The relationship between economic growth, energy consumption, and CO₂ emissions: Empirical evidence from China. *Science of the Total Environment*, 542(A): 360–371.

Wei, Y., and L. Liu. 2011. Study on Regional CO₂ Emissions Change in China. In Y. Wei. et al. (eds.) *Energy Economics: CO₂ Emissions in China*. *Science* Press Beijing and Springer-Verlag Berlin Heidelberg.

WRI – World Resources Institute. 2014. *6 Graphs Explain the World's Top 10 Emitters*. Available at: http://www.wri.org/blog/2014/11/6-graphs-explain-world%E2%80%99s-top-10-emitters, accessed on 28/01/2016.

Yuan, J., J. Kang, C. Yu, and Z. Hu. 2011. Energy conservation and emissions reduction in China: Progress and prospective. *Renewable and Sustainable Energy Reviews*. 15(9): 4334–4347.

Zhao, J. 2011. *Climate change mitigation in Beijing, China*. Case study prepared for Cities and Climate Change: Global report on Human Settlements 2011.

Zhou, N., M.D. Levine, and L. Price. 2010. Overview of current energy-efficiency policies in China. *Energy Policy* 38(1): 6439–6452.

CHAPTER 34

Breathe Easy? Local Nuances of Authoritarian Environmentalism in China's Battle Against Air Pollution

Anna L. Ahlers and Yongdong Shen

1 INTRODUCTION

Effective ecological, climate, and resource protection policies usually entail painful cuts in individual consumption and require sober revisions of all kinds of growth patterns. The concept of "authoritarian environmentalism" (hereafter abbreviated to AE) concedes that, in theory, authoritarian governments are better equipped with institutional and procedural features that allow for faster and more rigorous responses to environmental problems than are possible in democracies. In the words of Bruce Gilley,

> (…) authoritarian environmentalism can be provisionally defined as a public policy model that concentrates authority in a few executive agencies manned by capable and uncorrupt elites seeking to improve environmental outcomes. Public participation is limited to a narrow cadre of scientific and technocratic elites while others are expected to participate in state-led mobilization for the purposes of

This chapter is a reprint of an article previously published in The China Quarterly (no. 234, June 2018, pp. 299–319), slightly revised to fit the format of this volume.

A. L. Ahlers
University of Oslo, Oslo, Norway
e-mail: a.l.ahlers@ikos.uio.no

Y. Shen (✉)
School of Public Affairs, Zhejiang University, Hangzhou, Zhejiang, China
e-mail: yongdongshen@zju.edu.cn

© The Author(s) 2019
J. Yu, S. Guo (eds.), *The Palgrave Handbook of Local Governance in Contemporary China*, https://doi.org/10.1007/978-981-13-2799-5_34

implementation. The policy outputs that result include a rapid and comprehensive response to the issue and usually some limits on individual freedoms.[1]

It is argued (and expected) that "modern" authoritarian regimes, with a problem-focused eco-elite group, a policy-bound professional bureaucracy, and the rigid means to sanction individual behavior, have the ability to rapidly implement sweeping programs and wide-ranging measures. In the case of the People's Republic of China (PRC), Bruce Gilley later made two specific amendments:

> First, even with executive authority concentrated, implementation becomes highly dispersed in a large, decentralized system; in modern governance, much policy will be made at these downstream stages. Secondly, even when public participation is narrowly defined in official frameworks, there may be considerable mid-level activism within those narrow boundaries. Society does not become dormant even in an authoritarian model, but merely shifts its involvement towards acceptable areas.[2]

However, many other observers contend that the hailed effectiveness, or "authoritarian clout", of national-level environmental policy-making is usually offset by this very "dispersion of implementation". Under the auspices of the Chinese political system, they argue, local bureaucracies are often not incentivized enough to safeguard the comprehensive implementation of environmental policies.[3] Even advocates of Chinese AE, who have tried to trace it (primarily) in the field of climate politics, have come to the conclusion that, although policy responses have become increasingly swift and government activism (*output*) has been heightened during the last decade, actual results (*outcomes*) are still lacking.[4]

In this chapter, we do not intend to evaluate, from a macroscopic point of view, whether China's mode of governance functions exceptionally well or badly when it comes to tackling environmental challenges; rather, our study has been inspired by empirical observations in the field of air pollution[5] prevention and control policies (hereafter "air policy"). First of all, we take the basic assumptions ingrained in the concept of AE very seriously—especially those formulated for China by Beeson (2015) and Gilley (2012)—and examine these in the contexts in which they might be expected to play out most drastically,

---

[1] Gilley 2012, 288.

[2] Gilley 2012, 292.

[3] Kostka 2016; Kostka and Eaton 2014; Ran 2015.

[4] Beeson 2010; Gilley 2012.

[5] This study concentrates on "air pollution" as it is usually defined in a popular and political context in China. As the introduction to this special issue has explained, the type of air pollution that is currently receiving most attention is *atmospheric particulate pollution*. Greenhouse gas emissions, that is, climate change politics and so on, are usually treated separately. See, also, Ahlers and Hansen forthcoming.

that is, in the final processes of local policy implementation. In particular, we concentrate on one of the key assumptions of AE that has, as yet, been surprisingly under-researched in the case of China: how environmental policies are made and measures implemented by local authorities in consideration of, vis-à-vis, or 'against' the general public at the local level. The concept of AE implies the almost complete exclusion of public discussion on the input side, the authoritarian manner in which individual freedoms are targeted and restricted on the output side, and the state-led mobilization of relevant public parties for the sake of effective final policy implementation.[6] How this works in practice and the level of complexity this involves from a local state perspective have not yet been subjected to thorough study.

This chapter aims to fill the gap by refining some of the key aspects of Chinese AE presented in the existing literature. We emphasize that there are significant nuances of Chinese AE at the local level and draw attention to the conditions on the ground as well as to the strategies chosen by local authorities that have helped to produce them. Interestingly enough, we find that the choices on the continuum between coercive and more consultative means followed a rather counter-intuitive pattern: the more urgent and risky the conditions were perceived to be (i.e., the need for quick solutions which would affect the majority of the citizens, implying the potential risk of discontent and possibly "social destabilization"), the harsher and more exclusive were the strategies adopted by local implementers. In contrast, for more selective measures within a broader time frame, local authorities included the public in order to ensure smooth implementation and to deal with the often complex stakeholder relations and conflicts involved. However, we consider the more inclusive nuances of AE as still not necessarily equivalent to the features of "consultative authoritarianism" that are described in recent China studies literature. In both cases, although willing to accommodate limited public participation and opinions, the Chinese Communist Party (CCP) reserves the right to make the final decisions. But whereas the latter notion usually denotes a more open mode of searching for solutions, which includes the consultation or participation of the public or specific actors at the decision-making and formulation stage,[7] sometimes even the outsourcing of policy tasks to civic or corporate actors,[8] AE implies that a sacrosanct political authority takes the decisions it deems necessary to meet urgent environmental problems that are difficult to reach in a public and participatory manner and only allows for some flexibility, maybe participation, when it comes to effectively implementing them.

---

[6] See, also, Beeson 2015, 523. These measures can therefore be expected to go beyond the usual toolbox of environmental politics (e.g. Sterner and Coria 2012). Except for more coercive means than just merely legal sanctioning, they may also include more informal means of incentivizing (see, also, Schmitt in this issue).

[7] He and Thøgersen 2010, Truex 2014.

[8] Teets 2013.

Taking a microscopic approach to AE in the field of air policies, we have conducted three rounds of fieldwork in Hangzhou City, Zhejiang Province, and its surroundings between 2014 and 2016. The data collection method followed an approach employed for exploratory case studies, which included 41 semi-structured interviews with leading representatives of Party and government departments at the provincial and municipal levels, environmental NGOs, scholars (most notably in the fields of public administration, bio-chemistry, and environmental engineering), local business representatives, neighborhood committees, and individual residents, as well as an analysis of work reports and official documents at the central, provincial, and city levels, site visits, and a review of the relevant survey and research literature.

The chapter is organized as follows: the next section presents arguments for the new implications of the air pollution problem for the concept of AE in China in general. The chapter then zooms in on the local level, to Hangzhou City in Zhejiang Province. We provide a brief introduction to the prevailing situation in Hangzhou and the basic pillars of the municipal governments' ambitious air policy and then focus on two very different measures in Hangzhou City's local air policy portfolio that reveals considerable variation in the associated implementation strategies and the interfaces occurring between local authorities and the public: the city's attempts to curb motor vehicle driving and the (re)location of air-polluting industries. Altogether, a diverse picture emerges which, in conclusion, leads us to suggest some amendments to the AE concept in order to clarify what is actually on display in China's "modern" authoritarian approach to tackling these environmental challenges.

2   CHINA'S *AIRPOCALYPSE*: DRIVER OF RELOADED AUTHORITARIAN ENVIRONMENTALISM?

Public surveys show that environmental pollution, in particular, "air pollution", is among the top issues of concern among the Chinese population and usually only second to "corruption".[9] And although it is difficult to perceive any sort of silver lining in the thick blankets of smog, certain trends have emerged during the last few years that are worth mentioning. Air pollution control and prevention has become a crucial item on the Chinese governments' agenda, as is manifest, for example, in the national Action Plan on Prevention and Control of Air Pollution, the recently revised Air Pollution Prevention and Control Law and the very recently promulgated 13th Five-Year Plan (2016–2020). Leading Party and government cadre evaluation now includes

---

[9] Wike, Richard and Bridget Parker. 2015. "Corruption, Pollution, Inequality Are Top Concerns in China. Pew Research Center – Global Attitudes and Trends," 24 September, http://www.pewglobal.org/2015/09/24/corruption-pollution-inequality-are-top-concerns-in-china/. Accessed 01 October 2015. See, also, Tilt and Li in this issue.

environmental indicators such as air quality,[10] while political propaganda and public education has been fortified to evoke the spirit of "since we breathe together, we must also fight together".[11]

Although a comprehensive assessment of the results is not yet possible, these efforts have already had some initial tangible effects on particulate air pollution in China.[12]

> China's air pollution problem is slowly but surely receding, new data shows. More than three years on from its infamous 'airpocalypse', China's pollution levels are dropping at an average rate of 12% a year following emergency government action.[13]

Interestingly enough, in most of the related reports, analysts have attributed these fledgling successes to the harsh measures undertaken as part of the new governmental initiative and not just to the continuing economic slowdown and reduced production levels.[14] Could this all be taken as an indication that China's *airpocalypse*, with the reactions that this has provoked from the government and society, has the potential to be a game changer in China's environmental policy?

2.1 Societal Perception and Political Framing of the Air Pollution Problem

The perception and framing of problems are crucial elements of China's seemingly becoming AE in practice. Arguably, air pollution represents an environmental problem that actually meets the preconditions for "authoritarian responses" *better* than those previously described in the relevant literature on China. It embodies a challenge that both the general population and the authorities face in much more specific and immediate ways than the rather

---

[10] Ministry of Environmental Protection of the People's Republic of China (MEP). 2013. "Zhongzubu yinfa tongzhi gaijin zhengji kaohe gongzuo. Jiada huanjing sunhai deng zhibiao quanzhong" (Central Organization Department issues notice on the revision of evaluation work. Increases the weighting of environmental harm as a criterion). 11 December, http://edcmep.org.cn/hjxw/5762.html. Accessed 26 June 2015.

[11] Luo Sha et al. 2013. "Huanbao buzhang tan daqi wuran: 'jiran tong huxi jiu yao tong fendou'" (The Minister of Environment discusses air pollution: 'since we breathe together, we must fight together'), 15 June, http://news.sohu.com/20130615/n378878788.shtml. Accessed 26 June 2015.

[12] See also the introduction to this special issue by Aunan, Wang, and Hansen.

[13] Boren, Zachary Davies. 2015. "China Air Pollution. Things are getting better but 80% of cities are still super smoggy," Greenpeace Energydesk, 15 October, http://energydesk.greenpeace.org/2015/10/15/china-air-pollution-things-are-getting-better-but-80-of-cities-are-still-super-smoggy/. Accessed 16 October 2015.

[14] AFP. 2015. "Air Pollution Levels Drop in China: Greenpeace," Daily Mail Online, 21 April, http://www.dailymail.co.uk/wires/afp/article-3048298/Air-pollution-levels-drop-China-Greenpeace.html. Accessed 15 October 2015.

more diffuse threat of climate change which was the focal point of former analyses. For reasons of limited space,[15] we here emphasize only some of the characteristic aspects of air pollution as a perceived problem, including the ensuing social and political reactions to these that are of specific relevance for our description of Chinese AE in dialogue with the existing portrayals. Gilley (2012) and, to a lesser extent, Beeson (2015) point to the general lack of problem awareness and related "pressure to act" among the population as well as the lax policy mission and enforcement in the political system that, up to now, have rendered China's AE less than effective. It does not take much to argue that the story is somewhat different when it comes to the problem of air pollution.

First of all, the impact of the recent fear of the effects of ambient air pollution on Chinese society as a whole is remarkable. Seen as a health risk that can affect each individual member of society, air pollution now transgresses the usual boundaries between rulers and the ruled, policymakers, and policy addressees. These societal irritations can sometimes bear strange fruit: "Smog" (*wumai* 雾霾) and "$PM_{2.5}$" have become winged words among the young and old,[16] and everyday activities are often planned according to what mobile phone apps declare to be "good air" or "bad air" days. Although air pollution has not yet triggered large-scale public unrest or inspired a nationwide environmental movement in China, local communities have become increasingly aware of their rights and now demand increased environmental and health protection.[17] At the same time, during the last decade, the Chinese political authorities have shown themselves to be increasingly sensitive and responsive to public concerns and, as has been documented, even purely verbal demands can turn into a driving force for political action.[18] Anticipation of protest as well as general awareness that environmental problems can have a considerable effect on public health and China's economic performance should probably be regarded as the main drivers of governmental action against air pollution. We therefore hold that what is observable in China's air pollution drama supports Beeson's claim that "it is primarily domestic rather than international pressure that is forcing the Chinese government to act, as it is compelled to address the reality of a degraded environment that represents a failure of its developmental model and the leaders who guide it".[19]

It seems that ambient particulate pollution and the immediate challenges and effects this brings in terms of visibility and health strongly influence the perception of the situation by both the Chinese population and the authorities. Unlike the general climate protection framework, air quality protection requires

---

[15] For a more detailed analysis of major events and shifts in policy-making concerning ambient air pollution in China, see Ahlers and Hansen forthcoming.

[16] See Ahlers and Hansen forthcoming and Li and Svarverud in this issue.

[17] See, also, Hansen and Liu in this issue.

[18] Lewis-Beck, Tang, and Martini 2014; Wang 2008.

[19] Beeson 2015, 528.

local authorities to undertake measures against a complex problem that is much more immediate and graspable. Ambient air pollution's relative "measurability" in the context of performance evaluation[20] also pushes them to present quick and significant results. Air pollution reduction thus became a topic of national concern, a campaign, which required local adjustment and activism even before it was formally and legally upgraded by the central government's Action Plan for the Prevention and Control of Air Pollution (APAP) in 2013 and the accompanying revised law this year. By vigorously working to find ways to anticipate crucial and high-priority policies, and adding innovative features to enhance their local effectiveness, leaders of subnational governments are usually able to make a name for themselves.[21] These dynamic adjustments and extensions are among the main causes of the policy variation that is, to a remarkably high degree, observable in the field of local air policy implementation across China.

Finally, as our case studies show, in order to implement often contested measures under the umbrella of air policy, local authorities benefitted from the fact that these could be framed as inevitable necessities that had to be undertaken against a widely and publicly perceived environmental threat. Everything considered, we would go as far as to hypothesize that the intensification of eco-environment-related anxieties, accompanied by other social-engineering and educational means, can lead to the increased use and greater acceptance of top-down decision-making and more draconian implementation mechanisms in China.

3   In Focus: Hangzhou City Under the Dome … and Searching for Ways Out

For a study of the local implementation of China's new air policies, Hangzhou presents itself as a particularly interesting case for the following reasons: firstly, it is the capital of China's wealthiest province and features a well-developed economy with a strong service sector largely based on tourism. Hangzhou City can therefore 'afford'—and is specially motivated—to clean up its air and to manifest its green, "ecologically civilized", and "low-carbon" city image with nationwide appeal.[22] Secondly, it correspondingly represents a high level of socio-economic development with, among other things, one of China's most highly ranked universities (Zhejiang University), a thriving NGO community, innumerable IT start-ups, and a growing, cosmopolitan middle class and upper class.

---

[20] Environmental indicators are increasingly included in governments' target responsibility contracts and were recently strengthened in the leading cadre evaluation system, Caixin online. 2015. "China to Hold Officials Accountable for Life for Environmental Problems," 13 August 2015, http://english.caixin.com/2015-05-08/100807608.html. Accessed 10 October 2015.

[21] Ahlers and Hansen forthcoming.

[22] Delman 2014.

Hangzhou's poor air quality has long troubled its inhabitants as well as it tainted the city's reputation as a beautiful destination for tourism, and recreation and air pollution counter-measures were put in place even before the launch of the national APAP. For instance, since 2007, a number of air-polluting enterprises in Hangzhou were required to shut down or relocate—and in 2016, not least because of preparations for the G20 summit meeting in September, this work was extended. More specifically, since 2012, Annual Implementation Schemes for Combined Air Pollution Prevention (hereafter "Annual Scheme") have set targets for reducing nitrogen oxide emissions and have underwritten actions such as controlling the consumption of coal and other energy sources, motor vehicle exhaust emissions, industrial air pollution, urban dust and rural straw burning, and cooking oil fumes' emissions.

Following the promulgation of China's new national APAP in 2013, Hangzhou City government published its own "Action Plan on Prevention and Control of Air Pollution in Hangzhou (2014–2017)". It raised the target to a decrease in PM_{10} of more than 10% and to a decrease in $PM_{2.5}$ of more than 26% by 2017, as measured on the basis of figures calculated for 2013.[23] After a preliminary evaluation of the performance, a 2014 Annual Scheme was launched that called for the relocation of yet another group of enterprises and the scrapping of polluting motor vehicles. This scheme also included the goal of improving the city's air quality index (AQI) by 9% as compared with that of 2013.[24] The 2015 Annual Scheme further aimed to achieve a reduction in $PM_{2.5}$ of at least 9.1% during the course of only one year.

In addition to publishing new ambitious targets almost every year, Hangzhou's government representatives also take pride in the fact that their emission control indicators and evaluation targets have always been stricter than those laid down in central guidelines as well as those employed by other cities in China—a narrative that was supported by observers and local researchers.[25] In its evaluation of subordinate government levels, Hangzhou goes one step further and allocates maximum points only if 70% of the days during a one-year period have been classified as being of "excellent" or "good" air quality. Achieving less than 45% means obtaining zero points in this target category.[26] Hangzhou City government also introduced public surveys as part of the annual performance evaluation procedures. The "management of air pollution" ranked first among the topics that respondents wanted the city government to be more responsive to in the 2014 survey.[27]

---

[23] Hangzhou City Government 2014a.

[24] An "Air Quality Index" combines measurements of major ambient air pollutants and standardizes monitoring of air pollution in China since 2012 (Aunan, Wang, and Hansen in this issue).

[25] Interviews, Hangzhou, 13 and 17 January 2015.

[26] Interview with leading official from the Comprehensive Evaluation Office of Hangzhou City, Hangzhou, 13 March 2015.

[27] Delman 2015.

Air quality measurements conducted (or contracted) by superior-level evaluators are now seen as "hard facts" in China—notwithstanding all the whitewashing of data and the opacity that may still prevail especially vis-à-vis the public. While causes and effects are not always traceable and reproducible, this performance indicator creates stress among the relevant government bureaucracies and results in a great deal of serious activism in the search for effective smog-fighting tools.[28] It is therefore not surprising that a rather obvious drop in total $PM_{2.5}$ measures in 2014 led, literally, to gasps of relief in Hangzhou's environmental bureaucracy and among city leaders.[29] This improvement provided a kick start on the road toward achieving the city's three-year APAP goals, although the reasons for the decrease (scientifically speaking) cannot be directly related to specific types of short-term government interventions over the period of just one year.[30]

As in most other Chinese cities, analyses conducted by Hangzhou City's Environmental Protection Bureau had identified motor vehicle exhaust and industrial emissions as the two primary and consistent sources of $PM_{2.5}$ pollution. We shall now examine in greater detail two of the related core measures in the city's air policy portfolio, car ownership and driving controls and the relocation of polluting industries, in order to trace the nuances of local air policy implementation strategies.

4   NUANCES OF HANGZHOU CITY'S AIR POLICY IMPLEMENTATION

4.1   Case A: Car Policy—Against All Odds?

At noon, on 25 March 2014, Hangzhou municipal government held a press conference to announce that the number of new car license plates issued would from now on be limited and that this regulation would take effect just five hours after the announcement. Traffic authorities would not issue *any* new car license plates until 25 April 2014, when a lottery and auction system for obtaining new license plates would be launched. In addition, restrictions on vehicle use during the rush hour would be extended from 5 May in the same year.

What was behind this bold move? By the end of December 2011, the analysis of major $PM_{2.5}$ sources by Hangzhou's Environmental Monitoring Center had shown that motor vehicle exhaust emissions amounted to 39.5% of the overall $PM_{2.5}$ pollution in the urban areas of Hangzhou. The number of

---

[28] Interview with officials from the Economic and Information Technology Commission of Hangzhou City, Hangzhou, 16 March 2015.

[29] In general, during 2014, the average concentration of $PM_{2.5}$ went down to 64.6 μg/m³ (−7.7%) (Hangzhou EPB 2014). For the first three quarters of 2015, Greenpeace reported another drop of 11.7% in average $PM_{2.5}$ concentration in Hangzhou.

[30] Ahlers and Hansen forthcoming.

licensed cars in Hangzhou was already astronomical and was continuing to grow rapidly. By the end of April 2014, the number of motor vehicles had reached 1,897,527, that is, a further 18.11% increase on the figure of 1,606,638 in April 2013. This meant that Hangzhou was in first place in terms of cars per inhabitant (i.e., one car per three persons) and in seventh place out of 36 main Chinese cities with the highest total numbers of private cars.[31] One obvious result of this was heavy traffic congestion. In 2013, there were 35 days of serious traffic congestion with an average speed of below 20 km/h during rush hours.[32] These traffic jams, especially during peak times, were said to have resulted in even more vehicle exhaust emissions. Realizing the intrinsic contribution of motor vehicle emissions to particulate pollution, Hangzhou's municipal leadership decided to take immediate action, which meant, first and foremost, controlling the number of motor vehicles in the city in 2014. Backed by the Regulation for the Control of Motor Vehicle Exhaust Pollution in Zhejiang Province[33] and the national APAP, this step seemed to be an effective way of reducing both air pollution and the city's immense traffic congestion problems.

Before the official announcement of Hangzhou's new policy,[34] there had already been rumors about potential plans to limit the number of license plates for new cars, but the local authorities had consistently denied them, so that when the new system was finally introduced in such an ad hoc fashion, a torrent of criticism was unleashed. City residents complained that the new Temporary Regulation for Control of the Number of Private Cars in Hangzhou[35] had limited policy legitimacy since there had been neither notices to the public nor public hearings, which were by now a common feature in local drafting processes, and particularly widely used in Zhejiang Province, before the policy was published. As such, this was found to violate The Rule for the Management of Administrative Regulatory Documents in Zhejiang Province, which, for instance, states that,

[31] Xinhua Net. 2014. "Hangzhou shishi xiaokeche zongliang tiaokong guanli, xiangou xianxing shuangchong cuoshi" (Hangzhou's implements control and regulation of small passenger cars: two measures for license limitation and traffic control), 25 March, http://finance.sina.com.cn/roll/20140325/195818610408.shtml. Accessed 16 October 2015.

[32] Hangzhou Net. 2015. "Hangzhou shuangxian man yi nian, jiatong daodi gaishan le duoshao?" (Traffic controls have been in effect in Hangzhou for one year now. How much did the traffic situation improve?), 11 May, http://ori.hangzhou.com.cn/ornews/content/2015-05/11/content_5765344.htm. Accessed 16 October 2015.

[33] Standing Committee of the People's Congress of Zhejiang Province 2013.

[34] Only a few other cities across China had previously implemented similar controls of car ownership. Shanghai (2000), Beijing (2011), Guangzhou (2012), and Tianjin (2013) each introduced different systems for the obtainment of license plates, which basically meant auction or/and lottery. Hangzhou actually developed its strategy on the basis of the Tianjin model, combining a lottery and auction mode. See, also, Feng and Li 2013.

[35] Hangzhou City Government 2014b.

in the process of drafting administration regulations, the local government must take advice from the public; for the issue of advancing significant public interests, the local government should organize forums and public hearings and listen to stakeholders' suggestions (…).[36]

In this case, however, without any "warning", Hangzhou City government had announced a completely new regulation. Consequently, Zhejiang provincial government was publicly called upon to scrap Hangzhou's new regulation before it became valid. Even official media outlets, such as Xinhua News, criticized Hangzhou authority's sudden announcement, describing it as a "lose-lose situation", in which the city authorities had lost the citizens' trust and citizens had to rush out to pay additional amounts of money in order to buy new cars in the remaining five hours before the deadline expired.[37] Car dealers in Hangzhou confirmed during interviews that most of them had chosen to increase the price of cars just before the deadline came into effect. Nonetheless, many car salesrooms had to close down while others sought advice from colleagues in other cities, such as Beijing and Shanghai, where similar controls had been set up, and adjusted their business strategies accordingly.[38]

Against this chaotic backdrop, the Hangzhou City authorities saw themselves forced to provide some additional explanations but continued to implement the decisions. According to a leading representative of Hangzhou City's Transportation Department,

> limiting the number of car license plates issued was an administrative decision that we had to take this way. Had the government included the public to discuss the issue first, the number of new registered cars would have increased sharply in the meantime. But the purpose of the regulation was to reduce the number of new cars.[39]

The city government issued a public statement to the effect that there was nothing untoward concerning the legitimacy of the policy because it followed the Regulations for the Control of Motor Vehicle Exhaust Pollution in Zhejiang Province, which allows "municipal governments to take certain actions to control the number of motor vehicles in accordance with the city's conditions and size and the local air quality".[40] Concerning the problem of excluding the public throughout the policy drafting process, the same officer remarked further:

---

[36] Zhejiang Provincial Government 2010.

[37] Xinhua Net. 2014. "Hangzhou xianpai: Benyi suihao, naihe shuangshu?" (License limitations in Hangzhou: while the original idea is good, is there not actually a double loss?), 27 March, http://www.zj.xinhua.org/newscenter/headlines/2014-03/27/c_119964187.htm.   Accessed 16 October 2015.

[38] Interview with car sales manager, Hangzhou, 10 March 2015.

[39] Interview with leading official from the Transportation Department of Hangzhou City, Hangzhou, 10 March 2015.

[40] Standing Committee of People's Congress of Zhejiang Province 2013.

Table 34.1   The number and growth rate of registered cars in Hangzhou City

	Total number of registered cars	Growth rate (based on the figures from the previous year) (%)
April 2013	1,606,638	–
April 2014	1,897,527	18.11
April 2015	1,975,285	4.10
April 2016	2,055,106	4.04

Source: Official statistics, Hangzhou City Transportation Department, 2013–2016, http://xkctk.hzcb.gov.cn. Accessed 15 October 2016

Note: We extracted the data for the month of April for each year, since it was on 25 April 2014 that a lottery and auction system for obtaining new licenses was launched in Hangzhou

> Yes, the public was right that the government should have heard the public's suggestions in hearings which are a must when publishing ordinary administration regulations. But it is also in the regulations by Zhejiang Province that the decision-making process can be simplified (*jianhua zhiding chengxu* 简化制定程序) in exceptional cases and for security reasons. That was what we followed.[41]

Later, however, after the announcement had been made, Hangzhou City government published a draft version of the Regulations for the Control of the Number of Private Cars in Hangzhou and invited public discussion on the details of vehicle control by post, fax, email, and hotlines. But as a result the draft regulations were not meaningfully revised. On 29 April 2014, the city government finally promulgated the temporary regulations limiting the number of license plates issued which were supposed to be effective, first of all, for one year.

Hangzhou thus started to implement a multifaceted strategy by means of which it could control the number of license plates issued (*xianpai* 限牌) and gradually scrap the old and heavily polluting, or "yellow sticker", vehicles (*huangbiaoche* 黄标车). Since 5 May 2014, restrictions have been imposed on car driving by means of a temporary ban on specific license plate numbers (*weihao xianxing* 尾号限行) and non-Hangzhou-registered vehicles.[42] By these means, traffic in downtown areas is controlled during the weekday rush hour periods, and vehicular access to sightseeing and "ecological conservation" areas, for example, around the West Lake, is constrained. As expected, the new traffic control measures in Hangzhou led to a slower increase in the number of new cars. Official figures revealed that the number of cars registered in Hangzhou during the first year of the new policy increased from 1,897,527 in April 2014 to 1,975,285 in April 2015. The growth rate was therefore cut by 14.01% compared with that of 2013 (Table 34.1).

---

[41] Interview with leading official from the Transportation Department of Hangzhou City.

[42] This means that, for example, cars with license plate digits ending with the numbers "1" and "0" are not allowed to drive in downtown areas between 7:00–9:00 a.m. and 4:30–6:30 p.m. on Mondays. On Tuesdays, this refers to license plate numbers ending in "2" and "9" and so forth.

Not surprisingly, this also had positive effects on the degree of traffic congestion and air pollution in the city. Measurements have shown that traffic regulations during rush hour also contribute to the reduction of air pollution, although vehicle emissions are still the main source of particulate pollution.[43] Nevertheless, according to Hangzhou City's 2014 Environment Bulletin, the contribution of motor vehicle exhaust emissions to $PM_{2.5}$ pollution was reduced to 28% by the end of 2014.[44]

Altogether, measures to control vehicle emissions were implemented via a highly exclusive and centralized process. This is probably not overly surprising given that some interviewees referred to this policy innovation as a pet project of Zhejiang Province's Party Secretary. Once the decision was made that Hangzhou, as the provincial capital, should implement car usage restrictions in early 2014, the relevant municipal government departments were only allowed about one month to garner information about the handful of other cities in China which had introduced similar measures before and to draft implementation guidelines. Members of this task force were bound to the highest degree of confidentiality because of the extremely publicly contested nature of the project.[45]

At the time of our second visit in March 2015, the city government was in the process of revising the regulations after the first year. This was clearly still a highly sensitive issue for the city authorities, who were at the same time being subjected to intense pressure by both their superiors and the citizenry to improve public transportation and facilitate alternative or "greener" modes of motorized transportation, such as e-car rental or carpooling/sharing. Interestingly enough, despite the fact that the air pollution caused by diesel trucks, (mini)buses, and other similarly sized vehicles (as well as low-quality fuel in general) was publicly considered the main challenge to be tackled, restricting private car usage remained high on the political agenda.

Finally, Hangzhou was not the last city government to take this rather risky step. Several of the strategies that were tested there, such as shortening the deadline between the date of the announcement and the date that the policy came into effect, restricting car sales during this period, and strongly emphasizing the proportionately high contribution of vehicle exhaust emissions to air pollution in general, resulted in leaders from many other cities visiting Hangzhou on inspection tours.[46] On 29 December 2014, Shenzhen City followed suit and declared that it would immediately limit the number of car

---

[43] The other major components are estimated to be industrial pollution (22.8%), dust pollution (20.4%), coal burning (18.8%), and others (10%) (Hangzhou City EPB 2014).

[44] Hangzhou City EPB 2014.

[45] Interview with a leading official from the Traffic Police Department of Hangzhou City, Hangzhou, 9 March 2015.

[46] Interview with a leading official from the Transportation Department of Hangzhou City, Hangzhou, 10 March 2015.

license plates being issued, again without having a public hearing, and without even announcing a deadline.[47] Public protests against the measure were even louder in Shenzhen, but for Hangzhou at least, the anecdotal evidence that we gleaned from residents has indicated that the measures themselves are gradually accepted as time passes, because of a widely shared preference, not only for air quality improvement (a policy label that was mentioned by many interviewees) but also for congestion control.[48] Public discontent prevails with the way that these policies are implemented and with the inconveniences they entail.[49] But even interviewees who had to put up with the frustrating experience of not being able to buy and drive a car exactly how and when they wished to[50] agreed that now everyone simply had to contribute to improving the conditions in Hangzhou.

4.2   Case B: Public Dialogue vis-à-vis Air-Polluting Industries

By the end of 2006, the official data collected by the City Environmental Protection Bureau (hereafter EPB) showed that two old industrial regions in the urban areas of Hangzhou, the Banshan District 半山地区 and the Beidaqiao District 北大桥地区, made up 80% of the city's total coal consumption and produced more than 70% of the total pollution emissions.[51] Local residents appealed to government agencies and the media at different levels and even collectively protested against the industrial air pollution in their neighborhood.[52] There were around 1250 complaints addressed to Hangzhou City's EPB via hotlines, letters, and visits in 2006.[53] This conflict between local residents and polluting industries signified a potential risk to social stability and kept local authorities on high alert.

---

[47] Nanfang Dushibao (Southern Metropolis Daily). 2014. "Shenzhen tufa shuangxian ling" (Shenzhen announced to immediately limit the number of license plates issued), 30 December. http://paper.oeeee.com/nis/201412/30/312498.html. Accessed 16 October 2015.

[48] This was also found by Chen and Zhao (2013) in a survey about public perception of Shanghai City's car licensing policy.

[49] Horizon Key. 2015. "Shuzi jieshi 'xianxing buru jianliang'" (Numbers show 'limits do not equal reduction'), 13 January, http://www.horizonkey.com/c/cn/news/2015-01/13/news_2633.html. Accessed 13 June 2015.

[50] In the first year, from 1 May 2014, to 30 April 2015, the free lottery had an estimated success rate of 0.81–2.20%. Bidding for a license plate cost up to CNY47,785, which amounted to about one-third of the average price of a 2014 FAW Volkswagen Golf in China, Zhejiang News. 2015. "Shenqing yao bu yao jiashi? Hangzhou xianpai zhengce jiang tiaozheng 4 yue 30 ri qian fabu xingui" (Driving license required for applications? New regulations published before Hangzhou's [car] license limitation policy is adjusted on April 30th), 13 March, http://zjnews.zjol.com.cn/system/2015/03/13/020550157.shtml. Accessed 21 May 2015.

[51] Hangzhou EPB 2011, 13.

[52] Interview with a leading official from Hangzhou City's EPB, Hangzhou, 22 March 2015.

[53] Hangzhou EPB 2011, 57.

Following the Supervision and Management Measures for Environmental Pollution of Zhejiang Province,[54] Hangzhou City government promulgated a Comprehensive Environmental Pollution Regulation Scheme starting in 2007 for the two districts.[55] The declared target was to reduce industrial air pollution by 80%, relocate or shut down significantly polluting enterprises, and decrease the number of complaints made by local residents. However, putting these regulation schemes into action turned out to be far from straightforward and dragged on for years. Complications arose because many polluting plants were state-owned enterprises (SOEs) affiliated with local government agencies. For instance, one of them, the Wanli Chemical Factory, which produced washing powder, laundry detergent, and liquid soap, was attached to Hangzhou's Economic and Information Technology Commission. Most of these companies had operated in the urban areas of Hangzhou for more than 40 years and had contributed significantly to the city's gross domestic product (GDP). Any scheme to relocate or shut down these SOEs would, of course, not only lead to a reduction in local GDP growth but would also face resistance from groups with a vested interest, as a leading official of Hangzhou City's EPB recalled:

> [T]he state-owned enterprises were supported by certain government departments and that entailed many obstacles for us. In addition, laid-off workers in state-owned enterprises were another big problem.[56]

In the meantime, problems began to escalate, especially in Wanjia Huacheng Community, a residential area in Beidaqiao District, which had more than 2600 apartments and hosted primarily members from medium- to high-income groups, including young office workers, local civil servants, and businessmen. Most of the residents who had eagerly moved into these apartments in 2010 soon discovered that, where they were living, a noxious odor suffused the air. They quickly realized that this odor was actually due to the industrial waste gas that emanated from the Wanli Chemical Factory, located in the northeast of the residential area, less than 200 meters away as the crow flies. By the end of 2010, 60 residents had spontaneously formed a self-help organization to protest against the industrial air pollution. In early 2011 this group even marched into Hangzhou's EPB to demand the closure of the chemical factory.[57] Although the factory had been scheduled to relocate at the end of 2010, according to the Environmental Pollution Comprehensive Regulation Scheme, the relocation had been delayed due to the difficulties involved in finding an alternative site. Discontented with being continuously exposed to polluted air, the residents started to criticize the lack of action taken by Hangzhou City's

---

[54] Zhejiang Provincial Government 2006.
[55] Hangzhou EPB 2007; Hangzhou EPB 2009.
[56] Interview with a leading official of Hangzhou City's EPB.
[57] Interview with the former leader of the residents' self-help organization of Wanjia Huacheng Community, Hangzhou, 16 July 2015.

EPB, and petitioned the provincial government: "We didn't trust the local EPB anymore. We wanted to take collective action to draw the government leaders' attention and urge them to solve our problems".[58] In May 2011, over 30 residents of Wanjia Huacheng Community blocked the main entrance of the chemical plant and presented banners addressed to the Hangzhou EPB.

Faced with local residents' lack of confidence in the official relocation plan, Hangzhou City's EPB, in order to mollify the anger of the public and to put pressure on the polluting SOEs to relocate or to shut down as soon as possible, decided to embark on a new strategy by implementing a kind of communication mechanism described as a "dialogue platform between enterprises and residents" (*changqun duihua pingtai* 厂群对话平台). Representatives of the Wanli Chemical Factory enterprise and local residents as well as government agencies affiliated with the enterprise were invited to take part in the dialogue. Residents were encouraged to express their complaints and demands, while the companies' executives were expected to provide them with answers and to come up with plans for the reduction of industrial air pollution. Government agencies in charge of the polluting enterprise had to promise to enforce controls, while representatives of the local EPB acted as facilitators and witnesses.

During the first round of dialogue on 16 August 2011, the Hangzhou EPB pledged to local residents that the Wanli Chemical Factory would be forced to end production if it could not be relocated. The manager of the factory announced that the new factory site was in Jiande 建德 County (in Hangzhou's jurisdiction) and that the company would invest CNY 4,000,000 to upgrade filters in order to reduce the discharge of pollutants. According to our interviewees, many of the representatives of local residents openly showed their disbelief and lack of trust. To ease the situation a little, the director of Hangzhou City's EPB disclosed his private cell phone number and invited residents to call him if they had any problems. For the second session, a check on the factory's performance was promised. As a trade-off, residents were asked to stop interfering with the factory's current operations.

The second round of dialogue was held on 10 September 2011. Representatives of the local community were invited to pay an inspection visit to the factory's new site in Jiande County to learn about the completion date for the construction of the new site and so on. Upon seeing the site for the new factory, the residents reportedly felt somewhat relieved. But although the new factory was under construction, the completion date was still a long way off and local residents were still suffering from the heavy pollution produced by the original plant. On 25 October 2011, a third round of dialogue was held to try to deal with this problem. Local residents demanded that the factory, in order to reduce air pollution, should further reduce output. The local EPB, likewise, suggested that the factory should reduce production output or stop

---

[58] Interview with the former leader of the residents' self-help organization of Wanjia Huacheng Community.

production during the night hours and at weekends when most of the residents were at home. The factory managers, for their part, complained that, with the aim of continuing production, they had invested a great deal of extra money to upgrade the filters just two months earlier and that they would not be able to reach their production target if they only worked during the day on weekdays alone. Finally, however, weighing the costs against the benefits, the factory eventually gave way and accepted the local EPB's suggestion, promising to accelerate the relocation process with the support of specific government subsidies. The Wanli Chemical Plant was finally relocated to the new site in Jiande County at the beginning of 2012.

In this way, Hangzhou's EPB completed its first set of "dialogue" sessions between an enterprise and the residents and considered it a success. This led to the staging of further similar forums in the Banshan and the Beidaqiao districts: a thermal power plant was required to deal with the dark smoke that was coming out of its chimneys in early 2012, a steel plant had to stop highly polluting production procedures in late 2012, and a chemical factory was shut down due to serious dust emissions in 2013.[59] After 2014, this sort of dialogue mechanism was frequently adopted across Hangzhou municipality, not least because Hangzhou had launched a campaign to relocate all polluting industries from the city center in preparation for the G20 summit in September 2016. Furthermore, Hangzhou's experience was mentioned in national media reports and similar attempts at resolving conflict over air pollution between local community residents and polluting enterprises that took place under the aegis of local authorities are observable in other Chinese cities since the 2010s. Most recently, in 2015, a township belonging to Shanghai City founded a "dialogue platform" to resolve a conflict over industrial air and water pollution and undertook policy enforcement measures with direct reference to the "Hangzhou model".[60]

In Hangzhou, these dialogue mechanisms provided new channels through which the local authorities could distribute updated information about pollution regulations to aggrieved local residents and also use them as leverage to exert pressure on the problematic enterprises. This helped the government in its work toward achieving tangible policy results. By the end of 2012, the number of complaints made by local residents had fallen sharply to 413, compared to 1250 in 2006.[61] A total of 450 enterprises were shut down or relocated

[59] Hangzhou EPB 2013.

[60] Shanghai Maqiao Township Government Website. 2015. "Dajian jiaoliu pingtai, huajie changqun maodun" (Staging a communication platform: conciliating conflicts between factories and the public). 20 May, http://www.shmq.gov.cn/sites/maqiaozhen/maqiaozhen_content. aspx?ctgid=d4894652-c1ca-4d18-9be9-63cc7bc3a5b3&infoId=dee3e45e-f8a2-4c49-b020-0dc1a843203a. Accessed 16 October 2015.

[61] Hangzhou Net. 2013. "Liu nian zhengzhi, Banshan Beidaqiao diqu zhongdian wuran qiye huo guanting huo banqian" (Six years' of regulation: major polluting enterprises in Banshan and Beidaqiao districts were shut down or relocated), 28 November, http://hznews.hangzhou.com. cn/chengshi/content/2013-11/28/content_4981832.htm. Accessed 16 October 2015.

between 2007 and 2013, 24 of which were SOEs affiliated to Hangzhou municipal government and Zhejiang provincial government.[62]

5   CONCLUSIONS: CHINA'S AUTHORITARIAN ENVIRONMENTALISM 2.0?

China is trying to reduce heavy air pollution on a tremendously large scale and within a limited time frame. Preliminary successes have already been achieved, although there might still be a very long way to go before any real tangible and sustainable results can be gained. Our analysis was based on the notion that China's potential AE cannot be assessed by employing a macroscopic approach but requires more detailed analysis where ultimate policy implementation happens, that is, at the local level.

We began by observing that the focus on environmental problems in Chinese society has recently been intensified as a result of the heavy particulate air pollution in Chinese cities. By actually fulfilling more of the preconditions described in the usual AE concept than are found in climate change policies (in terms of the communication and perception of risks, the framing of counter-measures, the incentives for implementers, etc.), the air pollution problematique, arguably, gives new thrust on China's path toward developing an effective variant of AE.

Drawing on our studies of municipal-level "air policy" implementation, however, we have refined the Chinese AE narrative in certain respects. First, we take issue with the argument about the apparent existence of a general divide between macro/national-level effectiveness and micro/local-level sabotage that has appeared in studies of Chinese AE so far. The two case studies that we have undertaken have shown how different agencies at municipal levels came up with rather innovative steps under the banner of "air quality" policies. Indubitably, it was more often than not the national and provincial policies that lent legitimacy to the final implementation of contested measures; the channels and varying effects of "dispersed implementation", in particular, downstream adaptability and flexibility under the aegis of AE in China, require further investigation.

Our primary aim, however, was to describe the style of air policy implementation vis-à-vis the population as well as the complexity involved from a local state perspective. With regard to car licensing and driving restrictions, which affected Hangzhou's society as a whole, we found that the local government deliberately chose a highly centralized and exclusive implementation mode. Interestingly enough, notwithstanding the individual constraints and the dis-

[62] Hangzhou Daily. 2014. "Banshan yu Beidaqiao diqu wuran yao qingling, 2016 niandi zai guanting 7 jia daxing qiye" (Industrial pollution is projected to go down to zero in Banshan and Beidaqiao Districts, another 7 large enterprises will be shut down at the end of 2016), 7 September, http://biz.zjol.com.cn/system/2014/09/07/020243176.shtml. Accessed 16 October 2015.

satisfaction with governmental action that this gave rise to, the measures were apparently more acceptable to the public if labeled as "air quality protection" rather than as solutions to the problem of heavy traffic congestion. The extent to which these methods will actually contribute to the fight against smog in the city and whether Hangzhou will be able to comprehensively transform its transportation system are issues which will have to be closely examined in the coming years. In the case of public "dialogue platforms" for industrial relocation, the punctiform, goal-oriented mobilization and inclusion of various political, social, and economic interests were observable. As we showed, the local environmental bureaucracy was able to successfully employ public discontent to take action against SOEs within their jurisdictions. Here, as well, the long-term effects of these moves, including the conditions at the new industrial site, will need to be followed up. One of our core observations is that a "*mixture* of authoritarian *and* democratic features", which is, according to Bruce Gilley, common to "all environmental policy models",[63] was solely observable at the implementation stage, and only when it helped smoothen or accelerate the process. This kind of governmental outcome orientation, and all the different forms of public inclusion and exclusion that it entails, still needs to be given a greater emphasis in descriptions of a Chinese AE.

Ultimately, whether what is currently observable in China should be called "environmental-*ism*" at all, since this implies a universalist orientation and an over-prioritization of environmental goals over other goals, is, of course, highly questionable. What we can see, at the very least, is a remarkable environmental policy change, which reflects the accommodation, to a certain extent, of enormous public anxiety and mushrooming civil engagement, as well the acknowledgment of the health and economic risks posed by extreme air pollution, and which also entails considerable shifts in the interfaces and interactions of local governments, residents, and the business/industrial sector. Nevertheless, as the term "AE" also suggests, this is all happening against the background of an authoritarian political system in China, where the CCP Party state is, of course, not willing to relinquish its absolute monopoly over selecting, or at most tolerating, solutions as it sees fit.

References

Ahlers, Anna L., and Mette Halskov Hansen (forthcoming). "Air Pollution: How Will China Win its Self-Declared War Against it?" In Eva Sternfeld (ed.), *Routledge Handbook on Chinese Environmental Policy*. London: Routledge.

Beeson, Mark. 2015. "Authoritarian Environmentalism and China." In Teena Gabrielson, Cheryl Hall, John M. Meyer and David Schlosberg (eds.), *The Oxford Handbook of Environmental Political Theory*. Oxford: Oxford University Press, 520–532.

---

[63] Gilley 2012, 289; emphasis added.

Beeson, Mark. 2010. "The Coming of Environmental Authoritarianism." *Environmental Politics* 19(2), 276–294.

Chen, Xiaojie and Jinhua Zhao. 2013. "Bidding to Drive: Car License Auction Policy in Shanghai and Its Public Acceptance." *Transport Policy* 27, 39–52.

Delman, Jørgen. 2014. "Climate Change Politics and Hangzhou's 'Green City Making'." In Per Olof Berg and Björner Emma (eds.), *Branding Chinese mega-cities: policies, practices and positioning*. Cheltenham: Edward Elgar, 249–261.

Delman, Jørgen. 2015. "Performance Assessment, Social accountability and Sustainability Governance in Hangzhou: Leveraging the Implementation gap?" Paper to be presented at the workshop on *Governance for urban sustainability in China: Challenges and Practices*, University of Copenhagen, Denmark, 31 October–01 November 2015.

Feng, Suwei and Li, Qiang. 2013. "Car Ownership Control in Chinese Mega Cities: Shanghai, Beijing and Guangzhou." *Journeys*, 40–49.

Gilley, Bruce. 2012. "Authoritarian Environmentalism and China's Response to Climate Change." *Environmental Politics* 21(2), 287–307.

Hangzhou City Environmental Protection Bureau (EPB). 2007. "Hangzhoushi Banshan diqu huanjing wuran zonghe zhengzhi gongzuo fangan" (Scheme for the comprehensive regulation of environmental pollution in Banshan District).

Hangzhou City Environmental Protection Bureau (EPB). 2009. "Hangzhou shi Beidaqiao diqu huanjing wuran zonghe zhengzhi gongzuo fang'an" (Scheme for the comprehensive regulation of environmental pollution in Beidaqiao District).

Hangzhou City Environmental Protection Bureau (EPB). 2011. "Kuayue: Hangzhou shi huanjing wuran yonghe yhengzhi lichen" (Leap over: The progress of Hangzhou City's comprehensive regulation of environmental pollution in (2007–2011)).

Hangzhou City Environmental Protection Bureau (EPB). 2013. "Changqun duihua: huanbao zhili de chuangxin pingtai" (Dialogue between polluting enterprises and local residents: an innovative platform for environmental governance). *Hangzhou* 254(3), 43–44.

Hangzhou City Environmental Protection Bureau (EPB). 2014. "2014 nian Hangzhou shi huanjing zhuankuang gongbao" (Environment Bulletin of Hangzhou City for the year 2014).

Hangzhou City Government. 2014a. "Guanyu yinfa Hangzhou shi daqi wuran fangzhi xingdong jihua (2014–2017 nian) de tongzhi" (Circular on the implementation of Hangzhou City's action plan for air pollution control and prevention [2014–2017]). 15 May. Document No. 80.

Hangzhou City Government. 2014b. "Hangzhoushi xiaokeche zongliang tiaokong zanxing guanli guiding" (Temporary regulations for control of the number of private cars in Hangzhou). 29 April. Document No. 7.

He, Baogang and Stig Thøgersen. 2010. "Giving the People a Voice? Experiments with Consultative Authoritarian Institutions in China." *Journal of Contemporary China* 19(66), 675–692.

Kostka, Genia. 2016. "Command Without Control: The Case of China's Environmental Target System." *Regulation & Governance* 10(1), 58–74.

Kostka, Genia and Sarah Eaton. 2014. "Authoritarian Environmentalism Undermined? Local Leaders' Time Horizons and Environmental Policy Implementation in China." *The China Quarterly* 218, 359–380.

Lewis-Beck, Michael S., Wenfang Tang, and Nicholas F. Martini. 2014. "A Chinese Popularity Function Sources of Government Support." *Political Research Quarterly* 67(1), 16–25.

Ran, Ran. 2015. *Zhongguo difang huanjing zhengzhi: zhengce yu zhixing zhe jian de jilü* (*China's local environmental politics: discrepancies between policies and their implementation*). Beijing: Zhongyang bianyi chubanshe.

Shearman, David and Joseph Wayne Smith. 2007. *The Climate Change Challenge and the Failure of Democracy*. Westport: Praeger Publishers.

Standing Committee of the People's Congress of Zhejiang Province. 2013. "Zhejiangsheng jidongche paiqi wuran fangzhi tiaoli" (Regulation for the Control of Motor Vehicle Exhaust Pollution in Zhejiang Province). 22 November. Document No. 8.

Sterner, Thomas and Coria, Jessica. 2012. *Policy Instruments for Environmental and Natural Resource Management*. 2nd Edition. London: Routledge/RFF Press.

Teets, Jessica C. 2013. "Let Many Civil Societies Bloom: The Rise of Consultative Authoritarianism in China." *The China Quarterly* 213, 19–38.

Truex, Rory. 2014. "Consultative Authoritarianism and its Limits." *Comparative Political Studies*, https://doi.org/10.1177/0010414014534196.

Wang, Shaoguang. 2008. "Changing Models of China's Policy Agenda Setting." *Modern China* 34(1), 56–87.

Zhejiang Provincial Government. 2006. "Zhejiang sheng huanjing wuran jiandu guanli banfa" (Zhejiang Provinces' supervision management measures for environmental pollution). 13 July. Document No. 321.

Zhejiang Provincial Government. 2010. "Zhejiangsheng xingzheng guifanxing wenjian guanli banfa" (Rules for the management of administrative regulatory documents in Zhejiang Province). 20 July. Document No. 275.

Lightning Source UK Ltd.
Milton Keynes UK
UKHW021102200422
401759UK00003B/284